Child Development

ROBERT S. FELDMAN

University of Massachusetts at Amherst

Prentice Hall, Upper Saddle River, New Jersey 07458

Library of Congress Cataloging-in-Publication Data

Feldman, Robert S.,
Child development / Robert S. Feldman.
p. cm
Includes bibliographical references and index.
ISBN 0-13-348525-0
1. Child development. 2. Child psychology. 3. Adolescence.
4. Adolescent psychology. I. Title.
HQ772.F377 1998
305.231—dc21 97-14700
CIP

Editor-in-Chief: Nancy Roberts
Executive Editor: Bill Webber
Director of Production and Manufacturing: Barbara Kittle
Managing Editor: Bonnie Biller
Development Editor: Robert Weiss
Editorial/Production Supervision: Mary Rottino
Manufacturing Manager: Nick Sklitsis
Prepress and Manufacturing Buyer: Tricia Kenny
Creative Design Director: Leslie Osher
Interior and Cover Design: Joseph Rattan Design
Cover and Part Opening Art: Linda Holten
Electronic Illustrations: Joseph Rattan Design
Director, Image Resource Center: Lori Morris-Nantz
Photo Research Supervisor: Melinda Lee Reo
Image Permission Supervisor: Kay Dellosa
Photo Researcher: Eloise Donnelly
Editorial Assistants: Tamsen Adams and Emsal Hasan
Copyeditor: Lynn Buckingham

Acknowledgments for copyrighted material may be found beginning on p. 567, which constitutes an extension of this copyright page.

This book was set in Minion and Syntax Black by TSI Graphics and was printed by Von Hoffman Company. The cover was printed by Lehigh Press Colortronics.

Simon & Schuster/A Viacom Company
Upper Saddle River, New Jersey 07458

Printed in the United States of America
10 9 8 7 6 5 4 3 2 1

ISBN 0-13-348525-0

Prentice-Hall International (UK) Limited, *London*
Prentice-Hall of Australia Pty. Limited, *Sydney*
Prentice-Hall Canada, Inc. *Toronto*
Prentice-Hall Hispanoamericana, S.A., *Mexico*
Prentice-Hall of India Private Limited, *New Delhi*
Prentice-Hall of Japan, Inc. *Tokyo*
Simon & Schuster Asia Pte. Ltd., *Singapore*
Editoria Prentice-Hall do Brazil, Ltda., *Rio de Janeiro*

to my wonderful children

Brief Contents

PART 1–BEGINNINGS

PART 2–INFANCY

PART 3–THE PRESCHOOL YEARS

PART 4–MIDDLE CHILDHOOD

PART 5–ADOLESCENCE

Contents

PART 2–INFANCY

PART 4–MIDDLE CHILDHOOD

Preface

Child and adolescent development is a unique field of study, because each of us has experience with its subject matter in very personal ways. It is a discipline that deals not just with ideas and concepts and theories, but one that above all has at its heart the forces that have made each of us who we are.

This text, ***Child Development,*** seeks to capture the discipline in a way that sparks and nurtures and shapes readers' interest. It is meant to excite students about the field, to draw them into its way of looking at the world, and to mold their understanding of developmental issues. By exposing readers to both the current content and the promise inherent in child and adolescent development, the text is designed to keep interest in the discipline alive long after students' formal study of the field has ended.

Overview

Child Development provides a broad overview of the field of development. It covers the full range of childhood and adolescence, from the moment of conception through the end of adolescence. The text furnishes a broad, comprehensive introduction to the field, covering basic theories and research findings, as well as highlighting current applications outside the laboratory. It covers childhood and adolescence chronologically, encompassing the prenatal period, infancy and toddlerhood, the preschool years, middle childhood, and adolescence. Within these periods, it focuses on physical, cognitive, and social and personality development.

The book seeks to accomplish the following four major goals:

- First and foremost, the book is designed to provide a broad, balanced overview of the field of child and adolescent development. It introduces readers to the theories, research, and applications that constitute the discipline, examining both the traditional areas of the field as well as more recent innovations.

  The book pays particular attention to the applications developed by child and adolescent development specialists. While not slighting theoretical material, the text emphasizes what we know about development across childhood and adolescence rather than focusing on unanswered questions. It demonstrates how this knowledge may be applied to real-world problems.

  In sum, the book highlights the interrelationships among theory, research, and application, accentuating the scope and diversity of the field. It also illustrates how child and adolescent developmentalists use theory, research, and applications to help solve significant social problems.

- The second major goal of the text is to explicitly tie development to students' lives. Findings from the study of child and adolescent development have a significant degree of relevance to students, and this text illustrates how these findings can be applied in a meaningful, practical sense. Applications are presented in a contemporaneous framework, including current news items, timely world events, and contemporary uses of child and adolescent development that draw readers into the field. Numerous descriptive scenarios and vignettes reflect everyday situations in people's lives, explaining how they relate to the field.

  For example, each chapter begins with an opening prologue that provides a real-life situation relating to the chapter subject area. All chapters also have at least one "Informed Consumer of Development" section, which explicitly suggests ways to apply developmental findings to students' experience in a practical, hands-on way. Each chapter also includes a feature called "Directions in Development" that discusses ways that developmental research is being used to answer the problems that society faces. For instance, policy issues such as the effects of day care on child development are considered. Finally, every chapter has an interview ("Speaking of Development") with a person working in a profession related to the chapter's topic. These interviews illustrate how a background in child and adolescent development can be beneficial in a variety of vocations.

- The third goal of this book is to highlight both the commonalties and diversity of today's multicultural society. Consequently, every chapter has a "Developmental Diversity" section that considers how cultural factors relevant to development both unite and diversify our contemporary, global society. In addition, the book incorporates material relevant to diversity throughout every chapter.
- Finally, the fourth goal of the text is one that underlies the other three: making the field of child and adolescent development engaging, accessible, and interesting to students. Child and adolescent development is a joy both to study and teach, because so much of it has direct, immediate meaning to our lives. Because all of us are involved in our own developmental paths, we are tied in very personal ways to the content areas covered by the book. ***Child Development,*** then, is meant to engage and nurture this interest, planting a seed that will develop and flourish throughout readers' lifetimes.

  To accomplish this fourth goal, I have worked to make the book user-friendly. Written in a direct, conversational voice, the book replicates as much as possible a dialogue between author and student. The text is meant to be understood and mastered on its own. To that end, it includes a variety of pedagogical features. Each chapter contains a "Looking Ahead" overview that sets the stage for the chapter, a running glossary, a numbered summary, and a list of key terms and concepts. In addition each chapter has three "Review and Rethink" sections, which enumerate the key concepts and provide questions that promote and test critical thinking.

The Philosophy Behind *Child Development.* This text blends and integrates theory, research, and applications. It is *not* an applied development book, focused solely on techniques for translating the knowledge base of development into answers to societal problems. Nor does it concentrate primarily on the field's abstract theories. Instead, the focus of the text is on the scope and breadth of human development during childhood and adolescence. This focus permits the text to examine both the traditional core areas of the field, as well as evolving, nontraditional areas of development.

Furthermore, the book focuses on the here-and-now, rather than attempting to provide a detailed historical record of the field. Although it draws on the past where appropriate, it does so with a view toward delineating the field as it now stands and the directions toward which it is evolving. Similarly, although it describes classic studies, its emphasis is more on current research findings and trends.

Overall, then, the book seeks to provide a broad overview of child and adolescent development, integrating the theory, research, and applications of the discipline. It is meant to be a book that readers will want to keep in their personal libraries, one that they will take off the shelf when considering problems related to that most intriguing of questions: How do people get to be the way they are?

SPECIFIC FEATURES

CHAPTER-OPENING PROLOGUES

Each chapter begins with a short vignette, describing an individual or situation that is relevant to the basic developmental issues being addressed in the chapter. For instance, the chapter on birth describes several actual births, and one of the chapters on adolescence provides an account of Cedric Jennings' life as a student in an inner-city school.

PROLOGUE

A HIDDEN TIME BOMB

Michael Parseghian, 8, is brandishing a Power Rangers pistol as his sisters Marcia, 6, and Christa, 4, bounce on overstuffed leather couches, giggling helplessly. Watching the children romp around the sun-splashed living room of their Mediterranean-style house in the foothills of Arizona's Santa Catalina Mountains near Tucson, their maternal grandmother, Vickey Buesher, can't help smiling. But her eyes betray her sadness. "I've seen Michael deteriorate so much since I was here at Christmas," she says once the kids are out of earshot.

The kids, three of the four children of Michael and Cindy Parseghian, have a rare, incurable neurological condition that leads inexorably to paralysis and dementia. Children afflicted with the disease—called Niemann-Pick Type C—usually die in adolescence. Michael, a Cub Scout who takes karate and horseback-riding lessons, is the most seriously affected so far. His symptoms include vertical gaze palsy, which means that he can't easily raise his eyes. He has difficulty keeping his balance, and his speech is slurred. Marcia, whose passion is gymnastics, is just beginning to lose her coordination. Little Christa is so far symptom-free.

"The diagnosis is there; we can't do anything about that," says the children's paternal

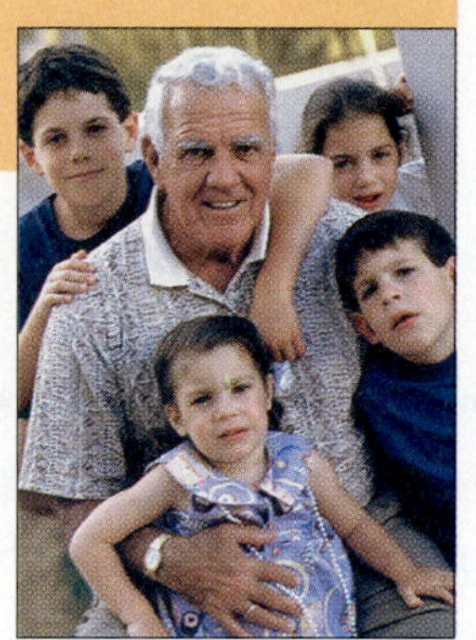

Several grandchildren of Ara Parseghian, former Notre Dame football coach, suffer from a rare genetic disease.

"LOOKING AHEAD"

These opening sections orient readers to the topics to be covered, linking the opening prologue to the remainder of the chapter and providing questions that draw students into the chapter content.

LOOKING AHEAD

Sadly, Parseghian was unable to reach his goal of finding a cure for the disease, and several years after the scene described above, Michael died. He was the victim of a hidden gene that had been present in his body from the moment of conception. Like a time bomb, this inherited gene activated a still little-understood process that ultimately led to his death at the age of 10.

The disease that haunts the Parseghian family is just one of a number that are produced by specific genetic problems, inherited from one (or both) of an individual's parents. Yet the same genetic processes that in some cases lead to deadly disease also permit our minds and bodies to function so effectively for the vast majority of our lives.

In this chapter, we'll examine what researchers in child development and other scientists have learned about ways that heredity and the environment work in tandem to shape human behavior. We begin with the basics of heredity, examining how we receive our genetic endowment. We'll consider a burgeoning area of study, behavioral genetics, that specializes in the consequences of heredity on behavior. We'll also discuss what happens when genetic factors cause development to go awry, such as with the Parseghian family, and how such problems are dealt with through genetic counseling.

Next, we'll turn to a discussion of the interaction of heredity and environment. We'll consider the relative influence of genes and environment on a variety of characteristics, including physical traits, intelligence, and even personality.

"DIRECTIONS IN DEVELOPMENT"

Each chapter includes a box that describes current developmental research or research issues, applied to everyday problems. These sections include discussions of ways of dealing with violence, training parents, and understanding the causes of eating disorders.

Directions in Development

Genetic Counseling: Predicting the Future from the Genes of the Present

The last thing Joey Paulowsky needs is another bout with cancer. Only 7 years old, the Dallas native has already fought off leukemia, and now his family worries that Joey could be hit again. The Paulowsky family carries a genetic burden—a rare form of inherited cancer of the thyroid. Deborah, Joey's mother, found a lump in her neck 6 years ago, and since then 1 family member has died of the cancer and 10 others have had to have their thyroids removed. "Do I have cancer?" Joey asks his mother. "Will it hurt?" The Paulowskys will know the answer next month, when the results of a genetic test will show whether their son carries the family's fateful mutation. (Brownlee, Cook, & Hardigg, 1994, p. 59)

The answer will be delivered by a member of a field that, just a few decades ago, was nonexistent: genetic counseling. **Genetic counseling** focuses on helping people deal with issues relating to inherited disorders.

"DEVELOPMENTAL DIVERSITY"

These sections highlight issues relevant to our multicultural society. Examples of these sections are discussions of cross-cultural differences in relationships, developing racial and ethnic awareness in childhood, adolescent race segregation, and racial differences in IQ and *The Bell Curve* controversy.

Developmental Diversity

Cultural Differences in Physical Arousal: Might a Culture's Philosophical Outlook Be Determined by Genetics?

The Buddhist philosophy, an inherent part of many Asian cultures, emphasizes harmony and peacefulness and suggests that one should seek the eradication of human desire. In contrast, some of the traditional philosophies of Western civilization, such as those of Mar-

"INFORMED CONSUMER OF DEVELOPMENT"

Every chapter includes information on specific uses that can be derived from research conducted by developmental investigators. For instance, the text provides concrete information on optimizing the prenatal environment, assessing language development, choosing a day-care provider, creating an atmosphere that promotes school success, dealing with drug and alcohol abuse, and deterring adolescent suicide.

The Informed Consumer of Development

Optimizing the Prenatal Environment

If you are contemplating ever having a child, by this point in the chapter you may be overwhelmed by the number of things that can go wrong. Don't be. Although the environment and genetics pose their share of risks, in the vast majority of cases, pregnancy and birth proceed without mishap. Moreover, there are several things that women can do—both before and during pregnancy—to optimize the probability that pregnancy will progress smoothly. Among them:

- For women who are planning to become pregnant, several precautions are in order. First, women should have nonemergency X-rays only during the first 2 weeks after

"SPEAKING OF DEVELOPMENT"

Each chapter includes an interview with a person working in a field that uses the findings of child and adolescent development. Among those interviewed are a toy designer, the chief of the marriage and family statistics branch of the U.S. Census Bureau, and a former U.S. secretary of education.

Speaking of Development

Lopa Malkan Wani, Genetic Counselor

Born: 1965

Education: Cornell University, B.A. in biology, with a concentration in genetics; Sarah Lawrence, M.S. in genetic counseling

Position: Genetic counselor for Genetrix, Inc.

Home: Newark, California

The field of genetics has not only advanced significantly our understanding of the way we are put together but also spawned a new occupation: genetic counselor. Genetic counselors help people deal with the potential consequences of the genes they carry.

Lopa Wani works in two major areas of the field. "The role of the genetic counselor is a dual one," she explains. "We are concerned with prenatal genetics and pediatric genetics, which deal with different issues.

"REVIEW AND RETHINK"

Interspersed throughout each chapter are three short recaps of the chapter's main points, followed by questions designed to provoke critical thinking.

Review and Rethink

REVIEW

- In humans, the male sex cell (the sperm) and the female sex cell (the ovum) provide the developing baby with 23 chromosomes each, through which the baby inherits characteristics from both mother and father.
- A genotype is the underlying combination of genetic material present in an organism, but invisible; a phenotype is the visible trait, the expression of the genotype. Within a range predetermined by the genotype, environmental factors play a significant role in determining the way in which that genotype will be expressed as a phenotype.
- The field of behavioral genetics, a combination of psychology and genetics, studies the effects of genetics on behavior.

Down syndrome *a disorder produced by the presence of an extra chromosome on the 21st pair; once referred to as mongolism*

sickle cell anemia *a blood disorder that gets its name from the shape of the red blood cells in those who have it*

Tay-Sachs disease *a disorder for which there is no treatment and which produces blindness and muscle degeneration prior to death*

Klinefelter's syndrome *a disorder resulting from the presence of an extra X chromosome that produces underdeveloped genitals, extreme height, and enlarged breasts*

RUNNING GLOSSARY

Key terms are defined in the margins of the page on which the term is presented.

What is our basic genetic endowment, and how do we receive it from our parents?

1. In humans, the adult female and male sex cells, or gametes, contain 23 chromosomes each. At fertilization, ovum and sperm unite to form a single new cell, called a zygote, in the female's uterus. The zygote receives a total of 46 chromosomes from its parents. Within the 46 chromosomes is the genetic blueprint—carried in some 100,000 genes—that will guide cell activity for the rest of the individual's life.
2. Gregor Mendel discovered an important genetic mechanism. In alleles, where genes for two competing traits are present but only one can be expressed, the offspring may receive either similar or dissimilar genes from each parent. If the offspring receives dissimilar genes (one dominant and one recessive), the dominant gene will be expressed. If the offspring receives similar genes (two dominant or two recessive genes), that gene will be expressed. Traits such as hair and eye color and the presence of phenylketonuria (PKU) are alleles and follow this pattern, but relatively few inherited traits are governed by a single pair of genes in this way.

END-OF-CHAPTER MATERIAL

Each chapter ends with a numbered summary and a list of key terms and concepts. This material is designed to help students study and retain the information in the chapter.

ANCILLARIES

Child Development is accompanied by a superb set of ancillary teaching materials. They include the following:

Instructor Supplements

Instructor's Resource Manual, by Gayla Preisser and Susy Horton of Mesa Community College. This thorough Manual contains a wealth of useful and practical teaching ideas. Contents for each chapter include the following: a one-page chapter organizer; detailed lecture outlines; additional Lecture and Discussion Topics; suggested Classroom Demonstrations and Student Activities; and a complete listing of Prentice Hall and other video resources.

Teaching Transparencies for Human Development. A full set of color transparencies add visual impact to the study of child development. Designed in large format for use in lecture hall settings, many of these high quality images are not found in the text.

Test Item File, by Vincent Punzo of Earlham College. Contains an average of 115 questions per chapter, including multiple choice, short answer and essay questions.

Prentice Hall Custom Tests for Windows, Macintosh, and DOS. A computerized version of the Test Item File, Prentice Hall's exclusive testing software supports a full range of editing and graphics options, network test administration capabilities, and greater ease-of-use than ever before. It offers a two-track design for constructing tests: Easytest for novice users and Fulltest for more advanced users. The Custom Testing also offers features such as On-Line Testing and Electronic Gradebook.

"800-Number" Telephone Test Preparation Service. A toll-free test preparation service is also available. Instructors may call an 800-number and select up to 200 questions from the Test Item File available with the text. Prentice Hall will format the test and provide an alternate version (if requested) and answer key(s), then mail it back within 48 hours, ready for duplication.

Videotape Support Materials

Speaking of Development Videos. This exclusive videotape program features interviews with several of the professionals highlighted within this text. Each segment visits the individual's workplace, and discusses their background in development issues and how it relates to their current job. The video may also provide students with some background information about future job opportunities.

ABC News/Prentice Hall Video Libraries
ABCNEWS
Lifespan Development, 1996
Child Development in Action, 1995
Human Development, 1993
Three video libraries consisting of feature segments from award-winning programs such as *Nightline, 20/20, PrimeTime Live,* and *The Health Show* are available to qualified adopters of ***Child Development.***

Student Supplements

Study Guide, by Kim Dolgin of Ohio Wesleyan University. The Study Guide is designed with an attractive visual format that incorporates line drawings and illustrations from the textbook. Each chapter includes unique features such as: an outline; thought-provoking chapter-opening questions; learning objectives; detailed guided reviews; cross-word puzzles; flash cards to reinforce concepts; and two practice multiple-choice tests with explanations of correct answers.

The New York Times

The New York Times* Supplement for Human Development.** When you adopt ***Child Development, Prentice Hall and the New York Times will provide you with a complimentary student newspaper in quantities for your class. This collection of articles is designed to supplement classroom lectures and improve student access to current real-world issues and research.

Website

In keeping with recent advances in technology, Prentice Hall has established a website for psychology. Please visit this site at: *http://www.prenhall.com/psychmap*

ACKNOWLEDGMENTS

I am grateful to the following reviewers who provided a wealth of comments, criticism, and encouragement: Dean Schroeder, Laramie County Community College; Prof. Lori Beasley, University of Central Oklahoma; Patricia Jarvis, Ph.D., Illinois State University; Professor Kevin Keating, Broward Community College; Dr. Judith Levine, State University of New York, Farmingdale; Dr. Robert Schultz, Fulton-Montgomery Community College; Dr. Marc Alcorn, University of Northern Colorado; and Prof. Joann Nelson, South Illinois University.

Many others deserve a great deal of thanks. I am indebted to the many people who provided me with a superb education, first at Wesleyan University and later at the University of Wisconsin. Specifically, Karl Scheibe, professor of psychology at Wesleyan University, played a pivotal role in my undergraduate education. The late Vernon Allen, my major professor at the University of Wisconsin, acted as mentor and guide through my graduate years. It was in graduate school that I learned about development, being exposed to such experts as Ross Parke, John Balling, Joel Levin, Herb Klausmeier, Frank Hooper, and many others.

My education continued when I became a professor. I am especially grateful to my colleagues at the University of Massachusetts, who make the university such a wonderful place in which to teach and do research.

Several people played central roles in the development of this book. Edward Murphy brought a keen intelligence and editorial eye to the process, and the book has been greatly strengthened by his considerable input. Lucy Rinehart and Erik Coats provided research assistance, and I am thankful for their help. Most of all, John Graiff was essential in juggling and coordinating the many aspects of producing a book, and I am very grateful for the substantial role he played.

I am also grateful to the superb Prentice Hall team that was instrumental in the inception and development of this book. Bill Webber and Nancy Roberts oversaw the project, always providing their wisdom, and creativity, and were ably assisted by Anita Castro, Tamsen Adams, and Emsal Hasan. Phil Miller stood behind the project, and I am grateful for his continuing support. Barbara Muller and Linda Youngman, development editors, and Bob Weiss, head of development for psychology, provided expertise and uncommon guidance. On the production end of things, Mary Rottino, the assistant managing editor, and Eloise Marion Donnelly, photo editor, helped in giving the book its distinctive look. Finally, I'd like to thank Mike Alread, the marketing manager, and his assistant, Aileen Ugural, whose skills I'm counting on.

I also wish to acknowledge the members of my family, who play such a pivotal role in my life. My brother, Michael, my sisters-in-law and brothers-in-law, my nieces and nephews, all make up an important part of my life. In addition, I am always indebted to the older generation of my family, who led the way in a manner I can only hope to emulate. I will always be obligated to Ethel Radler, Harry Brochstein, and the late Mary Vorwerk. Most of all, the list is headed by my father, the late Saul Feldman, and my mother, Leah Brochstein.

In the end, it is my immediate family who deserve the greatest thanks. My three terrific kids, Jonathan, Joshua, and Sarah, are my pride and joy. And ultimately my wife, Katherine Vorwerk, provides the love and grounding that makes everything worthwhile. I thank them, with all my love.

Robert S. Feldman
University of Massachusetts at Amherst

About the Author

Robert S. Feldman is professor of psychology at the University of Massachusetts in Amherst, where he is Director of Undergraduate Studies. He was educated as an undergraduate at Wesleyan University, graduating with high honors, and received an M.S. and Ph.D. from the University of Wisconsin in Madison, where he specialized in social and developmental psychology.

Among his more than 100 books, chapters, articles, and presentations, he has written *Development Across the Life Span* (Prentice Hall), edited *Development of Nonverbal Behavior in Children* (Springer-Verlag) and *Applications of Nonverbal Behavioral Theory and Research* (Erlbaum), and co-edited *Fundamentals of Nonverbal Behavior* (Cambridge University Press). He is the recipient of grants from the National Institute of Mental Health and the National Institute on Disability and Rehabilitation Research, which have supported his research on the development of nonverbal behavior in children. A past Fulbright lecturer and research scholar, he is a Fellow of the American Psychological Association and the American Psychological Society.

During the course of nearly two decades as a college instructor, he has taught both undergraduate and graduate courses at Mount Holyoke College, Wesleyan University, and Virginia Commonwealth University, in addition to the University of Massachusetts.

Professor Feldman is an avid, if not particularly accomplished, pianist and an excellent cook, despite his children's aversion to his experimentation with exotic cuisines. He lives with his three children and wife, a psychologist, in Amherst, Massachusetts, in a home overlooking the Holyoke mountain range.

Child Development

PART 1
Beginnings

n
waaa
N
g
S

CHAPTER 1

BEGINNINGS

An Introduction to Child Development

PROLOGUE
THE BRAVE NEW WORLDS OF CHILDHOOD

A few years ago, when Elizabeth Carr's class was learning how an egg combines with sperm in the mother's body to create a child, she felt compelled to interrupt.

"I piped up to say that not all babies are conceived like that and explained about sperm and eggs and petri dishes," said Elizabeth, now 14, the first child in the United States born through in vitro fertilization.

Because her mother's landmark pregnancy was documented in great detail by a film crew, Elizabeth has seen pictures of the egg and sperm that united to become her, the petri dish where she was conceived, the embryonic blob of cells that grew into the bubbly young woman who now plays field hockey and sings in the school chorus. . . .

Elizabeth, now an eighth grader in the Overlook Middle School in Westminster, Massachusetts, said that her parents—whose egg and sperm joined in a petri dish at the Jones Institute for Reproductive Medicine in Norfolk, Virginia—have always made it clear that she was created differently from other children. Although she said she had faced taunts of "test tube baby" or "weirdo" a few times at school, she said she had never felt resentful about her conception.

"I'm so grateful that they went through all this to have me. . . . Now I'm just a normal eighth grader trying to keep my room clean." (Rosenthal, 1995, A1, B8)

Elizabeth Carr, the first child in the United States born through in vitro fertilization.

LOOKING AHEAD

Welcome to the brave new world of childhood—or rather, just one of the brave new worlds. Issues ranging from so-called test-tube babies to the consequences of poverty on children to the prevention of AIDS raise significant concerns. Underlying these are even more fundamental issues: How do children develop physically? How does their understanding of the world grow and change over time? And how do their personalities and their social worlds develop as they move from birth through adolescence?

All of these questions, and the many others we'll encounter throughout this book, are central to the field of child development, and they underlie the lives of every human. Consider, for example, the range of approaches that different specialists in child development might take when considering the story of Elizabeth Carr:

- Child development researchers who investigate behavior at the level of biological processes might determine if Elizabeth's prenatal functioning was affected by her conception outside the womb.
- Specialists in child development who study genetics might examine how the biological endowment from Elizabeth's parents affects her later behavior.
- Child development experts who investigate the ways thinking changes over the course of childhood might examine Elizabeth's life in terms of how her understanding of the nature of her conception changed as she grew older.
- Other researchers in child development, who focus on physical growth, might consider whether her growth rate differed from children conceived more traditionally.
- Child development experts who specialize in the social world of children might look at the ways that Elizabeth interacted with other children and the kinds of friendships she developed.

Although their interests take many forms, all these specialists in child development share one concern: understanding the growth and change that occur during the course of childhood and adolescence. Taking many differing approaches, developmentalists study how both our biological inheritance from our parents and the environment in which we live jointly affect our behavior.

Some researchers in child development focus on explaining how our genetic background can determine not only how we look but also how we behave, how we relate to others, even our very personality. These professionals explore ways to identify how much of our potential as human beings is provided—or limited—by heredity. Other child development specialists look to the environment, exploring ways in which our lives are shaped by the world that we encounter. They investigate the extent to which we are molded by our early environments, and how our current circumstances influence our behavior in both subtle and evident ways.

Whether they focus on heredity or environment, all developmental specialists acknowledge that neither heredity nor environment alone can account for the full range of human development and change. Instead, our understanding of children and adolescents requires that we look at the joint effects of the interaction of heredity and environment, attempting to grasp how both, in the end, underlie human behavior.

In this chapter, we orient ourselves to the field of child development. We begin with a discussion of the scope of the discipline, illustrating the wide array of topics it covers and the full range of ages it examines, from the moment of conception through the end of adolescence. We also survey the key issues and controversies of the field.

Next, we continue with a consideration of the broad perspectives that guide the field, from a focus on people's inner, unconscious lives and the interior operation of their minds, to people's outward, overt behavior. Finally, we discuss the ways that specialists in child development use research to ask and answer questions. We discuss several research strategies, as well as ethical guidelines for conducting research. In sum, after reading this chapter, you will be able to answer these questions:

- What is child development, and what aspects of human life does it study?
- What are some of the basic influences on child development?
- What are the key issues in the field of child development?
- Which theoretical perspectives have guided thinking and research in child development?
- What role do theories and hypotheses play in child development?
- How are research studies in child development conducted?

AN ORIENTATION TO CHILD DEVELOPMENT

Have you ever marveled at the way an infant tightly grips your finger with tiny, perfectly formed hands? Or at how a preschooler methodically draws a picture? Or at the way an adolescent can make involved decisions about whom to invite to a party?

If you've ever wondered about such things, you are asking the kinds of questions that specialists working in the field of child development pose. The field of **child development** involves the scientific study of the patterns of growth, change, and stability that occur from conception through adolescence.

Although the definition of the field seems straightforward, the simplicity is somewhat misleading. In order to understand what child development is actually about, we need to look underneath the various parts of the definition.

In its study of growth, change, and stability, child development takes a *scientific* approach. Like members of other scientific disciplines, researchers in child development test their assumptions about the nature and course of human development by applying scien-

child development *the field that involves the scientific study of the patterns of growth, change, and stability that occur from conception through adolescence* tific methods. As we'll see later in the chapter, they develop theories about development, and they use methodical, scientific techniques to validate the accuracy of their assumptions systematically.

Child development focuses on *humans.* Although there are developmentalists who study the course of development in nonhuman species, the vast majority examine growth and change in people. Some seek to understand universal principles of development, while others focus on how cultural, racial, and ethnic differences affect the course of development. Still others aim to understand the unique aspects of individuals, looking at the traits and characteristics that differentiate one person from another. Regardless of approach, however, all child developmentalists view development as a continuing process throughout childhood and adolescence.

As developmental specialists focus on the ways people change and grow during their lives, they also consider stability in children's and adolescents' lives. They ask in which areas, and in what periods, people show change and growth, and when and how their behavior reveals consistency and continuity with prior behavior.

Finally, although child development focuses on growth, change, and stability during childhood and adolescence, developmentalists assume that the process of development persists throughout *every* part of people's lives, beginning with the moment of conception and continuing until death. Developmental specialists assume that in some ways people continue to grow and change right up to the end of their lives, while in other respects their behavior remains stable. At the same time, developmentalists believe that no particular, single period of life governs all development. Instead, they believe that every period of life contains the potential for both growth and decline in abilities, and that individuals maintain the capacity for substantial growth and change throughout their lives.

Characterizing Child Development: The Scope of the Field

Clearly, the definition of child development is broad and the scope of the field is extensive. Consequently, professionals in child development cover several quite diverse areas, and a typical developmentalist specializes in two ways: topical area and age range.

Topical Areas in Child Development. Some developmentalists focus on **physical development,** examining the ways in which the body's makeup—the brain, nervous system, muscles, and senses, and the need for food, drink, and sleep—helps determine behavior. For example, one specialist in physical development might examine the effects of malnutrition on the pace of growth in children, while another might look at how sexual maturation proceeds during adolescence.

Other developmental specialists examine **cognitive development,** seeking to understand how growth and change in intellectual capabilities influence a person's behavior. Cognitive developmentalists examine learning, memory, problem-solving, and intelligence. For example, specialists in cognitive development might want to see how intellectual abilities change over the course of childhood, or if cultural differences exist in the factors to which children attribute their academic successes and failures.

Finally, some developmental specialists focus on personality and social development. **Personality development** is the study of stability and change in the enduring characteristics that differentiate one person from another. **Social development** is the way in which individuals' interactions with others and their social relationships grow, change, and remain stable over the course of life. A developmentalist interested in personality development might ask whether there are stable, enduring personality traits throughout the life span, while a specialist in social development might examine dating patterns during adolescence. Personality and social developmentalists also focus on emotional development throughout childhood and adolescence. (The major approaches are summarized in Table 1-1.)

physical development *development involving the body's physical makeup, including the brain, nervous system, muscles, and senses, and the need for food, drink, and sleep*

cognitive development *development involving the ways that growth and change in intellectual capabilities influence a person's behavior*

personality development *development involving the ways that the enduring characteristics that differentiate one person from another remain stable or change over the life span*

social development *the way in which individuals' interactions with others and their social relationships grow, change, and remain stable over the course of life*

TABLE 1-1

TOPICAL AREAS IN CHILD DEVELOPMENT

Orientation	Defining Characteristics	Examples of Questions Asked*
Physical Development	Examines how brain, nervous system, muscles, sensory capabilities, and needs for food, drink, and sleep affect behavior	What determines the sex of a child? (2) What are the long-term results of premature birth? (3) What are the benefits of breastfeeding? (4) What are the consequences of child abuse? (7) What are the consequences of early or late sexual maturation? (13)
Cognitive Development	Examines intellectual abilities, including learning, memory, problem solving, and intelligence	What are the earliest memories that can be recalled from infancy? (5) What are the consequences of watching television? (8) Do spatial reasoning skills relate to music practice? (8) Are there benefits to bilingualism? (11) Are there ethnic and racial differences in intelligence? (11) How does an adolescent's egocentrism affect his/her view of the world? (14)
Personality and Social Development	Examines enduring characteristics that differentiate one person from another, and how interactions with others and social relationships grow and change over the lifetime	Do newborns respond differently to their mothers than to others? (3) What is the best procedure for disciplining children? (9) When does a child develop a sense of gender? (9) How can we promote cross-race friendships? (12) What are the causes of adolescent suicide? (15)

*Numbers in parentheses indicate in which chapter the question is addressed.

Age Ranges and Individual Differences. As they specialize in chosen topical areas, child developmentalists typically focus their study on particular age ranges. They usually divide childhood and adolescence into broad age ranges: the prenatal period (the period from conception to birth); infancy and toddlerhood (birth to age 3); the preschool period (ages 3 to 6); middle childhood (ages 6 to 12); and adolescence (ages 12 to 20).

Although most child developmentalists accept and employ these periods (and they are used to demarcate the major parts of this book), the age ranges themselves are in many ways arbitrary. Although some periods have one clear-cut boundary (infancy begins with birth, and the preschool period ends with entry into public school), others don't.

For instance, consider the separation between middle childhood and adolescence, which usually occurs around the age of 12. Because the boundary is based on a biological change—the onset of sexual maturation—which varies greatly from one individual to another, the specific age of entry into adolescence varies from one person to the next.

In short, there are substantial individual differences in the timing of events in people's lives. In part, this is a biological fact of life: People mature at different rates and reach developmental milestones at different points. However, environmental factors also play a significant role in determining the age at which a particular event is likely to occur. For example, the typical age at which people become romantically involved with members of the opposite sex varies substantially from one culture to another, depending in part on the way that male-female relationships are viewed in a given culture.

It is important to keep in mind, then, that when developmental specialists discuss age ranges, they are talking about averages—the times when people, on average, reach particular milestones. Some children will reach the milestone earlier, some later, and many—in fact, most—will reach it just around the time of the average. Such variation becomes noteworthy only when children show substantial deviation from the average.

Furthermore, as children grow older, they become more likely to deviate from the average and exhibit individual differences. In very young children a good part of developmental change is genetically determined and unfolds automatically, making development fairly similar across different children. But as children age, environmental factors become more potent, leading to greater variability and individual differences as time passes.

Developmentalists work in such diverse settings as this laboratory preschool on a college campus and in human service agencies.

The Links between Topics and Ages. Each of the broad topical areas of child development—physical, cognitive, and social and personality development—plays a role throughout childhood and adolescence. Consequently, some developmental experts focus on physical development during the prenatal period, and others during adolescence. Some might specialize in social development during the preschool years, while others look at social relationships in middle childhood. And still others might take a broader approach, looking at cognitive development through every period of childhood and adolescence (and beyond).

The variety of topical areas and age ranges studied within the field of child development means that specialists from many diverse backgrounds and areas of expertise consider themselves developmentalists. Psychologists (who study behavior and mental processes), educational researchers, geneticists, and physicians constitute only some of the people who specialize and conduct research in child development. Furthermore, developmentalists work in a variety of settings, including university departments of psychology, education, human development, and medicine, as well as nonacademic settings as varied as human service agencies and child-care centers. These diverse specialists bring a variety of perspectives and intellectual richness to the field of child development.

THE CONTEXT OF DEVELOPMENT: TAKING A BROAD PERSPECTIVE

Considering the course of development in terms of physical, cognitive, and personality and social factors has advantages and disadvantages. It allows us to divide developmental influences into reasonably neat and compact packages. But there is a real drawback to such a categorization: In the real world, none of these broad influences occurs in isolation from any other. Instead, there is a constant, ongoing interaction between the different types of influence. For instance, what occurs on a cognitive level has repercussions for personality, social, and physical development, while what is happening on a physical level has an impact on cognitive, personality, and social development.

The Ecological Approach to Development. In acknowledging the problem with traditional approaches to child development, psychologist Urie Bronfenbrenner (1979, 1989) has proposed an alternative perspective, which he calls the ecological approach. The **ecological approach** suggests that there are four levels of the environment that simultaneously influence individuals. Bronfenbrenner suggests that we cannot fully understand development without considering how a person fits into each of these levels (illustrated in Figure 1-1).

The *microsystem* is the everyday, immediate environment in which children lead their daily lives. Homes, caregivers, friends, and teachers all are examples of the influences that are part of the microsystem.

The *mesosystem* provides connections between the various aspects of the microsystem. Like links in a chain, the mesosystem binds children to parents, students to teachers, employees to bosses, friends to friends. It acknowledges the direct and indirect influences that bind us to one another. Family members, day-care workers, and neighborhood play groups are all part of the mesosystem.

ecological approach *the perspective suggesting that different levels of the environment simultaneously influence individuals*

FIGURE 1-1

BRONFENBRENNER'S APPROACH TO DEVELOPMENT

Urie Bronfenbrenner's ecological approach to development offers four levels of the environment that simultaneously influence individuals: the macrosystem, exosystem, mesosystem, and microsystem.

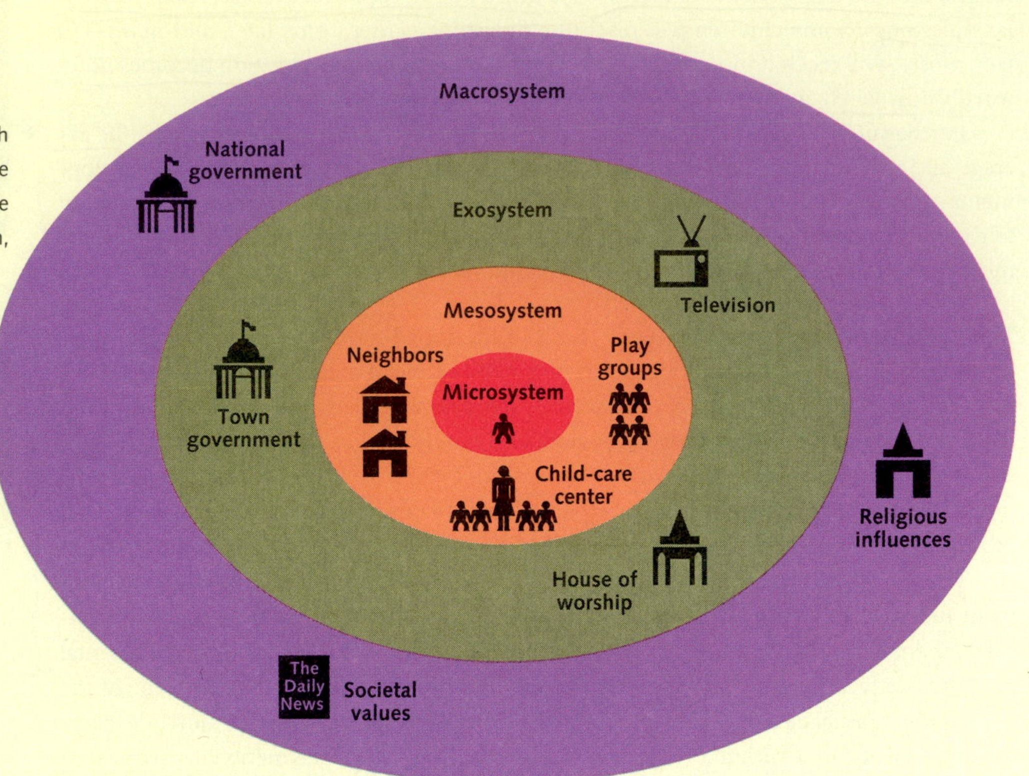

The *exosystem* represents broader influences, encompassing societal institutions such as local government, the community, schools, places of worship, and the local media. Each of these larger institutions of society can have an immediate, and major, impact on personal development, and each affects how the microsystem and mesosystem operate. For example, as we discuss in Chapter 8, the average child in the United States typically spends more time watching television than performing any other activity except sleeping for the first 18 years of life (Liebert & Sprafkin, 1988).

Finally, the *macrosystem* represents the larger cultural influences on an individual. Society in general, types of governments, religious systems, political thought, and other broad, encompassing factors are parts of the macrosystem.

There are several advantages to taking an ecological approach to development. For one thing, the ecological approach emphasizes the interconnectedness of the influences on development. Because the various levels are related to one another, a change in one part of the system has an impact on other parts of the system. For instance, a parent's loss of a job (involving the mesosystem) has an impact upon a child's microsystem.

Conversely, changes on one environmental level may make little difference if other levels are not also changed. For instance, improving the school environment may have a negligible effect on academic performance if children receive little support for academic success in their home environments.

The ecological approach also illustrates that the influences among different family members are multidirectional. As we'll consider in Chapter 6, the relationship between parent and child reflects not just the parent's behavior, but also what the child does to elicit responsiveness from the parent. For instance, infants who respond positively to parents

Governmental bodies such as this state assembly, illustrate the exosystem: societal institutions that influence personal development.

bring about more positive behaviors on the part of the parents, which in turn spark more positive responses from the infants (Cohn & Tronick, 1989; Nwokah & Fogel, 1993).

Finally, the ecological approach stresses the importance of broad cultural factors that affect development. Researchers in child development increasingly look at how membership in cultural and subcultural groups influences behavior. For instance, it is clear that, in general, Western cultures tend to be *individualistic,* emphasizing personal identity, uniqueness, freedom, and the worth of the individual. In contrast, Asian cultures are largely *collectivistic,* promoting the idea that the group or society is more important than the individual. As we'll see in Chapter 15, such broad cultural values play an important role in shaping the ways people view the world and behave (Kim et al., 1994).

Cohort and Normative Influences on Development: Developing with Others in a Social World. Bob, born in 1947, is a baby boomer; he was born soon after the end of World War II, when an enormous bulge in the birthrate occurred as soldiers returned to the United States from overseas. His adolescence was passed at the height of the Civil Rights movement and the beginning of protests against the Vietnam War. His mother, Leah, was born in 1922; she is part of the generation that passed its childhood and teenage years in the shadow of the depression. Bob's son, Jon, was born in 1975. Now in college, he is a member of what has been called Generation X.

These people are in part products of the social times in which they live. Each belongs to a particular **cohort,** a group of people born at around the same time in the same place. Such major social events as wars, economic upturns and depressions, famines, and epidemics (like the one due to the AIDS virus) work similar influences on members of a particular cohort.

Cohort effects provide an example of **normative history-graded influences,** which are biological and environmental influences associated with a particular historical moment (P. B. Baltes, 1987; P. B. Baltes, Reese, & Lipsitt, 1980). For instance, people who lived in Oklahoma City, Oklahoma, in 1995 shared both biological and environmental challenges due to the terrorist bombing of the federal building in that city.

Normative history-graded influences contrast with **normative age-graded influences,** biological and environmental influences that are similar for individuals in a particular age group, regardless of when or where they are raised. For example, biological events such as puberty and menopause are universal events that occur at relatively the same time throughout all societies. Similarly, a sociocultural event such as entry into formal education can be considered a normative age-graded influence because it occurs in most cultures around age six.

cohort *a group of people born at around the same time in the same place*

normative history-graded influences *biological and environmental influences associated with a particular historical moment*

normative age-graded influences *biological and environmental influences that are similar for individuals in a particular age group, regardless of when or where they are raised*

Development is also affected by normative sociocultural-graded influences. **Normative sociocultural-graded influences** represent the impact of social and cultural factors present at a particular time for a particular individual, depending on such variables as race, ethnicity, social class, and subcultural membership. For example, sociocultural-graded influences will be considerably different for children who are white and affluent than for children who are members of a minority group and living in poverty.

Finally, nonnormative life events also influence development. **Nonnormative life events** are specific, atypical events that occur in a particular person's life at a time when such events do not happen to most people. For instance, experiencing at an early age the death of both parents, being involved in a serious auto accident, coming down with a deadly disease, or having a physical disability are all nonnormative life events.

KEY ISSUES AND QUESTIONS: DETERMINING THE NATURE—AND NURTURE—OF CHILD DEVELOPMENT

As sciences go, child development is one of the new kids on the block. Although its roots can be traced back to the ancient Egyptians and Greeks, it didn't become established as a separate field until the late nineteenth and early twentieth centuries.

From the time of its establishment, several key issues and questions have dominated the field. Among the major issues (summarized in Table 1-2) are the nature of developmental change, the importance of critical periods, life-span approaches versus more focused approaches, and the nature-nurture issue (Kagan, 1994; R. Parke et al., 1994).

Continuous Change versus Discontinuous Change. One of the primary issues challenging child developmentalists is whether development proceeds in a continuous or discontinuous fashion (illustrated in Figure 1-2). In **continuous change,** development is gradual, with achievements at one level building on those of previous levels. Continuous change is quantitative in nature; the basic underlying developmental processes that drive change remain the same over the course of the life span. Continuous change, then, produces changes that are a matter of degree, but not kind.

In contrast, **discontinuous change** occurs in distinct steps or stages. Each stage brings about behavior that is assumed to be qualitatively different from behavior at earlier stages.

As we'll see throughout future chapters, proponents of continuous change have offered alternatives to theories of development that assume that change is discontinuous, and the predominant view today is that most developmental growth is continuous. Still, both approaches have their merits, and developmental experts in both branches of the debate continue to press their cases. In fact, some have argued that taking an either-or position on the issue is inappropriate. In their view, some types of developmental change may be continuous, while others are discontinuous. The debate, then, goes on (Flavell, 1994; Rutter, 1987).

Critical Periods: Gauging the Impact of Environmental Events. If a woman comes down with a case of rubella (German measles) in the eleventh week of pregnancy, the consequences for the child she is carrying are likely to be devastating: They include the potential for blindness, deafness, and heart defects. However, if she comes down with the exact same strain of rubella in the thirtieth week of pregnancy, damage to the child is unlikely.

The differing outcomes of the disease in the two periods demonstrate the concept of critical periods. A **critical period** is a specific time during development when a particular event has its greatest consequences. Critical periods occur when the presence of certain kinds of environmental stimuli are necessary for development to proceed normally.

Although early specialists in child development placed great emphasis on the importance of critical periods, more recent thinking suggests that in many realms individuals may be more malleable than was first thought, particularly in the domain of personality and social development.

normative sociocultural-graded influences *the impact of social and cultural factors present at a particular time for a particular individual, depending on such variables as race, ethnicity, social class, and subcultural membership*

nonnormative life events *specific, atypical events that occur in a particular person's life at a time when such events do not happen to most people*

continuous change *gradual development in which achievements at one level build on those of previous levels*

discontinuous change *development that occurs in distinct steps or stages, with each stage bringing about behavior that is assumed to be qualitatively different from behavior at earlier stages*

critical period *a specific time during development when a particular event has its greatest consequences*

TABLE 1-2

MAJOR ISSUES IN CHILD DEVELOPMENT

Issue	Explanation
Continuous change vs. discontinuous change	In continuous change, development is gradual; the achievements at one level build on the previous ones. The underlying developmental processes driving the change remain the same over the course of the life span. In contrast, discontinuous change occurs in distinct steps or stages, with each stage bringing about behavior that is assumed to be qualitatively different from that seen at earlier stages.
Critical periods	A critical period is a particular time during development in which a particular event has its greatest consequences. Although early developmentalists placed great emphasis on the importance of critical periods, more recent thinking suggests that in many realms individuals may be more malleable than was first thought, particularly in the area of personality and social development.
Life-span approaches vs. focus on particular periods	Earlier developmentalists focused attention primarily on the infancy and adolescence periods. Current thinking considers the entire period of childhood and adolescence as important for a number of reasons, including the discovery that developmental growth and change continues throughout every part of life.
Nature vs. nurture	Nature refers to traits, abilities, and capabilities that are inherited from one's parents. It encompasses any factor that is produced by the predetermined unfolding of genetic information. Nurture involves the environmental influences that shape behavior. Some may be biological, whereas others are more social in nature. Some influences are a result of larger societal-level factors, such as the socioeconomic opportunities available to members of minority groups.

For instance, rather than permanent damage being caused by a lack of certain kinds of early social experiences, there is increasing evidence that later experiences can overcome earlier deficits. Consequently, more recent formulations speak of **sensitive periods,** rather than critical periods. In a sensitive period, organisms are particularly susceptible to certain kinds of stimuli in their environments. Unlike a critical period, however, the absence of those stimuli does not always produce irreversible consequences (Bornstein, 1989a).

sensitive period *a specific time when organisms are particularly susceptible to certain kinds of stimuli in their environments*

Life-span Approaches versus a Focus on Particular Periods. On what part of the life span should child development focus its attention? For early developmentalists, the answers tended to be "infancy" and "adolescence." Most attention was clearly concentrated on those two periods, largely to the exclusion of other parts of childhood.

FIGURE 1-2

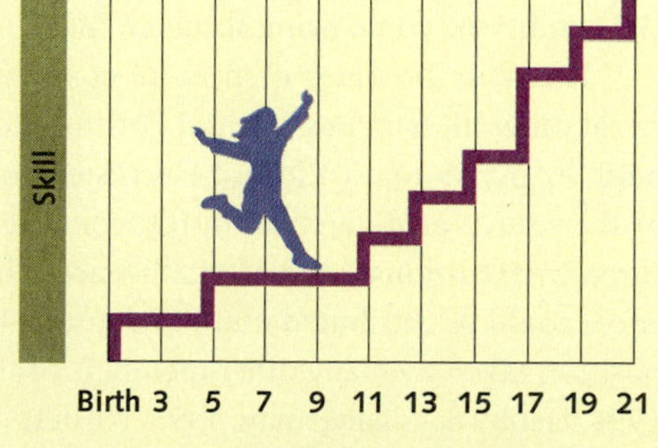

TWO APPROACHES TO DEVELOPMENTAL CHANGE

The two approaches to development are continuous change, which is gradual with achievements at one level building on those of previous levels, and discontinuous change, which occurs in distinct steps or stages.

Today, however, the story is different. The entire period encompassing conception through adolescence is now seen to be important, for several reasons. One is the discovery that developmental growth and change continue during every part of life—as we'll discuss throughout this book.

maturation *the process of the predetermined unfolding of genetic information*

Furthermore, it is clear that to understand fully the social influences on people of a given age, we need to understand the people who are in large measure providing those influences. For instance, to understand development in infants, we need to unravel the effects of their parents' ages on their social environments. It is likely that a 15-year-old mother will present parental influences of a very different sort from those presented by a 37-year-old mother. Consequently, infant development is in part a consequence of the development that the adults in the infant's environment are undergoing (Parke, 1989).

The Nature-Nurture Issue. One of the enduring questions of child development involves how much of people's behavior is due to their genetically determined nature and how much is due to nurture, the physical and social environment in which a child is raised. Having deep philosophical and historical roots, the issue has dominated much work in child development.

In this context, *nature* refers to traits, abilities, and capacities that are inherited from one's parents. It encompasses any factor that is produced by the predetermined unfolding of genetic information—a process known as **maturation.** These genetic, inherited influences are at work as we move from the one-cell organism that is created at the moment of conception to the billions of cells that make up a fully formed human. Nature influences whether our eyes are blue or brown, whether we have thick hair throughout life or go bald, and how good we are at athletics. Nature allows our brains to develop in such a way that we can read the words on this page.

In contrast, *nurture* refers to the environmental influences that shape behavior. Some of these influences may be biological, such as the impact on the unborn child of a pregnant woman's use of cocaine or the amount and kind of food available to children. Other environmental influences are more social, such as the ways in which parents discipline their children and the effects of peer pressure on an adolescent. Finally, some influences are a result of larger, societal-level factors, such as the socioeconomic circumstances in which people find themselves.

If our traits and behavior were determined solely by either nature or nurture, there would probably be little debate regarding the issue. However, for most critical behaviors this is hardly the case. Take, for instance, one of the most controversial arenas: intelligence. As we'll consider in detail in Chapter 11, the question of whether intelligence is determined primarily by inherited, genetic factors—nature—or is shaped by environmental factors—nurture—has caused lively and often bitter arguments. Largely because of its social implications, the issue has spilled out of the scientific arena and into the realm of politics and social policy.

Consider the implications of the issue: If the extent of one's intelligence is primarily determined by heredity and consequently is largely fixed at birth, then efforts to improve intellectual performance later in life may be doomed to failure. In contrast, if intelligence is primarily a result of environmental factors, such as the amount and quality of schooling and stimulation to which one is exposed, then we would expect that an improvement in social conditions could bring about an increase in intelligence.

The issue becomes even more controversial when we try to determine the cause of racial differences in intelligence. For instance, the publication in 1994 of *The Bell Curve*, a book by psychologist Richard Herrnstein and sociologist Charles Murray, raised the issue of the source of differences in IQ scores between whites and African Americans, as measured by traditional tests of intelligence. The controversy concerned whether such differences could be attributed more to nature—the argument of the authors—or nurture—the position taken by many other members of the research community (Herrnstein & Murray, 1994; Jacoby & Glauberman, 1995; Nisbett, 1994; Sternberg & Grigorenko, 1996).

The ferocity of the debate, and the importance of its resolution, illustrates the significance of issues that involve the nature-nurture question. As we address it in relation to several topical areas throughout this book, we should keep in mind that developmentalists reject the notion that behavior is the result solely of either nature *or* nurture. Instead, the question is one of degree. Furthermore, the interaction of genetic and environmental factors is complex, in part because certain genetically determined traits have not only a direct influence on children's behavior but also an indirect influence in shaping children's *environments* as well. For example, a child who is consistently cranky and who cries a great deal—a trait that may be produced by genetic factors—may influence its environment by making its parents so highly responsive to its insistent crying that they rush to comfort it whenever it cries. Their responsivity to the child's genetically determined behavior consequently becomes an environmental influence on the infant's subsequent development.

In sum, the question of how much of a given behavior is due to nature, and how much to nurture, is a challenging one. Ultimately, we should consider the two sides of the nature-nurture issue as opposite ends of a continuum, with particular behaviors falling somewhere between the two ends. Moreover, an analogous statement can be made regarding the other controversies that we have considered. For instance, continuous versus discontinuous development is not an either-or proposition; some forms of development fall toward the continuous end of the continuum, while others lie closer to the discontinuous end. In short, few statements about development involve either-or absolutes.

In the same way, a particular topical area can be approached on several different levels, and from several different angles, simultaneously. We discuss an example in the "Directions in Development" section.

Directions in Development

Violence: Dealing with a Modern-day Plague through Child Development

Garland Hampton

> *When other children were hearing fairy tales, Garland Hampton heard bedtime stories about the day Uncle Robert killed two Milwaukee police officers, or the time Grandma, with both barrels, blew away the father of two of her children back in '62. By the time he was 9, he had seen his mother kill her boyfriend.*
>
> *Now, at 15, locked up in the County Jail and awaiting trial on murder charges, Garland is still enough of a child that he is afraid he might cry when darkness falls.*
>
> *But he is old enough to have had a nasty past of his own, too: at 10, there was trouble about stolen bicycles; at 12, he was picked up for shooting and wounding a gang rival; at 14, for carrying a .357 Magnum and a bag of cocaine; and now, gunning down a fellow gang member. Prosecutors say he is an adolescent menace to society, who must pay for his sins like a man.*
>
> *Garland just says he is scared.*
>
> *"I guess I been scared all my life," said Garland, a stocky boy with a hint of a '70s-style Afro, who cried as he talked about his life. "For me, living has been the same as running through hell with a gasoline suit on. I don't want people feeling sorry for me, but I really ain't had nothing good happen to me. The ax fell heavy on my head."* (D. Terry, 1994, p. A1)

Garland's descent into violence is representative of the lives of many persons in the United States today. Many observers have called the level of violence nothing less than an epidemic. In fact, surveys find that violence and crime rank as the issue of greatest concern to most

U.S. citizens (Brossard, 1996; Mehran, 1996). How can we explain the level of violence? How do people learn to be violent? How can we control, and remedy, aggression? And how can we discourage violence from occurring in the first place?

Child development has sought to answer such questions from several different perspectives (American Psychological Association, 1993; Eron, Gentry, & Schlegel, 1994; Farley, 1993). This work, illustrated by some representative approaches noted below, exemplifies some of the ways in which the field can provide concrete solutions to pressing problems.

- *Explaining the roots of violence.* Some child developmentalists have looked at how early behavior problems may be associated with later difficulties in controlling aggression. For instance, Avashlom Caspi and colleagues are examining how a lack of control in early childhood is associated with later conduct disorders and antisocial behavior during adolescence (Caspi et al., 1995).

- *Dealing effectively with acts of aggression.* According to psychologist Arnold Goldstein (1994) of Syracuse University's Center for Research on Aggression, school teachers and administrators must be on the lookout for even mild forms of aggression, such as bullying and sexual harassment. Unless such forms of aggression are checked, they are likely to endure and to escalate into more blatant forms.

  Such "minor" forms of aggression are many. Name-calling, threats, thefts, extortion of lunch money, spreading of rumors, and racial and gender-based slurs all can have psychological and academic consequences. And major forms of aggression can have even more profound consequences—and are becoming increasingly commonplace. For instance, gun violence is seen in almost two-thirds of all high schools and about a quarter of junior high schools around the United States.

  To deal with such aggression, Goldstein (1994) has implemented a program that teaches students to "unlearn" aggression. Assuming that aggression is initially learned as a strategy—often successful—for dealing with conflict, the program teaches moral reasoning and new ways of controlling anger and handling conflict without aggression (Azar & McCarthy, 1994).

- *Seeking to prevent violence and other forms of juvenile delinquency.* Taking an ecological approach, some developmental experts have developed violence prevention programs based on the assumption that families, peers, schools, and the community as a whole must be taken into account.

  For instance, the Yale Child Welfare Research Program provided a randomly chosen group of poor families with child care, medical care, and parent education regarding child development for the 17 months following the birth of their first children. The families also received home visits to help them obtain food and housing and to offer general advice. Ten years later, their children had better school attendance and were rated less aggressive by their teachers than children in families who did not participate in the program. In addition, they were less likely than nonparticipants, in the eyes of their mothers, to stay out all night, steal, or be cruel to animals. According to developmental psychologist Edward Zigler (1994), the program was also cost-effective: For each of the children in the program, the annual cost of remedial and support services was more than $1,000 lower than for those in the control group.

As these examples illustrate, developmental researchers are making progress in dealing with the violence that is increasingly part of modern society. Furthermore, violence is just one example of the areas in which experts in child development are contributing their skills for the betterment of human society. As we'll see throughout this book, the field has much to offer.

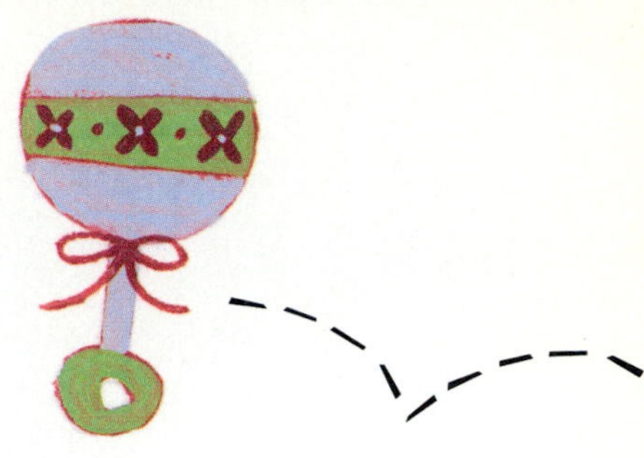

Review and Rethink

REVIEW

- Child development, a scientific approach to understanding human growth and change from conception to adolescence, encompasses physical, cognitive, and social and personality development.
- The ecological approach considers interrelationships among aspects of human development, and relationships between the individual and four levels of the environment.
- Membership in a cohort, based on age and place of birth, subjects people to influences based on historical events (normative history-graded influences). People are also subject to normative age-graded influences (experienced by all people at a given age), nonnormative life events (which are unique to an individual), and socio-cultural factors (normative sociocultural-graded influence).
- Four important issues in child development are continuity versus discontinuity in development, the importance of critical periods, whether to focus on certain periods or on the entire period of childhood, and the nature-nurture issue. Each is best seen not as an either-or choice, but as a continuum along which aspects of development can be placed.

RETHINK

- What sorts of questions would you expect a scientist studying cognitive development in children to ask? How about one studying personality or social development?
- What are some environmental factors that might influence the timing of a child's development?
- How might each of the four elements of the ecological approach influence a major developmental step, such as the decision to engage in premarital sex during adolescence?
- What are some events that might have a shared significance for members of your age cohort as normative history-graded influences? How might they produce different effects from events shared by members of different age cohorts?
- Can you think of one aspect of child development in each area (physical, cognitive, and personality and social) that is affected by both nature and nurture?

THEORETICAL PERSPECTIVES

Until the seventeenth century in Europe, there was no concept of "childhood." Instead, children were simply thought of as miniature adults. They were assumed to be subject to the same needs and desires as adults, to have the same vices and virtues as adults, and to warrant no more privileges than adults. They were dressed the same as adults, and their work hours were the same as adults'. Children also received the same punishments for misdeeds. If they stole, they were hanged; if they did well, they could achieve prosperity.

This view of childhood seems wrong-headed now, but at the time it was what passed for child development. From this perspective, there were no differences due to age; except for size, people were assumed to be virtually unchanging, at least on a psychological level, throughout most of the life span (Aries, 1962; Biemiller, 1995; Furnham & Weir, 1996; Hwang, Lamb, & Sigel, 1996).

Although, looking back over several centuries, it is easy to reject the medieval view of childhood, it is less clear how to formulate a contemporary substitute. Should our view of development focus on the biological aspects of change, growth, and stability during childhood? The cognitive or social aspects? Or some other factors?

Society's view of childhood, and what is appropriate to ask of children, has changed through the ages. These children worked full-time in mines in the early 1900s.

In fact, child development has produced a number of broad conceptual perspectives representing different approaches to development. Each broad perspective encompasses one or more **theories,** explanations and predictions concerning phenomena of interest. A theory provides a framework for understanding the relationships among an organized set of facts or principles (Thomas, 1996).

We'll consider three major perspectives used in child development: the psychodynamic, behavioral, and cognitive perspectives. Each emphasizes somewhat different aspects of development and steers developmentalists in particular directions. Furthermore, each perspective continues to evolve and change, as befits a growing and dynamic discipline.

THE PSYCHODYNAMIC PERSPECTIVE: FOCUSING ON THE INNER PERSON

When Janet was 6 months old, she was involved in a bloody automobile accident—or so her parents tell her, since she has no conscious recollection of it. Now, however, at age 24, she is having difficulty maintaining relationships, and her therapist is seeking to determine whether her current problems are a result of the earlier accident.

Looking for a such a link might seem a bit far-fetched, but to proponents of the **psychodynamic perspective,** it is not so improbable. Advocates of the psychodynamic perspective believe that behavior is motivated by inner forces, memories, and conflicts of which a person has little awareness or control. The inner forces, which may stem from one's childhood, continually influence behavior throughout the life span.

theories *explanations and predictions concerning phenomena of interest, providing a framework for understanding the relationships among an organized set of facts or principles*

psychodynamic perspective *the approach that states that behavior is motivated by inner forces, memories, and conflicts of which a person has little awareness or control*

psychoanalytic theory *the theory proposed by Freud that suggests that unconscious forces act to determine personality and behavior*

Freud's Psychoanalytic Theory. The psychodynamic perspective is most closely associated with a single person and theory: Sigmund Freud and his psychoanalytic theory. Freud, who lived from 1856 to 1939, was a Viennese physician whose revolutionary ideas about the unconscious determinants of behavior ultimately had a profound effect not only on the fields of psychology and psychiatry, but on Western thought in general.

Freud's **psychoanalytic theory** suggests that unconscious forces act to determine personality and behavior. To Freud, the *unconscious* is a part of the personality about which a person is unaware. It contains infantile wishes, desires, demands, and needs that are hidden, because of their disturbing nature, from conscious awareness. Freud suggested that the unconscious is responsible for a good part of our everyday behavior.

According to Freud, one's personality has three aspects: id, ego, and superego. The **id** is the raw, unorganized, inborn part of personality that is present at birth. It represents primitive drives related to hunger, sex, aggression, and irrational impulses. The id operates according to the *pleasure principle,* in which the goal is the immediate reduction of tension and the maximization of satisfaction.

The **ego** is the part of personality that is rational and reasonable. Providing a reality check for the demands of the id, the ego acts as a buffer between the outside world and the primitive demands of the id. The ego operates on the *reality principle,* in which instinctual energy is restrained in order to maintain the safety of the individual and help integrate the person into society.

Finally, Freud proposed that the **superego** represents a person's conscience, incorporating distinctions between right and wrong. It develops around age 5 or 6 and is learned from an individual's parents, teachers, and other significant figures.

In addition to providing an account of the various parts of the personality, Freud also suggested the ways in which personality developed during childhood. He argued that **psychosexual development** occurred as children passed through a series of stages in which pleasure, or gratification, was focused on a particular biological function and body part. As illustrated in Table 1-3, he suggested that pleasure shifted from the mouth (the *oral stage*) to the anus (the *anal stage*) and eventually to the genitals (the *phallic stage* and the *genital stage*).

If children are unable to gratify themselves sufficiently during a particular stage, or, conversely, if they receive too much gratification, fixation may occur. An adult with a **fixation** shows personality traits characteristic of an earlier stage of development because of an unresolved conflict from the earlier period. For instance, fixation at the oral stage might produce an adult unusually absorbed in oral activities—eating, talking, or chewing gum—or showing symbolic sorts of oral activities, such as "biting" sarcasm.

Sigmund Freud

Erikson's Psychosocial Theory. Psychoanalyst Erik Erikson, who lived from 1902 to 1990, provided an alternative view of how society and culture both challenge and shape us in his theory of psychosocial development. **Psychosocial development** encompasses changes in our interactions with and understandings of one another, as well as in our knowledge and understanding of ourselves as members of society (Erikson, 1963).

Erikson's theory suggests that developmental change occurs throughout our lives in eight distinct stages (see Table 1-3). The stages emerge in a fixed pattern and are similar for all people.

Erikson argues that each stage presents a crisis or conflict that the individual must resolve. Although no crisis is ever fully resolved, making life increasingly complicated, the individual must at least address the crisis of each stage sufficiently to deal with demands made during the next stage of development.

Unlike Freud, who regards development as relatively complete by adolescence, Erikson suggests that growth and change continue throughout the life span. For instance, he suggests that during middle adulthood people pass through the *generativity versus stagnation stage,* in which their contributions to family, community, and society can produce either positive feelings about the continuity of life—or a sense of stagnation and disappointment about what they are passing on to future generations.

Assessing the Psychodynamic Perspective. It is hard for us to grasp the full significance of psychodynamic theories, represented by Freud's psychoanalytic theory and Erikson's theory of psychosocial development. Freud's introduction of the notion that unconscious influences affect behavior was a monumental accomplishment, and the fact that it seems at all reasonable to us shows how far the idea of the unconscious has pervaded thinking in Western cultures. In fact, work by contemporary psychologists studying memory and learning suggests that we carry with us memories—of which we are not consciously

id *according to Freud, the raw, unorganized, inborn part of personality that is present at birth*

ego *according to Freud, the part of personality that is rational and reasonable*

superego *according to Freud, the aspect of personality that represents a person's conscience, incorporating distinctions between right and wrong*

psychosexual development *according to Freud, a series of stages that children pass through in which pleasure, or gratification, is focused on a particular biological function and body part*

fixation *behavior reflecting an earlier stage of development*

psychosocial development *the approach that encompasses changes in the understanding individuals have of their interactions with others and of others' behavior, and of themselves as members of society*

TABLE 1-3

FREUD'S AND ERIKSON'S THEORIES

Approximate Age	Freud's Stages of Psychosexual Development	Major Characteristics of Freud's Stages	Erikson's Stages of Psychosexual Development	Positive and Negative Outcomes of Erikson's Stages
Birth to 12–18 months	Oral	Interest in oral gratification from sucking, eating, mouthing, biting	Trust vs. mistrust	*Positive:* Feelings of trust from environmental support *Negative:* Fear and concern regarding others
12–18 months to 3 years	Anal	Gratification from expelling and withholding feces; coming to terms with society's controls relating to toilet training	Autonomy vs. shame and doubt	*Positive:* Self-sufficiency if exploration is encouraged *Negative:* Doubts about self, lack of independence
3 to 5–6 years	Phallic	Interest in the genitals; coming to terms with Oedipal conflict, leading to identification with same-sex parent	Initiative vs. guilt	*Positive:* Discovery of ways to initiate actions *Negative:* Guilt from actions and thoughts
5–6 years to adolescence	Latency	Sexual concerns largely unimportant	Industry vs. inferiority	*Positive:* Development of sense of competence *Negative:* Feelings of inferiority, no sense of mastery
Adolescence to adulthood (Freud) Adolescence (Erikson)	Genital	Reemergence of sexual interests and establishment of mature sexual relationships	Identity vs. identity confusion	*Positive:* Awareness of uniqueness of self, knowledge of role to be followed *Negative:* Inability to identify appropriate roles in life
Early adulthood (Erikson)			Intimacy vs. isolation	*Positive:* Development of loving, sexual relationships and close friendships *Negative:* Fear of relationships with others
Middle adulthood (Erikson)			Generativity vs. stagnation	*Positive:* Sense of contribution to continuity of life *Negative:* Trivialization of one's activities
Late adulthood (Erikson)			Ego-integrity vs. despair	*Positive:* Sense of unity in life's accomplishments *Negative:* Regret over lost opportunities of life

aware—that have a significant impact on our behavior (Jacoby & Kelley, 1992; Kihlstrom, 1987; Westen, 1990).

Some of the most basic principles of Freud's psychoanalytic theory have been called into question, however, because they have not been validated by subsequent research. In particular, the notion that people pass through stages in childhood that determine their adult personalities has little definitive research support. In addition, because much of Freud's theory was based on a limited population of upper-middle-class Austrians living during a strict, puritanical era, its application to broad, multicultural populations is questionable. Finally, because Freud's theory focuses primarily on male development, it has been criticized as sexist and may be interpreted as devaluing women. For such reasons, many developmental psychologists question Freud's theory (Brislin, 1993; Crews, 1993; Guthrie & Lonner, 1986).

Erikson's psychosocial theory has stood the test of time better than Freud's psychoanalytic theory. As we'll see in future chapters, Erikson's view that development continues throughout the life span is highly important—and has received considerable support. In fact, many of the specifics of Erikson's theory have been confirmed by later research (Hetherington & Weinberger, 1993; Peterson & Stewart, 1993; Whitbourne et al., 1992).

Erikson's theory also has its drawbacks, however. Like Freud's theory, it focuses more on men's than women's development. It is also vague in some respects, making it difficult for researchers to test rigorously. And, as is the case with psychodynamic theories in general, it is difficult to make definitive predictions about a given individual's behavior using the theory. In sum, then, the psychodynamic perspective provides good descriptions of past behavior, but imprecise predictions of future behavior.

Erik Erikson

The Behavioral Perspective: Considering the Outer Person

When Elissa Sheehan was 3, a large brown dog bit her, and she needed dozens of stitches and several operations. From the time she was bitten, she broke into a sweat whenever she saw a dog, and in fact never enjoyed being around any pet.

To a child development specialist using the behavioral perspective, the explanation for Elissa's behavior is straightforward: She has a learned fear of dogs. Rather than looking inside the organism at unconscious processes, the **behavioral perspective** suggests that the keys to understanding development are observable behavior and outside stimuli in the environment. If we know the stimuli, we can predict the behavior.

behavioral perspective *the approach that suggests that the keys to understanding development are observable behavior and outside stimuli in the environment*

classical conditioning *a type of learning in which an organism responds in a particular way to a neutral stimulus that normally does not bring about that type of response*

Behavioral theories reject the notion that people universally pass through a series of stages. Instead, people are assumed to be affected by the environmental stimuli to which they happen to be exposed. Developmental patterns, then, are personal, reflecting a particular set of environmental stimuli, and behavior is the result of continuing exposure to specific factors in the environment. Furthermore, developmental change is viewed in quantitative, rather than qualitative, terms. For instance, behavioral theories hold that advances in problem-solving capabilities as children age largely are a result of greater mental *capacities*, rather than changes in the *kind* of thinking that children are able to bring to bear on a problem.

Classical Conditioning: Stimulus Substitution.

> Give me a dozen healthy infants, well-formed, and my own specified world to bring them up in and I'll guarantee to take any one at random and train him to become any type of specialist I might select—doctor, lawyer, artist, merchant-chief, and yes, even beggar-man and thief, regardless of his talents, penchants, tendencies, abilities . . . . (Watson, 1925)

With these words, John B. Watson, one of the first American psychologists to advocate a behavioral approach, summed up the behavioral perspective. Watson, who lived from 1878 to 1958, believed strongly that we could gain a full understanding of development by carefully studying the stimuli that compose the environment. In fact, he argued that by effectively controlling a person's environment, it was possible to produce virtually any behavior.

John B. Watson, one of the first Americans to embrace the behavioral perspective, believed that by effectively controlling an individual's environment it was possible to produce almost any behavior.

As we'll consider further in Chapter 5, **classical conditioning** occurs when an organism learns to respond in a particular way to a neutral stimulus that normally does not evoke that type of response. For instance, if a dog is repeatedly exposed to the pairing of two stimuli, such

operant conditioning *a form of learning in which a voluntary response is strengthened or weakened, depending on its association with positive or negative consequences*

behavior modification *a formal technique for promoting the frequency of desirable behaviors and decreasing the incidence of unwanted ones*

as the sound of a bell and the presentation of meat, it may learn to react to the bell alone in the same way it reacts to the meat—by salivating and wagging its tail with excitement. Dogs don't typically respond to bells in this way; the behavior is a result of stimulus substitution.

The same process of classical conditioning explains how we learn emotional responses. In the case of dog-bite victim Elissa Sheehan, for instance, one stimulus has been substituted for another: Elissa's unpleasant experience with a particular dog (the initial stimulus) has been transferred to other dogs, and to pets in general.

Operant Conditioning. In addition to classical conditioning, other types of learning derive from the behavioral perspective. In fact, the learning approach that probably has had the greatest influence is operant conditioning. **Operant conditioning** is a form of learning in which a voluntary response is strengthened or weakened, depending on its association with positive or negative consequences.

In operant conditioning, formulated and championed by psychologist B. F. Skinner (1904–1990), individuals learn to act deliberately on their environments in order to bring about desired consequences (Skinner, 1975). In a sense, then, children *operate* on their environments to bring about a desired state of affairs.

Whether or not children will seek to repeat a behavior depends on whether it is followed by reinforcement. *Reinforcement* is the process by which a stimulus is provided that increases the probability that a preceding behavior will be repeated. Hence, a student is apt to work harder in school if he or she receives good grades; workers are likely to labor harder at their jobs if their efforts are tied to pay increases; and people are more apt to buy lottery tickets if they are reinforced by winning at least occasionally.

Behavior that is reinforced, then, is more likely to be repeated in the future, while behavior that receives no reinforcement is likely to be discontinued, or, in the language of operant conditioning, *extinguished*. Principles of operant conditioning are used in **behavior modification,** a formal technique for promoting the frequency of desirable behaviors and decreasing the incidence of unwanted ones. Behavior modification has been used in a variety of situations, ranging from teaching severely retarded people the rudiments of language to helping people stick to diets (Bellack, Hersen, & Kazdin, 1990; Malott, Whaley, & Malott, 1993; Sulzer-Azaroff & Mayer, 1991).

Social Learning Theory: Learning through Imitation. Beavis and Butt-head, cartoon characters on MTV, discuss how enjoyable it is to set fires. On at least one occasion, one of them lights the other's hair on fire using matches and an aerosol spray can. Not long after

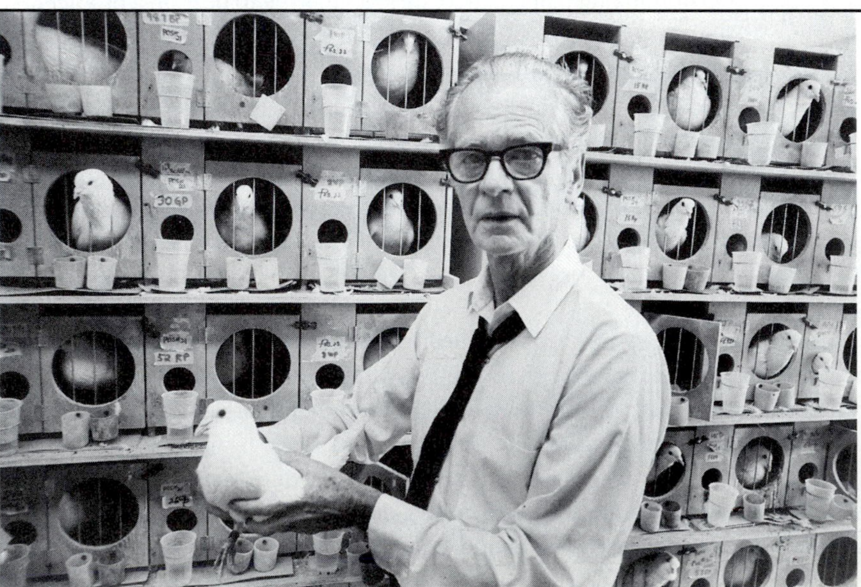

B. F. Skinner

seeing the show, 5-year-old Austin Messner sets his bed on fire with a cigarette lighter, starting a blaze that kills his younger sister.

Cause and effect? We can't know for sure, but it certainly seems possible, especially looking at the situation from the perspective of social learning theory. According to developmental psychologist Albert Bandura (1977) and colleagues, a significant amount of learning is in the form of **social learning,** which is learning by observing the behavior of another person, called a *model.*

Social learning theory holds that when we see the behavior of a model being rewarded, we are likely to imitate that behavior. For instance, in one classic experiment, children who were afraid of dogs were exposed to a model, nicknamed the "Fearless Peer," who was seen playing happily with a dog (Bandura, Grusec, & Menlove, 1967). After exposure, the children who previously had been afraid were more likely to approach a strange dog than children who had not seen the model.

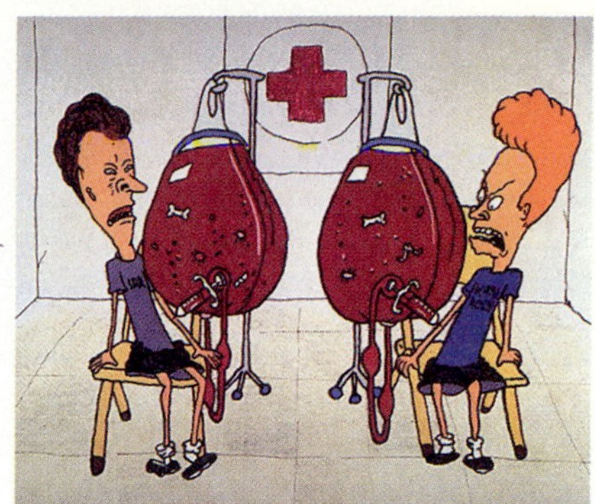

According to social learning theory, observation of shows such as *Beavis and Butt-head* can produce significant amounts of learning—not all of it positive, as this example suggests.

Bandura (1986) suggests that social learning proceeds in four steps. First, an observer must pay attention and perceive the most critical features of a model's behavior. Second, the behavior must be successfully recalled. Third, the behavior must be reproduced accurately. Finally, the observer must be motivated to learn and carry out the behavior. Rather than learning being a matter of trial and error, as it is with operant conditioning, in social learning theory behavior is learned through observation.

Assessing the Behavioral Perspective. Although they are part of the same general behavioral perspective, classical and operant conditioning on the one hand, and social learning theory on the other, disagree in some basic ways (Amsel, 1988). Both classical and operant conditioning consider learning in terms of external stimuli and responses, in which the only important factors are the observable features of the environment. In such an analysis, people and other organisms are "black boxes"; nothing that occurs inside the box is understood—nor much cared about, for that matter.

To social learning theorists, such an analysis is an oversimplification. They argue that what makes people different from rats and pigeons is mental activity, in the form of thoughts and expectations. A full understanding of people's development, they maintain, cannot occur without moving beyond external stimuli and responses.

In many ways, social learning theory has come to predominate over classical and operant conditioning theories in recent decades. In fact, another perspective that focuses explicitly on internal mental activity has become enormously influential. This is the cognitive approach, which we consider next.

THE COGNITIVE PERSPECTIVE: EXAMINING THE ROOTS OF UNDERSTANDING

When 3-year-old Jake is asked why it sometimes rains, he answers, "So the flowers can grow." When his 11-year-old sister Lila is asked the same question, she responds, "Because of evaporation from the surface of the Earth." And when their cousin Ajima, who is studying meteorology in her high school science class, considers the same question, her extended answer includes a discussion of cumulonimbus clouds, the Coriolis effect, and synoptic charts.

To a developmental theorist using the cognitive perspective, the difference in the sophistication of the answers is evidence of a different degree of knowledge and understanding, or cognition. The **cognitive perspective** focuses on the processes that allow people to know, understand, and think about the world.

The cognitive perspective emphasizes how people internally represent and think about the world. By using this perspective, developmental researchers hope to understand how children and adults process information, and how their ways of thinking and understanding affect their behavior. They also seek to learn how cognitive abilities change as people develop, and the degree to which cognitive development represents quantitative and qualitative growth in intellectual abilities.

social learning *learning by observing the behavior of another person, called a model*

cognitive perspective *the approach that focuses on the processes that allow people to know, understand, and think about the world*

Piaget's Theory of Cognitive Development. No single person has had a greater impact on the study of cognitive development than Jean Piaget. A Swiss psychologist who lived from 1896 to 1980, Piaget proposed that all people passed in a fixed sequence through a series of universal stages of cognitive development. In each stage, he suggested, not only did the quantity of information increase, but the quality of knowledge and understanding changed as well. His focus was on the change in cognition that occurred as children moved from one stage to the next (Piaget, 1952, 1962, 1983).

assimilation *the process in which people understand an experience in terms of their current stage of cognitive development and way of thinking*

accommodation *changes in existing ways of thinking that occur in response to encounters with new stimuli or events*

Although we'll consider Piaget's theory in detail beginning in Chapter 5, we can get a broad sense of it now by looking at some of its main features. Piaget suggested that human thinking is arranged into *schemes*, organized mental patterns that represent behaviors and actions. In infants, such schemes represent concrete behavior—a scheme for sucking, for reaching, and for each separate behavior. In older children, the schemes become more sophisticated and abstract. Schemes are like intellectual computer software that directs and determines how data from the world are looked at and dealt with (Achenbach, 1992).

Piaget suggests that the growth in children's understanding of the world can be explained by two basic principles. **Assimilation** is the process in which people understand an experience in terms of their current stage of cognitive development and way of thinking. In contrast, **accommodation** refers to changes in existing ways of thinking in response to encounters with new stimuli or events.

Assimilation occurs when current ways of thinking about and understanding the world are used to perceive and understand a new experience. For example, a young child who has not yet learned to count will look at a row of buttons that are closely spaced together and say there are fewer buttons in that row than in a row of the same number of buttons that are more spread out. The experience of counting buttons, then, is *assimilated* to already existing schemes that contain the principle "bigger is more."

Later, however, when the child is older and has had sufficient exposure to new experiences, the content of the scheme will undergo change. In understanding that the quantity of buttons is identical whether they are spread out or closely spaced, the child has *accommodated* to the experience. Assimilation and accommodation work in tandem to bring about cognitive development.

Assessing Piaget's Theory. Piaget was without peer in influencing our understanding of cognitive development, and he is one of the towering figures in child development. He provided masterful descriptions of how intellectual growth proceeds during childhood—descriptions which have stood the test of literally thousands of investigations. By and large, then, Piaget's broad view of the sequence of cognitive development is accurate (Gratch & Schatz, 1987).

However, the specifics of the theory, particularly in terms of change in cognitive capabilities over time, have been called into question. For instance, some cognitive skills clearly emerge earlier than Piaget suggested. Furthermore, the universality of Piaget's stages has been disputed. A growing amount of evidence suggests that the emergence of particular cognitive skills occurs according to a different timetable in non-Western cultures. And in every culture, some people never seem to reach Piaget's highest level of cognitive sophistication: formal, logical thought (Rogoff & Chavajay, 1995).

Ultimately, the greatest criticism leveled at the Piagetian perspective is that cognitive development is not necessarily as discontinuous as Piaget's stage theory suggests. Remember that Piaget argued that growth proceeded in distinct stages, in which the quality of cognition differed from one stage to the next. However, many developmental researchers argue that growth is considerably more continuous. These critics have suggested an alternative perspective, known as the information processing approach, that focuses on the processes that underlie learning, memory, and thinking throughout the life span.

Information Processing Approaches. Information processing approaches have become an important alternative to Piagetian approaches. **Information processing approaches** to cognitive development seek to identify the ways individuals take in, use, and store information. They assume that cognitive growth is typified more by quantitative than qualitative change (R. S. Siegler, 1991).

information processing approaches *approaches to cognitive development that seek to identify the ways individuals take in, use, and store information*

Information processing approaches grew out of developments in the electronic processing of information, particularly as carried out by computers. They assume that even complex behavior such as learning, remembering, categorizing, and thinking can be broken down into a series of individual, specific steps.

In contrast to Piaget's view that thinking undergoes qualitative advances as children age, information processing approaches assume that development is marked more by quantitative advances. With age, people are seen to change in their capacities to handle information, as well as in terms of the speed and efficiency of their processing. Furthermore, information processing approaches suggest that as people age, they are better able to control the nature of processing, and that they change in the strategies they choose to process information.

As we'll see in future chapters, information processing approaches have become important not only as an alternative to Piagetian approaches, but also as a central part of our understanding of development. They represent an increasingly influential means of studying children's behavior.

Which Approach Is Right? The Wrong Question

In our consideration of perspectives on development, we've looked at the three major ones: psychodynamic, behavioral, and cognitive. It would be natural to wonder which of the three—summarized in Table 1-4—provides the most accurate account of human development.

For several reasons, it is not entirely appropriate to question which perspective is most accurate. For one thing, each perspective emphasizes somewhat different aspects of development. For instance, the psychodynamic approach emphasizes emotions, motivational conflicts, and unconscious determinants of behavior. In contrast, behavioral perspectives emphasize overt behavior, paying far more attention to what people *do* than what goes on inside their heads, which is deemed largely irrelevant. Finally, the cognitive perspective takes quite the opposite tack, looking more at what people *think* than what they do.

Clearly, each perspective is based on its own premises and each focuses on different aspects of development. Furthermore, the same developmental phenomenon can be looked at from a number of perspectives simultaneously.

In short, we can think of the different perspectives as analogous to a set of maps of the same general geographical area. One map may contain detailed depictions of roads; another map may show geographical features; another may show political subdivisions, such as cities, towns, and counties; and still another may highlight particular points of interest, such as scenic areas and historical landmarks. Each of the maps is accurate, but each provides a different point of view and way of thinking. No one map is sufficient, but by considering them together, we can come to a fuller understanding of the area in which we are interested.

In the same way, the various theoretical perspectives provide us with different ways of looking at development. Considering them together paints a full portrait of the myriad ways in which human beings change and grow over the course of their lives. However, not all theories and claims derived from the various perspectives are accurate. How do we choose among competing explanations? The answer is *research,* which we consider in the final part of this chapter.

TABLE 1-4

MAJOR PERSPECTIVES ON CHILD DEVELOPMENT

Perspective	Description
Psychodynamic	Advocates of the *psychodynamic perspective* believe that behavior is motivated by inner, unconscious forces, memories, and conflicts over which a person has little awareness and control. The inner forces, which may stem from childhood experiences, continually influence behavior throughout our entire lives. Major proponents: Sigmund Freud and Erik Erikson.
Behavioral	The *behavioral perspective* suggests that the focus of understanding development rests on observable behavior and outside stimuli in the environment. If we know what those stimuli are, we can predict how people will behave. Major proponents: John B. Watson, B. F. Skinner, and Albert Bandura.
Cognitive	The *cognitive perspective* focuses on the processes that allow people to know, understand, and think about the world, and it emphasizes how people internally represent and think about the world. It emphasizes how children and adults process information, and how their ways of thinking and understanding affect their behavior. Major proponent: Jean Piaget.

Developmental Diversity

How Culture, Ethnicity, and Race Influence Development

> *South American Mayan mothers are certain that almost constant contact between themselves and their infant children is necessary for good parenting, and they are physically upset if contact is not possible. They are shocked when they see a North American mother lay her infant down, and they attribute the baby's crying to the poor parenting of the North American. (Morelli et al., 1992)*

Clearly, two views of good parenting are at odds in this passage. Is one correct and the other wrong?

Probably not, if we take into consideration the cultural context in which the mothers are operating. In fact, different cultures and subcultures have their own views of appropriate and inappropriate childrearing, just as they have different developmental goals toward which children are supposed to be aiming (P. Greenfield, 1995).

Consider, for instance, whether you agree that children should be taught that their classmates' assistance is indispensable to getting good grades in school, or that they should definitely plan to continue their fathers' businesses, or that children should follow their parents' advice in determining their career plans. If you have been raised in the most widespread North American culture, it is likely that you would disagree with all three statements, since they violate the premises of *individualism*, the dominant Western philosophy that emphasizes personal identity, uniqueness, freedom, and the worth of the individual.

The culture in which people are raised plays a central role in their development.

On the other hand, if you were raised in a traditional Asian culture, your agreement with the three statements is considerably more likely. The reason? The statements are indicative of the value orientation known as collectivism. *Collectivism* is the notion that the well-being of the group is more important than that of the individual. People raised in collectivistic cultures tend to emphasize the welfare of the groups to which they belong, sometimes even at the expense of their own personal well-being.

The individualism-collectivism spectrum is one of several dimensions along which cultures differ, and it illustrates differences in the cultural contexts in which people operate. One of the challenges developmentalists face is to take different cultural contexts into account.

Furthermore, they must consider more than just broad cultural differences, such as those that separate North American and Asian cultures. They must take into account finer ethnic, racial, and socioeconomic differences if they are to achieve an understanding of how people change and grow throughout childhood. If developmentalists succeed in doing so, not only can they achieve a better understanding of human development, but also they may be able to derive more precise applications for improving the human social condition.

Although the field of child development is increasingly concerned with issues of human diversity, its actual progress in this domain has been slow, and in some ways it has actually moved backwards. For instance, between 1970 and 1989, only 4.6 percent of the articles published in *Developmental Psychology*, the premier journal of the discipline, focused on African American participants. Moreover, the number of published studies involving African American participants actually declined over that 20-year period (S. Graham, 1992; MacPhee, Kreutzer, & Fritz, 1994).

Furthermore, the research community—as well as society at large—have sometimes used terms such as *race* and *ethnic group* in inappropriate ways. *Race* is a biological concept, which should be employed to refer to classifications based on physical and structural characteristics of species. In contrast, *ethnic group* and *ethnicity* are broader terms, referring to cultural background, nationality, religion, and language.

The concept of race has proven particularly problematic. Although it formally refers to biological factors, race has taken on substantially more meanings—many of them inappropriate—that range from skin color to religion to culture. Moreover, the concept of race is exceedingly imprecise; depending on how it is defined, there are between 3 and 300 races, and no race is biologically pure (Betancourt & Lopez, 1993).

In addition, there is little agreement about what names best reflect different races and ethnic groups. Should the term *African American*—which has geographical and cultural implications—be preferred over *black*, which focuses primarily on race and skin color? Is *Native American* preferable to *Indian*? Is *Hispanic* more appropriate than *Latino*? And how can researchers accurately categorize people with multiracial backgrounds? The choice of category has important implications for the validity (and usefulness) of research (Evinger, 1996).

Furthermore, it is important to keep in mind that race (a biological factor) does not occur independently from environmental and cultural contexts. Consequently, it is impossible to attribute a particular behavior or set of behaviors to race per se, without considering the environments in which people are developing.

In short, as the proportion of minorities in U.S. society continues to increase, it becomes increasingly crucial to take the complex issues associated with human diversity into account in order to fully understand development (Fowers & Richardson, 1996). In fact, it is only by looking for similarities and differences among various ethnic, cultural, and racial groups that developmental researchers can distinguish principles of development that are universal from ones that are culturally determined. In the years ahead, then, it is likely that child development will move from a discipline that primarily focuses on North American and European development to one that embodies development across the globe.

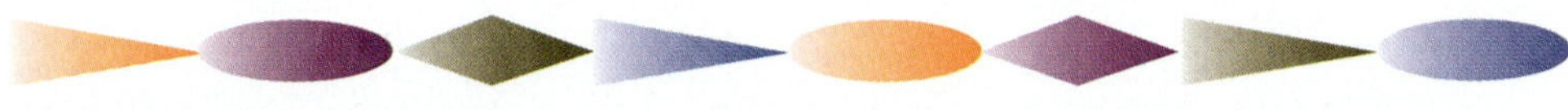

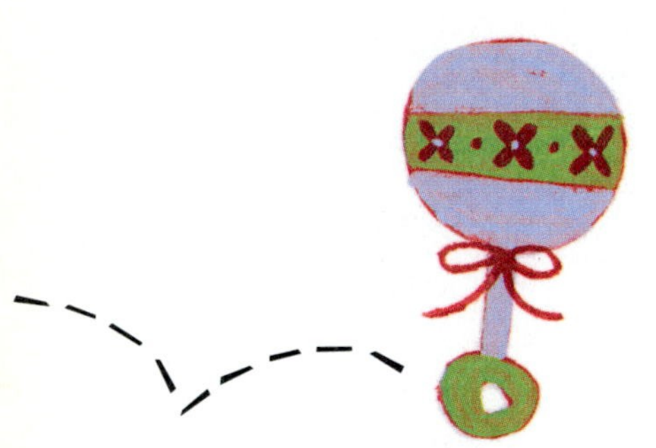

Review and Rethink

REVIEW

- Three major theoretical perspectives have dominated child development. The psychodynamic perspective looks primarily at the influence of internal, unconscious forces on development. Freud's psychoanalytic theory and Erikson's psychosocial theory are examples.
- A second perspective, the behavioral perspective, focuses on external, observable behaviors as the key to development. Classical conditioning, operant conditioning, and social learning theories are examples.
- The third major perspective is the cognitive perspective, which focuses on mental activity. Piaget's stage theory of development and information processing approaches to development are examples.
- All three perspectives are valuable and all are partial, with each providing a part of the total picture.
- Culture, too, plays an important role in development, both broad culture and aspects of culture, such as race, ethnicity, and socioeconomic status.

RETHINK

- How might a child's unconscious affect her or his behavior? How were such behaviors explained before the concept of the unconscious was devised?
- Can you think of examples of conditioned responses and reinforcement in everyday life?
- How do the concepts of social learning and modeling relate to the mass media?
- In general, what does each theoretical perspective contribute to our understanding of child development?
- Can you think of examples of the ways culture (either broad culture or aspects of culture) affects child development?

RESEARCH METHODS

> The Egyptians had long believed that they were the most ancient race on earth, and Psamtik [king of Egypt in the seventh century B.C.], driven by intellectual curiosity, wanted to prove that flattering belief. Like a good researcher, he began with a hypothesis: If children had no opportunity to learn a language from older people around them, they would spontaneously speak the primal, inborn language of humankind—the natural language of its most ancient people—which, he expected to show, was Egyptian.
>
> To test his hypothesis, Psamtik commandeered two infants of a lower-class mother and turned them over to a herdsman to bring up in a remote area. They were to be kept in a sequestered cottage, properly fed and cared for, but were never to hear anyone speak so much as a word. The Greek historian Herodotus, who tracked the story down and learned what he calls "the real facts" from priests of Hephaestus in Memphis, says that Psamtik's goal "was to know, after the indistinct babblings of infancy were over, what word they would first articulate."
>
> The experiment, he tells us, worked. One day, when the children were two years old, they ran up to the herdsman as he opened the door of their cottage and cried out "*Becos!*" Since this meant nothing to him, he paid no attention, but when it happened repeatedly, he sent word to Psamtik, who at once ordered the children brought to him. When he too heard them say it, Psamtik made inquiries and learned that *becos* was the Phrygian word for bread. He concluded that, disappointingly, the Phrygians were an older race than the Egyptians. (M. Hunt, 1993, pp. 1–2)

With the perspective of several thousand years, we can easily see the shortcomings—both scientific and ethical—in Psamtik's approach. Yet his procedure represents an improvement over mere speculation and, as such, is sometimes looked upon as the first developmental experiment in recorded history (M. Hunt, 1993).

THEORIES AND HYPOTHESES: POSING DEVELOPMENTAL QUESTIONS

Questions such as those raised by Psamtik lie at the heart of child development. Is language innate? What are the effects of malnutrition on later intellectual performance? How do infants form relationships with their parents, and does participation in day care disrupt such relationships? Why are adolescents susceptible to peer pressure?

To resolve such questions, specialists in development rely on the scientific method. The **scientific method** is the process of posing and answering questions using careful, controlled techniques that include systematic, orderly observation and the collection of data.

The scientific method involves the formulation of *theories,* broad explanations and predictions about phenomena of interest. All of us develop theories about development, based on our experience, folklore, and articles in magazines and newspapers. For instance, many people theorize that there is a crucial bonding period between parent and child immediately after birth, which is a necessary ingredient in forming a lasting parent-child relationship. Without such a bonding period, they believe, the parent-child relationship will be forever compromised.

Whenever we employ such explanations, we are developing our own theories. However, theories in child development are different. Whereas our own personal theories are built on unverified observations that are developed haphazardly, developmentalists' theories are more formal, based on a systematic integration of prior findings and theorizing. These theories allow developmental researchers to summarize and organize prior observations, and they allow them to move beyond existing observations to draw deductions that may not be immediately apparent.

Theories are used to develop hypotheses. A **hypothesis** is a prediction stated in a way that permits it to be tested. For instance, someone who subscribes to the general theory that bond-

scientific method *the process of posing and answering questions using careful, controlled techniques that include systematic, orderly observation and the collection of data*

hypothesis *a prediction stated in a way that permits it to be tested*

experimental research *research designed to discover causal relationships between various factors*

correlational research *research that seeks to identify whether an association or relationship between two factors exists*

experiment *a process in which an investigator, called an experimenter, devises two different experiences for subjects or participants*

treatment *a procedure applied by an investigator based on two different experiences devised for subjects or participants (See **experiment**)*

treatment group *the group receiving the treatment*

control group *the group that receives either no treatment or alternative treatment*

ing is a crucial ingredient in the parent-child relationship might derive the more specific hypothesis that adopted children whose adoptive parents never had the chance to bond with them immediately after birth may ultimately have less secure relationships with their adoptive parents. Others might derive other hypotheses, such as that effective bonding occurs only if it lasts for a certain length of time, or that bonding affects the mother-child relationship, but not the father-child relationship. (In case you're wondering: As we'll discuss in Chapter 3, these particular hypotheses have *not* been upheld; there are no long-term reactions to the separation of parent and child immediately following birth, even if the separation lasts several days.)

CHOOSING A RESEARCH STRATEGY: ANSWERING QUESTIONS

Once researchers have chosen a hypothesis to test, they must develop a strategy for testing its validity. There are two major categories of research: experimental research and correlational research. **Experimental research** is designed to discover *causal* relationships between various factors. In experimental research, researchers deliberately introduce a change in a situation in order to see the consequences of that change. For instance, a researcher conducting an experiment might vary the number of minutes that mothers and children interact immediately following birth, in an attempt to see whether the amount of bonding time affects the mother-child relationship.

In contrast, **correlational research** seeks to identify whether an association or relationship between two factors exists. Correlational research is unable to determine whether one factor causes changes in the other. For instance, correlational research could tell us if there is an association between the quality of a mother-child relationship when the child was 2 years old and the number of minutes that they were together just after birth. Such correlational research indicates if the two factors are *associated* or *related* to one another, but does not indicate if the initial contact caused the relationship to develop in a particular way.

Because experimental research is able to answer questions of causality, it represents the heart of developmental research. However, because some research questions cannot be answered through experiments, for either technical or ethical reasons, correlational research remains an important tool in the developmental researcher's toolbox.

Experiments: Determining Cause and Effect. In an **experiment,** an investigator, called an *experimenter*, typically devises two different experiences for *participants*, or *subjects*. These two different experiences are called treatments. A **treatment** is a procedure applied by an investigator. One group of participants receives one of the treatments, while another group of participants receives either no treatment or an alternative treatment. The group receiving the treatment is known as the **treatment group** (sometimes called the "experimental group"), while the no-treatment or alternative-treatment group is called the **control group.**

Although the terminology may seem daunting at first, there is an underlying logic to it that helps sort it out. Think in terms of a medical experiment in which the aim is to test the effectiveness of a new drug. In testing the drug, we wish to see if the drug successfully *treats* the disease. Consequently, the group that receives the drug would be called the *treatment* group. In comparison, another group of participants would not receive the drug treatment. Instead, they would be part of the no-treatment *control* group.

Similarly, suppose we wish to explore the consequences of exposure to movie violence on viewers' subsequent aggression. We might take a group of adolescents and show them a series of movies that contain a great deal of violent imagery. We would then measure their subsequent aggression. This group would constitute the treatment group. But we would also need another group—a control group. To fulfill this need, we might take a second group of adolescents, show them movies that contain no aggressive imagery, and then measure their subsequent aggression. This would be the control group.

By comparing the amount of aggression displayed by members of the treatment and control groups, we would be able to determine if exposure to violent imagery produces aggression in viewers. And this is just what a group of researchers found: Running an experiment of this very sort, psychologist Jacques-Philippe Leyens and colleagues of the University of Louvain in Belgium found that the level of aggression rose significantly for the adolescents who had seen the movies containing violence (Leyens et al., 1975).

The central feature of this experiment—and all experiments—is the comparison of the consequences of different treatments. The use of both treatment and control groups allows researchers to rule out the possibility that something other than the experimental manipulation produced the results found in the experiment. For instance, if a control group was not used, experimenters could not be certain that no other factor, such as the time of day the movies were shown, the need to sit still during the movie, or even the mere passage of time, produced the changes that were observed. By employing a control group, then, experimenters can draw accurate conclusions about causes and effects.

independent variable *the variable that is manipulated in the experiment by researchers*

dependent variable *the variable that is measured in an experiment and is expected to change as a result of the experimental manipulation*

The formulation of treatment and control groups represents the independent variable in an experiment. The **independent variable** is the variable that is manipulated in the experiment by researchers. In contrast, the **dependent variable** is the variable that is measured in an experiment and is expected to change as a result of the experimental manipulation. (One way to remember the difference: A hypothesis predicts how a dependent variable *depends* on the manipulation of the independent variable.) In an experiment studying the effects of taking a drug, for instance, manipulating whether participants receive or don't receive a drug is the independent variable. Measurement of the effectiveness of the drug or no-drug treatment is the dependent variable.

To consider another example, let's take the Belgian study of the consequences of observing filmed aggression on future aggression. In this experiment, the independent variable is the *level of aggressive imagery* viewed by participants—determined by whether they viewed films containing aggressive imagery (the treatment group) or devoid of aggressive imagery (the control group). The dependent variable in the study? It was what the experimenters expected to vary as a consequence of viewing a film: the *aggressive behavior* shown by participants after they had viewed the films, and measured by the experimenters. Every experiment has an independent and dependent variable.

Correlational Studies. There are some situations that a researcher, no matter how ingenious, simply cannot control. For instance, no researcher would be able to assign different groups of infants to parents of high and low socioeconomic status in order to learn the effects of such status on subsequent development. Similarly, we cannot control what a group

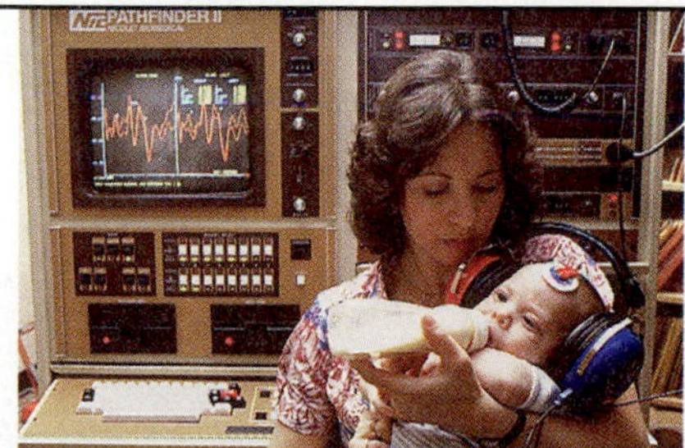

Researchers use a wide range of procedures to study human development.

of children watch on television throughout their childhood years in order to learn if exposure to televised aggression later leads to aggressive behavior.

Because some experiments are logistically or ethically impossible, developmentalists employ an alternative procedure—correlational research. As mentioned earlier, correlational research examines the relationship between two variables to determine whether they are associated, or *correlated*.

For instance, researchers interested in the relationship between televised aggression and subsequent behavior have found that children who watch a good deal of aggression on television—murders, crime shows, shootings, and the like—tend to be more aggressive than those who watch only a little. In other words, as we'll discuss in greater detail in Chapter 8, viewing of aggression and actual aggression are strongly associated, or correlated, with one another.

But does this mean we can conclude that the viewing of televised aggression *causes* the more aggressive behavior of the viewers? Not at all. Consider some of the other possibilities: It might be that being aggressive in the first place makes children more likely to choose to watch violent programs. In such a case, then, it is the aggressive tendency that causes the viewing behavior, and not the other way around.

Or consider another possibility. Suppose that children who are raised in poverty are more likely to behave aggressively *and* to watch higher levels of aggressive television than those raised in more affluent settings. In this case, it is socioeconomic status that causes *both* the aggressive behavior and the television viewing. (The various possibilities are illustrated in Figure 1-3.)

In short, finding that two variables are correlated proves nothing about causality. Although it is possible that the variables are linked causally, this is not necessarily the case.

FIGURE 1-3

CORRELATION AND CAUSATION

Finding a correlation between two factors does not imply that one factor *causes* the other factor to vary. For instance, suppose a study found that viewing television shows with high levels of aggression is correlated with actual aggression in children. The correlation may reflect at least three possibilities: (a) watching television programs containing high levels of aggression causes aggression in viewers; (b) children who behave aggressively choose to watch TV programs with high levels of aggression; or (c) some third factor, such as a child's socioeconomic status, leads both to high viewer aggression and to choosing to watch television programs with high levels of aggression.

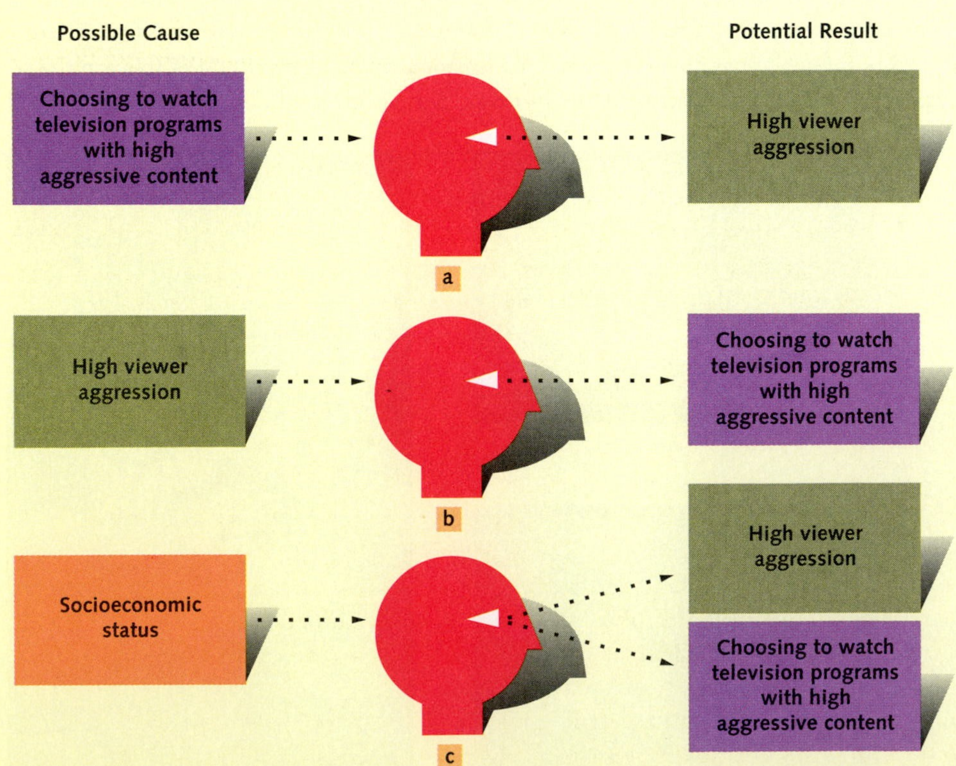

On the other hand, correlational studies can provide us with important information. For instance, as we'll see in later chapters, we know from correlational studies that the closer the genetic link between two people, the more highly associated is their intelligence. We have learned that the more parents speak to their young children, the more extensive are the children's vocabularies. And we know from correlational studies that the better the nutrition that infants receive, the fewer the cognitive and social problems they experience later (Hart & Risley, 1995; Plomin, 1994a; Pollitt et al., 1993).

There are actually several types of correlational studies. For example, **case studies** involve extensive, in-depth interviews with a particular individual or small group of individuals. They often are used not just to learn about the individual being interviewed, but also to derive broader principles or draw tentative conclusions that might apply to others.

Surveys represent another sort of correlational research. In **survey research,** a group of people chosen to represent some larger population are asked questions about their attitudes, behavior, or thinking on a given topic. For instance, surveys have been conducted about parents' use of punishment on their children and about attitudes toward breast-feeding. From the responses, inferences are drawn regarding the larger population represented by the individuals being surveyed.

case studies *extensive, in-depth interviews with a particular individual or small group of individuals*

survey research *research in which a group of people chosen to represent some larger population are asked questions about their attitudes, behavior, or thinking on a given topic*

sample *the group of participants chosen for an experiment; a subgroup of a population of interest*

laboratory study *a research investigation conducted in a controlled setting explicitly designed to hold events constant*

field study *a research investigation carried out in a naturally occurring setting*

naturalistic observation *studies in which researchers observe some naturally occurring behavior without intervening or making changes in the situation*

Choosing Participants and a Research Setting. Deciding who will particpate in research and where to conduct a study may be as important as determining what to do. In the Belgian experiment described earlier on the influence of exposure to media aggression, the researchers used a real-world setting—a group home for boys who had been convicted of juvenile delinquency. They chose this **sample,** the group of participants chosen for the experiment, because it was useful to have adolescents whose normal level of aggression was relatively high, and because they could incorporate showing the films into the everyday life of the home with minimal disruption.

In contrast, because it is typically more difficult to run an experiment in such real-world settings, most experiments in child development are conducted in laboratory settings. A **laboratory study** is a research investigation conducted in a controlled setting explicitly designed to hold events constant. The laboratory may be a room or building designed for research, as in a university's psychology or education department.

On the other hand, using a real-world setting like the one in the aggression experiment is the hallmark of a field study. A **field study** is a research investigation carried out in a naturally occurring setting. Field studies may be carried out in preschool classrooms, at community playgrounds, on school buses, or on street corners. (An example of the kind of information about children and families that can be obtained from field studies is provided in the "Speaking of Development" section.)

Field studies employ **naturalistic observation,** in which researchers observe some naturally occurring behavior without intervening or making changes in the situation. For instance, a researcher might examine behavior in a child-care center, or observe mothers interacting with their newborns in a hospital nursery, or view the groupings of adolescents in high school corridors. The crucial point is that researchers who conduct field studies using naturalistic observation do not intervene and change the situation. Instead, they seek to record what they find in as careful and unbiased a manner as possible.

Conducting Developmental Research: Choosing a Proper Strategy to Measure Change

For developmental researchers, an interest in how people grow and change through childhood and adolescence is central to their discipline. Consequently, one of the thorniest research issues they face concerns the measurement of change and differences over age and time.

Longitudinal studies: Measuring individual change. If you were interested in learning how a child's moral development changes between the ages of 3 and 5, the most direct approach would be to take a group of 3-year-olds and follow them until they were 5, testing them periodically.

longitudinal research *research in which the behavior of one or more individuals is measured as the subjects age*

Such a strategy illustrates longitudinal research. In **longitudinal research,** the behavior of one or more individuals is measured as the participants in the study age. Longitudinal research measures change over time. By following many individuals over time, researchers can understand the general course of change across some period of life.

The granddaddy of longitudinal studies, which has become a classic, is a study of gifted children begun by Lewis Terman in the 1920s. In the study—which has yet to be concluded—a group of 1,500 children with high IQs were tested about every 5 years. Now in their 80s, the participants—who call themselves "Termites"—have provided information on everything from intellectual accomplishment to personality and longevity (H. S. Friedman et al., 1995b; Terman & Oden, 1959).

Longitudinal studies can provide a wealth of information about change over time (M. Bullock, 1995). However, they have several drawbacks. For one thing, they require a tremendous investment of time, because researchers must wait for participants to become older. Furthermore, there is a significant possibility of participant *attrition,* or loss, over the course of the research. Participants may drop out of a study, they may move away, or they may become ill or even die as the research proceeds.

Speaking of Development

Donald J. Hernandez, Family Life Researcher

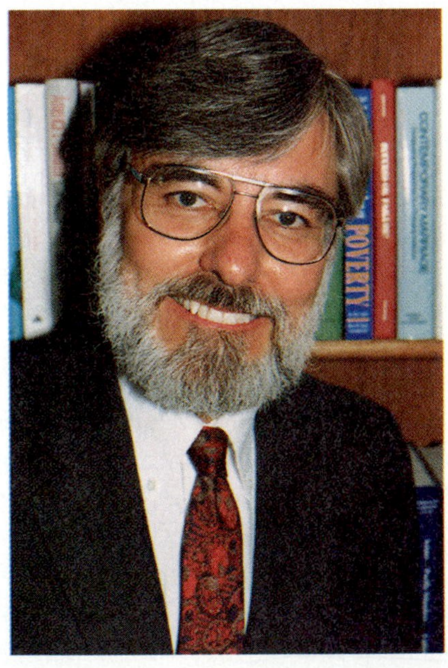

Born:	1948
Education:	University of Illinois at Urbana, B.A. in sociology University of California at Berkeley, M.A. and Ph.D. in sociology
Position:	Chief of the Marriage and Family Statistics branch of the U.S. Bureau of the Census
Home:	Silver Spring, Maryland

According to Donald J. Hernandez, when it comes to family life, there wasn't just one American Revolution. There have been five—and counting.

Hernandez, who conducts research on the evolution of the family, has uncovered statistics that put into clear perspective where the American family came from, and where it is today. Hernandez is the chief of the Marriage and Family Statistics branch of the U.S. Bureau of the Census, and he has published his research findings in a book entitled *America's Children: Resources from Family, Government and the Economy.*

Hernandez's findings indicate that over the past 150 years the family in America has been completely transformed by a series of revolutions. "Three of these revolutions started in the 1800s," he explains. "The first was caused by the rise in nonfarm work by the father of the family. In the mid-1800s most families were farm families. Fathers, mothers, and children worked together on the farm, day-in and day-out, to support themselves. But by the mid-1900s most fathers worked outside the home much of the day, earning income to support the family, while the mother's role became that of homemaker.

"During the same period," Hernandez continues, "a second revolution occurred—this one in family size. While most families in the mid-1800s had eight or more children, the figure dropped to two or three children in the 1930s. There was enormous pressure at the time to move off farms and to have fewer children."

Finally, participants who are observed or tested may become "test-wise" and perform better each time they are assessed, as they become more familiar with the procedure. Consequently, despite the benefits of longitudinal research, particularly its ability to look at change within individuals, developmental researchers often turn to other methods in conducting research. The alternative they choose most often: the cross-sectional study.

cross-sectional research *research in which people of different ages are compared at the same point in time*

Cross-sectional Studies. Let's return to the issue of moral development in children 3 to 5 years of age. Instead of using a longitudinal approach, and following the same children over several years, we might conduct the study by simultaneously looking at a group of 3-year-olds, 4-year-olds, and 5-year-olds.

Such an approach typifies cross-sectional research. In **cross-sectional research,** people of different ages are compared at the same point in time. Cross-sectional studies provide information about differences in development between different age groups.

Cross-sectional research is considerably more economical in terms of time than longitudinal research: Participants are tested at just one point in time. For instance, Terman's study conceivably might have been completed the same year it started if Terman had simply looked at a group of gifted 15-year-olds, 20-year-olds, 25-year-olds, and so forth, all the way through a group of 80-year-olds. Because the participants would not be periodically

---

"In 1940, 1 in 10 children had a working mother. Today about 60 percent of children have mothers who work for pay."

"Not once in the last 50 years have the majority of children lived in Ozzie and Harriet families."

The third major change, according to Hernandez, was a marked increase in schooling for America's children. "About half of children aged 5 to 19 were enrolled in school in 1870; but by the 1930s, 95 percent of children 7 to 13, and 79 percent of children 14 to 17, were enrolled."

The next two revolutions uncovered by Hernandez involve women's entry into the work force and the rise, since 1960, of the one-parent, mother-only family.

"In 1940, 1 in 10 children had a working mother. Today about 60 percent of children have mothers who work for pay," he explains. "Similarly, from 1940 to 1960 only 6 to 8 percent of children lived in a mother-only family. As of 1993 the figure was close to 23 percent."

A number of factors have contributed to the changes in the American family, says Hernandez, including the shift of the country's focus from agriculture to industry, new government policies, and the economy.

"There has been an increase of children born into poverty since the late 1970s. This is widely attributed to the rise in one-parent families, but the fact is that the economy and unemployment continue to be major contributors," he explains. "Parents face many obstacles. They don't have much money and they have to deal constantly with economic insecurity. This can lead to divorce. Economic factors have been very important influences on family changes, and on the poverty that results."

One statistic that amazed Hernandez clearly demonstrates that the so-called Ozzie and Harriet family is a myth. Hernandez defines such a family as one in which the father works full time, the mother is not in the paid labor force, and all the children are born after the parents' only marriage.

"Not once in the last 50 years have the majority of children lived in Ozzie and Harriet families," he says. "In 1940, 41 percent of children under 1 year of age lived in such families. The figure jumped a bit—to 43 percent—in 1960. Estimates today indicate that less than one-fourth of children under 1 year of age live in families that meet the definition.

"To me this was a surprise," Hernandez admits. "When I calculated the statistics, I believed I would find a large majority of Ozzie and Harriet kids, at least in the recent past. I believed in the myth, too. But even when Ozzie and Harriet were on television in the 1950s, that's what it was—a myth."

tested, there would be no chance that they would become test-wise, and problems of participant attrition would not occur. Why, then, would anyone choose to use a procedure other than cross-sectional research?

The answer is that cross-sectional research brings its own set of difficulties. We can start with cohort effects. Recall that every person belongs to a particular *cohort,* the group of people born at around the same time in the same place. If we find that people of different ages vary along some dimension, it may be due to differences in cohort membership, not age per se.

Consider a concrete example: If we find in a correlational study that people who are 15 years old perform better on a test of intelligence than those who are 75 years old, there are several explanations. Although the finding may be due to decreased intelligence in older people, it may also be attributable to cohort differences. The group of 75-year-olds may have had less education when they were younger than the 15-year-olds, because members of the older cohort were less likely to finish high school and attend college than members of the younger one. Or perhaps the older group performed less well because as infants they received less adequate nutrition than members of the younger group. In short, we cannot fully rule out the possibility that differences we find between people of different age groups in cross-sectional studies are due to cohort differences.

Cross-sectional studies have an additional disadvantage: They are unable to inform us about changes in individuals or groups. Although we can establish differences related to age, we cannot fully determine if such differences are related to change over time.

Cross-sequential Studies. Because both longitudinal and cross-sectional studies have their drawbacks, researchers have turned to some compromise techniques. Among the most frequently employed are cross-sequential studies, which are essentially a combination of longitudinal and cross-sectional studies.

In **cross-sequential studies,** researchers examine a number of different age groups over several points in time. For instance, an investigator might annually examine the moral behavior of a group of 3-, 4-, and 5-year-olds over a period of 3 years. During that time, the 3-year-olds would be tested at ages 3, 4, and 5; the 4-year-olds at ages 4, 5, and 6; and the 5-year-olds at ages 5, 6, and 7. Such an approach combines the advantages of longitudinal and cross-sectional research, and it permits developmental researchers to tease out the consequences of age *change* versus age *differences.* (The major research techniques for studying development are summarized in Figure 1-4.)

ETHICS AND RESEARCH: THE MORALITY OF RESEARCH

Return, for a moment, to the "study" conducted by Egyptian King Psamtik, in which two children were removed from their mothers and held in isolation in an effort to learn about the roots of language. Clearly, such an experiment raises blatant ethical concerns, and nothing like it would ever be done today.

But sometimes ethical issues are more subtle. For instance, in seeking to understand the roots of aggressive behavior, U.S. government researchers proposed holding a conference in the mid-1990s to examine possible genetic roots of aggression. Based on work conducted by biopsychologists and geneticists, some researchers had begun to raise the possibility that genetic markers might be found that would allow the identification of children as being particularly violence-prone. In such cases, it might be possible to track these violence-prone children and provide interventions that might reduce the likelihood of later violence.

Critics objected strenuously, however. They argued that such identification might lead to a self-fulfilling prophecy. In such a case, children labeled as violence-prone might be treated in a way that would actually *cause* them to be more aggressive than if they hadn't been so labeled. Ultimately, under intense political pressure, the conference was canceled (R. Wright, 1995).

cross-sequential studies *the process by which researchers examine a number of different age groups over several points in time*

FIGURE 1-4

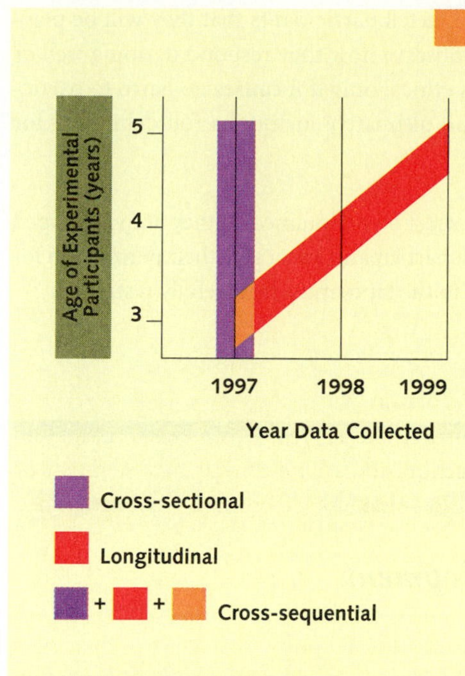

RESEARCH TECHNIQUES FOR STUDYING DEVELOPMENT

In a *cross-sectional study,* 3-, 4-, and 5–year-olds are compared at a similar point in time (1997). In *longitudinal research,* a set of participants who are 3 years old in 1997 are again studied when they are 4 years old (in 1998) and again when they are 5 years old (in 1999). Finally, a *cross-sequential study* combines cross-sectional and longitudinal techniques; here, a group of 3-year-olds would be compared initially in 1997 with 4- and 5-year-olds, but would also be studied 1 and 2 years later, when they themselves were 4 and 5 years old. Although the graph does not illustrate this, researchers carrying out this cross-sequential study might also choose to re-test the children who were 4 and 5 in 1997 for the next 2 years.

In order to help researchers deal with such ethical problems, the major organizations in child development, including the Society for Research in Child Development and the American Psychological Association, have developed comprehensive ethical guidelines for researchers. Among the basic principles that they must adhere to are those involving freedom from harm, informed consent, the use of deception, and maintenance of participants' privacy (American Psychological Association, 1992; Fisher & Fryrberg, 1994; Gurman, 1994; Rosnow, Rotheram-Borus, Ceci, Blanck, & Koocher, 1993).

Freedom from Harm. Participants must be protected from physical and psychological harm. Their welfare, interests, and rights come before those of researchers. In research, participants' rights always come first.

Informed Consent. Consent must be obtained from participants before their participation in a study. If they are above the age of 7, participants must voluntarily agree to be in a study. (In fact, many researchers feel that they should obtain some form of broad agreement from *any* participant who is able to provide it.) Furthermore, the parents or guardians of participants under 18 must also provide consent.

The requirement for informed consent raises some difficult issues. Suppose, for instance, researchers wish to learn the psychological consequences of abortion on adolescents. Although they may be able to obtain consent to participate from an adolescent who has had an abortion, the researchers will need to get her parents' permission as well if she is a minor. But suppose the parents haven't been told by their daughter that she had had an abortion. In such a case, the mere request for permission from the parents would violate the privacy of the adolescent—leading to an ethical violation

Use of Deception. Although deception to disguise the true purpose of the experiment is permissible, any experiment that uses deception must undergo careful scrutiny by an independent panel before it is conducted. Suppose, for example, we want to know the reaction of participants to success and failure. It is ethical to tell participants that they will be playing a game when the true purpose is actually to observe how they respond to doing well or poorly on the task. However, such a procedure is ethical only if it causes no harm to participants, has been approved by a review panel, and ultimately includes a full debriefing for participants when the study is over.

Maintenance of Privacy. Participants' privacy must be maintained. If they are videotaped during the course of a study, for example, research participants must give their permission for the videotapes to be viewed. Furthermore, access to the tapes must be carefully restricted.

The Informed Consumer of Development

Assessing Information on Development

If you immediately comfort crying babies, you'll spoil them.

If you let babies cry without comforting them, they'll be untrusting and clingy as adults.

***

Spanking is sometimes the best, most effective way to discipline your child.

Never hit your child.

***

If their parents' marriage is unhappy, children are better off if their parents divorce than if their parents stay together.

No matter how bad their marriage is, parents should avoid divorce for the sake of their children.

There is no lack of advice on the best way to raise a child or, more generally, to lead one's life. From bestsellers with unfathomable titles such as *Men Are from Mars, Women Are from Venus* to magazine and newspaper columns that provide advice on every imaginable topic, each of us is exposed to tremendous amounts of information.

Yet not all advice is equally valid. The mere fact that something is in print or on television does not automatically make it legitimate or accurate. Fortunately, there are ways to distinguish when recommendations and suggestions are reasonable and when they are not. Among the ways to determine if the advice should be accepted are the following:

- Consider the source of the advice. Recommendations from nationally respected organizations such as the American Medical Association, the American Psychological Association, and the American Academy of Pediatrics are likely to be the result of years of study, and their accuracy is probably high.
- Determine the credentials of the person providing advice. Information coming from established, acknowledged researchers and experts in a field is likely to be more accurate than that coming from a person whose credentials are obscure.
- Understand the difference between anecdotal evidence and scientific evidence. Anecdotal evidence is based on one or two instances of a phenomenon, haphazardly discovered or encountered. In contrast, scientific evidence is based on careful, systematic procedures. When evidence has been collected in a methodical, orderly manner, it is more apt to be reliable.

- Keep cultural context in mind. Although a pronouncement may be valid in some contexts, it may not be true in all. For example, it is typically assumed that providing infants the freedom to move about and exercise their limbs facilitates their muscular development and mobility. Yet in some cultures, infants' movements are very restricted, and in a few they spend most of their time closely bound to their mothers (H. Kaplan & Dove, 1987; Super, 1976; Tronick, Thomas, & Daltabuit, 1994). Although such infants may show initial delays in physical development, by late childhood they are indistinguishable from children raised in a less restrictive manner.
- Don't assume that because many people believe something, it is necessarily true. Scientific evaluation has often proven that some of the most basic presumptions about the effectiveness of various techniques are invalid. For instance, consider DARE, the Drug Abuse Resistance Education antidrug program that is used in about half the school systems in the United States. DARE is designed to prevent the spread of drug abuse through lectures and question-and-answer sessions run by specially trained police officers. One problem, though: Careful evaluation has found no evidence that the program works. Teachers, administrators, police officers, and taxpayers who support the program may like DARE—but it doesn't seem to reduce the use of drugs (Ennett et al., 1994).

In short, the key to evaluating information relating to child development is to maintain a healthy dose of skepticism. No source of information is invariably, unfailingly accurate. By keeping a critical eye on the statements you encounter, you'll be in a better position to determine the very real contributions made by the field of child development in understanding how we change and grow over the course of childhood and adolescence.

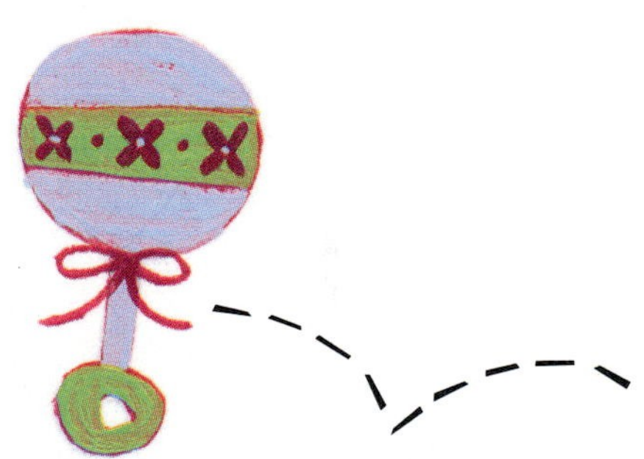

Review and Rethink

REVIEW

- Theories in child development are systematically derived explanations of facts or phenomena. Theories suggest hypotheses, which are predictions that can be tested.
- Experimental research seeks to discover cause-and-effect relationships by the use of a treatment group and a control group. Correlational studies examine relationships between factors without demonstrating causality.
- Research studies may be conducted in laboratories, where conditions can be controlled effectively, or in field settings, where participants are subject to natural conditions.
- Researchers measure age-related change by longitudinal studies (same participants at different ages), cross-sectional studies (different-age participants at one time), and cross-sequential studies (different-age participants at several times).
- Researchers in child development follow ethical guidelines relating to such issues as the prevention of harm in participants, informed consent, the use of deception, and the maintenance of privacy.

RETHINK

- Can you formulate a theory about one aspect of child development and a hypothesis that relates to it?

- What sort of research strategy would be appropriate for investigating each of the statements (about comforting babies, spanking, and divorce) at the beginning of the "Informed Consumer" section?
- Would a laboratory or a field setting be most appropriate for each research strategy you identified?
- Can you think of a correlation between two phenomena related to gender? What are some possible explanations for the correlation? How would you establish causality?
- What problems might affect a study of age-related changes in attitudes toward the police conducted at a single time among a cross section of children aged 5, 10, 15, and 20?

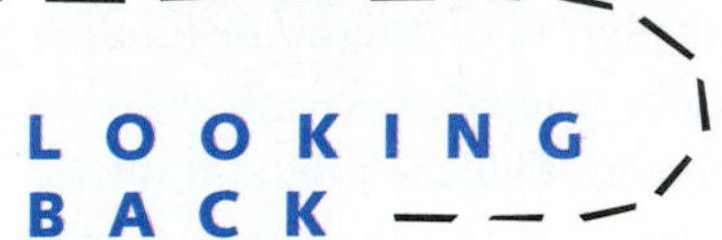

What is child development, and what aspects of human life does it study?

1. Child development is a scientific approach to questions about growth, change, and stability that occur from conception to adolescence. The scope of the field includes physical, cognitive, and social and personality development at all ages from conception through adolescence.
2. Childhood is generally divided for convenience into broad periods, including the prenatal period, infancy and toddlerhood, the preschool period, middle childhood, and adolescence. Individual and cultural differences affect the definition and application of these periods.

What are some of the basic influences on child development?

3. Because each area of development (physical, cognitive, social/personality) affects the others, some developmentalists take an ecological approach to development, which suggests that four levels of the environment simultaneously affect the individual: the microsystem, the mesosystem, the exosystem, and the macrosystem. The ecological approach stresses the interrelatedness of developmental areas and the importance of broad cultural factors in human development.
4. Each individual belongs to a cohort, a group of people born at around the same time and place and subject to similar influences. Membership in a cohort makes a person susceptible to normative history-graded influences, which contrast with normative age-graded influences (which occur at given ages to every cohort), nonnormative life events (which are individual), and normative sociocultural-graded influences.

What are the key issues in the field of child development?

5. Four key issues have been debated in the field of child development from its inception. One is whether developmental change in humans is continuous or discontinuous. Another is whether human development is largely governed by critical periods during which certain influences or experiences must occur for development to be normal. The third key issue is whether child development should focus on certain particularly important periods in human development (such as infancy or adolescence) or on the entire period.
6. The fourth, which has probably been the most enduring and heated major issue in child development, is the nature-nurture controversy: How much of human development is inherited (i.e., due to nature) and how much is learned through interactions with the environment (i.e., due to nurture)? This issue continues to be debated today.

7. Each of the four key issues is probably best regarded not as an either-or proposition, but as the ends of a continuum along which the various aspects of development are to be arrayed.

Which theoretical perspectives have guided thinking and research in child development?

8. Three major theoretical perspectives have dominated child development: the psychodynamic perspective (which focuses on inner, largely unconscious forces), the behavioral perspective (which focuses on external, observable actions), and the cognitive perspective (which focuses on intellectual, cognitive processes).

9. The psychodynamic perspective is exemplified by the psychoanalytic theory of Freud and the psychosocial theory of Erikson. Freud focused attention on the unconscious, distinguishing three main elements: the impulsive id, the rational ego, and the moral superego. He also identified stages, associated with body parts and biological functions, through which children must pass successfully to avoid harmful fixations. Erikson extended the psychodynamic time focus to include the whole life span, identifying eight distinct stages of development, each characterized by a conflict, or crisis, to work out.

10. The behavioral perspective typically concerns stimulus-response learning and is exemplified by classical conditioning (associating a neutral stimulus and a learned response), the operant conditioning of Skinner (in which voluntary responses are strengthened or weakened by reinforcement), and Bandura's social learning theory (in which people learn by observing the behavior of models).

11. Within the cognitive perspective, the most notable theorist is Piaget, who identified developmental stages through which all children are assumed to pass. Each stage involves qualitative differences in thinking. The two basic Piagetian principles are assimilation (fitting experiences into the current level of understanding) and accommodation (adjusting one's thinking to encompass new experiences). In contrast to the qualitative changes identified by Piaget, proponents of information processing approaches explain cognitive growth as quantitative changes in mental processes and capacities.

12. Each theory and each perspective has value, and each is incomplete. Child development has benefited by the presence of alternative explanations, and it is best to regard the varying perspectives as partial views of the truth which together can inform and enlighten one another and the field as a whole.

13. Culture is another important issue in child development. Many aspects of development are influenced not only by broad cultural differences, but by ethnic, racial, and socioeconomic differences within a particular culture.

What role do theories and hypotheses play in child development?

14. Theories in a science such as child development are broad explanations of facts or phenomena of interest, based on a systematic integration of prior findings and theories. Hypotheses are theory-based predictions that can be tested.

15. Hypotheses are tested by two primary research strategies. Experimental research, involving the controlled manipulation of a situation, is designed to discover cause-and-effect relationships. Correlational research is designed to determine if two factors are associated with one another.

How are research studies in child development conducted?

16. Experiments in child development typically are conducted on participants (subjects), who are divided into two groups, one of which—the treatment group—receives the experimental treatment and the other of which—the control group—does not. Following the treatment, differences between the treatment group and the control group

can help the experimenter determine the effects of the treatment. In experiments, the independent variable is the variable that is manipulated in the experiment by researchers; the dependent variable is the variable that is measured in an experiment and is expected to change as a result of the experimental manipulation.

17. Correlational studies typically focus on groups of participants with different characteristics, which are of interest because they are related to a researcher's hypothesis. If certain characteristics are found to be associated with other characteristics, a correlation is said to exist. While correlational studies can provide a great deal of information, they lead to no direct conclusions about cause and effect.
18. Research may be conducted in a laboratory or in a real-world setting. Experiments are typically conducted in laboratory settings because of the difficulty of controlling variables in real-world settings. In field studies, data are gathered from participants in naturally occurring settings.
19. To measure change over time, researchers use three major strategies: longitudinal studies of the same participants over time, cross-sectional studies of different-age participants conducted at one time, and cross-sequential studies of different-age participants at several points in time. Longitudinal and cross-sectional studies have disadvantages which cross-sequential studies help remedy.
20. Researchers must adhere to ethical guidelines pertaining, among other things, to the protection of participants from harm, informed consent of participants, limits on the use of deception, and the maintenance of privacy.

KEY TERMS AND CONCEPTS

child development (p. 6)
physical development (p. 7)
cognitive development (p. 7)
personality development (p. 7)
social development (p. 7)
ecological approach (p. 9)
cohort (p. 11)
normative history-graded influences (p. 11)
normative age-graded influences (p. 11)
normative sociocultural-graded influences (p. 12)
nonnormative life events (p. 12)
continuous change (p. 12)
discontinuous change (p. 12)
critical period (p. 12)
sensitive period (p. 13)
maturation (p. 14)
theories (p. 18)
psychodynamic perspective (p. 18)
psychoanalytic theory (p. 18)
id (p. 19)
ego (p. 19)
superego (p. 19)
psychosexual development (p. 19)
fixation (p. 19)
psychosocial development (p. 19)

behavioral perspective (p. 21)
classical conditioning (p. 21)
operant conditioning (p. 22)
behavior modification (p. 22)
social learning (p. 23)
cognitive perspective (p. 23)
assimilation (p. 24)
accommodation (p. 24)
information processing approaches (p. 25)
scientific method (p. 29)
hypothesis (p. 29)
experimental research (p. 30)
correlational research (p. 30)
experiment (p. 30)
treatment (p. 30)
treatment group (p. 30)
control group (p. 30)
indepedendent variable (p. 31)
dependent variable (p. 31)
case studies (p. 33)
survey research (p. 33)
sample (p. 33)
laboratory study (p. 33)
field study (p. 33)
naturalistic observation (p. 33)
longitudinal research (p. 34)
cross-sectional research (p. 35)
cross-sequential studies (p. 36)

CHAPTER 2

BEGINNINGS

The Start of Life: Prenatal Development

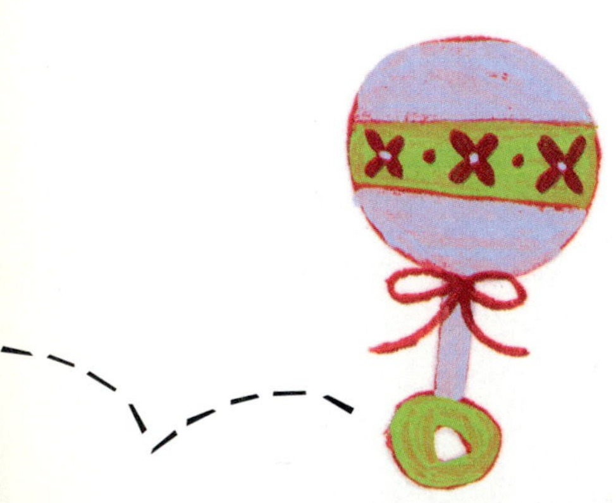

PROLOGUE

A HIDDEN TIME BOMB

Several grandchildren of Ara Parseghian, former Notre Dame football coach, suffer from a rare genetic disease.

Michael Parseghian, 8, is brandishing a Power Rangers pistol as his sisters Marcia, 6, and Christa, 4, bounce on overstuffed leather couches, giggling helplessly. Watching the children romp around the sun-splashed living room of their Mediterranean-style house in the foothills of Arizona's Santa Catalina Mountains near Tucson, their maternal grandmother, Vickey Buesher, can't help smiling. But her eyes betray her sadness. "I've seen Michael deteriorate so much since I was here at Christmas," she says once the kids are out of earshot.

The kids, three of the four children of Michael and Cindy Parseghian, have a rare, incurable neurological condition that leads inexorably to paralysis and dementia. Children afflicted with the disease—called Niemann-Pick Type C—usually die in adolescence. Michael, a Cub Scout who takes karate and horseback-riding lessons, is the most seriously affected so far. His symptoms include vertical gaze palsy, which means that he can't easily raise his eyes. He has difficulty keeping his balance, and his speech is slurred. Marcia, whose passion is gymnastics, is just beginning to lose her coordination. Little Christa is so far symptom-free.

"The diagnosis is there; we can't do anything about that," says the children's paternal grandfather, retired football coach and TV commentator Ara Parseghian. But the man who led Notre Dame to two national titles during his eleven seasons as head coach from 1964 to 1974 isn't comfortable letting fate rule his world. Parseghian, 72, is determined to raise money for research toward a cure that will be found in time to save his son's children. (Neill & Haederle, 1995, p. 45)

LOOKING AHEAD

Sadly, Parseghian was unable to reach his goal of finding a cure for the disease, and several years after the scene described above, Michael died. He was the victim of a hidden gene that had been present in his body from the moment of conception. Like a time bomb, this inherited gene activated a still little-understood process that ultimately led to his death at the age of 10.

The disease that haunts the Parseghian family is just one of a number that are produced by specific genetic problems, inherited from one (or both) of an individual's parents. Yet the same genetic processes that in some cases lead to deadly disease also permit our minds and bodies to function so effectively for the vast majority of our lives.

In this chapter, we'll examine what researchers in child development and other scientists have learned about ways that heredity and the environment work in tandem to shape human behavior. We begin with the basics of heredity, examining how we receive our genetic endowment. We'll consider a burgeoning area of study, behavioral genetics, that specializes in the consequences of heredity on behavior. We'll also discuss what happens when genetic factors cause development to go awry, such as with the Parseghian family, and how such problems are dealt with through genetic counseling.

Next, we'll turn to a discussion of the interaction of heredity and environment. We'll consider the relative influence of genes and environment on a variety of characteristics, including physical traits, intelligence, and even personality.

Finally, we'll focus on the very first stage of development, tracing prenatal growth and change. We'll talk about the stages of the prenatal period, and how the prenatal environment offers threats to—and the promise of—future growth.

In sum, after reading this chapter, you will be able to answer these questions:

- What is our basic genetic endowment, and how do we receive it from our parents?
- How can human development go wrong, and what can be done to prevent or remedy genetic problems?
- How do the environment and genetics work together to determine human characteristics?
- Which human characteristics are significantly influenced by heredity?
- What happens during the prenatal stages of development?
- What threats are there to the fetal environment and what can be done about them?

gametes *the sex cells from the mother and father that form a new cell at conception*

fertilization *the process by which a sperm and an ovum—the male and female gametes, respectively—join to form a single new cell*

zygote *the new cell formed by the process of fertilization*

HEREDITY

We humans begin the course of our lives simply.

Like individuals from tens of thousands of other species, we start as a single cell, a tiny speck probably weighing no more than one twenty-millionth of an ounce. But from this humble beginning, human development follows its own unique path, accomplishing a journey that leads to the flowering of humankind's vast potential.

What determines the process that transforms the single cell into something that we can more easily identify as a person? The answer is the human genetic code, transmitted at the moment of conception in the **gametes**, or sex cells, from the mother and father, and embedded in that single, first cell.

FERTILIZATION: THE MOMENT OF CONCEPTION

When most of us think about the facts of life, we tend to focus on the events that involve the moment when a male's *sperm* cells begin their journey towards a female's *ovum* (egg cell). Yet the act of sex that brings about the potential for conception is both the consequence and the start of a long string of events that precede and follow fertilization. **Fertilization**, or conception, is the process by which a sperm and an ovum—the male and female gametes, respectively—join to form a single new cell, called a **zygote**.

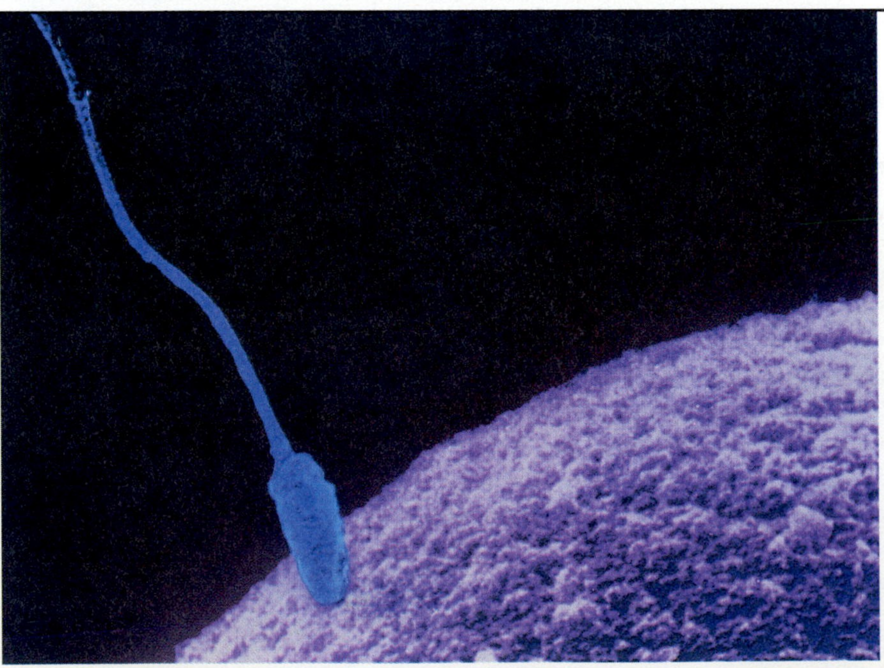

The moment of conception, when a sperm penetrates the egg at the point of fertilization.

Both the male's sperm and the female's ovum come with a history of their own. Females are born with around 400,000 ova located in the two ovaries (see Figure 2-1 for the basic anatomy of the female and male sex organs). However, the ova do not mature until the female reaches puberty. From that point until she reaches menopause, the female will ovulate about every 28 days. During ovulation, an egg is released from one of the ovaries and pushed by minute hair cells through the fallopian tube toward the uterus. If the ovum meets a sperm in the fallopian tube, fertilization takes place (Aitken, 1995).

Sperm, which look a little like microscopic tadpoles, have a shorter life span. They are created by the testicles at a rapid rate: An adult male typically produces several hundred million sperm a day. Consequently, the sperm ejaculated during sexual intercourse are of considerably more recent origin than the ovum to which they are heading.

When sperm enter the vagina, they begin a winding journey that takes them through the cervix, the opening into the uterus, and into the fallopian tube, where fertilization may take place. However, only a tiny fraction of the 300 million cells that are typically ejaculated during sexual intercourse ultimately survive the arduous journey. That's OK, though: It takes only one sperm to fertilize an ovum, and each sperm and ovum contain all the genetic data necessary to produce a new human.

Genes and Chromosomes: The Code of Life

Genes are the basic unit of genetic information. Composed of sequences of **DNA** (**deoxyribonucleic acid**) molecules, genes determine the nature of every cell in the body and how it will function. Genes are the biological equivalent of "software" that programs the future development of all parts of the body's "hardware."

Humans have some 100,000 genes. The genes are arranged in specific locations and in a specific order along 46 **chromosomes**, rod-shaped portions of DNA, that are organized in 23 pairs. Of the two chromosomes in each of the 23 pairs, one is provided by the mother and the other by the father at the time of fertilization. Through a cell replication process called *mitosis,* all the eventual cells of the body contain the same 46 chromosomes provided

genes *the basic unit of genetic information*

DNA (deoxyribonucleic acid) *the substance that genes are composed of that determines the nature of every cell in the body and how it will function*

chromosomes *rod-shaped portions of DNA that are organized in 23 pairs*

FIGURE 2-1

FEMALE AND MALE SEXUAL ANATOMY

The basic anatomy of the sexual organs is illustrated in these cutaway side views.

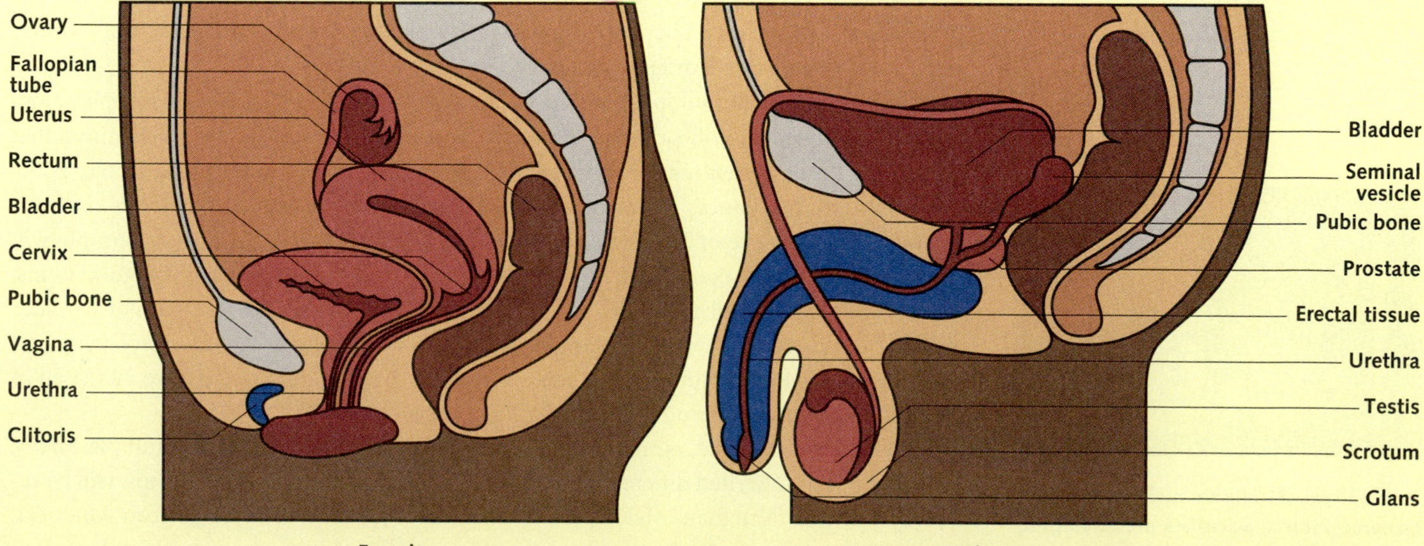

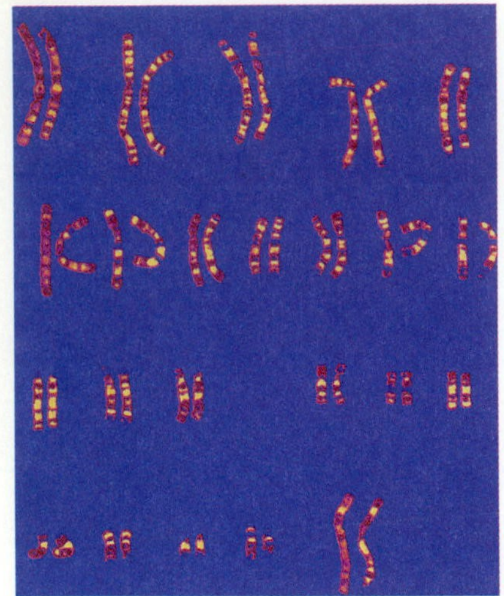

The 23 pairs of chromosomes, rod-shaped portions of DNA on which genes reside.

by the maternal and paternal gametes (sex cells). It is the uniting of the 23 maternal and 23 paternal chromosomes that provides the genetic blueprint that guides cell activity for the rest of the individual's life.

Specific genes in precise locations on the chain of chromosomes determine the nature and functioning of every cell in the body. For instance, genes determine which cells will ultimately become part of the heart and which will become part of the muscles of the leg. Genes also establish how different parts of the body will function: how rapidly the heart will beat, or how much strength a muscle will have. Each of these genes appears in a specific sequence on particular chromosomes, which molecular biologists are currently seeking to map in a massive, 15-year, $3-billion undertaking known as the Human Genome Project sponsored by the U.S. federal government (Beardsley, 1996; J. Marx, 1995).

If each parent provides just 23 chromosomes, where does the potential for the vast diversity of human beings come from? The answer resides primarily in the nature of the processes that underlie the cell division of the gametes. When gametes—sperm and ova—are formed in the adult human body in a process called *meiosis,* each gamete receives one of the (male or female) body's two pairs of 23 chromosomes. Because for each of the 23 pairs it is largely a matter of chance which member of the pair is contributed, there are 2^{23}, or some eight million, different combinations possible. Furthermore, other processes add to the variability of the genetic brew. The ultimate outcome: tens of *trillions* of possible genetic combinations.

With so many possible genetic mixtures provided by heredity, there is no likelihood that someday you'll bump into a genetic duplicate of yourself. There is one exception: an identical twin.

monozygotic twins *twins who are genetically identical*

dizygotic twins *twins who are produced when two separate ova are fertilized by two separate sperm at roughly the same time*

Multiple Births: Two—or More—for the Genetic Price of One. Although it doesn't seem surprising when dogs and cats give birth to several offspring at one time, in humans multiple births are cause for comment. They should be: Less than 2 percent of all pregnancies produces twins. But why do multiple births occur at all?

Some multiple births occur when a cluster of cells in the ovum splits off within the first 2 weeks following fertilization. The result is two genetically identical zygotes, which, because they come from the same original zygote, are called monozygotic. **Monozygotic twins** are twins who are genetically identical. Any differences in their future development can be attributed only to environmental factors, since genetically they are exactly the same.

There is a second, and actually more common, mechanism that produces multiple births. In these cases, two separate ova are fertilized by two separate sperm at roughly the same time. Twins produced in this fashion are known as **dizygotic twins.** Because they are the result of two separate ovum-sperm combinations, they are no more genetically similar than two siblings born at different times.

Of course, not all multiple births produce only two babies. Triplets, quadruplets, and even more single-birth offspring are produced by either (or both) of the mechanisms that yield twins. Thus, triplets may be some combination of monozygotic, dizygotic, or trizygotic.

Although the chances of having a multiple birth are typically slim, the odds rise considerably with the use of fertility drugs meant to improve the chances that a couple will conceive a child. For example, 1 in 10 couples using fertility drugs have dizygotic twins, compared to an overall figure of 1 in 86 for white couples in the United States. Older women, too, are more likely to have multiple births. The increased use of fertility drugs and rising average age of mothers giving birth has meant that multiple births have increased in the last 25 years (see Figure 2-2).

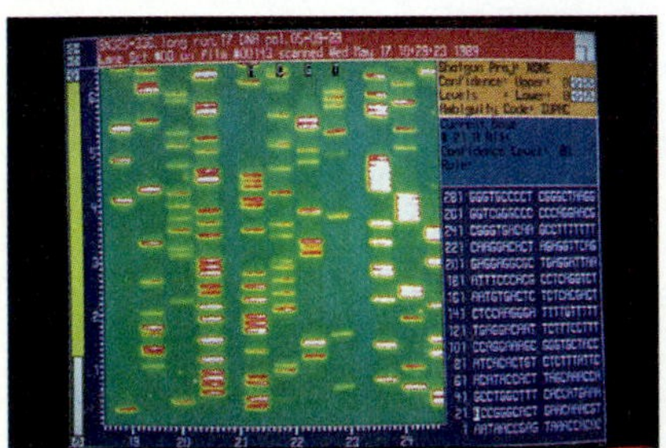

In a 15-year, $3-billion study, the Human Genome Project, scientists are attempting to map the entire sequence of human genes.

There are also racial, ethnic, and national differences in the rate of multiple births, probably due to inherited differences in the likelihood that more than one ovum will be released at a time (Vaughan, McKay, & Behrman, 1979). One out of 70 African American couples have dizygotic births, compared with the 1 out of 86 figure for white American

Twins attending the annual twin convention in Twinsburg, Ohio, are monozygotic (identical) and dizygotic (non-identical).

couples. On the other hand, in some groups multiple births are unusually rare. For instance, in China just 1 in every 300 births produces dizygotic twins, although these statistics may be suspect.

Boy or Girl? Establishing the Sex of the Child. Recall that there are 23 matched pairs of chromosomes. Each chromosome is similar to the other member of its pair, with one exception—the 23rd chromosome, which is the one that determines the sex of the child. In females, the 23rd pair consists of two matching, relatively large X-shaped chromosomes, appropriately identified as XX. In males, on the other hand, the members of the pair are dissimilar. One consists of an X-shaped chromosome, but the other is a smaller Y-shaped chromosome. This pair is identified as XY.

Because the production of gametes involves the receipt of only half of the chromosomal pairs in each parent, the ovum from the female will receive one of the two X chromosomes from the 23rd pair. However, because the male contributes either an X or a Y chromosome, the sperm will contain either an X or a Y from the 23rd pair.

The ultimate result of this process is that when an ovum and a sperm meet at fertilization, the ovum is sure to carry an X chromosome, but the sperm will carry either an X or a Y chromosome. If the sperm contributes an X chromosome, the child will have an XX pair-

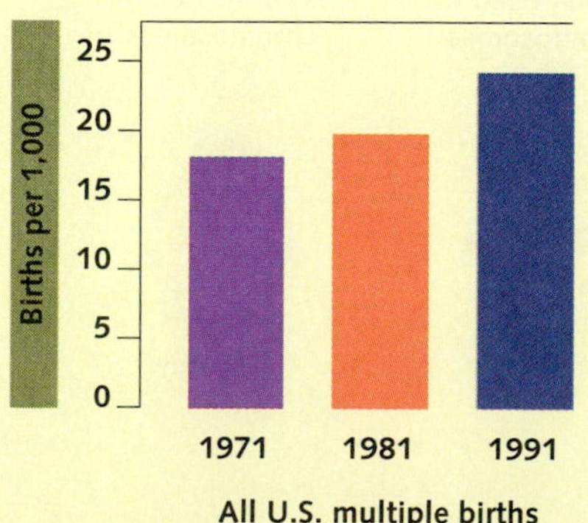

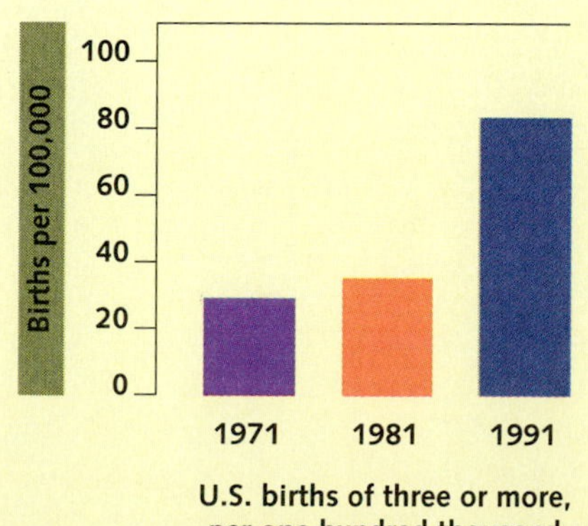

FIGURE 2-2

MULTIPLE BIRTH TRENDS

Multiple births have increased significantly over the last 25 years.

(Adapted from *USA Weekend*, 1995 p. 15)

ing on the 23rd chromosome—and will be a female. However, if the sperm contributes a Y chromosome, the result will be an XY pairing—a male (see Figure 2-3).

It is clear from this process that it is the father's sperm that determines the sex of the child. Curiously, our understanding of how sex is determined is consistent with Aristotle's ancient notion that it is the man who determines his child's sex. However, Aristotle's explanation couldn't have been more wrong: He argued that the more sexually excited the man was, the more apt he was to produce a son.

The Basics of Genetics: The Mixing and Matching of Heredity

What determined the color of your hair? Why are you tall or short? What made you susceptible to hay fever? And why do you have so many freckles? To answer these questions, we need to consider the basic mechanisms involved in the way that the genes we inherit from our parents transmit information.

We can start by examining the discoveries of an Austrian monk, Gregor Mendel, in the mid-1800s. In a series of simple yet convincing experiments, Mendel cross-pollinated pea plants that always produced yellow seeds with pea plants that always produced green seeds. The result was not, as one might guess, a plant with a combination of yellow and green seeds. Instead, all of the resulting plants had yellow seeds. At first it appeared that the green-seeded plants had had no influence.

However, additional research on Mendel's part proved that this was not true. When the plants that had been produced by the combination of yellow- and green-seeded parent plants were bred with one another, the consistent result was a ratio of three-quarters yellow seeds to one-quarter green seeds.

FIGURE 2-3

CHROMOSOME PAIRING RESULTS

When an ovum and sperm meet at the moment of fertilization, the ovum is certain to provide an X chromosome, while the sperm will provide either an X or a Y chromosome. If the sperm contributes its X chromosome, the child will have an XX pairing on the 23rd chromosome and will be a girl. If the sperm contributes a Y chromosome, the result will be an XY pairing—a boy.

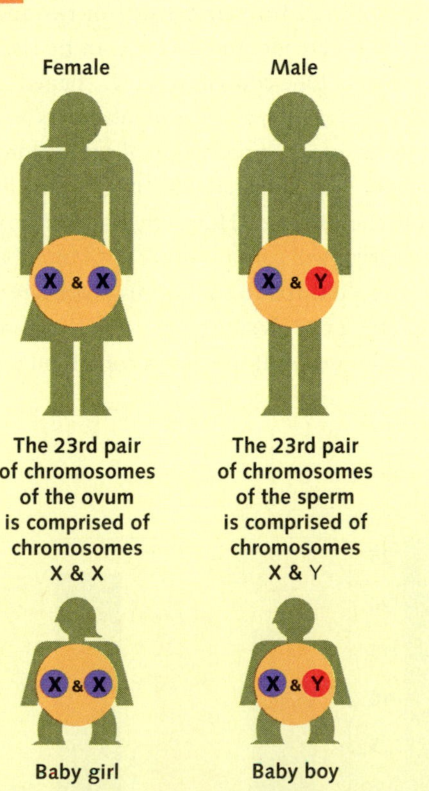

Why did this 3-to-1 ratio of yellow to green seeds appear so consistently? It was Mendel's genius to provide an answer. He argued that when two competing traits, such as a green or yellow coloring of seeds, were both present, only one could be expressed. The one that was expressed was called a **dominant trait**, while the one that was present in the organism but not expressed was called a **recessive trait**. In the case of the pea plants, when the two strains of purebred pea plants were bred, the offspring plants received genetic information from both parents. However, the yellow trait was dominant, and consequently the recessive (green) trait did not assert itself.

Keep in mind, however, that genetic material relating to both parent plants is present in the offspring, even though it cannot be seen. The genetic information is known as the organism's genotype. A **genotype** is the underlying combination of genetic material present (but outwardly invisible) in an organism. In contrast, a **phenotype** is the observable trait, the trait that actually is seen.

Although the offspring of the yellow-seeded and green-seeded pea plants all have yellow seeds (i.e., they have a yellow-seeded phenotype), the genotype consists of genetic information relating to both parents.

And what is the nature of the information in the genotype? To answer that question, let's turn from peas to people. In fact, the principles are the same not just for plants and humans, but for the majority of species.

Recall that parents transmit genetic information to their offspring via the chromosomes they contribute through the gamete they provide during fertilization. In cases of genes that govern *alleles*—genes for traits that may take alternate forms, such as hair or eye color—the offspring may receive similar or dissimilar genes from each parent. If the offspring receives similar genes, the organism is said to be **homozygous** for the trait. On the other hand, if the offspring receives different forms of the gene from its parents, it is said to be **heterozygous**. In the case of heterozygous alleles, the dominant characteristic is expressed. However, if the child happens to receive a recessive allele from each of its parents, and therefore lacks a dominant characteristic, it will display the recessive characteristic.

Gregor Mendel's pioneering experiments on pea plants provided the foundation for the study of genetics.

Transmission of Genetic Information in Humans. We can see this process at work in humans by considering the transmission of *phenylketonuria (PKU)*, an inherited disorder in which a child is unable to make use of phenylalanine, an essential amino acid present in proteins found in milk and other foods. If left untreated, PKU allows phenylalanine to build up to toxic levels, causing brain damage and mental retardation.

PKU, unlike most other characteristics, is produced by a single pair of genes in the offspring, inherited from a particular pair of genes in the mother and the father. As shown in Figure 2-4, we can think of the pair in terms of *P*, a dominant gene which causes the normal production of phenylalanine, and *p*, a recessive gene that produces PKU. In cases in which neither parent is a PKU carrier, both the mother's and the father's pairs of genes are the dominant form, symbolized as *PP*. Consequently, no matter which member of the pair is contributed by the mother and father, the resulting pair of genes in the child will be *PP*, and the child will not have PKU.

However, consider what happens if one of the parents has a recessive *p* gene. In this case, which we can we symbolize as *Pp*, the parent will not have PKU, since the normal *P* gene is dominant. But the recessive gene can be passed down to the child. This is not so bad: If the child has only one recessive gene, it will not suffer from PKU. But what if both parents carry a recessive *p* gene? In this case, although neither parent has the disorder, it is possible for the child to receive a recessive gene from both parents. The child's genotype for PKU then will be *pp*, and it will have the disorder.

Remember, though, that even children whose parents both have the recessive gene for PKU have only a 25 percent chance of inheriting the disorder. Due to the laws of probability,

dominant trait *the one trait that is expressed when two competing traits are present*

recessive trait *a trait within an organism that is present but is not expressed*

genotype *the underlying combination of genetic material present (but not outwardly visible) in an organism*

phenotype *an observable trait; the trait that actually is seen*

homozygous *inheriting similar genes from parents for a given trait*

heterozygous *inheriting different forms of a gene from parents for a given trait*

FIGURE 2-4

PHENYLKETONURIA (PKU)

PKU, a disease that causes brain damage and mental retardation, is produced by a single pair of genes inherited from one's mother and father. If neither parent carries a gene for the disease (a), a child cannot develop PKU. Even if one parent carries the recessive gene, but the other doesn't (b), the child cannot inherit the disease. However, if both parents carry the recessive gene (c), there is a 1 in 4 chance that the child will have PKU.

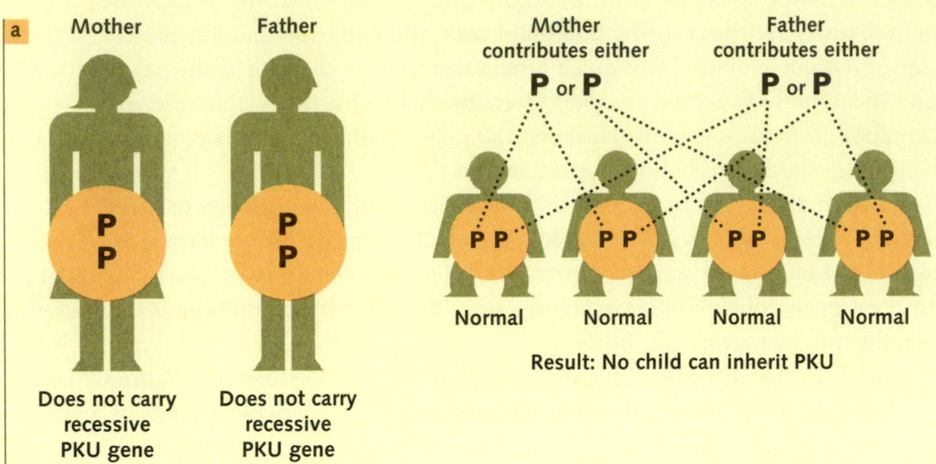

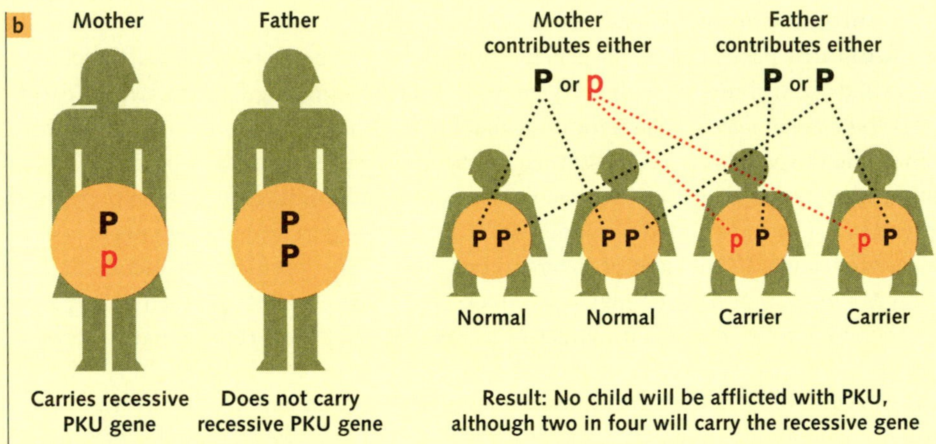

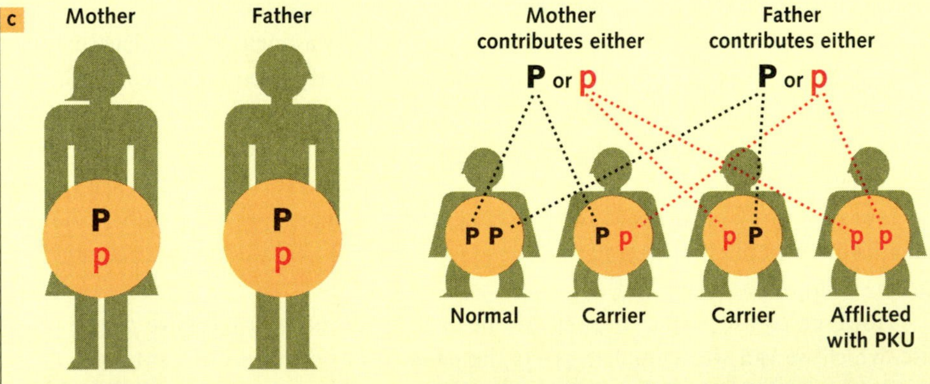

25 percent of children with *Pp* parents will receive the dominant gene from each parent (*PP*), and 50 percent will receive the dominant gene from one parent and the recessive gene from the other (*Pp* or *pP*). Only the unlucky 25 percent who receive the recessive gene from each parent and end up with the genotype *pp* will suffer from PKU.

The basic principles that explain the transmission of PKU underlie the transmission of all genetic information from parent to child. However, in some respects, the case of PKU is simpler than most cases of genetic transmission. Relatively few traits are governed by a single pair of genes. Instead, most traits are the result of polygenic inheritance. In **polygenic inheritance**, a combination of multiple gene pairs is responsible for the production of a particular trait.

Furthermore, some genes come in several alternate forms, and still others act to modify the way that particular genetic traits (produced by other alleles) are displayed. And some traits, such as blood type, are produced by genes in which neither pair of genes can be classified as purely dominant or recessive. Instead, the trait is expressed in terms of a combination of the two genes—such as type AB blood.

A number of recessive genes, called **X-linked genes**, are located only on the X chromosome. Recall that in females, the 23rd pair of chromosomes is an XX pair, while in males it is an XY pair. One result is that males have a higher risk for a variety of X-linked disorders, since males lack a second X chromosome that can counteract the genetic information that produces the disorder. For example, males are significantly more apt to have red-green colorblindness, a disorder produced by a set of genes on the X chromosome.

Similarly, *hemophilia,* a blood disorder, is produced by X-linked genes. Hemophilia has been a recurrent problem in the royal families of Europe, as illustrated in Figure 2-5, which shows the inheritance of hemophilia in many of the descendants of Queen Victoria of Great Britain.

Behavioral Genetics: Extending Mendel's Discoveries. Mendel's achievements in recognizing the basics of genetic transmission of traits were trailblazing. However, they mark only the beginning of our understanding of the ways that particular sorts of characteristics are passed on from one generation to the next. The most recent approach to deciphering the effect of heredity is through a rapidly burgeoning field known as behavioral genetics. As the name implies, **behavioral genetics** studies the effects of heredity on behavior. Rather than simply examining stable, unchanging characteristics such as hair or eye color, behavioral genetics takes a broader approach, considering how our personality and behavioral habits are affected by genetic factors. Behavioral genetics represents the melding of interests of

polygenic inheritance *inheritance in which a combination of multiple gene pairs is responsible for the production of a particular trait*

X-linked genes *genes that are considered recessive and located only on the X chromosome*

behavioral genetics *the study of the effects of heredity on behavior*

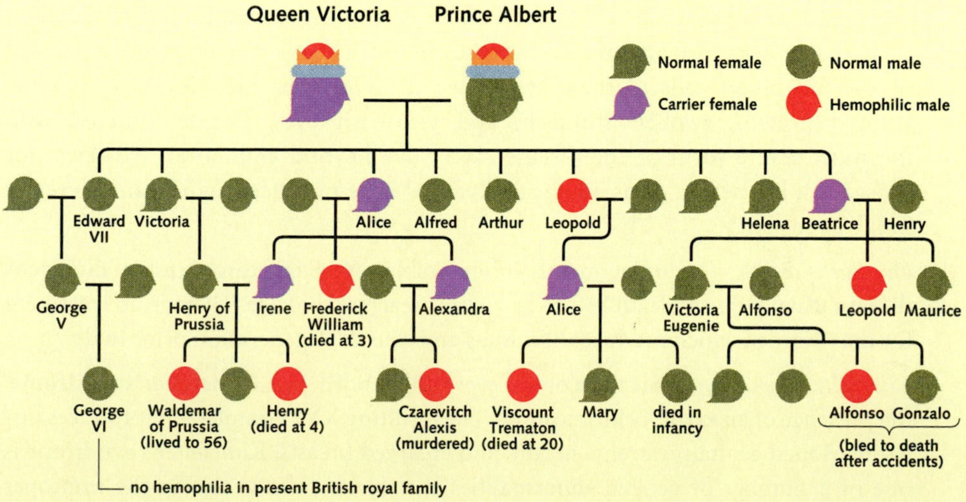

FIGURE 2-5

HEMOPHILIA IN A ROYAL FAMILY

Hemophilia, a blood clotting disorder, has been an inherited problem throughout the royal families of Europe, as illustrated by the descendants of Queen Victoria of Britain.

(Adapted from Kimball, 1983).

psychologists, who focus on the causes of behavior, and geneticists, who focus on the processes that permit the transmission of characteristics through heredity (T. J. Bouchard, 1994; Kimble, 1993; Lander & Schork, 1994; McClearn, 1993; Rowe, 1993).

The promise of behavioral genetics is substantial. For one thing, researchers working within the field have gained a better understanding of the specifics of the genetic code that underlie human behavior and development. Such advances have provided knowledge of the workings of genetics at a molecular and chemical level. Furthermore, scientists are learning how various behavioral difficulties, including psychological disorders such as schizophrenia, may have a genetic basis (Michel & Moore, 1995; Plomin, 1990b, 1994, 1995). Even more important, researchers are seeking to identify how genetic defects may be remedied. To understand how that possibility might come about, we need to consider the ways in which genetic factors, which normally cause development to proceed so smoothly, may falter.

Down syndrome *a disorder produced by the presence of an extra chromosome on the 21st pair; once referred to as mongolism*

sickle cell anemia *a blood disorder that gets its name from the shape of the red blood cells in those who have it*

Tay-Sachs disease *a disorder for which there is no treatment and which produces blindness and muscle degeneration prior to death*

Klinefelter's syndrome *a disorder resulting from the presence of an extra X chromosome that produces underdeveloped genitals, extreme height, and enlarged breasts*

INHERITED AND GENETIC DISORDERS: WHEN DEVELOPMENT GOES AWRY

Both PKU and Niemann-Pick Type C disease (the disorder described in the chapter-opening prologue) are examples of a number of ailments that may be inherited. Like a bomb that is harmless until its fuse is lit, a recessive gene responsible for a disorder may be passed on unknowingly from one generation to the next, revealing itself only when, by chance, it is paired with another recessive gene. It is only when two recessive genes come together like a match and a fuse that the gene will express itself and a child will inherit the genetic disorder.

But there is another way that genes are a source of concern: In some cases, genes become physically damaged. For instance, genes may break down due to wear-and-tear or chance events occurring during the cell division processes of meiosis and mitosis. Sometimes genes, for no known reason, spontaneously change their form, a process called *spontaneous mutation.* Alternatively, certain environmental factors, such as exposure to X-rays, may produce a malformation of genetic material. When such damaged genes are passed on to a child, the results can be disastrous in terms of future physical and cognitive development.

In addition to PKU, which occurs once in 10 to 20 thousand births, other inherited and genetic disorders include:

- *Down syndrome.* As we noted earlier, people have 46 chromosomes, arranged in 23 pairs. One exception is individuals with **Down syndrome**, a disorder produced by the presence of an extra chromosome on the 21st pair. Once referred to as mongolism, Down syndrome is the most frequent cause of mental retardation. It occurs in about 1 out of 500 births, although the risk is much greater in mothers who are unusually young or old (J. Carr, 1995; Cicchetti & Beeghly, 1990).
- *Sickle cell anemia.* Around one tenth of the African American population carry genes that produce sickle cell anemia, and 1 African American in 400 actually has the disease. **Sickle cell anemia** is a blood disorder that gets its name from the shape of the red blood cells in those who have it. Symptoms include poor appetite, stunted growth, swollen stomach, and yellowish eyes. People afflicted with the most severe form of the disease rarely live beyond childhood. However, for those with less severe cases, medical advances have produced significant increases in life expectancy.
- *Tay-Sachs disease.* Occurring mainly in Jews of eastern European ancestry, **Tay-Sachs disease** usually causes death before its victims reach school age. There is no treatment for the disorder, which produces blindness and muscle degeneration prior to death.
- *Klinefelter's syndrome.* One male out of every 400 is born with **Klinefelter's syndrome**, the presence of an extra X chromosome. The resulting XXY complement produces underdeveloped genitals, extreme height, and enlarged breasts. Klinefelter's syndrome is one of a number of genetic abnormalities that result from receiving the improper

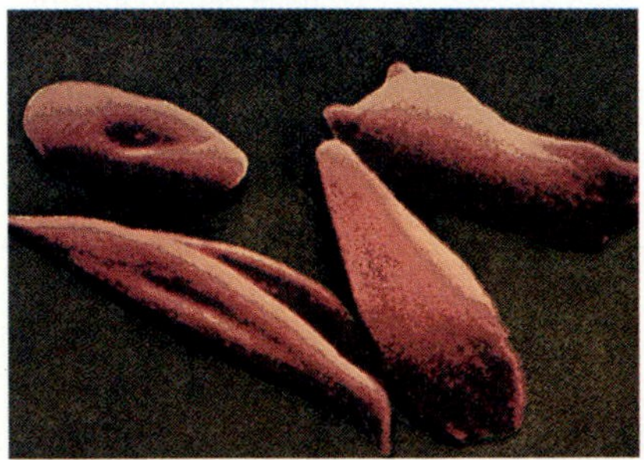

Sickle cell anemia, named for the presence of misshapen red blood cells, is carried in the genes of 1 in 10 African Americans.

number of sex chromosomes. For instance, there are disorders produced by an extra Y chromosome (XYY), a missing second chromosome (X0), and three X chromosomes (XXX). Such disorders are typically characterized by problems relating to sexual characteristics and by intellectual deficits (K. Sorenson, 1992).

It is important to keep in mind that just because a disorder has genetic roots, this does not mean that environmental factors do not also play a role. Consider, for instance, sickle cell anemia, which primarily afflicts people of African descent. Because the disease can be fatal in childhood, we'd expect that those who suffer from it would be unlikely to live long enough to pass it on. And this does seem true, at least in the United States: Compared with parts of West Africa, the incidence in the U.S. is much lower.

But why shouldn't the incidence of sickle cell anemia also be gradually reduced for people in West Africa? This question proved puzzling for many years, until scientists determined that carrying the sickle cell gene raises immunity to malaria, which is a common disease in West Africa (Allison, 1954). This heightened immunity meant that people with the sickle cell gene had a genetic advantage (in terms of resistance to malaria) that offset, to some degree, the disadvantage of being a carrier of the sickle cell gene.

The lesson of sickle cell anemia is that genetic factors are intertwined with environmental considerations, and they can't be looked at in isolation. Furthermore, we need to remember that although we've been focusing on inherited factors that can go awry, in the vast majority of cases, the genetic mechanisms with which we are endowed work quite well. Overall, just under 95 percent of children born in the United States are healthy and normal. For the some 250,000 who are born with some sort of physical or mental disorder, appropriate intervention often can help treat and, in some cases, cure the problem.

Moreover, due to advances in behavioral genetics, genetic difficulties increasingly can be forecast, anticipated, and planned for before a child's birth. In fact, as scientists' knowledge regarding the specific location of particular genes expands, predictions of what the genetic future may hold are becoming increasingly exact, as we discuss in the accompanying "Directions in Development" section (Cook-Deegan, 1994; Plomin, 1995).

Directions in Development

Genetic Counseling: Predicting the Future from the Genes of the Present

> *The last thing Joey Paulowsky needs is another bout with cancer. Only 7 years old, the Dallas native has already fought off leukemia, and now his family worries that Joey could be hit again. The Paulowsky family carries a genetic burden—a rare form of inherited cancer of the thyroid. Deborah, Joey's mother, found a lump in her neck 6 years ago, and since then 1 family member has died of the cancer and 10 others have had to have their thyroids removed. "Do I have cancer?" Joey asks his mother. "Will it hurt?" The Paulowskys will know the answer next month, when the results of a genetic test will show whether their son carries the family's fateful mutation. (Brownlee, Cook, & Hardigg, 1994, p. 59)*

The answer will be delivered by a member of a field that, just a few decades ago, was nonexistent: genetic counseling. **Genetic counseling** focuses on helping people deal with issues relating to inherited disorders.

Genetic counselors use a variety of data in their work (Lindhout, Frets, & Niermeijer, 1991). For instance, couples contemplating having a child may seek to determine the risks involved in a future pregnancy. In such a case, a counselor will take a thorough family history,

genetic counseling *the discipline that focuses on helping people deal with issues relating to inherited disorders*

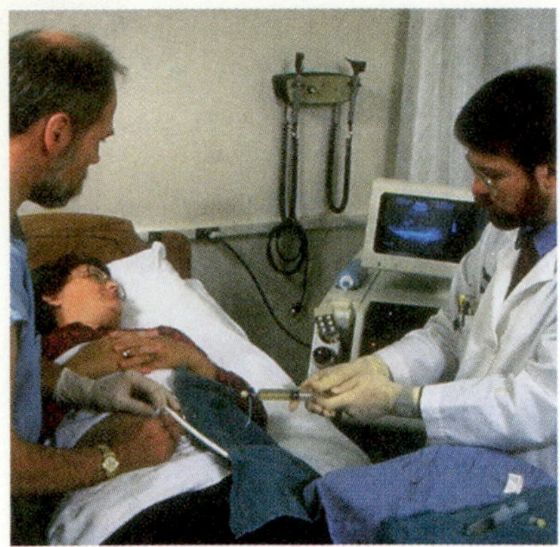

In amniocentesis, a sample of fetal cells is withdrawn from the amniotic sac and used to identify a number of genetic defects.

seeking any familial incidence of birth defects that might indicate a pattern of recessive or X-linked genes. In addition, the counselor will take into account factors such as the age of the mother and father and any previous abnormalities in other children they may have already had.

Typically, genetic counselors suggest a thorough physical examination. Such an exam may identify physical abnormalities which potential parents may have and not be aware of. In addition, samples of blood, skin, and urine may be used to isolate and examine specific chromosomes. Possible genetic defects, such as the presence of an extra sex chromosome, can be identified by assembling a *karyotype,* a chart containing enlarged photos of each of the chromosomes.

If the woman is already pregnant, testing of the unborn child itself is possible. In **amniocentesis**, a small sample of fetal cells is drawn by a tiny needle inserted into the amniotic fluid surrounding the unborn fetus. By analyzing the fetal cells, technicians can identify a variety of genetic defects. In addition, they can determine the sex of the child. Although there is always a danger to the fetus in such an invasive procedure, amniocentesis is generally safe when carried out between the twelfth and sixteenth weeks of pregnancy.

An additional test, **chorionic villus sampling (CVS)**, can be employed even earlier. The test involves taking small samples of hairlike material that surrounds the embryo. CVS can be done between the eighth and eleventh week of pregnancy. However, because it is riskier than amniocentesis and can identify fewer genetic problems, its use is relatively infrequent.

Other tests that are less invasive and therefore less risky are also possible. For instance, the unborn child may be examined through **ultrasound sonography**, in which high-frequency sound waves are used to bombard the mother's womb. These waves produce a rather indistinct, but useful, image of the unborn baby, whose size and shape can then be assessed. By using ultrasound sonography repeatedly, developmental patterns can be determined. After the various tests are complete and all possible information is available, the couple will meet with the genetic counselor again. Typically, counselors avoid giving specific recommendations. Instead, they lay out the facts and present various options, ranging from doing nothing to taking more drastic steps, such as terminating the pregnancy through abortion. Ultimately, it is the parents who must decide what course of action to follow.

The newest role of genetic counselors involves testing to identify whether an individual is susceptible to future disorders because of genetic abnormalities. For instance, *Huntington's disease,* a devastating, always fatal disorder marked by tremors and intellectual deterioration, typically does not appear until people reach their 40s. However, genetic testing can identify much earlier whether a person carries the flawed gene that produces Huntington's disease. Presumably, people's knowledge that they carry the gene can help them prepare themselves for the future.

In addition to Huntington's disease, there is an ever-increasing number of other disorders that can be predicted on the basis of genetic testing (see Table 2-1). Although such testing may bring welcome relief from future worries—if the results are negative—positive results may produce just the opposite effect. In fact, genetic testing raises difficult practical and ethical questions.

Suppose, for instance, a person who thought she was susceptible to Huntington's disease was tested in her 20s and found that she did not carry the defective gene. Obviously, she would experience tremendous relief. But suppose she found that she did carry the flawed gene and was therefore going to get the disease. She might well experience depression and remorse. In fact, some studies show that 10 percent of people who find they have the flawed gene that leads to Huntington's disease never recover fully on an emotional level (R. Nowak, 1994a).

Furthermore, genetic testing is a complicated issue. It rarely provides a simple yes or no answer. Typically it presents a range of probabilities, which many people find difficult to comprehend. For instance, many patients interpret "a risk of around 50 percent" as meaning that their chances are either zero or 100 percent. In addition, people are increasingly demanding the latest genetic test, even if evidence is scanty that they are at appreciable medical risk of having a particular disease (Brownlee, Cook, & Hardigg, 1994).

amniocentesis *the process of identifying genetic defects by examining a small sample of fetal cells drawn by a needle inserted into the amniotic fluid surrounding the unborn fetus*

chorionic villus sampling (CVS) *a test used to find genetic defects that involves taking samples of hairlike material that surrounds the embryo*

ultrasound sonography *a process in which high-frequency sound waves scan the mother's womb to produce an image of the unborn baby, whose size and shape can then be assessed*

TABLE 2-1

GENETIC TESTS

Disease	Description	Incidence	Cost
DNA Tests Available Now			
Adult polycystic kidney disease	Multiple kidney growths	1 in 1,000	$350
Alpha-1-antitrypsin deficiency	Can cause hepatitis, cirrhosis of the liver, emphysema	1 in 2,000 to 1 in 4,000	$200
Charcot-Marie-Tooth disease	Progressive degeneration of muscles	1 in 2,500	$250-$350
Familial adenomatous polyposis	Colon polyps by age 35, often leading to cancer	1 in 5,000	$1,000
Cystic fibrosis	Lungs clog with mucus; usually fatal by age 40	1 in 2,500 Caucasians	$125-$150
Duchenne/Becker muscular dystrophy	Progressive degeneration of muscles	1 in 3,000 males	$300-$900
Hemophilia	Blood fails to clot properly	1 in 10,000	$250-$350
Fragile X syndrome	Most common cause of inherited mental retardation	1 in 1,250 males; 1 in 2,500 females	$250
Gaucher's disease	Mild to deadly enzyme deficiency	1 in 400 Ashkenazic Jews	$100-$150
Huntington's disease	Lethal neurological deterioration	1 in 10,000 Caucasians	$250-$300
"Lou Gehrig's disease" (ALS)	Fatal degeneration of the nervous system	1 in 50,000, 10% familial	$150-$450
Myotonic dystrophy	Progressive degeneration of muscles	1 in 8,000	$250
Multiple endocrine neoplastia	Endocrine gland tumors	1 in 50,000	$900
Neurofibromatosis	Light brown spots to large tumors	1 in 3,000	$900
Retinoblastoma	Blindness; potentially fatal eye tumors	1 in 20,000	$1,500
Spinal muscular atrophy	Progressive degeneration of muscles	7 in 100,000	$100-$900
Tay-Sachs disease	Lethal childhood neurological disorder	1 in 3,600 Ashkenazic Jews	$150
Thalassemia	Mild to fatal anemia	1 in 100,000	$300
Tests of the Future			
Alzheimer's	Most likely multiple genes involved	4 million cases	Not available
Breast cancer	Five to 10% of all cases are thought to be hereditary	2.6 million cases	Not available
Diabetes	Most likely multiple genes involved	13-14 million cases	Not available
Nonpolyposis colon cancer	Several genes cause up to 20% of all cases	150,000 cases per year	Not available
Bipolar disorder	Most likely multiple genes involved	2 million cases	Not available

THE ROLE OF THE ENVIRONMENT IN DETERMINING THE EXPRESSION OF GENES: FROM GENOTYPES TO PHENOTYPES

It is important to keep in mind that the expression of particular traits is affected by factors other than genetics alone. The environment also plays a crucial role in determining the degree to which an individual's genotypic potential reaches fruition.

For instance, consider **temperament**, patterns of arousal and emotionality that represent consistent and enduring characteristics in an individual. Suppose we found—as increasing evidence suggests is the case—that a small percentage of children are born with temperaments that produce an unusual degree of physiological reactivity. Having a tendency to shrink from anything unusual, such infants react to novel stimuli with a rapid increase in heartbeat and unusual excitability of the limbic system of the brain (Gunnar, Porter, Wolf, Rigatuso, & Larson, 1995; Kagan & Snidman, 1991). Such heightened reactivity to stimuli at the start of life, which seems linked to inherited factors, is also likely to cause children, by the time they are 4 or 5, to be considered shy by their parents and teachers. But not always: Some of them behave indistinguishably from their peers at the same age (Rothbart, Ahadi, & Hershey, 1994; DiPietro et al., 1996).

temperament *patterns of arousal and emotionality that represent consistent and enduring characteristics in an individual*

multifactorial transmission *traits that are determined by a combination of both genetic and environmental factors in which a genotype provides a range within which a phenotype may be expressed*

What makes the difference? The answer seems to be the environment in which the children are raised. Children whose parents encourage them to be outgoing by arranging supportive opportunities for them to engage in new activities may overcome their shyness. In contrast, children raised in a stressful environment marked by marital discord or a prolonged illness may be more likely to retain their shyness later in life (Kagan, Arcus, & Snidman, 1993; Pedlow et al., 1993).

Such findings illustrate that many traits represent **multifactorial transmission**, meaning that they are determined by a combination of both genetic and environmental factors. In multifactorial transmission, a genotype provides a particular range within which a phenotype may achieve expression. For instance, people with a genotype that permits them to gain weight easily may never be slim, no matter how much they diet. They may be *relatively* slim, given their genetic heritage, but they may never be able to get beyond a certain degree of thinness. In many cases, then, it is the environment that determines the way in which a particular genotype will be expressed as a phenotype (Plomin, 1994c; Wachs, 1992, 1993).

On the other hand, certain genotypes are relatively unaffected by environmental factors. In such cases, development follows a preordained pattern, relatively independent of the specific environment in which a person is raised. For instance, research on pregnant women who were severely malnourished during famines caused by World War II found that their children were, on average, unaffected physically or intellectually as adults (Z. Stein, et al., 1975). Similarly, no matter how much health food people eat, they are not going to grow beyond certain genetically imposed limitations in height.

Ultimately, of course, it is the unique interaction of inherited and environmental factors that determines people's patterns of development. As Jerome Kagan writes:

> No human quality, psychological or physiological, is free of the contribution of events both within and outside the organism.... [E]very psychological quality is like a pale

Speaking of Development

Lopa Malkan Wani, Genetic Counselor

Born: 1965

Education: Cornell University, B.A. in biology, with a concentration in genetics; Sarah Lawrence, M.S. in genetic counseling

Position: Genetic counselor for Genetrix, Inc.

Home: Newark, California

The field of genetics has not only advanced significantly our understanding of the way we are put together but also spawned a new occupation: genetic counselor. Genetic counselors help people deal with the potential consequences of the genes they carry.

Lopa Wani works in two major areas of the field. "The role of the genetic counselor is a dual one," she explains. "We are concerned with prenatal genetics and pediatric genetics, which deal with different issues.

"Prenatal genetics is concerned with both the period before conception, when we focus on planned pregnancies, and the period preceding birth, when we mostly offer counseling about the risks that might be present, explain tests for genetic conditions, and explore the options that are available.

> gray fabric woven from thin black threads, which represent biology, and thin white ones, which represent experience. But it is not possible to detect any quite black or white threads in the gray cloth. (Bruner, Arcus, & Snidman, 1993, p. 209)

Alternate Routes to Pregnancy: Giving Nature a Boost

For some couples, conception presents a major challenge. In fact, some 15 percent of couples suffer from **infertility**, the inability to conceive after 12 to 18 months of trying to become pregnant.

Infertility is produced by several causes. In some cases, it is the age of the parents (the older the parents, the more likely infertility will occur), previous use of birth control pills, illicit drugs or cigarettes, or previous bouts of sexually transmitted diseases. In other cases, men have abnormally low sperm counts, which decreases the chances that a sperm will successfully fertilize an ovum. And still other cases of infertility are a result of the woman's *mother* taking certain drugs during pregnancy.

Whatever the cause of infertility, there are several approaches that provide alternate paths to conception. Some difficulties can be corrected through the use of drugs or surgery. Another option may be **artificial insemination**, in which a man's sperm is placed directly into a woman's vagina by a physician. In some situations, the woman's husband provides the sperm, while in others it is an anonymous donor from a sperm bank.

In other cases, in vitro fertilization is employed. **In vitro fertilization** (**IVF**) is a procedure in which a woman's ova are removed from her ovaries, and a man's sperm are used to fertilize the ova in a laboratory. The fertilized egg is then implanted in either the woman who provided the donor eggs or in a **surrogate mother**, a woman who agrees to carry the child to term. Surrogate mothers may also be used in cases in which the mother is unable to

infertility *the inability to conceive after 12 to 18 months of trying to become pregnant*

artificial insemination *a process of fertilization in which a man's sperm is placed directly into a woman's vagina by a physician*

in vitro fertilization (IVF) *a procedure in which a woman's ova are removed from her ovaries, and a man's sperm are used to fertilize the ova in a laboratory*

surrogate mother *a woman who agrees to carry a child to term in cases in which the mother who provides the donor eggs is unable to conceive*

"To some people a 4 percent risk factor is a large risk, while to others it isn't."

"If the person feels that the risk is great enough, we proceed to explore the types of testing that are available."

"In pediatric genetics, on the other hand, we work with a child who already has the problem or who may have a problem that needs to be identified."

The disorders that Wani and her colleagues deal with are primarily carried from one generation to the next by recessive genes. "When both parents carry the same nonworking gene, we refer to that as an autosomal recessive condition," explains Wani. "There is a 25 percent chance that the child of that sort of union will be affected by the disorder." Diseases carried by recessive genes include Tay-Sachs disease, cystic fibrosis, and sickle cell anemia, according to Wani.

"The first thing we assess is the parents' view of the condition—what their feelings are. Some people may not view the condition as serious. They might not want to go ahead with the tests for the condition," she explains. "We also have to be sure they understand the disorder, that they have an accurate perception of it."

According to Wani, risk assessment is very important—but equally important is the carrier's perception of the risk. "To some people a 4 percent risk factor is a large risk, while to others it isn't," she says. "If the person feels that the risk is great enough, we proceed to explore the types of testing that are available."

Staying in touch with parents and reading their signals carefully is a significant part of the counselor's work. "When a pregnancy is diagnosed as abnormal, people don't necessarily hear what you tell them the first time. They also have strong feelings of guilt and shame when they find out they are carrying a recessive gene," Wani concludes. "But there's nothing to be ashamed of. All of us carry about five to seven recessive genes that simply don't work right. Every one of us."

conceive; the surrogate mother is artificially inseminated by a father, agreeing to give up rights to the infant.

The use of a surrogate mother presents a variety of ethical and legal issues, as well as many emotional concerns. In some cases, surrogate mothers have decided to refuse to give up the child after its birth, while in others the surrogate mother has sought to have a role in the child's life. In such cases, the rights of the mother, father, surrogate mother, and ultimately the baby are in conflict.

How do children conceived using emerging reproductive technologies such as in vitro fertilization fare? As suggested by the case of Elizabeth Carr, whom we discussed at the beginning of Chapter 1, research shows that they do quite well. In fact, one study found that the quality of parenting in families who have used such techniques may even be superior to that of naturally conceived children. Furthermore, the later psychological adjustment of children conceived using in vitro fertilization and artificial insemination is no different from that of children conceived using natural techniques (Golombok et al., 1995).

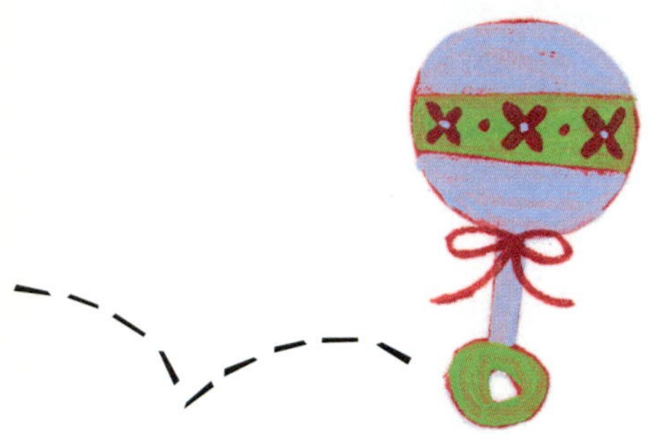

Review and Rethink

REVIEW

- In humans, the male sex cell (the sperm) and the female sex cell (the ovum) provide the developing baby with 23 chromosomes each, through which the baby inherits characteristics from both mother and father.
- A genotype is the underlying combination of genetic material present in an organism, but invisible; a phenotype is the visible trait, the expression of the genotype. Within a range predetermined by the genotype, environmental factors play a significant role in determining the way in which that genotype will be expressed as a phenotype.
- The field of behavioral genetics, a combination of psychology and genetics, studies the effects of genetics on behavior.
- Several inherited and genetic disorders are due to damaged or mutated genes, including phenylketonuria (PKU), Down syndrome, sickle cell anemia, Tay-Sachs disease, and Klinefelter's syndrome.
- Genetic counselors use a variety of data and techniques to advise future parents of possible genetic risks to their unborn children.
- Among the alternate routes to conception are artificial insemination and in vitro fertilization (IVF).

RETHINK

- How can the study of identical twins who were separated at birth help researchers determine the effects of genetic and environmental factors on human development? How might you design such a study?
- How can you inherit some traits from your mother and some from your father? How can you have some traits that are unlike either parent's? How might inherited characteristics "skip a generation," as they are often said to do?
- How might adopted children develop traits similar to those of their adoptive parents? What sorts of traits do you think might be shared or different in adoptive families?
- What are some ethical and philosophical questions that surround the issue of genetic counseling? Might it sometimes be unwise to know ahead of time about possible genetically linked disorders that might afflict your child or yourself?

- What are some examples of how the genotype might limit the expression of the phenotype? How might environment affect the ways in which the genotype is realized as the phenotype?

THE INTERACTION OF HEREDITY AND ENVIRONMENT

Nature versus nurture. Heredity versus environment. Genetic influences versus situational influences.

However we choose to state it, each of the previous statements reflects an enduring question that has intrigued and puzzled developmental researchers about the root causes of human behavior. Is behavior produced by inherited, genetic influences, or is it triggered by factors in the environment?

The answer is: There is no answer. As developmental research accumulates, it is becoming increasingly clear that to view behavior as due to *either* genetic *or* environmental factors is inappropriate. A given behavior is not caused just by genetic factors; nor is it caused solely by environmental forces. Instead, as we first discussed in Chapter 1, the behavior is the product of some combination of the two. The more appropriate question, then, is *how much* of the behavior is caused by genetic factors, and *how much* by environmental factors. (See, for example, the range of possibilities for the determinants of intelligence, illustrated in Figure 2-6.)

ANSWERING THE NATURE-NURTURE RIDDLE

Developmental researchers have used several strategies to try to resolve the question of the degree to which traits, characteristics, and behavior are produced by genetic and environmental factors, respectively. In seeking a resolution, they have turned to studies involving both nonhuman species and humans (Kimble, 1993; Plomin, 1994b; Plomin & McClearn, 1994).

FIGURE 2-6

NATURE-NURTURE CAUSES OF INTELLIGENCE

We can see that intelligence is produced by a range of possible causes, spanning the nature-nurture continuum.

Nature				Nurture
Intelligence is provided entirely by genetic factors; environment plays no role. Even a highly enriched environment and excellent education make no difference.	Although largely inherited, intelligence is affected by an extremely enriched or deprived environment.	Intelligence is affected both by a person's genetic endowment and environment. A person genetically predisposed to low intelligence may perform better if raised in an enriched environment or worse in a deprived environment. Similarly, a person genetically predisposed to higher intelligence may perform worse in a deprived environment, or better in an enriched environment.	Although intelligence is largely a result of environment, genetic abnormalities may produce mental retardation.	Intelligence depends entirely on the environment. Genetics plays no role in determining intellectual success.

Possible Causes

Nonhuman Studies: Controlling Both Genetics and Environment. One approach to understanding the relative contribution of heredity and environment makes use of nonhuman animals. It is relatively simple to develop breeds of animals that are genetically similar to one another in terms of specific traits. The people who raise Butterball turkeys for Thanksgiving do it all the time, producing turkeys that grow especially rapidly so that they can be brought to market inexpensively. Similarly, strains of laboratory animals can be bred to share similar genetic backgrounds.

By observing animals with similar genetic backgrounds in different environments, scientists can determine, with reasonable precision, the effects of specific kinds of environmental stimulation. Conversely, researchers can examine groups of animals that have been bred to have significantly *different* genetic backgrounds on particular traits. Then, by exposing such animals to identical environments, they can determine the role that genetic background plays.

Of course, the drawback to using nonhumans as research subjects is that we can't be sure how well the findings we obtain can be generalized to people. Still, the opportunities that animal research offers are substantial.

Human Studies: Exploiting Genetic Similarities and Dissimilarities. Obviously, researchers can't control either the genetic backgrounds or the environments of humans in the way they can with nonhumans. However, nature conveniently has provided the potential to carry out various kinds of "natural experiments"—in the form of twins.

Recall that identical, monozygotic twins share an identical genetic code. Because their inherited backgrounds are precisely the same, any variations in their behavior must be due entirely to environmental factors.

In a world devoid of ethics, it would be rather simple for researchers to make use of identical twins to draw unequivocal conclusions about the role of nature and nurture. For instance, by separating identical twins at birth and placing them in totally different environments, researchers could assess the impact of environment unambiguously. Obviously, ethical considerations make this impossible. However, there are a fair number of cases in which identical twins are put up for adoption at birth and are raised in substantially different environments. Such instances allow us to draw fairly confident conclusions about the relative contributions of genetics and environment (LaBuda, Gottesman, & Pauls, 1993; Lykken et al., 1993a).

Still, the data from monozygotic twins raised in different environments are not always without bias. Adoption agencies typically take the characteristics (and wishes) of birth mothers into account when they place babies in adoptive homes. For instance, children tend to be placed with families of the same race and religion. Consequently, even when monozygotic twins are placed in different adoptive homes, there are often similarities in the two home environments. The consequence is that researchers can't always unambiguously attribute differences in behavior to genetics or environment.

Dizygotic twins, too, present opportunities to learn about the relative contributions of heredity and situational factors. Recall that dizygotic twins are genetically no more similar than siblings in a family born at different times. It is possible to compare behavior within pairs of dizygotic twins with that of pairs of monozygotic twins (who are genetically identical). If monozygotic twins are more similar on a particular trait, on average, than dizygotic twins, we can assume that genetics plays an important role in determining the expression of that trait (M. Schulman, Keith, & Seligman, 1993).

Still another approach is to study people who are totally unrelated to one another and who therefore have dissimilar genetic backgrounds, but who share an environmental background. For instance, a family that adopts, at the same time, two very young unrelated children probably will provide them with quite similar environments throughout their childhood. In this case, similarities in the children's characteristics and behavior can be attributed with some confidence to environmental influences (N. L. Segal, 1993).

Finally, developmental researchers have examined groups of people in light of their degree of genetic similarity. For instance, if we find a high association on a particular trait between biological parents and their children, but a weaker association between adoptive parents and their children, we have evidence for the importance of genetics in determining the expression of that trait. On the other hand, if there is a stronger association on a trait between adoptive parents and their children than between biological parents and their children, we have evidence for the importance of the environment in determining that trait. In general, when a particular trait tends to occur at similar levels among genetically similar individuals, but tends to vary more among genetically more distant individuals, we can assume that genetics plays an important role in the development of that trait (Rowe, 1994).

Developmental researchers have used all these approaches, and more, to study the relative impact of genetic and environmental factors. What have they found? Before turning to their specific findings, it is important to state the general conclusion resulting from decades of research: Virtually all traits, characteristics, and behaviors are the joint result of the combination and interaction of nature and nurture. Like love and marriage and horses and carriages, genetic and environmental factors work in tandem to create the unique individual that each of us is and will become.

Some traits—like curly hair—have a clear genetic component.

Physical Traits: Family Resemblances

When patients entered the examining room of Dr. Cyril Marcus, they didn't realize that sometimes they were actually being treated by his identical twin brother, Dr. Stewart Marcus. So similar in appearance and manner were the twins that even long-time patients were fooled by this admittedly unethical behavior, which occurred in a bizarre case made famous in the film *Dead Ringers*.

Monozygotic twins are merely the most extreme example of the fact that the more genetically similar two people are, the more likely they are to share physical characteristics. Tall parents tend to have tall children, and short ones tend to have short children. Obesity, which is defined as being more than 20 percent above the average weight for a given height, also has a strong genetic component. For example, in one study, pairs of identical twins were put on diets that contained an extra 1,000 calories a day—and ordered not to exercise. Over a 3-month period, the twins gained almost identical amounts of weight. Moreover, different pairs of twins varied substantially in how much weight they gained, with some pairs gaining almost three times as much weight as other pairs (C. Bouchard et al., 1990). Other, less obvious physical characteristics also show strong genetic influences. For instance, blood pressure, respiration rates, and even the age at which life ends are more similar in closely related individuals than in those who are less genetically similar (Jost & Sontag, 1944; Price & Gottesman, 1991; Sorensen et al., 1988).

Intelligence: More Research, More Controversy

No other issue involving the relative influence of heredity and environment has generated more research than the topic of intelligence. Why? The main reason is that intelligence, generally measured in terms of an IQ score, is a core human characteristic. IQ is strongly related to success in scholastic endeavors and, somewhat less strongly, to other types of achievement.

Let's first consider the degree to which intelligence is related to genetic factors. The answer is unambiguous: Genetics plays a significant role in intelligence. Both overall intelligence and specific subcomponents of intelligence (such as spatial skills, verbal skills, and memory) show strong effects for heredity (Cardon et al., 1992; Cardon & Fulker, 1993; McGue et al., 1993; Pedersen et al., 1992). As can be seen in Figure 2-7, the closer the genetic link between two individuals, the greater the correspondence of their overall IQ scores.

Not only is genetics an important influence on intelligence, but the impact increases with age. For instance, as fraternal (i.e., dizygotic) twins move from infancy to adolescence, their IQ scores become less similar. In contrast, the IQ scores of identical (monozygotic)

FIGURE 2-7

GENETICS AND IQ

The closer the genetic link between two individuals, the greater the correspondence between their IQ scores.

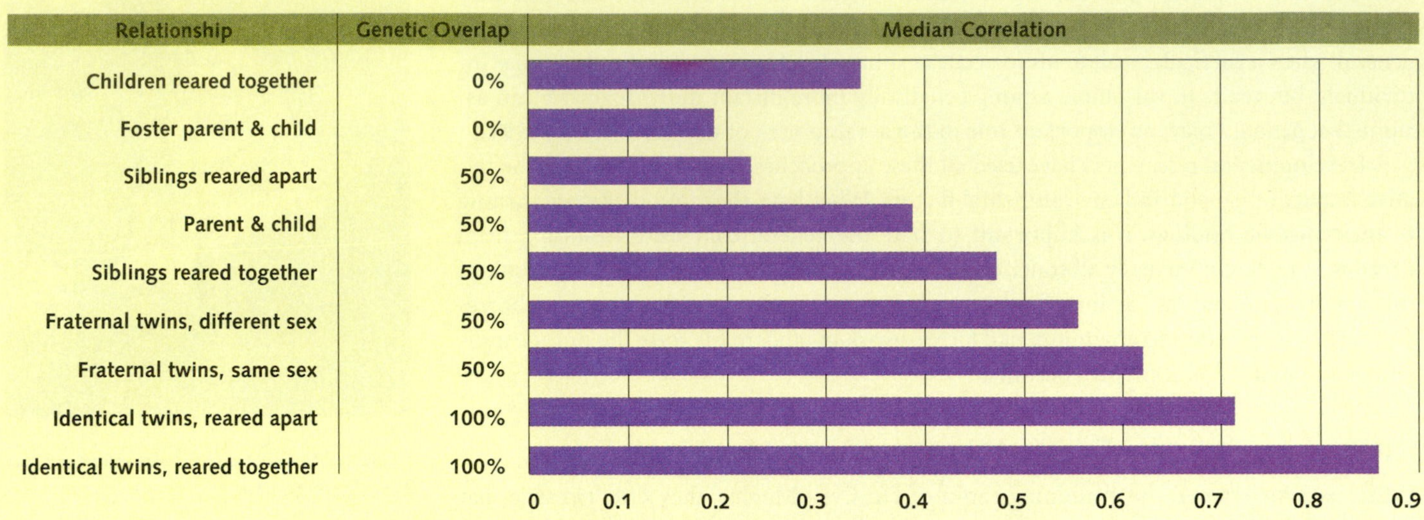

twins become increasingly similar over the course of time. These opposite patterns suggest the intensifying influence of inherited factors with increasing age (N. Brody, 1993; McGue et al., 1993; R. S. Wilson, 1983).

Although it is clear that heredity plays an important role in intelligence, investigators are much more divided on the question of how to quantify that role. Perhaps the most extreme view is held by psychologist Arthur Jensen (1969), who argues that as much as 80 percent of intelligence is a result of the influence of heredity. Others have suggested more modest figures, ranging from 50 to 70 percent (e.g., T. J. Bouchard, 1990; Herrnstein & Murray, 1994; Plomin, DeFries, & McClearn, 1990; Weinberg, 1989).

It is important to keep in mind that although heredity clearly plays an important role in intelligence, it is hardly the only factor. Even the most extreme estimates of the role of genetics still allow for environmental factors to play a significant role (Storfer, 1990). In fact, in terms of public policy for maximizing people's intellectual success, the issue is not whether primarily hereditary or environmental factors underlie intelligence. Instead, as developmental psychologist Sandra Scarr suggests, we should be asking what can be done to maximize the intellectual development of each individual (Scarr & Carter-Saltzman, 1982).

Genetic and Environmental Influences on Personality: Born to Be Outgoing?

Although it seems reasonable to most people that such characteristics as race and eye color are inherited, the notion that personality characteristics are affected by genetic factors seems less credible. However, increasing evidence supports the conclusion that at least some personality traits have at least some genetic components (T. J. Bouchard, 1994; Rowe, 1993, 1994; D. Smith, 1993).

For example, neuroticism and extroversion are among the personality factors that have been linked most directly to genetic factors. The term *neuroticism,* when considered in the context of personality, refers to the degree of moodiness, touchiness, or sensitivity an individual characteristically displays. In other words, neuroticism reflects emotional reactivity. *Extroversion* is the degree to which a person seeks to be with others, to behave in an outgoing manner, and generally to be sociable (Bergeman et al., 1993; Loehlin, 1992; Plomin, 1994a).

How do we know which personality traits reflect genetics? Some evidence comes from examination of genes. For instance, surprising recent evidence suggests that a specific gene partially determines risk-taking behavior. According to two teams of researchers, a novelty-seeking gene affects the production of the brain chemical dopamine, making some people more prone than others to seek out novel situations and to take risks (Benjamin et al., 1996; Ebstein et al., 1996).

Other evidence for the role of genetics in the determination of personality traits comes largely from studies of twins. For instance, in one large-scale study, personality psychologist Auke Tellegen and colleagues studied the personality traits of hundreds of pairs of twins. Because a good number of the twins were genetically identical but had been raised apart, it was possible to determine with some confidence the influence of genetic factors (Tellegen et al., 1988).

Tellegen found that certain traits reflected the contribution of genetics considerably more than others. As you can see in Figure 2-8, social potency (the tendency to be a masterful, forceful leader who enjoys being the center of attention) and traditionalism (strict endorsement of rules and authority) are strongly associated with genetic factors.

Other research has revealed genetic influences on other, less central personality traits. For example, a person's political attitudes, religious interests and values, and even attitudes toward human sexuality seem to have genetic components. Even the amount of television that people watch appears to have a genetic component (Coccaro, Bergeman, & McClearn, 1993; Eysenck, 1976; Loehlin, 1992; Lykken et al., 1993a; Plomin et al., 1990; Schulman et al., 1993; Waller et al., 1990).

It may seem far-fetched that factors such as television-viewing levels are affected by genetics. Admittedly, it is hardly likely that evolution has provided humans with a gene that controls TV viewing. How, then, could genetics play a role in a behavior that is so purely a part of contemporary life?

The answer comes from considering what is involved in watching television: It is a passive, solitary activity, one that largely precludes involvement in more social activities. Consequently, the influence of genetics may be indirect. For instance, we know that genetics plays an important role in determining a person's general level of extroversion. It may be

Recent research suggests that our preferences for risk taking may be genetically determined.

FIGURE 2-8

PERSONALITY AND GENETICS

These traits are among the personality factors that are related most closely to genetic factors. The higher the percentage, the greater the degree to which the trait reflects the influence of heredity.

(*Source:* Tellegen et al., 1988).

Trait	Percentage	Description
Social potency	61%	A person high in this trait is masterful, a forceful leader who likes to be the center of attention.
Traditionalism	60%	Follows rules and authority, endorses high moral standards and strict discipline.
Stress reaction	55%	Feels vulnerable and sensitive and is given to worries and is easily upset.
Absorption	55%	Has a vivid imagination readily captured by rich experience; relinquishes sense of reality.
Alienation	55%	Feels mistreated and used, that "the world is out to get me."
Well-being	54%	Has a cheerful disposition, feels confident and optimistic.
Harm avoidance	50%	Shuns the excitement of risk and danger, prefers the safe route even if it is tedious.
Aggression	48%	Is physically aggressive and vindictive, has taste for violence and is "out to get the world."
Achievement	46%	Works hard, strives for mastery, and puts work and accomplishment ahead of other things.
Control	43%	Is cautious and plodding, rational and sensible, likes carefully planned events.
Social closeness	33%	Prefers emotional intimacy and close ties, turns to others for comfort and help.

that people who are relatively extroverted are less likely to watch television, an activity that hinders social involvement with others. On the other hand, a more introverted person may be more apt to watch television largely because it involves only minimal social interaction.

Such reasoning helps illustrate the importance of inherited factors in determining personality. However, it also points out once again the critical interplay between nature and nurture. In homes that have a television set, an individual's personality tendencies that are shaped by genetic factors may be exhibited in a particular way. But in homes that lack a television set, these tendencies may be expressed in quite different behaviors. There is a constant interplay, then, between heredity and environment. In fact, the way in which nature and nurture interact may be reflected not just in the behavior of individuals, but in the very foundations of a culture, as we see next.

Developmental Diversity

Cultural Differences in Physical Arousal: Might a Culture's Philosophical Outlook Be Determined by Genetics?

The Buddhist philosophy, an inherent part of many Asian cultures, emphasizes harmony and peacefulness and suggests that one should seek the eradication of human desire. In contrast, some of the traditional philosophies of Western civilization, such as those of Martin Luther and John Calvin, accentuate the importance of controlling the anxiety, fear, and guilt that are thought to be basic parts of the human condition.

Could such philosophical approaches reflect, in part, genetic factors? That is the controversial suggestion made by developmental psychologist Jerome Kagan and his colleagues. They speculate that the underlying temperament of a given society, determined genetically, may predispose people in that society toward a particular philosophy (Kagan et al., 1993).

Kagan bases his admittedly speculative suggestion on well-confirmed findings that show clear differences in temperament between Caucasian and Asian children. For instance, one study that compared 4-month-old infants in China, Ireland, and the United States found several relevant differences. In comparison to the Caucasian-American babies and the Irish babies, the Chinese babies had significantly lower motor activity, irritability, and vocalization (see Table 2-2).

Kagan suggests that the Chinese, who enter the world temperamentally calmer, may find Buddhist philosophical notions of serenity more in tune with their natural inclinations. In contrast, Westerners, who are emotionally more volatile and tense, and who report higher levels of guilt, are more likely to be attracted to philosophies that articulate the necessity of controlling the unpleasant feelings that they are more apt to encounter in their everyday experience (Kagan et al., 1994).

It is important to note that this does not mean that one philosophical approach is necessarily better, or worse, than the other. Nor does it mean that either of the temperaments from which the philosophies are thought to spring is superior or inferior to the other. Similarly, we must keep in mind that any single individual within a culture can be more or less temperamentally volatile, and that the range of temperaments found even within a particular culture is vast. Finally, as we noted in our initial discussion of temperament, environmental conditions can have a significant effect on the portion of a person's temperament that is not genetically determined.

Still, the notion that the very basis of culture—its philosophical traditions—may be affected by genetic factors is intriguing. More research is necessary to determine just how the unique interaction of heredity and environment within a given culture may produce a framework for viewing and understanding the world.

TABLE 2-2

MEAN BEHAVIORAL SCORES FOR MOTOR ACTIVITY, CRYING, FRETTING, VOCALIZING, AND SMILING FOR CAUCASIAN-AMERICAN, IRISH, AND CHINESE 4-MONTH-OLD INFANTS

Behavior	American	Irish	Chinese
Motor activity	48.6	36.7	11.2
Crying (in seconds)	7.0	2.9	1.1
Fretting (% trials)	10.0	6.0	1.9
Vocalizing (% trials)	31.4	31.1	8.1
Smiling (% trials)	4.1	2.6	3.6

(*Source:* Kagan, J., Arcus, D., & Snidman, N., 1993)

PSYCHOLOGICAL DISORDERS: THE ROLE OF GENETICS AND ENVIRONMENT

> Lori Schiller began to hear voices when she was a teenager in summer camp. Without warning, the voices screamed, "You must die! Die! Die!" She ran from her bunk into the darkness, where she thought she could get away. Camp counselors found her screaming as she jumped wildly on a trampoline. "I thought I was possessed," she said later. (Bennet, 1992)

In a sense, she was possessed: possessed with schizophrenia, one of the most severe types of psychological disorder. Normal and happy through childhood, Schiller's world took a tumble during adolescence as she increasingly lost her hold on reality. For the next two decades, she would be in and out of institutions, struggling to ward off the ravages of the disorder.

What was the cause of Schiller's mental disorder? Increasing evidence suggests that schizophrenia is brought about by genetic factors. The disorder runs in families, with some families showing an unusually high incidence. Moreover, the closer the genetic links between someone with schizophrenia and another family member, the more likely it is that the other person will also develop schizophrenia. For instance, a monozygotic twin has close to a 50 percent risk of developing schizophrenia when the other twin develops the disorder (see Figure 2-9). On the other hand, a niece or nephew of a person with schizophrenia has less than a 5 percent chance of developing the disorder (Gottesman, 1991, 1993; Prescott & Gottesman, 1993).

However, these data also illustrate that genetics alone is not responsible for the disorder. If genetics were the sole cause, the risk for an identical twin would be 100 percent.

FIGURE 2-9

SCHIZOPHRENIA AND GENETICS

The psychological disorder of schizophrenia has clear genetic components. The closer the genetic links between someone with schizophrenia and another family member, the more likely it is that the other person will also develop schizophrenia.

(*Source:* Gottesman, 1991).

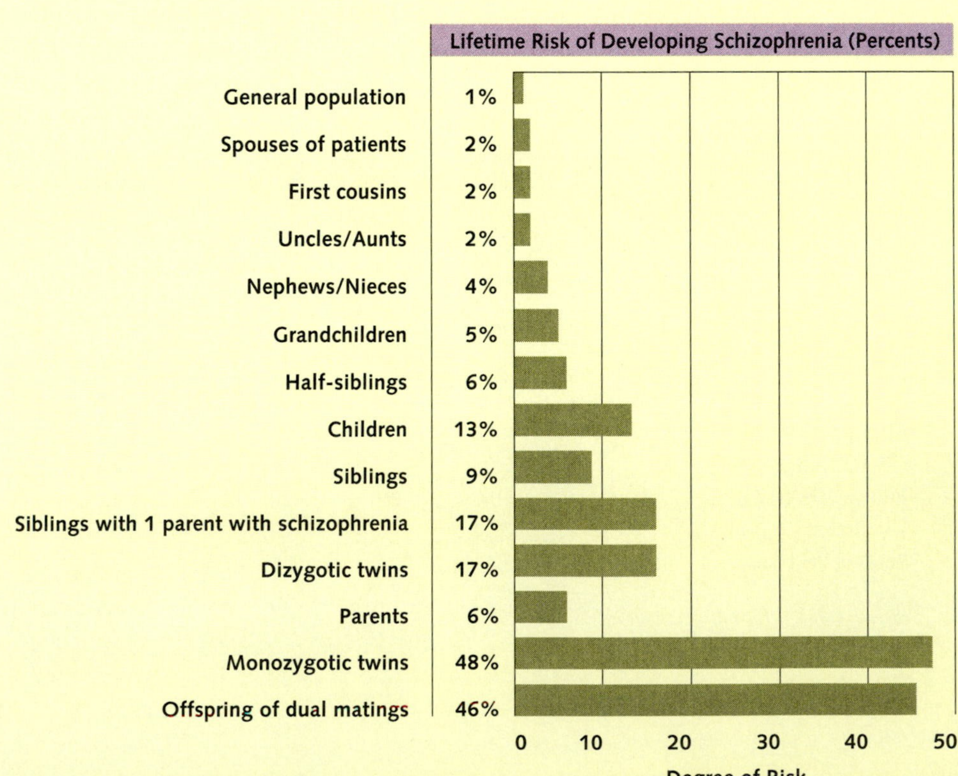

Developmental psychologist Sandra Scarr.

Consequently, other factors account for the disorder, ranging from structural abnormalities in the brain to a biochemical imbalance (Iacono & Grove, 1993; Wang et al., 1993).

It also seems that even if individuals harbor a genetic predisposition toward schizophrenia, they are not destined to develop the disorder. Instead, they may inherit an unusual sensitivity to stress in the environment. If stress is low, schizophrenia will not occur. But if stress is sufficiently strong, it will lead to schizophrenia. On the other hand, for someone with a strong genetic predisposition toward the disorder, even relatively weak environmental stressors may lead to schizophrenia (Fowles, 1992; Gottesman, 1991).

Several other psychological disorders have been shown to be related, at least in part, to genetic factors. For instance, major depression, alcoholism, autism, and attention-deficit hyperactivity disorder have significant inherited components (Eaves et al., 1993; McGue, 1993; McGuffin & Katz, 1993; Rutter et al., 1993; Shields, 1973).

The example of schizophrenia and other genetically related psychological disorders also illustrates a fundamental principle regarding the relationship between heredity and environment, one that underlies much of our previous discussion. Specifically, the role of genetics is often to produce preparedness for a future course of development. When and whether a certain behavioral characteristic will actually be displayed depends on the nature of the environment. Thus, although a predisposition for schizophrenia may be present at birth, typically people do not show the disorder until adolescence—if at all.

Similarly, certain other kinds of traits are more likely to be displayed as the influence of parents and other socializing factors declines. For example, adopted children may, early in their lives, display traits that are relatively similar to their adoptive parents', given the overwhelming influence of the environment on young children. In contrast, as they get older and their parents' influence declines, genetically influenced traits may begin to manifest themselves as unseen genetic factors begin to play a greater role (Caspi & Moffitt, 1991, 1993; Loehlin, 1992).

According to developmental psychologist Sandra Scarr (1992, 1993), the genetic endowment provided to children by their parents not only determines their genetic characteristics, but actively influences their environment. Because of **active genotype-environment effects**, children focus on those aspects of their environment that are most congruent with their genetically determined abilities. At the same time, they pay less attention to those aspects of the environment that are less compatible with their genetic endowment. For instance, a particularly well-coordinated child may be more apt to try out for Little League baseball, while her less-coordinated, but more musically endowed, friend might be more apt to try out for an after-school chorus. In each case, the child is actively producing an environment in which her genetically determined abilities can flourish.

But the relationship between genetics and environment can be more subtle. In some cases, there are **passive genotype-environment effects**, in which *parents'* genes are associated with the environment in which children are raised. For example, a particularly sports-oriented parent, who has genes that promote good physical coordination, may provide many opportunities for a child to play sports. Similarly, there are **evocative genotype-environment effects**, in which a child's genes elicit a particular type of environment. For instance, an infant's demanding behavior may cause parents to be more attentive to the infant's needs than they would if the infant were less demanding.

In sum, determining whether behavior is primarily attributable to nature or nurture is a bit like shooting at a moving target. Not only are behaviors and traits a joint outcome of genetic and environmental factors, but the relative influence of genes and environment for specific characteristics shifts over the course of people's lives. Although the pool of genes we inherit at birth sets the stage for our future development, the constantly shifting scenery and the other characters in our lives determine just how our development eventually plays out.

active genotype-environment effects *situations in which children focus on those aspects of their environment that are most congruent with their genetically determined abilities*

passive genotype-environment effects *situations in which parents' genes are associated with the environment in which children are raised*

evocative genotype-environment effects *situations in which a child's genes elicit a particular type of environment*

Review and Rethink

REVIEW

- Human characteristics and behavior are a joint outcome of genetic and environmental factors. The extent to which a given trait is caused by genetic factors or environmental factors varies from trait to trait and over time.
- Scientists use both nonhuman and human studies to analyze the different contributions of genetics and environment. Individuals with identical genetic backgrounds and different environmental influences and, conversely, individuals with different genetic backgrounds and highly similar environmental influences are studied to tease out the varying influences of nature and nurture.
- Genetic influences have been identified in physical characteristics, intelligence, personality traits and behaviors, and psychological disorders.
- There is some speculation that entire cultures may be predisposed genetically toward certain types of philosophical viewpoints and attitudes.

RETHINK

- How might a different environment from the one you experienced have affected the development of personality characteristics that you believe you inherited from one or both of your parents?
- Do you think dizygotic (i.e., fraternal) twins are likely to be more similar to one another than two siblings born of the same parents at different times? Why? What genetic or environmental factors help determine your answer?
- What sort of study might you design to examine whether "handedness" (the tendency to be either right-handed or left-handed) is determined more by genetics or environment?
- Some people have used the proven genetic basis of intelligence to argue against strenuous educational efforts on behalf of individuals with below-average IQs. Does this viewpoint make sense based on what you have learned about heredity and environment? Why or why not?
- A friend with a schizophrenic sister has just learned that her grandfather also had this disorder. Using your knowledge of the role of genetics and environment, what would you tell your friend about her chances of developing schizophrenia?

PRENATAL GROWTH AND CHANGE

From the moment of conception, development proceeds relentlessly, guided by the complex set of genetic guidelines inherited from the parents, and influenced from the start by environmental factors. Starting as a single cell produced by the alliance of ovum and sperm at the instant of conception, prenatal growth proceeds in an orderly, yet surprisingly rapid, pace.

THE STAGES OF THE PRENATAL PERIOD: THE ONSET OF DEVELOPMENT

The prenatal period consists of three phases: the germinal, embryonic, and fetal stages. They are summarized in Table 2-3.

germinal stage *the first—and shortest—stage of the prenatal period which takes place during the first 2 weeks following conception*

The Germinal Stage: Fertilization to 2 Weeks. The **germinal stage**, the first—and shortest—stage of the prenatal period, takes place during the first 2 weeks following conception. It is characterized by methodical cell division and the attachment of the organism to the wall of the uterus. Cell division gets off to a quick start: Three days after

TABLE 2-3

STAGES OF THE PRENATAL PERIOD

GERMINAL STAGE	EMBRYONIC STAGE	FETAL STAGE
Fertilization to 2 Weeks	**2 Weeks to 8 Weeks**	**8 Weeks to Birth**
The germinal stage is the first and shortest, characterized by methodical cell division and the attachment of the organism to the wall of the uterus. Three days after fertilization the zygote consists of 32 cells, a number that doubles by the next day. Within a week the zygote multiplies to 100 to 150 cells. The cells become specialized, with some forming a protective layer around the zygote.	In the embryonic stage, the zygote is now designated an embryo. The embryo develops three layers, which ultimately form a different set of structures as development proceeds. The layers are: Ectoderm: Skin, sense organs, brain, spinal cord. Endoderm: Digestive system, liver, respiratory system. Mesoderm: Muscles, blood, circulatory system. The embryo is 1 inch long.	The fetal stage formally starts when the differentiation of the major organs has occurred. Now called a fetus, the individual grows rapidly as length increases 20 times. At 4 months the fetus weighs an average of 4 ounces; at 7 months, 3 pounds; and at the time of birth, the average child weighs just over 7 pounds.

fertilization, the zygote consists of some 32 cells, and by the next day the number doubles. Within a week, the zygote is made up of 100 to 150 cells, and the number rises with increasing rapidity.

In addition to increasing in number, the cells of the zygote become increasingly specialized. For instance, some cells form a protective layer around the zygote, while others begin to establish the rudiments of a placenta and umbilical cord. When fully developed, the **placenta** serves as a conduit between the mother and fetus, providing nourishment and oxygen via the *umbilical cord.* In addition, waste materials from the developing child are removed through the umbilical cord.

placenta *a conduit between the mother and fetus, providing nourishment and oxygen via the umbilical cord*

embryonic stage *the period from 2 to 8 weeks following fertilization during which significant growth occurs in the major organs and body systems*

The Embryonic Stage: 2 Weeks to 8 Weeks. By the end of the germinal period—just 2 weeks after conception—the zygote is firmly secured to the wall of the mother's uterus. At this point, the child is called an *embryo.*

The **embryonic stage** is the period from 2 to 8 weeks following fertilization. During this time, significant growth occurs in the major organs and body systems. At the begin-

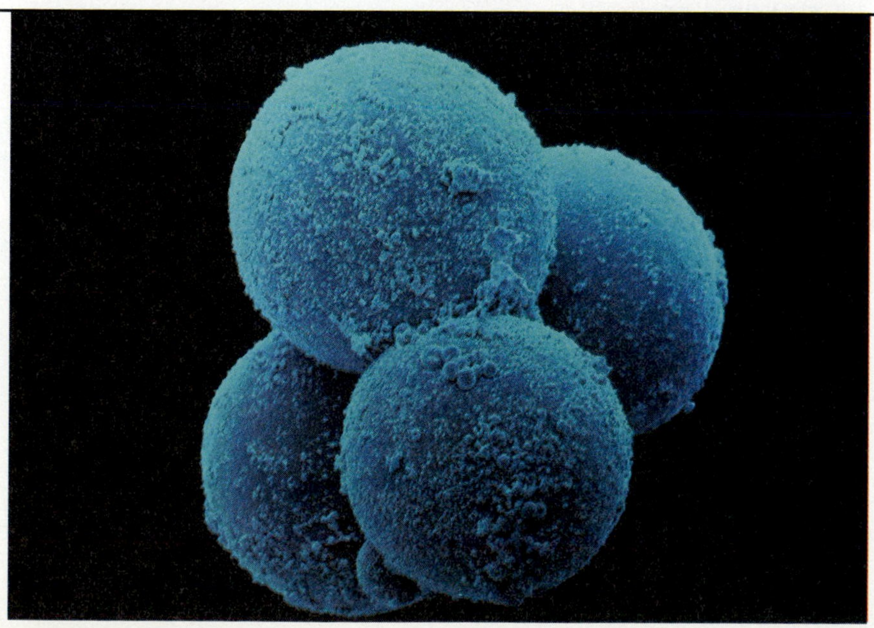

On the second day following fertilization, in the germinal stage, the organism consists of four cells.

ning of the embryonic stage, the developing child has three distinct layers, each of which will ultimately form a different set of structures as development proceeds.

fetal stage *the stage that begins at about 8 weeks after conception and continues until birth*

fetus *a developing child, from 8 weeks after conception until birth*

The outer layer of the embryo, the *ectoderm,* will form skin, hair, teeth, sense organs, and the brain and spinal cord. The *endoderm,* the inner layer, produces the digestive system, liver, pancreas, and respiratory system. Sandwiched between the ectoderm and endoderm is the *mesoderm,* from which the muscles, bones, blood, and circulatory system are forged. Every part of the body is formed from these three layers.

An observer looking at an embryo at the end of the embryonic stage would be hard-pressed to identify it as human. Only an inch long, an 8-week-old embryo has what appear to be gills and a taillike structure. On the other hand, a closer look reveals several familiar features. Rudimentary eyes, nose, lips, and even teeth can be recognized, and the embryo has stubby bulges that will form arms and legs.

The Fetal Stage: 8 Weeks to Birth. It is not until the final period of prenatal development, the fetal stage, that the developing child becomes instantly recognizable. The **fetal stage** starts at about 8 weeks after conception and continues until birth. The fetal stage formally starts when the differentiation of the major organs has occurred.

Now called a **fetus**, the developing child undergoes astoundingly rapid change during the fetal stage. For instance, it increases in length some 20 times, and its proportions change dramatically. At 2 months, around half the fetus is what will ultimately be its head; by 5 months, the head accounts for just over a quarter of its total size (see Figure 2-10). The fetus also increases in weight substantially. At 4 months, the fetus weighs an average of about 4 ounces; at 7 months, it weighs about 3 pounds; and at the time of birth, the average child weighs just over 7 pounds.

At the same time, the complexity of the organism increases rapidly. Organs become more differentiated and operational. By 3 months, the fetus swallows and urinates. In addition, the interconnections between the different parts of the body become more complex and integrated. Arms develop hands; hands develop fingers; fingers develop nails.

As this is happening, the fetus makes itself known to the outside world. Although mothers may at first be unaware in the earliest stages of pregnancy that they are, in fact, pregnant, the fetus now becomes increasingly active. By 4 months, a mother can feel the movement of her child, and several months later others can feel the baby's kicks through the mother's skin.

During the fetal stage, the fetus develops a wide repertoire of different types of activi-

FIGURE 2-10

HEAD SIZE IN FETAL PERIOD

During the fetal period, the proportions of the body change dramatically. At 2 months, the head represents about half the fetus, but by the time of birth, it is one quarter of its total size.

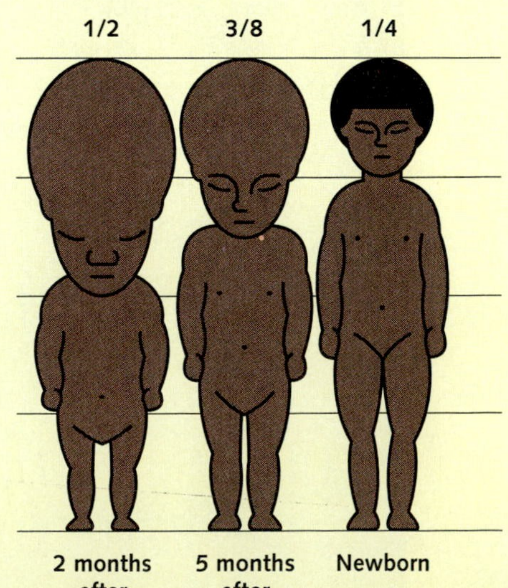

ties (Smotherman & Robinson, 1996). In addition to the kicks that alert its mother to its presence, the fetus can turn, do somersaults, cry, hiccup, clench its fist, open and close its eyes, and suck its thumb. It also is capable of hearing and can even respond to sounds that it hears repeatedly (Lecanuet, Granier-Deferre, & Busnel, 1995). For instance, researchers Anthony DeCasper and Melanie Spence (1986) asked a group of pregnant mothers to read aloud the Dr. Seuss story *The Cat in the Hat* two times a day during the latter months of pregnancy. Three days after the babies were born, they appeared to recognize the story they had heard, responding more to it than to another story that had a different rhythm.

Just as no two adults are alike, no two fetuses are the same. Although development during the prenatal period follows the broad patterns outlined here, there are significant differences in the specific nature of individual fetuses' behavior. Some fetuses are exceedingly active, while others are more sedentary. Some spend most of their time sucking their thumbs; others never do this at all. Some have relatively quick heart rates, while others' are slower, with the typical range varying between 120 to 160 beats per minute (Lecanuet et al., 1995).

Such differences in fetal behavior are due in part to genetic characteristics inherited at the moment of fertilization. Other kinds of differences, though, are brought about by the nature of the environment in which the child spends its first 9 months of life. As we will see, there are numerous ways in which the prenatal environment of infants affects their development—in good ways and bad.

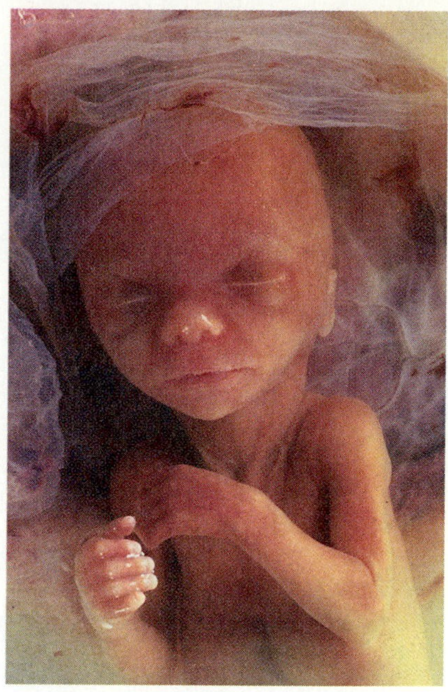

At 12 weeks, this fetus is clearly recognizable as a human.

The Prenatal Environment: Threats to Development

According to the Sirionο people of South America, if a pregnant woman eats the meat of certain kinds of animals, she runs the risk of having a child who may act and look like those animals. According to opinions offered on daytime television talk shows such as the Oprah Winfrey Show, a pregnant mother should avoid getting angry in order to spare her child from entering the world with anger (Cole, 1990).

Such views are largely the stuff of folklore. However, it is true that certain aspects of mothers' and fathers' behavior, both before and after conception, can produce lifelong consequences for the child. Some consequences show up immediately, while others, more insidious, may not appear until years after birth. In fact, half aren't apparent before birth (S. W. Jacobson et al., 1985; Leavitt & Goldson, 1996).

Some of the most profound consequences are brought about by teratogenic agents. A **teratogen** is a factor that produces a birth defect. Although it is the job of the placenta to keep teratogens from reaching the fetus, the placenta is not entirely successful at this, and probably every fetus is exposed to some teratogens. Furthermore, the timing of exposure to a teratogen is crucial. At some phases of prenatal development, a teratogen may have only a minimal impact. At other periods, however, the consequences may be profound (see Figure 2-11; Needleman & Bellinger, 1994; Bookstein et al., 1996; Rizzo et al., 1997).

Mother's Diet. Most of our knowledge of the environmental factors that affect the developing fetus comes from the study of the mother. For instance, a mother's diet clearly plays an important role in bolstering the development of the fetus. A mother who eats a varied diet high in nutrients is apt to have fewer complications during pregnancy, an easier labor, and a generally healthier baby than a mother whose diet is restricted in nutrients (J. L. Brown, 1987; Morgane et al., 1993).

The problem of diet is of immense global concern. In 1992 the World Food Council estimated that there were 550 million hungry people in the world. Even worse, the number of people vulnerable to hunger was thought to be close to one *billion.* Clearly, restrictions in diet that bring about hunger on such a massive scale affect millions of children born to women living in those conditions (United Nations, 1994; Pollitt et al., 1996).

Fortunately, there are ways to counteract the types of maternal malnourishment that affect prenatal development. Dietary supplements given to mothers can reverse some of the problems produced by a poor diet (Crosby, 1991; Prentice, 1991). Furthermore, research

teratogen *a factor that produces a birth defect*

FIGURE 2-11

SENSITIVITY TO TERATOGENS

Depending on their state of development, different parts of the body vary in their sensitivity to teratogens. (*Source:* Moore, 1974, p. 96).

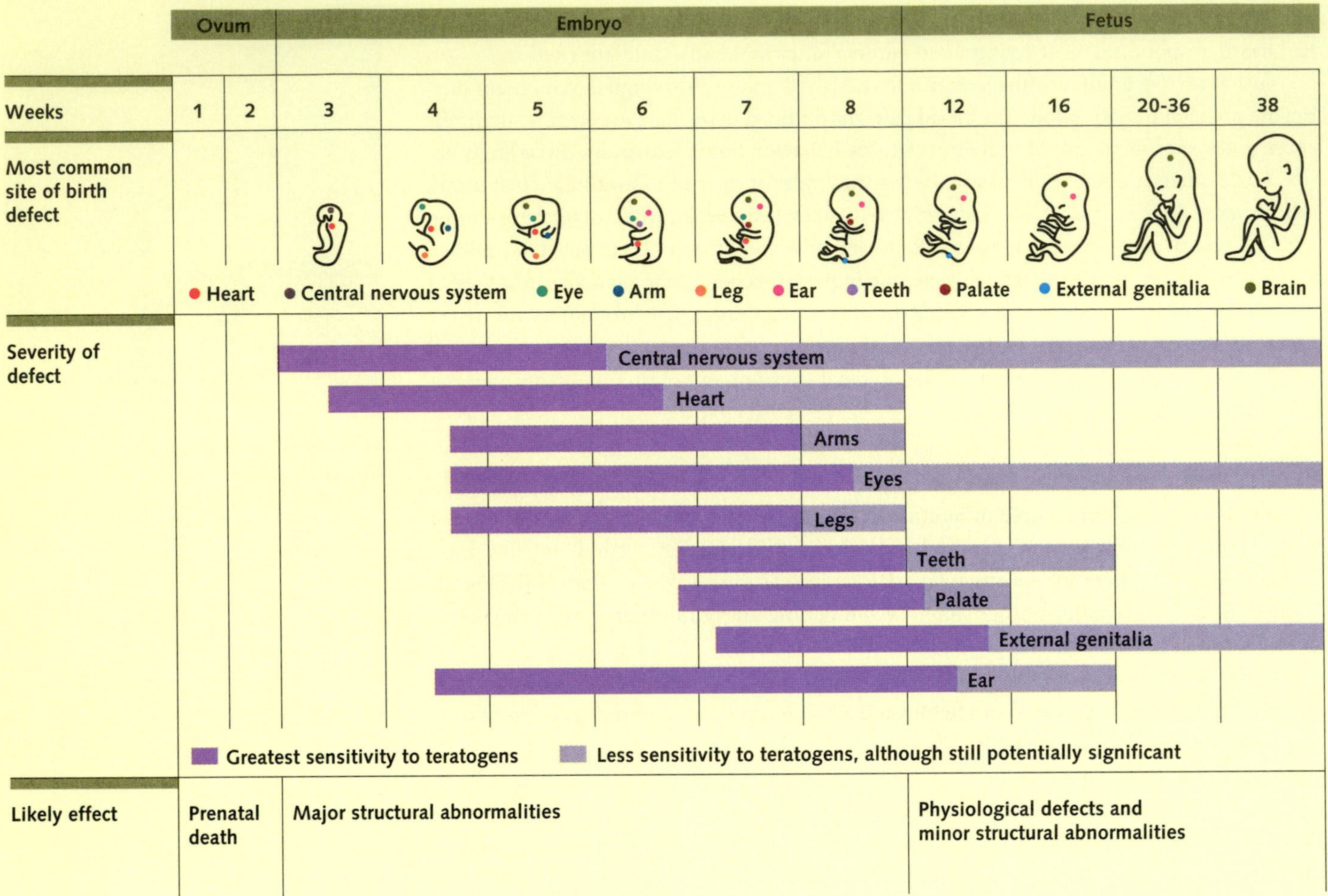

shows that babies who were malnourished as fetuses, but who are subsequently raised in enriched environments, can overcome some of the effects of their early malnourishment (Grantham-McGregor et al., 1994). However, the reality is that few of the world's children whose mothers were malnourished *before* their birth are apt to find themselves in enriched environments *after* birth (Garber, 1981; Ricciuti, 1993; Zeskind & Ramey, 1981).

Mother's Age. With a great deal of medical help from her physicians, a 63-year-old woman gave birth in 1997. At the time, she was the oldest woman ever known to have become a mother. Most of the media attention, which was substantial, focused on the potential psychological difficulties for a child whose mother would be so atypically old as well as the medical ethics of the case.

However, the mother's advanced age probably had an impact on physical aspects of her pregnancy and birth, as well as potentially on her child's future development. Women who give birth when over the age of 30 are at greater risk for a variety of pregnancy and birth complications than younger women. For instance, they are more apt to give birth prematurely, and their children are more likely to have low birth weights (G. S. Berkowitz et al., 1990; Cnattingius, Berendes, & Forman, 1993; Vercellini et al., 1993).

Furthermore, older mothers are considerably more likely to give birth to children with Down syndrome, a form of mental retardation. For mothers over 40, the incidence of Down syndrome is 1 percent; for mothers over 50, the incidence increases to 25 percent (Gaulden, 1992).

The risks involved in pregnancy are greater not only for unusually old mothers, but for atypically young women as well. Women who become pregnant during adolescence—and such pregnancies actually encompass 20 percent of all pregnancies—are more likely to have premature deliveries. Furthermore, the mortality rate of infants born to adolescent mothers is double that for mothers in their 20s.

Keep in mind, though, that the higher mortality rate for infants born to younger women may reflect more than just physiological problems related to the mothers' young age. The heightened mortality rate is also a consequence of adverse social and economic factors, which may have set the stage for the adolescent to become pregnant in the first place. Similarly, some researchers argue that older mothers are not automatically at risk for more pregnancy problems. For instance, one study found that when women in their 40s who had not experienced health difficulties were considered they were no more likely to have prenatal problems than those in their 20s (Ales, Druzin, & Santini, 1990).

Mother's Illness. Depending on when it strikes, an illness in a pregnant woman can have devastating consequences. For instance, the onset of *rubella* (German measles) in the mother prior to the 11th week of pregnancy is likely to cause serious consequences in the baby, including blindness, deafness, heart defects, or brain damage. In later stages of a pregnancy, however, adverse consequences of rubella become increasingly less likely.

Several other diseases may affect a developing fetus, again depending on when the illness is contracted. For instance, *chicken pox* may produce birth defects, while *mumps* may increase the risk of miscarriage.

Some sexually transmitted diseases such as *syphilis* can be transmitted directly to the fetus, who will be born suffering from the disease. In some cases, sexually transmitted diseases, such as *gonorrhea,* are communicated to the child as it passes through the birth canal to be born.

AIDS (acquired immune deficiency syndrome) is the newest, and probably the deadliest, of the diseases to affect a newborn. Mothers who have the disease or who merely are carriers of the virus may pass it on to their fetuses through the blood that reaches the placenta. If the fetuses contract the disease—and some 30 percent of infants born to mothers with AIDS are born with the virus—they face a devastating path. Many have birth abnormalities, including small, misshapen faces, protruding lips, and brain deterioration. Ninety percent experience neurological symptoms exemplified by intellectual delays and deficits, and loss of motor coordination, facial expressions, and speech. Because AIDS causes a breakdown of the immune system, these babies are extremely susceptible to infection. The long-term prognosis for infants born with AIDS is grim: Although drugs such as AZT and protease inhibitors may stave off the symptoms of the disease, survival beyond infancy is unusual (Brouwers et al., 1990; Nyhan, 1990; Harvard Mental Health Letter, 1994; Chin, 1994; Frenkel & Gaur, 1994).

Mother's Drug Use. A mother's use of many kinds of drugs—both legal and illegal—poses serious risks to the unborn child. Even over-the-counter remedies for common ailments can have surprisingly injurious consequences. For instance, aspirin taken for a headache can lead to bleeding in the fetus. Moreover, impairments in the physical development of 4-year-olds have been linked to the frequent use of aspirin during pregnancy (H. M. Barr et al., 1990; Griffith, Azuma, & Chasnoff, 1994).

Even drugs prescribed by medical professionals have sometimes proven to have disastrous consequences. In the 1950s, many women who were told to take *thalidomide* for morning sickness during their pregnancies gave birth to children with stumps instead of arms and legs. Although unknown to the physicians who prescribed the drug, thalidomide

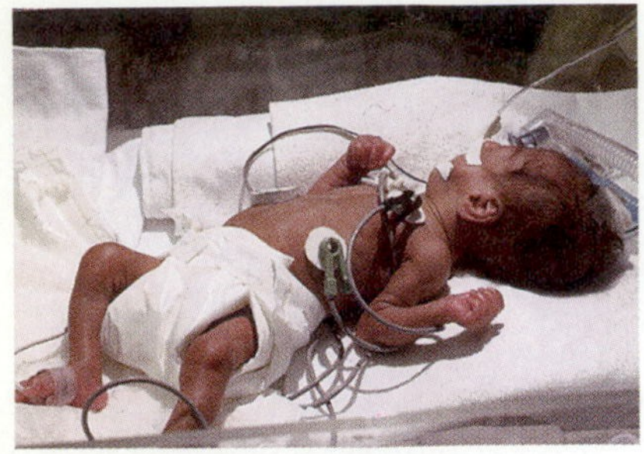

Children born to mothers who were addicted to crack cocaine, so-called crack babies, may themselves be addicted to the drug at birth.

inhibited the growth of limbs that normally would have occurred during the first 3 months of pregnancy.

Some drugs taken by mothers cause difficulties in their children literally decades after they were taken. As recently as the 1970s, the artificial hormone *DES (diethylstilbestrol)* was frequently prescribed to prevent miscarriage. Only later was it found that the daughters of mothers who took DES stood a much higher than normal chance of developing a rare form of vaginal or cervical cancer, and had more difficulties during their pregnancies (Herbst, 1981). Sons of the mothers who had taken DES had their own problems, including a higher rate than average of reproductive difficulties (Herbst, 1981).

Illicit drugs may pose equally great, and sometimes even greater, risks for the environments of prenatal children. For one thing, the purity of drugs purchased illegally varies significantly, so drug users can never be quite sure what specifically they are ingesting. Furthermore, the effects of some commonly used illicit drugs can be particularly devastating.

Consider, for instance, the use of *marijuana.* Certainly one of the most commonly used illegal drugs—millions of people in the United States have admitted trying it—marijuana used during pregnancy can restrict the oxygen that reaches the fetus. Its use can lead to infants who are irritable, nervous, and easily disturbed (Feng, 1993).

During the early 1990s, *cocaine* use by pregnant women led to an epidemic of thousands of so-called crack babies. Some estimates put the incidence of children born to mothers who have used cocaine during pregnancy at 1 in 50 (Julien, 1992; Sturner et al., 1992).

Cocaine produces an intense restriction of the arteries leading to the fetus, causing a significant reduction in the flow of blood and oxygen. This process increases the risks of fetal death. At birth, children whose mothers were addicted to cocaine may themselves be addicted to the drug and may have to suffer through the agonies of withdrawal. Even if not addicted, they may be born with significant problems. They are often shorter and weigh less than average, and they may have serious respiratory problems, visible birth defects, or seizures. They behave quite differently from other infants: Their reactions to stimulation are muted, but once they start to cry, it may be nearly impossible to soothe them (Alessandri et al., 1993; Mays et al., 1996; Gottwald & Thurman, 1994; Julien, 1992; M. Lewis & Bendersky, 1995).

It is difficult to focus on the long-term effects of mothers' cocaine use in isolation, because such drug use is often accompanied by poor nurturing following birth (G. A. Richardson & Day, 1994; Meyer et al., 1996). However, results of studies of crack babies who are just now entering school are discouraging. These children seem to have difficulty dealing with multiple stimuli and forming close attachments to others (Azuma & Chasnoff, 1993; Lewis & Bendersky, 1995; Rist, 1990).

Mother's Use of Alcohol and Tobacco. A pregnant woman who reasons that having a drink every once in a while or smoking an occasional cigarette has no appreciable effect on her unborn child is, in all likelihood, kidding herself: Increasing evidence suggests that even small amounts of alcohol and nicotine can disrupt the development of the fetus (Braun, 1996).

A mother's use of alcohol can have profound consequences for the unborn child. For instance, studies have found that maternal consumption of an average of just two alcoholic drinks a day during pregnancy is associated with lower intelligence in the offspring at age 7. Other research concurs, suggesting that relatively small quantities of alcohol taken during pregnancy can have future adverse effects on children's behavior and psychological functioning (R. G. Barr et al., 1991; Shriver & Piersel, 1994; Streissguth, Barr, & Sampson, 1990). Furthermore, the consequences of alcohol ingestion during pregnancy are long-lasting. For example, one study found that 14-year-olds' success on a test involving spatial and visual reasoning was related to their mothers' alcohol consumption during pregnancy. The more the mothers' reported drinking, the less accurately their children responded (E. Hunt, Streissguth, Kerr, & Olson, 1995).

The children of alcoholics, whose mothers consume substantial quantities of alcohol during pregnancy, are at an even greater risk. Approximately 1 out of every 750 infants is born with **fetal alcohol syndrome (FAS)**, a disorder that may include below-average intelligence and, sometimes, mental retardation, delayed growth, and facial deformities. FAS is now the primary preventable cause of mental retardation (Able & Sokol, 1987; Feng, 1993; Streissguth et al., 1990).

fetal alcohol syndrome (FAS) *a disorder caused by the pregnant mother consuming substantial quantities of alcohol during pregnancy, potentially resulting in mental retardation and delayed growth in the child*

Because of the risks associated with alcohol, physicians today counsel pregnant women (and even those who are trying to become pregnant) to avoid drinking any alcoholic beverages. In addition, they caution against another practice proven to have an adverse effect on an unborn child: smoking.

Smoking produces several consequences, none good. For starters, smoking reduces the oxygen content and increases the carbon monoxide of the mother's blood, which quickly reduces the oxygen available to the fetus. In addition, the nicotine and other toxins in cigarettes slow the respiration rate of the fetus and speed up its heart.

The ultimate result is an increased possibility of miscarriage and a higher likelihood of death during infancy. In fact, recent estimates suggest that smoking by pregnant women leads to 115,000 miscarriages and the deaths of 5,600 babies each year in the United States alone (DiFranza & Lew, 1995; Feng, 1993).

Smokers are two times as likely as nonsmokers to have babies with an abnormally low birth weight, and smokers' babies tend to be shorter, on average, than those of nonsmokers. Some studies have even found that language and intellectual development is delayed in children of mothers who smoked during pregnancy (Fried & Watkinson, 1990; Lefkowitz, 1981).

Do Fathers Affect the Prenatal Environment? It would be easy to reason that once the father has done his part in the sequence of events leading to fertilization, he would have no role in the *prenatal* environment of the fetus. In fact, developmental researchers have in the past generally shared this view, and there is little research investigating fathers' influence on the prenatal environment.

However, it is becoming increasingly clear that fathers also play a role in affecting the prenatal environment. For instance, the secondhand smoke from the cigarettes of fathers can affect both the mother and the unborn child. One study found that the greater the level of the father's smoking, the less the child weighed at birth (R. Lester & Van Theil, 1977; D. H. Rubin et al., 1986). Similarly, there are some associations between the development of certain kinds of tumors in a child and the nature of a father's occupation, although the explanation for the relationship is far from clear. Still, it does appear that fathers, and probably other family members as well, have an impact on the prenatal environment (J. Campbell, Poland, Waller, & Ager, 1992).

The Informed Consumer of Development

Optimizing the Prenatal Environment

If you are contemplating ever having a child, by this point in the chapter you may be overwhelmed by the number of things that can go wrong. Don't be. Although the environment and genetics pose their share of risks, in the vast majority of cases, pregnancy and birth proceed without mishap. Moreover, there are several things that women can do—both before and during pregnancy—to optimize the probability that pregnancy will progress smoothly. Among them:

- For women who are planning to become pregnant, several precautions are in order. First, women should have nonemergency X-rays only during the first 2 weeks after their menstrual periods. Second, women should be vaccinated against rubella (German measles) at least 3, and preferably 6, months before getting pregnant. Finally, women should avoid the use of birth control pills at least 3 months before trying to conceive, because of disruptions to hormonal production caused by the pills.

- Eat well, both before and during pregnancy (and after, for that matter!). Pregnant mothers are, as the old saying goes, eating for two. This means that it is more essential than ever to eat regular, well-balanced meals.
- Don't use alcohol and other drugs. The evidence is clear that many drugs pass directly to the fetus and may cause birth defects. It is also clear that the more one drinks, the greater the risk to the fetus. The best advice: Don't use *any* drug unless directed by a physician.
- Monitor caffeine intake. Although it is still unclear whether caffeine produces birth defects, it is known that the caffeine found in coffee, tea, and chocolate can pass to the fetus, acting as a stimulant. Because of this, you probably shouldn't drink more than a few cups of coffee a day.
- Whether pregnant or not, don't smoke. This holds true for mothers, fathers, and anyone else in the vicinity of the pregnant mother, since research suggests that smoke in the fetal environment can affect birth weight.
- Exercise regularly. In most cases, women can maintain their customary exercise level. According to a 1994 advisory from the American College of Obstetricians and Gynecologists, "There are no data in humans to indicate that pregnant women should limit exercise intensity and lower target heart rates because of potential adverse effects." On the other hand, extreme exercise should be avoided, especially on very hot or very cold days. "No pain, no gain" isn't applicable during pregnancy (J. Brody, 1994; Warrick, 1991).

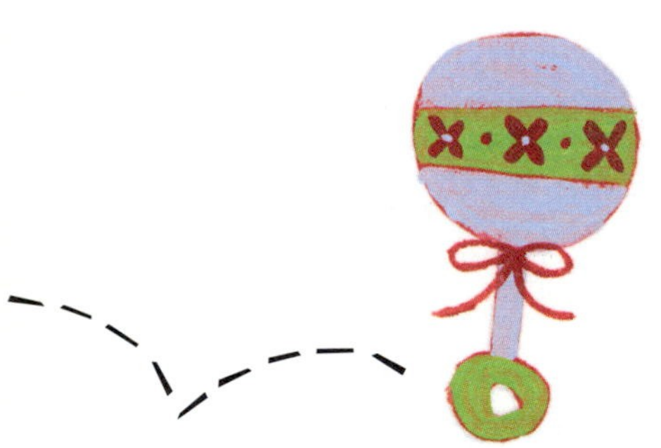

Review and Rethink

REVIEW

- The prenatal period consists of three stages: germinal, embryonic, and fetal.
- The prenatal environment significantly influences the development of the baby. The diet, age, and illnesses of mothers can affect their babies' health and growth.
- Mothers' use of drugs, alcohol, and tobacco can adversely affect the health and development of the unborn child. Fathers' and others' behaviors (e.g., smoking) can also affect the health of the unborn child.
- The vast majority of pregnancies and births proceed without mishap, and pregnant mothers can take positive steps to optimize their babies' chances for normal, healthy development.

RETHINK

- Based on your knowledge of prenatal development, do you think there is any truth in the opinion that pregnant women should avoid anger in order to spare their children from entering the world angry? Why or why not?
- Studies show that crack babies who are now entering school have significant difficulty dealing with multiple stimuli and forming close attachments. How might both genetic and environmental influences have combined to produce these results?

- In addition to avoiding smoking, do you think there are other steps fathers might take to help their unborn children develop normally in the womb? What are they and how might they affect the environment of the unborn child?
- Based on your knowledge of environmental influences on unborn children, what are some steps parents can take to give the fetus a healthy prenatal environment?

What is our basic genetic endowment, and how do we receive it from our parents?

1. In humans, the adult female and male sex cells, or gametes, contain 23 chromosomes each. At fertilization, ovum and sperm unite to form a single new cell, called a zygote, in the female's uterus. The zygote receives a total of 46 chromosomes from its parents. Within the 46 chromosomes is the genetic blueprint—carried in some 100,000 genes—that will guide cell activity for the rest of the individual's life.
2. Gregor Mendel discovered an important genetic mechanism. In alleles, where genes for two competing traits are present but only one can be expressed, the offspring may receive either similar or dissimilar genes from each parent. If the offspring receives dissimilar genes (one dominant and one recessive), the dominant gene will be expressed. If the offspring receives similar genes (two dominant or two recessive genes), that gene will be expressed. Traits such as hair and eye color and the presence of phenylketonuria (PKU) are alleles and follow this pattern, but relatively few inherited traits are governed by a single pair of genes in this way.

How can human development go wrong, and what can be done to prevent or remedy genetic problems?

3. Genes may become physically damaged due to wear and tear, environmental factors such as exposure to X-rays, or chance events during cell division. Sometimes genes spontaneously mutate, for no known reason. If damaged genes are passed on to the child, the result can be a genetic disorder such as Down syndrome, sickle cell anemia, Tay-Sachs disease, and Klinefelter's syndrome.
4. Behavioral genetics studies the genetic basis of human behavior. It focuses on personality characteristics and behaviors, as well as certain psychological disorders such as schizophrenia.
5. The study of genetic factors in behavior is leading to important discoveries relating to the minute workings of genetics at the molecular and chemical levels. The future promise is that researchers will learn how to remedy certain genetic defects.
6. Genetic counselors use data from many sources to identify potential genetic abnormalities in women and men who plan to have children. Tests, including amniocentesis, chorionic villus sampling (CVS), and ultrasound sonography, can also be performed on already developing fetuses.
7. Recently, genetic counselors have begun testing individuals for genetically based disorders that may eventually appear in the individuals themselves, rather than in their children. Ethical and practical issues relating to this sort of genetic counseling are complex and are still being worked out.
8. Infertility, the inability to conceive after 12 to 18 months of trying to become pregnant, occurs in some 15 percent of couples. Among the treatments are the use of drugs, surgery, artificial insemination, in vitro fertilization, and the use of surrogate mothers.

How do the environment and genetics work together to determine human characteristics?

9. Behavioral characteristics are often determined by a combination of genetics and environment. Genetically based traits represent a potential, called the genotype, which may be affected by the environment in different ways for different individuals. The actuality that is ultimately expressed is called the phenotype.

10. A disorder such as schizophrenia provides insight into the ways heredity and environment work together. Genetic factors alone do not produce schizophrenia, but they may produce a sensitivity toward environmental factors, such as stress, that can lead to schizophrenia. Other disorders, including alcoholism and autism, work similarly.

11. To work out the different influences of heredity and environment, researchers use nonhuman studies and human studies, particularly of twins. Identical twins adopted at birth and reared in different environments are especially helpful in such research. Other human studies compare the characteristics of dizygotic and monozygotic twins; the characteristics of unrelated children adopted together into the same environment; and the characteristics shared by adoptive parents and their children versus those shared by biological parents and their children.

Which human characteristics are significantly influenced by heredity?

12. The most important research finding is that virtually all human traits, characteristics, and behaviors are the result of the combination and interaction of nature and nurture.

13. Many physical characteristics, including height, obesity, blood pressure, respiration rate, and life span, show strong genetic influences.

14. Intelligence, one of the most studied—and controversial—topics, contains a strong genetic component, but can be significantly influenced by environmental factors.

15. Some personality traits, including neuroticism and extroversion, have been linked to genetic factors. Other aspects of personality, such as attitudes, values, and interests, also seem to have a genetic component. Some personal behaviors, such as preferences for leisure activities, may be genetically influenced through the mediation of inherited personality traits.

16. There has been some speculation that entire cultures may show a genetic predisposition toward one set of beliefs and values—one philosophy—over a different one.

What happens during the prenatal stages of development?

17. The germinal stage (fertilization to 2 weeks) is marked by rapid cell division and specialization, and the attachment of the zygote to the wall of the uterus. During the embryonic stage (2 to 8 weeks), three layers begin to grow and specialize. The ectoderm forms skin, hair, teeth, sense organs, and the brain and spinal cord. The mesoderm forms muscles, blood, and the circulatory system. The endoderm produces the digestive system, liver, pancreas, and respiratory system.

18. The fetal stage (8 weeks to birth) is characterized by a rapid increase in complexity and differentiation of the organs. The fetus becomes active and most of its systems operational. Even at the fetal stage, genetic differences produce differences in behavior.

What threats are there to the fetal environment and what can be done about them?

19. Mothers' characteristics and behaviors have the most direct influence on prenatal development. Factors in the mother that may affect the unborn child include diet; age; illnesses; and drug, alcohol, and tobacco use. The behaviors of fathers and others in the environment may also affect the health and development of the unborn child.

20. Pregnant women can give their unborn children the best chance of a healthy development by eating well; avoiding alcohol, unprescribed drugs, and cigarettes; limiting caffeine intake; and exercising regularly.

KEY TERMS AND CONCEPTS

gametes (p. 46)
fertilization (p. 46)
zygote (p. 46)
genes (p. 47)
DNA (deoxyribonucleic acid) (p. 47)
chromosomes (p.47)
monozygotic twins (p. 48)
dizygotic twins (p. 48)
dominant trait (p. 51)
recessive trait (p. 51)
genotype (p. 51)
phenotype (p. 51)
homozygous (p. 51)
heterozygous (p. 51)
polygenic inheritance (p. 53)
X-linked genes(p. 53)
behavioral genetics (p. 53)
Down syndrome (p. 54)
sickle cell anemia (p. 54)
Tay-Sachs disease (p. 54)
Klinefelter's syndrome (p. 54)
genetic counseling (p. 55)
amniocentesis (p. 56)
chorionic villus sampling (CVS) (p. 56)
ultrasound sonography (p. 56)
temperament (p. 57)
multifactorial transmission (p. 58)
infertility (p. 59)
artificial insemination (p. 59)
in vitro fertilization (IVF) (p. 59)
surrogate mother (p. 59)
active genotype-environment effects (p. 69)
passive genotype-environment effects (p. 69)
evocative genotype-environment effects (p. 69)
germinal stage (p. 70)
placenta (p. 71)
embryonic stage (p. 71)
fetal stage (p. 72)
fetus (p. 72)
teratogen (p. 73)
fetal alcohol syndrome (FAS) (p. 77)

CHAPTER 3

BEGINNINGS

Birth and the Newborn Infant

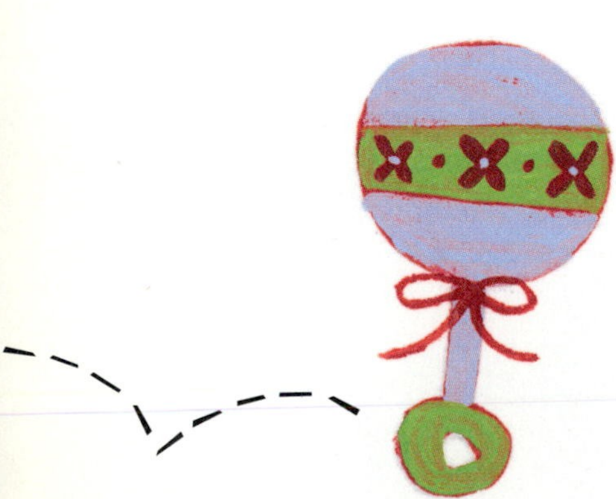

PROLOGUE

LABOR OF LOVE

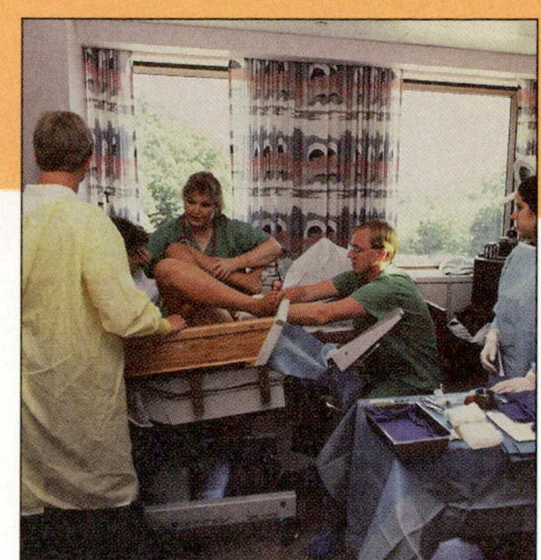

After carefully researching different techniques for childbirth, Anitra Ellis and her husband, Corelyou, picked a local family birthing center for the delivery of their twins. When Anitra went into labor, the Ellises drove the 15 miles to the Gentle Birth Center Medical Group, where four midwives were available to assist.

Labor was an active process for Anitra. Standing the entire time, she walked around and talked with her husband. She was encouraged to eat and drink whenever she wanted, and she was given a massage when her back started to feel sore.

Labor lasted some 18 hours, and the delivery was smooth. Corelyou Hayes Ellis IV was born first, followed by his sister, Erynn Emon Ellis. Just five hours after the birth, the whole family was at home, and Anitra and Corelyou were resting comfortably. As her parents watched, Erynn, the smaller of the two babies, used her arm to push herself over.

***

The experience of giving birth was likely very different for Anitra Ellis's mother. For her, the process probably began when she was wheeled into a hospital room crowded with women in various stages of labor. No husbands or other family members could be present, and standard operating procedure was to administer a strong dose of general anesthetic. Because of the drug, the mother was completely unaware of being taken to the delivery room and giving birth. The first time she saw her newborn, it was already several hours old and still groggy from the drugs administered during delivery (Knight, 1994).

LOOKING AHEAD

Despite variations in the processes of labor and delivery for Anitra and her mother, the birth undoubtedly brought equal joy to the parents. The entry into this world of a newborn, who so readily triggers the hopes, aspirations, and unconditional love of its parents, is a remarkable event.

Yet the excitement and wonder of the moment of birth is far overshadowed by the extraordinary nature of the newborn itself. It enters the world with a surprising array of capabilities, ready from the first moments of life outside the womb to respond to the world and the people in it.

In this chapter, we'll examine the events that lead to the delivery and birth of a child, and take an initial look at the newborn. We first consider labor and delivery, exploring how the process proceeds as well as several alternative approaches.

We next examine some of the possible complications of birth. Although most births progress without a hitch, we investigate the problems that sometimes occur, ranging from premature births to infant mortality.

Finally, we investigate the extraordinary range of capabilities of newborns. We'll look not only at their physical and perceptual abilities, but also at the way they enter the world with skills that help form the foundations of their future relationships with others.

In sum, after reading this chapter, you will be able to answer these questions:

- What is the normal process of labor?
- What happens immediately after the baby is born?
- What choices do parents have regarding the birthing process?

- What complications can occur at birth and what are their causes, effects, and treatments?
- What capabilities does the newborn have?

Birth

neonates *the term used for newborns*

> Her head was cone-shaped at the top. Although I knew this was due to the normal movement of the head bones as she came through the birth canal and that this would change in a few days, I was still startled. She also had some blood on the top of her head and was damp, a result of the amniotic fluid in which she had spent the last 9 months. There was some white, cheesy substance over her body, which the nurse wiped off just before she placed her in my arms. I could see a bit of downy hair on her ears, but I knew this, too, would disappear before long. Her nose looked a little as if she had been on the losing end of a fistfight: It was squashed into her face, flattened by its trip through the birth canal. But as she seemed to fix her eyes on me and grasped my finger, it was clear that she was nothing short of perfect. (Adapted from Brazelton, 1969.)

For those of us accustomed to thinking of newborns in the images of baby food commercials, this portrait of a typical newborn may be surprising. Yet most **neonates**—the term used for newborns—are born resembling this one. Make no mistake, however: Despite their temporary blemishes, babies are a welcome sight to their parents from the moment of their birth.

The neonate's outward appearance is caused by a variety of factors in its journey from the mother's uterus, down the birth canal, and out into the world. We can trace its passage, beginning with the release of the chemicals that initiate the process of labor.

Labor: The Process of Birth Begins

For the average mother, about 266 days after conception, an as-yet-unidentified factor triggers the process that leads to birth. At that point, the hormone *oxytocin* is released by the mother's pituitary gland. When the concentration of oxytocin becomes high enough, the uterus begins periodic contractions.

During the prenatal period, the uterus, which is composed of muscle tissue, slowly expands as the fetus grows. Although for most of the pregnancy it is inactive, after the fourth

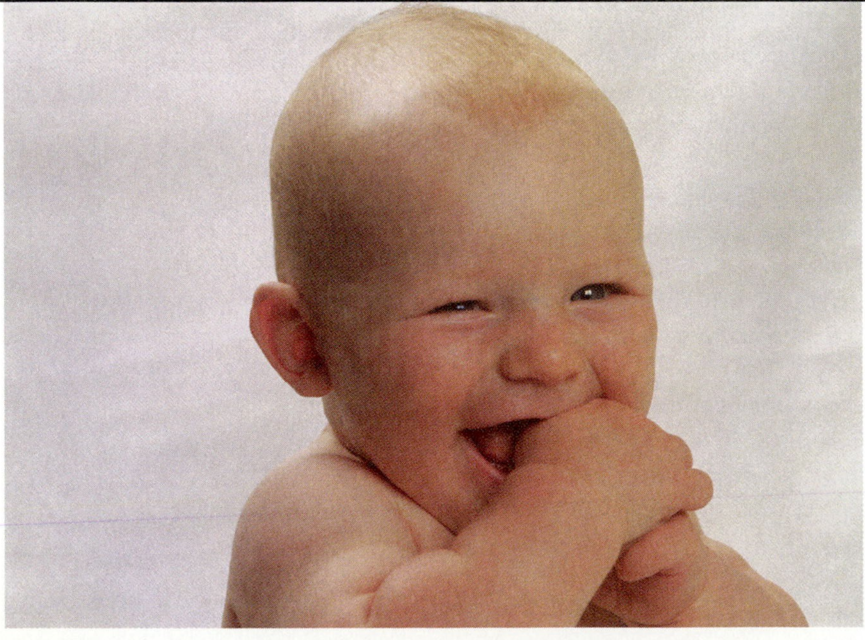

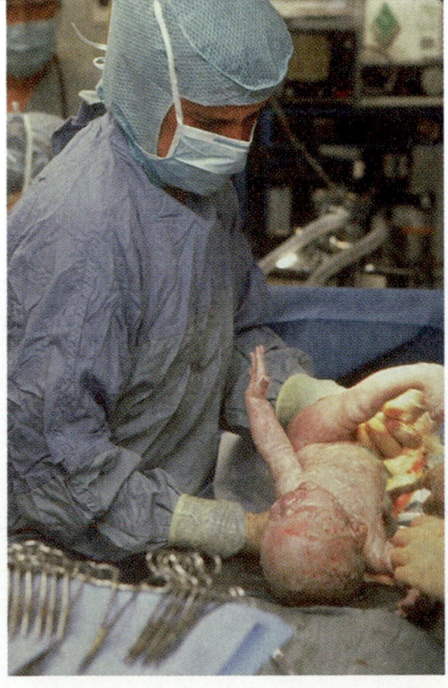

The image of newborns portrayed in commercials differs dramatically from reality.

month it occasionally contracts in order to ready itself for the eventual delivery. These contractions, called *Braxton-Hicks contractions,* are sometimes called "false labor," due to the fact that they do not necessarily signify that the baby will be born soon.

When birth is actually imminent, the uterus begins to contract intermittently. Its increasingly intense contractions act as if it were a vise, opening and closing to force the head of the fetus against the *cervix,* the neck of the uterus that separates it from the vagina. Eventually, the force of the contractions becomes strong enough to propel the fetus slowly down the birth canal until it enters the world as a newborn (Mittendorf et al., 1990).

Labor proceeds in three stages (see Figure 3-1). In the *first stage of labor,* the uterine contractions initially occur around every 8 to 10 minutes and last about 30 seconds. As labor proceeds, the contractions occur more frequently and last longer. Toward the end of labor, the contractions may occur every 2 minutes and last almost 2 minutes. During the final part of the first stage of labor, the contractions increase to their greatest intensity, a period known as *transition.* The mother's cervix fully opens, eventually expanding enough to allow the baby's head (the widest part of the body) to pass through.

This first stage of labor is the longest. Its duration varies significantly, depending on the mother's age, race, ethnicity, and number of prior pregnancies, and a variety of other factors involving both the fetus and the mother. Typically, labor takes 16 to 24 hours for firstborn children, but there are wide variations. Births of subsequent children usually involve shorter periods of labor.

During the *second stage of labor,* the baby's head starts to move through the cervix and birth canal. During this stage, which typically lasts around 90 minutes, the baby's head emerges more with each contraction, increasing the size of the vaginal opening. Because the area between the vagina and rectum must stretch a good deal, an incision called an **episiotomy** is sometimes made to increase the size of the opening of the vagina. However, this practice has been increasingly criticized in recent years as potentially causing more harm than good, and in developed areas of the world other than the United States episiotomies are uncommon (M. C. Klein et al., 1994).

episiotomy *an incision sometimes made to increase the size of the opening of the vagina to allow the baby to pass*

FIGURE 3-1

THE THREE STAGES OF LABOR

Stage 1

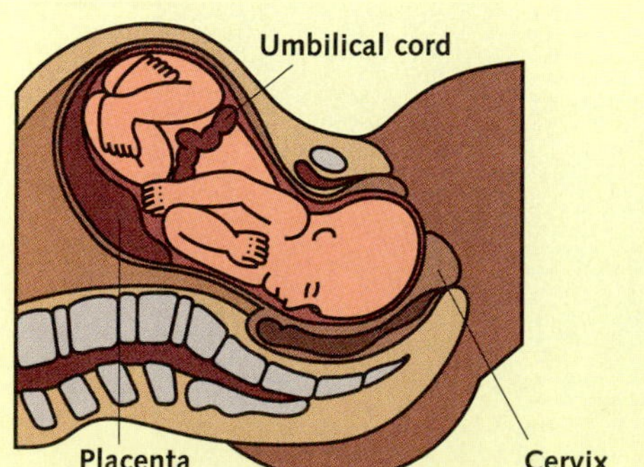

Uterine contractions initially occur every 8 to 10 minutes and last 30 seconds. Toward the end of labor, contractions may occur every 2 minutes and last as long as 2 minutes. As the contractions increase, the cervix, which separates the uterus from the vagina, becomes wider, eventually expanding to allow the baby's head to pass through.

Stage 2

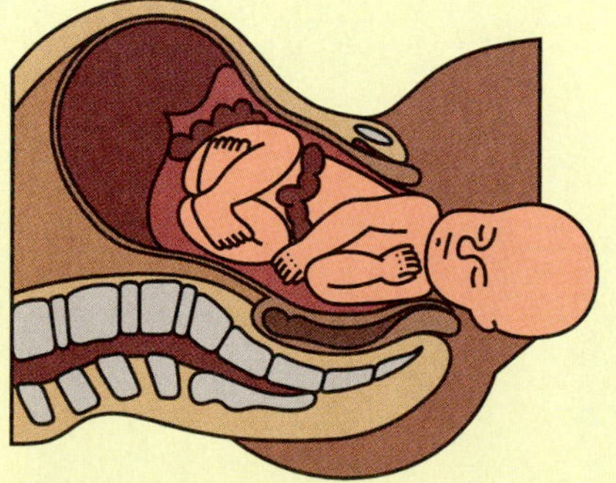

The baby's head starts to move through the cervix and birth canal. Typically lasting around 90 minutes, the second stage ends when the baby has completely left the mother's body.

Stage 3

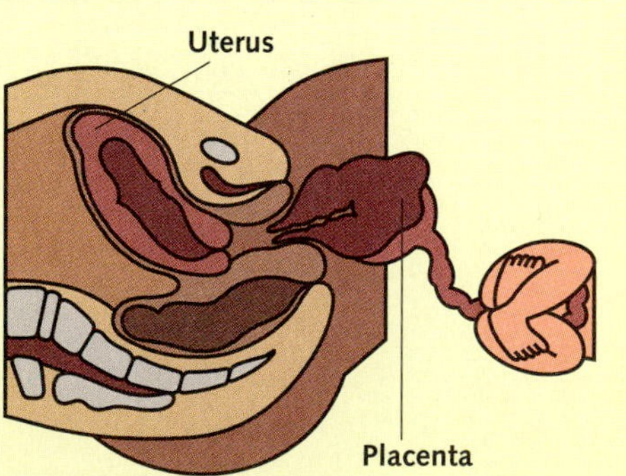

The child's umbilical cord (still attached to the neonate) and the placenta are expelled from the mother. This stage is the quickest and easiest, taking just a few minutes.

The second stage of labor ends when the baby has completely left the mother's body. Finally, the *third stage of labor* occurs when the child's umbilical cord (still attached to the neonate) and the placenta are expelled from the mother. This stage is the quickest and easiest, taking just a few minutes.

Apgar scale *a standard measurement system that looks for a variety of indications of good health in newborns*

The nature of a woman's reactions to labor reflect, in part, cultural factors. Although there is no evidence that the physiological aspects of labor differ among women of different cultures, expectations about labor and interpretations of its pain do vary significantly from one culture to another.

For instance, there is a kernel of truth to popular stories of pregnant women in certain societies putting down the tools with which they are tilling their fields, stepping aside and giving birth, and immediately returning to work with their neonates wrapped and bundled on their backs. Accounts of the !Kung people in Africa describe a woman in labor sitting calmly beside a tree and without much ado—or assistance—successfully giving birth to a child and quickly recovering. On the other hand, many societies regard childbirth as dangerous, and some even view it in terms befitting an illness. Such cultural perspectives color the way that people in a given society view the experience of childbirth (Chalmers, Enkin, & Keirse, 1989; Cole, 1992; Shostak, 1981).

BIRTH: FROM FETUS TO NEONATE

The exact moment of birth occurs when the fetus, having left the uterus through the cervix, passes through the vagina to emerge fully from its mother's body. In most cases, babies automatically make the transition from taking in oxygen via the placenta to using their lungs to breathe air. Consequently, as soon as they are outside the mother's body, most newborns spontaneously cry. This helps them to clear their lungs and to breathe on their own.

What happens next varies from situation to situation and from culture to culture. In Western cultures, health care workers are almost always on hand to assist with the birth. In the United States, 99 percent of births are attended by professional health care workers, but worldwide only about 50 percent of births have professional health care workers in attendance (United Nations, 1990).

The Apgar Scale. In most cases, the newborn infant first undergoes a quick visual inspection. Parents may be counting fingers and toes, but trained health care workers look for something more. Typically, they employ the **Apgar scale**, a standard measurement system that looks for a variety of indications of good health (see Table 3-1). Developed by physician Virginia Apgar in 1953, the scale directs attention to five basic qualities, recalled most easily

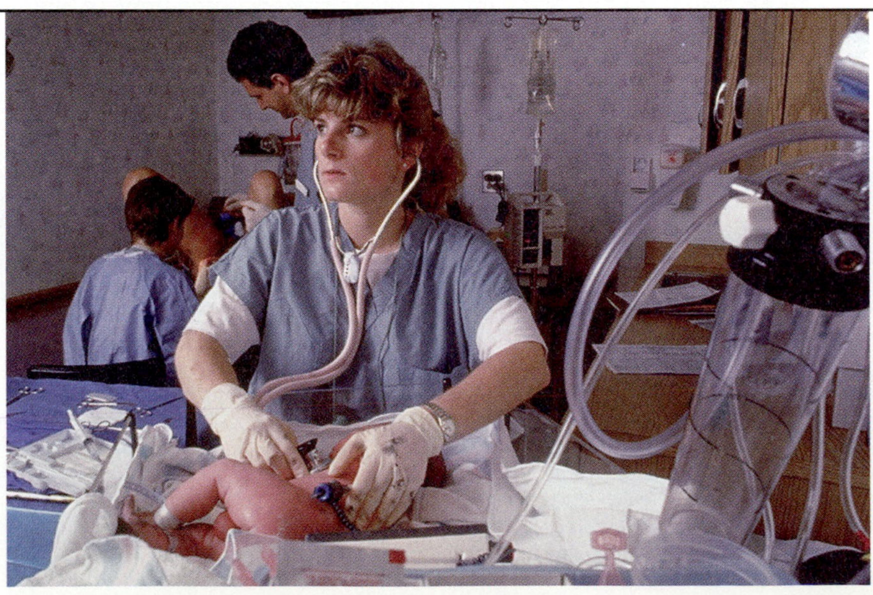

The Apgar scale is used at birth to measure several indications of good health.

TABLE 3-1

APGAR SCALE

Sign*	0	1	2
Appearance (color)	Blue, pale	Body pink, extremities blue	Entirely pink
Pulse (heart rate)	Absent	Slow (below 100)	Rapid (over 100)
Grimace (reflex irritability)	No response	Grimace	Coughing, sneezing, crying
Activity (muscle tone)	Limp	Weak, inactive	Strong, active
Respiration (breathing)	Absent	Irregular, slow	Good, crying

*Each sign is rated in terms of absence or presence from 0 to 2; highest overall score is 10.
(*Source:* Adapted from Apgar, 1953.)

by using Apgar's name as a guide: *a*ppearance (color), *p*ulse (heart rate), *g*rimace (reflex irritability), *a*ctivity (muscle tone), and *r*espiration (breathing).

Using the scale, health care workers assign the neonate a score ranging from 0 to 2 on each of the five qualities, producing an overall score that can range from 0 to 10. The vast majority of children score 7 or above. The 10 percent of neonates who score under 7 require help to start breathing. Newborns who score under 4 need immediate, lifesaving intervention. Scores that remain between 0 and 3 after 20 minutes indicate that severe problems are likely to be present. On the other hand, most of the components of the Apgar score are based on subjective factors, and parents sometimes place too much emphasis on the specific score (Jepson, Talashek, & Tichy, 1991).

Although low Apgar scores may indicate problems or birth defects that were already present in the fetus, the process of birth itself may sometimes cause difficulties. Among the most profound are those relating to a temporary deprivation of oxygen.

At various junctures during labor, the fetus may not get sufficient oxygen for any of a number of reasons. For instance, the umbilical cord may become pinched during a prolonged contraction, thereby cutting off the supply of oxygen to the fetus. The cord may also get wrapped around the neck of the fetus or another part of its body, or an unusual positioning of the fetus within the birth canal may cause the cord to be restricted. It is even possible that the stresses of traveling through the birth canal may cause the baby to grasp the umbilical cord and squeeze it (Bornstein & Lamb, 1992).

Lack of oxygen for a few seconds is not particularly harmful to the fetus, but deprivation for any longer time may cause serious harm. A restriction of oxygen, or **anoxia**, lasting a few minutes can produce brain damage as unoxygenated brain cells, which can never regenerate, die. Furthermore, anoxia can lead to such an increase in blood pressure that bleeding occurs in the brain.

Physical Appearance and Initial Encounters. After assessing the newborn's health, health care workers next deal with the remnants of the child's passage through the birth canal. You'll recall the description of the thick, greasy substance (like cheese) that covers the newborn. This material, called *vernix,* smoothes the passage through the birth canal; it is no longer needed once the child is born and is quickly cleaned away. Newborns' bodies are also covered with a fine, dark fuzz known as *lanugo;* this soon disappears. The newborn's eyelids may be puffy due to an accumulation of fluids during labor, and the newborn may have other blood or fluids on parts of its body.

After being cleansed, the newborn is usually returned to the mother and the father, if he is present. The everyday and universal occurrence of childbirth makes it no less miraculous to parents, and most cherish this time to make their first acquaintance with their child.

anoxia *a restriction of oxygen to the baby, lasting a few minutes, during the birth process, which can produce brain damage*

bonding *close physical and emotional contact between parent and child during the period immediately following birth, argued by some to affect later relationship strength*

However, the importance of the initial encounter between parent and child has become a matter of considerable controversy. Some psychologists and physicians argued in the 1970s and early 1980s that **bonding**, the close physical and emotional contact between parent and child during the period immediately following birth, was a crucial ingredient for forming a lasting relationship between parent and child. Their arguments were based in part on research conducted on nonhuman species such as ducklings. This work showed that there was a critical period just after birth when organisms showed a particular readiness to learn, or *imprint,* from other members of their species who happened to be present (Lorenz, 1957).

According to the concept of bonding applied to humans, a critical period begins just after birth and lasts only a few hours. During this period actual skin-to-skin contact between mother and child supposedly leads to deep, emotional bonding (deChateau, 1980; Klaus & Kennell, 1976). The corollary to this assumption is that if circumstances prevent such contact, the bond between mother and child will forever be lacking in some way. Because medical practices prevalent at the time often left little opportunity for sustained mother and child physical contact immediately after birth, the suggestion was received with alarm. The idea was taken seriously and generated a substantial amount of public attention (Eyer, 1992).

There was just one problem: Scientific evidence for the notion was lacking. When developmental researchers carefully reviewed the research literature, they found little support for the idea. Although it does appear that mothers who have early physical contact with their babies are more responsive to them than those who don't have such contact, the difference lasts only a few days. Furthermore, there are no lingering reactions to separations immediately following birth, even separations of several days. Such news is reassuring to parents whose children must receive immediate, intensive medical attention just after birth, as well as to parents who adopt children and are not present at all at their births (Eyer, 1994; Goldberg, 1983; M. Lamb, 1982; Myers, 1987).

APPROACHES TO CHILDBIRTH: WHERE MEDICINE AND ATTITUDES MEET

> Ester Iverem knew herself well enough to know that she didn't like the interaction she had with medical doctors. So she opted for a nurse-midwife at Manhattan's Maternity Center where she was free to use a birthing stool and to have her husband, Nick Chiles, by her side. When contractions began, Iverem and Chiles went for a walk, stopping periodically to rock—a motion, she says, "similar to the way children dance when they first learn how, shifting from foot to foot." That helped her work through the really powerful contractions.
>
> "I sat on the birthing chair [a Western version of the traditional African stool, which lies low to the ground and has an opening in the middle for the baby to come through] and Nick was sitting right behind me. When the midwife said 'Push!' the baby's head just went 'pop!,' and out he came." Their son, Mazi (which means "Sir" in Ibo) Iverem Chiles, was placed on Ester's breast while the midwives went to prepare for his routine examination. (Knight, 1994, p. 122)

For something as natural as giving birth, which occurs throughout the nonhuman animal world apparently without much thought, parents in the Western world have developed a variety of strategies—and some very strong opinions. Should the birth take place in a hospital or in the home? Should a physician, a nurse, or a midwife assist? Is the father's presence desirable? Should siblings and other family members be on hand to participate in the birth?

Most of these questions cannot be answered definitively, primarily because the choice of childbirth techniques often comes down to a matter of values and opinions. No single

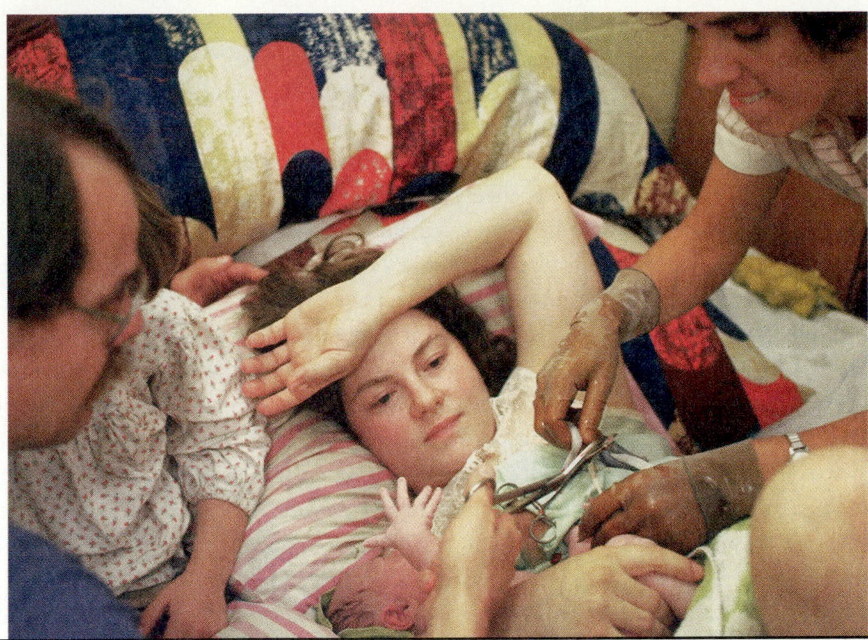

A midwife helps in this home delivery.

procedure will be effective for all mothers and fathers, and no conclusive research evidence has proven that one procedure is significantly more effective than another.

The abundance of choices is largely due to a reaction to traditional medical practices that had been prevalent in the United States until the early 1970s. Before that time, the typical procedure went something like this: A woman was placed in a room with many other women in labor, some of whom were screaming in pain. No fathers and other family members were allowed in the room. The mother's pubic hair was shaved, and she was given an enema. Just before delivery, she was rolled into a delivery room, where the birth took place. Often the woman was so drugged that she was not aware of the birth at all.

Physicians argued that such procedures were necessary to ensure the health of the newborn and the mother. However, critics charged that alternatives were available that not only would maximize the medical well-being of the participants in the birth, but would represent an emotional and psychological improvement as well (Pascoe, 1993).

Pain and Childbirth. Any woman who has delivered a baby will agree that childbirth is painful. But how painful, exactly, is it?

Such a question is largely unanswerable. One reason is that pain is a subjective, psychological phenomenon, one that cannot be easily measured. No one is able to answer the question of whether their pain is "greater" or "worse" than someone else's pain, although some studies have tried to quantify it. For instance, in one survey women were asked to rate the pain they experienced during labor on a 1-to-5 scale, with 5 being the most painful (L. Yarrow, 1992). Nearly half (44 percent) said "5," and an additional one-quarter said "4."

Furthermore, because pain is usually a sign that something is wrong in one's body, we have learned to react to pain with fear and concern. Yet during childbirth, pain is actually a signal that the body is working appropriately—that the contractions that are meant to propel the baby through the birth canal are doing their job. Consequently, the experience of pain during labor is difficult for women in labor to interpret, thereby potentially increasing their anxiety and making the contractions seem even more painful.

Ultimately, the nature of every woman's delivery depends on a complex series of factors. These factors encompass such variables as how much preparation and support she has before and during delivery, her culture's view of pregnancy and delivery, and the specific nature of the delivery itself (Davis-Floyd, 1994; Seibel & McCarthy, 1993).

Use of Anesthesia and Pain-reducing Drugs. Among the greatest advances of modern medicine is the ongoing discovery of drugs that reduce pain. However, the use of medication during childbirth is a practice that holds both benefits and pitfalls.

It is clear that drugs hold the promise of greatly reducing, and even eliminating, pain associated with labor, which can be extreme. However, pain reduction comes at a cost: the stronger the drug, the greater its effects on the fetus and neonate. The reason is pharmacologically simple: Drugs administered during labor reach not just the mother but the fetus as well. Because of the small size of the fetus relative to the mother, drug doses that might have only a minimal effect on the mother can have a magnified effect on the fetus.

Many studies have demonstrated the results of the use of anesthesia during delivery. Some consequences are immediate: Anesthetics may temporarily depress the flow of oxygen to the fetus and slow labor (Brackbill, 1979; Hollenbeck et al., 1984; Thorp et al., 1993). In addition, neonates whose mothers have been anesthetized are less physiologically responsive and show poorer motor control during the first days of life after birth. And the effects may be lasting: Research shows that during the course of the first year, progress in sitting up, standing, and other physical activities is somewhat slower for children whose mothers received drugs during labor (Brackbill & Broman, 1979; Douglas, 1991; Garbaciak, 1990; A. D. Murray et al., 1981).

The effects of drugs show up in other, less obvious ways. For example, anesthetic use can produce differences in the nature of the interactions between mother and child (Hollenbeck et al., 1984; Scanlon & Hollenbeck, 1983). Even after the physical effects of the drugs have worn off and the infants are behaving in the same way as infants whose mothers did not receive drugs, mothers report feeling differently about their babies. There may be several reasons for this difference. It may be that mothers who choose to avoid medication during delivery hold more positive attitudes toward giving birth and toward their babies in the first place. More probably, the presence or absence of drugs in the infants' systems causes behavioral differences in the infants themselves, which in turn elicit differing reactions from the mothers.

Not all studies, however, find that the use of drugs during labor invariably affects the neonate negatively. In fact, some researchers argue that drugs, as they are currently employed during labor, produce only minimal risks to the fetus and neonate. For instance, one study found no differences in strength, touch sensitivity, activity level, irritability, and sleep between children whose mothers had been given drugs during labor and those whose mothers had received no drugs (Kraemer, et al., 1985).

The wisdom of using drugs to control pain during labor is a difficult issue, pitting legitimate concerns regarding pain control against potential, and in many cases uncertain, concerns for the neonate. Joint guidelines issued by the American Academy of Pediatrics and the American College of Obstetricians and Gynecologists (AAP/ACOG, 1992) suggest that the proper use of minimal amounts of drugs for pain relief is reasonable and has no significant effect on a child's later well-being. Ultimately, the decision to use or not to use anesthetic drugs must be made by the mother, in conjunction with the father and medical care providers.

Post-delivery Hospital Stay: Deliver, Then Depart? When New Jersey mother Diane Mensch was sent home from the hospital just a day after the birth of her third child, she still felt exhausted. But her insurance company insisted that 24 hours was sufficient time to recover, and it refused to pay for more. Three days later, her newborn was back in the hospital, suffering from jaundice. Mensch is convinced the problem would have been discovered, and treated, sooner had she and her newborn been allowed to remain in the hospital longer (Begley, 1995).

Mensch's experience is not atypical. The average hospital stay following normal births has decreased from an average of 3.9 days in 1970 to 2 days in 1993, and many medical insurance companies are pushing for a reduction to 24 hours (see Figure 3-2).

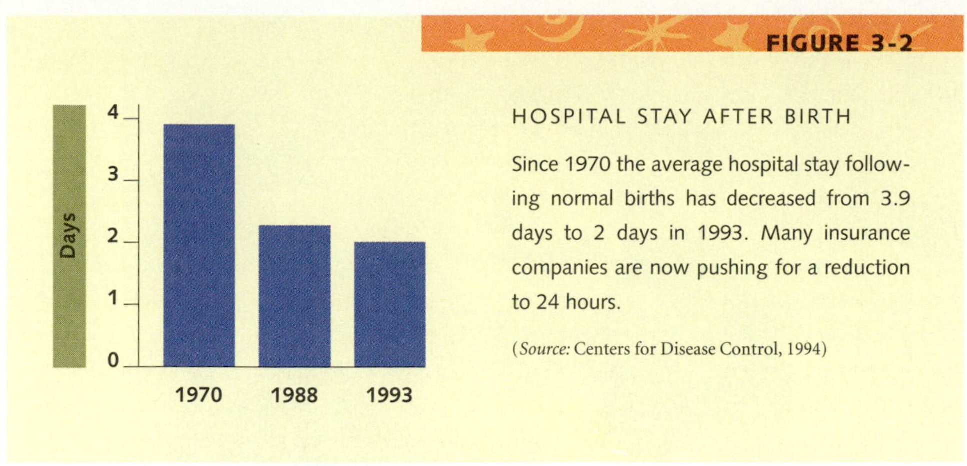

FIGURE 3-2

HOSPITAL STAY AFTER BIRTH

Since 1970 the average hospital stay following normal births has decreased from 3.9 days to 2 days in 1993. Many insurance companies are now pushing for a reduction to 24 hours.

(*Source:* Centers for Disease Control, 1994)

However, many medical care providers are fighting against this trend. Although the data are ambiguous on the specific consequences of early discharge, some medical professionals believe that there are definite risks involved, both for mothers and their newborns. For instance, mothers may begin to bleed if they tear tissue injured during childbirth. It is also riskier for newborns to be discharged prematurely from the intensive medical care that hospitals can provide.

In accordance with these views, the American Academy of Pediatrics issued a policy statement in 1995 stating that women should stay in the hospital no less than 48 hours after giving birth. It is unclear, however, how effective this pronouncement will be as it runs up against the realities of medical economics and managed medical care (American Academy of Pediatrics, 1995).

Of course, not all mothers give birth in hospitals, and not all births follow a traditional course. As we consider next, a number of alternatives now exist in birthing practices.

Alternative Birthing Procedures. Possible hazards because of the use of anesthetics during labor, as well as concerns about other traditional birth practices, have led to the development of several alternative strategies designed to minimize the need for anesthetics (Smith, 1990; J. J. Mathews & Zadak, 1991). The major strategies are described below:

- *Lamaze birthing techniques.* The Lamaze method has achieved widespread popularity in the United States. Based on the writings of Dr. Fernand Lamaze (1970), the method makes use of basic psychological techniques involving relaxation training. Typically, mothers-to-be undergo a series of weekly training sessions in which they learn exercises that help them relax various parts of the body on command. A "coach," most typically the father, is trained along with the future mother. The training allows women to cope with painful contractions with a relaxation response, rather than by tensing up, which may make the pain more acute. In addition, the women learn to focus on a relaxing stimulus, such as a tranquil scene in a picture. The goal is to learn how to deal positively with pain and to relax at the onset of a contraction.

  Does the procedure work? Most mothers, as well as fathers, report that a Lamaze birth is a very positive experience. They enjoy the sense of mastery that they gain over the process of labor, a feeling of control over what can be a formidable experience (Bing, 1983; M. C. Mackey, 1990; Wideman & Singer, 1984). On the other hand, we can't be sure that parents who choose the Lamaze method aren't already more highly motivated about the experience of childbirth than parents who do not choose the technique. It is therefore possible that the accolades they express after Lamaze births are due to their initial enthusiasm and not to the Lamaze procedures themselves.

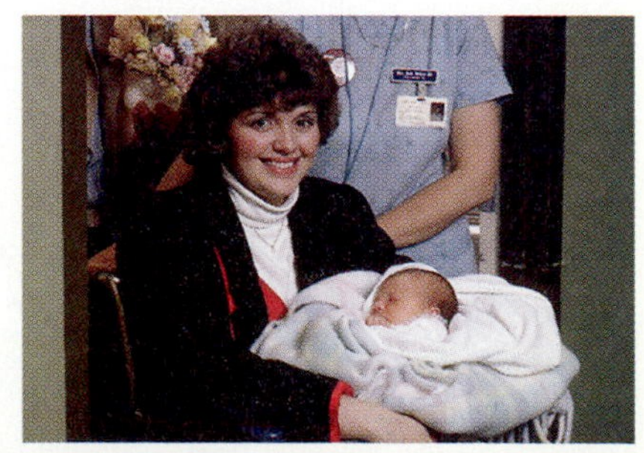

According to the American Academy of Pediatrics, women should not be released from the hospital until at least 48 hours after giving birth.

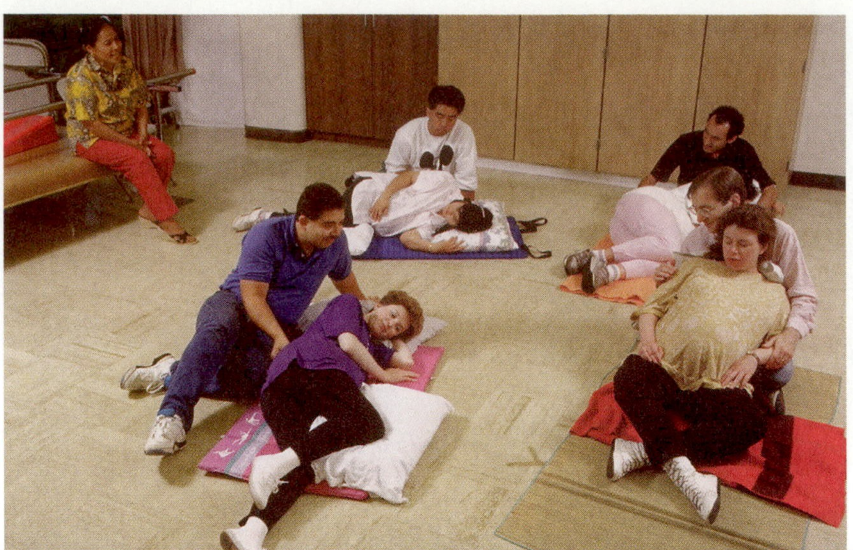

In Lamaze classes, parents are taught relaxation techniques to prepare for childbirth and to reduce the need for anesthetics.

Although it is not possible to pinpoint definitively the specific consequences of Lamaze preparation for childbirth, one thing is certain: Participation in Lamaze procedures—as well as other so-called *natural childbirth techniques* in which the emphasis is on educating the parents about the process of birth and minimizing the use of drugs—is relatively rare among members of lower income groups, including many members of ethnic minorities. Parents in these groups may not have transportation, time, or the financial resources to attend childbirth preparation classes. The result is that women in lower income groups tend to be less prepared for the events of labor and consequently may suffer more pain and anguish during childbirth (J. A. Ball, 1987).

- *The Leboyer method.* Consider the abrupt transition faced by a neonate. Accustomed to floating in a pool of warm water (the amniotic fluid) for 9 months, hearing only muffled sounds and seeing light only dimly, the newborn is violently thrust into a very different world outside the mother. How might this transition be facilitated?

    According to French physician Frederick Leboyer (pronounced "Leh-boy-AY"), the optimal approach is to maintain the environment of the womb as long as possible after birth (Leboyer, 1975). Under Leboyer's method, delivery rooms are kept softly lighted and a hushed atmosphere prevails. As soon as the baby is born, it is placed on the mother's stomach and then floated in a pool of warm water. The umbilical cord is not cut immediately after birth, as is traditionally done to compel the baby to breathe on its own. Instead, the cord is left intact, allowing the neonate to acclimate gradually to an air-breathing world.

    Although the Leboyer technique gained some popularity in the early 1980s, today only one remnant is seen frequently: Newborns are often placed on the warmth of the mother's stomach just after birth.

- *Family birthing centers.* When Jill Rakovich became pregnant for the third time, she and her husband, Milos, decided they wanted to find a less forbidding locale than the traditional delivery room. They had both found this setting uncomfortable and grim when their two older children were born.

    After researching the possibilities, Jill discovered a family birthing center located close to a nearby hospital. The center consisted of rooms decorated like homey bedrooms. Unlike the typical forbidding hospital room, these looked warm and inviting, although they also were equipped with several pieces of medical equipment. When labor began, Jill and Milos went to the birthing center and settled into

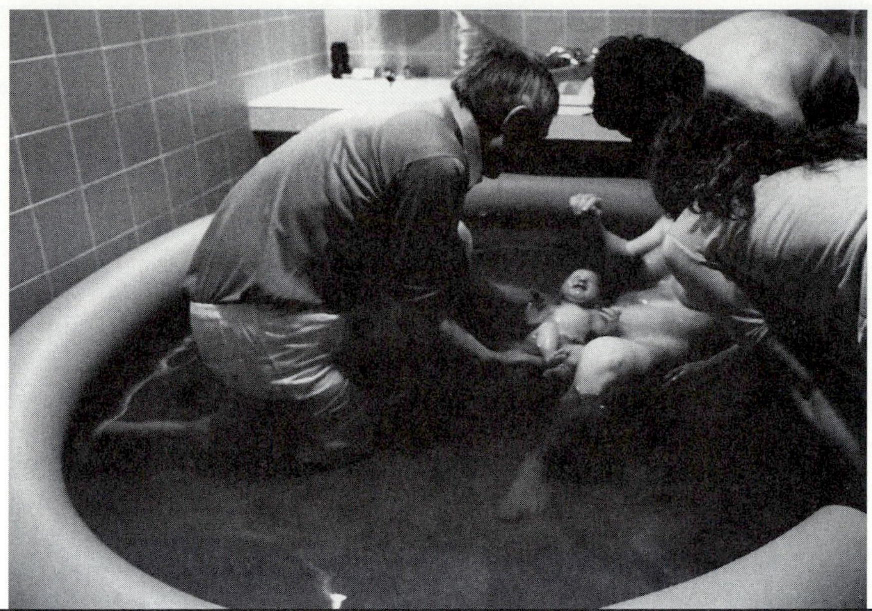

According to French physician Frederick Leboyer, methods that help sustain the environment of the womb after birth are most beneficial to the newborn.

one of the rooms. Labor proceeded smoothly, and, as her husband watched, Jill gave birth to her third child.

The decision to use a birthing center is becoming increasingly common. In the majority of cases labor and delivery are uneventful, permitting births to occur in the relatively relaxed, homelike setting the birthing center provides. Furthermore, in the event of complications, equipment is at hand. Supporters of birthing centers suggest that they provide a more comfortable, less stressful environment than a hospital room, offering a setting that may facilitate labor and delivery (Eakins, 1986).

Because of the popularity of the philosophy behind birthing centers, many hospitals have opened birthing rooms of their own. The increasing prevalence of birthing centers reflects the view that childbirth is a natural part of life that should not be rigidly isolated from its other aspects. Rather than medical events that involve a passive patient and a dictatorial physician, labor and delivery are now typically viewed as participatory experiences involving the mother, the father, other family members, and care providers acting jointly.

This philosophy also has implications for the choice of care provider. In place of a traditional *obstetrician*, a physician who specializes in delivering babies, some parents are turning to a *midwife*, a childbirth attendant who stays with the mother throughout labor and delivery. Midwives—often nurses specializing in childbirth—are used primarily for pregnancies in which no complications are expected. Although the use of midwives is increasing in the United States, they are employed in only a minority of births (DeClercq, 1992). In contrast, midwives help deliver some 80 percent of babies in other parts of the world. Moreover, in countries at all levels of economic development many births successfully take place at home. For instance, more than a third of all births in the Netherlands occur at home (Treffer et al., 1990).

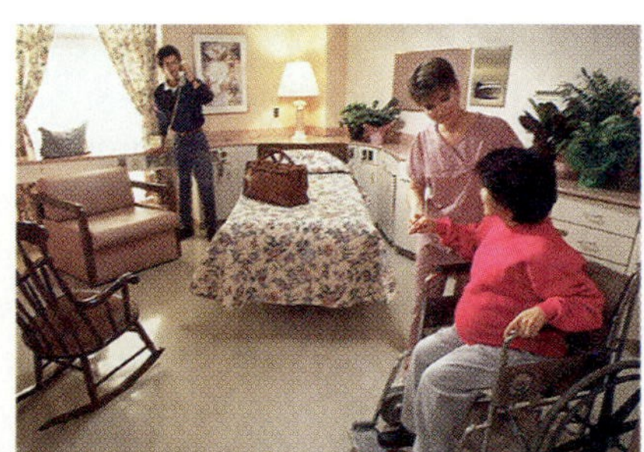

Family birthing centers, looking more like bedrooms than traditional delivery rooms, produce a more relaxed and less intimidating atmosphere than that typically found in hospitals.

What kind of setting and care provider are optimal? In the majority of cases, it does not make a great deal of difference. Naturally, arrangements for care should be made thoughtfully and in advance, and backup medical help should be on call. If a birth is to occur outside a traditional hospital, such a hospital should be no more than 5 to 10 minutes away. Furthermore, for pregnancies that stand a high risk of complications—such as those of women whose previous deliveries have been difficult—a hospital setting is preferable (Rusting, 1990). (For futher discussion, see the "Speaking of Development" interview.)

The Informed Consumer of Development

Dealing with Labor

Every woman who is soon to give birth has some fear of labor. Most have heard gripping tales of extended, 48-hour labors or vivid descriptions of the pain that accompanies labor. Still, few mothers would dispute the notion that the rewards of giving birth are worth the effort. Indeed, polls show that almost two thirds of women report feeling "very positive" about the births of their children (L. Yarrow, 1992).

There is no single right or wrong way to deal with labor. However, experts suggest several strategies that can help make the process as positive as possible (Salmon, 1993):

- *Be flexible.* Although you may have carefully worked out beforehand a scenario about what to do during labor, don't feel an obligation to follow through exactly. If a strategy is ineffective, turn to another one.

Speaking of Development

Kathy McKain, Nurse-Midwife

Born: 1958

Education: .... University of Pittsburgh, B.S. in Nursing; University of Pennsylvania, M.N.S. (Master of Nursing and Science)

Position: .... Coordinator of midwifery for Birthplace—Midwifery Services of Western Pennsylvania Hospital

Home: .... Pittsburgh, Pennsylvania

One of the most ancient of professions, midwifery, continues to fill a crucial niche in today's high-tech society, providing an alternative to a traditional in-hospital birth.

For the past 6 years, Kathy McKain has helped scores of women give birth, as a midwife and as coordinator of midwifery services at a modern urban hospital.

"Our basic idea as we approach the care of a woman and her family is a respect for the fact that this is her body, her pregnancy, and her experience," she explains. "We try hard to make the environment conducive to the family's developmental concerns. For instance,

- *Communicate with your health care providers.* Let them know what you are experiencing. They may be able to suggest ways to deal with what you are encountering. By examining you, they will also be able to explain just what stage of labor you are in.
- *Remember that labor is...laborious.* Labor is aptly named: It takes hard work and can be exhausting. Expect that you may become fatigued, but realize that as the final stages of labor occur, you may well get a second wind.
- *Accept your partner's support.* If a spouse or other partner is present, allow that person to make you comfortable and provide support. A partner's encouragement may be critical.
- *Be realistic and honest about your reactions to pain.* Even if you had planned an unmedicated delivery, realize that you may find the pain difficult to tolerate. At that point, consider the use of drugs. Above all, don't feel that asking for pain medication is a sign of failure. It isn't.
- *Focus on the big picture.* Keep in mind that labor is part of a process that ultimately leads to an event unmatched in the joy that it can bring.

"Our basic idea as we approach the care of a woman and her family is a respect for the fact that this is her body, her pregnancy, and her experience."

"We try hard to make the environment conducive to the family's developmental concerns."

many women who are giving birth already have children, and so we provide a comfortable waiting room and playroom, and we welcome the other children in to participate in their mother's visits. Incorporating family members into the process seems to work well.

"We discuss with the mother the fact that the pregnancy can be a life crisis or a major developmental milestone, rather than just a medical event," says McKain. "Along the way we talk about a lot of things in addition to the physical aspects of birth. We talk about the relationship between the woman and her partner, the planned or unplanned nature of the pregnancy, and the life changes that the pregnancy and the baby will cause. In many birthing processes, the mental side is neglected, but we consider it our responsibility to cover that side, too.

"Our goal is to keep the mother and baby together the entire time. While there could be an exception where the baby needs some separation, we generally see mother and child as a unit. We teach our midwives to deliver the baby right to the mother. They do their cleaning up and assessing of the baby right there, in the mother's arms.

"A great majority of women we see are planning to nurse their babies. We believe the baby is prepared at birth with the sucking and swallowing reflexes, and we capitalize on that fact."

In a typical year Birthplace sees more then 200 births and 450 annual checkups, according to McKain. Stays are generally no longer than 4 to 12 hours. Birthplace staff make a follow-up home visit with the newborn and mother.

Summing up her practice, McKain says, "There are so many issues that need to be addressed. We feel it is important to deal with the meaning of the birth to the mother."

Review and Rethink

REVIEW

- In the first stage of labor, contractions increase in frequency, duration, and intensity until the baby's head is able to pass through the cervix. In the second stage, the baby moves through the cervix and birth canal and leaves the mother's body. In the third stage, the umbilical cord and placenta emerge.
- Immediately after birth, birthing attendants usually examine the neonate using a measurement system such as the Apgar scale.
- Many birthing options are available to parents today. Parents may weigh the advantages and disadvantages of anesthetic drugs during birth, and they may choose alternatives to traditional hospital birthing, including the Lamaze method, the Leboyer method, the use of a birthing center, and the use of a midwife.

RETHINK

- Why might cultural differences exist in expectations and interpretations of labor? Do you think such cultural differences are due primarily to physical or psychological factors?
- While 99 percent of U.S. births are attended by professional medical workers or birthing attendants, this is the case in only about 50 percent of births worldwide. What do you think are some causal factors and implications of this statistic?
- What arguments have been advanced by those who consider the bonding process—close physical contact between parent and child immediately after birth—an essential ingredient in forming a normal parent-child relationship? Why might some parents have found this position alarming?
- What are some arguments for and against the use of pain-reducing drugs during birth? What advice would you give a mother-to-be about anesthetics, and why?
- Which elements of various birthing techniques, including more traditional and less traditional ones, do you think are most likely to contribute to the well-being of the newborn and its family? Why?

BIRTH COMPLICATIONS

> In addition to the usual complimentary baby supplies that most hospitals bestow on new mothers, the maternity nurses at Greater Southeast Hospital have become practiced in handing out "grief baskets."
>
> Inside are items memorializing one of [Washington, D.C.'s] grimmest statistics—an infant mortality rate that's more than twice the national average. The baskets contain a photograph of the dead newborn, a snip of its hair, the tiny cap it wore, and a yellow rose (P. Thomas, 1994, p. A14).

The infant mortality rate in Washington, D.C., capital of the richest country in the world, is 16.7 deaths per 1,000 births, exceeding the rate of countries such as Sri Lanka, Panama, Chile, and Jamaica. Overall, the United States ranks 22nd in the world in infant mortality, with 7.9 deaths for every 1,000 live births (Eberstadt, 1994; National Center for Health Statistics, 1993a; Singh & Yu, 1995).

Why is infant survival less likely in the United States than in other, less developed countries? To answer this question, we need to consider the nature of the problems that can occur during labor and delivery.

PRETERM INFANTS: TOO SOON, TOO SMALL

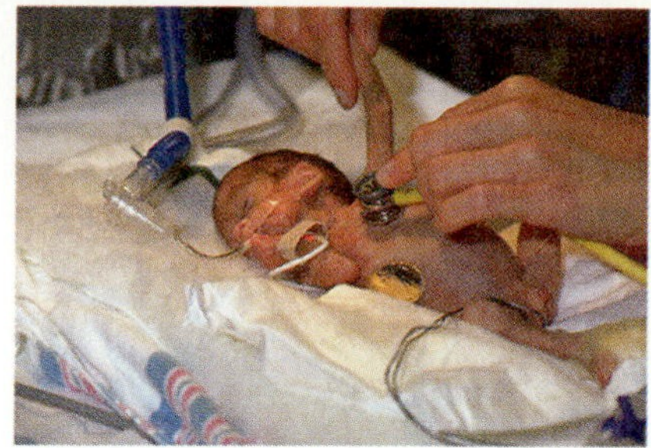

Briana McNeill was 18 weeks short of full term, yet survived.

> On the morning of January 7, as Jewel McNeill's labor pains grew stronger and stronger, a nurse came into the delivery room. Did the McNeills have any plans for burying their baby? she asked grimly. Would they want an autopsy? Jewel recalls her using the phrase "disposing of the fetus." Her husband, Michael, noticed a receptacle that looked like a trash can at the bottom of the table. This, he thought, would be his baby's only cradle. According to the hospital's calculations, Jewel was no more than 22 weeks pregnant—18 weeks short of full term. The baby would weigh barely a pound and its lungs would be too undeveloped to sustain life. The doctor told Jewel to start pushing. Better to end the agony. A few minutes later, at exactly 10:08 A.M., Briana Adia-Jewel McNeill was born.
>
> *Alive.*
>
> Her eyes were open, her arms and legs were wiggling, and she began to cry. To Jewel, it sounded like a cry for help. (Kantrowitz, 1988, p. 62.)

If Briana had been born only a decade or so earlier, her cry might have been ignored. Yet today, like the other 6 to 7 percent of infants in the United States who are born early, Briana has a significantly higher chance of survival.

Preterm infants, or premature infants, are born prior to 38 weeks after conception. Because they have not had time to develop fully as fetuses, preterm infants are at high risk for illness and death (D. L. Holmes, Reich, & Gyurke, 1989).

The extent of danger faced by preterm babies largely depends on the child's weight at birth, which has great significance as an indicator of the extent of the baby's development. Although the average newborn weighs around 3,400 grams (about 7.5 pounds), **low-birthweight infants** weigh less than 2,500 grams (around 5.5 pounds). Although only 7 percent of all newborns in the United States fall into the low-birthweight category, they account for the majority of newborn deaths.

Although most low-birthweight infants are preterm, some are small-for-gestational-age babies. **Small-for-gestational-age infants** are infants who, because of delayed fetal growth, weigh 90 percent (or less) of the average weight of infants of the same gestational age. Small-for-gestational-age infants are sometimes also preterm, but may not be (Meisels & Plunket, 1988; Shiono & Behrman, 1995).

If the degree of prematurity is not too great and weight at birth is not extremely low, the threat to the child's well-being is relatively minor. In such cases, the main treatment may be to keep the baby in the hospital to gain weight. Additional weight is critical because fat layers help prevent chilling in neonates, who are not particularly efficient at regulating body temperature.

Newborns who are born more prematurely and who have significantly below-average birthweights face a tougher road. For them, simply staying alive is a major task. For instance, low-birthweight infants are highly vulnerable to infection. Furthermore, because their lungs have not had sufficient time to develop completely, premature babies have problems taking in sufficient oxygen. As a consequence, they may experience *respiratory distress syndrome (RDS)*, with potentially fatal consequences.

To deal with respiratory distress syndrome, low-birthweight infants are often placed in incubators, enclosures in which temperature and oxygen content are controlled. The exact amount of oxygen is carefully monitored. Too low a concentration of oxygen will not provide relief, and too high a concentration can damage the delicate retinas of the eyes, leading to permanent blindness.

The immature development of preterm neonates makes them unusually sensitive to stimuli in their environment. They can easily be overwhelmed by the sights, sounds, and sensations they experience, and their breathing may be interrupted or their heart rates may slow. Furthermore, they are often unable to move smoothly; their arm and leg movements

preterm infants *infants who are born prior to 38 weeks after conception (also known as premature infants)*

low-birthweight infants *infants that weigh less than 2,500 grams (about 5.5 pounds) at birth*

small-for-gestational-age infants *infants who, because of delayed fetal growth, weigh 90 percent (or less) of the average weight of infants of the same gestational age*

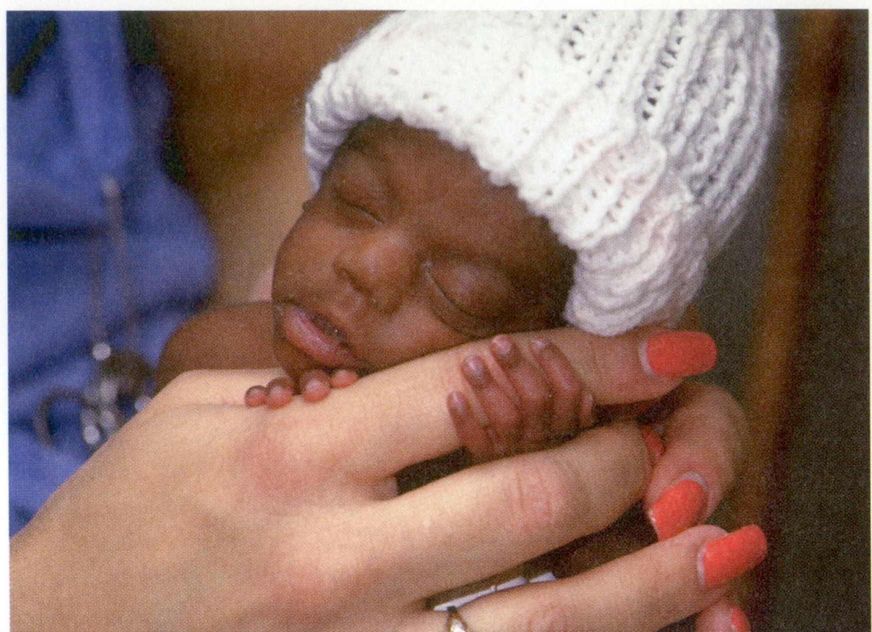

Preterm infants stand a much greater chance of survival today than they did even a decade ago.

are uncoordinated, causing them to jerk about and appear startled. Such behavior is quite disconcerting to parents (T. M. Field, 1990).

Despite the difficulties they experience at birth, the majority of preterm infants eventually develop normally in the long run. However, the tempo of development often proceeds more slowly for preterm children, compared to children born at full term, and more subtle problems sometimes emerge later. For example, by the end of 1 year, only 10 percent of prematurely born infants display significant problems, and only 5 percent are seriously disabled. By the age of 6, however, approximately 38 percent have mild problems that call for special educational interventions. For instance, some preterm children show learning disabilities, behavior disorders, or lower-than-average IQ scores. Others have difficulties with physical coordination. Still, around 60 percent of preterm infants are free of even minor problems (Bergman & Kimberlin, 1993; S. E. Cohen, 1996; Hack, Klein, & Taylor, 1995; H. Lee & Barratt, 1993; Liaw & Brooks-Gunn, 1993; Mandich et al., 1994; Menyuk, Liebergott, & Schultz, 1995).

Very-low-birthweight Infants: The Smallest of the Small. The story is less positive for the most extreme cases of prematurity—very-low-birthweight infants. **Very-low-birthweight infants** weigh less than 1,250 grams (around 2.25 pounds) or, regardless of weight, have been in the womb less than 30 weeks.

Very-low-birthweight infants not only are tiny, some fitting easily in the palm of the hand, they also hardly seem even to belong to the same species as full-term newborns. Their eyes may be fused shut and their earlobes may look like flaps of skin on the sides of their heads. Their skin is a darkened red color, whatever their race.

Very-low-birthweight babies are in grave danger from the moment they are born due to the immaturity of their organ systems. Before the last two decades, these babies would not have survived outside the mother. However, medical advances have led to a much higher chance of survival, pushing the **age of viability**, the point at which an infant can survive prematurely, to about 24 weeks—some 4 months earlier than the term of a normal delivery. At the same time, such advances have not been without their costs, both developmental and financial.

very-low-birthweight infants *infants who weigh less than 1,250 grams (around 2.25 pounds) or, regardless of weight, have been in the womb less than 30 weeks*

age of viability *the point at which an infant can survive a premature birth*

The physical and cognitive problems experienced by low birthweight and preterm babies are even more pronounced in very-low-birthweight infants, with astonishing financial consequences. For instance, the costs of keeping very-low-birthweight infants alive are enormous. A 3-month stay in an incubator in an intensive care unit can run hundreds of thousands of dollars, and not infrequently—some 50 percent of the time—the infant ultimately dies, despite massive medical intervention.

Even if a very-low-birthweight preterm infant survives, the medical costs can continue to mount. For instance, one estimate suggests that the average monthly cost of medical care for such infants during the first 3 years of life may be between 3 and 50 times higher than the medical costs for a full-term child. Such astronomical costs have raised significant ethical debate about the advisability of expending substantial financial and human resources in cases in which a positive outcome may be very unlikely (Beckwith & Rodning, 1991; Hille et al., 1994; Lewit et al., 1995; McCormick, 1992; I. K. Sung, Bohr, & Oh, 1993; Wallace et al., 1995).

The difficult issues surrounding very-low-birthweight infants are not likely to diminish in the years ahead. In fact, as medical capabilities progress, the age of viability is likely to be pushed even further back.

Developmental researchers, however, are formulating new strategies for dealing with preterm infants in the hope of improving their lives; and emerging evidence suggests that high-quality care can provide protection from some of the risks associated with prematurity. For instance, research shows that children who receive more responsive, stimulating, and organized care are apt to show more positive outcomes than those children whose care was not as good (Bradley et al., 1994). We consider some programs specifically designed to lower the risks for preterm infants in the "Directions in Development" section.

Directions in Development

Treating Preterm Infants: Effective Interventions

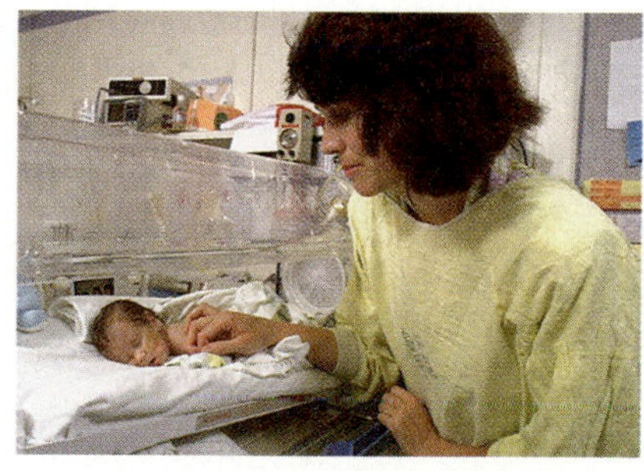

Massage of preterm infants triggers a complex chemical reaction that increases the chances that the infants will survive.

To most parents, stroking and soothingly caressing their babies seem to come naturally. What they probably don't know, though, is that touch does more than calm their babies: It triggers a complex chemical reaction that assists infants in their efforts to survive.

According to research conducted by developmental psychologist Tiffany M. Field (1988, 1995), a group of preterm infants who were massaged for 15 minutes three times a day gained weight some 50 percent faster than a group of preterm infants of the same age who were not stroked (see Figure 3-3). The massaged infants also were more active and responsive to stimuli. Ultimately, the preterm infants who were massaged were discharged earlier from the hospital, and their medical costs were significantly lower than infants in the unmassaged group.

The benefits of massage seem to stem from the physiological stimulation it provides. Preterm neonates housed in incubators often face a world consisting of the continuous sound of oxygen being pumped in and steady, bright lights overhead. The act of massage may provide environmental variation, and it may also stimulate the production of chemicals in the brain that instigate growth (T. M. Field, 1990, 1991, 1995; Schanberg & Field, 1987; Schanberg, Field, Kuhn, & Bartolome, 1993; Tronick, 1995; de Roiste & Bushnell, 1996).

Not every type of stimulation is successful in producing gains in preterm newborns, however. Stimulation that is too strong or rough can be harmful; stimulation that is too light can be irritating. Finally, in the case of very-low-birthweight infants, too much stimulation can overwhelm the infants' efforts to stabilize their internal physiological environments (Als, 1992; B. M. Lester & Tronick, 1990; Wheeden et al., 1993).

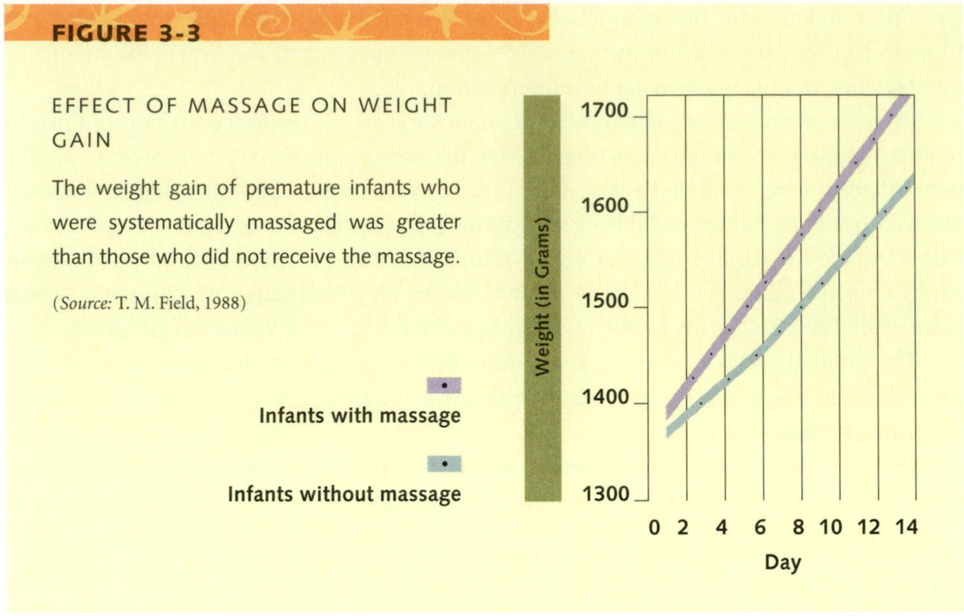

FIGURE 3-3

EFFECT OF MASSAGE ON WEIGHT GAIN

The weight gain of premature infants who were systematically massaged was greater than those who did not receive the massage.

(*Source:* T. M. Field, 1988)

Other approaches to improving the outcomes for low-birthweight and preterm newborns are geared to both parents and their children. For instance, in one successful program, close to one thousand preterm newborns, each weighing less than 5.5 pounds, were divided into two groups (R. T. Gross, Brooks-Gunn, & Spiker, 1992; Infant Health and Development Program, 1990). Parents of the children in one group received special instruction in their homes from health care experts. During the visit, the parents were given information on health and development and were provided with a program of games and activities meant to improve the cognitive, social, and language skills of their children. In addition, when the children reached 1 year of age, they were placed in a special educational day-care program, with one teacher for every three children. At age 2, the ratio changed to one teacher for every four children.

In comparison to children in the second group—in which the parents received no special training—the children in the treatment group achieved impressive results. Treated children had significantly higher IQ scores than those in the group that received no special treatment. Average IQ scores of the lightest babies, who had weighed less than 4.4 pounds at birth, were more than 13 points higher in the treated group than in the control group. Average IQ gains for the heavier babies, who weighed between 4.4 and 5.5 pounds at birth, were not as great—some 7 points higher—but still significant.

Results such as these have important implications for public policy. They suggest that intervention programs to help preterm and low-birthweight babies should begin at the very start of life. By intervening early, developmental specialists might well diminish—and possibly prevent—future problems.

Causes of Preterm and Low-birthweight Deliveries. Although half of preterm and low-birthweight births are unexplained, several known causes account for the remainder (S. L. Friedman & Sigman, 1992; Goldberg & DiVitto, 1983; Paneth, 1995; Radetsky, 1994). In some cases, difficulties relating to the mother's reproductive system cause such births. For instance, mothers carrying twins have unusual stress placed on them, leading to premature labor. In fact, most multiple births are preterm to some degree.

In other cases, preterm and low-birthweight babies are a result of the immaturity of the mother's reproductive system. Young mothers—under the age of 15—are more prone to deliver prematurely than older ones. In addition, a woman who has not had much time between pregnancies is more likely to deliver a preterm or low-birthweight infant than a woman who has given her reproductive system a chance to recover from a prior delivery.

Finally, factors that affect the general health of the mother, such as nutrition, level of medical care, amount of stress in the environment, and economic support, all are related to prematurity and low birthweight. Racial factors are also implicated, not because of race per se, but because members of racial minorities have disproportionately lower incomes. For instance, the percentage of low-birthweight infants born to African American mothers is double that for white American mothers (Cohen, 1995; Goldberg & DiVitto, 1983; J. C. Kleinman, 1992; National Center for Health Statistics, 1993b; Radetsky, 1994). A summary of the factors associated with increased risk of low birthweight is shown in Table 3-2.

postmature infants *infants still unborn 2 weeks after the mother's due date*

Postmature Babies: Too Late, Too Large

One might imagine that a baby who spends extra time in the womb might have some advantages, given the opportunity to continue growth undisturbed by the outside world. Yet the reality is different. **Postmature infants**—those still unborn 2 weeks after the mother's due date—face several risks.

For example, the blood supply from the placenta may become insufficient to nourish the fetus adequately. Consequently, the blood supply to the brain may be decreased, leading to the potential of brain damage. Similarly, labor becomes riskier (for both the child and the mother) as a fetus who may be equivalent in size to a 1-month-old infant has to make its way through the birth canal (Boylan, 1990).

TABLE 3-2

FACTORS ASSOCIATED WITH INCREASED RISK OF LOW BIRTHWEIGHT

I. Demographic Risks
- A. Age (less than 17; over 34)
- B. Race (minority)
- C. Low socioeconomic status
- D. Unmarried
- E. Low level of education

II. Medical Risks Predating Pregnancy
- A. Parity (0 or more than 4)
- B. Low weight for height
- C. Genitourinary anomalies/surgery
- D. Selected diseases such as diabetes, chronic hypertension
- E. Nonimmune status for selected infections such as rubella
- F. Poor obstetric history, including previous low birthweight infant, multiple spontaneous abortions
- G. Maternal genetic factors (such as low maternal weight at own birth)

III. Medical Risks in Current Pregnancy
- A. Multiple pregnancy
- B. Poor weight gain
- C. Short interpregnancy interval
- D. Hypotension
- E. Hypertension/preeclampsia/toxemia
- F. Selected infections such as asymptomatic bacteriuria, rubella,
- G. First or second trimester bleeding
- H. Placental problems such as placenta previa
- I. Hyperemesis
- J. Ologohydramnios/polyhydramnios
- K. Anemia/abnormal hemoglobin
- L. Isoimmunization
- M. Fetal anomalies
- N. Incompetent cervix
- O. Spontaneous premature rupture of membrane

IV. Behavioral and Environmental Risks
- A. Smoking
- B. Poor nutritional status
- C. Alcohol and other substance abuse
- D. DES exposure and other toxic exposure, including occupational hazards
- E. High altitude

V. Health Care Risks
- A. Absent or inadequate prenatal care
- B. Iatrogenic prematurity

VI. Evolving Concepts of Risks
- A. Stress, physical and psychosocial
- B. Uterine irritability
- C. Events triggering uterine contractions
- D. Cervical changes detected before onset of labor
- E. Selected infections such as Chlamydia trachomatis
- F. Inadequate plasma volume expansion
- G. Progesterone deficiency

(Adapted from Committee to Study the Prevention of Low Birthweight, 1985.)

Cesarean delivery *a birth in which the baby is surgically removed from the uterus, rather than traveling through the birth canal*

fetal monitors *devices that measure the baby's heartbeat during labor*

In some ways, difficulties involving postmature infants are more easily prevented than those involving preterm babies, since medical practitioners can induce labor artificially if the pregnancy continues too long. Not only can certain drugs bring on labor, but also physicians have the option of performing Cesarean deliveries, a form of delivery we consider next.

CESAREAN DELIVERY: INTERVENING IN THE PROCESS OF BIRTH

> As Elena entered her 18th hour of labor, the obstetrician who was monitoring her progress began to look concerned. She told Elena and her husband, Pablo, that the fetal monitor revealed that the fetus's heart rate had begun to repeatedly fall after each contraction. After trying some simple remedies, such as repositioning Elena on her side, the obstetrician came to the conclusion that the fetus was in distress. She told them that the baby should be delivered immediately, and to accomplish that, she would have to carry out a Cesarean delivery.

Elena became one of the almost one million mothers in the United States who have a Cesarean delivery each year. In a **Cesarean delivery**, the baby is surgically removed from the uterus, rather than traveling through the birth canal.

Several types of difficulties during the birthing process can lead to Cesarean deliveries. Fetal distress is the most frequent cause. For instance, if the fetus appears to be in some danger, as indicated by a sudden rise in its heart rate or if blood is seen coming from the mother's vagina during labor, a Cesarean may be performed. Cesarean deliveries are also used in some cases of *breech position,* in which the baby is positioned feet first in the birth canal, or *transverse position,* in which the baby lies crosswise in the uterus, or when the baby's head is so large it has trouble moving through the birth canal.

The routine use of **fetal monitors**, devices that measure the baby's heartbeat during labor, has contributed to a soaring rate of Cesarean deliveries. For instance, almost 25 percent of all children in the United States are born in this way, up some 500 percent from the early 1970s (National Center for Health Statistics, 1994). What benefits have resulted from this increase?

According to critics, very few. Other countries have substantially lower rates of Cesarean deliveries (see Figure 3-4), and there is no association between successful birth consequences and the rate of Cesarean deliveries (Notzon, 1990). In addition, Cesarean deliveries carry dangers. Cesarean delivery represents major surgery, and recovery can be relatively lengthy, particularly when compared to a normal delivery. In addition, the risk of maternal infection is higher with Cesarean deliveries (Mutryn, 1993; Shearer, 1993).

Finally, a Cesarean delivery presents some risks for the baby. Although Cesarean babies are spared the stresses of passing though the birth canal, their relatively easy passage into the world may deter the normal release of certain stress-related hormones, such as catecholamines, into the newborn's bloodstream. Because these hormones help prepare the neonate to deal with the stress of the world outside the womb, their absence may be detrimental to the newborn child. In fact, research indicates that babies who have not experienced labor due to a Cesarean delivery are more prone to initial breathing problems upon birth than those who experience at least some labor prior to being born via a Cesarean delivery (Hales, Morgan, & Thurnau, 1993; Lagercrantz & Slotkin, 1986).

Due in part to the increase in Cesarean deliveries that results from their use, fetal monitors are no longer employed routinely, in accordance with current recommendations from medical authorities. These experts cite research evidence that the outcomes are no better for newborns who have been monitored than for those who have not been monitored, and that monitors give false alarms regarding the presence of fetal distress with disquieting regularity (Albers & Krulewitch, 1993; Levano et al., 1986). On the other hand, monitors can play a critical role in high-risk pregnancies and in cases of preterm and postmature babies.

FIGURE 3-4

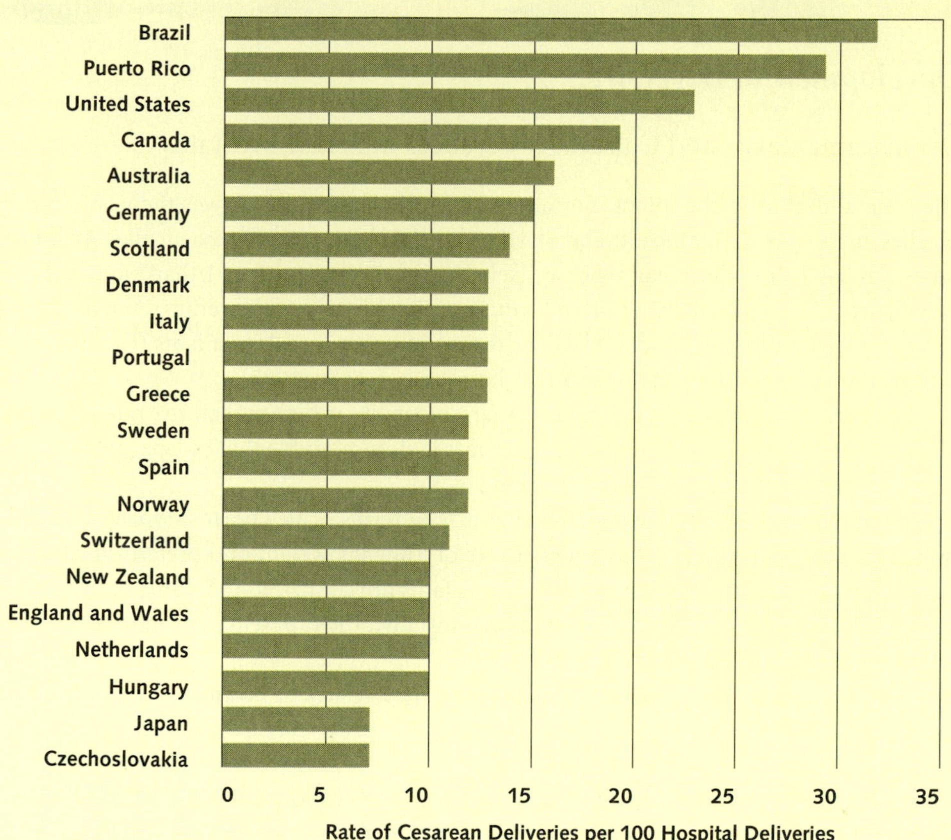

CESAREAN DELIVERIES IN U.S. AND ABROAD

The rate at which Cesarean deliveries are performed varies substantially from one country to another.

(*Source*: Notzon, 1990, p. 3287)

INFANT MORTALITY AND STILLBIRTH: THE TRAGEDY OF PREMATURE DEATH

The joy that accompanies the birth of a child is completely reversed when a newborn dies. The relative rarity of their occurrence makes infant deaths even harder for parents to bear.

Infant mortality is defined as death within the first year of life. In the 1990s the overall rate in the United States at this writing is 8.5 deaths per 1,000 live births. Infant mortality has been declining since the 1960s, and U.S. government officials expect to meet their goal of lowering the overall rate to 7 deaths per 1,000 live births (Guyer et al., 1995; Wegman, 1993).

Sometimes a child does not even live beyond its passage through the birth canal. **Stillbirth**, the delivery of a child who is not alive, occurs in less than 1 delivery out of 100. Sometimes the death is detected before labor begins. In this case, labor is typically induced, or physicians may carry out a Cesarean delivery in order to remove the body from the mother as soon as possible. In other cases of stillbirth, the baby dies during its travels through the birth canal.

Whether the death is a stillbirth or occurs after the child is born, the loss of a baby is a tragic occurrence. The impact on parents is significant: They move through the same stages of grief and mourning as they experience when an older loved one dies. In fact, the cruel juxtaposition of the first dawning of life and an unnaturally early death may make the death particularly difficult to accept and deal with. Depression is a common aftermath (DeFrain, et al., 1991; Brockington, 1992; Finkbeiner, 1996; J. Thomas, 1995; Lin & Lasker, 1996).

infant mortality *death within the first year of life*

stillbirth *the delivery of a child who is not alive, occurring in less than 1 delivery in 100*

Developmental Diversity

Overcoming Racial and Cultural Differences in Infant Mortality

The general decline in the infant mortality rate in the United States over the past several decades masks some significant, and startling, racial differences. In particular, African-American babies are more than twice as likely to die before the age of 1 than white babies (see Figure 3-5). In fact, if current trends continue, by the turn of the century, the mortality rate for African American infants will be three times that for white infants (Guyer et al., 1995; National Center for Health Statistics, 1993b; Singh & Yu, 1995).

Furthermore, the overall U.S. rate of infant mortality is higher than the rate in many other countries (see Figure 3-6). Its mortality rate is almost double that of Japan, which has the lowest mortality rate of any country in the world.

What makes the United States fare so poorly in terms of newborn survival? One answer is that the United States has a higher rate of low-birthweight and preterm deliveries than many other countries. In fact, when U.S. infants are compared to infants of the same weight who are born in countries with lower mortality, the differences in mortality rates disappear (Paneth, 1995; A. Wilcox et al., 1995).

Another reason for the higher U.S. mortality rate relates to economic diversity. The United States has a higher proportion of people living in poverty than many other countries. Because people in lower economic categories are less likely to have adequate medical care and be less healthy, the relatively high proportion of economically deprived individuals in the United States has an impact on the overall mortality rate (Aved et al., 1993).

Furthermore, many countries do a significantly better job providing prenatal care to mothers-to-be than the United States. For instance, low-cost and even free care, both before and after delivery, is often available in other countries. Paid maternity leave is frequently provided to pregnant women, lasting in some cases as long as 51 weeks (see Table 3-3). In certain European countries, women receive a comprehensive package of services involving general practitioner, obstetrician, and midwife. Pregnant women receive many privileges, such as transportation benefits for visits to health care providers. In Norway,

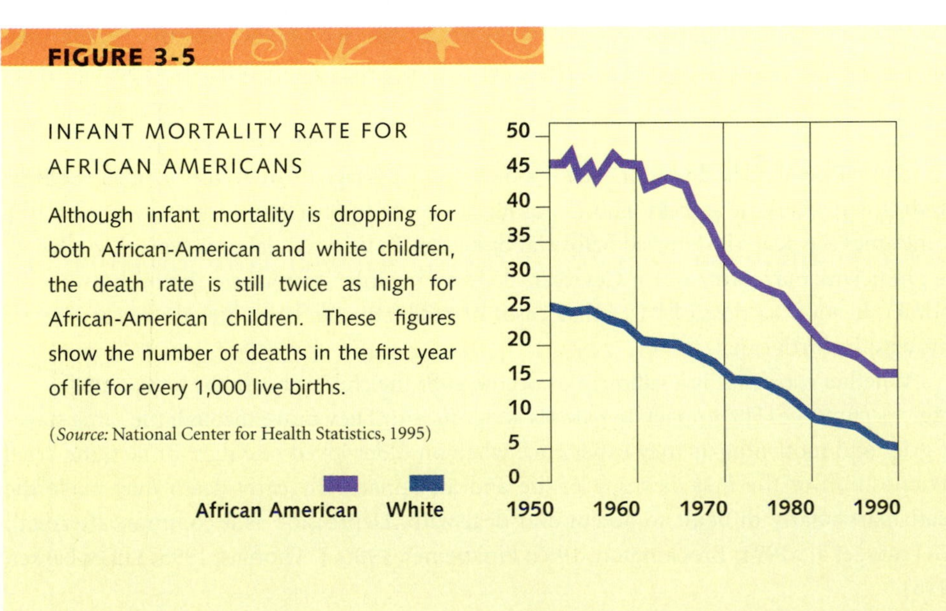

FIGURE 3-5

INFANT MORTALITY RATE FOR AFRICAN AMERICANS

Although infant mortality is dropping for both African-American and white children, the death rate is still twice as high for African-American children. These figures show the number of deaths in the first year of life for every 1,000 live births.

(*Source:* National Center for Health Statistics, 1995)

FIGURE 3-6

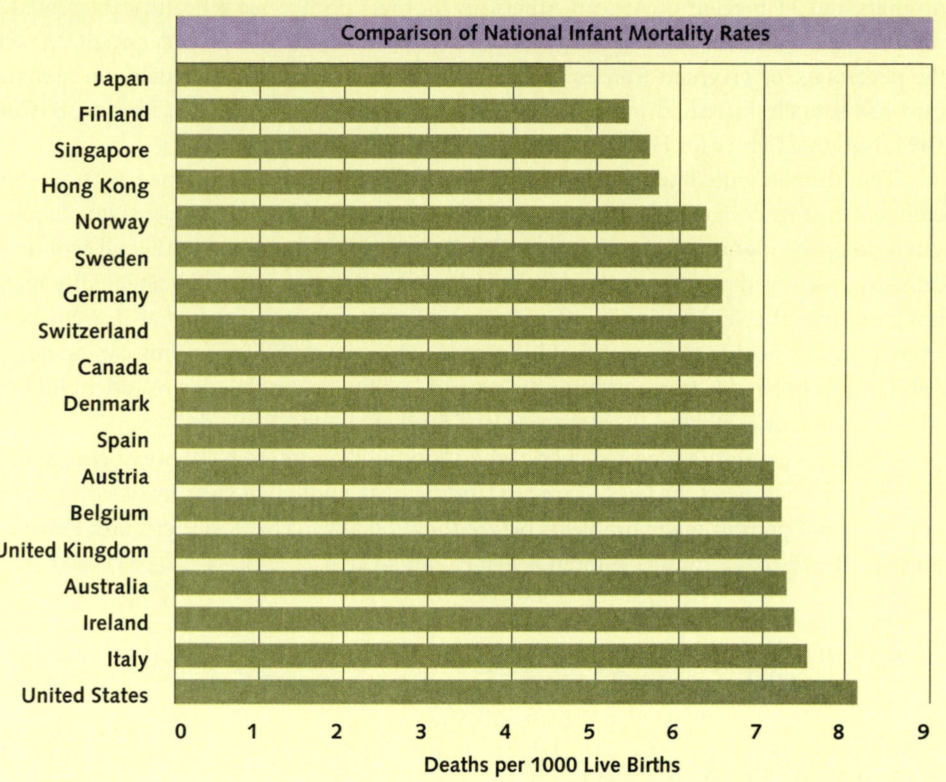

INFANT MORTALITY RATES

The rate of infant mortality is higher in the United States than for other industrialized countries.

(*Source: The World Factbook*, 1994)

pregnant women may be given living expenses for up to 10 days so they can be close to a hospital when it is time to give birth. And when their babies are born, new mothers receive, for just a small payment, the assistance of trained home helpers (C. A. Miller, 1987).

In the United States, the story is very different. The lack of national health care insurance or a national health care policy means that prenatal care is often haphazardly provided to the poor. About one out of every six pregnant women has insufficient prenatal

TABLE 3-3

MATERNITY-LEAVE POLICIES IN VARIOUS COUNTRIES

	Maximum Weeks Allowed	Percent of Salary Replaced
Sweden*	51	90
France	16-38	84
Italy	20	80
Britain	18	90
Canada	15	60
Germany	14	100
Japan	14	60
Netherlands	7	100

*For both parents combined.
(*Source:* Caminiti, 1992.)

care. Some 20 percent of white women and close to 40 percent of African American women who are pregnant receive no prenatal care early in their pregnancies. Five percent of white mothers and 11 percent of African American mothers do not see a health care provider until the last 3 months of pregnancy; some never see a health care provider at all. In fact, the percentage of pregnant women in the United States who receive virtually no prenatal care has actually increased in the 1990s from previous years (Johnson, Primas, & Coe, 1994; National Center for Health Statistics, 1993a; P. Thomas, 1994).

The ultimate outcome of the deficiency in prenatal services to women with low incomes is the higher likelihood of death for their infants. Yet this unfortunate state of affairs can be changed if greater support is provided. A start would be to ensure that all economically disadvantaged pregnant women have access to free or inexpensive high-quality medical care from the very beginning of pregnancy. Furthermore, barriers that prevent poor women from reaching such care should be reduced. For instance, programs can be developed that help pay for transportation to a health facility or for the care of older children while the mother is making a health care visit (Aved et al., 1993).

Finally, programs that provide basic education for all mothers-to-be are of paramount importance. Increasing the level of understanding of the potential risks involved in childbearing could prevent many problems before they actually occur (Carnegie Task Force on Meeting the Needs of Young Children, 1994; Fangman et al., 1994).

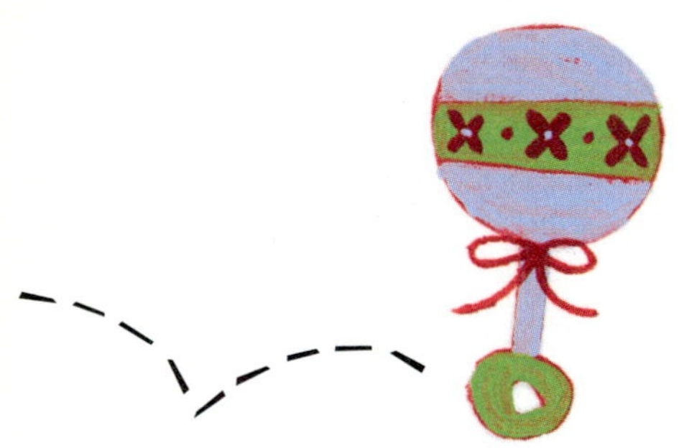

Review and Rethink

REVIEW

- Largely because of low birthweight, preterm infants may have substantial difficulties after birth and later in life, although most preterm babies ultimately develop normally.
- Very-low-birthweight infants are in special danger because of the immaturity of their organ systems. With massive intervention and at high cost, infants who have spent as little as 24 weeks in their mothers' bodies can now be helped to survive.
- Preterm and low-birthweight deliveries can be caused by health, age, and pregnancy-related factors in the mother. Income (and, because of its relationship with income, race) is also an important factor, with lower income leading to a higher incidence of low-birthweight babies.
- Cesarean deliveries, which occur with unusual frequency in the United States, are performed with postmature babies or when the fetus is in distress, in the wrong position, or unable to progress through the birth canal.
- Infant mortality rates can be affected by the availability of inexpensive health care and good education programs for mothers-to-be. The infant mortality rate in the United States is higher than the rate in many other countries, and higher for low-income families than higher-income families.

RETHINK

- What are some ethical considerations relating to the provision of intensive medical care to very-low-birthweight babies? Do you think such interventions should be routine practice? Why or why not?
- Effective educational programs have been devised for treating preterm infants. What are some public policy implications of this fact? What arguments, pro and con, can be made regarding such efforts?

- Why do you think the number of Cesarean deliveries has increased dramatically in the United States in recent years? What sort of policy for families and physicians would you design to govern the use of Cesarean procedures?
- Why do you think the United States lacks educational and health care policies that could reduce infant mortality rates overall and among poorer people? What arguments would you make to change this situation?

THE COMPETENT NEWBORN

In one sense, we are all born too soon.

The size of the brain of the average newborn is just one quarter what it will be at adulthood. In comparison, the brain of the macaque monkey, which is born after just 24 weeks of gestation, is 65 percent of its adult size. Because of the relative puniness of the infant human brain, some observers have suggested that we are propelled out of the womb some 6 to 12 months sooner than we ought to be.

In reality, evolution probably knew what it was doing: If we stayed inside our mothers' bodies an additional half-year to a year, our heads would be so large that we'd never manage to get through the birth canal (Gould, 1977; Kotre & Hall, 1990; A. H. Schultz, 1969).

The relatively underdeveloped brain of the human newborn helps explain the infant's apparent helplessness. Neonates arrive in the world quite incapable of successfully caring for themselves. Because of this, the earliest views of newborns focused on the things that they could not do, comparing them rather unfavorably to older members of the human species.

Today, however, such beliefs have taken a back seat to more favorable views of the neonate. As developmental researchers have begun to understand more about the nature of newborns, they have come to the realization that infants enter this world with an astounding array of capabilities.

PHYSICAL COMPETENCE: MEETING THE DEMANDS OF A NEW ENVIRONMENT

The world faced by a neonate is remarkably different from the one it experienced in the womb. Consider, for instance, the significant changes in functioning that the newly born Jamilla Castro, who weighed a robust 8 pounds 2 ounces at birth, encounters as she begins the first moments of life in her new environment (summarized in Table 3-4).

TABLE 3-4

JAMILLA CASTRO'S FIRST ENCOUNTERS UPON BIRTH

1. As soon as she is through the birth canal, Jamilla automatically begins to breathe on her own despite no longer being attached to the umbilical cord that provided precious air in the womb.
2. Reflexes–unlearned, organized involuntary responses that occur in the presence of certain stimuli–begin to take over. Sucking and swallowing reflexes permit Jamilla immediately to ingest food.
3. The rooting reflex, which involves turning in the direction of a source of stimulation, guides Jamilla toward potential sources of food that are near her mouth, such as her mother's nipple.
4. Jamilla begins to cough, sneeze, and blink–reflexes that help her avoid stimuli that are potentially bothersome or hazardous.
5. Her senses of smell and taste are highly developed. Physical activities and sucking increase when she smells peppermint. Her lips pucker when a sour taste is placed on her lips.
6. Objects with colors of blue and green seem to catch Jamilla's attention more than other colors, and she reacts sharply to loud, sudden noises. She will also continue to cry if she hears others newborns cry, but will stop if she hears a recording of her own voice crying.

Jamilla's most immediate task is to bring sufficient air into her body. Inside her mother, air was delivered through the umbilical cord, which also provided a means for the removal of carbon dioxide. The realities of the outside world are different: Once the umbilical cord is cut, Jamilla's respiratory system must begin its lifetime's work.

reflexes *unlearned, organized involuntary responses that occur automatically in the presence of certain stimuli*

For Jamilla, the task is automatic. As we noted earlier, most neonates begin to breathe on their own as soon as they are exposed to air. The ability to breathe immediately is a good indication that the respiratory system of the normal neonate is reasonably well developed, despite its lack of rehearsal in the womb.

Neonates emerge from the uterus more practiced in other types of physical activities. For example, newborns such as Jamilla show several **reflexes**—unlearned, organized involuntary responses that occur automatically in the presence of certain stimuli. Some of these reflexes are well rehearsed, having been present for several months before birth. The *sucking reflex* and the *swallowing reflex* permit the neonate to begin right away to ingest food. The *rooting reflex,* which involves turning in the direction of a source of stimulation (such as a light touch) near the mouth, is also related to eating. It guides the infant toward potential sources of food that are near its mouth, such as a mother's nipple.

Not all of the reflexes that are present at birth lead the newborn to seek out desired stimuli such as food. For instance, Jamilla can cough, sneeze, and blink—reflexes that help her to avoid stimuli that are potentially bothersome or hazardous.

Jamilla's sucking and swallowing reflexes, which help her to consume her mother's milk, are coupled with the new-found ability to digest nutriments. The neonate's digestive system initially produces *meconium,* a greenish-black material that is a remnant of the neonate's days as a fetus. The digestive tract immediately begins to process newly ingested nourishment.

Because their livers, a critical component of the digestive system, do not always work effectively at first, almost half of all newborns develop a distinctly yellowish tinge to their bodies and eyes. This change in color is a symptom of *neonatal jaundice.* It is most likely to occur in preterm and low-weight neonates, and it is typically not dangerous. Treatment most often consists of placing the baby under fluorescent lights or administering drugs.

SENSORY CAPABILITIES: EXPERIENCING THE WORLD

Just after Jamilla was born, her father was certain that she looked directly at him. Did she, in fact, see him?

Starting at birth, infants are able to distinguish different colors and even show preferences for particular ones.

This is a hard question to answer for several reasons. For one thing, when sensory experts talk of "seeing," they mean both a sensory reaction due to the stimulation of the visual sensory organs and an interpretation of that stimulation (the distinction, as you might recall from an introductory psychology class, between sensation and perception). Furthermore, as we'll discuss further when we consider sensory capabilities during infancy in Chapter 4, it is tricky, to say the least, to pinpoint the specific sensory skills of newborns who lack the ability to explain what they are experiencing.

Still, we do have some answers to the question of what newborns are capable of seeing and, for that matter, questions about their other sensory capabilities. For example, it is clear that neonates such as Jamilla can see to some extent. Although their visual acuity is not fully developed, newborns actively pay attention to certain types of information in their environment (M. M. Haith, 1980, 1991).

For instance, neonates pay closest attention to portions of scenes in their field of vision that are highest in information, such as objects that sharply contrast with the rest of their environment. Furthermore, infants can discriminate different levels of brightness. There is even evidence suggesting that newborns have a sense of size constancy, seemingly aware that objects stay the same size even though the size of the image on the retina varies with distance (Slater, Mattock, & Brown, 1990).

And not only can neonates distinguish different colors, they also seem to prefer particular ones. For example, they are able to distinguish between red, green, yellow, and blue, and they take more time staring at blue and green objects—suggesting a partiality for those colors (Adams, Mauer, & Davis, 1986).

Newborns are also clearly capable of hearing. They react to certain kinds of sounds, showing startle reactions to loud, sudden noises, for instance. The also exhibit familiarity with certain sounds. For example, newborns continue to cry when they hear other newborns crying. On the other hand, a crying newborn who hears a recording of its own crying is more likely to stop crying, as if it recognizes the familiar sound (G. B. Martin & Clark, 1982).

As with vision, however, the degree of auditory acuity is not as great as it will be later. The auditory system is not completely developed. Moreover, amniotic fluid, which is initially trapped in the middle ear, must drain out before the newborn can fully hear (Reinis & Goldman, 1980).

In addition to sight and hearing, the other senses also function quite adequately in the newborn. It is obvious that newborns are sensitive to touch. For instance, they respond to stimuli such as the hairs of a brush, and they are aware of puffs of air so weak that adults cannot notice them. The senses of smell and taste are also well developed. Newborns suck and increase other physical activity when the odor of peppermint is placed near the nose. They also pucker their lips when a sour taste is placed on them, and respond with suitable facial expressions to other tastes as well. Such findings clearly indicate that the senses of touch, smell, and taste are not only present at birth, but are also reasonably sophisticated (Jacklin, Snow, & Maccoby, 1981; Mistretta, 1990; Rosenstein & Oster, 1988; Sarnat, 1978).

In one sense, the sophistication of the sensory systems of newborns such as Jamilla is not surprising. After all, the typical neonate has had 9 months to prepare for his or her encounter with the outside world. As we discussed in Chapter 2, human sensory systems begin their development well before birth. Furthermore, some researchers suggest that the passage through the birth canal places babies in a state of heightened sensory awareness, preparing them for the world that they are about to encounter for the first time (Bornstein & Lamb, 1992).

Social Competence: Responding to Others

Soon after Jamilla was born, her older brother looked down at her in her crib and opened his mouth wide, pretending to be surprised. Jamilla's mother, looking on, was amazed when it appeared that Jamilla imitated his expression, opening her mouth as if she were surprised.

Developmental psychologist Tiffany Field.

Researchers registered surprise of their own when they first found that newborns did indeed have the capability to imitate others' behavior. Although infants were known to have all the muscles in place to produce facial expressions related to basic emotions, the actual appearance of such expressions was assumed to be largely random.

However, research beginning in the late 1970s suggested a different conclusion. For instance, developmental researchers demonstrated that when exposed to an adult modeling a behavior that the infant already performed spontaneously, such as opening the mouth or sticking out the tongue, the newborn was apt to imitate the behavior (Meltzoff & Moore, 1977).

Even more exciting were findings from a series of studies conducted by developmental psychologist Tiffany Field and her colleagues (T. M. Field, 1982; T. Field et al., 1984; T. Field & Walden, 1982). They initially showed that infants could discriminate between such basic facial expressions as happiness, sadness, and surprise. They then exposed newborns to an adult model with a happy, sad, or surprised facial expression. The results were clear: The newborns produced a reasonably accurate imitation of the adult's expression (see Figure 3-7).

Subsequent research, conducted just minutes after birth and in a variety of cultures, has shown that imitative capabilities appear to be a universal characteristic of newborns (Kaitz et al., 1988; Reissland, 1988). Imitative skills are more than a mere curiosity. Effective social interaction with others relies in part on the ability to react to other people in an appropriate manner and to understand the meaning of others' emotional states. Consequently, the imitative capability of newborns provides an important foundation for social interaction later in life (R. D. Phillips et al., 1990).

states of arousal *degree of sleep and wakefulness*

In addition to their imitative abilities, several other aspects of newborns' behavior act as forerunners for more formal types of social interaction that will develop more fully in the future. As shown in Table 3-5, certain characteristics of neonates mesh with parental behavior to help produce a social relationship between child and parent, as well as social relationships with others (Eckerman & Oehler, 1992).

For example, newborns cycle through various **states of arousal**, different degrees of sleep and wakefulness, that range from deep sleep to great agitation. Although immediately after birth these cycles are disrupted, they quickly become more regularized. Caregivers become involved when they seek to aid the infant in transitions from one state to another. For instance, a father who rhythmically rocks his crying daughter in an effort to calm her is engaged in a joint activity that is a prelude to future social interactions of different sorts.

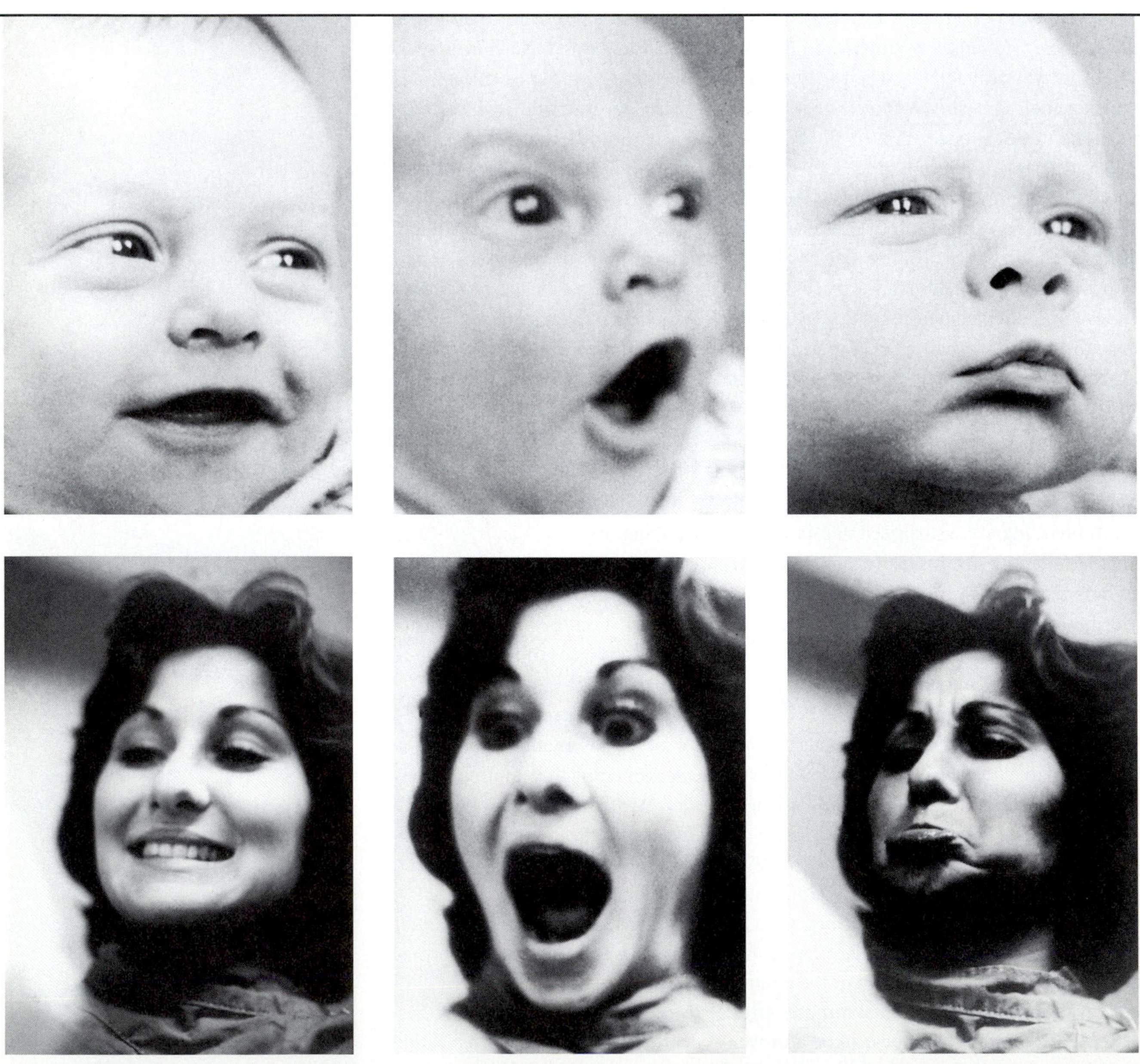

FIGURE 3-7 It is clear that this newborn infant is imitating the happy, surprised, and sad expressions of the adult model.

(Courtesy of Dr. Tiffany Field.)

TABLE 3-5

FACTORS THAT ENCOURAGE SOCIAL INTERACTION BETWEEN FULL-TERM NEWBORNS AND THEIR PARENTS

Full-Term Newborn	Parent
Has organized states	Helps regulate infant's states
Attends selectively to certain stimuli	Provides these stimuli
Behaves in ways interpretable as specific communicative intent	Searches for communicative intent
Responds systematically to parent's acts	Wants to influence newborn, feel effective
Acts in temporally predictable ways	Adjusts actions to newborn's temporal rhythms
Learns from, adapts to parent's behavior	Acts repetitively and predictably

(*Source:* Eckerman & Ochler, 1992.)

Similarly, newborns tend to pay particular attention to their mothers' voices (Hepper, Scott, & Shahidullah, 1993). In turn, parents and others modify their speech when talking to infants, using a different pitch and tempo than they use with older children and adults (A. DeCasper & Fifer, 1980; Fernald, 1984).

The ultimate outcome of the social interactive capabilities of the newborn infant, and the responses such behavior brings about from parents, is to pave the way for future social interactions. Just as the neonate shows remarkable skills on a physical and perceptual level, then, its social capabilities are no less sophisticated.

The Informed Consumer of Development

First Encounters: Interacting with a Newborn

If you are the relative or friend of a woman who has just given birth, you may be anticipating your initial encounter with the new baby with some degree of trepidation. In fact, people tend to interact with newborns in very different ways. Some approach newborns gingerly, acting as if they are confronting a representative of an alien society; others show no hesitation in touching and stroking them and hoisting them vigorously into the air.

Is there an optimal way of interacting with newborns? Although there are no hard and fast rules, several principles can guide your first encounters with a newborn:

- *Prepare yourself.* Newborns may look slightly "unfinished." As we discussed earlier, delivery is not an easy experience for a baby: Its head may be misshapen and its nose and ears squashed down. Hairlike material may cover its shoulder blades and spine, its skin may be wrinkled, and its color may be bluish or yellowish. Most of this will change in a few days.
- *Hold the baby securely.* Keep in mind that newborns have been in the close confines of the womb for 9 months, and they need to become accustomed to the newfound freedom of movement that the world provides. Consequently, they shouldn't be

dangled in the air or otherwise treated roughly. In fact, in some Native American cultures, newborns are routinely wrapped up firmly in blankets—a procedure called *swaddling.*

- *Speak gently.* Because the sense organs of babies are operative even before birth, they can readily hear voices and other sounds in their surroundings. In fact, because the stimulation from their passage through the birth canal may make them particularly sensitive to stimuli, you should take care not to speak too loudly. But do speak to the newborn: As we'll see in the next few chapters, linguistic stimulation is crucial to the development of language skills.
- *Keep to yourself any suspicions that something may be wrong with the child.* Unless you are a pediatrician or an expert in infant development, you don't have the knowledge to make such a pronouncement. Furthermore, what you are seeing may not be a true sample of the baby's behavior, particularly if the mother has received medication during labor. Remember that every baby is different, and that a baby's appearance and behavior on its first day of life will change substantially in just the next few days.

Review and Rethink

REVIEW

- Neonates, born with brains that are only a fraction of their ultimate size, are in many ways helpless. Nevertheless, studies of what newborns *can* do, rather than what they *can't* do, have revealed some surprising capabilities.
- Newborns' respiratory and digestive systems begin to function at birth. Newborns come equipped with an array of reflexes to help them eat, swallow, find food, and avoid unpleasant stimuli.
- Newborns' sensory competence includes the ability to distinguish objects in the visual field and to see color differences; the ability to hear and to discern familiar sounds; and sensitivity to touch, odors, and tastes.
- Newborns develop the foundations of social competence early. Sophisticated imitative capabilities help them react appropriately to other people's emotional states and to manage the beginnings of social interaction.

RETHINK

- Developmental researchers no longer view the neonate as a helpless, incompetent creature, but rather as a remarkably competent, developing human being. What do you think are some implications of this change in viewpoint for methods of childrearing and child care?
- How do newborns' reflexes help them in their new environment? How might the fetus have developed such organized responses to stimuli?
- How does the newborn's imitative capability help her or him to develop social competence later in life? In what ways might this process be different or similar for a baby born without sight?

- How should a person who is meeting a newborn for the first time act toward the baby and its parents? Why?

What is the normal process of labor?

1. Labor proceeds in three stages. The first stage begins with 30-second contractions occurring about every 8 to 10 minutes. The frequency, duration, and intensity of the contractions increase until the mother's cervix expands enough to permit the baby's head to pass through.
2. In the second stage of labor, which lasts about 90 minutes, the baby begins to move through the cervix and birth canal and ultimately leaves the mother's body.
3. In the third stage of labor, which lasts only a few minutes, the umbilical cord and placenta are expelled from the mother.

What happens immediately after the baby is born?

4. After it emerges, the newborn, or neonate, is usually inspected by health care workers using a standard measurement system such as the Apgar scale.
5. Health care workers inspect the newborn for signs of irregularities. One of the most serious problems that can be caused by the birth process itself is a temporary deprivation of oxygen, which can bring serious harm if it lasts longer than a few seconds.
6. After it is cleaned, the newborn is returned to its mother and father for its first encounter with those who will love and care for it.

What choices do parents have regarding the birthing process?

7. Parents today have a variety of options concerning the process of giving birth, including the use or nonuse of pain-suppressing drugs, and a range of alternative birthing techniques, including the Lamaze method, the Leboyer method, the use of birthing centers versus hospitals, and the use of midwives versus obstetricians.
8. Helpful strategies for women facing the pains of labor include maintaining a flexible mind about birthing methods, communicating frankly and frequently with health care workers, having realistic expectations about fatigue and pain, accepting the support of a partner, and focusing on the joyful event in which labor ends.

What complications can occur at birth and what are their causes, effects, and treatments?

9. Preterm, or premature, infants are born less than 38 weeks following conception. Preterm infants generally have low birthweight, which can cause chilling, vulnerability to infection, respiratory distress syndrome, and hypersensitivity to environmental stimuli.
10. Some children who were born prematurely may also show adverse effects later in life, including slowed development, learning disabilities, behavior disorders, below-average IQ scores, and problems with physical coordination.
11. Very-low-birthweight infants are in special danger because of the immaturity of their organ systems. However, medical advances have pushed the age of viability of the infant back to about 24 weeks following conception.

12. The costs of treating very-low-birthweight infants, at birth and later in life, are very high, a fact that raises serious ethical questions about the wisdom of such massive medical intervention.
13. Several treatment strategies for preterm infants appear to be effective, including regular massage and educational programs designed to improve cognitive, social, and language skills.
14. Causal factors in preterm and low-birthweight deliveries include multiple births, the young age of the mother, a short time between pregnancies, and general health factors in the mother.
15. Another factor in low birthweight is income. Women with lower incomes have a higher incidence of low-birthweight babies than those with higher incomes. The question of income also entails race, since members of racial minorities have disproportionately lower incomes.
16. Postmature babies, who spend extra time in their mothers' wombs, are also at risk. However, physicians can artificially induce labor or perform a Cesarean delivery to address this situation.
17. Cesarean deliveries are performed when the fetus is in distress, in the wrong position, or unable to progress through the birth canal. The United States has an unusually high incidence of Cesarean deliveries, which many critics consider unjustified because of dangers to mother and child from this procedure.
18. The infant mortality rate in the United States is higher than the rate in many other countries, and higher for low-income families than higher-income families. Improvements in the availability of high-quality but inexpensive medical care and in pregnancy-related education could change this situation.

What capabilities does the newborn have?

19. Although apparently helpless, human newborns have remarkable capabilities. They quickly master the breathing of air through the lungs, and they are equipped with reflexes to help them eat, swallow, find food, and avoid unpleasant stimuli.
20. Newborns' sensory capabilities are also sophisticated. Although their sensory systems will increase in acuity as they age, even as newborns they have some visual discrimination, can hear quite well, are sensitive to touch, and can smell and taste.
21. Newborns are able to imitate the behavior of others, a capability that helps them form social relationships and facilitates the development of social competence.

Key Terms and Concepts

neonates (p. 84)
episiotomy (p. 85)
Apgar scale (p. 86)
anoxia (p. 87)
bonding (p. 88)
preterm infants (p. 97)
low-birthweight infants (p. 97)
small-for-gestational-age infants (p. 97)
very-low-birthweight infants (p. 98)
age of viability (p. 98)
postmature infants (p. 101)
Cesarean delivery (p. 102)
fetal monitors (p. 102)
infant mortality (p. 103)
stillbirth (p. 103)
reflexes (p. 108)
states of arousal (p. 110)

PART 2 Infancy

CHAPTER 4

INFANCY

Physical Development in Infancy

PROLOGUE

FIRST STEPS

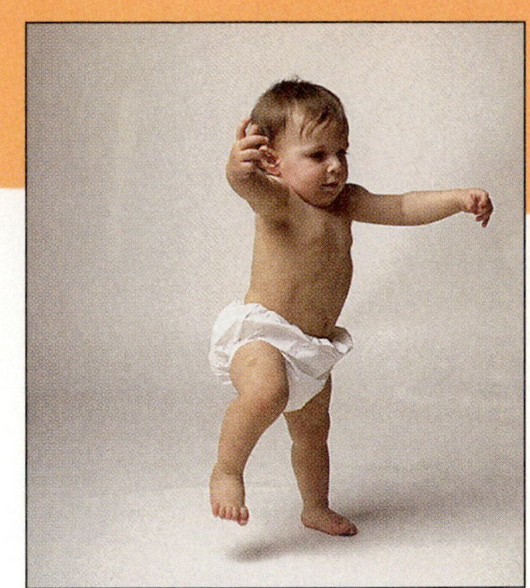

I was in the kitchen, on the phone, when my son Ben appeared in the doorway, his fingertips on the doorjamb for balance. Gradually he let go to toddle toward me, stringing one impossible step after another. He held his arms up in the air and moved his feet mechanically, stiffly stepping forward with slow deliberation at first and then awkwardly picking up speed, propelled by a force he couldn't quite control. His every step defied a law of motion, and he seemed poised to tumble, at any moment, in any direction. "He's walking!" I screamed to the long-distance operator on the other end of the line as Ben lunged for my knees in a moment of pure triumph. (Israeloff, 1991, p. 54)

LOOKING AHEAD

Ben Israeloff's first steps at the age of 9 months capped a succession of milestones that brought him closer to full mobility and caused his parents sheer joy. His accomplishment, however remarkable, was only one of many that characterize the dramatic physical attainments during infancy.

In this chapter we consider the nature of physical development during the period of infancy, which starts at birth and continues until the second birthday. We begin by considering the pace of growth during infancy: obvious changes in height and weight, but also less apparent changes in the nervous system. We also consider how infants quickly develop stable patterns in which their basic activities, such as sleeping, eating, and attending to the world, take on some degree of order.

Our discussion then turns to motor development, the development of skills that eventually will allow an infant to roll over, take the first step, and pick up a pin from the floor—skills that ultimately form the basis for later, even more complex behaviors. We start with basic, genetically determined reflexes and consider how even these may be modified on the basis of experience. We also discuss the nature and timing of the development of particular physical skills; we look at whether their emergence can be speeded up; and we consider the importance of early nutrition to their development.

Finally, we explore the development of the senses during infancy. We'll investigate how several individual sensory systems operate, and we'll look at how data from the sense organs are sorted out and transformed into meaningful information.

In sum, after reading this chapter, you'll be able to answer these questions:

- How do the human body and nervous system develop?
- Does the environment affect the pattern of development?
- What are reflexes and how are they useful?
- How universal are the schedule and sequence of motor development?
- What is the role of nutrition in physical development, and what food is best for infants?
- How do the senses develop, and what sensory capabilities do infants possess?

GROWTH AND STABILITY

The average newborn weighs in at just over 7 pounds, which is probably less than the weight of the turkey most of us ate last Thanksgiving. Its length is a mere 20 inches, shorter than a loaf of French bread. It is helpless; if left to fend for itself, it could not survive.

Yet after just a few years, the story is very different. Babies are much larger, they are mobile, and they become increasingly independent. How does this growth happen? We can answer this question first by describing the changes in weight and height that occur over the first 2 years of life, and then by examining some of the principles that underlie and direct that growth.

PHYSICAL GROWTH: THE RAPID ADVANCES OF INFANCY

Over the first 2 years of a human's life, growth occurs at a rapid pace (see Figure 4-1). By the age of 5 months, the average infant's birthweight has doubled to around 15 pounds. By the first birthday, the infant's weight has tripled to about 22 pounds. Although the pace of weight gain slows during the second year, it is still continuous. By the end of its second year, the average child weighs four times its birthweight.

The weight gains of infancy are matched by increased length. By the end of the first year, the typical baby stands a proud 30 inches tall, an average increase from birth of almost a foot. By its second birthday, it usually attains a height of 3 feet.

Not all parts of an infant's body grow at the same rate. For instance, as we saw first in Chapter 2, at birth the head accounts for one quarter of the newborn's entire body size. During the first 2 years of life, the rest of the body begins to catch up. By the age of 2 the baby's head is only one fifth of body length, and by adulthood it is only one eighth (see Figure 4-2). Furthermore, a growing body of evidence suggests that growth is not regular and continuous, as originally thought. Instead, recent research suggests that it occurs in short spurts, separated by periods of days in which there is little or no growth (Lampl et al., 1995).

The disproportionately large size of infants' heads at birth is an example of one of the major principles that govern growth: the cephalocaudal principle, which relates to the direction of growth. The **cephalocaudal principle** states that growth follows a pattern that begins with head and upper body parts and then proceeds to the rest of the body. Reflecting Greek and Latin roots meaning "head-to-tail," the cephalocaudal growth principle means that we develop visual abilities (located in the head) well before we master the ability to walk (closer to the end of the body). The cephalocaudal principle operates both prenatally and after birth.

cephalocaudal principle *the principle that growth follows a pattern that begins with head and upper body parts and then proceeds to the rest of the body*

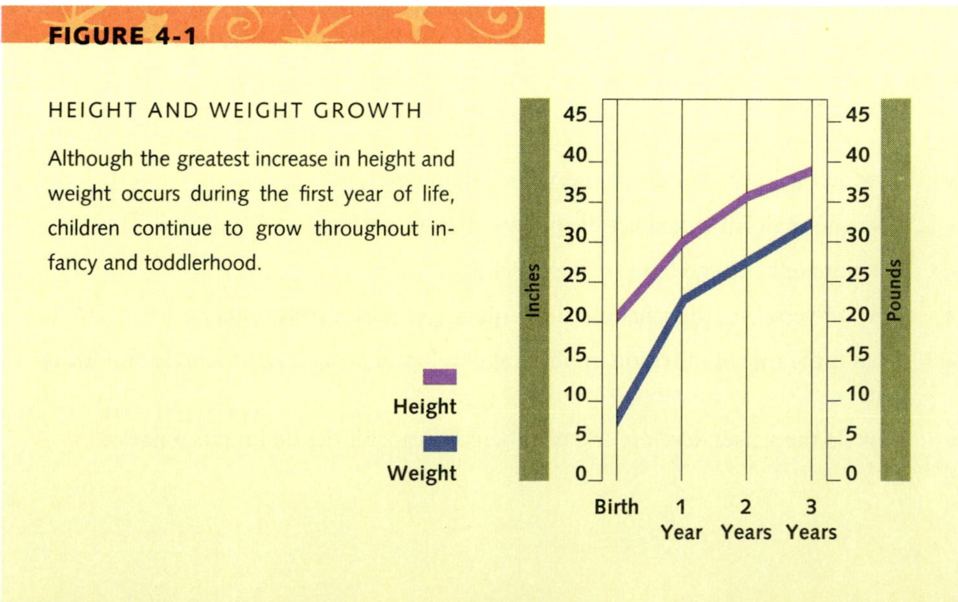

FIGURE 4-1

HEIGHT AND WEIGHT GROWTH

Although the greatest increase in height and weight occurs during the first year of life, children continue to grow throughout infancy and toddlerhood.

FIGURE 4-2

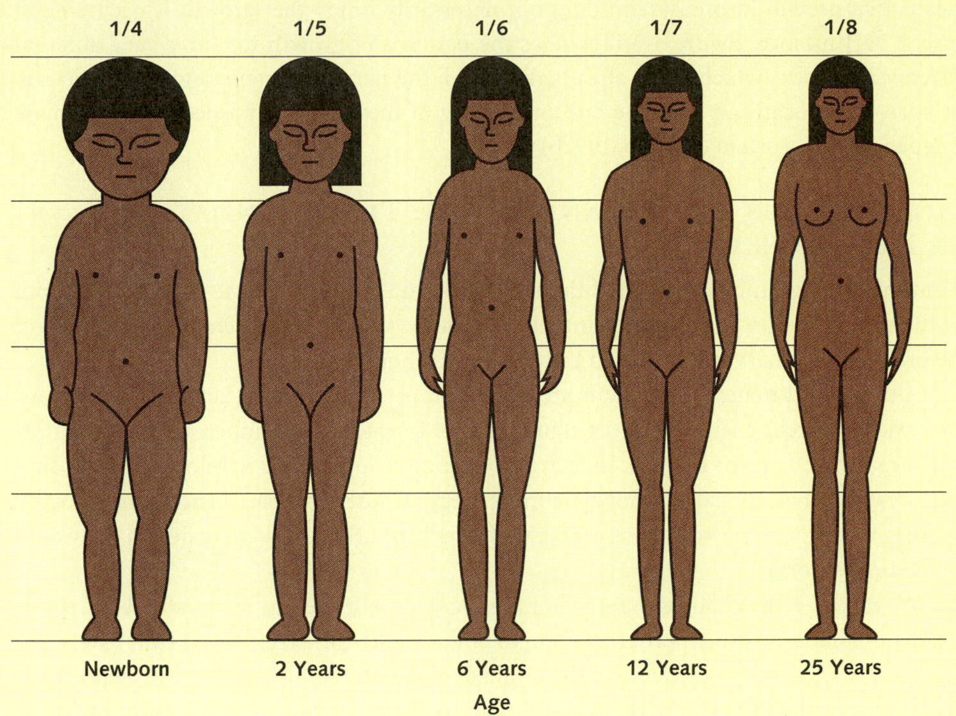

DECREASING PROPORTIONS

At birth, the head represents one quarter of the neonate's body. By adulthood, the head is only one eighth the size of the body.

Several other principles (summarized in Table 4-1) help explain the patterns by which growth occurs. The **proximodistal principle** states that development proceeds from the center of the body outward. Based on the Latin words for "near" and "far," the proximodistal principle means that the trunk of the body grows before the extremities of the arms and legs. Similarly, it is only after growth has occurred in the arms and legs that the fingers and toes can grow. Furthermore, the development of the ability to use various parts of the body also follows the proximodistal principle. For instance, the effective use of the arms precedes the ability to use the hands.

Another major principle of growth concerns the way complex skills build upon simpler ones. The **principle of hierarchical integration** states that simple skills typically develop separately and independently. Later, however, these simple skills are integrated into more complex ones. Thus, the relatively complex skill of grasping something in the hand cannot be mastered until the developing infant learns how to control—and integrate—the movements of the individual fingers.

proximodistal principle *the principle that development proceeds from the center of the body outward*

principle of hierarchical integration *the principle stating that simple skills typically develop separately and independently but are later integrated into more complex skills*

TABLE 4-1

MAJOR PRINCIPLES GOVERNING GROWTH

Cephalocaudal Principle	Proximodistal Principle	Principle of Hierarchical Integration	Principle of the Independence of Systems
Growth follows a pattern that begins with the head and upper body parts and then proceeds to the rest of the body. Based on Greek and Latin roots meaning "head-to-tail."	Development proceeds from the center of the body outward. Based on the Latin words for "near" and "far."	Simple skills typically develop separately and independently. Later they are integrated into more complex skills.	Different body systems grow at different rates.

Finally, the last major principle of growth is the **principle of the independence of systems**, which suggests that different body systems grow at different rates. This principle means that growth in one system does not necessarily imply that growth is occurring in others. For instance, Figure 4-3 illustrates the patterns of growth for three very different systems: body size, which we've already discussed, the nervous system, and sexual characteristics. As you can see, both the rate and timing of these different aspects of growth are independent (Bornstein & Lamb, 1992b).

principle of the independence of systems *the principle of growth that suggests that different body systems grow at different rates*

neurons *the basic nerve cells of the nervous system*

myelin *a fatty substance that helps insulate neurons and speeds the transmission of nerve impulses*

The Nervous System and Brain: The Foundations of Development

Whatever feelings, movements, and thoughts an infant may experience are brought about by the same complex network: the infant's nervous system. The *nervous system* comprises the brain and the nerves that extend throughout the body.

Although estimates vary, infants are born with between 100 and 200 billion **neurons,** the basic nerve cells of the nervous system. In order to reach this number, neurons multiply at an amazing rate prior to birth. In fact, at some points in prenatal development, cell division creates some 250,000 additional neurons every minute. This pace is necessary, though: Because virtually no new neurons are created after birth, the number created in the womb is a lifetime's worth.

We can liken the changes that the brain undergoes in its development after birth to the actions of a farmer who, in order to strengthen the vitality of a fruit tree, prunes away unnecessary branches. In the same way, the ultimate capabilities of the brain are brought about in part by a "pruning down" of unnecessary neurons. Neurons that do not become interconnected with other neurons as the infant's experience of the world increases become unnecessary. They eventually die out, increasing the efficiency of the nervous system. Unlike most other aspects of growth, then, the development of the nervous system proceeds most effectively through the loss of cells (Black & Greenough, 1986; Kolb, 1989, 1995; Lipsitt, 1986a).

Although the creation of neurons stops just after birth, neurons continue to increase in size. Neurons become coated with **myelin,** a fatty substance that helps insulate neurons and speeds the transmission of nerve impulses. The brain triples its weight in the first 2 years of life, and it reaches more than three quarters of its adult weight and size by the age

FIGURE 4-3

GROWTH RATE OF THREE DIFFERENT BODY SYSTEMS

Different body systems mature at different rates. For instance, the nervous system is highly developed during infancy, while the development of body size is considerably less developed. The development of sexual characteristics lag even more, maturing at adolescence.

(*Source:* Bornstein & Lamb, 1992b, p. 135.)

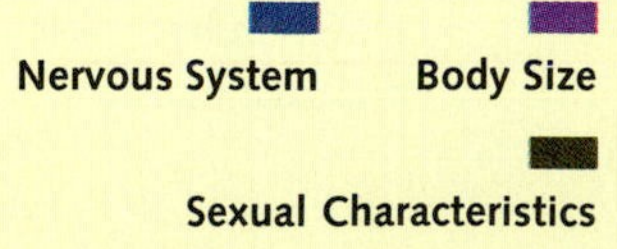

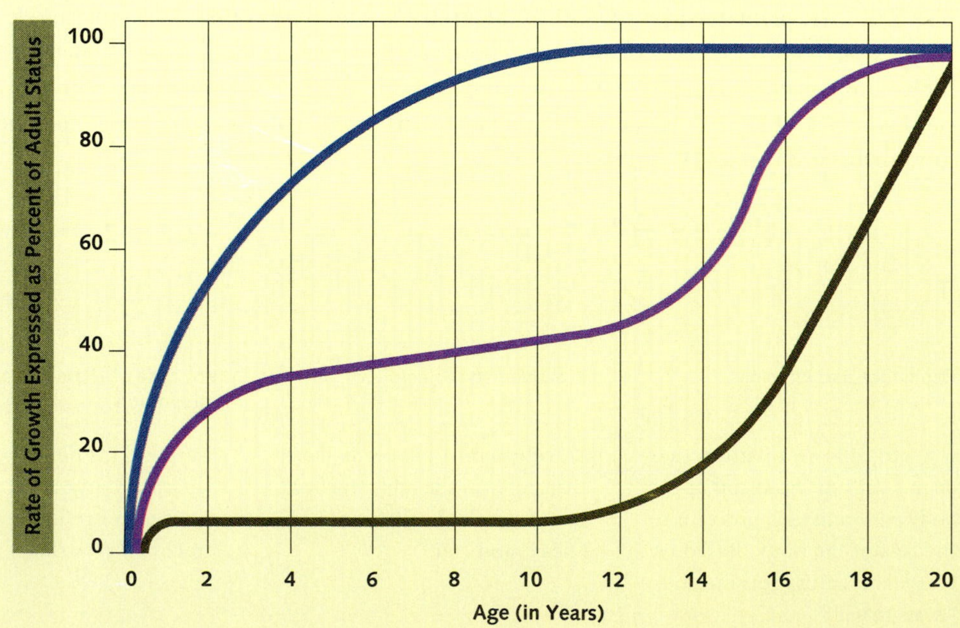

of 2. Furthermore, the network of neurons becomes increasingly complex, as illustrated in Figure 4-4 (Conel, 1930/1963). The intricacy of neural connections continues to increase throughout life.

As they grow, neurons become arranged by function. Some move into the **cerebral cortex,** the upper layer of the brain, while others move to *subcortical levels,* which are below the cerebral cortex. The subcortical levels, which regulate such fundamental activities as breathing and heart rate, are the most fully developed at birth. As time passes, however, the cells in the cerebral cortex, which are responsible for higher-order processes such as thinking and reasoning, become more developed and interconnected.

Brain development, much of which unfolds automatically because of genetically predetermined patterns, is also susceptible to environmental influences. **Plasticity,** the degree to which a developing structure or behavior is susceptible to experience, is relatively great for the brain. For instance, the nature of an infant's sensory experience affects both the size of individual neurons and the structure of their interconnections. Consequently, compared with those brought up in more enriched environments, infants raised in severely restricted settings are likely to show differences in brain structure and weight (Gottlieb, 1991; Kolb, 1995; Rosenzweig & Bennett, 1976).

Work with nonhumans has been particularly illuminating in revealing the nature of the brain's plasticity. For instance, some studies have compared rats raised in an unusually visually stimulating environment to those raised in more typical, and less interesting, cages. Results of such research show that areas of the brain associated with vision are both thicker and heavier for the rats reared in enriched settings (Black & Greenough, 1986).

On the other side of the coin, environments that are unusually barren or in some way restricted may impede the brain's development. Again, work with nonhumans provides some intriguing data. In one study kittens were fitted with goggles that restricted their vision so that they could view only vertical lines. When the cats grew up and had their goggles removed, they were unable to see horizontal lines, although they saw vertical lines perfectly well. Analogously, kittens whose goggles restricted their vision of vertical lines early in life were effectively blind to vertical lines during their adulthood—although their vision of horizontal lines was accurate (Hirsch & Spinelli, 1970).

On the other hand, when goggles are placed on older cats who have lived relatively normal kittenhoods, such results are not seen after the goggles are removed. The conclusion is that there is a sensitive period for the development of vision. As we noted in Chapter 1, a **sensitive period** is a specific but limited time, usually early in an organism's life, during

cerebral cortex *the upper layer of the brain*

plasticity *the degree to which a developing structure or behavior is susceptible to experience*

sensitive period *a specific but limited time, usually early in an organism's life, during which the organism is particularly susceptible to environmental influences relating to some particular facet of development*

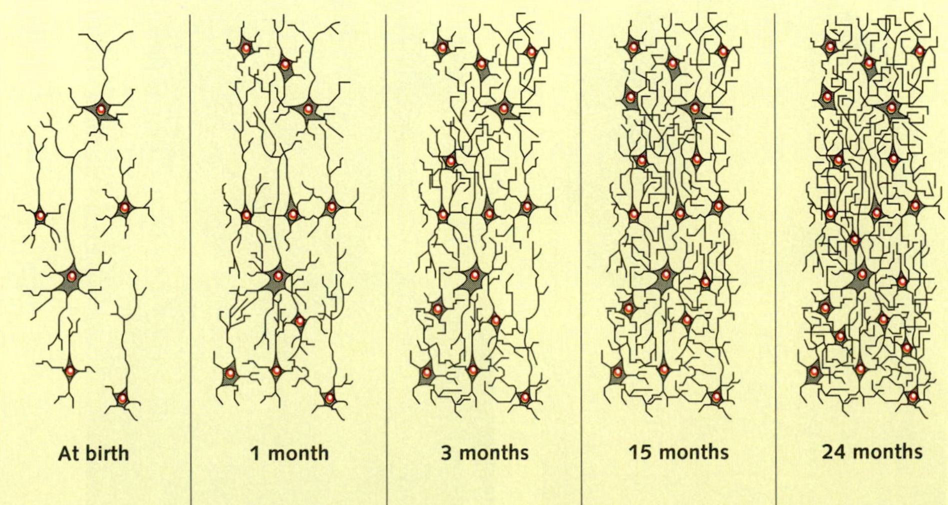

FIGURE 4-4

THE DEVELOPMENT OF NEURONS

Networks of neurons become increasingly complex and interconnected with age over the first 2 years of life.

(*Source:* Conel, J. L., 1930/1963.)

which the organism is particularly susceptible to environmental influences relating to some particular facet of development. A sensitive period may be associated with a behavior—such as the development of full vision—or with the development of a structure of the body, such as the configuration of the brain.

rhythms *repetitive, cyclical patterns of behavior*

The existence of sensitive periods raises several important issues. For one thing, it suggests that unless an infant receives a certain level of early environmental stimulation during a sensitive period, the infant may suffer damage or fail to develop capabilities that can never be fully remedied. If this is true, providing successful later intervention for such children may prove to be particularly challenging.

The opposite question also arises: Does an unusually high level of stimulation during sensitive periods produce developmental gains beyond what a more commonplace level of stimulation would provide?

Such questions have no simple answers. Determining how unusually impoverished or enriched environments affect later development is one of the central questions addressed by developmental researchers seeking to maximize opportunities for developing children (Fisher & Lerner, 1994; M. Lamb, 1994).

Integrating the Bodily Systems: The Life Cycles of Infancy

In the first days of life, the infant shows a jumble of different behavioral patterns. The most basic activities—sleeping, eating, crying, attending to the world—are controlled by a variety of bodily systems. Although each of these individual behavioral patterns may be functioning effectively, it takes some time and effort for infants to learn to integrate the separate systems. In fact, one of the neonate's major missions is to integrate its individual behaviors (Thoman, 1990; Thoman & Whitney, 1990).

Rhythms and States. One of the most important ways that behavior becomes integrated is through the development of various body **rhythms**, repetitive, cyclical patterns of behavior. Some rhythms are immediately obvious, such as the change from wakefulness to sleep. Others are more subtle, but still easily noticeable, such as breathing and sucking patterns. Still other rhythms may require careful observation to be noticed. For instance, newborns may go through periods in which they jerk their legs in a regular pattern every minute or so. Although some of these rhythms are apparent just after birth, others emerge slowly over the first year as the nervous system becomes more integrated (Robertson, 1982; Thelen, 1979).

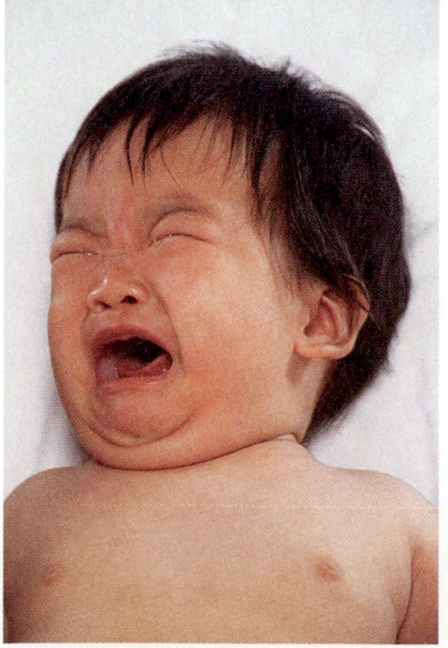

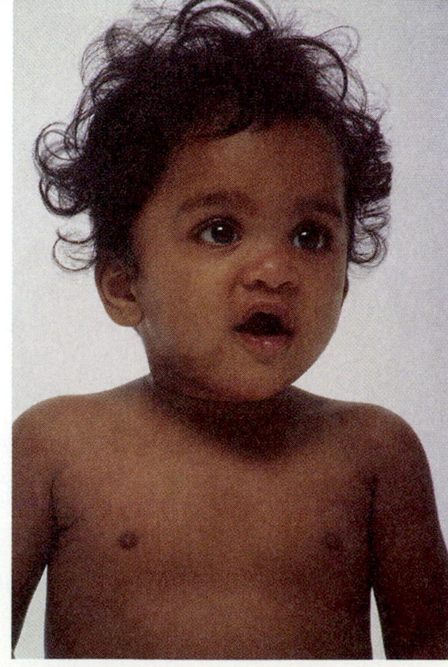

Infants cycle through various states, including crying and alertness. These states are integrated through bodily rhythms.

TABLE 4-2

PRIMARY BEHAVIORAL STATES FOR INFANTS

STATES	CHARACTERISTICS	PERCENTAGE OF TIME WHEN ALONE IN STATE
Awake States		
Alert	Attentive or scanning, the infant's eyes are open, bright, and shining.	6.7
Nonalert waking	Eyes are usually open, but dull and unfocused. Varied, but typically high motor activity.	2.8
Fuss	Fussing is continuous or intermittent, at low levels.	1.8
Cry	Intense vocalizations occurring singly or in succession.	1.7
Transition States between Waking and Sleeping		
Drowse	Infant's eyes are heavy-lidded, but opening and closing slowly. Low level of motor activity.	4.4
Daze	Open, but glassy and immobile eyes. State occurs between episodes of Alert and Drowse. Low level of activity.	1.0
Sleep-wake transition	Behaviors of both wakefulness and sleep are evident. Generalized motor activity; eyes may be closed, or they open and close rapidly. State occurs when baby is awakening.	1.3
Sleep States		
Active sleep	Eyes close; uneven respiration; intermittent rapid eye movements. Other behaviors: smiles, frowns, grimaces, mouthing, sucking, sighs, and sigh-sobs.	50.3
Quiet sleep	Eyes are closed and respiration is slow and regular. Motor activity limited to occasional startles, sigh-sobs, or rhythmic mouthing.	28.1
Transitional Sleep State		
Active-quiet transition sleep	During this state, which occurs between periods of Active Sleep and Quiet Sleep, the eyes are closed and there is little motor activity. Infant shows mixed behavioral signs of Active Sleep and Quiet Sleep.	1.9

One of the major body rhythms is that of an infant's **state**, the degree of awareness it displays to both internal and external stimulation. As can be seen in Table 4-2, such states include various levels of wakeful behaviors, such as alertness, fussing, and crying, and different levels of sleep as well. Each change in state brings about an alteration in the amount of stimulation required to get the infant's attention (Brazelton, 1973; Karmel, Gardner, & Magnano, 1991; Thoman & Whitney, 1990).

Some of the different states that infants experience produce changes in electrical activity in the brain. These changes are reflected in different patterns of electrical *brain waves*, which can be measured by a device called an *electroencephalogram*, or *EEG*. Starting at 3 months before birth, the nature of these brain wave patterns changes significantly until the infant reaches the age of 3 months, when a more mature pattern emerges and the brain waves stabilize (Parmelee & Sigman, 1983).

Sleep: Perchance to Dream? At the beginning of infancy, the major state that occupies a baby's time is sleep—much to the relief of exhausted parents, who often regard sleep as a welcome respite from caregiving responsibilities. On average, newborn infants sleep some 16 to 17 hours a day. However, there are wide variations. Some sleep more than 20 hours, while others sleep as little as 10 hours a day (Parmalee, Wenner, & Schulz, 1964).

state *the degree of awareness an infant displays to both internal and external stimulation*

rapid eye movement (REM) sleep *the period of sleep that is found in older children and adults and is associated with dreaming*

Even though infants sleep a lot, you probably shouldn't ever wish to "sleep like a baby," despite popular wisdom. For one thing, the sleep of infants comes in fits and starts. Rather than covering one long stretch, sleep initially comes in spurts of around 2 hours, followed by periods of wakefulness. Because of this, infants are "out of sync" with the rest of the world, for whom sleep comes at night and wakefulness during the day (Groome et al., 1997).

Luckily for their parents, infants eventually settle into a more adultlike pattern. After a week, babies sleep a bit more at night and are awake for slightly longer periods during the day. Typically, by the age of 16 weeks infants begin to sleep as much as 6 continuous hours at night, and daytime sleep falls into regular naplike patterns. Most infants sleep through the night by the end of the first year, and the total amount of sleep they need each day is down to around 15 hours (Thoman & Whitney, 1989).

Hidden beneath the supposedly tranquil sleep of infants is another cyclic pattern. During periods of sleep, infants' heart rates increase and become irregular, their blood pressure rises, and they begin to breathe more rapidly (Ferrarri, Kelsall, Rennie, & Evans, 1994; Schechtman & Harper, 1991). Sometimes, although not always, their closed eyes begin to move in a back-and-forth pattern, as if they were viewing an action-packed scene. This period of active sleep is similar, although not identical, to the **rapid eye movement,** or **REM, sleep** that is found in older children and adults and is associated with dreaming.

At first, this active, REM-like sleep takes up around one half of an infant's sleep, compared with just 20 percent of an adult's sleep (see Figure 4-5). However, the quantity of active sleep quickly declines, and by the age of 6 months, amounts to just one third of total sleep time (Coons & Guilleminault, 1982; Sandyk, 1992).

The appearance of active sleep periods that are similar to REM sleep in adults raises the intriguing question of whether infants dream during those periods. No one knows the answer, although it seems unlikely. First of all, young infants do not have much to dream about, given their relatively limited experiences. Furthermore, the brain waves of sleeping infants appear to be qualitatively different from those of adults who are dreaming. It is not until the baby reaches 3 or 4 months of age that the wave patterns become similar to those of dreaming adults, suggesting that young infants aren't dreaming during active sleep—or at least aren't doing so in the same way as adults do (McCall, 1979; Parmelee & Sigman, 1983).

Then what is the function of REM sleep in infants? Although we don't know for certain, some researchers think it provides a means for the brain to stimulate itself—a process

Infants sleep in spurts, often making them out of sync with the rest of the world.

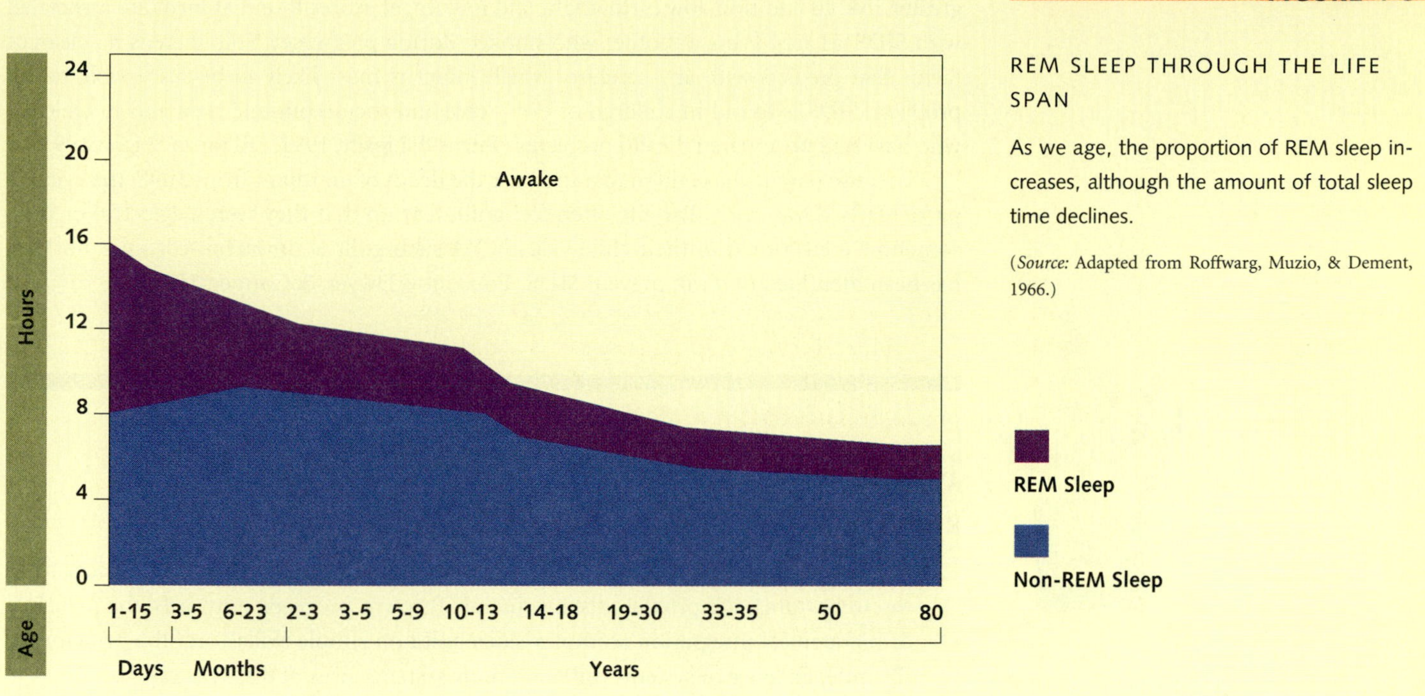

FIGURE 4-5

REM SLEEP THROUGH THE LIFE SPAN

As we age, the proportion of REM sleep increases, although the amount of total sleep time declines.

(*Source:* Adapted from Roffwarg, Muzio, & Dement, 1966.)

called *autostimulation* (Roffwarg, Muzio, & Dement, 1966). Stimulation of the nervous system would be particularly important in infants, who spend so much time sleeping and relatively little in alert states.

Although the patterns that infants show in their wakefulness-sleep cycles seem largely preprogrammed by genetic factors, environmental influences also play a part. For instance, both long- and short-term stressors in infants' environments can affect their sleep patterns. When environmental circumstances keep babies awake, sleep, when at last it comes, is apt to be less active (and quieter) than usual (Halpern, MacLean, & Baumeister, 1995).

Furthermore, cultural practices affect the sleep patterns of infants. For example, among the Kipsigis of Africa, infants sleep with their mothers at night and are allowed to nurse whenever they wake. In the daytime, they accompany their mothers during daily chores, often napping while strapped to their mothers' backs. The result of this practice is that infants among the Kipsigis don't sleep through the night until much later than babies in Western societies. In fact, for the first 8 months of life, Kipsigis infants don't sleep much longer than 3 hours at a stretch. In comparison, 8-month-old infants in the United States may sleep as long as 8 hours at a time (Anders & Taylor, 1994; Boismier, 1977; Cole, 1992; Super & Harkness, 1982).

SIDS: The Unanticipated Killer. For a tiny percentage of infants, the rhythm of sleep is interrupted by a deadly affliction: sudden infant death syndrome, or SIDS. **Sudden infant death syndrome (SIDS)** is a disorder in which seemingly healthy infants die in their sleep. Put to bed for a nap or for the night, an infant simply never wakes up.

No known cause has been found to explain SIDS, which afflicts some 2 of every 1,000 infants, or some 7,000 children in the United States each year. Although it seems to occur when the normal patterns of breathing during sleep are interrupted, scientists have been unable to discover why that might happen. It is clear that infants don't smother or choke; they die a peaceful death, simply ceasing to breathe. No means for preventing the syndrome have been found, which occurs most often for children under the age of 6 months. It is the leading cause of death in children under the age of 1 year (Burns & Lipsitt, 1991).

sudden infant death syndrome (SIDS) *the unexplained death during sleep of a seemingly healthy baby*

Certain factors increase the risk of SIDS. For instance, boys and African Americans are at greater risk. In addition, low birthweight and low Apgar scores found at birth are associated with SIDS, as are having a mother who smoked during pregnancy. Still, there is no clearcut factor that predicts with any certainty which infant is most likely to be susceptible to the problem. SIDS is found in children of every race and socioeconomic class and in children who have had no apparent health problems (Burns & Lipsitt, 1991; DiFranza & Lew, 1995).

Because parents have no preparation for the death of an infant from SIDS, the event is particularly devastating. Parents often feel guilt, fearing that they were neglectful or have somehow contributed to their child's death. Yet such guilt is unwarranted, since nothing has been identified that can prevent SIDS (Ponsonby, Dwyer, & Couper, 1997).

Review and Rethink

REVIEW

- The major principles of growth are the cephalocaudal principle (growth proceeds from top to bottom), the proximodistal principle (growth proceeds outward), the principle of hierarchical integration (complex skills build on simple skills), and the principle of the independence of systems (different body systems grow at different rates).
- The development of the nervous system entails first the development of billions of neurons, which mostly occurs before birth, and then the formation through the infant's experience of useful interconnections among the neurons.
- Brain development depends on both genetic and environmental factors. Plasticity, the susceptibility of a developing organism to environmental influences, is relatively high for the brain.
- Researchers have identified sensitive periods during the development of body systems and behaviors—limited periods when the organism is particularly susceptible to environmental influences. If environmental influences are disturbed during a sensitive period, development may also be disturbed.
- Babies integrate their individual behaviors by developing rhythms—repetitive, cyclical patterns of behavior. A major rhythm relates to the infant's state—the awareness it displays to internal and external stimulation.

RETHINK

- The cephalocaudal principle seems to imply that babies should learn how to talk before they learn how to walk, and yet most babies can walk long before they can form understandable utterances. How does another major growth principle explain this apparent contradiction?
- Research indicates that there is a sensitive period during childhood for normal language acquisition. Persons deprived of normal language stimulation as babies and children may never use language with the same skill as others who were not so deprived. For babies who are born deaf, what are the implications of this research finding, particularly with regard to signed languages?
- This chapter describes sensitive periods during which infants may be either helped or harmed in their development by their exposure to environmental influences. What are the implications of such sensitive periods for public policy relating to infant care?
- What are some cultural influences on infants' daily patterns of behavior that operate in the culture of which you are a part? How do they differ from the influences of other cultures (either within or outside the United States) of which you are aware?

Motor Development

Suppose you were hired by a genetic engineering firm to redesign newborns and were charged with replacing the current version with a new, more mobile one. The first change you'd probably consider in carrying out this (luckily fictitious) job would be in the conformation and composition of the baby's body.

The shape and proportions of newborn babies are simply not conducive to easy mobility. Their heads are so large and heavy that young infants lack the strength to raise them. Because their limbs are short in relation to the rest of the body, their movements are further impeded. Furthermore, their bodies are mainly fat, with a limited amount of muscle; the result is that they lack strength (Illingworth, 1973).

Fortunately, it doesn't take too long before infants begin to develop a remarkable amount of mobility. In fact, even at birth they have an extensive repertoire of behavioral possibilities brought about by innate reflexes, and their range of motor skills grows rapidly during the first 2 years of life.

Reflexes: Our Inborn Physical Skills

When her father pressed 3-day-old Christina's palm with his finger, she responded by tightly winding her small fist around his finger and grasping it. When he moved his finger upward, she held on so tightly that it seemed he might be able to lift her completely off her crib floor.

The Basic Reflexes. In fact, her father was right: Christina probably could have been lifted in this way. The reason for her resolute grip was activation of one of the dozens of reflexes with which infants are born. **Reflexes** are unlearned, organized involuntary responses that occur automatically in the presence of certain stimuli. As we first noted in Chapter 3, when we discussed reflexes relating to the intake of food, newborns enter the world with an expansive repertoire of behavioral patterns that, when activated, help them adapt to their new surroundings and serve to protect them.

As we can see from the list of reflexes in Table 4-3, many reflexes clearly represent behavior that has survival value, helping to ensure the well-being of the infant. For instance, the *swimming reflex* makes a baby who is lying face down in a body of water paddle and kick in a sort of swimming motion. The obvious consequence of such behavior is to help the baby move from danger and survive until a caregiver can come to its rescue. Similarly, the *eye blink reflex* seems designed to protect the eye from too much direct light, which might damage the retina.

Given the protective value of many reflexes, it might seem beneficial for them to remain with us for our entire lives. In fact, some do: The eye blink reflex remains functional throughout the full life span. On the other hand, quite a few reflexes, such as the swimming reflex, disappear after a few months. Why should this be the case?

reflexes *unlearned, organized involuntary responses that occur automatically in the presence of certain stimuli*

(a) 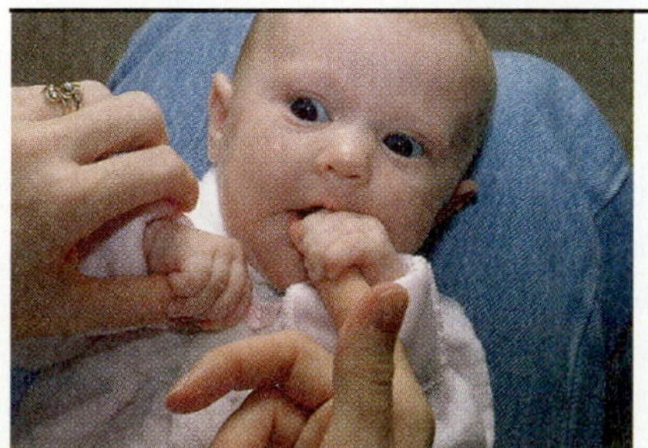
(b) 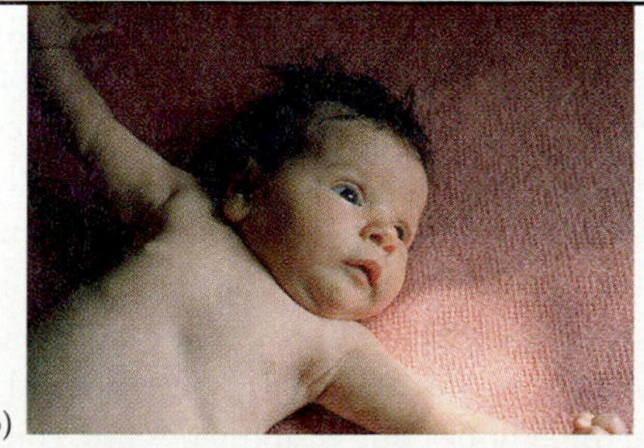
(c) 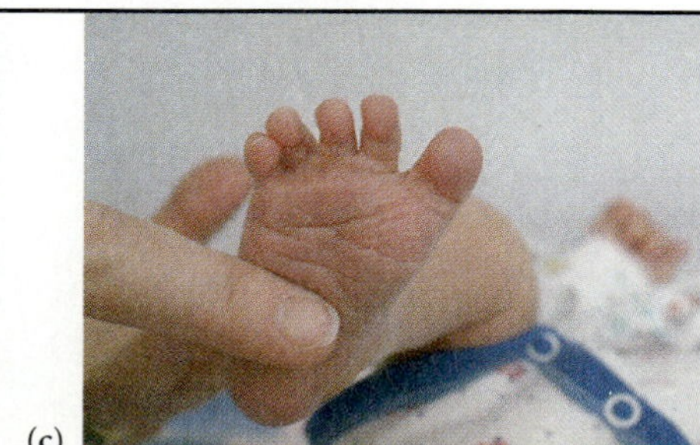

Infants showing (a) the rooting and grasping reflex, (b) the startle reflex, and (c) the Babinski reflex.

TABLE 4-3

SOME BASIC REFLEXES IN INFANTS

Reflex	Approximate Age of Disappearance	Description	Possible Function
Rooting reflex	3 weeks	Neonate's tendency to turn its head toward things that touch its cheek.	Food intake
Stepping reflex	2 months	Movement of legs when held upright with feet touching the floor.	Prepares infants for independent locomotion
Swimming reflex	4-6 months	Infant's tendency to paddle and kick in a sort of swimming motion when lying face down in a body of water.	Avoidance of danger
Moro reflex	6 months	Arms of the infant are thrust outward and then appear to grasp on to something when support for the neck and head is suddenly removed.	Similar to primates' protection from falling
Babinski reflex	8-12 months	Infant fans out its toes in response to a stroke on the outside of its foot.	Unknown
Startle reflex	Remains in different form	Infant, in response to a sudden noise, flings out its arms, arches its back, and spreads its fingers.	Protection
Eye blink reflex	Remains	Rapid shutting and opening of eye on exposure to direct light.	Protection of eye from direct light
Sucking reflex	Remains	Infant's tendency to suck at things that touch its lips.	Food intake
Gag reflex	Remains	Infant's reflex to clear its throat.	Prevents choking

Most researchers attribute the gradual disappearance of reflexes to the increase in voluntary control over behavior that occurs as infants become more able to control their muscles. In addition, it may be that reflexes form the foundation for future, more complex behaviors. As these more intricate behaviors become well learned, they subsume the earlier reflexes (Minkowski, 1967; Myklebust & Gottlieb, 1993; Touwen, 1984).

It may even be that the use of reflexes stimulates parts of the brain responsible for more complex behaviors. For example, some researchers argue that exercise of the stepping reflex helps the brain's cortex later develop the ability to walk. As evidence, developmental psychologist Philip R. Zelazo and his colleagues conducted a study in which they provided 2-week-old infants practice in walking for four sessions of 3 minutes each over a 6-week period. The results showed that the children who had the walking practice actually began to walk unaided several months earlier than those who had had no such practice. Zelazo suggests that the training produced stimulation of the stepping reflex, which in turn led to stimulation of the brain's cortex, readying the infant earlier for independent locomotion (N. Zelazo et al., 1993; P. R. Zelazo, Zelazo, & Kolb, 1972; P. R. Zelazo, 1983).

Do these findings suggest that parents should make out-of-the-ordinary efforts to stimulate their infant's reflexes? Probably not. Although the evidence shows that intensive practice may produce an earlier appearance of certain motor activities, there is no evidence that the activities are performed qualitatively any better in practiced infants than in unpracticed infants. Furthermore, even when early gains are found, they do not seem to produce ultimately an adult who is more proficient in motor skills.

In fact, structured exercise may do more harm than good: According to the American Academy of Pediatrics (1988), structured exercise for infants may lead to muscle strain, fractured bones, and dislocated limbs, consequences that far outweigh the unproven benefits that may come from the practice.

The Universality of Reflexes. Although reflexes are, by definition, genetically determined and universal throughout all infants, there are actually some cultural variations in the ways they are displayed. For instance, consider the *Moro reflex,* which is activated when support for the neck and head is suddenly removed. The Moro reflex consists of the infant's arms thrusting outward and then appearing to seek to grasp on to something. Most scientists feel that the Moro reflex represents a leftover response that we humans have inherited from our nonhuman ancestors. The Moro reflex is an extremely useful behavior for monkey babies, who travel about by clinging to their mothers' backs. If they lose their grip, they fall down unless they are able to grasp quickly on to their mother's fur—in a Morolike reflex (Prechtl, 1982).

Although the Moro reflex is found in all humans, it appears with significantly different vigor in different children. Some differences reflect cultural and ethnic variations. For instance, Caucasian infants show a pronounced response to situations that produce the Moro reflex. Not only do they fling out their arms, but they also cry and respond in a generally agitated manner. In contrast, Navajo babies react to the same situation much more calmly. Their arms do not flail out as much, and they cry only rarely (Freedman, 1979).

In some cases, reflexes can serve as helpful diagnostic tools for pediatricians. Because reflexes emerge and disappear on a regular timetable, their absence—or presence—at a given point of infancy can provide a clue that something may be amiss in an infant's development. (Even for adults, physicians include reflexes in their diagnostic bags of tricks, as anyone knows who has had his or her knee tapped with a rubber mallet to see if the lower leg jerks forward.)

Although some reflexes may be remnants from our prehuman past and seemingly have little usefulness in terms of survival today, they still may serve a very contemporary function. According to some developmental researchers, some reflexes may promote caregiving and nurturance on the part of adults in the vicinity. For instance, Christina's father, who found his daughter gripping his finger tightly when he pressed her palm, probably cares little that she is simply responding with an innate reflex. Instead, he will more likely view his daughter's action as responsiveness to him, a signal perhaps of increasing interest and affection on her part. As we will see in Chapter 6, when we discuss the social and personality development of infants, such apparent responsiveness can help cement the growing social relationship between an infant and its caregivers (S. M. Bell & Ainsworth, 1972; Belsky, Rovine, & Taylor, 1984).

Motor Development in Infancy: Landmarks of Physical Achievement

Probably no physical changes are more obvious—and more eagerly anticipated—than the increasing array of motor skills that babies acquire during infancy. Most parents can remember their child's first steps with a sense of pride and awe at how quickly she or he changed from a helpless infant, unable even to roll over, into a person who could navigate quite effectively in the world (Thelen, 1995).

Gross Motor Skills. Even though the motor skills of newborn infants are not terribly sophisticated, at least compared with attainments that will soon appear, infants still are able to accomplish some kinds of movement. For instance, when placed on their stomachs they wiggle their arms and legs and may try to lift their heavy heads. As their strength increases, they are able to push hard enough against the surface on which they are resting to propel their bodies in different directions. They often end up moving backwards rather than forwards, but by the age of 6 months they become rather accomplished at moving themselves in particular directions. These initial efforts are the forerunners of crawling, in which they coordinate the motions of their arms and legs and propel themselves forward. Crawling appears typically between 8 and 10 months. (Figure 4-6 provides a summary of some of the milestones of normal motor development.)

This 5-month-old girl demonstrates her gross motor skills.

By 4 months of age, infants are able to reach toward an object with some degree of precision.

Walking comes later. At around 9 to 11 months of age, most infants are able to walk by supporting themselves on furniture, and by the time of their first birthday, most can walk fairly well on their own.

At the same time infants are learning to move around, they are perfecting the ability to remain in a stationary sitting position. At first, babies cannot remain seated upright without support. But they quickly master this ability, and most are able to sit without support by the age of 6 months.

Fine Motor Skills. As infants are perfecting their gross motor skills, such as sitting upright and walking, they are also making advances in their finer motor skills (see Table 4-4). For instance, by the age of 3 months, infants show some ability to coordinate the movements of their limbs (Thelen, 1994).

Furthermore, although infants are born with a rudimentary ability to reach toward an object, this ability is neither very sophisticated nor very accurate, and it disappears around

FIGURE 4-6

MILESTONES OF MOTOR DEVELOPMENT

(*Source:* Adapted from Shirley, 1993.)

0 month: fetal posture	1 month: chin up	2 months: chest up	3 months: reach and miss
4 months: sit with support	5 months: sit on lap, grasp object	6 months: sit on high chair, grasp dangling object	7 months: sit alone
8 months: stand with help	9 months: stand holding furniture	10 months: creep	11 months: walk when led
12 months: pull to stand by furniture	13 months: climb stair steps	14 months: stand alone	15 months: walk alone

TABLE 4-4

MILESTONES OF FINE MOTOR DEVELOPMENT

Age (months)	Skill
3	Opens hand prominently
3.5	Grasps rattle
8.5	Grasps with thumb and finger
11	Holds crayon adaptively
14	Builds tower of two cubes
16	Places pegs in board
24	Imitates strokes on paper
33	Copies circle

(*Source:* Adapted from Frankenburg et al., 1992, and Bayley, 1969.)

the age of 4 weeks. A different, more precise, form of reaching appears at 4 months. It takes some time for infants to coordinate successful grasping after they reach out, but in fairly short order they are able to reach out and hold on to an object of interest (Mathew & Cook, 1990; Rochat & Goubet, 1995; Berthier, 1996).

The sophistication of fine motor skills continues to grow. By the age of 11 months, infants are able to pick up off the ground objects as small as marbles—presenting care providers with issues of safety, since the place such objects often go next is the mouth. And by the time they are 2 years old, children can carefully hold a cup, bring it to their lips, and take a drink without spilling a drop.

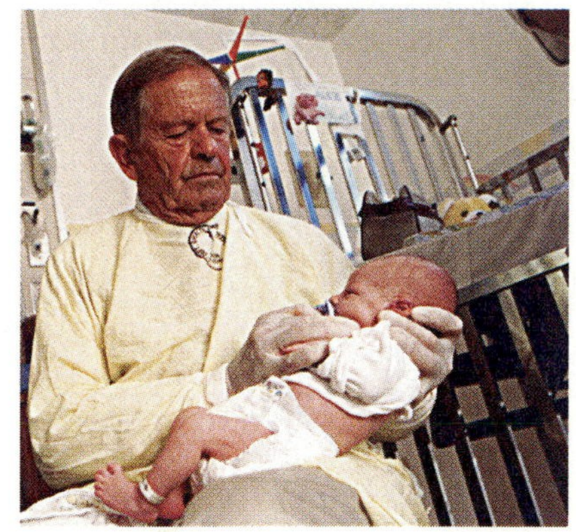

T. Berry Brazelton devised the Brazelton Neonatal Behavior Assessment Scale (NBAS), which measures infants' neurological and behavioral responses.

Developmental Norms: Comparing the Individual to the Group. It is important to keep in mind that the timing of the milestones that we have been discussing is based on norms. **Norms** represent the average performance of a large sample of children of a given age. They permit comparisons between a particular child's performance on a particular behavior and the average performance of the children in the norm sample.

For instance, one of the most widely used techniques to determine infants' normative standing is the **Brazelton Neonatal Behavior Assessment Scale (NBAS),** a measure designed to determine infants' neurological and behavioral responses to their environment.

The NBAS provides a supplement to the traditional Apgar test (discussed in Chapter 3) that is given immediately following birth. Taking about 30 minutes to administer, the NBAS includes 27 separate categories of responses that constitute four general aspects of infants' behavior: interactions with others (such as alertness and cuddliness), motor behavior, physiological control (such as the ability to be soothed after being upset), and responses to stress (Brazelton, 1973, 1990; Brazelton, Nugent, & Lester, 1987; Davis & Emory, 1995).

Although the norms provided by scales such as the NBAS are useful in making broad generalizations about the timing of various behaviors and skills, they must be interpreted with caution. Because norms are averages, they mask substantial individual differences in the times when children attain various achievements. They also may hide the fact that the sequence in which various behaviors are achieved may differ somewhat from one child to another.

Furthermore, norms are useful only to the extent that they are based on data from a large, heterogeneous, culturally diverse sample of children. Unfortunately, many of the norms on which developmental researchers have traditionally relied have been based on groups of infants who are predominantly white and from the middle and upper socioeconomic strata (e.g., Gesell, 1946).

This limitation would not be critical if no differences existed in the timing of development in children from different cultural, racial, and social groups. But they do. For example, as

norms *the average performance of a large sample of children of a given age*

Brazelton Neonatal Behavioral Assessment Scale (NBAS) *a measure designed to determine infants' neurological and behavioral responses to their environment* a group, African American babies show more rapid motor development than white babies throughout infancy. Moreover, there are significant variations related to cultural factors, as we discuss next (Brazelton, 1991; Keefer et al., 1991; Rosser & Randolph, 1989; Werner, 1972).

Developmental Diversity

The Cultural Dimensions of Motor Development

Among the Ache people, who live in the rain forest of South America, infants face an early life of physical restriction. Because the Ache lead a nomadic existence, living in a series of tiny camps in the rain forest, open space is at a premium. Consequently, for the first few years of life, infants spend nearly all their time in direct physical contact with their mothers. Even when they are not physically touching their mothers, they are permitted to venture no more than a few feet away.

***

Infants among the Kipsigis people, who live in a more open environment in rural Kenya, Africa, lead quite a different existence. Their lives are filled with activity and exercise. Parents seek to teach their children to sit up, stand, and walk from the earliest days of infancy. For example, very young infants are placed in shallow holes in the ground designed to keep them in an upright position. Parents begin to teach their children to walk starting at the eighth week of life. The infants are held with their feet touching the ground, and they are pushed forward.

Clearly, the infants in these two societies lead very different lives (Kaplan & Dove, 1987; Super, 1976). But do the relative lack of early motoric stimulation for Ache infants and the efforts of the Kipsigis to encourage motoric development really matter?

The answer is both yes and no. Yes, in that Ache infants tend to show delayed motor development, relative both to Kipsigis infants and to children raised in Western societies. Although their social abilities are no different, Ache children tend to begin walking at around 23 months, about a year later than the typical child in the United States. In contrast, Kipsigis children, who are encouraged in their motor development, learn to sit up and walk several weeks earlier, on average, than U.S. children.

In the long run, however, the differences between Ache, Kipsigis, and Western children disappear. By late childhood, there is no evidence of differences in general, overall motor skills among Ache, Kipsigis, and Western children.

Variations in the timing of motor skills seem to depend in part on parental expectations of what is the "appropriate" schedule for the emergence of specific skills. For instance, one study examined the motor skills of infants who lived in a single city in England, but whose mothers varied in ethnic origin. In the research, English, Jamaican, and Indian mothers' expectations were first assessed regarding several markers of their infants' motor skills. The Jamaican mothers expected their infants to sit and walk significantly earlier than the English and Indian mothers, and the actual emergence of these activities was in line with their expectations. The source of the Jamaican infants' earlier mastery seemed to lie in the treatment of the children by their parents. For instance, Jamaican mothers gave their children practice in stepping quite early in infancy (Hopkins & Westra, 1989, 1990).

In sum, the time at which specific motor skills appear is in part determined by cultural factors. Activities that are an intrinsic part of a culture are more apt to be purposely taught to infants in that culture, leading to the potential for their earlier emergence (Nugent, Lester, & Brazelton, 1989).

It is not all that surprising that children in a given culture who are expected by their parents to master a particular skill, and who are taught components of that skill from an early age, are more likely to be proficient in that skill earlier than children from other cultures with no such expectations and no such training. The larger question, however, is whether the earlier emergence of a basic motor behavior in a given culture has lasting consequences for specific motor skills and for achievements in other domains. On this issue, the jury is still out (Bloch, 1989).

What is clear, however, is that there are certain genetically determined constraints on how early a skill can emerge. It is physically impossible for 1-month-old infants to stand and walk, regardless of the encouragement and practice they may get within their culture. Parents who are eager to accelerate their infants' motoric development, then, should be cautioned not to hold overly ambitious goals. In fact, they might well ask themselves whether it matters if an infant acquires a motor skill a few weeks earlier than his or her peers.

The most reasonable answer is "no." Although some parents may take pride in a child who walks earlier than other babies (just as some parents may be concerned over a delay of a few weeks), in the long run the timing of this activity will probably make no difference.

Nutrition in Infancy: Fueling Motor Development

The rapid physical growth that occurs during infancy is fueled by the nutrients that infants receive. Without proper nutrition, infants not only cannot reach their physical potential, but they suffer cognitive and social consequences as well (Pollitt, 1994; Pollitt et al., 1993).

Malnutrition. *Malnutrition,* the condition of having an improper amount and balance of nutrients, produces several results, none good. For instance, children living in many developing countries—where they are more susceptible to malnourishment and at greater risk for disease than children in more industrialized, affluent countries—begin to show a slower growth rate by the age of 6 months. By the time they reach the age of 2 years, their height and weight are only 95 percent the height and weight of children in more industrialized countries.

Furthermore, children who have been chronically malnourished during infancy later score lower on tests of IQ and tend to do less well in school. These effects may linger even if the children's diets have improved substantially (Barrett & Frank, 1987; Gorman & Pollitt, 1992; Grantham-McGregor et al., 1994; M. Sigman et al., 1989).

The problem of malnutrition is greatest in underdeveloped countries, where almost 10 percent of infants are severely malnourished. In the Dominican Republic, for instance, 13 percent of children under 3 years of age are underweight, and 21 percent have stunted growth. In other areas, the problem is even worse. In South Asia, for example, almost 60 percent of all children are underweight (World Food Council, 1992; see Figure 4-7).

Problems of malnourishment are not restricted to developing countries, however. In the United States, the richest country in the world, some 14 million children live in poverty, which puts them at risk for malnutrition. In fact, although overall poverty rates are no worse than they were 20 years ago, the poverty rate for children under the age of 3 has increased. Some one quarter of families who have children 2 years old and younger live in poverty. And, as we can see in Figure 4-8, the rates are even higher for African American and Hispanic families, as well as for single-parent families (Carnegie Task Force on Meeting the Needs of Young Children, 1994; Einbinder, 1992).

Although these children rarely become severely malnourished, due to adequate social safety nets, they remain susceptible to *undernutrition,* in which there is some deficiency in diet. In fact, some surveys find that as many as a quarter of 1- to 5-year-old children in the

FIGURE 4-7

UNDERWEIGHT CHILDREN IN DEVELOPING COUNTRIES, 1990

The number of underweight children under the age of 5 years in developing countries is substantial.

(*Source:* World Food Council, 1992.)

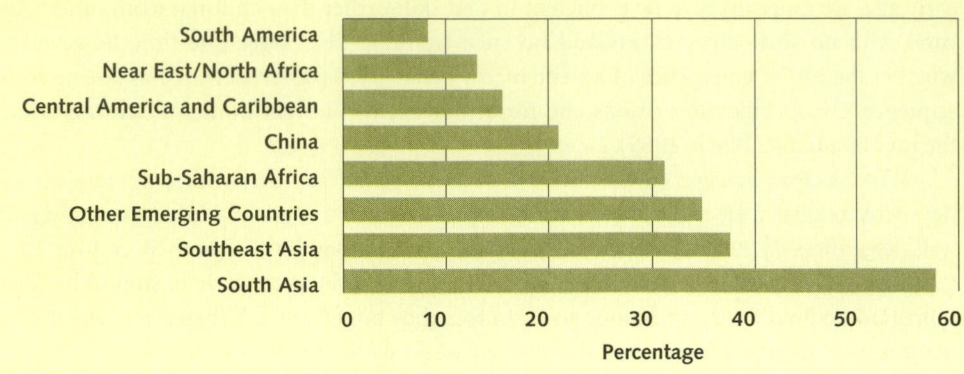

marasmus *a disease characterized by the cessation of growth*

United States have diets that fall below the minimum caloric intake recommended by nutritional experts (Barrett & Frank, 1987; U.S. Bureau of the Census, 1992).

Severe malnutrition during infancy may lead to several disorders. Malnutrition during the first year can produce **marasmus,** a disease characterized by the cessation of growth.

Speaking of Development

J. Kenneth Whitt, Nutrition Expert

Born: 1946

Education: .... University of Virginia, B.A. in psychology
University of Texas, Ph.D. in clinical psychology

Position: .... Associate professor of psychiatry and pediatrics at the University of North Carolina School of Medicine

Home: .... Temple Hill, North Carolina

While malnutrition in infants is often thought of as a condition more prevalent in underdeveloped countries, it can also be found in the richest of nations such as the United States.

But the causes of malnutrition, in many cases, are not what they may appear to be on the surface, and a further diagnosis can reveal the root problem and provide treatment that will restore the infant's development.

According to Dr. Kenneth Whitt, an associate professor of psychiatry and pediatrics, when children show abnormally slow growth and development in their first 3 years, it is known as *failure to thrive.*

"Traditionally, failure to thrive was considered to have either an organic or nonorganic basis," Whitt explained. While organic failure to thrive is produced by a physical cause such as malnutrition or the inability to digest food properly, "nonorganic failure to thrive was considered to be produced by caregiver neglect or psychopathology of the caregiver."

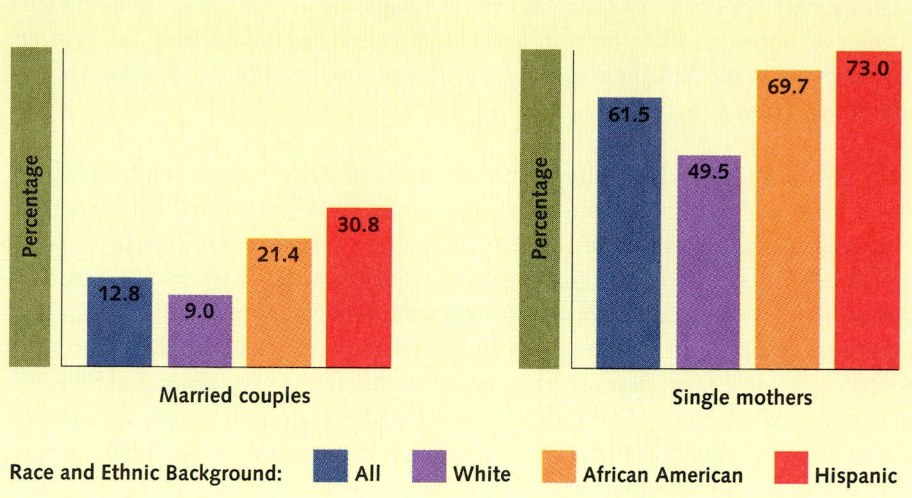

FIGURE 4-8

CHILDREN LIVING IN POVERTY

The incidence of poverty among children under the age of 3 is particularly high in minority and single-parent households. (Figures are shown only for single mothers and not fathers because 97 percent of all children under 3 who live with a single parent live with their mothers; only 3 percent live with their fathers.)

(*Source:* Einbinder, 1992).

Marasmus, attributable to a severe deficiency in proteins and calories, causes the body to waste away and ultimately results in death. Older children are susceptible to **kwashiorkor,** a disease in which a child's stomach, limbs, and face swell with water. To a casual observer, it appears that a child with kwashiorkor is actually chubby. However, this is an illusion: The child's body is in fact struggling to make use of the few nutrients that are available.

kwashiorkor *a disease in which a child's stomach, limbs, and face swell with water*

"While at first it appeared to be a simple eating disorder, something didn't seem to fit. Why would a child develop this pattern of behavior? There was nothing in the infant's social history that would indicate a reason for it."

"One of the ways we use our understanding of child development is to provide a rationale to families so as to decrease struggles over feeding."

Determining the cause of failure to thrive has proved challenging. For instance, looking at the point where a child's growth begins to show a change may be only a starting point in finding the ultimate reason for the malnutrition, according to Whitt.

"If we notice that a child begins to fall off the growth curve, but does not fit 'failure to thrive' until much later we have to trace back to where the failure to thrive began," he said.

Whitt noted that there have been numerous cases in which the caregiver was initially considered to have been the source of failure to thrive, but after closer scrutiny a different cause emerged. "For instance, a series of infants were admitted who had nonorganic failure to thrive, but it was found that a number of the cases didn't fit with the history from a social/emotional perspective."

For example, one case of failure to thrive occurred in an 11-month-old where it seemed as if the child was simply refusing to eat. As Whitt explained, "His refusing to eat appeared to be a behavior problem. However, after talking with the child's caregivers, it was discovered that this problem had been occurring since the infant was 5 or 6 months of age.

"While at first it appeared to be a simple eating disorder, something didn't seem to fit. Why would a child develop this pattern of behavior? There was nothing in the infant's social history that would indicate a reason for it."

Ultimately, Whitt identified the true cause. "It was found that the child had lactose intolerance and was unable to digest milk properly. Within a few days after changing the formula, he began to recover," Whitt said.

Understanding how feeding emerges in normal development is an important part of understanding failure to thrive and malnutrition, according to Whitt. "Kids of all ages are trying to be competent," Whitt explained. "One of the ways we use our understanding of child development is to provide a rationale to families so as to decrease struggles over feeding.

"Have them look at finger feeding, allowing the child to feed him or herself and not worry about the mess. It's a beginning to help families to plug into the normal developmental process, and a way to help them and physicians in treating eating disorders."

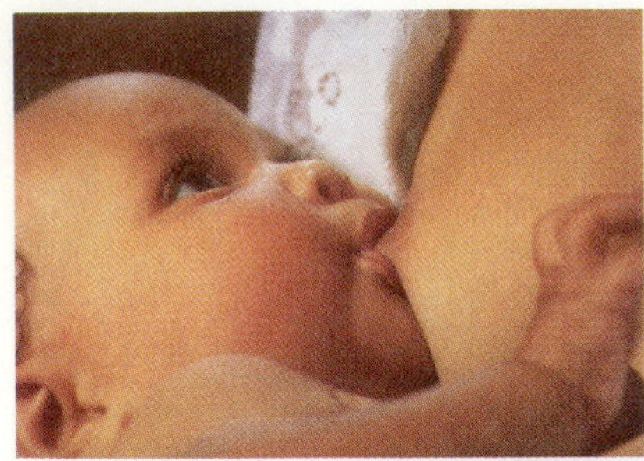

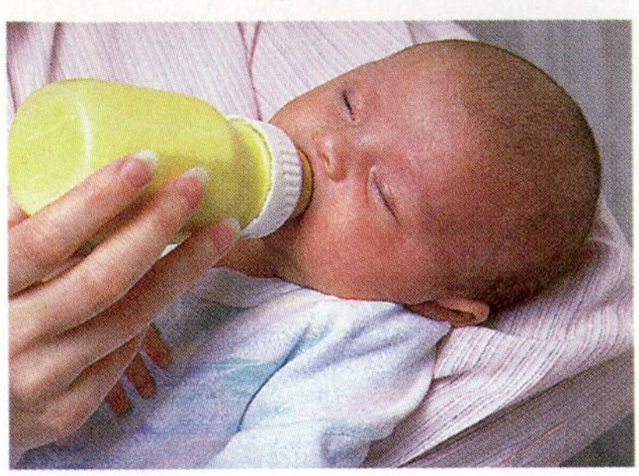

Breast or bottle? Although infants receive adequate nourishment from breast- or bottle-feeding, most authorities agree "breast is best."

Although the consequences are not as severe as those of malnutrition, undernutrition also has its long-term costs. For instance, there is increasing evidence that children's later cognitive development is affected by even mild to moderate undernutrition (M. Sigman, 1995). (For more on the difficulties associated with malnutrition, see the "Speaking of Development" interview.)

Obesity. While it is clear that malnourishment during infancy has potentially disastrous consequences for an infant, the effects of *obesity,* defined as weight greater than 20 percent above the average for a given height, are less clear. For one thing, there appears to be no correlation between obesity during infancy and obesity at the age of 16 years. (There is an association between obesity after the age of 6 and adult weight, however.)

Furthermore, although some research suggests that overfeeding during infancy may lead to the creation of unnecessary fat cells, which remain in the body throughout life, it is not clear that an abundance of fat cells necessarily leads to adult obesity. In fact, genetic factors are an important determinant of obesity (C. Bouchard et al., 1990; Fabsitz, Carmelli, & Hewitt, 1992; Knittle, 1975).

In sum, obesity during infancy is not a major concern. On the other hand, the societal view that "a fat baby is a healthy baby" is not necessarily correct, either. Rather than focusing on their infant's weight, parents should concentrate on providing appropriate nutrition. At least during the period of infancy, concerns about weight need not be central, as long as infants are provided with an appropriate diet.

Although everyone agrees on the importance of receiving proper nutrition during infancy, just how to reach that goal is a source of controversy. Because infants are not born with the ability to eat or digest solid food, at first they exist solely on a liquid diet. But just what should that liquid be—a mother's breast milk or a formula of commercially processed cow's milk with vitamin additives? The answer has been a major source of contention.

Breast or Bottle: Which Is Better? Some 40 to 50 years ago, if a mother asked her pediatrician whether breast-feeding or bottle-feeding was better, she would have received a simple and clear-cut answer: Bottle-feeding was the preferred method. Starting around the 1940s, the general belief among child-care experts was that breast-feeding was an obsolete method that put children unnecessarily at risk.

With bottle-feeding, the argument went, parents could keep track of the amount of milk their baby was receiving and could thereby ensure that the child was taking in sufficient nutrients. In contrast, mothers who breast-fed their babies could never be certain just how much milk their infants were getting. Furthermore, use of the bottle was said to help mothers keep their feedings to a rigid schedule of one bottle every 4 hours, at that time the recommended procedure.

Today, however, a mother would get a very different answer to the same question. Child care authorities agree: For the first 4 to 6 months of life, there is no better food for an infant than breast milk (American Academy of Pediatrics, 1982). Breast milk not only contains all the nutrients necessary for growth, but it also seems to offer some degree of immunity to a variety of childhood diseases, such as respiratory infections and diarrhea. Breast milk is more easily digested than cow's milk or formula, and it is sterile, warm, and convenient for the mother to dispense (Eiger, 1987; Howie et al., 1990). And, as we discuss in the "Directions in Development" feature, it may even hold health-related advantages for mothers.

Breast-feeding also holds significant emotional advantages for both mother and child. Most mothers report that the experience of breast-feeding brings about feelings of intimacy and closeness that are incomparable to any other experiences with their infants (K. Epstein, 1993). At the same time, infants, whose rooting and sucking reflexes are genetically well designed to find nourishment and satisfaction from breast-feeding, seem to be calmed and soothed by the experience (Eiger & Olds, 1987).

Directions in Development

Understanding the Benefits of Breast-feeding

"Breast is Best."

This slogan has been widely publicized by groups seeking to increase the use of breast-feeding. The notion that breast-feeding is superior to bottle-feeding recently has taken on new credibility, as research by developmental specialists has found new benefits—not only for infants, but for mothers as well.

For instance, recent research suggests that women who breast-feed may have lower rates of ovarian cancer and breast cancer prior to menopause. Furthermore, the hormones produced during breast-feeding help shrink the uteruses of women following birth, enabling their bodies to return more quickly to a prepregnancy state. These hormones also may inhibit ovulation, potentially preventing pregnancy and helping to space the birth of additional children. Breast-feeding even helps mothers react to stress better: Research shows that the level of stress hormones is lower in mothers who breast-feed their infants than those who bottle-feed them (Altemus et al., 1995; Herbst, 1994; R. K. Ross & Yu, 1994).

Although it is clear that mothers benefit from breast-feeding, it is their infants who are helped the most, in ways that are only now becoming apparent. Although it has been known for some time that breast-feeding helps provide some protection from respiratory and stomach illnesses, new evidence suggests that breast milk has other, more subtle virtues.

For instance, several recent studies have found that breast-fed infants have higher levels of docosahexaenoic acid (DHA) in their brains and retinas than those who have been bottle-fed (Neuringer, 1993). Because research with nonhumans suggests that a deficit of DHA leads to irreversible changes, it is possible—although highly speculative—that higher levels of the chemical may enhance the brain functioning of children who have been breast-fed (Rogan & Gladen, 1993).

Much current work is focused on understanding how other components of breast milk may enhance growth. For instance, some researchers are examining how an epidermal growth factor present in breast milk may advance the development of the digestive and respiratory systems in infants. Furthermore, there is evidence that preterm infants ultimately may do better cognitively as a result of being fed breast milk during infancy (J. E. Brody, 1994; Lucas et al., 1992).

Obviously, breast-feeding is not the solution to every problem faced by infants, and the millions of individuals who have been raised on formula should not be concerned that they have suffered irreparable harm. But it does continue to be clear that the slogan "Breast is Best" is right on target.

Despite the advantages of breast-feeding, only about half of all new mothers in the United States employ it. This is actually a decline from the peak that was reached in 1982, when almost two thirds of all new mothers breast-fed their babies (see Figure 4-9). Although recent figures suggest that breast-feeding may once again be on the rise, the decline that occurred in the 1980s was significant (Ross Laboratories, 1993; Ryan, 1997).

Issues of age, social status, and race influence the decision whether to breast-feed. The rates of breast-feeding are highest among women who are older, have better educations,

FIGURE 4-9

BREAST-FEEDING TRENDS

Beginning in the early 1970s and extending for the next 10 years, the percentage of mothers who were breast-feeding increased steadily. However, the rate has declined since that point, except for a slight rise at the beginning of the 1990s. In addition, the rate of mothers who breast-feed has been more than twice as high for white women as for African-American women.

(*Source:* Ross Laboratories, 1993.)

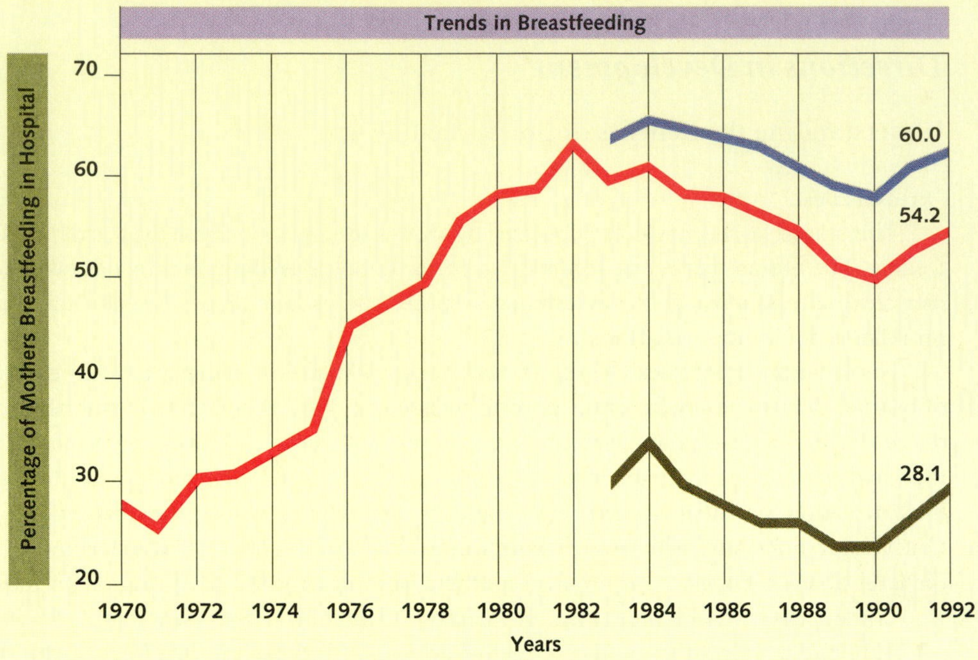

and are of higher socioeconomic status (V. Richardson & Champion, 1992). Moreover, there are ethnic and racial group differences. For instance, breast-feeding among white mothers in the United States occurs at a rate almost double that for African-American mothers (Maternal and Child Health Bureau, 1994).

If authorities are in agreement about the benefits of breast-feeding, why in so many cases do women not breast-feed? In some cases, they can't. Some women have difficulties producing milk, while others are taking some type of medicine or have an infectious

"I forgot to say I was breast-fed."

Drawing by M. Twohy; © 1996 The New Yorker Magazine, Inc.

disease such as AIDS that could be passed on to their infants through breast milk. Sometimes, infants are too ill to nurse successfully. And in many cases of adoption, where the birth mother is unavailable after giving birth, the adoptive mother has no choice but to bottle-feed.

In other cases, the decision not to breast-feed is based on practical considerations. Women who hold jobs outside the home may not have sufficiently flexible schedules to breast-feed their infants. This problem is particularly true with less affluent women who may have less control over their schedules. Such problems also may account for the lower rate of breast-feeding among mothers of lower socioeconomic status.

Education is also an issue: Some women simply do not receive adequate information and advice regarding the advantages of breast-feeding, and they choose to use formula because it seems an appropriate choice. Indeed, some hospitals may inadvertently encourage the use of formula by including it in the gift packets new mothers receive as they leave the hospital.

In developing countries, the use of formula is particularly problematic. Because formula often comes in powdered form that has to be mixed with water, local pollution of the water supply can make formula particularly dangerous. Yet until the early 1980s, manufacturers aggressively sold formula in developing countries, touting it as the "modern" choice. It took a massive, worldwide boycott of products manufactured by the Nestlé company, a major manufacturer of formula, to end their promotion of bottle-feeding (J. L. Fox, 1984). Formula containers now include labels that advertise the benefits of breast-feeding and the dangers associated with bottle-feeding, and free samples are no longer supplied to mothers.

Infants generally start solid foods at around 4 to 6 months, gradually working their way up to a variety of foods.

Educational, social, and cultural support for breast-feeding is particularly important. For instance, physicians need to educate their patients about the importance of the practice and to provide specific information on just how to breast-feed. (Although breast-feeding is a natural act, mothers require a bit of practice to learn how to hold the baby properly, position the nipple correctly, and deal with such potential problems as sore nipples.)

Introducing Solid Foods: When and What? Although pediatricians agree that breast milk is the ideal initial food, at some point infants require more nutrients than breast milk alone can provide. The American Academy of Pediatrics (1992) suggests that babies benefit from solids starting at around 4 to 6 months.

Solid foods are introduced into an infant's diet gradually, one at a time. Most often cereal comes first, followed by strained fruits. Vegetables typically are introduced next, and ultimately other kinds of food, such as eggs, fish, and meat, are added.

The exact amount of solid foods is hard to specify. In part, it depends on the activity level of the particular infant. Highly active children require more calories than those who are relatively sedentary.

The timing of *weaning,* the cessation of breast-feeding, varies greatly. In developed countries such as the United States, weaning typically occurs as early as 3 or 4 months. On the other hand, in certain subcultures within the U.S., breast-feeding may continue for 2 or 3 years. Recommendations from the American Academy of Pediatrics (1992) suggest that infants be fed breast milk for the first 6 to 12 months.

Review and Rethink

REVIEW

- Reflexes, which are universal, genetically acquired physical behaviors, have many uses. Some reflexes help the infant survive and remain safe in its new environment, others serve as the basis of later-learned behaviors such as walking, and others seem to help infants and caregivers form intimate social relationships.

- During infancy children achieve a series of landmarks in their physical development. The schedule and order of these landmarks are generally consistent across children. However, significant individual and cultural variations exist, and any norms used to describe the timing of developmental milestones should be regarded with caution.
- Training and cultural expectations can affect the timing of the development of motor skills. Whether such manipulation of the developmental schedule produces lasting effects remains an open question.
- Nutrition strongly affects physical development. Malnutrition, which is a problem especially in developing countries, can slow growth, affect intellectual performance, and cause diseases such as marasmus and kwashiorkor. Negative effects are also suffered by the victims of undernutrition, which exists even in developed countries.
- The advantages of breast-feeding are numerous, including nutritional, immunological, emotional, and physical benefits for the infant, and physical and emotional benefits for the mother as well. Factors of age, education, socioeconomic status, health, and practicality influence mothers' willingness and ability to breast-feed.

RETHINK

- What are some examples of reflexive behaviors not mentioned in this chapter that are part of your physical repertoire? How are they useful? Are the behaviors you named really innate, automatic reflexes, or are they learned responses?
- In what ways does the practice of training infants to accelerate their motor skill development recall the relationship between genotype and phenotype (discussed in Chapter 2)? What sorts of constraints might there be on the results of such training?
- What advice might you give a friend who is concerned about the fact that her infant is still not walking at 14 months, when every other baby she knows started walking by the first birthday?
- How would you design an experiment to determine whether early development of physical skills produces lasting effects? Why do you think a definitive answer to this question has not yet been found? How would you eliminate factors other than early development from your study?
- Given that malnourishment negatively affects physical growth, how can it also adversely affect IQ scores and school performance, as reported in this chapter?

THE DEVELOPMENT OF THE SENSES

According to William James, one of first persons who can be accurately labeled a "psychologist" and one of the founders of the field, the world of the infant was a "blooming, buzzing confusion" (James, 1890/1950). Was he right?

In this case, James's wisdom failed him. The newborn's world does lack the clarity and stability that we can distinguish as adults, but day by day the world grows increasingly comprehensible as the infant's ability to sense and perceive the environment develops.

The processes that underlie infants' understanding of the world around them are sensation and perception. **Sensation** is the stimulation of the sense organs, and **perception** is the sorting out, interpretation, analysis, and integration of stimuli involving the sense organs and brain. Sensation is the responsiveness of the sense organs to stimulation, while perception is the interpretation of that stimulation. Sorting out infants' capabilities in the realm of sensation and perception presents a challenge to the ingenuity of investigators (D. G. K. Nelson et al., 1995).

sensation *the stimulation of the sense organs*

perception *the sorting out, interpretation, analysis, and integration of stimuli involving the sense organs and brain*

Visual Perception: Seeing the World

From the time of little Lee Eng's birth, everyone who met him felt that he gazed at them intently. His eyes seemed to meet those of visitors. They seemed to bore deeply, and knowingly, into the faces of people who were looking at him.

How good in fact was Lee's vision, and what, precisely, could he make out of his environment? Quite a bit.

According to some estimates, a newborn's distance vision ranges from 20/200 to 20/600, which means that an infant cannot discern visual material beyond 20 feet that an adult with normal vision is able to see from a distance of between 200 and 600 feet (M. M. Haith, 1991).

These figures indicate that infants' distance vision is some 10 to 30 times poorer than the average adult's, perhaps suggesting that the vision of infants is inadequate. However, looking at the figures from a different perspective suggests a revised interpretation: The vision of newborns provides the same degree of distance acuity as the uncorrected vision of many adults who wear eyeglasses or contact lenses. (If you wear glasses or contact lenses, remove them to get a sense of what an infant can see of the world.) Furthermore, infants' distance vision grows increasingly acute. By 6 months of age, the average infant's vision is already 20/20—in other words, identical to that of adults (Aslin, 1987; K. Simons, 1993).

Other visual abilities grow rapidly. For instance, *binocular vision*, the ability to combine the images coming to each eye to see depth and motion, is achieved at around 14 weeks.

Depth perception is a particularly useful ability, as a classic study on the topic indicates. In this study, carried out by developmental psychologists Eleanor Gibson and Richard Walk (1960), infants were placed on a sheet of heavy glass. A checkered pattern appeared under one half of the glass sheet, making it seem that the infant was on a stable floor. However, in the middle of the glass sheet, the pattern dropped down several feet, forming an apparent "visual cliff." The question Gibson and Walk asked was whether infants would willingly crawl across the cliff when called by their mothers (see Figure 4-10).

The results were unambiguous. Most of the infants in the study, who ranged in age from 6 to 14 months, could not be coaxed over the apparent cliff. Clearly the ability to perceive depth had already developed in most of them by that age. On the other hand, the experiment did not pinpoint when depth perception emerged, since only infants who had

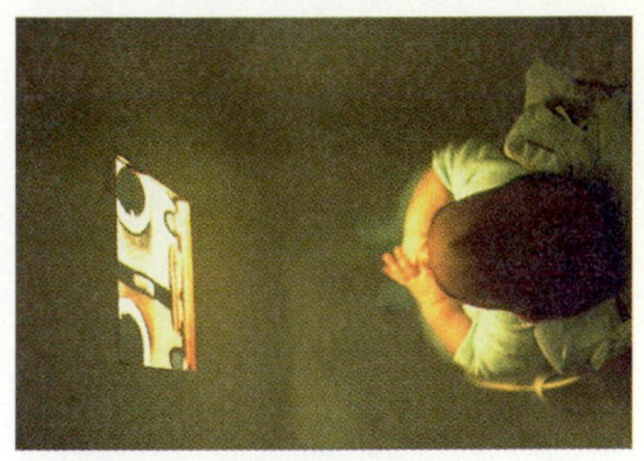

Using a testing chamber similar to this, developmental psychologist Robert Fantz was able to demonstrate the visual preferences of infants.

FIGURE 4-10 THE VISUAL CLIFF
The "visual cliff" examines the depth perception of infants. Most infants in the age range of 6 to 14 months cannot be coaxed to cross the cliff, apparently responding to the fact that the patterned area drops several feet.

already learned to crawl could be tested. But other experiments, in which infants of 2 and 3 months were placed on their stomachs above the apparent floor and above the visual cliff, revealed differences in heart rate between the two positions (Campos, Langer, & Krowitz, 1970).

Still, such findings do not permit us to know whether infants are responding to depth itself, or merely to the *change* in visual stimuli that occurs when they are moved from a lack of depth to depth.

Infants also show clear visual preferences, preferences that are present from birth. For example, when given a choice, infants reliably prefer to look at stimuli that include patterns than to look at simpler stimuli (see Figure 4-11). How do we know? Developmental psychologist Robert Fantz (1963) created a classic test. He built a chamber in which babies could lie on their backs and see pairs of visual stimuli above them. Fantz could determine which of the stimuli the infants were looking at by observing the reflections of the stimuli in their eyes.

Fantz's work was the impetus for a great deal of research on the preferences of infants, most of which points to a critical conclusion: Infants are genetically preprogrammed to prefer particular kinds of stimuli. For instance, just minutes after birth, they show preferences for certain colors, shapes, and configurations of various stimuli. Such capabilities may be a reflection of the existence of highly specialized cells in the brain that react to stimuli of a particular pattern, orientation, shape, and direction of movement (Colombo, 1995; Gallant, Braun, & VanEssen, 1993; Haith, 1991a; Hubel & Wiesel, 1979).

However, genetics is not the sole determinant of infant visual preferences. Just a few hours after birth, infants have already learned to prefer their own mother's face to other faces. Such findings provide another clear piece of evidence of how heredity and environmental experiences are woven together to determine an infant's capabilities (Field et al., 1984; R. Gelman & Au, 1996; Pascalis et al., 1995).

Auditory Perception: The World of Sound

What is it about a mother's lullaby that helps soothe a crying, fussy baby? Some clues emerge when we look at the capabilities of infants in the realm of auditory sensation and perception.

It is clear that infants hear from the time of birth—and even before. As we noted in Chapter 3, the ability to hear begins prenatally. Even in the womb, the fetus responds to sounds outside of its mother.

Because they have had some practice in hearing before birth, it is not surprising that infants have reasonably good auditory perception after they are born. In fact, for certain very high and very low frequencies, infants actually are more sensitive to sound than adults—a sensitivity that seems to increase during the first 2 years of life. On the other

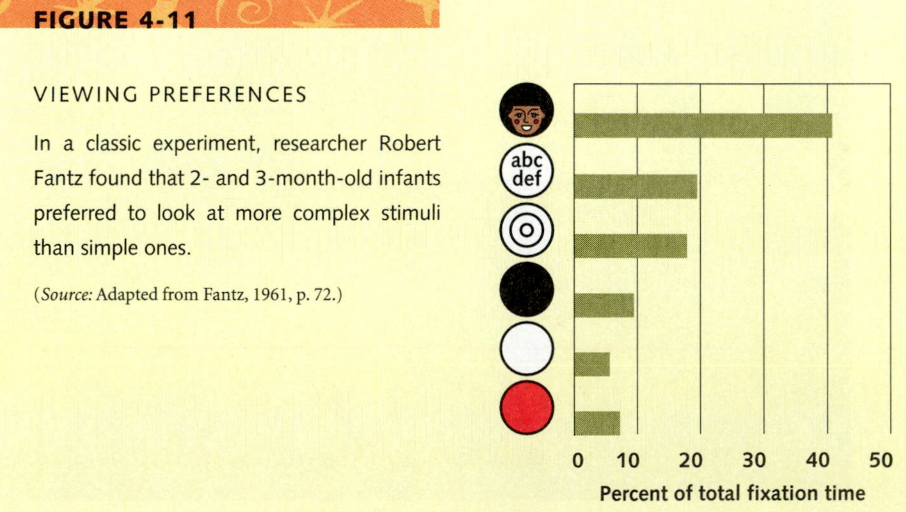

FIGURE 4-11

VIEWING PREFERENCES

In a classic experiment, researcher Robert Fantz found that 2- and 3-month-old infants preferred to look at more complex stimuli than simple ones.

(*Source:* Adapted from Fantz, 1961, p. 72.)

hand, infants are initially less sensitive than adults to middle-range frequencies. Eventually, however, their capabilities within the middle range improve (Fenwick & Morrongiello, 1991; L. A. Werner & Marean, 1996).

It is not fully clear what leads to the improvement during infancy in sensitivity to sounds, although it may be related to the maturation of the nervous system. More puzzling is why after infancy, children's ability to hear very high and low frequencies gradually declines. One explanation may be that exposure to high levels of noise may diminish capacities at the extreme ranges (Kryter, 1983; B. A. Schneider, Trehub, & Bull, 1980; Trehub et al., 1988, 1989).

In addition to the ability to detect sound, infants need several other abilities in order to hear effectively. For instance, *sound localization* permits infants to discern the direction from which a sound is emanating. Compared to adults, infants have a slight handicap in this task because effective sound localization requires the use of the slight difference in the times at which a sound reaches our two ears. Because infants' heads are smaller than those of adults, the difference in timing of the arrival of sound at the two ears is less than it is in adults.

However, despite the potential limitation brought about by their smaller heads, infants' sound localization abilities are actually fairly good even at birth, and they reach adult levels of success by the age of 1 year (Clifton, 1992). Interestingly, their improvement is not steady: Although we don't know why, the accuracy of sound localization actually declines between birth and 2 months of age, but then begins to increase (Aslin, 1987; Schneider, Bull, & Trehub, 1988; Trehub et al., 1989).

Infant discrimination of groups of different sounds, in terms of their patterns and other acoustical characteristics, is also quite good. For instance, the change of a single note in a six-tone melody can be detected by infants as young as 6 months old. They also react to changes in musical key (Trehub, Thorpe, & Morrongiello, 1985). In sum, they listen with a keen ear to the melodies of lullabies sung to them by their mothers and fathers!

Even more important to their ultimate success in the world, young infants are capable of making the fine discriminations that their future understanding of language will require (Bijeljac-Babic, Bertoncini, & Mehler, 1993). For instance, in one classic study, a group of 1- to 4-month-old infants sucked on nipples that activated a recording of a person saying "ba" every time they sucked (Eimas et al., 1971). At first, their interest in the sound made them suck vigorously. Soon, though, they became acclimated to the sound (through a process called *habituation,* discussed in Chapter 5) and sucked with less energy. On the other hand, when the experimenters changed the sound to "pa," the infants immediately showed new interest and sucked with greater vigor once again. The clear conclusion: Infants as young as a month old could make the distinction between the two similar sounds (Eimas et al., 1971; J. C. Goodman & Nusbaum, 1994; J. L. Miller & Eimas, 1995).

Even more intriguingly, young infants are able to discriminate certain characteristics that differentiate one language from another. By the age of 4-½ months, infants are able to discriminate their own names from other, similar-sounding, words. By the age of 5 months, they can distinguish the difference between English and Spanish passages, even when the two are similar in meter, number of syllables, and speed of recitation. In fact, some evidence suggests that even 2-day-olds show preferences for their native language (Bahrick & Pickens, 1988; Best, 1994; Mandel, Jusczyk, & Pisoni, 1995; Moon, Cooper, & Fifer, 1993).

Given their ability to discriminate a difference in speech as slight as the difference between two consonants, it is not surprising that infants can distinguish different people on the basis of voice. In fact, from an early age they show clear preferences for some voices over others. For instance, in one experiment newborns were allowed to suck a nipple that turned on a recording of a human voice reading a story. The infants sucked significantly longer when the voice was that of their mother than when the voice was that of a stranger (DeCasper & Fifer, 1980; Fifer, 1987).

How do such preferences arise? One hypothesis is that prenatal exposure to the mother's voice is the key. As support for this conjecture, researchers point to the fact that

Infants react to unpleasant tastes from birth.

newborns do not show a preference for their fathers' voices over other male voices. Furthermore, newborns prefer listening to melodies sung by their mothers before they were born to melodies that were not sung before birth. It seems, then, that the prenatal exposure to their mothers' voices—although muffled by the liquid environment of the womb—helps shape infants' listening preferences (DeCasper & Prescott, 1984; Panneton, 1985).

Smell and Taste

What do infants do when they smell a rotten egg? Pretty much what adults do—crinkle their noses and generally look unhappy. On the other hand, the scent of bananas and butter produces a pleasant reaction on the part of infants (Steiner, 1979).

The sense of smell is so well developed, even among very young infants, that at least some 12- to 18-day-old babies can distinguish their mothers on the basis of smell alone. For instance, in one experiment infants were exposed to the smell of gauze pads worn under the arms of adults the previous evening. Infants who were being breast-fed were able to distinguish their mothers' scent from those of other adults. However, not all infants could do this: Those who were being bottle-fed were unable to make the distinction. Moreover, both breast-fed and bottle-fed infants were unable to distinguish their fathers on the basis of odor (Cernoch & Porter, 1985; R. H. Porter, Bologh, & Makin, 1988).

Taste, like smell, shows surprising sophistication during infancy—in part because the two capabilities are related. Some taste preferences are well developed at birth, such as disgust over bitter tastes. At the same time, infants seem to have an innate sweet tooth—even before they have teeth: Very young infants smile when a sweet-tasting liquid is placed on their tongues. They also suck harder at a bottle if it is sweetened (Crook, 1978, 1987; Porges & Lipsitt, 1993; Rosenstein & Oster, 1988; Steiner, 1979; Mattes et al., 1996).

Sensitivity to Pain and Touch

When Eli Rosenblatt was 8 days old, he participated in the ancient Jewish ritual of circumcision. As he lay nestled in his father's arms, the foreskin of his penis was removed. Although Eli shrieked in what seemed to his anxious parents as pain, he soon settled down and went back to sleep. Others who had watched the ceremony assured his parents, with great authority, that at Eli's age babies don't really experience pain, at least not in the same way that adults do.

Were Eli's relatives accurate in saying that young infants don't experience pain? In the past, many medical practitioners would have agreed. In fact, because they assumed that infants didn't experience pain in truly bothersome ways, many physicians routinely carried out medical procedures, and even some forms of surgery, without the use of painkillers or anesthesia. Their argument was that the risks from the use of anesthesia outweighed the potential pain that the young infants experienced.

Contemporary Views on Infant Pain. Today, however, it is widely acknowledged that infants are born with the capacity to experience pain. Obviously, no one can be sure if the experience of pain in children is identical to that in adults, any more than we can tell if an adult friend who complains of a headache is experiencing pain that is more or less severe than our own pain when we have a headache.

What we do know is that pain produces signs of distress in infants, such as a rise in heartbeat, sweating, facial expressions indicative of discomfort, and changes in the intensity and tone of crying (Johnston, 1989). Such evidence indicates that infants do, in fact, experience pain. There also seems to be a developmental progression in reactions to pain.

For example, a newborn infant who has her heel pricked for a blood test responds with signs of distress, but it takes her several seconds to show the response. In contrast, only a few months later, the same procedure brings a much more immediate response. It is possible that the delayed reaction in infants is produced by the relatively slower transmission of information within the newborn's nervous system (Anand & Hickey, 1987, 1992; Axia, Bonichini, & Benini, 1995; Bornstein & Lamb, 1992b; F. L. Porter, Porges, & Marshall, 1988).

In response to increasing support for the notion that infants experience pain, medical experts now endorse the use of anesthesia and painkillers during surgery for even the youngest infants. According to the American Academy of Pediatrics, painkilling drugs are appropriate in most types of surgery, although minor surgical procedures—such as circumcision—still may be done without their use.

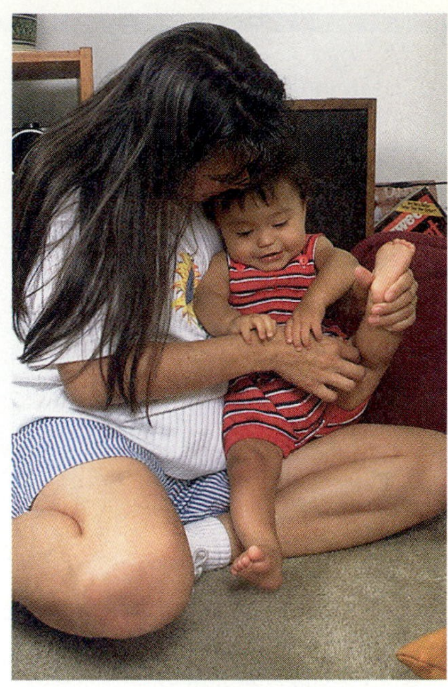

Touch is one of the most highly developed sensory systems from the time of birth.

Responding to Touch. It clearly does not take the sting of pain to get an infant's attention. Even the youngest infants respond to gentle touches, such as a soothing caress, which can calm a crying, fussy infant (Stack & Muir, 1992).

In fact, touch is one of the most highly developed sensory systems in a newborn. It is also one of the first to develop; there is evidence that by 32 weeks after conception, the entire body is sensitive to touch. Furthermore, several of the basic reflexes present at birth, such as the rooting reflex, require touch sensitivity to operate: An infant must sense a touch near the mouth in order to seek automatically a nipple to suck (M. M. Haith, 1986).

Infants' abilities in the realm of touch are particularly helpful in their efforts to explore the world. Several theorists have suggested that one of the ways children gain information about the world is through touching. For instance, at the age of 6 months, infants are apt to place almost any object in their mouths, apparently taking in data about its configuration from their sensory responses to the feel of it in their mouths (Ruff, 1989).

Multimodal Perception: Combining Individual Sensory Inputs

When Eric Pettigrew was 7 months old, his grandparents presented him with a squeaky rubber doll. As soon as he saw it, he reached out for it, grasped it in his hand, and listened as it squeaked. He seemed delighted with the gift.

One way of considering Eric's sensory reaction to the doll is to focus on each of the senses individually: what the doll looked like to Eric, how it felt in his hand, and what it sounded like. In fact, this approach has dominated the study of sensation and perception in infancy.

However, we might take another approach: We might examine how the various sensory responses are integrated with one another. Instead of looking at each individual sensory response, we could consider how the responses work together and are combined to produce Eric's ultimate reaction. The **multimodal approach to perception** considers how information that is collected by various individual sensory systems is integrated and coordinated.

Although the multimodal approach is a relatively recent innovation in the study of how infants understand their sensory world, it raises some fundamental issues about the development of sensation and perception. For instance, some researchers argue that sensations are initially integrated with one another in the infant, while others maintain that the infant's sensory systems are initially separate and that development leads to increasing integration (Bahrick, 1989; Legerstee, 1990; Lewbowicz & Lickliter, 1994; P. C. Quinn & Eimas, 1996; Rose & Ruff, 1987; Streri, 1994).

We don't yet know which view is correct. However, it does appear that by an early age infants are able to relate what they have learned about an object through one sensory channel to what they have learned about it through another. For instance, even 1-month-old infants are able to recognize by sight objects that they have previously held in their mouths but never seen (Meltzoff, 1981; Streri & Spelke, 1988). Clearly, some cross-talk between various sensory channels is already possible a month after birth.

The success of infants at multimodal perception is another example of the sophisticated perceptual abilities of infants, which continue to grow throughout the period of infancy. These increasing capabilities are mirrored by the growth of cognitive abilities, which we'll consider in the next chapter.

multimodal approach to perception *the approach that considers how information that is collected by various individual sensory systems is integrated and coordinated*

The Informed Consumer of Development

Exercising Your Infant's Body and Senses

We've seen how the kind of experiences infants encounter as they grow is reflected in their motor and sensory development. For instance, recall how cultural expectations and environments affect the age at which various physical milestones, such as the timing of the first step, occur. Does this suggest that parents are well advised to try to accelerate their infants' timetables?

Although experts disagree, most feel that such acceleration yields little advantage. No data suggest that a child who walks at 10 months ultimately has any advantage over one who walks at 15 months.

On the other hand, it does seem reasonable for parents to ensure that their infants receive some level of physical and sensory stimulation. The goal, according to Jane Clark, an expert in kinesiology (the science of human anatomy and movement), is not to get children to achieve motoric milestones early, but "to raise active, confident children who will become healthy, active adults who feel good about their bodies and who value physical activity for its intrinsic benefits and rewards" (Israeloff, 1991). There are several specific ways to accomplish this goal:

- Carry a baby in different positions—in a backpack, in a frontpack, or in a football hold with the infant's head in the palm of your hand and its feet lying on your arm.
- Let infants explore their environment. Don't contain them too long in a barren environment. Let them crawl or wander around an environment—after first making it "childproof" by removing dangerous objects.
- Engage in "rough-and-tumble" play. Wrestling, dancing, and rolling around on the floor—if not violent—are activities that are fun and that stimulate older infants' motoric and sensory systems.
- Let babies touch their food and even play with it. Infancy is too early to start teaching infants very much about the etiquette of table manners.
- Provide toys that stimulate the senses. For instance, brightly colored, textured toys with movable parts are enjoyable and help hone infants' senses.

Above all, don't focus so much on the goal of stimulating an infant's motoric and sensory abilities that you miss out on the joy and wonder of his or her continuing development.

Review and Rethink

REVIEW

- Sensation refers to the activation of the sense organs by external stimuli. Perception is the sorting out, interpretation, analysis, and integration of sensations.

- Infants' abilities in the sensory realm are surprisingly well developed at or shortly after birth. Their perceptions through sight, hearing, smell, taste, and touch help them explore and begin to make sense of the world.
- Very early, infants can see depth and motion, distinguish colors and patterns, localize and discriminate sounds, recognize the sound of their mothers' voices, and discern their mothers by smell alone. Moreover, infants can relate some perceptions received through one sensory channel to those received through another.
- Infants are sensitive to pain and to touch. Most medical authorities now subscribe to procedures, including anesthesia, that minimize infants' pain.
- Parents and caregivers should help infants engage in physical activities that will help them grow into healthy adults who feel confident about their bodies.

RETHINK

- Given what was said earlier in this chapter about the way the brain and nervous system develop, what sort of sensory environment would probably be most conducive to healthy neural development in the infant? Why?
- Are the processes of sensation and perception always linked? Is it possible to sense without perceiving? To perceive without sensing? How?
- In this chapter it was said that the nervous system develops by "pruning down" unnecessary neurons that do not form links with other neurons. Do you think an infant's early preference for the sounds of its home language gives evidence that such a process operates in the area of language development? How?
- The "ba"-"pa" experiment described in this chapter—in which sucking intensity decreased once babies became used to the "ba" sound, and then increased again when "ba" was changed to "pa"—was used to show that infants can discriminate highly similar sounds. Another conclusion might be that infants prefer novelty. How might a preference for novelty facilitate infant development?
- Persons who are born without the use of one sense often develop unusual abilities in one or more other senses. Do you think this phenomenon might relate to the argument about whether integration of the senses precedes differentiation, or vice versa? How?

How do the human body and nervous system develop?

1. Human babies grow rapidly, especially during the first 2 years of life. By the end of that time, the average baby in the United States has grown from 20 to 36 inches in height and from 7 to about 27 pounds.
2. The nervous system, which includes the brain and the nerves of the body, contains a huge number of neurons, virtually all of which grow before birth. For neurons to survive and become useful, they must form interconnections with other neurons based on the infant's experience of the world.
3. Major principles that govern human growth include the cephalocaudal principle (growth proceeds from upper body to lower), the proximodistal principle (growth proceeds from the center of the body outward), the principle of hierarchical integration (simple skills are grasped first and then integrated into more complex ones), and

the principle of the independence of systems (different body systems grow at different rates).

Does the environment affect the pattern of development?

4. Brain development, largely predetermined genetically, also contains a strong element of plasticity—a susceptibility to environmental influences.
5. Studies have shown that many aspects of development, including both behaviors and body structures, occur during sensitive periods when the organism is particularly susceptible to environmental influences. If interactions between baby and environment are affected during the sensitive period, development may be affected as well.
6. One of the primary tasks of the infant is the development of rhythms—cyclical patterns that integrate individual behaviors. An important rhythm pertains to the infant's state—the degree of awareness it displays to stimulation. The infant experiences various states during both sleep and wakefulness. Normal rhythms can be disturbed, as evidenced by sudden infant death syndrome, or SIDS.

What are reflexes and how are they useful?

7. Reflexes are unlearned, automatic responses to stimuli that help newborns survive and protect themselves. Some reflexes also have value as the foundation for future, more conscious behaviors.
8. Reflexes, although genetically determined and universal, are susceptible to some cultural variations. Reflexes also have utility as diagnostic devices for doctors and even as facilitators to promote caregiving and nurturing emotions in adults.

How universal are the schedule and sequence of motor development?

9. The development of gross and fine motor skills proceeds along a generally consistent timetable in normal children. However, caution should be applied to the interpretation of norms used to describe "average" behavior. Not only do individual variations exist, but cultural factors influence development and may not be reflected in norms that are not carefully determined to include cultural variations.
10. The development of motor skills reflects cultural differences. Within limits that are set genetically, the onset of certain motor skills can be speeded up or slowed down, depending on cultural expectations and practices. In the long term, it is unclear whether such differences in timing have lasting effects on the ultimate level of motor skill achieved by the individual.

What is the role of nutrition in physical development, and what food is best for infants?

11. Adequate nutrition is essential for physical development. Malnutrition and undernutrition affect physical aspects of growth and also may affect IQ and school performance.
12. Breast-feeding has distinct advantages over bottle-feeding, including the nutritional completeness of breast milk, its provision of a degree of immunity to certain childhood diseases, and its easy digestibility. In addition, breast-feeding offers significant physical and emotional benefits to both child and mother.
13. The decision whether to breast-feed or bottle-feed depends on a number of factors, including age, socioeconomic status, health issues, practical constraints, and level of knowledge of the benefits of breast-feeding.

How do the senses develop, and what sensory capabilities do infants possess?

14. Sensation, the stimulation of the sense organs, differs from perception, the interpretation and integration of sensed stimuli.

15. Infants' visual perception is quite good. Although infants' vision is less acute than adults' at first, within 6 months infants achieve adult levels of distance acuity. Moreover, the early achievement of binocular vision permits sophisticated perception of depth and motion by infants.

16. Auditory perception, which begins in the womb, is well developed in infants. They can localize sound, discriminate sound patterns and tones, and make fine sound discriminations that will be essential in the later development of language.

17. The senses of smell and taste are surprisingly sophisticated in infants. Infants react as adults do to pleasant and unpleasant odors and tastes, and even very young infants can recognize their mothers' scents.

18. The nature of infants' experiences of pain is not entirely clear, but it is clear that infants react negatively to painful stimuli. Infants use their highly developed sense of touch to explore and experience the world.

19. Whether all sensations are initially integrated in infants and later become differentiated, or whether initially separate senses later become increasingly integrated, is an unresolved issue. However, infants are clearly able to relate perceptions from one sensory source to those from another.

20. Although attempts to accelerate infants' achievement of motoric milestones are probably unwise and fruitless, parents should encourage and participate with their babies in physical activity and provide room for them to explore. Such activity can help them become healthy, active, and confident adults.

Key Terms and Concepts

cephalocaudal principle (p. 120)
proximodistal principle (p. 121)
principle of hierarchical integration (p. 121)
principle of the independence of systems (p. 122)
neurons (p. 122)
myelin (p. 122)
cerebral cortex (p. 123)
plasticity (p. 123)
sensitive period (p. 123)
rhythms (p. 124)
state (p. 125)
rapid eye movement (REM) sleep (p. 126)
sudden infant death syndrome (SIDS) (p. 127)
reflexes (p. 129)
norms (p. 133)
Brazelton Neonatal Behavioral Assessment Scale (NBAS) (p. 133)
marasmus (p. 136)
kwashiorkor (p. 137)
sensation (p. 142)
perception (p. 142)
multimodal approach to perception (p. 147)

CHAPTER 5

INFANCY

Cognitive Development in Infancy

PROLOGUE
THE FORGOTTEN MEMORIES OF SIMONA YOUNG

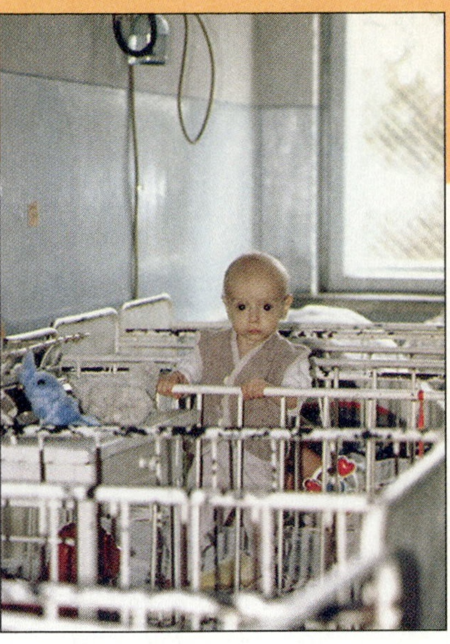

Children in this Romanian orphanage had virtually no human contact.

Simona Young was fated to spend her infancy with virtually no human contact. For up to 20 hours each day, she was left alone in a crib in a squalid Romanian orphanage. Cold bottles of milk were propped above her small body, which she would clutch to get nourishment. She would rock back and forth, rarely feeling any soothing touch or hearing words of comfort. Alone in her bleak surroundings, she would rock back and forth for hours on end.

Simona's story, however, has a happy ending. After being adopted by a Canadian couple when she was 2, Simona's life is now filled with the usual activities of childhood involving friends, classmates, and above all, a loving family. In fact, now, at age 6, she can remember almost nothing of her miserable life in the orphanage. It is as if she has entirely forgotten the past. (Blakeslee, 1995, p. C1)

LOOKING AHEAD

Has Simona really forgotten the first 2 years of her life, or do her memories still exist, hidden behind more current—and pleasant—recollections? Will she ever recall her past? Will any memories of her infancy be accurate?

Such questions go to the heart of the nature of memory in infancy. Clearly, infants remember *some* information, because without memory they would be unable to speak, recognize others, or, more generally, show the enormous advances in cognitive development that routinely occur throughout infancy. Yet it is still not entirely clear how accurate our earliest recollections are, and when—and how—our earliest memories are formed.

We address these and related questions in this chapter as we consider cognitive development during the first years of life. To do this, we consider the work of developmental researchers who seek to understand how infants develop their knowledge and understanding of the world. We first discuss the work of Swiss psychologist Jean Piaget, whose theory of developmental stages served as a highly influential impetus for a considerable amount of work on cognitive development. We'll look at both the limitations and the contributions of this important developmental theorist.

We then turn to the basic processes by which cognitive growth occurs. After considering how learning takes place, we turn to memory in infants and the ways in which infants process, store, and retrieve information. We discuss the controversial issue of the recollection of events that occurred during infancy. We also address individual differences in intelligence.

Finally, we consider language, the medium by which infants develop communication with others. We look at the roots of language in prelinguistic speech and trace the milestones indicating the development of language skills in the progression from first words to first phrases and sentences. We also look at the characteristics of communication addressed to infants, and examine some surprising universals in the nature of such communication across different cultures.

In sum, after reading this chapter, you'll be able to answer these questions:

- What can we learn about children's views of the world from Piaget's theories of cognitive development?

- How do infants process information and learn about the world?
- What sorts of memories do infants have?
- How can we measure infant intelligence, and how does it relate to adult intelligence?
- By what processes do children learn to use language?
- How do children influence the language that adults use to address them?

PIAGET'S APPROACH TO COGNITIVE DEVELOPMENT

ACTION = KNOWLEDGE.

In certain ways, this equation sums up the view of Swiss psychologist Jean Piaget (1896–1980) of how infants attain an understanding of the world. He argues that infants do not acquire knowledge from facts communicated by others, nor through sensation and perception. Instead, Piaget suggests that knowledge is the product of direct motor behavior. Although many of his basic explanations and propositions have been challenged by subsequent research, as we'll discuss later, the view that in significant ways infants learn by doing remains unquestioned (Piaget, 1952, 1962, 1983).

As we first noted in Chapter 1, Piaget's theory is based on a stage approach to development. He assumes that all children pass through a series of universal stages in a fixed order. He also believes that not only does the quantity of information acquired in each stage increase, but—even more importantly—the quality of knowledge and understanding grows as well. Some approaches to cognition focus on the content of an individual's knowledge about the world, such as might be assessed in a traditional intelligence test. In contrast, Piaget's theory suggests that the focus should be on the change in understanding that occurs as the child moves from one stage to another.

For instance, several kinds of changes in knowledge about what can and cannot occur in the world develop during infancy. Consider an infant who, during an experiment, is exposed to an impossible event, such as seeing her mother simultaneously in three identical versions (due to some clever trickery with mirrors). A 3-month-old infant shows no disturbance over the multiple apparitions and in fact will interact happily with each. However, by 5 months of age, the child becomes quite agitated at the sight of multiple mothers. Apparently by this time the child has figured out that she has but one mother, and viewing three at a time is thoroughly alarming (T. G. R. Bower, 1977). To Piaget, such reactions indicate growth in an underlying mastery of principles regarding the way the world operates.

According to Piaget, such cognitive development occurs in an orderly fashion. Children pass through four major stages as they move from birth through adolescence: sensorimotor, preoperational, concrete operational, and formal operational. Piaget suggests that movement from one stage to the next occurs when a child reaches an appropriate level of physical maturation and is exposed to relevant types of experience. Without such experience, children are assumed to be incapable of reaching their cognitive potential.

Piaget gives a name to the shifting patterns of understanding that characterize infancy: schemes. In infancy, a **scheme** is an organized pattern of sensorimotor functioning, a representation in the nervous system of action upon the world. Although at first schemes are related to physical activity, as children develop, their schemes move to a mental level, reflecting thought. Schemes are like computer programs: They direct and determine how data from the world are considered and dealt with (Achenbach, 1992).

Schemes may be illustrated by the way in which an infant reacts when given a new cloth book. The infant will touch it, mouth it, perhaps try to tear it or bang it on the floor. To Piaget, each of these actions may be representative of a scheme, and they are the infant's way of gaining knowledge and understanding of the book. Adults, on the other hand, would use a different scheme upon encountering the book. Far from picking it up and

scheme *an organized pattern of sensorimotor functioning* putting it in their mouths or banging it on the floor, they would probably be drawn to the letters on the page, seeking to understand the book through the meaning of the printed words—a very different approach.

In newborns, schemes are primarily limited to reflexes, such as sucking and rooting. Quickly, however, schemes become more sophisticated as infants become more advanced in their motor capabilities—to Piaget, a signal of the potential for more advanced cognitive development.

Piaget contends that two principles underlie the growth in children's schemes: assimilation and accommodation. **Assimilation** is the process in which people understand an experience in terms of their current stage of cognitive development and way of thinking. Assimilation occurs, then, when a stimulus or event is acted upon, perceived, and understood in accordance with existing patterns of thought. For example, an infant who tries to suck on any toy in the same way is assimilating the objects to her existing sucking scheme. Similarly, a child who encounters a flying squirrel at a zoo and calls it a "bird" is assimilating the squirrel to his existing scheme of bird.

In contrast, **accommodation** refers to changes in existing ways of thinking that occur in response to encounters with new stimuli or events. When existing ways of behaving, thinking, and understanding become altered to fit or match novel experiences, accommodation takes place. For instance, when a child modifies the way she sucks on a toy according to the particular shape of the toy, she is accommodating her sucking scheme to the special characteristics of the toy. In the same way, a child who sees a flying squirrel and calls it "a bird with a tail" is beginning to accommodate to new knowledge, modifying his scheme of "bird."

Because the sensorimotor stage of development begins at birth and continues until the child is about 2 years old, we'll consider it here in detail. (In future chapters, we'll discuss development during the other stages.) In considering the specific substages of the sensorimotor period, it may at first appear that they unfold with great regularity, as infants reach a particular age and smoothly proceed into the next substage. However, the reality of cognitive development, Piaget admits, is somewhat different. First, the ages at which infants actually reach a particular stage vary a good deal among different children. The exact timing of a stage reflects an interaction between the infant's level of physical maturation and the nature of the social environment in which the child is being raised. Consequently, although Piaget contends that the order of the substages does not change from one child to the next, the timing can and does vary to some degree.

Furthermore, Piaget argues that development is a more gradual process than the demarcation of different stages might seem to imply. Specifically, infants do not go to sleep one night in one substage and wake up the next morning in the next one. Instead, there is a rather steady shift in behavior as a child moves toward the next stage of cognitive development. Infants also pass through periods of transition in which some aspects of their behavior reflect the next higher stage while other aspects are indicative of their current stage (see Figure 5-1).

assimilation *the process in which people understand an experience in terms of their current stage of cognitive development and way of thinking*

accommodation *changes in existing ways of thinking that occur in response to encounters with new stimuli or events*

sensorimotor stage *the initial major stage of cognitive development; can be broken down into six substages*

The Sensorimotor Period: Charting the Course of Early Cognitive Growth

Piaget suggests that the **sensorimotor stage,** the initial major stage of cognitive development, can be broken down into six substages (summarized in Table 5-1), described here in turn.

Substage 1: Simple Reflexes. The first substage of the sensorimotor period is *Substage 1: Simple reflexes,* encompassing the first month of life. During this time, the various reflexes that determine the nature of the infant's interactions with the world are at the center of its cognitive life. For example, the sucking reflex causes the infant to suck at anything placed in its lips. This sucking behavior, according to Piaget, provides the newborn with information about objects—information that paves the way to the next substage of the sensorimotor period.

FIGURE 5-1

TRANSITIONS

Infants do not suddenly shift from one stage of cognitive development to the next. Instead, Piaget argues that there is a period of transition in which some behavior reflects one stage while other behavior reflects the more advanced stage.

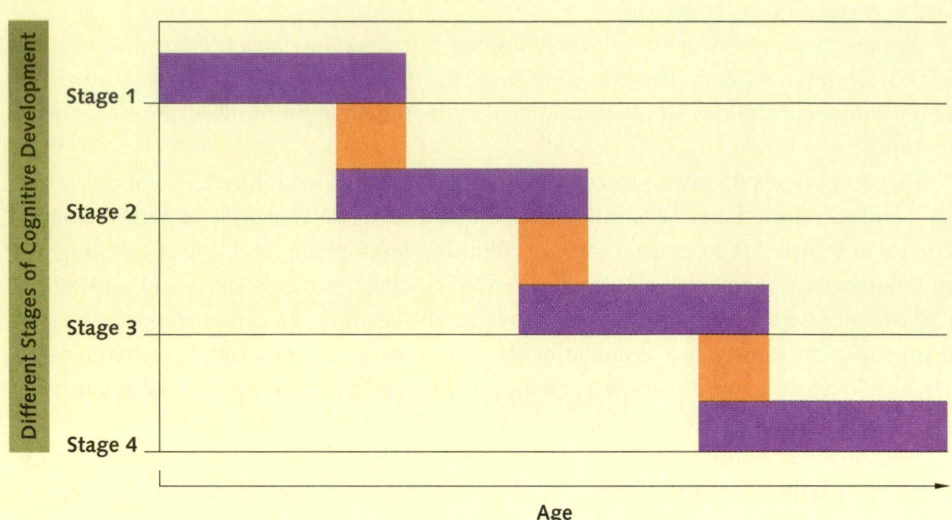

At the same time, some of the reflexes become modified as a result of the infant's experience with the nature of the world. For instance, an infant who is being breast-fed, but who also receives supplemental bottles, may begin to make modifications in how it sucks depending on whether the nipple it is sucking is on a breast or a bottle.

Substage 2: First Habits and Primary Circular Reactions. The second substage of the sensorimotor period, *Substage 2: First habits and primary circular reactions,* occurs from 1 to 4 months of age. In this period, infants begin to coordinate what were separate actions into single, integrated activities. For instance, an infant might combine grasping an object with sucking on it, or staring at something while touching it.

If an activity engages children's interests, they may repeat it over and over, simply for the sake of continuing to experience it. A **circular reaction** permits the construction of cognitive schemes through the repetition of a chance motor event. *Primary circular reactions* are schemes reflecting an infant's repetition of interesting or enjoyable actions, just for the enjoyment of doing them. Thus, when an infant first puts his thumb in his mouth and begins to suck, it is a mere chance event. However, when he repeatedly sucks his thumb in the future, it represents a primary circular reaction which he is repeating because the sensation of sucking is pleasurable.

Substage 3: Secondary Circular Reactions. The next period, *Substage 3: Secondary circular reactions,* occurs from 4 to 8 months of age. During this period, infants take major strides in shifting their cognitive horizons beyond themselves and begin to act upon the outside world. For instance, when infants, through chance activities, produce an enjoyable event in their environment, they now seek to repeat that event. A child who repeatedly picks up a rattle in her crib and shakes it in different ways to see how the sound changes is demonstrating her ability to modify her cognitive scheme about shaking rattles. She is engaging in what Piaget calls secondary circular reactions.

Secondary circular reactions are schemes regarding repeated actions meant to bring about a desirable consequence. The major difference between primary circular reactions and secondary circular reactions is whether the infant's activity is focused on the infant and his or her own body (primary circular reactions) or involves actions relating to the world outside (secondary circular reactions).

circular reaction *an activity that permits the construction of cognitive schemes through the repetition of a chance motor event*

TABLE 5-1

PIAGET'S SIX SUBSTAGES OF THE SENSORIMOTOR STAGE

Substage	Age	Description	Example
SUBSTAGE 1: Simple reflexes	Birth-1 month	During this period, the various reflexes that determine the nature of the infant's interactions with the world are at the center of its cognitive life.	The sucking reflex causes the infant to suck at anything placed in its lips.
SUBSTAGE 2: First habits and primary circular reactions	1-4 months	At this age, infants begin to coordinate what were separate actions into single, integrated activities.	An infant might combine grasping an object with sucking on it, or staring at something with touching it.
SUBSTAGE 3: Secondary circular reactions	4-8 months	During this period, infants take major strides in shifting their cognitive horizons beyond themselves and begin to act upon the outside world.	A child who repeatedly picks up a rattle in her crib and shakes it in different ways to see how the sound changes is demonstrating her ability to modify her cognitive scheme about shaking rattles.
SUBSTAGE 4: Coordination of secondary circular reactions	8-12 months	In this stage, infants begin to use more calculated approaches to producing events, coordinating several schemes to generate a single act. They achieve object permanence during this stage.	An infant will push one toy out of the way to reach another toy that is lying, partially exposed, under it.
SUBSTAGE 5: Tertiary circular reactions	12-18 months	At this age, infants develop what Piaget regards as the deliberate variation of actions that bring desirable consequences. Rather than just repeating enjoyable activities as in Substage 4, infants appear to carry out miniature experiments to observe the consequences.	A child will drop a toy repeatedly, varying the position from which he dropped it, carefully observing each time to see where it fell.
SUBSTAGE 6: Beginnings of thought	18 months-2 years	The major achievements of Substage 6 is the capacity for mental representation or symbolic thought. Piaget argued that only at this stage can infants imagine where objects that they cannot see might be.	Children can plot in their heads unseen trajectories of objects, so that if a ball rolls under a piece of furniture, they can figure out where it is likely to emerge on the other side.

During the third substage, the degree of vocalization increases substantially as infants come to notice that if they make noises, other people around them will respond with noises of their own. Similarly, infants begin to imitate the sounds made by others. Vocalization becomes a secondary circular reaction that ultimately helps lead to the development of language and the formation of social relationships.

Substage 4: Coordination of Secondary Circular Reactions. One of the major leaps forward in terms of cognitive development comes as infants move through the next substage, *Substage 4: Coordination of secondary circular reactions,* which lasts from around 8 months to 12 months. Before this stage, behavior involved direct action on objects. When something caught an infant's interest, she attempted to repeat the event using a single scheme. However, in Substage 4, infants begin to use more calculated approaches to producing events. They employ **goal-directed behavior** in which several schemes are combined and coordinated to generate a single act to solve a problem. For instance, they will push one toy out of the way to reach another toy that is lying, partially exposed, under it. They also begin to anticipate upcoming events. For instance, Piaget tells of his son Laurent, who at 8 months "recognizes by a certain noise caused by air that he is nearing the end of his feeding and, instead of insisting on drinking to the last drop, he rejects his bottle" (Piaget, 1952, pp. 248–249).

goal-directed behavior *behavior in which several schemes are combined and coordinated to generate a single act to solve a problem*

Infants' newfound purposefulness, their ability to use means to attain particular ends, and their skill in anticipating future circumstances, owe their appearance in part to the developmental achievement of object permanence that emerges in Substage 4. **Object permanence** is the realization that people and objects exist even when they cannot be seen. It is a simple principle, but its mastery has profound consequences.

object permanence *the realization that people and objects exist even when they cannot be seen*

Consider, for instance, how a 7-month-old infant named Chu, who has yet to learn the idea of object permanence, reacts when his father, who has been shaking a rattle in front of him, takes the rattle and places it under a blanket. To Chu, who has not mastered the concept of object permanence, the rattle no longer exists, and he will make no effort to look for it.

Several months later, when he is in Substage 4, the story is quite different (see Figure 5-2). This time, as soon as his father places the rattle under the blanket, Chu tries to toss the cover aside, eagerly searching for the rattle. Chu clearly has learned that the object continues to exist even when it cannot be seen. For the infant who achieves an understanding of object permanence, then, out of sight is decidedly not out of mind.

The attainment of object permanence extends not only to inanimate objects, but to people, too. It gives Chu the security that his father and mother still exist even when they have left the room. This awareness is likely a key element in the development of social attachments, which we'll consider in Chapter 6. The recognition of object permanence also feeds infants' growing assertiveness: As they realize that an object taken away from them doesn't just cease to exist, but is merely somewhere else, their only-too-human reaction may be to want it back—and want it back quickly.

Although the understanding of object permanence emerges in Substage 4, it is only a rudimentary understanding. It takes several months for the concept to be fully comprehended, and infants continue for several months to make certain kinds of errors relating to object permanence. For instance, they often are fooled when they watch as a toy is hidden first under one blanket and then under a second blanket. In seeking out the toy, Substage 4 infants most often turn to the first hiding place, ignoring the blanket under which the toy is currently located—even though the hiding was done in plain view.

Substage 5: Tertiary Circular Reactions. At around the age of 12 months, infants reach *Substage 5: Tertiary circular reactions,* which extends to 18 months. As the name of the stage indicates, during this period infants develop what Piaget labeled *tertiary circular reactions,*

FIGURE 5-2

OBJECT PERMANENCE

Before an infant has understood the idea of object permanence, he will not search for an object that has been hidden right before his eyes. But several months later, he will search for it, illustrating that he has attained object permanence.

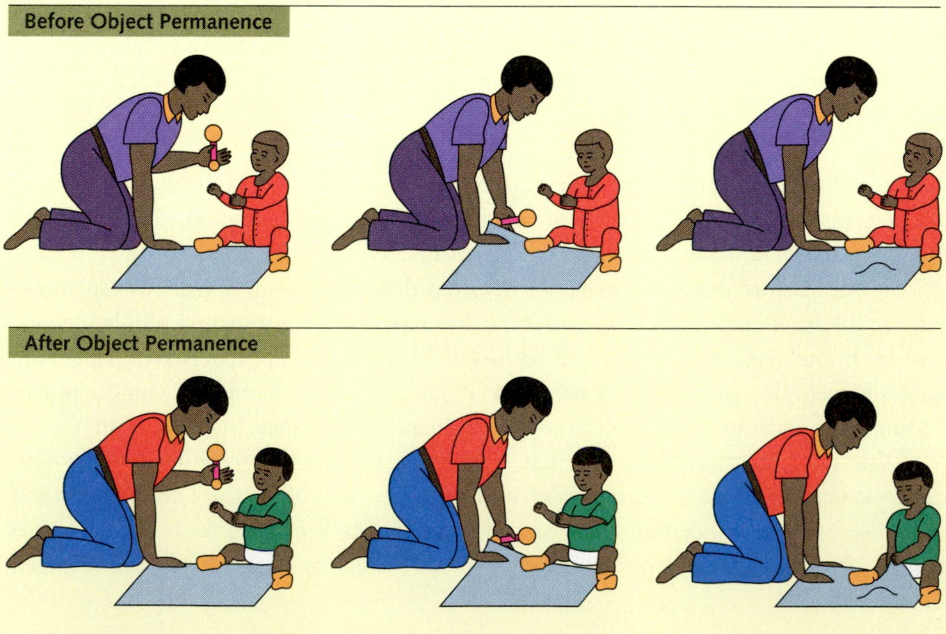

Before Object Permanence

After Object Permanence

schemes regarding the deliberate variation of actions that bring desirable consequences. Rather than just repeating enjoyable activities, as they do with secondary circular reactions, infants appear to carry out miniature experiments to observe the consequences.

For example, Piaget observed his son Laurent dropping a toy swan repeatedly, varying the position from which he dropped it, carefully observing each time to see where it fell. Instead of just repeating the action each time (as in a secondary circular reaction), Laurent made modifications in the situation to learn about their consequences. As you may recall from our discussion of research methods in Chapter 1, this behavior represents the essence of the scientific method: An experimenter varies a situation in a laboratory to learn the effects of the variation. To infants in Substage 5, the world is their laboratory, and they spend their days leisurely carrying out one miniature experiment after another.

What is most striking about infants' behavior during Substage 5 is their interest in the unexpected. Unanticipated events are treated not only as interesting, but also as something to be explained and understood. Infants' discoveries can lead to newfound skills, some of which may cause a certain amount of chaos. For instance, an infant may pull at a tablecloth in order to reach a plate of cookies or throw a water toy into the tub with increasing vigor to see how high the water splashes.

mental representation *an internal image of a past event or object*

deferred imitation *an act in which a person who is no longer present is imitated later by children after they have witnessed the person's actions*

Substage 6: Beginnings of Thought. The final stage of the sensorimotor period is *Substage 6: Beginnings of thought,* which lasts from around 18 months to 2 years. The major achievement of Substage 6 is the capacity for mental representation or symbolic thought. A **mental representation** is an internal image of a past event or object. Piaget argued that only at this stage can infants imagine where objects that they cannot see might be. They can even plot in their heads unseen trajectories of objects, so if a ball rolls under a piece of furniture, they can figure out where it is likely to emerge on the other side.

Because of children's new abilities to create internal representations of objects, their understanding of causality also becomes more sophisticated. For instance, consider Piaget's description of his son Laurent's efforts to open a garden gate:

> Laurent tries to open a garden gate but cannot push it forward because it is held back by a piece of furniture. He cannot account either visually or by any sound for the cause that prevents the gate from opening, but after having tried to force it he suddenly seems to understand; he goes around the wall, arrives at the other side of the gate, moves the armchair which holds it firm, and opens it with a triumphant expression. (Piaget, 1954, p. 296)

The attainment of mental representation also permits another important development: the ability to pretend. Using the skill of what Piaget refers to as **deferred imitation,** in which a person who is no longer present is imitated later, children are able to pretend that they are driving a car, feeding a doll, or cooking dinner long after they have witnessed such scenes played out in reality.

Appraising Piaget: Support and Challenges

Most developmental researchers would probably agree that, in many significant ways, Piaget's descriptions of how cognitive development proceeds during infancy are quite accurate (P. L. Harris, 1983, 1987). Yet, when many of the specifics of Piagetian theory are considered, there is substantial disagreement over the validity of the theory and its predictions.

Let's start with what is clearly correct about the Piagetian approach. Piaget was a masterful reporter of children's behavior, and his descriptions of their growth during infancy remain a monument to his powers of observation. Furthermore, literally thousands of studies have supported Piaget's view that children learn much about the world by acting on objects in their environment. Finally, the broad outlines sketched out by Piaget of the sequence of cognitive development and the increasing cognitive accomplishments that occur during infancy are generally accurate (Gratch & Schatz, 1987).

On the other hand, specific aspects of the theory have come under increasing scrutiny—and criticism—in the decades since Piaget carried out his pioneering work. For example, some researchers question the stage conception that forms the basis of Piaget's theory. To critics, development proceeds in a much more continuous fashion than Piaget's stage theory suggests. Rather than showing major leaps of competence at the end of one stage and the beginning of the next, improvement comes in more gradual increments, growing step by step in a skill-by-skill manner.

For instance, developmental researcher Robert Siegler (1995) suggests that cognitive development proceeds not in stages but in "waves." According to him, children don't one day drop a mode of thinking and the next take up a new form. Instead, there is an ebb and flow of cognitive approaches used to understand the world. One day children may use one form of cognitive strategy, while another day they may choose a less advanced strategy—moving back and forth over a period of time. Although one strategy may be used most frequently at a given age, children still may have access to alternative ways of thinking. Siegler thus sees cognitive development as in constant flux.

Other critics dispute Piaget's notion that cognitive development is grounded in motor activities. Some developmental specialists charge that such a view ignores the importance of the sophisticated sensory and perceptual systems that are present from a very early age in infancy—systems about which Piaget knew little, since so much of the research illustrating their sophistication was done relatively recently (Butterworth, 1994). (See, for instance, the accompanying "Directions in Development" section on infants' mathematical skills.) Critics also point to studies involving children born without arms and legs due to their mothers' use during pregnancy of drugs that, unbeknownst to them at the time, could cause birth defects. These studies show that such children develop quite normally on a cognitive level, despite their lack of practice with motor activities (Decarrie, 1969).

To bolster their views, Piaget's critics also point to recent studies that cast doubt on Piaget's view that infants are incapable of mastering the concept of object permanence until they are close to a year old. For instance, some work suggests that younger infants may not appear to understand object permanence because the techniques used to test their abilities are too insensitive (Baillargeon & DeVos, 1991).

It may be that a 4-month-old doesn't search for a rattle hidden under a blanket because she hasn't learned the motor skills necessary to do the searching—not because she

With the attainment of the cognitive skill of deferred imitation, children are able to imitate people and scenes they have witnessed in the past.

Directions in Development

Mathematical Skills: The Pluses and Minuses of Infancy

Can 5-month-old infants add and subtract?

Surprisingly, yes, according to recent research—yielding an answer that contradicts Piaget's view of infants' cognitive capabilities. Based on data collected by developmental psychologist Karen Wynn (1992, 1995), infants as young as 5 months can calculate the outcome of simple addition and subtraction problems.

To arrive at this conclusion, Wynn developed an ingenious procedure. As illustrated in the photo in Figure 5-3, infants first were shown an object—a 4-inch-high Mickey Mouse statuette. A screen then came up, hiding the statuette. Next, the experimenter showed the infants a second, identical Mickey Mouse, and then placed it behind the same screen.

Finally, depending on the experimental condition, one of two outcomes occurred. In the "correct addition" condition, the screen dropped, revealing the two statuettes (analogous to 1 + 1 = 2). But in the "incorrect addition" condition, the screen dropped to reveal just one statuette (analogous to the incorrect 1 + 1 = 1).

Because infants look longer at unexpected occurrences than at expected ones, the researchers examined the pattern of infants' gaze in the different conditions. In support of the notion that infants can distinguish between correct and incorrect addition, the infants in the experiment gazed longer at the incorrect result than at the correct one. In a similar procedure, infants looked longer at incorrect subtraction problems than at correct ones. The conclusion: Infants have rudimentary mathematical skills.

These results suggest that infants may have an innate ability to comprehend certain basic mathematical functions. This inborn proficiency may form the basis of future understanding of more complex mathematics. Furthermore, the presence of such early mathematical skills lends weight to the notion that other basic skills may have innate components, and calls into question some of Piaget's fundamental views of the infants' capabilities (Canfield & Smith, 1996).

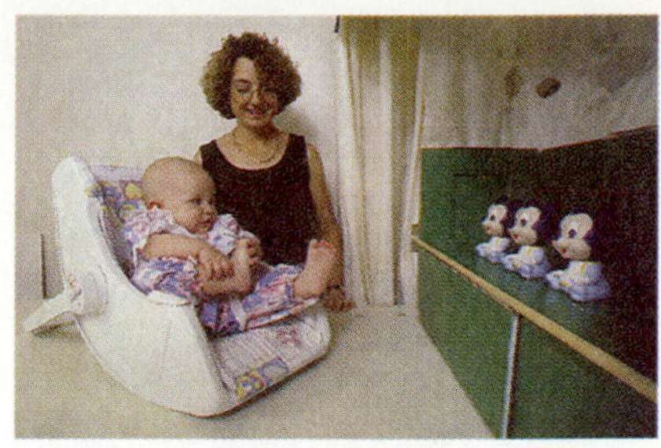

FIGURE 5-3 MICKEY MOUSE MATH Researcher Karen Wynn found that 5-month-olds like Michelle Follet, pictured here, reacted differently according to whether the number of Mickey Mouse statuettes they saw represented correct or incorrect addition.

doesn't understand that the rattle still exists. Similarly, the apparent inability of young infants to comprehend object permanence may reflect more about their memory deficits than their lack of understanding of the concept: The memories of young infants may be poor enough that they simply do not recall the earlier concealment of the toy (Diamond, 1991). In fact, when more age-appropriate tasks were employed, some researchers found indications of object permanence in children as young as 3½ months old (Baillargeon, 1987; Mandler, 1990; E. S. Spelke, 1991).

Other types of behavior likewise seem to emerge earlier than Piaget suggested. For instance, recall the ability of neonates to imitate basic facial expressions of adults just hours after birth, as we discussed in Chapter 3. The presence of such a skill at such an early age contradicts Piaget's view that initially infants are able to imitate only behavior that they see in others, using parts of their own body that they can plainly view—such as the hands and feet. In fact, facial imitation suggests that humans are born with a basic, innate capability for imitating others' actions, a capability that depends on certain kinds of environmental experiences (Meltzoff & Moore, 1989), but one that Piaget believed develops later in infancy.

Some of the most powerful evidence against Piaget's views emerges from work with children in non-Western cultures. For instance, some evidence suggests that the timing of the emergence of various cognitive skills among children in non-Western cultures differs from the timing observed in children living in Europe and the United States. Infants raised in the Ivory Coast of Africa, for example, reach the various substages of the sensorimotor period at an earlier age than infants reared in France (Dasen et al., 1978). This is not altogether surprising, since parents in the Ivory Coast tend to emphasize motor skills more heavily than parents in Western societies, thereby providing greater opportunity for practice of those skills (Dasen et al., 1978; Rogoff & Chavajay, 1995).

Despite the problems we've addressed regarding Piaget's view of the sensorimotor period, even his most passionate critics concede that he has provided us with a masterful description of the broad outlines of sensorimotor development during infancy. His failings seem to be in underestimating the capabilities of younger infants and in his claims that sensorimotor skills develop in a consistent, fixed pattern. Still, his influence has been enormous, and although the focus of many contemporary developmental researchers has shifted to newer information-processing approaches that we discuss next, Piaget remains a towering and pioneering figure (Beilin & Pufall, 1992; Demetriou, Shayer, & Efklides, 1993; R. S. Siegler, 1994).

Review and Rethink

REVIEW

- Jean Piaget's theory of human cognitive development involves a succession of stages through which children progress from birth to adolescence.
- As humans move from one stage to another, the way they understand the world changes as a function of their maturation and their experiences.
- The sensorimotor stage, from birth to about 2 years, involves a gradual progression through simple reflexes, single coordinated activities, interest in the outside world, purposeful combinations of activities, manipulation of actions to produce desired outcomes, and symbolic thought.
- Piaget, whose influence has been substantial, is respected as a careful observer of children's behavior and a generally accurate interpreter of the way human cognitive development proceeds.
- Critics of Piaget fault him for underestimating infants' capabilities and for regarding as universal some aspects of human development that appear to be subject to cultural and individual variations.

RETHINK

- In this chapter, an individual's approach to a book is used as an example of a difference in scheme between children and adults. Can you think of other examples of different ways that adults and children understand and interpret objects or events in their worlds?
- Can you think of examples of the principles of assimilation and accommodation at work in child development? Do these principles function in adult human learning?
- In what ways do you think the concept of object permanence might foster the infant's social and emotional development?

- Why is the emergence of a capacity for mental representation essential for the development of thought? In what ways do you think the mental representations of a blind infant differ from those of a sighted infant? In what ways might they be the same?
- In general, what are some implications for childrearing practices of Piaget's observations about the ways children gain an understanding of the world?

Information-Processing Approaches to Cognitive Development

At the age of 3 months, Amber Nordstrom breaks into a smile as her brother Marcus stands over her crib, picks up a doll, and makes a whistling noise through his teeth. In fact, Amber never seems to tire of Marcus's efforts at making her smile, and soon whenever Marcus appears and simply picks up the doll, her lips begin to curl into a smile.

Clearly, Amber remembers Marcus and his humorous ways. But how did she learn this? What is it that makes Marcus distinctive to her? How does she come to associate Marcus's presence with previous entertaining encounters?

To answer questions such as these, we need to diverge from the road that Piaget laid out for us. Rather than seeking to identify the universal milestones in cognitive development through which all infants pass, as Piaget tried to do, we must consider the processes by which individuals acquire and use the information to which they are exposed. We need, then, to focus less on the qualitative changes in infants' mental lives and consider more closely their quantitative capabilities.

Information-processing approaches to cognitive development seek to identify the ways that individuals take in, use, and store information (R. S. Siegler, 1991). According to this approach, the quantitative changes in infants' abilities to organize and manipulate information represent the hallmarks of cognitive development.

Taking this perspective, cognitive growth is characterized by increasing sophistication in information processing, similar to the way a computer program becomes more sophisticated and useful as the programmer modifies it and as the size of the computer's memory and its computational sophistication increase. Information-processing approaches, then, focus on the types of "mental programs" that people use when they seek to solve problems (Mehler & DuPoux, 1994).

The Basics of Learning: Starting Simply

Six-month-old Michael Samedi was on a car ride with his family when a thunderstorm suddenly began. The storm rapidly became violent, and flashes of lightning were quickly followed by loud thunderclaps. Michael was clearly disturbed and began to sob. With each new thunderclap, the pitch and fervor of his crying increased. Unfortunately, before very long it wasn't just the sound of the thunder that would raise Michael's anxiety; the sight of the lightning alone was enough to make him bawl in fear. In fact, even as an adult, Michael feels his chest tighten and his stomach churn at the mere sight of lightning.

Classical Conditioning. The source of Michael's fear is classical conditioning, a basic type of learning first identified by Russian Physiologist Ivan Pavlov (1849–1936). In **classical conditioning** an organism learns to respond in a particular way to a neutral stimulus that normally does not bring about that type of response.

You've probably heard of the initial demonstration of classical conditioning, which involved Pavlov's research with dogs. Pavlov discovered that by repeatedly pairing two stimuli, such as the sound of a bell and the arrival of meat, he could make hungry dogs learn to respond (in this case by salivating) not only when the meat was presented, but even when the bell was sounded without the presence of meat (Pavlov, 1927).

information-processing approaches *approaches to cognitive development that seek to identify the ways that individuals take in, use, and store information*

classical conditioning *a type of learning in which an organism responds in a particular way to a neutral stimulus that normally does not bring about that type of response*

Ivan Pavlov's research with dogs laid the groundwork for our understanding of classic conditioning.

The key feature of classical conditioning is stimulus substitution, in which a stimulus that doesn't naturally bring about a particular response is paired with a stimulus that does evoke that response. Repeatedly presenting the two stimuli together results in the second stimulus taking on the properties of the first. In effect, the second stimulus is substituted for the first.

Classical conditioning underlies the learning of both pleasurable and undesired responses. For example, our earlier example of Amber Nordstrom, who smiles when her brother Marcus picks up her doll, may be viewed as an example of classical conditioning: The mere presence of Marcus brings the same reaction to the now-conditioned Amber as would Marcus's earlier playing with her doll. On the other hand, Michael Samedi's fear of lightning is also brought about by classical conditioning: The lightning has become a substitute stimulus for thunder, and each stimulus now evokes the response of fear.

One of the earliest examples of the power of classical conditioning in shaping human emotions was demonstrated in the case of an 11-month-old infant called Little Albert in the research report (Watson & Rayner, 1920). Although he initially adored furry animals and showed no fear of rats, he learned to fear them when, during a laboratory demonstration, a loud noise was sounded every time he played with a cute and harmless white rat. In fact, the fear generalized to other furry objects, including rabbits and even a Santa Claus mask. (By the way, such a demonstration would be considered unethical today, and it would never be conducted.)

Infants are capable of learning very early through classical conditioning. For instance, 1- and 2-day-old newborns who are stroked on the head just before being given a drop of a sweet-tasting liquid soon learn to suck and to turn their heads at the head-stroking alone (Blass, Ganchrow, & Steiner, 1984). Clearly, classical conditioning is in operation from the time of birth.

Operant Conditioning. But classical conditioning is not the only mechanism through which infants learn; they also respond to operant conditioning. As we discussed first in Chapter 1, **operant conditioning** is a form of learning in which a voluntary response is strengthened or weakened, depending on its association with positive or negative consequences. In operant conditioning, infants learn to act deliberately on their environments in order to bring about some desired consequence. An infant who learns that crying in a certain way is apt to bring her parents' immediate attention is displaying operant conditioning.

operant conditioning *a form of learning in which a voluntary response is strengthened or weakened, depending on its association with positive or negative consequences*

Like classical conditioning, operant conditioning functions from the earliest days of life. For instance, researchers have found that even newborns readily learn through operant conditioning to keep sucking on a nipple when it permits them to continue hearing their mothers read a story or to listen to music (Butterfield & Siperstein, 1972; DeCasper & Fifer, 1980; Lipsitt, 1986b).

Habituation. Probably the most primitive form of learning is habituation. **Habituation** is the decrease in the response to a stimulus that occurs after repeated presentations of the same stimulus.

habituation *the decrease in the response to a stimulus that occurs after repeated presentations of the same stimulus*

Habituation in infants relies on the fact that the presentation of a novel stimulus typically produces an orienting response, in which the infant quiets, becomes attentive, and experiences a slowed heart rate. But when the novelty wears off due to repeated exposure to the stimulus, the infant no longer reacts with an orienting response. However, when a new and different stimulus is presented, the infant once again reacts with an orienting response. When this happens, we can say that the infant has learned to recognize the original stimulus and to distinguish it from others.

Habituation occurs in every sensory system of infants, and researchers have studied the phenomenon in several ways. One is to examine changes in sucking, which stops temporarily when a new stimulus is presented. This reaction is not unlike that of an adult who temporarily puts down his knife and fork when a dinner companion makes an interesting statement to which he wishes to pay particular attention. Other study techniques include measuring heart rate, respiration rate, and the length of time an infant looks at a particular stimulus.

The ability to learn through habituation is clearly present at birth, and it becomes more pronounced over the first 12 weeks of infancy. As a consequence, habituation is linked to physical and cognitive maturation, and difficulties involving habituation represent a signal of developmental problems (Braddick, 1993; C. K. Rovee-Collier, 1987; Tamis-LeMonda & Bornstein, 1993).

Are There Limits on Learning? Although the three basic processes of learning that we've considered—classical conditioning, operant conditioning, and habituation (summarized in Table 5-2)—are all present at birth, they face considerable constraints. According to researchers Marc Bornstein and Michael Lamb (1992b), three factors limit the success of learning during infancy. One is the *behavioral state* of the infant. In order for learning to occur, infants must be in a sufficiently attentive state to sense, perceive, and recognize the relationship between various stimuli and responses. Without at least a minimal level of attentiveness, learning will not be possible (Papousek & Bernstein, 1969).

Natural constraints on learning are a second limiting factor. Not all behaviors are physically possible for an infant, and infants' perceptual systems, which are not fully developed at birth, may not be sufficiently refined to respond to, or even notice, a particular stimulus. Consequently, certain types of classical and operant conditioning that are possible with older individuals are ineffective with infants.

Finally, *motivational constraints* may limit learning. In order for learning to occur, the response involved must not be so taxing on infants that they simply are unmotivated to respond. If the response is too demanding, learning may fail to appear not because the infants haven't learned an association between a stimulus and a response, but because they just don't have the energy or skills to proceed (C. K. Rovee-Collier, 1987).

Despite these limitations, infants show great capacities to learn. But just how far do the capabilities of infants extend beyond the basic learning processes? Research on memory in infants illustrates just how competent infants are in other regards.

Memory During Infancy: They Must Remember This . . .

Think back to the story of Simona, the Romanian orphan, described at the beginning of the chapter. How likely is it that Simona truly remembers nothing of her infancy? And if she ever does recall her first 2 years of life, how accurate will her memories be? To answer these questions, we need to consider the qualities of memory that exist during infancy.

TABLE 5-2

THREE BASIC PROCESSES OF LEARNING

Type	Description	Example
Classical conditioning	A situation in which an organism learns to respond in a particular way to a neutral stimulus that normally does not bring about that type of response.	1-and 2-day-old newborns are stroked on the head just before being given a drop of a sweet-tasting liquid. They soon learn to suck and turn their heads at the head-stroking alone.
Operant conditioning	A form of learning in which a voluntary response is strengthened or weakened, depending on its positive or negative consequences.	An infant who learns that crying in a certain way is apt to bring her parents' immediate attention is displaying operant conditioning.
Habituation	The decrease in the response to a stimulus that occurs after repeated presentations of the same stimulus. The most primitive form of learning, habituation occurs in every sensory system of infants.	The presentation of a novel stimulus, such as a new, unusual-looking toy, typically produces an orienting response, in which the infant quiets, becomes attentive, and experiences a slowed heart rate. However, after repeated exposure to the toy, the response diminishes.

Memory Capabilities in Infancy. Certainly, infants have **memory** capabilities, defined as the process by which information is initially recorded, stored, and retrieved. As we've seen, the ability of infants to distinguish new stimuli from old, as illustrated by habituation, implies that some memory of the old must be present. Unless the infants had some memory of an original stimulus, it would be impossible for them to recognize that a new stimulus differed from the earlier one (Newcombe, Drummey, & Lie, 1995).

However, infants' capability to habituate and show other basic forms of learning tells us little about how age brings about changes in the capacities of memory and in its fundamental nature. Consider the question of capacity: Do infants' memory capabilities increase as they get older? The answer is clearly affirmative. In one study, infants were taught that they could move a mobile hanging over the crib by kicking (see Figure 5-4). It took only a few days for 2-month-old infants to forget their training, but 6-month-old infants still remembered for as long as 3 weeks (C. Rovee-Collier, 1993; C. K. Rovee-Collier, 1984).

Furthermore, infants who were later prompted to recall the association between kicking and moving the mobile showed evidence that the memory continued to exist even longer. Infants who had received just two training sessions lasting 9 minutes each still recalled about a week later, as illustrated by the fact that they began to kick when placed in the crib with the mobile. Two weeks later, however, they made no effort to kick, suggesting that they had forgotten entirely.

But they hadn't: When a reminder was given—a look at a moving mobile—the memory was apparently reactivated. In fact, the infants could remember the association, following prompting, for as long as an additional month (Sullivan, Rovee-Collier, & Tynes, 1979). Other evidence confirms these results, suggesting that hints can reactivate memories that at first seem lost, and that the older the infant, the more effective such prompting is (Enright et al., 1983; Hayne & Rovee-Collier, 1995; C. K. Rovee-Collier, 1987; C. K. Rovee-Collier & Hayne, 1987).

memory *the process by which information is initially recorded, stored, and retrieved*

Is the nature of memory in infants different from that in older children and adults? Some researchers suggest that memory during infancy is dependent on particular neurological systems in the brain—specifically, the hippocampus—and that memory in later life involves additional structures of the brain (C. A. Nelson, 1995).

On the other hand, although the nature of information and the parts of the brain involved in memory may differ during infancy, other researchers suggest that information is processed similarly throughout the life span. According to memory expert Carolyn Rovee-Collier (1993), people, regardless of their age, gradually lose memories, although they may regain them if reminders are provided. Moreover, the more times a memory is retrieved, the more enduring the memory becomes.

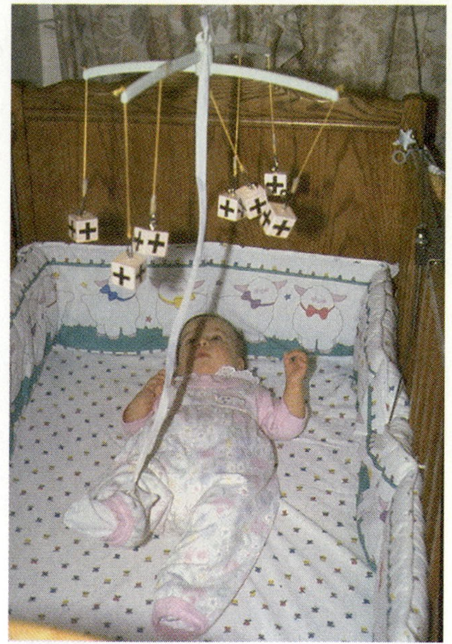

FIGURE 5-4 EARLY SIGNS OF MEMORY Infants who had learned the association between a moving mobile and kicking showed surprising recall ability if they were exposed to a reminder.

The Duration of Memories. Although the processes that underlie memory retention and recall seem similar throughout the life span, the quantity of information stored and recalled does differ markedly as infants develop. Older infants can remember information longer, and they can retrieve it more rapidly.

Researchers disagree on the age from which memories can be retrieved. Some research supports the notion of **infantile amnesia,** the lack of memory for experiences that occurred prior to 3 years of age. For instance, consider whether you can recall the birth of a younger brother or sister. For most college students, if the birth happened before they reached the age of 3, they can remember virtually nothing about the event (Sheingold & Tenney, 1982).

However, other research shows surprising retention in infants (Mandler & McDonough, 1995). For example, Nancy Myers and her colleagues exposed a group of 6-month-old children to an unusual series of events in a laboratory, such as intermittent periods of light and dark and unusual sounds. When the children were later tested at the age of 1½ years or 2½ years, they demonstrated clear evidence that they had some memory of their participation in the earlier experience. Not only did particular behaviors, such as reaching, reflect their earlier participation, but they seemed more familiar with the testing situation itself, showing more willingness to remain in the situation than a control group of same-age children (N. A. Myers, Clifton, & Clarkson, 1987; Perris, Myers, & Clifton, 1990).

Such findings are consistent with evidence that the physical record of a memory in the brain appears to be relatively permanent, suggesting that memories, even from infancy, may be enduring (Newcombe & Fox, 1994). However, because memories may be stored somewhere in the recesses of the brain, they may not be easily, or accurately, retrieved. Memories are susceptible to interference from other, newer information, which may displace or block out the older information, thereby preventing its recall (Potter, 1990). Furthermore, recall of memories is sensitive to the environmental context in which the memories were initially formed. If changes have occurred in the context relating to the initial memories, then recall may be difficult, if not impossible (Ceci & Hembrooke, 1993; C. Rovee-Collier, 1993).

Ultimately, the issue of whether memories formed during infancy are retained into adulthood remains an open—and controversial—issue (Bauer, 1996). Although infants' memories may be highly detailed and can be enduring if the infants experience repeated reminders, it is still not clear how accurate those memories remain over the course of the life span. In fact, research shows that early memories are susceptible to misrecollection if people are exposed to related, and contradictory, information following the initial formation of the memory. Not only does such new information potentially impair recall of the original material, but the new material may be inadvertently incorporated into the original memory, thereby corrupting its accuracy (Fivush, 1995; C. Rovee-Collier et al., 1993).

In sum, the data suggest that, at least theoretically, it is possible for memories to remain intact from a very young age—if subsequent information does not interfere with them. This is a big "if," because most memories are likely to involve experiences that are somehow related to subsequent experiences and therefore susceptible to interference. Ultimately,

infantile amnesia *The lack of memory for experiences that occurred prior to 3 years of age*

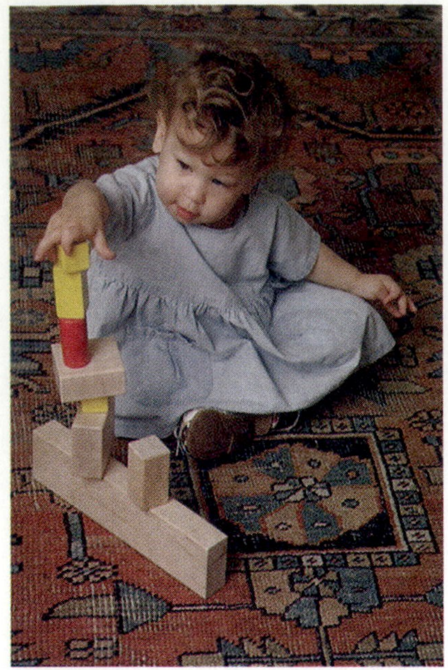

Determining what is meant by intelligence in infants represents a major challenge for developmentalists.

it may be that the validity of recollections of memories from infancy needs to be evaluated on a case-by-case basis.

Individual Differences in Intelligence: Is One Infant Smarter than Another?

> Maddy Rodriguez is a bundle of curiosity and energy. At 6 months of age, she cries heartily if she can't reach a toy, and when she sees a reflection of herself in a mirror, she gurgles and seems, in general, to find the situation quite amusing.
>
> ***
>
> Jared Lynch, at 6 months, is a good deal more inhibited than Maddy. He doesn't seem to care much when a ball rolls out of his reach, losing interest in it rapidly. And, unlike Maddy, when he sees himself in a mirror, he pretty much ignores the reflection.

As anyone who has spent any time at all observing more than one baby can tell you, not all infants are alike. Some are full of energy and life, apparently displaying a natural-born curiosity, while others seem, by comparison, somewhat less interested in the world around them. Does this mean that such infants differ in intelligence?

Answering questions about how and to what degree infants vary in their underlying intelligence is not easy. Although it is clear that different infants show significant variations in their behavior, the issue of just what types of behavior may be related to cognitive ability is complicated. Interestingly, the examination of individual differences between infants was the initial approach taken by developmental specialists to understand cognitive development, and such issues still represent an important focus within the field.

What Is Infant Intelligence? Before we can address whether and how infants may differ in intelligence, we need to consider what is meant by the term *intelligence.* Educators, psychologists, and other experts on development have yet to agree upon a general definition of intelligent behavior, even among adults. Is it the ability to do well in scholastic endeavors? Competence in navigating across treacherous seas, such as that shown by peoples of the South Pacific, who have no knowledge of Western navigational techniques? Proficiency in business negotiations?

The problem of defining intelligence in infants is even more problematic than with adults. Is it the speed with which a new task is learned through classical or operant conditioning? The rapidity of habituation? The age at which an infant learns to crawl or walk? Furthermore, even if we are able to identify particular behaviors that seem validly to differentiate one infant from another in terms of intelligence during infancy, we need to address a further, and probably more important, issue: How well do measures of infant intelligence relate to eventual adult intelligence?

Clearly such questions are not simple, and no simple answers have been found. However, developmental specialists have devised several approaches (summarized in Table 5-3) to illuminate the nature of individual differences in intelligence during infancy.

Developmental Scales. Developmental psychologist Arnold Gesell (1946) formulated the earliest measure of infant development, which was designed to screen out normally developing babies from those with atypical development. Gesell based his scale on examinations of hundreds of babies. He compared their performance at different ages to learn what behaviors were most common at a particular age. If an infant varied significantly from the norms of a given age, he or she was considered to be developmentally delayed or advanced.

Gesell's primary motivation in developing his norms was to screen out abnormally developing infants for purposes of adoption. Following the lead of researchers who sought to quantify intelligence through a specific score (known as an intelligence quotient, or IQ, score), Gesell developed a developmental quotient, or DQ. The **developmental quotient** is

developmental quotient *an overall developmental score that relates to performance in four domains: motor skills, language use, adaptive behavior, and personal-social*

TABLE 5-3

APPROACHES USED TO DETECT DIFFERENCES IN INTELLIGENCE DURING INFANCY

Developmental quotient	Formulated by Arnold Gesell, the developmental quotient is an overall developmental score that relates to performance in four domains: motor skills (balance and sitting), language use, adaptive behavior (alertness and exploration), and personal-social domains (feeding and dressing).
Bayley Scales of Infant Development	Developed by Nancy Bayley, the Bayley Scales of Infant Development evaluate an infant's development from 2 to 30 months. The Bayley Scales focus on two areas: mental (senses, perception, memory, learning, problem solving, and language), and motor abilities (fine and gross motor skills).
Visual-recognition memory measurement	Measures of visual-recognition memory, the memory of and recognition of a stimulus that has been previously seen, relate to intelligence. The more quickly an infant can retrieve a representation of a stimulus from memory, the more efficient, presumably, is that infant's information processing.

an overall developmental score that relates to performance in four domains: motor skills (for example, balance and sitting), language use, adaptive behavior (such as alertness and exploration), and personal-social domains (for example, feeding and dressing).

Later researchers were motivated by different goals. For instance, Nancy Bayley (1969) developed one of the most widely used measures for infants. The **Bayley Scales of Infant Development** evaluate an infant's development from 2 to 30 months. The Bayley Scales focus on two areas: mental and motor abilities. The mental scale focuses on the senses, perception, memory, learning, problem solving, and language, while the motor scale evaluates fine and gross motor skills (see Table 5-4). Like Gesell's approach, the Bayley yields a developmental quotient (DQ). A child who scores at an average level—meaning average performance for other children at the same age—receives a score of 100.

The Bayley Scales of Infant Development are used to assess mental and motor abilities in children between the ages of 2 and 30 months.

The virtue of approaches such as those taken by Gesell and Bayley is that they provide a good snapshot of an infant's current developmental level. Using these scales, we can tell in an objective manner whether a particular infant falls behind or is ahead of his or her same-age peers. The scales are particularly useful in identifying infants who are substantially behind their peers, and who therefore need immediate special attention (Culbertson & Gyurke, 1990).

On the other hand, except in extreme cases, such scales are not very good at all in predicting a child's future course of development. A child whose development at the age of 1 year is relatively slow, as identified by these measures, does not necessarily display slow development at age 5, or 12, or 25. The association between most measures of behavior during infancy and adult intelligence, then, is minimal (Bornstein & Sigman, 1986; DiLalla et al., 1990; L. S. Siegel, 1989).

Because it is difficult with these global measures to obtain measures of infant intelligence that are related to later intelligence, investigators have turned in the last decade to other techniques that may help assess intelligence in a meaningful way. Some have proven to be quite useful.

Information-processing Approaches to Individual Differences in Intelligence. When we speak of intelligence in everyday parlance, we often differentiate between "quick" individuals and those who are "slow." Actually, according to research on the

Bayley Scales of Infant Development *a measure that evaluates an infant's development from 2 to 30 months*

TABLE 5-4

SAMPLE ITEMS FROM THE BAYLEY SCALES OF INFANT DEVELOPMENT

MENTAL SCALE		MOTOR SCALE	
Age (in months)	**Item**	**Age (in months)**	**Item**
0.1	Responds to sound of rattle	0.1	Lifts head when held at shoulder
1.5	Social smile	1.8	Turns: side to back
2.0	Visually recognizes mother	2.3	Sits with support
3.8	Turns head to sound	3.2	Turns: back to side
4.1	Reaches for cube	5.3	Pulls to sitting
4.8	Discriminates stranger	6.4	Rolls: back to stomach
6.0	Looks for fallen spoon	6.6	Sits alone steadily
7.0	Vocalizes four different syllables	8.1	Pulls to standing
9.1	Responds to verbal request	9.6	Walks with help
13.4	Removes pellet from bottle	11.7	Walks alone
14.2	Says two words	14.6	Walks backward
18.8	Uses words to make wants known	16.1	Walks upstairs with help
19.3	Names one picture (e.g., dog)	23.4	Jumps off floor

(*Source:* Adapted from N. Bayley, 1969.)

speed of information processing, such terms hold some truth. Contemporary approaches to infant intelligence suggest that the speed with which infants process information may correlate most strongly with later intelligence, as measured by IQ tests administered during adulthood.

For instance, infants who process information efficiently ought to be able to learn about stimuli more quickly, and thus we would expect that they would turn their attention away from a given stimulus more rapidly than those who are less efficient at information processing. Similarly, measures of **visual-recognition memory,** the memory of and recognition of a stimulus that has been previously seen, also relate to IQ. The more quickly an infant can retrieve a representation of a stimulus from memory, the more efficient, presumably, is that infant's information processing (Tamis-LeMonda & Bornstein, 1993).

Research using an information-processing framework is clear in suggesting a relationship between information processing and cognitive abilities: Measures of how quickly infants lose interest in stimuli that they have previously seen, as well as their responsiveness to new stimuli, correlate moderately well with later measures of intelligence. Infants who are more efficient information processors during the 6 months following birth tend to have higher intelligence scores between 2 and 12 years of age, as well as higher scores on other measures of cognitive competence (Perleth, Lehwald, & Browder, 1993; Rolfe, 1994; Rose & Feldman, 1995; Rose, Feldman, & Wallace, 1992; Sigman et al., in press; Slater, 1995; L. A. Thompson, Fagen, & Fulker, 1991).

Other research suggests that abilities related to the *multimodal approach to perception,* which we considered in Chapter 4, may offer clues about later intelligence. For instance, the information-processing skill of cross-modal transference is associated with intelligence. **Cross-modal transference** is the ability to identify a stimulus that has previously been experienced through only one sense by using another sense. For instance, a baby who is able to recognize by sight a screwdriver that she has previously only touched, but not seen, is displaying cross-modal transference. Research has found that the degree of cross-modal

visual-recognition memory *the memory of and recognition of a stimulus that has been previously seen*

cross-modal transference *the ability to identify a stimulus that has previously been experienced through only one sense by using another sense* transference displayed by an infant at age 1—which requires a high level of abstract thinking—is associated with intelligence scores several years later (Rose et al., 1991; Rose & Ruff, 1987; E. Spelke, 1987).

Although information-processing efficiency and cross-modal transference abilities during infancy relate moderately well to later IQ scores, we need to keep in mind two qualifications. First, even though there is an association between early information-processing capabilities and later measures of IQ, the correlation is only moderate in strength. Other factors, such as the degree of environmental stimulation, also play a crucial role in helping to determine adult intelligence. Consequently, we should not assume that intelligence is somehow permanently fixed in infancy.

Second, and perhaps even more important, intelligence measured by traditional IQ tests relates to a particular type of intelligence, one that emphasizes abilities that lead to academic, and certainly not artistic or professional, success. Consequently, predicting that a child may do well on IQ tests later in life is not the same as predicting that the child will be successful later in life.

Still, the relatively recent finding that an association exists between efficiency of information processing and later IQ scores has changed how we view the consistency of cognitive development across the life span. Whereas the earlier reliance on scales such as the Bayley led to the misconception that little continuity existed, the more recent information-processing approaches suggest that cognitive development unfolds in a more orderly, continuous manner from infancy to the later stages of life.

The Informed Consumer of Development

What Can You Do to Promote Infants' Cognitive Development?

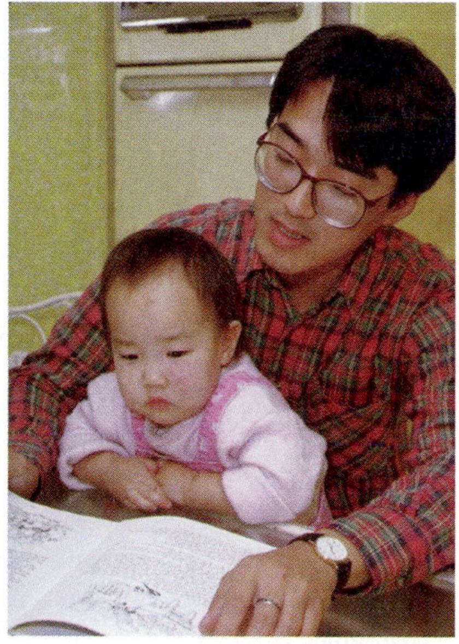

Even if they don't understand the meaning of the words, infants still benefit from being read to.

All parents want their children to reach their full cognitive potential, but sometimes efforts to reach this goal take a bizarre path. For instance, some parents pay hundreds of dollars to enroll in workshops on topics such as "How to Multiply Your Baby's Intelligence" and to buy books with titles such as "How to Teach Your Baby to Read" (Sharpe, 1994).

Do such efforts ever succeed? Although some parents swear they do, there is no scientific support for the efficacy of such programs. For example, despite the many cognitive skills of infants, it should be clear that no infant skill will permit a child actually to read. Furthermore, "multiplying" a baby's intelligence is impossible, and organizations such as the American Academy of Pediatrics and the American Academy of Neurology have denounced programs that claim to do so.

On the other hand, there are things that can be done to promote cognitive development in infants. The following suggestions, based upon findings of developmental researchers, offer a starting point (Meyerhoff & White, 1986; M. Schulman, 1991; Schwebel, Maher, & Fagley, 1990):

- Provide infants the opportunity to explore the world. As Piaget suggests, children learn by doing, and they need the opportunity to explore and probe their environment. Make sure that environment contains a variety of toys, books, and other sources of stimulation. (Also see the "Speaking of Development" interview.)
- Be responsive to infants, on both a verbal and a nonverbal level. Try to speak *with* babies, as opposed to *at* them. Ask questions, listen to their responses, and provide further communication.

- Read to your infants. Although they may not understand the meaning of your words, they will respond to your tone of voice and the intimacy provided by the activity. Reading together also begins to create a lifelong reading habit.
- Keep in mind that you don't have to be with an infant 24 hours a day. Just as infants need time to explore their world on their own, parents and other caregivers need time off from child-care activities.
- Don't push infants and don't expect too much too soon. Your goal should not be to create a genius; it should be to provide a warm, nurturing environment that will allow an infant to reach his or her potential.

Review and Rethink

REVIEW

- Information-processing approaches to the study of cognitive development complement qualitative approaches such as Piaget's by considering quantitative changes in children's abilities to organize and use information.

Speaking of Development

Ellen Sackoff, Toy Designer

Born:	1949
Education:	Hood College, B.A. in art City University of New York, M.A. in developmental psychology
Position:	Managing partner for the Discovery Group
Home:	New York, New York

How would you like to blend your educational background and personal interests and end up in a job developing, evaluating, and marketing kids' toys? That's exactly what Ellen Sackoff did.

Armed with an art degree, Sackoff started her worklife as a textile designer. But she wanted something more. She was determined to combine her art background with her interest in human behavior. So she started a company that designs and develops toys for infants.

As a managing partner of the Discovery Group, Sackoff uses her background in child development to alert parents about the best toys of the year and to test toys for the Children's Television Workshop.

"One might wonder why the field of child development would be involved in making toys for infants," she observes. "The reason is that play has long been a major area of research in psychology. Psychologists look at the play of animals and humans, and they think about what constitutes play and what its role is in development.

- Even young infants are capable of learning through such simple means as classical conditioning, operant conditioning, and habituation.
- Infants clearly have memory capabilities from a very early age, although the duration and accuracy of such memories over the long term are unresolved questions.
- Traditional measures of infant intelligence focus on behavioral attainments, which can help identify developmental delays or advances. However, these measures are not strongly related to measures of adult intelligence.
- Information-processing approaches to assessing intelligence rely on variations in the speed with which infants process information. Infants' speed of information processing correlates moderately with adult measures of IQ.

RETHINK

- According to this chapter, classical conditioning relies on stimulus substitution. Can you think of examples of the use of classical conditioning on adults in everyday life, in such areas as entertainment, advertising, or politics?
- What information from this chapter could you use to refute the claims of books or educational programs that promise to help parents multiply their babies' intelligence or instill advanced intellectual skills in infants?
- This chapter refers to the issue of the duration and accuracy of early childhood memories as "controversial." What sorts of controversies arise out of this issue? Can such controversies be resolved? How?

"People now are focusing more and more on making toys that tune into children's developmental stages."

"If toys are truly tools for play, then let's give babies tools that work well, tools that keep their attention."

"For infants, play serves an important function in their exploration of the world. It is all they do. Through their explorations, infants learn about their world."

Involving child development experts in the design of toys for infants is a relatively new phenomenon, but already there appears to be considerable demand for it.

"Play contributes to all aspects of development," Sackoff explains. "People now are focusing more and more on making toys that tune into children's developmental stages. We make use of the fact that the development of a child follows a fairly universal course.

"In the first few months, we know that infants rely on their eyes and ears, but particularly their eyes. Babies focus more on objects that have sharp contrasts, and that is why there has been a proliferation of black-and-white toys. A lot of bold primary colors are used as well, but pastels are not used much because infants do not see their lack of contrast well."

Another development fact used by toy developers in the creation of new products is that babies like to look at faces, largely because faces are in constant movement.

"Things that move are fascinating to infants. The constant movement and changing of a face are what keep a baby's attention," Sackoff notes. "Many toys incorporate images of faces even though the image is static."

A toy with high play value, according to Sackoff, is one that will sustain infants' interest over time. Children tend to get bored playing with the same toy all the time.

"We test toys largely through observation of kids. We try to see which features are used and which are not," she adds. "This is the basis for removing weak features and emphasizing strong ones.

"Play is important, and good toys are therefore important," she says. "If toys are truly tools for play, then let's give babies tools that work well, tools that keep their attention."

- In what ways is the use of such developmental scales as Gesell's or Bayley's helpful? In what ways is it dangerous? How would you maximize the helpfulness and minimize the danger?
- Information-processing speed in infants correlates moderately well with one sort of adult intelligence. Might there be other indicators in infants that correlate with other adult skills or intelligences? Of what use would such indicators be? What would be their limitations?

THE ROOTS OF LANGUAGE

Mama. No. Cookie. Dad. Jo.

When an infant utters his or her first word, no matter what it is, it marks the start of a transformation: from an entity seemingly not so different from animals of many other species to an entity with skills that are, arguably, unique to human beings.

But those initial words are just the first and most obvious manifestations of language. Many months earlier, infants have been using language to comprehend the world around them. How does this linguistic ability develop? What is the pattern and sequence of language development? And how does the use of language mark a transformation in the cognitive world of infants and their parents? We'll consider these questions, and others, as we address the development of language during the first years of life.

THE FUNDAMENTALS OF LANGUAGE: FROM SOUNDS TO SYMBOLS

Language, the systematic, meaningful arrangement of symbols, provides the basis for communication. But it does more than that: It closely relates to the way infants think and understand the world. It enables them to reflect on people and objects, and to convey their thoughts to others.

In considering the development of language, we need to distinguish between linguistic *comprehension,* the understanding of speech, and linguistic *production,* the use of language to communicate. One principle underlies the relationship between the two: Comprehension precedes production. An 18-month-old may be able to understand a complex series of directions ("pick up your coat from the floor and put it on the chair by the fireplace") but may not yet have strung more than two words together. Comprehension, then, begins earlier than production, and throughout infancy comprehension increases at a faster rate than production. For instance, during infancy comprehension of words expands at a rate of 22 new words a month, while production of words increases at a rate of about 9 new words a month (Benedict, 1979). Other forms of language ability show the same pattern, with comprehension consistently preceding production (see Figure 5-5).

Prelinguistic Communication. Consider the following "dialogue" between a mother and her 3-month-old child (Snow, 1977a):

Mother	*Infant*
	[Smiles]
Oh, what a nice little smile! Yes, isn't that pretty? There now. There's a nice little smile.	
	[Burps]
What a nice wind as well! Yes, that's better, isn't it? Yes. Yes.	

language *the systematic, meaningful arrangement of symbols, which provides the basis for communication*

FIGURE 5-5

COMPREHENSION PRECEDES PRODUCTION

Throughout infancy, the comprehension of speech precedes the production of speech. (*Source:* Adapted from Bornstein & Lamb, 1992a).

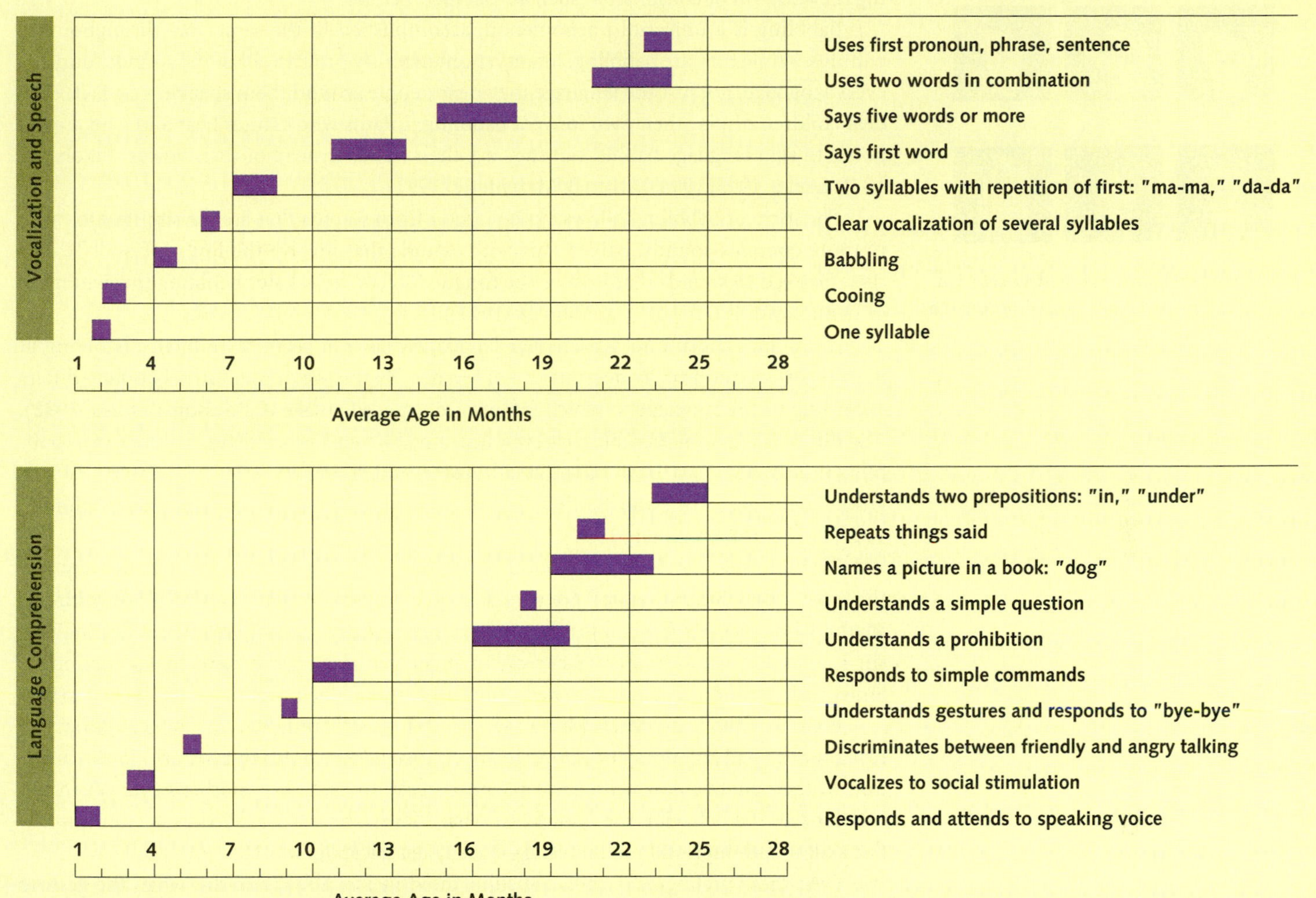

[Vocalizes]

Yes!
There's a nice noise.

Although we tend to think of language in terms of the production first of words and then of groups of words, infants actually begin to communicate linguistically well before they say their first word. Spend 24 hours with even a very young infant and you will hear a variety of sounds: cooing, crying, gurgling, murmuring, and assorted types of other noises. These sounds, although not meaningful in themselves, play an important role in linguistic development, paving the way for true language (Bloom, 1993).

Prelinguistic communication is communication through sounds, facial expressions, gestures, imitation, and other nonlinguistic means. When a father responds to his daughter's "ah" with an "ah" of his own, and then the daughter repeats the sound, and the father responds once again, they are engaged in prelinguistic communication. Clearly, the "ah" sound has no particular meaning. However, its repetition, which mimics the give-and-take of conversation, teaches the infant something about turn taking (Dromi, 1993).

prelinguistic communication *communication through sounds, facial expressions, gestures, imitation, and other nonlinguistic means*

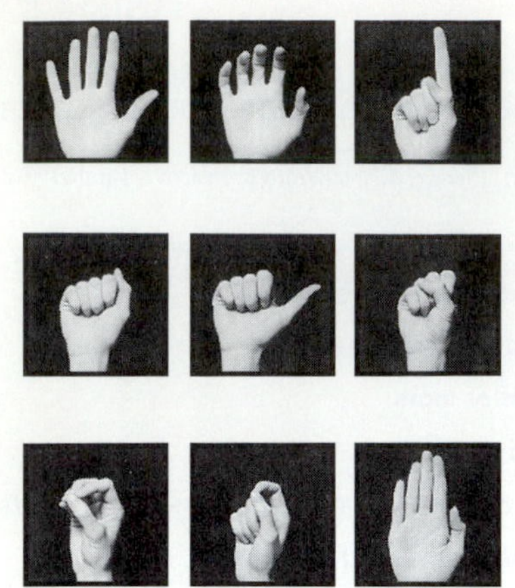

Deaf infants who are exposed to sign language do their own type of babbling, related to the use of signs.

The most obvious manifestation of prelinguistic communication is babbling. **Babbling,** making speechlike but meaningless sounds, starts at the age of 2 or 3 months and continues until around the age of 1 year. When they babble, infants repeat the same vowel sound over and over, changing the pitch from high to low (as in "ee-ee-ee," repeated at different pitches). After the age of 5 months, the sounds of babbling begin to expand, reflecting the addition of consonants (such as "bee-bee-bee-bee").

Babbling is a universal phenomenon, accomplished in the same way throughout all cultures. While they are babbling, infants spontaneously produce all of the sounds found in every language, not just the language they hear people around them speaking. In fact, even deaf children display their own form of babbling: Infants who cannot hear and who are exposed to sign language babble, but they use their hands instead of their voices (Jakobson, 1971; Locke, 1993, 1994; Petitto & Marentette, 1991).

The form of babbling follows a progression from sounds that are the simplest to make to more complex sounds. Babies start with sounds that involve the lips ("p" or "b"), and then proceed to sounds that involve the tongue ("d" or "n"). Later babbling involves nasal or dental sounds ("m" or "t") (Menyuk, 1995).

Although exposure to a particular language does not seem to influence babbling at first, experience eventually does make a difference. By the age of 6 months, babbling differs according to the language to which infants are exposed (Blake & Boysson-Bardies, 1992). The difference is so noticeable that even untrained listeners can distinguish between babbling infants who have been raised in cultures in which French, Arabic, or Cantonese languages are spoken (Boysson-Bardies, Sagart, & Durand, 1984; Boysson-Bardies & Vihman, 1991; Locke, 1983; Vihman, 1991).

Babbling may be the most obviously languagelike achievement of early infancy, but there are other indications of prelinguistic speech. For instance, consider 5-month-old Marta, who spies her red ball just beyond her reach. After reaching for it and finding that she is unable to get to it, she makes a cry of anger that alerts her parents that something is amiss, and her mother hands it to her. Communication, albeit prelinguistic, has occurred.

Four months later, when Marta faces the same situation, she no longer bothers to reach for the ball and doesn't respond in anger. Instead, she holds out her arm in the direction of the ball, but now, with great purpose, seeks to catch her mother's eye. When her mother sees the behavior, she knows just what Marta wants. Clearly, Marta's communicative skills—although still prelinguistic—have taken a leap forward.

Even these prelinguistic skills are supplanted in just a few months, when the gesture gives way to a new communicative skill: producing an actual word. Marta's parents clearly hear her say "ball."

First Words. When a mother and father first hear their child say "Mama" or "Dada," which may occur as early as 9 months, it is hard to be anything but delighted. But their initial enthusiasm may be dampened a bit when they find that the same sound is used to ask for a cookie, a doll, and a ratty old blanket.

First words generally are spoken somewhere around the age of 10 to 14 months. Linguists differ on just how to recognize that a first word has actually been uttered. Some say it is when an infant clearly understands words and can produce a sound that is close to a word spoken by adults, such as a child who uses "mama" for any request she may have. Other linguists use a stricter criterion for the first word; they restrict "first word" to cases in which children give a clear, consistent name to a person, event, or object. In this view, "mama" counts as a first word only if it is consistently applied to the same person, seen in a variety of situations and doing a variety of things, and is not used to label other people (Bornstein & Tamis-LeMonda, 1989; Kamhi, 1986).

Although there is disagreement over when we can say a first word has been uttered, there is no disputing the fact that once an infant starts to produce words, the rate of increase in vocabulary is rapid. By the age of 15 months, the average child has a vocabulary of

babbling *making speechlike but meaningless sounds*

10 words. The child's vocabulary methodically expands until the one-word stage of language development ends at around 18 months. Around that time, a sudden spurt in vocabulary occurs. In just a short period—a few weeks somewhere between 16 and 24 months of age—a child's vocabulary typically increases from 50 to 400 words (E. Bates, Bretherton, & Snyder, 1988; Fenson et al., 1994; Gleitman & Landau, 1994).

holophrases *one-word utterances that depend on the particular context in which they are used to determine meaning*

As you can see from the list in Table 5-5, the first words in children's early vocabularies typically regard objects and things, both animate and inanimate. Most often they refer to people or objects who constantly appear and disappear ("Mama"), to animals ("kitty"), or to temporary states ("wet"). These first words are often **holophrases,** one-word utterances that depend on the particular context in which they are used to determine meaning. For instance, a youngster may use the phrase "ma" to refer to his mother's coming in and out or to ask for something to eat (E. Clark, 1983; Dromi, 1987; K. Nelson, 1981).

First Sentences. When Aaron was 19 months old, he heard his mother coming up the back steps, as she did every day just before dinner. Aaron turned to his father and distinctly said, "Ma come." In stringing those two words together, Aaron took a giant step in his language development.

The increase in vocabulary that comes at around 18 months is accompanied by another accomplishment: the linking together of individual words into sentences that convey a single thought. Although there is a good deal of variability in the time at which children first create two-word phrases, it is generally around 8 to 12 months after they say their first word.

The linguistic advance represented by two-word combinations is important because the linkage not only provides labels for things in the world, but also indicates the relations between them. For instance, the combination may declare something about possession ("Mama

TABLE 5-5

COMPREHENSION AND PRODUCTION OF WORDS

	Comprehension Percentage	Production Percentage
1. *Nominals (words referring to "things")*	56	61
Specific (people, animals, objects)	17	11
General (words referring to all members of a category)	39	50
Animate (objects)	9	13
Inanimate (objects)	30	37
Pronouns (e.g., this, that, they)	1	2
2. *Action words*	36	19
Social action games (e.g., peekaboo)	15	11
Events (e.g., "eat")	1	NA
Locatives (locating or putting something in specific location)	5	1
General action and inhibitors (e.g., "don't touch")	15	6
3. *Modifiers*	3	10
Status (e.g., "all gone")	2	4
Attributes (e.g., "big")	1	3
Locatives (e.g., "outside")	0	2
Possessives (e.g., "mine")	1	1
4. *Personal-social*	5	10
Assertions (e.g., "yes")	2	9
Social expressive (e.g., "bye-bye")	4	1

Note: Percentage refers to percentage of children who include this type of word among their first 50 words.
(*Source:* Adapted from Benedict, 1979.)

telegraphic speech *speech in which words not critical to the message are left out*

underextension *the act of using words too restrictively, common among children just mastering spoken language*

overextension *the act of using words too broadly, overgeneralizing their meaning*

key") or recurrent events ("Dog bark"). Interestingly, most early sentences don't represent demands or even necessarily require a response. Instead, they are often merely comments and observations about events occurring in the child's world (Halliday, 1975; Slobin, 1970).

Two-year-olds using two-word combinations tend to employ particular sequences that are similar to the ways in which adult sentences are constructed. For instance, sentences in English typically follow a pattern in which the subject of the sentence comes first, followed by the verb, and then the object ("Josh threw the ball.") Children's speech most often uses a similar order, although not all the words are initially included. Consequently, a child might say "Josh threw" or "Josh ball" to indicate the same thought. What is significant is that the order is typically not "threw Josh" or "ball Josh," but rather the usual order of English, which makes the utterance much easier for an English speaker to comprehend (R. Brown, 1973; Hirsh-Pasek & Michnick-Golinkoff, 1995; Maratsos, 1983).

Although the creation of two-word sentences represents an advance, the language used by children still is by no means adultlike. For instance, 2-year-olds produce **telegraphic speech,** in which words not critical to the message are left out, similar to the way we might write a telegram for which we were paying by the word. Rather than saying, "I showed you the book," a child using telegraphic speech might say, "I show book." "I am drawing a dog" might become "Drawing dog" (see Table 5-6).

Early language has other characteristics that differentiate it from the language used by adults. For instance, consider Sarah, who refers to the blanket she sleeps with as "blankie." When her Aunt Ethel gives her a new blanket, Sarah refuses to call the new one a "blankie," restricting the word to her original blanket.

Sarah's inability to generalize the label of "blankie" to blankets in general is an example of **underextension,** using words too restrictively, which is common among children just mastering spoken language. Underextension occurs when language novices think that a word refers to a specific concept, instead of to all examples of the concept (Caplan & Barr, 1989).

As infants grow more adept with language, the opposite phenomenon sometimes occurs. In **overextension,** words are used too broadly, overgeneralizing their meaning. For example, when Sarah referred to buses, trucks, and tractors as "cars," she was guilty of overextension, making the assumption that any object with wheels must be a car. Although overextension reflects speech errors, it also shows that advances are occurring in the child's thought processes: The child is beginning to develop general mental categories and concepts (Behrend, 1988).

The Origins of Language Development. The immense strides in language development during the preschool years raise a fundamental question: How does proficiency in language come about? Linguists are deeply divided on how to answer this question.

TABLE 5-6

CHILDREN'S IMITATION OF SENTENCES SHOWING DECLINE OF TELEGRAPHIC SPEECH

	Eve, 25.5 Months	Ivan, 28.5 Months	Soshanna, 30 Months	Miguel, 31.5 Months	Jimmy, 32 Months	Simona, 35.5 Months
I showed you the book.	I show book.	(I show) book.	C	I show you the book.	C	Show you the book.
I am very tall.	(My) tall.	I (very) tall.	I very tall.	I'm very tall.	Very tall.	I very tall.
It goes in a big box.	Big box.	Big box.	In big box.	It goes in the box.	C	C
I am drawing a dog.	Drawing dog.	I draw dog.	I drawing dog.	Dog.	C	C
I will read the book.	Read book.	I will read book.	I read the book.	I read the book.	C	C
I can see a cow.	See cow.	I want see cow.	C	Cow.	C	C
I will not do that again.	Do again.	I will that again.	I do that.	I again.	C	C

C = correct imitation.
(*Source:* Adapted from Brown & Fraser, 1963.)

One response comes from the basic principles of learning. According to the **learning theory approach,** language acquisition follows the basic laws of reinforcement and conditioning discussed earlier. For instance, a child who articulates the word "da" may be hugged and praised by her father, who jumps to the conclusion that she is referring to him. This reaction reinforces the child, who is more likely to repeat the word. In sum, the learning theory perspective on language acquisition suggests that children learn to speak by being rewarded for making sounds that approximate speech. Through the process of *shaping,* language becomes more and more similar to adult speech (Skinner, 1957).

learning theory approach *the theory that language acquisition follows the basic laws of reinforcement and conditioning*

universal grammar *a similar underlying structure shared by all the world's languages, according to linguist Noam Chomsky's theory*

language-acquisition device (LAD) *a neural system of the brain hypothesized to permit understanding of language structure and provide strategies for learning the particular characteristics of a language*

There's a problem, though, with the learning theory approach. It doesn't seem to explain adequately how readily children acquire the rules of language. For instance, novice users of language are reinforced not only when they use grammatically impeccable language, but also when they make errors. Parents are apt to be just as responsive if their child says, "Why the dog won't eat?" as they are if the child phrases the question more correctly ("Why won't the dog eat?"). Both forms of the question are understood correctly, and both elicit the same response; reinforcement is provided for both correct and incorrect language usage. Under such circumstances, learning theory is hard put to explain how children learn to speak properly.

Still other problems exist with learning theory explanations. For instance, research shows that children are able to move beyond specific utterances they have heard, and produce novel phrases, sentences, and constructions. Furthermore, children can apply rules to nonsense words. In one study, 4-year-old children heard the nonsense verb "to pilk" in the sentence "the bear is pilking the horse." Later, when asked what was happening to the horse, they responded by placing the nonsense verb in the correct tense and voice: "He's getting pilked by the bear."

Such conceptual difficulties with the learning theory approach have led to the development of an alternative approach, championed by the linguist Noam Chomsky (1968, 1978, 1991). Chomsky argues that there is a genetically determined, innate mechanism that directs the development of language. He suggests that people are born with an innate capacity to use language that emerges, more or less automatically, due to maturation.

Chomsky's analysis of different languages suggests that all the world's languages share a similar underlying structure, which he calls **universal grammar.** In this view, the human brain is wired with a neural system called the **language-acquisition device,** or **LAD,** that both permits the understanding of language structure and provides a set of strategies and techniques for learning the particular characteristics of the language to which a child is exposed. In this view, language is uniquely human, made possible by a genetic predisposition to both comprehend and produce words and sentences (Lust, Hermon, & Kornfilt, 1994; Lust, Suner, & Whitman, 1995).

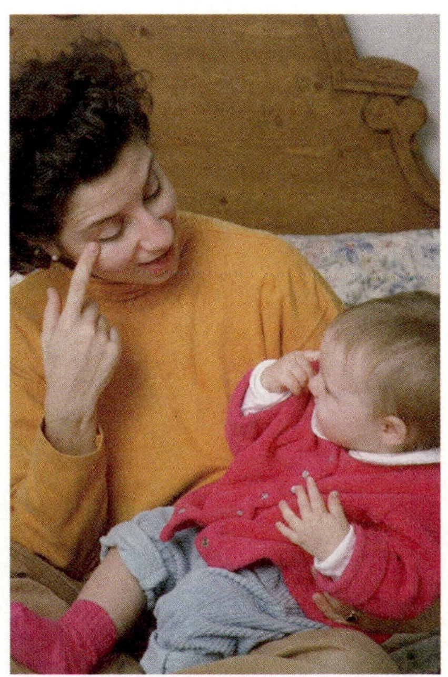

Motherese or, more precisely, infant-directed speech, includes the use of short, simple sentences and is said in a pitch that is higher than that used with older children and adults.

Like the learning theory approach, the view that language represents an innate ability unique to humans has its critics. For instance, some researchers argue that certain primates are able to learn at least the basics of language, an ability that calls into question the uniqueness of the human linguistic capacity. Other critics suggest that we must identify mechanisms other than either a language-acquisition device or learning theory principles if we are to understand fully the processes that underlie language development. In short, the origins of language remain a hotly contested question (MacWhinney, 1991; Savage-Rumbaugh et al., 1993).

Speaking to Children: The Language of Motherese

Say the following sentence aloud: Do you like the apple dumpling?

Now pretend that you are going to ask the same question of an infant, and speak it as you would for the child's ears.

Chances are several things happened when you translated the phrase for the infant. First of all, the wording probably changed, and you may have said something like, "Does baby like the apple dumpling?" At the same time, the pitch of your voice probably rose, your general intonation most likely had a singsong quality, and you probably separated your words carefully.

motherese *a type of speech directed toward infants that is characterized by short, simple sentences*

Motherese, or Infant-directed Speech. The shift in your language was due to an attempt to use what has been called **motherese,** a style of speech directed toward infants. Motherese is characterized by short, simple sentences, and it typically refers to concrete objects in the baby's environment. Pitch becomes higher, the range of frequencies increases, and intonation is more varied. There is also repetition of words, and topics are restricted to items that are assumed to be comprehensible by infants.

Sometimes motherese includes amusing sounds that are not even words, imitating the prelinguistic speech of infants. In other cases, it has little formal structure, but is similar to the kind of telegraphic speech that infants use as they develop their own language skills. Even deaf mothers use a form of motherese: When communicating with their infants, deaf mothers use signed language at a significantly slower tempo than when communicating with adults, and they frequently repeat the signs (Masataka, 1993; Swanson, Leonard, & Gandour, 1992).

Motherese changes as children become older. Around the end of the first year, motherese takes on more adultlike qualities. Sentences become longer and more complex, although individual words are still spoken slowly and deliberately. Pitch is also used to focus attention on particularly important words.

Because it is inexactly named—fathers and other adults use the same kind of speech with infants, not just mothers—motherese has come to be called *infant-directed speech.* Whatever name is used, however, the way in which adults speak to children plays an important role in infants' acquisition of language. Newborns prefer such speech to regular language, a fact that suggests that they may be particularly receptive to it (Fernald, 1991; Hepper et. al., 1993). Furthermore, some research suggests that unusually extensive exposure to motherese early in life is related to the comparatively early appearance of first words and earlier linguistic competence in other areas (Bornstein & Ruddy, 1984; Cooper & Aslin, 1990, 1994; Hampson & Nelson, 1993; Hoff-Ginsberg, 1986).

Gender Differences. To a girl, a bird is a birdie, a blanket a blankie, and a dog a doggy. To a boy, a bird is a bird, a blanket a blanket, and a dog a dog.

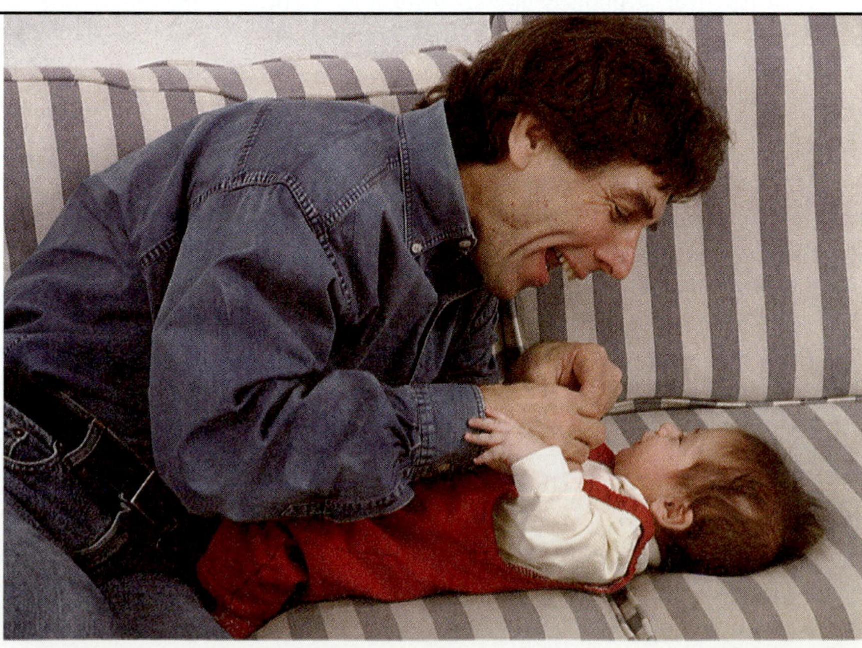

Infant-directed speech plays an important role in infants' acquisition of language.

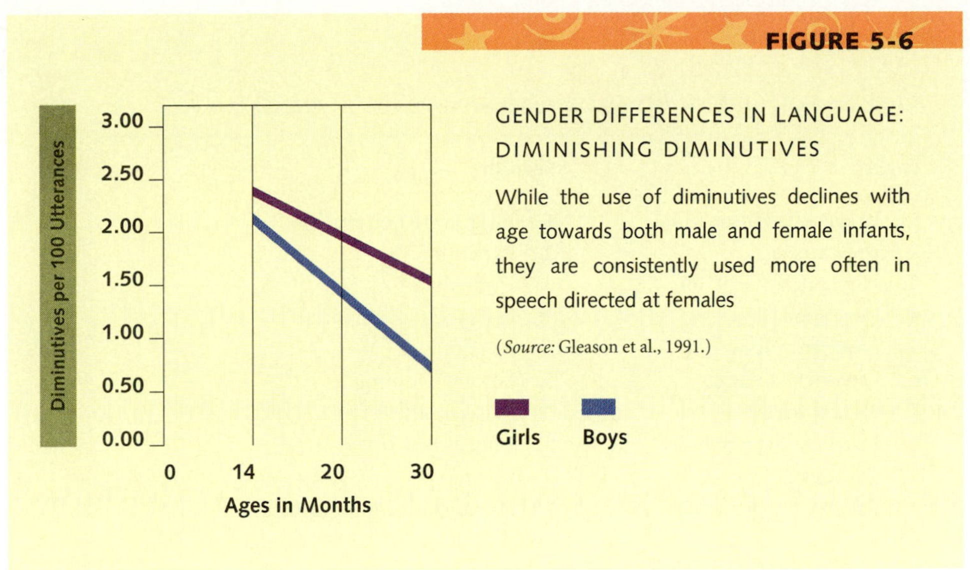

FIGURE 5-6

GENDER DIFFERENCES IN LANGUAGE: DIMINISHING DIMINUTIVES

While the use of diminutives declines with age towards both male and female infants, they are consistently used more often in speech directed at females

(*Source:* Gleason et al., 1991.)

At least that's what parents of boys and girls appear to think, as illustrated by the language they use toward their sons and daughters. Virtually from the time of birth, the language parents employ with their children differs depending on the child's sex, according to research conducted by developmental psychologist Jean Berko Gleason (1987; Gleason et al., 1984, 1991).

Gleason found that, by the age of 32 months, girls hear twice as many diminutives (words such as "kitty" or "dolly" instead of "cat" or "doll") as boys hear. Although the use of diminutives declines with increasing age, their use consistently remains higher in speech directed at girls than in that directed at boys (see Figure 5-6).

Parents also are more apt to respond differently to children's requests depending on the child's gender. For instance, when turning down a child's request, mothers are likely to respond with a firm "no" to a male child, but to soften the blow to a female child by providing a diversionary response ("Why don't you do this instead?") or by somehow making the refusal less direct. Consequently, boys tend to hear firmer, clearer language, while girls are exposed to warmer phrases, often referring to inner emotional states (Perlmann & Gleason, 1990).

Do such differences in language directed at boys and girls during infancy affect their behavior as adults? Although there is no direct evidence that plainly supports such an association, it is clear that men and women use different sorts of language as adults. For instance, as adults, women tend to use more tentative, less assertive language than men. While we don't know if these differences are a reflection of early linguistic experiences, such findings are certainly intriguing (Matlin, 1987; Tannen, 1991).

Developmental Diversity

Is Infant-directed Speech Similar Across All Cultures?

Do mothers in the United States, Japan, and Italy speak the same way to their infants?

In some respects, they clearly do. Although the words themselves differ across languages, the way the words are spoken is quite similar. According to a growing body of research, there are basic similarities across cultures in the nature of infant-directed speech (Grieser & Kuhl, 1988; Papousek & Papousek, 1991).

TABLE 5-7

RANKINGS OF 10 MOST COMMON FEATURES IN ENGLISH AND SPANISH

English	Spanish
1. Exaggerated intonation	1. Exaggerated intonation
2. Breathiness	2. Repetition
3. High pitch	3. High pitch
4. Repetition	4. Instructional emphasis
5. Lowered volume	5. Attentionals
6. Lengthened vowels	6. Lowered volume
7. Creaky voice	7. Raised volume
8. Instructional emphasis	8. Lengthened vowels
9. Tenseness	9. Fast tempo
10. Falsetto	10. Personal pronoun substitution

(*Source:* Adapted from Blount, 1982.)

Consider, for instance, the comparison in Table 5-7 of the major characteristics of speech directed at infants used by native speakers of English and Spanish. Of the 10 most frequent features, 6 are common to both: exaggerated intonation, high pitch, repetition, lowered volume, lengthened vowels, and instructional emphasis (that is, heavy stress on certain key words, such as emphasizing the word "ball" in the sentence, "No, that's a *ball*") (Blount, 1982).

More precise comparisons, across a broader range of languages, reveal other similarities. For instance, Figure 5-7 shows the remarkable similarities in speech pitch among speakers of different languages when they are directing speech to infants, as opposed to adults (Fernald et al., 1989). It is particularly interesting that in every case mothers raise their pitch more than fathers when speaking to infants. Furthermore, speakers of American English show the greatest differences between speech to an infant and speech to an adult.

The cross-cultural similarities in infant-directed speech are so great, in fact, that they appear in some facets of language specific to particular types of interactions. For in-

FIGURE 5-7

INFANT-DIRECTED SPEECH

Across a variety of cultures, both mothers and fathers use speech pitch of a higher frequency when speaking to infants than to other adults. (*Source:* Fernald et al., 1989.)

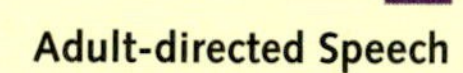

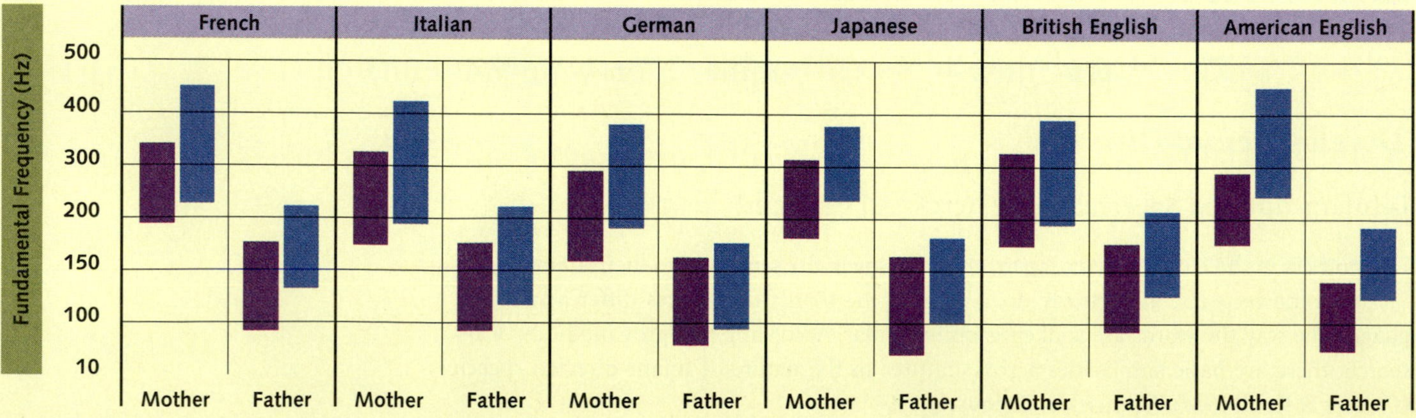

stance, evidence comparing American English, German, and Mandarin Chinese speakers shows that in each of the languages, pitch rises when a mother is attempting to get an infant's attention or produce a response, while pitch falls when she is trying to calm an infant (Papousek & Papousek, 1991).

Why do we find such similarities across very different languages? One hypothesis is that the characteristics of infant-directed speech activate innate responses in infants. For instance, infants seem to prefer infant-directed speech over adult-directed speech, suggesting that their perceptual systems may be more responsive to such characteristics. Another explanation is that infant-directed speech facilitates language development, providing cues as to the meaning of speech before infants have developed the capacity to understand the meaning of words (Fernald, 1989; Fernald & Kuhl, 1987).

The Informed Consumer of Development

Assessing Language Development

Given the critical role that language plays in cognitive development, parents often are concerned that their infant's language development proceeds on schedule. Although there are no hard and fast rules, given the wide variability in the timing of children's first words and the ways their vocabularies develop (Shore, 1994), there are several guidelines that indicate whether language development is normal. An infant who shows the following abilities is probably developing normally, according to psycholinguist Anne Dunlea (W. Fowler, 1990; Yarrow, 1990):

- Understanding at least some things that are heard. This means that, at the minimum, the child has some receptive language and is capable of hearing. For instance, most children can discriminate between friendly and angry speech by the age of 6 months.
- Producing sounds, such as a raspberry noise, at around 6 or 7 months of age. Children who are deaf may end prelinguistic speech at this point, even if they produced it earlier, because they cannot hear themselves.
- Using gestures to communicate. Pointing and reaching are often forerunners of language. Most children look towards an object pointed to by an adult by the age of 9 months, and most use pointing themselves before the end of their first year.
- Pretending to use language. Even if the words make no sense, children may pretend to use language before they actually begin to speak, indicating that they at least know how language functions.

What if a child does not demonstrate any of these abilities? It would be reasonable to have a pediatrician evaluate the child. Keep in mind, however, the wide range of variations in language development among different children and the fact that the vast number of children develop quite normally.

Review and Rethink

REVIEW

- Before they speak their first words, infants understand many adult utterances and engage in several forms of prelinguistic communication, including the use of facial expressions, gestures, and babbling.
- Children typically produce their first words between 10 and 14 months, and rapidly increase their vocabularies from that point on, especially during a spurt at about 18 months.
- Children's language development proceeds through a pattern of holophrases, two-word combinations, and telegraphic speech. Their linguistic development reflects their growing sense of the relations between objects in the world, and their acquisition of general mental categories and concepts.
- Learning theorists believe that basic learning processes adequately account for language development, while Noam Chomsky and his followers argue that humans have an innate language capacity that naturally facilitates language development.
- When talking to infants, adults of all cultures tend to use infant-directed speech, or motherese. This type of speech seems to appeal to infants and to facilitate their linguistic development.
- According to some research, adults tend to speak more indirectly to girls and more directly to boys, which may contribute to behavioral differences later in life.

RETHINK

- What are some ways in which children's linguistic development reflects their acquisition of new ways of interpreting and dealing with their world?
- If Chomsky is correct about the language-acquisition device, why do children raised in isolation not develop language naturally? Why do adults have such difficulty learning a second language?
- American Sign Language (ASL) is generally regarded as a true language. What characteristics must ASL have to fit Chomsky's conception of a language? Do you think humans are genetically predisposed to acquire a language such as ASL?
- What are some implications of differences in the ways adults speak to boys and girls? How might such speech differences contribute to later differences not only in speech, but also in attitudes?

LOOKING BACK

What can we learn about children's views of the world from Piaget's theories of cognitive development?

1. Jean Piaget, a Swiss developmental psychologist, was a highly influential theorist and experimenter most noted for his pioneering work in child development. His basic premise is that infants achieve their understanding of the world through direct motor behavior, rather than from other people or through sensation and perception.

2. Piaget's stage theory asserts that children pass through stages of cognitive development in a fixed order. The stages represent changes not only in the quantity of knowledge infants gain, but in the quality of that knowledge as well. Their schemes, or organized patterns of understanding aspects of the world, shift as they progress from stage to stage.

3. According to Piaget, all children pass gradually through the four major stages of cognitive development (sensorimotor, preoperational, concrete operational, and formal operational) and their various substages when the children are at an appropriate level of maturation and are exposed to relevant types of experiences.

4. In the Piagetian view, children's understanding grows through assimilation of their experiences into their current way of thinking or through accommodation of their current way of thinking to their experiences.

5. During the sensorimotor period, which stretches from birth to about 2 years old, and which Piaget divides into six substages, infants progress from the use of simple reflexes, through the development of repeated and integrated actions that gradually increase in complexity, to the ability to generate purposeful effects from their actions. By the end of the sixth substage of the sensorimotor period, infants are beginning to engage in symbolic thought.

6. An important concept in the Piagetian view is object permanence, the realization that people and objects continue to exist even when they are not seen. This concept is regarded as developing during the fourth substage of the sensorimotor period.

7. Piaget's theories have had great influence on the field of child development. Modern researchers agree that Piaget was an unparalleled observer of child behavior, that his insights into the ways children learn are correct, and that the broad outlines of his stages of development are accurate. However, they criticize his underestimation of infants' abilities and his assumption that the pattern of cognitive development is universal, instead of potentially influenced by cultural and other factors.

How do infants process information and learn about the world?

8. Information-processing approaches to the study of cognitive development seek to learn how individuals receive, organize, store, and retrieve information. Such approaches differ from and supplement qualitative approaches such as Piaget's by considering quantitative changes in children's abilities to process information.

9. From birth, infants learn through such simple means as habituation (a decreased response due to familiarity), classical conditioning (a response displaced from one stimulus to another), and operant conditioning (an increased response due to association with a desirable effect).

10. For all their abilities, infants' learning is clearly limited by their behavioral state, by natural constraints, and by motivational factors influenced by the demands of the learning task.

What sorts of memories do infants have?

11. Infants have memory capabilities from their earliest days, as evidenced by their ability to habituate and to learn in other basic ways. With prompting, they can retrieve memories after considerable intervals.

12. The accuracy of infant memories is a matter of debate. There is evidence that some information taken in by the infant at a very early age can be successfully stored and retrieved. However, there is also evidence that infant memories are susceptible to interference from later experiences and memories.

How can we measure infant intelligence, and how does it relate to adult intelligence?

13. Traditional measures of infant intelligence, such as Gesell's developmental quotient and the Bayley Scales of Infant Development, focus on average behavior observed at particular ages in large numbers of children. Such measures can help identify developmental delays or advances at given points in time. However, they do not effectively predict adult intelligence.
14. Information-processing approaches to assessing intelligence rely on variations in the speed with which infants process information. Infants' speed of information processing appears to correlate moderately well with adult measures of IQ. However, this finding has limited application because intelligence is not a fixed quantity during the life span, is influenced by environmental factors, and includes aspects and components not measured by IQ tests.

By what processes do children learn to use language?

15. Prelinguistic communication involves the use of sounds, gestures, facial expressions, imitation, and other nonlinguistic means to express thoughts and states. Babbling is a form of prelinguistic communication, which proceeds through regular stages and, with other forms of prelinguistic communication, prepares the infant for speech.
16. Infants typically produce their first words between the ages of 10 and 14 months. Thereafter, vocabulary increases rapidly, especially during a spurt at around 18 months. At about the same time, children typically begin to link words together into primitive sentences that express single thoughts.
17. Beginning speech is characterized by the use of holophrases, in which a single word conveys more complex meaning based on its context; telegraphic speech, in which only essential sentence components are used; underextension, in which an overly restrictive meaning is assigned to a word; and overextension, in which an overly generalized meaning is assigned to a word.
18. Features of the child's native language begin to emerge as early as the babbling stage, when sounds other than those of the home language gradually disappear. In addition, the structure of the home language begins to be reflected even in telegraphic speech, when word order mirrors that used by mature speakers of the home language.
19. One theory of how humans develop language is the learning theory approach, which assumes that adults and children use basic behavioral processes—such as conditioning, reinforcement, and shaping—in language learning. A radically different approach is proposed by Chomsky, who holds that humans are genetically endowed with a language acquisition device, which permits them to detect and use the principles of universal grammar that underlie all languages.

How do children influence the language that adults use to address them?

20. Adult language is influenced by the children to whom it is addressed. Infant-directed speech (also called motherese) takes on characteristics, surprisingly invariant across cultures, that make it appealing to infants and that probably facilitate language development.
21. Adult language also exhibits differences based on the gender of the child to whom it is directed. For example, some research indicates that adult speech addressed to boys is more direct than that addressed to girls. It is possible that gender differences in the language heard during infancy may have effects that emerge later in life.

Key Terms and Concepts

scheme (p. 154)
assimilation (p. 155)
accommodation (p. 155)
sensorimotor stage (of cognitive development) (p. 155)
circular reaction (p. 156)
goal-directed behavior (p. 157)
object permanence (p. 158)
mental representation (p. 159)
deferred imitation (p. 159)
information-processing approaches (p. 163)
classical conditioning (p. 163)
operant conditioning (p. 164)
habituation (p. 165)
memory (p. 166)
infantile amnesia (p. 167)
developmental quotient (p. 168)
Bayley Scales of Infant Development (p. 169)
visual-recognition memory (p. 170)
cross-modal transference (p. 170)
language (p. 174)
prelinguistic communication (p. 175)
babbling (p. 176)
holophrases (p. 177)
telegraphic speech (p. 178)
underextension (p. 178)
overextension (p. 178)
learning theory approach (p. 179)
universal grammar (p. 179)
language-acquisition device (LAD) (p. 179)
motherese (p. 180)

CHAPTER 6

INFANCY

Social and Personality Development in Infancy

PROLOGUE

THE VELCRO CHRONICLES

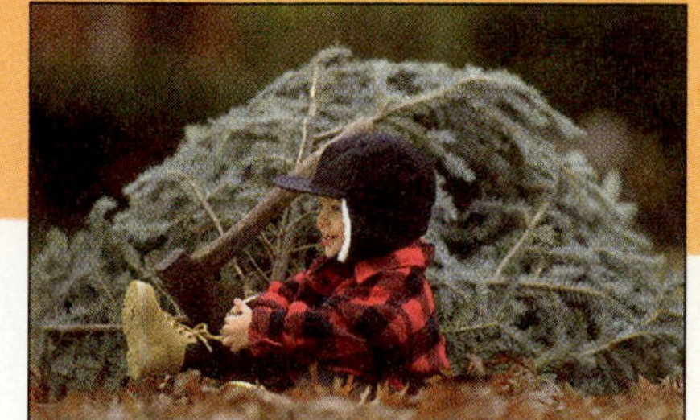

It was during the windy days of March that the problem in the day-care center first arose. Its source: 10-month-old Russell Ruud. Otherwise a model of decorum, Russell had somehow learned how to unzip the Velcro chin strap to his winter hat. He would remove the hat whenever he got the urge, seemingly oblivious to the potential health problems that might follow.

But that was just the start of the real difficulty. To the chagrin of the teachers in the day-care center, not to speak of the children's parents, soon other children were following his lead, removing their own caps at will.

Russell's mother, made aware of the anarchy at the day-care center—and the other parents' distress over Russell's behavior—pleaded innocent. "I never showed Russell how to unzip the Velcro," claimed his mother, Judith Ruud, an economist with the Congressional Budget Office in Washington, D.C. "He learned by trial and error, and the other kids saw him do it one day when they were getting dressed for an outing." (Goleman, 1993, C10)

By then, however, it was too late for excuses: Russell, it seems, was an excellent teacher. Keeping the children's hats on their heads proved to be no easy task. Even more ominous was the thought that if the infants could master the Velcro straps on their hats, would they soon be undoing the Velcro fasteners on their shoes and removing *them*?

LOOKING AHEAD

Russell's behavior embodies what recent research suggests is a heretofore unsuspected outcome of infants' participation in day care: the acquisition of new skills and abilities from more "expert" peers. Infants, as we will see, have an amazing capacity to learn from other children, and their interactions with others can play a central role in their developing social and emotional worlds.

In this chapter we consider social and personality development in infancy. We begin by examining the emotional lives of infants, considering which emotions they feel and how well they can decode others' emotions. We also consider how infants use others to determine how to react, and their views of their own and others' mental lives.

We then turn to a consideration of social relationships. We look at how bonds of attachment are forged, and the ways in which infants interact with family members and peers.

Finally, we will cover the characteristics that differentiate one infant from another. We'll discuss differences in the way children are treated depending on their gender. We'll consider the nature of family life at the close of the twentieth century and how it differs from earlier eras. The chapter closes with a look at the benefits and costs of infant day care outside the home, a child-care option increasingly employed.

In sum, after reading this chapter, you'll be able to answer these questions:

- Do infants have emotions?
- How do infants interpret the emotions of others?
- What are some characteristics of infants' mental life?
- What is attachment in infancy, and how does it relate to the future social competence of individuals?
- What roles do mothers, fathers, and infants play in social development?

- What sorts of interactions do infants engage in with caregivers and other children?
- What are some of the ways that infants differ from one another?
- How are societal changes reflected in family life and child-care practices?
- Is day care beneficial or harmful for infants?

FORMING THE ROOTS OF SOCIABILITY

Germaine smiles when he catches a glimpse of his mother. Tawanda looks angry when her mother takes away the spoon that she is playing with. Sydney scowls when a loud plane flies overhead.

A smile. A look of anger. A scowl. The emotions of infancy are written all over a baby's face. Yet do infants experience emotions in the same way that adults do? When do they become capable of understanding what others are experiencing emotionally? And how do they use others' emotional states to make sense of their environment? We consider some of these questions as we seek to understand how infants develop emotionally and socially.

EMOTIONS IN INFANCY: DO INFANTS EXPERIENCE EMOTIONAL HIGHS AND LOWS?

Anyone who spends any time at all around infants knows they display facial expressions that seem indicative of their emotional states. In situations in which we expect them to be happy, they seem to smile; when we might assume they are frustrated, they show anger; and when we might expect them to be unhappy, they look sad.

In fact, these basic facial expressions are remarkably similar across the most diverse cultures. Whether we look at babies in India, the United States, or the rain forests of New Guinea, the expression of basic emotions is the same (see Figure 6-1). Furthermore, the

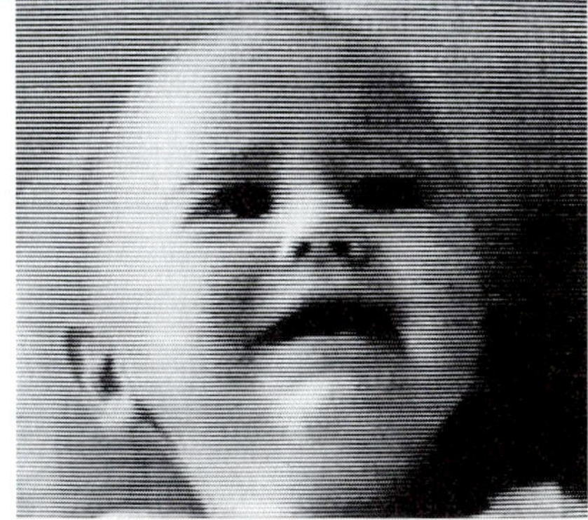
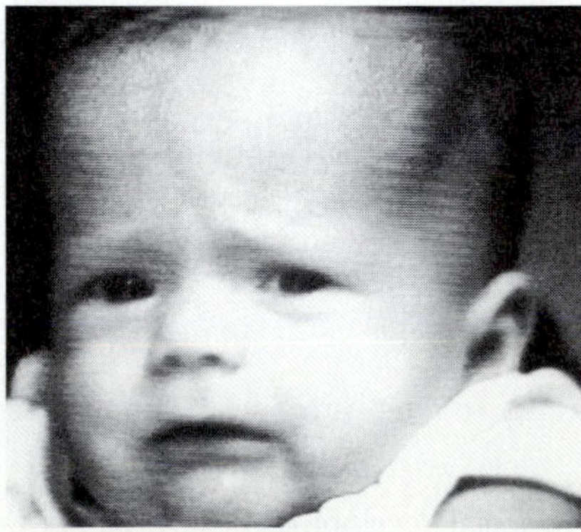

FIGURE 6-1 Across every culture, infants show similar facial expressions relating to basic emotions.

nonverbal expression of emotion, called *nonverbal encoding*, is fairly consistent throughout the life span. These consistencies have led researchers to conclude that the capacity to display basic emotions is innate (Camras, Malatesta, & Izard, 1991; Ekman & O'Sullivan, 1991; R. S. Feldman, 1982; C. E. Izard et al., 1995).

Infants appear to display a fairly wide range of emotional expressions. According to research on what mothers see in their children's nonverbal behavior, almost all think that by the age of 1 month, their babies have expressed interest and joy. In addition, 84 percent of mothers think their infants have expressed anger; 75 percent, surprise; 58 percent, fear; and 34 percent, sadness (Johnson et al.,1982).

differential emotions theory *the theory that emotional expressions not only reflect emotional experiences, but also help in the regulation of emotion itself*

stranger anxiety *the caution and wariness displayed by infants when encountering a strange person; begins at around 6 months of age*

Experiencing Emotions. Yet does the capability of infants to encode emotions nonverbally in a consistent, reliable manner mean that they actually *experience* emotions, and—if they do—is the experience similar to that of adults? These questions are not easy to answer.

The fact that children display nonverbal expressions in a manner similar to that of adults does not necessarily mean that the actual experience is identical. In fact, if the nature of such displays is innate, it is possible that facial expressions can occur spontaneously, without any emotional experience accompanying them. Nonverbal expressions, then, might be emotionless in young infants, in much the same way that our knee reflexively jerks forward, without the involvement of emotions, when a physician taps it.

However, most developmental researchers think otherwise: They argue that the nonverbal expressions of infants represent emotional experiences. In fact, developmental psychologist Carroll Izard suggests in his **differential emotions theory** that emotional expressions not only reflect emotional experiences, but also help in the regulation of emotion itself. Izard suggests that infants are born with an innate repertoire of emotional expressions, reflecting basic emotional states. These basic expressions are expanded and modified as infants and children grow older and become more adept at controlling their nonverbal behavioral expressions and more sophisticated in their ability to experience a wider array of emotions (Camras, et. al., 1991: C. E. Izard, 1977; C. Izard & Malatesta, 1987).

In sum, infants do appear to experience emotions, although the range of emotions at birth is fairly restricted. However, as they get older, infants both display and experience a wider range of increasingly complex emotions (N. F. Fox, 1994; Sroufe, 1996).

Stranger Anxiety and Separation Anxiety. "She used to be such a friendly baby," thought Erika's mother. "No matter who she encountered, she had a big smile. But now, I don't know what's happened. Almost the day she turned 7 months old, she began to react to strangers as if she were seeing a ghost. Her face crinkles up with a frown, and she either turns away or stares at them with suspicion. And she doesn't want to be left with anyone she doesn't already know. It's as if she has undergone a personality transplant."

What happened to Erika is, in fact, quite typical. By the end of the first year, infants often develop both stranger anxiety and separation anxiety. **Stranger anxiety,** which begins at around 6 months of age, is the caution and wariness displayed by infants when encountering a strange person.

What brings on stranger anxiety? One basic cause is the increased cognitive abilities of infants, allowing them to separate who they know from who they don't. The same cognitive advances that allow them to respond so positiviely to those people with whom they are familiar also means that they are able to recognize people who are unfamiliar. Furthermore, between the ages of 6 to 9 months, infants begin to try to make sense of their world. When they can't–such as with the appearance of an unknown person–they experience fear. It's as if an infant has a question, but they are unable to answer it (M. D. S. Ainsworth, 1973; Kagan, Kearsley, & Zelazo, 1978).

Although stranger anxiety is common after the age of 6 months, significant differences exist between children. Some infants, particularly those who have a lot of experience with strangers, tend to show less anxiety than those whose experience with strangers is

Separation anxiety, the distress displayed by infants when their customary care provider departs, usually starts at about 8 or 9 months and peaks at around 14 months of age.

limited. Furthermore, not all strangers evoke the same reaction. For instance, infants tend to show less anxiety with strangers who are female than those who are male. In addition, strangers who are children are reacted to more positively than adults, perhaps because their size is less intimidating (Brooks & Lewis, 1976; Lenssen, 1973; R. A. Thompson & Limber, 1990).

Separation anxiety is the distress displayed by infants when a customary care provider departs. Separation anxiety starts a little later than stranger anxiety, usually begining at about 8 or 9 months. It peaks around 14 months, and then slowly decreases. Separation anxiety is produced largely by the same causes as stranger anxiety: Infants' growing cognitive skills allow them to ask questions with no readily apparent answers: "Why is my mother leaving?" "Where is she going?" and "Will she come back?"

Stranger anxiety and separation anxiety represent important social progress. They reflect both cognitive advances and the growing emotional and social bond between infants and their caregivers—bonds that we'll consider later in the chapter when we discuss infants' social relationships.

separation anxiety the distress displayed by infants when a customary care provider departs; usually begins at about 8 or 9 months of age

social smile smiling in response to other individuals

Smiling. As Luz lay sleeping in her crib, her mother and father caught a glimpse of the most beautiful smile crossing her face. Her parents were sure that Luz was having a pleasant dream. Were they right?

Probably not. The earliest smiles expressed during sleep probably have little meaning, although no one can be absolutely sure. However, by 6 to 9 weeks it is clear that babies begin to smile reliably at the sight of stimuli that please them, including toys, mobiles, and—to the delight of parents—people. Smiling in response to other individuals is considered a **social smile**, in comparison to smiling at nonhuman stimuli.

Actually, the first smiles tend to be relatively indiscriminate, as infants first begin to smile at the sight of almost anything they find amusing. However, as they get older, they become more selective in their smiles, and their social smiles become directed toward particular individuals, not just anyone (Wolff, 1963).

Furthermore, by the age of 18 months, social smiling, directed more toward mothers and other caregivers, becomes more frequent than smiling directed toward nonhuman objects. Moreover, if an adult is unresponsive to a child, the amount of smiling decreases. In sum, by the end of the second year children are quite purposefully using smiling to communicate their positive emotions, and they are sensitive to the emotional expressions of others (Jones, Collins, & Hong, 1991; Jones & Raag, 1989; Toda & Fogel, 1993).

True social smiles emerge by the age of 6 to 9 weeks.

Decoding Others' Facial and Vocal Expressions. You may recall from Chapter 3 that neonates are able to imitate adults' facial expressions, a capability that is apparent even minutes after birth (Kaitz et al., 1988; Reissland, 1988). Although their imitative abilities certainly do not mean that they can understand the meaning of others' facial expressions, such imitation does pave the way for future *nonverbal decoding* abilities, which begin to emerge fairly soon. Using these abilities, infants can interpret others' facial and vocal expressions that carry emotional meaning.

Although relatively little attention has been given to infants' perception of vocal expressions, it does appear that they are able to discriminate happy and sad vocal expressions at the age of 5 months. Infants also seem to be able to discriminate vocal expressions of emotion at a slightly earlier age than they discriminate facial expressions (Walker-Andrews & Grolnick, 1983; Walker-Andrews & Lennon, 1991).

Scientists know more about the *sequence* in which nonverbal facial decoding ability progresses. In the first 6 to 8 weeks, infants' visual precision is sufficiently limited that they cannot pay much attention to others' facial expressions. But they soon begin to discriminate among different facial expressions of emotion and even seem to be able to respond to differences in emotional intensity conveyed by facial expressions. They also respond to unusual facial expressions. For instance, they show distress when their mothers pose bland, unresponsive, neutral facial expressions (Klinnert et al., 1983; Kuchuk, Vibbert, & Bornstein, 1986; M. E. Lamb, Morrison, & Malkin, 1987; C. A. Nelson, 1987).

By the time they reach the age of 4 months, infants may already have begun to understand the emotions that lie behind the facial and vocal expressions of others. How do we know this? One important clue comes from a study in which 7-month-old infants were shown a pair of facial expressions relating to joy and sadness and, simultaneously, heard a vocalization representing either joy (a rising tone of voice) or sadness (a falling tone of voice). The infants paid more attention to the face that matched the tone, suggesting that they had at least a rudimentary understanding of the emotional meaning of facial expressions and voice tones (R. D. Phillips et al., 1990).

In sum, infants learn early both to encode and to decode emotions. Such abilities play an important role not only in helping them experience their own emotions, but also—as we see next—in using others' emotions to understand the meaning of ambiguous social situations.

Social Referencing: Feeling What Others Feel

> When 23-month-old Stephania watches as her mother and father loudly argue with one another, she glances at her older brother. He appears unperturbed by the scene, having witnessed it all too often in the past, and he wears a small smile of embarrassment on his face. On seeing this, Stephania smiles slightly, too, mimicking her brother's facial expression.

Like Stephania, most of us have been in situations in which we feel uncertain. In such cases, we sometimes turn to others to see how they are reacting. This reliance on others, known as social referencing, helps us decide what an appropriate response ought to be.

Social referencing is the intentional search for information to help explain the meaning of uncertain circumstances and events. Social referencing is used to clarify the meaning of a situation by reducing our uncertainty about what is occurring (Campos & Stenberg, 1981; Klinnert, 1984).

Social referencing first tends to occur around the age of 8 or 9 months (Walden & Ogan, 1988). It is a fairly sophisticated social ability: Infants need it not only to understand the significance of others' behavior, such as their facial expressions, but also to realize that others' behavior has meaning with reference to specific circumstances (Rosen, Adamson, & Bakeman, 1992).

social referencing *the intentional search for information to help explain the meaning of uncertain circumstances and events*

Infants make particular use of facial expressions in their social referencing. For instance, in one study infants were given an unusual toy to play with. The amount of time they played with it depended on their mothers' facial expressions. When their mothers displayed disgust, they played with it significantly less than when their mothers appeared pleased. Furthermore, when given the opportunity to play with the same toy later, the infants revealed lasting consequences of their mothers' earlier behavior, despite the mothers' now neutral-appearing facial reactions (Hornik, Risenhoover, & Gunner, 1987; Hornik & Gunner, 1988).

Although it is clear that social referencing begins fairly early in life, researchers are still not certain *how* it operates. Consider, for instance, one possibility: It may be that observing someone else's facial expression brings about the emotion the expression represents. That is, an infant who views someone looking sad may come to feel sad herself, and her behavior may be affected. On the other hand, it may be the case that viewing another's facial expression simply provides information. In this case, the infant does not experience the particular emotion represented by another's facial expression; she simply uses the display as data to guide her own behavior.

Both explanations for social referencing have received support, and so we still don't know which is correct. What we do know is that social referencing is most likely to occur when a situation breeds uncertainty and ambiguity. Furthermore, infants who reach the age when they are able to use social referencing become quite upset if they receive conflicting nonverbal messages from their mothers and fathers. Mixed messages, then, are a real source of stress for an infant (Camras & Sachs, 1991; Hirshberg, 1990; Hirshberg & Svejda, 1990; Walden & Baxter, 1989).

THE DEVELOPMENT OF SELF: DO INFANTS KNOW WHO THEY ARE?

Elysa, 8 months old, crawls past the full-length mirror that hangs on a door in her parents' bedroom. She barely pays any attention to her reflection as she moves by. On the other hand, her cousin Brianna, who is almost 2 years old, stares at herself in the mirror as she passes and laughs as she touches her forehead with her fingers.

Perhaps you've had the experience of catching a glimpse of yourself in a mirror and noticing a hair out of place. You probably reacted by attempting to push the unruly hair back into place. Your reaction shows more than that you care about how you look. It implies that you have a sense of yourself, the awareness and knowledge that you are an independent social entity to which others react and which you attempt to present to the world in ways that reflect favorably upon you.

We aren't, however, born with the knowledge that we exist independently from others and the larger world. Although it is difficult to demonstrate, the youngest infants—like all animals other than some apes—don't seem to have a sense of themselves as individuals. They do not recognize likenesses of themselves, whether in photos or in mirrors, and they show no evidence of being able to distinguish themselves from other people (G. G. Gallup, 1977).

The roots of **self-awareness**, knowledge of oneself, begin to grow at around the age of 12 months. We know this from a simple but ingenious experimental technique known as the *mirror-and-rouge task.* In it, an infant's nose is secretly colored with a dab of red rouge, and the infant is seated in front of a mirror. If infants touch their noses or attempt to wipe off the rouge, we have evidence that they have at least some knowledge of their physical characteristics. For them, this awareness is one step in developing an understanding of themselves as independent objects.

Although some infants as young as 12 months seem startled on seeing the rouge spot, for most a reaction does not occur until between 17 and 24 months of age. It is also around this age that children begin to show awareness of their own capabilities. For instance, infants between the ages of 23 and 25 months sometimes begin to cry when asked in experi-

self-awareness *knowledge of oneself*

ments to imitate a complicated sequence of behaviors involving toys, although they readily accomplish simpler ones. According to developmental psychologist Jerome Kagan (1981) their reaction suggests that they are conscious that they lack the capability to carry out difficult tasks, and are unhappy about it—a reaction that provides a clear indication of self-awareness (Asendorpf & Baudonniere, 1993; Asendorpf, Warkentin, & Baudonniere, 1996; M. Lewis & Brooks-Gunn, 1979; Lipka & Brinthaupt, 1992).

In sum, by the time they reach the age of 18 to 24 months, infants have developed at least the rudiments of awareness of their own physical characteristics, and they understand that their appearance is stable over time. Although it is not clear how far this awareness extends, it is becoming increasingly evident that, as we discuss next, infants have not only a basic understanding of themselves, but also the beginnings of an understanding of how the mind operates—what has come to be called a "theory of mind" (Damon & Hart, 1992).

By the age of 2, children demonstrate the foundations of empathy, an emotional response that corresponds to the feelings of another person.

Theory of Mind: Infants' Perspectives on the Mental Lives of Others—and Themselves

What are infants' thoughts about thinking? According to developmental psychologist John Flavell, infants begin to understand certain things about the mental processes of themselves and others at quite an early age. Flavell has investigated children's **theory of mind**, their knowledge and beliefs about the mental world. Theories of mind represent the explanations that children use to explain how others think.

For instance, cognitive advances during infancy permit older infants to come to see people in ways that are very different from other objects. They learn to see others as *compliant agents,* beings similar to themselves who behave under their own power and who have the capacity to respond to infants' requests (Flavell, 1993; Flavell, Green, & Flavell, 1995; C. Lewis & Mitchell, 1994).

In addition, children's capacity to understand intentionality and causality grows during infancy. They begin to understand that others' behaviors have some meaning and that the behaviors they see people enacting are designed to accomplish particular goals, in contrast to the "behaviors" of inanimate objects (S. A. Gelman & Kalish, 1993; Golinkoff, 1993; Parritz, Mangelsdorf, & Gunar, 1992).

By the age of 2, infants begin to demonstrate the rudiments of empathy. **Empathy** is an emotional response that corresponds to the feelings of another person. At 24 months of age, infants sometimes comfort others or show concern for them (Zahn-Waxler, Robinson, & Emde, 1992). In order to do this, they need to be aware of others' emotional states. Further, during their second year, infants begin to use deception, both in games of "pretend" and in outright attempts to fool others. A child who plays "pretend" and who uses falsehoods must be aware that others hold beliefs about the world—beliefs that can be manipulated (J. Dunn, 1991; Leslie, 1987).

In sum, by the end of infancy children have developed the rudiments of a theory of mind. This theory represents a kind of folk psychology. It helps them understand the actions of others and it affects their own behavior (Moses & Chandler, 1992; Wellman, 1990).

theory of mind *a child's knowledge and beliefs about the mental world*

empathy *an emotional response that corresponds to the feelings of another person*

Review and Rethink

REVIEW

- Infants appear both to express and to experience emotions, at first displaying a limited range, and then a wider range reflecting increasingly complex emotional states.
- Infants experience stranger anxiety starting at about 6 months, and separation anxiety starting at around 8 months of age.

- Infants from different cultures use similar facial expressions to express basic emotional states. As the infant matures, the meaning of an expression such as the smile grows increasingly specific, with a more limited range of applicability.
- The ability to decode the nonverbal facial and vocal expressions of others develops early in infants. By 8 or 9 months, infants begin to use such nonverbal decoding to clarify situations of uncertainty and determine appropriate responses, an ability termed *social referencing*.
- Infants are not at first aware that they exist separately from the rest of the world. They develop self-awareness gradually, starting after 12 months of age.
- By the age of 2, children have developed the rudiments of a theory of mind, including a realization that people are essentially different from inanimate objects, a growing sense of intentionality and causality, fundamental feelings of empathy, and the ability to pretend and to deceive.

RETHINK

- If the facial expressions that convey basic emotions are similar across cultures, how do such expressions arise? Can you think of facial expressions that are culture-specific? How do they arise?
- Why might the ability to discriminate vocal expressions emerge earlier than the ability to discriminate facial expressions?
- In what situations do adults rely on social referencing to work out appropriate responses? How might social referencing be used to manipulate individuals' responses?
- How might a child's developing sense of empathy be fostered by parents and other caregivers?
- How do Flavell's ideas about a growing sense of causality, pretense, and deception in children compare to Piaget's notions of experimentation and deferred imitation by children?

FORGING RELATIONSHIPS

> Louis became the center of attention on the way home [from the hospital]. His father brought Martha, aged 5, and Tom, aged 3, to the hospital with him when Mrs. Moore was discharged. Martha rushed to see "her" new baby and ignored her mother. Tom clung to his mother's knees in the reception hall of the hospital.
>
> A hospital nurse carried Louis to the car, placing him in Mrs. Moore's arms for the ride home. The two older children immediately climbed over the seat and swamped mother and baby with their attention. Both children stuck their faces into his, smacked at him, and talked to him. They soon began to fight over him with loud voices. The loud argument and the jostling of his mother upset Louis and he started to cry. He let out a wail that came like a shotgun blast into the noisy car. The children quieted immediately and looked with awe at this new infant. His insistent wails drowned out their bickering. He had already asserted himself in their eyes. Martha's lip quivered as she watched her mother attempt to comfort Louis, and she added her own soft cooing in imitation of her mother. Tom squeezed even closer to his mother, put his thumb in his mouth, and closed his eyes to shut out the commotion. (Brazelton, 1983, p. 48)

The arrival of a newborn brings a dramatic change to a family's dynamics. No matter how welcome a baby's birth, it causes a fundamental shift in the roles that people play within the family. The mother and father must start to build a relationship with their infant, and older children must adjust to the presence of a new member of the family and build their own alliance with their infant brother or sister.

Although the process of social development during infancy is neither simple nor automatic, it is crucial: The bonds that grow between infants and their parents, family, and others provide the foundation for a lifetime's worth of social relationships.

attachment *the positive emotional bond that develops between a child and a particular individual*

Ainsworth Strange Situation *a sequence of staged episodes that illustrate the strength of attachment between a child and (typically) his or her mother*

ATTACHMENT: FORMING SOCIAL BONDS

The most important form of social development that takes place during infancy is attachment. **Attachment** is the positive emotional bond that develops between a child and a particular individual. The nature of our attachment during infancy has repercussions for how we relate to others throughout the rest of our lives (Greeberg, Cicchetti, & Cummings, 1990; Kochanska, 1995).

To understand attachment, the earliest researchers turned to the bonds that form between parents and children in the nonhuman animal kingdom. For instance, ethologist Konrad Lorenz (1965) studied the poultry equivalent of attachment by observing newborn goslings, who have an innate tendency to follow their mother, the first moving object to which they typically are exposed after birth. Lorenz found that goslings whose eggs were raised in an incubator and who viewed *him* after hatching would follow *his* every movement, as if he were their mother. He labeled this process *imprinting:* behavior that takes place during a critical period and involves attachment to the first moving object that is observed.

Lorenz's findings suggested that attachment was based on biologically determined factors, and other theorists agreed. For instance, Freud suggested that attachment grew out of a mother's ability to satisfy a child's oral needs.

On the other hand, the ability to provide food and other physiological needs is not as crucial as Freud and other theorists first thought. In a classic study, psychologist Harry Harlow gave infant monkeys the choice of cuddling a wire "monkey" that provided food or a soft, terry cloth "monkey" that was warm but did not provide food (see Figure 6-2). Their preference was clear: They would spend most of their time clinging to the cloth "monkey," although they made occasional expeditions to the wire monkey to nurse. Harlow suggested that the preference for the warm cloth "monkey" provided *contact comfort* (Harlow & Zimmerman, 1959).

Harlow's work clearly illustrates that food alone is insufficient to bring about attachment. Furthermore, these findings are congruent with the research we discussed in Chapter 3 showing no evidence for the existence of a critical bonding period between human mothers and infants immediately after birth.

The earliest work on human attachment, which is still highly influential, was carried out by John Bowlby (1951). Bowlby's theorizing about attachment had a biological basis, although it was supplemented by observations of emotionally disturbed children with whom he worked in a London clinic.

In Bowlby's view, attachment is based primarily on infants' needs for safety and security—their genetically determined motivation to avoid predators. As they develop, infants come to learn that their safety is best provided by a particular individual, a realization that ultimately leads to the development of a special relationship, typically with the mother. He suggests that this single relationship is qualitatively different from the bonds formed with others, including the father—a suggestion that, as we'll see later, has been a source of some subsequent dispute.

Bowlby also suggests, somewhat ironically, that attachment—which has its roots in the desire to seek the protective security of the mother—is critical in allowing an infant to explore the world. According to his view, having strong, firm attachment provides a kind of home base away from which growing children can progressively roam as they become more independent.

FIGURE 6-2 Harlow's research showed that monkeys preferred the warm, soft "monkey" over the wire "monkey" that provided food.

Using Bowlby's theorizing as a base, developmental psychologist Mary Ainsworth developed a widely used experimental technique to measure attachment (M. D. S. Ainsworth et al., 1978). The **Ainsworth Strange Situation** consists of a sequence of staged episodes that illustrate the strength of attachment between a child and (typically) his or her mother.

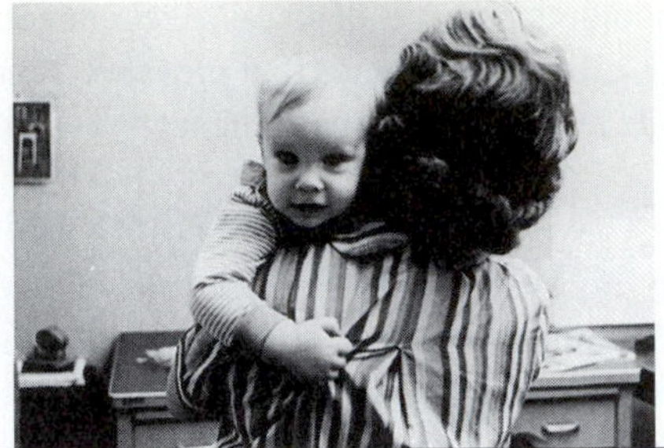

In this illustration of the strange situation, the infant first explores the playroom on his own, as long as his mother is present. But when she leaves, he begins to cry. On her return, however, he is immediately comforted and stops crying. The conclusion: he is securely attached.

securely attached children *children who use the mother as a kind of home base and are at ease when she is present; when she leaves they become upset and go to her as soon as she returns; about two thirds of children fall into the securely attached category*

avoidant children *children who do not seek proximity to the mother; after the mother has left they seem to avoid her when she returns as if they are angered by her behavior; 20 percent of children fall into this category*

ambivalent children *children who display a combination of positive and negative reactions to their mothers; they show great distress when the mother leaves, but upon her return they may simultaneously seek close contact but also hit and kick her; about 12 percent of children fall into the category of ambivalent*

The "strange situation" follows this general eight-step pattern: (1) The mother and baby enter an unfamiliar room; (2) the mother sits down, leaving the baby free to explore; (3) an adult stranger enters the room and converses first with the mother and then with the baby; (4) the mother exits the room, leaving the baby alone with the stranger; (5) the mother returns, greeting and comforting the baby, and the stranger leaves; (6) the mother departs again, leaving the baby alone; (7) the stranger returns; and (8) the mother returns and the stranger leaves (M. D. S. Ainsworth et al., 1978).

Infants' reactions to the various aspects of the Ainsworth Strange Situation vary considerably, depending on the nature of their attachment to their mothers. One-year-olds show three major patterns, labeled *securely attached, avoidant,* and *ambivalent* (summarized in Table 6-1). **Securely attached children** use the mother as a kind of home base, at ease in the Strange Situation as long as she is present. They explore independently, returning to her occasionally. When she leaves, though, they act upset, and they go to her as soon as she returns. Most children—about two thirds—fall into the securely attached category.

In contrast, children labeled **avoidant children** do not seek proximity to the mother, and after the mother has left, they seem to avoid her when she returns. It is as if they are angered by her behavior. Some 20 percent of children are found to be in the avoidant category at 1 year of age.

Finally, the third group of children is labeled **ambivalent children**, displaying a combination of positive and negative reactions to their mothers. Ambivalent children are in such close contact with the mother that they may not explore their environment much. They may be anxious even before the mother leaves, and when she does they show great distress. But upon her return, they show ambivalent reactions, simultaneously seeking close contact but also hitting and kicking her. About 12 percent of 1-year-olds fall into the ambivalent classification (Cassidy & Berlin, 1994).

TABLE 6-1

CLASSIFICATIONS OF INFANT ATTACHMENT

	CLASSSIFICATION CRITERIA				
Label	**Proximity Seeking**	**Contact Maintaining**	**Proximity Avoiding**	**Contact Resisting**	**Crying**
Securely attached	High	High (if distressed)	Low	Low	Low (preseparation), high or low (separation), low (reunion)
Avoidant	Low	Low	High	Low	Low (preseparation), high or low (separation), low (reunion)
Ambivalent	High	High (often preseparation)	Low	High	Occasionally (preseparation), high (separation), moderate to high (reunion)

(*Source:* Waters, 1978. © The Society for Research in Child Development, Inc.)

Although Ainsworth identified only three categories, a more recent expansion of her work suggests that there is a fourth category: disorganized-disoriented. **Disorganized-disoriented children** show inconsistent, often contradictory behavior, such as approaching the mother when she returns but not looking at her. Their confusion suggests that they may be the least securely attached children of all (Egeland & Farber, 1984; M. J. O'Connor, Sigman, & Brill, 1987).

disorganized-disoriented children *children who show inconsistent, often contradictory behavior, such as approaching the mother when she returns but not looking at her; they may be the least securely attached children of all*

The explicit classification of a child into an attachment style would be of only minor consequence were it not for the fact that the nature of attachment between infants and their mothers seems to have significant consequences for relationships at later stages of life. For example, research has found that boys who were securely attached at the age of 1 year showed fewer psychological difficulties at older ages than did avoidant or ambivalent children. Similarly, children who were securely attached as infants tended to be more socially and emotionally competent later than those with the other attachment styles, and others viewed them more positively. Ultimately, some research suggests that the nature of romantic relationships in adult life is associated with the kind of attachment style developed during infancy (M. D. Ainsworth, 1989; M. D. Ainsworth & Bowlby, 1991; J. Holmes, 1994; Seifer, Schiller, & Sameroff, 1996; P. R. Shaver, Hazan, & Bradshaw, 1988; Shaw & Vondra, 1995; van IJzendoorn, 1995).

On the other hand, we cannot say that having something other than a secure attachment style as a child invariably leads to difficulties later in life, nor that having a secure attachment at age 1 always leads to good adjustment later on (N. A. Fox, 1995; M. E. Lamb et al., 1984). In fact, some evidence suggests that children with avoidant and ambivalent attachment—as measured by the Ainsworth Strange Situation—do quite well, particularly when we look at experimental findings from different cultures.

Developmental Diversity

Are There Cross-cultural Differences in Attachment?

Recall that the work on attachment was initially inspired by John Bowlby's observations of the biologically motivated efforts of the young of other species to seek safety and security. From these observations, Bowlby suggested that seeking attachment was a biological universal, one that we should find not only in other species, but among humans as well. Such reasoning suggests that we should see attachment strivings in all humans, regardless of their culture.

However, research has brought this contention into question. For example, one study of German infants showed that most fell into the avoidant category (K. E. Grossmann et al, 1982). Other studies, conducted in Israel and Japan, have found a smaller proportion of infants who were securely attached than in the United States (Sagi, 1990; Sagi, et al., 1985; Takahashi, 1986).

More recent analyses confirm not only that there are differences in the distribution of infants into the various types of attachment, but that subcultural differences also exist even within particular societies (van IJzendoorn & Kroonenberg, 1988; Sagi, van IJzendoorn, & Koren-Karie, 1991; Sagi et al., 1994, 1995). Do such findings suggest that we should abandon the notion that attachment is a universal biological tendency?

Not necessarily. Most of the data on attachment have been obtained by using the Ainsworth Strange Situation, which may not be the most appropriate measure in non-Western cultures. For example, Japanese parents seek to avoid separation and stress during infancy, and they don't strive to foster independence to the same degree as parents in many

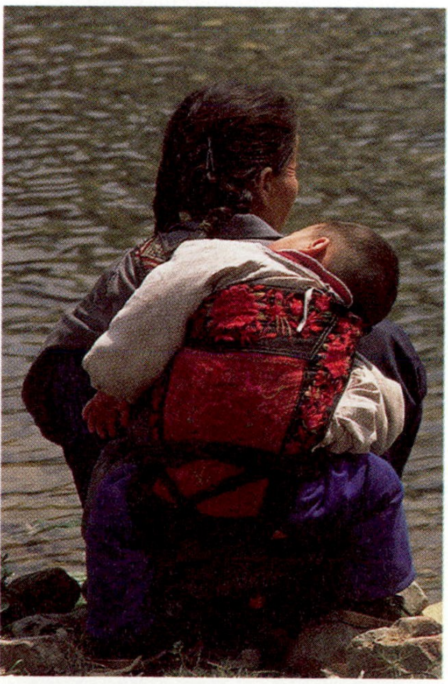

Japanese parents seek to avoid separation from their infants and do not strive to foster independence. Such childrearing practices may produce the appearance of less secure attachment using the Strange Situation. If other measurement techniques are used, however, Japanese children might well score higher in attachment.

Western societies. Because of their relative lack of prior experience in separation, then, infants placed in the Strange Situation may experience unusual stress—producing the appearance of less secure attachment in Japanese children. If a different measure of attachment were to be used, one that might be administered later in infancy, more Japanese infants could well be classified as secure (Nakagawa, Lamb, & Miyaki, 1992; Posada, et al., 1995; Takahashi, 1990).

In sum, it may be that cross-cultural and within-cultural differences in attachment reflect the nature of the measure employed. On the other hand, it is still possible that Bowlby's claim that the desire for attachment is universal was too strongly stated. In fact, more recent approaches view attachment as not entirely biologically determined, but rather as susceptible to cultural norms and expectations.

Specifically, some developmental specialists suggest that attachment should be viewed as a general tendency, but one that is modifiable according to how actively caregivers in a society seek to instill independence in their children. Consequently, secure attachment may be seen earliest in cultures that promote independence, but may be delayed in societies in which independence is a less important cultural value (Harwood, Miller, & Irizarry, 1995; van IJzendoorn & Tavecchio, 1987).

PRODUCING ATTACHMENT: THE ROLES OF THE MOTHER, FATHER, AND INFANT

> As 5-month-old Annie cries passionately, her mother comes into the room and gently lifts her from her crib. After just a few moments, as her mother rocks Annie and speaks softly, Annie's cries cease, and she cuddles in her mother's arms. But the moment her mother places her back in the crib, Annie begins to wail again, leading her mother to pick her up once again.

The pattern is familiar to most parents. The infant cries, the parent reacts, and the child responds in turn. Yet such seemingly insignificant sequences as these, repeatedly occurring in the lives of infants and parents, help pave the way for the development of relationships between children, their parents, and the rest of the social world. We'll consider how each of the major caregivers and the infant play a role in the development of attachment.

Mothers and Attachment. Sensitivity to their infants' needs and desires is the hallmark of mothers of securely attached infants. Such a mother tends to be aware of her child's moods, and she takes into account her child's feelings as she interacts with it. She is also responsive during face-to-face interactions, provides feeding "on demand," and is warm and affectionate to her infant (M. S. Ainsworth, 1993; T. M. Field, 1987; Isabella, 1993; Pederson et al., 1990).

It is not only a matter of responding in *any* fashion to their infants' signals that separates mothers of securely attached and insecurely attached children. Mothers of secure infants tend to provide the appropriate level of response. For instance, research has shown that overly responsive mothers are just as likely to have insecurely attached children as under-responsive mothers (Belsky et al., 1984).

The research showing the correspondence between mothers' sensitivity to their infants and the security of the infants' attachment is consistent with Ainsworth's arguments that attachment depends on how mothers react to their infants' social overtures. Ainsworth suggests that mothers of securely attached infants respond rapidly and positively to their infants. In contrast, the way for mothers to produce insecurely attached infants, according to Ainsworth, is to ignore their behavioral cues, to behave inconsistently with them, and to ignore or reject their social efforts.

But how do mothers know how to respond to their infants' cues? One answer is that they learn from their own mothers. For instance, infants tend to develop attachment styles that are similar to those of their mothers. In fact, some research finds substantial stability in attachment patterns from one generation to the next (Benoit & Parker, 1994).

On the other hand, it is important to keep in mind that mothers' (and others') behavior toward infants is, in part, a reaction to the children's ability to provide effective cues. A mother may not be able to respond effectively to a child whose own behavior is unrevealing, misleading, or ambiguous. As we will see, the kind of cues a child gives off may in part determine how successful the mother will be in responding to the infant.

Attachment styles are stable from one generation to the next.

Infants' Behavior and Attachment. As we first noted in Chapter 2, and as we'll discuss in greater detail later in this chapter, infants are born with particular temperaments—patterns of arousal and emotionality that represent consistent and enduring characteristics. Do such temperamental differences, as well as other individual differences, affect attachment?

The evidence is mixed. Some researchers find associations between attachment and temperament, while others do not. Most evidence seems to suggest that there is some relationship, although it is not particularly strong. For instance, one study examined infants' temperaments at 2 days of age, as determined by their behavior when a dummy was withdrawn from them. The results showed an association between their early reactions and whether they later were securely or insecurely attached. It may be that temperament relates to the manner in which infants demonstrate their security or insecurity, but that temperament has only minor effects on actual attachment (Belsky & Rovine, 1987; Calkins & Fox, 1992; Goldsmith & Harman, 1994; Vaughn et al., 1989; Vaughn et al., 1992; Belsky et al., 1996).

Other individual differences between infants are likely related to attachment. For example, infants vary considerably in how much emotion they display nonverbally. Some are "poker-faced," showing little expressivity, while others' reactions tend to be much more easily decoded (R. S. Feldman & Rime, 1991; Field et al., 1982). It seems reasonable to assume that more expressive infants provide more easily discernible cues to others, thereby easing the way for caregivers to be more successful in responding to their needs.

Fathers and Attachment. Up to now, we've barely touched upon one of the key players involved in the upbringing of a child: the father. In fact, if you looked at the early theorizing and research on attachment, you'd find little mention of the father and his potential contributions to the life of the infant (Russell & Radojevic, 1992).

There are at least two reasons for this. First, John Bowlby, who provided the initial theory of attachment, suggested that there was something unique about the mother-child relationship. He saw the mother as uniquely equipped, biologically, to provide sustenance for the child, and he concluded that this capability led to the development of a special relationship between mothers and children. Second, the early work on attachment was influenced by the traditional social views of the time, which considered it "natural" for the mother to be the primary caregiver, while the father's role was to work outside the home to provide a living for his family.

Several factors led to the demise of this view. One was that societal norms changed, and fathers began to take a more active role in childrearing activities. More important, it became increasingly clear from research findings that—despite societal norms that relegated fathers to secondary childrearing roles—some infants formed their primary initial relationship with their fathers. Moreover, many infants had strong attachment relationships with more than one individual (Goossens & van IJzendoorn, 1990; Lamb, 1982b; Volling & Belsky, 1992).

For example, one study found that although most infants formed their first primary relationship with one person, around one third had multiple relationships, and it was difficult to determine which attachment was primary (Schaffer & Emerson, 1964). Furthermore, by the time the infants were 18 months old, most had formed multiple relationships. In sum, infants may develop attachments not only to their mothers, but to a variety of others as well (N. Fox, Kimmerly, & Schafer, 1991; R. D. Parke & Tinsley, 1987).

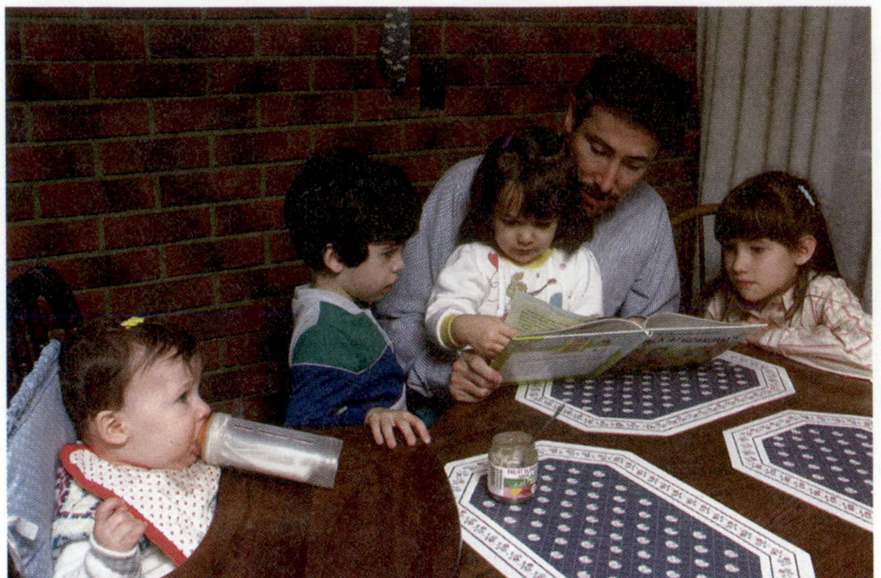

Some children form their primary initial relationship with their fathers, and some have more than one strong attachment relationship.

Still, the nature of attachment between infants and mothers, on the one hand, and infants and fathers, on the other hand, is not identical (Cox, Owen, Henderson, & Margand, 1992; Pipp, Easterbrooks, & Brown, 1993). For example, when they are in unusually stressful circumstances, infants prefer to be soothed by their mothers, rather than by their fathers (M. E. Lamb, 1977).

One reason for qualitative differences in attachment involves the differences in what fathers and mothers do with their children. Mothers spend a greater proportion of their time feeding and directly nurturing their children. In contrast, fathers spend more time, proportionally, playing with infants. Nevertheless, almost all fathers do contribute to child care: Surveys show that 95 percent say they do some child-care chores every day. But they still, on average, do less than mothers. For instance, 30 percent of fathers with wives who work do 3 or more hours of daily child care, in comparison with 74 percent of employed married mothers who spend that amount of time in child-care activities (see Figure 6-3; Bailey, 1994; Jacobsen & Edmondson, 1993; National Survey of Families and Households, 1988; R. D. Parke, 1981).

FIGURE 6-3

WHO'S CARING FOR THE KIDS?

It's mostly not fathers: Even in families in which the mother works outside the home, only 30 percent of fathers put in more than 3 hours each day caring for their preschooler.

(*Source*: National Survey of Families and Households [NSFH]/American Demographics.)

Average for all married fathers with a preschooler

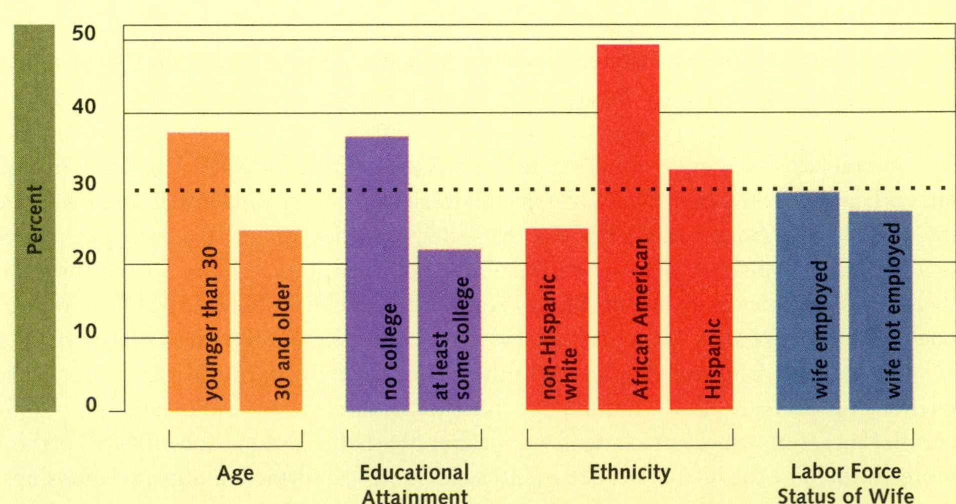

Furthermore, the nature of fathers' play with their infants is often quite different from that of mothers. Fathers engage in more physical, rough-and-tumble activities with their children. In contrast, mothers play traditional games such as peekaboo and games with more verbal elements (M. E. Lamb, 1986; R. D. Parke, 1990; Power & Parke, 1982).

These differences in the ways that fathers and mothers play with their children occur even in the minority of families in the United States in which the father is the primary caregiver. Moreover, the differences occur in very diverse cultures: Fathers in Australia, Israel, India, and Japan all engage more in play than in caregiving, as do fathers of the Aka Pygmy tribe in central Africa (M. E. Lamb, 1987; Roopnarine, 1992).

mutual regulation model *the model in which infants and parents learn to communicate emotional states to one another and to respond appropriately*

reciprocal socialization *a process in which infants' behaviors invite further responses from parents and other caregivers*

Infant Interactions: Developing a Working Relationship

It is clear that infants may develop multiple attachment relationships, and that over the course of time the specific individuals with whom the infant is primarily attached may change. These variations in attachment highlight the fact that the development of relationships is an ongoing process, not only during infancy, but also throughout childhood.

What processes underlie the development of relationships during infancy? One answer comes from studies that examine how parents interact with their children. For instance, across almost all cultures, mothers behave in typical ways with their infants. They tend to exaggerate their facial and vocal expressions—the nonverbal equivalent of the "motherese" that they use when they speak to infants (as we discussed in Chapter 5). Similarly, they often imitate their infants' behavior, responding to distinctive sounds and movements by repeating them. There are even types of games, such as peekaboo, itsy-bitsy spider, and patty-cake, that are nearly universal (T. Field, 1990; T. Field, 1979).

According to the **mutual regulation model**, infants and parents learn to communicate emotional states to one another and to respond appropriately. For instance, both infant and parent act jointly to regulate turn-taking behavior, with one individual waiting until the other completes a behavioral act before starting another. Consequently, when infants are 3 months old, they and their mothers have about the same influence on each other's behavior. Interestingly, by the age of 6 months, infants have more control over turn taking, although both partners once again become roughly equivalent in terms of mutual influence when infants are 9 months old (Cohn & Tronick, 1988, 1989; Nwokah & Fogel, 1993; Tronick & Gianino, 1986; Kochanska, 1997).

One of the ways in which infants and parents signal each other when they interact is through facial expressions. Even quite young infants are able to read, or decode, the facial expressions of their caregivers, and they react to those expressions (Camras et al., 1991; Lelwica & Haviland, 1983).

For example, an infant whose mother, during an experiment, displays a stony, immobile facial expression reacts by making a variety of sounds, gestures, and facial expressions of her own in response to such a puzzling situation—and possibly to elicit some new response from her mother. Infants also show more happiness themselves when their mothers appear happy, and they look at their mothers longer. On the other hand, infants are apt to respond with sad looks and to turn away when their mothers display unhappy expressions (Termine & Izard, 1988).

In sum, the development of attachment in infants does not merely represent a reaction to the behavior of the people around them. Instead, there is a process of **reciprocal socialization**, in which infants' behaviors invite further responses from parents and other caregivers. In turn, the caregivers' behaviors bring about a reaction from the child, continuing the cycle. Ultimately, these actions and reactions lead to an increase in attachment, forging and strengthening bonds between infants and caregivers. Figure 6-4 summarizes the sequence of infant-caregiver interaction (Ainsworth & Bowlby, 1991; S. M. Bell & Ainsworth, 1972; Bradley & Caldwell, 1995; Egeland, Pianta, & O'Brien, 1993).

FIGURE 6-4

SEQUENCE OF INFANT-CAREGIVER INTERACTION

The actions and reactions of caregivers and infants influence one another in complex ways.

(*Source*: Adapted from S. M. Bell & Ainsworth, 1972; Tomlinson-Keasey, 1985).

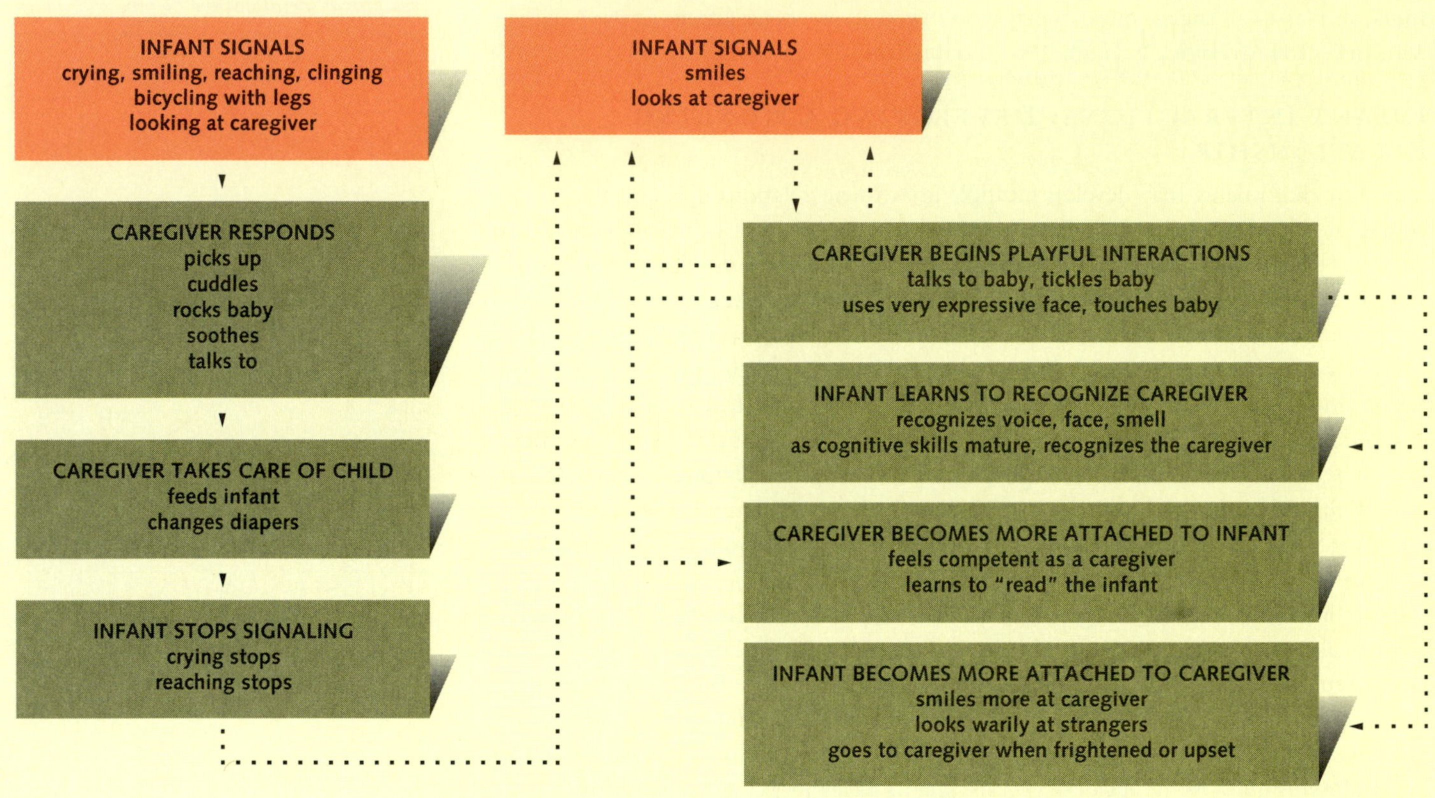

Infants' Sociability with Their Peers: Infant-Infant Interaction

How sociable are infants with other children? Although it is clear that they do not form "friendships" in the traditional sense, they do react positively to the presence of peers from early in life, and they engage in rudimentary forms of social interaction (T. Field, 1990).

Infants' sociability is expressed in several ways. From the earliest months of life they smile, laugh, and vocalize while looking at their peers. They show more interest in peers than in inanimate objects, and pay greater attention to other infants than they do to a mirror image of themselves (T. Field & Roopnarine, 1982; T. Field, 1981; Fogel, 1980).

On the other hand, infants are not consistently sociable. For one thing, by the end of the first year they start to show more interest in inanimate toys as they become better able to manipulate objects and to move around in the world. Furthermore, they begin to show preferences for people with whom they are familiar compared with those they don't know. For example, studies of identical twins show that twins exhibit a higher level of social behavior toward each other than toward an unfamiliar infant (T. Field, 1990; T. Field & Roopnarine, 1982).

Still, an infant's level of sociability generally rises as it gets older. Nine- to 12-month-olds mutually present and accept toys, particularly if they know each other. They also play social games, such as peekaboo or crawl-and-chase (Endo, 1992; Vincze, 1971). Such behavior is important, as it serves as a foundation for future social exchanges involving the elicitation of responses from others and the offering of reactions to those responses (C. Brownell, 1986; Howes, 1987).

Finally, as infants age, they begin to imitate each other (Russon & Waite, 1991). For instance, 14-month-old infants who are familiar with one another sometimes reproduce each other's behavior (E. Mueller & Vandell, 1979). Not only does such imitation serve a social function, but it can be a powerful teaching tool, as we discuss in the accompanying "Directions in Development" section.

Directions in Development

Infants Teaching Infants: When Babies Become Experts

"Expert" infants can teach their peers how to play with complicated toys, according to researcher Andrew Meltzoff and colleagues.

Think back to the story of 10-month-old Russell Ruud at the start of the chapter. He showed the other children in his day-care center how he could remove his hat by unfastening the Velcro straps, and soon others were following his lead.

According to Andrew Meltzoff, a developmental psychologist at the University of Washington, Russell's ability to impart this information is only one example of how so-called expert babies are able to teach skills and information to other infants. And, according to the research of Meltzoff and his colleagues, the abilities learned from the experts are retained and later utilized to a remarkable degree (Hanna & Meltzoff, 1993; Meltzoff & Moore, 1994).

In an innovative series of studies, Meltzoff and his colleagues devised a procedure to illustrate the sophistication of the teaching process. In one study, for instance, they created five toys, each attractive to a 1-year-old. Although simple to play with, each toy had to be worked in a particular manner in order for it to function correctly. For example, one toy was a plastic cup that would contract only if pushed in a particular way.

The experimenters then demonstrated to a group of infants, all around 17 months old, how to play with one of the five toys. The infants were allowed to play with it on their own until they had mastered it.

The next phase of the study was conducted in a day-care center. The infants—now expert in the use of the toy—were allowed to play with it while other 1-year-olds watched. However, the observers were not immediately given the opportunity to use the toy; they could only observe the "expert" play with it.

Two days later, however, when they were by themselves in their own homes, the observer infants got their opportunity to play with the toy. The result was that nearly three quarters of the observer babies were able to play correctly with the toy. In comparison, only one quarter of a control group of infants who had not seen an expert's demonstration were able to play appropriately with it (Hanna & Meltzoff, 1993).

The results are clear in suggesting the importance of exposure to other children's activities in promoting learning. Moreover, learning by exposure is a powerful phenomenon, one that starts early in life. For example, recent evidence shows that even 6-week-old infants perform delayed imitation of a novel stimulus to which they have earlier been exposed, such as an adult sticking the tongue out the side of the mouth (Meltzoff & Moore, 1994).

Finding that infants learn new behaviors, skills, and abilities due to exposure to other children has several implications. For one thing, it suggests that interactions between infants provide more than social benefits; they may have an impact on children's future cognitive development as well. Even more important, these findings illustrate a possible benefit that infants derive from participation in day care (which we consider later in this chapter). Although we don't know for sure, the opportunity to learn from their peers may prove to be a lasting advantage for infants in group day-care settings.

Review and Rethink

REVIEW

- Attachment, the positive emotional bond between an infant and a significant individual, may be genetically based, and different patterns of attachment seem to relate to a person's later social competence as an adult.
- Mothers and their babies generally form the primary social attachment in infancy, and the quality of the attachment is related to the warmth and effectiveness of the mother's responses to her baby's social overtures. Typically, the father's role has been seen as less central, and the nature of fathers' and mothers' attachments to their babies is qualitatively different.
- By the amount of emotion they display nonverbally, infants to some extent may affect the nature and quality of their caregivers' responses to them and, consequently, the quality of the attachment between themselves and their caregivers.
- Infants and the persons with whom they interact engage in reciprocal socialization as they mutually adjust to one another's interactions.
- Infants react differently to other children than to inanimate objects, and gradually they engage in increasing amounts of peer social interaction, even participating in reciprocal teaching and learning.

RETHINK

- In what sort of society might the attachment style labeled avoidant be encouraged by cultural attitudes toward childrearing? In such a society, would characterizing the infant's consistent avoidance of its mother as anger be an accurate interpretation?
- In what ways might overly responsive and underresponsive caregivers equally contribute to insecure attachment in their infants?
- Does the importance of infants' early attachment to primary caregivers have social policy implications relating to working parents? Do current policies reveal societal assumptions pertaining to the different roles of mothers and fathers?
- Can you discern a relationship between reciprocal socialization and operant conditioning?
- Why do you think that learning from their peers is so effective for young children? Does this finding have implications for educational practices?

DIFFERENCES AMONG INFANTS

"It's a boy." "It's a girl."

One of these two statements, or some variant, is probably the first announcement made in the delivery room after the birth of a child. Why does this differentiation occur, and what are the implications of dividing children so rigorously according to their gender?

We turn now to such questions as we consider some of the differences we find among infants and the lives they lead—differences not only in gender, but also in their overall personality and temperament, the nature of infants' families, and the ways in which infants are cared for.

Personality Development: The Characteristics That Make Infants Unique

The origins of **personality**, the sum total of the enduring characteristics that differentiate one individual from another, begin during infancy. From birth onward, infants begin to show unique, stable traits and behaviors that ultimately lead to their development as distinct, special individuals (Halverson, Kohnstamm, & Martin, 1994).

According to psychologist Erik Erikson, whose approach to personality development we first discussed in Chapter 1, infants' early experiences are responsible for shaping one of the key aspects of their personalities: whether they will be basically trusting or mistrustful.

Erikson's theory of psychosocial development considers how individuals come to understand themselves and the meaning of others'—and their own—behavior (Erikson, 1963). The theory suggests that developmental change occurs throughout people's lives in eight distinct stages, the first of which occurs in infancy.

According to Erikson, infancy marks the time of the **trust-versus-mistrust stage**, encompassing birth to 1½ years. During this period, infants develop a sense of trust or mistrust, largely depending on how well their needs are met by their caregivers. Erikson suggests that if infants are able to develop trust, they experience a sense of hope, which permits them to feel as if they can fulfill their needs successfully. On the other hand, feelings of mistrust lead infants to see the world as harsh and unfriendly, and they may have later difficulties in forming close bonds with others.

During the end of infancy, children enter the **autonomy-versus-shame-and-doubt stage**, which lasts from around 1½ to 3 years. During this period, children develop independence and autonomy if parents encourage exploration and freedom. On the other hand, if they are restricted and overprotected, children feel shame, self-doubt, and unhappiness.

Erikson argues that personality is primarily shaped by infants' experiences. However, as we discuss next, other developmentalists concentrate on consistencies of behavior that are present at birth. These consistencies are viewed as largely genetically determined and as providing the raw material of personality.

personality *the sum total of the enduring characteristics that differentiate one individual from another, beginning during infancy*

Erikson's theory of psychosocial development *the theory that considers how individuals come to understand themselves and the meaning of others'—and their own—behavior*

trust-versus-mistrust stage *the period from birth to 1½ years during which infants develop a sense of trust or mistrust, largely depending on how well their needs are met by their caregivers*

autonomy-versus-shame-and-doubt stage *the period during which toddlers (ages 18 months to 3 years) develop independence and autonomy if exploration and freedom are encouraged or shame and self-doubt if they are restricted and overprotected*

temperament *patterns of arousal and emotionality that represent consistent and enduring characteristics in an individual*

Temperament: Stabilities in Infant Behavior

Sarah's parents thought there must be something wrong. Unlike her older brother Josh, who had been so active as an infant that he seemed to never be still, Sarah was much more placid. She took long naps and was easily soothed on those relatively rare occasions when she became agitated. What could be producing her extreme calmness?

The most likely answer: The difference between Sarah and Josh reflected differences in temperament. As we first discussed in Chapter 2, **temperament** encompasses patterns of arousal and emotionality that represent consistent and enduring characteristics in an individual.

Temperament refers to *how* children behave, as opposed to *what* they do or *why* they do it (A. Thomas & Chess, 1977). As we first noted in Chapter 2, infants show temperamental differences in general disposition from the time of birth. These differences appear to be largely determined by genetic factors, although there is also evidence that the prenatal environment and the nature of a child's birth may also have some influence. Regardless of cause, temperament is quite consistent, with longitudinal studies showing stability from infancy well into adolescence (Caspi et al., 1995; Guerin & Gottfried, 1994; Gunnar et al., 1995; Pedlow et al., 1993; Riese, 1990; Sanson et al., 1994).

easy babies *babies who have a positive disposition; their body functions operate regularly, and they are adaptable; about 40 percent of all babies are in this category*

difficult babies *babies who have negative moods and are slow to adapt to new situations; when confronted with a new situation, they tend to withdraw; about 10 percent of all babies belong in this category*

slow-to-warm babies *babies who are inactive, showing relatively calm reactions to their environment and are generally negative, withdrawing from new situations and adapting slowly; around 15 percent of infants are slow-to-warm*

Several dimensions of behavior reflect temperament. One central dimension is *activity level,* which reflects the degree of overall movement. Some babies (like Sarah) are relatively placid, and their movements are slow and almost leisurely. In contrast, the activity level of other infants (like Josh) is quite high, with strong, restless movements of the arms and legs.

Another important dimension of temperament is the nature and quality of an infant's mood, and in particular a child's *irritability.* Some infants are easily disturbed and cry easily, while others are relatively easygoing. Irritable infants fuss a great deal, and they are easily upset. They are also difficult to soothe when they do begin to cry. Such irritability is relatively stable: Researchers find that infants who are irritable at birth remain irritable at the age of 1, and even at age 2 they are still more easily upset than infants who were not irritable just after birth (Riese, 1987; Worobey & Bajda, 1989). (Other aspects of temperament are listed in Table 6-2).

Categorizing Temperament: Easy, Difficult, and Slow-to-Warm Babies. Because temperament can be viewed along so many dimensions, some researchers have asked whether there are broader categories that can be used to describe children's overall behavior. According to Alexander Thomas and Stella Chess (1984), who carried out a large-scale study of a group of infants that has come to be known as the *New York Longitudinal Study,* babies can be described according to one of several profiles:

- *Easy babies.* **Easy babies** have a positive disposition. Their body functions operate regularly, and they are adaptable. They are generally positive, showing curiosity about new situations; and their emotions are moderate or low in intensity. This category applies to about 40 percent (the majority) of infants.
- *Difficult babies.* **Difficult babies** have more negative moods, and they are slow to adapt to new situations. When confronted with a new situation, they tend to withdraw. About 10 percent of infants belong in this category.
- *Slow-to-warm babies.* **Slow-to-warm babies** are inactive, showing relatively calm reactions to their environment. Their moods are generally negative, and they withdraw from new situations, adapting slowly. Around 15 percent of infants are slow-to-warm.

As for the remaining 35 percent, they cannot be consistently categorized. These children show a variety of combinations of characteristics. For instance, one infant may have relatively sunny moods, but react negatively to new situations, or another may show little stability of any sort in terms of general temperament.

TABLE 6-2

DIMENSIONS OF TEMPERAMENT

Dimension	Description
Activity level	Proportion of active time periods to inactive time periods
Approach-withdrawal	The response to a new person or object, based on whether the child accepts the new situation or withdraws from it
Adaptability	How easily the child is able to adapt to changes in his or her environment
Quality of mood or irritability	The contrast of the amount of friendly, joyful, and pleasant behavior with unpleasant, unfriendly behavior
Attention span and persistence	The amount of time the child devotes to an activity and the effect of distraction on that activity
Distractibility	The degree to which stimuli in the environment alter behavior
Rhythmicity (regularity)	The regularity of basic functions such as hunger, excretion, sleep, and wakefulness
Intensity of reaction	The energy level or reaction of the child's response
Threshold of responsiveness	The intensity of stimulation needed to elicit a response

(*Source:* Thomas & Chess, 1984.)

The Consequences of Temperament: Does Temperament Matter? The obvious question to emerge from the findings of the relative stability of temperament is whether a particular kind of temperament is beneficial. The answer seems to be that no single type of temperament is invariably good or bad. Instead, children's long-term adjustment depends on the **goodness of fit** of their particular temperament and the nature and demands of the environment in which they find themselves. For instance, children with a low activity level and low irritability may do particularly well in an environment in which they are left to explore on their own and allowed to largely direct their own behavior. In contrast, high-activity-level, highly irritable children may do best with greater direction, which permits them to channel their energy in particular directions (Bornstein & Lamb, 1992b; Mangelsdorf et al., 1990; A. Thomas & Chess, 1977, 1980).

goodness of fit *the notion that children's long-term adjustment is dependent on the degree of match between their temperament and the nature and demands of the environment in which they are being raised*

gender *the sense of being male or female*

Some research does suggest that certain temperaments are, in general, more adaptive than others. For instance, Thomas, Chess , and Birch (1968) found that difficult children, in general, were more likely to show behavior problems by school age than those who were classified as easy children in infancy. But not all difficult children do experience problems. The key determinant seems to be the way in which parents react to their infants' difficult behavior. If they react by showing anger and inconsistency—which their child's difficult, demanding behavior readily evokes—then the child is ultimately more likely to experience behavior problems. On the other hand, parents who display more warmth and consistency in their responses are more likely to have children who avoid later problems (Belsky, Fish, & Isabella, 1991; Crockenberg, 1986).

Cultural differences also have a major influence on the consequences of a particular temperament. For instance, children who would be described as "difficult" in Western cultures actually seem to have an advantage in the East African Masai culture. The reason? Since mothers offer their breast to their infants only when they fuss and cry, the irritable, more difficult infants are apt to receive more nourishment than the more placid easy infants. Particularly when environmental conditions are bad, such as during a drought, difficult babies are apt to have an advantage (M. W. deVries, 1984).

Recent approaches to temperament grow out of the framework of behavioral genetics that we discussed in Chapter 2. For instance, Arnold Buss and Robert Plomin (1984) argue that temperamental characteristics represent inherited traits that are fairly stable during childhood and across the entire life span. These traits are seen as making up the core of personality and playing a substantial role in future development.

Gender: Why Do Boys Wear Blue and Girls Wear Pink?

From the moment of birth, girls and boys are treated differently. Their parents send out different kinds of birth announcements. They are given different clothes to wear and different-colored blankets. The toys that are chosen for them differ (Bridges, 1993).

Parents play with them differently: From birth on, fathers tend to interact more with sons than daughters, while mothers interact more with daughters (R. D. Parke & Sawin, 1980). Because, as we noted earlier in the chapter, mothers and fathers play in different ways (with fathers typically engaging in more physical, rough-and-tumble activities and mothers in traditional games such as peekaboo), male and female infants are clearly exposed to different styles of activity and interaction from their parents (Grant, 1994; Lamb, 1986; R. D. Parke, 1990; Power & Parke, 1982).

The behavior exhibited by girls and boys is interpreted in very different ways by adults. For instance, in one experiment researchers showed adults a video of an infant whose name was given as either "John" or "Mary" (Condry & Condry, 1976). Although it was the same baby performing a single set of behaviors, adults perceived "John" as adventurous and inquisitive, while "Mary" was fearful and anxious. Clearly adults view the behavior of children through the lens of **gender**, the sense of being male or female. ("Gender" and "sex" are not the same: *sex* typically refers to sexual anatomy and sexual behavior, while *gender* refers

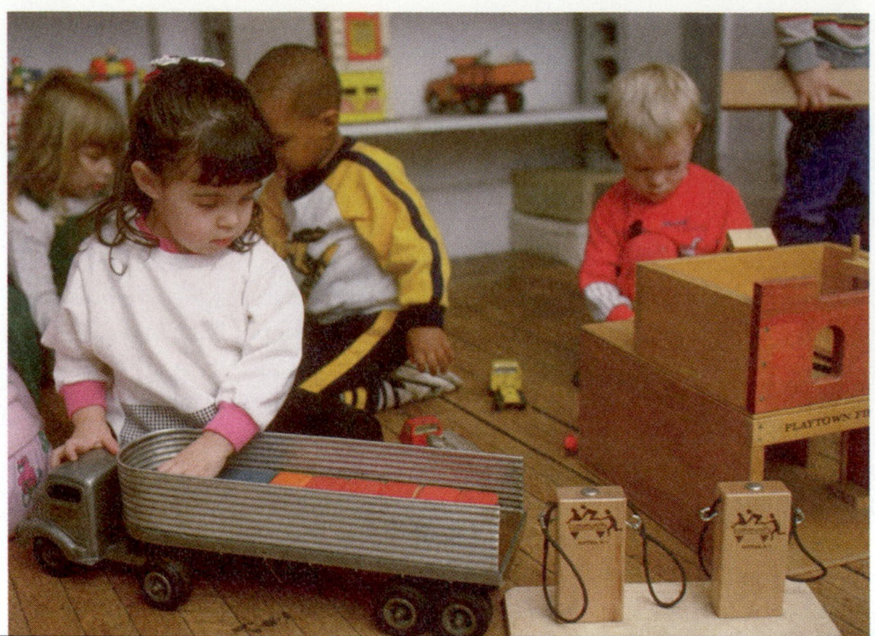

Parents of girls who play with toys related to activities associated with boys are apt to be less concerned than parents of boys who play with toys typically associated with girls.

to the perception of maleness or femaleness related to membership in a particular society) (Burnham & Harris, 1992; A. Pomerleau, Bolduc, Malcuit, & Cossette, 1990; M. Stern & Karraker, 1989).

Although it is obvious that boys and girls live, to some extent, in different worlds due to their respective gender, there is a considerable amount of argument over both the extent and causes of such gender differences. Some gender differences are fairly clear from the time of birth. For example, male infants tend to be more active and fussier than female infants. Boys grimace more, although no gender difference exists in the overall amount of crying, and boys' sleep tends to be more disturbed than that of girls. There is also some evidence that male newborns are more irritable than female newborns, although the findings are inconsistent (Eaton & Enns, 1986; Moss, 1974; Phillips, King, & DuBois, 1978).

However, the overall differences between male and female infants are generally minor. In fact, in most ways infants seem so similar that usually adults cannot discern whether a baby is a boy or girl. Furthermore, it is important to keep in mind that the differences among individual boys, and the differences among individual girls, are much more extensive than the average differences found when boys and girls are compared (Beal, 1994; Langlois et al., 1991; Unger & Crawford, 1992).

Gender differences emerge more clearly as children age–and become increasingly influenced by the gender roles that society sets out for them. For instance, by the age of 1 year, infants are able to make distinctions between males and females. Furthermore, girls prefer to play with dolls or stuffed animals, while boys seek out blocks and trucks. Often, of course, these are the only options available to them, due to the choices their parents and other adults have made in the toys they provide (Poulin-Dubois et al., 1994).

Children's preferences for certain kinds of toys are reinforced by their parents, although parents of boys are more apt to be concerned about their child's choices than are parents of girls. For example, 1-year-old boys receive more positive reactions for playing with transportation and building toys than do girls. Moreover, the amount of reinforcement boys receive for playing with toys that society deems appropriate increases with age, and boys receive increasing discouragement for playing with toys that society views as more acceptable for girls. On the other hand, girls who play with toys seen by society as "masculine" are less discouraged for their behavior than boys who play with toys seen as "feminine" (Eisenberg et al., 1985; Fagot & Hagan, 1991).

By the time they reach the age of 2, boys behave more independently and less compliantly than girls. Much of this behavior can be traced to parental reactions to earlier behav-

The view of the family, as reflected in media depictions ranging from Ozzie and Harriet to Roseanne, has changed radically from the 1950s to the present.

ior. For instance, when a child takes his or her first steps, parents tend to react differently, depending on the child's gender: Boys are encouraged more to go off and explore the world, while girls are hugged and kept close. In general, exploratory behavior tends to be encouraged more in boys than in girls. It is hardly surprising, then, that by 2 years, girls tend to show less independence and greater compliance (Brooks-Gunn & Matthews, 1979; Fagot, 1978; Kuczynski, & Kochanska, 1990).

In sum, differences in behavior between boys and girls begin in infancy, and—as we will see in future chapters—continue to be seen throughout childhood (and beyond). Although gender differences have complex causes, representing some combination of innate, biologically related factors and environmental factors, they play a profound role in the social and emotional development of infants. Boys and girls are treated differently on the basis of gender from birth onward, and this differential treatment produces dissimilar worlds for members of the two sexes, even during infancy.

Family Life in the 1990s: Ozzie and Harriet Go the Way of the Dinosaurs

A look back at television shows of the 1950s (such as *Ozzie and Harriet* and *Leave It to Beaver*) finds a world of families portrayed in a way that today seems oddly old-fashioned and quaint: mothers and fathers, married for years, and their good-looking children making their way in a world that seems to have few, if any, serious problems.

As we discussed in Chapter 1, even in the 1950s such a view of family life was overly romantic and unrealistic. Today, however, it is broadly inaccurate, representing only a minority of families in the United States. A quick review of statistics collected by the U.S. Census Bureau tells the story (Bird & Melville, 1994; Carnegie Task Force on Meeting the Needs of Young Children, 1994; Gelles, 1994):

- The number of single-parent families has increased dramatically in the last two decades, as the number of two-parent households has declined. Around 56 percent of white children live with both parents, while just one quarter of African American children and one third of Hispanic children live with both parents. If current trends continue, 60 percent of all children will live at some time during their lives with a single parent (Demo & Acock, 1991; U.S. Bureau of the Census, 1991c).

- The average size of families is shrinking. Today there are 2.6 persons in the average household, compared to 2.8 in 1980. The number of people living in nonfamily households (without any relatives) is close to 30 million.
- In 1960, 5 percent of all births in the United States were to unmarried mothers. By the 1990s, more than 25 percent of births were to unmarried mothers.
- Every minute, an adolescent in the United States gives birth.
- More than 5 million children under the age of 3 are cared for by other adults while their parents work, and more than half of mothers of infants work outside the home.
- In 1990, one quarter of families with children under 3 years of age lived in poverty in the United States. The rates are even higher for African American and Hispanic families and for single-parent families of young children. More children under 3 live in poverty than do older children, adults, or the elderly (Einbinder, 1992).

Such statistics are disheartening. At the very least, they suggest that infants are being raised in environments in which substantial stressors are present, factors that make raising children, never easy even under the best circumstances, an unusually difficult task.

On the other hand, society is adapting to the new realities of family life in the 1990s. Several kinds of social support exist for the parents of infants, and society is evolving new institutions to help in their care. One example is the growing array of child-care provisions available to help working parents.

INFANT DAY CARE: ASSESSING THE CONSEQUENCES

Should infants be placed in day care?

For many parents, there is little choice: Economic realities, or the desire to maintain a career, require that their children be left in the care of others for a portion of the day, typically in infant day-care settings. In fact, recent figures indicate that almost 25 percent of preschool children whose mothers work outside the home spend their days in day-care centers (see Figure 6-5). Do such arrangements have any discernible effects on infant development?

The answer, while not definitive, is reassuring: High-quality day care seems to produce only minor differences from home care, in most respects, and may even enhance certain aspects of development. For example, most research finds little or no difference in the strength of parental attachment bonds of infants who have been in day care compared with infants raised solely by their parents. Furthermore, various studies have found clear benefits from participation in day care. For instance, compared with children not in day care, children who participated in day care during their first year showed higher levels of play, laughing, and touching;

FIGURE 6-5

WHERE ARE CHILDREN CARED FOR?

Although most children spend their days at home, almost one quarter of children younger than 5 years of age whose mothers work outside the home spend their days in day-care centers.

(*Source*: U.S. Bureau of the Census, 1991c; Child Health USA '93, 1993.)

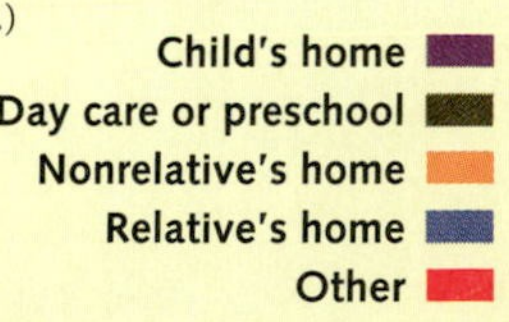

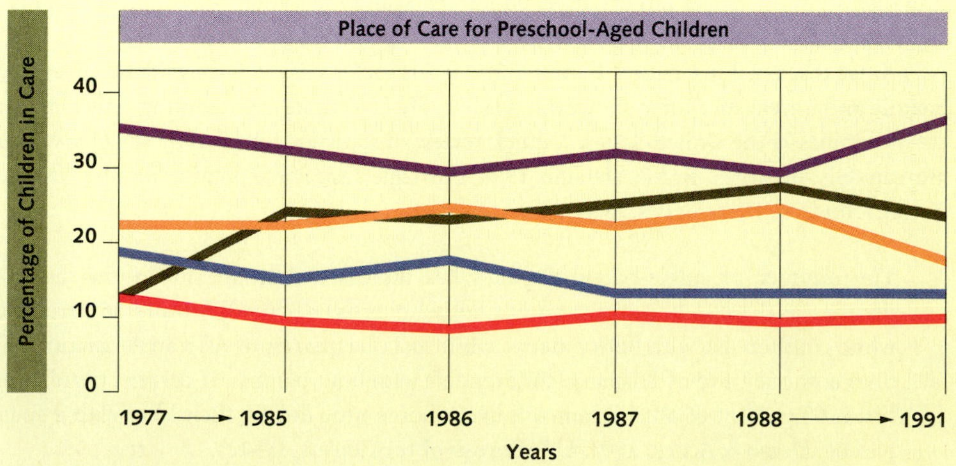

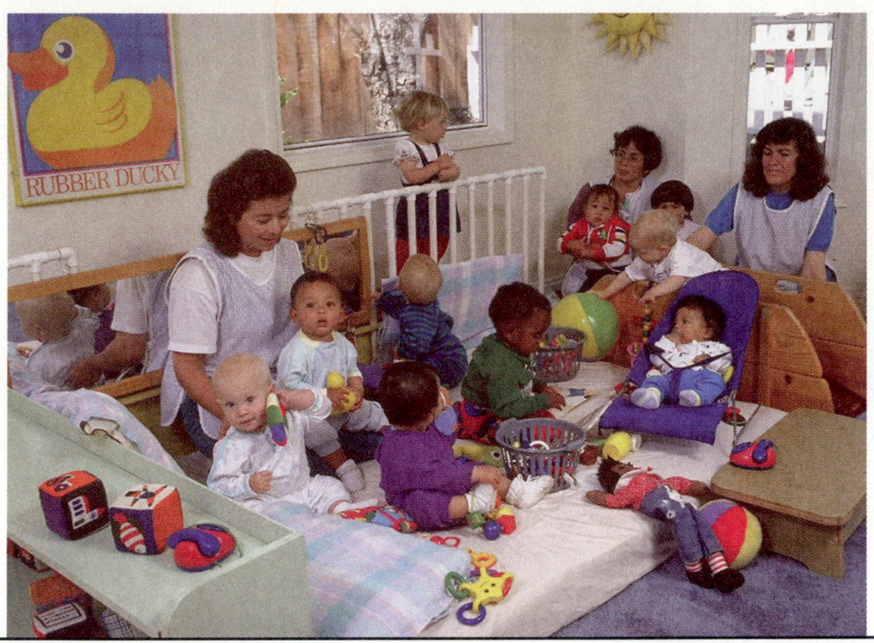

High-quality infant day care seems to produce only minor differences from home care in most respects, and some aspects of development may even be enhanced.

they kicked and pushed less; and they were found to be more sociable and cooperative (Haskins, 1985; Phillips et al., 1987; T. Field et al., 1988; Howes, Phillips, & Whitebook, 1992; Fein, Gariboldi, & Boni, 1993; Volling & Feagans, 1995).

In addition, infant day care may have lasting beneficial effects. For instance, research examining chldren from low-income families who had participated in day care from infancy through 3 years of age found advantages in terms of cognitive and academic achievement at the age of 12 (F. A. Campbell & Ramey, 1994).

On the other hand, some research has yielded mixed, and some negative, results regarding the outcomes of infant day care (Matlock & Green, 1990). For example, one study found that high-risk, poor children who had secure attachment to their mothers showed negative, avoidant, and more aggressive behavior several years after participating in infant day care. However, the results were not uniformly negative: For insecurely attached infants, participation in infant day care was associated with more positive outcomes. Apparently, involvement in day care acted as a protective factor for the children who had come from insecurely attached backgrounds (Egeland & Hiester, 1995).

Other research finds that participation in infant day care may actually produce less secure attachment. For instance, one study found that infants involved in care outside the home for more than 20 hours a week during their first year show less secure attachment to their mothers than those who have not been in day care. Moreover, boys in day care for 35 or more hours a week show some evidence of less secure attachment to their fathers (Belsky & Rovine, 1988; Chase-Lansdale & Owen, 1987).

Other research points to further potential drawbacks of day care—at least in extensive quantities—during infancy. For instance, infants who spend their first year in full-time day care have sometimes been found to exhibit more aggression, less obedience, and more negative reactions to frustration than those who were cared for at home. Furthermore, some studies suggest that children who spend more time in day care may adjust less successfully when they get to kindergarten (J. E. Bates et al., 1994; Haskins, 1985; Rubenstein, Howes, & Boyule, 1981).

Although such findings are troubling, their implications may be less far-reaching than we might at first assume. For instance, not all of the children in the studies were enrolled in high-quality day-care settings; many were in less than optimal situations. Furthermore, some of the findings may not be entirely negative: The greater aggression and lower compliance found in some studies may simply reflect increased assertiveness among children who have more experience in the company of groups of other children (Aviezer et al., 1994; Howes et al., 1992).

Finally, there is no assurance that the personalities and socioeconomic status of children who are in day care are similar to those of children who are raised in the home by parents. Although the use of day care is prevalent throughout all segments of society, it is likely that certain groups are overrepresented in day-care centers. Consequently, until more research is done on just who makes use of day care and how it is used by members of different segments of society, we won't be able to understand fully the consequences of participation. Furthermore, research must take into account the quality of day-care centers and the specific activities they engage in to optimize the potential benefits and minimize the negative consequences of care outside the home (Appelbaum, 1995; Clarke-Stewart, Gruber, & Fitzgerald, 1994).

The Informed Consumer of Development

Choosing the Right Infant Care Provider

If there is one finding that emerges with crystal clarity from research conducted on the consequences of infant day care, it is that benefits occur only when day care is of high quality (Volling & Feagans, 1995; Zigler & Styfco, 1994). But what distinguishes high-quality day care from low-caliber programs?

The American Psychological Association suggests considering these questions in choosing a program (Committee on Children, Youth, and Families, 1994):

- Are there enough providers? A desirable ratio is one adult for every three to four infants.

Speaking of Development

Melinda Rauch, Child-Care Provider

Born: 1966

Education: University of Colorado at Denver, B.A. in psychology

Position: Infant/toddler teacher for HeartsHome Early Learning Center in Houston, Texas

Home: Spring, Texas

Upon graduation from college, Melinda Rauch answered an ad for a preschool teacher, expecting that it would be just a temporary job. As it turned out, her love of children had guided her to her current vocation.

For the past 4-½ years, Rauch has worked with infants and toddlers at HeartsHome, providing far more than basic day-care services.

"We meet our children's basic needs by making sure they're happy, clean, dry, and fed; but we also meet their developmental needs by teaching them to take turns, get along with others, and accept that they don't always get their own way," Rauch says.

- Are group sizes manageable? Even with several providers, a group of infants should not be larger than eight.
- Do the individuals providing the care seem to like what they are doing? You should find out what their motivation is. Is day care just a temporary job, or is it a career? Are they experienced? Do they seem happy in the job, or is offering day care just a way to earn money?
- What do the caregivers do during the day? They should spend their time playing with, listening and talking to, and paying attention to the children. They should seem genuinely interested in the children, rather than merely going through the motions of caring for them.
- Are the children safe and clean? The environment should be one in which infants can move around and not be endangered. The equipment and furniture should be in good repair. Moreover, the providers should adhere to the highest levels of cleanliness. After changing a baby's diaper, providers should wash their hands.
- What training do the providers have in caring for children? They should know the basics of infant development, having an understanding of how normal children develop and being alert to signs that development may depart from normal patterns.
- Finally, is the environment happy and cheerful? Day care is not just a baby-sitting service: For the time an infant is there, it is the child's whole world. You should feel fully comfortable and confident that the day-care center is a place where your infant will be treated as an individual.

In addition to following these guidelines, you may contact the National Association for the Education of Young Children, from which you may be able to get the name of a

"We also meet their developmental needs by teaching them to take turns, get along with others."

Activities that include learning opportunities are an integral part of an infant's day at HeartsHome, according to Rauch. "We work with infants from 6 weeks to 3 years old, and we vary the activities by age group. We do a lot of sensory play with different substances, such as rice, cornmeal, and water. When we do artwork, we don't focus on the products that the child creates so much as on the process the child uses in creating.

"Everything is a hands-on experience," she explains. "Basically, I take a crayon and model what to do with it. Then I put the crayon in their hands and help them make the same motions. Often they'll stick it in their mouths, and so we'll have a learning experience that crayons aren't food. We can go through several learning experiences just using crayons."

Getting along with others is an important socialization task, and Rauch says she works with children as young as 18 months on the concept of sharing.

"We don't expect them to learn the concept completely at 18 months, but we will use a popular toy like mini-basketballs to teach sharing. There may be more than one of a particular item, but it's still a problem when all the children want to do the same thing at the same time. I try to explain turn taking, and then I might take the child who doesn't have the item and guide him or her to read a book or play with another toy. It's important to give them a sense that there are alternatives."

"When we do artwork, we don't focus on the products that the child creates so much as on the process the child uses in creating."

resource and referral agency in your area. Write (enclosing a self-addressed, stamped envelope) to NAEYC Information Service, 1509 16th Street NW, Washington, DC 20036-1426; or call (800) 424-2460.

Review and Rethink

REVIEW

- Personality is the sum total of the enduring characteristics that differentiate one individual from another. According to Erikson, infants move from the first stage of psychosocial development, the trust-versus-mistrust stage, to the second, the autonomy-versus-shame-and-doubt stage.
- Temperament encompasses enduring levels of arousal and emotionality that are characteristic of an individual.
- Gender differences become more pronounced as infants age, due mostly to environmental influences, especially the different expectations, attitudes, and actions displayed by parents and other adults toward boys and girls.
- Substantial changes in the nature of the family have brought about corresponding adjustments in the ways children are nurtured and reared.
- Day care can have neutral, positive, or negative effects on the social development of children, depending largely on its quality.
- Research on the effects of day care must take into account the varying quality of different day-care settings and the social characteristics of the parents who tend to use day care.

RETHINK

- Does the concept of social referencing, studied in this chapter, help explain the development of gender-based behavioral differences in young children? How?
- The "John" and "Mary" video experiment described in this section demonstrates how identical actions of boys and girls can be interpreted differently. Can you think of examples of the same phenomenon occurring in adulthood?
- What are some social implications of the changes in family life described in this chapter? What sorts of family policies might be instituted to address these changes?
- Can you relate the issue of day care to the phenomenon of attachment studied earlier in this chapter? What factors complicate the relationship between day care and attachment?
- How might social attitudes toward such issues as women's careers and alternative lifestyles influence studies of the effects of day care and the interpretation of their findings?

LOOKING BACK

Do infants have emotions?

1. Infants display a variety of facial expressions that appear to reflect their basic emotional states. This is called nonverbal encoding. The basic facial expressions that infants display are similar across cultures.

2. By the end of the first year, infants often develop both stranger anxiety and separation anxiety. Stranger anxiety, which begins at around 6 months of age, is the caution and wariness displayed by infants when encountering a strange person. Separation anxiety is the distress displayed by infants when a customary care provider departs. Separation anxiety starts a little later than stranger anxiety, usually begining at about 8 or 9 months. It peaks around 14 months, and then slowly decreases.
3. Infants experience emotions that correspond to their facial displays. A basic repertoire of expressions and emotional states appears to be innate and to grow in sophistication and complexity as the child ages and gradually experiences a wider array of emotions.

How do infants interpret the emotions of others?

4. Early on infants develop the capability of nonverbal decoding: determining the emotional states of others based on their facial and vocal expressions.
5. Through a process called social referencing, infants from the age of 8 or 9 months use the expressions of others to clarify ambiguous situations and learn appropriate reactions to them.

What are some characteristics of infants' mental life?

6. Although at first infants are not aware that they exist independently from others and the larger world, they begin to develop self-awareness from about the age of 12 months.
7. Infants are also developing a theory of mind at this time: knowledge and beliefs about how they and others think. Their theory of mind gradually helps them understand that humans differ from other entities, that humans act with a sense of purpose and intentionality, that the emotions of others can be shared through empathy, and that beliefs can be manipulated through pretense and deception.

What is attachment in infancy, and how does it relate to the future social competence of individuals?

8. Attachment, a strong, positive emotional bond that forms between an infant and one or more significant persons, is a crucial factor in enabling individuals to develop social relationships. Bowlby's theory that attachment is based primarily on infants' genetic motivation to seek safety from predators and Lorenz's theory that infants are biologically driven to "imprint" on a caregiving individual—typically the mother—during a critical period soon after birth suggest that attachment is a genetically determined trait, although some would contend that it has significant cultural aspects.
9. The Ainsworth Strange Situation measure classifies infants into one of three major attachment patterns: securely attached, avoidant, and ambivalent. A fourth pattern, disorganized-disoriented, was added later. Research suggests an association between an infant's attachment pattern and his or her adult social and emotional competence. Cultural factors probably affect interpretation of this measure.

What roles do mothers, fathers, and infants play in social development?

10. Mothers' interactions with their babies have been found to be particularly important for social development. Mothers who respond effectively to their babies' social overtures appear to contribute to the babies' ability to become securely attached.
11. Infants' temperamental differences have at most a slight association with their attachment patterns, but infants who tend to display their emotions nonverbally provide cues that facilitate caregiver responses conducive to secure attachment.
12. Infants may form primary attachments with their fathers, but this is less usual than with their mothers. Furthermore, attachments to fathers differ qualitatively from

attachments to mothers, at least partly because fathers and mothers interact differently with their babies.

What sorts of interactions do infants engage in with caregivers and other children?

13. Through a process of reciprocal socialization, infants and caregivers interact and affect one another's behavior, which strengthens their mutual relationship.
14. From an early age, infants engage in rudimentary forms of social interaction with other children, and their level of sociability rises as they age, eventually encompassing the ability to learn effectively from one another. Social interactions with other children serve as a foundation for future social exchanges and relationships.

What are some of the ways that infants differ from one another?

15. The origins of personality, the sum total of the enduring characteristics that differentiate one individual from another, are found during infancy. According to Erikson's theory of psychosocial development, infants are initially in the trust-versus-mistrust stage, encompassing birth to 1½ years. During this period, infants develop a sense of trust or mistrust, largely depending on how well their needs are met by their caregivers. They then enter the autonomy-versus-shame-and-doubt stage (1½ to 3 years), in which they either develop independence and autonomy or feel shame, self-doubt, and unhappiness.
16. Temperament encompasses enduring levels of arousal and emotionality that are characteristic of an individual. Several dimensions, such as activity level and irritability, reflect temperament. Temperamental differences are reflected in the broad classification of infants into easy, difficult, and slow-to-warm categories.
17. Although biologically based behavioral differences between boy and girl infants exist, they are minor compared to their behavioral similarities. However, as infants age, gender differences become more pronounced, mostly due to the influence of environmental factors.
18. Differences between boys and girls are accentuated by parental expectations and behavior. For instance, mothers and fathers display different interaction patterns with their children. Furthermore, the toy and play preferences of boys and girls differ and are differently encouraged by parents, and boys' and girls' actions are interpreted differently by parents and other adults.

How are societal changes reflected in family life and child-care practices?

19. Family life in the United States is rapidly changing. The size of the average family has decreased, and there are now more single-parent families, more unmarried and very young mothers, more working parents, and more children born into poverty than ever before.

Is day care beneficial or harmful for infants?

20. Day care, a social response to the changing nature of the family, can be beneficial to the social development of children, fostering social interaction and cooperation, if it is of high quality.
21. On the other hand, some research has found negative outcomes from day care, including increased levels of aggression and disobedience in children placed in day care and a decreased ability among young infants to form secure attachments to their parents. These findings pertain to children involved in large amounts of day care each week.

22. Studies of the effects of day care should increasingly take into account factors related to the quality of the day care provided and to the characteristics of the parents who tend to use day care as a childrearing strategy.
23. High-quality day care appears to have few or no negative effects on children and may even have positive effects in terms of social development. High-quality day care can be recognized by the ratio of providers to children, the quality of the facilities, the nature of the activities provided, and the attitudes and expertise of the providers.

KEY TERMS AND CONCEPTS

differential emotions theory (p. 191)
stranger anxiety (p. 191)
separation anxiety (p. 192)
social smile (p. 192)
social referencing (p. 193)
self-awareness (p. 194)
theory of mind (p. 195)
empathy (p. 195)
attachment (p. 197)
Ainsworth Strange Situation (p. 197)
securely attached children (p. 198)
avoidant children (p. 198)
ambivalent children (p. 198)
disorganized-disoriented children (p. 199)
mutual regulation model (p. 203)
reciprocal socialization (p. 203)
personality (p. 207)
Erikson's theory of psychosocial development (p. 207)
trust-versus-mistrust stage (p. 207)
autonomy-versus-shame-and-doubt stage (p. 207)
temperament (p. 207)
easy babies (p. 208)
difficult babies (p. 208)
slow-to-warm babies (p. 208)
goodness-of-fit (p. 209)
gender (p. 209)

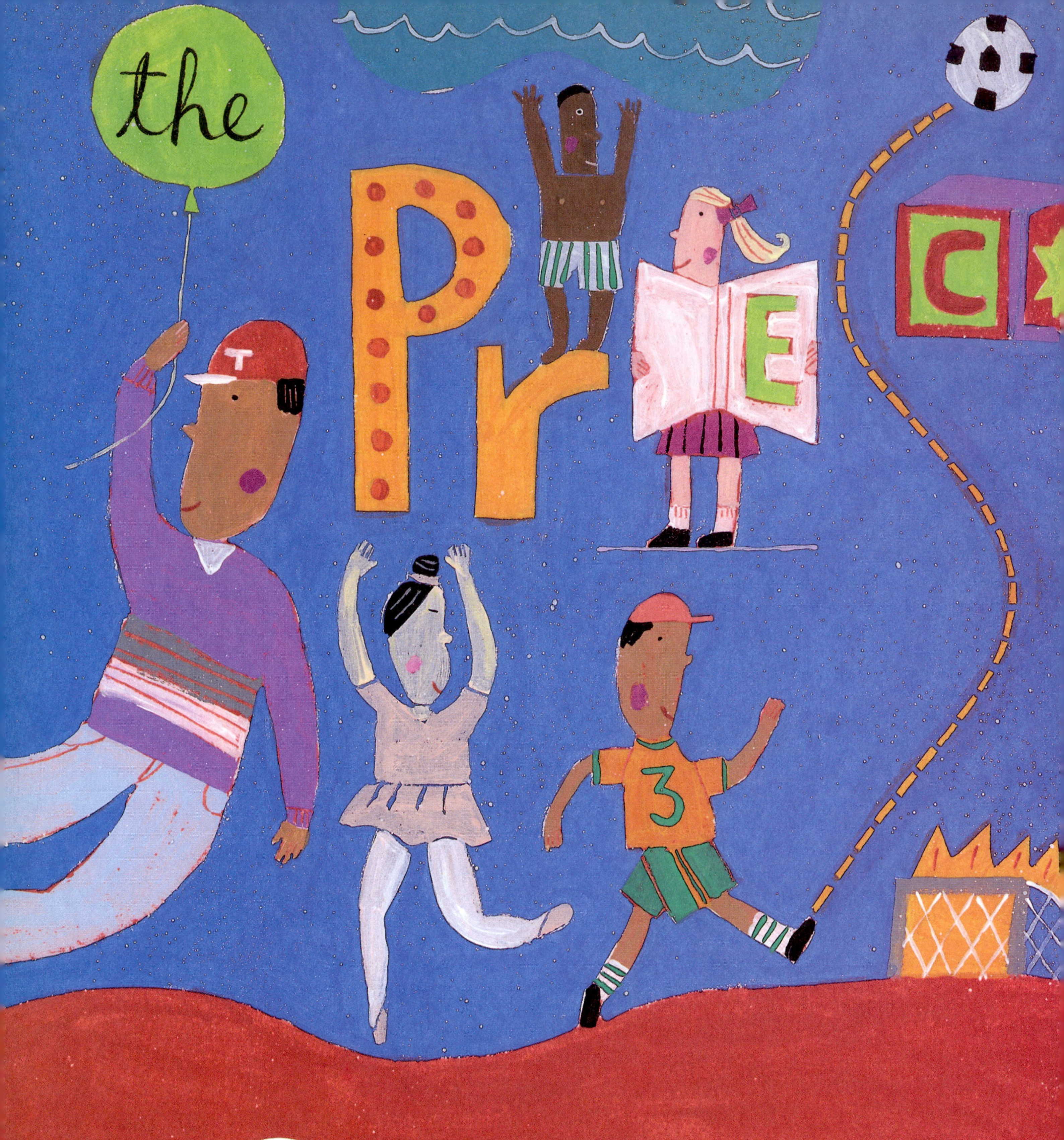

PART 3

The Preschool Years

yum!
meow
years

CHAPTER 7

THE PRESCHOOL YEARS

Physical Development in the Preschool Years

ROLOGUE

THE SHORT LIFE AND SLOW DEATH OF ELISA IZQUIERDO

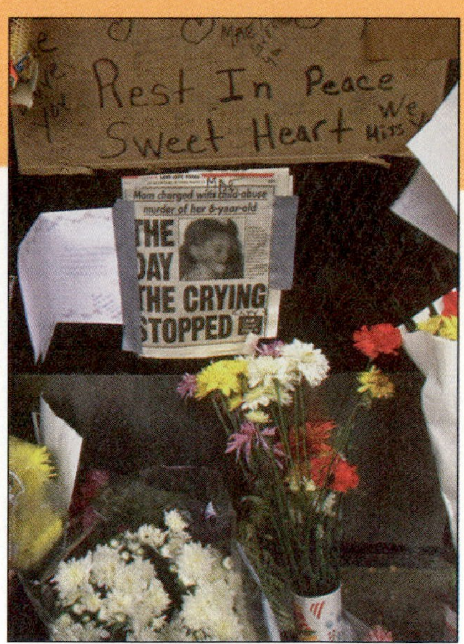

In one sense, she was just another statistic: Elisa Izquierdo—born 1989, died 1995. But her death put a face on what some experts call a public health epidemic of child abuse—and a system of protection that often fails those most in need.

The facts of Elisa's case are nothing less than horrifying. Conceived in a homeless shelter, she was probably a victim of abuse from the earliest years of her life. Her mother, estranged from her father, was a crack cocaine addict, and she somehow became convinced that her daughter had been put under a spell and harbored evil spirits. With twisted logic, her mother tried to batter the supposed evil out of Elisa through years of beatings and violations of every part of her body. The abuse culminated one November evening with her mother forcing Elisa to eat feces, mopping the floor with her head, and throwing her against a concrete wall. When Elisa was found by authorities, there was no part of her body that was not cut or bruised.

What set Elisa's case apart was not only its severity, but also, in some ways even more chilling, the repeated missed opportunities that might have saved her. Child welfare officials were told on many occasions that Elisa may have been the victim of abuse. A school administrator called them. An emergency room physician called. School social workers called repeatedly. Yet the child welfare system, overburdened and understaffed, let Elisa down, in a failure that is a painful commentary on our society's inability to protect its children. (Bernstein & Bruni, 1995; van Biema, 1995)

LOOKING AHEAD

Elisa's death at the hand of a parent is not, unfortunately, a very rare occurrence. Some 3 million children are abused or neglected in the United States each year, and some 2,000 die as a result of violence. According to some experts, the incidence of violence aimed at young children has reached the level of a public health crisis (Ards & Harrell, 1993; Mones, 1995; U.S. Advisory Board on Child Abuse and Neglect, 1995).

Happily, however, most children do not experience such violence. The vast majority pass through the preschool years not as victims, but as beneficiaries of the love and support of their families and society. These years are, in fact, an exciting time in children's lives. In one sense, the preschool years mark a time of preparation: a period spent anticipating and getting ready for the start of a child's formal education, where society begins to pass on its intellectual tools to a new generation.

But it is a mistake to take the label "preschool" too literally. The years between 3 and 6 are hardly a mere way station in life, an interval spent waiting for the next, more important period to start. Instead, the preschool years are a time of tremendous change and growth, where physical, intellectual, and social development proceeds at a rapid pace.

In this chapter, we focus on the physical changes that occur during the preschool years. We begin by considering the nature of growth during those years. We discuss the rapid changes in the body's weight and height, as well as developmental changes in the brain and its neural byways. We also consider some intriguing findings relating to the ways the brain functions across genders and cultures.

Next, we focus on health and wellness in the preschool years. After discussing the nutritional needs of preschoolers, we examine the risk of illness and injury that they face. We

Only a few years earlier, these tireless preschoolers were not able to walk or crawl.

also look at the grimmer side of some children's lives: child abuse and psychological maltreatment.

Finally, the chapter ends with a discussion of the development of gross and fine motor skills. We consider the significant changes that occur during the preschool period in motor performance, and what these changes allow children to accomplish. We also look at the impact of being right- or left-handed, and discuss how artistic abilities develop during the preschool years.

After reading this chapter, then, you'll be able to answer the following questions:

- What changes in the body and the brain do children experience in the preschool years?
- What are the nutritional needs of preschool children, and what causes obesity?
- What threats to their health and wellness do preschool children experience?
- What are child abuse and psychological maltreatment, what factors contribute to them, and can anything be done about them?
- In what ways do children's gross and fine motor skills develop during the preschool years?
- How do handedness and artistic expression develop during these years?

PHYSICAL GROWTH

It is an unseasonably warm spring day at the Cushman Hill Preschool, one of the first nice days after a long winter. The children in Mary Scott's class have happily left their winter coats in the classroom for the first time this spring, and they are excitedly playing outside. Jessie plays a game of catch with Germaine, while Sarah and Molly climb up the slide. Craig and Marta chase one another, while Jesse and Bernstein try, with gales of giggles, to play leapfrog. Virginia and Ollie sit across from each other on the teeter-totter, successively bumping it so hard into the ground that they both are in danger of being knocked off. Erik, Jim, Scott, and Paul race around the perimeter of the playground, running for the sheer joy of it.

These same children, now so active and mobile, were unable even to crawl or walk just a few years earlier. The advances in their physical abilities that have occurred in such a short time are nothing short of astounding. Just how far they have developed is apparent when we look at the specific changes they have undergone in their size, shape, and physical abilities.

THE GROWING BODY

Two years after birth, the average child in the United States weighs in at around 25 to 30 pounds and is close to 36 inches tall—around half the height of the average adult. Children grow steadily during the preschool period, and by the time they are 6 years old they weigh, on average, about 46 pounds and stand 46 inches tall (see Figure 7-1).

Individual Differences in Height and Weight. These averages mask great individual differences in height and weight. For instance, 10 percent of 6-year-olds weigh 55 pounds or more, and 10 percent weigh 36 pounds or less. Furthermore, average differences in height and weight between boys and girls increase during the preschool years. Although at age 2 the differences are relatively small, by the age of 6 boys begin to be taller and heavier, on average, than girls.

Furthermore, profound differences in height and weight exist between children in economically developed countries and those in developing countries. The better nutrition and health care received by children in developed countries translates into significant differ-

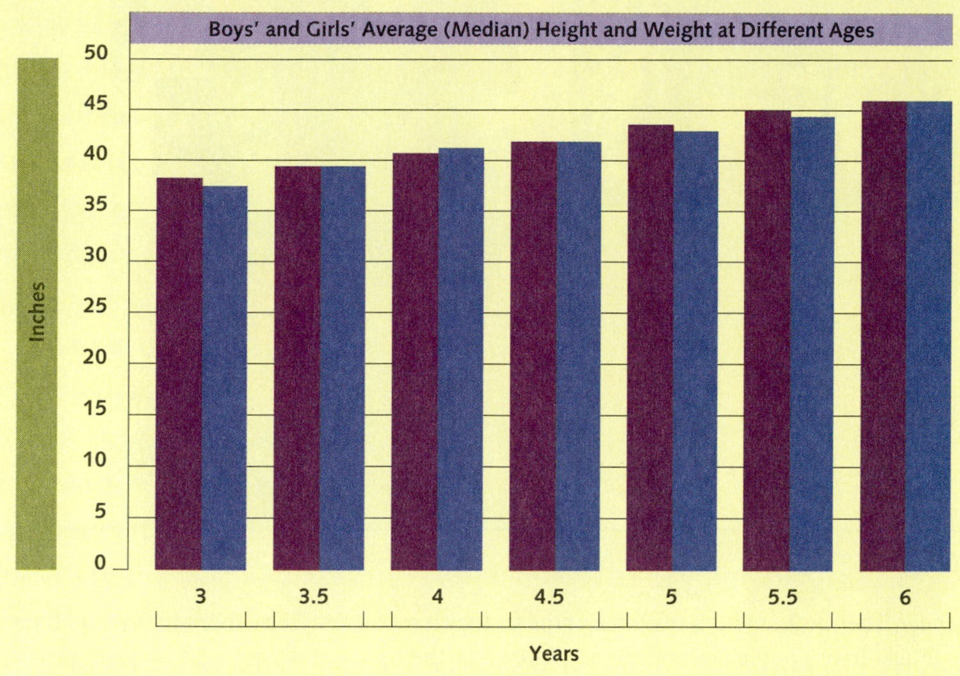

GAINING HEIGHT AND WEIGHT

The preschool years are marked by steady increases in height and weight. The graphs show the median point for boys and girls at each age, in which 50 percent of children in each category are above this height or weight level and 50 percent are below.

(*Source:* Adapted from Lowrey, 1986.)

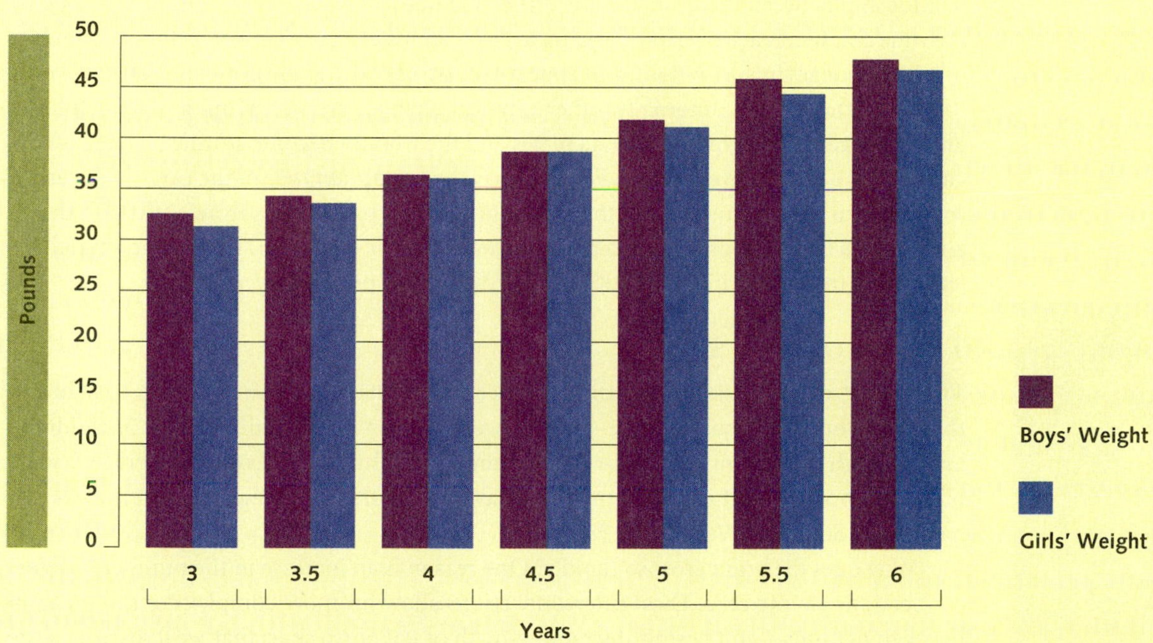

ences in growth. For instance, the average Swedish 4-year-old is as tall as the average 6-year-old in Bangladesh (United Nations, 1990).

Differences in height and weight reflect economic factors within the United States, as well. For instance, more than 10 percent of children in the United States whose family incomes are below the poverty level are among the shortest 5 percent of all preschool-age children (Barrett & Frank, 1987; Egan, 1994; Sherry, Springer, Connell, & Garrett, 1992).

Changes in Body Shape and Structure. If we compare the bodies of a 2-year-old and a 6-year-old, we find that the bodies vary not only in height and weight, but also in shape. During the preschool years, boys and girls become less chubby and roundish and more

This 2 and 6-year-old demonstrate the changes that occur in body shape during the preschool years. During this period, boys and girls become more slender and less roundish, and their arms and legs lengthen, making the size relationship between the head and the rest of the body more adultlike.

myelin *protective insulation that surrounds parts of neurons*

lateralization *the process in which certain functions are located more in one hemisphere of the brain than the other*

slender. They begin to burn off some of the fat they have carried from their infancy, and they no longer have a potbellied appearance. Moreover, their arms and legs lengthen, and the size relationship between the head and the rest of the body becomes more adultlike. In fact, by the time children reach 6 years of age, their proportions are quite similar to those of adults.

The changes in size, weight, and appearance we see during the preschool years are only the tip of the iceberg. Internally, other physical changes are occurring as well. Children grow stronger as their muscle size increases and their bones become sturdier. The sense organs continue their development. For instance, the *eustachian tube* in the ear, which carries sounds from the external part of the ear to the internal part, moves from a position that is almost parallel to the ground at birth to a more angular position. This change sometimes leads to an increase in frequency of earaches during the preschool years.

THE GROWING BRAIN

The brain grows at a faster rate than any other part of the body. Two-year-olds have brains that are about three quarters the size and weight of an adult brain. By age 5, children's brains weigh 90 percent of average adult brain weight. In comparison, the average 5-year-old's total body weight is just 30 percent of average adult body weight (Lowrey, 1986; Nihart, 1993; Schuster & Ashburn, 1986).

Why does the brain grow so rapidly? One reason is an increase in the number of interconnections among cells. These interconnections allow for more complex communication between neurons—and permit the rapid growth of cognitive skills that we'll discuss in the next chapter. In addition, the amount of **myelin**—protective insulation that surrounds parts of neurons—increases, which speeds the transmission of electrical impulses along brain cells but also adds to brain weight.

The two halves of the brain also begin to become increasingly differentiated and specialized. **Lateralization,** the process in which certain functions are located more in one hemisphere than the other, becomes more pronounced during the preschool years. (See Figure 7-2.)

For almost all right-handed individuals, and a majority of left-handed people, the left hemisphere concentrates on tasks that necessitate verbal competence, such as speaking, reading, thinking, and reasoning. The right hemisphere develops its own strengths, especially in nonverbal areas such as comprehension of spatial relationships, recognition of patterns and drawings, music, and emotional expression (Hellige, 1994; Kitterle, 1991; Zaidel, 1994).

HEARING WORDS

SPEAKING WORDS

FIGURE 7-2 These scans show how different parts of the brain are activated during particular tasks, illustrating the increasing specialization of the brain.

Each of the two hemispheres begins to process information in a slightly different manner. Whereas the left hemisphere considers information sequentially, one piece of data at a time, the right hemisphere processes information in a more global manner, reflecting on it as a whole (Gazzaniga, 1983; S. P. Springer & Deutsch, 1989).

Despite the specialization of the hemispheres, we need to keep in mind that in most respects the two hemispheres of the brain act in tandem. They are interdependent, and the differences between the two are minor. Furthermore, there are many individual differences in the nature of lateralization. For example, many of the 10 percent of people who are left-handed or ambidextrous (able to use both hands interchangeably) have language centered in their right hemispheres or have no specific language center.

Developmental Diversity

Are Gender and Culture Related to the Structure of the Brain?

Among the most controversial findings relating to the specialization of the hemispheres of the brain involves evidence that lateralization is related to gender and culture. For instance, starting during the first year of life and continuing in the preschool years, boys and girls show some hemispheric differences associated with lower body reflexes and the processing of auditory information (Grattan et al., 1992; Shucard et al., 1981). Furthermore, males clearly tend to show greater lateralization of language in the left hemisphere; among females, in contrast, language is more evenly divided between the two hemispheres (Gur et al., 1982). Such differences may help explain why—as we'll see in the next chapter—females' language development proceeds at a more rapid pace during the preschool years than males' language development.

We still don't know the source of the difference in lateralization between females and males. One explanation is genetic: that female and male brains are predisposed to function in slightly different ways. Such a view is supported by data suggesting that there are minor structural differences between males' and females' brains. For instance, a section of the **corpus callosum,** a bundle of fibers that connects the hemispheres of the brain, is proportionally larger in women than in men. Furthermore, studies conducted among other species, such as primates, rats, and hamsters, have found size and structural differences in the brains of males and females (Allen et al., 1989; Hammer, 1984; Witelson, 1989).

Before we accept a genetic explanation for the differences between female and male brains, we need to consider an equally plausible alternative: It may be that verbal abilities emerge earlier in girls because girls receive greater encouragement for verbal skills than boys do. For instance, there is evidence suggesting that, even as infants, girls are spoken to more than boys. Such higher levels of verbal stimulation may produce growth in particular areas of the brain that does not occur in boys. Consequently, environmental factors rather than genetic ones may lead to the gender differences we find in brain lateralization (Fagot, 1987; Maccoby & Jacklin, 1974; Unger & Crawford, 1996).

Even more tentative is evidence that suggests that the culture in which one is raised may be related to brain lateralization. For instance, native speakers of Japanese process information related to vowel sounds primarily in the left hemisphere of the brain. In comparison, North and South Americans and Europeans—as well as people of Japanese ancestry who learn Japanese as a second language—process vowel sounds primarily in the brain's right hemisphere.

The explanation for this cultural difference in processing of vowels seems to rest on the nature of the Japanese language. Specifically, the Japanese language allows for the

corpus callosum *a bundle of fibers that connects the hemispheres of the brain* expression of complex concepts using only vowel sounds. Consequently, a specific type of brain lateralization may develop while learning and using Japanese at a relatively early age (Tsunoda, 1985).

On the other hand, such an explanation, which is speculative, does not rule out the possibility that some type of subtle genetic difference may also be at work in determining the difference in lateralization. Once again, then, we find that teasing out the relative impact of heredity and environment is a challenging task.

In evaluating findings relating to the lateralization of the brain, it is important to keep in mind that the two halves of the brain do not work in isolation from one another. The two hemispheres are interdependent, and information, no matter of what sort, is typically processed simultaneously, to at least some degree, by both hemispheres.

Furthermore, the brain has remarkable resiliency. Even when the hemisphere that specializes in a particular type of information is damaged, the other hemisphere can take up the slack. For instance, when young children suffer brain damage to the left side of the brain (which specializes in verbal processing) and initially lose language capabilities, the linguistic deficits are often not permanent. In such cases, the right side of the brain pitches in and may be able to compensate substantially for the damage to the left hemisphere (Hellige, 1993, 1994; Hoptman & Davidson, 1994; Wiederhold, 1982).

SENSORY DEVELOPMENT

The increasing development of the brain permits improvements in the senses during the preschool period. For instance, brain maturation leads to better control of eye movements and focusing. Still, preschoolers' eyes are not as capable as they will be in later stages of development. Specifically, preschool-age children are unable to easily and precisely scan groupings of small letters, as is required when reading small print. Consequently, preschoolers who start to read often focus on just the initial letter of a word and guess at the rest—leading, as you might expect, to relatively frequent errors. It is not until they are approximately 6 years of age that children can effectively focus and scan. Even at this point, however, they still don't have the capabilities of adults (Aslin, 1987; Rayner & Pollatsek, 1989; Vurpillot, 1968; Willows, Kruk, & Corcos, 1993).

Preschool-age children also begin a gradual shift in the way they view objects made up of multiple parts. For instance, consider the rather unusual vegetable-fruit-bird combination shown in Figure 7-3 (Elkind, 1978). Rather than identifying it as a bird, as most adults do, preschool-age children see the figure in terms of the parts that make it up ("carrots" and "an apple" and "cherries" and "a pear"). It is not until they reach middle childhood, about the age of 7 or 8, that they begin to look at the figure in terms of both its overall organization and its parts ("a bird made of fruit").

Preschoolers' judgments of objects may reflect the way in which their eyes move when perceiving figures (Zaporozhets, 1965). Up until the age of 3 or 4, preschoolers devote most of their looking to the insides of two-dimensional objects they are scanning, concentrating on the internal details and largely ignoring the perimeter of the figure. In contrast, 4- and 5-year-olds begin to look more at the surrounding boundaries of the figure, and at 6 and 7 years of age they look at the outside systematically, with far less scanning of the inside. The result is a greater awareness of the overall organization of the figure.

Of course, vision is not the only sense that improves during the preschool period. For instance, *auditory acuity,* or the sharpness of hearing, improves as well. However, because hearing is more fully developed at the start of the preschool period, the improvement is not as significant as with vision.

FIGURE 7-3

SENSORY DEVELOPMENT

This odd vegetable-fruit-bird combination is seen by preschool-age children in terms of the parts that make it up. It is not until they reach middle childhood that they begin to look at the figure as a whole as well as its parts.

(*Source:* Elkind, 1978.)

One area in which preschoolers' auditory acuity does show some deficits is in the ability to isolate specific sounds when many sounds are heard simultaneously (Moores & Meadow-Orlans, 1990). This deficiency may account for why some preschoolers are easily distracted by competing sounds in group situations such as classrooms.

Sleep

No matter how tired they may be, it is often difficult for active preschoolers to make the passage from the excitement of the day to settling down for a night's rest. Consequently, there may be friction between caregivers and preschoolers over when it is time to go to bed. Children may object to being told to sleep, and it may take them some time before they are able to fall asleep.

Although most children settle down fairly easily and drift off into sleep, for some sleep presents a real problem. As many as 20 to 30 percent of preschoolers experience difficulties lasting more than an hour in getting to sleep. Furthermore, they may wake in the night and call to their parents for comfort (Lozoff, Wolf, & Davis, 1985).

Once they do get to sleep, most preschoolers sleep fairly soundly through the night. However, between 10 and 50 percent of children age 3 to 5 experience nightmares, with the frequency higher in boys than girls. **Nightmares** are vivid bad dreams, usually occurring towards morning. Although an occasional nightmare is no cause for concern, when they occur repeatedly and cause a child anxiety during waking hours, they may be indicative of a problem (Mindell & Cashman, 1995).

Night terrors produce intense physiological arousal and cause a child to wake up in an intense state of panic. After waking from a night terror, children are not easily comforted, and they cannot say why they are so disturbed and cannot recall having a bad dream. But the following morning, they cannot remember anything about the incident. Night terrors are much less frequent than nightmares, occurring in just 1 to 5 percent of children (Bootzin et al., 1993).

The most common sleep-related difficulty is **enuresis,** or a lack of bladder control past the age when most children are toilet trained. When it occurs, it usually involves bed-wetting during the night, making it a sleeping problem.

nightmares *vivid bad dreams, usually occurring towards morning*

night terrors *intense physiological arousal that causes a child to wake up in an intense state of panic*

enuresis *a lack of bladder control past the age when most children are toilet trained*

More common in boys than girls, enuresis is not, by itself, a sign of emotional difficulties. In fact, most instances spontaneously disappear as children mature and attain greater control over the muscles relating to urination. However, it can be a cause for concern if a child is upset about it or if it makes the child a target of ridicule from siblings or peers. In such cases, several types of treatments have proven effective. In particular, treatments in which children are rewarded for staying dry or are awakened by a battery device that senses when they have wet the bed are often effective (American Psychiatric Association, 1994; W. G. Wagner, Smith, & Norris, 1988).

Review and Rethink

REVIEW

- During the preschool period, the body grows steadily in height and weight, with individual differences varying widely around the average.
- Preschool children's bodies change in shape and structure, as well as size, becoming more slender and long-limbed, and developing body proportions generally similar to adults'.
- The brain grows at a very fast rate during the preschool years, largely due to an increase in cell interconnections and the amount of myelin in the brain. In addition, lateralization, a tendency of the two hemispheres to adopt somewhat specialized functions, becomes more pronounced.
- There is some evidence of gender and cultural differences in brain structure, including brain lateralization and language processing.
- The senses, especially vision and hearing, improve during the preschool years. Control of eye movements, focusing, and the processes of visual perception all develop. Auditory acuity improves too, although the ability to isolate individual sounds from a multitude of sounds is not yet fully developed.
- Sleep-related problems include nightmares, night terrors, and enuresis.

RETHINK

- How might biology and environment combine to affect the physical growth of a child adopted as an infant from a developing country and reared in a more industrialized one?
- Can you propose both a *cultural* and a *genetic* explanation for the fact that girls show less lateralization of language in the left hemisphere than boys?
- Does it make sense for a parent to coach a 3-year-old to recognize letters in order to induce early reading skills?
- Is the ability to perceive the perimeter of a figure advantageous to a human child? Why? Might this ability relate to lateralization?

HEALTH AND WELLNESS

For the average child in the United States, a runny nose due to the common cold is the most frequent—and happily, the most severe—kind of health problem during the preschool years. In fact, the majority of children in the United States are quite healthy during this period. The major threats to health and wellness come not from disease but, as we'll see, from injuries due to accidents.

Providing preschoolers with a variety of foods helps ensure good nutrition.

Nutrition: Eating the Right Foods

Nutritional needs change during the preschool years. Because the rate of growth during this period is slower than during infancy, preschoolers need less food to maintain their growth. The change in food consumption may be so noticeable that parents sometimes worry that their preschooler is not eating enough. However, children tend to be quite adept at maintaining an appropriate intake of food, if provided with nutritious meals. In fact, anxiously encouraging children to eat more than they seem to want naturally may lead them to increase their food intake beyond an appropriate level.

Ultimately, some children's food consumption can become so high as to lead to **obesity,** which is defined as a body weight more than 20 percent above the average weight for a person of a given age and height. Obesity is brought about by both biological and social factors. There is a clear genetic component of obesity, illustrated by the fact that adopted children tend to have weights that are more similar to those of their birth parents than those of their adoptive parents. In addition, children who are obese during the preschool years tend to have responded more to sweet tastes at birth and to have been more responsive at birth to environmental stimuli (Biron, Mongeau, & Bertrand, 1977; Rodin & Hall, 1987; Schlicker, Borra, & Regan, 1994; Unger, Kreeger, & Christoffel, 1990; Ogden, 1997).

The degree of encouragement—or discouragement—parents provide on the subject of eating also plays a role in obesity. For instance, some parents may strongly encourage their preschoolers to eat in the mistaken belief that their children are not eating enough. Conversely, other parents may place strong restraints on children's food intake in order to prevent obesity.

In either case, such behavior may prevent children from developing their own internal controls over eating. Without such controls, children may become less aware of their internal hunger cues—and may ultimately become obese. For instance, a study of a group of children aged 3 to 5 found that those with the highest proportion of body fat had mothers who exerted the greatest level of control over the amount of food their children ate (Johnson & Birch, 1994). Furthermore, the more control the mothers in the study reported exerting, the less self-regulation of food intake their children exhibited. In sum, strong parental involvement in what children eat may suppress the children's natural ability to monitor and control their food intake, and may lead to obesity and even to more severe eating problems in the future (Brownell & Rodin, 1994; Rodin & Hall, 1987).

How do parents ensure that their children have good nutrition without turning mealtimes into a tense, adversarial situation? In most cases, the best strategy is to make sure that a variety of foods, low in fat and high in nutritional content, is available. Foods that have a relatively high iron content are particularly important: Iron deficiency anemia, which causes chronic fatigue, is one of the prevalent nutritional problems in developed countries such as the United States. High-iron foods include dark green vegetables (such as broccoli), whole grains, and some kinds of meat (Ranade, 1993).

On the other hand, preschool children, like adults, will not find all foods equally appealing, and children should be given the opportunity to develop their own natural preferences. As long as a child's overall diet is adequate, no single food is indispensable.

Minor Illnesses of Preschoolers

The average preschooler has seven or eight minor colds and other minor respiratory illnesses in each of the years from age 3 to 5 (Denny & Clyde, 1983). Although the sniffles and coughs that are the symptoms of such illnesses are certainly distressing to children, the unpleasantness is usually not too severe and the illnesses usually last only a few days.

obesity *a body weight more than 20 percent above the average weight for a person of a given age and height*

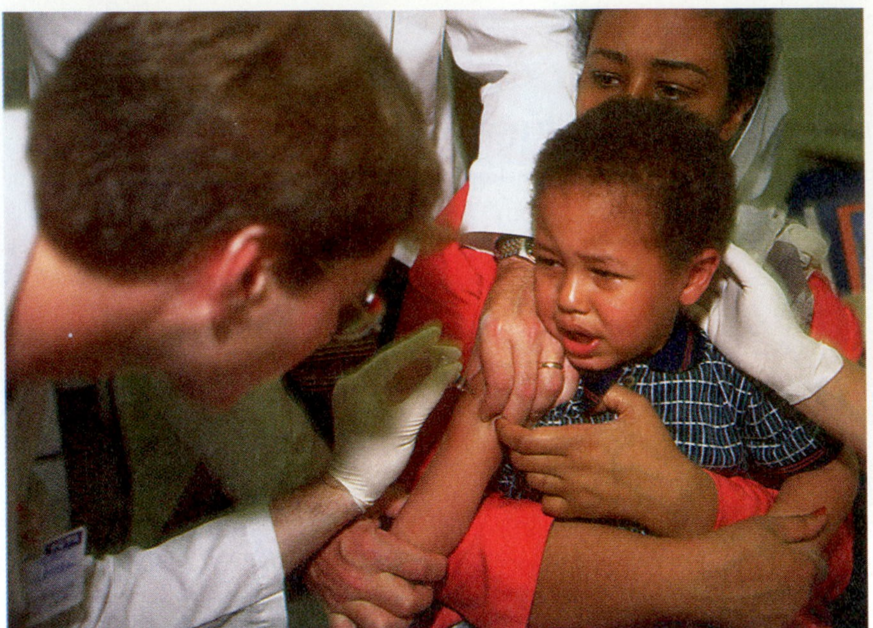

The discovery of vaccines and the routine immunization of children have made the preschool years a considerably less dangerous period than for earlier generations.

Actually, such minor illnesses may offer some unexpected benefits: Not only may they help children build up immunity to more severe illnesses to which they may be exposed in the future, but they also may provide some emotional benefits. Specifically, some researchers argue that minor illness permits children to understand their bodies better. It also may permit them to learn coping skills that will help them deal more effectively with future, more severe diseases. Furthermore, it gives them the ability to understand better what others who are sick are going through. This ability to put oneself in another's shoes, known as empathy, may teach children to be more sympathetic and better caretakers (Parmalee, 1986).

MAJOR ILLNESSES OF PRESCHOOLERS

The preschool years were not always a period of relatively good health. Before the discovery of vaccines and the routine immunization of children, the preschool period was a dangerous time. Even today, this period is risky in many parts of the world, as well as in certain lower socioeconomic segments of the U.S. population. In fact, probably because of a combination of the lack of a national health care policy and complacency on the part of government officials, the proportion of children immunized in the United States has fallen during some portions of the last two decades—at the same time as it has been rising in many third-world countries (B. C. Williams, 1990).

Preventing Major Disease through a "Supervaccine." The goal of many scientists is to prevent major diseases from occurring in the first place, rather than having to treat them. Consequently, some researchers are turning their efforts toward the development of a so-called supervaccine that will protect every child in the world from all the major preventable childhood diseases.

To accomplish this daunting task, the Children's Vaccine Initiative (CVI) was begun in the early 1990s with the backing of leaders of many countries around the globe and a confederation of international organizations, such as the United Nations Children's Fund and the World Health Organization. The CVI was designed to attack a problem that has kept millions of children from being vaccinated against the diseases of childhood.

The problem has been that today's vaccines, while effective, must be administered in six separate doses—something that is simply impossible to accomplish in most developing countries. In addition, many vaccines require refrigeration and must be administered by injection. In this context, a supervaccine that simultaneously could prevent all major childhood diseases, could last some period without refrigeration, and could be administered orally in a single dose would clearly be an important accomplishment. With such a vaccine it would become at least theoretically feasible to provide protection for all the world's children (Gibboins, 1994).

The need certainly exists for such a supervaccine. More than 2 million children needlessly die each year from measles, influenza, polio, tetanus, diphtheria, tuberculosis, and other diseases that can be prevented.

For the moment, a supervaccine remains more a goal than a reality. Several preliminary problems must be overcome. For instance, it is unclear how many antibodies a child is capable of accepting at a single time. Moreover, vaccines differ in stability, which means that, for purposes of preservation, different vaccines require different preparations. To produce a supervaccine, some means must be discovered to preserve simultaneously several different types of vaccine.

On the other hand, the goal does not seem to be unattainable. Several combined vaccines are already on the market. For instance, one vaccine now being sold in Europe combines diphtheria, tetanus, pertussis, and polio protection. In light of such developments, the goal of creating a supervaccine for the next century seems achievable.

Cancer and AIDS. The most frequent major illness to strike preschoolers is cancer, particularly in the form of leukemia. Leukemia causes the bone marrow to produce an excessive amount of white blood cells, inducing severe anemia and, potentially, death. Although just two decades ago a diagnosis of leukemia was the equivalent of a death sentence, today the story is quite different. Due to advances in treatment, more than 70 percent of victims of childhood leukemia survive (American Cancer Society, 1993).

One childhood disease that presents a far more discouraging picture is childhood AIDS, or acquired immune deficiency syndrome. Because it is ultimately fatal and because it often produces significant developmental delays, children with this disease face many difficulties. For instance, even though there is virtually no risk of spreading the disease through everyday contact, children with AIDS may be shunned by others. Furthermore, because their parents may suffer from the disease themselves—children with AIDS typically have contracted the disease prenatally from their mothers—there are often severe disruptions in the family due to a parent's death (American Academy of Pediatrics [AAP] Task Force on Pediatric AIDS, 1991; Frenkel & Gau, 1994).

Reactions to Hospitalization. For ill preschoolers who must spend time in the hospital, the experience is quite difficult. The most frequent reaction of 2- to 4-year-olds is anxiety, most typically brought about by the separation from their parents. At slightly older ages, preschoolers may become upset because they interpret their hospitalization, on some level, as due to desertion or even rejection by their family. Their anxiety may result in the development of new fears, such as fear of the dark or of hospital staff (Taylor, 1991).

One of the ways that hospitals deal with the anxieties of young patients is to allow a parent to stay for lengthy periods of time with the child, even, in some cases, permitting parents to spend the night on a cot in the child's room. But it does not have to be a parent who can alleviate a child's fears; research has shown that assigning children a "substitute mother," a nurse or other health care provider who is supportive and nurturant, can go a long way toward reducing children's concerns (Branstetter, 1969).

In short, it is important for parents and medical caregivers to keep in mind how difficult a hospital stay can be for children. Not fully understanding why they are in the hospital in the first place, preschoolers require warmth and nurturance to get through the rigors of hospitalization.

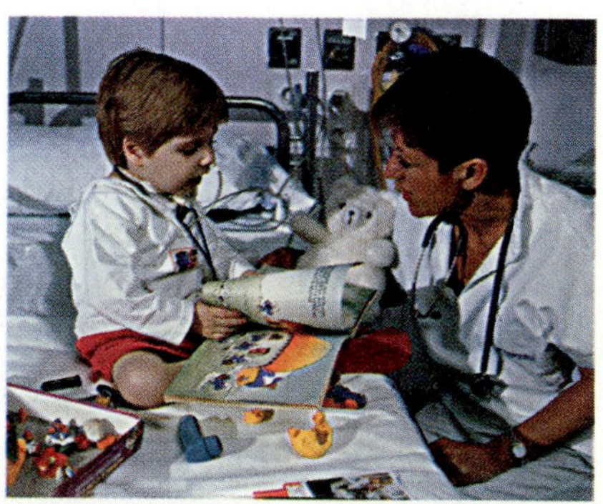

The fears that young hospital patients experience can be reduced by the presence of "substitute mothers," health care providers who are supportive and nurturing.

Preschoolers' high level of physical activity and their curiosity increase the risk of injury.

INJURIES DURING THE PRESCHOOL YEARS: PLAYING IT SAFE

Aaron, a wildly energetic 3-year-old, was trying to stretch far enough to reach the bowl of cookies sitting on the kitchen counter. Because the bowl was just beyond his grasp, he pushed a chair from the kitchen table over to the counter, and was able to pick out a cookie. As he tried to get down, however, the chair slid away from the counter, and Aaron fell to the floor, twisting, and fracturing, his arm. His wails brought his father on the run from the next room.

In some ways, Aaron was lucky, for some injuries sustained by preschoolers are far more serious, resulting in permanent disfigurement or even death. In fact, statistically speaking, the greatest risk that preschoolers face comes from neither illness nor nutritional problems but from accidents: Children have twice the likelihood of dying from an injury than from an illness before the age of 10. In fact, children in the United States have a 1 in 3 likelihood every year of receiving an injury that requires medical attention (National Safety Council, 1989).

The danger of injuries during the preschool years is in part a result of the children's high levels of physical activity. A 3-year-old might think that it is perfectly reasonable to climb on a chair to get something that is out of reach, and a 4-year-old might enjoy holding on to a low tree branch and swinging her legs up and down. At the same time, children lack the judgment to know that their activities may hold some danger, and they are less likely than older children to be careful.

Furthermore, some children are more apt to take risks than others, and such preschoolers are more likely to be injured than their more cautious peers. Boys, who are both more active than girls and tend to take more risks, have a higher rate of injuries. Ethnic differences, probably due to differences in cultural norms about how closely children need to be supervised, can also be seen in accident rates. Asian American children in the United States, who tend to be supervised particularly strictly by their parents, have one of the lowest accident rates for children. Economic factors also play a role. Children raised under conditions of poverty in urban areas, whose inner-city neighborhoods may contain more hazards than more affluent areas, are two times as likely to die of injuries than children living in affluence.

The range of dangers that preschoolers face is wide. Injuries come from falls, burns from stoves and fires, drowning in bathtubs indoors and standing water outdoors, and suffocation in places such as abandoned refrigerators. Auto accidents also account for a large number of injuries. Finally, children face injuries from poisonous substances such as household cleaners or, as we discuss in the "Directions in Development" section, long-term exposure to poisons such as lead.

The sad part of the fact that children face such injuries is that many can be prevented, or at least the chance of sustaining one can be reduced. Poisons, medicines, household cleaners, and other potentially dangerous substances can be removed from the house or kept under lock and key. To reduce the risk of injuries from auto accidents, parents can strap their children into car seats whenever they take them along for a ride. Because drowning can occur in just a few inches of water and in a short time, young children should never be left unattended in the bathtub or a wading pool. Finally, children can be taught basic safety rules from the earliest age (Mathews et al., 1987).

Obviously, we can never completely prevent accidents and injuries. But adults can attempt to reduce the risks to preschoolers (Garbarino, 1988). Rather than focusing on preventing "accidents"—which implies a random act in which no one is at fault—safety experts suggest that adults instead concentrate on "injury control," which is a more realistic goal.

Directions in Development

The Silent Danger: Lead Poisoning in Young Children

> *At the age of 3, Tory couldn't sit still. He was unable to watch a television show for more than 5 minutes, and sitting still while his mother read to him seemed to be an impossibility. He was often irritable, and he impulsively took risks when he was playing with other children.*
>
> *When his behavior reached a point where his parents thought that there was something seriously wrong with him, they took him to a pediatrician for a thorough physical examination. After testing Tory's blood, the pediatrician found that his parents were right: Tory was suffering from lead poisoning.*

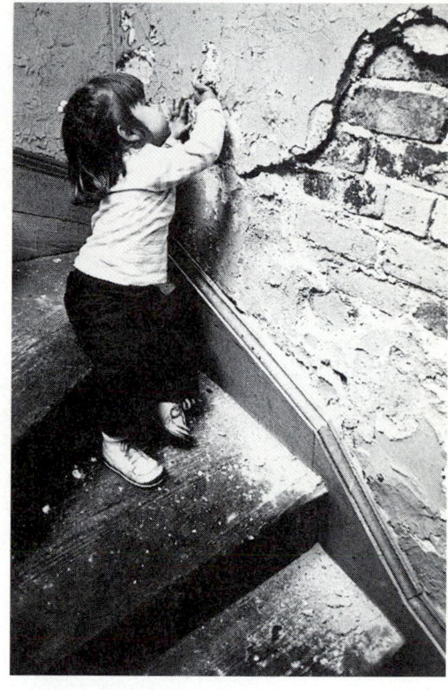

Exposure to lead paint represents the most hazardous health threat to children under the age of 6.

Some 14 million children are at risk for lead poisoning due to exposure to potentially toxic levels of lead, according to the Centers for Disease Control (1991). Although there are stringent legal restrictions on the amount of lead in paint and gasoline, lead is found on painted walls and window frames—particularly in older homes—in gasoline, ceramics, lead-soldered pipes, and even in dust and water. People who live in areas of substantial air pollution due to automobile and truck traffic may also be exposed to high levels of lead. The U.S. Department of Health and Human Services has called lead poisoning the most hazardous health threat to children under the age of 6 (Centers for Disease Control, 1991; Tesman & Hills, 1994).

Even tiny amounts of lead can permanently harm children. Exposure to lead has been linked to lower intelligence, problems in verbal and auditory processing, and—as in the case of Tory—hyperactivity and distractibility. High lead levels have also been linked to higher levels of antisocial behavior, including aggression and delinquency in school-age children (see Figure 7-4). At yet higher levels of exposure, lead poisoning results in illness and death (Leviton et al., 1993; Needleman et al., 1996; Tomson et al., 1989).

Poor children are particularly susceptible to lead poisoning, and the results of poisoning tend to be worse for them than for children from more affluent families. Children living in poverty are more apt to reside in housing that contains peeling and chipping lead paint or to live near heavily trafficked urban areas with high levels of air pollution. At the same time, many families living in poverty may be less stable and unable to provide consistent opportunities for intellectual stimulation that might serve to offset some of the cognitive problems caused by the poisoning. Consequently, poorer children may be particularly susceptible to the negative effects of lead poisoning (Harvey et al., 1984; Tesman & Hills, 1994).

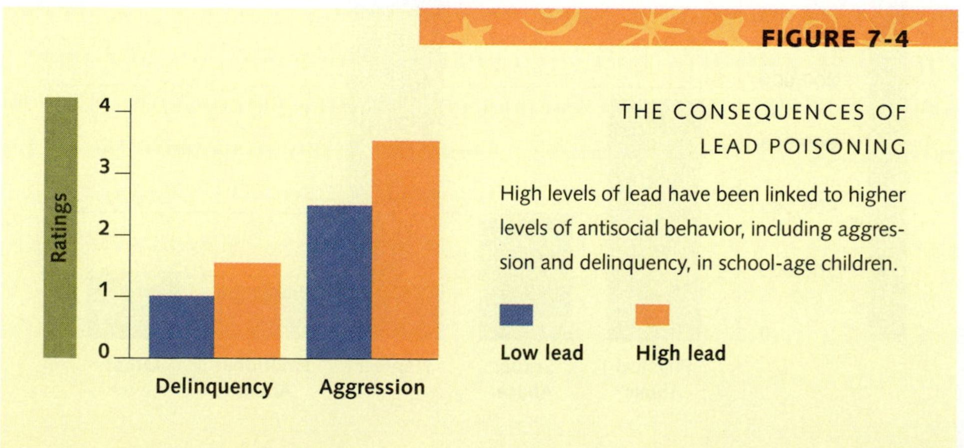

FIGURE 7-4

THE CONSEQUENCES OF LEAD POISONING

High levels of lead have been linked to higher levels of antisocial behavior, including aggression and delinquency, in school-age children.

Efforts to reduce the incidence of lead poisoning have taken many forms. One approach is through legislation that mandates the removal of paint that contains lead in dwellings in which children reside. Another is through parent education.

child abuse *the physical or psychological maltreatment or neglect of children*

In one program, for example, parents who lived near a previously functioning lead smelter, and whose pre-1920s homes still contained high levels of lead, were trained to take several precautionary measures. For instance, they were taught to wash their children's hands before mealtime and bedtime, to clip their children's fingernails short, and to furnish their children with a good diet. In addition, they were taught to take precautions in the home, such as removing peeling paint and cordoning off high-lead areas. The program was effective: Over a 4-month period, the lead levels in the bodies of the children in the study, who ranged in age from 6 months to 6 years, declined significantly (Kimbrough, LeVois, & Webb, 1994; Tesman & Hills, 1994).

Still, the problem of potentially dangerous levels of lead in many children's surroundings persists. The question that must be addressed is how to remove such dangers and what the costs will be. Clearly, there is no easy solution to the problem.

CHILD ABUSE AND PSYCHOLOGICAL MALTREATMENT: THE GRIM SIDE OF FAMILY LIFE

The figures are gloomy and disheartening: At least 5 children are killed by their parents or caregivers every day, and 140,000 others are physically injured every year. Overall, each year more than 3 million children in the United States are the victims of **child abuse,** the physical or psychological maltreatment or neglect of children. Violence claims the lives of at least 2,000 children annually (Ards & Harrell, 1993; Briere et al., 1996; Mones, 1995; U.S. Advisory Board on Child Abuse and Neglect, 1995). The abuse takes several forms, ranging from actual physical abuse to psychological mistreatment (see Figure 7-5).

Physical Abuse. Although child abuse can occur in any household, regardless of economic well-being or the social status of the parents, it is most frequent in families living in

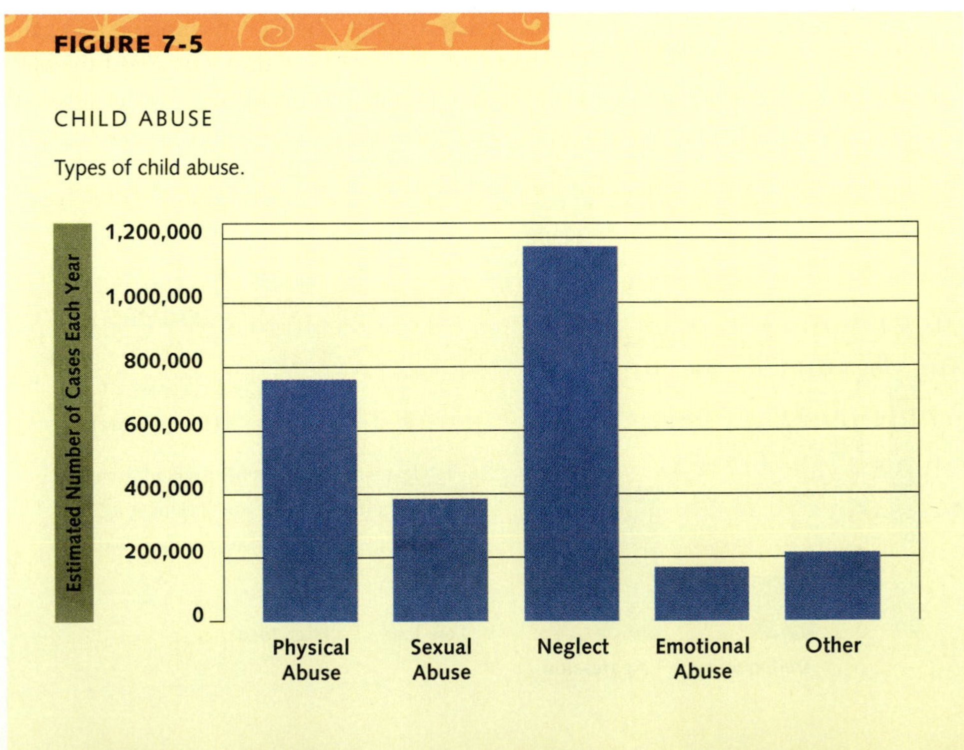

FIGURE 7-5

CHILD ABUSE

Types of child abuse.

stressful environments. Conditions of poverty, single-parent households, and families with higher-than-average levels of marital conflict create such environments. Child abuse is also related to the presence of violence between spouses, and children are more likely the victims of abuse at the hands of stepparents than their genetic parents (Coulton et al., 1995; M. Daly & Wilson, 1996; Dodge, Bates, & Pettit, 1990; Margolin, 1995; McCloskey, Figueredo, & Koss, 1995; Milner, 1995).

Children with certain characteristics are more prone to be the victims of child abuse. Abused children are more likely to be fussy, resistant to control, and not readily adaptable to new situations. They have more headaches and stomachaches, experience more bedwetting, are generally more anxious, and may show developmental delays. Moreover, victims are most vulnerable to abuse at certain ages: Three- and 4-year-olds, as well as 15- to 17-year-olds, are the most likely to be abused by their parents (Gelles & Cornell, 1990; Gil, 1970; Putnam, 1995; Steinmetz, 1987; Straus & Gelles, 1990).

It is critical to keep in mind that labeling children as being at higher risk for receiving abuse does not make them responsible for their abuse; the family members who carry out the abuse are at fault. Statistical findings simply suggest that children with such characteristics tend to be at greater risk of being the recipients of family violence.

Why does physical abuse occur? Most parents certainly don't intend to abuse their children. In fact, most parents who abuse their children later express bewilderment and dismay at their own behavior.

One reason for child abuse is the vague demarcation between permissible and impermissible forms of physical violence. Societal folklore says that spanking is not merely acceptable, but often necessary and desirable. For example, one survey found that almost half of mothers with children less than 4 years of age had spanked their child in the previous week, and close to 20 percent of mothers believe it is appropriate to spank a child less than 1 year of age (Holden, Coleman, & Schmidt, 1995; Socolar & Stein, 1995).

Unfortunately, the line between "spanking" and "beating" is not clear, and spankings begun in anger can escalate easily into abuse. Furthermore, despite common wisdom, the use of physical punishment of any sort is *not* recommended by child-care experts (Committee for Rights and Legal Matters, 1989; Greven, 1990; Welker, 1991). (For a guide to when punishment crosses the line into abuse, see Table 7-1.)

Many other societies do not make the distinctions between acceptable violence and abuse that we find in the United States. For instance, Sweden outlaws *any* form of physical punishment directed toward a child. In many other countries, such as China, social norms work against the use of physical punishment, and its use is rare (Kessen, 1979). In contrast,

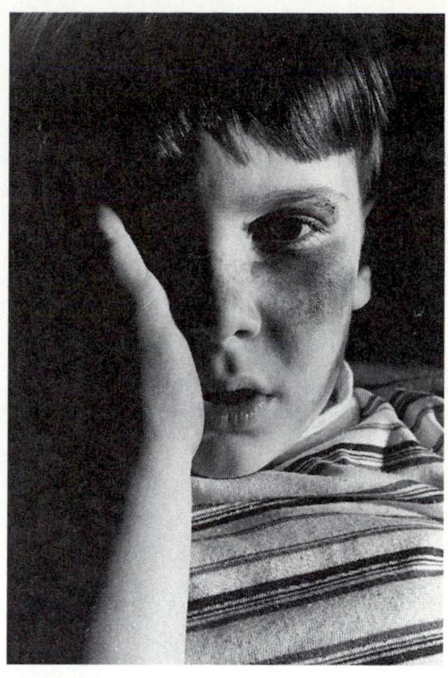

Each year, more than 3 million children in the United States are victims of child abuse.

TABLE 7-1

IDENTIFYING CHILD ABUSE

Because child abuse is typically a secret crime, identifying the victims of abuse is particularly difficult. Still, there are several signs in a child that indicate that he or she is the victim of violence (Robbins, 1990):

- Visible, serious injuries that have no reasonable explanation
- Bite or choke marks
- Burns from cigarettes or immersion in hot water
- Feelings of pain for no apparent reason
- Fear of adults or care providers
- Inappropriate attire in warm weather (long sleeves, long pants, high-necked garments)–possibly to conceal injuries to the neck, arms, and legs
- Extreme behavior–highly aggressive, extremely passive, extremely withdrawn
- Fear of physical contact

If you suspect a child is a victim of aggression, it is your responsibility to act. Call your local police or the department of social services in your city or state, or call the National Center on Child Abuse and Neglect (Washington, D.C.) at (202)727-0995. Talk to a teacher or a member of the clergy. Remember, by acting decisively you can literally save someone's life.

the values of personal freedom and responsibility prevalent in the United States foster a social climate in which high levels of child abuse occur.

cycle-of-violence hypothesis the theory that the abuse and neglect that children suffer predispose them as adults to abuse and neglect their own children

Another factor that leads to high rates of abuse is the privacy with which child care is conducted in Western societies. Unlike in many other cultures, where childrearing is seen as the joint responsibility of several people and even of society as a whole, in most Western cultures—and particularly the United States—children are raised in private, isolated households. Because child care is seen as the sole responsibility of the parent, other people are typically not available when a parent's patience is tested.

One additional source of abuse is insensitivity to age norms. Abusive parents and caregivers may have unrealistically high expectations regarding children's abilities to be quiet and compliant at particular ages. Their children's failure to meet these unrealistic expectations may provoke abuse (L. Peterson, 1994).

Finally, abuse inflicted on children is often associated with violence that the abusers themselves have suffered as children. According to the **cycle-of-violence hypothesis,** the abuse and neglect that children suffer predispose them as adults to abuse and neglect their own children (Dodge et al., 1990; Widom, 1989).

The cycle of violence hypothesis suggests that victims of abuse have learned from their childhood experiences that violence is an appropriate and acceptable form of discipline. Violence is consequently perpetuated from one generation to another, as each generation learns to behave abusively through its participation in an abusive, violent family (Feshbach, 1980; Ney, Fung, & Wickett, 1993; Straus & Gelles, 1990).

On the other hand, although there are many cases in which abusive parents have themselves suffered abuse as children, being abused as a child does not inevitably lead to abuse

Speaking of Development

David S. Kurtz, Child Abuse Counselor

Born: 1960

Education: University of California at Irvine, B.S. in biology and B.A. in psychology
California State University in Fullerton, M.A. in experimental psychology
California School of Professional Psychology at Los Angeles, M.A. and Ph.D. in clinical psychology

Position: Associate Director of the Childhelp Los Angeles Center

Home: Glendale, California

What is it like to pick up the phone and hear the voice of an abused child reaching out for help? Dr. David Kurtz knows.

For most of his 8 years with the Childhelp Los Angeles Center, Dr. Kurtz worked in crisis intervention. He was one of the many counselors working the phones at the National Child Abuse Hotline located at Childhelp.

Currently the associate director of the Center, Dr. Kurtz still finds occasion to provide help and support via the phone lines.

"Those who call us with a child abuse issue may be the parents of an abused child, a neighbor who has witnessed child abuse, or an adult who was a victim of abuse 20 or 30 years ago," says Dr. Kurtz. "But children who call in, or those who represent them, are given priority. They are put at the front of the line.

of one's own children. In fact, statistics show that only about one third of people who were abused or neglected as children abuse their own children; the remaining two thirds of people abused as children do not turn out to be child abusers. Clearly, suffering abuse as a child is not the full explanation for child abuse in adults.

psychological maltreatment *maltreatment in which parents or other caregivers harm children's behavioral, cognitive, emotional, or physical functioning*

child neglect *neglect in which parents ignore their children or act emotionally unresponsive to them*

Psychological Maltreatment. Child abuse does not necessarily take the form of direct physical injury. In fact, sometimes neglect can be as devastating.

Unlike physical abuse, in which children suffer actual bodily injury and punishment, **psychological maltreatment** occurs when parents or other caregivers harm children's behavioral, cognitive, emotional, or physical functioning. Psychological maltreatment may occur through either overt behavior or neglect (S. N. Hart & Brassard, 1987; Iwaniec, 1995).

For example, abusive parents may frighten, belittle, or humiliate their children, thereby intimidating and harassing them. Children may be made to feel like disappointments or failures, or they may be constantly reminded that they are a burden to their parents. Parents may tell their children that they wish they had never had children and specifically that they wish that their children had never been born. Children may be threatened with abandonment or even death. In other instances, older children may be exploited. They may be forced to seek employment and then to give their earnings to their parents.

In other cases of psychological maltreatment, the abuse takes the form of neglect. In **child neglect,** parents ignore their children or act emotionally unresponsive to them. In such cases, children may be given unrealistic responsibilities or may be left to fend for themselves.

"Often we find that a significant part of parents' frustration is attributable to their unrealistic expectations of what children are capable of doing at a given age."

"A child is going to be very, very scared and will be dealing with confused feelings of shame, guilt, and fear that the abuser—who is usually a close family member—is going to get into trouble."

"For younger children the caller is usually a sibling or an adult who is representing the abused child," he says, adding that there are also occasions when a parent may call about his or her own frustrations with a very young child.

"We often explore developmental issues when parents call us," he notes. "Often we find that a significant part of parents' frustration is attributable to their unrealistic expectations of what children are capable of doing at a given age.

"An example of this is a highly frustrated woman who called us after returning from a grocery shopping trip with her child. She had a very strong impulse to slap the child, and she was afraid she would lose control. The child kept pulling items off the shelves at the store, and she was convinced the child was doing it purposefully to upset her.

"When we asked how old the child was, she said 10 months. We explained that her child was much too young to be acting purposefully in that way, and that the child was not trying to get at her. Clearly, this parent was not alone. Many parents who have to deal with some sort of disciplinary issue would benefit from a better understanding of child development."

Dr. Kurtz emphasizes the importance of establishing as trusting a relationship as possible with the stressed people who are looking for help on this issue. "When people call, it's essential to build a rapport with them. The general policy at the Hotline is that the counselors do not give their names, but with children we make an exception," he says. "A child is going to be very, very scared and will be dealing with confused feelings of shame, guilt, and fear that the abuser—who is usually a close family member—is going to get into trouble."

resilience *the ability to overcome circumstances that place a child at high risk for psychological or physical damage*

No one knows how much psychological maltreatment occurs each year, because figures separating psychological maltreatment from other types of abuse are not routinely gathered. The lack of trustworthy statistics stems from obstacles that stand in the way of unambiguously identifying cases of psychological maltreatment. Most such maltreatment occurs in the privacy of people's homes. Furthermore, psychological maltreatment typically causes no physical damage, such as bruises or broken bones, to alert physicians, teachers, and other authorities. Consequently, many cases of psychological maltreatment probably are not identified.

What are the consequences of psychological maltreatment? Although some children are sufficiently resilient to survive the abuse and grow into psychologically healthy adults, in many cases lasting damage results. For example, psychological maltreatment has been associated with low self-esteem, lying, misbehavior, and underachievement in school. In extreme cases, it can produce criminal behavior, aggression, and murder. In other instances, children who have been psychologically maltreated become depressed and even commit suicide (Leiter & Johnsen, 1994; Malinosky-Rummell & Hansen, 1993; Perez & Widom, 1994; Trickett & McBride-Chang, 1995; Vondra, Barnett, & Cicchetti, 1990).

RESILIENCE: OVERCOMING THE ODDS

Not all children succumb to the mistreatment and abuse that life thrusts on them. In fact, some do surprisingly well, considering the types of problems they have encountered. What enables some children to overcome stress and trauma that may scar others for life?

Resilience refers to the ability to overcome circumstances that place a child at high risk for psychological or physical damage. Several factors seem to reduce and, in certain cases, eliminate the effects on some children of difficult environments—extremes of poverty, parental stress, or homes racked with violence or other forms of social disorder. Yet these same environments can produce profoundly negative consequences in other children.

According to developmental psychologist Emmy Werner (1995), resilient children have temperaments that evoke positive responses from a wide variety of caregivers. They tend to be affectionate, easygoing, and good-natured. They are easily soothed as infants, and they are able to elicit care from the most nurturant people in the environment—whatever it is—in which they find themselves. In short, because of their pleasant temperaments, they can evoke whatever support is present in a given setting. In a sense, then, resilient children are able to create their own environments by drawing out from others behavior that is necessary for their own successful development.

Similar traits are associated with resilience in older children. The most resilient school-age children are those who are socially pleasant, outgoing, and have good communication skills. They tend to be relatively intelligent, and they are independent, feeling that they can shape their own fate and are not dependent on others or on luck (Werner, 1993, 1995; Werner & Smith, 1992).

The characteristics of resilient children suggest ways of increasing the chances of success for children who are at risk from a variety of developmental threats. For instance, in addition to decreasing their exposure to factors that put them at risk in the first place, we may need to increase their competence and teach them ways of dealing with their situation. In fact, programs that have been successful in helping especially vulnerable children have a common thread: They provide competent and caring adult models who can teach problem-solving skills and help children communicate their needs to people who are in a position to help them (Haggerty et al., 1994; E. M. Hetherington & Blechman, 1996; Schorr, 1988).

Review and Rethink

REVIEW

- Nutritional needs change during the preschool years, with children needing less food to maintain growth. In general, children who can choose from a variety of nutritious foods develop their own internal controls over eating, avoid obesity, and develop healthful food preferences.
- Illness in preschoolers is generally mild, since most major illnesses (with the exception of childhood leukemia and AIDS) have been controlled by immunization. Injury presents a far greater health risk during this period than illness.
- Due largely to cultural factors, child abuse is comparatively prevalent in the United States. Abuse may be physical or psychological, is associated with both social and personal factors, and can have long-term effects.
- According to the cycle-of-violence hypothesis, child abuse may be perpetuated across generations because persons who were abused as children show a tendency to be abusers as adults.
- Resilience is a personal characteristic that permits some children to avoid damage from environments of risk. Resilient children tend to be easygoing and develop the ability to exercise control over their environments by eliciting nurturant behavior from others.

RETHINK

- What evidence can you offer that obesity is determined by both genetic and environmental factors?
- In addition to eating, can other areas of children's behavior be negatively influenced by excessive parental control? Can you give examples and reasons?
- Some people believe that researching the personality traits of abused children, such as fussiness or failure to adapt to new situations, contributes to a tendency to blame the victim. What do you think? Why are such studies conducted?
- If a societal emphasis on family privacy contributes to the prevalence of child abuse, what sorts of social policies regarding privacy do you think are appropriate? Why?
- What are some ways that increased understanding of issues relating to the physical development of preschoolers might help parents and caregivers in their care of children?

MOTOR DEVELOPMENT

As their parents watched from the edge of the summer school playground, 3-year-old Jorge tore after Henry, with Cary in hot pursuit. Eleanor and Heidi threw a ball to each other. Mick and Satra sat at a bench, painstakingly using a scissors to cut out paper flowers for a party that afternoon. It was hard for their parents to recall that just a few years earlier, these same children were not even able to lift up their heads or roll over, let alone walk.

In their motor development, preschool children have come a long way since birth. Both their gross and fine motor skills have become increasingly fine-tuned.

TABLE 7-2

GROSS MOTOR SKILLS

3-Year-Olds	4-Year-Olds	5-Year-Olds
Cannot turn or stop suddenly or quickly	Have more effective control of stopping, starting, and turning	Start, turn, and stop effectively in games
Jump a distance of 15 to 24 inches	Jump a distance of 24 to 33 inches	Can make a running jump of 28 to 36 inches
Ascend a stairway unaided, alternating the feet	Descend a long stairway alternating the feet, if supported	Descend a long stairway alternating the feet, without support
Can hop, using largely an irregular series of jumps with some variations added	Hop 4 to 6 steps on one foot	Easily hop a distance of 16 feet

(*Source:* Corbin, 1973.)

GROSS MOTOR SKILLS

By the time they are 3, children have mastered a variety of skills: jumping, hopping on one foot, skipping, and running. By 4 and 5, their skills have become more refined, as they gain increasing control over their muscles. For instance, at 4 children can throw a ball with enough accuracy that a friend can catch it, and by age 5 they can toss a ring and have it land on a peg 5 feet away. Five-year-olds can learn to ride bikes, climb ladders, and ski downhill—activities that all require a good bit of coordination (J. E. Clark & Humphrey, 1985). (Table 7-2 summarizes major gross motor skills that emerge during the preschool years.)

Activity Level. One reason motor skills develop at such a rapid clip during the preschool years is that children spend a great deal of time practicing them. During this period, the general level of activity is extraordinarily high: Preschoolers seem to be perpetually in motion. In fact, the activity level is higher at age 3 than at any other point in the entire life span (Eaton & Yu, 1989; Poest et al., 1990).

Despite generally high activity levels, there are also significant variations between individual children. Some differences are related to inherited temperament. Due to temperamental factors, children who are unusually active during infancy tend to continue in this way during the preschool years, while those who are relatively docile during infancy generally remain fairly docile during those years. Furthermore, monozygotic (identical) twins tend to show more similar activity levels than dizygotic twins, a fact that suggests the importance of genetics in determining activity level (Goldsmith & Gottesman, 1981).

Of course, genetics is not the sole determinant of preschoolers' activity levels. Environmental factors, such as a parent's style of discipline and, more broadly, a particular culture's view of what is appropriate and inappropriate behavior, also play a role. Some cultures are much more lenient in allowing preschoolers to play vigorously, whereas others are considerably more restrictive.

Ultimately, a combination of genetic and environmental factors determines just how active an individual child will be. But regardless of their individual levels of activity during preschool, the period generally represents the peak of activity across the entire life span.

Gender Differences in Gross Motor Skills. Girls and boys differ in several aspects of gross motor coordination. In part, this difference is produced by variations in muscle strength, which is somewhat greater in boys than in girls. For instance, boys can typically throw a ball better and jump higher. Furthermore, boys' overall activity levels are generally greater than girls' (Eaton & Yu, 1989).

Although they are not as strong as boys and have lower overall activity levels, girls generally surpass boys in tasks that involve the coordination of their arms and legs. For instance, at the age of 5, girls are better than boys at doing jumping jacks and balancing on one foot (Cratty, 1979).

The differences between preschoolers on some tasks involving gross motor skills are due to a number of factors. In addition to genetically determined differences in strength and activity levels, social factors likely play a role. As we will discuss further in Chapter 9, gender increasingly determines the sorts of activities that are seen by society as appropriate for girls and appropriate for boys. For instance, suppose that the games and toys that are seen as socially acceptable for preschool boys tend to involve gross motor skills, while the games and toys seen as appropriate for girls are less apt to involve gross motor skills. If this supposition is correct, then boys will have more practice in gross motor activities—and ultimately be more proficient than girls (Golombok & Fivush, 1994; Yee and Brown, 1994).

Regardless of their gender, however, both boys and girls typically show significant improvement in their gross motor skills during the preschool years. Such improvement permits them by the time they are 5 to climb ladders, play follow the leader, and snowboard with relative ease.

Fine Motor Skills

At the same time that gross motor skills are developing, children are progressing in their ability to use fine motor skills, which involve smaller, more delicate body movements. Fine motor skills encompass such varied activities as using a fork and spoon, cutting with scissors, tying one's shoelaces, and playing the piano.

The skills involved in fine motor movements require a good deal of practice, as anyone knows who has watched a 4-year-old struggling painstakingly to copy letters of the alphabet. Yet fine motor skills show clear developmental patterns (see Table 7-3). At the age of 3, children can undo their clothes when they go to the bathroom. They can put a simple jigsaw puzzle together, and they can fit blocks of different shapes into matching holes. On the other hand, they do not show much polish in accomplishing such tasks; for instance, they may try to force puzzle pieces into place.

By the age of 4, their fine motor skills are considerably better. For example, they can fold paper into triangular designs and some can print their name with a crayon. And by the time they are 5, most children are able to hold and manipulate a thin pencil properly.

TABLE 7-3

FINE MOTOR SKILLS SHOW CLEAR DEVELOPMENTAL PATTERNS

3-4 Year-Olds	4-5 Year-Olds	5-6 Year-Olds
Cuts paper	Folds paper into triangles	Folds paper into halves and quarters
Pastes using finger	Prints name	Draws triangle, rectangle, circle
Builds bridge with three blocks	Strings beads	Uses crayons effectively
Draws 0 and +	Copies X	Creates clay objects
Draws doll	Builds bridge with five blocks	Copies letters
Pours liquid from pitcher without spilling	Pours from various containers	Copies two short words
Completes simple jigsaw puzzle	Opens and positions clothespins	

Handedness: Separating Righties from Lefties

handedness *a clear preference for the use of one hand over the other*

By the end of the preschool years, almost all children show a clear preference for the use of one hand over the other—the development of **handedness.** Actually, some signals of future handedness are seen early in infancy, when infants may show a preference for one side of their bodies over another. By the age of 7 months, some infants seem to favor one hand by grabbing more with it than the other (G. L. Michel, 1981; Ramsay, 1980). Many children, however, show no preference until the end of the preschool years.

By the age of 5, most children display a clear-cut tendency to use one hand rather than the other, with 90 percent being right-handed and 10 percent left-handed. Furthermore, more boys than girls are left-handed.

Much speculation has been devoted to the meaning of handedness, fueled in part by longstanding myths about the sinister nature of left-handedness. (In fact, the word *sinister* itself is derived from the Latin word meaning "on the left.") In Islamic cultures, for instance, the left hand is generally used in going to the toilet, and it is considered uncivilized to serve food with that hand. Furthermore, many artistic portrayals of the devil show him as left-handed.

However, there is no scientific basis for myths that suggest that there is something wrong with being left-handed. In fact, some evidence exists that left-handedness may be associated with certain advantages. For example, a study of 100,000 students who took the Scholastic Aptitude Test (SAT) showed that 20 percent in the highest-scoring category were left-handed, double the proportion of left-handed people in the general population. Moreover, such individuals as Michelangelo, Leonardo da Vinci, Benjamin Franklin, and Pablo Picasso were left-handed (B. Bower, 1985).

Although some educators of the past tried to force left-handed children to use the right hand, particularly when learning to write, thinking has changed. Most teachers now encourage children to use whichever hand they prefer. Still, most left-handed people will agree that the design of desks, scissors, and most other everyday objects favors those who are right-handed. In fact, the world is so "right biased" that it may prove to be a dangerous place for those who are left-handed: Left-handed people have more accidents and are likely to die younger than right-handed people (Coren, 1989; Coren & Halpern, 1991).

Art: The Picture of Development

It is a basic feature of many kitchens: the refrigerator covered with recent art created by the children of the house.

Yet the art that children create is far more important than mere kitchen decoration. Developmentalists suggest that art plays an important role in honing fine motor skills, as well as in several other aspects of development.

At the most basic level, the production of art involves practice with tools such as paintbrushes, crayons, pencils, and markers. As preschoolers learn to manipulate these tools, they gain motor control skills that will help them as they learn to write.

But art also teaches several important lessons. For example, children learn the importance of planning, restraint, and self-correction. When 3-year-olds pick up a brush, they tend to swish it across the page, with little thought of the ultimate product. By the time they are 5, however, children spend more time thinking about and planning the final product. They are more likely to have a goal in mind when they start out; and when they are finished, they examine their creation to see how successful they have been. Older children also will produce the same artwork over and over, seeking to overcome their previous errors and improve the final product.

According to developmental psychologist Howard Gardner (1980), the rough, unformed art of preschoolers represents the equivalent of linguistic babbling in infants. He argues that the random marks that young preschoolers make contain all the building blocks of more sophisticated creations that will be produced later.

FIGURE 7-6 As preschoolers enter the pictorial stage between the ages of 4 and 5 their drawings begin to approximate recognizable objects.

Other researchers suggest that children's art proceeds through a series of stages during the preschool years (Kellogg, 1970). The first is the *scribbling* stage, in which the end product appears to be random scrawls across a paper. But this is not the case: Instead, scribbles can be categorized into 20 distinct types, such as horizontal lines and zigzags.

The *shape* stage, which is reached around the age of 3, is marked by the appearance of shapes such as squares and circles. Here, children draw shapes of various sorts, as well as ×'s and plus signs. After reaching this stage, they soon move into the *design* stage, which is characterized by the ability to combine more than one simple shape into a more complex one.

Finally, preschoolers enter the *pictorial* stage between the ages of 4 and 5. At this point, drawings begin to approximate recognizable objects (see Figure 7-6).

The depiction of recognizable, real-world objects, known as representational art, may appear to be a substantial advance over previous art, and adults often strongly encourage its creation. However, in some respects this change to representational art is regrettable, for it marks a shift in focus away from an interest in form and design. Because form and design are important, and in some ways essential, a focus on representation ultimately may have its disadvantages. As the great artist Pablo Picasso once remarked, "it has taken me a whole lifetime to learn to draw like children" (Winner, 1986, 1989).

The Informed Consumer of Development

Keeping Preschoolers Healthy

There's no way around it: Even the healthiest preschooler occasionally gets sick. Social interactions with others ensure that illnesses are going to be passed from one child to another. However, some diseases are preventable, and others can be minimized if simple precautions are taken:

- Preschoolers should eat a well-balanced diet containing the proper nutrients, particularly foods with sufficient protein. (The recommended energy intake for children aged 2 to 4 is about 1,300 calories a day, and for those aged 4 to 6, it is around 1,700 calories a day.) Because preschoolers' stomachs are small, they may need to eat as often as five to seven times a day.
- Children should get as much sleep as they wish. Being run-down from lack of either nutrition or sleep makes children more susceptible to illness.
- Children should avoid contact with others who are ill. Parents should make sure that children wash their hands after playing with other kids who are obviously sick. Cold germs are often carried from one person to another via the hands.
- Ensure that children follow an appropriate schedule of immunizations. As illustrated in Table 7-4 on page 246, current recommendations are that a child should have received nine different vaccines and other preventive medicines in five to seven separate visits to the doctor.
- Finally, if a child does get ill, remember this: Minor illnesses during childhood sometimes provide immunity to more serious illnesses later on.

TABLE 7-4

RECOMMENDED CHILD VACCINATION SCHEDULE OF THE PUBLIC HEALTH SERVICE'S IMMUNIZATION PRACTICES ADVISORY COMMITTEE

				HIB[1]		HBV[2]	
Age	DTP[3]	Poliomyelitis[4]	MMR[5]	Option 1	Option 2	Option 1	Option 2
Birth	-	-	-	-	-	x	-
1–2 months	-	-	-	-	-	x	x
2 months	x	x	-	x	x	-	-
4 months	x	x	-	x	x	-	x
6 months	x	-	-	x	-	-	-
6–8 months	-	-	-	-	-	x	x
12 months	-	-	-	-	x	-	-
15 months	x[6]	x[6]	x[7]	x	-	-	-
4–6 years[8]	x	x	x[9]	-	-	-	-

[1]HIB = Haemophilus b conjugate vaccine. HIB vaccine is given in either a 4-dose schedule (option 1) or a 3-dose schedule (option 2), depending on the type of vaccine used.
[2]HBV = Hepatitis B vaccine. HBV can be given simultaneously with DTP, poliomyelitis, MMR, and Haemophilus b conjugate vaccine at the same visit.
[3]DTP = Diphtheria, tetanus, and pertussis vaccine, combined.
[4]Poliomyelitis vaccine may be live oral polio vaccine in drops (OPV) or killed (inactivated) polio vaccine by injection (IPV).
[5]MMR = Measles, mumps, and rubella vaccine, combined.
[6]Many experts recommend this vaccine at 18 months of age.
[7]In some areas, this dose of MMR vaccine may be given at 12 months.
[8]Before school entry.
[9]Many experts recommend this dose of MMR vaccine be given at entry to middle or junior high school.
Source: Child Health USA '93.

Review and Rethink

REVIEW

- Gross motor development advances rapidly during the preschool years, a time of uniquely high activity levels. Activity level is subject to environmental and genetic influences.
- Gender differences in gross motor development emerge during this period, with boys excelling in activities involving strength and girls in those involving coordination. These differences have both genetic and environmental roots.
- Fine motor skills, producing smaller, more delicate movements and requiring practice, begin to advance in this period.
- By the end of the preschool years, most children have developed handedness, a phenomenon that is little understood. Right-handedness is by far more prevalent and is favored in society in many practical ways, although left-handedness may offer certain advantages.
- The development of artistic expression follows a fairly regular pattern, progressing through the scribbling, shape, design, and pictorial stages.

RETHINK

- Do you think environmental influences can overcome the strength advantages of boys and the coordination advantages of girls? Would this be desirable? Why or why not?

- Assuming that left-handers perform disproportionately well on tests of scholastic aptitude, should parents train their children to become left-handed? Why or why not?
- How might culture influence activity level in children? Do you think there are long-term effects on children influenced in this way?
- Can you offer some explanations for the fact that left-handed people tend to die younger than right-handed people?
- Do you think the stages of artistic development mirror the stages of linguistic development? Does the shift to representation from form and design have a linguistic parallel?

What changes in the body and the brain do children experience in the preschool years?

1. Children's physical growth during the preschool period proceeds steadily. Differences in height and weight reflect individual differences, gender, and economic status.
2. In addition to gaining height and weight, the body of the preschooler undergoes changes in shape and structure. Children grow more slender and their bones and muscles strengthen.
3. Brain growth is particularly rapid during the preschool years, with the number of interconnections among cells and the amount of myelin around neurons increasing greatly. Through the process of lateralization, the two halves of the brain begin to specialize in somewhat different functions. However, despite lateralization, the two hemispheres function as a unit and in fact differ only slightly.
4. There is some evidence that the structure of the brain differs across genders and cultures. For instance, boys and girls show some hemispheric differences in lower body reflexes, the processing of auditory information, and language. Furthermore, some studies suggest that such structural features as the processing of vowel sounds may show cultural differences.
5. Brain development permits improvements in sensory processing during the preschool years, including better control of eye movements and focusing, and improved visual perception and auditory acuity.
6. Although most children sleep well at night, sleep presents real difficulties for some. Sleep-related problems include nightmares, night terrors, and enuresis.

What are the nutritional needs of preschool children, and what causes obesity?

7. Preschoolers need less food than they did in the early years. Primarily, they require balanced nutrition. If parents and caregivers provide a good variety of healthful foods, children will generally achieve an appropriate intake of nutrients.
8. Obesity is caused by both genetic and environmental factors. One strong environmental influence appears to be parents and caregivers, who may substitute their own interpretations of their children's food needs for the children's internal tendencies and controls.

What threats to their health and wellness do preschool children experience?

9. Children in the preschool years generally experience only minor illnesses, but they are susceptible to some dangerous diseases, including childhood leukemia and AIDS.

10. In the economically developed world, immunization programs have largely controlled most life-threatening diseases during these years. However, in economically disadvantaged sectors of the world—and of the United States—immunization is not completely effective.
11. Preschool children are more at risk from accidents than from illness or nutritional problems. The danger is partly due to children's high activity levels and partly to environmental hazards, such as lead poisoning.

What are child abuse and psychological maltreatment, what factors contribute to them, and can anything be done about them?

12. Child abuse may take highly physical forms, but it may also be more subtle. Psychological maltreatment may involve neglect of parental responsibilities, emotional negligence, intimidation or humiliation, unrealistic demands and expectations, or exploitation of children. Psychological maltreatment may have lasting behavioral and psychological effects.
13. Child abuse occurs with alarming frequency in the United States and other countries, especially in stressful home environments. Firmly held notions regarding family privacy and a folklore that supports the use of physical punishment in childrearing contribute to the high rate of abuse in the United States.
14. The cycle-of-violence hypothesis points to the likelihood that persons who were abused as children may turn into abusers as adults.
15. Resilience is a personal characteristic that permits some children at risk for abuse to overcome their dangerous situations. Resilient children tend to be affectionate and easygoing, able to elicit a nurturant response from people in their environment. Programs that teach the skills associated with resilience promise to help otherwise vulnerable children deal with their situations.

In what ways do children's gross and fine motor skills develop during the preschool years?

16. Gross motor skills advance rapidly during the preschool years, a time when the activity levels of children are at their peak. Genetic and cultural factors determine how active an individual child will be.
17. During these years, gender differences in gross motor skill levels begin to emerge clearly, with boys displaying greater strength and activity levels, and girls showing greater coordination of arms and legs. Both genetic and social factors probably play a role in determining these differences.
18. Fine motor skills also develop during the preschool years, with increasingly delicate movements being mastered through extensive practice.

How do handedness and artistic expression develop during these years?

19. Handedness also asserts itself, with the great majority of children showing a clear preference for the right hand by the end of the preschool years.
20. The meaning of handedness is unclear, but myths about the sinister nature of left-handers are growing less prevalent. Right-handers have certain practical advantages because of the "right bias" of the world, but left-handers may have certain intellectual and artistic advantages.
21. The development of artistic expression progresses during the preschool years through the scribbling, shape, design, and pictorial stages. Artistic expression entails the development of important related skills, including planning, restraint, and self-correction.

Key Terms and Concepts

myelin (p. 226)
lateralization (p. 226)
corpus callosum (p. 227)
nightmare (p. 229)
night terrors (p. 229)
enuresis (p. 229)
obesity (p. 231)
child abuse (p. 236)
cycle-of-violence hypothesis (p. 238)
psychological maltreatment (p. 239)
child neglect (p. 239)
resilience (p. 240)
handedness (p. 244)

CHAPTER 8

THE PRESCHOOL YEARS

Cognitive Development in the Preschool Years

PROLOGUE

THE LONG GOODBYE

The separations that occur during the first day of school can be difficult for both parent and child.

Samantha Sterman doesn't know it yet, but she has just taken a giant stride on the road to independence. The curly haired tot is mixing well with the other 3-year-olds kneading Play-Doh and bathing dolls at West Village Nursery School in Greenwich Village.

For her father, Bruce Sterman, the first day of nursery school is a bit more stressful. Squirming in his tiny chair in a corner of the classroom, . . . he is going to spend his mornings here in the classroom, easing Samantha's oh-so-gradual transition into school.

This is an autumn ritual known as "separation," the weaning of child from parent—and vice versa—that transpires at the beginning of preschool. For countless parents whose children attend developmentally sensitive nursery schools, it is a time of high anxiety and disrupted work schedules. The protracted parting sometimes can go on for weeks—a far cry from the kiss-and-run approach of years gone by . . . .

At West Village Nursery, the day of reckoning dawns the third week of September. Paint pots and crayons at the ready, the teachers throw the door open to welcome the first shift. The coatroom, a boisterous tumble of denim and plaid, is ablaze with flashbulbs, as parents capture for a lifetime the first meeting of teacher and child. Jack Kamine clings to his mother's leg. Nina Boyd clutches a well-worn doll.

But the classroom beckons, and as the children scamper off, their parents give each other meaningful, misty glances. "I feel like chopped liver," Mr. Sterman jokes—both proud and rueful—as he takes up his station in the corner. (E. Graham, 1994, p. A1)

LOOKING AHEAD

For both preschoolers and their parents, the experience of attending school for the first time produces a combination of apprehension, exhilaration, and anticipation. It marks the start of an intellectual, as well as social, journey that will continue for many years and shape the development of children in significant ways.

In this chapter, we focus on the cognitive and linguistic growth that occurs during the preschool years. We begin by examining the major approaches to cognitive development, including Piaget's theory, information-processing approaches, and an increasingly influential view of cognitive development that takes culture into account.

Next, we turn to the important advances in language development that occur during the preschool years. We consider several different explanations for the rapid increase in language abilities that characterizes the preschool period, and consider the ways that poverty is related to language development.

Finally, we discuss two of the major factors that influence cognitive development during the preschool years: schooling and television. We consider the different types of child-care and preschool programs, examining their impact on children's development. We end the chapter with a discussion of how exposure to television affects preschool viewers.

After reading this chapter, then, you'll be able to answer the following questions:

- How does Piaget interpret cognitive development during the preschool years?
- How do other views of cognitive development differ from Piaget's?
- How do children's linguistic abilities develop in the preschool years, and what is the importance of early linguistic development?

- What kinds of preschool educational programs are available in the United States, and what effects do they have?
- What effects does television have on preschoolers?

INTELLECTUAL DEVELOPMENT

Three-year-old Sam was talking to himself. As his parents listened with amusement from another room, they could hear him using two very different voices. "Find your shoes," he said in a low voice. "Not today. I'm not going. I hate the shoes," he said in a higher-pitched voice. The lower voice answered, "You are a bad boy. Find the shoes, bad boy." The higher-voiced response was "No, no, no."

Sam's parents realized that he was playing a game with his imaginary friend, Gill. Gill was a bad boy who often disobeyed his mother, at least in Sam's imagination. In fact, according to Sam's musings, Gill often was guilty of misdeeds for which his parents blamed Sam.

preoperational stage *the stage of cognitive development which lasts from age 2 until around age 7 when children's use of symbolic thinking grows, mental reasoning emerges, and the use of concepts increases*

operations *organized, formal, logical mental processes*

symbolic function *the ability to use a mental symbol, a word, or an object to stand for or represent something that is not physically present*

In some ways, the intellectual sophistication of 3-year-olds is astounding. Their creativity and imagination leap to new heights, their language is increasingly complex, and they reason and think about the world in ways that would have been impossible even a few months earlier. But what underlies the dramatic advances in intellectual development that start early in the preschool years and continue throughout that period? We can consider several approaches to answering this question, starting with a look at Piaget's findings on the cognitive changes that characterize the preschool years.

PIAGET'S STAGE OF PREOPERATIONAL THINKING

The Swiss psychologist Jean Piaget, whose stage approach to cognitive development we discussed in Chapter 5, saw the preschool years as a time of both stability and great change. According to Piaget, the preschool years fit entirely into a single stage of cognitive development—the preoperational stage—which lasts from age 2 until around age 7.

During the **preoperational stage,** children's use of symbolic thinking grows, mental reasoning emerges, and the use of concepts increases. Children become better at representing events internally, and they grow less dependent on the use of direct sensorimotor activity to understand the world around them. Yet they are still not capable of **operations:** organized, formal, logical mental processes. It is only at the end of the preoperational stage that the ability to carry out operations comes into play.

Swiss psychologist Jean Piaget.

According to Piaget, a key aspect of preoperational thought is **symbolic function,** the ability to use a mental symbol, a word, or an object to stand for or represent something that is not physically present. For example, during this stage, preschoolers can use a mental symbol for a car (the word "car"), and they likewise understand that a small toy car is representative of the real thing. Because of their ability to use symbolic function, children have no need to get behind the wheel of an actual car to understand its basic purpose and use.

Symbolic function is at the heart of one of the major advances that occur in the preoperational period: the increasingly sophisticated use of language. As we'll discuss later in this chapter, children make substantial progress in language skills during the preschool period.

It is important to consider Piaget's approach to cognitive development within the appropriate historical context and in light of more recent research findings. Recall, as we discussed in Chapter 5, that Piaget's theory is based on extensive observations of relatively few children. Despite his insightful and groundbreaking observations, recent experimental investigations suggest that, in certain regards, Piaget underestimated children's capabilities. Nevertheless, the broad outlines of his approach, which we'll consider here, provide a useful means of thinking about the advances in cognitive ability that occur during the preschool years.

The Relation Between Language and Thought. Piaget suggests that language and thinking are inextricably intertwined, and that the advances in language that occur during the preschool years offer several improvements over the type of thinking that is possible during the earlier sensorimotor period. For instance, thinking embedded in sensorimotor activities is relatively slow, since it depends on actual movements of the body that are bound by human physical limitations. In contrast, the use of symbolic thought allows preschoolers to represent actions symbolically, permitting much greater speed.

Even more important, the use of language allows children to think beyond the present to the future. Consequently, rather than being grounded in the immediate here and now, preschoolers can imagine future possibilities through language. A third advantage provided by the use of language is that preschoolers in the preoperational period can use language to consider several possibilities at the same time (Piaget & Inhelder, 1969; Wadsworth, 1971). In contrast, sensorimotor thought progresses in a linear, step by step way—the same way that children in the sensorimotor stage move from one sequential activity to the next.

Do the increased language abilities of preschoolers lead to increased thinking proficiency, or do the improvements in thinking during the preoperational period lead to enhancements in language ability? This question—whether thought determines language or language determines thought—is one of the enduring and most controversial questions within the fields of psychology and development. Piaget's answer is that language grows out of cognitive advances, rather than the other way around. He argues that improvements during the earlier sensorimotor period are necessary for language development, and that continuing growth in cognitive ability during the preoperational period provides the foundation for language ability. Consequently, Piaget argues that language development is based on the development of more sophisticated modes of thinking—and not the other way around.

centration *the process of concentrating on one limited aspect of a stimulus and ignoring other aspects*

Centration: What You See Is What You Think. Place a dog mask on a cat and what do you get? According to 3- and 4-year-old preschoolers, a dog. To them, a cat with a dog mask ought to bark like a dog, wag its tail like a dog, and eat dog food. In every respect, the cat has been transformed into a dog (deVries, 1969).

Piaget suggests that the root of this belief is centration, a key element, and limitation, of the thinking of children in the preoperational period. **Centration** is the process of concentrating on one limited aspect of a stimulus and ignoring other aspects.

Preschoolers are unable to consider all available information about a stimulus. Instead, they focus on superficial, obvious elements that are within their sight. These external elements come to dominate preschoolers' thinking, leading to inaccuracy in thought.

For example, consider what preschoolers say when they are shown two rows of buttons, one with 10 buttons that are closely spaced, and the other with 8 buttons spread out to form a longer row (see Figure 8-1). If asked which of the rows contains more buttons,

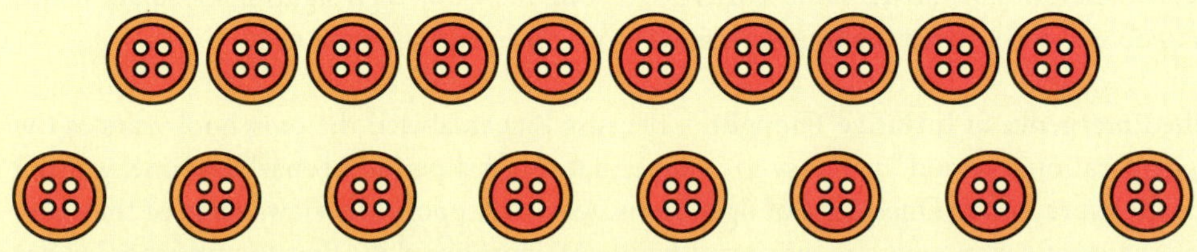

FIGURE 8-1

WHICH ROW CONTAINS MORE BUTTONS?

When preschoolers are shown these two rows and asked the question of which row has more buttons, they usually respond that the lower row of buttons contains more, because it looks longer. They answer in this way even though they know quite well that 10 is greater than 8.

children who are 4 or 5 usually choose the row that looks longer, rather than the one that actually contains more buttons. This occurs in spite of the fact that children this age know quite well that 10 is more than 8.

The cause of the children's mistake is that the visual image dominates their thinking. Rather than taking into account their understanding of quantity, they focus on appearance. To a preschooler, appearance is everything.

egocentric thought *thinking that does not take into account the viewpoints of others*

transformation *the process in which one state is changed into another*

Egocentrism: The Inability to Take Others' Perspectives. One hallmark of the preoperational period is egocentric thinking. **Egocentric thought** is thinking that does not take into account the viewpoints of others. Preschoolers do not understand that others have different perspectives from their own. Egocentric thought takes two forms: the lack of awareness that others see things from a different physical perspective, and the failure to realize that others may hold thoughts, feelings, and points of view that differ from theirs. (Note what egocentric thought does *not* imply: that preoperational children intentionally think in a selfish or inconsiderate manner.)

Egocentric thinking underlies children's lack of concern over their nonverbal behavior and the impact it has on others. For instance, a 4-year-old who is given an unwanted gift of socks when he was expecting something more desirable may frown and scowl as he opens the package, unaware that his face can be seen by others and may reveal his true feelings about the gift (Feldman, 1992).

Egocentrism lies at the heart of several types of behavior during the preoperational period. For instance, preschoolers may talk to themselves, even in the presence of others, and at times they simply ignore what others are telling them. Rather than being a sign of eccentricity, such behavior illustrates the egocentric nature of preoperational children's thinking: the lack of awareness that their behavior acts as a trigger to others' reactions and responses. Consequently, a considerable amount of verbal behavior on the part of preschoolers has no social motivation behind it but is meant for the preschoolers' own consumption.

Similarly, egocentrism can be seen in hiding games with children during the preoperational stage. In a game of hide-and-seek, 3-year-olds may attempt to hide by covering their faces with a pillow—even though they remain in plain view. Their reasoning: If they cannot see others, others cannot see them. They assume that others share their view.

Incomplete Understanding of Transformation. Children in the preoperational period are unable to understand the notion of transformation. **Transformation** is the process in which one state is changed into another. For instance, adults know that if a pencil that is held upright is allowed to fall down, it passes through a series of successive stages until it reaches its final, horizontal resting spot (see Figure 8-2). In contrast, children in the preoperational period are unable to envision or recall the successive transformations that the pencil followed in moving from the upright to the horizontal position. If asked to reproduce the sequence in a drawing, they draw the pencil upright and lying down, with nothing in between. Basically, they ignore the intermediate steps.

Similarly, a preoperational child who sees several slugs during a walk in the woods may believe that they are all the same slug. The reason: She views each sighting in isolation and is unable to reconstruct the transformation from one sighting to the next.

The Emergence of Intuitive Thought. Because Piaget labeled the preschool years as the "*pre*operational period," it is easy to assume that this is a period of marking time, waiting for the more formal emergence of operations. As if to support this view, many of the characteristics of the preoperational period highlight cognitive skills that the preschooler has yet to master. However, the preoperational period is far from idle. Cognitive development proceeds steadily, and in fact several new types of ability emerge. A case in point: the development of intuitive thought.

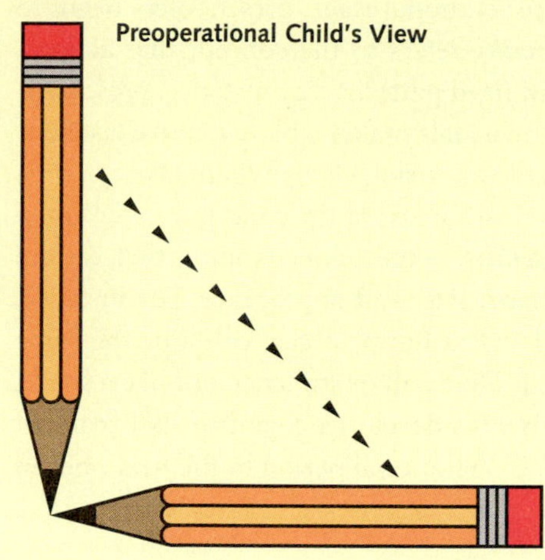

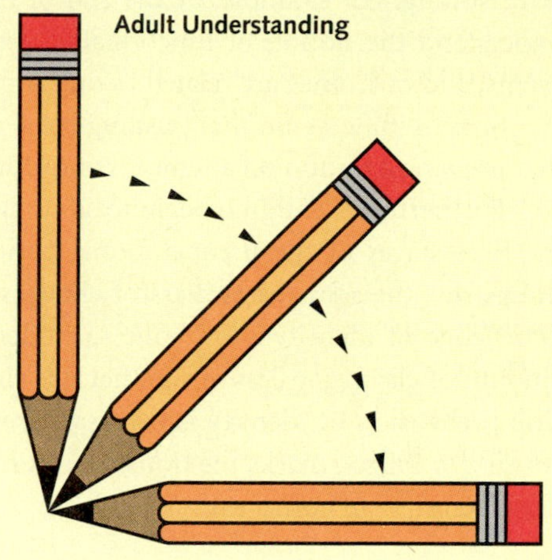

FIGURE 8-2

THE FALLING PENCIL

Children in Piaget's preoperational stage do not understand that as a pencil falls from the upright to the horizontal position it moves through a series of intermediary steps. Instead, they think that there are no intermediate steps in the change from the upright to horizontal position.

Intuitive thought reflects preschoolers' use of primitive reasoning and their avid acquisition of knowledge about the world. From about age 4 through age 7, children's curiosity blossoms. They constantly seek out the answers to a wide variety of questions.

At the same time, children may act as if they are authorities on particular topics, feeling certain that they have the correct—and final—word on an issue. If pressed, they are unable to back up their reasoning, and they are inattentive to how they know what they know. In other words, their intuitive thought leads them to believe that they know answers to all kinds of questions, but there is little or no logical basis for this confidence in their understanding of the way the world operates.

intuitive thought *thinking that reflects preschoolers' use of primitive reasoning and their avid acquisition of knowledge about the world*

"It sounds a little too perfect. What's the downside?"

conservation *the knowledge that quantity is unrelated to the arrangement and physical appearance of objects*

On the other hand, the intuitive thinking that children display in the late stages of the preoperational period has certain qualities that prepare them for more sophisticated forms of reasoning. For example, by the end of the preoperational stage, preschoolers begin to understand the notion of functionality. *Functionality* refers to the concept that actions, events, and outcomes are related to one another in fixed patterns. For instance, preschoolers come to understand that pushing harder on the pedals makes a bicycle move faster, or that pressing a button on a remote control makes the television change channels.

Furthermore, children begin to show an initial awareness of the concept of identity in the later stages of the preoperational period. *Identity* is the understanding that certain things stay the same, regardless of changes in shape, size, and appearance. For instance, knowledge of identity allows one to understand that a lump of clay contains the same amount of clay regardless of whether it is clumped into a ball or stretched out like a snake. Comprehension of identity is necessary for children to develop a cognitive skill that, according to Piaget, marks the transition from the preoperational period to the next one: an understanding of conservation.

Conservation: Learning that Appearances Are Deceiving. Consider the following scenario:

> Four-year-old Jaime is shown two drinking glasses of different shapes. One is short and broad, the other tall and thin. A teacher half-fills the short, broad glass with apple juice. The teacher then pours the juice into the tall, thin glass. The juice fills the tall glass almost to the brim. The teacher asks Jaime a question: Is there more juice in the second glass than there was in the first?

If you view this as an easy task, so do children like Jaime. They have no trouble answering the question. However, they almost always get the answer wrong.

Most 4-year-olds respond that there is more apple juice in the tall, thin glass than there was in the short, broad one. In fact, if the juice is poured back into the shorter glass, they are quick to say that there is now less juice than there was in the taller glass (see Figure 8-3).

The reason for the error in judgment is that children of this age do not understand the principle of conservation. **Conservation** is the knowledge that quantity is unrelated to the arrangement and physical appearance of objects. During the preoperational period, preschoolers are unable to understand that changes in one dimension (such as appearance) do not necessarily mean that other dimensions (such as quantity) are changed.

Children who do not yet understand the principle of conservation feel quite comfortable in asserting that the amount of liquid changes as it is poured between glasses of different sizes. They simply are unable to realize that the transformation in appearance does not imply a transformation in quantity.

The inability to conserve manifests itself in several ways during the preoperational period. For example, if 5-year-olds are shown a row of checkers and are asked to build a row that is "the same," the row they typically build will be identical in length—but it may vary

FIGURE 8-3 Which container contains more? Even after seeing that the amount of liquid in the two cups is identical (left), and watching while the liquid in one cup is poured into the glass, most 4-year-olds believe the glass contains more liquid than the cup (right).

in the number of checkers. Similarly, if shown two rows of checkers, each with the same number of checkers, but one with the checkers more spread out, children in the preoperational stage will reason that the two rows are not equal.

The lack of conservation also manifests itself in children's understanding of area, as illustrated by Piaget's cow-in-the-field problem (Piaget, Inhelder, & Szeminska, 1960). In the problem, two sheets of green paper, equal in size, are shown to a child, and a toy cow is placed in each field. Next, a toy barn is placed in each field, and children are asked which cow has more to eat. The typical—and, so far, correct—response is that the cows have the same amount.

In the next step, a second toy barn is placed in each field. But in one field, the barns are placed adjacent to one another, while in the second field, they are separated from one another. Children who have not mastered conservation usually say that the cow in the field with the adjacent barns has more grass to eat than the cow in the field with the separated barns. In contrast, children who have mastered conservation answer, correctly, that the amount available is identical. (Some other conservation tasks are shown in Figure 8-4).

Why do children in the preoperational stage make errors on tasks that require conservation? Piaget suggests that the main reason is that their tendency toward centration prevents them from focusing on the relevant features of the situation. Furthermore, they cannot follow the sequence of transformations that accompanies changes in the appearance of a situation.

Evaluating Piaget's Approach to Cognitive Development. Piaget, a masterful observer of children's behavior, provides a detailed portrait of preschoolers' cognitive abilities. His rich description of how children view the world is simply unmatched by most other accounts of cognitive development.

However, Piaget's portrait is both incomplete and, in certain respects, flawed. Several aspects of his theory considerably underestimate children's capabilities. Take, for instance, Piaget's views of how children in the preoperational period understand numbers. He contends that preschoolers' thinking is seriously handicapped, as evidenced by their performance on tasks involving conservation. Yet recent experimental work suggests otherwise. For instance, as we'll discuss in greater detail later, developmental psychologist Rochel Gelman (1972) has found in her research that children as young as 3 can readily discern the difference between rows of two and three toy animals, regardless of the animals' spacing. Furthermore, older children are able to note differences in number, performing tasks such as identifying which of two numbers is larger. In fact, we as noted in Chapter 5, some developmentalists find evidence that even infants can calculate simple addition and subtraction problems (Wynn, 1992).

Based on such evidence, Gelman concludes that children have an innate ability to count, one akin to the ability to use language that some theorists see as universal and genetically determined. Such a conclusion is clearly at odds with Piagetian notions, which suggest that children's numerical abilities do not blossom until after the preoperational period.

Some developmentalists also believe that cognitive skills develop in a more continuous manner than Piaget's stage theory implies. Rather than thought changing in quality, as Piaget argues, critics of Piaget suggest that developmental changes are more quantitative in nature. The underlying processes that produce cognitive skill are regarded by such critics as undergoing only minor changes with age (Case, 1991: Gelman & Baillargeon, 1983).

There are further difficulties with Piaget's view of cognitive development. His contention that conservation does not emerge until the end of the preoperational period or, in some cases, even later has not stood up to careful experimental scrutiny. For instance, performance on conservation tasks can be improved by providing preoperational children with certain kinds of training and experiences. The mere possibility of enhancing performance argues against the Piagetian view that children in the preoperational period have not reached a level of cognitive maturity that would permit them to understand conservation (Field, 1987; Siegler, 1995).

FIGURE 8-4

COMMON TESTS OF CHILDREN'S UNDERSTANDING OF THE PRINCIPLE OF CONSERVATION

Type of Conservation	Modality	Change in Physical Appearance	Average Age Invariance is Grasped
Number	Number of elements in a collection 	Rearranging or dislocating elements 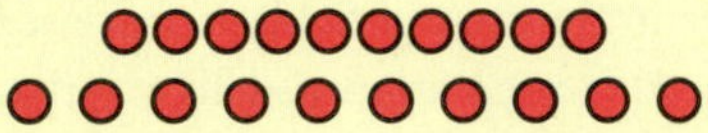	6–7 years
Substance (mass)	Amount of a malleable substance (e.g., clay or liquid) 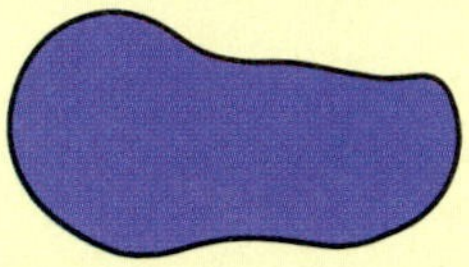	Altering shape 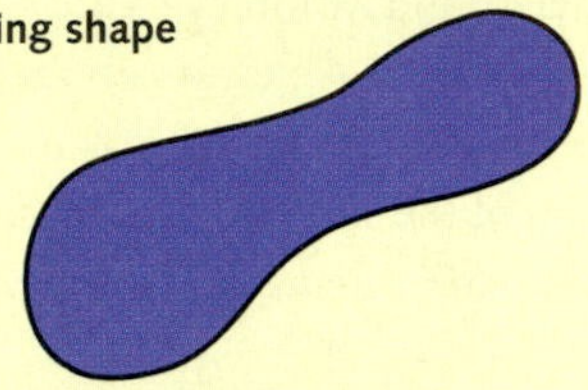	7–8 years
Length	Length of a line or object 	Altering shape or configuration 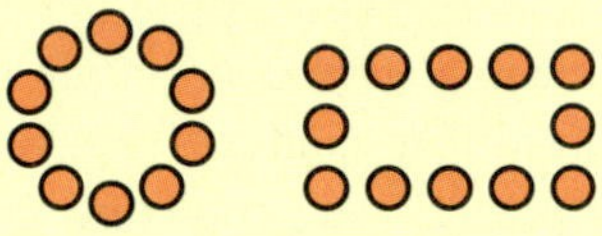	7–8 years
Area	Amount of surface covered by a set of plane figures 	Rearranging the figures 	8–9 years
Weight	Weight of an object 	Altering shape 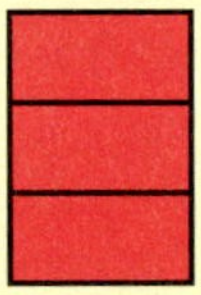	9–10 years
Volume	Volume of an object (in terms of water displacement) 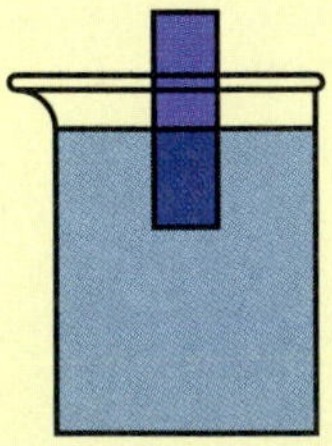	Altering shape 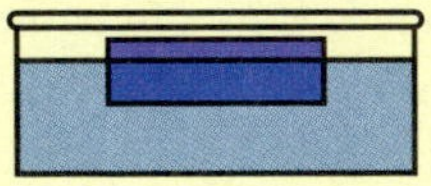	14–15 years

Clearly, children are more capable at an earlier age than Piaget's account would lead us to believe. Why did Piaget underestimate children's cognitive abilities? One answer is that he tended to concentrate on preschoolers' *deficiencies* in thinking, focusing his observations on children's lack of logical thought. In contrast, more recent theorists have focused more on children's competence. By shifting the question, they have found increasing evidence for a surprising degree of cognitive expertise in preschoolers.

autobiographical memory *memory of particular events from one's own life*

scripts *general representations in memory of a sequence or series of events*

Information-processing Approaches to Cognitive Development

> Even as an adult, Paco has clear recollections of his first trip to a farm, which he took when he was 3 years old. He was visiting his godfather, who lived in Puerto Rico, and the two of them went to a nearby farm. Paco recounts seeing what seemed like hundreds of chickens, and he clearly recalls his fear of the pigs, who seemed huge, smelly, and frightening. Most of all he recalls the thrill of riding on a horse with his godfather.

That Paco has a clear memory of his farm trip is not surprising: Most people have unambiguous, and seemingly accurate, memories dating as far back as the age of 3. But are the processes used to form memories during the preschool years similar to those that operate later in life? More broadly, what general changes in the processing of information occur during the preschool years?

Memory: Recalling the Past. Think back to your own earliest memory. If you are like most people, it probably is of an event that occurred after the age of 3.

According to Katherine Nelson (1989, 1992), **autobiographical memory,** memory of particular events from one's own life, doesn't achieve much accuracy until after 3 years of age. Accuracy then increases gradually and slowly throughout the preschool years.

Preschool children's recollections of events that happened to them are sometimes, but not always, accurate. For instance, 3-years-olds can remember fairly well central features of routine occurrences, such as the sequence of events involved in eating at a restaurant. In addition, preschoolers are typically accurate in their responses to open-ended questions, such as "What rides did you like best at the amusement park?" (Goodman & Reed, 1986; K. Nelson, 1986; Price & Goodman, 1990).

One important determinant of the accuracy of preschoolers' autobiographical memories is how soon they are assessed. Unless an event is particularly vivid or meaningful, it is not likely to be remembered at all. Moreover, not all autobiographical memories last into later life. For instance, the first day of preschool may be remembered by a 3-year-old 6 months later, but the event may not be recalled at all later in life.

Furthermore, preschoolers' autobiographical memories not only fade, but the ones that are remembered may not be wholly accurate. For instance, preschoolers have difficulty describing certain kinds of information, such as complex causal relationships, and may oversimplify recollections. Their memories are also susceptible to the suggestions of others. For example, if preschoolers are repeatedly asked questions about an event they do not at first remember, the question itself may send them the message that they "ought" to remember it. Consequently, they may feel obliged to report recalling the event, even if they really don't (Ceci & Bruck, 1993, 1995; Ceci & DeSimone, 1992; Lewis et al., 1995; Marche & Howe, 1995).

Finally, the memories of preschoolers often are recalled in terms of **scripts,** general representations in memory of a sequence or series of events. When preschoolers experience the same activity or event repeatedly—such as being driven to preschool five days a week—the activity becomes remembered in terms of a general script. Subsequently, unless something unusual occurs, such as seeing an accident, it is difficult to recall anything specific about any particular ride to school, because it is remembered in terms of the general script.

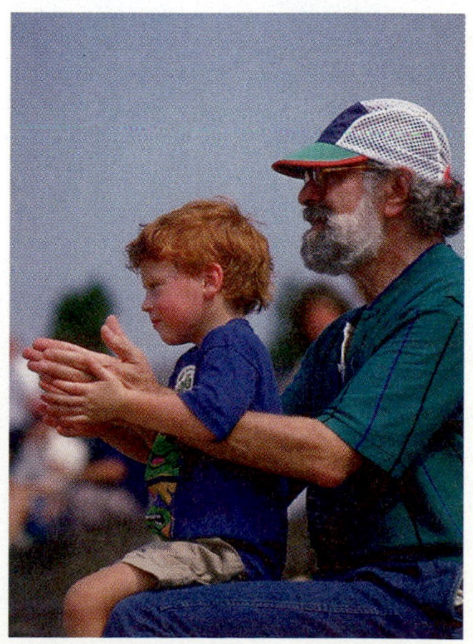

How specific and accurate will this preschooler's memory of this event be in the future?

Preschoolers' Understanding of Number. Researchers using information-processing approaches to cognitive development have found increasing evidence for the sophistication of preschoolers' understanding of numbers. The average preschooler not only is able to count, but to do so in a fairly systematic, consistent manner (Siegler, 1991).

For instance, developmental psychologist Rochel Gelman (1972; Gelman & Gallistel, 1978) suggests that preschoolers follow a number of principles in their counting. When shown a group of several items, they know they should assign just one number to each item, and that each item should be counted only once. Moreover, even when they get the *names* of numbers wrong, they are consistent in their usage. For instance, a 4-year-old who counts three items as "1, 3, 7" will say "1, 3, 7" when counting another group of different items. And she will probably say that there are 7 items in the group, if asked how many there are.

In short, preschoolers may demonstrate a surprisingly sophisticated understanding of number, although their understanding is not totally firm. Still, by the age of 4, most are able to carry out simple addition and subtraction problems by counting, and they are able to compare different quantities quite successfully. (For a discussion of another type of information-processing skill in preschoolers, see the accompanying "Directions in Development" feature.)

Directions in Development

Spatial Reasoning Skills: Music to a Preschooler's Ear?

Some research suggests that preschoolers' spatial reasoning abilities improve as a result of musical training.

Learning the notes on a piano may do more than produce the ability to make music: It may also lead to an increase in spatial abilities.

At least that is the conclusion of a team of researchers who studied the effects of teaching preschoolers to play the piano, as well as involving them in organized singing activities. In the research, Frances Rauscher and colleagues reasoned that musical activity is associated with particular neural firing patterns in the brain related to spatial reasoning skills (Rauscher et al., 1994).

To test the hypothesis, the researchers taught a group of 3- and 4-year-olds to play the piano over an 8-month period, instructing them in the fundamentals of the keyboard and rudimentary music theory. In addition, the children participated in daily 30-minute group singing sessions.

In comparison to a control group of preschoolers who did not receive musical training, the musically sophisticated children performed better on measures of spatial reasoning that involved assembling objects into a whole. In contrast, there was no difference between the two groups on tasks that did not involve spatial reasoning.

Although more work is needed to validate these findings and to determine if the effects of musical training are lasting, the results are intriguing. Not only do they suggest that certain kinds of training in one domain, such as music, can have consequences for skills in other areas, such as spatial skills, but they also have applied implications. For instance, they argue that so-called educational frills, which are the activities that are often the first to be jettisoned by school systems facing financial crises, might well promote significant basic skills.

Information-Processing and the Continuities of Cognitive Development. According to information-processing approaches, cognitive development consists of gradual improvements in the ways people perceive, understand, and remember information. With age and practice, preschoolers process information more efficiently and with greater sophistication, and they are able to handle increasingly complex problems. In the eyes of proponents of information-processing approaches, it is these quantitative advances in information processing—and not the qualitative changes suggested by Piaget—that constitute cognitive development (Case, 1991).

For instance, dramatic changes in the nature of attention occur as preschoolers become older: They have longer attention spans, can pay attention to more than one dimension of an object simultaneously, and can monitor and plan what they are attending to more effectively (Flavell, 1979; Kail, 1991; Siegler, 1989). Such increasing attentional abilities place some of Piaget's findings in a different light. For instance, increased attention allows older children to attend to both the height *and* the width of tall and short glasses into which liquid is poured. This permits them to understand that the amount of liquid in the glasses stays the same when it is poured back and forth. Preschoolers, in contrast, are unable to attend to both dimensions simultaneously, and thus are less able to conserve.

In sum, information-processing approaches view the changes that occur in children's cognitive abilities during the preschool years as analogous to the way a computer program becomes more sophisticated as a programmer modifies it on the basis of experience. These approaches focus on changes in the kinds of "mental programs" that children invoke when approaching problems. By focusing on the improvements in cognitive performance that these changes bring about, we can come closer to understanding the hallmarks of developmental change during the preschool years (Mehler & Dupoux, 1994; R. S. Siegler, 1994).

VYGOTSKY'S VIEW OF COGNITIVE DEVELOPMENT: TAKING CULTURE INTO ACCOUNT

> As her daughter watches, a member of the Chilcotin Indian tribe prepares a salmon for dinner. When the daughter asks a question about a small detail of the process, the mother takes out another salmon and repeats the entire process. According to the tribal view of learning, understanding and comprehension can come only from grasping the total procedure, and not from learning about the individual subcomponents of the task (Tharp, 1989).

The Chilcotin view of how children learn about the world stands in contrast to the prevalent view of Western society, in which the general assumption is that only by mastering the separate parts of a problem can one fully comprehend it. Do differences in the ways different cultures and societies approach problems have an influence on cognitive development? According to Russian developmental psychologist Lev Vygotsky, the answer is a clear "yes."

In an increasingly influential view, Vygotsky argues that the focus of cognitive development should be on a child's social and cultural world. Instead of concentrating on individual performance, as do both Piagetian and information-processing approaches, Vygotsky focuses on the social aspects of development and learning. He holds that cognitive development proceeds as a result of social interactions in which partners jointly work to solve problems. Because of the assistance that such adult and peer partners provide, children gradually grow intellectually and begin to function on their own (Vygotsky, 1979; Wertsch & Tulviste, 1992).

Vygotsky argues that the nature of the partnership that adults and peers provide is determined largely by cultural and societal factors. For instance, culture and society establish the institutions, such as preschools and play groups, that promote development by providing opportunities for cognitive growth. Furthermore, by emphasizing particular tasks, culture and society shape the nature of specific cognitive advances. Unless we look at what is important and meaningful to members of a given society, we may seriously underestimate the nature and level of cognitive abilities that ultimately will be attained (Belmont, 1995).

Russian psychologist Lev Vygotsky, who died at the age of 38, suggested that children's social and cultural worlds have a significant influence on development.

Vygotsky proposes that a child's cognitive abilities increase through exposure to information that resides within the child's zone of proximal development. The **zone of proximal development,** or **ZPD,** is the level at which a child can *almost,* but not fully, comprehend or perform a task on her or his own. When appropriate instruction occurs within the ZPD, students are able to increase their understanding or master new tasks. In order for cognitive development to occur, then, new information must be presented—by parents, teachers, or more skilled peers—within the zone of proximal development (Rogoff, 1990; Steward, 1995).

zone of proximal development (ZPD) *according to Vygotsky the level at which a child can* almost, *but not fully, comprehend or perform a task on her or his own*

scaffolding *the support for learning and problem solving that encourages independence and growth*

The assistance provided by others has been termed scaffolding. **Scaffolding** is the support for learning and problem solving that encourages independence and growth. To Vygotsky, not only does scaffolding promote the solution of specific problems, it also aids in the development of overall cognitive abilities.

In sum, Vygotsky's view is that the specific nature of cognitive development cannot be understood without taking the cultural and social context of a society into account. The focus of preschoolers' comprehension of the world, the specific sequence in which their cognitive development proceeds, and the nature of their understanding are all outcomes of their interactions with their parents, peers, and other members of society.

Review and Rethink

REVIEW

- According to Piaget, children in the preoperational stage develop symbolic function, a qualitative change in their thinking that is the foundation of further cognitive advances, including the development of language and intuitive thought.
- Children in the preoperational stage use intuitive thought to explore and draw conclusions about the world, and their thinking begins to encompass the important notions of functionality and identity.
- Recent developmentalists, while acknowledging Piaget's gifts and contributions, take issue with his emphasis on children's limitations and his underestimation of their capabilities.
- Proponents of information-processing approaches argue that quantitative changes in children's processing skills, such as memory and attention, largely account for their cognitive development.
- Vygotsky believes that children develop cognitively within a context of culture and society that influences the path and sequence of their development.

RETHINK

- In your view, how do thought and language interact in preschoolers' development? Is it possible to think without language? How do children who are born deaf think?
- Do you believe that development of the ability to conserve is the result of qualitative changes in the ways people think (as Piaget believed) or quantitative changes in information processing (as information-processing proponents believe)? Why? Can an experiment be devised to resolve this question?
- Are there cultural aspects to intuitive thought? Do you think children in all cultures develop logical thinking identically, or are there cultural differences? Why?
- How might learning in one skill, such as music, work to improve performance in a skill such as spatial understanding? Might there be other such links between seemingly different cognitive areas?
- Do you agree with Vygotsky's view that cognitive development and learning are social and cultural phenomena rather than strictly individual achievements? Why or why not? What implications does Vygotsky's view have for schooling?

THE GROWTH OF LANGUAGE

> I tried it out and it was very great!
> This is a picture of when I was running through the water with Mommy.
> Where you are going when I go to the fireworks with Mommy and Daddy?
> I didn't know creatures went on floats in pools.
> We can always pretend we have another one.
> And the teacher put it up on the counter so no one could reach it.
> I really want to keep it while we're at the park.
> You need to get your own ball if you want to play "hit the tree."
> When I grow up and I'm a baseball player, I'll have my baseball hat, and I'll put it on, and I'll play baseball. (Schatz, 1994, p. 179)

Listen to Ricky, at the age of 3. In addition to recognizing most letters of the alphabet, printing the first letter of his name, and writing the word *HI,* he is readily capable of producing the complex sentences quoted above.

During the preschool years, children's language skills reach new heights of sophistication. They begin the period with reasonable linguistic capabilities, although with significant gaps in both comprehension and production. In fact, no one would mistake the language used by a 3-year-old for that of an adult. However, by the end of the preschool years, they can hold their own with adults, both comprehending and producing language that has many of the qualities of adults' language. How does this transformation occur?

LANGUAGE ADVANCES DURING THE PRESCHOOL YEARS

The two-word utterances of the 2-year-old soon increase in both number of words and scope. Indeed, language blooms so rapidly between the late 2s and the mid-3s that researchers have yet to understand the exact pattern. What is clear is that sentence length increases at a steady pace, and the ways in which children at this age combine words and phrases to form sentences—known as **syntax**—doubles each month. By the time a preschooler is 3, the various combinations reach into the thousands (see Table 8-1 for an example of one child's growth in the use of language; Pinker, 1994).

In addition to the increasing complexity of sentences, there are enormous leaps in the number of words children use. By age 6 the average child has a vocabulary of around 14,000 words. To reach this number, preschoolers acquire vocabulary at a rate of nearly one new word every 2-½ hours, 24 hours a day (Clark, 1983). They manage this feat through a process known as **fast mapping,** in which new words are associated with their meaning after only a brief encounter (Fenson et al., 1994).

By the age of 3, preschoolers routinely use plurals and possessive forms of nouns (such as "boys" and "boy's"), and they use articles ("the" and "a"). They can ask, and answer, complex questions ("Where did you say my book is?" and "Those are trucks, aren't they?"). They also employ the past tense, adding "ed" to verbs to change from present to past tense ("walk" and "walked"). On the other hand, their mental rules about language sometimes lead them into trouble: They may use "singed" for the past tense of "sing" (Marcus, 1996).

Preschoolers' skills extend to the appropriate formation of words that they have never before encountered. For example, in one classic experiment, preschool children were shown cards with drawings of a cartoonlike bird, such as those shown in Figure 8-5 (Berko, 1958). The experimenter told the children that the figure was a "wug," and then showed them a card with two of the cartoon figures. "Now there are two of them," the children were told; and they were then asked to supply the missing word in the sentence, "There are two ____" (the answer to which, as *you* no doubt know, is "wugs").

Not only did children show that they knew rules about the plural forms of nouns, but they understood possessive forms of nouns and the third-person singular and past-tense

syntax *the combining of words and phrases to form sentences*

fast mapping *the process in which new words are associated with their meaning after only a brief encounter*

TABLE 8-1

GROWING SPEECH CAPABILITIES

Over the course of just a year, the sophistication of the language of a boy named Adam increases amazingly, as these speech samples show:

2 years, 3 months:	Play checkers. Big drum. I got horn. A bunny-rabbit walk.
2 years, 4 months:	See marching bear go? Screw part machine. That busy bulldozer truck.
2 years, 5 months:	Now put boots on. Where wrench go? Mommy talking 'bout lady. What that paper clip doing?
2 years, 6 months:	Write a piece of paper. What that egg doing? I lost a shoe. No, I don't want to sit seat.
2 years, 7 months:	Where piece a paper go? Ursula has a boot on. Going to see kitten. Put the cigarette down. Dropped a rubber band. Shadow has hat just like that. Rintintin don't fly, Mommy.
2 years, 8 months:	Let me get down with the boots on. Don't be afraid a horses. How tiger be so healthy and fly like kite? Joshua throw like a penguin.
2 years, 9 months:	Where Mommy keep her pocket book? Show you something funny. Just like turtle make mud pie.
2 years, 10 months:	Look at that train Ursula brought. I simply don't want put in chair. You don't have paper. Do you want little bit, Cromer? I can't wear it tomorrow.
2 years, 11 months:	That birdie hopping by Missouri in bag. Do want some pie on your face? Why you mixing baby chocolate? I finish drinking all up down my throat. I said why not you coming in? Look at that piece a paper and tell it. Do you want me tie that round? We going turn light on so you can't see.
3 years, 0 months:	I going come in fourteen minutes. I going wear that to wedding. I see what happens. I have to save them now. Those are not strong mens. They are going sleep in wintertime. You dress me up like a baby elephant.
3 years, 1 month:	I like to play with something else. You know how to put it back together. I gon' make it like a rocket to blast off with. I put another one on the floor. You went to Boston University? You want to give me some carrots and some beans? Press the button and catch it, sir. I want some other peanuts. Why you put the pacifier in his mouth? Doggies like to climb up.
3 years, 2 months:	So it can't be cleaned? I broke my racing car. Do you know the light wents off? What happened to the bridge? When it's got a flat tire it's need a go to the station. I dream sometimes. I'm going to mail this so the letter can't come off. I want to have some espresso. The sun is not too bright. Can I have some sugar? Can I put my head in the mailbox so the mailman can know where I are and put me in the mailbox? Can I keep the screwdriver just like a carpenter keep the screwdriver?

(*Source:* Pinker, 1994.)

forms of verbs—all for words that they never had previously encountered, since they were nonsense words with no real meaning.

Preschoolers also learn what *can't* be said as they acquire the principles of grammar. **Grammar** is the system of rules that determine how our thoughts can be expressed. For instance, preschoolers come to learn that "I am sitting" is correct, while the similarly structured "I am knowing [that]" is incorrect. Although they still make frequent mistakes of one sort or another, 3-year-olds follow the principles of grammar most of the time. Some errors are very noticeable—such as the use of "mens" and "wents"—but these errors are actually quite rare, occurring between 0.1 percent and 8 percent of the time. Put another way, more than 90 percent of the time young preschoolers are correct in their grammatical constructions (deVilliers & deVilliers, 1992; Hirsh-Pasek & Michnick-Golinkoff, 1996; Marcus, 1996; Pinker, 1994).

grammar *the system of rules that determine how our thoughts can be expressed*

pragmatics *the aspect of language relating to communicating effectively and appropriately with others*

Finally, preschoolers' pragmatic abilities grow. **Pragmatics** is the aspect of language relating to communicating effectively and appropriately with others. The development of pragmatic abilities permits children to understand the basics of conversations—turn tak-

This is a wug.
Now there is another one.
There are two of them.
There are two ________.

FIGURE 8-5

FORMING PLURALS

Even though preschoolers—like the rest of us—are unlikely to have ever before encountered a wug, they are able to produce the appropriate word to fill in the blank (which, for the record, is *wugs*).

(*Source:* Adapted from Berko, 1958.)

ing; sticking to a topic; and what should and should not be said, according to the conventions of society. When children are taught that the appropriate response to receiving a gift is "thank you," they are learning the pragmatics of language.

Private Speech and Social Speech. Over the course of the preschool years, children's use of **private speech,** spoken language that is not intended for others, is common. As much as 20 to 60 percent of what children say is private speech, and such speech is a normal practice during even later stages of childhood. In fact, some research suggests that its use grows over the preschool years, peaking between the ages of 4 and 7. On the other hand, private speech becomes more secretive as children grow older and realize that talking to oneself is discouraged by society. Consequently, older children tend to whisper private speech or silently move their lips, rather than speaking out loud (Berk, 1992; Berk & Landau, 1993; Quay & Blaney, 1992; Flavell et al., 1997).

Some developmentalists suggest that private speech performs an important function. For instance, Lev Vygotsky (1962, 1986) suggests that it facilitates children's thinking and that they use it to help them control their behavior. (Have you ever said to yourself, "Take it easy" or "Calm down" when trying to control your anger over some situation?) In Vygotsky's view, then, private speech ultimately serves an important social function, allowing children to solve problems and reflect upon difficulties they encounter. He suggests further that private speech is a forerunner to the internal dialogues that we use when we reason with ourselves during thinking. Clearly, Vygotsky's views are at odds with those of Piaget, who suggests that private speech is egocentric and a sign of immature thought and ultimately a failure to communicate effectively.

The preschool years also mark the growth of social speech. **Social speech** is speech directed toward another person and meant to be understood by that person. Before the age of 3, children may seem to be speaking only for their own entertainment, apparently uncaring whether anyone else can understand. However, during the preschool years, children begin to direct their speech to others, wanting others to listen and becoming frustrated when they cannot make themselves understood. As a result, they begin to adapt their speech to others. Recall that Piaget contended that most speech during the preoperational period was egocentric: Preschoolers were seen as taking little account of the effect their speech was having on others. However, more recent experimental evidence suggests that children are somewhat more adept in taking others into account than Piaget initially suggested.

private speech *spoken language that is not intended for others and is commonly used by children during the preschool years*

social speech *speech directed toward another person and meant to be understood by that person*

The language that children hear spoken in affluent homes may differ significantly from the language spoken in lower-income homes, and this difference has consequences for language development.

POVERTY AND LANGUAGE DEVELOPMENT

The language that preschoolers hear at home has profound implications for future cognitive success, according to results of a landmark study by psychologists Betty Hart and Todd Risley (1995). The researchers studied the language used over a 2-year period by a group of parents of varying levels of affluence as they interacted with their children. Coding some 1,300 hours of everyday interactions between parents and children produced several major findings:

- The rate at which language was addressed to children varied significantly according to the economic level of the family. As can be seen in Figure 8-6, the greater the affluence of the parents, the more they spoke to their children.
- In a typical hour, parents classified as professionals spent almost twice as much time interacting with their children as parents who received welfare assistance.
- By the age of 4, children in families that received welfare assistance were likely to have been exposed to some 13 million fewer words than those in families classified as professionals.
- There were differences in the kind of language used in the home by the various types of families. Children in families that received welfare assistance were apt to hear prohibitions ("no" or "stop," for example) twice as frequently as those in families classified as professionals.

FIGURE 8-6

DIFFERENT LANGUAGE EXPOSURE

Parents at differing levels of economic affluence provide different language experiences. Professional parents and working parents address more words to their children, on average, than parents on welfare.

(*Source:* Hart & Risley, 1995, p. 239.)

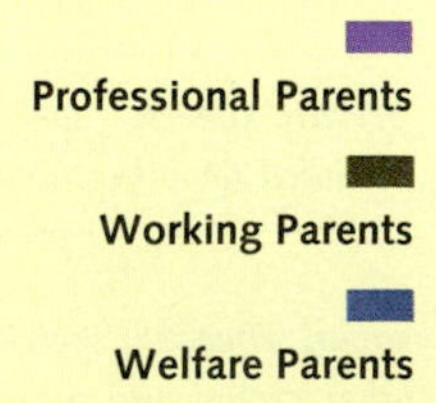

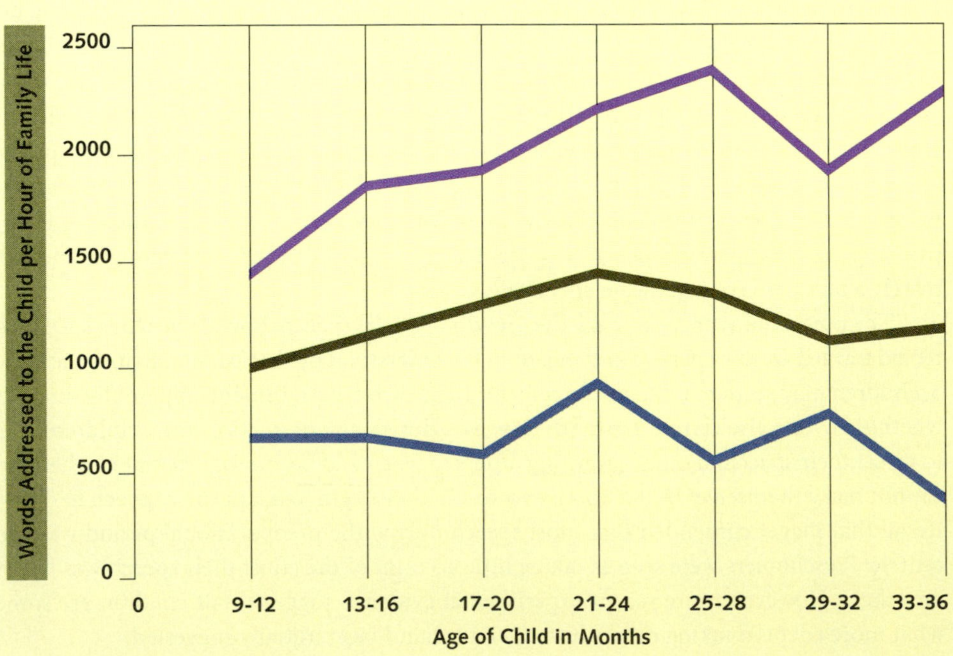

Ultimately, the study found that the type of language to which children were exposed was associated with their performance on tests of intelligence. The greater the number and variety of words children heard, for instance, the better their performance at age 3 on a variety of measures of intellectual achievement.

Although the findings are correlational, and thus cannot be interpreted in terms of cause-and-effect, they clearly suggest the importance of early exposure to language, in terms of both quantity and variety. They also suggest that intervention programs that teach parents to speak to their children more often and use more varied language may be useful in alleviating some of the potentially damaging consequences of poverty.

The research is also consistent with an increasing body of evidence that family income and poverty have powerful consequences for children's general cognitive development and behavior. By the age of 5, children raised in poverty tend to have lower IQ scores and perform less well on other measures of cognitive development than children raised in affluence. Furthermore, the longer children live in poverty, the more severe are the consequences. Poverty not only reduces the educational resources available to children, it also has such negative effects on *parents* that it limits the psychological support they can provide their families. In short, the consequences of poverty are severe, and they linger (Bolger et al., 1995; Duncan, Brooks-Gunn, & Klebanov, 1994).

Review and Rethink

REVIEW

- In the preschool years, linguistic ability increases rapidly. Substantial advances are made in sentence length, vocabulary, syntax, and use of forms such as plurals and possessives.
- Children also develop a strong sense of the grammar of their language, knowing which forms and utterances are permissible and which are not.
- Another linguistic development is a gradual shift from private to social speech. Piaget regards private speech as a sign of immaturity and egocentrism; Vygotsky views it as a useful cognitive mechanism that ultimately serves a social function.
- Economic factors in the home have a significant influence on language development. Children raised in affluence hear a greater quantity and variety of language from their parents than children of poverty, with positive effects on later measures of intellectual achievement.

RETHINK

- Is private speech egocentric or useful? Do adults ever use private speech? What functions does it serve?
- What do you think are the underlying reasons for differences between poor and more affluent households in the use of language?
- If parents living in poverty are given instruction in using a greater quantity and variety of language in the home, do you think their children will achieve equality with more affluent children in linguistic and cognitive areas? Why or why not?

Schooling and Society

It's a Thursday afternoon at Unitel Studio on Ninth Avenue, where *Sesame Street* is taping its 19th season. Hanging back in the wings is a newcomer on the set, a compact young woman with short blond hair named Judy Sladky. Today is her screen test.

> Other performers come to New York aspiring to be actresses, dancers, singers, comedians. But Sladky's burning ambition is to be Alice, a shaggy mini-mastodon who will make her debut later this season as the devoted baby sister of Aloysius Snuffle-upagus, the biggest creature on the show. (Hellman, 1987, p. 50)

Ask almost any preschooler, and she or he will be able to identify Snuffle-upagus, as well Big Bird, Bert, Ernie, and a host of other characters as the members of the cast of *Sesame Street. Sesame Street* is the most successful television show in history targeted at preschoolers, with an audience in the millions.

However, preschoolers do more than watch TV. Many spend a good portion of their day involved in some form of child-care setting outside their own homes, designed, in part, to enhance their cognitive development. What are the consequences of these activities? We turn now to a consideration of how early childhood education and television are related to preschool development.

Early Childhood Education: Taking the "Pre" Out of the Preschool Period

The term *preschool period* is something of a misnomer: Almost three quarters of children in the United States are enrolled in some form of care outside the home, much of which is designed either explicitly or implicitly to teach skills that will enhance intellectual, as well as social, abilities. There are several reasons for the prevalence of such care arrangements, but one major factor is the rise in the number of families in which both parents work outside the home. For instance, a high proportion of fathers work outside the home, and close to 60 percent of mothers with children under 6 are employed, most of them full-time (Gilbert, 1994).

However, there is another reason, one less tied to the practical considerations of child care: Developmentalists have found increasing evidence that children can benefit substantially from involvement in some form of educational activity before they enroll in formal schooling, which typically takes place at age 5 or 6 in the United States. When compared to children who stay at home and have no formal educational involvement, those children enrolled in *good* preschools experience clear cognitive and social benefits (Clarke-Stewart, 1993; Haskins, 1989; McCartney, 1984).

The Varieties of Early Education. The variety of early education alternatives is vast. Some outside-the-home care for children is little more than babysitting, while other options are designed to promote intellectual and social advances. Among the major choices of the latter type are the following:

- *Day care.* **Day-care centers** typically provide care for children all day, while their parents are at work. Although many day-care centers were first established as safe, warm environments where children could be cared for and could interact with other children, today their purpose tends to be broader, aimed at providing some form of intellectual stimulation. Still, their primary purpose tends to be more social and emotional than cognitive.

  Some day care is provided in family day-care centers, small operations run in private homes. Because such centers are often unlicensed, the quality of care can be uneven, and parents should investigate these carefully before enrolling their children. In contrast, providers of center-based care—which is offered in institutions such as school classrooms, community centers, and churches and synagogues—are licensed and regulated by governmental authorities. Because teachers in such programs are more often trained professionals than those who provide family day care, the quality of care is often higher and more stable.

day-care centers *places that typically provide care for children all day, while their parents are at work*

"Oh, yes, indeed. We all keep a sharp eye out for those little clues that seem to whisper 'law' or 'medicine.'"

- *Preschools or nursery schools.* **Preschools** (or **nursery schools**) are more explicitly designed to provide intellectual and social experiences for children. Because they tend to be more limited in their schedules, typically providing care for only 3 to 5 hours per day, preschools mainly serve children from middle and higher socioeconomic levels.

  As do day-care centers, preschools vary enormously in the activities they provide. Some emphasize social skills, while others focus on intellectual development. Some do both. For instance, Montessori preschools, which use a method developed by Italian educator Maria Montessori, employ a carefully designed set of materials to create an environment that fosters sensory, motor, and language development.

- *School day care.* **School day care** is provided by some local school systems in the United States. Almost half the states in the United States fund prekindergarten programs for 4-year-olds, often targeted at disadvantaged children. Because they typically are staffed by better-trained teachers than are less-regulated day care centers, school day-care programs are often of higher quality than other early education alternatives.

How effective are such programs? According to developmental psychologist Alison Clarke-Stewart (1993), who has studied the issue extensively, preschoolers enrolled in day-care centers show intellectual development that at least matches that of children at home, and often is better. For instance, some studies find that day-care preschoolers are more verbally fluent, show memory and comprehension advantages, and even achieve higher IQ scores than at-home children (Kontos, Hsu, & Dunn, 1994). Other studies find that early participation in day care is particularly helpful for children from impoverished home environments or who are otherwise at risk (Caughy, DiPietro, & Strobino, 1994; Reynolds, 1994).

preschools (nursery schools) *child-care facilities designed to provide intellectual and social experiences for children*

school day care *child-care programs provided by some local school systems in the United States*

Analogous advantages are found in social development. Children in high-quality programs tend to be more self-confident, independent, and knowledgeable about the social world in which they live than those who do not participate. On the other hand, not all the outcomes of outside-the-home care are positive: Children in day care have been found to be less polite, less compliant, less respectful of adults, and sometimes more competitive and aggressive than their peers (Bates et al., 1991; Belsky, Steinberg, & Walker, 1982; Thornburg et al., 1990).

It is important to keep in mind that not all early childhood care programs are equally effective. As we observed of infant day care in Chapter 6, one key factor is program *quality:* High-quality care provides intellectual and social benefits; low-quality care is unlikely to furnish benefits, and poor programs may actually harm children (Burchinal et al., 1996; D. A. Phillips et al., 1994).

How can we define "high quality"? Several characteristics are important; they are analogous to those that pertain to infant day care (see Chapter 6). For example, high-quality facilities have well-trained care providers. Furthermore, both the overall size of the group and the ratio of care providers to children are critical. Single groups should not have many more than 14 to 20 children, and there should be no more than five to ten 3-year-olds per caregiver, or seven to ten 4- or 5-year-olds per caregiver. Finally, the curriculum of a child-care facility should not be left to chance, but should be carefully planned and coordinated among the teachers (Cromwell, 1994; National Research Council, 1991).

No one knows how many programs in the United States can be considered "high quality," but there are many fewer than desirable. In fact, the United States lags behind almost every other industrialized country in the quality of its day care, as well as in its quantity and affordability.

Preschool curricula typically include both intellectual and social components.

Developmental Diversity

Preschools around the World: Why Does the United States Lag Behind?

In France and Belgium, accessibility to preschool is a legal right. In Sweden and Finland, preschoolers whose parents work have day care provided, if it is wanted. Russia has an ex-

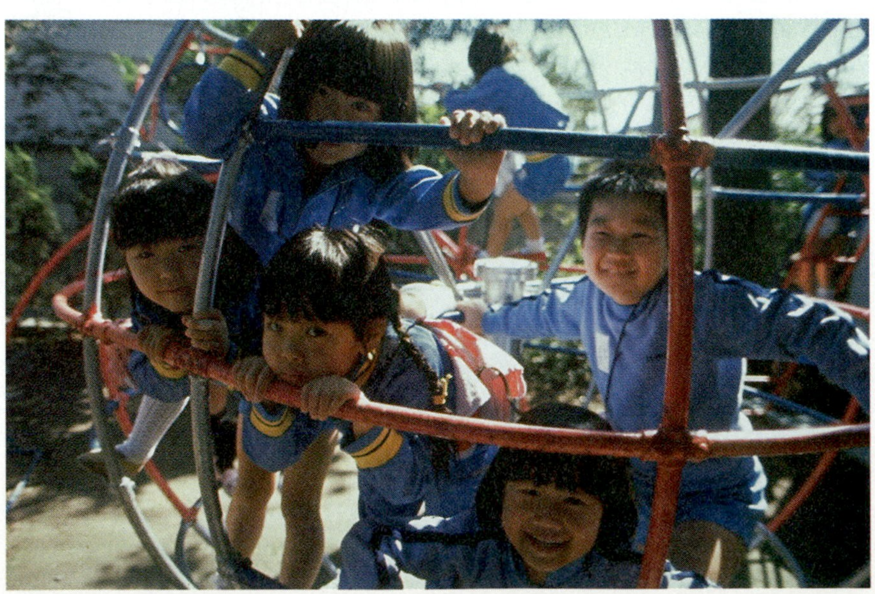

In many industrialized countries other than the United States, preschool education receives significantly more national support.

tensive system of state-run *yasli-sads*, nursery schools and kindergartens, attended by 75 percent of children age 3 to 7 in urban areas.

In contrast, the United States has no coordinated national policy on preschool education—or on the care of children in general. There are several reasons for this. For one, decisions about education have traditionally been left to the states and local school districts. For another, the United States has no tradition of teaching preschoolers, unlike other countries which have for decades enrolled preschool-age children in formal programs. Finally, the status of preschools in the United States has been traditionally low. Consider, for instance, that preschool and nursery school teachers are the lowest paid of all teachers. (Teacher salaries increase as the age of students rises. Thus, college and high school teachers are paid most, while preschool and elementary school teachers are paid least.)

Finally, the quantity and nature of preschools may differ from one country to another according to the views that different societies hold of the purpose of early childhood education (M. E. Lamb et al., 1992; Thyssen, 1995). For instance, in a cross-country comparison of preschools in China, Japan, and the United States, researchers found that parents in the three countries view the purpose of preschools very differently. Whereas parents in China tend to see preschools primarily as a way of giving children a good start academically, Japanese parents view them primarily as a way of giving children the opportunity to be members of a group. In the United States, in comparison, parents regard the primary purpose of preschools as making children more independent and self-reliant, although obtaining a good academic start and having group experience are also important (see Figure 8-7; Tobin, Wu, & Davidson, 1989).

FIGURE 8-7

THE PURPOSE BEHIND PRESCHOOL

Although parents in China see preschools mainly as a way of giving children a good start academically, parents in Japan see them primarily as a means of giving children the experience of being a member of a group. In contrast, parents in the United States view preschools as a way of making children more independent, although obtaining a good academic start and group experience are also important.

(*Source:* Tobin, Wu, & Davidson, 1989.)

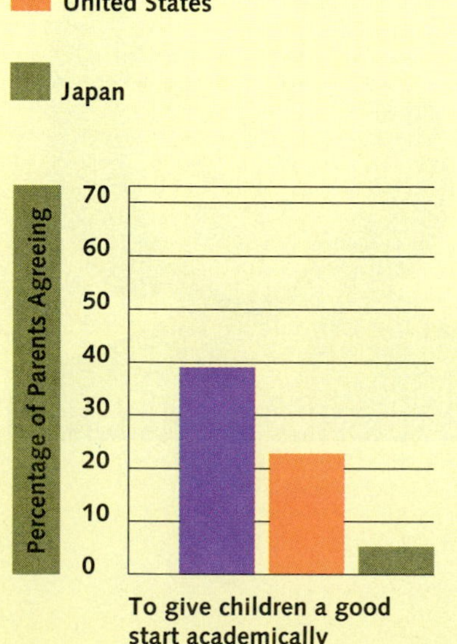

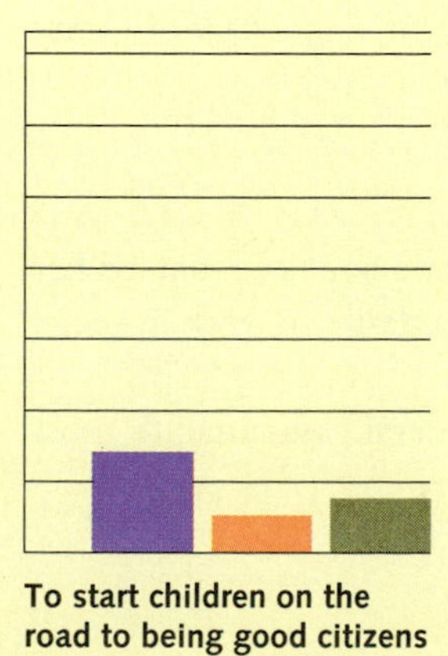

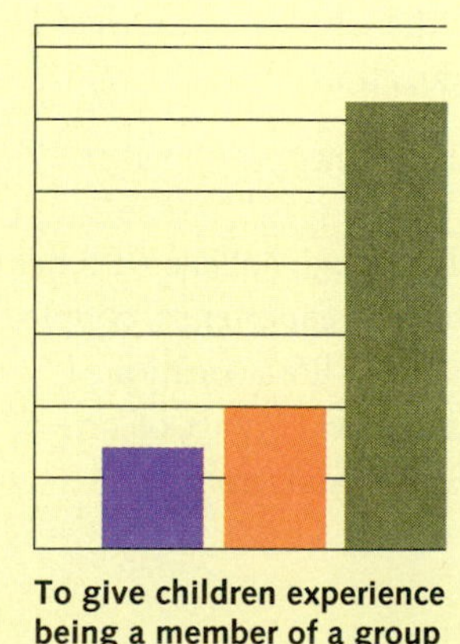

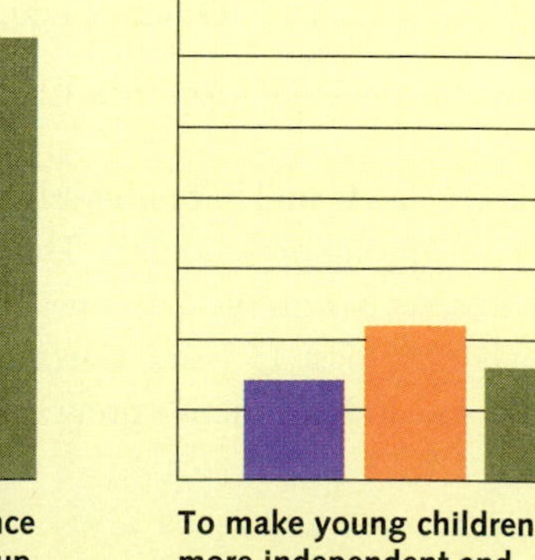

Parents of preschoolers in Asian countries are more apt to view preschool as an opportunity to learn to be members of a group, whereas parents in the United States see preschool as promoting independence and self-reliance.

Preparing Preschoolers for Academic Pursuits: Does Head Start Truly Provide a Head Start? Although many programs designed for preschoolers focus primarily on social and emotional factors, some programs are geared primarily toward promoting cognitive gains and preparing preschoolers for the more formal instruction that they will experi-

Speaking of Development

Yolanda Garcia, Head Start Advocate

Born:	1952
Education:	University of California at Santa Barbara, B.A. in combined social sciences (history, sociology, and political science) University of Chicago School of Social Services, M.A. in administration, child welfare, and public policy San Jose State University, M.A. in education administration
Position:	Director of the Children's Services Department, Santa Clara County Office of Education
Home:	San Jose, California

Yolanda Garcia had to put herself through college with her own money, a need that led her to a job among preschoolers. That job experience, coupled with a desire to work in social services, set her on the path toward her life's vocation.

For the past 15 years, Garcia has been part of one of the federal government's most successful and productive programs: Head Start.

ence when they start kindergarten. In the United States, the best-known program designed to promote future academic success is **Head Start.** Born in the 1960s when the United States declared a War on Poverty, the program has served more than 13 million children and their families. Although it was designed to serve the "whole child," including children's physical health, self-confidence, social responsibility, and social and emotional development, the program has been scrutinized most closely in relation to the goal of improving cognitive processes (U.S. Department of Education, 1992; Zigler & Styfco, 1994; Zigler, Styfco, & Gilmar, 1993).

Head Start *a program begun in the United States in the 1960s, designed to serve the "whole child" and promote future academic success*

Whether Head Start is seen as successful or not depends on the lens through which one is looking. If, for instance, the program is expected to provide long-term increases in IQ scores, it is a disappointment. Although graduates of Head Start programs tend to show immediate IQ gains, these increases do not last. On the other hand, it is clear that preschoolers who participate in Head Start are more ready for future schooling than those who do not. Furthermore, graduates of Head Start programs have better future school adjustment than their peers, and they are less likely to be in special education classes or to be retained in grade. Finally, some research suggests that ultimately Head Start graduates show higher academic performance at the end of high school, although the gains are modest (Hebbeler, 1985; Lee et al., 1990; McKey et al., 1985).

In addition, results from other types of preschool readiness programs indicate that those who participate and graduate are less likely to repeat grades, and they complete school more frequently than those who are not in the program. Moreover, according to a cost-benefit analysis of one preschool readiness program, for every $1 spent on the program, taxpayers saved $7 by the time the graduates reached the age of 27 (Schweinhart, Barnes, & Weikart, 1993). (For more on Head Start, see the "Speaking of Development" interview.)

"Children learn by doing, with the teacher helping them develop cognitive skills and reinforcing their interest areas."

"Teachers will guide the child through processes that build on their level of cognitive development."

As director of the Children's Services Department in the Santa Clara County Office of Education, Garcia is responsible for a Head Start program that serves 1,799 children at 56 facilities in two counties. Garcia is proud of her program and of its approach to children and to learning.

"In Head Start classes children learn by doing," she explains, "with the teacher helping them develop cognitive skills and reinforcing their interest areas. The teacher guides the children, led by their interests, and sets up an environment that is conducive to their pursuit of those interests.

"For instance, in teaching prereading and premath skills we focus on the recognition of symbols. Children love symbols and have an intuitive sense of them. Every item in the learning center has a symbol attached to it. This is to help the child see and make a connection between the object and the symbol," she says. "The child learns that there is a name, a symbol, and a place for every object. This growing sense of connection and order is very important for future learning."

Much of the teaching and planning in Head Start programs is done in conjunction with the children through a variety of learning activities, according to Garcia.

"We utilize an open framework of learning where teachers plan with the children. The teacher becomes the observer, recorder, and guide from one step in the learning process to the next," she explains. "Teachers will guide the child through processes that build on their level of cognitive development."

A ratio of one teacher to seven students is the goal of each Head Start program, according to Garcia. This, she says, allows for a very high quality of interaction.

"It also allows the teacher to individualize the teaching. We can focus on each child and his or her interests and level of development. Even group activities are based on what the teacher knows about the individual children in the group."

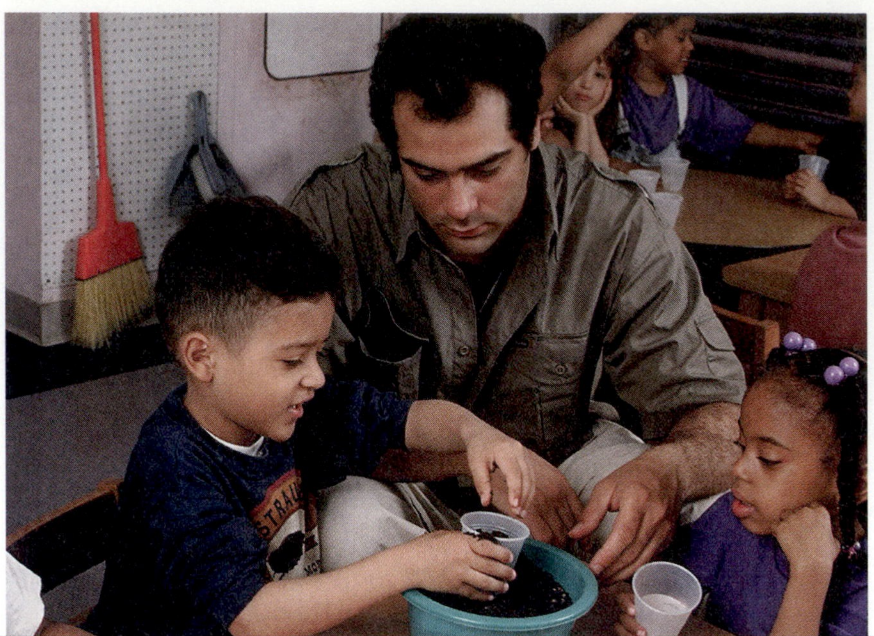

Head Start, one of the most extensive national preschool programs, has served more than 13 million children.

Should We Seek to Improve Cognitive Skills during the Preschool Years? Not everyone agrees that programs that seek to enhance academic skills during the preschool years are a good thing. In fact, according to developmental psychologist David Elkind (1984, 1988), U.S. society tends to push children so rapidly that they begin to feel stress and pressure at a young age.

Elkind argues that academic success is largely dependent upon factors out of parents' control, such as inherited abilities and a child's rate of maturation. Consequently, children of a particular age cannot be expected to master educational material unless their current level of cognitive development is taken into account.

Rather than arbitrarily expecting children to master material at a particular age, Elkind suggests that a better strategy is to provide an environment in which learning is encouraged, but not pushed. By creating an atmosphere in which learning is facilitated—for instance, by reading to preschoolers or taking them on visits to museums—parents will allow children to proceed at their own pace, rather than a pace that pushes them beyond their limits.

Although Elkind's suggestions are appealing—it is certainly hard to argue that increases in children's anxiety levels and stress should be avoided—they are not without their detractors. For instance, some educators have argued that pushing children is largely a phenomenon of the middle and higher socioeconomic levels, possible only if parents are relatively affluent. For poorer children, whose parents may not have substantial resources available to push their children or the easy ability to create an environment that promotes learning, the benefits of formal programs that promote learning are likely to outweigh their drawbacks.

Television: Learning from the Media

Almost every home in the United States has a television, and more than half of all households own more than one. Statistics show that there are more televisions than toilets in this country.

These televisions do not sit idle: It has been estimated that the average American child spends more time watching television than talking to adults, playing with siblings, or attending school. In fact, the average preschooler watches some 20 to 30 hours of TV a week (Liebert & Sprafkin, 1988; Rosemond, 1988; VanEvra, 1990).

Television: Ubiquitous Presence, Uncertain Consequences. Despite television's ubiquitous presence, the consequences of watching so much television are not entirely clear. For instance, research suggests that children do not fully understand the plots of the stories they are viewing, particularly in longer programs. They are unable to recall significant story details after viewing a program, and the inferences they make about the motivations of characters are limited and often erroneous. Moreover, preschool children may have difficulty separating fantasy from reality in television programming (Anderson & Collins, 1988; Parke & Slaby, 1983; Rule & Ferguson, 1986; Wright, Huston, Reitz, & Piemyat, 1994).

On the other hand, some kinds of information are likely to be understood relatively well by children. For instance, preschoolers are able to decode the facial expressions they see on television. However, the emotional displays that they view differ from what they find in the everyday, nontelevised world. For instance, one examination of the nonverbal behavior on the television shows viewed most frequently by children found that nonverbal displays of emotion occurred at the surprisingly high rate of some 200 emotional expressions per hour. Furthermore, although a wide range of emotions was observed, depictions of certain emotions (such as happiness and sadness) were displayed considerably more frequently than others (for instance, fear and disgust). Consequently, televised displays of emotion occur at high frequencies and diverge from what happens in the real world (Coats & Feldman, 1995; Houle & Feldman, 1991).

In sum, preschool children's understanding of what they see on television is typically incomplete and not fully accurate. This problem is compounded by the fact that much of what they view on TV is not representative of what actually happens in the real world. On the other hand, as they get older and their information-processing capabilities improve, preschoolers' understanding of the material they see on television improves (J. C. Wright et al., 1994). They remember things more accurately, and they become better able to focus on the central message of a show. This suggests that the powers of the medium of television may be harnessed to bring about cognitive gains—exactly what the producers of *Sesame Street* set out to do (VanEvra, 1990).

***Sesame Street:* A Teacher in Every Home?** *Sesame Street* is, without a doubt, the most popular educational program for children in the United States. Almost half of all preschoolers in the United States watch the show, and it is broadcast in almost 100 different countries and in 13 foreign languages. Characters like Big Bird and Kermit the Frog have become familiar throughout the world, to both adults and preschoolers (Liebert & Sprafkin, 1988).

Sesame Street was devised with the express purpose of providing an educational experience for preschoolers. Its specific goals include teaching letters and numbers, increasing vocabulary, and teaching preliteracy skills. Has *Sesame Street* achieved its goals? Most evidence suggests that it has.

For example, a 2-year longitudinal study compared three groups of 3- and 5-year-olds: those who watched cartoons or other programs, those who watched the same amount of *Sesame Street,* and those who watched little or no TV. Children who watched *Sesame Street* had significantly larger vocabularies than those who watched other programs or those who watched little television. These findings held regardless of the children's gender, family size, and parental education and attitudes. Such findings are consistent with earlier evaluations of the program, which concluded that viewers showed dramatic improvements in skills that were directly taught, such as alphabet recitation, and improvements in other areas that were not directly taught, such as reading words (Bogatz & Ball, 1972; Rice et al., 1990).

A recent evaluation of the show found not only that preschool viewers of the show who live in lower-income households are better prepared for school than those who do not

Careful research suggests that *Sesame Street* has met its goal of teaching letters and numbers, increasing vocabulary, and teaching preliteracy skills.

watch it, but also that they perform significantly higher on several measures of verbal and mathematics ability at ages 6 and 7 (see Figure 8-8). Furthermore, viewers of *Sesame Street* spend more time reading than nonviewers. And by the time they are 6 and 7, viewers of *Sesame Street* and other educational programs tend to be better readers and judged more positively by their teachers (Huston & Wright, 1995).

On the other hand, *Sesame Street* has not been without its critics. For instance, some educators claim the frenetic pace at which different scenes are shown makes viewers less receptive to the traditional forms of teaching that they will experience when they begin school. Traditional teaching moves at a slower pace and the lessons are typically less visually appealing than those presented on *Sesame Street.* However, careful evaluations of the program find no evidence that viewing *Sesame Street* leads to declines in enjoyment of traditional schooling (VanEvra, 1990).

In sum, the results of research on the consequences of watching *Sesame Street* are largely positive. Still, it is important to keep in mind the difficulties of carrying out evaluations of the effects of viewing. For instance, parents who encourage their children to watch a show reputed to improve academic performance may also encourage their children's academic performance in other spheres. Consequently, it may be the parents' high level of encouragement, and not the program itself, that leads to the children's improved cognitive performance. Without the use of true experiments—which are difficult, if not impossible, to carry out because it is hard to maintain experimental control of what children watch in their homes—conclusions about the consequences of TV viewing remain uncertain.

FIGURE 8-8

THE BENEFITS OF SESAME STREET

Children who watched more of *Sesame Street* and other informative shows during the preschool years scored better at age 7 than nonviewers. In contrast those who watched cartoons predominately are at a disadvantage at age 7.

(*Source:* Adapted from Huston & Wright, 1995.)

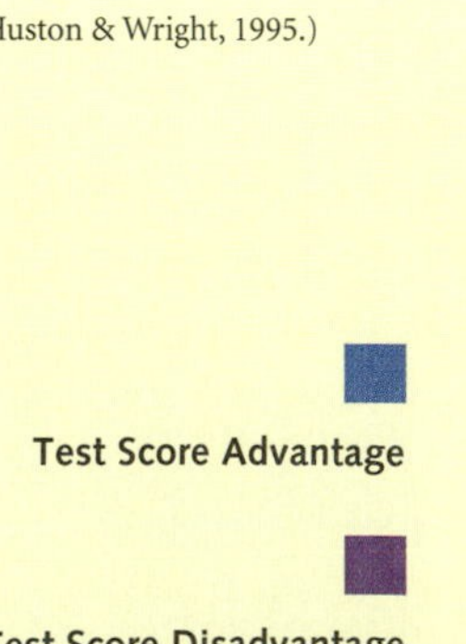

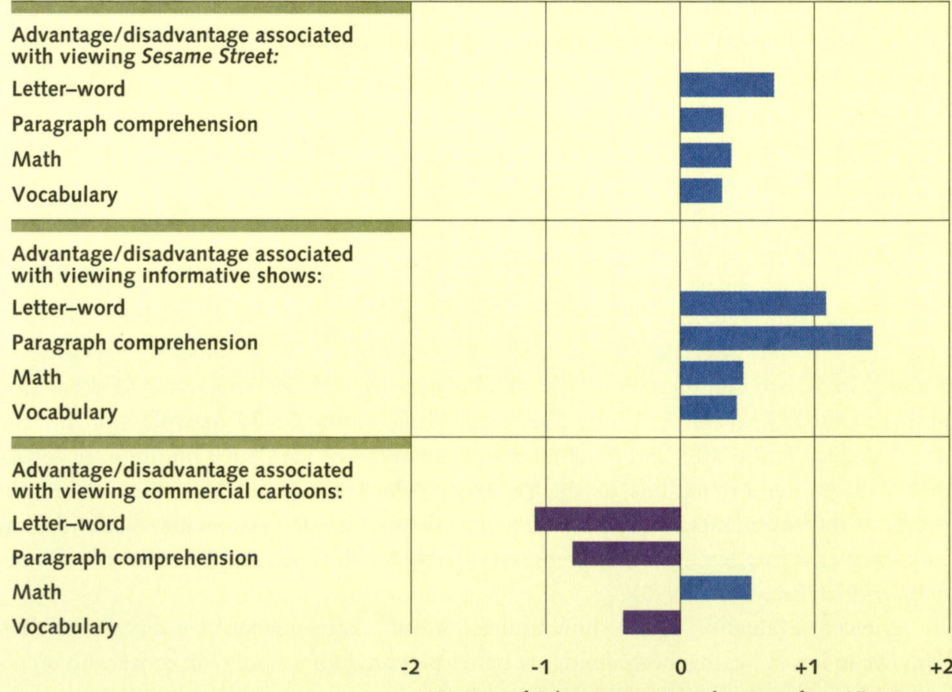

The Informed Consumer of Development

Promoting Cognitive Development in Preschoolers: From Theory to the Classroom

We've considered the notion that one focus of the preschool period should be on promoting future academic success, and we've also discussed the alternative view that pushing children too hard academically may be hazardous to their well-being.

There is, however, a middle ground. Drawing on research conducted by developmentalists who examine cognitive development during the preschool years, we can make the following suggestions for parents and preschool teachers who wish to improve the academic readiness of children without creating undue stress:

- Both parents and teachers should be aware of the stage of cognitive development, with its capabilities and limitations, that each individual child has reached. Unless they are aware of a child's current level of development, it will be impossible to provide appropriate materials and experiences.
- Instruction should be at a level that reflects—but is just slightly higher than—each student's current level of cognitive development. Piaget, for instance, suggests that cognitive growth is more likely to occur when information and material are of moderate novelty. With too little novelty, children will be bored; with too much, they will be confused.
- Instruction should be individualized as much as possible. Because children of the same age may hover around different levels of cognitive development, curriculum materials that are prepared individually stand a better chance of success.
- Students should be kept actively engaged in learning, and they should be allowed to pace themselves as they move through new material.
- Opportunities for social interaction—both with other students and with adults—should be provided. By receiving feedback from others and observing how others react in given situations, preschoolers learn new approaches and ways of thinking about the world.
- Students should be allowed to make mistakes. Cognitive growth often flows from confronting errors.
- Because cognitive development can occur only when children have achieved the appropriate level of maturation, preschoolers should not be pushed too far ahead of their current state of cognitive development. For instance, although it may be possible through intensive training to get preoperational children to recite, in a rote manner, the correct response to a conservation problem, this does not mean that they will have true comprehension of what they are verbalizing.

Ultimately, keep in mind that children require **developmentally appropriate educational practice,** which is education that is based on both typical development and the unique characteristics of a given child (Bredekamp, 1989; Cromwell, 1994).

developmentally appropriate educational practice *education that is based on both typical development and the unique characteristics of a given child*

Review and Rethink

REVIEW

- Enrollments are on the rise in many different kinds of preschool programs, primarily due to increased numbers of families in which both parents work outside the home. Some families that do not have to employ preschool programs do so anyway for the perceived social and educational benefits of the experience.
- Preschool programs can be beneficial if they are of high quality, with trained staff, good curriculum, proper group sizes, and low student-staff ratios.
- With the exception of the successful Head Start program, the U. S. government pays little attention to preschool education. This contrasts with many other countries and reflects U. S. traditions and values with respect to education.
- The effects of television on preschoolers are unclear. Some people are concerned about the excessive emotionalism and distorted reality presented by television, while others are hopeful about the potential for facilitating cognitive gains in preschoolers through programs like *Sesame Street.*
- While some people oppose attempts to improve preschoolers' cognitive skills, it is likely that preschool children can benefit from developmentally appropriate, individualized, and supportive efforts to improve academic readiness.

RETHINK

- Do you think that children with certain personality or cognitive characteristics might benefit more from preschool programs than children with different characteristics? What sorts of characteristics might make a difference?
- Should the United States adopt a more definite preschool policy? If so, what sort of policy? If not, why not?
- What might be some effects on preschoolers of television's overemphasis on emotional expression? How would you test your hypotheses? What difficulties would you encounter?
- What are some examples of developmentally appropriate and developmentally inappropriate educational practices for the preschool years?
- Should children participate in formal programs that enhance academic skills during the preschool years? Why do some people criticize this practice, while others argue that opposing the practice may reflect a biased attitude?

LOOKING BACK

How does Piaget interpret cognitive development during the preschool years?

1. The intellectual development of preschoolers, which is rapid and dramatic, has been observed and interpreted by numerous theoreticians. Among the most influential is Jean Piaget, whose preoperational stage of cognitive development coincides with these years.

2. During Piaget's preoperational stage, children are as yet unable to perform mental operations: organized, formal, logical thinking. However, their cognitive abilities involve symbolic function, which permits quicker and more effective thinking than previously. According to Piaget, improved cognitive abilities in the preoperational period enable significant improvements in language.
3. Piaget focuses on certain limitations of children's thinking during the preoperational stage, including centration (concentration on limited aspects of stimuli), egocentric thought (thinking that fails to take into account others' viewpoints), and an imperfect understanding of transformation (the interim processes involved in changes of state).
4. According to Piaget, children in the preoperational stage do engage in intuitive thought for the first time, actively applying rudimentary reasoning skills to the acquisition of world knowledge. Their intuitive thinking leads to other advances—such as an understanding of the concepts of functionality and identity—that position them for the major cognitive changes that attend the next stage of development. Their main deficit is in failing to grasp conservation, the notion that the quantity of objects is unaffected by changes in their appearance.

How do other views of cognitive development differ from Piaget's?

5. More recent work by developmentalists suggests that Piaget's views of children's development, though based on gifted intuitions and intensive observations, focused excessively on children's limitations rather than on their capabilities. These researchers have found evidence of significantly greater cognitive capabilities in preschoolers than Piaget proposed.
6. A different approach to cognitive development is taken by proponents of information-processing theories. One focus of these researchers is on ways preschoolers store and recall information in the form of memories. These theorists find that preschool children's autobiographical memories, inaccessible or unreliable at first, begin to achieve some degree of accuracy after age 3.
7. Another important focus of information-processing theorists is on the effects that quantitative changes in information-processing abilities (such as attention) have on cognitive development. Such theorists conclude that changes in preschoolers' cognitive abilities are more gradual and more purely quantitative than Piaget theorized.
8. Lev Vygotsky's view of children's learning is becoming increasingly influential. He proposes that the nature and progress of children's cognitive development are dependent on the children's social and cultural context. According to Vygotsky, children's cognitive abilities are developed in socially supported ways as children and others work together to solve problems that reside in the children's zone of proximal development (ZPD)—the level of cognitive skill at which the children can almost, but not quite, perform a task.

How do children's linguistic abilities develop in the preschool years, and what is the importance of early linguistic development?

9. The burst in language ability that occurs during the preschool years is dramatic. Children rapidly progress from two-word utterances to longer, more sophisticated expressions that reflect their growing vocabularies, sense of syntax, and emerging grasp of grammar. They also proceed along a continuum from private speech to more social speech.
10. Language development and economic circumstances are significantly linked. Preschool children living in poverty tend to hear a smaller quantity and variety of

language from their parents and caregivers than children of affluence. This linguistic difference in turn is linked to later differential performance on a variety of measures of intellectual achievement.

What kinds of preschool educational programs are available in the United States, and what effects do they have?

11. Educational and social programs for young children, including day care, preschools or nursery schools, and school day care, are growing ever more popular as families increasingly follow the two-working-parent pattern.
12. Good preschool programs can lead to cognitive and social advances. The quality of such programs is largely a factor of high staff expertise, sound curriculum, low group size, and good caregiver-child ratios.
13. The United States lacks a coordinated national policy on preschool education, an unusual characteristic among industrialized nations. Federal neglect in this area reflects systemic factors relating to the federal-state division of responsibility, tradition, and the low status of preschools in the United States.
14. The major federal initiative in U. S. preschool education has been the Head Start program. Head Start, aimed at less advantaged children, has yielded mixed but generally positive results: no permanent gains in IQ scores, but an increased likelihood of good school adjustment and somewhat higher academic performance, and a decreased likelihood of retention in grade and assignment to special education classes.
15. While it may not be either advisable or effective to push preschool children aggressively toward higher academic achievement, providing an individually tailored educational program that is developmentally appropriate and set in a good social context creates a supportive atmosphere in which children can pursue their own learning and increase their academic readiness.

What effects does television have on preschoolers?

16. Television has become a ubiquitous presence in children's lives in the United States and other industrialized countries. The effects of television on preschool children are mixed. While children's comprehension of television storylines is imperfect, they can decode facial expressions accurately. Preschoolers' sustained exposure to emotions and situations that are not representative of the real world has raised concerns about children's television viewing.
17. On the other hand, television can be a positive influence. The fact that preschoolers can derive meaning from television programs has led to such targeted programs as *Sesame Street,* a highly successful venture designed to bring about cognitive gains in children.

Key Terms and Concepts

preoperational stage (p. 252)
operations (p. 252)
symbolic function (p. 252)
centration (p. 253)
egocentric thought (p. 254)
transformation (p. 254)
intuitive thought (p. 255)
conservation (p. 256)
autobiographical memory (p. 259)
scripts (p. 259)
zone of proximal development (ZPD) (p. 262)
scaffolding (p. 262)
syntax (p. 263)
fast mapping (p. 263)
grammar (p. 264)
pragmatics (p. 264)
private speech (p. 265)
social speech (p. 265)
day-care centers (p. 268)
preschools (nursery schools) (p. 269)
school day care (p. 269)
Head Start (p. 273)
developmentally appropriate educational practice (p. 277)

CHAPTER 9

THE PRESCHOOL YEARS

Social and Personality Development in the Preschool Years

PROLOGUE CAUTION: MORPHING MAY BE HAZARDOUS TO A TEACHER

It's 8:30 a.m. and 30 preschoolers are kicking and karate-chopping their way into Fannie Elliott's classroom.

Ms. Elliott, a teacher at Kedren Headstart Preschool in Los Angeles, is aghast. "Why," she asks the 4-year-olds, "do you do what you do?" Still breathless from their romp, they shout almost in unison: "We are the Power Rangers."

Like many grown-ups these days, Ms. Elliott lives in a strange world in which, at any moment, small children may suddenly turn into frenzied, brawling boxers. Emulating the teenage heroes of the hit television show *Mighty Morphin Power Rangers,* legions of tots are fighting in classrooms. . . .

"One simply has to say 'Trini' [a ranger's name] and abracadabra, the little curmudgeons transform before my very eyes into an entire martial-arts army," Ms. Elliott says. First come grunts and groans, then cries of "Hi-Yah!" as the children's eyes take on a bewitched glint. Soon the classroom erupts into a Bruce Lee festival, she says, as the children "tumble and run around so the enemy won't attack them." (Pereira, 1994, p. A1)

LOOKING AHEAD

Ms. Elliott's experience is not unique: a poll of preschool teachers found that 96 percent had witnessed a Morphin-inspired act of aggression (Carlsson-Paige & Levin, 1994).

Why is the aggression displayed by characters such as the *Mighty Morphin Power Rangers* so appealing to preschool-age viewers, and does observing fictional violence lead to actual aggression? More broadly, what are the factors that determine how preschoolers interact with one another, and how does social and personality development proceed during this period?

These and many other questions are addressed in this chapter. We begin by examining how preschool-age children continue to form a sense of self, focusing on how they develop their self-concepts. We especially examine issues of self relating to gender, a central aspect of children's views of themselves and others.

Preschoolers' social lives are the focus of the next part of the chapter. We look at how children play with one another, examining the various types of play. We consider how parents and other authority figures use discipline to shape children's behavior.

Finally, we examine two key aspects of preschoolers' social behavior: moral development and aggression. We consider how children develop a notion of right and wrong, and how that development can lead them to be helpful to others. We also look at the other side of the coin—aggression—and examine the factors that lead preschoolers to behave in a way that hurts others. We end on an optimistic note: considering how we may help preschoolers to be more moral, and less aggressive, individuals.

In sum, after reading this chapter, you'll be able to answer these questions:

- How do preschool-age children develop a concept of themselves?
- How do children develop a sense of racial identity and gender?
- In what sorts of social relationships do preschoolers engage?
- How do the nature and function of play change over time?
- What sorts of disciplinary styles do parents employ, and what effects do they have?

- How do children develop a moral sense?
- Is aggression normal in preschoolers, and how does it develop?

FORMING A SENSE OF SELF

Although the question "Who am I?" is not explicitly posed by most preschoolers, it underlies a considerable amount of development during the preschool years. During this period, children wonder about the nature of the self, and the way they answer the "Who am I?" question may affect them for the rest of their lives.

SELF-CONCEPT IN THE PRESCHOOL YEARS: THINKING ABOUT THE SELF

If you ask preschoolers to specify what makes them different from other kids, they readily respond with answers such as, "I'm a good runner" or "I like to color" or "I'm a big girl." Such answers relate to **self-concept**—their identity, or their set of beliefs about what they are like as individuals (Breakwell, 1992; Eder, 1990; Hattie, 1992).

The statements that compose children's self-concepts are not necessarily accurate. In fact, preschool children typically overestimate their skills and knowledge across all domains of expertise. Consequently, their view of the future is quite rosy: They expect to win the next game they play, to beat all opponents in an upcoming race, and even to write great stories when they grow up. Even when they have just experienced failure at a task, they are likely to expect to do well in the future (Damon & Hart, 1988; Ruble, 1983; Stipek & Hoffman, 1980).

Preschoolers also begin to develop a view of self that reflects the way their particular culture considers the self. Such views pervade a culture, sometimes in subtle ways. For instance, one well-known saying in Western cultures states that "the squeaky wheel gets the grease." On the other hand, children in Asian cultures are exposed to a different perspective; they are told that "the nail that stands out gets pounded down." Such adages represent two very different views of the world. In the view that predominates in Western cultures, one should seek to get the attention of others by standing out and making one's needs known. In contrast, the predominant Asian perspective suggests that individuals should attempt to blend in and refrain from making themselves distinctive (Markus & Kitayama, 1991; H. C. Triandis, 1995).

Such varying philosophies may lead to differences in how children begin to view the self during the preschool years. Asian societies tend to have a **collectivistic orientation,** promoting the notion of interdependence. People in such cultures tend to regard themselves as parts of a larger social network in which they are interconnected with others.

In contrast, children in Western cultures are more likely to develop an independent view of the self, reflecting an **individualistic orientation** that emphasizes personal identity and the uniqueness of the individual. They are more apt to see themselves as self-contained and autonomous, in competition with others for scarce resources. Consequently, children in Western cultures are more likely to focus on their uniqueness and what sets them apart from others—what makes them special.

Of course, it is important to note that even within a culture there is great heterogeneity in terms of orientation. Furthermore, members of subcultural minority groups may sometimes reflect their ethnicity and family backgrounds, rather than the culture at large. For example, cross-cultural psychologist Harry C. Triandis (1994) suggests that Asian Americans are more collectivistic than European Americans (H. Triandis et al., 1986).

In short, preschoolers' self-concepts are a result of more than how their parents treat them. Additional influences are the views of their society and their exposure to the philosophy of the culture in which they are being reared (Marjoribanks, 1994).

self-concept *one's identity, or set of beliefs about what one is like as an individual*

collectivistic orientation *a philosophy that promotes the notion of interdependence*

individualistic orientation *a philosophy that emphasizes personal identity and the uniqueness of the individual*

PSYCHOSOCIAL DEVELOPMENT: RESOLVING THE CONFLICTS

According to psychoanalyst Erik Erikson (1963), by the time they reach the preschool years, children have already passed through several stages of psychosocial development. As we discussed in Chapter 6, **psychosocial development** encompasses changes both in the understanding individuals have of themselves as members of society, and in their comprehension of the meaning of others' behavior.

Erikson suggests that throughout life, society and culture present particular challenges, which shift as people age. As we noted in Chapter 6, Erikson suggests that people pass through eight distinct stages, each of which necessitates resolution of a crisis or conflict.

In the early part of the preschool period, children are ending the autonomy-versus-shame-and-doubt stage, which lasts from around 1-½ to 3 years. In this period, children either become more independent and autonomous if their parents encourage exploration and freedom or experience shame and self-doubt if they are restricted and overprotected.

The preschool years largely encompass the **initiative-versus-guilt stage,** which lasts from around age 3 to age 6. It is during this period that children's views of themselves undergo major change as preschoolers face conflicts between, on the one hand, the desire to act independently of their parents and, on the other hand, the guilt that comes from the unintended consequences of their actions. In essence, preschoolers come to realize that they are persons in their own right, and they begin to make decisions and to shape the kind of persons that they will become.

Parents who react positively to this transformation toward independence can help their children resolve the opposing forces of taking initiative and experiencing guilt that is characteristic of this period. By providing their children with opportunities to act self-reliantly, while still giving them direction and guidance, parents can support and encourage their children's initiative. On the other hand, parents who discourage their children's efforts to seek independence may contribute to a sense of guilt that persists throughout their lives.

psychosocial development *according to Erikson, development that encompasses changes both in the understandings individuals have of themselves as members of society and in their comprehension of the meaning of others' behavior*

initiative-versus-guilt stage *the period during which children age 3 to 6 years experience conflict between independence of action and the sometimes negative results of that action*

race dissonance *the phenomenon in which minority children indicate preferences for majority values or people*

Developmental Diversity

Developing Racial and Ethnic Awareness

The preschool years mark an important turning point for children. Their answer to the question of who they are begins to take into account their racial and ethnic identity.

For most preschoolers, racial awareness comes relatively early. Certainly, even infants are able to distinguish different skin colors; their perceptual abilities allow for such color distinctions quite early in life. However, it is only later that children begin to attribute meaning to different racial characteristics. By the time they are 3 or 4 years of age, preschoolers distinguish between African Americans and whites and begin to understand the significance that society places on racial membership.

At the same time, some preschoolers start to experience ambivalence over the meaning of their racial and ethnic identity. Some preschoolers experience **race dissonance,** the phenomenon in which minority children indicate preferences for majority values or people. For instance, some studies find that as many as 90 percent of African American children, when asked about their reactions to drawings of black and white children, react more negatively to the drawings of black children than to those of white children. However, these negative reactions did not translate into lower self-esteem for the African American subjects. Instead, their preferences appear to be a result of the powerful influence of the dominant white culture, rather than a disparagement of their own racial characteristics (Holland, 1994).

By the time they are 3 or 4 years of age, preschoolers distinguish between members of different races and begin to understand the significance of race in society.

Ethnic identity emerges somewhat later. For instance, in one study of Mexican American ethnic awareness, preschoolers displayed only a limited knowledge of their ethnic identity. However, as they became older, their understanding of their racial background grew in both magnitude and complexity. In addition, those preschoolers who were bilingual, speaking both Spanish and English, were most apt to be aware of their racial identity (Bernal, 1994).

Gender Identity: Developing Femaleness and Maleness

> Boys' awards: Very Best Thinker, Most Eager Learner, Most Imaginative, Most Enthusiastic, Most Scientific, Best Friend, Mr. Personality, Hardest Worker, Best Sense of Humor.
>
> Girls' awards: All-Around Sweetheart, Sweetest Personality, Cutest Personality, Best Sharer, Best Artist, Biggest Heart, Best Manners, Best Helper, Most Creative.

What's wrong with this picture? To one parent, whose daughter received one of the girls' awards during a kindergarten graduation ceremony, quite a bit. While the girls were getting pats on the back for their pleasing personalities, the boys were receiving awards for their intellectual and analytic skills (Deveny, 1994).

Such a situation is not rare: Girls and boys often live in very different worlds. Differences in the ways in which males and females are treated begin at birth (as we noted in Chapter 6), continue during the preschool years, and—as we'll see later—extend into adolescence and beyond.

Gender, the sense of being male or female, is well established by the time children reach the preschool years. (As we first noted in Chapter 6, "gender" and "sex" do not mean the same thing. *Sex* typically refers to sexual anatomy and sexual behavior, while *gender* refers to the perception of maleness or femaleness related to membership in a given society). By the age of 2, children consistently label themselves and those around them as male or female (Fagot & Leinbach, 1993; Poulin-Dubois et al., 1994; Signorella, Bigler, & Liben, 1993).

One way in which gender is manifested is in play. During the preschool years, boys increasingly play with boys and girls with girls, a trend that increases during middle childhood. Actually, girls begin the process of preferring same-sex playmates a little earlier than boys. Girls first have a clear preference for interacting with other girls at age 2 while boys don't show much preference for same-sex partners until age 3 (Benenson, 1994; Fagot, 1991; Lloyd & Duveen, 1991; Ramsey, 1995; Serbin et al., 1991).

Such same-sex preferences appear in many cultures. For instance, studies of kindergartners in mainland China show no examples of mixed-gender play. Similarly, gender "outweighs" ethnic variables when it comes to play: A Hispanic boy would rather play with a white boy than with a Hispanic girl (Fishbein & Imai, 1993; Martin, 1993; Shepard, 1991; Turner, Gervai, & Hinde, 1993; Whiting & Edwards, 1988).

Preschoolers also begin to hold expectations about appropriate behavior for girls and boys. In fact, their expectations about gender-appropriate behavior are even more rigid and gender-stereotyped than those of adults, and may be less flexible during the preschool years than at any other point in the life span. For instance, beliefs in gender stereotypes become more pronounced up to age 5 and have already started to become somewhat less rigid by age 7. On the other hand, gender expectations do not disappear, and the content of gender stereotypes held by preschoolers is similar to that held traditionally by adults in society (Golombok & Fivush, 1994; Urberg, 1982; Yee & Brown, 1994).

During the preschool period, differences in play, relating to gender, become more pronounced. In addition, boys tend to play with boys, and girls with girls.

And what is the nature of preschoolers' gender expectations? Like adults, preschoolers expect that males are more apt to have traits involving competence, independence, forcefulness, and competitiveness. In contrast, women are viewed as more likely to have traits such as warmth, expressiveness, nurturance, and submissiveness. Although these are *expectations,* and say nothing about the way that men and women actually behave, such expectations both provide the lens through which preschoolers view the world and affect their own behavior and the way they interact with their peers and with adults (Signorella et al., 1993).

The prevalence and strength of preschoolers' gender expectations, and differences in behavior between boys and girls, have proven puzzling. Why should gender play such a powerful role during the preschool years (as well as during the rest of the life span)? Developmentalists have proposed several explanations.

Biological Perspectives. Recall that gender relates to the sense of being male or female, while sex refers to the physical characteristics that differentiate males and females. It would hardly be surprising to find that the physical characteristics associated with sex might themselves lead to gender differences, and this in fact has been shown to be true.

For example, some research has focused on girls whose mothers had, prior to being aware that they were pregnant, taken drugs that contained high levels of *androgens* (male hormones) due to certain medical problems. These androgen-exposed girls are more likely to display behaviors associated with male stereotypes than are their sisters who were not exposed to androgens (Money & Ehrhardt, 1972). Androgen-exposed girls preferred boys as playmates and spent more time than other girls playing with toys associated with the male role, such as cars and trucks. Similarly, boys prenatally exposed to unusually high levels of female hormones are apt to display more behaviors that are stereotypically female than is usual (Berenbaum & Hines, 1992; Hines & Kaufman, 1994).

Moreover, as we first noted in Chapter 7, some research suggests that biological differences exist in the structure of female and male brains. For instance, part of the *corpus callosum,* the bundle of nerves that connects the hemispheres of the brain, is proportionally larger in women than in men (Witelson, 1989). To some theoreticians, evidence such as this suggests that gender differences may be produced by biological factors.

Before accepting such contentions, however, it is important to note that alternative explanations abound. For example, it may be that the corpus callosum is proportionally larger in women as a result of certain kinds of experiences that influence brain growth in particular ways. If this is true, environmental experience produces biological change—and not the other way around.

identification *the process in which children attempt to be similar to their same-sex parent, incorporating the parent's attitudes and values*

In sum, as in many other domains that involve the interaction of inherited, biological characteristics and environmental influences, it is difficult to attribute behavioral characteristics unambiguously to biological factors. Because of this difficulty, we must consider other explanations for gender differences.

Psychoanalytic Perspectives. You may recall from Chapter 1 that Freud's psychoanalytic theory suggests that we move through a series of stages related to biological urges. To Freud, the preschool years encompass the *phallic stage,* in which the focus of a child's pleasure relates to genital sexuality.

Freud argued that the end of the phallic stage is marked by an important turning point in development: the Oedipal conflict. According to Freud, the *Oedipal conflict* occurs at around the age of 5, when the anatomical differences between males and females become particularly evident. Boys begin to develop sexual interests in their mothers, viewing their fathers as rivals. As a consequence, boys conceive a desire to kill their fathers—just as Oedipus did in the ancient Greek tragedy. However, because they view their fathers as all-powerful, boys develop a fear of retaliation, which takes the form of *castration anxiety.* In order to overcome this fear, boys repress their desires for their mothers and instead begin to identify with their fathers, attempting to be as similar to them as possible. **Identification** is the process in which children attempt to be similar to their same-sex parent, incorporating the parent's attitudes and values.

Girls, according to Freud, go through a different process. They begin to feel sexual attraction toward their fathers and experience *penis envy*—a view that not unexpectedly has led to accusations that Freud viewed women as inferior to men. In order to resolve their penis envy, girls ultimately identify with their mothers, attempting to be as similar to them as possible.

In the cases of both boys and girls, the ultimate result of identifying with the same-sex parent is that the children adopt their parents' gender attitudes and values. In this way, says Freud, society's expectations about the ways females and males "ought" to behave are perpetuated into new generations.

If you are like many people, you may find it difficult to accept Freud's elaborate explanation of gender differences. So do most developmentalists, who believe that gender development is best explained by other mechanisms. In part, they base their criticisms of Freud on the lack of scientific support for his theories. For example, children learn gender stereotypes much earlier than the age of 5. Furthermore, this learning occurs even in single-parent households. On the other hand, some aspects of psychoanalytic theory have been supported, such as findings indicating that preschoolers whose same-sex parents support sex-stereotyped behavior tend to demonstrate that behavior also. Still, far simpler processes can account for this phenomenon, and many developmentalists have searched for explanations of gender differences other than Freud's (Maccoby, 1980; Mussen, 1969).

Social Learning Approaches. According to social learning approaches, children learn gender-related behavior and expectations from their observation of others. In this view, children watch the behavior of their parents, teachers, and even peers. Their observation of the rewards that these others attain for acting in a gender-appropriate manner leads them to conform to such behavior themselves.

The media, and in particular television, also play a role in perpetuating traditional views of gender-related behavior from which preschoolers may learn. For instance, television shows typically define female characters in terms of their relationships with males.

According to social learning approaches, children observe the behavior of same-sex adults and come to imitate it.

Furthermore, females are more apt to appear with males, whereas female-female relationships are relatively uncommon. Also, females appear as victims far more often than do males (Condry, 1989; Mackey & Hess, 1982; Signorelli, 1987).

Television also presents men and women in traditional gender roles. Although such shows as *ER* and *Murphy Brown* portray women in atypical, counterstereotypical roles, these shows generally go unwatched by preschoolers. Instead, preschoolers are often exposed to repeats of older shows such as *Leave It to Beaver* and *The Brady Bunch,* which portray women and men in highly traditional roles. And contemporary programming is, by and large, little better. For instance, analyses of the most popular television shows find that male characters outnumber female characters by 2 to 1. Furthermore, women are much less likely to be illustrated as decision-makers or productive, and more likely to be portrayed as interested in romance, their homes, and their families. Such models, according to social learning theory, are apt to have a powerful influence on preschoolers' definitions of appropriate behavior (Atken, Moorman, & Linn, 1991; Signorelli, 1990; VandeBerg & Streckfuss, 1992).

In some cases, learning of social roles does not involve models, but occurs more directly. For example, most of us have heard preschoolers being told by their parents to act like a "little lady" or "little man." What this generally means is that girls should behave politely and courteously and that boys should be tough and stoic—traits associated with society's traditional stereotypes of women and men. Such direct training sends a clear message about the behavior expected of a preschooler.

Cognitive Approaches. In the view of some theorists, the desire to form a clear sense of identity leads children to establish a **gender identity**, a perception of themselves as male or female. To do this, they develop a **gender schema,** a cognitive framework that organizes information relevant to gender (Bem, 1987; Stangor et al., 1992).

Gender schemas are developed early in life, forming a lens through which preschoolers view the world. For instance, preschoolers use their increasing cognitive abilities to develop "rules" about what is right, and what is inappropriate, for males and females. Thus, some girls decide that wearing pants is inappropriate for a female, and apply the rule so rigidly that they refuse to wear anything but dresses. Or a preschool boy may reason that since makeup is typically worn by females, it is inappropriate for

gender identity *the perception of oneself as male or female*

gender schema *a cognitive framework that organizes information relevant to gender*

gender constancy the belief that people are permanently males or females, depending on fixed, unchangeable biological factors

androgynous a state in which gender roles encompass characteristics thought typical of both sexes

him to wear makeup even when he is in a preschool play and all the other boys and girls are wearing it.

According to *cognitive-developmental theory,* proposed by Lawrence Kohlberg (1966), this rigidity is in part an outcome of changes in preschoolers' understanding of gender. Initially, gender schemas are influenced by erroneous beliefs about sex differences. Specifically, young preschoolers believe that sex differences are based not on biological factors but on differences in appearance or behavior. Employing this view of the world, a girl may reason that she can be a father when she grows up, or a boy may think he could turn into a girl if he put on a dress and tied his hair in a ponytail. However, by the time they reach the age of 4 or 5, children develop an understanding of **gender constancy,** the belief that people are permanently males or females, depending on fixed, unchangeable biological factors.

Although research has supported the notion that the understanding of gender constancy changes during the preschool period, it has been less supportive of the idea that this understanding is the cause of gender-related behavior. In fact, the appearance of gender schemas occurs well before gender constancy is understood. Even young preschoolers assume that certain behaviors are appropriate–and others are not–on the basis of stereotypical views of gender (Bussey & Bandura, 1992; Maccoby, 1990).

Can we reduce the objectionable consequences of viewing the world in terms of gender schemas? According to Sandra Bem (1987), one way is to encourage children to be **androgynous,** a state in which gender roles encompass characteristics thought typical of both sexes. For instance, androgynous males may be encouraged to be assertive (typically viewed as a male-appropriate trait) but at the same time to be warm and tender (usually viewed as female-appropriate traits). Similarly, girls might be encouraged to be both empathetic and tender (typically seen as female-appropriate traits) and competitive, assertive, and independent (typical male-appropriate traits).

Like the other approaches to gender development (summarized in Table 9-1), the cognitive perspective does not imply that differences between the two sexes are in any way improper or inappropriate. Instead, it suggests that preschoolers should be taught to treat others as individuals. Furthermore, preschoolers need to learn the importance of fulfilling their own talents, acting as individuals and not as representatives of a particular gender.

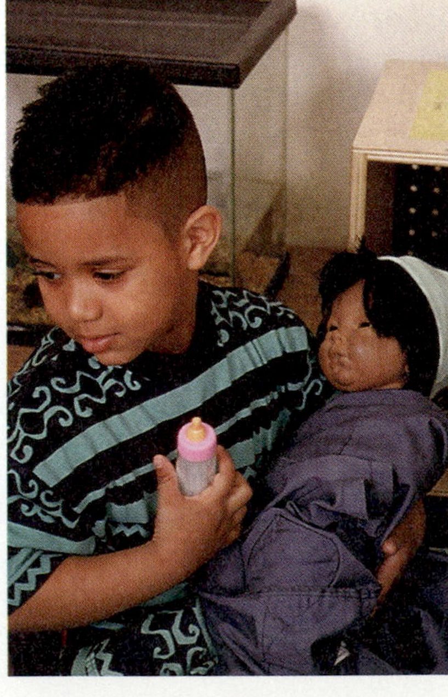

According to Sandra Bem, one way to encourage children to be androgynous is to provide them with toys that are typically played with by children of the other sex.

TABLE 9-1

FOUR APPROACHES TO GENDER DEVELOPMENT

Perspective	Key Concepts
Biological	Inborn, genetic factors produce gender differences.
Psychoanalytic	Gender development is the result of moving through a series of stages related to biological urges.
Social learning	Children learn gender-related behavior and expectations from their observation of others' behavior.
Cognitive	Through the use of gender schemas, developed early in life, preschoolers form a lens through which they view the world. They use their increasing cognitive abilities to develop "rules" about what is appropriate for males and females.

Review and Rethink

REVIEW

- During the preschool years, children develop their self-concepts, beliefs about themselves that they derive from their own perceptions, their parents' behaviors, and society.
- According to Erikson's psychosocial development theory, preschool children move from the autonomy-versus-shame-and-doubt stage to the initiative-versus-guilt stage.
- Racial and ethnic awareness begins to form in the preschool years. Members of minority groups may experience race dissonance before establishing a sense of identity regarding their race and ethnicity.
- Gender awareness also develops in the preschool years. Explanations of this phenomenon that emphasize the action of universal factors within the individual include purely biological explanations and psychoanalytical explanations such as Freud's.
- While the social learning approach to explaining gender expectations focuses on the influence of society, the cognitive approach focuses on the individual's formation of a cognitively based gender schema.

RETHINK

- Is an individual's self-concept fully formed by the time he or she reaches adulthood? What processes might influence an adult's self-concept?
- How would you relate Erikson's stages of trust-versus-mistrust, autonomy-versus-shame-and-doubt, and initiative-versus-guilt to the issue of secure attachment discussed in Chapter 6?
- How might the Black Power and Black Pride movements of the 1960s and 1970s have addressed issues of self-concept for African Americans? In what ways might these movements have affected white Americans' self-concepts?
- What are the distinctions among gender differences, gender expectations, and gender stereotypes? How are they related?
- Why do cognitive approaches to gender differences appear to offer the most hope of causing changes in gender expectations? What is a gender schema, what are its contents, and how might a schema change over time?

Preschoolers' Social Lives

To Nicole and Diana Schoo, the movie *Home Alone* probably didn't seem too funny. For them, the tale of a child mistakenly left behind by his vacationing parents was all too similar to their own experience. In their case, though, their abandonment was no comic error: Their parents intentionally left them behind.

Diana, age 4, and her older sister Nicole, age 9, were found at home—alone—while their parents were on a 9-day vacation in Acapulco, Mexico. It was not the first time the girls had been left unattended; their parents had left them unaccompanied while they went off on a 4-day visit to Massachusetts the previous summer.

Local authorities who learned of the girls' plight arrested the Schoo parents on their return from Acapulco. The Schoos faced charges on two felony counts of child abandonment and cruelty to children, and a misdemeanor charge of child endangerment.

For an increasing number of preschoolers, life does not mirror what we see in reruns of *The Cosby Show* or *Leave It to Beaver*. Many face the realities of an increasingly complicated world. For instance, as we'll discuss in more detail in Chapter 12, children are increasingly likely to live with only one parent. In 1960, less than 10 percent of all children under the age of 18 lived with one parent; by 1989, almost a quarter lived in a single-parent household. In fact, in 1993, almost 50 percent of all children experienced their parents' divorce and lived with one parent for an average of 5 years (Carnegie Task Force, 1994).

Still, for most children the preschool years are not a time of upheaval and turmoil. Instead, the period encompasses a growing interaction with the world at large. For instance, preschoolers begin to develop genuine friendships with other children, in which close ties emerge.

Preschool Social Life: The Development of Friendships

When Juan was 3, he had his first best friend, Emilio. Juan and Emilio, who lived in the same apartment building in San Jose, were inseparable. They played incessantly with toy cars, racing them up and down the apartment hallways until some of the neighbors began to complain about the noise. They pretended to read to one another, and sometimes they slept over at each other's home—a big step for a 3-year-old. Neither

The parents of Diana and Nicole Schoo, shown here following their hearing on child abandonment, left their 4- and 9-year-old daughters unattended while they vacationed for 9 days in Mexico.

boy seemed more joyful than when he was with his "best friend"—the term each used of the other.

Around the age of 3, children develop real friendships. Although they play together earlier, much of their activity involves simply being in the same place at the same time, without real social interaction.

Something changes around age 3. Peers come to be seen not as miniature, less powerful adults, but as individuals who hold some special qualities and rewards. While preschoolers' relations with adults reflect children's needs for care, protection, and direction, their relations with peers are based more on the desire for companionship, play, and entertainment.

Furthermore, as they get older, preschoolers' conception of friendship gradually evolves. With age, they come to view friendship as a continuing state, a stable relationship that has meaning beyond the immediate moment, and that bears implications for future activity (Furman & Bierman, 1983).

The quality of interactions that children have with friends changes during the preschool period. The focus of friendship in 3-year-olds is the enjoyment of carrying out shared activities—doing things together and playing jointly. Older preschoolers, however, pay more attention to abstract concepts such as trust, support, and shared interests (Park, Lay, & Ramsay, 1993).

Even at the age of 3, preschoolers are interested in maintaining smooth social relations with their friends. They try to create a sense of agreement with one another and attempt to avoid disagreement. In fact, they are more concerned with avoiding disagreement than older preschoolers, who more readily accept dissension as the occasional outcome of a social relationship (Gottman & Parkhurst, 1980).

Why are Some Children More Popular than Others? Not all preschoolers form close friendships with others in the way that Juan and Emilio did. In fact, some children have relatively few friends, experiencing difficulty in interacting with others and forming stable relationships.

Several qualities are associated with popularity during the preschool years, an association that in many cases persists throughout much of the life span. For instance, one unfortunate byproduct of society's emphasis on physical attractiveness is the "beautiful is good" stereotype, which suggests that physical attractiveness is linked to other positive qualities. Not only are physically attractive preschoolers judged more likable, by both peers and adults, than less attractive preschoolers, but their behavior is interpreted in light of their attractiveness. As a result, physically attractive children who misbehave are judged more leniently than those who are less attractive. In sum, those who are physically attractive are responded to more favorably than those who are unattractive, beginning as early as infancy and continuing into old age (K. K. Dion, 1972; Hatfield & Sprecher, 1986; Langlois, et al., 1995).

But it is not only physical attractiveness that determines popularity. Preschoolers' social skills and behavior play an even more important role. For instance, disliked children are more likely to display aggressive behavior, to be disruptive, and to impose themselves on their peers. They are less cooperative, and they do not take turns (Mendelson, Aboud, & Lanthier, 1994; Newcomb, Bukowski, & Pattee, 1993).

In contrast, children who are more popular are more outgoing and sociable. They speak more, and nonverbally they are more positive, smiling more often than those who are less popular. In general, they have a greater understanding of others' emotions and are more sensitive to the meaning of others' nonverbal behavior (Dunn, 1995; Garner, Jones, & Miner, 1994; Philippot, Feldman, & McGee, 1992; Roopnarine & Honig, 1985).

Improving Children's Social Skills. Are unpopular preschoolers destined for a life with few friends? Not necessarily. The social skills that make some children more popular than others can be promoted by parents and preschool teachers.

For instance, children can be taught to be more cooperative, to share with others, and to play with others in appropriate ways. At the same time, they can be encouraged to decrease the incidence of aggressive behaviors that put others off, and to avoid taking things from others (Bierman, Miller, & Stabb, 1987; Ogilvy, 1994; Roopnarine & Honig, 1985).

functional play *play that involves simple, repetitive activities typical of 3-year-olds*

constructive play *play in which children manipulate objects to produce or build something*

In addition, parents can promote positive peer relations by providing a warm, supportive home environment. A good deal of research evidence shows that children with parents who were rejecting or authoritarian tend to be less socially skilled than those with more parental support. The evidence suggests that strong, positive relationships between parents and children facilitate children's relationships with others (Hartup, 1989; Hinde, Tamplin, & Barrett, 1993; Sroufe, 1994).

PLAYING BY THE RULES: THE WORK OF PLAY

In Minka Arafat's class of 3-year-olds, Minnie bounces her doll's feet on the table as she sings softly to herself. Ben pushes his toy car across the floor, making motor noises. Sarah chases Abdul around and around the perimeter of the room.

Categorizing Play. These 3-year-olds are engaged in **functional play**—simple, repetitive activities typical of 3-year-olds. Functional play may involve objects, such as dolls or cars, or repetitive muscular movements like skipping, jumping, or rolling and unrolling a piece of clay. Functional play, then, involves doing something for the sake of being active, rather than with the aim of creating some end product (Rubin, Fein, & Vandenberg, 1983).

As children get older, functional play declines. By the time they are 4, children become involved in a more sophisticated form of play. In **constructive play** children manipulate objects to produce or build something. A child who builds a house out of Legos or puts a puzzle together is involved in constructive play: He or she has an ultimate goal—the production of something. Such play is not necessarily aimed at creating something novel, since children may repeatedly build a house of blocks, let it fall into disarray, and then rebuild it.

Constructive play permits children to test their developing physical and cognitive skills and to practice their fine muscle movements. They gain experience in solving problems about the ways and the sequences in which things fit together (Tegano et al., 1991). They also learn to cooperate with others—a development we observe as the social nature of play shifts during the preschool period.

The Social Aspects of Play. If two preschoolers are sitting at a table side by side, each putting a different puzzle together, are they engaged jointly in play?

In parallel play, children play with similar toys, in a similar manner, but don't necessarily interact with one another.

According to pioneering work done by Mildred Parten (1932), the answer is "yes." She suggests that these preschoolers are engaged in **parallel play,** in which children play with similar toys, in a similar manner, but do not interact with each other. Parallel play is typical for children during the early preschool years. Preschoolers also engage in another form of play, a highly passive one: onlooker play. In **onlooker play,** children simply watch others at play but do not actually participate themselves. They may look on silently, or they may make comments of encouragement or advice.

As they get older, however, preschoolers engage in more sophisticated forms of social play that involve a greater degree of interaction. In **associative play,** two or more children actually interact with one another by sharing or borrowing toys or materials, although they do not do the same thing. In **cooperative play,** children genuinely play with one another, taking turns, playing games, or devising contests. (The various types of play are summarized in Table 9-2.)

Although associative and cooperative play do not typically become prevalent until children reach the end of the preschool years, the amount and kind of social experience children have had significantly influences the nature of play. For instance, children who have had substantial preschool experience are apt to engage in more social forms of behavior, such as associative and cooperative play, fairly early in the preschool years than those with less experience (J. L. Roopnarine, Johnson, & Hooper, 1994).

Furthermore, solitary and onlooker play continue in the later stages of the preschool period. There are simply times when children prefer to play by themselves. And when newcomers join a group, one strategy for becoming part of the group—often successful—is to engage in onlooker play, waiting for an opportunity to join the play more actively (Howes, Unger, & Seidner, 1989; P. K. Smith, 1978).

The nature of pretend or make-believe play also changes during the preschool period. In some ways, pretend play becomes increasingly *un*realistic, as preschoolers change from using only realistic objects to less concrete ones. Thus, at the start of the preschool period, children may pretend to listen to a radio only if they actually have a plastic radio that looks realistic. Later, however, they are more likely to use an entirely different object, such as a large cardboard box, as a pretend radio (Corrigan, 1987).

parallel play *action in which children play with similar toys, in a similar manner, but do not interact with each other*

onlooker play *action in which children simply watch others at play but do not actually participate themselves*

associative play *play in which two or more children actually interact with one another by sharing or borrowing toys or materials, although they do not do the same thing*

cooperative play *play in which children genuinely interact with one another, taking turns, playing games, or devising contests*

TABLE 9-2

PRESCHOOLERS' PLAY

Type of Play	Definition
Functional play	Functional play involves simple, repetitive activities typical of 3-year-olds. It may involve objects, such as dolls or cars, or repetitive muscular movements like skipping, jumping, or rolling and unrolling a piece of clay.
Constructive play	By the time they are 4, children become involved in more sophisticated play in which they manipulate objects to produce or build something. A child who builds a house out of Legos or puts together a puzzle is involved in constructive play. This type of play permits children to test their developing physical and cognitive skills as well as practice their fine muscle movements.
Parallel play	Children who engage in parallel play use similar toys, in a similar manner, but do not interact with each other. This form of play is typical of children during the early preschool years.
Onlooker play	In onlooker play, children simply watch others at play, but do not actually participate themselves. They may look on silently, or they may make comments of encouragement or advice. This type of play is common among preschoolers.
Associative play	As they grow older, preschoolers are involved in the greater degree of interaction of associative play. Here, two or more children actually interact with one another by sharing or borrowing toys or materials, although they do not do the same thing.
Cooperative play	In cooperative play, children genuinely play with one another, taking turns, playing games, or devising contests.

authoritarian parents parents who are controlling, punitive, rigid, and cold; their word is law, and they value strict, unquestioning obedience from their children and do not tolerate expressions of disagreement

permissive parents parents who provide lax and inconsistent feedback and require little of their children

Russian developmental psychologist Lev Vygotsky (1930/1978) argued that pretend play, particularly that involving social play, is an important means for expanding preschoolers' cognitive skills. Through make-believe play, children are able to "practice" activities that are a part of their particular culture and broaden their understanding of the way the world functions.

Children's cultural backgrounds also result in different styles of play. For example, comparisons of Korean Americans and Anglo-Americans find that Korean American children engage in a higher proportion of parallel play than their Anglo-American counterparts, while Anglo-American preschoolers are involved in more pretend play (Farver, Kim, & Lee, 1995; see Figure 9-1).

Discipline: Teaching Desired Behavior

While no one is looking—she thinks—Maria goes into her brother Alejandro's bedroom, where he has been saving the last of his Halloween candy. Just as Maria takes Alejandro's last Reese's Peanut Butter Cup, the children's mother walks into the room and immediately takes in the situation.

If you were Maria's mother, which of the following reactions seems most reasonable?

1. Tell Maria that she must go to her room and stay there for the rest of the day, and that she is going to lose access to her favorite blanket, the one she sleeps with every night and during naps.
2. Mildly tell Maria that what she did was not such a good idea, and she shouldn't do it in the future.
3. Explain why her brother Alejandro was going to be upset, and tell her that she must go to her room for an hour as punishment.

Each of these three alternative responses represents one of the three major parenting styles that, according to classic research by Diana Baumrind (1971, 1980), characterize most parents' patterns of discipline. **Authoritarian parents** are controlling, punitive, rigid, cold. Their word is law, and they value strict, unquestioning obedience from their children. They also do not tolerate expressions of disagreement.

Permissive parents, in contrast, provide lax and inconsistent feedback. They require little of their children, and they don't see themselves as holding much responsibility for how their children turn out.

FIGURE 9-1

COMPARING PLAY COMPLEXITY

An examination of Korean American and Anglo-American preschoolers' play complexity finds clear differences in patterns of play.

(*Source:* Adapted from Farver, Kim, & Lee, 1995.)

Korean American

Anglo-American

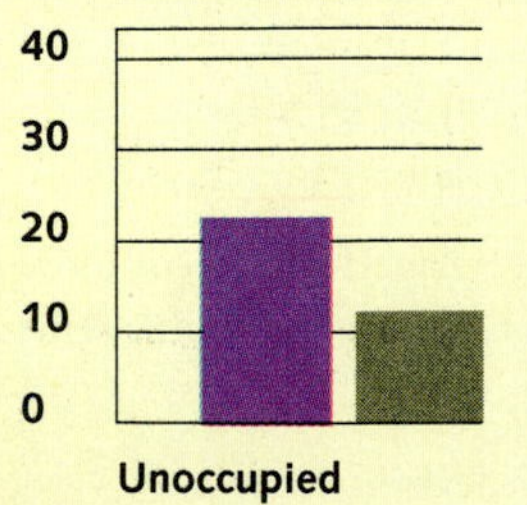

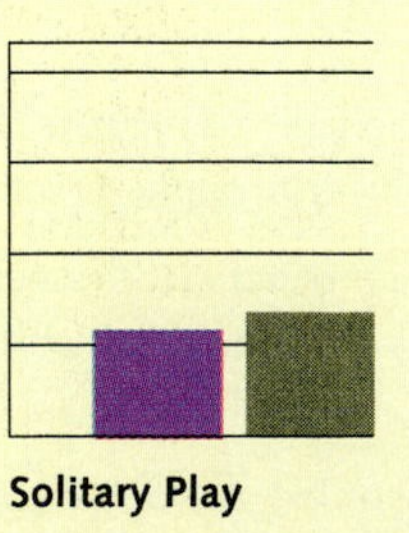

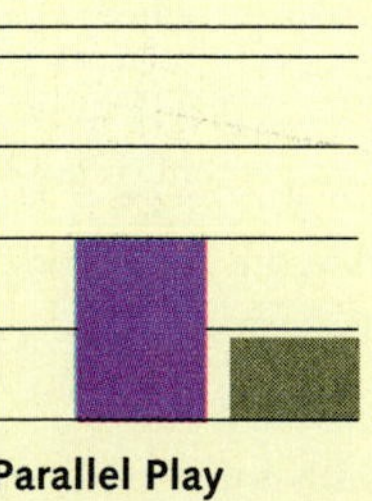

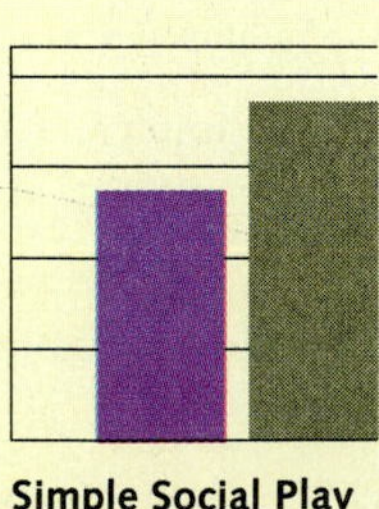

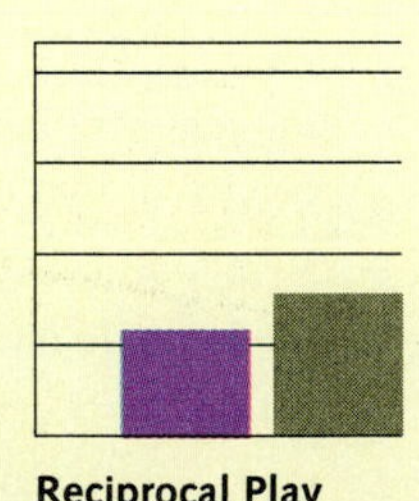

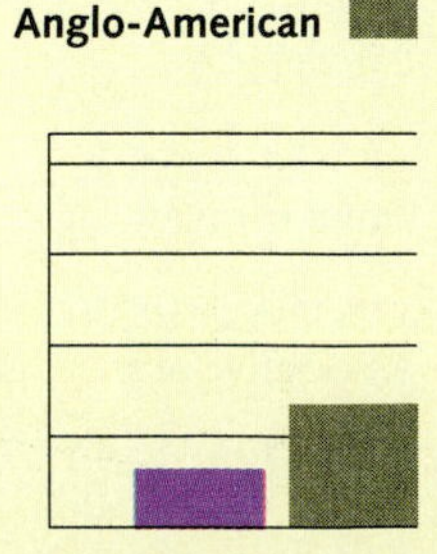

The way in which children are disciplined has important consequences for children's development in a variety of areas.

There are actually two types of permissive parents. *Permissive-indifferent* parents are unusually uninvolved in their children's lives; they show little interest or concern with their children's well-being. In contrast, *permissive-indulgent* parents are more involved with their children, but they place little or no limits or control on their children's behavior.

authoritative parents *parents who are firm, setting clear and consistent limits, but try to reason with their children, giving explanations for why they should behave in a particular way*

Finally, **authoritative parents** are firm, setting clear and consistent limits. Although they tend to be relatively strict, like authoritarian parents, they are more receptive to disagreement from their children. They also try to reason with their children, giving explanations for why the children should behave in a particular way and communicating the rationale for any punishment they may impose. The children of authoritative parents are encouraged to be independent. (The three patterns are summarized in Table 9-3.)

Does the particular style of parental discipline result in differences in children's behavior? The answer, according to Baumrind, is very much "yes"—although, as you might expect, there are many exceptions.

Children of authoritarian parents tend to be withdrawn, showing relatively little sociability. They are not very friendly, often behaving uneasily around their peers. Girls who are raised by authoritarian parents are especially dependent on their parents, whereas boys are unusually hostile.

TABLE 9-3

PARENTAL DISCIPLINE STYLES

Type	Characteristics	Relationship with Children
Authoritarian	Controlling, punitive, rigid, cold	Their word is law, and they value strict, unquestioning obedience from their children. They also do not tolerate expressions of disagreement.
Permissive-indifferent	Lax and inconsistent feedback	They are usually uninvolved in their children's lives; they show little interest or concern with their children's well-being.
Permissive-indulgent	Lax and inconsistent feedback	They are more involved with their children, but they place little or no limits or control on their children's behavior.
Authoritative	Firm, setting clear and consistent limits	They tend to be relatively strict, like authoritarian parents, but they are more receptive to disagreement from their children and encourage them to be independent. They also try to reason with their children, giving explanations for why the children should behave in a particular way and communicating the rationale for any punishment they may impose.

Permissive parents have children who, in many ways, share the undesirable characteristics of children of authoritarian parents. Children with permissive-indifferent parents tend to be dependent and moody, and low in social skills and self-control. Permissive-indulgent parenting results in children who have lower self-control and feel that they are especially privileged. Such children also have lower social skills.

Children of authoritative parents fare best. They generally are independent, friendly with their peers, self-assertive, and cooperative. They have strong motivation to achieve, and they are typically successful and likable.

Clearly, authoritative parents appear to be the most likely to produce successful children. But not always. For instance, in a significant number of cases the children of authoritarian and permissive parents develop quite successfully. Moreover, parents are not entirely consistent: Although the authoritarian, permissive, and authoritative patterns describe general styles, sometimes parents switch from their dominant mode to one of the others. For instance, when a child darts into the street, even the most laid-back and permissive parent is likely to react in an authoritarian manner, laying down strict demands about safety. In such cases, authoritarian styles may be most effective (Bayer & Cegala, 1992; Darling & Steinberg, 1993; Kuczynski, 1984; Steinberg et al., 1994).

Furthermore, the findings regarding childrearing styles are chiefly applicable to Western society. As we discuss in the "Directions in Development" section, the style of parenting that is most successful may depend quite heavily on the norms of a particular culture—and what parents in a particular culture are taught regarding appropriate childrearing practices (Papps et al., 1995).

According to developmental psychologist Ruth Chao, Asian traditions suggest that parents should be strict and firm and that they should train their children to adhere to rigid standards of behavior.

Directions in Development

Successful Parenting: Teaching Parents to Parent

Chiao shun. Guan.

When parents in China seek advice on the best childrearing practices, they are likely to encounter these two terms, and unlikely to hear about the virtues of authoritative parenting with which parents in Western societies are apt to be regaled. The reason relates not only to differences in parenting advice, but to a wide cultural gulf between Eastern and Western conceptions of childrearing practices.

According to developmental psychologist Ruth Chao (1994), the concept of *chiao shun* suggests that parents should be strict, firm, and in tight control of their children's behavior. Parents are seen to have a duty to train their children to adhere to socially and culturally desirable standards of behavior, particularly those manifested in good school performance. Furthermore, children's acceptance of such an approach to discipline is seen as a sign of parental respect.

The notion of rigid control of children grows out of the concept of *guan,* which literally means "to govern." But the concept is broader than the literal meaning; it encompasses notions of caring for and loving children. Thus, to provide strict control is a measure of parents' involvement with their children and concern for their welfare. This philosophy derives from the teachings of Confucius, who emphasized the importance of maintaining harmonious relations with others.

Chiao shun and *guan* result in views of the most appropriate childrearing practices that are very different from their Western counterparts. Parents in China are encouraged to be highly directive with their children, pushing them to excel and controlling their behavior to a considerably higher degree than parents typically do in Western countries. And it works: Children of Asian parents tend to be quite successful, particularly academically (Steinberg, Dornbusch, & Brown, 1992).

In contrast, the childrearing advice given to parents in the United States conveys a very different message. Parents are generally advised to use authoritative methods and explicitly to avoid authoritarian measures. Interestingly, it wasn't always this way. Until World War II, the point of view that dominated the advice literature was authoritarian, apparently founded on Puritan religious influences that suggested that children had "original sin" or that they needed to have their wills broken (Smuts & Hagen, 1985).

In sum, the childrearing practices that parents are urged to follow reflect cultural perspectives about the nature of children, as well as about the appropriate role of parents. No single parenting pattern or style, then, is likely to be universally appropriate or likely invariably to produce successful children. Instead, cultural context must be taken into account.

The Informed Consumer of Development

Disciplining Children

The question of how best to discipline children has been raised for generations. Answers coming from developmentalists today include the following advice (Grusec & Goodnow, 1994b; M. E. Lamb, Ketterlinus, & Fracasso, 1992; O'Leary, 1995; Wierson & Forehand, 1994):

- For most children in Western cultures, authoritative parenting is best. Parents should be firm and consistent, providing clear direction for desirable behavior. Reprimands for misbehavior should be immediate and brief. Authoritative disciplinarians provide rules, but they explain why those rules make sense in language that children can understand.
- Spanking is never an appropriate discipline technique, according to the American Academy of Pediatrics. Not only is spanking less effective than other techniques in curbing undesirable behavior, but it leads to additional, unwanted outcomes. For instance, children who are spanked are significantly more aggressive toward their peers than those who have not been spanked (Strassberg et al., 1994).
- Parents should tailor discipline to the characteristics of the child and the situation. As we first discussed in Chapter 2, children have different temperaments that may predispose them to be more or less accepting of discipline. Parents ought to keep the child's particular personality qualities in mind, and adapt discipline to it.
- A related suggestion is more controversial. Lawrence Steinberg and his colleagues (1994) cite evidence that the consequences of authoritarian parenting styles do not appear to be as negative among minority youth as they are among majority youth. These researchers suggest that some children from economically disadvantaged families may benefit from more authoritarian styles of parenting. They believe that authoritarianism may be beneficial for children in unusually difficult living situations. It also may be the case that ethnic and cultural factors lead to differences in the perception of parental authoritarianism. However, this view remains controversial.

- Difficult situations can be defused with humor and playfulness and by providing alternative activities. Some parents and children engage in repetitive battles, in which each participant vies to be the winner and to make the other party the loser. For instance, bedtime can be the source of a nightly struggle between a resistant child and an insistent parent. Parental strategies for gaining compliance that involve making the situation enjoyable—such as reading a bedtime story or engaging in a nightly "wrestling" match with the child—can defuse potential battles and turn bedtime into an opportunity for fun.

Review and Rethink

REVIEW

- In the preschool years, children develop their first true friendships on the basis of personal characteristics, trust, and shared interests. They begin to view friendship as a stable relationship with meaning beyond the moment.
- Popularity among preschool-age children is influenced by physical and social characteristics, and by the nature of relationships with parents. Improving social skills can increase popularity.
- The character of preschoolers' play changes over time, growing more sophisticated, interactive, and cooperative, and relying increasingly on social skills.
- There are several distinct childrearing styles. In the United States, parents may be classified as authoritarian, permissive, or authoritative, with the authoritative style being in most cases the most effective.
- Childrearing styles show strong cultural influences. In cultures that value strict adherence to socially desirable standards of behavior, the culturally endorsed style of parenting is highly authoritarian.

RETHINK

- Do you believe the association between physical attractiveness and popularity is caused by biological or environmental factors? Why?
- Which comes first: popularity or cooperative social behaviors? Why? Can this question be answered by research?
- Are the styles and strategies of preschool-age children's play, such as parallel play and onlooker play, mirrored in adult life in realms of interaction other than play?
- Why might the children of authoritarian and of permissive parents equally tend to have sociability problems as adults?
- What cultural and environmental factors in the United States may have contributed to the shift in the dominant childrearing style from authoritarian to authoritative since World War II? Is another shift underway?

MORAL DEVELOPMENT AND AGGRESSION

During snack time at preschool playmates Jan and Meg inspected the goodies in their lunch boxes. Jan found two appetizing cream-filled cookies. Meg's snack offered a less tempting carrot and celery sticks. As Jan began to munch on one of her cookies, Meg

> looked at the cut-up vegetables and burst into tears. Jan responded to Meg's distress by offering her companion one of her cookies, which Meg gladly accepted. Jan was able to put herself in Meg's place, understand Meg's thoughts and feelings, and act compassionately. (L. G. Katz, 1989, p. 213)

In this short scenario we see many of the key elements of morality, as it is played out among preschoolers. Changes in children's views of morality and their helpfulness to others are an important element of growth during the preschool years.

Yet, at the same time these changes are occurring, the degree and nature of aggressive behavior displayed by preschoolers are also changing. We can consider the development of morality and aggression as two sides of the coin of human conduct.

Developing Morality: Following Society's Rights and Wrongs

Moral development refers to changes in people's sense of justice and of what is right and wrong, and in their behavior related to moral issues. Developmentalists have considered moral development in terms of children's reasoning about morality, their attitudes toward moral transgressions, and their behavior when faced with moral issues. In the process of studying moral development, several approaches have evolved (Langford, 1995).

Piaget's View of Moral Development. Consider the following exchange:

> Q. *How did you get to know the rules [of the game of marbles]?*
> A. When I was quite little my Daddy showed me.
>
> Q. *And how did your daddy know?*
> A. My Daddy just knew. No one told him . . .
>
> Q. *Who invented the game of marbles?*
> A. My Daddy did . . . . (Piaget, 1932, p. 55)

When a preschooler feels, as does this 5-year-old, that a game was invented by no less an authority figure than his father, it is no wonder that he would adhere rigidly to its rules. According to Jean Piaget (1932), who was one of the first to study questions of moral development, the view expressed by the child quoted above is representative of a broad form of moral thinking known as heteronomous morality.

The initial stage of moral development is **heteronomous morality,** in which rules are seen as unchangeable and never varying. During this stage, which lasts from around age 4 through age 7, children play games rigidly, assuming that there is one, and only one, way to play, and that every other way is wrong. At the same time, though, preschoolers may not even fully grasp game rules. Consequently, a group of children may be playing together, with each child playing according to a slightly different set of rules. Nevertheless, they enjoy playing with others. Piaget suggests that every child may "win" such a game, because winning is equated with having a good time, as opposed to truly competing with others.

Heteronomous morality ultimately is replaced by two later stages of morality: incipient cooperation and autonomous cooperation. In the *incipient cooperation stage,* which lasts from around age 7 to age 10, children's games become more clearly social. Children actually learn the formal rules of games, and they play according to this shared knowledge. Consequently, rules are still seen as largely unchangeable. There is a "right" way to play the game, and children play according to these formal rules.

It is not until the *autonomous cooperation stage,* which begins at around age 10, that children become fully aware that formal game rules can be modified if the people who play them agree. The later transition into more sophisticated forms of moral development—

moral development *the changes in people's sense of justice and of what is right and wrong, and in their behavior related to moral issues*

heteronomous morality *the stage of moral development in which rules are seen as unchangeable and never varying*

imminent justice *the notion that rules that are broken earn immediate punishment*

prosocial behavior *helping behavior that benefits others*

which we will consider in Chapter 12—also is reflected in school-age children's understanding that rules of law are created by people and are subject to change according to the will of people.

Until these later stages are reached, however, children's reasoning about rules and issues of justice is bounded in the concrete. For instance, consider the following two stories:

> A little boy who is called John is in his room. He is called to dinner. He goes into the dining room. But behind the door there was a chair, and on the chair there was a tray with 15 cups on it. John couldn't have known there was all this behind the door. He goes in, the door knocks against the tray, bang go the 15 cups, and they all get broken!
>
> ***
>
> Once there was a little boy whose name was Marcello. One day when his mother was out he tried to get some jam out of the cupboard. He climbed up onto a chair and stretched out his arm. But the jam was too high up and he couldn't reach it and have any. But while he was trying to get it he knocked over a cup. The cup fell down and broke. (Piaget, 1932, p. 122)

Piaget found that a preschool child, in the heteronomous morality stage, judges the child who broke the 15 cups worse than the one who broke just one. In contrast, children who have moved beyond the heteronomous morality stage consider the child who broke the one cup naughtier. The reason: Children in the heteronomous morality stage do not take *intention* into account.

Children in the heteronomous stage of moral development also believe in imminent justice. **Imminent justice** is the notion that rules that are broken earn immediate punishment. Preschool children believe that if they do something wrong, they will be punished instantly—even if no one sees them carrying out their misdeeds. In contrast, older children understand that punishments for misdeeds are determined and meted out by people. Other people are seen as making judgments about the severity of a transgression, and as taking intentionality into account in determining the nature of the penalty to be imposed.

Evaluating Piaget's Approach to Moral Development. Recent research suggests that although Piaget was on the right track in his description of how moral development proceeds, his approach suffers from the same problem we encountered in his theory of cognitive development. Specifically, Piaget underestimated the age at which children's moral skills are honed.

It is now clear that preschool children understand the notion of intentionality by about age 3, and this allows them to make judgments based on intent at an earlier age than Piaget supposed. Specifically, when provided with moral questions that emphasize intent, preschool children judge someone who is intentionally bad as more "naughty" than someone who is unintentionally bad, but who creates more objective damage. Moreover, by the age of 4, they judge intentional lying wrong (Bussey, 1992; Yuill & Perner, 1988).

Social Learning Approaches to Morality. Social learning approaches to moral development stand in stark contrast to Piaget's approach. While Piaget emphasizes how limitations in preschoolers' cognitive development lead to particular forms of moral *reasoning*, social learning approaches focus more on how the environment in which preschoolers operate produces **prosocial behavior,** helping behavior that benefits others.

According to social learning approaches, the best predictor of children's prosocial behavior is whether they have received positive reinforcement for acting in a morally appropriate way. For instance, when Claire's mother tells her she has been a "good girl" for sharing a box of candy with her brother Dan, Claire's behavior has been reinforced. As a consequence, she is more likely to engage in sharing behavior in the future.

Not all prosocial behavior has to be directly performed, and subsequently reinforced, for learning to occur. According to social learning approaches, children also learn moral behavior by observing the behavior of others, called *models* (Bandura, 1977). Models who are seen to receive reinforcement for their behavior are imitated, and ultimately observers learn to perform the behavior themselves. For example, when Claire's friend Jake watches Claire share her candy with her brother, Jake is more likely to engage in sharing behavior himself at some later point.

abstract modeling *the process in which modeling paves the way for the development of more general rules and principles of behavior*

empathy *an emotional response that corresponds to the feelings of another person*

Quite a few studies illustrate the power of models, and of social learning more generally, in producing prosocial behavior in preschoolers. For example, experiments have shown that children who view someone behaving generously or unselfishly are apt to follow the model's example, subsequently behaving in a generous or unselfish manner themselves when put in a similar situation (Kim & Stevens, 1987; Midlarsky & Bryan, 1972). Furthermore, the reverse holds true: If a model behaves selfishly, children who observe such behavior tend to behave more selfishly themselves (Grusec, 1982, 1991; Staub, 1977).

Not all models are equally effective in producing prosocial responses. For instance, preschoolers are more apt to model the behavior of warm, responsive adults than of adults who appear colder. Furthermore, models viewed as highly competent or high in prestige are more effective than others (Bandura, 1977; Yarrow, Scott, & Waxler, 1973).

Children do more than simply mimic unthinkingly behavior that they see rewarded in others. By observing moral conduct, they are reminded of society's norms about the importance of moral behavior, as conveyed by parents, teachers, and other powerful authority figures. The observation of others demonstrating moral conduct illustrates the connection between particular situations and certain kinds of behavior. This increases the likelihood that similar situations will elicit similar behavior in the observer.

Consequently, modeling paves the way for the development of more general rules and principles in a process called **abstract modeling.** Rather than always modeling the particular behavior of others, older preschoolers begin to develop generalized principles that underlie the behavior that they observe. After observing repeated instances in which a model is rewarded for acting in a morally desirable way, children begin the process of inferring and learning the general principles of moral conduct (Bandura, 1991).

Empathy and Moral Behavior. According to some developmentalists, **empathy**—the understanding of what another individual feels—lies at the heart of some kinds of moral behavior. Consider, for example, a scene in a city playground. Four-year-old Ezra sees his playmate Ned trip, fall, and begin to cry. Ezra goes to Ned, telling him not to feel bad, and offers to push him on a swing. In order for Ezra to understand that Ned needed comforting, it was necessary for Ezra to feel empathy with Ned's unhappiness—to realize that he was hurt and warranted sympathy.

The roots of empathy grow early. One-year-old infants cry when they hear other infants crying. By 2 and 3, toddlers will offer gifts and spontaneously share toys with other children and adults, even if they are strangers (Stanjek, 1978; Radke-Yarrow, Zahn-Waxler, & Chapman, 1983; Zahn-Wexler & Radke-Yarrow, 1990).

During the preschool years, empathy continues to grow. Some theorists believe that increasing empathy—as well as other positive emotions such as sympathy and admiration—leads children to behave in a more moral fashion. In addition, some negative emotions—such as anger at an unfair situation or shame over previous transgressions—also may promote moral behavior (Damon, 1988; Farver & Branstetter, 1994).

The notion that negative emotions may promote moral development is one that Freud first suggested in his theory of psychoanalytic personality development (first discussed in Chapter 1). Freud argued that a child's *superego,* the part of the personality that represents societal dos and don'ts, is developed through resolution of the *Oedipal conflict.* Children come to identify with their same-sex parent, incorporating that parent's standards of morality in order to avoid unconscious guilt raised by the Oedipal conflict.

"Have you been a moral child?"

Drawing by M. Hamilton. © 1995 The New Yorker Magazine, Inc.

Whether or not we accept Freud's account of the Oedipal conflict and the guilt it produces—and most developmentalists do not, as we saw in Chapter 1—it is consistent with more recent findings. These suggest that preschoolers' attempts to avoid experiencing negative emotions sometimes lead them to act in more moral, helpful ways. For instance, one reason that children help others is to avoid the feelings of personal distress that they experience when they are confronted with another person's unhappiness or misfortune (Eisenberg & Fabes, 1991).

AGGRESSION AND VIOLENCE IN PRESCHOOLERS: SOURCES AND CONSEQUENCES

> Four-year-old Duane couldn't hold his anger and frustration in anymore. Although he usually was mild-mannered, when Eshu began to tease him about the split in his pants and kept it up for several minutes, Duane finally snapped. Rushing over to Eshu, Duane pushed him to the ground and began to hit him with his small, closed fists. Because he was so distraught, Duane's punches were not terribly effective, but they were severe enough to hurt Eshu and bring him to tears before the preschool teachers could intervene.

Although violence of this sort is relatively rare among preschoolers, aggression is not uncommon. The potential for verbal hostility, shoving matches, kicking, and other forms of aggression is present throughout the preschool period, although the degree to which aggression is acted out changes as children become older.

Aggression is intentional injury or harm to another person (Berkowitz, 1993). Infants don't act aggressively; it is hard to contend that their behavior is *intended* to hurt others, even if they inadvertently manage to do so. On the other hand, by the time they reach preschool age, children demonstrate true aggression.

During the early preschool years, some of the aggression is addressed at attaining a desired goal, such as getting a toy away from another person or using a particular space occu-

aggression *intentional injury or harm to another person*

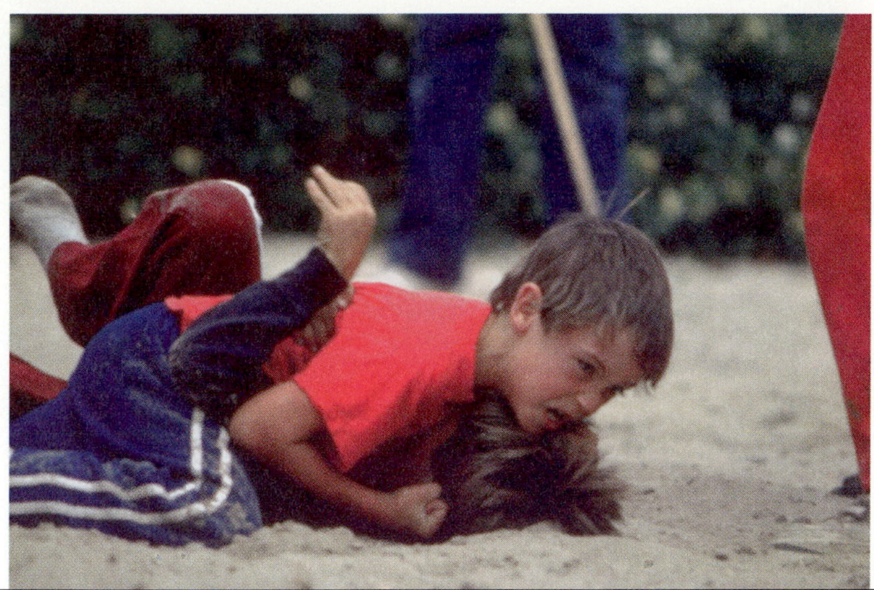

Aggression, both physical and verbal, is present throughout the preschool period.

pied by another person. Consequently, in some ways the aggression is inadvertent, and minor scuffles may in fact be a typical part of early preschool life.

On the other hand, extreme and sustained aggression is a cause for concern. In most children, the amount of aggression declines as they move through the preschool years. Most learn to use language to express their wishes, and they become increasingly able to negotiate with others. Typically, the frequency and average length of episodes of aggressive behavior decline in the preschool years (Cummings, Iannotti, & Zahn-Waxler, 1989).

Although declines in aggression are typical, some children remain aggressive throughout the preschool period. Furthermore, aggression is a relatively stable characteristic: The most aggressive preschoolers tend to be the most aggressive children during the school-age years, and the least aggressive preschoolers tend to be the least aggressive school-age children (Minde, 1992; Olewus, 1982; Parke & Slaby, 1983). Still, it is the rare child who does not demonstrate at least an occasional act of aggression.

The Roots of Aggression. How can we explain the aggression of preschoolers? Some theoreticians suggest that to behave aggressively is an instinct, part and parcel of the human condition. For instance, Freud's psychoanalytic theory suggests that we all have a death drive, which leads us to act aggressively toward others as we turn our inward hostility outward (Freud, 1920). According to ethologist Konrad Lorenz (1966, 1974), an expert in animal behavior, animals—including humans—share a fighting instinct that stems from primitive urges to preserve territory, maintain a steady supply of food, and weed out weaker animals.

Similar arguments are made by **sociobiologists,** scientists who consider the biological roots of social behavior. They argue that aggression facilitates the goal of strengthening the species and its gene pool as a whole. As a result, aggressive instincts promote the survival of one's genes to pass on to future generations (McKenna, 1983; Reiss, 1984).

Although instinctual explanations of aggression are logical, most developmentalists believe they are not the whole story (Bandura, 1978). Not only do instinctual explanations fail to take into account the increasingly sophisticated cognitive abilities that humans develop as they get older, but they also have relatively little experimental support. Moreover, they provide little guidance in determining when and how children, as well as adults, will behave aggressively, other than noting that aggression is an inevitable part of the human condition. Consequently, developmentalists have turned to other approaches to explain aggression and violence.

sociobiologists *scientists who consider the biological roots of social behavior*

Social learning explanations of aggression suggest that children's observation of aggression on television can result in actual aggression.

Social Learning Approaches to Aggression. The day after Duane lashed out at Eshu, Lynn, who had watched the entire scene, got into an argument with Ilya. They verbally bickered for a while, and suddenly Lynn balled her hand into a fist and tried to punch Ilya. The preschool teachers were stunned: It was rare for Lynn to get upset, and she had never displayed aggression before.

Is there a connection between the two events? Most of us would answer "yes," particularly if we subscribed to the view, suggested by social learning approaches, that aggression is largely a learned behavior. Social learning approaches to aggression contend that aggression is based on prior learning. To understand the causes of aggressive behavior, then, we should look at the system of rewards and punishments that exists in a child's environment.

Social learning approaches to aggression emphasize how social and environmental conditions teach individuals to be aggressive. For instance, preschoolers may learn that they can continue to play with the most desirable toys by declining aggressively their classmates' requests for sharing. In the parlance of social learning theory, they have been reinforced for acting aggressively, and they are more likely to behave aggressively in the future.

Reinforcement also comes in less direct ways. A good deal of research suggests that exposure to aggressive models leads to increased aggression, particularly if the observers are themselves angered, insulted, or frustrated. For example, Albert Bandura and his colleagues illustrated the power of models in a classic study of preschoolers (Bandura, Ross, & Ross, 1963). One group of children watched a film of an adult playing aggressively and violently with a Bobo doll (a large, inflated plastic dummy that always returns to an upright position after being pushed down). In comparison, children in another group watched a film of an adult playing sedately with a set of Tinkertoys (see Figure 9-2). Later, the preschoolers were allowed to play with a number of toys, which included both the Bobo doll and the Tinkertoys. But first, the children were led to feel frustration by being refused the opportunity to play with a favorite toy.

Consistent with social learning approaches, the preschoolers modeled the behavior of the adult. Those who had seen the aggressive model playing with the Bobo doll were considerably more aggressive than those who had watched the calm, unaggressive model playing with the Tinkertoys.

Later research has supported this early study, and it is clear that exposure to aggressive models increases the likelihood that aggression on the part of observers will follow. These findings have profound consequences, particularly for children who live in communities in which violence is prevalent. For instance, one survey conducted in a city public hospital

FIGURE 9-2 This series of photos is from Albert Bandura's classic Bobo doll experiment, designed to illustrate social learning of aggression. The photos clearly show how the adult model's aggressive behavior (in the first row) is imitated by children who had viewed the aggressive behavior (second and third rows).

found that 1 in 10 children under the age of 6 said they had witnessed a shooting or stabbing. Other research indicates that one third of the children in some urban neighborhoods have seen a homicide and that two thirds have seen a serious assault (Bell & Jenkins, 1991, 1993; Groves et al., 1993; Osofsky, 1995; also see the "Speaking of Development" interview on page 308).

Even children who are not witnesses to real-life violence— the majority of preschoolers—are apt to be exposed to aggression via the medium of television, particularly in light of the high levels of viewing in which most preschoolers engage. The average preschooler watches 3 hours of television each day, and even children whose parents don't own television sets watch from 1 to 2 hours a day—at friends' homes (Condry, 1989).

Although television has a clear impact on cognitive development, as we discussed in Chapter 8, it has other, and perhaps even more important, consequences for frequent viewers. In particular, because it contains so much violent content (see Figure 9-3 on page 310), the medium can have a powerful influence on the subsequent aggressive behavior of viewers (Liebert & Sprafkin, 1988; Sanson & diMuccio, 1993; W. Wood, Wong, & Chachere, 1991).

As we noted in the prologue to this chapter, programs such as *Mighty Morphin Power Rangers* are watched by millions of preschoolers, who later imitate the Rangers' violent behavior during play. This is no surprise, given social learning theory. But does the playful enactment of aggression later turn into the real thing, producing children (and later adults) who demonstrate more actual—and ultimately deadly—aggression?

It is hard to answer the question definitively, primarily because no true experiments outside laboratory settings have been conducted. Although it is clear that laboratory observation of aggression on television leads to higher levels of aggression, evidence showing that real-world viewing of aggression is associated with subsequent aggressive behavior is correlational. (Think, for a moment, of how we might conduct a true experiment involving children's viewing habits. It would require that we control children's viewing of television in their homes for extended periods, exposing some to a steady diet of violent shows and others to nonviolent ones—something that most parents would not agree to.)

Despite the fact that the results are primarily correlational and therefore inconclusive, the weight of research evidence is clear in suggesting that observation of televised aggression does lead to subsequent aggression. For example, in one longitudinal study, children's preferences for violent television shows at age 8 were related to the seriousness of criminal convictions by age 30 (Huesmann, 1986). Other evidence supports the notion that observation of media violence can lead to a greater readiness to act aggressively and to an insensitivity to the suffering of victims of violence (Bushman & Geen, 1990; Comstock & Strasburger, 1990; Gadow & Sprafkin, 1993; Linz, Donnerstein, & Penrod, 1988).

Fortunately, the same principles of social learning theory that lead preschoolers to learn aggression from television suggest ways of reducing the negative influence of the medium. For instance, children can be explicitly taught critical viewing skills that influence their interpretation of televised models. In such training, they are taught that violence is not representative of the real world, that the viewing of violence is objectionable, and that they should refrain from imitating the behavior they have seen on television (Eron & Huesmann, 1985; Farhi, 1995; Huesmann et al., 1983; Zillman, 1993).

Furthermore, just as exposure to aggressive models leads to aggression, observation of *non*aggressive models can *reduce* aggression. Preschoolers don't learn from others only how to be aggressive; they can also learn how to avoid confrontation and to control their aggression, as we'll discuss later.

Speaking of Development

Joy D. Osofsky, Violence Authority

Born: 1944

Education: Syracuse University, B.A., M.A., and Ph.D. in psychology

Position: Professor of pediatrics and psychiatry at Louisiana State University School of Medicine; Director of the Violence Intervention Project for Children and Families.

Home: New Orleans, Louisiana

As the incidence of violence has increased over the years, its effects on children have become a major concern. More and more children now either are victims of violence themselves, or have witnessed a violent act in their homes or neighborhoods.

As the Director of the Violence Intervention Project for Children and Families in New Orleans, Joy Osofsky works to educate the community in ways to prevent violence and provide help for children affected by violence, whom she calls its "invisible victims."

"It is very important that we work with parents, particularly on the issue of trauma," Osofsky says. "In order for children to deal with the trauma they experience when they witness violent acts, they need, first and foremost, to feel safe and be in a supportive environment at home."

In her work with more than 250 children a year, Osofsky finds that it is not unusual to find that the lack of a supportive home environment contributes to the trauma that the child experiences following an act of violence.

"In the most extreme cases we see signs of post-traumatic stress disorder similar to the symptoms of soldiers returning from war. We see a numbing effect in children who have been traumatized: They do not show the normal range of emotions. We also see hyper-

Cognitive Approaches to Aggression: The Thoughts Behind Violence. Two children, waiting for their turn in a game of kickball, inadvertently knock into each other. One child's reaction is to apologize; the other's is to shove, saying angrily, "Cut it out."

Despite the fact that each child bears the same responsibility for the minor event, very different reactions result. The first child interprets the event as an accident, while the second sees it as a provocation, and reacts with aggression.

The cognitive approach to aggression suggests that the key to understanding moral development is to examine preschoolers' interpretations of others' behavior and of the environmental context in which a behavior occurs. According to developmental psychologist Kenneth Dodge and his colleagues, some children are more prone than others to assume that actions are aggressively motivated. They are unable to pay attention to the appropriate cues in a situation, and unable to interpret the behaviors in a given situation accurately. Instead, they assume—often erroneously—that what is happening is related to others' hostility. Subsequently, in deciding how to respond, they base their behavior on their inaccurate interpretation of others' behavior. In sum, they may behave aggressively in response to a situation that never in fact existed (Dodge & Coie, 1987; Dodge & Crick, 1990).

Although the cognitive approach to aggression provides a description of the process that leads some children to behave aggressively, it is less successful in explaining how certain children come to be inaccurate perceivers of situations in the first place. Furthermore,

---

"In order for children to deal with the trauma they experience when they witness violent acts, they need, first and foremost, to feel safe and be in a supportive environment at home."

"We see a numbing effect in children who have been traumatized: They do not show the normal range of emotions."

arousal, aggressive and out-of-control behaviors, and withdrawn and depressed behavior as well."

As part of the treatment of children who have been traumatized, Osofsky stresses the importance of psychologist Erik Erikson's perception that the development of trust in childhood is the initial step that helps a person form healthy relationships with others throughout life.

"Obviously if you witness the murder of somebody close to you, or see that person become a victim of domestic violence, it can shatter your sense of trust. This is especially true in cases of domestic violence, where both the victim and the abuser are likely to be in the caregiver role. Your family members are the first people you are supposed to trust," says Osofsky. "If they are engaged in violent acts, your trust can be endangered, and with it your ability to form healthy relationships beyond the family.

"We try to help parents and caregivers understand the very great importance of trust in a child's development."

Through the Violence Intervention Project, Osofsky also works closely with police, educators, and community members.

"We regard the issue of prevention as a major goal of the overall program," she explains. "We work with the many service providers who come into contact with children who may be exposed to violence—teachers, day-care providers, pediatricians, hospital workers. But above all we work with the police.

"We do a lot of education with police officers, who are most often first on the scene of a violent act. We focus on how violence affects children and how police officers might be sensitive to the needs and reactions of children. We address developmental issues such as the formation of trust and mistrust, and we combine education with mental health crisis referral and consultation."

Osofsky's work with the police is based on a study her group conducted in New Orleans that revealed the somewhat surprising finding that most children trusted police officers as the first people they would go to if they were lost or needed help.

"The majority of children under 12 said they would go to a police officer for help. If little kids trust police officers, we feel we have an obligation to build on that trust," she says.

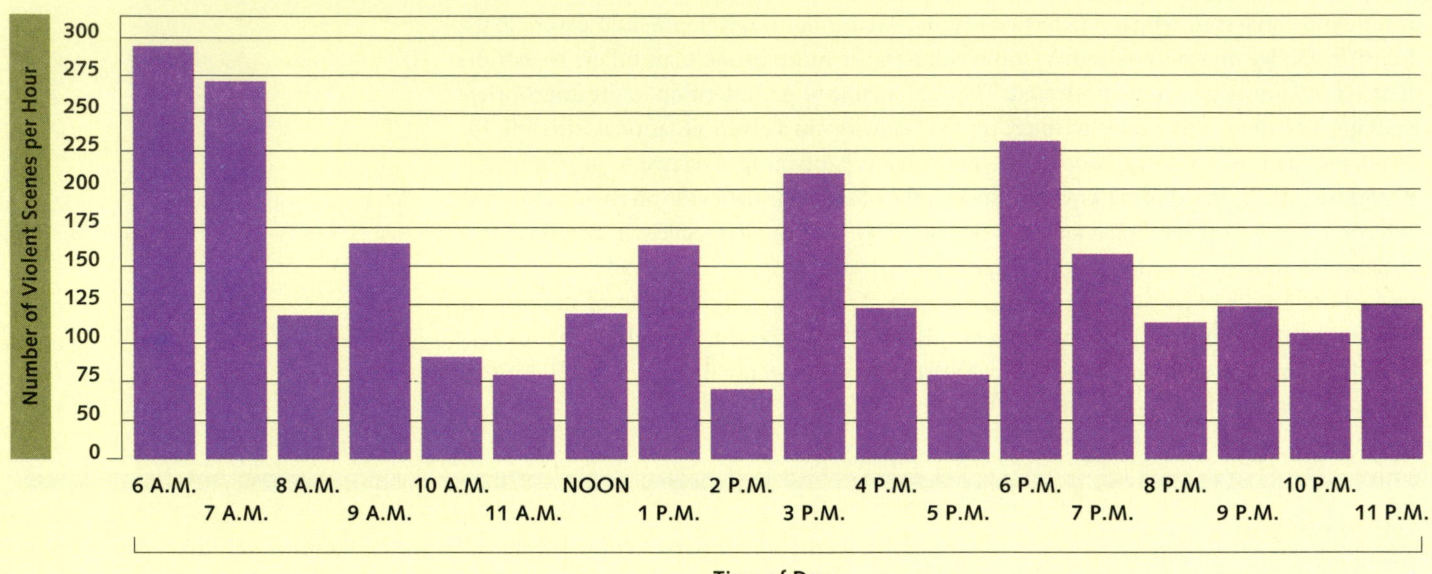

An analysis of the violence shown on the major TV networks and several cable channels in Washington, D.C., on just one particular weekday found acts of violence during every time period. (*Source:* Center for Media and Public Affairs, 1995.)

it doesn't tell why such inaccurate perceivers so readily respond with aggression and why they assume that aggression is an appropriate and even desirable response.

On the other hand, cognitive approaches to aggression are useful in pointing out a means to reduce aggression: By teaching preschoolers to be more accurate interpreters of a situation, we can induce them to be less prone to view others' behavior as motivated by hostility and consequently less likely to respond with aggression themselves.

The Informed Consumer of Development

Increasing Moral Behavior and Reducing Aggression in Preschoolers

Based on our discussions of moral development and the roots of aggression, we can identify several methods for encouraging preschoolers' moral conduct and reducing the incidence of aggression. Among the most practical and readily accomplished are the following (Bullock, 1988; Lifton, 1997):

- Provide opportunities for preschoolers to observe others acting in a cooperative, helpful, prosocial manner. Furthermore, encourage them to interact with peers in joint activities in which they share a common goal. Such cooperative activities can teach the importance and desirability of working with—and helping—others.

- Don't ignore aggressive behavior. Parents and teachers should intervene when they see aggression in preschoolers and send a clear message that aggression is an unacceptable means to resolve conflicts.
- Help preschoolers devise alternative explanations for others' behavior. This is particularly important for children who are prone to aggression and who may be apt to view others' conduct as more hostile than it actually is. Parents and teachers should help such children see that the behavior of their peers has several possible interpretations.
- Monitor preschoolers' television viewing, particularly the violence that they view. There is good evidence that observation of televised aggression results in subsequent increases in children's levels of aggression. At the same time, encourage preschoolers to watch particular shows that are designed, in part, to increase the level of moral conduct, such as *Sesame Street, Mister Rogers' Neighborhood,* and *Barney and Friends.*
- Help preschoolers understand their feelings. When children become angry—and there are times when almost all children do—they need to learn how to deal with their feelings in a constructive manner. Tell them *specific* things they can do to improve the situation ("I see you're really angry with Jake for not giving you a turn. Don't hit him, but tell him you want a chance to play with the game.")
- Explicitly teach reasoning and self-control. Preschoolers can understand the rudiments of moral reasoning, and they should be reminded why certain behaviors are desirable. For instance, explicitly saying "If you take all the cookies, others will have no dessert" is preferable to saying "Good children don't eat all the cookies."

Review and Rethink

REVIEW

- Piaget believed that preschoolers are in the heteronomous morality stage of moral development, which includes the sense that rules of conduct are unchangeable and beyond human control and that actions, not intentions, determine morality.
- Social learning approaches to moral development emphasize the importance of reinforcement for moral actions and the observation of models of moral conduct.
- While some developmentalists place the emergence of empathy at the heart of a child's moral development, negative emotions such as anger at unfairness and shame over previous misdeeds may also be important.
- Aggression, which in mild forms is normal in preschoolers and in extreme forms is unusual and disturbing, typically declines in frequency and duration as children become more able to use language to negotiate disputes.
- Ethologists and sociobiologists regard aggression as an innate human characteristic, while proponents of social learning and cognitive approaches focus on learned aspects of aggression and on ways to teach nonaggressive behavior.

RETHINK

- If high-prestige models of behavior are particularly effective in influencing moral attitudes and actions, are there implications for individuals in such industries as sports, advertising, and entertainment?

- How does the process of abstract modeling operate in the development of moral principles?
- Do empathy, anger at unfairness, and shame continue to operate in the moral development of adults? How?
- Why are biological explanations of aggression insufficient? What more is needed?
- If television and aggression are ever conclusively linked, what will be the social policy implications? Why do children enjoy watching acts of aggression and violence on television?

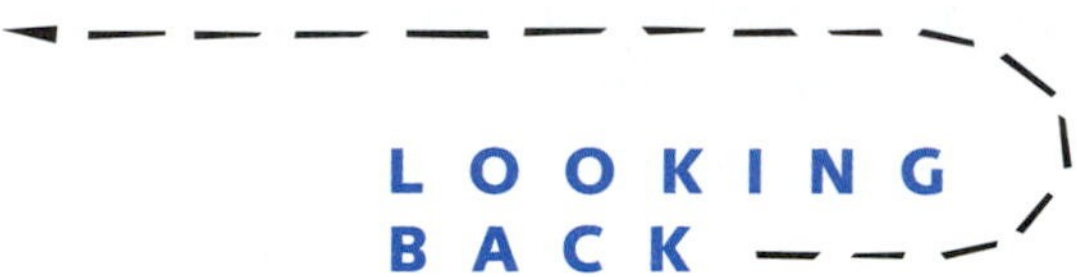

How do preschool-age children develop a concept of themselves?

1. An important issue during the preschool years is the development of self-concept. Preschoolers' self-concepts are formed partly from their own perceptions and estimations of their characteristics, partly from their parents' behavior toward them, and partly from cultural influences.
2. According to Erik Erikson, individuals pass through eight stages of psychosocial development. During the preschool years, they initally are in the autonomy-versus-shame-and-doubt stage (1½ to 3 years), in which children develop independence and mastery over their physical and social worlds, or feel shame, self-doubt, and unhappiness.
3. Later, in the initiative-versus-guilt stage (age 3 to age 6), preschoolers face conflicts between the desire to act independently of their parents and the guilt that comes from the unintended consequences of their actions.

How do children develop a sense of racial identity and gender?

4. Two human traits of which preschoolers become aware are race/ethnicity and gender. Each presents complex issues to resolve. Racial attitudes are formed largely in response to the children's environment, including parents and other influences. Preschool-age children of minority backgrounds may experience race dissonance, in which their own race appears to them to be less desirable than the majority race; only later will they develop racial and ethnic identity.
5. Gender differences emerge early in the preschool years as children form expectations about what is appropriate and inappropriate for each sex. Their expectations generally conform to widely held societal stereotypes.
6. The reason for the strong gender differences in preschoolers is unclear. Some researchers point to genetic factors, such as hormones and brain structures, as evidence for a biological explanation of gender expectations. Freud's psychoanalytic theories used the concepts of Oedipal urges, castration anxiety, identification, and penis envy to explain gender expectations, a framework that many later researchers have found cumbersome and inaccurate.
7. Social learning theorists believe that environmental influences, including parents, teachers, peers, and the media, cause preschoolers to develop their stereotyped understandings of gender. Another approach is more cognitive: that children form gender schemas, cognitive frameworks that organize information that the children gather about gender.

In what sorts of social relationships do preschoolers engage?

8. Preschool social relationships begin to encompass genuine friendship, which develops from children's emerging appreciation of other children as particularly enjoyable persons and which takes on a dimension of stability and trust.
9. Popularity among preschoolers is linked to physical characteristics, such as attractiveness, and behavioral characteristics, such as social skill and sensitivity to others. Some of the characteristics that tend to make children popular can be taught; others may relate to the type of home environment the child experiences.

How do the nature and function of play change over time?

10. The nature of play changes during these years. Children progress from repetitive functional play to more creative constructive play. In addition, the social nature of play changes, progressing through parallel play, onlooker play, associative play, and cooperative play, with increasing demands for organization and social skill.

What sorts of disciplinary styles do parents employ, and what effects do they have?

11. Disciplinary styles differ both individually and culturally. In the United States and other Western societies, parents' styles tend to be mostly authoritarian, permissive, or authoritative, with the last being regarded as the most effective.
12. In some Asian countries, an emphasis on social harmony provides support for a more authoritarian style of childrearing, which can be quite effective in its home setting.
13. Children of authoritarian and permissive parents in the United States may suffer consequences in terms of sociability. Dependency, hostility, and low self-control are often effects of these parenting styles. Children of authoritative parents tend to be more independent, friendly, self-assertive, and cooperative.

How do children develop a moral sense?

14. The process of moral development during the preschool years has been studied by several researchers. Piaget believed that children at this age are in the heteronomous morality stage of moral development, characterized by a belief in external, unchangeable rules of conduct. These rules do not take intention into account, merely acts. The belief in imminent justice—sure, immediate punishment for all misdeeds—is also a characteristic of this stage.
15. In contrast, social learning approaches to morality emphasize interactions between environment and behavior in moral development. According to these approaches, models of behavior play an important role in development, providing not only specific examples of appropriate actions, but also the basis for establishing abstract principles of moral behavior.
16. Some developmentalists believe that a child's development of empathy, which begins early in life, underlies many kinds of moral behavior. Other emotions, including the negative emotions of anger and shame that were emphasized in Freud's psychoanalytic theories of personality development, may also promote moral behavior.

Is aggression normal in preschoolers, and how does it develop?

17. Aggression, which involves intentional harm to another person, begins to emerge in the preschool years. Mild forms of aggression appear to be virtually universal, but extreme aggression, which occurs infrequently, is cause for concern. As children age and improve their language skills, acts of aggression typically decline in frequency and duration, although aggressive or nonaggressive tendencies in the individual are relatively stable throughout the school years.

18. Whether aggression is innate or learned is a topic of theory and research. Some ethologists, such as Konrad Lorenz, believe that aggression is simply a biological fact of human—and all animal—life, a belief held also by many sociobiologists, who focus on the individual's instinctual desire to pass genes on to the next generation, a desire that leads to aggressive intraspecies competition.

19. On the other hand, social learning theorists, disturbed by the lack of experimental support for the view that aggression is innate—and by its failure to account for cognition and to explain in detail how aggression operates—focus on learned aspects of aggressive behavior. In their view, the role of the environment, including models of behavior and social reinforcement, is of primary importance. The hypothesis that television can induce aggressive behavior has been studied and has found experimental support.

20. The cognitive approach to aggression emphasizes the role of interpretations of the behaviors of others in determining aggressive or nonaggressive responses. By teaching children to consider multiple interpretations of others' acts and to use problem-solving skills, proponents of the cognitive approach hope to reduce aggressive responses.

KEY TERMS AND CONCEPTS

self-concept (p. 284)
collectivistic orientation (p. 284)
individualistic orientation (p. 284)
psychosocial development (p. 285)
initiative-versus-guilt stage (p. 285)
race dissonance (p. 285)
identification (p. 288)
gender identity (p. 289)
gender schema (p. 289)
gender constancy (p. 290)
androgynous (p. 290)
functional play (p. 294)
constructive play (p. 294)
parallel play (p. 295)
onlooker play (p. 295)
associative play (p. 295)
cooperative play (p. 295)
authoritarian parents (p. 296)
permissive parents (p. 296)
authoritative parents (p. 297)
moral development (p. 301)
heteronomous morality (p. 301)
imminent justice (p. 302)
prosocial behavior (p. 302)
abstract modeling (p. 303)
empathy (p. 303)
aggression (p. 304)
sociobiologists (p. 305)

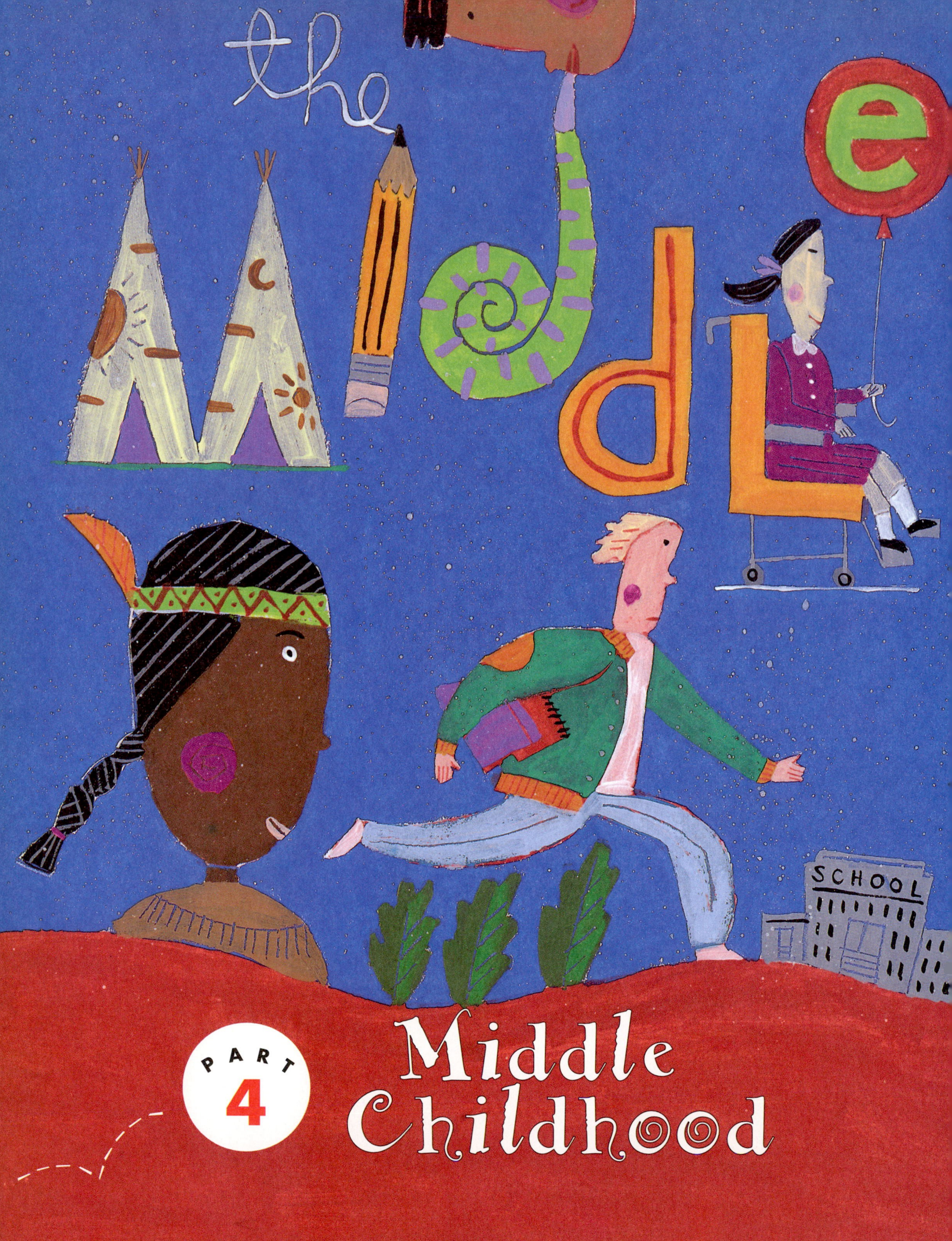
the
Middle
SCHOOL
PART
4
Middle
Childhood

years

CHAPTER 10

MIDDLE CHILDHOOD

Physical Development in Middle Childhood

PROLOGUE

DUSTY NASH

Dusty Nash, an angelic-looking blond child of 7, awoke at 5 one recent morning in his Chicago home and proceeded to throw a fit. He wailed. He kicked. Every muscle in his 50-pound body flew in furious motion. Finally, after about 30 minutes, Dusty pulled himself together sufficiently to head downstairs for breakfast. While his mother bustled about the kitchen, the hyperkinetic child pulled a box of Kix cereal from the cupboard and sat on a chair.

But sitting still was not in the cards this morning. After grabbing some cereal with his hands, he began kicking the box, scattering little round corn puffs across the room. Next he turned his attention to the TV set, or rather, the table supporting it. The table was covered with checkerboard Con-Tact paper, and Dusty began peeling it off. Then he became intrigued with the spilled cereal and started stomping it to bits. At this point his mother interceded. In a firm but calm voice she told her son to get the stand-up dustpan and broom and clean up the mess. Dusty got out the dustpan but forgot the rest of the order. Within seconds he was dismantling the plastic dustpan, piece by piece. His next project: grabbing three rolls of toilet paper from the bathroom and unraveling them around the house. (Wallis, 1994, p. 43)

LOOKING AHEAD

It was only 7:30 A.M.

Dusty suffers from a disorder that just a few decades ago no one had heard of: attention-deficit hyperactivity disorder (ADHD). Although not common, occurring in only 3 to 5 percent of the school-age population, the disorder represents one of several special challenges that some children may face as they pass through middle childhood.

Yet even in children without identifiable difficulties, the range of skills and abilities that their development encompasses is enormous. In this chapter, we focus on the physical aspects of middle childhood, both in typical children and in children, like Dusty, with special needs. Beginning at age 6 and continuing to the start of adolescence at around age 12, middle childhood is often referred to as the "school years" because for most children, these years coincide with the elementary school period. These are also years of significant physical, cognitive, and social growth.

We begin our consideration of middle childhood by focusing on physical development. We first discuss how children's bodies change during these years. We also consider the twin problems of malnutrition and—the other side of the coin—childhood obesity.

Next, we turn to motor development. We discuss the growth of gross and fine motor skills, and the role that physical competence plays in children's lives. We also discuss threats to children's safety—including a new one that enters the home through the personal computer.

Finally, the chapter ends with a discussion of some of the special needs that affect the sensory and physical abilities of exceptional children. It concludes by focusing on the question of how children with special needs should be integrated into society.

In sum, after reading this chapter, you will be able to answer these questions:

- In what ways do children grow during the school years, and what factors influence their growth?

- What are the nutritional needs of school-age children, and what are some causes and effects of improper nutrition?
- What sorts of health threats do school-age children face?
- What are the characteristics of motor development during middle childhood, and what advantages do improved physical skills bring?
- What safety threats affect school-age children, and what can be done about them?
- What sorts of special needs manifest themselves in the middle childhood years, and how can they be met?

THE GROWING BODY

Slow but steady.

If three words could characterize the nature of growth during middle childhood, it would be these. Especially when compared to the swift growth during the first 5 years of life and the remarkable growth spurt characteristic of adolescence, middle childhood is relatively tranquil. On the other hand, the body has not shifted into neutral. Physical growth continues, although at a more stately pace than it did during the preschool years.

HEIGHT AND WEIGHT CHANGES: CONTINUING GROWTH

While they are in elementary school, children in the United States grow, on average, 2 to 3 inches a year. By the age of 11, the average girl is 4 feet, 10 inches tall and the average boy is slightly shorter at 4 feet, 9½ inches tall. This is the only time during the life span when girls are, on average, taller than boys. This height difference reflects the slightly more rapid physical development of girls, who start their adolescent growth spurt around the age of 10.

Weight gain follows a similar pattern. During middle childhood, both boys and girls gain around 5 to 7 pounds a year. Weight also becomes redistributed. As the rounded look of "baby fat" disappears, children's bodies become more muscular and their strength increases.

Average height and weight increases disguise significant individual differences, as anyone who has seen a line of fourth-graders walking down a school corridor has doubtless noticed. Variations of a half-foot between children of the same age are not unusual and well within normal ranges.

Significant individual differences exist in children's height during middle childhood.

Children in poorer areas of cities, such as these youngsters in Calcutta, are shorter and weigh less than those raised in more affluent places.

Children who are well above or below the average height of their classmates may feel stigmatized by their size. In fact, concerns about shortness have led some children and their parents to seek out medical remedies, as we discuss in the "Directions in Development" box.

Because most children in North America receive sufficient nutrients to reach their full potential, most height and weight differences among North American children are due to genetically determined variability. In other parts of the world, inadequate nutrition and disease take a greater toll, producing children who are shorter and who weigh less than they would if they had sufficient nutrients. The discrepancies can be dramatic: Children in poorer areas of cities such as Calcutta, Hong Kong, and Rio de Janeiro are smaller than their counterparts in affluent areas of the same cities.

Other variations in height and weight are the result of genetic factors relating to ethnicity background. For instance, children from Asian and Oceanic Pacific backgrounds tend to be shorter, on average, than those with northern and central European heritages. However, even within particular ethnicities there is significant variation. Furthermore, ethnic differences should not be attributed solely to inherited factors, because dietary customs, as well as possible variations in levels of affluence, also may contribute to the differences.

Directions in Development

Promoting Growth with Hormones: Should Short Children Be Made to Grow?

The makers of Protropin, an artificial human growth hormone that can make short children taller, had a problem: To promote the use of their drug, they needed to find short children. One of the ways they solved their problem was by paying for surveys to identify short children in schools.

Although such practices are legal, they are on the fringe of ethical conduct, at least according to some child developmentalists. The problem is not so much whether the drug is effective in increasing the growth of unusually short children—it is—but whether drug manufacturers are being overly aggressive in their quest to market the drug to potential patients (Kolata, 1994).

The problem is a new one: Artificial hormones to promote growth have become available only in the last decade. Today some 20,000 children who have insufficient levels of natural growth hormone are taking such drugs. But some observers question whether shortness is a serious enough problem to warrant the use of the drug, which is costly and has potential side effects. For instance, the drug makes some children more susceptible to infection. Furthermore, in some cases, the drug may lead to the premature onset of puberty, which may—ironically—restrict later growth. In fact, no evidence confirms that children given the growth hormone when they are young end up any taller as adults than they would have been had they not been given the drug.

On the other hand, there is no denying that artificial growth hormones are effective in increasing children's height. In fact, for those children whose height is projected to be well below normal, the effect of such drugs can be dramatic. In some cases the drug has added well over a foot in height to extremely short children, placing them within normal height ranges.

However, the American Academy of Pediatrics (1983) urges caution. It suggests that the growth hormone be used only with children who have naturally occurring levels of growth hormone that are below normal, and not just to boost the height of children who are, by virtue of their genetic background, simply short.

NUTRITION: LINKS TO OVERALL FUNCTIONING

The level of nutrition children experience during their lives significantly affects many aspects of their behavior. For instance, longitudinal studies over many years in Guatemalan villages show that children's nutritional backgrounds are related to several dimensions of social and emotional functioning at school age. Children who had received more nutrients were more involved with their peers, showed more positive emotion, had less anxiety, and had more moderate activity levels than their peers who had received less adequate nutrition. Furthermore, the children with a better nutritional history were more eager to explore new environments, showed more persistence in frustrating situations, were more alert on some types of activities, and generally displayed higher energy levels and more self-confidence (Barrett & Frank, 1987; see Figure 10-1).

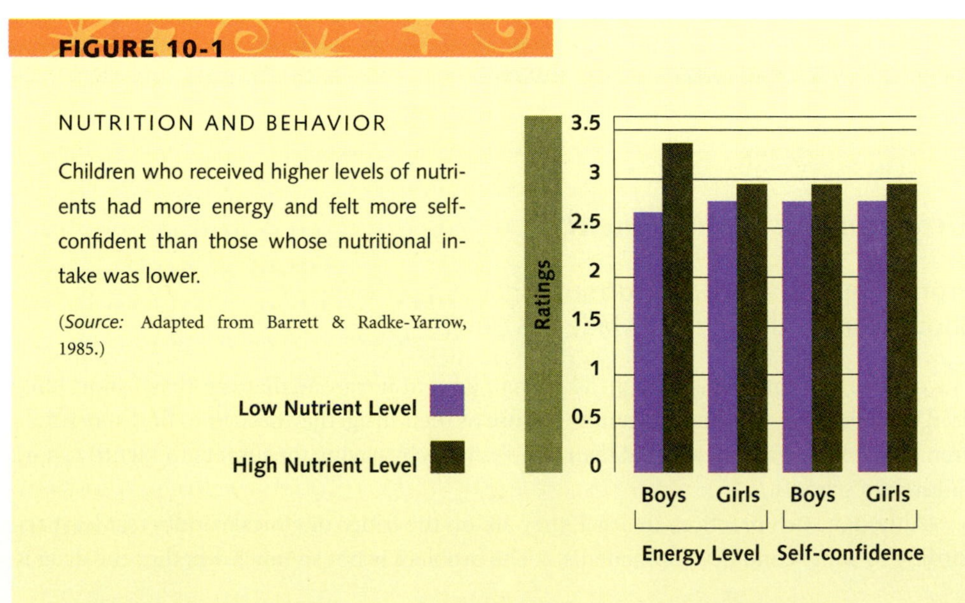

FIGURE 10-1

NUTRITION AND BEHAVIOR

Children who received higher levels of nutrients had more energy and felt more self-confident than those whose nutritional intake was lower.

(*Source:* Adapted from Barrett & Radke-Yarrow, 1985.)

Nutrition is also linked to cognitive performance. For instance, in one study, children in Kenya who were well nourished performed better on a test of verbal abilities and on other cognitive measures than those who had mild to moderate undernutrition. Other research suggests that malnutrition may influence cognitive development by dampening children's curiosity, responsiveness, and motivation to learn (McDonald et al., 1994; Ricciuti, 1993; Sigman et al., 1989; Brown & Pollitt, 1996).

Although undernutrition and malnutrition clearly lead to physical, social, and cognitive difficulties, in some cases *over*nutrition—the intake by a child of too many calories—presents problems of its own, particularly when it leads to childhood obesity.

Childhood Obesity: Genetic and Social Factors

When Ruthellen's mother asks if she would like a piece of bread with her meal, Ruthellen replies that she better not—she thinks that she may be getting fat. Ruthellen, who is of normal weight and height, is 6 years old.

Although height can be of concern to both children and parents during middle childhood, maintaining the appropriate weight is an even greater worry for some. In fact, concern about weight can border on an obsession, particularly among girls. For instance, many 6-year-old girls worry about becoming "fat," and they try to avoid foods that they think are likely to make them put on weight. Why? Their concern is probably due to the U.S. preoccupation with being slim, which permeates every sector of society (Feldman, Feldman, & Goodman, 1988).

What is ironic about the widely held view that thinness is a virtue is that increasing numbers of children are becoming obese. *Obesity* is defined as body weight that is more than 20 percent above the average for a person of a given age and height. By this definition, some 10 percent of all children are obese—a proportion that is growing. In fact, since the 1960s, obesity among children ages 6 to 11 has risen by 54 percent (Gortmaker, Dietz, Sobol, & Welher, 1987; D. R. Lamb, 1984; Troiano et al., 1995; Ungrady, 1992; Steinberg, 1996).

Several factors account for childhood obesity. As we first noted in Chapter 7, obesity is caused by a combination of genetic and social characteristics. For instance, increasing evidence suggests that particular inherited genes are related to obesity and predispose certain children to be overweight (Y. Zhang, et al., 1994).

At the same time, obesity cannot be attributable solely to inherited factors, since it is hard to link the rise in obesity over the past several decades to changes in the gene pool. Clearly, various social factors must also enter into children's weight problems.

In addition to society's preoccupation with slimness as a sign of beauty, an additional social ingredient in obesity is parental worry about their children's weight. Parents who are particularly involved in their children's eating habits, and who exhibit controlling behavior regarding them, may produce children who lack internal controls to regulate their own food intake (Brownell & Rodin, 1994; Johnson & Birch, 1994).

Another important social factor that determines obesity is exercise—or rather, the lack of exercise (Epstein, 1992). School-age children, by and large, tend to engage in relatively little exercise and are not particularly fit (Wolf et al., 1993). For instance, around 40 percent of boys ages 6 to 12 are unable to do more than one pull-up, and a quarter can't do any. Furthermore, school fitness surveys reveal that American children have shown little or no improvement in the amount of exercise they get, despite national efforts to increase the level of fitness of school-age children. In one survey, for example, two thirds of children tested failed to meet minimum standards set by the U.S. President's Council on Physical Fitness and Sports (Ungrady, 1992).

Why, when our visions of childhood include children running happily on school playgrounds, playing sports, and chasing one another in games of tag, is the actual level of exercise relatively low? One answer is that many kids are closeted in their homes, watching television.

Television viewing is associated with obesity, in part because watching TV replaces more social activities that involve physical exercise.

The correlation between television viewing and obesity is strong: The more television children watch, the more likely they are to be overweight (Dietz, 1987). There are several reasons for this pattern. For one thing, television viewing is a passive activity; few children engage in vigorous exercise while watching TV. Furthermore, TV viewing replaces the social play with friends that typically would involve physical activity. Even worse, children often snack while watching television, thereby increasing their caloric intake beyond their nutritional needs. Finally, repeated exposure to commercials for food products may entice habitual television viewers to be overly interested in food and eating (Gortmaker et al., 1996).

Regardless of the causes of childhood obesity, treatment is tricky, because creating too strong a concern about food and dieting needs to be avoided. In most cases, the goal of treatment for obesity is to temporarily maintain a child's current weight through an improved diet and increased exercise, rather than actually seeking to lose weight. In time, obese children's normal growth in height will result in their weight becoming more normal.

HEALTH DURING MIDDLE CHILDHOOD

Imani was miserable. Her nose was running, her lips were chapped, and her throat was sore. Although she had been able to stay home from school and spend the day watching old reruns on TV, she still felt that she was suffering mightily.

Despite her misery, Imani is not too badly off. She'll get over the cold in a few days and be no worse for having experienced it. In fact, she may be a little *better* off, for she is now immune to the specific cold germs that made her ill in the first place.

For Imani, as well as most children, a cold or other type of upper respiratory infection is just about the most serious illness that occurs during middle childhood. For most children, this is a period of great health, and most of the ailments they do contract tend to be mild and brief.

On the other hand, illness is not uncommon. For instance, more than 90 percent of children are likely to have at least one serious medical condition over the 6-year period of middle childhood, according to the results of one large survey. And, although most children have short-term illnesses, about one in nine has a chronic, persistent condition, such as repeated migraine headaches (Starfield, 1991; Starfield et al., 1984).

Routine immunizations during childhood have produced a considerably lower incidence of the life-threatening illnesses that 50 years ago claimed the lives of a significant number of children. Despite these gains, however, some illnesses are becoming more prevalent.

Asthma. Asthma is among the diseases that have shown a significant increase in prevalence over the last several decades. **Asthma** is a chronic condition characterized by periodic attacks of wheezing, coughing, and shortness of breath. More than 7 percent of children under age 18 suffer from the disorder—a rate that has almost doubled over the last decade.

Asthma occurs when the airways leading to the lungs constrict, partially blocking the passage of oxygen. Because the airways are obstructed, more effort is needed to push air through them, making breathing more difficult. Furthermore, as air is forced through the obstructed airways, it makes the whistling sound called wheezing.

Not surprisingly, children are often exceedingly frightened by asthma attacks, and the anxiety and agitation produced by their breathing difficulties may actually make the attack worse. In some cases, breathing becomes so difficult that further physical symptoms develop, including sweating, an increased heart rate, and—in the most severe cases—a blueness in the face and lips due to a lack of oxygen.

Asthma attacks are triggered by a variety of factors. Among the most common are respiratory infections (such as colds or flu), allergic reactions to airborne irritants (such as pollution, cigarette smoke, dust mites, and animal dander and excretions), stress, and exercise. Sometimes even a sudden change in air temperature or humidity is enough to bring on an attack.

Although asthma can be serious, treatment is increasingly effective for those who suffer from the disorder. Some children who experience frequent asthma attacks use a small aerosol container with a special mouthpiece to spray drugs into the lungs. Other patients take tablets or receive injections (Rosen, 1997).

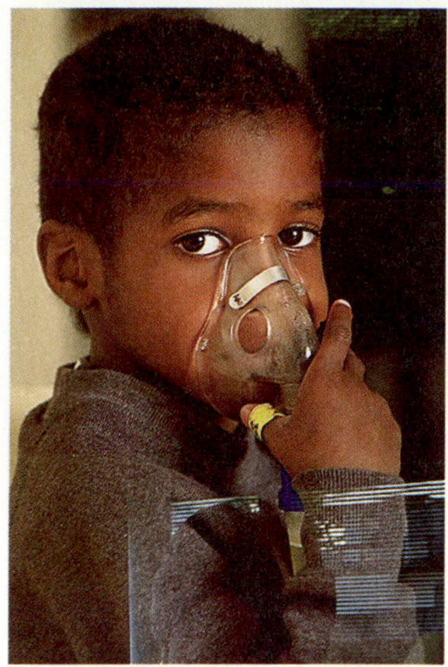

The incidence of asthma, a chronic respiratory condition, has increased dramatically over the last several decades.

One of the most puzzling questions about asthma is why the incidence has increased over the last 2 decades. Some researchers suggest that increasing air pollution has led to the rise; others believe that cases of asthma that might have been missed in the past are simply being identified more accurately. Still others have suggested that exposure to "asthma triggers," such as dust, may be increasing, because new buildings are more weatherproof—and therefore less drafty—than old ones, and consequently the flow of air within them is more restricted.

Finally, poverty may play an indirect role. Children living in poverty have a higher incidence of asthma than other children, probably due to poorer medical care and less sanitary living conditions. For instance, poor youngsters are more likely than more affluent ones to be exposed to triggering factors that are associated with asthma, such as dust mites, cockroach feces and body parts, and rodent feces and urine (Nossiter, 1995).

Psychological Disorders. Jackson had always been a quiet child and had, since his days as a toddler, seemed less exuberant than most other children. But when his third-grade teacher called his parents to report that Jackson seemed increasingly withdrawn from his classmates and had to be coaxed into going out to the playground, the parents thought they might have a serious problem on their hands. They were right: A psychologist diagnosed Jackson as suffering from *childhood depression.*

For years most people neglected the symptoms of childhood depression, and even today parents and teachers may overlook its presence. In part, their neglect is due to the fact that its symptoms are not entirely consistent with the ways adults express depression. Rather than being manifested in a profound sadness or hopelessness, a negative outlook on life, and, in extreme cases, suicidal thoughts, as adult depression is, childhood depression may instead be characterized by the expression of exaggerated fears, clinginess, or avoidance of everyday activities. In older children, childhood depression may produce sulking, school problems, and even acts of delinquency (Mitchell et al., 1988; Prieto, Cole, & Tageson, 1992; Wenar, 1994).

The incidence of childhood depression is surprisingly high. Experts suggest that between 2 and 5 percent of school-age children suffer from the disorder. In some children it is particularly severe: Around 1 percent are so depressed that they express unmistakable suicidal ideas (Cohen et al., 1993; Larsson & Melin, 1992).

asthma *a chronic condition characterized by periodic attacks of wheezing, coughing, and shortness of breath*

It is important to keep in mind that all children are occasionally sad, and short periods of unhappiness should not be mistaken for childhood depression. The distinguishing characteristics of childhood depression are its depth, which can be truly profound, and its duration, which can extend for days or even weeks.

Like adult depression, childhood depression can be treated effectively through a variety of approaches. In addition to psychological counseling, drugs are sometimes prescribed, although they can cause undesirable side effects. Whatever treatment is chosen, it is important that childhood depression not be ignored, particularly because children who are depressed are at risk for mood disorders during adulthood (Alloy, Acocella, & Bootzin, 1996; Harrington et al., 1990; Kazdin, 1990).

In addition to depression, several other psychological disorders may appear during middle childhood. For example, some 8 to 9 percent of children suffer from *anxiety disorders,* in which they experience intense, uncontrollable anxiety about situations that most people would not find bothersome. For instance, some children have strong fears about specific stimuli–such as a fear of germs or of school–while others have bouts of generalized anxiety, the source of which they cannot pinpoint (Bernstein & Borchardt, 1991; Wenar, 1994).

The Informed Consumer of Development

Keeping Children Fit

> *Here is a brief portrait of a contemporary American: Sam works all week at a desk and gets no regular physical exercise. On weekends he spends many hours sitting in front of the TV, often snacking on sodas and sweets. Both at home and at restaurants, his meals feature high-calorie, fat-saturated foods. (Segal & Segal, 1992, p. 235)*

Although this sketch could apply to many adult men and women, Sam is actually a 6-year-old. He is one of many school-age children in the United States who get little or no regular exercise, and who consequently are physically unfit and at risk for obesity and other health problems. Many children appear to find exercise unappealing.

However, parents and teachers can take several approaches to encourage children to become more physically active (O'Neill, 1994; Squires, 1991):

- *Make exercise fun.* In order for children to build the habit of exercising, they must find exercise enjoyable. Activities that keep children on the sidelines or that are overly competitive may give children with inferior skills a lifelong distaste for exercise.
- *Gear activities to the child's physical level and motor skills.* For instance, use child-sized equipment that can make participants feel successful.
- *Encourage the child to find a partner.* It could be a friend, a sibling, or a parent. Exercising can involve a variety of activities, such as roller-skating or hiking, but almost all activities are carried out more readily if someone else is doing them too.
- *Start slowly.* Sedentary children—those who haven't habitually engaged in physical activity—should start off gradually. For instance, they could start with 5 minutes of exercise a day, 7 days a week. Over 10 weeks, they could move toward a goal of 30 minutes of exercise 3 to 5 days a week.

- *Urge, but don't push too hard, participation in organized sports activities.* Not every child is athletically inclined, and pushing too hard for involvement in organized sports may backfire. Make participation and enjoyment the goals of such activities, not winning.
- *Keep exercise positive.* Don't make physical activity, such as jumping jacks or push-ups, a punishment for unwanted behavior.
- *Encourage children to participate in an organized physical fitness program.* For instance, the Cooper Institute for Aerobics Research has designed a program called the *Fitness*gram, which is used by 2 million children in 6,000 schools around the United States. (For more information, write Cooper Institute for Aerobics Research, 12330 Preston Road, Dallas, TX 75230 or call 800-635-7050.)

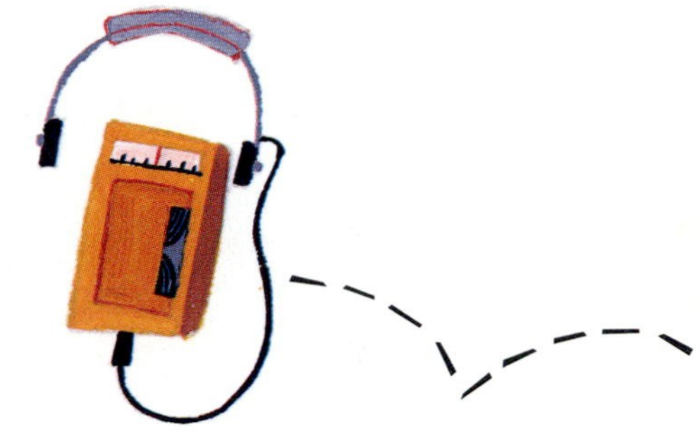

Review and Rethink

REVIEW

- During middle childhood, height and weight increase gradually and the body loses its baby fat. Girls tend to develop a little more quickly than boys and stand on average about ½ inch taller.
- Differences in average height and weight relate partly to affluence and poverty. Furthermore, ethnic differences are attributable not only to genetic factors, but also to cultural and economic differences.
- Nutrition is important not only for physical growth, but also because it affects many aspects of social, emotional, and cognitive functioning.
- Obesity in children, which can be caused by genetic and social factors, can be a serious problem. Anxiety about obesity can be equally serious, especially if it leads to an obsession about slimness.
- The health of children in middle childhood is generally good, with few major health worries. However, the incidence of asthma among children in this period is surprisingly high, as is the incidence of psychological disorders such as childhood depression and anxiety disorders.

RETHINK

- Under what circumstances would you recommend the use of a growth hormone such as Protropin? Is shortness primarily a physical or a cultural problem?
- What evidence is there that an individual's height is due to both genetic and cultural factors?
- Do proven links among affluence, nutrition, and the development of cognitive and social skills provide insight into the persistence of poverty from one generation to another? How might such a "cycle of poverty" be broken?
- What are some aspects of U.S. culture that may contribute to fitness and nutritional problems among school-age children?
- In what ways can childhood depression be distinguished from simple sadness in school-age children?

MOTOR DEVELOPMENT AND SAFETY

> When my son's friend Owen was 9 years old, everybody at school knew the shameful truth about him: He was a whiz at math but a lousy football player.
>
> Nobody was more aware of this than Owen. "He knew he wasn't as good at sports as the others," says his mother, Cheryl. "It really got him down. Even when we told him, 'You have to get out there, you have to try,' as soon as he made a mistake, he would just walk away. Owen's schoolwork was good, so he felt okay about himself. But because he didn't play sports, he didn't have as many friends as most kids did."
>
> Then one day, just after he turned 10, when Owen happened to be at a nearby mall, he saw a demonstration of a martial art called tae kwon do. "That's what I want to do," he immediately told his mother. "Can you sign me up?"
>
> He now takes lessons several times a week, and according to Cheryl, the changes are remarkable. "Owen's mood has improved, he's sleeping better, he's even better about doing homework," she says. "And when he got his yellow belt, he was over the moon." (Heath, 1994, p. 127–128)

During middle childhood, children's athletic abilities play an important role in determining how they see themselves, as well as how they are viewed by others. This is also a time when such physical proficiencies develop substantially.

MOTOR SKILLS: CONTINUING IMPROVEMENT

Watching a softball player pitch a ball past a batter to her catcher, or a runner reach the finish line in a race, it is hard not to be struck by the huge strides that children have made since the more awkward days of preschool. In terms of both their gross and their fine motor skills, children improve significantly.

Gross Motor Skills. During middle childhood, children master many types of skills that earlier they could not perform well. For instance, riding a bike, ice-skating, swimming, and skipping rope are readily mastered by most school-age children (Cratty, 1986; see Figure 10-2).

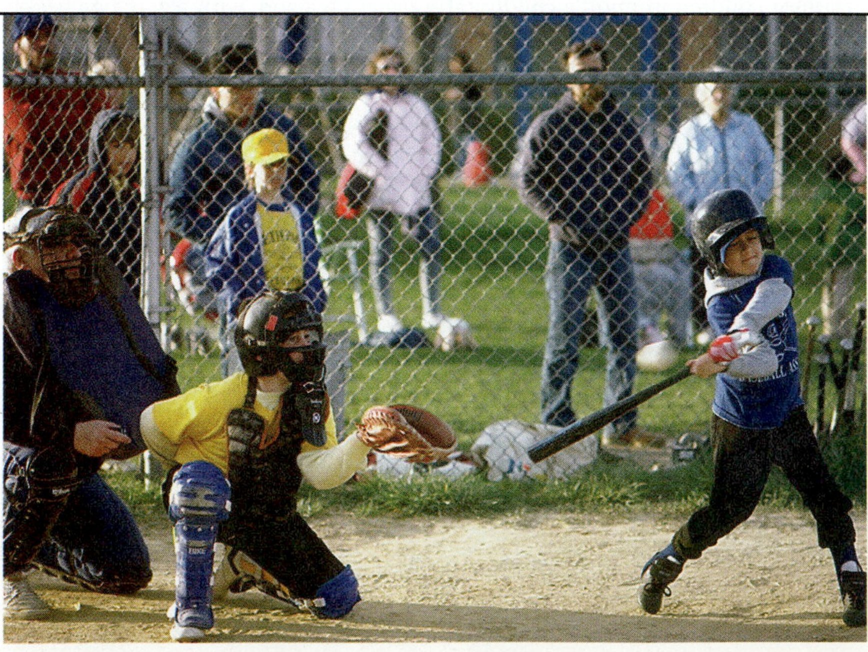

Baseball involves a variety of gross motor skills, many of which could not be performed by these children only a few years earlier.

FIGURE 10-2

GROSS MOTOR SKILLS DEVELOPED BY CHILDREN BETWEEN THE AGES OF 6 AND 12 YEARS (*Source:* Adapted from Cratty, 1982.)

6 Years	7 Years	8 Years	9 Years	10 Years	11 Years	12 Years
Girls superior in accuracy of movement; boys superior in more forceful, less complex acts. Can throw with the proper weight shift and step. Acquire the ability to skip.	Can balance on one foot with eyes closed. Can walk on a 2-inch-wide balance beam without falling off. Can hop and jump accurately into small squares (hopscotch). Can correctly execute a jumping-jack exercise.	Can grip objects with 12 pounds of pressure. Can engage in alternate rhythmical hopping in a 2-2, 2-3, or 3-3 pattern. Girls can throw a small ball 33 feet; boys can throw a small ball 59 feet. The number of games participated in by both sexes is the greatest at this age.	Girls can jump vertically 8.5 inches over their standing height plus reach; boys can jump vertically 10 inches. Boys can run 16.6 feet per second and throw a small ball 41 feet; girls can run 16 feet per second and throw a small ball 41 feet.	Can judge and intercept directions of small balls thrown from a distance. Both girls and boys can run 17 feet per second .	Boys can achieve standing broad jump of 5 feet; girls can achieve standing broad jump of 4.5 feet.	Can achieve high jump of 3 feet.

Do boys and girls differ in their motor skills? Traditionally, developmental researchers have concluded that gender differences in gross motor skills become increasingly pronounced during these years, with boys outperforming girls (Espenschade, 1960). However, more recent research casts some doubt on this conclusion. When comparisons are made between boys and girls who regularly take part in similar activities—such as softball—gender variations in gross motor skills are minimized (Hall & Lee, 1984).

Why? Performance differences were probably found in the first place because of differences in motivation and expectations. Society told girls that they would do worse than boys in sports, and the girls' performance reflected that message.

Today, however, society's message has changed somewhat, at least officially. For instance, the American Academy of Pediatrics suggests that boys and girls should engage in the same sports and games, and that they can do so together in mixed-gender groups. There is no reason to separate the sexes in physical exercise and sports until puberty, when the smaller size of females begins to make them more susceptible than males to injury in contact sports (American Academy of Pediatrics Committee on Sports Medicine and Committee on School Health, 1989).

Improvements in fine motor skills are significant during middle childhood, almost reaching the level of proficiency of adults.

Fine Motor Skills. Typing at a computer keyboard. Writing in cursive with pen and pencil. Drawing detailed pictures. These are just a few of the accomplishments that depend on improvements in fine motor coordination that occur during early and middle childhood. Six- and 7-year-olds are able to tie their shoes and fasten buttons; by age 8, they can manipulate different things simultaneously with their hands; and by 11 and 12, they can manipulate objects with almost as much capability as they will show in adulthood.

One of the reasons for advances in fine motor skills is that the amount of myelin in the brain increases significantly between the ages of 6 and 8 (Lecours, 1982). You may recall from Chapter 7 that *myelin* provides protective insulation that surrounds parts of nerve cells. Because increased levels of myelin raise the speed at which electrical impulses travel between neurons, messages can reach muscles more rapidly and control them better.

The Social Benefits of Physical Competence. Is Matt, a fifth-grader who is a clear standout on his Saturday morning soccer team, more popular as a result of his physical talents? He may well be. According to a long history of research on the topic, school-age children who perform well physically are often more accepted and liked by their peers than those who perform less well (Cratty, 1986; Pintney, Forlands, & Freedman, 1937).

However, the link between physical competence and popularity is considerably stronger for boys than for girls. The reason for this sex difference most likely relates to differing societal standards for appropriate male and female behavior. Despite the increasing evidence that girls and boys do not differ substantially in athletic performance, a lingering "physical toughness" norm, or standard, still exists for males but not females. Regardless of age, males who are bigger, stronger, and more physically competent are seen as more desirable than those who are smaller, weaker, and less physically competent. In contrast, standards for females are less supportive of physical success. In fact, women receive less admiration for physical prowess than men do throughout the life span. Although these societal standards may be changing, with women's participation in sports activities becoming more frequent and valued, gender biases remain (Burn, 1996).

Although the social desirability of athletically proficient boys increases throughout elementary school and continues into secondary school, at some point the positive consequences of motor ability begin to diminish. Presumably, other traits become increasingly important in determining social attractiveness—some of which we'll discuss in Chapter 12.

Furthermore, it is difficult to sort out the extent to which advantages from exceptional physical performance are due to actual athletic competence, as opposed to being a result of earlier maturation. Boys who physically mature at a more rapid pace than their peers, or who happen to be taller, heavier, and stronger, tend to perform better at athletic activities due to their relative size advantage. Consequently, it may be that early physical maturity is ultimately of greater consequence than physical skills per se.

Still, it is clear that athletic competence, and motoric skills in general, play a notable role in school-age children's lives. However, it is important to help children avoid overemphasizing the significance of physical ability. Participation in sports should be fun, not something that separates one child from another and raises children's and parents' anxiety levels. In fact, some forms of organized sports, such as Little League baseball, occasionally are criticized for the emphasis they sometimes place on winning at any cost. When children feel that success in sports is the sole goal, the pleasure of playing the game is diminished, particularly for those children who are not naturally athletic and do not excel.

In sum, the goals of participation in sports and other physical activities should be to maintain physical fitness, to learn physical skills, and to become comfortable with one's body. And, ultimately, children should have fun in the process.

The increasing independence that occurs during middle childhood makes children more susceptible to accidents.

THREATS TO CHILDREN'S SAFETY: ON-LINE AND OFF

The increasing independence and mobility of school-age children lead to new safety issues. In fact, the rate of injury for children increases between the ages of 5 and 14 (see Figure 10-3). Furthermore, boys are more apt to be injured than girls, probably because their overall level of physical activity is greater (Schor, 1987)

Accidents. The most frequent source of injury to children is automobile-related injuries. Auto crashes annually kill 5 out of every 100,000 children between the ages of 5 and 9. Fires and burns, drowning, and gun-related deaths follow in frequency (Maternal and Child Health Bureau, 1994).

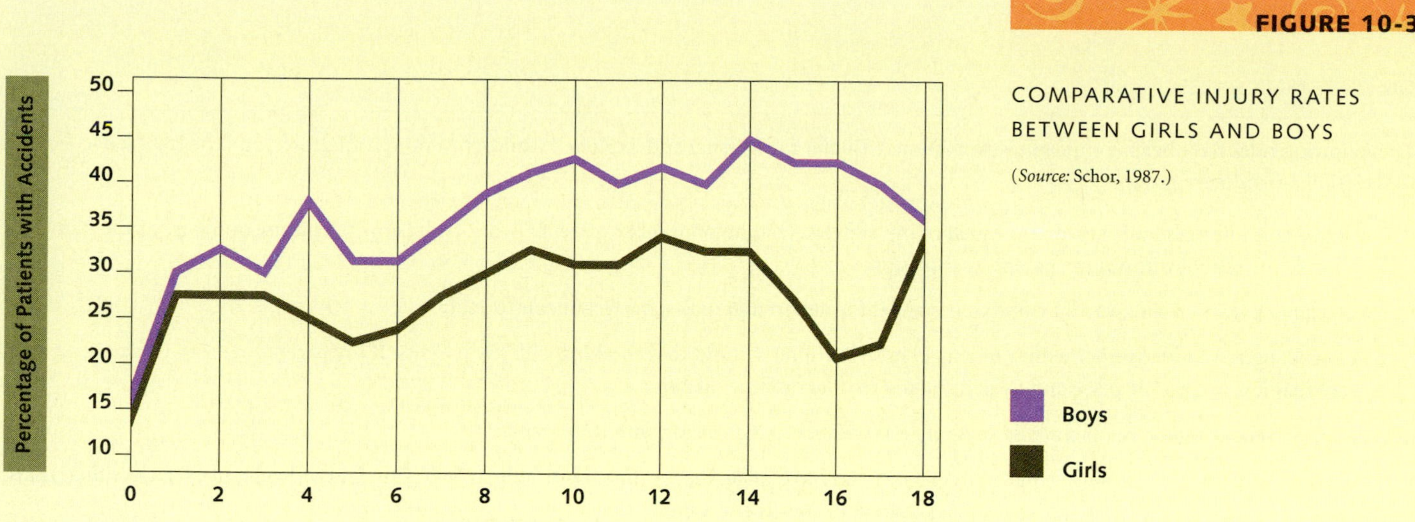

FIGURE 10-3

COMPARATIVE INJURY RATES BETWEEN GIRLS AND BOYS

(*Source:* Schor, 1987.)

The increased mobility of school-age children causes other accidents. For instance, children who regularly walk to school on their own, many traveling such a distance alone for the first time in their lives, face the risk of being hit by cars and trucks. Because of their lack of experience, they may misjudge distances when calculating just how far they are from an oncoming vehicle. Furthermore, bicycle accidents pose an increasing risk, particularly as children more frequently venture out onto busy roads.

Two ways to reduce motion-related injuries considerably are to use seat belts consistently inside the car and to wear appropriate protective gear outside. Bicycle helmets have significantly reduced head injuries, and in many localities their use is mandatory. Similar protection is available for other activities; for example, knee and elbow pads have proven to be important sources of injury reduction for roller-blading and skateboarding (American Academy of Pediatrics Committee on Accident and Poison Prevention, 1990).

Some injuries occur during organized sports activities—most often because of differences in participants' size. Younger players—generally outweighed and outperformed by older children—are often injured during organized games. Many such injuries could be avoided if games were limited to players of approximately the same weight, age, and skill level.

Safety in Cyberspace. The newest threat to the safety of school-age children comes from a source that just a decade ago was unheard of: the Internet and the World Wide Web. Although claims that cyberspace is overrun with pornography and child molesters are clearly exaggerated, it is true that cyberspace makes available material that many parents find objectionable (Lohr, 1996; also see the "Speaking of Development" interview on page 330).

Although computer software developers are working on programs that will block particular computer sites, most experts feel that the most reliable safeguard is close supervision by parents. According to the National Center for Missing and Exploited Children (1995), a nonprofit organization that works with the U.S. Department of Justice, parents should warn their children never to provide personal information, such as home addresses or telephone numbers, to people on public computer "bulletin boards" or in "chat rooms." In addition, children should not be allowed to hold face-to-face meetings with people they "meet" via computer, at least not without a parent being present.

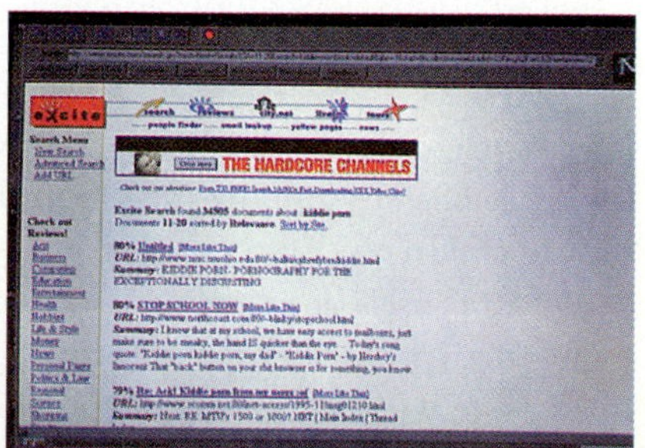

A new threat to children's well-being may come from the World Wide Web, where material can be found that many parents would find objectionable.

It is too early to have clear statistics that provide a true sense of the risk presented by exposure to cyberspace. But certainly a potential hazard exists, and parents must offer their children guidance in the use of this computer resource. It would be erroneous to think that,

TABLE 10-1

ON-LINE SAFETY RULES

The following rules have been compiled by the National Center for Missing and Exploited Children, a nonprofit group, and the Interactive Services Association, an industry group:

- I will not give out personal information such as my address, telephone number, parents' work address or telephone number, or the name and location of my school without my parents' permission.
- I will tell my parents right away if I come across any information that makes me feel uncomfortable.
- I will never agree to get together with someone I "meet" on-line without first checking with my parents. If my parents agree to the meeting, I will be sure that it is in a public place and I will bring my mother or father along.
- I will never send a person my picture or anything else without first checking with my parents.
- I will not respond to any messages that are mean or in any way make me feel uncomfortable. It is not my fault if I get a message like that. If I do, I will tell my parents right away so that they can contact the on-line service.
- I will talk with my parents so that we can set up rules for going on-line. We will decide upon the time of day that I can be on-line, the length of time I can be on-line, and appropriate areas for me to visit. I will not break these rules or access other areas without their permission.

(*Source:* National Center for Missing and Exploited Children, 1995.)

Speaking of Development

Kathryn C. Montgomery, Media Educator

Born:	1947
Education:	California State University at Los Angles, B.A. in American studies and M.A. in mass communications University of California at Los Angeles, Ph.D. in film and television
Position:	Cofounder and president of the Center for Media Education
Home:	Washington, D.C.

The Internet is being touted as one of the great frontiers of high technology, and some predict it will change our lives completely. But the currently untamed medium is also being regarded with caution, especially by those who are watching its effects on children.

Kathryn Montgomery, president of the Center for Media Education in Washington, D.C., has been examining the use of the Internet by companies that target their products toward children.

"At precisely the time when this new medium is emerging, children have become a highly desirable target for advertisers," says Montgomery, who with Shelley Pasnik conducted and wrote about a 1996 study on the subject, entitled "Web of Deception."

"The Internet differs from television in the way children relate to it," Montgomery adds. "On-line services and computers are much more personal than television, parents can't monitor them as easily, and they are interactive. The child can actually enter into a relationship with the computer.

just because children are in the supposed safety of their own rooms, logged on to home computers, they are truly safe. (For a list of on-line safety rules, see Table 10-1).

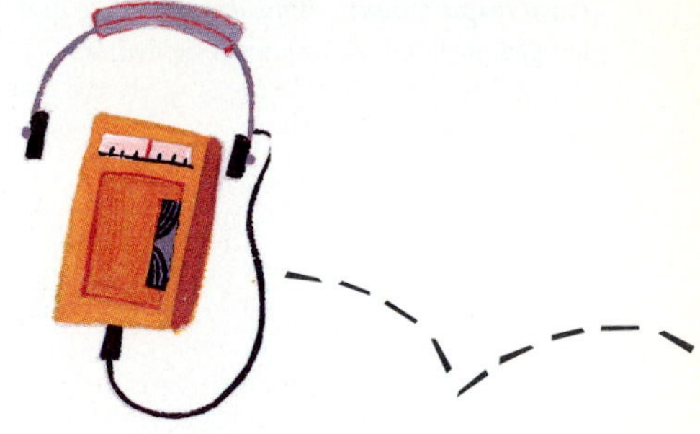

Review and Rethink

REVIEW

- School-age children experience continuing improvement in gross motor skills. Gross motor performance differences that tend to favor boys may be due in large part to cultural norms that have limited girls' motivation and expectations.
- Fine motor skills improve steadily during middle childhood, with children developing nearly adult levels of coordination by the end of the period. This is facilitated by increases in myelin, the protective insulation around nerve cells.
- Physical competence plays a large part in school-age children's lives and social success. Boys especially experience social benefits from physical competence that are not shared by less competent boys (or by physically competent girls).
- Threats to safety in middle childhood include accidents that can result from increased independence and mobility and, increasingly, children's unsupervised access to the confusing and stimulating world of cyberspace.

"Some of the factors that have made children a prime target for advertisers are the very same social and economic trends that many people are concerned about, such as children growing up in single-parent households or households in which both parents work outside the home."

"There are completely new forms of advertising on-line—a whole new set of advertising practices that are part of some very innovative development work. But serious questions arise when children are the targets."

"Some of the factors that have made children a prime target for advertisers are the very same social and economic trends that many people are concerned about, such as children growing up in single-parent households or households in which both parents work outside the home. In some of these cases, children have become highly involved in shopping, and hence their appeal to advertisers."

Montgomery notes that the advertising industry makes use of the expertise of anthropologists and psychologists to become aware of the developing stages of children and to capture their attention. "There are completely new forms of advertising on-line—a whole new set of advertising practices that are part of some very innovative development work. But serious questions arise when children are the targets," she says. "In broadcast television, limits have been set on advertising, especially for children, but on-line you can have commercials in which kids can easily become involved—and stay involved forever."

Following the release of the "Web of Deception" study and the publicity that followed, some major companies decided to review their policies regarding on-line advertising directed to children. But, Montgomery says, more still must be done to protect children.

"We would like to work to educate health professionals and educators about the problem, and we have filed petitions with the Federal Communications Commission to investigate the entire issue," Montgomery says. "Our goal is not to ban advertising, but to see it regulated. We also would like to urge the industry to develop its own guidelines."

RETHINK

- How would you design an experiment to examine the roots of gender differences in gross motor skills? What impediments would there be to conducting such an experiment?
- What societal changes would have to occur for physically competent women to experience the same desirability as physically competent men? Are such changes occurring? Would this be a good thing?
- How can the ideas of fun and competition be reconciled in sports? Can organized competitive sports be fun for both physically more competent and less competent individuals? Why or why not?
- Do you think using blocking software or computer chips to screen potentially offensive content on the Internet is a practical idea? A good idea? Are such controls the best way to keep children safe in cyberspace?
- What advice would you give parents regarding modeling and competition to encourage their children to engage in physical exercise?

visual impairment *difficulties in seeing that may include blindness or partial sightedness*

CHILDREN WITH SPECIAL NEEDS

What would it be like if every letter that is underlined in this sentence appeared to you to be reversed? To children with one form of learning disability, called dyslexia, this is in fact the case every time they try to read or write.

Dyslexia is just one of several types of special needs that school-age children can have. Although every child has different specific capabilities, children with *special needs* differ significantly from typical children in terms of physical attributes or learning abilities. Furthermore, their needs present major challenges for both care providers and teachers.

We turn now to the most prevalent exceptionalities that affect children of normal intelligence. We'll consider sensory difficulties, learning disabilities, and attention-deficit disorders. (The special needs of children who are significantly below and above average in intelligence will be discussed in Chapter 11.)

SENSORY DIFFICULTIES: VISUAL, AUDITORY, AND SPEECH PROBLEMS

Anyone who has temporarily lost eyeglasses or a contact lens has had a glimpse of how difficult even basic, everyday tasks must be for those with sensory impairments. To function with less than typical vision, hearing, or speech can be a tremendous challenge (Wang, Reynolds, & Walberg, 1996).

Auditory impairments can produce both academic and social difficulties, and they may lead to speech difficulties.

Visual impairment, difficulties in seeing that may include blindness or partial sightedness, can be considered in either a legal or an educational sense. The definition of legal impairment is quite straightforward: Blindness is visual acuity of less than 20/200 after correction (meaning the inability to see even at 20 feet what a typical person can see at 200 feet), while *partial sightedness* is visual acuity of less than 20/70 after correction.

Even when the legal limits of impairment are not reached, however, visual impairment in an educational sense can be present. For one thing, the legal criterion pertains solely to distance vision, while most educational tasks require close-up vision. In addition, the legal definition does not consider abilities in the perception of color, depth, and light—all of which might influence a student's educational success. About 1 student in 1,000 requires special education services relating to a visual impairment.

Although most severe visual problems are identified fairly early, it sometimes happens that an impairment goes undetected. Furthermore, visual problems can emerge gradually as children develop physiologically and changes occur in the visual apparatus of the eye. Parents must be aware of the signals of visual problems in their children. Frequent eye irritation (redness, sties, or infection); continual blinking and facial contortions when reading; holding reading material unusually close to the face; difficulty in writing; and frequent headaches, dizziness, or burning eyes are some of the signs of visual problems.

Another relatively frequent special need relates to **auditory impairment,** involving the loss of hearing or some aspect of hearing. Not only do auditory impairments cause academic problems, but they can produce social difficulties as well, since considerable peer interaction takes place through informal conversation. Hearing loss, which affects some 1 to 2 percent of the school-age population, is not simply a matter of not hearing enough. Rather, auditory problems can vary along a number of dimensions (U.S. Department of Education, 1987).

In some cases of hearing loss, only a limited range of frequencies, or pitches, is affected. For example, the loss may be great at pitches in the normal speech range yet quite minor in other frequencies, such as those of very high or low sounds. In addition, a child may require different levels of amplification at different frequencies. For this reason, a hearing aid that indiscriminately amplifies all frequencies equally may be ineffective.

The age of onset of a hearing loss is critical in determining the degree to which a child can adapt to the impairment. If the loss of hearing occurs in infancy, the effects will probably be much more severe than if it occurs after the age of 3. The reason relates to the critical role that hearing plays in the development of language. Children who have had little or no exposure to the sound of language are unable to understand or produce oral language themselves. On the other hand, loss of hearing after a child has learned language will not have serious consequences for subsequent linguistic development.

Severe and early loss of hearing is also associated with difficulties in abstract thinking. Because hearing-impaired children may have limited exposure to language, abstract concepts that can be understood fully only through the use of language may be less well understood than concrete concepts that can be illustrated visually (Fischgrund, 1996; Hewett & Forness, 1974).

Auditory difficulties are sometimes accompanied by speech impairments. A speech impairment is one of the most public types of exceptionality: Every time the child speaks aloud, the impairment is obvious to listeners. In fact, the definition of **speech impairment** suggests that speech is impaired when it deviates so much from the speech of others that it calls attention to itself, interferes with communication, or produces maladjustment in the speaker (Van Riper, 1972). In other words, if a child's speech sounds impaired, it probably is. Speech impairments are present in around 3 to 5 percent of the school-age population (U.S. Department of Education, 1987).

Stuttering, which entails substantial disruption in the rhythm and fluency of speech, is the most common speech impairment. Despite a great deal of research on the topic, no single cause has been identified. Although the disfluencies of stuttering are relatively normal in young children—and occasionally occur in normal adults—chronic stuttering can be a severe problem. Not only does stuttering hinder communication, but it also can produce embarrassment and stress in children, who may become inhibited from conversing with others and speaking aloud in class.

Parents and teachers can adopt several strategies for dealing with stuttering. For starters, attention should not be drawn to the stuttering. Furthermore, children should be given sufficient time to finish what they begin to say, no matter how protracted the statement becomes. It does not help stutterers to finish their sentences for them or otherwise correct their speech. Finally, stuttering can be helped through speech therapy (Onslow, 1992).

auditory impairment *a special need that involves the loss of hearing or some aspect of hearing*

speech impairment *speech that deviates so much from the speech of others that it calls attention to itself, interferes with communication, or produces maladjustment in the speaker*

stuttering *substantial disruption in the rhythm and fluency of speech; the most common speech impairment*

LEARNING DISABILITIES: DISCREPANCIES BETWEEN ACHIEVEMENT AND CAPACITY TO LEARN

learning disabilities *difficulties in the acquisition and use of listening, speaking, reading, writing, reasoning, or mathematical abilities*

attention-deficit hyperactivity disorder (ADHD) *a learning disability marked by inattention, impulsiveness, a low tolerance for frustration, and a great deal of inappropriate activity*

Some 2.3 million school-age children in the United States are officially labeled as having learning disabilities. **Learning disabilities** are characterized by difficulties in the acquisition and use of listening, speaking, reading, writing, reasoning, or mathematical abilities. A somewhat ill-defined, grab-bag category, learning disabilities are diagnosed when there is a discrepancy between children's actual academic performance and their apparent potential to learn (Lyon, 1996; National Joint Committee on Learning Disabilities, 1989; Roush, 1995; Wong, 1996).

Such a broad definition encompasses a wide and heterogeneous variety of difficulties. For instance, some children suffer from *dyslexia,* a reading disability that can result in the reversal of letters during reading and writing, confusion between left and right, and difficulties in spelling. Although the causes of dyslexia are unknown, increasing evidence suggests that visual information may reach the brain in an improper sequence, producing the kinds of reversals and confusions typical of the disability.

The causes of learning disabilities are not well understood. Although they are generally attributed to some form of brain dysfunction, probably due to genetic factors, some experts suggest that they are produced by such environmental causes as poor early nutrition or allergies (Mercer, 1992).

ATTENTION-DEFICIT HYPERACTIVITY DISORDER

Attention-deficit hyperactivity disorder, or **ADHD,** is marked by inattention, impulsiveness, a low tolerance for frustration, and generally a great deal of inappropriate activity. Although all children show such traits some of the time, for those diagnosed with ADHD such behavior is common and interferes with their home and school functioning (Barkley, 1995; Sandberg, 1996).

Although it is hard to know how many children have the disorder, most estimates put the number at from 3 to 5 percent of the school-age population, or some 3.5 million Americans under the age of 18. What is clear is that a child who has ADHD is likely to have difficulty staying on task and working toward goals, have limited self-control, be easily distracted, and—above all—be physically active. An ADHD child can be a whirlwind of activity, exhausting the energy and patience of parents, teachers, and even peers (Baker, 1994; Wender, 1995; Barkley, 1997).

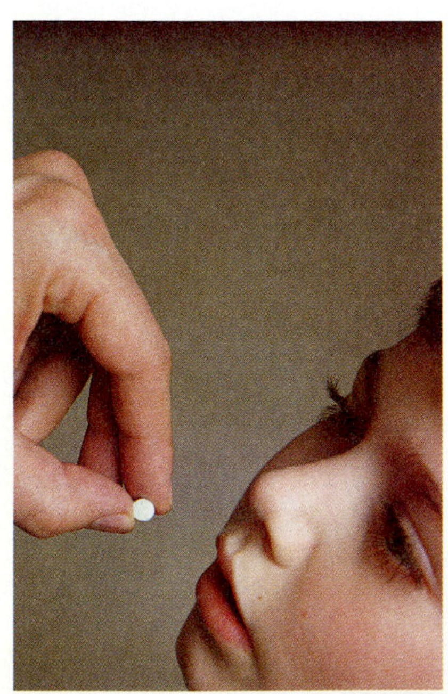

For some children, taking drugs for attention-deficit hyperactivity disorder is a routine occurrence.

The treatment of children with ADHD has been a source of considerable controversy. Because it has been found that doses of Ritalin or Dexadrine (which, paradoxically, are stimulants) reduce activity levels in hyperactive children, many physicians routinely prescribe drug treatment (Rief, 1995).

Although in many cases such drugs are effective in increasing attention span and compliance, in some cases the side effects are considerable, and the long-term health consequences of this treatment are unclear. Furthermore, although in the short run drugs often help scholastic performance (Weber, Frankenberger, & Heilman, 1992), the long-term evidence for continuing improvement is mixed. In fact, some studies suggest that after a few years, children treated with drugs do not perform academically any better than untreated children (McDaniel, 1986).

What are the most common signs of ADHD? Although it is often difficult to distinguish between children who simply have a high level of activity and those with ADHD, some of the most common symptoms include persistent difficulty in finishing tasks, following instructions, and organizing work; inability to watch an entire television program; frequent interruption of others; and a tendency to jump into a task before hearing all the instructions (see Table 10-2). If a child is suspected of having ADHD, he or she should be evaluated by a specialist.

TABLE 10-2

IS THIS A CASE OF ADHD?
SYMPTOMS OF ATTENTION-DEFICIT HYPERACTIVITY DISORDER

If eight of the following statements describe a child—or you as a child—it is reasonable to suspect attention-deficit hyperactivity disorder. Of course, examination by a specialist is necessary before a diagnosis can be made.

1. Often fidgets or squirms in seat.
2. Has difficulty remaining seated.
3. Is easily distracted.
4. Has difficulty awaiting turn in groups.
5. Often blurts out answers to questions.
6. Has difficulty following instructions.
7. Has difficulty sustaining attention to tasks.
8. Often shifts from one uncompleted activity to another.
9. Has difficulty playing quietly.
10. Often talks excessively.
11. Often interrupts or intrudes on others.
12. Often does not seem to listen.
13. Often loses things necessary for tasks.
14. Often engages in physically dangerous activities without considering consequences.

(*Source:* Wallis, 1994, p. 49.)

Developmental Diversity

Mainstreaming Children with Special Needs

Are exceptional children best served by providing specialized services that separate them from their peers who do not have special needs, or do they benefit more from being integrated with their peers to the fullest extent?

If you had asked that question 2 decades ago, the answer would have been quick and simple: Exceptional children were assumed to do best when removed from their regular classes and placed in a class taught by a special needs teacher. Such classes—which often accommodated a hodgepodge of afflictions, including emotional difficulties, severe reading problems, and physical disabilities such as multiple sclerosis—traditionally kept students segregated and apart from the regular educational process.

However, all that changed in 1975, when Congress passed Public Law 94–142, the Education for All Handicapped Children Act. The intent of the law—an intent that has been largely realized—was to ensure that children with special needs received a full education in the **least restrictive environment,** the setting most similar to that of children without special needs.

In practice, the law has meant that children with special needs must be integrated into regular classrooms and regular activities to the greatest extent possible, as long as doing so is educationally beneficial. Children are to be isolated from the regular classroom only for those subjects that are specifically affected by their exceptionality; for all other subjects they are to be taught with nonexceptional children in regular classrooms. Of course, some children with severe handicaps still need a mostly or entirely separate education, depending on

least restrictive environment *the educational setting that is most similar to that of children without special needs* the extent of their condition. But the goal of the law is to integrate exceptional children and typical children to the fullest extent possible (Yell, 1995).

mainstreaming *an educational approach in which exceptional children are integrated as much as possible into the traditional educational system and are provided with a broad range of educational alternatives*

This educational approach to special education, designed to end the segregation of exceptional students to the greatest extent feasible, has come to be called mainstreaming. In **mainstreaming,** exceptional children are integrated as much as possible into the traditional educational system and are provided with a broad range of educational alternatives (Hocutt, 1996).

In many respects, the introduction of mainstreaming—while clearly increasing the complexity of classroom teaching—was a reaction to failures of traditional special education. For one thing, there was little research support for the advisability of special education for exceptional students. Research that examined such factors as academic achievement, self-concept, social adjustment, and personality development generally failed to discern any advantages for special needs children placed in special, as opposed to regular, education classes (Dunn, 1968; M. C. Wang, Peverly, & Catalano, 1987). Furthermore, systems that compel minorities to be educated separately from majorities historically tend to be less effective—as an examination of schools that were once segregated on the basis of race clearly demonstrates (Wang et al., 1996).

An additional important argument in favor of mainstreaming concerns the issue of labeling students into such categories as "mentally deficient," "emotionally disturbed," or a host of other classifications. Labeling students, which is frequently done with little precision, often produces negative expectations regarding the students' capabilities, which in turn can lead to behavior in the students and others that actually causes the expectations to be fulfilled. Furthermore, being labeled negatively can lead to a decrease in peer acceptance and self-concept. For example, research has found that a behavior is viewed more negatively when it is carried out by a student labeled "mentally retarded" than when the same behavior is performed by a presumably "normal" student (Archibald, 1974; Cook & Wollersheim, 1976; Walker et al., 1989).

Ultimately, though, the most compelling argument in favor of mainstreaming is philosophical: Because special needs students must ultimately function in a normal environment, greater experience with their peers ought to enhance their integration into society, as well as positively affect their learning. Mainstreaming, then, provides a mechanism to equalize the opportunities available to all children. The ultimate objective of mainstreaming is to ensure that all persons, regardless of ability or disability, will have—to the greatest extent possible—opportunities to choose their goals on the basis of a full education, enabling them to obtain a fair share of life's rewards (Fuchs & Fuchs, 1994).

Does the reality of mainstreaming live up to its promise? To some extent the benefits extolled by proponents have been realized, at least where mainstreaming is done with care and classroom teachers receive substantial support. Furthermore, mainstreaming provides important benefits not only for exceptional children, but for typical children as well. For instance, typical children in mainstreamed classes come to understand the nature of others' disabilities better and, at least potentially, come to hold more positive attitudes toward persons with disabilities. In short, everyone—typical and exceptional children alike—can potentially benefit from mainstreaming (Daly & Feldman, 1994; Kauffman, 1993; Scruggs & Mastropieri, 1994).

The proven benefits of mainstreaming have led some professionals to promote an alternative educational model known as full inclusion. *Full inclusion* is the integration of all students, even those with the most severe disabilities, into regular classes. In such a system, separate special education programs would cease to operate. Full inclusion is controversial, and it remains to be seen how widespread such a practice will become (Hocutt, 1996; Siegel, 1996).

Review and Rethink

REVIEW

- Visual impairments, which can escape immediate detection, can affect many aspects of life, including education. Auditory impairments can affect the development of language (if they arise early in life), learning, and social relationships.
- Speech impairments, which sometimes but not always accompany hearing difficulties, can impede effective oral communication and have serious social consequences.
- Learning disabilities, a term that includes difficulties in the acquisition and use of listening, speaking, reading, writing, reasoning, or mathematical abilities, seem to be attributable to some form of brain dysfunction that may have either genetic or environmental causes.
- Attention-deficit hyperactivity disorder (ADHD), marked by inattention, impulsiveness, a low tolerance for frustration, and very high activity levels, affects from 3 to 5 percent of the school-age population. The most effective treatment, which involves drugs, is highly controversial.
- Mainstreaming—accommodating students with and without exceptionalities in the same classrooms—can benefit both sorts of children by emphasizing strengths instead of weaknesses and promoting social interaction skills.

RETHINK

- Do you think early hearing loss affects the ability to learn to read? How?
- If hearing is associated with abstract thinking, how do people who were born deaf think? Would the early acquisition of a signed language such as ASL affect this process?
- In general, are social attitudes toward people with speech impairments supportive? How would you advise children to treat a child with a noticeable speech impairment?
- Before accepting drug treatment for a child with ADHD, what questions should be answered about the child and the drugs?
- What are the advantages of mainstreaming? What challenges does it present? Are there situations in which you would not support mainstreaming?

LOOKING BACK

In what ways do children grow during the school years, and what factors influence their growth?

1. The middle childhood years are characterized by slow and steady growth, with children gaining, on average, about 5 to 7 pounds per year and 2 to 3 inches. Weight is redistributed as baby fat disappears.
2. In part, growth is genetically determined, but societal factors such as affluence, dietary habits, nutrition, and disease also contribute significantly.
3. Growth can be artificially induced by hormones such as Protropin, but the use of drugs for this purpose raises ethical questions. Use of artificial growth hormones should be limited to cases where levels of natural growth hormone are below normal.

What are the nutritional needs of school-age children, and what are some causes and effects of improper nutrition?

4. Adequate nutrition is important because of its many effects on children in the school years. In addition to enjoying purely physical benefits, well-nourished children generally show better social and emotional functioning and cognitive performance.

5. Obesity can be a problem in middle childhood. Although partially influenced by genetic factors, obesity also is associated with excessive parental interference with children's development of internal controls over eating, overindulgence in sedentary activities such as television viewing, and lack of physical exercise.

What sorts of health threats do school-age children face?

6. The health of children in the school years is generally good, and few health hazards arise. However, the incidence of some diseases that affect children, such as asthma, is on the rise, probably due to environmental conditions relating to airborne asthma triggers.

7. School-age children can suffer from psychological disorders as well as physical ones, including childhood depression. Because childhood depression can lead to adult mood disorders or even to suicide, it should be taken seriously and treated either by psychological counseling or through careful use of drug therapies.

What are the characteristics of motor development during middle childhood, and what advantages do improved physical skills bring?

8. During the middle childhood years, great improvements occur in gross motor skills in both boys and girls. Cultural expectations, rather than actual genetic differences, probably underlie most gross motor skill differences between boys and girls.

9. Fine motor skills also develop rapidly, with coordination achieving nearly adult levels by the end of the period. This is largely attributable to increases in the level of myelin in the brain.

10. Physical competence is important for a number of reasons, some of which relate to self-esteem and confidence. Physical competence also brings social benefits during this period, especially for males.

11. Because of their importance in school-age children's lives, physical skills should be encouraged. Children can be helped to place emphasis less on competition and more on achieving physical fitness, learning physical skills, and becoming comfortable with their bodies.

What safety threats affect school-age children, and what can be done about them?

12. Threats to safety in middle childhood relate mainly to children's increasing independence and mobility. Accidents account for most injuries, especially those related to automobiles, other "vehicles" (such as bicycles, skateboards, and roller-blades), and sports. In most cases, the use of proper protective gear (for example, seat belts or helmets) could greatly reduce injuries.

13. An emerging area of potential danger for children is cyberspace. Unsupervised access to the Internet and the World Wide Web can induce children to explore offensive areas and come into contact with people who might take advantage of them. Children should be given both supervision and appropriate guidance on using these resources safely.

What sorts of special needs manifest themselves in the middle childhood years, and how can they be met?

14. Children with special needs represent a significant proportion of the population. Developmental difficulties can relate to such areas as sensation, learning, and attention.

Because they can lead to academic and social problems, these needs must be met with sensitivity and appropriate assistance.

15. Visual impairments come in many forms and can affect a student's chances of educational success. Because visual difficulties tend to emerge gradually as children develop and can therefore go unnoticed, caregivers and teachers should be aware of the signals of such difficulties.

16. Auditory impairments can also be hard to detect and can bring serious consequences. Because conversation is a primary mode of peer interaction, hearing loss can negatively affect social development. If it comes early enough, hearing loss can even interfere with the development of oral language and cognitive skills.

17. Speech impairments, which are often associated with hearing impairments, can also interfere with communication and social development. Caregivers and teachers should adopt strategies for dealing with speech impairments and for helping others deal with them as well.

18. Learning disabilities, characterized by difficulties in the acquisition and use of listening, speaking, reading, writing, reasoning, or mathematical abilities, affect a sizable proportion of the population. Although the causes of learning disabilities are not well understood, some form of brain dysfunction, which may have genetic or environmental roots, seems to be involved.

19. Children with attention-deficit hyperactivity disorder exhibit another form of special need. ADHD is characterized by inattention, impulsiveness, failure to complete tasks, lack of organization, and excessive amounts of uncontrollable activity. Treatment of ADHD by drugs is highly controversial because of unwanted side effects and doubts about long-term consequences.

20. Today's thinking focuses on placing children with exceptionalities in the least restrictive environment, typically the regular classroom. If done properly, this strategy—called mainstreaming—can benefit all students by permitting them to focus on strengths rather than weaknesses and gain useful skills of social interaction.

Key Terms and Concepts

asthma (p. 325)
visual impairment (p. 334)
auditory impairment (p. 335)
speech impairment (p. 335)
stuttering (p. 335)
learning disabilities (p. 336)
attention-deficit hyperactivity disorder (ADHD) (p. 336)
least restrictive environment (p. 337)
mainstreaming (p. 338)

CHAPTER 11

MIDDLE CHILDHOOD

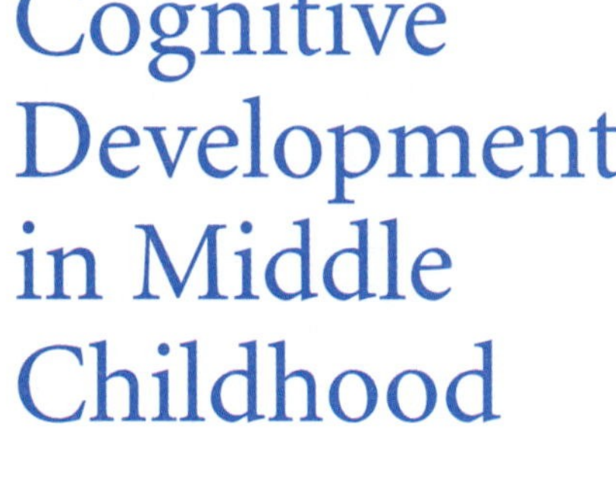

Cognitive Development in Middle Childhood

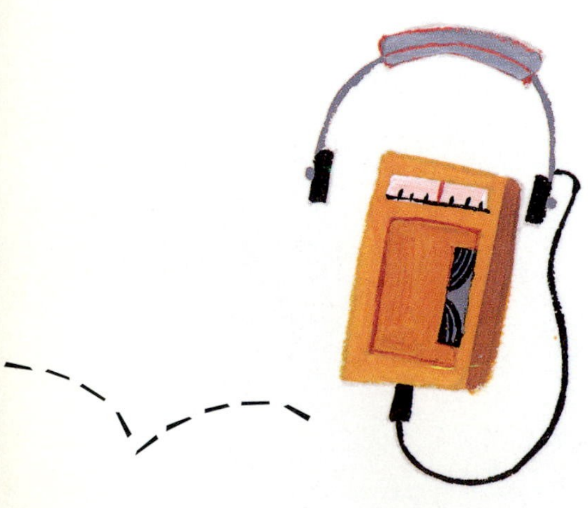

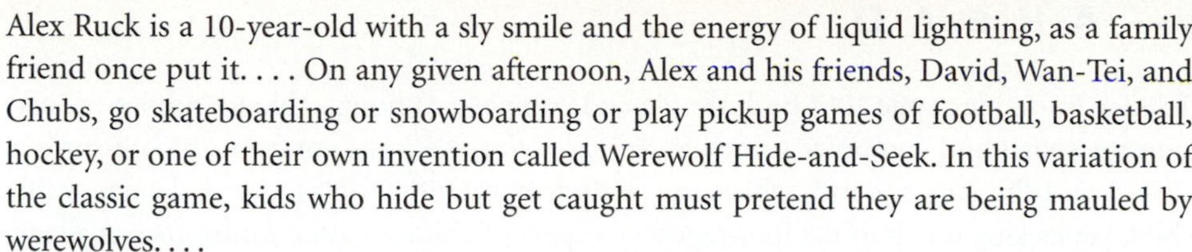

PROLOGUE

ALEX RUCK

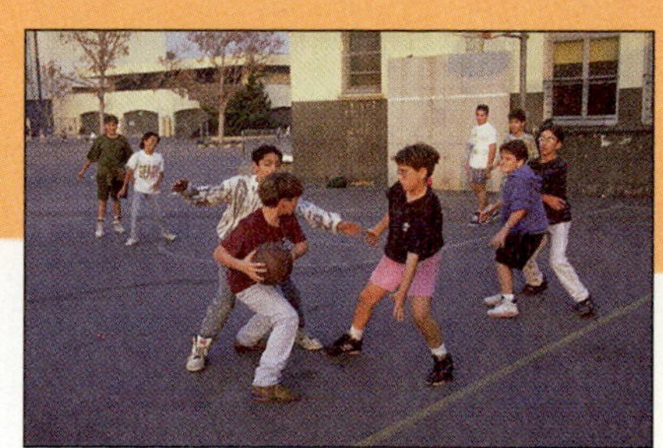

Alex Ruck is a 10-year-old with a sly smile and the energy of liquid lightning, as a family friend once put it. . . . On any given afternoon, Alex and his friends, David, Wan-Tei, and Chubs, go skateboarding or snowboarding or play pickup games of football, basketball, hockey, or one of their own invention called Werewolf Hide-and-Seek. In this variation of the classic game, kids who hide but get caught must pretend they are being mauled by werewolves. . . .

Like many 10-year-olds, Alex plays Little League baseball every spring, usually as a shortstop or pitcher. He's just an "OK" player, he says. When he reads—usually before going to bed at 9 P.M.—he favors books like *Fangs of Evil* or *Zombie Camp*. He dresses in baggy T-shirts, sweats, and flannel shirts, along with a well-worn pair of Converse high tops. . . .

School is getting tough for Alex—he usually finishes his 6-hour school day with an hour or two of homework ahead. Sports are becoming more competitive, too. He's on a community-center swim team and practices three times a week, all year round; his coaches say he swims better than most kids in his age group.

Alex's daily school-bus ride takes him from his stable, mostly white neighborhood to a public magnet school, East Hills International Studies Academy, in the middle of a housing project. It is a few miles and half a world from his house. East Hills is about 60 percent black, and has students from Russia, Africa, China, and the Middle East. Both privileged and poor families send their kids to East Hills; about 70 percent of its student body is bused in. Alex mixes with a wide variety of kids in classes and at lunch. The school has an aggressive mediation program that defuses fights before they get out of control; serious arguments break out very rarely. The children find common ground in TV shows, new computer games, or hated teachers.

There are harsher truths, too. Two bodies have been found within several hundred yards of the school in the past 2 years. Last year, when a tree branch fell on Alex's school bus, the children hit the floor screaming: They thought it was a gunshot. Alex won't wear a red, black, and white Starter jacket he got last year to school because, he says, those are gang colors. "I don't want to get shot," he explains matter-of-factly. . . .

He is generally attentive and quiet in class, sometimes placing his head on the desk as he listens. One recent day starts in science and takes him through two math classes, where Alex struggles through a test on fractions and works some negative numbers on a calculator.

In reading class, the kids are excited to learn they will hear a narrative version of *Hamlet,* read by their teacher, Carol Beavers, who has been telling them the stories of Shakespeare this year. "All right, Hamlet!" one student yells. But the narrative is very literal, summarizing the stage actions as well as the story. Some children listen closely, but others seem to lose track of the story. Ms. Beavers admits some of her pupils probably forget what they heard the minute they walk out the door. "But my objective is to foster an interest, to try to get them to understand the plot," she says. "I just want to lay a groundwork."

In science, Alex studies birds on a computer program, and late in the day he appalls some girls by balancing his bubble gum on his nose.

"That's disgusting," one of them snipes.

Alex smiles. . . . (M. Murray, 1995, pp. B1–B2)

LOOKING AHEAD

To Alex Ruck, life at age 10 is both simple and complex. Although able to indulge his passion for sports and computer games, at the same time he must confront the pressures of school and the larger world, which can include substantial violence and danger. Still a child, yet lacking much of the innocence we expect of children, Alex confronts a challenging world—one that will tax his abilities to the fullest extent.

In this chapter, we consider the cognitive advances made by children during middle childhood. After beginning with Piaget's explanation for intellectual development, we turn to information-processing approaches. We discuss the development of memory, as well as how memory can be improved.

Next, we turn to the important strides that occur in language development during the preschool years. We focus on increases in linguistic skill, as well as on the consequences of bilingualism, the use of more than one language to communicate.

We then discuss schooling and the ways in which society transmits knowledge, beliefs, values, and wisdom to a new generation. We consider such topics as how children explain their academic performance and how teachers' expectations can affect student achievement.

Finally, the chapter ends by focusing on intelligence. It highlights what developmentalists mean when they speak of intelligence, how intelligence is related to school success, and the ways in which children differ from one another in terms of intelligence.

In sum, after reading this chapter, you will be able to answer the following questions:

- In what ways do children develop cognitively during the years of middle childhood?
- How does language develop during the middle childhood period, and what special circumstances pertain to children for whom English is not the first language?
- What trends are affecting schooling worldwide and in the United States?
- How do subjective interpretations of successes and failures, by oneself and by others, contribute to school outcomes?
- How can intelligence be measured, what are some issues in intelligence testing, and how are children who fall outside the normal range of intelligence educated?

INTELLECTUAL AND LANGUAGE DEVELOPMENT

Jared's parents were delighted when he came home from kindergarten one day and explained that he had learned why the sky is blue. He talked about the earth's atmosphere—although he didn't pronounce the word correctly—and how tiny bits of moisture in the air reflect the sunlight. Although his explanation had rough edges (he couldn't quite grasp what the "atmosphere" was), he still had the general idea, and that, his parents felt, was quite an achievement for their 5-year-old.

***

Fast-forward 6 years. Jared, now 11, had already spent an hour laboring over his evening's homework. After completing a two-page worksheet on multiplying and dividing fractions, he had begun work on his U.S. Constitution project. He was taking notes for his report, which would explain what political factions had been involved in the writing of the document and how the Constitution had been amended since its creation.

Jared, of course, is not alone in having made vast intellectual advances during his middle childhood. In this period, cognitive abilities broaden, and children become increasingly able to understand and master complex skills. At the same time, though, their thinking is still not fully adultlike.

What are the advances, and the limitations, in thinking during childhood? Several perspectives provide us with an understanding of what goes on cognitively during middle childhood.

concrete operational stage *the period of cognitive development between 7 and 12 years of age, which is characterized by the active, and appropriate, use of logic*

decentering *the ability to take multiple aspects of a situation into account*

Piagetian Approaches to Cognitive Development: The Rise of Concrete Operational Thought

Let's return for a moment to Jean Piaget's view of the preschooler, which we considered in Chapter 8. From Piaget's perspective, the preschooler thinks *preoperationally.* This type of thinking is largely egocentric, and preoperational children lack the ability to use *operations*—organized, formal, logical mental processes.

Concrete Operational Thought. All this changes, according to Piaget, during the concrete operational period, which broadly coincides with the elementary school years. The **concrete operational stage,** which occurs between 7 and 12 years of age, is characterized by the active, and appropriate, use of logic. Concrete operational thought involves applying *logical operations* to concrete problems. For instance, when children in the concrete operational stage are confronted with a conservation problem (such as determining whether the amount of liquid poured from one container to another container of a different shape stays the same), they use cognitive and logical processes to answer, no longer being influenced solely by appearance. Consequently, they easily—and correctly—solve conservation problems. Because they are less egocentric, they can take multiple aspects of a situation into account, an ability known as **decentering.**

The shift from preoperational thought to concrete operational thought does not happen overnight, of course. During the 2 years before children move firmly into the concrete operational period, they shift back and forth between preoperational and concrete operational thinking. For instance, they typically pass through a period when they can answer conservation problems correctly but can't articulate why they did so. When asked to explain the reasoning behind their answers, they may respond with an unenlightening, "Because."

However, once concrete operational thinking is fully engaged, children show several cognitive advances. For instance, they attain the concept of *reversibility,* which is the notion that processes that transform a stimulus can be reversed, returning it to its original form. Grasping reversibility permits children to understand that a ball of clay that has been

Cognitive development makes substantial advances during middle childhood.

squeezed into a long, snakelike rope can be returned to its original state. More abstractly, it allows school-age children to understand that if 3 + 5 equals 8, then 5 + 3 also equals 8—and, later during the period, that 8 – 3 equals 5.

In addition, the ability to use concrete operations permits children to understand the concepts of identity and compensation. *Identity* is the understanding that despite changes in shape, amount remains the same. *Compensation* is the knowledge that an increase in one dimension (such as length) is canceled out by a decrease in another dimension (such as width).

Concrete operational thinking also permits children to understand such concepts as the relationship between time and speed. For instance, consider the problem shown in Figure 11-1, in which two cars start and finish at the same points in the same amount of time, but travel different routes. Children who are just entering the concrete operational period reason that the cars are traveling at the same speed. However, between the ages of 8 and 10, children begin to draw the right conclusion: that the car traveling the longer route must be moving faster if it arrives at the finish point at the same time as the car traveling the shorter route.

On the other hand, despite the advances that occur during the concrete operational stage, children still experience one critical limitation in their thinking. They remain tied to concrete, physical reality. Furthermore, they are unable to understand truly abstract or hypothetical questions, or ones that involve formal logic.

Piaget in Perspective: Piaget Was Right, Piaget Was Wrong. As we've seen in our prior consideration of Piaget's views in Chapters 5 and 8, researchers following in Piaget's footsteps have found much to cheer about—as well as much to criticize.

Piaget was a virtuoso observer of children, and his many books contain pages of brilliant, careful observations of children at work and play. Furthermore, his theories have powerful educational implications, and many schools employ principles derived from his views to guide the nature and presentation of instructional materials (Flavell, 1985, 1996; Ravitch, 1985; Lourenco & Machado, 1996; Siegler & Ellis, 1996).

In some ways, then, Piaget's approach was quite successful in describing cognitive development. At the same time, though, critics have raised compelling, and seemingly legitimate, grievances about his approach. As we have noted before, many researchers argue that Piaget underestimated children's capabilities, in part because of the limited nature of the mini-experiments he conducted. When a broader array of experimental tasks is used, children show less consistency within stages than Piaget would predict (Siegler, 1994).

Furthermore, Piaget seems to have misjudged the age at which children's cognitive abilities emerge. As might be expected from our earlier discussions of Piaget's stages, in-

FIGURE 11-1

SAMPLE PROBLEM IN CONCRETE OPERATIONAL THINKING

After being told that the two cars traveling Routes 1 and 2 start and end their journeys in the same amount of time, children who are just entering the concrete operational period still reason that the cars are traveling at the same speed. Later, however, they reach the correct conclusion: that the car traveling the longer route must be moving at a higher speed if it starts and ends its journey at the same time as the car traveling the shorter route.

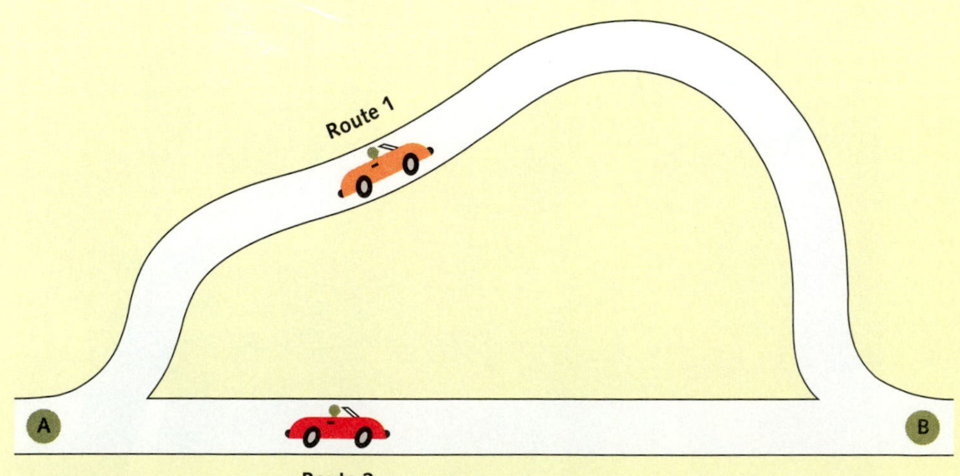

creasing evidence suggests that children's capabilities emerge earlier than Piaget envisioned. Some children show evidence of a form of concrete operational thinking before the age of 7, the time at which Piaget suggested these abilities first appear.

The opposite phenomenon also seems to occur: Cross-cultural research implies that some children never leave the preoperational stage, failing to master conservation and to develop concrete operations. For example, pioneering work by Patricia Greenfield (1966) found that among the Wolof children in Senegal, a West African country, only half of children aged 10 to 13 understood conservation of liquid. Studies in other non-Western areas such as the jungles of New Guinea and Brazil and remote villages in Australia confirmed her findings: When a broad sample of children are studied—children who have had very different experiences from the Western European children on whom Piaget based his theory—not everyone reaches the concrete operational stage (Dasen, 1977). It appears, then, that Piaget's claims that his stages provided a universal description of cognitive development were exaggerated.

On the other hand, we should not entirely dismiss the Piagetian approach. For one thing, sometimes the use of research materials inappropriate to a particular culture has led to an underestimation of the degree to which children from different cultures are actually similar in their cognitive performance. In addition, research has found that when given training in conservation, children in non-Western cultures who do not conserve can readily learn to do so. For instance, in one study, urban Australian children—who develop concrete operations on the same timetable as Piaget suggested—were compared to rural Aborigine children, who typically do not demonstrate an understanding of conservation at the age of 14 (Dasen, Ngini, & Lavallee, 1979). When the rural Aborigine children were given training, they began to conserve in the same way as their urban counterparts, although with a time lag of around 3 years (see Figure 11-2).

Such research suggests that in some ways Piaget may have been more right than wrong: Although school-age children in some cultures may differ from Westerners in the demonstration of certain cognitive skills, it is unlikely that they lack the ability to

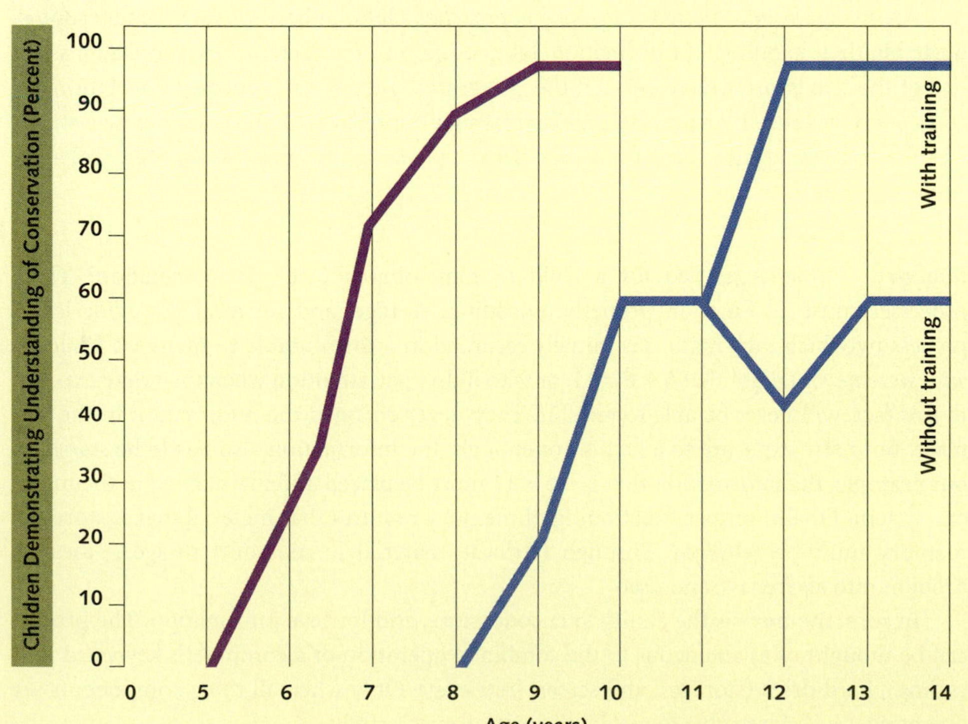

FIGURE 11-2

UNDERSTANDING OF CONSERVATION AMONG URBAN AND ABORIGINAL AUSTRALIAN CHILDREN

Rural Australian Aborigine children trail their urban counterparts in the development of their understanding of conservation, but with training they later catch up. Without training, around half of 14-year-old Aborigines do not have an understanding of conservation.

(*Source:* Adapted from Dasen, Ngini, & Lavallee, 1979.)

Urban Australians

Rural Australian Aborigines

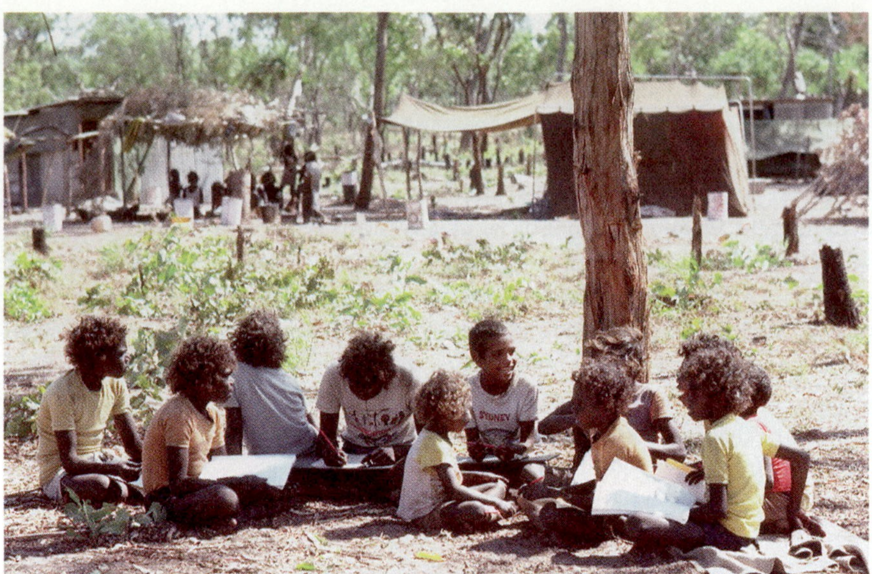

Research conducted in such places as remote areas of Australia shows that, contrary to Piaget's assertion, not everyone reaches the concrete operational stage.

perform concrete operations. Instead, the most probable explanation of the difference is that the non-Western children have had different sorts of experiences from those that permit children in Western societies to perform well on Piagetian measures of conservation and concrete operations. The progress of cognitive development, then, cannot be understood without looking at the nature of a child's culture (Beilin & Pufall, 1992; Jahoda & Lewis, 1988).

INFORMATION PROCESSING IN MIDDLE CHILDHOOD

memory *the process by which information is recorded, stored, and retrieved*

It is a real feat for first-graders to learn basic math tasks, such as addition and subtraction of single-digit numbers, as well as the spelling of simple words such as *dog* and *run.* But by the time they reach the sixth grade, children are able to work with fractions and decimals, and *exhibit* and *residence* are typical spelling words.

According to *information-processing approaches,* children become increasingly sophisticated in their handling of information. Like computers, they can process more data as the size of their memories increases and the "programs" they use to process information become more advanced. As they become increasingly sophisticated, they develop new strategies for processing information and acquiring knowledge (Kuhn, Garcia-Mila, Zohar, & Andersen. 1995).

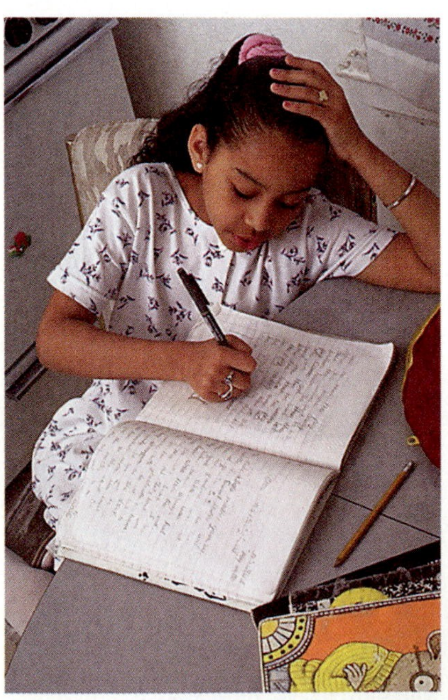

Memory requires three steps: recording, storing, and retrieving material.

Memory. What is needed for a child to remember a piece of information? Three processes must all function properly: encoding, storage, and retrieval. *Encoding* is the process by which information is initially recorded in a form usable to memory. Children who were never taught that 5 + 6 = 11, or who didn't pay attention when they were exposed to this fact, will never be able to recall it. They never encoded the information in the first place. But mere exposure to a fact is not enough; the information also has to be *stored.* In our example, the information that 5 + 6 = 11 must be placed and maintained in the memory system. Finally, proper functioning of memory requires that material that is stored in memory must be *retrieved.* Through retrieval, material in memory storage is located, brought into awareness, and used.

In sum, **memory** is the ability to encode, store, and retrieve information. The process can be thought of as analogous to the combined operation of a computer's keyboard (encoding), hard drive (storage), and screen (retrieval). Only when all three components are operating are children able to recall information successfully.

During middle childhood, short-term memory capacity improves significantly. For instance, children are increasingly able to hear a string of digits ("1-5-6-3-4") and then repeat the string in reverse order ("4-3-6-5-1"). At the start of the preschool period, they can remember and reverse only about two digits; by the beginning of adolescence they can perform the task with as many as six digits. In addition, they use more sophisticated strategies for recalling information, which can be improved with training (Ardila & Rosselli, 1994; Bjorklund, et al., 1994; Halford et al., 1994; Roodenrys, Hulme, & Brown, 1993).

metamemory *an understanding about the processes that underlie memory, which emerges and improves during middle childhood*

Memory capacity may shed light on another issue in cognitive development. Some developmentalists suggest that the difficulty children experience in solving conservation problems just before the preschool period may stem from memory limitations (Siegler & Richards, 1982). They argue that young children simply may not be able to recall all the necessary pieces of information that enter into the correct solution of conservation problems.

Metamemory, an understanding about the processes that underlie memory, also emerges and improves during middle childhood. By the time they enter first grade, children have a general notion of what memory is, and that some people have "good" memories and others "bad" memories (Lewis & Mitchell, 1994; Schneider & Pressley, 1989).

School-age children's understanding of memory becomes more sophisticated as they grow older and increasingly engage in *control strategies*—conscious, intentionally used tactics to improve cognitive processing. For instance, school-age children are aware that rehearsal, the repetition of information, is a useful strategy for improving memory, and they increasingly employ it over the course of middle childhood. Similarly, they progressively make more effort to organize material into coherent patterns, a strategy that permits them to recall it better. For instance, when faced with remembering a list including cups, knives, forks, and plates, older school-age children are more likely to group the items into coherent patterns—cups and plates, forks and knives—than children just entering the school-age years (Howe & O'Sullivan, 1990; Pressley & VanMeter, 1993; Weed, Ryan, & Day, 1990).

Improving Memory. Can children be trained to be more effective in the use of control strategies? The answer is decidedly "yes." School-age children can be taught to apply particular strategies, although such teaching is not a simple matter. For instance, children need to know not only how to use a memory strategy, but also when and where to use it most effectively. But if such information is conveyed by teachers and parents, it can be a genuine boon to children (O'Sullivan, 1993).

Take, for example, an innovative technique called the keyword strategy, which can help students learn the vocabulary of a foreign language, the capitals of the states, or other information in which two sets of words or labels are paired. In the *keyword strategy,* one word is paired with another that sounds like it. For instance, in learning foreign language vocabulary, a foreign word is paired with a common English word that has a similar sound. The English word is the keyword. Thus, to learn the Spanish word for duck (*pato,* pronounced *pot-o*), the keyword might be *pot;* for the Spanish word for horse (*caballo,* pronounced *cob-eye-yo*), the keyword might be *eye.* Once the keyword is chosen, children then form a mental image of the two words interacting with one another. For instance, a student might use an image of a duck taking a bath in a pot to remember the word *pato,* or a horse with bulging eyes to remember the word *caballo* (Pressley, 1987; Pressley & Levin, 1983).

Language Development: Mastering the Mechanics

Listen to two school-age children conversing with one another. Their speech, at least at first hearing, probably doesn't sound too different from that of adults.

In reality, however, the apparent similarity is deceiving. The linguistic sophistication of children—particularly at the start of the school-age period—still requires refinement to reach adult levels of expertise.

For instance, vocabulary continues to grow during the school years. Although children know thousands of words, they continue to add new words to their vocabularies, and at a fairly rapid clip. For instance, the average 6-year-old has a vocabulary of from 8,000 to 14,000 words, and the vocabulary grows by another 5,000 words between the ages of 9 and 11.

Furthermore, school-age children's mastery of grammar improves. For instance, the use of the passive voice (as in "The dog was walked by Lee") is rare during the early school-age years compared with the active-voice ("Lee walked the dog"). Six- and 7-year-olds only infrequently use conditional sentences, such as "If Sarah will set the table, I will wash the dishes." However, over the course of middle childhood, the use of both passive voice and conditional sentences increases. In addition, children's understanding of *syntax,* the rules that indicate how words and phrases can be combined to form sentences, grows during middle childhood.

By the time they reach first grade, most children pronounce words quite accurately. However, certain *phonemes,* units of sound, remain troublesome. For instance, the ability to pronounce *j, v, th,* and *zh* sounds develops later than the ability to pronounce other phonemes.

School-age children also may have difficulty decoding sentences when the meaning depends on *intonation,* or tone of voice. For example, consider the sentence, "George gave a book to Roberto and he gave one to Bill." If the word "he" is emphasized, the meaning is "George gave a book to Roberto and Roberto gave a different book to Bill." But if the intonation emphasizes the word "and," then the meaning changes to "George gave a book to Roberto and George also gave a book to Bill." Such subtleties are not easily sorted out by school-age children (Moshman, Glover, & Bruning, 1987; Woolfolk, 1993).

Children also become more competent during the school years in their use of *pragmatics,* the rules governing the use of language to communicate in a social context. Pragmatics concern children's ability to use appropriate and effective language in a given social setting.

For example, although children are aware of the rules of conversational turn taking at the start of the early childhood period, their use of these rules is sometimes primitive. Consider the following conversation between 6-year-olds Yonnie and Ali:

Yonnie: My dad drives a Fedex truck.

Ali: My sister's name is Molly.

Yonnie: He gets up really early in the morning.

Ali: She wet her bed last night.

Later, however, conversations show more give-and-take, with the second child actually responding to the comments of the first. For instance, this conversation between 11-year-olds Mia and Yan reflects a more sophisticated mastery of pragmatics:

Mia: I don't know what to get Claire for her birthday.

Yan: I'm getting her earrings.

Mia: She already has a lot of jewelry.

Yan: I don't think she has that much.

metalinguistic awareness *an understanding of one's own use of language*

The increase in metalinguistic skills during middle childhood allows children to enter into the give-and-take of conversation more successfully.

Metalinguistic Awareness: Learning Self-control. One of the most significant developments in middle childhood is the increasing metalinguistic awareness of children. **Metalinguistic awareness** is an understanding of one's own use of language. By the time they are 5 or 6, children understand that language is governed by a set of rules. Whereas in the early years these rules are learned and comprehended implicitly, during middle childhood children come to understand them more explicitly (Kemper & Vernooy, 1994).

Metalinguistic awareness helps children achieve comprehension when information is fuzzy or incomplete. For instance, when preschoolers are given ambiguous or unclear information, they rarely ask for clarification, and they tend to blame themselves if they do not understand. By the time they reach the age of 7 or 8, children realize that miscommunication may be due to factors attributable not only to themselves, but to the person communicating with them as well. Consequently, school-age children are more likely to ask for clarification of information that is unclear to them (Beal & Belgrad, 1990; Kemper & Vernooy, 1993).

The growing sophistication of their language also helps school-age children control their behavior. For instance, in one experiment, children were told that they could have one marshmallow treat if they chose to eat one immediately, but two treats if they waited. Most of the children, who ranged in age from 4 to 8, chose to wait, but the strategies they used while waiting differed significantly.

The 4-year-olds often chose to look at the marshmallow treats while waiting, a strategy that was not terribly effective. In contrast, 6- and 8-year-olds used language to help them overcome temptation, although in different ways. The 6-year-olds spoke and sang to themselves, reminding themselves that if they waited they would get more treats in the end. The 8-year-olds focused on aspects of the marshmallow treats that were not related to taste, such as their appearance, which helped them to wait.

BILINGUALISM: SPEAKING IN MANY TONGUES

> For picture day at New York's P.S. 217, a neighborhood elementary school in Brooklyn, the notice to parents was translated into five languages. That was a nice gesture, but insufficient: More than 40 percent of the children are immigrants whose families speak any one of twenty-six languages, ranging from Armenian to Urdu. (Leslie, 1991, p. 56)

From the smallest towns to the biggest cities, the voices with which children speak are changing. In seven states, including Texas, New York, and Colorado, more than a quarter of the students are not native English speakers. In fact, English is the second language for more than 32 million Americans (U.S. Census Bureau, 1993; see Figure 11-3).

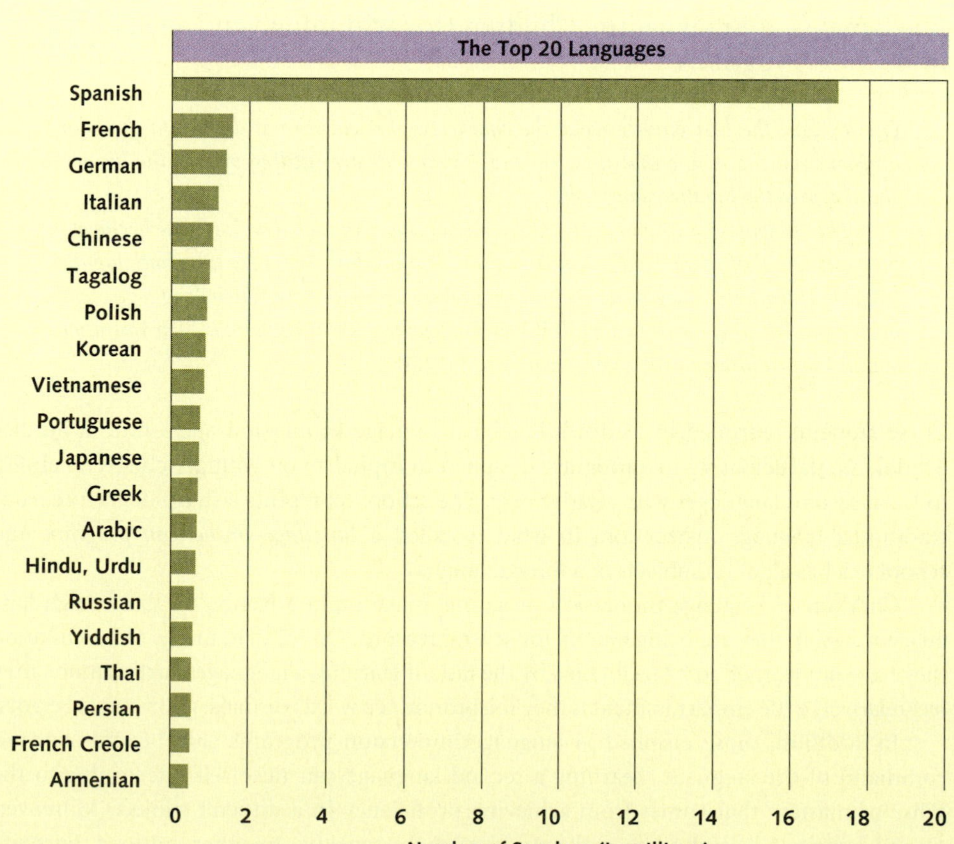

FIGURE 11-3

THE TOP 20 LANGUAGES OTHER THAN ENGLISH SPOKEN IN THE UNITED STATES

The graph shows the number of U.S. residents over the age of 5 who speak a language other than English at home.

(*Source:* U.S. Bureau of the Census, 1993.)

bilingualism *the use of more than one language*

Although **bilingualism** (use of more than one language) presents a challenge to the teachers of children who speak English either haltingly or, initially, not at all, increasing evidence suggests that knowing more than one language may present distinct cognitive advantages.

For instance, speakers of two languages show greater cognitive flexibility. Because they have a wider range of linguistic possibilities to choose from as they assess a situation, they can solve problems with greater creativity and versatility (Romaine, 1994).

Bilingual students often have greater metalinguistic awareness, understanding the rules of language more explicitly. They even may score higher on tests of intelligence, according to some research. For example, one survey of French- and English-speaking schoolchildren in Canada found that bilingual students scored significantly higher on both verbal and nonverbal tests of intelligence than those who spoke only one language (Genesee, 1994; Hakuta & Garcia, 1989; Lambert & Peal, 1972; Ricciardelli, 1992).

Finally, because many linguists contend that universal processes underlie language acquisition, as we noted in Chapter 8, instruction in a native language may enhance instruction in a second language. Consequently, students who enter school speaking no English may be successfully taught in their native languages, while at the same time learning English. There is no evidence that children will be overwhelmed cognitively by simultaneous instruction in their native languages and in English. In fact, as we discuss in the "Directions in Development" box, many educators believe that second-language learning should be a regular part of elementary schooling (Lindholm, 1991; Perozzi & Sanchez, 1992; Yelland, Pollard, & Mercuri, 1993).

Directions in Development

The Benefits of Bilingualism: Children Do Swimmingly in Language-Immersion Programs

> *One by one, the first graders recite the characters the teacher has drawn on the board. Only it's not the ABC's that these 6- and 7-year-olds are rattling off but the hiragana characters of the Japanese language.*
>
> *The students in this inner-city public-school classroom have no Japanese heritage. In fact, almost all of them are African American. But all day long, they hear only Japanese from their teachers. They recite their math problems in Japanese. Their language readers open from left to right as in Japan. When the teacher asks in Japanese, "Do you understand?" the children chirp, "Hai." (Reitman, 1994, B1)*

These students, enrolled in Detroit's Foreign Language Immersion and Cultural Studies School, are participating in a program designed to capitalize on younger children's ability to learn second languages with relative ease. The school represents a sharp departure from traditional language instruction. In what is called a *language immersion program,* the school teaches all of its subjects in a foreign language.

Children in language immersion programs make rapid advances in the foreign language in which they are being taught, for several reasons. One is that, unlike older children, they have not learned to be frightened by the task of learning a language. Furthermore, they feel relatively little embarrassment if they mispronounce words or make grammatical errors.

In addition, those enrolled in language immersion programs gain benefits beyond command of the language. Learning a second language can raise self-esteem due to the sense of mastery that comes from achieving proficiency in a difficult subject. Moreover, second-language learning can make students more sensitive to other cultures. Furthermore, although parents sometimes worry that their children's progress in English will be limited by their concentration on a foreign language, such concerns seem misplaced. Research suggests that children in immersion programs perform as well as their peers, and sometimes even better, in English grammar, reading comprehension, and tests of English vocabulary (Larsen-Freeman & Long, 1991; Bochner, 1996).

In bilingual classrooms, children are taught in both their native language and English.

On the other hand, not all language immersion programs are successful. The most positive results have come from programs in which majority-group children are learning languages that are not spoken by the dominant culture. In contrast, when minority-group children who enter school knowing only a language other than English are immersed in English-only programs, the results are less positive. In fact, children from minority language backgrounds enrolled in English-only programs sometimes perform worse in both English *and* their native languages than same-age peers (Genesee, 1994).

Clearly, the effectiveness of language immersion programs varies widely. Furthermore, such programs are difficult to operate administratively. Finding an adequate number of bilingual teachers can be difficult, and teacher and student attrition can be a problem. Still, the results of participation in immersion programs can be impressive, particularly as knowledge of multiple languages becomes less of a luxury and more of a necessity in today's multicultural world.

The Ebonics Controversy: Is Black English a Separate Language from Standard English?

Although the word "Ebonics" had been in use since the 1970s, few people had heard of it before the Oakland, California, school board declared it a distinctive language. Their decision affirmed that Ebonics—a word derived from a combination of the words "ebony" and "phonics"—was a separate language from English. According to the school board's declaration, Ebonics was a distinct language with roots in Africa, one spoken by many African Americans in inner-cities. The school board ordered that students who spoke Ebonics should receive their initial classroom instruction using Ebonics, and not standard English (Applebome, 1996).

The school board's decision provoked a national controversy, and within a month the board had reversed itself. Members of the board said that they had never meant for students to learn anything other than standard English, and that they had merely wanted recognition for the fact that many African-American students needed instruction to make the leap from Ebonics they spoke at home to standard English.

The controversy raised several issues, none of which have had definitive resolutions. For instance, linguists vary in their views of the legitimacy of Ebonics. According to linguist Dennis Baron, most linguists consider what they call African-American Vernacular English, or sometimes Black English, as a dialect or variety of standard English. Although it has some characteristics that are derived from African languages, it can be understood fairly well by speakers of standard English. Furthermore, certain features of Ebonics, such as the use of different conjugations of the verb "to be" (as in "I be going") are evidence that it is not a separate language, but a dialect of English (Baron, 1997; Sanchez, 1997).

On the other hand, it is also clear that non-standard English operates according to a set of consistent rules and conventions. Although in the past African-American Vernacular English has been treated as a form of speech disability, one that required the intervention of speech pathologists or special-education teachers, today's educators have become more accepting. Probably most educators would argue that non-standard English is not an *inferior* form of language, but one that is *different*—an important distinction. Furthermore, they point out that many words that have their origins in Black English have entered the mainstream of standard English, including "hip," "cool," "chill out," "slick," and "rip-off" (Sanchez, 1997).

Still, the issues revolving around "Ebonics" or "Black English" or "African-American Vernacular English"—or whatever else it may be called—are not likely to go away soon. Not only does the controversy raise important linguistic issues, but it raises many social ones as well.

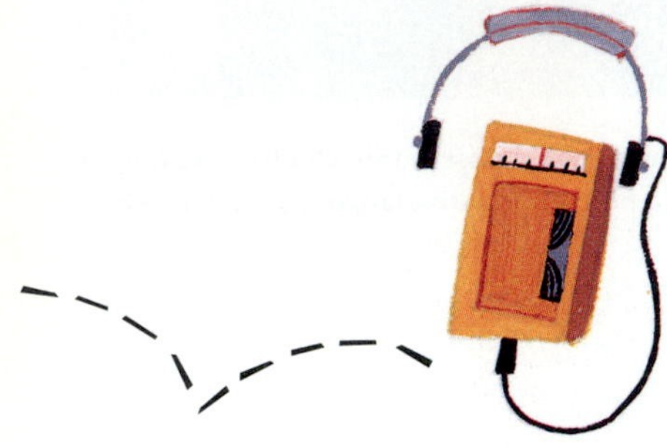

Review and Rethink

REVIEW

- According to Piaget, individuals in middle childhood are in the concrete operational stage of cognitive development, characterized by the application of logical processes to concrete problems and by "decentering," the ability to take multiple aspects of a situation into account.
- Information-processing approaches attribute cognitive development during middle childhood to quantitative improvements in memory and the increased sophistication of the mental programs that children use.
- The three processes of memory—encoding, storage, and retrieval—come under increasing control during middle childhood, and the development of metamemory permits the use of control strategies to improve cognitive processing and memorization.
- Language development in middle childhood is characterized by improvements in vocabulary, syntax, and pragmatics; by the use of language as a self-control device; and by the growth of metalinguistic awareness.
- Bilingualism, the ability to speak more than one language, can produce improvements in cognitive flexibility, metalinguistic awareness, and even IQ test performance, but simple immersion in the language of the dominant culture can be problematic for children of other cultures.

RETHINK

- Do you think a non-Western Piaget working in a different culture might have developed a theory of stages involving cognitive tasks that Western children would have difficulty performing without explicit instruction? Why?
- Why do control strategies such as grouping into patterns and using keywords work? What do they tell us about memory?
- This chapter discusses two rules of pragmatics that govern the social uses of language: (1) that speakers should take turns, and (2) that speakers should address the same topic. Can you think of other rules of pragmatics?
- Do adults use language as a self-control device? How?
- Why might instruction in one's first language enhance instruction in another language, such as English? Do the notions of metalinguistic awareness and universal grammar relate to this phenomenon?

SCHOOLING: THE THREE R'S (AND MORE) OF MIDDLE CHILDHOOD

As the eyes of the six other children in his reading group turned to him, Glenn shifted uneasily in his chair. Reading had never come easily to him, and he always felt anxious when it was his turn to read aloud. But as his teacher nodded in encouragement, he plunged in, hesitantly at first, then gaining momentum as he read the story about a mother's first day on a new job. He found that he could read the passage quite nicely, and he felt a surge of happiness and pride at his accomplishment. When he was done, he broke into a broad smile as his teacher said simply, "Well done, Glenn."

It is small moments such as these, repeated over and over, that make—or break—a child's educational experience. Schooling marks a time when society formally attempts to transfer its accumulated body of knowledge, beliefs, values, and wisdom to new generations. The success with which this transfer is managed determines, in a very real sense, the future fortunes of the world.

Schooling around the World: Who Gets Educated?

In the United States, as in most developed countries, a primary school education is both a universal right and a legal requirement. Virtually all children are provided with a free education through the 12th grade.

Children in other parts of the world are not so fortunate. In 1990, more than 100 million children, 60 percent of them female, did not have access to even a primary school education. An additional 100 million children did not complete a basic education, and overall more than 960 million individuals (two thirds of them women) were illiterate throughout their lives (see Figure 11-4). Projections suggest that by the year 2000 more than 160 million of the world's children will not have access to even a primary school education (World Conference on Education for All, 1990).

In almost all developing countries, fewer females receive formal education than males, a discrepancy found at every level of schooling. Even in developed countries, women lag behind men in their exposure to science and technological topics. These differences reflect widespread and deeply held cultural and parental biases that favor males over females.

Readiness: What Equips Children for School?

Do children who are younger than most of the other children in their grade suffer as a result? According to traditional wisdom, the answer is "yes." Because younger children are assumed to be slightly less advanced developmentally than their peers, it has been assumed that such children would be at a competitive disadvantage.

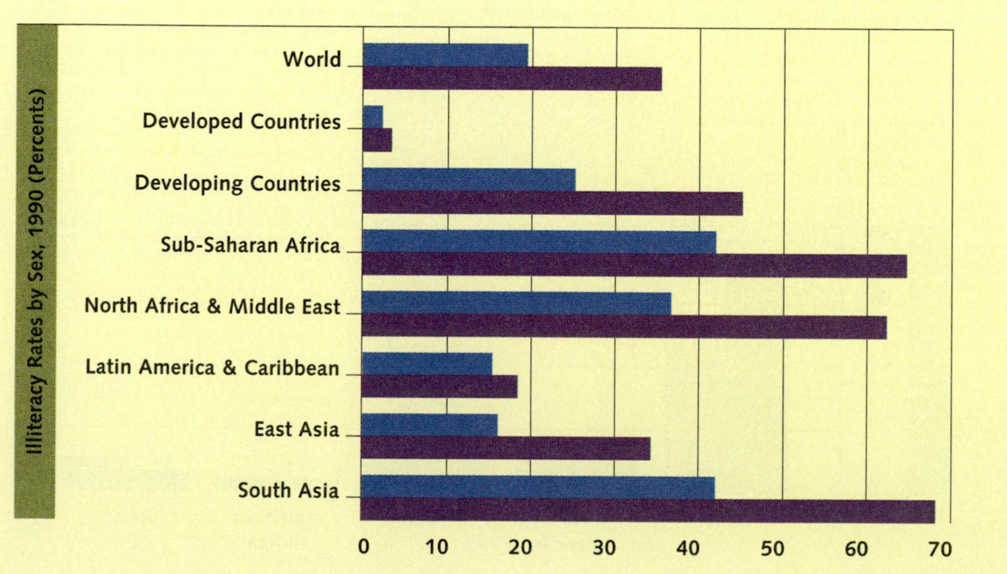

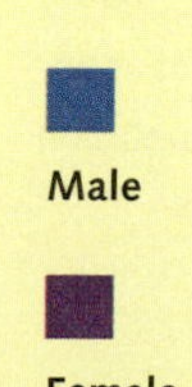

FIGURE 11-4

ILLITERACY RATES BY SEX, 1990

Illiteracy remains a significant problem worldwide, particularly among women. Across the world, close to a billion people are illiterate throughout their lives.

(*Source:* UNESCO, 1990.)

However, recent research has begun to dispel this view. According to a massive study conducted by developmental psychologist Frederick Morrison (1993), children who are among the youngest in first grade progress at the same rate as the oldest. Although they were slightly behind older first-graders in reading, the difference was negligible. It was also clear that parents who chose to hold their children back in kindergarten, thereby ensuring that they would be among the oldest in first grade and after, were not doing their children a favor. These older children did no better than their younger classmates (DeAngelis, 1994).

Clearly, then, age relative to same-grade peers is not, by itself, a particularly important factor in determining school success. If age does not matter, what did have an impact on school success? It turned out that several factors relating to parental influence played a large role. For example, parents' attitude toward reading was important, as were parents' intelligence and educational background.

In sum, evidence suggests that age, per se, is not a critical indicator of when children should start school. Instead, the start of formal schooling is more reasonably tied to overall developmental readiness, the product of a complex combination of several factors.

EDUCATIONAL TRENDS: BEYOND THE THREE R'S

Schooling in the 1990s is very different from what it was as recently as a decade ago. U.S. schools are experiencing a definite return to the educational fundamentals embodied in the traditional three R's (reading, writing, and arithmetic). As can be seen in the model curriculum promoted by the U.S. Department of Education (Table 11-1), the emphasis on educational basics is strong. This trend marks a departure from the 1970s and 1980s, when the emphasis was on socioemotional issues and on allowing students to choose study topics on the basis of their interests, instead of in accordance with a set curriculum.

The elementary classrooms of the 1990s also stress individual accountability. Teachers are more likely to be held responsible for their students' learning, and both students and teachers are more likely to be required to take tests, developed at the state or national level, to assess their competence (Woolfolk, 1993).

Furthermore, increased attention is being paid to issues involving student diversity and multiculturalism. And with good reason: The demographic makeup of students in the United States is undergoing an extraordinary shift. For instance, the proportion of Hispanics will in all likelihood more than double in the next 50 years. Moreover, by the year 2050, Caucasians will make up just over half of the total population of the United States (U.S. Bureau of the Census, 1993; see Figure 11-5). Consequently, educators have been taking multicultural matters more and more seriously.

FIGURE 11-5

THE CHANGING FACE OF AMERICA

Current projections of the population makeup of the United States show that by the year 2050, the proportion of non-Hispanic whites will decline as the proportion of minority group members increases.

(*Source:* U.S. Bureau of the Census, 1993.)

Year 2000 Year 2050

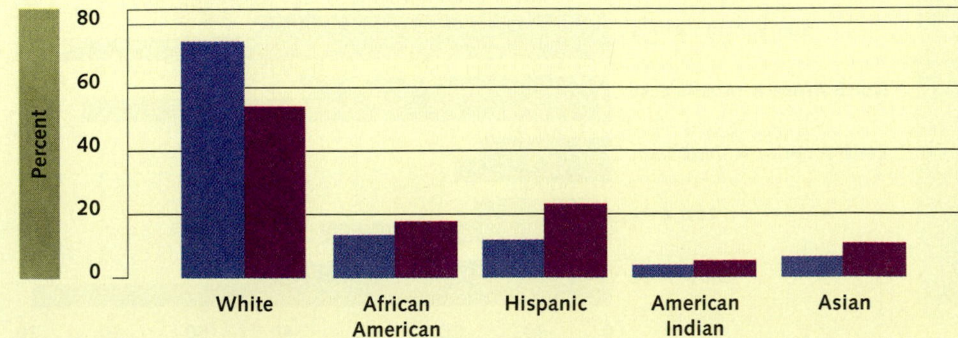

TABLE 11-1

JAMES MADISON ELEMENTARY SCHOOL: A MODEL CURRICULUM FOR KINDERGARTEN THROUGH GRADE 6

SUBJECT	KINDERGARTEN THROUGH GRADE 3	GRADES 4 THROUGH 6
ENGLISH	*INTRODUCTION TO READING AND WRITING* (phonics, silent and oral reading, basic rules of grammar and spelling, vocabulary, writing and penmanship, elementary composition, and library skills)	*INTRODUCTION TO CRITICAL READING* (children's literature, independent reading and book reports, more advanced grammar, spelling and vocabulary, and composition skills)
SOCIAL STUDIES	*INTRODUCTION TO HISTORY, GEOGRAPHY, AND CIVICS* (significant Americans; explorers; Native Amricans; American holidays, customs, and symbols; citizenship; and landscape, climate and mapwork)	Grade 4: *U.S. HISTORY TO CIVIL WAR* Grade 5: *U.S. HISTORY SINCE 1865* Grade 6: *WORLD HISTORY TO THE MIDDLE AGES*
MATHEMATICS	*INTRODUCTION TO MATHEMATICS* (numbers; basic operations; fractions and decimals; rounding; geometric shapes; measurement of length, area, and volume; bar graphs; and estimation and elementary statistics)	*INTERMEDIATE ARITHMETIC AND GEOMETRY* (number theory, negative numbers, percentages, and exponents, line graphs, the Pythagorean theorem, and basic probability)
SCIENCE	*INTRODUCTION TO SCIENCE* (plants and animals, the food chain, the solar system, rocks and minerals, weather, magnets, energy and motion, properties of matter, and simple experiments)	Grade 4: *EARTH SCIENCE AND OTHER TOPICS* Grade 5: *LIFE SCIENCE AND OTHER TOPICS* Grade 6: *PHYSICAL SCIENCE AND OTHER TOPICS*
FOREIGN LANGUAGE	*(OPTIONAL)*	*INTRODUCTION TO FOREIGN LANGUAGE* (basic vocabulary, grammar, reading, writing, conversation, and cultural material)
FINE ARTS	*MUSIC AND VISUAL ART* (songs, recordings, musical sounds and instruments, painting, craftmaking, and visual effects)	*MUSIC AND VISUAL ART* (great composers, musical styles and forms, elementary music theory, great painters, interpretation of art, and creative projects)
PHYSICAL EDUCATION AND HEALTH	*PHYSICAL EDUCATION AND HEALTH* (body control; fitness; sports, games, and exercises; sportsmanship; safety; hygiene; nutrition; and drug prevention education)	*PHYSICAL EDUCATION AND HEALTH* (team and individual sports, first aid, drug prevention education, and appropriate sex education)

(*Source:* U.S. Department of Education, 1988.)

Multicultural educational practices seek to maintain positive group identities relating to students' cultural origins.

Developmental Diversity

Multicultural Education

Since the earliest period of formal education in the United States, classrooms have been populated by individuals from a broad range of backgrounds and experiences. Yet it is only relatively recently that variations in student backgrounds have been viewed as one of the major challenges—and opportunities—that educators face.

In fact, the diversity of background and experience in the classroom relates to a fundamental objective of education, which is to provide a formal mechanism to transmit the information a society holds important. As the famous anthropologist Margaret Mead (1942) once said:

> In its broadest sense, education is the cultural process, the way in which each newborn human infant, born with a potentiality for learning greater than that of any other mammal, is transformed into a full member of a specific human society, sharing with the other members a specific human culture. (p. 633)

Culture, then, can be thought of as a set of behaviors, beliefs, values, and expectations shared by members of a particular society. But although culture is often thought of in a relatively broad context (as in "Western culture" or "Asian culture"), it is also possible to focus on particular *subcultural* groups within a larger, more encompassing culture. For example, we can consider particular racial, ethnic, religious, socioeconomic, or even gender groups within the United States as manifesting characteristics of a subculture.

Membership in a cultural or subcultural group might be of only passing interest to educators were it not for the fact that students' cultural backgrounds have a substantial impact on the way that they—and their peers—are educated. In fact, in recent years a considerable amount of thought has gone into establishing **multicultural education,** a form of education in which the goal is to help minority students develop competence in the culture of the majority group while maintaining positive group identities that build on their original cultures (Grant & Sleeter, 1986).

Cultural Assimilation or Pluralistic Society? Multicultural education developed in part as a reaction to a **cultural assimilation model,** which fostered the view of American society as the proverbial melting pot. According to this view, the goal of education was to assimilate individual cultural identities into a unique, unified American culture. In practical terms this meant that students were discouraged from speaking their native tongues and were totally immersed in English.

In the early 1970s, however, educators and members of minority groups began to suggest that the cultural assimilation model ought to be replaced by a **pluralistic society model.** According to this conception, American society is made up of diverse, coequal cultural groups that should preserve their individual cultural features.

The pluralistic society model grew in part from the belief that teachers, by discouraging children's use of their native tongues, denigrated their cultural heritages and lowered their self-esteem. Furthermore, because instructional materials inevitably feature culture-specific events and understandings, children who were denied access to their own cultural materials might never be exposed to important aspects of their backgrounds. For example, English-language texts rarely present some of the great themes that appear throughout Spanish literature and history (such as the search for the Fountain of Youth and the Don

multicultural education *a form of education in which the goal is to help students from minority cultures develop competence in the culture of the majority group while maintaining positive group identities that build on their original cultures*

cultural assimilation model *the model that fostered the view of American society as the proverbial melting pot*

pluralistic society model *the concept that American society is made up of diverse, coequal cultural groups that should preserve their individual cultural features*

Juan legend). Hispanic students immersed in such texts might never come to understand important components of their own heritage.

Ultimately, educators began to argue that the presence of students representing diverse cultures enriched and broadened the educational experience of all students. Pupils and teachers exposed to people from different backgrounds could better understand the world and gain greater sensitivity to the values and needs of others.

bicultural identity *the maintenance of one's original cultural identity while becoming integrated into the dominant culture*

Fostering a Bicultural Identity. Today, most educators agree that the pluralistic society model is the most valid one for schooling, and that minority children should be encouraged to develop a **bicultural identity.** They recommend that children be supported in maintaining their original cultural identities while they integrate themselves into the dominant culture. This view suggests that an individual can live as a member of two cultures, with two cultural identities, without having to choose one over the other (LaFromboise, Coleman, & Gerton, 1993).

However, the means of achieving the goal of biculturalism are far from clear. Consider, for example, children who enter a school speaking only Spanish. The traditional "melting pot" technique would be to immerse the children in classes taught in English while providing a crash course in English language instruction (and little else) until the children demonstrate a suitable level of proficiency. Unfortunately, the traditional approach has a considerable drawback: Until the children master English, they fall further and further behind their peers who entered school already knowing English (First & Cardenas, 1986).

More contemporary approaches emphasize a bicultural strategy, in which children are encouraged to maintain simultaneous membership in more than one culture. Instruction begins in the child's native language, and shifts as rapidly as possible to include English.

Even after the children have mastered English, some instruction in the native language continues. At the same time, the school conducts a program of multicultural education for all students, in which teachers present material on the cultural backgrounds and traditions of speakers of all the languages spoken in the school (Grant & Sleeter, 1986). Such instruction is designed to enhance the self-image of students from both majority and minority cultures (Buriel, 1993).

Successful bicultural programs also attempt to bring multiple languages into the context of everyday social interactions. Children are encouraged to use a variety of languages in their social relationships and to become equally adept at several languages.

Although most educational experts favor bicultural approaches, the general public does not always agree. For instance, a national "English only" movement has as one of its goals the prohibition of school instruction in any language other than English. Whether such a perspective will prevail remains to be seen.

Do Attributions for Academic Performance Explain Academic Success?

Consider two students, Ben and Hannah, each performing poorly in school. Suppose you thought that Ben's poor performance was due to unalterable, stable causes, such as a lack of intelligence, while Hannah's was produced by temporary causes, such as a lack of hard work. Who would you think would ultimately do better in school?

If you are like most people, you'd probably predict that the outlook was better for Hannah. After all, Hannah could always work harder, but it is hard for someone like Ben to develop higher intelligence.

attributions *understandings of the causes behind someone's behavior*

According to psychologist Harold Stevenson, this reasoning lies at the heart of the superior school performance of Asian students, compared with students in the United States. Stevenson argues that teachers, parents, and students in the United States are likely to hold different kinds of **attributions,** understandings of the causes behind someone's behavior, than people in Asian countries. Specifically, his research suggests that people in Western countries, such as the United States, tend to attribute school performance to stable, internal causes, while people in Japan, China, and other East Asian countries are more likely to see temporary, situational factors as the cause of their performance. The Asian view, which stems in part from ancient Confucian writings, tends to accentuate the necessity of hard work and perseverance (Stevenson & Lee, 1990).

This cultural difference in attributional styles is revealed in several ways. For instance, surveys show that mothers, teachers, and students in Japan and Taiwan all believe strongly that students in a typical class tend to have the same amount of ability. In contrast, mothers, teachers, and students in the United States are apt to disagree, arguing that there are significant differences in ability among the various students (see Figure 11-6).

It is easy to imagine how such different attributional styles can influence teaching approaches. If, as in the United States, students and teachers seem to believe that ability is fixed and locked in, poor academic performance will be greeted with a sense of failure and reduced motivation to work harder to overcome it. In contrast, Japanese teachers and students are apt to see failure as a temporary setback, due to their lack of hard work. After making such an attribution, they are more apt to expend increased effort on future academic activities.

Some researchers have suggested that these different attributional orientations may explain the fact that Asian students frequently outperform American students in international comparisons of student achievement (Geary, Fan, & Bow-Thomas, 1992). Because Asian students tend to assume that academic success results from hard work, they may put greater effort into their schoolwork than American students, who believe that their inherent abilities determine their performance. These arguments suggest that the attributional style of students and teachers in the United States might well be maladaptive (Stevenson, 1992; Stevenson & Stigler, 1992; Stevenson, Chen, & Lee, 1992; Chen & Stevenson, 1995).

Race and gender also are related to children's attributions. For example, African Americans are less likely than whites to attribute success to internal rather than external causes. Specifically, African-American children sometimes feel that task difficulty and luck (external causes) are the major determinants of their performance outcomes and that even if they put in maximum effort, prejudice and discrimination will prevent them from succeeding (Ogbu, 1988; Graham, 1990, 1997).

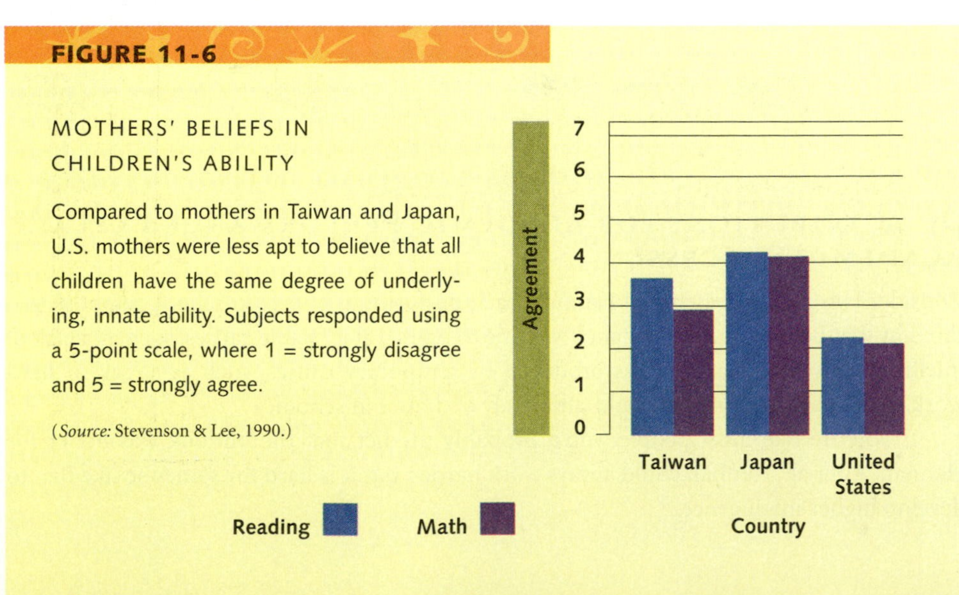

FIGURE 11-6

MOTHERS' BELIEFS IN CHILDREN'S ABILITY

Compared to mothers in Taiwan and Japan, U.S. mothers were less apt to believe that all children have the same degree of underlying, innate ability. Subjects responded using a 5-point scale, where 1 = strongly disagree and 5 = strongly agree.

(*Source:* Stevenson & Lee, 1990.)

Doonesbury BY GARRY TRUDEAU

In addition, women are more prone to attribute their unsuccessful performance to low ability, an uncontrollable factor. Ironically, though, they do not attribute successful performance to high ability, but to factors outside their control. This belief pattern leads to the conclusion that even with future effort, success will be unattainable. Females who subscribe to this pattern of beliefs may be less inclined to expend the effort necessary to improve their rate of success (Dweck, 1991; Dweck & Bush, 1976; Phillips & Zimmerman, 1990).

Expectation Effects: How Others' Expectancies Influence Children's Behavior

Suppose you were an elementary school teacher and were told at the beginning of a new school year that the children in your class were about to take a test as part of a research study described in this way:

> All children show hills, plateaus, and valleys in their scholastic progress. A study being conducted at Harvard with the support of the National Science Foundation is interested in those children who show an unusual forward spurt of academic progress. These spurts can and do occur at any level of academic and intellectual functioning. When these spurts occur in children who have not been functioning too well academically, the result is familiarly referred to as "late blooming."

> As part of our study we are further validating a test which predicts the likelihood that a child will show an inflection point or "spurt" within the near future. This test which will be administered in your school will allow us to predict which youngsters are most likely to show an academic spurt. . . . The development of the test for predicting inflections or "spurts" is not yet such that *every* one of the top 20 percent will show the spurt or "blooming" effect. But the top 20 percent of the children *will* show a more significant inflection or spurt within the next year or less than will the remaining 80 percent of the children. (Rosenthal & Jacobson, 1968, p. 66)

Consider your reaction to the children on the list of bloomers later identified by the test. Would you treat them differently than the children who were not so designated?

If the results of a classic, but controversial, study are any guide, your answer should be affirmative: Teachers do, in fact, seem to treat children for whom they have expectations of improvement differently from those for whom they have no such expectations (R. Rosenthal & Jacobson, 1968). In the experiment, elementary school teachers were told at the beginning of a new school year that five children in their classes would be likely to "bloom" in the upcoming year, based on the test described above. In reality, however, the information was bogus: The names of the children had simply been picked at random, although the teachers didn't know that. The teachers received no further details from the experimenters for the rest of the year.

At the end of the year, the children completed an intelligence test that was identical to one taken a year earlier. According to the experimenters, the results showed that clear differences existed in the intellectual growth of the so-called bloomers, compared with that of the other members of their classes. Those randomly designated as likely to make significant gains did, in fact, improve more than the other children. However, the results were not uniform: The greatest differences were found in first- and second-grade children, with smaller differences for children in grades three through six.

When the findings of the experiment, reported in a book dubbed *Pygmalion in the Classroom,* were published, they caused an immediate stir among educators—and among the public at large. The reason for this furor was the implication of the results: If merely holding high expectations is sufficient to bring about gains in achievement, wouldn't holding low expectations lead to slowed achievement? And since teachers sometimes may hold low expectations about children from lower socioeconomic and minority backgrounds, did this mean that children from such backgrounds were destined to show low achievement throughout their educational careers?

Although the original experiment has been criticized on methodological and statistical grounds (R. Snow, 1969; Wineburg, 1987), enough new evidence has been amassed to make it clear that the expectations of teachers are communicated to their students and can in fact bring about the expected performance. The phenomenon has come to be called the **teacher expectancy effect**—the cycle of behavior in which a teacher transmits an expectation about a child and thereby actually brings about the expected behavior (Babad, 1992).

The teacher expectancy effect can be viewed as a special case of a broader concept known as the *self-fulfilling prophecy,* in which a person's expectation is capable of bringing about an outcome (Snyder, 1974). For instance, physicians have long known that providing patients with placebos (fake, inactive drugs) can sometimes "cure" them, simply because the patients expect the medicine to work.

In the case of teacher expectancy effects, the basic explanation seems to be that teachers, after forming an initial expectation about a child's ability, transmit it to the child through a complex series of verbal and nonverbal cues. These communicated expectations in turn indicate to the child what behavior is appropriate, and the child behaves accordingly (Harris & Rosenthal, 1986; Rosenthal, 1987, 1994).

teacher expectancy effect *the cycle of behavior in which a teacher transmits an expectation about a child and thereby actually brings about the expected behavior*

Once teachers have developed expectations about a child, by what method do they transmit them? Generally, four major factors relate to the transmission of expectations (Harris & Rosenthal, 1986; Rosenthal, 1994):

- *Classroom social-emotional climate.* Teachers create a warmer, more accepting environment for children for whom they hold high expectations than for those from whom they expect less. They convey more positive attitudes by smiling and nodding more often, and they look at high-expectation children more frequently.
- *Feedback.* When teachers hold high expectations for a child, they provide more positive evaluations of the child's work and they are more accepting of the child's ideas. In contrast, low-expectation children receive more criticism and little or no feedback in some situations. Even when low-expectation children do well, the kind of feedback teachers offer is less positive than when a high-expectation child does well.
- *Input to children.* Children who are expected to do well receive greater quantities of material from their teachers, and they are asked to complete more difficult material. Consequently, they are given more opportunities to perform well.
- *Output from teachers.* Teachers initiate more contacts with high-expectation children, and the overall number of contacts between teachers and high-expectation children is higher than with low-expectation children. As a result, high-expectation children have more opportunities to respond in class.

The final link in the chain of events that encompasses the teacher expectancy effect is the child. And given the range of teacher behaviors brought about by teacher expectations, it is hardly surprising that children's performance would be significantly affected. Clearly, children who encounter a warm socioemotional climate, who are the recipients of more feedback from their teachers, who are given more material to complete, and who have more contact with teachers are going to develop more positive self-concepts, be more motivated, and work harder than those who receive negative treatment or neglect. Ultimately, the high-expectation children are likely to perform better in class.

The cycle, then, is complete: A teacher who expects a child to do better treats that child more positively. The child responds to such treatment and eventually performs in accord with the teacher's expectations. But note that the cycle does not stop there: Once children behave congruently with the teacher's expectations, the expectations are reinforced. As a consequence, a child's behavior ultimately may cement the expectation initially held by the teacher (see Figure 11-7).

We should also note that expectations are an omnipresent phenomenon in classrooms and are not the province of teachers alone. For instance, children develop their own expectations about their teacher's competence, based on rumors and other bits of information, and they communicate their expectations to the teacher. In the end, a teacher's behavior may be brought about in significant measure by children's expectations (Feldman & Prohaska, 1979; Feldman & Theiss, 1982; Jamieson et al., 1987).

It is also important to keep in mind that the classroom is not the only place in which expectations operate. Any setting in which one person holds an expectation about a child, and vice versa, may produce analogous expectation effects. Clearly, children's views of themselves and of their behavior are in part a consequence of what others expect of them (Eden, 1990; Harris et al., 1992).

FIGURE 11-7

HOW TEACHER EXPECTATIONS CAN AFFECT STUDENT PERFORMANCE

Teachers who hold a positive or negative expectation about a student can actually bring about positive or negative performance in the student due to their expectation.

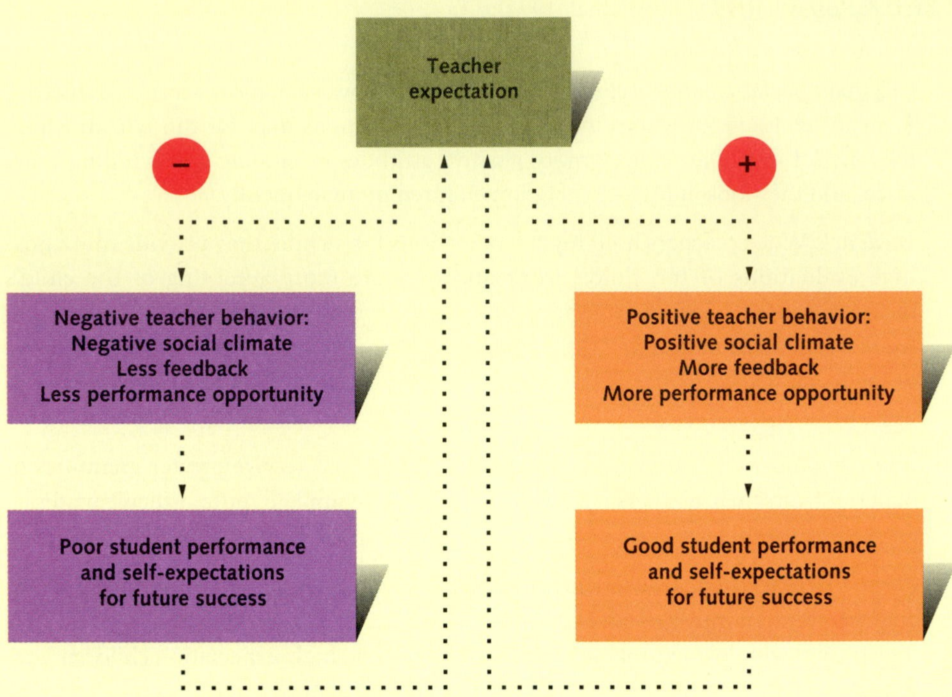

Speaking of Development

Lauro F. Cavazos, Educator

Born:	1927
Education:	Texas Tech University, B.A. and M.A. Iowa State University, Ph.D.
Position:	United States Secretary of Education, 1988–90
Home:	Concord, Massachusetts

By the year 2000 many facets of society in America will change, and much of that change will be the result of education, according to Lauro F. Cavazos, former Secretary of Education in the administration of President George Bush.

In his cabinet position Cavazos worked toward three main goals: raising the expectations of students, teachers, and parents; providing access to quality education for all students, especially those most at risk of failing; and promoting the notion that quality education is the responsibility of every member of society. This was a tremendous task, considering the growing diversity of the student population.

"First of all, we're finally starting to recognize that there is cultural diversity and acknowledge it in a serious fashion," says the sixth-generation Texan. "Already some 30 percent of the students in elementary and secondary public education are Hispanic or African American, and these numbers are going to continue to grow as we approach the turn of the century."

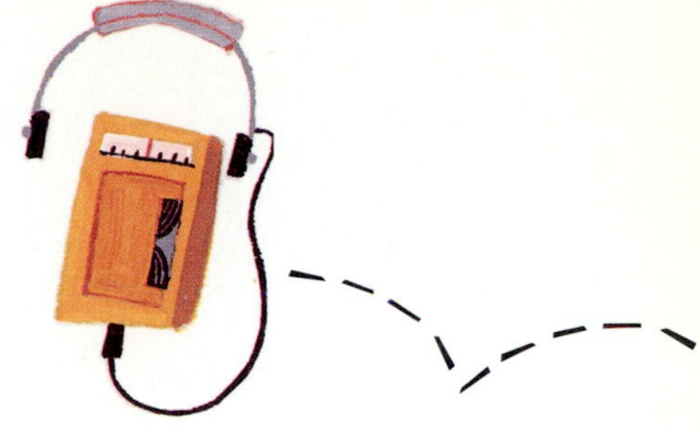

Review and Rethink

REVIEW

- Schooling in the United States, which is nearly universally available, has recently focused on the basic academic skills, student and teacher accountability, and multiculturalism.
- Success in school does not appear to be a factor of age relative to same-grade peers. Readiness for schooling seems to relate to a child's overall developmental level, which is the product of a complex combination of situational factors.
- Multicultural education is in transition from a melting pot model, based on cultural assimilation, to a pluralistic society model, in which coexisting cultures are respected for their unique contributions to the whole.
- Attributions for success and failure, which differ on the basis of culture, race, and gender, cause people to attribute performance either to temporary, situational factors or to stable, internal causes, with different consequences.
- The teacher expectancy effect causes teachers to hold and to communicate different expectations for different students, which can cause the students to fulfill those expectations.

RETHINK

- Is an educational focus on the basic academic skills appropriate? What sorts of skills and abilities does the basics movement emphasize? What gets left out? What are the implications?

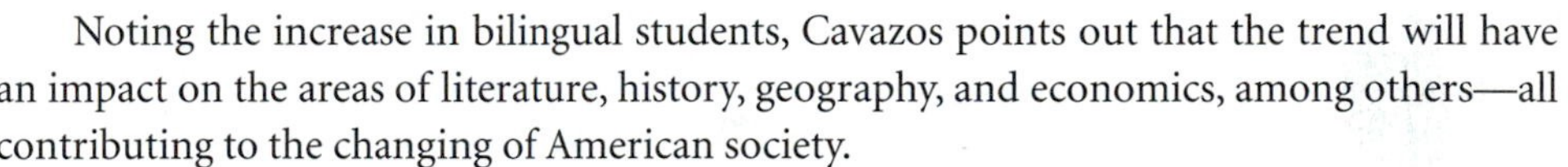

"We're finally starting to recognize that there is cultural diversity and acknowledge it in a serious fashion."

"We need to recognize that diversity is a bonus in America."

Noting the increase in bilingual students, Cavazos points out that the trend will have an impact on the areas of literature, history, geography, and economics, among others—all contributing to the changing of American society.

"We need to recognize that diversity is a bonus in America," he notes. "I'm a strong supporter of bilingual education, but certain conditions need to be met in order for it to work. First, I think non-English-speaking students need to learn English as quickly as possible, hopefully within a year, but at most 3 years. Second, they should retain their original language, whatever that language is—Cambodian, Spanish, or whatever. And third, each group should be expected to add to the culture of America, because America is an amalgamation of many different cultures. We need to recognize that America is already a pluralistic society."

Maintaining that one of America's biggest problems is an education deficit, Cavazos stresses the importance of the educational development of children.

"Some 27 million Americans are illiterate, and 40 to 50 million Americans read at the fourth-grade level," he says. "We have 600,000 to 700,000 youngsters who drop out of school each year, and we haven't had a significant increase in SAT scores in years. I call that the education deficit.

"Our first major goal is to help those students who are in need—the minorities, handicapped, students in special education, and so forth. Our second central goal is to support good research. I've had tremendous resistance to some of the things I've said, and some people really take offense," Cavazos states. "But if we don't change things, in one or two generations this nation is going to be in serious trouble."

- Should instruction be provided to children in the United States in their home languages at first or should they be immersed in English from the start? Why?
- How are attributions related to expectancies?
- Are people subject to expectancies outside the school? How might expectancies operate in a home or business setting?
- Is the Pygmalion study described in this chapter ethical? What concerns, if any, do you have about such a study and other studies that involve human subjects?

INTELLIGENCE: DETERMINING INDIVIDUAL STRENGTHS

intelligence *the capacity to understand the world, think with rationality, and use resources effectively when faced with challenges*

"Why should you tell the truth?" "How far is Los Angeles from New York?" "A table is made of wood; a window of ______."

As 10-year-old Hyacinth sat hunched over her desk, trying to answer a long series of questions like these, she tried to guess the point of the test she was taking in her fifth-grade classroom. Clearly, the test didn't cover material that her teacher, Ms. White-Johnston, had talked about in class.

"What number comes next in this series: 1, 3, 7, 15, 31, ______?"

As she continued to work her way through the questions, she gave up trying to guess the rationale for the test. She'd leave that to her teacher, she sighed to herself. Rather than attempting to figure out what it all meant, she simply tried to do her best on the individual test items.

Hyacinth might be surprised to learn that she was not alone in questioning the meaning and import of the items on the test she was taking. For although the test items were painstakingly prepared, many developmentalists would admit to harboring their own doubts as to whether questions such as these are appropriate to the task of assessing what they are designed to measure: intelligence.

Understanding just what is meant by the concept of intelligence has proven to be a major challenge for researchers interested in delineating what separates intelligent from unintelligent behavior. Although nonexperts have their own conceptions of intelligence (one survey found, for instance, that laypersons believe that intelligence consists of three components: problem-solving ability, verbal ability, and social competence), it has been more difficult for experts to concur (Davidson, 1990; Sternberg et al., 1981; Weinberg, 1989). Still, a general definition of intelligence is possible: **Intelligence** is the capacity to understand the world, think with rationality, and use resources effectively when faced with challenges (Wechsler, 1975).

Part of the difficulty in defining intelligence stems from the many—and sometimes unsatisfactory—paths that have been followed over the years in the quest to distinguish more intelligent people from less intelligent ones. To understand how researchers have approached the task of devising batteries of assessments, called *intelligence tests,* we need to consider some of the historical milestones in the area of intelligence.

The French educator Alfred Binet originated the intelligence test.

INTELLIGENCE BENCHMARKS: DIFFERENTIATING THE INTELLIGENT FROM THE UNINTELLIGENT

The Paris school system was faced with a problem at the turn of the twentieth century: A significant number of children were not benefiting from regular instruction. Unfortunately, these children—many of whom we would now call mentally retarded—were generally not identified early enough to shift them to special classes. The French minister of instruction approached psychologist Alfred Binet with the problem of devising a technique for the early identification of students who might benefit from instruction outside the regular classroom.

Binet tackled his task in a thoroughly practical manner. His years of observing school-aged children suggested to him that previous efforts to distinguish intelligent from unintelligent students—some of which were based on reaction time or keenness of sight—were off the mark. Instead, he launched a trial-and-error process in which items and tasks were administered to students who had been previously identified by teachers as being either "bright" or "dull." Tasks that the bright students completed correctly and the dull students failed to complete correctly were retained for the test. Tasks that did not discriminate between the two groups were discarded. The end result of this process was a test that reliably distinguished students who had previously been identified as fast or slow learners.

mental age *the typical intelligence level found for people of a given chronological age*

chronological (physical) age *the actual age of the person taking the intelligence test*

intelligence quotient (IQ) *a score that takes into account a person's mental and chronological ages*

Binet's pioneering efforts in intelligence testing left three important legacies. The first was his pragmatic approach to the construction of intelligence tests. Binet did not have theoretical preconceptions about what intelligence was. Instead, he used a trial-and-error approach to psychological measurement that continues to serve as the predominant approach to test construction today. His definition of intelligence as *that which his test measured* has been adopted by many modern researchers, and it is particularly popular among test developers who respect the widespread utility of intelligence tests but wish to avoid arguments about the underlying nature of intelligence.

Our second inheritance from Binet stems from his focus on linking intelligence and school success. Binet's procedure for constructing an intelligence test ensured that intelligence—defined as performance on the test—and school success would be virtually one and the same. Binet's intelligence test and its current successors, then, have become reasonable indicators of the degree to which students possess attributes that contribute to successful school performance. Unfortunately, they do not provide particularly useful information regarding a vast number of other attributes that are largely unrelated to academic proficiency.

Finally, Binet developed a procedure of assigning each intelligence test score to a **mental age,** the age of the children taking the test who, on average, achieved that score. For example, if a 6-year-old girl received a score of 30 on the test, and this was the average score received by 10-year-olds, her mental age would be considered 10 years. Similarly, a 15-year-old boy who scored a 90 on the test—thereby matching the mean score for 15-year-olds—would be assigned a mental age of 15 years.

Although assigning a mental age to students provides an indication of whether or not they are performing at the same level as their peers, it does not permit adequate comparisons between students of different **chronological** (or **physical**) **ages.** By using mental age alone, for instance, it would be assumed that a 15-year-old responding with a mental age of 17 years would be as bright as a 6-year-old responding with a mental age of 8 years, when actually the 6-year-old would be showing a much greater *relative* degree of brightness.

A solution to this problem comes in the form of the **intelligence quotient,** or **IQ,** a score that takes into account a student's mental *and* chronological age. The traditional method of calculating an IQ score uses the following formula, in which MA stands for mental age and CA for chronological age:

$$\mathit{IQ\ SCORE} = \frac{\text{MA}}{\text{CA}} \times 100$$

As a bit of trial and error with this formula demonstrates, people whose mental age (MA) is equal to their chronological age (CA) will always have an IQ of 100. Furthermore, if the chronological age exceeds the mental age—implying below-average intelligence—the score will be below 100; and if the chronological age is lower than the mental age—suggesting above-average intelligence—the score will be above 100.

Using this formula, we can return to our earlier example of a 15-year-old who scores at a 17-year-old mental age. This student's IQ is 17/15 × 100, or 113. In comparison, the IQ of a 6-year-old scoring at a mental age of 8 is 8/6 × 100, or 133—a higher IQ score than the 15-year-old's.

Stanford-Binet Intelligence Scale *an oral test that consists of a series of problems that get progressively more difficult and that vary according to the age of the person being tested*

Wechsler Intelligence Scale for Children-III (WISC-III) *a test for children that provides separate measures of verbal and performance (or nonverbal) skills, as well as a total score*

Wechsler Adult Intelligence Scale-III (WAIS-III) *a test for adults that provides separate measures of verbal and performance (or nonverbal) skills, as well as a total score*

Kaufman Assessment Battery for Children (K-ABC) *a children's intelligence test which measures the ability to integrate different kinds of stimuli simultaneously and to use step-by-step thinking; it permits unusual flexibility in its administration*

fluid intelligence *the ability to deal with new problems and situations*

While the basic principles behind the calculation of an IQ score still hold, scores today are calculated in a more mathematically sophisticated manner and are known as *deviation IQ scores.* The average deviation IQ score remains set at 100, but tests are now devised so that the degree of deviation from this score permits the calculation of the proportion of people who have similar scores. For instance, approximately two thirds of all people fall within 15 points of the average score of 100, achieving scores between 85 and 115. As scores rise or fall beyond this range, the percentage of people in the same score category falls significantly.

Measuring IQ: Present-day Approaches to Intelligence. Although tests of intelligence have become increasingly sophisticated since the time of Binet in terms of the accuracy with which they measure IQ, most of them can still trace their roots to his original work in one way or another. For example, one of the most widely used tests—the **Stanford-Binet Intelligence Scale**—began as an American revision of Binet's original test. The test consists of a series of items that vary according to the age of the person being tested. For instance, young children are asked to answer questions about everyday activities or to copy complex figures. Older people are asked to explain proverbs, solve analogies, and describe similarities between groups of words. The test is administered orally and test takers are given progressively more difficult problems until they are unable to proceed.

The **Wechsler Intelligence Scale for Children-III (WISC-III)** and its adult version, the **Wechsler Adult Intelligence Scale-III (WAIS-III),** are two other widely used intelligence tests. The tests provide separate measures of verbal and performance (or nonverbal) skills, as well as a total score. As you can see from the sample items in Figure 11-8, the verbal tasks are traditional word problems that test skills such as understanding a passage, while typical nonverbal tasks are copying a complex design, arranging pictures in a logical order, and assembling objects. The separate portions of the test allow for easier identification of any specific problems a test taker may have. For example, significantly higher scores on the performance part of the test than on the verbal part may indicate difficulties in linguistic development.

The **Kaufman Assessment Battery for Children (K-ABC)** takes a different approach from the Stanford-Binet, WISC-III, and WAIS-III. In it, children are tested on their ability to integrate different kinds of stimuli simultaneously and to use step-by-step thinking. A special virtue of the K-ABC is its flexibility. It allows the person giving the test to use alternate wording or gestures, or even to pose questions in a different language, in order to maximize a test taker's performance.

What do the IQ scores derived from IQ tests mean? For most children, IQ scores are reasonably good predictors of their school performance. That's not surprising, given that the initial impetus for the development of intelligence tests was to identify children who were having difficulties in school.

But when it comes to performance outside of academic spheres, the story is different. For instance, although people with higher IQ scores are apt to finish more years of schooling, once this is statistically controlled for, IQ scores are not closely related to income and later success in life. Furthermore, IQ scores are frequently inaccurate when it comes to predicting a particular individual's future success. Because of these difficulties with traditional IQ scores, researchers have turned to alternative approaches to intelligence (McClelland, 1993).

What IQ Tests Don't Tell: Alternative Conceptions of Intelligence. The intelligence tests used most frequently in school settings today share an underlying premise: Intelligence is composed of a single, unitary mental ability factor, commonly called *g* (Spearman, 1927). The *g* factor is assumed to underlie performance on every aspect of intelligence, and it is the *g* factor that intelligence tests presumably measure.

However, many theorists dispute the notion that intelligence is unidimensional (Neisser et al., 1996; Weinberg, 1989). For example, some developmentalists suggest that in fact two kinds of intelligence exist: fluid intelligence and crystallized intelligence (Catell, 1967, 1987). **Fluid intelligence** is the ability to deal with new problems and situations. For

FIGURE 11-8

SAMPLE ITEMS FOUND ON THE WECHSLER INTELLIGENCE SCALES FOR CHILDREN (WISC-III)

NAME	GOAL OF ITEM	EXAMPLE
VERBAL SCALE		
Information	Assess general information	Where does honey come from?
Comprehension	Assess understanding and evaluation of social norms and past experience	Why do we use an umbrella when it rains?
Arithmetic	Assess math reasoning through verbal problems	Alice found three baseballs in a field. She gives two to her friend Jocelyn. How many baseballs does Alice have left?
Similarities	Test understanding of how objects or concepts are alike, tapping abstract reasoning	In what way are birds and airplanes alike?
PERFORMANCE SCALE		
Digit symbol	Assess speed of learning	Match symbols to numbers using key. 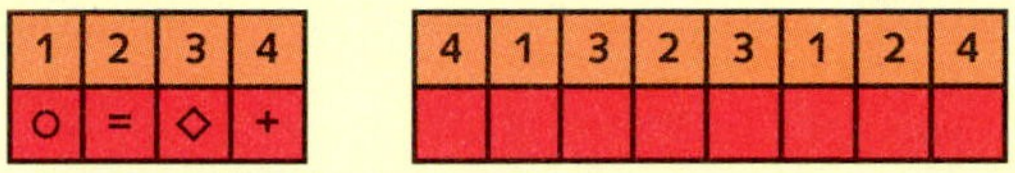 1 2 3 4 / ○ = ◇ + 4 1 3 2 3 1 2 4
Picture completion	Visual memory and attention	Identify what is missing. 
Object assembly	Test understanding of relationship of parts to wholes	Put pieces together to form a whole. 

example, a student asked to group a series of letters according to some criterion or to remember a set of numbers would be using fluid intelligence. In contrast, **crystallized intelligence** is the store of information, skills, and strategies that people have acquired through education and prior experiences and through their use of fluid intelligence. A student would likely be relying on crystallized intelligence to solve a puzzle or deduce the solution to a mystery, in which it was necessary to draw on past experience.

crystallized intelligence *the store of information, skills, and strategies that people have acquired through education and prior experiences and through their previous use of fluid intelligence*

Other theorists divide intelligence into an even greater number of parts. For example, psychologist Howard Gardner suggests that we have seven distinct intelligences, each relatively independent (see Table 11-2). Gardner suggests that these separate intelligences operate not in isolation, but together, depending on the type of activity in which we are engaged (Gardner & Hatch, 1989; Kronhaber, Krechevsky, & Gardner, 1990).

The Russian psychologist Lev Vygotsky, whose approach to cognitive development we first discussed in Chapter 8, takes a very different approach to intelligence. He suggests that

TABLE 11-2

GARDNER'S SEVEN INTELLIGENCES

1. *Musical intelligence* (skills in tasks involving music). Case example:
   When he was 3, Yehudi Menuhin was smuggled into the San Francisco Orchestra concerts by his parents. The sound of Louis Persinger's violin so entranced the youngster that he insisted on a violin for his birthday and Louis Persinger as his teacher. He got both. By the time he was 10 years old, Menuhin was an international performer.
2. *Bodily kinesthetic intelligence* (skills in using the whole body or various portions of it in the solution of problems or in the construction of products or displays, exemplified by dancers, athletes, actors, and surgeons). Case example:
   Fifteen-year-old Babe Ruth played third base. During one game, his team's pitcher was doing poorly and Babe loudly criticized him from third base. Brother Mathias, the coach, called out, "Ruth, if you know so much about it, *you* pitch!" Babe was surprised and embarrassed because he had never pitched before, but Brother Mathias insisted. Ruth said later that at the very moment he took the pitcher's mound, he *knew* he was supposed to be a pitcher.
3. *Logical mathematical intelligence* (skills in problem solving and scientific thinking). Case example:
   Barbara McClintock won the Nobel Prize in medicine for her work in microbiology. She describes one of her breakthroughs, which came after thinking about a problem for half an hour…"Suddenly I jumped up and ran back to the (corn) field. At the top of the field (the others were still at the bottom) I shouted, 'Eureka, I have it!'"
4. *Linguistic intelligence* (skills involved in the production and use of language). Case example:
   At the age of 10, T. S. Elliot created a magazine called *Fireside*, to which he was the sole contributor. In a 3-day period during his winter vacation, he created eight complete issues.
5. *Spatial intelligence* (skills involving spatial configurations, such as those used by artists and architects). Case example:
   Navigation around the Caroline Islands…is accomplished without instruments…. During the actual trip, the navigator must envision mentally a reference island as it passes under a particular star and from that he computes the number of segments completed, the proportion of the trip remaining, and any corrections in heading.
6. *Interpersonal intelligence* (skills in interacting with others, such as sensitivity to the moods, temperaments, motivations, and intentions of others). Case example:
   When Anne Sullivan began instructing the deaf and blind Helen Keller, her task was one that had eluded others for years. Yet, just 2 weeks after beginning her work with Keller, Sullivan achieved a great success. In her words, "My heart is singing with joy this morning. A miracle has happened! The wild little creature of 2 weeks ago has been transformed into a gentle child."
7. *Intrapersonal intelligence* (knowledge of the internal aspects of oneself; access to one's own feelings and emotions). Case example:
   In her essay "A Sketch of the Past," Virginia Woolf displays deep insight into her own inner life through these lines, describing her reaction to several specific memories from her childhood that still, in adulthood, shocked her: "Though I still have the peculiarity that I receive these sudden shocks, they are now always welcome; after the first surprise, I always feel instantly that they are particularly valuable. And so I go on to suppose that the shock-receiving capacity is what makes me a writer."

(*Source:* Adapted from Walters & Gardner, 1986.)

to assess intelligence, we should not only look at those cognitive processes that are fully developed; in addition, those cognitive processes that are currently being developed should also be assessed. To do this, Vygotsky (1976) contends that assessment tasks should involve cooperative interaction between the individual who is being assessed and the person who is doing the assessment—a process called *dynamic assessment.* In short, intelligence is seen as being reflected not only in how children can perform on their own, but in terms of how well they perform when helped by adults (Campione & Brown, 1987; Carlson & Wiedl, 1992; Daniels, 1996; Kozulin & Falik, 1995).

triarchic theory of intelligence *the model that states that intelligence consists of three aspects of information processing: the componential element, the experiential element, and the contextual element*

Taking yet another approach, psychologist Robert Sternberg (1987, 1990) suggests that intelligence is best thought of in terms of information processing. In this view, the way in which people store material in memory and later use it to solve intellectual tasks provides the most precise conception of intelligence. Rather than focusing on the structure of intelligence in the form of its various subcomponents, then, information-processing approaches examine the processes that underlie intelligent behavior.

Researchers who have broken tasks and problems into their component parts have noted critical differences in the nature and speed of problem solving processes between those who score high and those who score low on traditional IQ tests. For instance, when verbal problems such as analogies are broken into their component parts, it becomes clear that people with higher intelligence levels differ from others not only in the number of problems they ultimately are able to solve, but in their method of solving the problems as well. People with high IQ scores spend more time on the initial stages of problem solving, retrieving relevant information from memory. In contrast, those who score lower on traditional IQ tests tend to spend less time on the initial stages, instead skipping ahead and making less-informed guesses. The processes used in solving problems, then, may reflect important differences in intelligence (Deary & Stough, 1996; Sternberg, 1982, 1990).

Sternberg's work on information-processing approaches to intelligence has led him to develop the **triarchic theory of intelligence.** According to this model, intelligence consists of three aspects of information processing: the componential element, the experiential element, and the contextual element. The componential aspect of intelligence reflects how efficiently people can process and analyze information. Efficiency in these areas allows people to infer relationships among different parts of a problem, solve the problem, and then evaluate their solution. People who are strong on the componential element score highest on traditional tests of intelligence (Sternberg, 1996).

The experiential element is the insightful component of intelligence. People who have a strong experiential element can easily compare new material with what they already know, and can combine and relate facts that they already know in novel and creative ways. Finally, the contextual element of intelligence concerns practical intelligence, or ways of dealing with the demands of the everyday environment.

In Sternberg's view (1985a, 1991), people vary in the degree to which each of these three elements is present, and a person's success on a given task reflects the match between the task and the person's specific pattern of strength on the three components of intelligence.

Racial Differences in IQ and *The Bell Curve* Controversy

A "jontry" is an example of a

(a) rulpow
(b) flink
(c) spudge
(d) bakwoe

If you were to find an item such as this on an intelligence test that you were taking, your immediate—and quite legitimate—reaction would likely be to complain. How could a test that purports to measure intelligence include test items that incorporate meaningless terminology?

But suppose, instead, that the following item was on a test:

A "handkerchief head" is

(a) a cool cat
(b) a porter
(c) an "Uncle Tom"
(d) a hoddi

Equally invalid? Actually, there is considerably more of a rationale for including this second question on an intelligence test than the first question. For unlike the first example, which was made up of words with no meaning, the second example employs meaningful language used in predominately African-American areas of certain cities and rural sections of the United States. In fact, one might argue that an intelligence test including the second example would be more appropriate than a traditional test for people who routinely use non-standard English.

The second item (the correct answer to which is *c*, by the way) is drawn from a series of questions devised by sociologist Adrian Dove (1968), as part of a pseudo-intelligence test designed to make a point. Dove contended that cultural experience played a crucial role in determining intelligence test scores, and he suggested that traditional measures of intelligence were biased in favor of white, upper- and middle-class students and against groups with different cultural experiences.

The Racial Debate. Dove created his "test" in reaction to a longstanding debate among researchers regarding the finding that members of certain racial groups consistently score lower on IQ tests than members of other groups. For example, the mean score of African Americans tends to be about 15 IQ points lower than the mean score of whites—although the measured difference varies a great deal depending on the particular IQ test employed (e.g., Vance, Hankins, & Brown, 1988).

The question that emerges from such differences, of course, is whether they reflect actual differences in intelligence or, instead, are caused by bias in the intelligence tests themselves in favor of majority groups and against minorities. For example, if whites perform better on an IQ test than African Americans because of their greater familiarity with the language used in the test items, the test hardly can be said to provide a fair measure of the intelligence of African Americans. Similarly an intelligence test that used language such as that used in Dove's test could not be considered an impartial measure of intelligence for whites.

The question of how to interpret differences between intelligence scores of different cultural groups lies at the heart of one of the major controversies in child development: To what degree is an individual's intelligence determined by heredity, and to what degree by environment? The issue is crucial because of its social implications. For instance, if intelligence is primarily determined by heredity and is therefore largely fixed at birth, attempts to alter intelligence later in life will meet with limited success. On the other hand, if intelligence is largely environmentally determined, modifying social conditions is a more promising strategy for bringing about increases in intelligence (Sternberg & Grigorenko, 1996).

***The Bell Curve* Controversy.** Although investigations into the relative contributions of heredity and environment to intelligence have been conducted for decades, the smoldering debate became a raging fire with the publication in 1994 of a book by Richard J. Herrnstein and Charles Murray called *The Bell Curve*. In the book, Herrnstein and Murray argue that the average 15-point IQ difference between whites and African Americans is due primarily to heredity rather than environment. Furthermore, they argue that this IQ difference accounts for the higher rates of poverty, lower employment rates, and higher use of welfare among minority groups, as compared with majority groups.

"I don't know anything about the bell curve, but I say heredity is everything."

Drawing by C. Barsotti; ©1994 The New Yorker Magazine, Inc.

Herrnstein and Murray contend that whites score higher than African Americans on traditional IQ tests even when socioeconomic status (SES) is taken into account. Specifically, middle- and upper-SES African Americans tend to score lower than middle- and upper-SES whites, just as lower-SES African Americans score lower on average than lower-SES whites. Herrnstein and Murray use this evidence to argue that the IQ score difference between whites and African Americans is primarily due to genetic factors.

The conclusions reached by Herrnstein and Murray raised a storm of protest, and many researchers who examined the data reported in the book came to conclusions that were quite different. Most researchers responded by arguing that the differences between races in measured IQ can be explained by environmental differences in their backgrounds. Furthermore, critics maintain that, despite what Herrnstein and Murray contend, little evidence suggests that IQ accounts for poverty and other social ills. Indeed, some researchers go further, suggesting that IQ scores are unrelated in meaningful ways to later success in life; they suggest that little evidence shows that high IQ scores produce either financial or social success (e.g., Jacoby & Glauberman, 1995; McClelland, 1993; Nisbett, 1994; Sternberg & Wagner, 1993; Sternberg, 1995).

Herrnstein and Murray's critics base their conclusions on several pieces of evidence. For one thing, even when socioeconomic conditions are supposedly held constant, wide variations remain in the home environments among different households. Thus, living conditions of African Americans and whites are hardly identical, even when their socioeconomic status seems apparently to be similar. Consequently, we cannot rule out the possibility that significant environmental differences exist between white and African-American families. In fact, a recent study finds that when a variety of indicators of economic and social factors (and not just socioeconomic status) are statistically taken into account simultaneously, mean IQ scores between African American and white children turn out to be actually quite similar (Brooks-Gunn, Klebanov, & Duncan, 1996).

Finally, members of cultural and social minority groups may score lower than members of the majority group due to the nature of the intelligence tests themselves. As we discussed earlier, traditional intelligence tests may discriminate against minority groups who have not had exposure to the same environment as majority group members (Miller-Jones, 1989).

In sum, most members of the research community believe that Herrnstein and Murray came to a conclusion about the source of racial IQ differences that is not supported by evidence. Still, the view set forth in *The Bell Curve* remains noteworthy, and it is likely to continue to influence both political and scientific agendas.

mental retardation *a significantly subaverage level of intellectual functioning that occurs with related limitations in two or more skill areas*

FALLING BELOW AND ABOVE THE INTELLIGENCE NORMS: MENTAL RETARDATION AND THE INTELLECTUALLY GIFTED

> Although Curry kept pace with her classmates in kindergarten, by the time she reached first grade she was academically the slowest in almost every subject. It was not that she didn't try, but rather that it took her longer than other students to catch on to new material, and she regularly required special attention to keep up with the rest of the class.
>
> On the other hand, in some areas she excelled: When asked to draw or produce something with her hands, she not only matched her classmates' performance but exceeded it, producing beautiful work that was much admired by her classmates. Although the other students in the class felt that there was something different about Curry, they were hard pressed to identify the source of the difference, and in fact they didn't spend much time pondering the issue.

Curry's parents and teacher, though, knew what made her special. Extensive testing in kindergarten had shown that Curry's intelligence was well below normal, and she was officially classified as mentally retarded.

Below the Norm: Mental Retardation. Around 1 to 3 percent of the school-age population is considered to be mentally retarded (U.S. Department of Education, 1987). The wide variation in these incidence estimates stems from the breadth of the most widely accepted definition of mental retardation, which leaves ample room for interpretation. According to the American Association on Mental Retardation (AAMR, 1992), **mental retardation** refers to "substantial limitations in present functioning" characterized by "significantly subaverage intellectual functioning, existing concurrently with related limitations in two or more of the following applicable adaptive skill areas: communication, self-care, home living, social skills, community use, self-direction, health and safety, functional academics, leisure and work. Mental retardation manifests before age 18."

While "subaverage intellectual functioning" can be measured in a relatively straightforward manner—using standard IQ tests—it is more difficult to determine how to gauge limitations in "applicable adaptive skills." Ultimately, this imprecision leads to a lack of uniformity in the ways experts apply the label of "mental retardation." The result has been significant variation in the abilities of people who are categorized as mentally retarded. Accordingly, mentally retarded people range from those who can be taught to work and function with little special attention to those who are virtually untrainable and who never develop speech or such basic motor skills as crawling or walking (Matson & Mulick, 1991).

In addition, even when objective measures such as IQ tests are used to identify mentally retarded individuals, discrimination may occur against children from ethnically diverse backgrounds. Most traditional intelligence tests are standardized using white, English-speaking, middle-class populations. As a result, children from different cultural backgrounds may perform poorly on the tests—not because they are retarded, but because the tests use questions that are culturally biased in favor of majority group members. In fact, one classic study found that in one California school district, Mexican American students were 10 times more likely to be placed in special education classes than whites (Mercer, 1973). More current findings show that nationally twice as many African-American students as white students are classified as mildly retarded, a difference that experts attribute primarily to cultural bias and poverty (Reschly, 1996; Terman, Larner, Stevensen, & Behrman, 1996).

This boy, who has been identified as mentally retarded, is mainstreamed into this fifth grade classroom.

The vast majority of the mentally retarded—some 90 percent—have relatively low levels of deficits. Classified with **mild retardation,** they score in the range of 50 or 55 to 70 on IQ tests. Typically their retardation is not even identified before they reach school, although their early development often is slower than average. Once they enter elementary school, their retardation and their need for special attention usually become apparent. With appropriate training, these students can reach a third- to sixth-grade educational level, and although they cannot carry out complex intellectual tasks, they are able to hold jobs and function quite independently and successfully.

Intellectual and adaptive limitations become more apparent, however, at higher levels of mental retardation. People whose IQ scores range from around 35 or 40 to 50 or 55 are classified with **moderate retardation.** Composing between 5 and 10 percent of those classified as mentally retarded, the moderately retarded display distinctive behavior early in their lives. They are slow to develop language skills, and their motor development is also affected. Regular schooling is usually not effective in training the moderately retarded to acquire academic skills, because generally they are unable to progress beyond the second-grade level. Still, they are capable of learning occupational and social skills, and they can learn to travel independently to familiar places. Typically, they require moderate levels of supervision.

At the most significant levels of retardation—those who are classified with **severe retardation** (IQs ranging from around 20 or 25 to 35 or 40) and **profound retardation** (IQs below 20 or 25)—the ability to function is severely limited. Usually, such people have little or no speech, have poor motor control, and may need 24-hour nursing care. At the same time, though, some people with severe retardation are capable of learning basic self-care skills, such as dressing and eating, and they may even develop the potential to become partially independent as adults. Still, the need for relatively high levels of care continues throughout the life span, and most severely and profoundly retarded people are institutionalized for the majority of their lives.

mild retardation *retardation with IQ scores in the range of 50 or 55 to 70*

moderate retardation *retardation with IQ scores from around 35 or 40 to 50 or 55*

severe retardation *retardation with IQ scores that range from around 20 or 25 to 35 or 40*

profound retardation *retardation with IQ scores below 20 or 25*

No less than children below the norm, children who are gifted and talented warrant special attention.

Above the Norm: The Gifted and Talented. Consider this situation:

> I was standing at the front of the room explaining how the earth revolves and how, because of its huge size, it is difficult for us to realize that it is actually round. All of a sudden, Spencer blurted out, "The earth isn't round." I curtly replied, "Ha, do you think it's flat?" He matter-of-factly said, "No, it's a truncated sphere." I quickly changed the subject. Spencer said the darnedest things. (Payne, Kauffman, Brown, & DeMott, 1974, p. 94)

It sometimes strikes people as curious that the gifted and talented are considered to have a form of exceptionality. Yet—as the above quote suggests—the 3 to 5 percent of school-age children who are gifted and talented present special challenges of their own.

What students are considered to be **gifted and talented**? Because of the breadth of the term, little agreement exists among researchers on a single definition. However, the federal government considers the term "gifted" to include "children who give evidence of high performance capability in areas such as intellectual, creative, artistic, leadership capacity, or specific academic fields, and who require services or activities not ordinarily provided by the school in order to fully develop such capabilities" (Sec. 582, P.L. 97-35). Intellectual capabilities, then, represent only one type of exceptionality; unusual potential in areas outside the academic realm are also included in the concept. Gifted and talented children have so much potential that they, no less than students with low IQs, warrant special concern (Azar, 1995; Sparrow, 1985; Gottfried et al., 1994).

Although the stereotypic description of the gifted—particularly those with exceptionally high intelligence—would probably include adjectives such as "unsociable," "poorly adjusted," and "neurotic," such a view is far off the mark. In fact, most research suggests that highly intelligent people also tend to be outgoing, well adjusted, and popular (Stanley, 1980).

For instance, one landmark, long-term study of 1,500 gifted students, which began in the 1920s, found that the gifted did better than the nongifted in virtually every dimension studied. Not only were they smarter than average, but they were healthier, better coordinated, and psychologically better adjusted than their less intelligent classmates. Furthermore, their lives played out in ways that most people would envy. The subjects received more awards and distinctions, earned more money, and made many more contributions in art and literature than the average person. For instance, by the time they had reached the age of 40, they had collectively produced more than 90 books, 375 plays and short stories, and 2,000 articles, and they had registered more than 200 patents. Perhaps not surprisingly, they reported greater satisfaction with their lives than the nongifted (Sears, 1977; Shurkin, 1992; Terman & Oden, 1959).

Yet being gifted or talented is no guarantee of success in school, as we can see if we consider the particular components of the category. For example, the verbal abilities that allow the eloquent expression of ideas and feelings can equally permit the expression of glib and persuasive statements that happen to be inaccurate. Furthermore, teachers may sometimes misinterpret the humor, novelty, and creativity of unusually gifted children, considering their intellectual fervor to be disruptive or inappropriate. And peers are not always sympathetic: Some very bright children try to hide their intelligence in an effort to fit in better with other students (Feldman, 1982).

Two main approaches to educating the gifted and talented have been devised: acceleration and enrichment (Feldhusen, 1989). **Acceleration** allows gifted students to move ahead at their own pace, even if this means skipping to higher grade levels. The materials that students receive under acceleration programs are not necessarily different from what other students receive; they simply are provided at a faster pace than for the average student.

An alternative approach is **enrichment,** through which students are kept at grade level but are enrolled in special programs and given individual activities to allow greater depth of study on a given topic. In enrichment, the material provided to gifted students differs

gifted and talented *children who show evidence of high performance capability in intellectual, creative, or artistic areas; in leadership capacity; or in specific academic fields*

acceleration *special programs that allow gifted students to move ahead at their own pace, even if this means skipping to higher grade levels*

enrichment *an approach through which students are kept at grade level but are enrolled in special programs and given individual activities to allow greater depth of study on a given topic* not only in the timing of its presentation, but in its sophistication as well. Thus, enrichment materials are designed to provide an intellectual challenge to the gifted student, encouraging higher-order thinking.

Both acceleration and enrichment programs can be remarkably effective. For example, most studies show that gifted students in acceleration programs who begin school even considerably earlier than their age-mates do as well as or better than those who begin at the traditional age (Rimm & Lovance, 1992; VanTassel-Baska, 1986). One of the best illustrations of the benefits of acceleration is the "Study of Mathematically Precocious Youth," an ongoing program at Johns Hopkins University in Baltimore. In this program, seventh- and eighth-graders who have unusual abilities in mathematics participate in a variety of special classes and workshops. The results have been nothing short of sensational, with students successfully completing college courses and sometimes even enrolling in college early. Some students have even graduated from college before the age of 18 (Brody & Benbow, 1987; Stanley & Benbow, 1983; Southern, Jones, & Stanley, 1993).

The Informed Consumer of Development

Creating an Atmosphere that Promotes School Success

What makes children succeed in school? Although there are many factors, some of which we'll be discussing in the next chapter, there are several practical steps that can be taken to maximize children's chances of success. Among them:

- *Promote a "literacy environment."* Parents should read to their children and familiarize them with books and reading. Adults should provide reading models: Children should see that reading is an important activity in the lives of the adults with whom they interact.
- *Talk to children.* Discuss events in the news, talk about their friends, and share hobbies. Getting children to think about and discuss the world around them is one of the best preparations for school.
- *Provide a place for children to work.* This can be a desk, a corner of a table, or an area of a room. What's important is that it be a separate, designated area.
- *Encourage children's problem-solving skills.* To solve a problem, they should learn to identify their goal, what they know, and what they don't know; to design and carry out a strategy; and finally to evaluate their result.

Review and Rethink

REVIEW

- The measurement of intelligence has traditionally involved testing skills that promote academic success, and calculating the ratio of mental age (measured in relation to average test performance by age group) to chronological age.

- The traditional view of intelligence may be insufficient. In fact, several kinds of intelligence (for example, fluid and crystallized) or several components of intelligence (for example, componential, experiential, and contextual) might reflect different ways of processing information.
- To a significant degree, racial differences in intelligence test results reflect environmental differences in the lives of people of different races, rather than genetic factors.
- Most persons with mental retardation have a mild form that permits effective schooling to as high as the sixth-grade level and allows independent living and functioning. Persons with more severe forms require significant amounts of care.
- Gifted and talented persons can benefit from either acceleration programs (in which they proceed through their education at a fast rate) or enrichment programs (in which they remain with their age peers but receive "enriched" materials and instruction).

RETHINK

- How do fluid and crystallized intelligence interact? Which of the two is likely to be more influenced by genetic factors, and which by environmental factors? Why?
- In what ways might differences in the environments experienced by two middle-class families, one white and the other nonwhite, affect IQ test performance?
- If IQ test scores are associated primarily with school performance, but don't relate closely to ultimate success in life, why do people bother to give IQ tests? In light of the inability of IQ scores to predict success, what are the implications for the relationship between the concept of intelligence and IQ test scores?
- Some people argue that expending additional resources on gifted and talented children is wasteful, since they will succeed anyway. Do you agree? Why or why not?

LOOKING BACK

In what ways do children develop cognitively during the years of middle childhood?

1. Intellectually, middle childhood is a time of substantial growth. According to Piaget, children entering the concrete operational period become capable for the first time of applying logical thought processes to concrete problems.
2. Other cognitive advances that emerge in Piaget's concrete operational stage are the ability to "decenter" (to take multiple aspects of a situation into account), to grasp the notion of reversibility, and to understand concepts such as the relationship between speed and time.
3. Piaget's view has limitations due to his tendency to underestimate the capabilities of children and to overestimate the universality of his stages (which appear to have a significant cultural dimension). Nevertheless, the notion of concrete operational thinking has found clear applications in Western cultures and has influenced educational principles and practices positively.
4. According to information-processing approaches, intellectual development in middle childhood is more quantitative than qualitative. The rapid cognitive development of the period is attributed to substantial increases in memory capacity and in the sophistication of the "programs" children can handle.
5. Children's memory, including the ability to encode, store, and retrieve information, increases dramatically during the school years, and their increased understanding of

the processes that underlie memory (metamemory) enables them to use control strategies to improve cognitive processing and memorization.

How does language develop during the middle childhood period, and what special circumstances pertain to children for whom English is not the first language?

6. The language development of children in the school years is substantial, with improvements in vocabulary, syntax, and pragmatics. Despite these advances, school-age children's language is still not as proficient as it will become in adulthood, and some pronunciation and comprehension difficulties are normal.
7. Improvements in language help children control their behavior through linguistic strategies. Moreover, their growing metalinguistic awareness permits them to realize that language use is rule-governed and is subject to breakdowns for which they are not solely responsible, and which can be remedied by seeking clarification.
8. Bilingualism is an increasingly prevalent phenomenon in the school years. There is evidence that many children who are taught all subjects in the first language, with simultaneous instruction in English, experience few deficits and several linguistic and cognitive advantages.
9. Immersion programs work well when majority children are immersed during the school day in a minority language, but do not work as well the other way around: when minority children are immersed in the language of the majority.

What trends are affecting schooling worldwide and in the United States?

10. Schooling, which is available to nearly all children in most developed countries, is not as accessible to children (especially girls) in many less developed countries. The time at which schooling begins should be determined by the child's overall developmental readiness, rather than by age.
11. Schooling in the United States appears to be moving from a socioemotional focus on the student to a stronger emphasis on academic basics and student and teacher accountability.
12. Multiculturalism and diversity are significant issues in U.S. schools, where the traditional "melting pot" society, in which minority cultures were assimilated to the majority culture, is being replaced by the pluralistic society, in which individual cultures maintain their own identities while participating in the definition of a larger culture.
13. For children from minority cultures, the most promising contemporary approach is to encourage a bicultural identity, simultaneous membership in both the home culture and the new culture. In a school that supports this approach, instruction begins in the home language and shifts as quickly as possible to English.

How do subjective interpretations of successes and failures, by oneself and by others, contribute to school outcomes?

14. People attach attributions to their academic successes and failures, relating them to either internal, unchangeable factors, such as intelligence, or to external, changeable factors, such as luck or a failure to work hard. Differences in attributional patterns appear to be influenced by culture, race, and gender. Some attributional patterns that overemphasize uncontrollable factors may be maladaptive.
15. The expectancies of others, particularly teachers, can produce outcomes that conform to those expectancies. Expectancies can cause differences in the ways teachers deal with students, which may lead to modified behavior on the part of students, which in turn may confirm the teachers' initial expectancies.

How can intelligence be measured, what are some issues in intelligence testing, and how are children who fall outside the normal range of intelligence educated?

16. Intelligence testing has traditionally focused on factors that differentiate successful academic performers from unsuccessful ones. The intelligence quotient, or IQ, reflects the ratio of a person's mental age to his or her chronological age, based on average test performance for persons of a given chronological age.

17. More recently, other conceptualizations of intelligence have emerged, focusing on different types of intelligence (for example, fluid and crystallized intelligence, and Gardner's seven distinct intelligences) or on different aspects of the information-processing task (for example, Sternberg's triarchic theory, encompassing componential, experiential, and contextual aspects of intellectual processing).

18. The issue of possible cultural bias in IQ testing and the relationship among race, socioeconomic status, and IQ are highly controversial and hotly debated. In 1994, a book called *The Bell Curve* ignited a controversy by suggesting that low IQ scores are due to heredity, and account for poverty and other social ills. In fact, race differences in IQ scores most likely reflect environmental differences in the backgrounds of persons of different races.

19. The vast majority of persons with mental retardation suffer from a mild form and can profit from elementary education and eventually lead independent lives. People with more severe cases require significant assistance and care.

20. Gifted and talented children, whatever their advantages, appear to need special educational programs and materials to permit their gifts to flourish. These have been made available mainly through acceleration programs and enrichment programs.

Key Terms and Concepts

concrete operational stage (p. 345)
decentering (p. 345)
memory (p. 348)
metamemory (p. 349)
metalinguistic awareness (p. 350)
bilingualism (p. 352)
multicultural education (p. 358)
cultural assimilation model (p. 358)
pluralistic society model (p. 358)
bicultural identity (p. 359)
attributions (p. 360)
teacher expectancy effect (p. 362)
intelligence (p. 366)
mental age (p. 367)
chronological (physical) age (p. 367)
intelligence quotient (IQ) (p. 367)
Stanford-Binet Intelligence Scale (p. 368)
Wechsler Intelligence Scale for Children-III (WISC-III) (p. 368)
Wechsler Adult Intelligence Scale-III (WAIS-III) (p. 368)
Kaufman Assessment Battery for Children (K-ABC) (p. 368)
fluid intelligence (p. 368)
crystallized intelligence (p. 370)
triarchic theory of intelligence (p. 371)
mental retardation (p. 374)
mild retardation (p. 375)
moderate retardation (p. 375)
severe retardation (p. 375)
profound retardation (p. 375)
gifted and talented (p. 376)
acceleration (p. 376)
enrichment (p. 376)

CHAPTER 

MIDDLE CHILDHOOD

Social and Personality Development in Middle Childhood

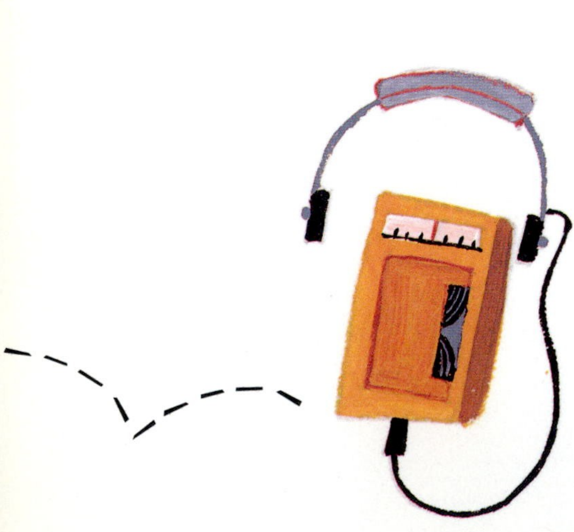

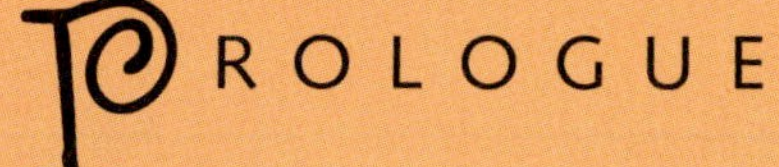

PROLOGUE

KEVIN

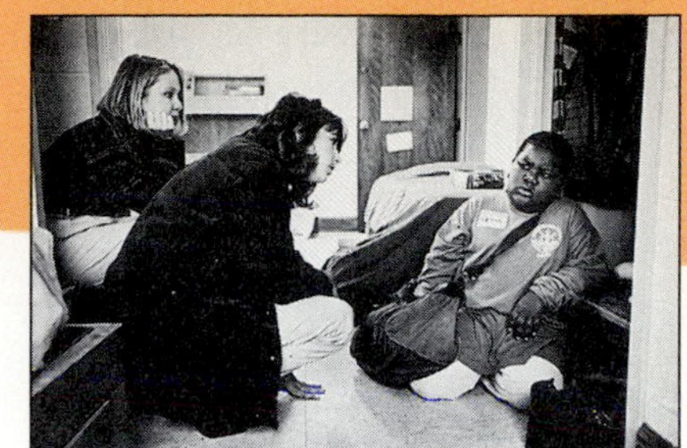

It is a cold, bleak Friday afternoon in Kansas City, and inside this second-floor dorm room at the Gillis Center, the atmosphere seems no less gloomy. Emily McLane, 24, one of the center's 42 child-care specialists, is getting Kevin ready for the weekend. "Okay, time to pack up," she tells him cheerfully. "You're going home." Suddenly the first-grader explodes in anger, scowling and clenching his fists. Although these weekend trips home to his grandmother's are routine, they still mean leaving the orderly world of Gillis for the chaos of home, where his mother's drug problems have shattered the family's stability. "Kevin," McLane asks as the boy's anger gradually subsides, "do you need a *hug?*" Kevin's face softens. "Yes," he says, melting into the young woman's arms. (Arias, 1995, p. 35–36)

LOOKING AHEAD

Like many residential treatment centers, the Gillis Center serves a variety of children. Some of them have severe emotional and behavioral problems, while others are orphans—children without parents whose problems keep them from being adopted. Others have families lost to crime, drugs, or violence and unable to care adequately for children.

Of course, children like Kevin are the exception. For most children in the United States, home is with their biological fathers and mothers, and a more typical array of relationships with friends and family affects development.

But regardless of their circumstances and fortune, children face a range of challenges during middle childhood that can affect their social and personality development, which we consider in this chapter. We start by examining the changes that occur in the ways children see themselves. We discuss how they view their personal characteristics, and we examine the complex issue of self-esteem.

Next, the chapter turns to relationships during middle childhood. We discuss the stages of friendship and the ways gender and ethnicity affect how and with whom children interact. We also look at how to improve children's social competence.

The last part of the chapter examines the central societal institution in children's lives: the family. We consider the consequences of divorce, self-care children, and the phenomenon of group care.

In sum, after reading this chapter, you will be able to answer the following questions:

- In what ways do children's views of themselves change during middle childhood?
- How do children in this period develop a sense of self-esteem?
- What sorts of relationships and friendships are typical of middle childhood?
- What are the causes and effects of popularity and unpopularity?
- How do gender and race affect friendships?
- How do today's diverse family and care arrangements affect children?

The Developing Self

> Nine-year-old Karl Haglund is perched in his eagle's nest, a treehouse built high in the willow that grows in his backyard. Sometimes he sits there alone among the tree's spreading branches, his face turned toward the sky, a boy clearly enjoying his solitude. Sometimes he's with his friend, engrossed in the kind of talk that boys find fascinating.
>
> This morning Karl is busy sawing and hammering. "It's fun to build," he says. "I started the house when I was 4 years old. Then when I was about 7, my dad built me this platform. 'Cause all my places were falling apart and they were crawling with carpenter ants. So we destroyed them and then built me a deck. And I built on top of it. It's stronger now. You can have privacy here, but it's a bad place to go when it's windy 'cause you almost get blown off." (Kotre & Hall, 1990, p. 116)

Karl's growing sense of competence is reflected in the passage above, as he describes how he and his father built his treehouse. Conveying what psychologist Erik Erikson calls industriousness, Karl's quiet pride in his accomplishment illustrates one of the ways in which children's views of themselves evolve.

Understanding One's Self: A New Response to "Who Am I?"

During middle childhood, children continue their efforts to answer the question "Who am I?" as they seek to understand the nature of the self. Although the question does not yet have the urgency it will assume in adolescence, elementary-school-age children still seek to pin down their place in the world.

The Shift in Self-understanding from the Physical to the Psychological. Several changes in children's views of themselves during middle childhood illustrate the quest for self-understanding. For one thing, they begin to view themselves less in terms of external, physical attributes and more in terms of psychological traits (Aboud & Skerry, 1983).

For instance, 6-year-old Carey describes herself as "a fast runner and good at drawing"—both characteristics dependent on skill in external, motoric activities. In contrast, 11-year-old Meiping characterizes herself as "pretty smart, friendly, and helpful to my friends." Meiping's portrayal is based on psychological characteristics, inner traits that are more abstract than the younger child's descriptions. The use of inner traits to determine self-concept results from the child's increasing cognitive skills, a development that we discussed in Chapter 11.

In addition to shifting focus from external characteristics to internal, psychological traits, children's views of self become more differentiated. As they get older, children discover that they may be good at some things and not so good at others. Ten-year-old Ginny, for instance, comes to understand that she is good at arithmetic but not very good at spelling; 11-year-old Alberto determines that he is good at softball but doesn't have the stamina to play soccer very well.

Furthermore, children's self-concepts become divided into personal and academic spheres. In fact, research on students' self-concepts in English, mathematics, and nonacademic realms has found that the separate self-concepts are not always correlated, although there is overlap among them.

Furthermore, as can be seen in Figure 12-1, self-concept in each of four domains—academic, social, emotional, and physical—can be further broken down. For instance, the nonacademic self-concept includes the components of physical appearance, peer relations, and physical ability. In sum, self-concept becomes increasingly differentiated as children mature (Marsh, 1990; Marsh & Holmes, 1990).

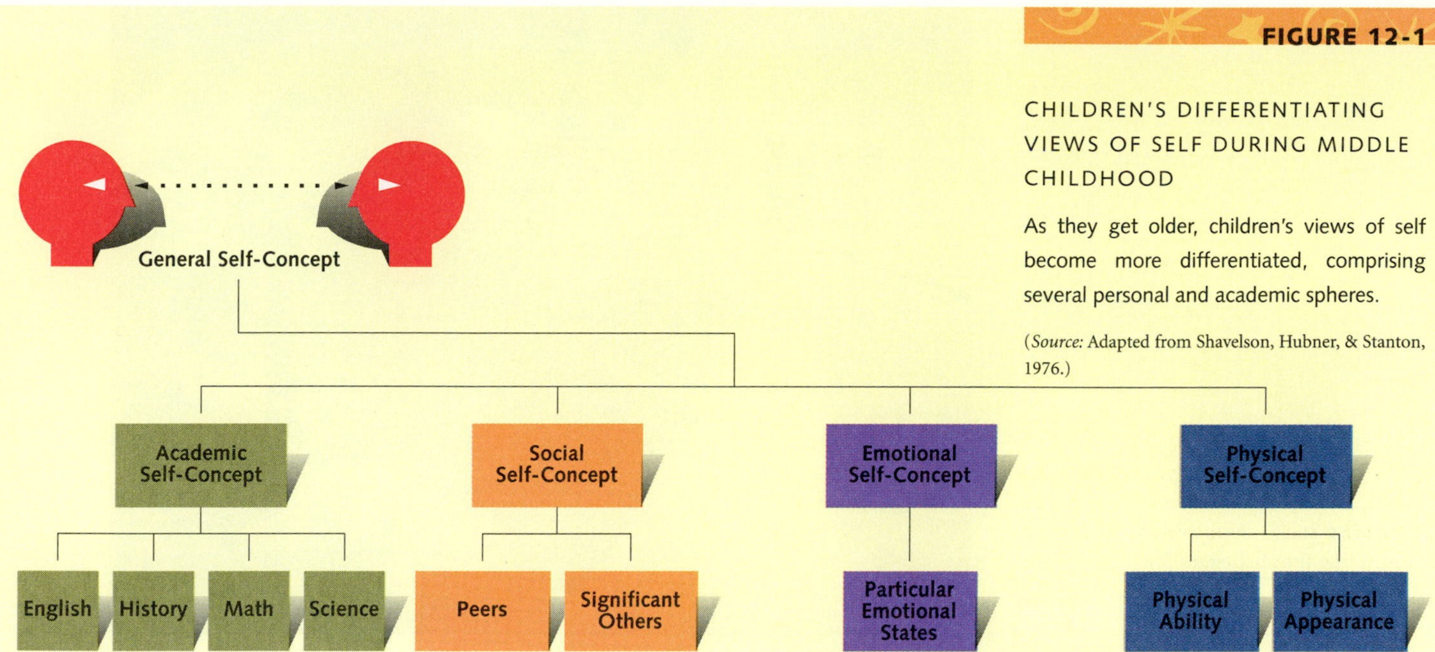

FIGURE 12-1

CHILDREN'S DIFFERENTIATING VIEWS OF SELF DURING MIDDLE CHILDHOOD

As they get older, children's views of self become more differentiated, comprising several personal and academic spheres.

(*Source:* Adapted from Shavelson, Hubner, & Stanton, 1976.)

Social comparison. If someone asks you how good you are at math, how would you respond? Most of us would compare our performance to others who are roughly of the same age and educational level. It is unlikely that we'd answer the question by comparing ourselves either to Albert Einstein or to a kindergartner just learning about numbers.

Elementary-school-age children begin to follow the same sort of reasoning when they seek to understand how able they are. Whereas earlier they tended to consider their abilities in terms of absolutes, now they begin to use social comparison processes to determine their levels of accomplishment during middle childhood.

Social comparison is the desire to evaluate one's own behavior, abilities, expertise, and opinions by comparing them to those of others. According to a theory first suggested by psychologist Leon Festinger (1954), when concrete, objective measures of ability are lacking, people turn to *social reality* to evaluate themselves. Social reality refers to understanding that is derived from how others act, think, feel, and view the world.

But who provides the most adequate comparison? Generally, children compare themselves to persons who are similar along relevant dimensions. Consequently, when they cannot objectively evaluate their ability, children during middle childhood increasingly look to others who are similar to themselves (Ruble et al., 1989; Suls & Wills, 1991; Wood, 1989).

Although children typically compare themselves to similar others, in some cases—particularly when their self-esteem is at stake—they choose to make *downward social comparisons* with others who are obviously less competent or successful (Pyszczynski, Greenberg, & LaPrelle, 1985).

Downward social comparison protects self-image. By comparing themselves to those who are less able, children ensure that they will come out on top and thereby preserve an image of themselves as successful.

Downward social comparison helps explain why some students in elementary schools that have low achievement levels are found to have stronger academic self-esteem than very capable students in schools with high achievement levels. The reason seems to be that students in the low-achievement schools observe others who are not doing terribly well academically, and they feel relatively good by comparison. In contrast, students in the high-achievement schools may find themselves competing with a more academically proficient group of students, and their perception of their performance may suffer in comparison. In some ways, then, it is better to be a big fish in a small pond than a small fish in a big one (Marsh & Parker, 1984).

social comparison *the desire to evaluate one's own behavior, abilities, expertise, and opinions by comparing them to those of others*

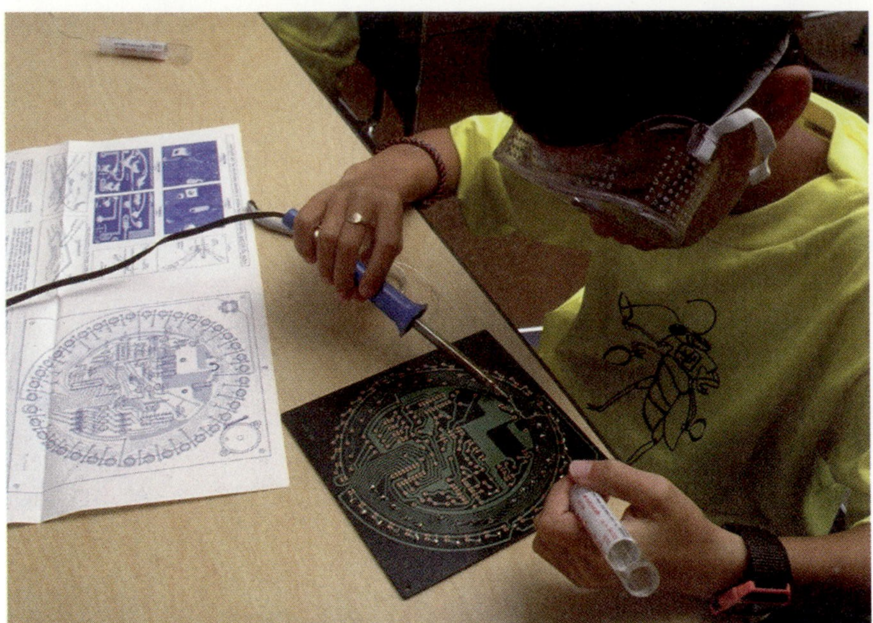

According to Erik Erikson, middle childhood encompasses the industry-versus-inferiority stage, characterized by a focus on meeting the challenges presented by the world.

PSYCHOSOCIAL DEVELOPMENT IN MIDDLE CHILDHOOD: INDUSTRY VERSUS INFERIORITY

According to Erik Erikson, whose approach to psychosocial development we've considered in earlier chapters, middle childhood encompasses the **industry-versus-inferiority stage.** Lasting from roughly age 6 to age 12, the industry-versus-inferiority stage is characterized by a focus on efforts to attain competence in meeting the challenges presented by parents, peers, school, clubs and groups to which they belong, and the other complexities of the modern world.

As they move through middle childhood, children direct their energies not only to mastering what they are presented in school–an enormous body of information–but also to making a place for themselves in their social worlds. Success in those efforts brings with it feelings of mastery and proficiency and a growing sense of competence.

On the other hand, difficulties in this stage lead to feelings of failure and inadequacy. Children may come to feel unskilled and incapable. As a result, they may withdraw both from academic pursuits, showing less interest and motivation to excel, and from interactions with peers.

Developing industriousness during the middle childhood years has lasting consequences. For example, one study examined how childhood industriousness and hard work were related to adult behavior by following a group of 450 men over a 35-year period, starting in early childhood. The men who were most industrious and hard-working during childhood were most successful as adults, both in occupational attainment and in their personal lives. In fact, childhood industriousness was more closely associated with adult success than was intelligence or family background (Vaillant & Vaillant, 1990).

industry-versus-inferiority stage *the period from age 6 to 12 characterized by a focus on efforts to attain competence in meeting the challenges presented by parents, peers, school, clubs and groups, and the other complexities of the modern world*

self-esteem *an individual's overall and specific positive and negative self-evaluation*

SELF-ESTEEM: DEVELOPING A POSITIVE—OR NEGATIVE—VIEW OF ONESELF

Children don't dispassionately view themselves just in terms of an itemization of physical and psychological characteristics. Instead, they think of themselves as being good, or bad, in particular ways. **Self-esteem** is an individual's overall and specific positive and negative self-evaluation. Whereas self-concept reflects beliefs and cognitions about the self, self-esteem is more emotionally oriented (Baumeister, 1993).

Self-esteem develops in important ways during middle childhood. Children increasingly compare themselves to others, and as they do, they assess how well they measure up to society's standards. In addition, they increasingly develop their own, internal standards of success, and they can see how well they compare to those.

One of the advances that occurs during middle childhood is an increasing differentiation of self-esteem. At the age of 7, most children have self-esteem that reflects a global, undifferentiated view of themselves. If their overall self-esteem is positive, they assume that they are relatively good at all things. Conversely, if their overall self-esteem is negative, they assume that they are inadequate at most things (Harter, 1990b; Marsh & Shavelson, 1985). As children progress into the middle childhood years, however, their self-esteem becomes differentiated: higher for some areas that they evaluate, and lower for others.

Change and Stability in Self-esteem. Generally, the self-esteem of most children tends to increase during middle childhood, with a brief decline around the age of 12. Although there are probably several reasons for the decline, the main one appears to be the school transition that typically occurs around this age: Students leaving elementary school and entering either middle school or junior high school show a decline in self-esteem, which then gradually rises again (Eccles et al., 1989).

Children with chronically low self-esteem face a tough road, in part because their self-esteem becomes enmeshed in a cycle of failure that grows increasingly difficult to break. Assume, for instance, that Harry, a student with chronically low self-esteem, is facing an important test. Because of his low self-esteem, he expects to do poorly. As a consequence, he is quite anxious—so anxious that he is unable to concentrate well and study effectively. Furthermore, he may decide not to study much, because he figures that if he's going to do badly anyway, why bother studying?

Ultimately, of course, Harry's high anxiety and lack of effort bring about the result he expected: He does poorly on the test. This failure, which confirms Harry's expectation, reinforces his low self-esteem, and the cycle of failure continues (see Figure 12-2).

The importance of self-esteem in helping to determine academic success, as well as in other domains, has led some experts to suggest that raising self-esteem is critical in solving a variety of academic and social problems. However, as we discuss in the "Directions in Development" box, holding oneself in high esteem may not be without its drawbacks.

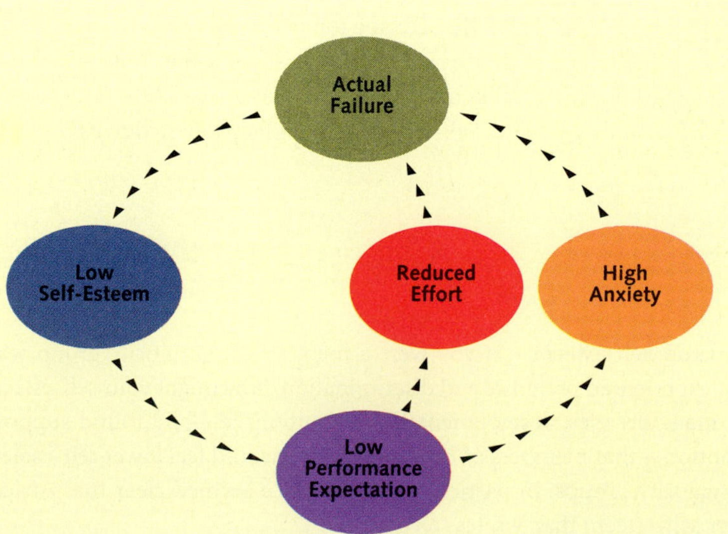

FIGURE 12-2

THE CYCLE OF LOW SELF-ESTEEM

Because children with low self-esteem may expect to do poorly on a test, they may experience high anxiety and not work as hard as those with higher self-esteem. As a result, they actually do perform badly on the test, which in turn confirms their negative view of themselves.

According to recent findings, high self-esteem may actually be associated with higher levels of aggression than low self-esteem.

Directions in Development

Self-esteem, Violence, and Aggression: The Downside of High Self-esteem

> *Leigh is on the road to trouble. Even as a fifth grader, he is cutting school, stealing from local stores, and participating in fights. The local police already are well acquainted with him, and his parents have told his teacher that he barely listens to them. His teacher, however, thinks she has a solution: raise Leigh's self-esteem, which, because of his behavior, she is sure must be exceptionally low. Surely, she believes, helping him to feel better about himself will make him less aggressive and hostile.*

If such a solution seems reasonable to you, you are not alone: Many experts feel that bolstering the self-esteem of children can cure a variety of societal ills, most particularly violence and other forms of antisocial behavior (e.g., California Task Force, 1990).

However, according to new research conducted by psychologists Roy Baumeister, Laura Smart, and Joseph Boden (1996), such an approach not only may be wrong, but also may actually make the problem worse. In a comprehensive review of studies of aggression, they found that *high* self-esteem is often associated with violence and aggression.

In their review of a massive amount of literature from many disciplines, the researchers found that perpetrators of violence frequently not only see themselves in a favorable light, but in fact have an inflated view of themselves. Even in the face of contrary evidence, such as school failure, the inability to get along with peers, and family strife, some individuals hold surprisingly positive views of themselves, and in fact it is these positive views that lead to violence.

According to this argument, when individuals with unusually high self-esteem are challenged, they vigorously seek to maintain their view of themselves as superior, frequently through violent means. In contrast, people with lower self-esteem are less prone to lash out at others when attacked or challenged, because such threats to their self-worth are more in keeping with their more negative view of themselves.

In short, individuals with unusually high self-esteem are motivated to maintain their high level of self-regard. When challenged by others or by various circumstances in which they find themselves, they direct their anger toward others or toward the situation. In turn, this tactic allows them to avoid revising their view of themselves in a negative direction.

Of course, these findings do not mean that every person high in self-esteem is likely to act violently. Nor do they mean that seeking to bolster the self-esteem of perpetrators of violence is necessarily a poor strategy. But they do suggest that raising self-esteem to levels that are incongruent with reality may not be the best approach to dealing with individuals who are violent and aggressive. Self-esteem may, in fact, have a downside.

Ethnicity and Self-esteem. If you were a member of a minority group whose members routinely experienced prejudice and discrimination, how might your self-esteem be affected?

For many decades, developmentalists hypothesized—and found supportive evidence for the notion—that members of minority groups would feel lower self-esteem than members of majority groups. In particular, the evidence seemed clear that African Americans had lower self-esteem than whites (Deutsch, 1967).

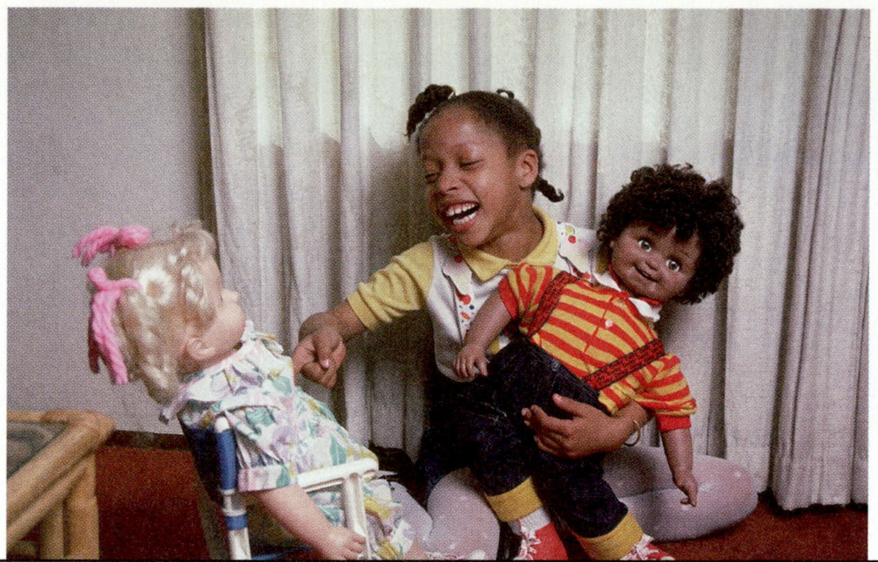

In pioneering research conducted several decades ago, African-American girls' preference for white dolls was viewed as an indicator of low self-esteem. More recent evidence, however, suggests that whites and African-American children show little difference in self-esteem.

Some of the first evidence was found in a set of pioneering studies more than a generation ago, in which African-American children were shown a black doll and a white doll (Clark & Clark, 1947). In the study, the children received a series of requests, including "Give me the doll that looks bad" and "Give me the doll that is a nice color." In every case, the African-American children preferred white dolls over black ones. The interpretation that was drawn from the study: The self-esteem of the African-American children was low.

Subsequent research in the 1950s and 1960s supported the notion that children showed lower self-esteem as a consequence of being members of minority groups that were discriminated against. In fact, some research even suggested that members of minority groups preferred members of majority groups to members of their own groups, and that they rejected membership in their own groups, showing a form of self-hatred due to minority-group status (Miner, 1983).

More recent theorizing, however, sheds a different light on the issue of self-esteem and racial group membership. According to French psychologist Henri Tajfel (1982), members of a minority group are likely to accept the negative views held by a majority group only if they perceive that there is little realistic possibility of changing the power and status differences between the groups.

On the other hand, if the existing differences between majority and minority group members are viewed as illegitimate, unstable, and potentially changeable, then minority group members will place the blame for the prejudice and discrimination they experience on societal forces and prejudice, and not on themselves. In this case, self-esteem between African Americans and whites should not differ.

In fact, societal attitudes favoring group pride and ethnic awareness for minority group members, as well as increased sensitivity to the importance of multiculturalism in general, have become considerably more widespread in the last several decades. Such attitudes have resulted in a narrowing of measured differences in self-esteem between members of different ethnic groups (Duckitt, 1994; Garbarino, 1985; Harter, 1990a).

Self-efficacy: Expecting to Be Capable

"Will I do well in arithmetic?" "How will I be able to complete this project?" "Can I make the after-school basketball team?"

These questions are typical of those that children ask themselves during the elementary school years. How each is answered depends in large measure on a child's self-efficacy. **Self-efficacy** refers to learned expectations that one is capable of carrying out a behavior or producing a desired outcome in a particular situation (Bandura, 1988, 1993; Schunk, 1991).

self-efficacy *learned expectations that one is capable of carrying out a behavior or producing a desired outcome in a particular situation*

Self-efficacy is critical to children's success because it motivates greater effort and persistence in the face of a challenging task. As a result, children with high self-efficacy are more likely to be successful, whether the realm is academics or athletics (Bandura & Schunk, 1981; Scheier & Carver, 1992; M. S. Taylor et al., 1991).

Self-efficacy develops over the course of middle childhood. By observing their prior successes and failures on particular tasks, children begin to develop a sense of how well they can expect to do within a particular domain. For instance, a child who has even moderate success roller-blading for the first time is on the road to developing self-efficacy in that domain and is more likely to try it in the future. In contrast, a child who has little initial success is less likely to try it in the future.

There are other sources of children's self-efficacy. For instance, observation of others' success (or failure) in an activity can affect a child's sense of self-efficacy. Direct reinforcement from others, in the form of praise or encouragement, is also an important determinant (Bandura, 1988).

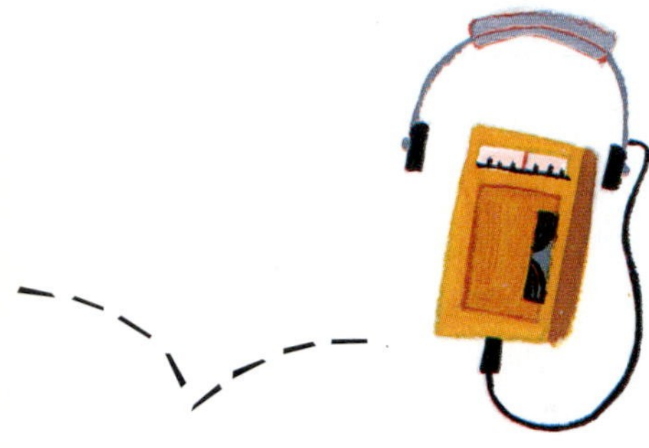

Review and Rethink

REVIEW

- In the middle childhood years, children begin to use social comparison to develop self-concepts involving psychological rather than physical characteristics and differentiation into distinct domains.
- According to Erikson, children at this time are in the industry-versus-inferiority stage, with a focus on achieving competence and meeting increasingly complex challenges.
- During middle childhood, self-esteem develops significantly through comparisons with others and the formation of internal standards of success. If self-esteem is low, a cycle of failure can result. If self-esteem is excessively high, challenges to it may produce violent reactions.
- Members of racial minorities can have low self-esteem if they feel powerless to change a discriminatory status and power structure. However, if that structure is viewed as illegitimate and changeable, minority group members can have high self-esteem as they fight discrimination.
- Self-efficacy—a sense of one's capabilities—develops over the course of middle childhood through reflections on one's own performance, observations of others, and feedback.

RETHINK

- In what ways do the cognitive advances of middle childhood, discussed in the previous chapter, support developmental changes in self-understanding and self-concept?
- Does the fact that students in low-achievement schools often have higher academic self-esteem than students in high-achievement schools argue against high-achievement schools? Why or why not?
- If industriousness is a more accurate predictor of future success than IQ, how might industriousness be measured? How might an individual's industriousness be improved? Should this be a focus of schooling?
- What might be some reasonable approaches to dealing with a violent person who has inflated self-esteem?
- Does the "cycle of failure" concept in the realm of self-esteem also apply to self-efficacy? Is it possible to break the cycle? If so, how?

Relationships: Building Friendship in Middle Childhood

Put yourself in 6-year-old Jamillah Johnson's shoes, as she eats lunch during her first day in a new school:

> In Lunch Room Number Two, Jamillah and her new classmates chew slowly on sandwiches and sip quietly on straws from cartons of milk. They huddle into their seats, staring blankly ahead, in awe of what's happening. The school principal moves among them with a microphone. "We eat quietly and we eat in our seats. No one gets up." On this day, no one seems inclined to test him. Boys and girls look timidly at the strange faces across the table from them, looking for someone who might play with them in the schoolyard, someone who might become a friend. (Kotre & Hall, 1990, p. 112–113)

peer group *Children who are about the same age and developmental level as one another*

For Jamillah and her classmates, the task of finding and making friends is central to their lives. In fact, building and maintaining friendships comes to play an increasingly important role during middle childhood. Children grow progressively more sensitive to the importance of their **peer group,** children who are about the same age and developmental level as themselves, and building and maintaining friendships becomes a large part of children's social lives.

The formation of friendships influences children's development in several ways. For instance, friendships provide children with information about the world and other people, as well as about themselves. Friends provide emotional support that allows children to respond more effectively to stress. Friends can teach children how to manage and control their emotions, and help them interpret their own emotional experiences. Friendships also provide a training ground for communicating and interacting with others, and they can foster intellectual growth. Finally, friendships allow children to practice their skills in forming close relationships with others—skills that will become increasingly important in their future lives (Asher & Parker, 1991; Hartup, 1992, 1996; Bukowski, Newcomb, & Hartup, 1996).

Stages of Friendship: Changing Views of Friends

During middle childhood, children's conception of the nature of friendship undergoes some profound changes. According to developmental psychologist William Damon (1977; Damon & Hart, 1988), children's view of friendship passes through three distinct stages.

In the first stage, which ranges from around 4 to 7 years of age, children see friends as others who like them and with whom they share toys and other activities. They view the children with whom they spend the most time as their friends. For instance, a kindergartner who was asked, "How do you know that someone is your best friend?" responded in this way:

> I sleep over at his house sometimes. When he's playing ball with his friends he'll let me play. When I slept over, he let me get in front of him in 4-squares. He likes me. (Damon, 1983, p. 140)

What children in this first stage don't do much of, however, is to take others' personal qualities into consideration. For instance, they don't see their friendships as being based upon their peers' unique positive personal traits. Instead, they use a very concrete approach to deciding who is a friend, primarily dependent upon others' behavior. They like those who share and with whom they can share, while they don't like those who don't share, who hit, or who don't play with them. In sum, in the first stage, friends are viewed largely in terms of presenting opportunities for pleasant interactions.

In the next stage, however, children's view of friendship becomes more complicated. Lasting from around age 8 to age 10, this stage covers a period in which children take

Friendships provide children with emotional support as well as information about others and themselves.

others' personal qualities and traits into consideration. In addition, friends are viewed in terms of the kinds of rewards they provide. For instance, consider how an 8-year-old girl explains why another girl is her "best friend":

> She never disagrees, she never eats in front of me, she never walks away when I'm crying, and she helps me on my homework. (Damon, 1988, p. 80–81)

Clearly, this girl's view of friendship is based on the responsivity of her "best friend" to her needs, not just on how often they engage in shared activities. In fact, the centerpiece of friendship in this second stage is mutual trust. Friends are seen as those who can be counted on to help out when they are needed. This means that violations of trust are taken very seriously, and friends cannot make amends for such violations just by engaging in positive play, as they might at earlier ages. Instead, the expectation is that formal explanations and formal apologies must be provided before a friendship can be re-established.

The third stage of friendship begins toward the end of middle childhood, from 11 to 15 years of age. During this period, children begin to develop the view of friendship that they hold during adolescence. Although we'll discuss this perspective in detail in Chapter 15, the main criteria for friendship shift toward intimacy and loyalty. Friendship is characterized by psychological closeness, mutual disclosure, and exclusivity. By the time they reach the end of middle childhood, children seek out friends who will be loyal (Newcomb & Bagwell, 1995).

Consider, for instance, the following sixth-grader's response to the question "How do you know that someone is your best friend?":

> If you can tell each other things that you don't like about each other. If you get in a fight with someone else, they'd stick up for you. If you can tell them your phone number and they don't give you crank calls. If they don't act mean to you when other kids are around. (Damon, 1983, p. 140)

The twin themes of intimacy and loyal support are clearly sounded in this child's response. By the end of middle childhood, then, children come to view friendship not so much in terms of shared activities as in terms of the psychological benefits that friendship brings.

Children also develop clear ideas about which behaviors they seek in their friends—and which they dislike. As can be seen in Table 12-1, fifth- and sixth-graders most enjoy others who invite them to participate in activities and who are helpful, both physically and psychologically. In contrast, displays of physical or verbal aggression, among other behaviors, are disliked.

STATUS AMONG SCHOOL-AGE CHILDREN: ESTABLISHING A PECKING ORDER

Who's on top? Although school-age children are not likely to articulate such a question, the reality of children's friendships is that they exhibit clear hierarchies in terms of status. **Status** is the evaluation of a role or person by other members of a group or society. Children who have higher status have greater access to available resources, such as games, toys, books, and information. In contrast, lower-status children are more likely to follow the lead of children of higher status.

Status is an important determinant of children's friendships. Higher-status children tend to form friendships with higher-status individuals, while lower-status children are more likely to have friends of lower status. The number of friends a child has is also related to status: Higher-status children are more apt to have a greater number of friends than those of lower status.

But it is not only quantity of social interactions that separates higher-status children from lower-status children; the nature of their interactions is different. Higher-status chil-

status *the evaluation of a role or person by other members of a group or society*

TABLE 12-1

THE MOST-LIKED AND LEAST-LIKED BEHAVIORS THAT CHILDREN NOTE IN THEIR FRIENDS, IN ORDER OF IMPORTANCE

MOST-LIKED BEHAVIORS	LEAST-LIKED BEHAVIORS
Having a sense of humor	Verbal aggression
Being nice or friendly	Expressions of anger
Being helpful	Dishonesty
Being complimentary	Being critical or criticizing
Inviting one to participate in games, etc.	Being greedy or bossy
Sharing	Physical aggression
Avoiding unpleasant behavior	Being annoying or bothersome
Giving one permission or control	Teasing
Providing instructions	Interfering with achievements
Loyalty	Unfaithfulness
Performing admirably	Violating rules
Facilitating achievements	Ignoring others

Adapted from Zarbatany, Hartmann, & Rankin (1990).

dren are more likely to be viewed as friends by other children. They are more likely to form cliques, groups that are viewed as exclusive and desirable, and they tend to interact with a greater number of other children. In contrast, children of lower status are more likely to play with younger or less popular children (Ladd, 1983).

Popularity, then, is a reflection of children's status. School-age children who are average to high in status are more likely to initiate and coordinate joint social behavior, making their general level of social activity higher than that of children low in social status (Erwin, 1993).

Individual Differences in Friendship: What Makes a Child Popular?

Why is it that some children are the schoolyard equivalent of the life of the party, while others are social isolates, whose overtures to others are dismissed or disdained?

Developmental researchers have attempted to answer this question by examining individual differences in popularity, seeking to identify the reasons why some children climb the ladder of popularity while others remain firmly on the ground (Bigelow, Tesson, & Lewko, 1996).

What Personal Characteristics Lead to Popularity? Popular children share several personality characteristics. They are usually helpful, cooperating with others on joint projects. They are also funny, tending to have good senses of humor and to appreciate others' attempts at humor. Compared with children who are less popular, they are better able to understand others' emotional experiences by more accurately reading their nonverbal behavior. In sum, popular children are high in **social competence,** the collection of specific social skills that permit individuals to perform successfully in social settings (Erwin, 1993; Feldman, Philippot, & Custrini, 1991; Hubbard & Coie, 1994).

Popular children are not totally self-sufficient. They show interest in others, and they are not afraid to ask for others' help when necessary. At the same time, though, they are not overly reliant on others. Consequently, popular children maintain a balance between independence and dependence (Hartup, 1970; Rubin, Daniels-Beirness, & Hayvren, 1982).

social competence *the collection of specific social skills that permit individuals to perform successfully in social settings*

neglected children *children who receive relatively little attention, in the form of either positive or negative interactions, from their peers*

rejected children *children who are actively disliked and whose peers may react to them in an obviously negative manner*

When they enter a new social situation, popular children have a sense of what is occurring and learn to adapt their behavior to the situation. They are aware that it takes time to build relationships and that they may only gradually become a full member of a new group (Asher, 1983; Putallaz, 1983).

Children who are unpopular, in contrast, can be sad figures, for school-age children can be particularly unwelcoming to social outcasts. Unpopular children may be the last chosen to participate in activities with other children, or they may be actively discriminated against in classroom activities.

On the other hand, unpopular children are not always unhappy children, and they often have at least some friends. For example, one study showed that only a moderate association existed between unpopularity in school and children's reports of how lonely they were. One explanation may be that the children who are unpopular in school compensate by playing with neighborhood friends or siblings (Asher, Hymel, & Renshaw, 1984; Vandell & Hembree, 1994).

What makes some children unpopular? Some are unliked because they are immature, acting silly or in ways that are more appropriate to younger children. Others are overly aggressive, showing hostility to their peers or acting in an overbearing manner, while still others are so withdrawn that they permit little interaction. Some children are unpopular because they are far from society's stereotypes of physical attractiveness. Consequently, children who are unusually obese or thin, who "look funny," or who are extremely slow academically may find themselves in the unenviable role of class outcast (Crick & Grotpeter, 1995; Dodge & Crick, 1990).

Lack of popularity may take one of two forms (Asher & Parker, 1991). **Neglected children** are those who receive relatively little attention from their peers. They are not necessarily disliked; they just do not receive much attention in the form of either positive or negative interactions. It turns out, however, that neglected children do not fare all that badly. Although they see themselves as less socially competent than other children, they often don't feel less happy or accepted than their more popular peers. Morevoer, they tend to do well academically (Erwin, 1993; Wentzel & Asher, 1995).

On the other hand, a second form of unpopularity—active rejection—is more harmful. **Rejected children** are actively disliked, and their peers may react to them in an obviously negative manner. Rejected children are disruptive, aggressive, uncooperative, short-tempered, and unfriendly. In general, they lack social competence. Moreover, their behavior is often seen as a problem not only by other children, but by adults as well (Boivin, Dodge, & Coie, 1995; DeRosier, Kupersmidt, & Patterson, 1994; Volling, Mackinnon-Lewis, Rabiner, & Baradaran, 1993).

A variety of factors lead some children to be unpopular and socially isolated from their peers.

The long-term outcomes for rejected children can be quite negative. Rejected children are more likely to be poorly adjusted and to show delinquency in their later lives than popular or neglected children. Of course, it is not clear whether these difficulties are caused by their rejection by their peers or by behavior problems that may have led them to become rejected in the first place.

social problem solving *the use of strategies for solving social conflicts in ways that are satisfactory both to oneself and to others*

Social Problem-solving Abilities. Another factor that relates to children's popularity is their skill at social problem solving. **Social problem solving** refers to the use of strategies for solving social conflicts in ways that are satisfactory both to oneself and to others. Because social conflicts among school-age children are a not infrequent occurrence—even among the best of friends—successful strategies for dealing with them are an important element of social success (Hay, 1984).

According to developmental psychologist Kenneth Dodge, successful social problem solving proceeds through a series of steps that correspond to children's information-processing strategies (see Figure 12-3). Dodge argues that the manner in which children solve social problems is a consequence of the decisions that they make at each point in the sequence (Dodge, 1985b; Dodge, Pettit, McClasky, & Brown, 1986; Dodge & Crick, 1990; Dodge & Price, 1994).

By carefully delineating each of the stages, Dodge provides a means by which interventions can be targeted toward a specific child's deficits. For instance, some children routinely misinterpret the meaning of other children's behavior (Step 2) and then respond according to their misinterpretation.

Consider, for example, Frank, a fourth-grader, who is playing a game with Bill. While playing the game, Bill begins to get angry because he is losing. If Frank mistakenly assumes that Bill is angry not because he is losing but because of something that Frank has done, Frank's misunderstanding may lead *him* to react with anger, making the situation more

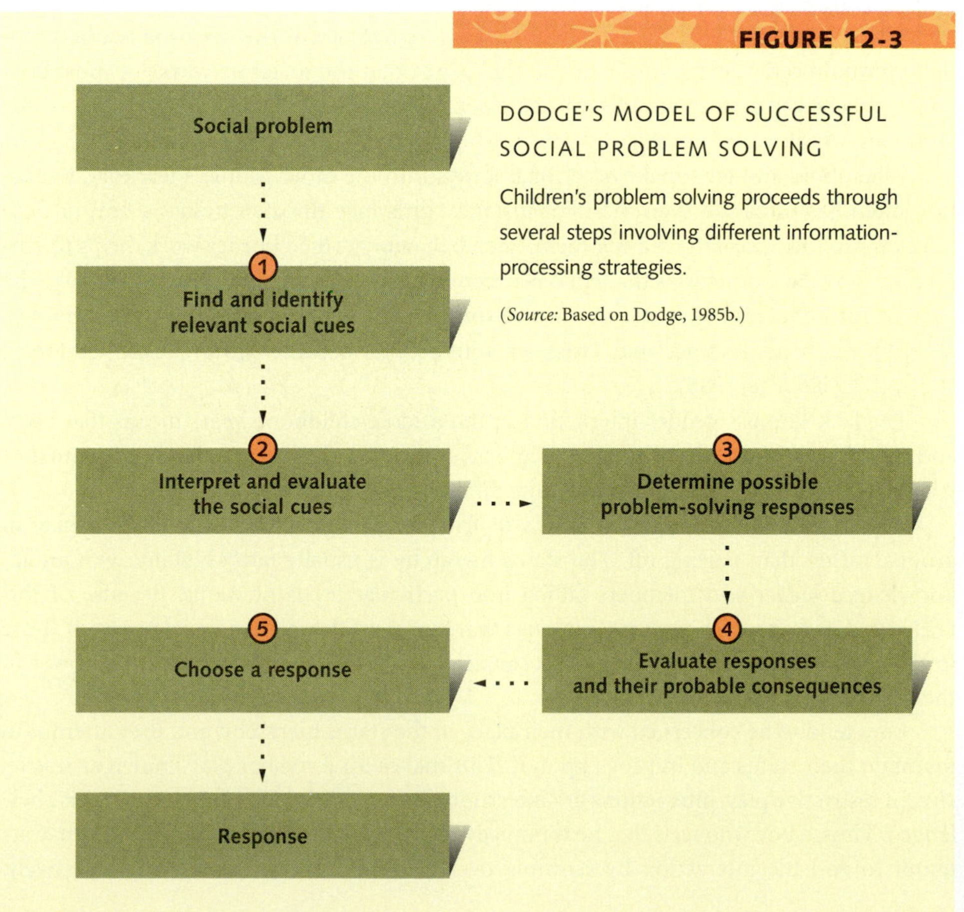

FIGURE 12-3

DODGE'S MODEL OF SUCCESSFUL SOCIAL PROBLEM SOLVING

Children's problem solving proceeds through several steps involving different information-processing strategies.

(*Source:* Based on Dodge, 1985b.)

volatile. If Frank had interpreted the source of Bill's anger more accurately, Frank might have been able to behave in a more effective manner, thereby defusing the situation.

dominance hierarchy *rankings that represent the relative social power of those in a group*

Generally, children who are popular are better at interpreting the meaning of others' behavior. Furthermore, they possess a wider inventory of techniques for dealing with social problems. In contrast, less popular children tend to be less effective at understanding the causes of others' behavior, and their strategies for dealing with social problems are more limited (Vitaro & Pelletier, 1991).

Teaching Social Competence. Can anything be done to help unpopular children learn social competence? Happily, the answer appears to be "yes." Several programs have been developed to teach children a set of social skills that seem to underlie general social competence. For example, in one experimental program, a group of unpopular fifth- and sixth-graders were taught the skills that underlie such abilities as holding a conversation with friends. They were taught ways to disclose material about themselves, to learn about others by asking questions, and to offer help and suggestions to others in a nonthreatening way. Compared with a group of children who did not receive such training, the children who were in the experiment interacted more with their peers, held more conversations, developed higher self-esteem, and—most critically—were more accepted by their peers than before training (Bierman & Furman, 1984).

Similarly, children in another program were taught to be more adept at decoding the meaning of facial expressions, thereby becoming more sensitive to others' emotions and moods. As a result of their training, some children in the program became noticeably better at making friends and getting along with their teachers (Nowicki & Duke, 1994).

GENDER AND FRIENDSHIPS: THE SEX SEGREGATION OF MIDDLE CHILDHOOD

Boys are idiots. Girls have cooties.

At least those are the typical views offered by girls and boys regarding members of the opposite sex during the elementary school years. Avoidance of the opposite sex becomes quite pronounced during those years, to the degree that the social networks of most boys and girls consist almost entirely of same-sex groupings (Adler, Kless, & Adler, 1992; Gottman, 1986).

When boys and girls make occasional forays into the other gender's territory, the action often has romantic overtones. For instance, girls may threaten to kiss a boy, or boys might try to lure girls into chasing them. Such behavior, termed border work, helps to emphasize the clear boundaries that exist between the two sexes. In addition, it may pave the way for future interactions that do involve romantic or sexual interests, when school-age children reach adolescence and cross-sex interactions become more socially endorsed (Beal, 1994; Thorne, 1986).

The lack of cross-gender interaction in the middle childhood years means that boys' and girls' friendships are restricted to members of their own gender. However, the nature of friendships within the two genders is quite different.

Boys, who typically have a larger network of friends than girls, usually have a fairly rigid dominance hierarchy in the groups in which they interact.

Boys typically have larger networks of friends than girls, and they tend to play in groups, rather than pairing off. The status hierarchy is usually fairly blatant, with an acknowledged leader and members falling into particular levels of status. Because of this fairly rigid **dominance hierarchy,** rankings that represent the relative social power of those in the group, members of higher status can safely question and oppose children lower in the hierarchy (Beal, 1994).

Boys tend to be concerned with their place in the status hierarchy, and they attempt to maintain their status and improve upon it. This makes for a style of play known as *restrictive.* In restrictive play, interactions are interrupted when a child feels that his status is challenged. Thus, a boy who feels that he is unjustly challenged by a peer of lower status may attempt to end the interaction by scuffling over a toy or otherwise behaving assertively.

Consequently, boys' play tends to come in bursts, rather than in more extended, tranquil episodes (Benenson & Apostoleris, 1993; Boulton & Smith, 1990).

The language of friendship used among boys reflects their concern over status and challenge. For instance, consider this conversation between two boys who were good friends:

Child 1: Why don't you get out of my yard.

Child 2: Why don't you *make* me get out the yard.

Child 1: I *know* you don't want that.

Child 2: You're not gonna make me get out the yard 'cuz you can't.

Child 1: Don't force me.

Child 2: You can't. Don't force me to hurt you *(snickers)* (Goodwin, 1990, p. 37).

Friendship patterns among girls are quite different. Rather than having a wide network of friends, school-age girls focus on one or two "best friends" who are of relatively equal status. In contrast to boys, who seek out status differences, girls tend to avoid differences in status, preferring to maintain friendships at equal-status levels.

Conflicts among school-age girls are solved through compromise, by ignoring the situation, or by giving in, rather than by seeking to make one's own point of view prevail. In sum, the goal is to smooth over disagreements, making social interaction easy and nonconfrontational (Goodwin, 1990).

According to developmental psychologist Carole Beal (1994), the motivation of girls to solve social conflict indirectly does not stem from a lack of self-confidence or from apprehension over the use of more direct approaches. In fact, when school-age girls interact with other girls who are not considered friends or with boys, they can be quite confrontational. However, among friends their goal is to maintain equal-status relationships—ones lacking a dominance hierarchy.

The language used by girls tends to reflect their view of relationships. Rather than blatant demands ("Give me the pencil"), girls are more apt to use language that is less confrontational and directive. Girls tend to use indirect forms of verbs, such as "Let's go to the movies" or "Would you want to trade books with me?" rather than "I want to go to the movies" or "Let me have these books" (Goodwin, 1980, 1990).

Interestingly, the segregation of friendships according to gender occurs in almost all societies. Why should this be? In nonindustrialized societies, same-gender segregation may be the result of the types of activities that children engage in. For instance, in many cultures, boys are assigned one type of chore and girls another. Segregation in activities leads to the development of same-gender friendships (Harkness & Super, 1985; Whiting & Edwards, 1988).

Developmental Diversity

Promoting Friendships across Racial and Ethnic Lines: Integration in and out of the Classroom

Are friendships colorblind? For the most part, the answer is "no." Children's closest friendships tend largely to be with others of the same race and ethnicity. In fact, as children age there is a decline in the number and depth of friendships outside their own racial group. By

Although closest friendships tend to be with others of the same race, members of different racial and ethnic groups can show a high degree of mutual acceptance, particularly in schools with ongoing integration efforts.

the time they are 11 or 12, it appears that African-American children become particularly aware of and sensitive to the prejudice and discrimination directed toward members of their race, and they are more apt to make in-group, out-group distinctions (Hartup, 1983; Singleton & Asher, 1979).

For instance, when third-graders from one long-time integrated school were asked to name a best friend, around one quarter of white children and two thirds of African-American children chose a child of the other race. In contrast, by the time they reached 10th grade, less than 10 percent of whites and 5 percent of African Americans named a different-race best friend (Asher, Singleton, & Taylor, 1982; Singleton & Asher, 1979).

On the other hand, although they may not choose each other as best friends, whites and African Americans—as well as members of other minority groups—can show a high degree of mutual acceptance. This pattern is particularly true in schools with ongoing integration efforts. This makes sense: A good deal of research supports the notion that contact between majority and minority group members can reduce prejudice and discrimination.

Contact between different racial groups is effective for several reasons. For one thing, people may find that they have more in common with members of other racial groups than they had expected. This realization leads to greater attraction. In addition, as people learn more about members of other racial groups, their previously held but inaccurate biases may be reduced (Gaertner et al., 1990; Stephan, 1985).

Contact among members of different ethnic groups and races can open access to information about a broader range of educational and occupational opportunities, as well as cultural and leisure choices. It can also reduce anxieties and fears that members of both minority and majority groups hold about people outside their group. Finally, contact offers the opportunity to view members of other racial and ethnic groups as individuals rather than as representatives of some vague, distant, and homogeneous group (Desforges et al, 1991; Wells & Crain, 1994).

On the other hand, contact between members of majority and minority groups does not invariably increase cross-racial acceptance. Contact is effective only if several important conditions are met (Cook, 1984). First, the contact must occur in equal-status settings. It hardly seems realistic to expect, for instance, that hiring an African-American custodian in a school will reduce the prejudice of white students; placing white and African American same-status students together in the same classes would be of greater benefit.

A second important factor concerns the intimacy of the interaction between group members. Majority and minority group members must be cooperatively involved in activities that are important to them. They need to know each other on an informal basis and as individuals.

Finally, the situation must support interracial interaction and favor equality. It must allow the disconfirmation of negative stereotypes and permit individuals to interact under a variety of circumstances (Gerard, 1988; N. Miller & Brewer, 1990; Stephan, 1985, 1986).

In sum, contact can be an effective means of promoting acceptance and friendship among school-age children, as long as the conditions outlined in this section are met. Fortunately, in most elementary-school settings, this can be the case. Students in the same class can be made to feel that they are of relatively equal status; they can be guided, through various teaching techniques, to interact closely and cooperatively; and teachers can communicate the importance of interracial interaction and equality.

In addition, majority and minority group interaction can spill over outside of school once it occurs in the classroom. For example, students attending schools with a substantial minority population report relatively frequent interracial contacts after school. However, there remains a higher likelihood that a minority group member will have a majority group friend than that a majority group member will have a minority group friend. This tendency is not surprising, particularly in schools in which the minority group population is proportionately small relative to the majority group. In such cases, on a statistical basis alone we'd expect fewer opportunities for majority group members to interact with minority group members (DuBois & Hirsch, 1990; Howes & Wu, 1990).

The Informed Consumer of Development

Increasing Children's Social Competence

It is clear that building and maintaining friendships is critical in children's lives. Is there anything that parents and teachers can do to increase children's social competence?

The answer is a clear "yes." Among the strategies that can work are the following:

- Encourage social interaction. Teachers can devise ways in which children are led to take part in group activities, and parents can encourage membership in groups such as Brownies and Cub Scouts or participation in team sports.
- Teach listening skills to children. Show them how to listen carefully and respond to the underlying meaning of a communication as well as its overt content.
- Make children aware that people display emotions and moods nonverbally and that consequently they should pay attention to others' nonverbal behavior, not only to what they are saying on a verbal level.
- Teach conversational skills, including the importance of asking questions and self-disclosure. Encourage students to use "I" statements in which they clarify their own feelings or opinions, and avoid making generalizations about others.
- Don't ask children to choose teams or groups publicly. Instead, assign children randomly. It works just as well in ensuring a distribution of abilities across groups and avoids the public embarrassment of a situation in which some children are chosen last.

Review and Rethink

REVIEW

- Children pass through stages in their understanding of the nature of friendship, from the sharing of enjoyable activities, through the consideration of personal traits that can meet their needs, to a focus on intimacy and loyalty.
- Friendships in childhood display status hierarchies, with popular, high-status children manifesting social competence and engaging in more relationships; low-status

children becoming followers; and unpopular children being either neglected or rejected by their peers.

- Because social competence affects popularity, improvements in such abilities as social problem solving and social information processing can lead to better interpersonal skills and greater popularity.
- Boys and girls engage increasingly in same-sex friendships, with boys' friendships involving group relationships, dominance hierarchies, and restrictive play, and girls' friendships characterized by equal-status pairings, cooperation, compromise, and the avoidance of confrontation.
- Interracial friendships decrease in frequency as children age, but equal-status contacts among members of different races can promote mutual acceptance and appreciation.

RETHINK

- Do you think the stages of friendship are a childhood phenomenon, or do adults' friendships display similar stages?
- Is there a "cycle of success" in the relationship between social competence and popularity? A "cycle of failure" in their opposites?
- How does the increasing sophistication of cognitive skills contribute to social competence? Does social competence relate to one of Howard Gardner's seven intelligences discussed in Chapter 11?
- Do you think boys' and girls' different approaches to friendship are primarily genetic or environmental? In what ways might they be influenced by cultural factors?
- Is it possible to decrease the segregation of friendships along racial lines? What factors would have to change in individuals or in society?

FAMILY LIFE

> The routine is similar every day. Five days a week, after school gets out, 10-year-old Marlene O'Connor gets off the school bus and trudges up the hill to her home. She takes the house key, which she keeps on a string around her neck to avoid losing it, and opens the front door to her empty home. Locking the door behind her, she turns on the television and calls her mother, who is at work as a service representative for an Ohio electric utility. After chatting briefly with her mother, assuring her that she is well, Marlene turns her attention to the television as she eats a snack she has found in the kitchen. She watches TV until her mother and father return home a few hours later.

Is Marlene paying a price because both her parents work outside the home? This question is one of several that we need to address as we consider how children's home situations profoundly affect their lives during middle childhood.

FAMILIES IN THE 1990S: THE CHANGING WORLD OF FAMILY LIFE

> The original plot goes like this: First comes love. Then comes marriage. Then comes Mary with a baby carriage. But now there's a sequel: John and Mary break up. John moves in with Sally and her two boys. Mary takes the baby Paul. A year later Mary meets Jack, who is divorced with three children. They get married. Paul, barely 2 years old, now has a mother, a father, a stepmother, a stepfather, and five stepbrothers and stepsisters—as well as four sets of grandparents (biological and step) and countless aunts and uncles. And guess what? Mary's pregnant again. (Katrowitz & Wingert, 1990, p. 24)

We've already noted in earlier chapters the changes that have occurred in the structure of the family over the last few decades. With a soaring divorce rate, an increase in the number of parents who both work outside of the home, and a rise in single-parent families, the environment faced by children passing through middle childhood in the 1990s is very different from the one prior generations faced.

coregulation *a transitional stage during middle childhood in which children and parents jointly control the children's behavior*

One of the basic challenges facing children and their parents is to navigate the independence that increasingly characterizes children's behavior during middle childhood. During the period, children move from being almost completely controlled by their parents to increasingly controlling their own destinies–or at least their everyday conduct. Middle childhood, then, is a period of **coregulation,** in which children and parents jointly control behavior. Increasingly, parents provide broad, general guidelines for conduct, while children have control over their everyday behavior. For instance, parents may urge their daughter to buy a balanced, nutritious school lunch each day, but their daughter's decision to regularly buy pizza and two desserts is very much her own.

While coregulation is of concern to children in every family situation, it is particularly difficult for children with parents who have divorced. In fact, divorce produces the potential for several kinds of difficulties.

The Consequences of Divorce. Having divorced parents is no longer very distinctive. Only around half the children in the United States spend their entire childhoods living in the same household with both their parents (Jacobson, 1987). The rest will live in single-parent homes; or with stepparents, grandparents, or other non-parental relatives; and some will end up in foster care.

How do children react to divorce? The answer depends on how soon you ask the question following a divorce, as well as how old the children are at the time. Immediately after a divorce, the results can be quite devastating. Both children and parents may show several types of psychological maladjustment for a period that may last from 6 months to 2 years. For instance, children may be anxious, experience depression, or show sleep disturbances and phobias. Even though children most often live with their mothers following a divorce, the quality of the mother-child relationship declines in the majority of cases (Gottman, 1993; Guttman, 1993).

During the early stage of middle childhood, children whose parents are divorcing often blame themselves for the breakup. By the age of 10, children feel pressure to choose sides, taking the position of either the mother or the father. They thereby experience some degree of divided loyalty (Wallerstein & Blakeslee, 1989).

The consequences of divorce become less devastating from 18 months to 2 years later. After reaching a low point at around 1 year following the divorce, most children begin to return to their predivorce state of psychological adjustment. Still, compared to children whose parents have remained married, twice as many children of divorced parents require psychological counseling (Hetherington, Stanley-Hagan, & Anderson, 1989; Zill, 1983; Chase-Lansdale, Cherlin, & Kiernan, 1995).

Several factors relate to how children react to divorce. One is the economic standing of the family the child is living with. In many cases, divorce brings a decline in both parents' standards of living. When this occurs, children may be thrown into poverty, which can have a negative effect on many aspects of their upbringing.

In other cases, the negative consequences of divorce are less severe than they might otherwise be because the divorce reduces the hostility and anger in the home. Because the predivorce household typically was overflowing with parental strife, in some cases the relative lack of conflict of a postdivorce household may be beneficial to children. This is particularly true for children who maintain a close, positive relationship with the parent with whom they do not live. Consequently, for some children, living with parents who have an intact but unhappy marriage, high in conflict, has more and stronger negative consequences than experiencing a parental divorce (Booth & Edwards, 1989; Cherlin, 1993; Davies & Cummings, 1994; Gelles, 1994; Gottfried & Gottfried, 1994).

Living in Blended Families. For many children, the aftermath of divorce includes the subsequent remarriage of one or both parents. In fact, more than 10 million households in the United States contain at least one spouse who has remarried. More than five million remarried couples have at least one stepchild living with them in what has come to be called **blended families.** Experts predict that by the year 2000, over 50 percent of children born in the last decade will be stepdaughters and stepsons (Glick, 1989; U.S. Bureau of the Census, 1991b).

blended families *remarried couples who have at least one stepchild living with them*

Living in a blended family is challenging for the children involved. There often is a fair amount of *role ambiguity,* in which roles and expectations are unclear. Children may be uncertain about their responsibilities, how to behave to stepparents and stepsiblings, and how to make a host of decisions that have wide-ranging implications for their role in the family. For instance, a child in a blended family may have to choose which parent to spend each vacation and holiday with, or to decide between the conflicting suggestions they have received from biological parent and stepparent. Thus, even though a parent's life may improve because of a remarriage, their children may not be happier (Cherlin, 1993; Dainton, 1993; Wallerstein & Blakeslee, 1990).

How do school-age children in blended families fare? In many cases, surprisingly well. In comparison to adolescents, who have more difficulties, school-age children often adjust relatively smoothly to blended arrangements, for several reasons. For one thing, the family's financial situation is often improved after a parent remarries. In addition, in a blended family more people are available to share the burden of household chores. Finally, the fact that the family contains more individuals can increase the opportunities for social interaction (Hetherington & Clingempeel, 1992; Hetherington, Stanley-Hagan, & Anderson, 1989).

On the other hand, not all children adjust well. Some find the disruption of routine and of established networks of family relationships difficult. For instance, a child who is used to having her mother's complete attention may find it difficult to observe her mother showing interest and affection to a stepchild. The blending of families does not always proceed smoothly.

When Both Parents Work. In most cases, children whose parents both work full time outside of the home fare quite well. Most research suggests that children whose parents are loving, are sensitive to their children's needs, and provide appropriate substitute care de-

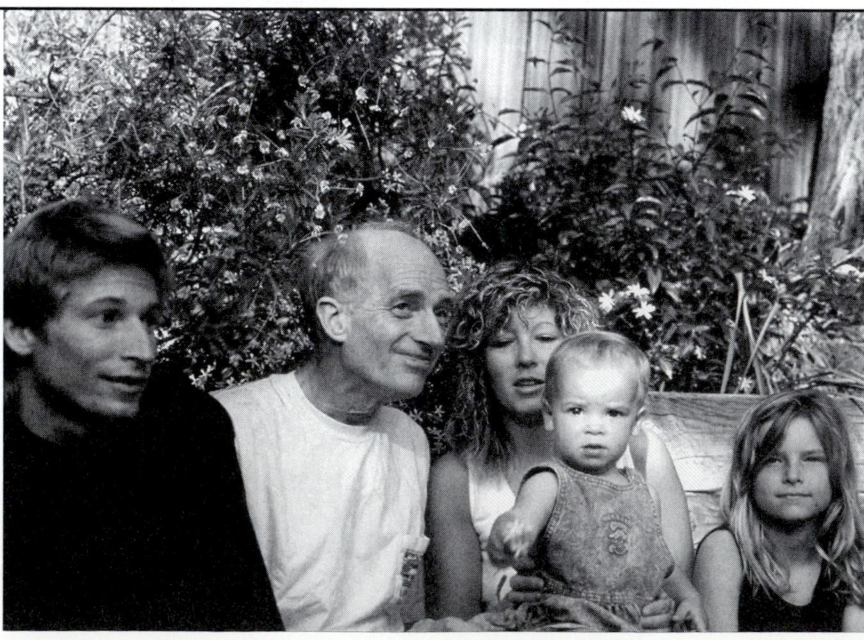

"Blended" families occur when previously married husbands and wives remarry.

velop no differently than children in families in which one of the parents does not work (Hoffman, 1989; Kamerman & Hayes, 1982).

One reason that children whose mothers and fathers both work develop no differently relates to the psychological adjustment of the parents. In general, women who are satisfied with their lives tend to be more nurturing with their children. When work provides a high level of satisfaction, then mothers who work outside of the home may be more psychologically supportive of their children. Thus, it is not so much a question of whether a mother chooses to work full-time, to stay at home, or to arrange some combination of the two. What matters is how satisfied she is with the choices she has made (Barnett & Rivers, 1992; Gilbert, 1994; Scarr, Phillips, & McCartney, 1989).

self-care children *children who let themselves into their homes after school and care for themselves until their parents return from work*

Although we might expect that children whose parents both work would spend comparatively less time with their parents than children with one parent at home full-time, research suggests otherwise. Children with mothers and fathers who work full-time spend essentially the same amount of time with family, in class, with friends, and alone as children in families where one parent stays at home (Galambos & Dixon, 1984; Richards & Duckett, 1991, 1994).

Furthermore, as much time is spent on family meals and evening activities for children in families in which mothers are employed as in families in which mothers are not employed. In fact, some evidence suggests that working parents try to compensate for time that they are away from home, spending even more time in the evenings with their children than parents who do not both work.

On the other hand, the parent with whom children spend their time may be different. For instance, one survey of 10- to 13-year-olds found that children whose mothers were employed full time spent more time alone with their fathers than children whose mothers were not so employed (Richards & Duckett, 1994).

Self-care Children. Although children in families in which both parents work typically fare well, their success is due in part to the availability of adequate substitute care. For many children, however, no care is available, and they return after school to empty houses. These are **self-care children,** children who let themselves into their homes after school and wait alone until their parents return from work.

Concern about self-care children has centered on their lack of supervision and the emotional costs of being alone. In fact, such children were previously called *latchkey children,* raising connotations of sad, pathetic, and neglected children. However, research has not identified many differences between self-care children and children who return to homes with parents. Although many children report negative experiences while at home by themselves (such as loneliness), they seem emotionally undamaged by the experience. In addition, if they stay at home by themselves rather than "hanging out" unsupervised with friends, they may avoid involvement in activities that can lead to difficulties (Long & Long, 1983; Rodman & Cole, 1987; Steinberg, 1986).

In sum, the consequences of being a self-care child are not necessarily harmful. In fact, children may develop an enhanced sense of independence and competence. Furthermore, the time spent alone provides an opportunity to work uninterrupted on homework or school projects. Some findings even suggest that children with employed parents can have higher self-esteem because they feel they are contributing to the household in significant ways (Hoffman, 1989).

The consequences of being a so-called self-care child are not necessarily harmful, and may even lead to a greater sense of independence and competence.

Single-parent Families. Almost one quarter of all children under the age of 18 in the United States live with only one parent. If present trends continue, almost three quarters of American children will spend some portion of their lives in a single-parent family before they are 18 years old. For minority children, the numbers are even higher: Some 60 percent of African-American children and 35 percent of Hispanic children under the age of 18 live in single-parent homes (Demo & Acock, 1991; U.S. Bureau of the Census, 1990b, 1994).

FIGURE 12-4

THE COMPOSITION OF SINGLE-PARENT FAMILIES

For both African Americans and Caucasians, the single parent who is present is most often the mother.

(*Source:* Suro, 1992).

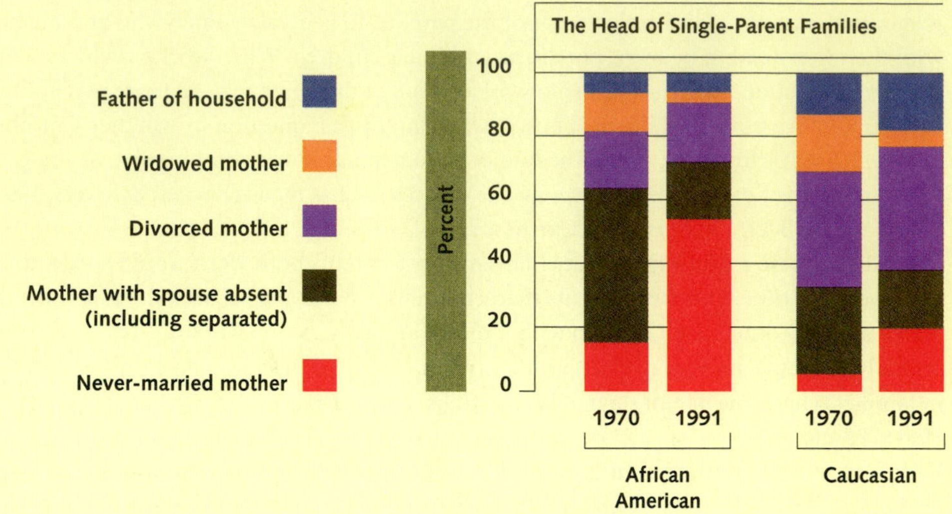

Single-parent households reflect several situations (see Figure 12-4). The most prevalent are cases in which there never was a spouse (that is, the mother never married), the spouses have divorced, or the spouse is absent. In the vast majority of cases, the single parent who is present is the mother.

What consequences are there for children living in homes with just one parent? This is a difficult question to answer. Much depends on whether a second parent was present earlier and, if so, whether the two parents got along with each other or were constantly fighting. In cases of high parental strife, the decrease in overall tension and anxiety in a household reduced to a single parent may actually enhance a child's adjustment (Gongla & Thompson, 1987; Gottman & Katz, 1989).

Furthermore, the economic status of the single-parent family plays a role in determining the consequences on children. Living in relative poverty—and single-parent families are often less well-off financially than two-parent families—has a negative impact on children.

In short, the impact of living in a single-parent family is not, by itself, invariably negative or positive. Given the large number of single-parent households, the stigma that once existed toward such families has largely declined. The ultimate consequences for children depend on a variety of factors that accompany single parenthood, such as the economic status of the family, the amount of time that the parent is able to spend with the child, and the degree of stress in the household.

THE CONSEQUENCES OF GROUP CARE: ORPHANAGES IN THE 1990S

The term *orphanage* evokes images of pitiful youngsters clothed in rags, eating porridge out of tin cups, and housed in huge, prisonlike institutions.

The reality today is different. Even the term *orphanage* is rarely used, having been replaced by *group home* or *residential treatment center.* Typically housing a relatively small number of children, group homes are used for children—like Kevin, described at the beginning of this chapter—whose parents are no longer able to care for them adequately.

Although orphanages of the early 1900s were crowded and institutional (left), today the equivalent, called group homes or residential treatment centers (right), are much more pleasant.

Group care has grown significantly in the last decade. In fact, in just the 4-year period from 1987 to 1991, the number of children in foster care increased by more than 50 percent. Today, close to one-half million children in the United States live in foster care (Carnegie Task Force on Meeting the Needs of Young Children, 1994).

About three quarters of children in group care have been victims of neglect and abuse. Most of them can be returned to their homes, following intervention with their families by social service agencies. But the remaining one quarter are so psychologically damaged due to abuse or other causes that, once they are placed in group care, they are likely to remain there throughout childhood. With severe problems, such as high levels of aggression or anger, they are largely unadoptable. No family wants to house them even temporarily in a foster home (Fanshel, Finch, & Grundy, 1990; Sugden, 1995).

Although some politicians have suggested that an increase in group care is a solution to complex social problems associated with unwed mothers who become dependent on welfare, experts in providing social services and psychological treatment are not so sure. For one thing, group homes cannot always consistently provide the support and love potentially available in a family setting. Moreover, group care is hardly cheap: It can cost some $40,000 per year to support a child in group care—about 10 times the cost of maintaining a child in foster care or on welfare (Cox & Cox, 1985; Fanshel, Finch, & Grundy, 1990, 1992).

Other experts argue that group care is neither inherently good nor bad. Instead, the consequences of living away from one's family may be quite positive, depending on the particular characteristics of the staff of the group home and whether child- and youth-care workers are able to develop an effective, stable, and strong emotional bond with a specific child. (Table 12-2 shows the personal characteristics of the best—and worst—child- and youth-care workers.) On the other hand, if a worker is unable to form a meaningful relationship with a child in a group home, the results may well be unfavorable (Shealy, 1995). (For one view of group care, see the "Speaking of Development" interview.)

TABLE 12-2

PERSONAL CHARACTERISTICS OF THE BEST AND WORST CHILD AND YOUTH CARE WORKERS

THE BEST WORKERS	*THE WORST WORKERS*
Flexible	Exhibit pathology
Mature	Selfish
Integrity	Defensive
Good judgment	Dishonest
Common sense	Abusive
Appropriate values	Abuse drugs/alcohol
Responsible	Uncooperative
Good self-image	Poor self-esteem
Self-control	Rigid
Responsive to authority	Irresponsible
Interpersonally adept	Critical
Stable	Passive-aggressive
Unpretentious	Inappropriate boundaries
Predictable/consistent	Unethical
Nondefensive	Authoritarian/coercive
Nurturant/firm	Inconsistent/unpredictable
Self-aware	Avoidant
Empowering	Don't learn from experience
Cooperative	Poor role model
Good role models	Angry/explosive

(*Source:* Adapted from Shealy, 1995.)

Speaking of Development

Sam Schmidt, Group Home Teacher

Born: 1966

Education: University of Nebraska at Lincoln, B.A. in business administration

Position: Family teacher at Boys Town

Home: Boys Town, Nebraska

Following graduation from college, Sam and Kristin Schmidt became house parents, or as they are called at Boys Town, family teachers, in one of the 76 individual homes at Boys Town.

"Many of the kids who come to Boys Town have been physically or sexually abused, and almost all of them have been emotionally abused," Schmidt says. "They have a distorted perception of how to treat other children and adults. We try to teach them appropriate boundaries and help them learn gradually to build relationships to the point where they are comfortable and confident with other people.

"A major problem in our children is their behavior patterns, which they have learned in a dysfunctional family setting or in and around their neighborhoods. Boys Town combines a family style environment with skill-based training to help remediate these learned behaviors," says Schmidt. "We teach them a number of different skills, such as how to follow instructions, accept criticism, and agree and disagree appropriately with adults."

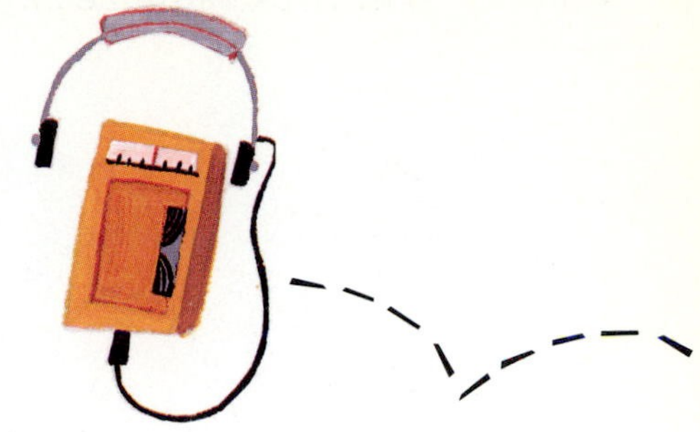

Review and Rethink

REVIEW

- Divorce can cause psychological difficulties in school-age children, but the consequences depend on such factors as financial circumstances and the comparative levels of tension in the family before and after the divorce.
- Despite the awkward choices and role ambiguity that living with stepparents and stepsiblings can cause, most school-age children in blended families fare well because of improved family finances and the presence of new siblings with whom to interact and share chores.
- Children whose parents work outside the home usually receive about the same amount of parental attention and care as children with an at-home parent, and self-care children may gain independence and enhanced self-esteem from their experience.
- Single parenthood may have either positive or negative effects on children, depending on family finances, the amount of parent-child interaction, and the level of tension in the family.
- Most children in group care have been victims of neglect and abuse; following professional intervention with their families, most can return home. However, about one quarter of children in group care have been so severely damaged psychologically that they are likely to remain in group care throughout childhood.

"A major problem in our children is their behavior patterns, which they have learned in a dysfunctional family setting or in and around their neighborhoods."

Boys Town has its own elementary school and high school, and many of the same techniques are applied there as are used in the home, according to Schmidt. One of the basic approaches is called SODAS, or *S*ituation, *O*ptions, *D*isadvantages, *A*dvantages, and *S*olution.

"We start by asking the individuals to write down what the situation is—say, taking out the trash," Schmidt explains. "They then think of two or three options, such as 'I will do it' and 'I won't do it.' Then they write down the advantages and disadvantages of each option and think about them. This process usually helps them arrive at a solution."

Another important tool at Boys Town is a point system used to motivate the kids to behave appropriately. Positive points are awarded for appropriate behavior and point fines are assessed for irresponsible behaviors.

"Once a day the point cards are totaled, and if the kids have enough points they get privileges like watching television, going to the gym, or using the telephone," Schmidt says. "If they don't make the point total, they are assigned to work with the family teachers to learn the skills that caused them to lose their privileges. We accomplish this by doing role plays with the youths, providing them with rationales for understanding, and we continue to practice these skills to help ensure more success in the future.

"When they come here they learn the basic skills, and usually they respond to them very well," he adds. "Many of them practice the skills over time, until, gradually, appropriate behavior becomes internalized and they do it without thinking about it."

"Gradually, appropriate behavior becomes internalized and they do it without thinking about it."

RETHINK

- How might the development of self-esteem in middle childhood be affected by a divorce? By a family situation characterized by constant hostility and tension between parents?
- In what ways might cognitive changes in middle childhood help children adjust to life in a blended family?
- How might being a self-care child affect self-efficacy, self-concept, and self-esteem?
- If children whose parents both work at satisfying jobs fare well, is the same true of children whose parents do not find satisfaction in their work, but are forced to work anyway?
- Politicians often speak of "family values." How does this term relate to the diverse family situations covered in this chapter?

In what ways do children's views of themselves change during middle childhood?

1. In middle childhood, children begin to view themselves in terms of psychological characteristics rather than physical ones. In addition, they begin to differentiate their self-concepts into several distinct areas.
2. Children use social comparison as an important means of arriving at an evaluation of their behavior, abilities, expertise, and opinions. Generally, they measure themselves against relevant others in their environment.
3. According to Erikson, children in the middle childhood years are in the industry-versus-inferiority stage, during which they focus on achieving competence and responding to a wide range of personal challenges. Their success or failure at meeting these challenges affects their sense of competence and can have lifelong consequences.

How do children in this period develop a sense of self-esteem?

4. In addition to working on their self-concepts, children in the middle childhood years are also developing self-esteem, an evaluation of their overall worth as individuals. While in general self-esteem grows steadily during these years, a temporary dip appears at around age 12, most likely attributable primarily to the transition from elementary school to the next higher school level.
5. Children with chronically low self-esteem can become trapped in a cycle of failure in which low self-esteem feeds on itself by producing low expectations and poor performance. On the other hand, children with excessively high self-esteem may have a tendency to react with violence to perceived threats to their self-esteem.
6. Members of minority groups that are the objects of discrimination may have low self-esteem unless they are convinced that the discrimination they experience are illegitimate and can be changed.
7. Children develop a sense of self-efficacy during middle childhood, using reflections on their own behavior, observations of the behavior of others, and feedback from others to form expectations about what they are capable of doing and achieving.

What sorts of relationships and friendships are typical of middle childhood?

8. Children's understanding of friendship passes through stages, from a focus on mutual

liking and time spent together, through a consideration of personal traits and the rewards that friendship provides, to an appreciation of intimacy and loyalty.

9. Children's friendships display clear status hierarchies, with high status leading to a greater number of friendships and interactions, access to more desirable resources, and membership in preferred social groupings.

What are the causes and effects of popularity and unpopularity?

10. Popularity in children is related to traits that underlie social competence, including cooperation, humor, understanding, adaptability, and skill at social problem solving. Unpopularity can result from socially unacceptable behavior, physical unattractiveness, or extreme academic slowness.

11. Popular children engage in activities that promote social development and skill. Unpopular children may be simply neglected by their peers, in which case they may not suffer serious consequences, or they may be rejected by their peers, in which case their ultimate social adjustment is endangered.

12. Because of the importance of social interactions and friendships, developmental researchers have engaged in efforts to improve social skills. The focus on improving social problem-solving skills has utilized the information-processing approach of psychologist Kenneth Dodge. This intervention technique targets deficits in children's processing of social information that affect their exercise of social skills.

How do gender and race affect friendships?

13. Gender is a significant factor in friendship. Not only do boys and girls increasingly prefer same-gender friendships, but friendships among males have different characteristics than friendships among females. Male friendships are characterized by groups of more than two, status hierarchies, and restrictive play to address status challenges. Female friendships tend to involve one or two close relationships, equal status among friends, and a reliance on cooperation, compromise, and the avoidance of confrontation.

14. Race also influences the formation of friendships, with cross-race friendships diminishing in frequency as children age. Nevertheless, equal-status interactions among members of different racial groups can lead to improved understanding, mutual respect and acceptance, and a decreased tendency to stereotype.

How do today's diverse family and care arrangements affect children?

15. Immediately after a divorce, the effects on school-age children can be serious, but they tend to diminish after about 18 to 24 months. If the divorce occurs during the early stage of middle childhood, children may blame themselves for it; if it occurs later in the period, they may feel pressure to choose sides.

16. Major factors in the seriousness of the consequences of divorce for children in this period are the financial condition of the family and the hostility level between spouses before the divorce.

17. The blended families that often result from divorce and remarriage present challenges to the child, including role ambiguity and awkward choices involving their parents, but blended families can also offer opportunities for increased social interaction and sharing of chores.

18. Children in families in which both parents work outside the home generally fare well, because their parents' sense of career fulfillment often translates into satisfaction in the home and because most working parents try hard to spend time with their children. When both parents work, their children (known as self-care children) often must fend for themselves in an empty home after school, a requirement that can lead to independence and a sense of competence and contribution.

19. Living in a single-parent family does not in itself lead to negative consequences. The factors that affect children in single-parent families are the same as those that affect children of divorce: the financial condition of the family and, if there had been two parents, the level of hostility that existed between them.
20. Children in group care, whose numbers are increasing, tend to have been victims of neglect and abuse before their group-care placement. Many can be helped and placed with their own or other families, but about 25 percent of them are so psychologically damaged that they will never be adopted or taken into a foster home and will spend the remainder of their childhood years in group care.

Key Terms and Concepts

social comparison (p. 385)
industry-versus-inferiority stage (p. 386)
self-esteem (p. 386)
self-efficacy (p. 389)
peer group (p. 391)
status (p. 392)
social competence (p. 393)
neglected children (p. 394)
rejected children (p. 394)
social problem solving (p. 395)
dominance hierarchy (p. 396)
coregulation (p. 401)
blended families (p. 402)
self-care children (p. 403)

PART 5

Adolescence

JOLT

CHAPTER 13

ADOLESCENCE

Physical Development in Adolescence

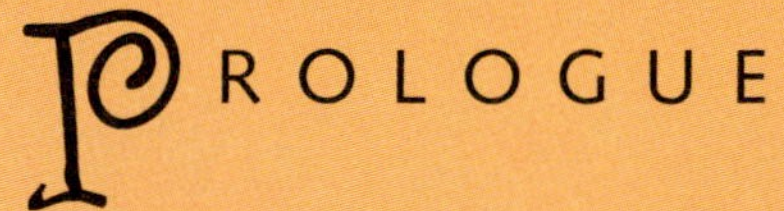

PROLOGUE

AGAINST THE ODDS

Recently, a student was shot dead by a classmate during lunch period outside Frank W. Ballou Senior High. It didn't come as much of a surprise to anyone at the school, in this city's most crime-infested ward. Just during the current school year, one boy was hacked by a student with an ax, a girl was badly wounded in a knife fight with another female student, five fires were set by arsonists, and an unidentified body was dumped next to the parking lot.

But all is quiet in the echoing hallways at 7:15 A.M., long before classes start on a spring morning. The only sound comes from the computer lab, where 16-year-old Cedric Jennings is already at work on an extra-credit project, a program to bill patients at a hospital. Later, he will work on his science-fair project, a chemical analysis of acid rain.

He arrives every day this early and often doesn't leave until dark. The high-school junior with the perfect grades has big dreams: He wants to go to Massachusetts Institute of Technology. (Suskind, 1994, p. 1)

LOOKING AHEAD

Cedric is one of a tiny group of students who have an average of B or better at their huge inner-city high school in Washington, D.C. This cadre of achievers is a lonely group, the frequent target of threats and actual violence. Yet Cedric perseveres, intent on getting a college education and succeeding academically and, ultimately, in life.

adolescence *the developmental stage that lies between childhood and adulthood*

Why do students such as Cedric overcome the extremes of poverty and violence that they face, while others are less successful? More broadly, what are the challenges that all adolescents face, and how do they confront those challenges?

In this chapter and the ones that follow, we consider the basic issues and questions that underlie adolescence. **Adolescence** is the developmental stage that lies between childhood and adulthood. It begins and ends imprecisely, starting just before the teenage years and ending just after them. This imprecision reflects the nature of society's treatment of the period: Adolescents are considered to be no longer children, but not yet adults. Clearly, though, adolescence is a time of considerable physical, cognitive, and social growth and change (Hoffman, 1996).

This chapter focuses on physical growth during adolescence. We begin by considering the extraordinary physical maturation that occurs during adolescence, triggered by the onset of puberty. We then discuss the consequences of early and late maturation and how they differ for males and females. We also consider nutrition during adolescence. After discussing the causes—and consequences—of obesity, we discuss eating disorders, which are surprisingly common during the period.

We then turn to stress and coping. We examine the causes of stress during adolescence, as well as the short- and long-term consequences of stress. We also discuss the ways in which people can cope with it.

The chapter concludes with a discussion of several of the major threats to adolescents' well-being. We'll focus on drug, alcohol, and tobacco use, as well as sexually transmitted diseases.

After reading this chapter, then, you'll be able to answer the following questions:

- What physical changes do adolescents experience?

- What are the consequences of early and late maturation?
- What are the nutritional needs and concerns of adolescents?
- What are the effects of stress, and what can be done about it?
- What are some threats to the well-being of adolescents?
- What dangers do adolescent sexual practices present, and how can these dangers be avoided?

PHYSICAL MATURATION

adolescent growth spurt *a period of very rapid growth in height and weight during adolescence*

puberty *the period of maturation during which the sexual organs mature, beginning earlier for girls than for boys*

For the male members of the Awa tribe, the beginning of adolescence is marked by an elaborate and—to Western eyes—gruesome ceremony signaling the transition from childhood to adulthood. First the boys are whipped for 2 or 3 days with sticks and prickly branches. Through the whipping, the boys atone for their previous infractions and honor tribesmen who were killed in warfare.

But that's just for starters. In the next phase of the ritual, sharpened sticks are punched into the boys' nostrils, producing a considerable amount of blood. Then, adults force a 5-foot length of vine into the boys' throats, causing them to choke and vomit. Finally, deep cuts are made in the boys' genitals. Jeering onlookers poke at the cuts to make them bleed even more.

Most of us probably feel gratitude that we did not have to endure such physical trials when we entered adolescence. But members of Western cultures do have their own rites of passage into adolescence, admittedly less fearsome, such as bar mitzvahs and bat mitzvahs at age 12 or 13 for Jewish boys and girls, and confirmation ceremonies in many Christian denominations (Dunham, Kidwell, & Wilson, 1986; Myerhoff, 1982).

Regardless of the nature of the ceremonies celebrated by various cultures, their underlying purpose tends to be similar from one culture to the next: symbolically celebrating the onset of the physical changes that take a child to the doorstep of adulthood.

GROWTH DURING ADOLESCENCE: THE RAPID PACE OF PHYSICAL AND SEXUAL MATURATION

The growth in height and weight during adolescence can be breathtaking. In only a few months, an adolescent can grow several inches and require an almost entirely new wardrobe. In fact, boys and girls undergo a surprisingly rapid transformation, at least in physical appearance, from children to young adults.

The dramatic changes during adolescence constitute the **adolescent growth spurt,** a period of very rapid growth in height and weight. During the adolescent growth spurt, height and weight increase as quickly as they did during infancy. On average, boys grow 4.1 inches a year and girls 3.5 inches a year. Some adolescents grow as much as 5 inches in a single year (J. Tanner, 1972).

Boys' and girls' adolescent growth spurts begin at different times. On average, girls start their spurts two years earlier than boys, and they complete them earlier as well. As you can see in Figure 13-1, girls begin their spurts around age 10, while boys don't start until about age 12. For the 2-year period starting at age 11, girls tend to be a bit taller than boys. This doesn't last, however: By the age of 13, boys, on average, are taller than girls—a state of affairs that persists for the remainder of the life span.

In Liberia, girls traditionally participate in a ritual painting ceremony to mark the beginning of adolescence.

Puberty: The start of sexual maturation. As with the growth spurt, **puberty,** the period during which the sexual organs mature, begins earlier for girls than for boys. Girls start puberty at around age 11 or 12, and boys begin at around age 13 or 14. However, there are wide variations among individuals. For example, some girls begin puberty as early as 8 or 9 or as late as 16 years of age.

FIGURE 13-1

AVERAGE CHANGES IN BOYS' AND GIRLS' HEIGHT DURING ADOLESCENCE

The first figure shows height at a given age, while the second shows the height *increase* that occurs from birth through the end of adolescence. These figures illustrate how girls begin their growth spurt around age 10, while boys don't start until about age 12. However, by the age of 13, boys tend to be taller than girls.

(*Source:* Adapted from Cratty, 1986.)

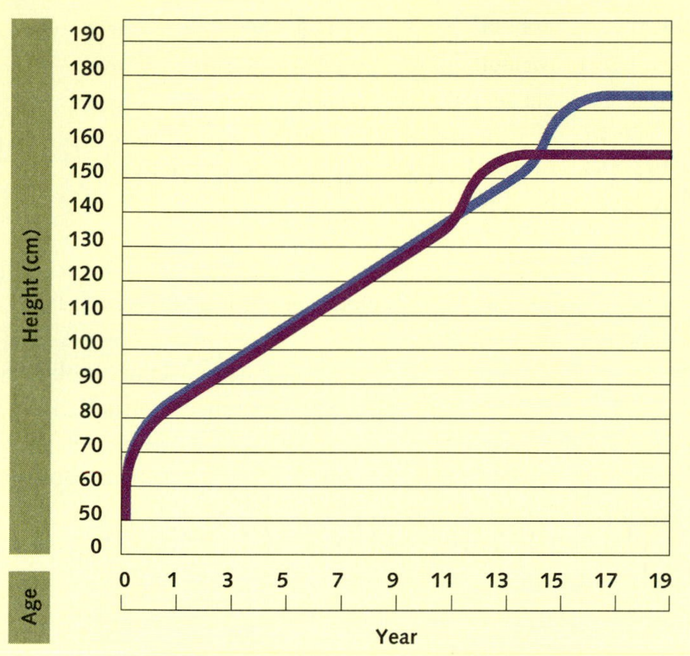

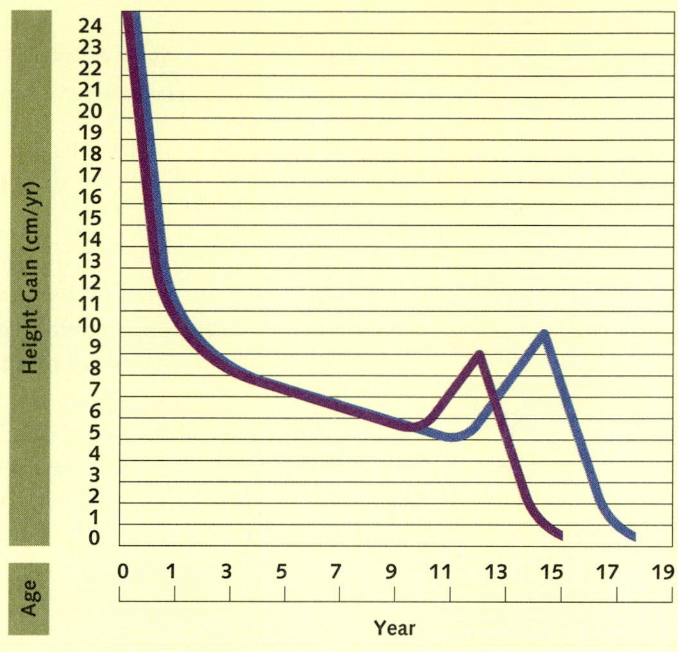

Puberty begins when children's bodies begin to produce androgens (male hormones) or estrogens (female hormones) at adult levels. This surge in the production of hormones leads to the growth spurt and puberty.

What triggers the start of puberty? Although we know what happens when it begins, no one has yet identified the reason that it begins at a particular time. However, it is clear that environmental and cultural factors play a role. For example, **menarche,** the onset of menstruation, and probably the most conspicuous signal of puberty in girls, varies greatly in different parts of the world. In poorer, developing countries, menstruation begins later than in more economically advantaged countries. Even within wealthier countries, girls in more affluent groups begin to menstruate earlier than less affluent girls (see Figure 13-2). Consequently, it appears that girls who are better nourished and healthier are more apt to start menstruation at an earlier age than those who suffer from malnutrition or chronic disease.

Other factors can affect the timing of menarche. For instance, environmental stress can bring about an earlier onset. To illustrate, one recent study found that girls from divorced families or families high in interparental conflict tended to begin menstruation earlier than girls from families with lower levels of stress (Graber, Brooks-Gunn, & Warren, 1995; Wierson, Long, & Forehand, 1993).

Within the United States, historical patterns of menarche are congruent with what we find in other cultures. Near the end of the nineteenth century, menstruation began, on average, around age 14 or 15, compared with today's 11 or 12.

The earlier onset of menarche is reflected in other indicators of puberty. In fact, for the past 100 years or so, the age at which adult height and sexual maturity are reached has been declining—an example of a significant secular trend. A **secular trend** is a statistical tendency

menarche *the onset of menstruation*

secular trend *a statistical tendency observed over several generations*

FIGURE 13-2

THE TIMING OF MENSTRUATION

The onset of menstruation occurs earlier in more economically advantaged countries than in those that are poorer. But even in wealthier countries, girls living in more affluent circumstances begin to menstruate earlier than those living in less affluent situations.

(*Source:* Adapted from Eveleth & Tanner, 1976.)

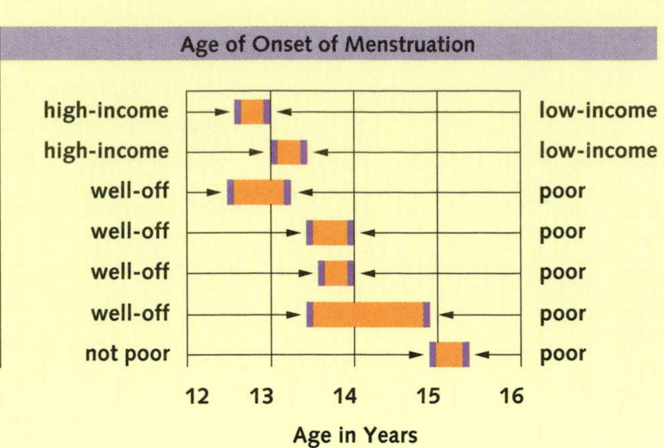

primary sex characteristics *characteristics that are associated with the development of the organs and structures of the body that directly relate to reproduction*

secondary sex characteristics *the visible signs of sexual maturity that do not involve the sex organs directly*

observed over several generations. The secular trend in earlier onset of maturation is likely the result of reduced disease and improved nutrition.

Does this mean that the age at which puberty starts will continue to decline? Probably not. It is likely that there is a genetically determined limit on how early menstruation can occur. In fact, we may have reached it already: For the last few decades, despite generally rising health and affluence, there has been no further decline in the age at which puberty begins (Bullough, 1981; Dreyer, 1982; Malina, 1979).

Menstruation is just one of several changes in puberty that are related to the development of primary and secondary sex characteristics. **Primary sex characteristics** are associated with the development of the organs and structures of the body that directly relate to reproduction. In contrast, **secondary sex characteristics** are the visible signs of sexual maturity that do not involve the sex organs directly.

For instance, girls experience development of primary sex characteristics through changes in the vagina and uterus as a result of maturation. Secondary sex characteristics include the development of breasts and pubic hair. Breasts begin to grow at around the age of 10, and pubic hair beings to appear at about age 11. Underarm hair is seen about two years later.

Boys' sexual maturation follows a somewhat different course. In terms of primary sex characteristics, the penis and scrotum begin to grow at an accelerated rate around the age of 12, and they reach adult size about three or four years later. By the age of 14, the average boy is able to have his first ejaculation, although his body has already been producing sperm for a few years. At the same time, the secondary sex characteristics are developing. Pubic hair begins to grow around the age of 12, followed by the growth of underarm and facial hair. Finally, boys' voices deepen as the vocal cords become longer and the larynx larger. (Figure 13-3 summarizes the changes that occur in sexual maturation during early adolescence.)

Both males and females undergo significant bodily changes during adolescence, and they show increased interest in physical appearance.

Body Image: Reactions to physical changes in adolescence. Unlike infants, who also undergo extraordinarily rapid growth, adolescents are well aware of what is happening to their bodies, and they may react with horror or joy. Few, though, are neutral about the changes they are witnessing.

For instance, menarche produces several psychological consequences. Western society has in the past emphasized the more negative aspects of menstruation, such as the potential for cramps and messiness, and girls tended to react to menarche with anxiety (Ruble & Brooks-Gunn, 1982). Today, however, society's view of menstruation tends to be more positive, in part because menstruation has been demystified and discussed more openly. (For instance, television commercials for tampons are commonplace.) As a consequence, menarche is typically accompanied by a rise in self-esteem, status, and self-awareness (Brooks-Gunn & Reiter, 1990).

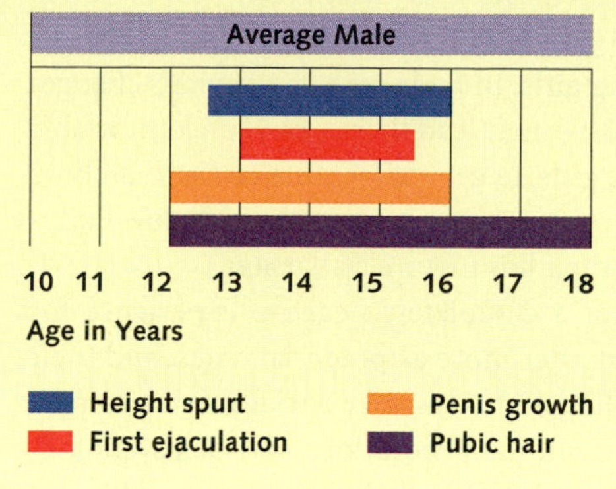

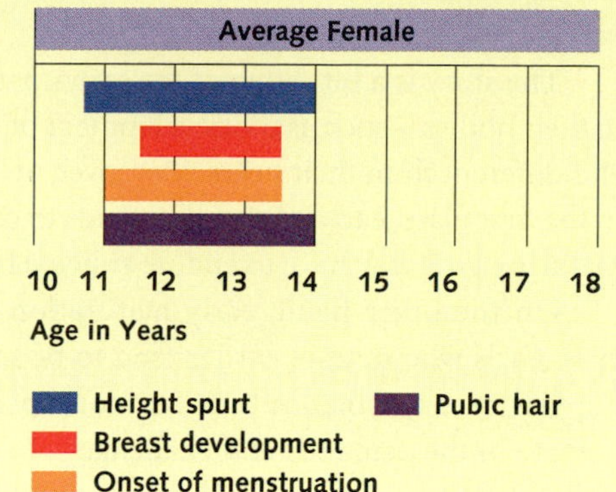

SEXUAL MATURATION

The changes in sexual maturation that occur for males and females during early adolescence.

(*Source:* Adapted from Tanner, 1978.)

In some ways, a boy's first ejaculation is roughly equivalent to menarche in a girl. However, while girls generally tell their mothers about the onset of menstruation, boys rarely mention their first ejaculation to either their parents or their friends (J. H. Stein & Reiser, 1994). Moreover, there is little evidence that the first ejaculation causes boys much anxiety or worry (Gaddis & Brooks-Gunn, 1985). There are several possible explanations for this: It may be that the event is actually of little concern or interest to boys, and therefore not worthy of mention. However, it seems more likely that boys see the first ejaculation as part of their sexuality, an area about which they are quite uncertain and which they are therefore reluctant to discuss with others.

Menstruation and ejaculations are private affairs, but changes in body shape and size are quite public. Consequently, teenagers entering puberty are frequently embarrassed by the changes that are occurring.

Girls, in particular, are often unhappy with their new bodies. This dissatisfaction is likely due to strong societal pressures regarding the ideal female shape, which frequently has little to do with the reality of mature women's bodies. Specifically, the unrealistic thinness that societal standards call for is quite different from the actual shape of most women. Puberty brings a considerable increase in the amount of fatty tissue, as well as enlargement of the hips and buttocks—a far cry from the slenderness that society seems to demand (Attie & Brooks-Gunn, 1989; Tobin-Richards, Boxer, & Petersen, 1983; Unger & Crawford, 1996).

How children react to the onset of puberty depends, in part, on when it happens. Girls and boys who mature either earlier or later than most of their peers are especially affected by the timing of puberty.

The Timing of Puberty: The Consequences of Early and Late Maturation. What are the social consequences of early or late maturation? One of the most persistent questions addressed by developmentalists who specialize in adolescence is whether early and late maturation bring with them any particular advantages or disadvantages. The answer, it turns out, differs for boys and girls.

For boys, early maturation is largely a plus. Early-maturing boys tend to be more successful at athletics, presumably because of their larger size. Furthermore, they tend to be more popular and to have a more positive self-concept.

On the other hand, early maturation in boys does have a downside. Boys who mature early are more apt to have difficulties in school, and they are more likely to become involved in delinquency and substance abuse. The reason: Their larger size makes it more likely that they will seek out the company of older boys who may involve them in activities that are inappropriate for their age.

Overall, though, early maturation appears to be generally beneficial for boys. Ultimately, early maturers end up being more responsible and cooperative in later life (Andersson & Magnusson, 1990; Duncan, Ritter, Dornbusch, Gross, & Carlsmith, 1985; Livson & Peskin, 1980).

The story is a bit different for early-maturing girls. In their case, the obvious changes in their bodies—such as the development of breasts—may lead them to feel uncomfortable and different from their peers. Moreover, because girls, in general, mature earlier than boys in the first place, early maturation tends to come at a very young age in the girl's life. Early-maturing girls may have to endure ridicule from their less mature classmates.

On the other hand, early maturation is not a completely negative experience for girls. Girls who mature earlier tend to be sought after more as potential dates, and their popularity may enhance their self-concepts. Still, they may not be socially ready to participate in the demands and challenges of dating, and such situations may be psychologically challenging for early-maturing girls. Moreover, the distinctiveness of their deviance from their later-maturing classmates may have a negative effect on them (Simmons & Blyth, 1987).

Whether girls face difficulties with early maturation depends in part on cultural norms and standards. For instance, in the United States, the notion of female sexuality is looked upon with a degree of ambivalence. Consequently, the outcome of early maturation may be negative. On the other hand, in countries in which attitudes about sexuality are more liberal, the results of early maturation may be more positive. For example, in Germany, which has a more open view of sex, early-maturing girls have higher self-esteem than such girls in the United States. Furthermore, the consequences of early maturation vary even within the United States, depending on the views of girls' peer groups and on prevailing community standards regarding sex (A. Petersen, in press; Richards et al., 1990; Silbereisen et al., 1989).

As with early maturation, the situation with late maturation is mixed, although in this case boys fare worse than girls. For instance, boys who are smaller and lighter than their more mature peers tend to be viewed as less attractive. Because of their smaller size, they are at a disadvantage when it comes to sports activities. Furthermore, because of the social convention that boys should be taller than their dates, the social lives of late-maturing boys may suffer. Ultimately, these difficulties may lead to a decline in self-concept. In fact, the disadvantages of late maturation for boys may extend well into adulthood (Livson & Peskin, 1980; Mussen & Jones, 1957).

The picture for late-maturing girls, on the other hand, is a bit more complicated. Girls who mature later may be overlooked in dating and other mixed-sex activities during junior high school and middle school, and they may have relatively low social status (Apter et al., 1981; Clarke-Stewart & Friedman, 1987). However, by the time they are in 10th grade and have begun to mature visibly, late-maturing girls' satisfaction with themselves and their bodies may be greater than that of early maturers. In fact, late-maturing girls may end up with fewer emotional problems. The reason? Late-maturing girls are more apt to fit the societal ideal of a slender, "leggy" body type than early maturers, who tend to look heavier in comparison (Simmons & Blythe, 1987; Petersen, 1988).

In sum, the reactions to early and late maturation present a complex picture. Some developmentalists suggest that the concern over early and later maturation, and over the effects of puberty in general, may have been overemphasized in the past (Paikoff & Brooks-Gunn, 1990; Petersen & Crockett, 1985). Rather than focusing on the growth spurt and sexual maturation that occur during adolescence, they suggest that other factors, such as changes in peer groups, family dynamics, and particularly schools and other societal institutions, may be more pertinent in determining an adolescent's behavior. As we've seen repeatedly, we need to take into consideration the complete constellation of factors affecting individuals in order to understand their development.

Nutrition and Food: Fueling the Growth of Adolescence

The rapid physical growth of adolescence is fueled by an increase in food consumption. Particularly during the growth spurt, most adolescents eat substantial quantities of food, increasing their intake of calories rather dramatically. During the teenage years, the average girl requires some 2,200 calories a day, and the average boy 2,800.

Of course, not just any calories help nourish adolescents' growth. Several key nutrients are essential, including in particular calcium and iron. The calcium provided by milk helps bone growth, which may prevent the later development of osteoporosis—the thinning of bones—that affects 25 percent of women later in their lives. Similarly, iron is necessary to prevent iron-deficiency anemia, an ailment that is not uncommon among teenagers.

For most adolescents, the major nutritional issue is ensuring the consumption of a sufficient balance of appropriate foods. But for a substantial minority, nutrition can be a major concern and can create a real threat to health.

The most common nutritional concern during adolescence is obesity. As we discussed in earlier chapters (see Chapters 4, 7, and 10), *obesity* is defined as body weight that is more than 20 percent above the average for a given age and height. Under this definition, some 5 percent of adolescents are formally classified as obese, and an additional 15 percent are overweight to some degree (Gans, 1990).

Although adolescents are obese for the same reasons as younger children, the psychological consequences may be particularly severe during a time of life when body image is of special concern. Furthermore, the potential health consequences of obesity during adolescence are also problematic. For instance, obesity taxes the circulatory system, increasing the likelihood of high blood pressure and diabetes. Finally, obese adolescents stand an 80 percent chance of becoming obese adults.

For some individuals, the quest to avoid obesity is an obsession and becomes a life-threatening disorder, as we consider in the accompanying "Directions in Development" box.

anorexia nervosa *a severe eating disorder (primarily afflicting women age 12 to 40) in which individuals refuse to eat, while denying that their behavior and appearance, which may become skeletonlike, are out of the ordinary*

Directions in Development

Anorexia Nervosa and Bulimia: The Frightening World of Eating Disorders

> *A rice cake in the afternoon, an apple for dinner. That was Heather Rhodes's typical diet her freshman year at St. Joseph's College in Rensselaer, Indiana, when she began to nurture a fear (exacerbated, she says, by the sudden death of a friend) that she was gaining weight. But when Rhodes, now 20, returned home to Joliet, Illinois, for summer vacation a year and a half ago, her family thought she was melting away. "I could see the outline of her pelvis in her clothes . . ." says Heather's mother . . . , so she and the rest of the family confronted Heather one evening, placing a bathroom scale in the middle of the family room. "I told them they were attacking me and to go to hell," recalls Heather, who nevertheless reluctantly weighed herself. Her 5′7″ frame held a mere 85 pounds—down 22 pounds from her senior year in high school. "I told them they rigged the scale," she says. It simply didn't compute with her self-image. "When I looked in the mirror," she says, "I thought my stomach was still huge and my face was fat." (Sandler, 1994, p. 56)*

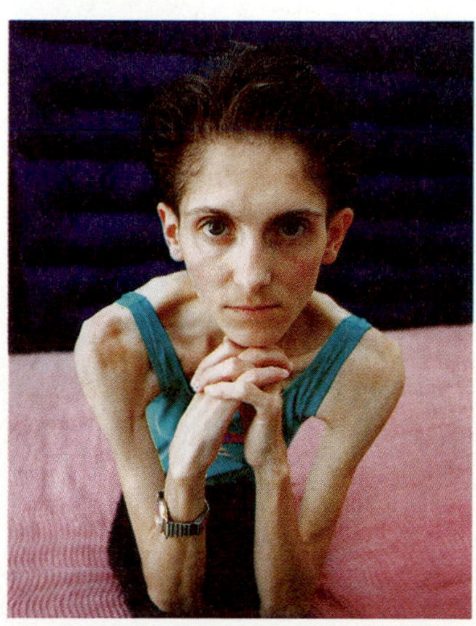

Those who suffer from anorexia nervosa, a severe eating disorder in which people refuse to eat, deny that their behavior and appearance are out of the ordinary.

Heather's problem: the eating disorder of anorexia nervosa. **Anorexia nervosa** is a severe eating disorder in which individuals refuse to eat, while denying that their behavior and appearance, which may become skeletonlike, are out of the ordinary.

__bulimia__ an eating disorder that primarily afflicts adolescent girls and young women and is characterized by binges on large quantities of food, followed by purges of the food through vomiting or the use of laxatives

Anorexia is a serious psychological disorder with grave consequences: Some 15 to 20 percent of its victims literally starve themselves to death. It primarily afflicts women between the ages of 12 and 40. Those most susceptible are intelligent, successful, and attractive white adolescent girls from affluent homes (Button, 1993; Hsu, 1990).

Anorexics' lives become centered on food. Even though they eat little, they may go shopping often, collect cookbooks, talk about food, or cook huge meals for others. Although they may be incredibly thin, their body images are so distorted that they see their reflections in mirrors as disgustingly fat, and they try to lose more and more weight. Even when they look like skeletons, they are unable to see what they have become.

Bulimia, another eating disorder that primarily afflicts adolescent girls and young women, is characterized by binges on large quantities of food, followed by purges of the food through vomiting or the use of laxatives. Bulimics may eat an entire gallon of ice cream or a whole package of tortilla chips. But after such a binge, sufferers experience powerful feelings of guilt and depression, and they intentionally rid themselves of the food.

Although the weight of a person with bulimia remains fairly normal, the disorder is quite hazardous. The constant vomiting and diarrhea of the binge-and-purge cycles may produce a chemical imbalance that can lead to heart failure.

The exact reasons for the occurrence of eating disorders are not clear, although several factors appear to be implicated. For one thing, girls who mature earlier than their peers and who have a higher level of body fat are more susceptible to eating disorders during later adolescence. In addition, several psychological problems are also associated with subsequent eating disorders. Girls who show clinical levels of depression are more likely to develop eating disorders later (Graber, Brooks-Gunn, Paikoff, & Warren, 1994; Lavigueur, Tremblay & Saucier, 1995; Nagel & Jones, 1992).

Some theorists suggest that a biological cause lies at the root of both anorexia nervosa and bulimia. In fact, there appear to be genetic components to the disorders, and in some cases doctors have found hormonal imbalances in sufferers (Condit, 1990; Gold et al., 1986; Holland, Sicotte, & Treasure, 1988; Irwin, 1993; Treasure & Tiller, 1993).

Other attempts at explaining the eating disorders emphasize psychological and social factors. For instance, some experts suggest that the disorders are a result of overdemanding parents or byproducts of other family difficulties (Miller, McCluskey-Fawcett, & Irving, 1993).

In addition, the societal preference for slender bodies and disapproval of obesity may contribute to the disorder. Interestingly, the obsession with thinness that is characteristic of U.S. society today is of relatively recent vintage, and society's views of ideal weight have changed significantly over time. A survey of the ideal figure, as exemplified by fashion models in popular magazines, reveals that the standard of slenderness popular today is matched historically in only one other recent period, the mid-1920s (Crandall & Biernat, 1990; Rothblum, 1990; Silverstein et al., 1986; Sohlberg & Strober, 1994; J. K. Thompson, 1996; see Figure 13-4).

Culture also plays a role in eating disorders. Anorexia nervosa, for instance, is found only in cultures that idealize slender female bodies. Because in most places such a standard does not hold, anorexia is not prevalent outside the United States. Consequently, no cases of anorexia are found in all of Asia, with two interesting exceptions: the upper classes of Japan and of Hong Kong, where Western influence is greatest. Furthermore, anorexia nervosa is a fairly recent disorder. It was not seen in the seventeenth and eighteenth centuries, when the ideal of the female body was a plump corpulence (Carson, Butcher, & Coleman, 1988; Kleinman, 1991).

Because anorexia nervosa and bulimia are products of both biological and environmental causes, treatment, which is successful in the majority of cases, typically involves multiple approaches. For instance, both psychological therapy and dietary modifications are likely to be needed for successful treatment (Fairburn et al., 1993; Lask & Bryant-Waugh, 1993; Schmidt & Treasure, 1993).

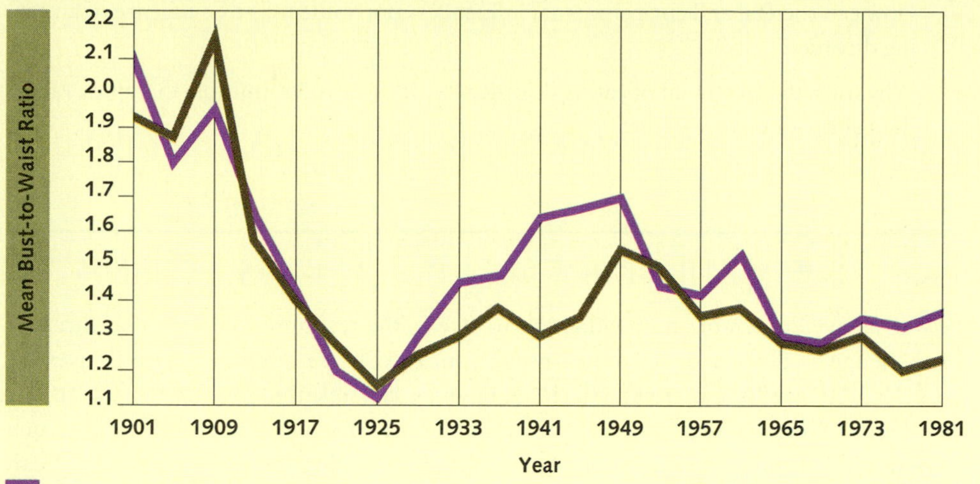

FIGURE 13-4

IDEAL WOMEN'S PROPORTIONS, AS REFLECTED BY FASHION MODELS IN TWO POPULAR MAGAZINES

During the course of the twentieth century, norms regarding women's body types have changed significantly. This graph shows the mean "bust-to-waist" ratio, a measure of full-figuredness, of models appearing in *Vogue* and *Ladies' Home Journal* during the course of the twentieth century. As depicted in these magazines, slenderness has been in style in only two periods: the mid-1920s and in recent decades. In other times, societal standards supported relatively full figures.

(*Source:* Silverstein et al., 1986.)

Review and Rethink

REVIEW

- Adolescence is a period of rapid physical growth, including the hormonal and bodily changes associated with puberty. Girls typically begin their growth spurts and puberty about 2 years earlier than boys.
- Puberty, whose timing is due to a combination of biological, cultural, and environmental factors, can cause reactions in adolescents ranging from confusion to increased self-esteem.
- Early or late maturation can bring advantages and disadvantages. The disadvantages are largely due to dissonance between physical maturity and emotional and psychological maturity.
- Adequate nutrition is essential in adolescence because it fuels physical growth. Changing physical needs and environmental pressures can induce obesity—or an obsession with avoiding obesity that can manifest itself as an eating disorder.
- The two most common eating disorders among adolescent girls, anorexia nervosa and bulimia, are serious and involve multiple causes. Both must be treated with a combination of physical and psychological therapies.

RETHINK

- Why do you think the passage to adolescence is regarded in many cultures as such a significant transition that it calls for unique ceremonies?
- What are some of the educational implications of the variations in maturation rate among adolescents? How can a teacher help students deal with the wide variety of changes they are witnessing and experiencing?

- In what ways might the popularity of early-developing boys and girls offer both benefits and threats?
- How can societal and environmental influences contribute to the emergence of an eating disorder?
- Why must the treatment of eating disorders typically involve multiple therapies, rather than simply a change in diet?

STRESS AND COPING

stress *the response to events that threaten or challenge us*

Few of us need much of an introduction to **stress,** the response to events that threaten or challenge us. Stress is a part of nearly everyone's existence, and most people's lives are crowded with events and circumstances, known as *stressors,* that produce threats to our well-being. Stressors need not be unpleasant events: Even the happiest events, such as obtaining admission to a sought-after college or graduating from high school can produce stress for adolescents (Brown & McGill, 1989; Sarason, Johnson, & Siegel, 1978).

Stress produces several outcomes. The most immediate is typically a biological reaction, as certain hormones, secreted by the adrenal glands, cause a rise in heart rate, blood pressure, respiration rate, and sweating. In some situations, these immediate effects may be beneficial because they produce an "emergency reaction" in the sympathetic nervous system by which people are better able to defend themselves from a sudden, threatening situation. A person challenged by a snarling, ferocious dog, for instance, would want all the bodily preparedness possible to deal with the emergency situation.

On the other hand, long-term, continuous exposure to stressors may result in a reduction of the body's ability to deal with stress. As stress-related hormones are constantly secreted, the heart, blood vessels, and other body tissues may deteriorate. As a consequence, people become more susceptible to diseases as their ability to fight off germs declines (Cohen, Tyrell, & Smith, 1993; Kiecolt-Glaser & Glaser, 1986; Schneiderman, 1983).

THE ORIGINS OF STRESS: REACTING TO LIFE'S CHALLENGES

Not every situation produces stress. What makes some stressful? According to psychologists Richard Lazarus and Susan Folkman, people move through a series of stages, depicted in Figure 13-5, that determine whether they will experience stress (Lazarus, 1968, 1991; Lazarus & Folkman, 1984).

Primary appraisal is the first step—the assessment of an event to determine whether its implications are positive, negative, or neutral. If the event is seen as primarily negative, it is appraised in terms of the harm that it has caused in the past, how threatening it is likely to be, and how likely it is that the challenge can be resisted successfully.

Even the happiest of events, such as graduating from high school, can produce stress.

Secondary appraisal follows. *Secondary appraisal* is the assessment of whether one's coping abilities and resources are adequate to overcome the harm, threat, or challenge posed by the potential stressor. At this point in the process, people try to determine whether they will be able to meet the dangers in the situation. If resources are lacking and the potential threat is great, they will experience stress.

Stress, then, follows from primary and secondary appraisal. This appraisal process makes the determination of what is stressful very personal. Some adolescents find hang gliding and rock climbing diverting and entertaining; for others, the very thought of such activities brings about a good deal of stress.

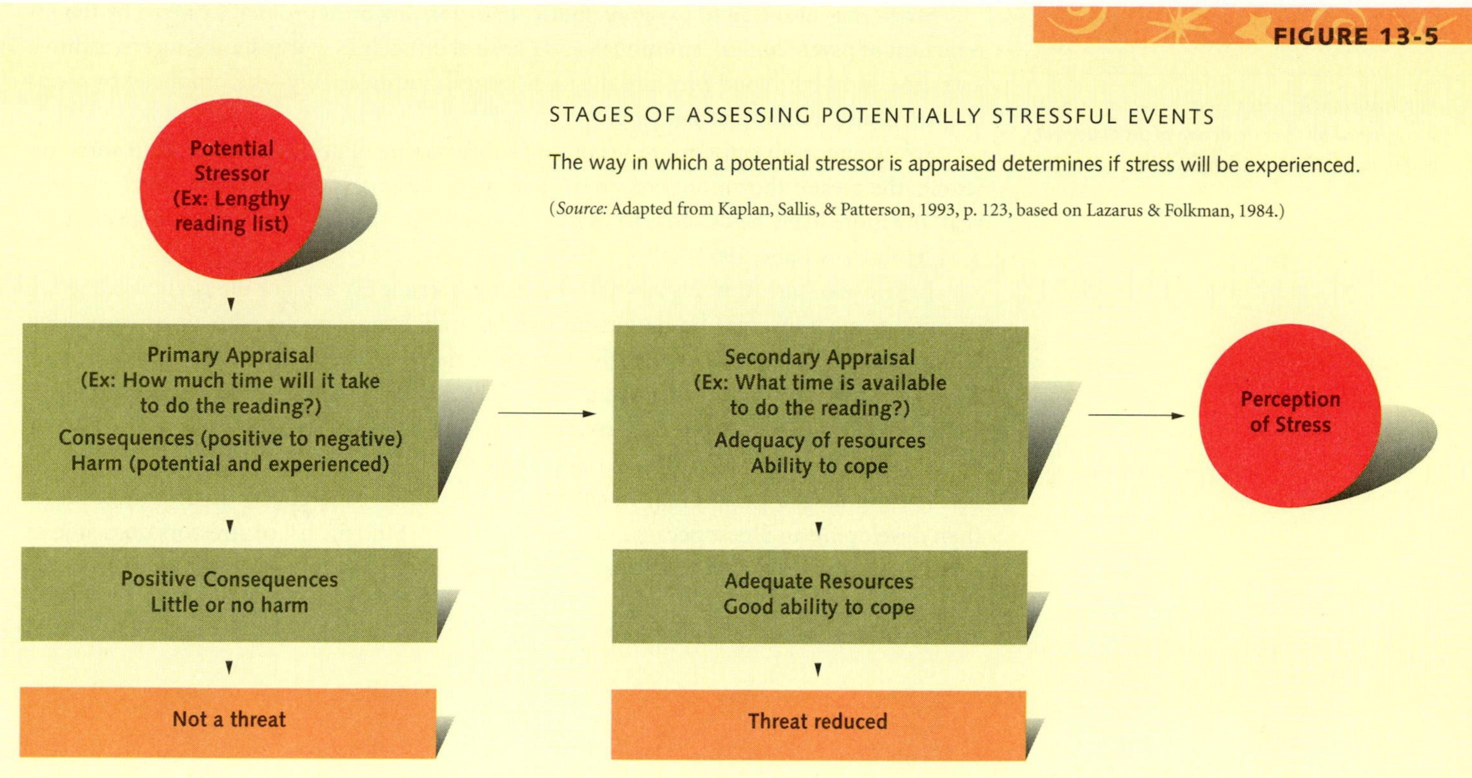

FIGURE 13-5

STAGES OF ASSESSING POTENTIALLY STRESSFUL EVENTS

The way in which a potential stressor is appraised determines if stress will be experienced.

(*Source:* Adapted from Kaplan, Sallis, & Patterson, 1993, p. 123, based on Lazarus & Folkman, 1984.)

Still, some general principles help predict when an event will be appraised as stressful. Psychologist Shelley Taylor (1991) suggests the following:

- Events and circumstances that produce negative emotions are more likely to lead to stress than events that are positive. For example, memorizing one's lines for a large role in a school play is likely to produce less stress than juggling the demands of five different high school classes.
- Situations that are uncontrollable or unpredictable are more likely to produce stress than those that can be controlled and predicted. Teachers who give surprise quizzes in their classes, then, probably produce more stress in their students than those whose quizzes are scheduled in advance.
- Events and circumstances that are ambiguous and confusing produce more stress than those that are unambiguous and clear. If people cannot easily understand a situation, they must struggle simply to comprehend it, rather than dealing with it directly.
- Adolescents who face many demands simultaneously that strain their capabilities are more likely to experience stress than those who have fewer things to do.

The Consequences of Stress: Physical and Psychological Wear and Tear

If adolescents experience enough stress in a short time span, they can pay formidable costs. Over the long run, the constant wear and tear caused by the physiological arousal that occurs as the body tries to fight off stress produces negative effects. For instance, headaches, backaches, skin rashes, indigestion, chronic fatigue, and even the common cold are stress-related illnesses (Cohen et al., 1993; Kiecolt-Glaser & Kiecolt-Glaser, 1991).

psychosomatic disorders *medical problems caused by the interaction of psychological, emotional, and physical difficulties*

Stress may also lead to **psychosomatic disorders,** medical problems caused by the interaction of psychological, emotional, and physical difficulties. For instance, ulcers, asthma, arthritis, and high blood pressure may—although not invariably—be produced by stress (Lepore, Palsane, & Evans, 1991).

Stress may even cause more serious, life-threatening, illnesses. According to some research, the greater the number of stressful events a person experiences over the course of a year, the more likely he or she is to have a major illness (see Table 13-1; Coddington, 1984; T. H. Holmes & Rahe, 1967).

Before you start computing whether you are overdue for a major illness, however, keep in mind some important limitations to the research. Not everyone who experiences high stress becomes ill, and the weights given to particular stressors probably vary from one person to the next. Furthermore, there is a kind of circularity to such enumerations of stressors as in Table 13-1: Because the research is correlational, it is possible that someone who has a major illness to begin with is more likely to experience some of the stressors on the list. For example, a person may have lost a job *because* of the effects of an illness, rather than developing an illness because he or she lost a job. Still, the list of stressors does at least provide a way to consider how most people react to various potentially stressful events in their lives.

TABLE 13-1

ASSESSING PERSONAL DEGREE OF STRESS

Using the following scale, you can assess the degree of stress in your life (Rahe & Arthur, 1978). To do this, take the stressor value given beside each event you have experienced and multiply it by the number of occurrences over the past year (up to a maximum of four), then add up the scores.

Value	Event
87	Experienced the death of a spouse
77	Got married
77	Experienced the death of a close family member
76	Got divorced
74	Experienced a marital separation
68	Experienced the death of a close friend
68	Experienced pregnancy or fathered a pregnancy
65	Had a major personal injury or illness
62	Were fired from work
60	Ended a marital engagement or a steady relationship
58	Had sexual difficulties
58	Experienced a marital reconciliation with your mate
57	Had a major change in self-concept or self-awareness
56	Experienced a major change in the health or behavior of a family member
54	Became engaged to be married
53	Had a major change in financial status
52	Took on a mortgage or loan of less than $10,000
52	Had a major change in use of drugs
50	Had a major conflict or change in values
50	Had a major change in the number of arguments with your spouse
50	Gained a new family member
50	Entered college
50	Changed to a new school
50	Changed to a different line of work
49	Had a major change in amount of independence and responsibility
47	Had a major change in responsibilities at work
46	Experienced a major change in use of alcohol
45	Revised personal habits
44	Had trouble with school administration
43	Held a job while attending school
43	Had a major change in social activities
42	Had trouble with in-laws
42	Had a major change in working hours or conditions
42	Changed residence or living conditions
41	Had your spouse begin or cease work outside the home
41	Changed your choice of major field of study
41	Changed dating habits
40	Had an outstanding personal achievement
38	Had trouble with your boss
38	Had a major change in amount of participation in school activities
37	Had a major change in type and/or amount of recreation
36	Had a major change in church activities
34	Had a major change in sleeping habits
33	Took a trip or vacation
30	Had a major change in eating habits
26	Had a major change in the number of family get-togethers
22	Were found guilty of minor violations of the law

A total score of 1,435 or higher places you in a high-stress category. According to M. B. Marx, Garrity, & Bowers (1975), a high score increases the chances of experiencing a future stress-related illness, although it certainly does not guarantee it.

Coping with Stress: Meeting the Challenge of Stress

Some adolescents are better than others at **coping,** the effort to control, reduce, or learn to tolerate the threats that lead to stress. What is the key to successful coping?

coping *the effort to control, reduce, or learn to tolerate the threats that lead to stress*

Some individuals use *problem-focused coping,* by which they attempt to manage a stressful problem or situation by directly changing the situation to make it less stressful. For example, a high school student who is having academic difficulties may speak to his teachers and ask that they extend the deadlines for assignments, or a worker who is dissatisfied with what her employer assigns her can ask that she be assigned other tasks.

Other adolescents employ *emotion-focused coping,* which involves the conscious regulation of emotion. For instance, a teenager who is having problems getting along with her boss in her after-school job may tell herself that she should look at the bright side: At least she has a job in the first place (Folkman & Lazarus, 1980, 1988).

Coping is also aided by the presence of *social support,* assistance and comfort supplied by others. Turning to others in the face of stress can provide both emotional support (in the form of a shoulder to cry on) and practical, tangible support (such as an advance of one's allowance) (Croyle & Hunt, 1991; Lepore, Evans, & Schneider, 1991; Lepore, Palsane et al., 1991; Sarason, Sarason, & Pierce, 1991; Spiegel, 1993).

Finally, even if adolescents don't consciously cope with stress, some psychologists suggest that they may unconsciously use defensive coping mechanisms that aid in stress reduction. *Defensive coping* involves the unconscious use of strategies that distort or deny the true nature of a situation. For instance, a person may deny the seriousness of a threat, trivializing a life-threatening illness or telling oneself that academic failure on a series of tests is unimportant. The problem with such defensive coping is that it does not deal with the reality of the situation, but merely avoids or ignores the problem.

The Informed Consumer of Development

Coping with Stress

Although no single formula can cover all cases of stress, some general guidelines can help everyone cope with the stress that is part of our lives. Among them are the following (Greenglass & Burke, 1991; Holahan & Moos, 1987, 1990; Kaplan, Sallis, & Patterson, 1993; Sacks, 1993):

- *Seek control over the situation producing the stress.* Putting yourself in charge of a situation that is producing stress can take you a long way toward coping with it.
- *Redefine "threat" as "challenge."* Changing the definition of a situation can make it seem less threatening. "Look for the silver lining" isn't bad advice.
- *Get social support.* Almost any difficulty can be faced more easily with the help of others. Friends, family members, and even telephone hotlines staffed by trained counselors can provide significant support. (For help in identifying appropriate hotlines, the U.S. Public Health Service maintains a "master" toll-free number that can provide phone numbers and addresses of many national groups. Call 800-336-4797.)
- *Use relaxation techniques.* Procedures that reduce the physiological arousal brought about by stress can be particularly effective. A variety of techniques that produce relaxation, such as transcendental meditation, Zen and yoga, progressive muscle relaxation, and even

hypnosis, have been shown to be effective in reducing stress. One that works particularly well was devised by physician Herbert Benson and is illustrated in Table 13-2.

- *Realize stress is natural.* If all else fails, keep in mind that a life without any stress at all would be a dull one. Stress is a natural part of life, and successfully coping with it can be a gratifying experience.

TABLE 13-2

HOW TO ELICIT THE RELAXATION RESPONSE

There are several approaches to eliciting the relaxation response. Here is one standard set of instructions:

Step 1. Pick a focus word or short phrase that's firmly rooted in your personal belief system. For example, a nonreligious individual might choose a neutral word like *one* or *peace* or *love.* A Christian person desiring to use a prayer could pick the opening words of Psalm 23, *The Lord is my shepherd;* a Jewish person could choose *Shalom.*
Step 2. Sit quietly in a comfortable position.
Step 3. Close your eyes.
Step 4. Relax your muscles.
Step 5. Breathe slowly and naturally, repeating your focus word or phrase silently as you exhale.
Step 6. Throughout, assume a passive attitude. Don't worry about how well you're doing. When other thoughts come to mind, simply say to yourself, "Oh, well," and gently return to the repetition.
Step 7. Continue for 10 to 20 minutes. You may open your eyes to check the time, but do not use an alarm. When you finish, sit quietly for a minute or so, at first with your eyes closed and later with your eyes open. Do not stand for 1 or 2 minutes.
Step 8. Practice the technique once or twice a day.

Some general advice on regular practice of the relaxation response:

- Try to find 10 to 20 minutes in your daily routine; before breakfast is a good time.
- Sit comfortably.
- For the period you will practice, try to arrange your life so you won't have distractions. Put the phone on the answering machine, and ask someone else to watch the kids.
- Time yourself by glancing periodically at a clock or watch (but don't set an alarm). Commit yourself to a specific length of practice, and try to stick to it.

(*Source:* Benson, 1993.)

Review and Rethink

REVIEW

- Stress, which is a healthy reaction in small doses, can be harmful to body and mind if it is frequent or long-lasting.
- The body's immediate reactions to stress include a hormone-induced rise in heart rate, blood pressure, respiration rate, and sweating. These effects produce an "emergency response" that assists in the defense against threats.
- Long-term exposure to stressors may cause deterioration in the heart, blood vessels, and other body tissues. Stress is linked to many common ailments, to psychosomatic disorders, and even to more serious, life-threatening illnesses.

- People faced with potential stressors perform first a primary appraisal of the event, its implications, and their past experiences with similar events, and then a secondary appraisal of their coping abilities and resources.
- Strategies for coping with stress include problem-focused coping, emotion-focused coping, the use of social support, and defensive coping.

RETHINK

- In what circumstances can stress be an adaptive, helpful response? In what circumstances is it maladaptive?
- Are there periods of life that are relatively stress-free, or do people of all ages experience stress? Do stressors differ from age to age?
- Why are there individual differences in people's reactions to stress? Are there cultural differences as well?
- What factors determine whether a person will use problem-focused or emotion-focused coping strategies? Is it a matter of personal style? Of the situation? Both?
- The evidence that stress causes disease is termed "correlational." What does this mean? Is it possible to design an experiment that would conclusively establish a causal link?

Threats to Adolescents' Well-being

> Like most parents, I had thought of drug use as something you worried about when your kids got to high school. Now I know that, on the average, kids begin using drugs at 11 or 12, but at the time that never crossed our minds. Ryan had just begun attending mixed parties. He was playing Little League. In the eighth grade, Ryan started getting into a little trouble—one time he and another fellow stole a fire extinguisher, but we thought it was just a prank. Then his grades began to deteriorate. He began sneaking out at night. He would become belligerent at the drop of a hat, then sunny and nice again. By then he was pretty heavy into drugs, but we were denying what we saw. You build up this trust with your child, and the last thing you want to do is break it. But looking back, there were signs everywhere. His room was filled with bottles of eye drops, to cover the redness from smoking marijuana. Money was missing from around the house, and he began burning incense in his room.
>
> It wasn't until Ryan fell apart at 14 that we started thinking about drugs. He had just begun McLean High School, and to him, it was like going to drug camp every day. Back then, everything was so available. He began cutting classes, a common tip-off, but we didn't hear from the school until he was flunking everything. It turned out that he was going to school for the first period, getting checked in, then leaving and smoking marijuana all day (Shafer, 1990, p. 82)

Ryan's parents learned all too soon that marijuana was not the only drug Ryan was using. As his friends later admitted, Ryan was what they called a "garbage head." He'd try anything, including cocaine, PCP, alcohol, and LSD. Despite efforts to curb his use of drugs, he never succeeded in stopping. He died at the age of 16, hit by a passing car after wandering into the street during an episode of drug use.

Although most cases of adolescent drug use produce far less extreme results, the use of drugs, as well as other kinds of substance use and abuse, represents a primary threat to health during adolescence, which is usually one of the healthiest periods of life.

In our discussion of threats to adolescents' well-being, we'll focus on some of the preventable problems of adolescence, such as drug, alcohol, and tobacco use, as well as sexually transmitted diseases.

The use of marijuana among high school students has increased significantly since the early 1990s.

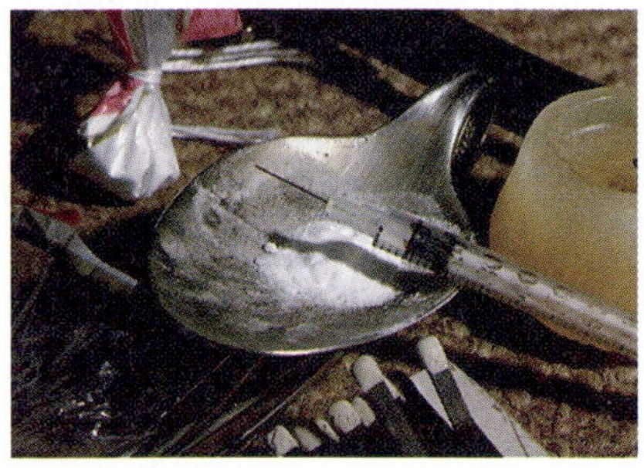

The use of cocaine, crack, heroin, and other illegal drugs has increased over the last decade.

ILLEGAL DRUGS

How prevalent is illegal drug use during the adolescent period? Very prevalent, and rising. For instance, the most recent annual survey of nearly 50,000 U.S. high-school students showed that one in four high-school sophomores and one in three seniors said they had smoked marijuana at least once within the last year. Even eighth graders are using the drug: Some 13 percent said they had smoked the drug during the past year, and 8 percent said they had smoked it within the last 30 days (see Figure 13-6). Almost half of high-school seniors have used an illegal drug at least once in their lives (O'Malley, Johnston, & Bachman, 1995).

The use of marijuana and other illegal drugs is rising. Although drug use declined in the 1980s—the "just say no" campaigns seem to have been effective—it began to rise again in the 1990s. For instance, 1995 figures on marijuana usage were almost double what they were in 1991. Furthermore, the number of high-school seniors who disapprove of the occasional use of marijuana dropped from 79 percent to 69 percent.

The use of other illegal drugs has also grown recently. In contrast to the early 1990s, more high-school students report having used cocaine, crack, hallucinogenic drugs, heroin, and stimulants at least once during the previous year. On the other hand, the use of drugs by adolescents is less prevalent than it was in the late 1970s and early 1980s. During that period, surveys found that more than 50 percent of high school seniors had used marijuana.

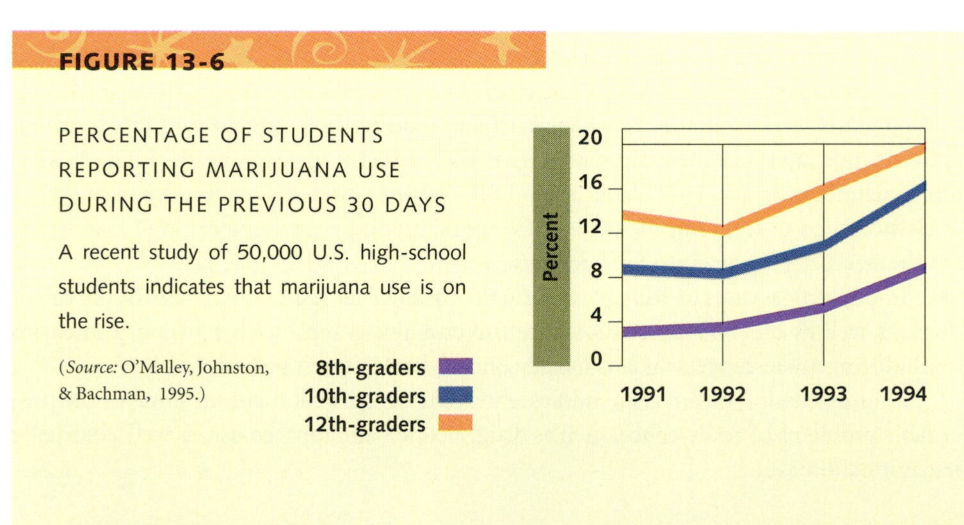

FIGURE 13-6

PERCENTAGE OF STUDENTS REPORTING MARIJUANA USE DURING THE PREVIOUS 30 DAYS

A recent study of 50,000 U.S. high-school students indicates that marijuana use is on the rise.

(*Source:* O'Malley, Johnston, & Bachman, 1995.)

Why do adolescents use drugs? There are multiple reasons. Some relate to the perceived pleasurable experience drugs may provide, and others to the escape from the pressures of everyday life that drugs temporarily permit. Some adolescents try drugs simply for the thrill of doing something illegal. Especially in adolescence, the alleged drug use of well-known role models—such as movie star River Phoenix or Washington, D.C., mayor Marion Barry (who served time in prison for the use of cocaine)—may also contribute. Finally, peer pressure plays a role: Adolescents, as we'll discuss in greater detail in Chapter 15, are particularly susceptible to the perceived standards of their peer groups (Dinges & Oetting, 1993; Epstein et al., 1995; McDonald & Towberman, 1993; Mounts & Steinberg, 1995; Petraitis, Flay, & Miller, 1995; Segal & Stewart, 1996).

addictive drugs *drugs that produce a biological or psychological dependence in users, leading to increasingly powerful cravings for them*

alcoholics *people who have learned to depend on alcohol and are unable to control their drinking*

The use of illegal drugs is dangerous in several respects. For instance, some drugs are addictive. **Addictive drugs** are drugs that produce a biological or psychological dependence in users, leading to increasingly powerful cravings for them. When drugs produce a *biological addiction*, their presence in the body becomes so common that the body is unable to function in their absence. Drugs can also produce a *psychological addiction*. In such cases, people grow to depend on drugs as a way of coping with the everyday stress of life, or they become hooked on the pleasurable feelings produced by a drug.

In addition, if drugs are used as an escape, they may keep adolescents from confronting—and potentially solving—the problems that led them to drug use in the first place. Finally, drugs may be dangerous because even casual users of less hazardous drugs can "graduate" to more dangerous forms of substance abuse. For instance, those who smoke marijuana are 85 times more likely to use cocaine than those who don't (Toch, 1995). (For more on efforts to deal with adolescent drug use, see the "Speaking of Development" feature.)

ALCOHOL: USE AND ABUSE

More than 75 percent of college students have something in common: They've consumed at least one alcoholic drink during the last 30 days. More than 40 percent say they've had five or more drinks within the past 2 weeks, and some 16 percent drink 16 or more drinks per week. High-school students, too, are drinkers: Some 76 percent of high-school seniors report having had an alcoholic drink in the last year, and in some subgroups—such as male athletes—the proportion of drinkers is even higher (Carmody, 1990; C. N. Carr, Kennedy, & Dimick, 1996; Center on Addiction and Substance Abuse, 1994; National Institute on Alcohol Abuse and Alcoholism [NIAAA], 1990).

One of the most troubling patterns is the frequency of binge drinking among college students. Binge drinking is defined for men as drinking five or more drinks in one sitting; for women, who tend to weigh less and whose bodies absorb alcohol less efficiently, binge drinking is defined as four drinks in one sitting.

Recent surveys find that some 50 percent of male college students and 39 percent of female college students say they participated in binge drinking during the previous 2 weeks (see Figure 13-7). Even for lighter drinkers and nondrinkers, this high level of drinking among their peers affects their college experience. For instance, two thirds of lighter drinkers reported that they had had their studying or their sleep disturbed by drunk students. Around a third had been insulted or humiliated by a drunk student, and 25 percent of women said they had been the target of an unwanted sexual advance by a drunk classmate (Wechsler et al., 1994).

Why do adolescents start to drink? Some believe it is the "adult" thing to do. Others drink for the same reason that they use drugs: It releases inhibitions and tension and reduces stress (Fromme & Rivet, 1994). Of course, the same chemical reaction that produces these results can also make adolescents feel depressed, cloud their judgment, impair memory, and reduce motoric skills necessary for driving. These consequences are the greatest danger of alcohol use.

For some adolescents—perhaps as many as a third—alcohol use becomes a habit that cannot be controlled. **Alcoholics** are people who have learned to depend on alcohol and are unable to control their drinking. They also become increasingly immune to the consequences of drinking, and therefore need to drink ever-larger amounts of liquor in order to bring about the positive effects they crave. Some drink throughout the day, while others go on binges in which they consume huge quantities of alcohol (Boyd, Howard, & Zucker, 1995; Morse & Flavin, 1992; NIAAA, 1990).

The reasons why some adolescents become alcoholics are not fully known. Genetics plays a role: Alcoholism runs in families. On the other hand, not all alcoholics have others in their family who drink too much. In cases such as these, alcoholism may be triggered by efforts to deal with environmental stress (Boyd et al., 1995; Bushman, 1993).

TOBACCO: THE DANGERS OF SMOKING

Even though most adolescents are well aware of its dangers, many still indulge in smoking. While recent figures show that, overall, a smaller proportion of adolescents smoke than in prior decades, the numbers remain substantial. Furthermore, within certain groups the numbers are increasing. For instance, smoking is more prevalent among girls, and in several countries, including Austria, Norway, and Sweden, the proportion of girls who smoke is higher than the proportion of boys (Bartecchi, MacKenzie, & Schrier, 1995; Chollat-Traquet, 1992).

Speaking of Development

Doreen Gail Branch, Public Program Analyst

Born: ·················· 1958

Education: ········· Howard University, B.S. and M.A. in psychology

Position: ············· Research Associate for the National Public Service Research Institute

Home: ················ Greenbelt, Maryland

Substance abuse (the abuse of alcohol, tobacco, and drugs) cuts across all segments of the population, but one group that is particularly vulnerable is adolescents. In an effort to create effective preventive programs, Doreen Branch is working as part of a community services coalition project in Maryland's Prince Georges County. The coalition serves adolescents between the ages of 12 and 18.

"We are currently looking at the community to see how the different parts of it can band together to battle alcohol, tobacco, and other drug abuse problems, as well as other problems associated with the use of these substances," says Branch.

After starting college as a premedical student, Branch decided to try her hand at psychology. She was immediately attracted to the discipline, finding that it emphasized thought and creativity instead of including a heavy emphasis on textbook memorization. Her new interest ultimately led her to a master's degree in psychology, and shortly after achieving that degree she joined the National Public Service Research Institute.

One major goal of her work is to provide youth with alternatives to drug use by introducing them to other activities. "Many people are familiar with midnight basketball programs," she says, "but our efforts go beyond programs like that. For instance, one of the activities we are developing is a tennis program that not only teaches tennis, but also provides mentoring to at-risk adolescents." She notes that such a program emphasizes that there are other things to do with one's time than use drugs.

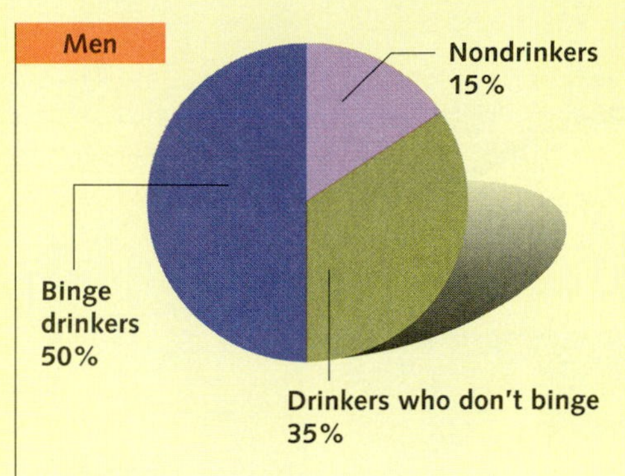

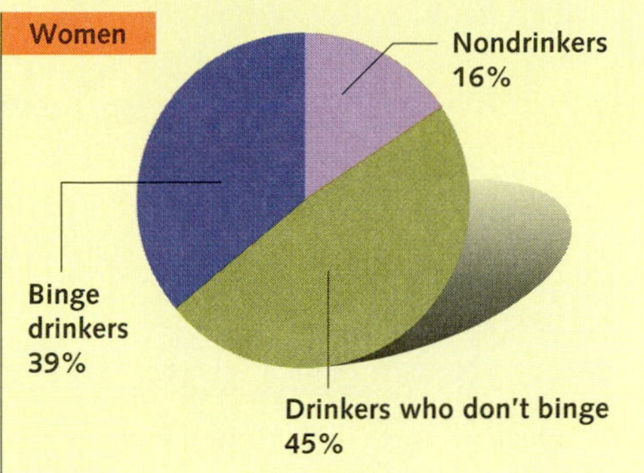

LEVELS OF ALCOHOL CONSUMPTION AMONG COLLEGE STUDENTS

For men, binge drinking was defined as consuming five or more drinks in one sitting; for women, the total was four or more.

(*Source:* H. Wechsler, Davenport et al., 1994.)

"We have to educate students on drugs, and we need to inform them of the dangers of even a little drug use."

"Many adolescents that we deal with do not believe that marijuana, and sometimes even cocaine, are harmful."

"We have to educate students on drugs, and we need to inform them of the dangers of even a little drug use. Many adolescents that we deal with do not believe that marijuana, and sometimes even cocaine, are harmful," Branch adds.

Branch is also studying how tobacco and alcohol manufacturers use advertising to influence teenagers. "One of the things that we are trying to do is change local policies affecting billboards that cater to cigarette and alcohol advertisements. While many of these advertisements are in the poorest sections of town, all teenagers can be influenced by them," she says.

One tactic she has used to deter adolescents' drug use has been to ask them to write, produce, and act in their own commercials on the dangers of drug and alcohol abuse. Another tactic was to provide funding for a large meeting, the Kiamsha Youth Empowerment Conference. With the help of adult mentors, Maryland adolescents organized the meeting largely by themselves.

"The issues discussed at the conference included drugs, sex, violence, and spirituality," says Branch. "The whole conference was planned and conducted by teenagers. They hit on a lot of issues that kids have to deal with, and—in part because it was planned by the adolescents themselves—it was a great success."

Drawing by R. Chast; ©1995 The New Yorker Magazine, Inc.

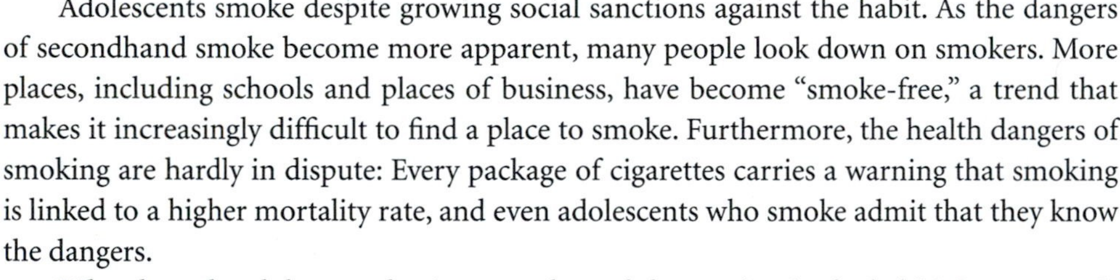

Adolescents smoke despite growing social sanctions against the habit. As the dangers of secondhand smoke become more apparent, many people look down on smokers. More places, including schools and places of business, have become "smoke-free," a trend that makes it increasingly difficult to find a place to smoke. Furthermore, the health dangers of smoking are hardly in dispute: Every package of cigarettes carries a warning that smoking is linked to a higher mortality rate, and even adolescents who smoke admit that they know the dangers.

The portrayal of Joe Camel as a hip and smooth character has helped to maintain the image of smoking as a "cool" activity.

Why, then, do adolescents begin to smoke and then maintain the habit? One reason is that smoking is still considered sexy and hip. Advertisements for cigarettes depict attractive individuals smoking, and clever ads, such as the highly successful "Joe Camel" series, make an effective pitch to young males. In fact, children as young as 6 identify Joe Camel as readily as Mickey Mouse (Bartecchi et al., 1995; Lipman, 1992; Ono, 1995).

There are other reasons, too. Nicotine, the active chemical ingredient of cigarettes, can produce biological and psychological dependency: Smoking it produces a pleasant emotional state that smokers seek to maintain (Nowak, 1994b; Pomerlau & Pomerlau, 1989). Furthermore, exposure to parents and peers who smoke increases the chances that an adolescent will take up the habit (Botvin et al., 1994; Webster, Hunter, & Keats, 1994). Finally, smoking is sometimes seen as an adolescent rite of passage: Trying cigarettes is looked upon as a sign of growing up. Although one or two cigarettes do not usually produce a lifetime smoker, it doesn't take much more. In fact, people who smoke as few as 10 cigarettes early in their lives stand an 80 percent chance of becoming habitual smokers (Bowen et al., 1991; Salber, Freeman, & Abelin, 1968; Stacy et al., 1992).

Developmental Diversity

Pushing Smoking to the Less Advantaged

> *In Dresden, Germany, three women in miniskirts offer passers-by a pack of Lucky Strikes and a leaflet that reads: "You just got hold of a nice piece of America." Says a local doctor, "Adolescents time and again receive cigarettes at such promotions."*
>
> *A Jeep decorated with the Camel logo pulls up to a high school in Buenos Aires. A woman begins handing out free cigarettes to 15- and 16-year-olds during their lunch recess.*
>
> *At a video arcade in Taipei, free American cigarettes are strewn atop each game. At a disco filled with high school students, free packs of Salems are on each table. (Ecenbarger, 1993, p. 50)*

In order to increase sales of their product, cigarette manufacturers are aggressively advertising in developing countries.

If you are a cigarette manufacturer and you find that the number of people using your product is declining, what do you do? U.S. companies have sought to carve out new markets by turning to the least advantaged groups of people, both at home and abroad. For instance, in the early 1990s the R. J. Reynolds tobacco company designed a new brand of cigarettes it named "Uptown." The advertising used to herald its arrival made clear who the target was: African Americans living in urban areas (Quinn, 1990). Because of subsequent protests, the tobacco company withdrew "Uptown" from the market.

In addition to seeking new converts in the United States, tobacco companies aggressively recruit adolescent smokers abroad. In many developing countries the number of smokers is still low. Tobacco companies are seeking to increase this number through marketing strategies designed to hook adolescents on the habit by means of free samples. In addition, in countries where American culture and products are held in high esteem, advertising suggests that the use of cigarettes is an American—and consequently prestigious—habit (Sesser, 1993).

The strategy is effective. For instance, in some Latin American cities as many as 50 percent of teenagers smoke. According to the World Health Organization, smoking will prematurely kill some 200 million of the world's children and adolescents, and overall, 10 percent of the world's population will die because of smoking (Ecenbarger, 1993).

DYING IN ADOLESCENCE: THE RISK OF DEATH

When an adolescent dies, most of the time it is not from natural causes. Instead, most deaths—some three quarters of them—stem from behavior-related problems, such as motor vehicle and other accidents, gun-related homicides and mishaps, suicide, abuse of drugs, and AIDS (Carnegie Council on Adolescent Development, 1995; see Figure 13-8).

The most frequent cause of death in adolescence is from accidents, most often related to motor vehicle use. Teenage boys are involved in most of the accidental injuries, accounting for four out of five of them. In addition, the overall death rate is three times higher for teenage boys than girls.

Violence presents an increasing risk to adolescents. For example, the homicide rate from guns for 10- to 14-year-olds more than doubled between 1985 and 1992 (from 0.8 to

FIGURE 13-8

LEADING CAUSES OF DEATH IN ADOLESCENTS

Most of the time the death of an adolescent is not from natural causes, but rather from behavior-related problems.

(*Source:* National Center for Health Statistics, 1994.)

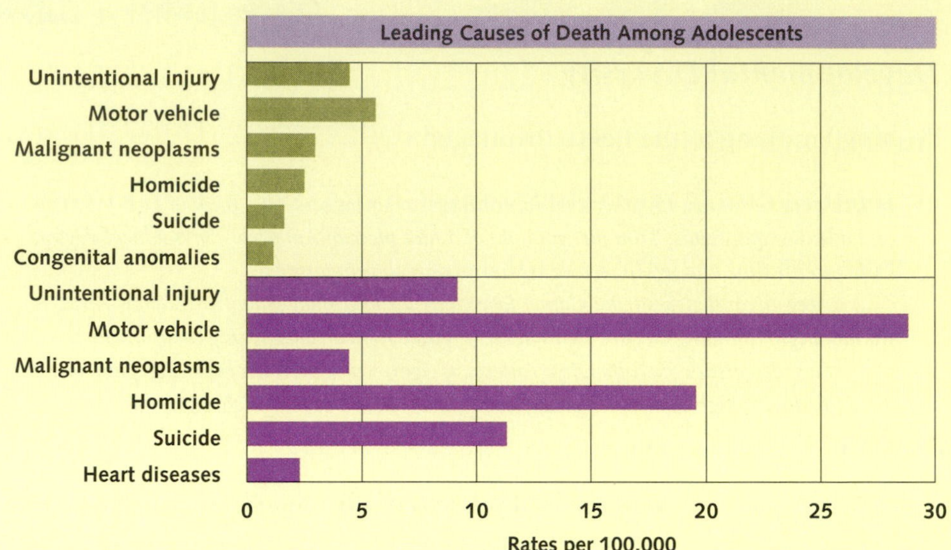

Note: A recent addition to the leading causes of death for adolescents ages 15–19 is infection with the human immunodeficiency virus (HIV). HIV infection was the 10th leading cause of death for this age group, at a rate of 0.3 per 100,000.

1.9 per 100,000). For African-American males, the rate almost tripled, increasing from 3.0 to 8.4 per 100,000 during the same period. Furthermore, 12- to 15-year-olds were victims of assault more than any other age group. Homicide is now the second leading cause of death for older adolescents (Carnegie Council on Adolescent Development, 1995; O'Donnell, 1995).

Finally, suicide represents a major cause of death for adolescents. As we'll consider in detail in Chapter 15, the rate of adolescent suicide has tripled in the last 30 years, and it now ranks as the third most frequent cause of death during adolescence.

Krista Blake contracted AIDS at the age of 16. She later died from the disease.

SEXUALLY TRANSMITTED DISEASES: ONE COST OF SEX

> In the fall of 1990, Krista Blake was 18 and looking forward to her first year at Youngstown State University in Ohio. She and her boyfriend were talking about getting married. Her life was, she says, "basic, white-bread America." Then she went to the doctor, complaining about a backache, and found out she had the AIDS virus.
>
> Blake had been infected with HIV, the virus that causes AIDS, 2 years earlier by an older boy, a hemophiliac. "He knew that he was infected, and he didn't tell me," she says. "And he didn't do anything to keep me from getting infected, either." (Becahy, 1992, p. 49)

AIDS. Krista Blake is not alone: **Acquired immunodeficiency syndrome,** or **AIDS,** is now the leading cause of death among young people. AIDS has no cure and ultimately brings death to those who are infected with the HIV virus that produces the disease.

Because AIDS is spread primarily through sexual contact, it is classified as a **sexually transmitted disease (STD).** Experts estimate that the United States will have more than 1 million reported cases by the year 2000, and the figure is expected to reach 10 million worldwide. Minorities have been particularly hard hit: African Americans and Hispanics account for some 40 percent of AIDS cases, although they make up only 18 percent of the population. AIDS is the tenth leading cause of death for adolescents aged 15 to 19 (National Center for Health Statistics, 1994).

acquired immunodeficiency syndrome (AIDS) *a sexually transmitted disease, produced by the HIV virus, that has no cure and ultimately causes death*

sexually transmitted disease (STD) *a disease that is spread through sexual contact*

Although most adolescents are well aware of the importance of safer sex practices, their feelings of invulnerability sometimes lead them to believe that their chances of contracting a sexually transmitted disease are minimal—especially when they are well acquainted with their partner.

Furthermore, the worldwide cumulative total of people with the virus that causes AIDS, *human immunodeficiency virus,* or *HIV,* is projected to stand at a mind-boggling 30 to 40 million by 2000. Unless a cure for the disease is discovered, all of them will die from the disease (Harvard Mental Health Letter, 1994; World Health Organization, 1993, 1995; Doyle, 1996).

AIDS and Adolescent Behavior. Although it is no secret how AIDS is transmitted—through the exchange of bodily fluids, including semen and blood—it has proven difficult to motivate teenagers to employ safer sex practices that can prevent its spread. On the one hand, the use of condoms during sexual intercourse has increased, and people are less likely to engage in casual sex with new acquaintances (Catania et al., 1992; Kelly, 1995; Kolata, 1991).

On the other hand, the use of safer sex practices is far from universal. Adolescents, who—as we will discuss in the next chapter—are prone to engage in risky behavior due to feelings of invulnerability, are likely to believe that their chances of contracting AIDS are minimal. This is particularly true when adolescents perceive that their partner is "safe"—someone they know well and with whom they are involved in a relatively long-term relationship (Kelly, 1995; Moore & Rosenthal, 1991; Rosenthal & Shepherd, 1993).

Unfortunately, unless an individual knows the complete sexual history and HIV status of a partner, unprotected sex remains risky business. And learning a partner's complete sexual history is difficult. It is often inaccurately communicated out of embarrassment, a sense of privacy, or simply forgetfulness.

Short of celibacy, a solution regarded as improbable for many adolescents involved in relationships, there is no certain way to avoid AIDS. However, health experts suggest several strategies for making sex safer; these are listed in Table 13-3.

Other Sexually Transmitted Diseases. Although AIDS is the deadliest of sexually transmitted diseases, others are far more common (see Figure 13-9). In fact, one in four adolescents contracts an STD before graduating from high school. Overall, around 2.5 million teenagers contract an STD each year (Alan Guttmacher Institute, 1993a; Barringer, 1993; Gans, 1990).

Chlamydia, a disease caused by a parasite, is the most common STD. Initially it has few symptoms, but later it causes burning urination and a discharge from the penis or vagina. It can lead to pelvic inflammation and even to sterility. Although not bacterial in origin, chlamydial infections can be treated successfully with antibiotics.

chlamydia *the most common sexually transmitted disease, caused by a parasite*

TABLE 13-3

GUIDELINES TO HELP PREVENT THE SPREAD OF AIDS

Health psychologists and educators have devised several guidelines to help prevent the spread of AIDS. Among them are the following:

- *Use condoms.* The use of condoms greatly reduces the risk of transmission of the virus that produces AIDS, which occurs through exposure to bodily fluids such as semen or blood.
- *Avoid high-risk behaviors.* Such practices as unprotected anal intercourse or the sharing by drug users of needles greatly increase the risk of AIDS.
- *Know your partner's sexual history.* Knowing your sexual partner and his or her sexual history can help you to evaluate the risks of sexual contact.
- *Consider abstinence.* Although not always a practical alternative, the only certain way of avoiding AIDS is to refrain from sexual activity altogether.

Another common STD is **genital herpes,** a virus not unlike the cold sores that sometimes appear around the mouth. The first symptoms of herpes are often small blisters or sores around the genitals, which may break open and become quite painful. Although the sores may heal after a few weeks, the disease often recurs after an interval, and the cycle repeats itself. When the sores reappear, the disease, for which there is no cure, is contagious.

genital herpes *a common sexually transmitted disease which is a virus and not unlike cold sores that sometimes appear around the mouth*

Several other STDs are frequent among adolescents. Trichomoniasis, an infection in the vagina or penis, is caused by a parasite. Initially without symptoms, it can eventually cause a painful discharge. Gonorrhea and syphilis are the STDs that have been recognized for the longest time; cases were recorded by ancient historians. Until the advent of antibiotics, both diseases were deadly; today both can be treated quite effectively.

FIGURE 13-9

COMMON SEXUALLY TRANSMITTED DISEASES

Best estimates for sexually transmitted diseases (STDs) among adolescents.

(Source: Alan Guttmacher Institute, 1993a.)

3 million teenagers, about 1 person in 8 aged 13–19 and about 1 in 4 of those who have had sexual intercourse, acquire an STD every year. Among the most common:

Chlamydia: Chlamydia is more common among teenagers than among older men and women; in some studies, 10 to 29 percent of sexually active adolescent girls and 10 percent of teenage boys have been found to be infected with chlamydia.

Genital herpes: A viral disease that is incurable, often indicated first by small blisters or sores around the genitals. It is periodically contagious.

Trichomoniasis: An infection of the vagina or penis, caused by a parasite.

Gonorrhea: Adolescents aged 15–19 have higher rates of gonorrhea than do sexually active men and women in any 5-year age group between 20–44.

Syphillis: Infectious syphillis rates more than doubled between 1986 and 1990 among women aged 15–19.

The Informed Consumer of Development

Hooked on Drugs or Alcohol?

Although it is not always easy to determine if an adolescent has a drug or alcohol abuse problem, there are some signals (Frank & Brownstone, 1991). Among them:

Identification with the drug culture

- Drug-related magazines or slogans on clothing
- Conversation and jokes that are preoccupied with drugs
- Hostility discussing drugs
- Collection of beer cans

Signs of physical deterioration

- Memory lapses, short attention span, difficulty concentrating
- Poor physical coordination, slurred or incoherent speech
- Unhealthy appearance, indifference to hygiene and grooming
- Bloodshot eyes, dilated pupils

Dramatic changes in school performance

- Marked downturn in grades—not just from C's to F's, but from A's to B's and C's; assignments not completed
- Increased absenteeism or tardiness

Changes in behavior

- Chronic dishonesty (lying, stealing, cheating), trouble with the police
- Changes in friends, evasiveness in talking about new ones
- Possession of large amounts of money
- Increasing and inappropriate anger, hostility, irritability, secretiveness
- Reduced motivation, energy, self-discipline, self-esteem
- Diminished interest in extracurricular activities and hobbies

If an adolescent—or anyone else, for that matter—fits any of these descriptors, help is probably needed. It is possible to get advice from a national hotline. For help with drug problems, the National Drug Information, Treatment, and Referral Hotline is (800) 662-4357. The National Council on Alcoholism and Drug Dependence can be reached at (800) 622-2255 or by writing 12 West 21 Street, New York, NY 10010, for help with alcohol and drug problems. In addition, those who need advice can find a local listing for Alcoholics Anonymous, Narcotics Anonymous, or Cocaine Anonymous in the telephone book.

Review and Rethink

REVIEW

- Illegal drug use is prevalent among adolescents, who may regard drugs as a way to find pleasure, avoid pressure, or gain the approval of peers. Drug use can escalate, become addictive, and prevent the confrontation of problems.
- Alcohol also is widely used by adolescents, often out of a desire to appear grown up or to lessen inhibitions. Impaired judgment and motor control are major dangers of alcohol use.
- A third substance that constitutes a serious health hazard to adolescents is tobacco. Despite the well-known dangers of smoking, adolescents often engage in the practice to enhance their images or emulate adults.
- AIDS is the most serious of the sexually transmitted diseases, ultimately causing death. Safe sex or sexual abstinence—strategies often ignored by adolescents—can prevent AIDS.
- Other sexually transmitted diseases that affect adolescents are chlamydia, genital herpes, trichomoniasis, gonorrhea, and syphilis.

RETHINK

- In what ways might characteristics of adolescent physical development contribute to the decision to use drugs? Is stress a factor?
- Do you think patterns of alcohol use in adolescence are culture-related? What cultural and environmental conditions might contribute to alcohol use?
- How can adolescents clearly know the hazards of smoking and yet engage in the practice? Do efforts to restrict access to tobacco products decrease the desire to smoke?
- Why do many adolescents find it difficult to engage in only protected sex? Is the issue of protected sex perceived differently by males and females?
- What are the responsibilities of people who are aware that their friends are engaging in hazardous practices?

LOOKING BACK

What physical changes do adolescents experience?

1. The adolescent years are marked by a physical growth spurt that mirrors the rapid growth rate of infancy. Girls' growth spurts begin around age 10, about 2 years earlier than boys'.
2. The most significant event during adolescence is the onset of puberty, which begins for most girls at around age 11 or 12 and for most boys at around age 13 or 14. As puberty commences, the body begins to produce male or female hormones at adult levels, the sex organs develop and change, menstruation and ejaculation begin, and other body changes occur.

3. The timing of puberty is linked to cultural and environmental factors, as well as biological ones. Compared with the past, girls in the United States today experience menarche—the onset of menstruation—at the significantly younger age of 11 or 12, most likely because of better nutrition and overall health.

4. The physical changes that accompany puberty, which adolescents usually experience with keen interest, often have psychological effects, which may involve an increase in self-esteem and self-awareness, as well as some confusion and uncertainty about sexuality.

What are the consequences of early and late maturation?

5. Those who mature either early or late experience mixed consequences. For boys, early maturation can lead to increased athleticism, greater popularity, and a more positive self-concept. For girls, although early maturation can lead to increased popularity and an enhanced social life, they may also experience embarrassment over the changes in their bodies that differentiate them from their peers. Furthermore, early physical maturation can lead both boys and girls into activities and situations for which they are not adequately prepared.

6. Late maturation, because it results in smaller size, can put boys at a distinct physical and social disadvantage, which can affect self-concept and have lasting negative consequences. Girls who mature late may suffer neglect by their peers of both sexes, but ultimately they appear to suffer no lasting ill effects and may even benefit from late maturation.

What are the nutritional needs and concerns of adolescents?

7. While most adolescents have no greater nutritional worries than fueling their growth with appropriate foods, some are obese or overweight and may suffer psychological and physical consequences. Furthermore, a substantial number are excessively concerned about obesity, to the point of contracting an eating disorder.

8. Two major eating disorders that affect adolescent girls are anorexia nervosa—a refusal to eat because of a perception of being overweight—and bulimia—a cycle of binge eating followed by purges of food. Both biological and environmental factors appear to contribute to these disorders, and treatment typically involves psychological therapy and dietary changes.

What are the effects of stress, and what can be done about it?

9. Moderate, occasional stress is biologically healthy, producing physical reactions that facilitate the body's defense against threats; but long exposure to stressors produces damaging physical and psychosomatic effects.

10. Stress has been linked to many common ailments, including headaches, back pains, rashes, indigestion, and even the common cold. It has also been linked to psychosomatic disorders, such as ulcers, asthma, arthritis, and high blood pressure, and to more serious, even life-threatening, illnesses.

11. People pass through two stages in reacting to potentially stressful situations: primary appraisal of the situation itself and secondary appraisal of their own coping abilities.

12. People cope with stress in a number of ways, including problem-focused coping, by which they attempt to modify the stressful situation, and emotion-focused coping, by which they attempt to regulate the emotional response to stress.

13. Coping is aided by social support from others. Defensive coping, which is the unconscious resort to a strategy of denial, is less successful because it represents a failure to deal with the reality of the situation.

What are some threats to the well-being of adolescents?

14. The use of illicit drugs is alarmingly prevalent among adolescents, who are motivated by pleasure seeking, pressure avoidance, the desire to flout authority, or the imitation of role models.

15. Drug use is dangerous not only because it can escalate and lead to addiction, but also because an adolescent's escape into drugs as a way to avoid underlying problems can have serious effects.

16. Alcohol use is also prevalent among adolescents, who may view drinking as a way to lower inhibitions or to manifest adult behavior. The impairment of judgment and motor skills is one of the main dangers of alcohol consumption, although secondary dangers to others—including personal and sexual aggression—are also serious.

17. Even though the dangers of smoking are well known and accepted by adolescents, tobacco use continues. Despite a reduction in smoking among adolescents in general, smoking within some groups has actually increased, including among girls. Adolescents who smoke appear to be motivated by a desire to look "cool" or act like adults.

18. Among the warning signs that an adolescent may have a problem with drugs or alcohol are identification with the drug culture, evidence of physical deterioration, dramatic declines in school performance, and significant changes in behavior.

What dangers do adolescent sexual practices present, and how can these dangers be avoided?

19. AIDS is now the leading cause of death among young people in the United States, affecting minority populations with particular severity. Adolescent behavior patterns and attitudes, such as shyness and a belief in personal invulnerability, work against the use of safer sex practices that can prevent the disease.

20. Other sexually transmitted diseases, including chlamydia, genital herpes, trichomoniasis, gonorrhea, and syphilis, occur frequently among the adolescent population and can also be prevented by safer sex practices or abstinence.

Key Terms and Concepts

adolescence (p. 415)
adolescent growth spurt (p. 416)
puberty (p. 416)
menarche (p. 417)
secular trend (p. 417)
primary sex characteristics (p. 418)
secondary sex characteristics (p. 418)
anorexia nervosa (p. 421)
bulimia (p. 422)
stress (p. 424)
psychosomatic disorders (p. 426)
coping (p. 427)
addictive drugs (p. 431)
alcoholics (p. 431)
acquired immunodeficiency syndrome (AIDS) (p. 436)
sexually transmitted disease (STD) (p. 436)
chlamydia (p. 437)
genital herpes (p. 438)

CHAPTER 14

ADOLESCENCE

Cognitive Development in Adolescence

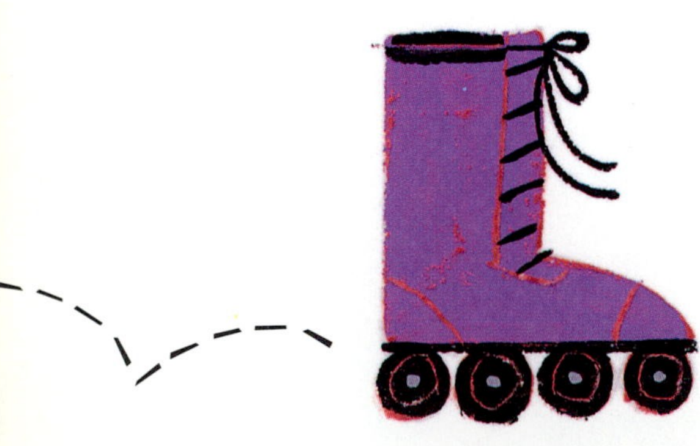

ROLOGUE

ALEKSANDR KHAZANOV

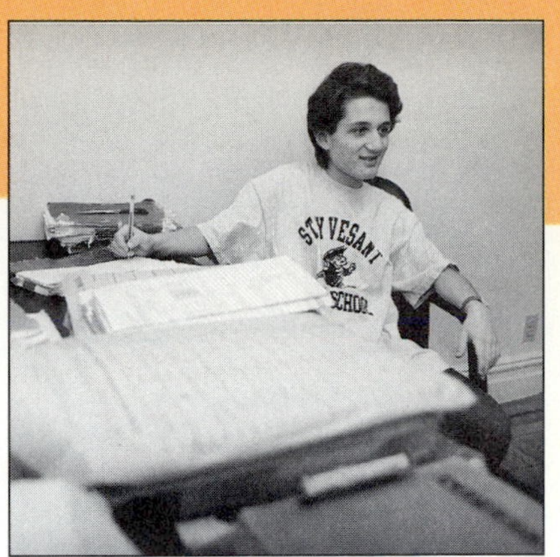

The bedtime stories Aleksandr Khazanov's father told him were multiplication tables and long division.

When Aleksandr was 14—a little over a year after his family immigrated to Brooklyn as refugees from Russia—his math teacher at Stuyvesant High School watched him whiz through differential equations and felt the boy was so advanced that he could learn more studying on his own.

Last summer, at 15, long before he was old enough to get his driver's license, Aleksandr took qualifying exams for Pennsylvania State University's doctoral program in math. He passed all three tests on the first try.

So when Aleksandr submitted a paper to the Westinghouse Science Talent Search competition, the most prestigious science contest for high school students, the Stuyvesant coordinator for contest entries, Stan Teitel, took an extraordinary step.

"I had the audacity to call up Westinghouse and question them as to whether they had someone advanced enough to understand his paper," Mr. Teitel said. "I'm telling you, this kid is way above the rest of us." (Belluck, 1995, p. A1)

LOOKING AHEAD

The people at Westinghouse must have agreed: Khazanov was named a finalist in the contest.

Although most adolescents do not reach the heights of mathematical sophistication that Aleksandr attained—nor do most adults, for that matter—their intellectual abilities do make significant gains during adolescence. In fact, by the end of the period, adolescents' cognitive proficiencies match those of adults in major respects.

In this chapter, we examine cognitive development during adolescence. The chapter begins with an examination of several theories that seek to explain cognitive development. We first consider the Piagetian approach, discussing the way in which adolescents use what Piaget calls "formal operations" to solve problems. We then turn to the increasingly influential alternative, information-processing perspectives, which provide a different point of view. We consider the growth of metacognitive capabilities, through which adolescents become increasingly aware of their own thinking processes.

The chapter then turns to the development of moral reasoning and behavior. We consider two major approaches, both of which seek to explain the ways adolescents differ from one another in their moral judgments.

Finally, the chapter ends with an examination of school performance and career choices. After discussing the profound impact that socioeconomic status has on school achievement, we consider school performance and ethnicity. We close with a discussion of the ways in which adolescents make career choices.

After reading this chapter, then, you'll be able to answer these questions:

- How does cognitive development proceed during adolescence?
- What aspects of cognitive development cause difficulties for adolescents?
- Through what stages does moral development progress during childhood and adolescence?

- What factors affect adolescent school performance?
- Who attends college, and how is the college experience different for men and women?
- How do adolescents make career choices, and what influence do ethnicity and gender have on career opportunities?

Intellectual Development

What is it that sets adolescents' thinking apart from that of younger children? One of the major changes is the ability to think beyond the concrete current situation to what *might* or *could* be. Adolescents are able to keep in their heads a variety of abstract possibilities, and they can see issues in relative, as opposed to absolute, terms. Instead of viewing problems as having black-and-white solutions, they are capable of perceiving shades of gray (Keating, 1980, 1990).

As was the case with other stages of life, we can use several approaches to explain adolescents' cognitive development. We'll begin by returning to Piaget's theory, which has had a significant influence on how developmentalists think about thinking during adolescence.

Piagetian Approaches to Cognitive Development: Using Formal Operations

Fourteen-year-old Aleigh is asked to solve a problem that anyone who has seen a grandfather's clock may have pondered: What determines the speed at which a pendulum moves back and forth? In the version of the problem that she is asked to solve, Aleigh is given a weight hanging from a string. She is told that she can vary several things: the length of the string, the weight of the object at the end of the string, the amount of force used to push the string, and the height to which the weight is raised in an arc before it is released.

Aleigh doesn't remember, but she was asked to solve the same problem when she was 8 years old. At that time, she was in the concrete operational period, and her efforts to solve the problem were not very successful. For instance, she approached the problem haphazardly, with no systematic plan of action. She simultaneously tried to push the pendulum harder *and* shorten the length of the string *and* increase the weight on the string. Because she was varying so many factors at once, when the speed of the pendulum changed she had no way of knowing which factor or factors made a difference.

Now, however, Aleigh is much more systematic. Rather than immediately beginning to push and pull at the pendulum, she stops a moment and thinks. Then, just like a scientist conducting an experiment, she varies only one factor at a time. By examining each variable separately and systematically, she is able to come to the correct solution: The length of the string determines the speed of the pendulum.

Using Formal Operations to Solve Problems. Aleigh's approach to the pendulum question, a problem devised by Piaget, illustrates that she has moved into the formal operational period of cognitive development (Piaget & Inhelder, 1958). The **formal operational stage** is the stage at which people develop the ability to think abstractly. Most people reach it at the start of adolescence, around the age of 12.

By bringing formal principles of logic to bear on problems they encounter, adolescents in the formal operational stage are able to consider problems in the abstract rather than only in concrete terms. They are able to test their understanding by systematically carrying out rudimentary experiments on problems and situations, and observing what their experimental "interventions" bring about.

formal operational stage *the stage of cognitive development at which people develop the ability to think abstractly*

Adolescents in the formal operational stage use *hypothetico-deductive reasoning,* in which they start with a general theory about what produces a particular outcome, and then deduce explanations for what has brought about the outcome. Like scientists who form hypotheses, they can then test their theories. What distinguishes this kind of thinking from earlier cognitive stages is the ability to start with abstract possibilities and move to the concrete; in previous stages, children are tied to the concrete here and now.

Although Piaget proposed that children enter the formal operational stage at the beginning of adolescence, you may recall that he also hypothesized that—as with all the stages of cognitive development—full capabilities do not emerge suddenly, at one stroke. Instead, they gradually unfold through a combination of physical maturation and environmental experiences. According to Piaget, it is not until adolescents are around 15 years old that they are fully settled in the formal operational stage.

In fact, some evidence suggests that a sizable proportion of people hone their formal operational skills at a later age, and in some cases, never fully employ formal operational thinking at all. For instance, most studies show that only 40 to 60 percent of college students and adults achieve formal operational thinking completely, and some estimates run as low as 25 percent. But many of those adults who do not show formal operational thought in every domain are fully competent in *some* aspects of formal operations (Keating & Clark, 1980; Sugarman, 1988).

One of the reasons adolescents differ in their use of formal operations relates to the culture in which they are raised. For instance, people who live in isolated, scientifically unsophisticated societies and who have little formal education are less likely to perform at the formal operational level than formally educated persons living in more technologically sophisticated societies (Jahoda, 1980; Segall et al., 1990).

Does this mean that adolescents (and adults) from cultures in which formal operations tend not to emerge are incapable of attaining them? Not at all. A more probable conclusion is that the scientific reasoning that characterizes formal operations is not equally valued in all societies. If everyday life does not require or promote a certain type of reasoning, it is irrational to expect people to employ that type of reasoning when confronted with a problem (Greenfield, 1976; Shea, 1985).

Evaluating Piaget's Approach. Each time we've considered Piaget's theory in previous chapters, several concerns have cropped up. Let's summarize some of the issues here:

- Piaget suggests that cognitive development proceeds in universal, steplike advances that occur at particular stages. Yet we find significant differences in cognitive abilities from one person to the next, especially when we compare individuals from different cultures. Furthermore, we find inconsistencies in the performance of tasks even within the same individual—tasks that, if Piaget were correct, a person ought to perform uniformly well once she or he reaches a given stage (Siegler, 1994).
- The notion of stages proposed by Piaget suggests that cognitive abilities do not grow gradually or smoothly. Instead, the stage point of view implies that cognitive growth is typified by relatively rapid shifts from one stage to the next. In contrast, many developmentalists argue that cognitive development proceeds in a more continuous fashion, increasing not so much in qualitative leaps forward as in quantitative accumulations. They also contend that Piaget's theory is better at *describing* behavior at a given stage than *explaining* why the shift from one stage to the next occurs (Case, 1991; Gelman & Baillargeon, 1983).
- Because of the nature of the tasks Piaget employed to measure cognitive abilities, critics suggest that he underestimated the age at which certain capabilities emerge. It is now widely accepted that infants and children are more sophisticated at an earlier age than Piaget asserted (Bornstein & Sigman, 1986).
- Piaget had a relatively narrow view of what is meant by *thinking* and *knowing*. To Piaget knowledge consists primarily of the kind of understanding displayed in the pendulum problem. However, as we discussed in Chapter 11, developmentalists such as

Howard Gardner suggest that we have many kinds of intelligence, separate from and independent of one another (Gardner & Hatch, 1989; Kronhaber et al., 1991).

These criticisms of Piaget's approach to cognitive development have considerable merit. On the other hand, Piaget made momentous contributions to our understanding of cognitive development, and his work remains highly influential. He was a brilliant observer of children's and adolescents' behavior, and his portrayal of children as actively constructing and transforming information about their world has had a substantial impact on the way we view children and their cognitive capabilites.

Piaget's theory has been the impetus for an enormous number of studies on the development of thinking capacities and processes, and it also spurred a good deal of classroom reform. Finally, his bold statements about the nature of cognitive development provided a fertile soil from which many opposing positions on cognitive development bloomed, such as the information-processing perspective, to which we turn next (Demetriou et al., 1993; Elkind, 1996).

Information-processing Perspectives: Gradual Transformations in Abilities

To proponents of information-processing approaches to cognitive development, growth in mental abilities proceeds gradually and continuously. Unlike Piaget's view that the increasing cognitive sophistication of the adolescent is a reflection of stagelike spurts, the *information-processing perspective* sees changes in cognitive abilities as gradual transformations in the capacity to take in, use, and store information.

In this view, increases in information-processing capabilities lie at the heart of the advances in mental ability that are seen during adolescence. Developmental advances are brought about by progressive changes in the ways people organize their thinking about the world, develop strategies for dealing with new situations, sort facts, and achieve advances in memory capacity and perceptual abilities (Burbules & Linn, 1988; Gagne, 1985; Keating & Clark, 1980; Wellman & Gelman, 1992).

And the cognitive strides made during adolescence are considerable. Although general intelligence—as measured by traditional IQ tests—remains stable, dramatic improvements evolve in the specific mental abilities that underlie intelligence. Verbal, mathematical, and spatial abilities increase. Memory capacity grows, and adolescents become more adept at effectively dividing their attention across more than one stimulus at a time—such as simultaneously studying for a biology test and listening to a Fugees CD.

Furthermore, adolescents grow increasingly sophisticated in their understanding of problems, their ability to grasp abstract concepts and to think hypothetically, and their comprehension of the possibilities inherent in situations. They know more about the world, too; their store of knowledge increases as the amount of material to which they are exposed grows and their memory capacity enlarges (Pressley, 1987). Taken as a whole, the mental abilities that underlie intelligence show a marked improvement during adolescence, peaking at around age 20 (see Figure 14-1).

According to information-processing explanations of cognitive development during adolescence, one of the most important reasons for advances in mental abilities is the growth of metacognition. **Metacognition** is the knowledge that people have about their own thinking processes, and their ability to monitor their cognition.

For example, as adolescents improve their understanding of their memory capacity, they get better at gauging how long they need to study a particular kind of material to memorize it for a test. Furthermore, they can judge when they have fully memorized the material considerably more accurately than when they were younger. These improvements in metacognitive abilities permit adolescents to comprehend and master school material more effectively (Flavell, 1979; Garner & Alexander, 1989; Nelson, 1990, 1994).

metacognition *the knowledge that people have about their own thinking processes, and their ability to monitor their cognition*

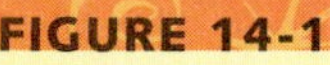

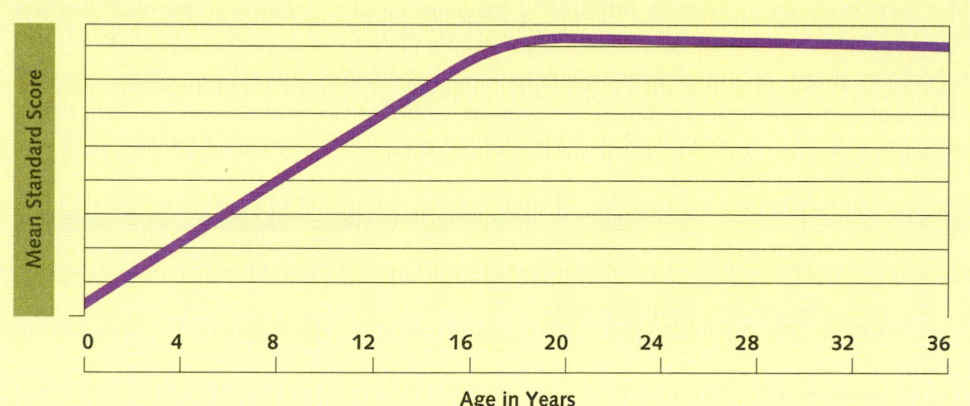

GROWTH OF ONE INDIVIDUAL'S MENTAL ABILITIES

The mental abilities that underlie intelligence show a marked improvement during adolescence, peaking at around age 20.

(*Source:* Adapted from Bayley, 1949.)

On the other hand, advances in metacognition do not always produce positive results. For instance, metacognition may make adolescents particularly introspective and self-conscious—two hallmarks of the period which, as we see next, may produce a high degree of egocentrism.

EGOCENTRISM IN THINKING: ADOLESCENTS' SELF-ABSORPTION

Carlos is furious at his parents. He sees them as totally unfair because, when he borrows their car, they insist that he call home and let them know where he is. Eleanor is angry at Molly because Molly, by chance, bought earrings just like hers, and Molly insists on sometimes wearing them to school. Lu is upset with his biology teacher, Ms. Sebastian, for giving a long, difficult midterm exam on which he didn't do well.

Each of these adolescents is furious, angry, or upset over what may seem like not-so-unreasonable behavior on the part of others. Why? It is quite possible that the cause lies in the egocentrism that may sometimes dominate adolescents' thinking.

According to developmental psychologist David Elkind (1967, 1985) this period of life fosters **adolescent egocentrism,** a state of self-absorption in which the world is viewed from one's own point of view. Egocentrism makes adolescents highly critical of authority figures such as parents and teachers, unwilling to accept criticism, and quick to find fault with others' behavior.

The kind of egocentrism we see in adolescence helps explain why adolescents sometimes perceive that they are the focus of everyone else's attention. In fact, adolescents may develop what has been called an **imaginary audience,** fictitious observers who pay as much attention to the adolescents' behavior as adolescents do themselves.

Because of adolescents' newly sophisticated metacognitive abilities, they readily imagine that others are thinking about them, and they may construct elaborate scenarios about others' thoughts. Unfortunately, these scenarios may suffer from the same kind of egocentrism as the rest of their thinking. The imaginary audience is usually perceived as focusing on the one thing that adolescents think most about: themselves. For instance, a student sitting in a class may be sure a teacher is focusing on her, and a teenager at a basketball game may just know that everyone around is focusing on the pimple on his chin.

Egocentrism leads to a second distortion in thinking: the notion that one's experiences are unique. Adolescents develop **personal fables,** the view that what happens to them is unique, exceptional, and shared by no one else. For instance, teenagers whose romantic relationships have ended may feel that no one has ever experienced the hurt they feel, that no one has ever been treated so badly, that no one can understand what they are going through.

adolescent egocentrism *a state of self-absorption in which the world is viewed from one's own point of view*

imaginary audience *fictitious observers who pay as much attention to adolescents' behavior as adolescents do themselves*

personal fables *the view held by some adolescents that what happens to them is unique, exceptional, and shared by no one else*

Adolescents' egocentrism leads to the belief that what happens to them is unique and to feelings of invulnerability—producing risky behavior.

Personal fables also may make adolescents feel invulnerable to the risks that threaten others. They may think that there is no need to use condoms during sex, since the personal fables they construct make them immune to pregnancy and to sexually transmitted diseases such as AIDS. They may drive after drinking, because their personal fables paint them as careful drivers, always in control. In short, adolescents' risk-taking may well be traced to the personal fables they construct for themselves (Arnett, 1995; Dolcini et al., 1989; Lightfoot, 1997).

Review and Rethink

REVIEW

- As they enter Piaget's formal operational stage, adolescents begin to think abstractly, use logic, and perform systematic experiments to answer questions.
- Because there are individual and cultural differences in formal operations, Piaget's theory has been questioned. In contrast, the information-processing perspective attributes cognitive advances to quantitative gains in the ability to take in, use, and store information.
- Information-processing gains, including memory and perceptual advances, permit individuals to organize their thinking more effectively, use their increased store of world knowledge, develop strategies for dealing with new situations, sort facts, think hypothetically, and divide their attention across multiple tasks.
- Through metacognition, one of the most important cognitive advances of the stage, adolescents can monitor their thinking and assess with accuracy the cognitive resources they will need to perform mental tasks.
- Adolescent egocentrism, an excessively self-centered perspective on the world, can cause problems, including consciousness of an imaginary audience and the development of personal fables that imply individual uniqueness and immunity to risks.

RETHINK

- When faced with complex problems, do adults routinely use formal operations? Under what circumstances do you think they use and don't use formal operational approaches?
- What sorts of cognitive processes might people of less scientifically oriented societies develop that do not usually emerge among people in more technologically sophisticated societies?
- Why do individual and cultural differences in such cognitive abilities as formal operations argue against a qualitative stage theory like Piaget's?
- Why does IQ remain stable in adolescence despite dramatic advances in mental abilities and cognitive functioning?
- In what ways does adolescent egocentrism complicate adolescents' social and family relationships? Do adults entirely outgrow egocentric thought and personal fables?

MORAL DEVELOPMENT

Your wife is near death from an unusual kind of cancer. One drug exists that the physicians think might save her—a form of radium that a scientist in a nearby city has recently developed. The drug, though, is expensive to manufacture, and the scientist is charging 10 times what the drug costs him to make. He pays $1,000 for the radium and charges $10,000 for a small dose. You have gone to everyone you know to borrow money, but you can get together only $2,500—one quarter of what you need. You've told the scientist that your wife is dying and asked him to sell it more cheaply or let you pay later. But the scientist has said, "No, I discovered the drug and I'm going to make money from it." In desperation, you consider breaking into the scientist's laboratory to steal the drug for your wife.

Should you do it?

KOHLBERG'S THEORY OF MORAL DEVELOPMENT: DESCRIBING MORAL REASONING

According to developmental psychologist Lawrence Kohlberg and his colleagues, the answer that children give to this question reveals central aspects of their sense of morality and justice. He suggests that people's responses to moral dilemmas such as this one reveal the stage of moral development they have attained—as well as yielding information about their general level of cognitive development (Colby & Kohlberg, 1987; Kohlberg, 1984).

Kohlberg contends that people pass through a series of stages in the evolution of their sense of justice and in the kind of reasoning they use to make moral judgments. Primarily due to cognitive characteristics that we discussed earlier, school-age children tend to think either in terms of concrete, unvarying rules ("It is always wrong to steal" or "I'll be punished if I steal") or in terms of the rules of society ("Good people don't steal" or "What if everyone stole?").

By the time they reach adolescence, however, individuals are able to reason on a higher plane, typically having reached Piaget's stage of formal operations. They are capable of comprehending abstract, formal principles of morality, and they consider cases such as the one presented earlier in terms of broader issues of morality and of right and wrong ("Stealing may be justifiable if you are following your own standards of conscience").

Kohlberg suggests that moral development can best be understood within the context of a three-level sequence, which is further subdivided into six stages (see Table 14-1). At the lowest level, *preconventional morality* (Stages 1 and 2), people follow unvarying rules based on rewards and punishments. For example, a child at the preconventional level might evaluate the moral dilemma posed in the story by saying that it was not worth stealing the drug because if you were caught, you would go to jail.

In the next level, that of *conventional morality* (Stages 3 and 4), people approach moral problems in terms of their own position as good, responsible members of society. Thus, children who decide *against* stealing the drug because they think they would feel guilty or dishonest, and those who decide *in favor of* stealing the drug because if they did nothing in this situation they would be unable to face others, would be reasoning at the conventional level of morality.

Finally, individuals using *postconventional morality* (Stages 5 and 6) invoke universal moral principles that are considered broader than the rules of the particular society in which they live. Students who feel that they would condemn themselves if they did not steal the drug because they would not be living up to their own moral principles would be reasoning at the postconventional level.

Kohlberg's theory proposes that people move through the periods of moral development in a fixed order and that they are unable to reach the highest stage until about the age of 13, due to deficits in cognitive development that are not overcome until then (Kurtines & Gewirtz, 1987). However, not everyone is presumed to reach the highest stages: Kohlberg has found that only about 25 percent of all adults rise above the fourth stage of his model, into the level of postconventional morality.

Unfortunately, although Kohlberg's theory provides a good account of the development of moral *judgments*, it is less adequate in predicting moral *behavior* (Malinowski & Smith, 1985; Snarey, 1985). For example, one experiment found that 15 percent of students who reasoned at the postconventional level of morality—the highest category—

TABLE 14-1

KOHLBERG'S SEQUENCE OF MORAL REASONING

LEVEL	STAGE	IN FAVOR OF STEALING	AGAINST STEALING
LEVEL 1 Preconventional morality: At this level, the concrete interests of the individual are considered in terms of rewards and punishments.	*STAGE 1* Obedience and punishment orientation: At this stage, people stick to rules in order to avoid punishment, and obedience occurs for its own sake.	"If you let your wife die, you will get in trouble. You'll be blamed for not spending the money to save her, and there'll be an investigation of you and the scientist for your wife's death."	"You shouldn't steal the drug because you'll get caught and sent to jail if you do. If you do get away, your conscience will bother you thinking how the police will catch up with you at any minute."
	STAGE 2 Reward orientation: At this stage, rules are followed only for a person's own benefit. Obedience occurs because of rewards that are received.	"If you do happen to get caught, you could give the drug back and you wouldn't get much of a sentence. It wouldn't bother you much to serve a little jail term, if you have your wife when you get out."	"You may not get much of a jail term if you steal the drug, but your wife will probably die before you get out, so it won't do much good. If your wife dies, you shouldn't blame yourself; it isn't your fault she has cancer."
LEVEL 2 Conventional morality: At this level, people approach moral problems as members of society. They are interested in pleasing others by acting as good members of society.	*STAGE 3* "Good boy" morality: Individuals at this stage show an interest in maintaining the respect of others and doing what is expected of them.	"No one will think you're bad if you steal the drug, but your family will think you're an inhuman husband if you don't. If you let your wife die, you'll never be able to look anybody in the face again."	"It isn't just the scientist who will think you're a criminal; everyone else will, too. After you steal the drug, you'll feel bad thinking how you've brought dishonor on your family and yourself; you won't be able to face anyone again."
	STAGE 4 Authority and social-order-maintaining morality: People at this stage conform to society's rules and consider that "right" is what society defines as right.	"If you have any sense of honor, you won't let your wife die just because you're afraid to do the only thing that will save her. You'll always feel guilty that you caused her death if you don't do your duty to her."	"You're desperate and you may not know you're doing wrong when you steal the drug. But you'll know you did wrong after you're sent to jail. You'll always feel guilty for your dishonesty and law-breaking."
LEVEL 3 Postconventional morality: At this level, people use moral principles which are seen as broader than those of any particular society.	*STAGE 5* Morality of contract, individual rights, and democratically accepted law: People at this stage do what is right because of a sense of obligation to laws which are agreed upon within society. They perceive that laws can be modified as part of changes in an implicit social contract.	"You'll lose other people's respect, not gain it, if you don't steal. If you let your wife die, it will be out of fear, not out of reasoning. So you'll just lose self-respect and probably the respect of others, too."	"You'll lose your standing and respect in the community and violate the law. You'll lose respect for yourself if you're carried away by emotion and forget the long-range point of view."
	STAGE 6 Morality of individual principles and conscience: At this final stage, a person follows laws because they are based on universal ethical principles. Laws that violate the principles are disobeyed.	"If you don't steal the drug, and if you let your wife die, you'll always condemn yourself for it afterward. You won't be blamed and you'll have lived up to the outside rule of the law but you won't have lived up to your own standards of conscience."	"If you steal the drug, you won't be blamed by other people, but you'll condemn yourself because you won't have lived up to your own conscience and standards of honesty."

(*Source:* Adapted from Kohlberg, 1969.)

cheated on a task, although they were not as prone to cheating as those at lower levels: Some 55 percent of those at the conventional level and 70 percent of those at the preconventional level also cheated (Kohlberg, 1975; Kupfersmid & Wonderly, 1980). Clearly, though, knowing what is morally right does not always mean acting that way (Killen & Hart, 1995).

Still, a good deal of research suggests that some aspects of moral conduct are clearly related to Kohlberg's levels of moral reasoning, although the results are often complex and not easy to interpret. For instance, children who reason at Stage 1 and Stage 3 tend to be the best behaved in school, while those who reason at Stage 2 are more apt to exhibit poor social behavior in school settings. Such findings suggest that we have not heard the last word on Kohlberg's stages (Bear & Rys, 1994; Langford, 1995; Richards, Bear, Stewart, & Norman, 1992).

Carol Gilligan argues that boys and girls view morality differently, with boys seeing it primarily in terms of broad principles, and girls considering it in terms of personal relationships and responsibility towards individuals.

Gilligan's Theory of Moral Development: Focusing on Girls

An aspect of Kohlberg's theory that has proved particularly problematic is the difficulty it has explaining *girls'* moral judgments. Because the theory initially was based largely on data from males, some researchers have argued that it does a better job describing boys' moral development than girls'.

In fact, psychologist Carol Gilligan (1982, 1987) has suggested an alternative account of the development of moral behavior in girls. She suggests that differences in the ways boys and girls are raised in our society lead to basic distinctions in how men and women view moral behavior. According to her, boys view morality primarily in terms of broad principles such as justice or fairness, while girls see it in terms of responsibility towards individuals and willingness to sacrifice themselves to help specific individuals within the context of particular relationships. Compassion for individuals, then, is a more prominent factor in moral behavior for women than it is for men (Gilligan, Lyons, & Hammer, 1990; Gilligan, Ward, & Taylor, 1988).

Because Kohlberg's theory considers moral behavior largely in terms of principles of justice, it is inadequate in describing the moral development of females. This accounts for the surprising finding that women typically score at a lower level than men on tests of moral judgment using Kohlberg's stage sequence. In Gilligan's view, a female's morality is centered more on individual well-being than on moral abstractions, and the highest levels of morality are represented by compassionate concern for the welfare of others.

Gilligan views morality as developing among females in a three-stage process (summarized in Table 14-2). In the first stage, called *orientation toward individual survival,* females first concentrate on what is practical and best for them, gradually making a transition from selfishness to responsibility, in which they think about what would be best for others. In the second stage, termed *goodness as self-sacrifice,* females begin to think that they must sacrifice their own wishes to what other people want, ultimately making the transition from "goodness" to "truth," in which they take into account their own needs plus those of others. Finally, in the third stage, *morality of nonviolence,* women come to see that hurting anyone—including themselves—is immoral. This realization establishes a moral equivalence between themselves and others and represents, according to Gilligan, the most sophisticated level of moral reasoning.

Obviously, Gilligan's sequence of stages is quite different from that of Kohlberg. However, some researchers have suggested that her rejection of Kohlberg's work is too sweeping and that gender differences are not as pronounced as first thought (Colby & Damon, 1987). For instance, some studies have found that both males and females use similar "justice" and "compassion" orientations in making moral judgments. Clearly, the question of how boys and girls differ in their moral orientations is far from settled (Jadack et al., 1995; McGraw & Bloomfield, 1987; Perry & McIntire, 1995).

TABLE 14-2

GILLIGAN'S THREE STAGES OF MORAL DEVELOPMENT FOR WOMEN

Stage	Major Characteristics	Samples of Reasoning Used by Women Contemplating Having an Abortion
STAGE 1 Orientation toward individual survival	In this first stage a woman initially concentrates on what is practical and best for her, gradually making a transition from selfishness to responsibility, in which she thinks about what would be best for others.	Having a baby would prevent her "from doing other things " but would be "the perfect chance to move away from home."
STAGE 2 Goodness as self-sacrifice	In the second stage she begins to think that she must sacrifice her own wishes to what other people want, ultimately making the transition from goodness to truth, in which she takes into account her own needs plus those of others.	"I think what confuses me is a choice of either hurting myself or hurting other people around me. What is more important?"
STAGE 3 Morality of nonviolence	In the final stage, she comes to see that hurting anyone—including herself—is immoral. This realization establishes a moral equivalence between herself and others and, according to Gilligan, represents the most sophisticated level of moral reasoning.	"The decision has got to be, first of all, something that the woman can live with, and it must be based on where she is at and where other significant people in her life are."

(*Source:* Gilligan, 1982.)

Review and Rethink

REVIEW

- In Kohlberg's first level of moral development, preconventional morality, children think in terms of concrete, unvarying rules of reward and punishment.
- In adolescence, Kohlberg's level of conventional morality, people understand abstract, formal principles of morality and justice that reflect their position as responsible members of society.
- In the third level, postconventional morality, which few people reach, individuals invoke universal moral principles, which are broader than the rules of their particular society, to solve moral dilemmas.
- The ability to make moral judgments does not invariably lead to moral behavior, but there is a relationship between moral reasoning and moral behavior.
- Psychologist Carol Gilligan finds that females view morality in terms of responsibility and self-sacrifice on behalf of others, in contrast to the broad principles of justice that characterize males' moral reasoning.

RETHINK

- In what ways are cognitive development and moral development interrelated? What cognitive abilities underlie the stages of moral development described by Kohlberg and Gilligan?
- Why might children who reason at Kohlberg's Stage 1 and Stage 3 tend to be well behaved in school? Why are those who reason at Stage 2 less well behaved?

- Do nations and their leaders show differences in moral reasoning? Could the levels of morality postulated by Kohlberg and Gilligan apply to nations?
- What levels of moral reasoning might prove easiest and most difficult for a society to accommodate?
- Are Kohlberg's and Gilligan's three levels of moral development comparable or distinct? In which level of either theory do you think the greatest differences between males and females would be observed?

SCHOOL PERFORMANCE AND COGNITIVE DEVELOPMENT

Do the considerable advances that occur in cognitive abilities during adolescence translate into improvements in school performance? Curiously, the answer is "no," at least if we use U.S. students' grades as the measure of school performance. On average, students' grades *decline* during the course of schooling (Schulenberg, Asp, & Petersen, 1984; Simmons & Blyth, 1987).

The reason for this decline is not entirely clear. Obviously, the nature of the material to which students are exposed becomes increasingly complex and sophisticated as adolescence proceeds. But the growing cognitive abilities of adolescents might be expected to compensate for the increased sophistication of the material. Thus, we need to look to other causes to account for the grade decline.

A better explanation relates to teachers' grading practices. It turns out that teachers grade older adolescents more stringently than younger ones. Consequently, even though students may be demonstrating greater competence as they continue with their schooling, their grades don't necessarily reflect the improvement because teachers are grading them more strictly (Simmons & Blyth, 1987).

SOCIOECONOMIC STATUS AND SCHOOL PERFORMANCE: INDIVIDUAL DIFFERENCES IN ACHIEVEMENT

Despite the ideal that all students are entitled to the same opportunity in the classroom, it is very clear that certain groups have more educational advantages than others. One of the most telling indicators of this reality is the relationship between educational achievement and socioeconomic status (SES).

Middle- and high-SES students earn higher grades, score higher on standardized tests of achievement, and complete more years of schooling than students from lower-SES homes. This disparity does not, of course, start in adolescence; the same findings hold for children in lower grades. However, by the time students are in high school, the effects of socioeconomic status become even more pronounced (Garbarino & Asp, 1981).

Why do students from middle- and high-SES homes show, in general, greater academic success? There are several explanations, most involving environmental factors. For one thing, children living in poverty lack many of the advantages enjoyed by other children. Their nutrition and health may be less adequate. Often living in crowded conditions, they may have few places to do homework. Their homes may lack the books and computers that are found in more economically advantaged households.

Furthermore, parents living in poverty are less likely to be involved in their children's schooling—a factor that is related to school success. Poorer adolescents, who may live in impoverished areas of cities with high levels of violence, may also attend older and generally inadequate schools with run-down facilities and a higher incidence of violence. Taken together, these factors clearly result in a less-than-optimal learning environment (Garbarino et al., 1992; Grolnick & Slowiaczek, 1994).

Although most developmentalists reject the approach, some researchers point to genetic factors as a source of SES differences in educational attainment. According to the controversial argument put forward by the authors of *The Bell Curve* (discussed in Chapter 11), lower school performance of children living in poverty may be due to inherited differences in intelligence levels. According to this argument, the parents' lower IQ scores lead them into poorer-paying professions and a life of poverty. The children, inheriting their parents' low IQ and subject to the harsh conditions of poverty, are unlikely to do well in school. So goes the argument (Herrnstein & Murray, 1994).

There are several reasons to reject this reasoning. For one thing, there is substantial variation in school performance *within* a particular SES level—often, in fact, more than the variation *between* students of different SES. Put another way, there are many low-SES students who perform far better than the average performance of higher-SES students. Likewise, many higher-SES students perform well below the average performance of lower-SES students.

More important, the consequences of environment are particularly potent. Students from impoverished backgrounds may be at a disadvantage from the day they begin their schooling for the reasons discussed earlier. Consequently, they may perform less well initially than their more affluent peers. As they grow older, their school performance may continue to lag, and in fact their disadvantage may snowball. Because later school success builds heavily on basic skills presumably learned early in school, children who experience problems early may find themselves falling increasingly behind the academic eight ball as adolescents (Huston, 1991; Phillips et al., 1994).

ETHNICITY AND SCHOOL ACHIEVEMENT

Does ethnicity relate to school performance? Although the answer is fairly simple—it is "yes, it does"—reasons for the differences are as hard to come by as they were when we examined socioeconomic differences in school performance (Dornbusch, Ritter, & Steinberg, 1992).

Achievement differences between ethnic groups are significant, and they paint a troubling picture of American education. For instance, data on school achievement indicate that, on average, African-American and Hispanic students tend to perform at lower levels, receive lower grades, and score lower on standardized tests of achievement than Caucasian students (see Table 14-3). In contrast, Asian-American students tend to receive higher grades than Caucasian students.

TABLE 14-3

TEST SCORES AMONG U.S. STUDENTS OF DIFFERENT ETHNIC BACKGROUNDS

READING, 1987-88	**9-YEAR-OLDS**	**13-YEAR-OLDS**	**17-YEAR-OLDS**
National average	211.8	257.5	290.1
White	217.7	261.3	294.7
African American	188.5	242.9	274.4
Hispanic	193.7	240.1	270.8
WRITING, 1988	**4TH GRADERS**	**9TH GRADERS**	**11TH GRADERS**
National average	173.3	208.2	220.7
White	180.0	213.1	225.3
African American	150.7	190.1	206.9
Hispanic	162.2	197.2	202.0
MATHEMATICS, 1985-86	**9-YEAR-OLDS**	**13-YEAR-OLDS**	**17-YEAR-OLDS**
National average	222.0	269.0	302.0
White	227.0	274.0	308.0
African American	202.0	249.0	279.0
Hispanic	205.0	254.0	283.0

National Assessment of Educational Progress scales in reading, writing, and mathematics range from 0 to 500. (*Source:* National Center for Education Statistics, 1991.)

Moreover, as shown in Figure 14-2, the high-school dropout rate, which stands overall at about 12 percent, differs according to ethnicity. For instance, although the dropout rate for all ethnicities has been declining somewhat over the last two decades, Hispanics and African-American students still are more likely to leave high school before graduating than white students. On the other hand, not all minority groups show higher dropout rates: Asians, for instance, drop out at a lower rate than Caucasians (Carnegie Council on Adolescent Development, 1995).

What is the source of such ethnic differences in academic achievement? Clearly, much of the difference is due to socioeconomic factors: Because more African-American and Hispanic families live in poverty, their economic disadvantage may be reflected in children's school performance. In fact, when we take socioeconomic levels into account by comparing different ethnicities at the same socioeconomic level, achievement differences diminish (Luster & McAdoo, 1994, 1996; Steinberg et al., 1992; Woolfolk, 1993).

But socioeconomic factors are not the full story. For instance, anthropologist John Ogbu (1988, 1992) argues that members of certain minority groups may perceive school success as relatively unimportant. They may believe that societal prejudice in the workplace will dictate that they will not succeed, no matter how much effort they expend. The conclusion is that hard work in school will have no eventual payoff.

Furthermore, Ogbu suggests that members of minority groups who enter a new culture voluntarily are more likely to be successful in school than those who are brought into a new culture against their will. For instance, he notes that Korean children who are the sons and daughters of voluntary immigrants to the United States tend to be, on average, quite successful in school. On the other hand, Korean children in Japan, whose parents were forced to immigrate during World War II and work as forced laborers, tend to do relatively poorly in school. The reason for the disparity? The process of involuntary immigration apparently leaves lasting scars, reducing the motivation to succeed in subsequent generations (Gallagher, 1994; Ogbu, 1992).

Another factor in the differential success of various ethnic group members has to do with attributions for academic success. As we discussed in Chapter 11, students from many Asian cultures tend to view achievement as the consequence of temporary situational factors, such as how hard they work. In contrast, African-American students are more apt to view success as the result of external causes over which they have no control, such as luck or

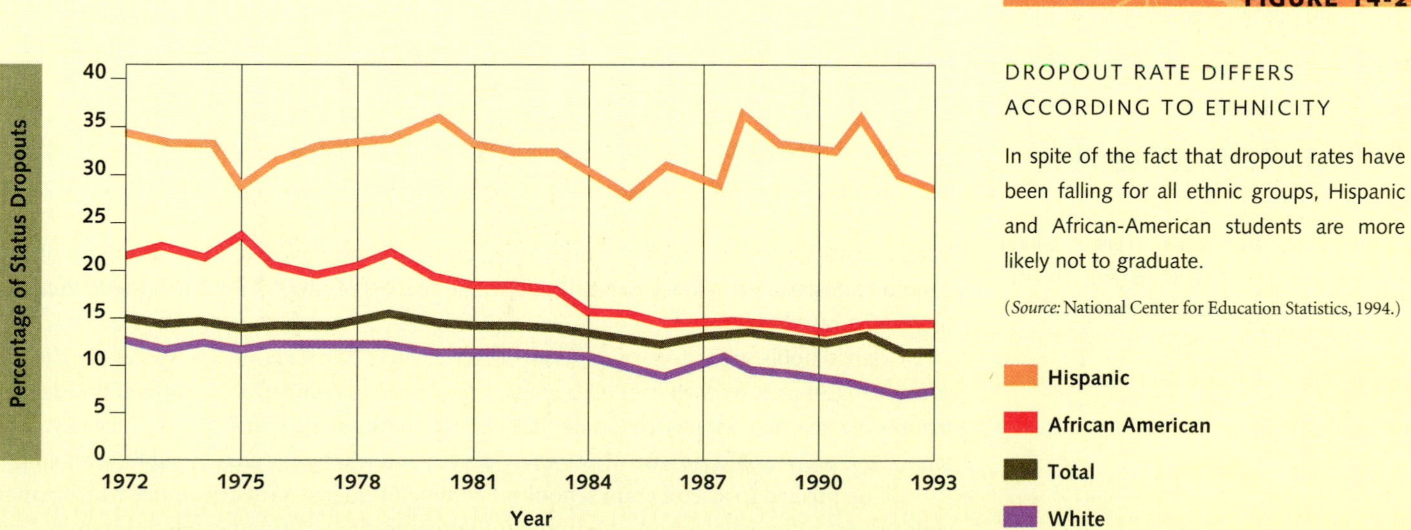

FIGURE 14-2

DROPOUT RATE DIFFERS ACCORDING TO ETHNICITY

In spite of the fact that dropout rates have been falling for all ethnic groups, Hispanic and African-American students are more likely not to graduate.

(*Source:* National Center for Education Statistics, 1994.)

Note: Status rates measure the proportion of the population who have not completed high school and are not enrolled at one point in time, regardless of when they dropped out.

societal biases. Students who subscribe to the belief that effort will lead to success, and then expend that effort, are more likely to do better in school than students who believe that effort makes less of a difference (Graham, 1990; Stevenson et al., 1992; Stevenson & Stigler, 1992).

Another explanation for ethnic differences in adolescent performance comes from developmental psychologist Laurence Steinberg. He and his colleagues (Steinberg et al., 1992) suggest that differences in adolescents' beliefs about the consequences of not doing well in school may account for ethnic differences in school performance.

Specifically, Steinberg argues that African-American and Hispanic students tend to believe that they can succeed *despite* poor school performance. This belief may cause them to put less effort into their studies. In contrast, Asian-American students tend to believe that if they don't do well in school, they are unlikely to get good jobs and be successful. Asian Americans, then, are motivated to work hard in school by a fear of the consequences of poor academic performance.

The research on ethnicity and achievement suggests a strategy for improving the performance of groups that do less well in school. If, in fact, the root of the problem is the belief that poor school performance brings few negative consequences, society needs to provide a clearer message about the value of education and to make the point that school failure clearly has negative consequences. More broadly, adolescent minority group members need to believe that their future success depends, in part, on their academic performance, and that—despite the societal hurdles they face—they can overcome such barriers and succeed.

Developmental Diversity

Are There Psychological Costs to Academic Achievement? It Depends on Your Culture

Students in Asian cram schools sometimes spend hours after their regular school closes and on weekends being taught material beyond what is covered in their public school classes.

On a brisk Saturday morning, while most of their friends were relaxing at home, 16-year-old Jerry Lee and eight other Asian teenagers huddled over their notebooks and calculators for a full day of math and English lessons.

During the week, they all attend public schools in the city. But every Saturday, they go to a Korean hag-won, or cram school, in Flushing to spend up to seven hours immersed in the finer points of linear algebra or Raymond Chandler.

"I complain, but my mom says I have to go," said Jerry, a Stuyvesant High School student from Sunnyside, Queens, who has already scored a 1520 on the Scholastic Assessment Test for college, but is shooting for a perfect 1600. "It's like a habit now." (Dunn, 1995, p. 1)

Long a tradition in Korea, Japan, and China, cram schools have begun to spring up in the United States as Asian parents, committed to the success of their children, demand them in increasing numbers.

Cram schools are a fixture in Asian society, where competition for success begins as young as age 4 or 5. By the time children reach adolescence, competition to attend prestigious schools has reached fever pitch. Some high-school-age students spend hours every day after school and on weekends in instruction that goes beyond what is covered in public schooling.

Being pushed to attend cram school is one type of intense pressure under which Asian children are often placed. In fact, although the scholastic performance of children in Asia typically exceeds that of children in the United States, critics suggest that such success comes at the price of increased stress, psychological burdens, and depression (e.g., Holman, 1991; Watanabe, 1992).

Not so—at least according to recent research that casts doubt on the critics' contentions. Developmental psychologist David Crystal and his colleagues (1994) examined psychological adjustment in a group of 11th-grade students in the United States, China, and Japan. Compared with the U.S. students, the Asian students reported that their parents held higher expectations for their academic achievement and were less satisfied with their academic success.

However, despite the higher parental pressure, both Japanese and Chinese students experienced lower levels of stress than their U.S. counterparts. As can be seen in Figure 14-3, almost three-quarters of U.S. students said they felt stress once a week or almost every day. In comparison, far fewer Japanese and Chinese students reported such frequent stress.

Furthermore, Japanese students were less depressed and in general had lower academic anxiety than their U.S. counterparts. Chinese students, too, reported lower levels of anxiety regarding academic performance than U.S. students, although they did suffer somewhat more often from depression and health-related problems than U.S. and Japanese students.

Why should U.S. students experience greater stress and anxiety than Asian students, who experience significantly greater demands from their parents? One explanation may be that students in the United States view academics as only one of many spheres in which they need to achieve. As we'll discuss more in the next chapter, social relationships play a major role in U.S. adolescents' lives. In addition, many adolescents experience pressures about dating or part-time jobs. Consequently, pressures and competition between academic and social pursuits may contribute to U.S. students' high levels of stress.

In contrast, Asian students perceive that the major task they face during adolescence is achieving high levels of academic success. Other demands are clearly secondary. As a consequence, they may be more focused on the pursuit of academic excellence and feel less conflict from competing demands.

Although the full explanation for these findings remains to be discovered, one lesson is clear: High academic achievement of the sort attained by students in Japan and China does not necessarily come at the expense of psychological adjustment.

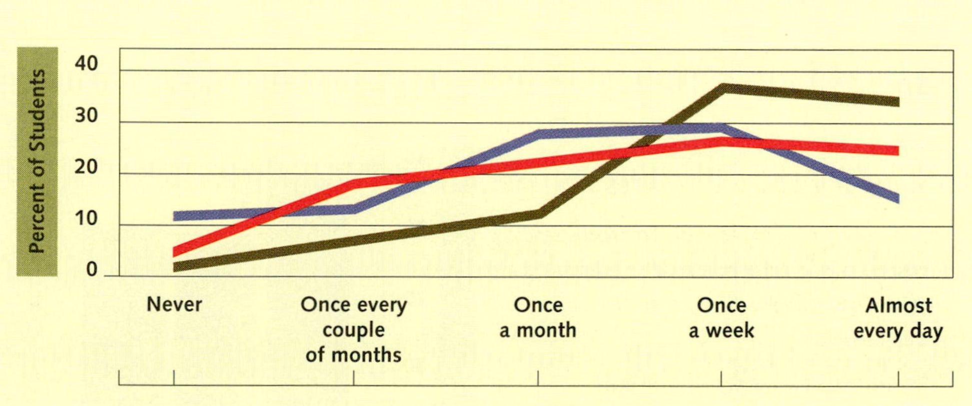

FIGURE 14-3

THE EXPERIENCE OF STRESS

Although almost three-quarters of U.S. students say they feel stress once a week or almost every day, far fewer Japanese and Chinese students report such frequent stress.

(*Source:* Crystal et al., 1994, p. 745.)

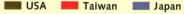

USA Taiwan Japan

COLLEGE: PURSUING HIGHER EDUCATION

For Enrico Vasquez, there was never any doubt: He was headed for college. Enrico, the son of a wealthy Cuban immigrant who had made a fortune in the medical supply business after fleeing Cuba 5 years before Enrico's birth, had had the importance of education constantly drummed into him by his family. In fact, the question was never *whether* he would go to college, but what college he would be able to get into. As a consequence, Enrico found high school to be a pressure cooker: Every grade and extracurricular activity was seen as helping—or hindering—his chances of admission to a "good" college.

***

Armando Williams' letter of acceptance to Dallas County Community College is framed on the wall of his mother's apartment. To her, the letter represents nothing short of a miracle, an answer to her prayers. Growing up in a neighborhood saturated with drugs and drive-by shootings, Armando had always been a hard worker and a "good boy," in his mother's view. But when he was growing up she never even entertained the possibility of his making it to college. To see him reach this stage in his education fills her with joy.

Whether a student's enrollment seems almost inevitable or signifies a triumph over the odds, attending college is a significant accomplishment. Although students already enrolled may feel that college attendance is nearly universal, this is not the case at all: Nationwide, only a minority of high school graduates enter college.

THE DEMOGRAPHICS OF HIGHER EDUCATION

Who goes to college? As in the U.S. population as a whole, U.S. college students are primarily white and middle class. Although nearly 40 percent of white high school graduates enter college, just 29 percent of African-American and 31 percent of Hispanic graduates enter college (see Figure 14-4).

Even more striking, although the absolute number of minority students enrolled in college has increased, the overall *proportion* of the minority population that does enter college has *decreased* over the last decade—a decline that most education experts attribute to changes in the availability of financial aid.

Furthermore, the proportion of students who enter college but ultimately never graduate is substantial. Only around 40 percent of those who start college finish 4 years later with a degree. Although about half of those who don't receive a degree in 4 years eventually

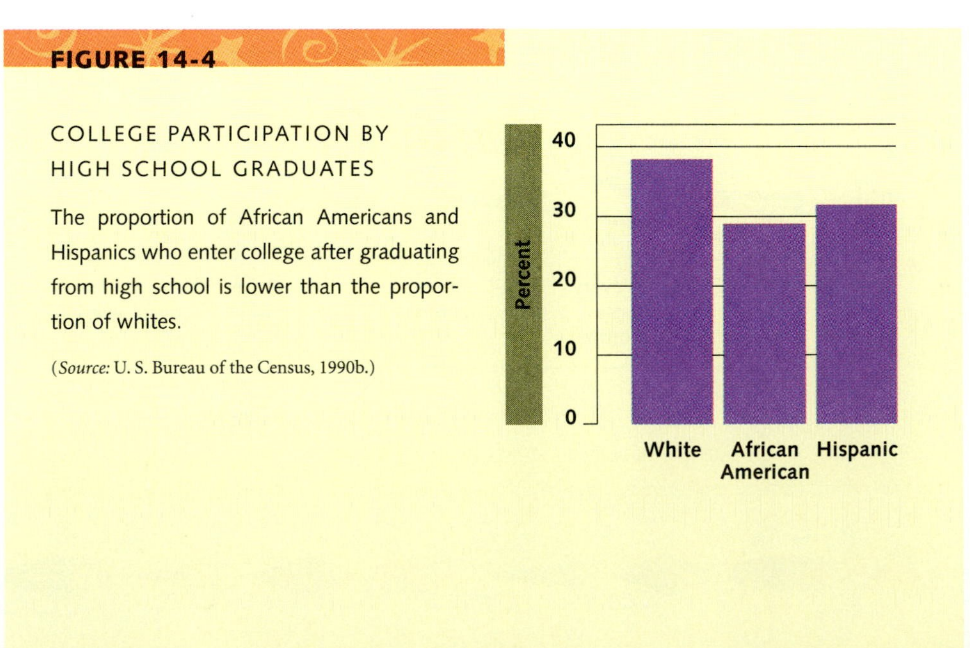

FIGURE 14-4

COLLEGE PARTICIPATION BY HIGH SCHOOL GRADUATES

The proportion of African Americans and Hispanics who enter college after graduating from high school is lower than the proportion of whites.

(*Source:* U. S. Bureau of the Census, 1990b.)

do finish, the other half never obtain a college degree. For minorities, the picture is even worse: The national dropout rate for African-American college students stands at 70 percent (Minorities in Higher Education, 1995).

On the other hand, the sheer number of minority students attending college is rising dramatically, and minority students make up an increasingly larger proportion of the college population. These trends, reflecting changes in the ethnic composition of the United States, are significant, since higher education remains an important way for families to improve their economic well-being (Kates, 1995).

For instance, by the year 2000, the U.S. Department of Education (1992) projects an increase of 13 percent in African-American college attendance and 22 percent in Hispanic college attendance over levels 10 years earlier. Over the same period, enrollment of whites is projected to rise only 6 percent. Already at some colleges, such as the University of California at Berkeley, whites have shifted from the majority to the minority, as what is traditionally called "minority" representation has increased significantly.

Even though they may be unaware of it, both male and female professors treat men and women in their classes differently. For example, they typically call on men in class more frequently than women.

Gender and College Performance

> I registered for a calculus course my first year at DePauw. Even 20 years ago I was not timid, so on the very first day I raised my hand and asked a question. I still have a vivid memory of the professor rolling his eyes, hitting his head with his hand in frustration, and announcing to everyone, "Why do they expect me to teach calculus to girls?" I never asked another question. Several weeks later I went to a football game, but I had forgotten to bring my ID. My calculus professor was at the gate checking IDs, so I went up to him and said, "I forgot my ID but you know me, I'm in your class." He looked right at me and said, "I don't remember you in my class." I couldn't believe that someone who changed my life and whom I remember to this day didn't even recognize me. (Sadker & Sadker, 1994, p. 162)

Although such incidents of blatant sexism are less likely to occur today, prejudice and discrimination directed at women are still a fact of college life. For instance, the next time you are in class, consider the gender of your classmates—and the subject matter of the class. Although men and women attend college in roughly equal proportions, there is significant variation in the classes they take. Classes in education and the social sciences, for instance, typically have a larger proportion of women than men; and classes in engineering, the physical sciences, and mathematics tend to have more men than women.

Even women who start out in mathematics, engineering, and the physical sciences are more likely than men to drop out. For instance, the attrition rate for all women in such fields during the college years is 2 1/2 times greater than the rate for men. Ultimately, although white women make up 43 percent of the U.S. population, they earn just 22 percent of the bachelor of science degrees and 13 percent of the doctorates, and they hold only 10 percent of the jobs in physical science, math, and engineering. Nonwhite women, who hold "double minority" status, also hold fewer positions in science than nonwhite men (Cipra, 1991).

The differences in gender distribution and attrition rates across subject areas are no accident. They reflect the powerful influence of gender stereotypes that operate throughout the world of education—and beyond. For instance, when women in their first year of college are asked to name a likely career choice, they are much less apt to choose careers that have traditionally been dominated by men, such as engineering or computer programming, and more likely to choose professions that have traditionally been populated by women, such as nursing and social work (Cooperative Institutional Research Program of the American Council on Education [CIRE], 1990; Glick, Zion, & Nelson, 1988).

These initial expectations about the fields that are of interest to them are reflected in students' anticipation of their starting salaries when they leave college and their eventual peak salaries. Women expect to earn less than men, both when they start their careers and when they are at their peaks (Jackson, Gardner, & Sullivan, 1992; Major & Konar, 1984; Martin, 1989). These expectations jibe with reality: On average, women earn 70 cents for every dollar that men earn. Moreover, women who are members of minority groups do even worse: African-American women earn 62 cents for every dollar men make, while for Hispanic women the figure is 54 cents (U.S. Bureau of Labor Statistics, 1993).

Male and female college students also have different expectations regarding their areas of competence. For instance, one survey asked first-year college students whether they were above or below average on a variety of traits and abilities. As can be seen in Figure 14-5, men were more likely than women to think of themselves as above average in overall academic and mathematical ability, competitiveness, and emotional health.

Both male and female college professors treat men and women differently in their classes, even though the different treatment is largely unintentional and the professors are unaware of their actions. For instance, professors call on men in class more frequently than women, and they make more eye contact with men than with women. Furthermore, male students are more likely to receive extra help from their professors than women. Finally, the quality of the responses received by male and female students differs, with male students receiving more positive reinforcement for their comments than female students—exemplified by the startling illustration in Table 14-4 (AAUW, 1992; Epperson, 1988; Sadker & Sadker, 1994).

The different treatment of men and women in the college classroom has led some educators to argue in favor of single-sex colleges for women. They point to evidence that the rate of participation and ultimately the success of women in the sciences is greater for graduates of women's colleges than for graduates of coeducational institutions. Furthermore, some research suggests that women who attend same-sex colleges may show higher self-esteem than those attending coeducational colleges, although the evidence is not entirely consistent on this count (Miller-Bernal, 1993; Smith, 1990).

Why might women do better in single-sex colleges? One reason is that they receive more attention than they would in coeducational settings, where professors are affected, however inadvertently, by societal biases. In addition, women's colleges tend to have more

FIGURE 14-5

SELF-ASSESSMENTS IN VARIOUS CATEGORIES BY MALE AND FEMALE COLLEGE STUDENTS

During their first year of college, men, compared to women, are more apt to view themselves as above average on several spheres relevant to academic success.

(*Source:* Higher Education Research Institute, 1991.)

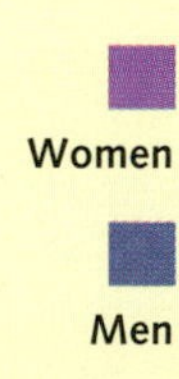

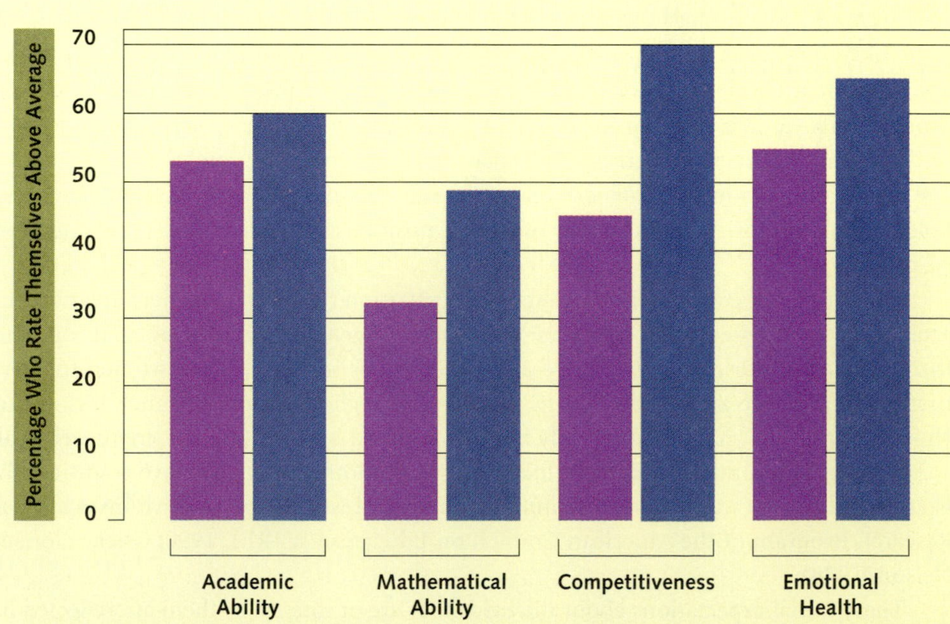

TABLE 14-4

SAMPLE PROFESSOR REACTIONS TO MALE AND FEMALE STUDENTS

The course on the U.S. Constitution is required for graduation, and more than 50 students, approximately half male and half female, file in. The professor begins by asking if there are questions on next week's midterm. Several hands go up.

BERNIE: Do we have to memorize names and dates in the book? Or will the test be more general?
PROFESSOR: You do have to know those critical dates and people. Not every one but the important ones. If I were you, Bernie, I would spend time learning them. Ellen?
ELLEN: What kind of short-answer questions will there be?
PROFESSOR: All multiple choice.
ELLEN: Will we have the whole class time?
PROFESSOR: Yes, we'll have the whole class time. Anyone else?
BEN (calling out): Will there be an extra-credit question?
PROFESSOR: I hadn't planned on it. What do you think?
BEN: I really like them. They take some of the pressure off. You can also see who is doing extra work.
PROFESSOR: I'll take it under advisement. Charles?
CHARLES: How much of our final grade is this?
PROFESSOR: The midterm is 25 percent. But remember, class participation counts as well. Why don't we begin?

The professor lectures on the Constitution for 20 minutes before he asks a question about the electoral college. The electoral college is not as hot a topic as the midterm, so only four hands are raised. The professor calls on Ben.

BEN: The electoral college was created because there was a lack of faith in the people. Rather than have them vote for the president, they voted for the electors.
PROFESSOR: I like the way you think. (He smiles at Ben, and Ben smiles back.) Who could vote? (Five hands go up, 5 out of 50.) Angie?
ANGIE: I don't know if this is right, but I thought only men could vote.
BEN (calling out): That was a great idea. We began going downhill when we let women vote. (Angie looks surprised but says nothing. Some of the students laugh, and so does the professor. He calls on Barbara.)
BARBARA: I think you had to be pretty wealthy, own property—
JOSH (not waiting for Barbara to finish, calls out): That's right. There was a distrust of the poor, who could upset the democracy. But if you had property, if you had something at stake, you could be trusted not to do something wild. Only property owners could be trusted.
PROFESSOR: Nice job, Josh. But why do we still have electors today? Mike?
MIKE: Tradition, I guess.
PROFESSOR: Do you think it's tradition? If you walked down the street and asked people their views of the electoral college, what would they say?
MIKE: Probably they'd be clueless. Maybe they would think that it elects the Pope. People don't know how it works.
PROFESSOR: Good, Mike. Judy, do you want to say something? (Judy's hand is at "half-mast," raised but just barely. When the professor calls her name, she looks a bit startled.)
JUDY (speaking very softly): Maybe we would need a whole new constitutional convention to change it. And once they get together to change that, they could change anything. That frightens people, doesn't it? (As Judy speaks, a number of students fidget, pass notes, and leaf through their books; a few even begin to whisper.)

(*Source:* Sadker & Sadker, 1994.)

female professors than coeducational institutions, and they thereby provide more role models for women. Finally, women attending women's colleges may receive more encouragement for participation in nontraditional subjects such as mathematics and science than women in coeducational colleges.

In fact, the apparent effect of encouragement on women's mathematics achievement is illustrated in a striking experiment involving women's expectations about a mathematics test, as discussed in the accompanying "Directions in Development" box.

Directions in Development

Overcoming Gender and Racial Barriers to Achievement

When women take college classes in math, science, and engineering, they are more likely to do poorly than men who enter college with the same level of preparation and identical SAT scores. Strangely, however, this phenomenon does not hold true for other areas of the curriculum, where men and women perform at similar levels (Steele, 1992).

According to psychologist Claude Steele (Steele & Aronson, 1995), the reason has to do with women's acceptance of stereotypes about achievement in certain domains. Steele suggests that women are no strangers to society's dominant view that some subjects are more appropriate areas of study for women than others are. In fact, the pervasiveness of the stereotype makes women who attempt to achieve in traditionally "inappropriate" fields highly vulnerable.

Specifically, because of the strength and pervasiveness of such stereotypes, the performance of women seeking to achieve in nontraditional fields may be hindered as they are distracted by worries about the failure that society predicts for them. In some cases, a woman may decide that failure in a male-dominated field, because it would confirm societal stereotypes, would be so unpalatable that the struggle to succeed is not worth the effort. In that instance, the woman may not even try very hard.

On the other hand, there is a bright side to Steele's analysis: If women can be convinced that societal stereotypes regarding achievement are invalid, their performance might well improve. And in fact, this is just what Steele found in a series of experiments he conducted at the University of Michigan and Stanford University (Steele, 1992).

In one study male and female college students were told they would be taking two math tests: one in which there were gender differences—men supposedly performed better than women—and a second in which there were no gender differences. In reality, the tests were entirely similar, drawn from the same pool of difficult items. The reasoning behind the experimental manipulation was that women would be vulnerable to societal stereotypes on a test that they thought supported those stereotypes, but would not be vulnerable on a test supposedly lacking gender differences.

The results fully supported Steele's reasoning. When the women were told there were gender differences in the test, they greatly underperformed the men. But when they were told there were no gender differences, they performed virtually the same as the men.

In short, the evidence from this study and others clearly suggests that women are vulnerable to expectations regarding their future success, whether the expectations come from societal stereotypes or from information about the prior performance of women on similar tasks. More encouraging, the evidence suggests that if women can be convinced that others have been successful in given domains, they may overcome even longstanding societal stereotypes.

We should also keep in mind that women are not the only group susceptible to society's stereotyping. Members of minority groups, such as African Americans and Hispanic Americans, are also vulnerable to stereotypes about academic success. In fact, Steele suggests that African Americans may "disidentify" with academic success by putting forth less effort on academic tasks and generally downgrading the importance of academic achievement. Ultimately, such disidentification may act as a self-fulfilling prophecy, increasing the chances of academic failure (Steele & Aronson, 1995).

In sum, until society's stereotypes change, women and members of minority groups run the risk of academic failure because of their vulnerability to those stereotypes.

Review and Rethink

REVIEW

- School success is related to socioeconomic status (SES), with low-SES students achieving less academic success than others. Environmental factors associated with SES are probably at the root of this situation.
- Ethnicity also influences academic achievement and college attendance, due in part to SES differences and in part to a belief by some members of minority groups that hard work in school is unrelated to later career success because of societal biases.
- In college, women tend to choose and remain in different courses and majors than men. This is largely due to gender stereotypes that affect teachers' and students' expectations.

RETHINK

- What would account for the finding that children whose parents immigrate voluntarily to a new country perform better in school than children whose parents were forced to immigrate?
- If it were proved that no link existed between academic success and later career success, would there be any justification for working hard in school? Why or why not?
- Some people advocate same-sex (and even same-ethnicity) high schools and colleges as a way to combat the disadvantages of discrimination. Would this work? What effects would it have on males and members of majority cultures?

Picking an Occupation: Choosing Life's Work

Some people know from childhood that they want to be physicians or actors or go into business, and they follow invariant paths toward that goal. For others, the choice of a career is very much a matter of chance, of turning to the want ads and seeing what's available.

Ginzberg's Career Choice Theory

According to Eli Ginzberg (1972), people typically move through a series of stages in choosing a career. The first stage is the **fantasy period,** which lasts until a person is around 11. During the fantasy period, career choices are made, and discarded, without regard to skills, abilities, or available job opportunities. Instead, choices are made solely on the basis of what sounds appealing. Thus, a child may decide she wants to be a veterinarian—despite the fact that she is allergic to dogs and cats.

People begin to take practical considerations into account during the tentative period. During the **tentative period,** which spans adolescence, people begin to think in pragmatic terms about the requirements of various jobs and how their own abilities might fit with them. They also consider their personal values and goals, exploring how well a particular occupation might satisfy them.

Finally, in early adulthood, people enter the realistic period. In the **realistic period,** young adults explore specific career options either through actual experience on the job or through training for a profession. After initially exploring what they might do, people begin to narrow their choices to a few alternative careers and eventually make a commitment to a particular one.

fantasy period *according to Ginzberg, the period when career choices are made, and discarded, without regard to skills, abilities, or available job opportunities*

tentative period *the second stage of Ginzberg's theory, which spans adolescence, in which people begin to think in pragmatic terms about the requirements of various jobs and how their own abilities might fit with them*

realistic period *the stage in late adolescence and early adulthood during which people explore career options through job experience or training, narrow their choices, and eventually make a commitment to a career*

Although Ginzberg's theory makes sense, critics have charged that it oversimplifies the process of choosing a career. Because Ginzberg's research was based on subjects from middle socioeconomic levels, it may overstate the choices and options available to people in lower socioeconomic levels. Furthermore, the ages associated with the various stages may be too rigid. For instance, a person who does not attend college but begins to work immediately after high-school graduation is likely to be making serious career decisions at a much earlier point than a person who attends college.

Holland's Personality Type Theory

Other theories of career choice emphasize how an individual's personality affects decisions about a career. According to John Holland, for instance, certain personality types match particularly well with certain careers. If the correspondence between personality and career is good, people will enjoy their careers more and be more likely to stay in them; but if the match is poor, they will be unhappy and more likely to shift into other careers (Gottfredson & Holland, 1990; Holland, 1973, 1987).

According to Holland, six personality types are relevant to career choice:

- *Realistic.* These people are down-to-earth, practical problem solvers, and physically strong, but their social skills are mediocre. They make good farmers, laborers, and truck drivers.

Speaking of Development

Henry Klein, Career Counselor

Born:	1918
Education:	University of Pennsylvania, B.A. in English University of Pennsylvania, M.A. in sociology Temple University, Ph.D. in psychoeducational processes
Position:	Founder and director of the American College and Career Counseling Center
Home:	Philadelphia, Pennsylvania

At one time or another everyone has pondered the question of which career to pursue, or whether to change a current job. For those facing that decision there are people like Henry Klein.

In 1962 Klein founded the American College and Career Counseling Center in Philadelphia. Its purpose is to help people find professions that are right for them.

A former columnist who wrote for 20 years on careers and education for several Philadelphia newspapers, Klein has also published a book that answers questions about getting into, and staying in, college.

Career counseling at Klein's center, which lasts about five sessions, begins with a basic interview and proceeds to the point where the counselor and the client have identified specific companies to pursue and outlined concrete strategies for approaching them.

"Before people come to me for career counseling I ask them to send me their résumés and, if they're close to graduation, copies of their transcripts," Klein explains. "I look through the transcript to find the strongest subject areas and try to get a baseline from that.

- *Intellectual.* Intellectual types are oriented toward the theoretical and abstract. Although not particularly good with people, they are well suited to careers in math and science.
- *Social.* The traits associated with the social personality type are related to verbal skills and interpersonal relations. Social types are good at working with people, and consequently make good salespersons, teachers, and counselors.
- *Conventional.* Conventional individuals prefer highly structured tasks. They make good clerks, secretaries, and bank tellers.
- *Enterprising.* These individuals are risk takers and take-charge types. They are good leaders and may be particularly effective as managers or politicians.
- *Artistic.* Artistic types use art to express themselves, and they often prefer the world of art to interactions with people. They are best suited to occupations involving art.

According to John Holland, personality factors play a major role in career decisions.

Although Holland's enumeration of personality types is sensible, it suffers from a central flaw: Not everyone fits neatly into one particular personality type. Furthermore, there are certainly exceptions to the typology, with jobs being held successfully by people who don't have the particular personality that Holland would predict. Still, the basic notions of the theory have been validated, and they form the foundation of several measures designed to assess the occupational options for which a given person is particularly suited (Randahl, 1991). (See the "Speaking of Development" interview.)

"We will try to find out if there's any common thread, no matter how small, that runs through each of the jobs—and there is usually some*thing there that I can grab on to."*

"You can't talk in terms of just one occupation; you have to think in terms of a career."

I then look over the résumés to get a sense of the progression of jobs the person has passed through, as well as the functions and skills that the person has practiced.

"I look for a particular trend in a field, and if there are no negatives, we go in that direction," he adds.

While a fairly clear trend line is easier to work with, the person with a scattered, inconsistent history is more of a challenge, according to Klein.

"If the person's experience is scattered and there's no particular trend, we almost have to start from zero. In that case we have to ask a lot of basic questions, such as 'What kind of person are you?' and 'Where are you in your development?'

"We won't throw away all the things a person has been doing. We will try to find out if there's any common thread, no matter how small, that runs through each of the jobs—and there is usually *something* there that I can grab on to," he notes. "There might be a clue inside each job. It could be only a part of each of the jobs people have had, but they couldn't see it because they were always looking at the job as a whole."

While it is important to look at academic and work background, Klein points out that a person's character and development are equally important, if not more so.

"A person with a fairly stable life, who hasn't moved around a lot or job-hopped, produces a trend in careers and vocations that we can use," he says. "You have to work on personal development before you can commit to something in the longer term.

"Even if you fell into the perfect job, your personal development might push you out sooner or later if you were not up to a long-term career commitment. You can't talk in terms of just one occupation; you have to think in terms of a career."

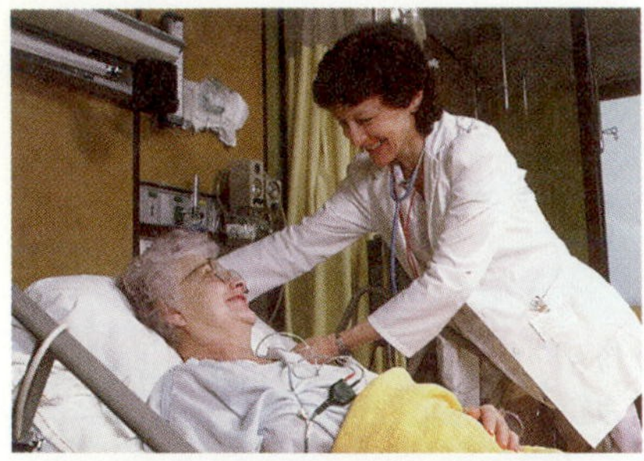

Women were traditionally considered most appropriate for communal professions, which are occupations associated with relationships. In contrast, men were traditionally thought to be best suited for agentic professions, those associated with getting things done.

GENDER AND CAREER CHOICES: WOMEN'S WORK

> WANTED: Full-time employee for small family firm. DUTIES: Including but not limited to general cleaning, cooking, gardening, laundry, ironing and mending, purchasing, bookkeeping and money management. Child care may also be required. HOURS: Avg. 55/wk but standby duty required 24 hours/day, 7 days/wk. Extra workload on holidays. SALARY AND BENEFITS: No salary, but food, clothing, and shelter provided at employer's discretion; job security and benefits depend on continued good will of employer. No vacation. No retirement plan. No opportunities for advancement. REQUIREMENTS: No previous experience necessary, can learn on the job. Only women need apply. (Unger & Crawford, 1992, p. 446)

Just two decades ago, many women entering early adulthood assumed that this admittedly exaggerated job description matched the work for which they were best suited and to which they aspired: housewife. Even those women who sought work outside the home were relegated to certain professions. For instance, until the 1960s employment ads in newspapers throughout the United States were almost always divided into two sections: "Help Wanted: Male" and "Help Wanted: Female." The men's job listings encompassed such professions as police officer, construction worker, and legal counsel; the women's listings were for secretaries, teachers, cashiers, and librarians.

The breakdown of jobs deemed appropriate for men and women reflected society's traditional view of what the two genders were best suited for. Traditionally, women were considered most appropriate for **communal professions,** occupations associated with relationships. In contrast, men were perceived as best suited for agentic professions. **Agentic professions** are associated with getting things accomplished. It is probably no coincidence that communal professions typically have lower status and lower salaries than agentic professions (Eagly & Steffen, 1984, 1986).

Although discrimination based on gender is far less blatant today than it was several decades ago—it is now illegal, for instance, to advertise a position specifically for a man or a woman—remnants of traditional gender role prejudice persist. As we discussed earlier in this chapter, women are less likely to be found in traditionally male-dominated professions such as engineering and computer programming. As shown in Figure 14-6, women in many professions earn less than men in identical jobs. Although the discrepancy has been reduced in the last decade, this change has more to do with men's wages falling because of the disappearance of highly paid manufacturing jobs than with rises in women's wages (CIRE, 1990; U.S. Bureau of Labor Statistics, 1993).

Despite status and pay that are often lower than men's, more women are working outside the home than ever before. Between 1950 and 1990, the percentage of the female population (aged 16 and over) in the U.S. labor force overall increased from around 35 percent to nearly 60 percent, and women today make up around 46 percent of the labor force. Almost all women expect to earn a living, and almost all do at some point in their lives. Furthermore, in about one half of U.S. households, women earn about as much as their husbands (Lewin, 1995).

Furthermore, opportunities for women are in many ways considerably greater than they were in earlier years. Women are more likely to be physicians, lawyers, insurance agents, and bus drivers than they were in the past. However, within specific job categories, sex discrimination still occurs. For example, female bus drivers are more apt to have part-time school bus routes, while men hold better-paying full-time routes in cities. Similarly, female pharmacists are more likely to work in hospitals, while men work in higher-paying jobs in retail stores (England & McCreary, 1987; Unger & Crawford, 1992).

In the same way, women—and minorities, too—in high-status, visible professional roles may hit what has come to be called the glass ceiling. The *glass ceiling* is an invisible barrier within an organization that, because of discrimination, prevents individuals from being promoted beyond a certain level. It operates subtly, and often the people responsible for keeping the glass ceiling in place may not be aware of how their actions perpetuate discrimination

communal professions *occupations associated with relationships*

agentic professions *occupations associated with getting things accomplished*

FIGURE 14-6

PERCENTAGE OF MEN'S SALARIES EARNED BY WOMEN IN IDENTICAL JOBS

The median wages of women in a given profession as a proportion of the wages that men receive.

(*Source:* U.S. Bureau of Labor Statistics, 1993.)

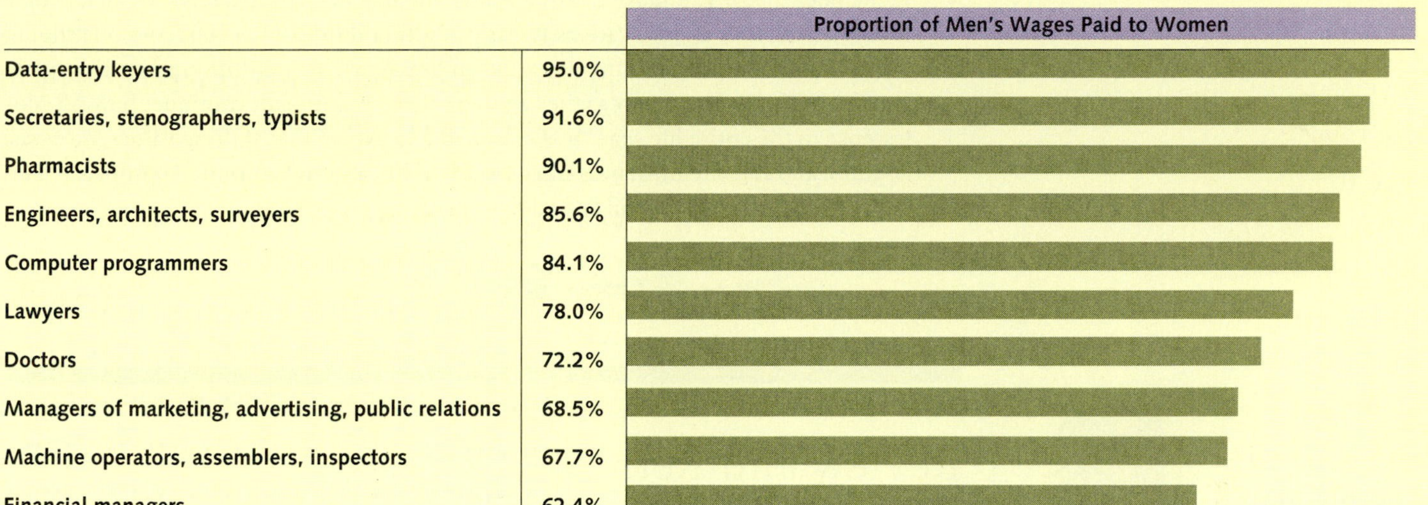

against women and minorities. For instance, a male supervisor in the oil exploration business may conclude that a particular task is too dangerous for a female employee. As a consequence of his decision, he may be preventing her from obtaining the experience that she needs in order to get promoted (Kilborn, 1995; Larwood, Szwajkowski, & Rose, 1988; Morrison & von Gilnow, 1990; Snyder, Verderber, Langmeyer, & Myers, 1992).

Proportion of Men's Wages Paid to Women
Data-entry keyers 95.0%
Secretaries, stenographers, typists 91.6%
Pharmacists 90.1%
Engineers, architects, surveyers 85.6%
Computer programmers 84.1%
Lawyers 78.0%
Doctors 72.2%
Managers of marketing, advertising, public relations 68.5%
Machine operators, assemblers, inspectors 67.7%
Financial managers 62.4%

The Informed Consumer of Development

Choosing a Career

One of the greatest challenges people face in late adolescence is making a decision that will have lifelong implications: the choice of a career. Although there is no single correct choice—most people can be happy in any of several different jobs—the options can be daunting. Here are some guidelines for at least starting to come to grips with the question of what occupational path to follow:

- Systematically evaluate a variety of choices. Libraries contain a wealth of information about potential career paths, and most colleges and universities have career centers that can provide occupational data and guidance.
- Know yourself. Evaluate your strengths and weaknesses, perhaps by completing a questionnaire at a college career center that can provide insight into your interests, skills, and values.
- Create a "balance sheet," listing the potential gains and losses that you will incur from a particular profession. First list the gains and losses that you will experience directly,

and then list the gains and losses for others. Next, write down the projected social approval or disapproval you are likely to receive from others. By systematically evaluating a set of potential careers according to each of these criteria, you will be in a better position to compare different possibilities.

- "Try out" different careers through paid or unpaid internships. By seeing a job firsthand, interns are able to get a better sense of what an occupation is truly like.
- Remember that if you make a mistake, it is possible to change careers. In fact, people today increasingly change careers in early adulthood or even beyond. No one should feel locked in to a decision made earlier in life. As we've seen throughout this book, people develop substantially as they age, and this development continues beyond adolescence to the entire life span. It is reasonable to expect that shifting values, interests, abilities, and life circumstances might make a different career more appropriate later in life than the one chosen in late adolescence.

Review and Rethink

REVIEW

- According to Eli Ginzberg, people pass through three stages in considering careers: the fantasy period, the tentative period, and the realistic period. Other theories of career choice, such as John Holland's, attempt to match personality types to suitable careers.
- Gender influences career choice and attitudes and behaviors on the job. Traditionally, women have been considered more appropriate for communal professions, which pay less than the agentic professions to which men were considered better suited.

RETHINK

- How does the division of jobs into communal and agentic types relate to traditional views of male-female differences?
- What sorts of behaviors and attitudes on the part of supervisors and coworkers contribute to the glass ceiling that affects women and minorities in the workplace?
- How might we encourage girls as they are growing up to begin thinking about professions without regard to traditional views concerning their gender-role appropriateness?

LOOKING BACK

How does cognitive development proceed during adolescence?

1. Cognitive growth during adolescence is rapid and substantial, with notable gains in the ability to think abstractly, to reason accurately, and to view possibilities in relative rather than absolute terms.
2. Adolescence coincides with Piaget's formal operational stage of development, the stage at which people begin to engage in abstract thought and experimental reasoning.
3. In this area as in others, Piaget is now regarded as having ignored individual and cultural differences, underestimated children's capabilities, overemphasized the qualitative nature of cognitive advances, and too narrowly defined cognition.

4. According to information-processing approaches, cognitive growth during adolescence is gradual and quantitative, involving improvements in mental organization and strategies; memory capacity; perceptual abilities; verbal, mathematical, and spatial abilities; attention; problem solving; and knowledge.
5. Another major area of cognitive development, according to the information-processing view, is the growth of metacognition, which permits adolescents to monitor their thought processes and accurately assess their cognitive capabilities.

What aspects of cognitive development cause difficulties for adolescents?

6. Hand in hand with the development of metacognition is the growth of adolescent egocentrism, a self-absorption that makes it hard for adolescents to accept criticism and tolerate authority figures.
7. Adolescents may play to an imaginary audience of critical observers, and they may develop personal fables, which emphasize the uniqueness of their experiences and plight, and their supposed invulnerability to risks.

Through what stages does moral development progress during childhood and adolescence?

8. Adolescents develop morally as well as in other ways. According to Lawrence Kohlberg, people pass through three major levels and six stages of moral development, as their sense of justice and their moral reasoning evolve.
9. Kohlberg's levels of moral development include preconventional morality (motivated by rewards and punishments), conventional morality (motivated by social reference), and postconventional morality (motivated by a sense of universal moral principles)—a level that may be reached during adolescence but that many people never attain.
10. Although Kohlberg's theory provides a good account of moral judgments, it is less adequate in predicting moral behavior. The ability to make moral judgments does not mean, then, that people invariably behave morally.
11. There appear to be gender differences in moral development not reflected in Kohlberg's work. Carol Gilligan has sketched out an alternative progression for girls, from an orientation toward individual survival, through goodness as self-sacrifice, to the morality of nonviolence.
12. Neither Kohlberg's nor Gilligan's conception of moral development may be entirely accurate and complete, and the issue of gender differences is far from settled.

What factors affect adolescent school performance?

13. School performance during the adolescent years declines, probably because of increased demands placed on students and more stringent grading practices than before.
14. Socioeconomic status is directly related to school achievement levels, largely because environmental factors relating to health, nutrition, living conditions, parental availability, and deteriorating schools negatively affect students of lower socioeconomic status.
15. Ethnicity is also related to school achievement. Differences are linked to socioeconomic factors, the circumstances under which a minority group enters the majority culture, attributional patterns regarding success factors, and belief systems regarding the link between school success and success in life.

Who attends college, and how is the college experience different for men and women?

16. College attendance is also influenced by ethnicity. A larger proportion of white high school-graduates enters and completes college than African-American or Hispanic high-school graduates. Nevertheless, minority students make up an increasingly larger proportion of the U.S. college population each year.

17. The college experience differs for men and women. Differences are evident in courses and majors chosen and in expectations for financial success upon graduation. The differences appear to be attributable to gender stereotypes that operate in college to affect teachers' and students' expectations.

How do adolescents make career choices, and what influence do ethnicity and gender have on career opportunities?

18. According to Eli Ginzberg, people proceed through stages as they consider careers, from the fantasy period, in which dream choices are made without regard to practical factors, through the tentative period, which spans adolescence and involves pragmatic thought about job requirements and personal abilities and goals, to the realistic period of early adulthood, in which career options are explored through actual experience and training. Other theories of career choice, such as John Holland's, link personality characteristics and career options.
19. Career choice and attitudes and behaviors on the job are influenced by gender. Traditionally, women have been associated with communal professions, which tend to be lower-paid, and men with agentic professions, which pay better.
20. Women and minorities in professional roles may find themselves hitting the "glass ceiling," an invisible barrier within an organization that, because of conscious or unconscious discrimination, prevents career advancement beyond a certain level.

Key Terms and Concepts

formal operational stage (p. 446)
metacognition (p. 448)
adolescent egocentrism (p. 449)
imaginary audience (p. 449)
personal fables (p. 449)
fantasy period (p. 465)
tentative period (p. 465)
realistic period (p. 465)
communal professions (p. 468)
agentic professions (p. 468)

CHAPTER 15

ADOLESCENCE

Social and Personality Development in Adolescence

PROLOGUE

NUKET CURRAN

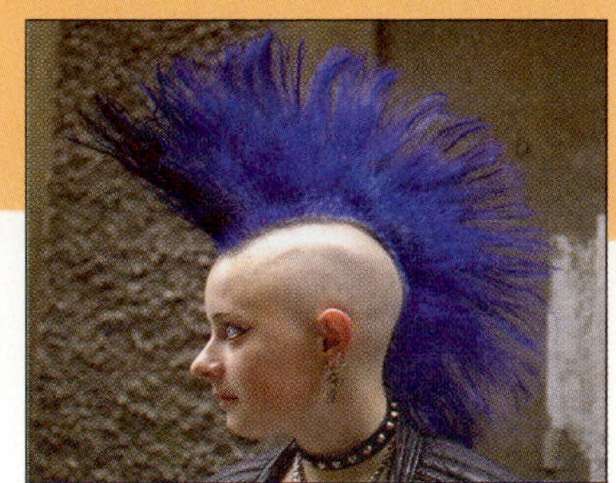

The first thing you notice about 17-year-old Nuket Curran is her hair. Her light brown locks are trimmed close on the back and sides—like those of a typical male in the 1950s. The entire top is roached, standing straight up for about an inch and a half. From the right side, just above and behind her ear, hangs a long, very thin braid.

"I started out looking like everyone else," she says. "In ninth grade I was more, like preppy. Had the bob, it was down to here—just standard-looking. And then I got an undercut; it was called a wedge. Then I cut one side off and then I shaved it off and then I just had long, long bangs and black in my hair. It was, like, striped black and my natural color. Then it was red—cherry cola red—and black. Then it was orange and black. I looked like Halloween. Then it was blond and black. I just felt like doing it, you know, and I can't do that when I'm 35. I can't get a job looking like that. So why not just do it now?

"People said, 'Well, she's dyeing her hair to be different.' In a way that's true. I mean, it's just a different way of expressing myself. I don't like to call it punk or new wave or any other terminology. It's a way of showing that I'm just another human being that's different from every other human being. I'm so bored with how everyone dresses the same. They have plain hair and plain everything. It's just monotonous. They're afraid to, like, stand out, to be themselves. And I just felt like I was being myself." (Kotre & Hall, 1990, pp. 178–179)

LOOKING AHEAD

No one would mistake Nuket—named by her parents for the Turkish word meaning "mountain flower"—for plain and monotonous. A nonconformist by nature, she epitomizes the rebelliousness that traditionally has been thought to typify the adolescent period.

Yet Nuket is less of a rebel than her appearance would suggest—a characterization that recent evidence suggests applies to most adolescents. Research increasingly shows that most people pass through adolescence without much turmoil in their lives. Although they may "try on" different roles and flirt with activities that their parents find objectionable, the majority of adolescents pass through the period in relative tranquillity (Petersen, 1988; Steinberg, 1993).

This is not to say that the transitions adolescents pass through are less than highly challenging (Compas, Hinden, & Gerhardt, 1995; Crockett & Crouter, 1995; Eccles et al., 1993; Laursen & Collins, 1994). As we'll see in this chapter, in which we examine the personality and social developments of the period, adolescence brings about major changes in the ways in which individuals must deal with the world.

We begin by considering how adolescents form their views of themselves. We look at self-concept and self-esteem, and at identity development. We also examine two major psychological difficulties: depression and suicide.

Next, we discuss relationships during adolescence. We consider how adolescents reposition themselves within the family, and how the influence of family members declines in some spheres as peers take on new importance. We also examine the ways in which adolescents interact with their friends, and the determinants of popularity and rejection.

Finally, we will consider dating and sexual behavior. We look at the role of dating in adolescents' lives, and we consider sexual behavior and the standards that govern adolescents' sex lives. We conclude by looking at teenage pregnancy, and at programs that seek to prevent unwanted pregnancy.

In sum, after reading this chapter, you'll be able to answer these questions:

- How does the development of self-concept, self-esteem, and identity proceed during adolescence?
- What dangers do adolescents face as they deal with the stresses of adolescence?
- How does the quality of relationships with family and peers change during adolescence?
- What are gender, race, and ethnic relations like in adolescence?
- What does it mean to be popular and unpopular in adolescence, and how do adolescents respond to peer pressure?
- What are the functions and characteristics of dating during adolescence?
- How does sexuality develop in the adolescent years?
- Why is teenage pregnancy a particular problem in the United States, and what can be done about it?

IDENTITY: ASKING "WHO AM I?"

> Turning 13 was an important period of my life. It was the time when I started to mature physically. It also was the time when more girls started to notice me. My personality changed a lot from a boring nerd to an energetic, funny, and athletic kid.
>
> As my year went on as a 13-year-old, as if things couldn't get better, they surprisingly did! My life as a child had ended. I was now a teenager. This just goes to show you that turning 13 meant turning into a new person.
>
> Patrick Backer (1993, p. 2)

> As you go to school, things get harder. You sort of realize that you're getting older. Adults treat you like an adult and don't give you the breaks you got when you're a child.
>
> To be 13 you have journeyed only half way to the *real* world. Then you notice that you're going to high school and think of the next 4 years and then college. Next you vote, a house, job, and kids. It seems your life passes right before your eyes.
>
> Mieko Ozecki (1993, p. 2)

> When I turned 13 it was like starting a new life. It was the year I was finally going to be allowed to do more things. For one thing I was able to hang out later. I wasn't a child anymore. I knew it and my parents knew it, too.
>
> I really can't think of a more important birthday besides your first one.
>
> Dmitri Ponomarev (1993, p. 2)

These voices of adolescents resonate with a common theme: a keen awareness and self-consciousness regarding their newly forming place in society and life. During adolescence, questions like "Who am I?" and "Where do I belong in the world?" begin to take a front seat.

Why should issues of identity become so important during adolescence? One reason is that adolescents' intellectual capacities become more adultlike. They can now understand—and appreciate—such abstract issues as the importance of establishing their position in society and the need to form a sense of themselves as individuals. Another reason is that the dramatic physical changes during puberty make adolescents acutely aware of their own bodies—and of the fact that others are reacting to them in ways to which they are unaccustomed.

Whatever the cause, adolescence often brings substantial changes in teenagers' self-concepts and self-esteem—in sum, their notions of their own identity.

Self-concept: Characterizing the Characteristics of Adolescence

Ask Louella to describe herself, and she says, "Others look at me as laid-back, relaxed, and not worrying too much. But really, I'm often nervous and emotional."

The fact that Louella distinguishes others' views of her from her own perceptions represents a developmental advance of adolescence. In childhood, Louella would have characterized herself according to a list of traits that would not differentiate her view of herself and others' perspectives. However, adolescents are able to make the distinction, and when they try to describe who they are, they take both their own and others' views into account (Harter, 1990a).

This broadening view of themselves is one aspect of adolescents' increasing discernment and perception in their understanding of who they are. The view of the self becomes more organized and coherent, and they can see various aspects of the self simultaneously. Furthermore, they look at the self from a psychological perspective, viewing traits not as concrete entities but as abstractions.

In some ways, however, the increasing differentiation of self-concept is a mixed blessing, especially during the earlier years of adolescence. At that time, adolescents may be troubled by the multiple aspects of their personalities. During the beginning of adolescence, for instance, teenagers may want to view themselves in a certain way ("I'm a sociable person and love to be with people"), and they may become concerned when their behavior is inconsistent with that view ("Even though I want to be sociable, sometimes I can't stand being around my friends and just want to be alone"). By the end of adolescence, however, teenagers accept the fact that different situations elicit different behaviors and feelings (Harter, 1990a; Pyryt & Mendaglio, 1994).

Self-esteem: Evaluating Oneself

Knowing who you are and *liking* who you are represent two different things. Although adolescents become increasingly accurate in understanding who they are (their self-concept), this knowledge does not guarantee that they like themselves (their self-esteem) any better. In fact, their increasing accuracy in understanding themselves permits them to see themselves fully—warts and all.

The same cognitive sophistication that allows adolescents to differentiate various aspects of the self also leads them to evaluate those aspects in different ways. For instance, an adolescent may have high self-esteem in terms of academic performance, but lower self-esteem in terms of relationships with others. Or it may be just the opposite, as articulated by this adolescent:

> How much do I *like* the kind of person I am? Well, I like some things about me, but I don't like others. I'm glad that I'm popular since it's really important to me to have friends. But in school I don't do as well as the really smart kids. That's OK, because if you're too smart you'll lose your friends. So being smart is just not that important. Except to my parents. I feel like I'm letting them down when I don't do as well as they want. (Harter, 1990, p. 364)

What determines an adolescent's self-esteem? Several factors make a difference. One is gender: Particularly during early adolescence, girls' self-esteem tends to be lower and more vulnerable than boys' (Cairns, McWhirter, Duffy, & Barry, 1990; Simmons, Brown, Bush, & Blyth, 1978; Simmons & Rosenberg, 1975). One reason is that, compared to boys, girls are more highly concerned about physical appearance and social success—in addition to academic achievement. Although boys are also concerned about these things, their attitudes are often more casual. Moreover, traditional societal messages may be interpreted as suggesting that female academic achievement is a roadblock to social success. Girls hearing such messages, then, are in a difficult bind: If they do well academically, they jeopardize their social success. No wonder that the self-esteem of adolescent girls is more fragile than that of boys (Unger & Crawford, 1992).

Socioeconomic status (SES) and ethnicity also influence self-esteem. Adolescents of higher SES generally have higher self-esteem than those of lower SES, particularly during middle and later adolescence. It may be that the social status factors that especially enhance one's standing and self-esteem—such as having more expensive clothes or a car—become more conspicuous in the later periods of adolescence (Savin-Williams & Demo, 1983; Van-Tassel-Baska, Olszewski-Kubilius, & Kulieke, 1994).

Ethnicity also plays a role in self-esteem, although the findings are not entirely consistent. Early studies argued that minority status would lead to lower self-esteem. This finding led to the hypothesis—initially supported—that African Americans and Hispanics would have lower self-esteem than Caucasians. Researchers' explanations for this finding were straightforward: Societal prejudice would be incorporated into the self-concepts of the targets of the prejudice, making them feel disliked and rejected.

However, more recent research paints a different picture. Most findings now suggest that African Americans differ little from whites in their levels of self-esteem (Harterb, 1990). Why should this be? One explanation is that social movements within the African-American community that bolster racial pride help support African-American adolescents. In fact, research finds that a stronger sense of racial identity is related to a higher level of self-esteem in African Americans and Hispanics (Phinney, Lochner, & Murphy, 1990).

Another reason for overall similarity in self-esteem levels between minority and majority adolescents is that teenagers in general focus their preferences and priorities on those aspects of their lives at which they are best. Consequently, African-American youths, as with any others, may concentrate on the things that they find most satisfying, and gain self-esteem from being successful at them (Hunt & Hunt, 1975; Phinney & Alipura, 1990).

Finally, self-esteem may be influenced not by ethnicity alone, but by a complex combination of factors. For instance, some developmentalists have considered ethnicity and gender simultaneously, coining the term *ethgender* to refer to the joint influence of ethnicity and gender. One study that simultaneously took both ethnicity and gender into account found that African-American and Hispanic males had the highest levels of self-esteem, while Asian and Native American females had the lowest levels (Dukes & Martinez, 1994; Martinez & Dukes, 1991).

IDENTITY FORMATION IN ADOLESCENCE: CHANGE OR CRISIS?

According to Erik Erikson (1963), whose theory we last discussed in Chapter 12, the search for identity inevitably leads some adolescents into substantial psychological difficulties as they encounter the adolescent identity crisis. Erikson's theory regarding this stage, which is summarized with his other stages in Table 15-1, suggests that adolescence is the time of the **identity-versus-identity-confusion stage.**

During the identity-versus-identity-confusion stage, teenagers seek to determine what is unique and distinctive about themselves. They strive to discover their particular strengths and weaknesses and the roles they can best play in their future lives. In short, they seek to understand their identity.

identity-versus-identity-confusion stage *the period during which teenagers seek to determine what is unique and distinctive about themselves*

In Erikson's view, adolescents who stumble in their efforts to find a suitable identity may follow several dysfunctional courses. They may adopt socially unacceptable roles, such

TABLE 15-1

A SUMMARY OF ERIKSON'S STAGES

STAGE	APPROXIMATE AGE	POSITIVE OUTCOMES	NEGATIVE OUTCOMES
1. Trust vs. mistrust	Birth–1.5 years	Feelings of trust from environmental support	Fear and concern regarding others
2. Autonomy vs. shame and doubt	1.5–3 years	Self-sufficiency if exploration is encouraged	Doubts about self, lack of independence
3. Initiative vs. guilt	3–6 years	Discovery of ways to initiate actions	Guilt from actions and thoughts
4. Industry vs. inferiority	6–12 years	Development of sense of competence	Feelings of inferiority, no sense of mastery
5. Identity vs. identity confusion	Adolescence	Awareness of uniqueness of self, knowledge of role to be followed	Inability to identify appropriate roles in life
6. Intimacy vs. isolation	Early adulthood	Development of loving, sexual relationships and close friendships	Fear of relationships with others
7. Generativity vs. stagnation	Middle adulthood	Sense of contribution to continuity of life	Trivialization of one's activities
8. Ego integrity vs. despair	Late adulthood	Sense of unity in life's accomplishments	Regret over lost opportunities of life

(*Source:* Erikson, 1963.)

as that of deviant, or they may have difficulty forming and maintaining long-lasting close personal relationships later on in life. In general, their sense of self becomes "diffuse," failing to organize around a central, unified core identity.

On the other hand, those who are successful in forging an appropriate identity set a course that provides a foundation for future psychosocial development. They learn their unique capabilities, and they develop an accurate sense of who they are. They are prepared to set out on a path that takes full advantage of what their unique strengths permit them to do (Archer & Waterman, 1994; Blustein & Palladino, 1991; Kahn, Zimmerman, Csikczentmihalyi, & Getzels, 1985; Adams, Montemayer, & Gullotta, 1996).

Societal pressures are high during the identity-versus-identity-confusion stage, as any student knows who has been repeatedly asked by parents and friends "What's your major?" and "What are you going to do when you graduate?" Adolescents feel pressure to make choices about what their life's work will be, or—at the very least—to decide whether their post-high-school plans include work or college. These are new choices, because up to this point, at least in the United States, society has laid out a universal educational track for all students. However, the track ends at high school, and consequently, adolescents face difficult choices about which of several possible future paths they will follow.

During the identity-versus-identity-confusion period, adolescents increasingly rely on their friends and peers as sources of information. At the same time, their dependence on adults declines. As we'll discuss later in the chapter, this increasing dependence on the peer group enables adolescents to forge close relationships. It also helps them to clarify their own identities as they compare themselves to others.

Because of the pressures of the identity-versus-identity-confusion period, Erikson suggests that many adolescents pursue a "psychological moratorium." The *psychological moratorium* is a period during which adolescents take time off from the upcoming responsibilities of adulthood and explore various roles and possibilities.

On the other hand, many adolescents cannot, for practical reasons, pursue a psychological moratorium involving a relatively leisurely exploration of various identities. For instance, some adolescents, for economic reasons, must work part-time after school and then take jobs immediately after graduation from high school. As a result, they have little time to experiment with identities and engage in a psychological moratorium. Does this mean such adolescents will be psychologically damaged in some way? Probably not. In fact, the satisfaction that can come from successfully holding a part-time job while attending school may be a sufficient psychological reward to outweigh the inability to try out various roles.

identity achievement *the particular identity to which teenagers commit following a period of crisis during which they consider various alternatives*

identity foreclosure *the state of adolescents who prematurely commit to an identity without adequately exploring alternatives*

identity diffusion *the category in which adolescents consider various identity alternatives but never commit to one, or never even consider identity options in any conscious way*

MARCIA'S APPROACH TO IDENTITY DEVELOPMENT: UPDATING ERIKSON

Using Erikson's theory as a springboard, psychologist James Marcia (1966, 1980) suggests that identity can be seen in terms of four categories, called statuses. The identity statuses depend on whether each of two characteristics—crisis and commitment—is present or absent. *Crisis* is a period of identity development in which an adolescent consciously chooses between various alternatives and makes decisions. *Commitment* is psychological investment in a course of action or an ideology.

By conducting lengthy interviews with adolescents, Marcia proposed four categories of adolescent identity (see Table 15-2):

(1) **Identity achievement.** Following a period of crisis during which they consider various alternatives, adolescents commit to a particular identity. Teenagers of this identity status have successfully thought through who they are and what they want to do. They tend to be the most psychologically healthy, higher in achievement motivation and moral reasoning than adolescents of any other status.

(2) **Identity foreclosure.** These are adolescents who have committed to an identity, but who did not do it by passing through a period of crisis in which they explored alternatives. Instead, they accepted others' decisions about what was best for them. Typical adolescents in this status are a son who enters the family business because it is expected of him, and a daughter who decides to become a physician simply because her mother is one. Although foreclosers are not necessarily unhappy, they tend to have what can be called rigid strength: Happy and self-satisfied, they also have a high need for social approval and tend to be authoritarian.

(3) **Identity diffusion.** Some adolescents in this status consider various alternatives but never commit to one. Others in this category never even get that far, not even considering their options in any conscious way. They tend to be flighty, shifting from one thing to the next. While they may seem carefree, their lack of commitment impairs their ability to form close relationships. In fact, they are often socially withdrawn.

TABLE 15-2

MARCIA'S FOUR CATEGORIES OF ADOLESCENT DEVELOPMENT

		COMMITMENT	
		PRESENT	ABSENT
CRISIS	PRESENT	Identity achievement	Moratorium
	ABSENT	Identity foreclosure	Identity diffusion

(*Source:* Marcia, 1980.)

(4) **Moratorium.** Although adolescents in the moratorium category have explored various alternatives to some degree, they have not yet committed themselves. As a consequence, they show relatively high anxiety and experience psychological conflict. On the other hand, they are often lively and appealing, seeking intimacy with others. Adolescents of this status typically settle on an identity, but only after something of a struggle.

moratorium *the category in which adolescents may have explored various identity alternatives to some degree but have not yet committed themselves*

It is important to note that adolescents are not necessarily stuck in one of the four categories. For instance, even though a foreclosure may have settled upon a career path during early adolescence with little active decision making, he or she may reassess the choice later and move into another category. For some individuals, then, identity formation may take place beyond the period of adolescence (Flum, 1994; Marcia, 1980; Kroger, 1995).

On the other hand, most research suggests that identity gels by the age of 18. In fact, the freshman year of college is, for many individuals, a time of considerable movement toward establishing an identity (Waterman, 1982; Waterman & Waterman, 1981).

DEPRESSION AND SUICIDE: PSYCHOLOGICAL DIFFICULTIES IN ADOLESCENCE

Although by far the majority of teenagers weather the search for identity—as well as the other challenges presented by the period—without major psychological difficulties, some find adolescence particularly stressful. Some, in fact, develop severe psychological problems. Two of the most vexing are adolescent depression and suicide.

Adolescent Depression. No one is immune to periods of sadness and bad moods, and adolescents are no exception. The end of a relationship, failure at an important task, the death of a loved one—all may produce profound feelings of sadness, loss, and grief. In situations such as these, depression is a fairly typical reaction.

How common are feelings of depression in adolescence? Although figures are hard to come by, some estimates suggest that 20 to 35 percent of boys and 25 to 40 percent of girls report having experienced depressed moods in the previous 6 months. Reports of feeling "sad and hopeless" are even higher: Almost two thirds of teenagers say they have experienced such feelings at one time or another (see Figure 15-1). Furthermore, although more than 30 percent have thought about committing suicide, only a small minority of adolescents—some 3 percent—experience *major depression,* a full-blown psychological disorder in which depression is severe and lingers for long periods (Boehm & Campbell, 1995; Culp,

Between 25 and 40 percent of girls, and 20 to 35 percent of boys, experience occasional episodes of depression during adolescence, although the incidence of major depression is far lower.

FIGURE 15-1

ADOLESCENTS' REPORTING OF FEELINGS OF SADNESS AND HOPELESSNESS

(*Source:* Adapted from J. Gans, 1990, National Adolescent Student Health Survey.)

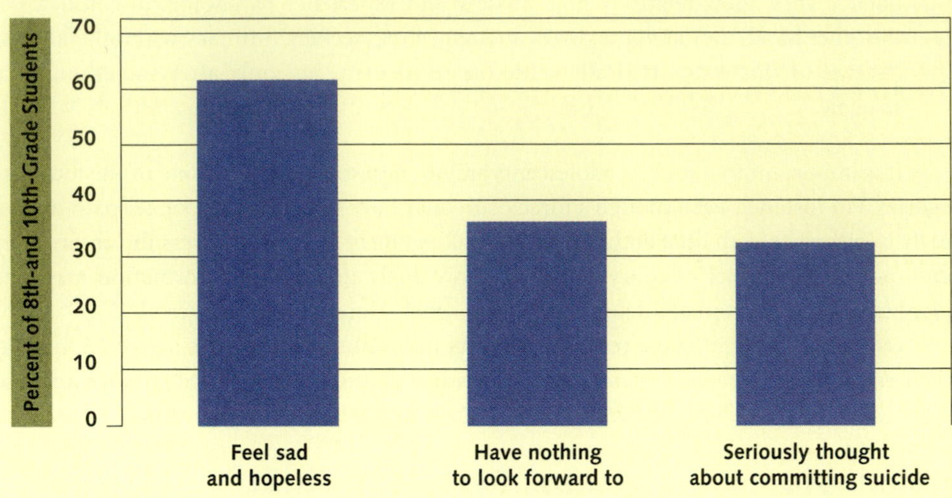

Clyman, & Culp, 1995; J. E. Gans, Blyth, Elsby, & Gaveras, 1990; Petersen, Compas, & Brooks-Gunn, 1991; Petersen et al., 1993).

Gender, ethnic, and racial differences also are found in depression rates. As is the case among adults, adolescent females, on average, experience depression more often than males. Furthermore, some studies have found that African-American adolescents have higher rates of depression than white adolescents, although not all research supports this conclusion. Native Americans, too, appear to have higher rates of depression (Fleming & Offord, 1990; Nettles & Pleck, 1990).

Depression has several causes. In cases of severe, long-term depression, biological factors are often involved. Some adolescents, for instance, seem to be genetically predisposed to experience depression (Brooks-Gunn, Petersen, & Compas, 1994; Ehlers, Frank, & Kupfer, 1988).

However, environmental and social factors relating to the extraordinary changes in the social lives of adolescents are also an important cause (Aseltine, Gore, & Colten, 1994). Thus, an adolescent who experiences the death of a loved one or grows up with a depressed parent is at a higher risk of depression (Hammen, 1991). In addition, being unpopular, having few close friends, and experiencing rejection are associated with adolescent depression (Vernberg, 1990).

One of the most puzzling questions about depression is why its incidence is higher among girls than boys. Some psychologists speculate that stress is more pronounced for girls than for boys in adolescence, due to the many, sometimes contradictory, aspects of the traditional female gender role, such as the inconsistency between academic success and popularity which some girls perceive.

There may also be other causes of girls' generally higher levels of depression during adolescence. They may be more apt than boys to react to stress by turning inward, thereby experiencing a sense of helplessness and hopelessness. In contrast, boys more often react by externalizing the stress and acting more impulsively or aggressively, or by turning to drugs and alcohol. One factor that doesn't seem to cause the higher incidence of female depression is female hormones: Little evidence links hormonal production in adolescent girls to depression (Gjerde, Block, & Block, 1988; Lewinsohn et al., 1994; Nolen-Hoeksema & Girgus, 1994; A. C. Petersen, Sarigiani, & Kennedy, 1991; Rutter & Garmezy, 1983; Hammond & Romney, 1995).

Adolescent Suicide. Elyssa Drazin was 16. Although her grades had gone down in the previous 6 months, she was still a pretty good student. Her social life had picked up over the last 2 years, and she had been involved with Hector Segool. In the past month, however, the relationship had cooled considerably, and Hector had told her he wanted to date other girls. Elyssa was devastated, and—as she wrote in a note that was found on her desk—she could not bear the thought of seeing Hector holding hands with another girl. She took a large quantity of sleeping pills and became one of the thousands of adolescents who take their own lives each year.

cluster suicide *a situation in which one suicide leads to attempts by others to kill themselves*

The rate of adolescent suicide in the United States has tripled in the last 30 years. In fact, one teenage suicide occurs every 90 minutes, for an annual rate of 12.2 suicides per 100,000 adolescents. Moreover, the reported rate may actually understate the true number of suicides; parents and medical personnel are often reluctant to report a death as suicide, preferring to label it an accident. Even with underreporting, suicide is the third most common cause of death among 15- to 24-year-olds, after accidents and homicide (Henry, Stephenson, Hanson, & Hargett, 1993).

The rate of suicide is higher for boys than girls, although girls *attempt* suicide more frequently. Males are more successful because of the methods they use: Boys tend to use more violent means, such as guns, while girls are more apt to choose the more peaceful strategy of drug overdose. Some estimates suggest that there are as many as 200 attempted suicides for every successful one (Berman & Jobes, 1991; Gelman, 1994; Hawton, 1986).

The reasons behind the increase in adolescent suicide over past decades are unclear. The most obvious explanation is that the stress experienced by teenagers has increased, leading those who are most troubled to be more likely to commit suicide (Elkind, 1984). But why should stress have increased just for adolescents? The suicide rate for other segments of the population has remained fairly stable over the same time period.

Although an explanation for the increase in adolescent suicide has not been found, it is clear that certain factors heighten the risk of suicide. One factor is depression. Depressed teenagers who are experiencing a profound sense of hopelessness are at greater risk of committing suicide. In addition, social inhibition, perfectionism, and a high level of anxiety are related to a greater risk of suicide (Lewinsohn, Rohde, & Seeley, 1994; Petersen et al., 1993).

Some cases of suicide are associated with family conflicts and adjustment difficulties. Others follow a history of abuse and neglect. The rate of suicide among drug and alcohol abusers is also relatively high. As can be seen in Figure 15-2, those contemplating suicide cite several other factors as well (Brent, Perper, Moritz, & Liotus, 1994; Garland & Zigler, 1993).

Some suicides appear to be caused by exposure to the suicide of others. In **cluster suicide,** one suicide leads to attempts by others to kill themselves. For instance, some high schools have experienced a series of suicides following a well-publicized case. As a result,

The rate of adolescent suicide has tripled in the last 30 years. These girls console one another following the suicide of a classmate in their New Jersey high school.

FIGURE 15-2

SUICIDE-RELATED PROBLEMS

These problems were the ones most frequently cited by callers to a suicide-prevention hotline who were contemplating suicide.

(*Source:* Samaritans, 1989.)

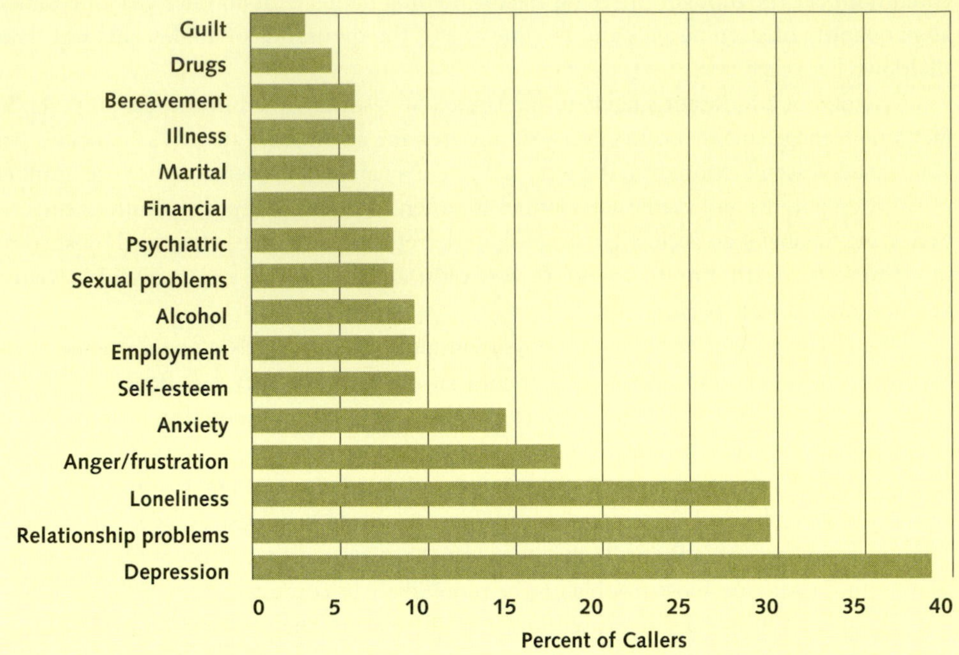

many schools have established crisis intervention teams to counsel students when one student commits suicide (Hazell, 1993).

There are several warning signs that should sound an alarm regarding the possibility of suicide. Among them:

- Direct or indirect talk about suicide, such as "I wish I were dead" or "You won't have me to worry about any longer"
- School difficulties, such as missed classes or a decline in grades
- Making arrangements as if preparing for a long trip, such as giving away prized possessions or arranging for the care of a pet
- Writing a will
- Loss of appetite or excessive eating
- General depression, including a change in sleeping patterns, slowness and lethargy, and uncommunicativeness
- Dramatic changes in behavior, such as a shy person suddenly acting outgoing
- Preoccupation with death in music, art, or literature

The Informed Consumer of Development

Deterring Adolescent Suicide

If you suspect that an adolescent, or anyone else for that matter, is contemplating suicide, don't stand idly by. Act! The U.S. Public Health Service makes several suggestions for what to do (based on Franck & Brownstone, 1991):

- Talk to the person, listening without judging, and giving the person an understanding forum in which to try to talk things through.
- Talk specifically about suicidal thoughts, such as: Does the person have a plan? Has he or she bought a gun? Where is it? Has he or she stockpiled pills? Where are they? The Public Health Service notes that, "contrary to popular belief, such candor will not give a person dangerous ideas or encourage a suicidal act."
- Evaluate the situation, trying to distinguish between general upset and more serious danger, as when suicide plans *have* been made. If the crisis is acute, *do not leave the person alone.*
- Be supportive, letting the person know you care and trying to break down his or her feelings of isolation.
- Take charge of finding help, without concern about invading the person's privacy. Do not try to handle the problem alone; get professional help immediately.
- Make the environment safe, removing from the premises (not just hiding) weapons such as guns, razors, scissors, medication, and other potentially dangerous household items.
- Do not keep suicide talk or threats secret; these are calls for help and warrant immediate action.
- Do not challenge, dare, or use verbal shock treatment. They can have tragic effects.
- Make a contract with the person, getting a promise or commitment, preferably in writing, not to make any suicidal attempt until you have talked further.
- Beware of elevated moods and seemingly quick recoveries; sometimes they are illusory, reflecting the relief of finally deciding to commit suicide or the temporary release of talking to someone, though the underlying problems have not been resolved.

For immediate help with a suicide-related problem, call (800) 621-4000, a national hotline staffed with trained counselors.

Review and Rethink

REVIEW

- Self-concept during adolescence grows more differentiated as the view of the self becomes more organized, broader, and more abstract, and takes account of the views of others.
- Self-esteem, too, grows increasingly differentiated as the adolescent develops the ability to place different values on different aspects of the self. Factors of gender, ethnicity, and socioeconomic status appear to influence self-esteem.
- Both Erikson's identity-versus-identity-confusion stage and Marcia's four identity statuses focus on the adolescent's struggle to determine an identity and a role in society. Adolescents tend to rely on friends and peers in the face of societal pressures, may react in dysfunctional ways, and may seek a psychological moratorium to explore role possibilities.

- One of the dangers that adolescents face is depression, a psychological disorder with biological, environmental, and social causes, which affects girls more than boys.
- Suicide is the third most common cause of death among 15- to 24-year-olds. Those who deal with adolescents should familiarize themselves with the warning signs of suicide and with ways to prevent it.

RETHINK

- How does an adolescent's changing self-concept relate to changes in his or her cognitive development?
- What are some consequences of the shift from reliance on adults to reliance on peers? Are there advantages? Dangers?
- Do you believe that all four of Marcia's identity statuses can lead to reassessment and different choices later in life? Do you think some statuses are more likely than others to produce this type of rethinking? Why?
- Why are females more likely to experience depression than males? How would you design a study to explore the possible effects of biological versus environmental factors?
- What obligations do you have to a friend who confides in you the intention to commit suicide and asks you to respect confidentiality?

RELATIONSHIPS: FAMILY AND FRIENDS

> Slim and dark, with a passing resemblance to actress Demi Moore, Leah is dressed up and ready to go to the first real formal dance of her life. True, the smashing effect of her short beaded black dress is marred slightly by the man's shirt she insists on wearing to cover her bare shoulders. And she is in a sulk. Her boyfriend, Sean Moffitt, is 4 minutes late, and her mother, Linda, refuses to let her stay out all night at a coed sleepover party after the dance.
>
> When Sean arrives with his mother, Pam, Leah reluctantly sheds the work shirt. She greets Sean shyly, not sure he'll approve of that afternoon's makeover by hairdresser and manicurist. Sean, an easygoing youth with dimples and rosy cheeks, squirms in his tuxedo. Leah recombs his hair and makes him remove his earring. "None of the guys are wearing them to the dance," she declares. (She's wrong. A few moments later, their friends Melissa and Erik arrive, and Erik is wearing his earring.)
>
> Leah's father, George, suggests a 2 A.M. curfew: Leah hoots incredulously. Sean pitches the all-nighter, stressing that the party will be chaperoned. Leah's mother has already talked to the host's mother, mortifying Leah with her offhand comment that a coed sleepover seemed "weird." Rolling her eyes, Leah persists: "It's not like anybody's really going to sleep!" Sean asks his mother for another $20. "Why did the amount suddenly jump?" she asks, digging into her purse. (E. Graham, 1995, p. B1)

This snapshot of the life of 16-year-old Leah Brookner of Norwalk, Connecticut, provides a glimpse of some of the complex, interdependent relationships in which adolescents are involved. As Leah juggles parents, friends, and romantic partners, her life—and those of other adolescents—seems, at times, like an intricate jigsaw puzzle in which not all the pieces fit together perfectly.

The social world of adolescents is considerably wider than that of younger children. As adolescents' relationships with people outside the home grow increasingly important, their interactions with their families evolve and take on a new, and sometimes difficult, character (Montemayor, Adams, & Gulotta, 1994).

FAMILY TIES: REASSESSING RELATIONS WITH RELATIONS

When Pepe Lizzagara entered junior high school, his relationship with his parents changed drastically. Although relations were quite good previously, by the middle of seventh grade, tensions grew. In Pepe's view, his parents always seemed to be "on his case." Instead of giving him more freedom, which he felt he deserved at age 13, they actually seemed to be getting more restrictive.

Pepe's parents would probably suggest that they were not the source of the tension in the household—Pepe was. From their point of view, Pepe, with whom they'd established what seemed to be a stable relationship throughout much of his childhood, suddenly seemed transformed. Like Nuket Curran (described in the chapter prologue), whose hair color shifted almost as frequently as her moods, Pepe presented novel, and often bewildering, behavior.

autonomy *independence and a sense of control over one's life*

generation gap *a divide between parents and children in attitudes, values, aspirations, and worldviews*

The Quest for Autonomy. Parents are sometimes angered, and even more frequently puzzled, by adolescents' conduct. Children who have previously accepted their parents' judgments, declarations, and guidelines begin to question—and sometimes rebel against—their parents' views of the world.

One reason for these clashes is the shift in the roles that both children and parents must deal with during adolescence. Adolescents increasingly seek **autonomy,** independence and a sense of control over their lives. Most parents intellectually realize that this shift is a normal part of adolescence, representing one of the primary developmental tasks of the period, and in many ways they welcome it as a sign of their children's growth. However, in many cases the day-to-day realities of adolescents' increasing autonomy may prove difficult for them to deal with (Smetana, 1995).

In most families, teenagers' autonomy grows gradually over the course of adolescence. For instance, one study of changes in adolescents' views of their parents found that increasing autonomy led them to perceive parents less in idealized terms and more as persons in their own right. At the same time, adolescents came to depend more on themselves, and to feel more like separate individuals (see Figure 15-3).

The increase in adolescent autonomy is reflected in the relationship between parents and teenagers. At the start of adolescence, the relationship tends to be asymmetrical: Parents hold most of the power and influence over the relationship. By the end of adolescence, however, power and influence have become more balanced, and parents and children end up in a more symmetrical, or egalitarian, relationship. Power and influence are shared, although parents typically retain the upper hand.

The degree of autonomy that is eventually achieved varies from one family to the next. Furthermore, cultural factors play an important role. In Western societies, which tend to value individualism, adolescents seek autonomy at a relatively early stage of adolescence. In contrast, Asian societies are *collectivistic*; they promote the idea that the well-being of the group is more important than that of the individual. In such societies, adolescents' aspirations to achieve autonomy are less pronounced (Feldman & Rosenthal, 1990; Kim et al., 1994).

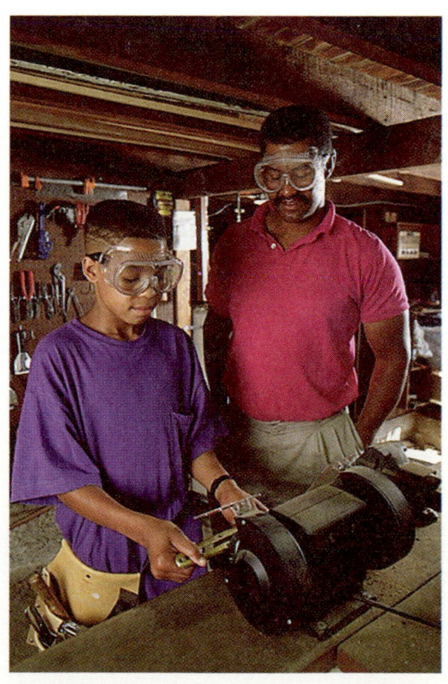

Although parents hold most of the power and influence over their relationship with their children at the start of adolescence, by the end of the period the relationship is more egalitarian.

The Myth of the Generation Gap. It might be thought that one factor motivating adolescents' efforts to attain autonomy is the discrepancy between parents' and teenagers' views of the world. According to this argument, there is a **generation gap,** a deep divide between parents and children in attitudes, values, aspirations, and worldviews.

The reality, however, is quite different. The generation gap, when it exists, is really quite narrow. Adolescents and their parents tend to see eye-to-eye in a variety of domains. Republican parents generally have Republican children; members of the Christian right have children who espouse similar views; parents who advocate for abortion rights have children who are pro-abortion. On social, political, and religious issues, parents and

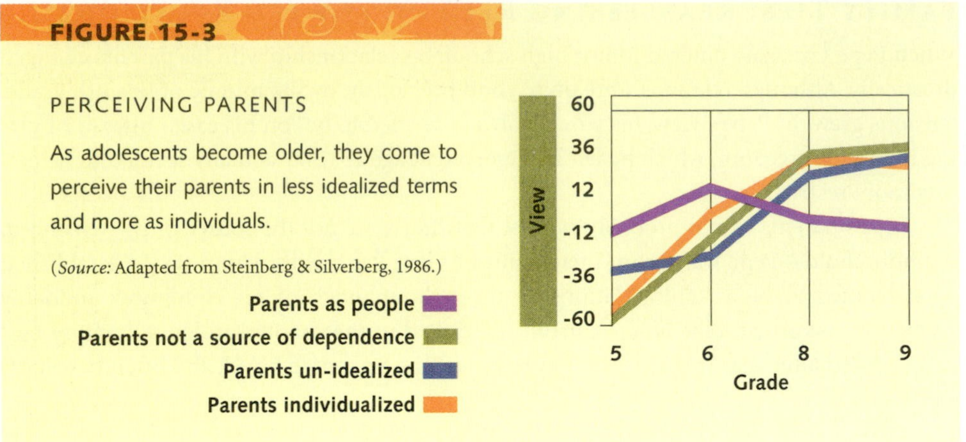

adolescents tend to be in sync, and children's worries mirror those of their parents. They also have similar career aspirations and attitudes about work. In fact, on most issues of attitudes and values, the differences between one adolescent and another are far greater than the differences between parents and their adolescent children (Chira, 1994; Conger, 1977; Feather, 1980; Youniss, 1989).

Similarly, there is typically no generation gap in the value that parents and adolescents place on the relationship they have with one another. Despite their quest for autonomy and independence, most adolescents have deep love, affection, and respect for their parents—reciprocating the feelings that their parents have for them. Although there are notable exceptions, with some parent-adolescent relationships marked by significant strife, the majority of relationships are more positive than negative. Furthermore, even though adolescents spend decreasing amounts of time with their families in general, the amount of time they spend alone with each parent remains remarkably stable across adolescence (see Figure 15-4). In short, there is no evidence suggesting that family problems are worse during adolescence than at any other stage of development (Larson et al., 1996; Steinberg, 1990, 1993).

On the other hand, parents' and adolescents' relationships are not always sweetness and light. For instance, parents and adolescents often hold different views on matters of personal taste, such as music preferences and styles of dress. Significant strife may occur between parents and adolescents, particularly during early adolescence, when conflicts between children's efforts to achieve autonomy and parental reactions are more pronounced than at any other time.

More conflict between parents and their children occurs during the early stages of adolescence than at later stages of the period.

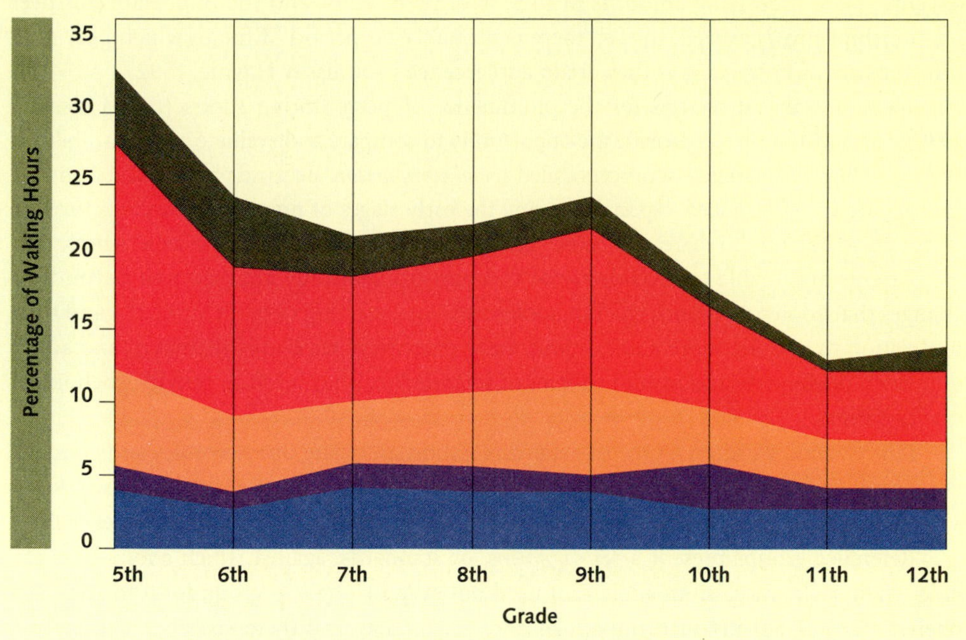

FIGURE 15-4

TIME SPENT BY ADOLESCENTS WITH PARENTS REMAINS STABLE

Despite their quest for autonomy and independence, most adolescents have deep love, affection, and respect for their parents; and the amount of time they spend alone with each parent remains remarkably stable across adolescence.

(*Source*: Larson et al., 1996.)

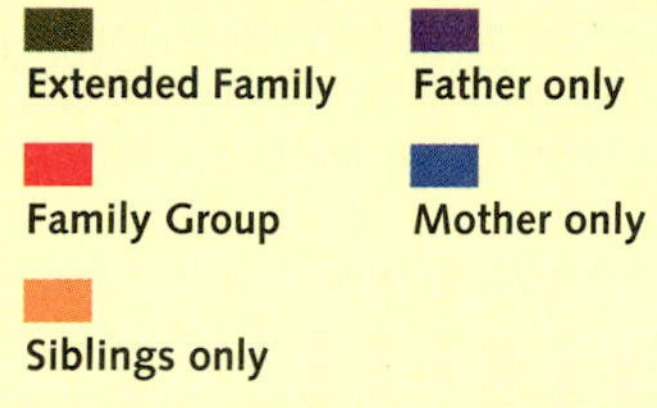

Why should strife be greater during early adolescence than at later stages of the period? According to developmental psychologist Judith Smetana, the reason involves differing definitions of, and rationales for, appropriate and inappropriate conduct. Parents may feel, for instance, that getting one's ear pierced in three places is inappropriate because society traditionally deems it inappropriate. On the other hand, adolescents may view the issue in terms of personal choice (Smetana, 1988, 1989; J. Smetana, Yau, & Hanson, 1991).

Furthermore, the newly sophisticated reasoning of adolescents (discussed in the previous chapter) leads teenagers to think about parental rules in more complex ways. Consequently, arguments that were convincing to a school-age child ("Do it because I tell you to do it") are less compelling to an adolescent.

Although at first the argumentativeness and assertiveness of early adolescence may lead to an increase in conflict, in many ways they play an important role in the evolution of parent-child relationships. While parents may at first react defensively to the challenges that their children present, and may grow inflexible and rigid, in most cases they eventually come to realize that their children *are* growing up.

Parents also come to see that their adolescent children's arguments are often compelling and not so unreasonable, and that their daughters and sons can, in fact, be trusted with more freedom. Consequently, they become more yielding, allowing and eventually perhaps even encouraging independence. As this process occurs during the middle stages of adolescence, the combativeness of early adolescence declines.

Of course, this pattern does not hold for all adolescents. Although the majority of teenagers maintain stable relations with their parents throughout adolescence, as many as 20 percent pass through a fairly rough time (Dryfoos, 1990). We'll consider some of the factors that place adolescents at risk later in the chapter.

Relationships with Peers: The Importance of Belonging

In the eyes of numerous parents, the most fitting symbol of adolescence is the telephone. For many of their children, it appears to be an indispensable lifeline, sustaining ties to friends with whom they may have already spent many hours earlier in the day.

Communicating with friends becomes increasingly important during adolescence as peer relationships take on new prominence.

reference groups *groups of people with whom one compares oneself*

cliques *groups of from 2 to 12 people whose members have frequent social interactions with one another*

crowds *larger groups than cliques, composed of individuals who share particular characteristics but who may not interact with one another*

The seemingly compulsive need to communicate with friends is symbolic of the role that peers play in adolescence. Continuing the trend that began in middle childhood, adolescents spend increasing amounts of time with their peers, and the importance of peer relationships grows as well. In fact, there is probably no period of life in which peer relationships are as important as they are in adolescence (Youniss & Haynie, 1992).

There are several reasons for the prominence of peers during adolescence (Coleman, 1980). For one thing, peers provide the opportunity to compare and evaluate opinions, abilities, and even physical changes—a process called *social comparison.* Because physical and cognitive changes are so pronounced, especially during the early stages of puberty, adolescents turn increasingly to others who share, and consequently can shed light on, their own experiences.

Parents are unable to provide social comparison. Not only are they well beyond the changes that adolescents undergo, but adolescents' questioning of adult authority and their motivation to become more autonomous make parents, other family members, and adults in general inadequate and invalid sources of knowledge. Who is left to provide such information? Peers.

Finally, adolescence is a time of experimentation, of trying out new roles and conduct. Peers provide information about what roles and behavior are most acceptable by serving as a reference group. **Reference groups** are groups of people with whom one compares oneself.

Reference groups present a set of *norms,* or standards, against which adolescents can judge their social success. An adolescent need not even belong to a group for it to serve as a reference group. For instance, unpopular adolescents may find themselves belittled and rejected by members of a popular group yet use that more popular group as a reference group.

Cliques and Crowds: Belonging to a Group. Even if they do not belong to the group they use for reference purposes, adolescents typically are part of some identifiable group. In fact, one of the consequences of the increasing cognitive sophistication of adolescents is the ability to group others in more discriminating ways. Rather than defining people in concrete terms relating to what they do ("football players" or "musicians"), adolescents use more abstract terms packed with greater subtleties ("jocks" or "the artsy-craftsy crowd") (Brown, 1990; Montemayor et al., 1994).

What are the typical groups to which adolescents belong? There are actually two types: cliques and crowds. **Cliques** are groups of from 2 to 12 people whose members have frequent social interactions with one another. In contrast, **crowds** are larger and comprise individuals who share particular characteristics but who may not interact with one another. For instance, "toughs," "jocks," and "brains" are separate crowds currently found in the typical high school.

The sex segregation of childhood continues during the early stages of adolescence. However, by the time of middle adolescence, this segregation decreases, and the boys' and girls' cliques begin to converge.

There is a surprisingly high level of agreement among adolescents regarding the characteristics of members of particular groups. For instance, one study found that "jocks" and "normals" were seen as dressing casually, while "populars" were viewed as more stylish dressers. "Normals" and "jocks" were perceived as friendly, while "populars" and "jocks" were cliquish. "Populars" and "jocks" tried hard in school, while "druggies" and "toughs" hated it (Brown, Lohr, & Trujillo, 1983; see Figure 15-5).

Of course, these descriptions are merely stereotypes, and they do not necessarily represent the actual characteristics of individual group members. Still, the stereotypes are powerful and widespread, and the expectation that people in a particular crowd behave in a certain way may constrain members' behavior. In fact, the stereotype may actually bring about the expected behavior—another example of a self-fulfilling prophecy.

sex cleavage *sex segregation in which boys interact primarily with boys, and girls primarily with girls*

Gender Relations. At the very start of adolescence, groups tend to mirror the makeup of middle childhood groups in that they are composed almost universally of same-sex individuals. Boys hang out with boys; girls hang out with girls. Technically, this sex segregation is called the **sex cleavage.**

However, the situation changes in short order as members of both sexes enter puberty. Both the hormonal surge that marks puberty and causes the maturation of the sex organs and societal pressures suggesting that the time is appropriate for romantic involvement lead to a change in the ways the opposite sex is viewed. Rather than seeing every member of the opposite sex as "annoying" and "a pain," boys and girls begin to regard each other with greater interest, in terms of both personality and sexuality.

When this change occurs, boys' and girls' cliques, which previously had moved along parallel but separate tracks, begin to converge. Adolescents begin to attend boy-girl dances or parties, although most of the time the boys still spend their time with boys, and the girls with girls (Csikszentmihalyi & Larson, 1984). (Think back to your own early adolescence, and perhaps you'll recall dances with boys lined up on one side of the room and girls on the other.)

A little later, however, adolescents increasingly spend time with members of the opposite sex (Dunphy, 1963). New cliques emerge, composed of both males and females. Not everyone participates initially: Early on, the teenagers who are leaders of the same-sex cliques and who have the highest status pilot the way. Eventually, however, most adolescents find themselves in cliques that include boys and girls.

Cliques and crowds undergo yet another transformation at the end of adolescence: They become less powerful and may, in fact, succumb to the increased pairing off that occurs between males and females. Rather than the clique being the center of adolescents' social lives, then, boy-girl interaction becomes the focus.

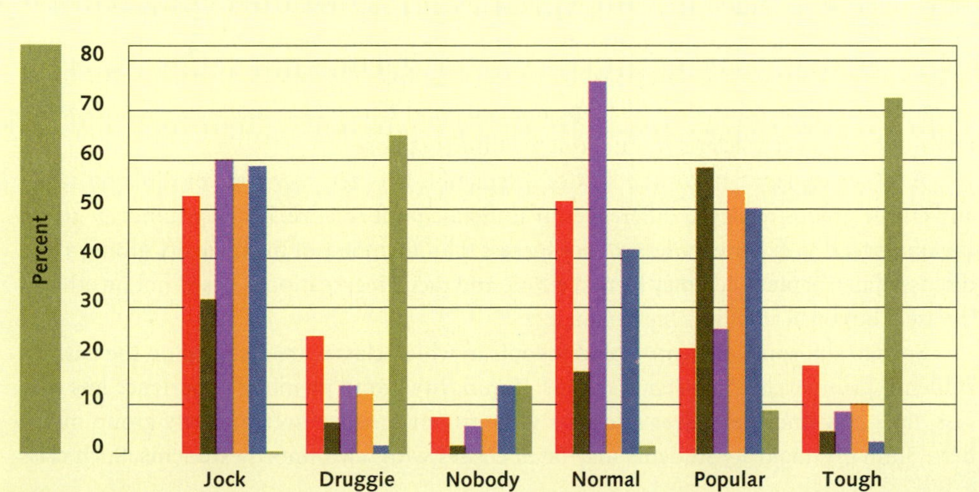

FIGURE 15-5

CHARACTERISTICS OF MEMBERS OF PARTICULAR GROUPS, AS IDENTIFIED BY OTHER ADOLESCENTS

Various high-school groups are seen as having particular characteristics.

(*Source:* Adapted from B. Brown et al., 1983.)

- Casual, athletic dress
- Stylish dress and grooming
- Friendly
- Cliquish
- Enjoy, try hard at academics
- Hate school

Even in schools that are racially integrated, members of different races interact relatively little.

Developmental Diversity

Race Segregation: The Great Divide of Adolescence

> *When Philip McAdoo, a [student] at the University of North Carolina, stopped one day to see a friend who worked on his college campus, a receptionist asked if he would autograph a basketball for her son. Because he was African American and tall, "she just assumed that I was on the basketball team," recounted McAdoo.*
>
> *Jasme Kelly, an African-American sophomore at the same college, had a similar story to tell. When she went to see a friend at a fraternity house, the student who answered the door asked if she was there to apply for the job of cook.*
>
> *White students, too, find racial relations difficult and in some ways forbidding. For instance, Jenny Johnson, a white 20-year-old junior, finds even the most basic conversation with African-American classmates difficult. She describes a conversation in which African-American friends "jump at my throat because I used the word 'black' instead of African American. There is just such a huge barrier that it's really hard . . . to have a normal discussion." (Sanoff & Minerbrook, 1993, p. 58)*

The pattern of race segregation found at the University of North Carolina is repeated over and over in schools and colleges throughout the United States: Even when they attend desegregated schools with a high proportion of minority students, people of different ethnicities and races interact very little. Moreover, even if they have a friend of a different ethnicity within the confines of a school, most adolescents don't interact with that friend outside of school (DuBois & Hirsch, 1990).

It doesn't start out this way. During elementary school and even during early adolescence, there is a fair amount of integration among students of differing ethnicities. However, by middle and late adolescence, the amount of segregation is striking (Shrum, Cheek, & Hunter, 1988; Spencer, 1991; Spencer & Dornbusch, 1990).

Why should race and ethnic segregation be the rule, even in schools that have been desegregated for some time? One reason is that minority students may actively seek support from others who share their minority status. Furthermore, by associating primarily with other members of their own minority group, they are able to affirm their own identity.

Other explanations for campus segregation are less positive. For instance, socioeconomic status (SES) differences between people of different races and ethnicities may keep integration at low levels. Racial and ethnic differences tend to mirror SES differences: People from minority groups are overrepresented in lower SES groups (J. Coleman, 1961), just as people from the majority group are overrepresented in higher SES groups. Because cliques tend to comprise members who are of similar SES, they also display very little racial integration. It is possible, then, that apparent ethnic differences in interaction patterns are really due to SES characteristics, and not to ethnicity per se.

Another explanation for the lack of interaction between members of different racial and ethnic groups relates to differences in academic performance. Because minority group members tend to experience less school success than members of the majority group, as we discussed in Chapter 14, it may be that ethnic and racial segregation is based not on ethnicity itself, but on academic achievement.

Specifically, some students attend schools in which classes are assigned on the basis of students' prior levels of academic success. If minority group members experience less success, they may find themselves in classes with proportionally fewer majority group members. Similarly, majority students may be in classes with few minority students. Such class assignment practices, then, may inadvertently maintain and promote race and ethnic segregation. This pattern would be particularly prevalent in schools where rigid academic tracking is practiced, with students assigned to "low," "medium," and "high" tracks depending on their prior achievement (Hallinan & Williams, 1989).

Finally, the lack of racial and ethnic interaction in school may reflect negative attitudes held by both majority and minority students. Minority students may feel that the white majority is prejudiced, discriminatory, and hostile; and they may prefer to stick to same-race groups. Conversely, majority students may assume that minority group members are antagonistic and unfriendly. Such mutually destructive attitudes reduce the likelihood that meaningful interaction can take place (N. Miller & Brewer, 1984).

Is the voluntary segregation along racial and ethnic lines found during adolescence inevitable? No. For instance, adolescents who have had extensive interactions with members of different races earlier in their lives are more likely to have friends of different races. Furthermore, schools that actively promote contact between members of different ethnicities in mixed-ability classes may create an environment in which cross-race friendships can flourish (Schofield & Francis, 1982).

Still, the task is daunting. Many societal pressures act to keep members of different races from interacting with one another. Furthermore, cliques may actively promote norms that discourage group members from crossing racial and ethnic lines to form new friendships.

Popularity and Rejection: Adolescent Likes and Dislikes

Most adolescents have well-tuned antennae when it comes to determining who is popular and who is not. In fact, for some teenagers, concerns over popularity—or lack of it—may be a central focus of their lives.

Actually, the social world of adolescents is divided not only into popular and unpopular individuals; the differentiations are more complex (see Figure 15-6). For instance,

FIGURE 15-6

SOCIAL DIFFERENTIATIONS AMONG ADOLESCENTS

(*Source:* Adapted from Franzoi et al., 1994.)

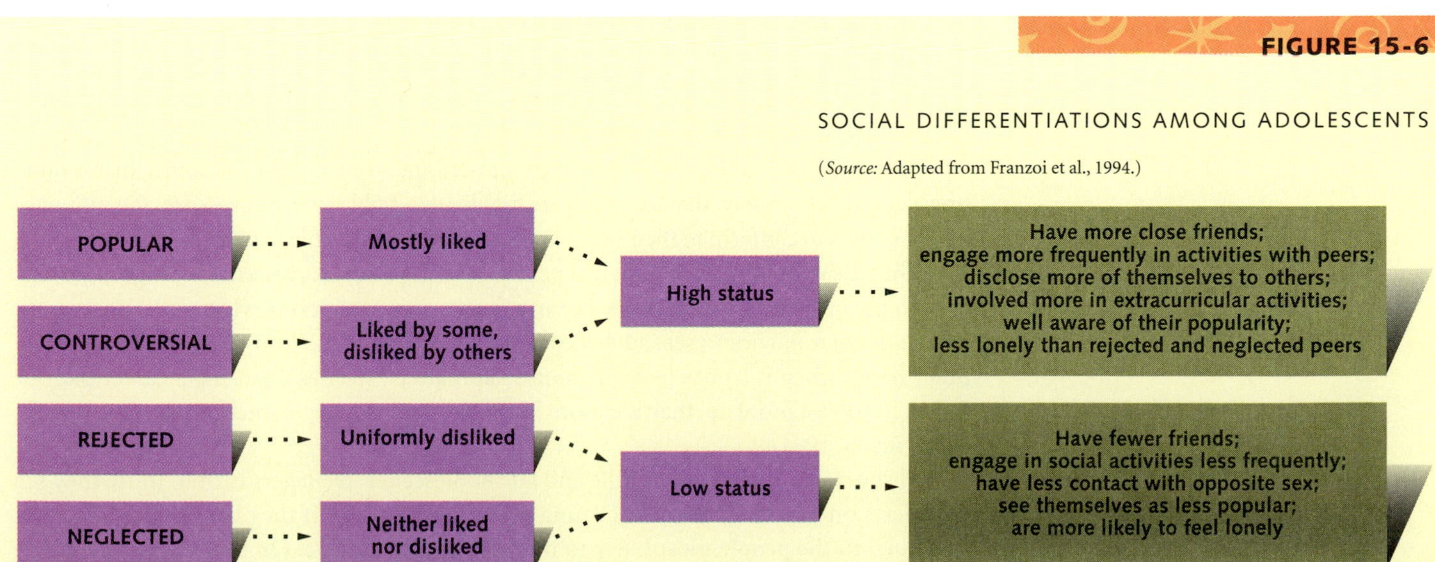
POPULAR
Mostly liked
CONTROVERSIAL
Liked by some, disliked by others
High status
Have more close friends; engage more frequently in activities with peers; disclose more of themselves to others; involved more in extracurricular activities; well aware of their popularity; less lonely than rejected and neglected peers
REJECTED
Uniformly disliked
NEGLECTED
Neither liked nor disliked
Low status
Have fewer friends; engage in social activities less frequently; have less contact with opposite sex; see themselves as less popular; are more likely to feel lonely

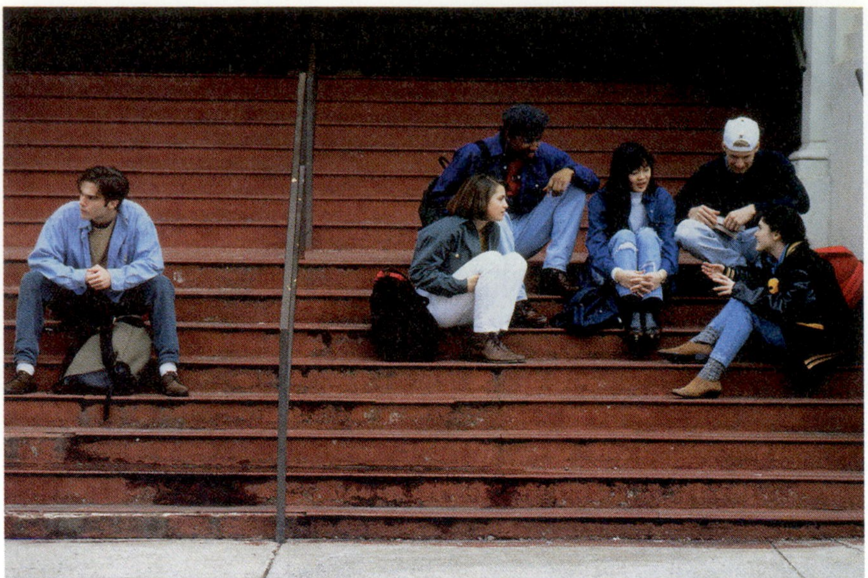

Unpopular adolescents fall into several categories. Controversial adolescents are liked by some and disliked by others; rejected adolescents are uniformly disliked; and neglected adolescents are neither liked nor disliked.

Although adolescents are particularly susceptible to peer pressure in social areas, they are more likely to be influenced by experienced adults when it comes to nonsocial matters such as choosing a career or solving a problem.

some adolescents are controversial; in contrast to *popular* adolescents, who are mostly liked, *controversial* adolescents are liked by some and disliked by others. Furthermore, there are *rejected* adolescents, who are uniformly disliked, and *neglected* adolescents, who are neither liked nor disliked. In most cases, however, popular and controversial adolescents tend to be similar in that their overall status is higher, while rejected and neglected adolescents share a generally lower status.

For instance, popular and controversial adolescents have more close friends, engage more frequently in activities with their peers, and disclose more about themselves to others than less popular students. They are also more involved in extracurricular school activities. In addition, they are well aware of their popularity, and they are less lonely than their less popular classmates (Franzoi, Davis, & Vasquez-Suson, 1994).

In contrast, the social world of rejected and neglected adolescents is considerably more negative. They have fewer friends, engage in social activities less frequently, and have less contact with the opposite sex. They see themselves—accurately, it turns out—as less popular, and they are more likely to feel lonely.

CONFORMITY: PEER PRESSURE IN ADOLESCENCE

Whenever Aldos Henry said he wanted to buy a particular brand of sneakers or a certain style of shirt, his parents complained that he was just giving in to peer pressure and told him to make up his own mind about things.

In arguing with Aldos, his parents were subscribing to a view of adolescence that is quite prevalent in U.S. society: that teenagers are highly susceptible to **peer pressure,** the influence of one's peers to conform to their behavior and attitudes. Were his parents correct?

The research suggests that it all depends. In some cases, adolescents *are* highly susceptible to the influence of their peers. For instance, when considering what to wear, whom to date, and what movies to see, adolescents are apt to follow the lead of their peers. On the other hand, when it comes to many nonsocial matters, such as choosing a career path or trying to solve a problem, they are more likely to turn to an experienced adult (Phelan, Yu, & Davidson, 1994).

In short, particularly in middle and late adolescence, teenagers turn to those they see as experts on a given dimension (Young & Ferguson, 1979). If they have social concerns, they turn to the people most likely to be experts—their peers. On the other hand, if the problem is one about which parents or other adults are most likely to have expertise, teenagers tend to turn to them for advice and are most susceptible to their opinions.

peer pressure *the influence of one's peers to conform to their behavior and attitudes*

Overall, then, it does not appear that susceptibility to peer pressure suddenly soars during adolescence. Instead, adolescence brings about a change in the people to whom an individual conforms. Whereas children conform fairly consistently to their parents during childhood, in adolescence conformity shifts to encompass the peer group.

Ultimately, however, adolescents conform less to both peers *and* adults as they develop increasing autonomy over their lives. As they grow in confidence and in the ability to make their own decisions, adolescents are more apt to remain independent and to reject pressures from others, no matter who those others are (Crockett & Crouter, 1995; Steinberg, 1993; Steinberg & Silverberg, 1986).

undersocialized delinquents *adolescent delinquents who are raised with little discipline or with harsh, uncaring parental supervision; they typically begin criminal activities at an early age*

socialized delinquents *adolescent delinquents who know and subscribe to the norms of society and who are fairly normal psychologically; they engage in petty crimes but do not continue lawbreaking into adulthood*

Juvenile Delinquency: The Crimes of Adolescence

Although the vast majority of them are law-abiding citizens, adolescents, along with young adults, are more likely to commit crimes than any other age group. Some of the reason for this state of affairs has to do with the definition of certain behaviors (such as drinking), which are illegal for adolescents but not for older individuals. But even when such crimes are disregarded, adolescents are disproportionately involved in violent crimes, such as murder, assaults, and rape, and property crimes, involving theft, robbery, and arson.

For example, almost 20 percent of serious violent crimes are committed by adolescents, either alone or in groups. Another 8 percent are committed by adolescents in conjunction with older offenders. Overall, a quarter of all serious violent crime involves an adolescent. Furthermore, the numbers are growing. Over the past decade, the arrest rate for violent crimes rose almost 60 percent among adolescents. Experts predict that if present trends continue, by the year 2010 the number of arrests of juveniles for violent crimes will more than double (Juvenile Justice Clearinghouse, 1995).

Why do adolescents become involved in criminal activity? Some offenders are known as **undersocialized delinquents,** adolescents who are raised with little discipline or with harsh, uncaring parental supervision. These children have never been appropriately socialized and simply have not learned standards of conduct to regulate their own behavior. Undersocialized delinquents typically begin criminal activities at an early age, well before the onset of adolescence.

Undersocialized delinquents share several characteristics. They tend to be relatively aggressive and violent fairly early in life, characteristics that lead to rejection by peers and academic failure. They also are more likely to have been diagnosed with attention deficit disorder as children and tend to be less intelligent than average (Patterson, DeBaryshe, & Ramsey, 1989).

Undersocialized delinquents often suffer from psychological difficulties, and as adults fit a psychological pattern called antisocial personality disorder. They are relatively unlikely to be successfully rehabilitated, and many undersocialized delinquents live on the margins of society throughout their lives (Farrington, 1991; Lewis et al., 1994; Rönkä & Pulkkinen, 1995; Tate, Reppucci, & Mulvey, 1995).

On the other hand, most adolescent offenders are socialized delinquents. **Socialized delinquents** know and subscribe to the norms of society; they are fairly normal psychologically. For them, transgressions committed during adolescence do not lead to a life of crime. Instead, most socialized delinquents pass through a period during adolescence when they engage in some petty crimes, but they do not continue lawbreaking into adulthood.

Socialized delinquents are typically highly influenced by their peers, and their delinquency often occurs in groups. In addition, some research suggests that parents of socialized delinquents supervise their children's behavior less closely than other parents (Dornbusch et al., 1985; Fletcher, Darling, Steinberg, & Dornbusch, 1995; Miller, 1958; Windle, 1994).

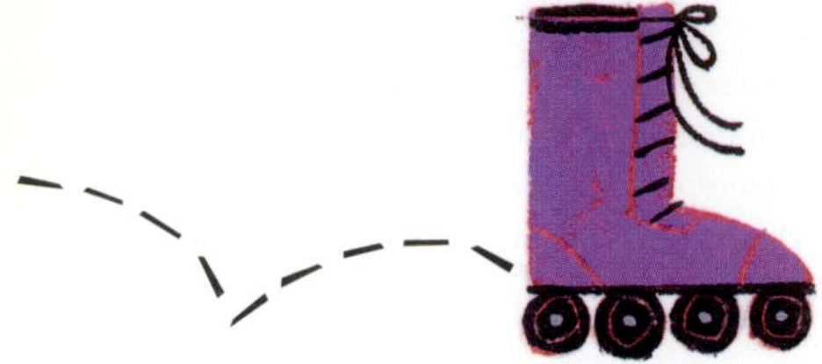

Review and Rethink

REVIEW

- The search for autonomy causes a sometimes painful readjustment in relations between teenagers and their parents, due partly to different definitions of appropriate and inappropriate behavior. However, the gender gap is actually less wide than is generally thought.
- Belonging becomes a significant issue in adolescence, with cliques and crowds serving as reference groups and offering a ready means of social comparison. Sex cleavage gradually diminishes, until boys and girls begin to pair off.
- Racial separation increases during adolescence, bolstered by socioeconomic status differences, different academic experiences, and mutually distrustful attitudes.
- Degrees of popularity in adolescence include popular, controversial, neglected, and rejected adolescents. More popular adolescents engage in more friendships, activities, and intergender relationships than less popular adolescents.
- Adolescents tend to conform to their peers, and to be susceptible to peer pressure, in areas in which they regard their peers as experts, and to conform to adults in areas of perceived adult expertise. In general, conformity to others decreases during adolescence.
- Adolescents are disproportionately involved in criminal activities, although most do not commit crimes. Juvenile delinquents can be categorized as undersocialized or socialized delinquents.

RETHINK

- In what ways do you think parents with the different parenting styles discussed in Chapter 9—authoritarian, permissive, and authoritative—tend to react to adolescents' attempts to establish autonomy?
- Why does there appear to be no real generation gap in most attitudes, despite adolescents' need to question authority?
- In what ways does membership in cliques or crowds constrain behavior? Do such groupings disappear in adulthood?
- What school policies do you think would be most effective in decreasing racial segregation?
- How do the findings about conformity and peer pressure reported in this chapter relate to adolescents' developing cognitive abilities?

DATING, SEXUAL BEHAVIOR, AND TEENAGE PREGNANCY

Night has eased into day, but it is all the same for Tori Michel, 17. Her 5-day-old baby, Caitlin, has been fussing for hours, though she seems finally to have settled into the pink-and-purple car seat on the living-room sofa. "She wore herself out," explains Tori, who lives in a two-bedroom duplex in this St. Louis suburb with her mother, Susan, an aide to handicapped adults. "I think she just had gas."

Motherhood was not in Tori's plans for her senior year at Fort Zumwalt South High School—not until she had a "one-night thing" with James, a 21-year-old she met through friends. She had been taking birth-control pills but says she stopped after breaking up with a long-term boyfriend. "Wrong answer," she now says ruefully.

> When she learned she was pregnant last January, Tori decided against having an abortion. "It just doesn't seem right," she says. Her mother, who divorced her husband Robert 2 years ago, supported her daughter's decision. James is no longer in the picture. . . . Tori cannot help but admit she's a bit shell-shocked. Finishing school, she insists, is her priority. "Ever since I've had Caitlin, I haven't felt like a teenager. I've felt like a mom," she says. "I think it happened too fast." (Gleick, Reed, & Schindehette, 1994, p. 40)

Three A.M. feedings, diaper changes, and visits to the pediatrician are not part of most people's vision of adolescence. Yet millions of teenagers become mothers, a problematic trend in the United States, with ramifications for every segment of society.

In the remainder of this chapter, we'll consider several aspects of adolescents' relationships with one another. Just as one thing sometimes leads to another in the real world, we'll first consider dating, then sexual behavior, and then adolescent pregnancy.

DATING: BOY MEETS GIRL IN THE 1990S

It took him almost a month, but Sylvester Chiu finally got up the courage to ask Jackie Durbin to go to the movies. It was hardly a surprise to Jackie, though: Sylvester had first told his friend Erik about his resolve to ask Jackie out, and Erik had told Jackie's friend Cynthia about Sylvester's plans. Cynthia, in turn, had told Jackie, who was primed to say "yes" when Sylvester finally did call.

Welcome to the complex world of dating, an important ritual of adolescence. By the time most girls are 12 or 13, and boys 13 or 14, they begin to engage in dating. By the age of 16, more than 90 percent of teenagers have had at least one date, and by the end of high school, some three quarters of adolescents have been steadily involved with someone (Dickenson, 1975; McCabe, 1984).

The Functions of Dating. Although on the surface dating may seem to be simply part of a pattern of courtship that can potentially lead to marriage, it actually serves other functions as well. For instance, dating is a means of learning how to establish intimacy with other individuals. Furthermore, it can provide entertainment and, depending on the status of the person one is dating, prestige. It can even be used in developing a sense of one's own identity (Sanderson & Cantor, 1995; Savin-Williams & Berndt, 1990; Skipper & Nass, 1966).

Just how well dating serves such functions, particularly the development of psychological intimacy, is an open question. What specialists in adolescence do know, however, is surprising: Dating in early and middle adolescence is not terribly successful at facilitating intimacy. On the contrary, dating is often a superficial activity in which the participants so rarely let down their guards that they never become truly close and never expose themselves emotionally to each other. Psychological intimacy may be lacking even when sexual activity is part of the relationship (Douvan & Adelson, 1966; Savin-Williams & Berndt, 1990).

True intimacy becomes more common during later adolescence. At that point, the dating relationship may be taken more seriously by both participants, and it may be seen as a means of selecting a mate and as a potential prelude to marriage.

Dating in Minority Groups. Cultural influences affect dating patterns among minority adolescents, particularly those whose parents have come to the United States from other countries. Minority parents may try to control their children's dating behavior in an effort to preserve the minority group's traditional values (Spencer & Dornbusch, 1990).

For example, Asian parents may be especially conservative in their attitudes and values, in part because they themselves may have had no experience of dating. (In many cases, the parents' marriage was arranged by others, and the entire concept of dating is unfamiliar.) They may insist that dating be conducted with chaperones, or not at all. As a consequence, they may find themselves involved in substantial conflict with their children (Sung, 1985).

masturbation *sexual self-stimulation*

SEXUAL RELATIONSHIPS: PERMISSIVENESS WITH AFFECTION

The maturation of the sexual organs during the start of adolescence opens a new range of possibilities in relations with others: sexuality. In fact, sexual behavior and thoughts are among the central concerns of adolescents. Almost all adolescents think about sex, and many think about it a good deal of the time (Coles & Stokes, 1985).

Masturbation. For most adolescents, their initiation into sexuality comes from **masturbation,** sexual self-stimulation. Almost half of all adolescent boys and a quarter of adolescent girls report that they have engaged in masturbation. The frequency of masturbation shows a sex difference: Male masturbation is most frequent in the early teens and then begins to decline, while females begin more slowly and reach a maximum later (Oliver & Hyde, 1993).

Although masturbation is widespread, it still may produce feelings of shame and guilt. There are several reasons for this. One is that adolescents may believe that masturbation signifies the inability to find a sexual partner—an erroneous assumption, since statistics show that three quarters of married men and 68 percent of married women report masturbating between 10 and 24 times a year (Hunt, 1974). Another reason is the legacy of shame remaining from misguided past views. For instance, nineteenth-century physicians and lay persons warned of horrible effects of masturbation, including "dyspepsia, spinal disease, headache, epilepsy, various kinds of fits . . . , impaired eyesight, palpitation of the heart, pain in the side and bleeding at the lungs, spasm of the heart, and sometimes sudden death" (Gregory, 1856). Suggested remedies included bandaging the genitals, covering them with a cage, tying the hands, male circumcision without anesthesia (so that it might better be remembered), and for girls, the administration of carbolic acid to the clitoris. One physician, J. W. Kellogg, believed that certain grains would be less likely to provoke sexual excitation—leading to his invention of corn flakes (Michael, Gagnon, Laumann, & Kolata, 1994).

The reality is different. Today, experts on sexual behavior view masturbation as a normal, healthy, and harmless activity (Leitenberg, Detzer, & Srebnik, 1993). In fact, some suggest that it provides a useful means of learning about one's own sexuality.

Sexual Intercourse. Although it may be preceded by many different types of sexual intimacy, including deep kissing, massaging, petting, and oral sex, sexual intercourse remains a major milestone in the perceptions of most adolescents. Consequently, the focus of researchers investigating sexual behavior has been on the act of intercourse.

The age at which adolescents first have sexual intercourse has been steadily declining over the last 50 years. Overall, around half of adolescents begin having intercourse between the ages of 15 and 18, and at least 80 percent have had sex before the age of 20 (Seidman & Rieder, 1994).

There are racial and gender differences in the timing of first intercourse (Leigh, Morrison, Trocki, & Temple, 1994). For instance, half of all African-American men have intercourse by the time they are 15, and half of all Hispanic men by the time they are around 16½. In comparison, it is not until age 17 that half of white males have had sexual intercourse. The pattern is a little different for women: Although half of black women have intercourse by the time they are around 17, half of white women and half of Hispanic women have intercourse by the time they are just about 18 (Michael et al., 1994; see Figure 15-7).

Clearly, sexual activities are taking place earlier during adolescence than they did in prior eras. This is in part a result of a change in societal norms governing sexual conduct.

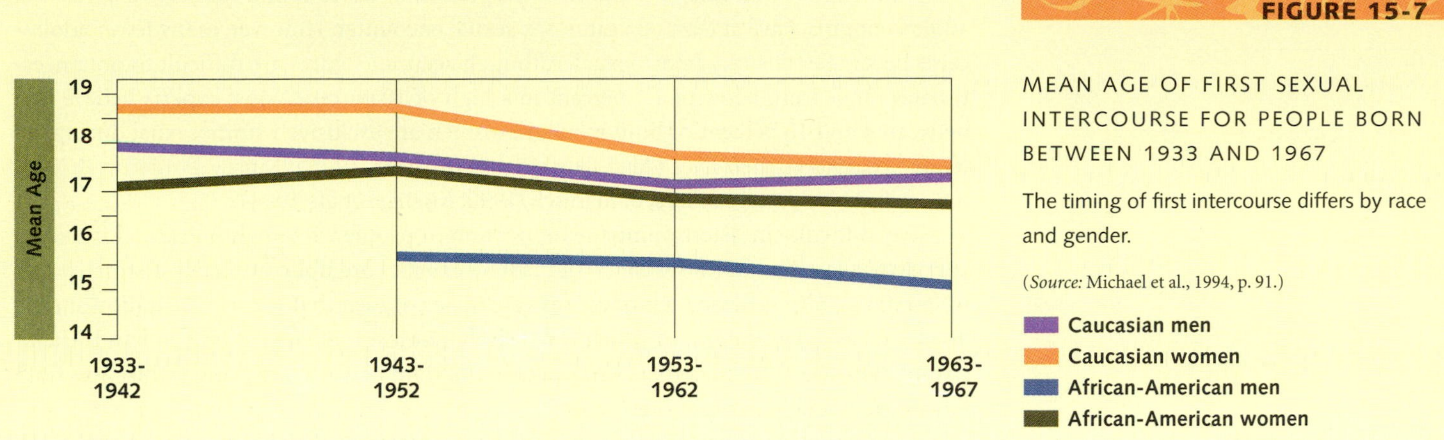

FIGURE 15-7

MEAN AGE OF FIRST SEXUAL INTERCOURSE FOR PEOPLE BORN BETWEEN 1933 AND 1967

The timing of first intercourse differs by race and gender.

(*Source:* Michael et al., 1994, p. 91.)

- Caucasian men
- Caucasian women
- African-American men
- African-American women

The prevailing norm several decades ago was the *double standard,* in which premarital sex was considered permissible for males but not for females. Women were told by society that "nice girls don't," while men heard that premarital sex was permissible—although they should be sure to marry virgins.

Today, however, the double standard has largely been supplanted by a new norm, called *permissiveness with affection.* According to this standard, premarital intercourse is viewed as permissible for both men and women if it occurs in the context of a long-term, committed, or loving relationship (Hyde, 1994; Reiss, 1960).

On the other hand, the demise of the double standard has not been complete. Attitudes toward sexual conduct are typically more lenient for males than for females. The nature of this difference extends across very different cultures. For instance, in Mexico, where there are strict standards against premarital sex, males are considerably more likely than females to have premarital sex (Johnson et al., 1992; Liskin, 1985; Spira, 1992).

Sexual Orientation: Heterosexuality and Homosexuality

When we consider adolescents' sexual development, the most frequent pattern is *heterosexuality,* sexual attraction and behavior directed to the other sex. Yet some teenagers do not follow this path. Instead, they experience *homosexual* feelings, sexual attraction to members of their own sex.

The stresses of adolescence are magnified for homosexuals, who often face societal prejudice. Eventually, however, most adolescents come to grips with their sexual orientation, as these students at a symposium exemplify.

At one time or another, around 20 to 25 percent of adolescent boys, and 10 percent of adolescent girls, have at least one same-sex sexual encounter. However, many fewer adolescents become exclusively homosexual. Although accurate figures are difficult to obtain, estimates range from a low of 1.1 percent to a high of 10 percent. Most experts believe that between 4 and 10 percent of both men and women are exclusively homosexual during extended periods of their lives (Alan Guttmacher Institute, 1993b; Kinsey, Pomeroy, & Martin, 1948; McWhirter, Sanders, & Reinisch, 1990; Michael et al., 1994).

The difficulty in determining the proportion of people who are homosexual is due, in part, to the fact that homosexuality and heterosexuality are not completely distinct sexual orientations. Alfred Kinsey, a pioneer sex researcher, argued that sexual orientation should be viewed as a continuum, in which "exclusively homosexual" was at one end and "exclusively heterosexual" at the other (Kinsey et al., 1948). In between are people who show both homosexual and heterosexual behavior.

The factors that induce people to develop as heterosexual or homosexual are not well understood. Increasing evidence suggests that genetic and biological factors may play an important role. For instance, evidence from studies of twins shows a higher joint incidence of homosexuality in identical twins than in nontwins. Other research finds that various structures of the brain are different in homosexuals and heterosexuals, and hormone production also seems to be linked to sexual orientation (Berenbaum & Snyder, 1995; Gladue, 1994; LeVay, 1993; Meyer-Bahlburg et al., 1995).

On the other hand, evidence of a biological cause is not yet conclusive, given that most findings are based on small samples (Byne & Parsons, 1994). Consequently, some researchers have suggested that family or peer environmental factors play a role. For example, Freud argued that homosexuality was the result of inappropriate identification with the opposite-sex parent (Freud, 1922/1959).

The difficulty with Freud's theoretical perspective and other, similar perspectives that followed his is that there simply is no evidence to suggest that any particular family dynamic or childrearing practice is consistently related to sexual orientation. Similarly, explanations based on learning theory, which suggest that homosexuality arises because of rewarding, pleasant homosexual experiences and unsatisfying heterosexual ones, do not appear to be the complete answer (Bell & Weinberg, 1978; Isay, 1990).

In short, there is no accepted explanation for why some adolescents develop a heterosexual orientation and others a homosexual orientation. Most experts believe that sexual orientation develops out of a complex interplay of genetic, physiological, and environmental factors (Gladue, 1994).

What is clear is that adolescents who find themselves attracted to members of the same sex face a difficult time (Anderson, 1994). U.S. society still harbors great ignorance and prejudice regarding homosexuality, persisting in the belief that people have a choice in the matter—which they don't. The result is that adolescents who find themselves to be homosexual are at greater risk for depression, and suicide rates are significantly higher for homosexual adolescents than heterosexual adolescents (Rotheram-Borus et al., 1995).

Ultimately, though, most adolescents come to grips with their sexual orientation. Once they are past adolescence, homosexuals have the same overall degree of mental and physical health as heterosexuals. Homosexuality is not considered a psychological disorder by any of the major psychological or medical associations, and all of them endorse efforts to reduce discrimination against homosexuals (Bersoff & Ogden, 1991; Herek, 1993; C. J. Patterson, 1994).

TEENAGE PREGNANCY: A PROBLEM OF EPIDEMIC PROPORTIONS

Every minute of the day, an adolescent in the United States gives birth. Every year, over 1 million women under the age of 20—one in every 10 teenage girls—become pregnant, and the pregnancy rate among teenage women aged 15 to 19 has increased 23 percent in the last 2 decades. Around half of all adolescent mothers are unmarried, and in some inner cities,

80 percent of teenagers who have babies are not married. Frequently, a mother must care for her child without the help of the father (Alan Guttmacher Institute, 1994; Stevens-Simon & White, 1991).

The results of an unintended pregnancy can be devastating to both mother and child. Without financial or emotional support, a mother may have to abandon her own education, and consequently she may be relegated to unskilled, poorly paying jobs for the rest of her life. In other cases, she may develop long-term dependency on welfare. An adolescent mother's physical and mental health may suffer as she faces unrelenting stress due to continual demands on her time (Ambuel, 1995; Baldwin, 1993; B. C. Miller, 1992; Prodromidis et al., 1994). (See the "Speaking of Development" box.)

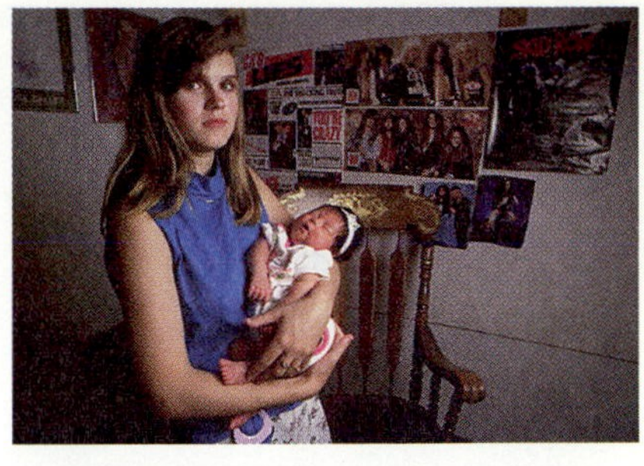

This 16-year-old mother and her child are representative of a major social problem: teenage pregnancy. Each year, 1 in 10 teenage girls becomes pregnant.

The children of teenage mothers also do not fare well when compared to children of older mothers. They are more likely to suffer from poor health and to show poorer school performance. Later, they are more likely to become teenage parents themselves, creating a cycle of pregnancy and poverty from which it is very difficult to extricate themselves (Carnegie Task Force, 1994; Furstenberg, Brooks-Gunn, & Morgan, 1987).

The severity of the problem of teenage pregnancies is peculiarly American. If we look at other industrialized countries, we find much lower rates of teenage pregnancy (Alan Guttmacher Institute, 1988; see Figure 15-8). Although it might be suspected that the higher rate of pregnancy in the United States is due to more frequent or earlier sexual activity, that is not the case. For instance, there is little difference among industrialized countries in the age at which adolescents first have sexual intercourse.

What does differ is the use of birth control. Teenage girls in the United States are much less likely to use contraception than teenagers in other countries. And even when they do use birth control, teenagers in the United States are less likely to use effective methods (Musick, 1993).

However, ineffective birth control is only part of the answer. An additional factor is that, despite increasing rates of premarital sexual behavior, people in the United States remain basically intolerant of premarital sex, and they are unwilling to provide the type of sex education that might reduce the rate of teenage pregnancies.

Consequently, sex education is considerably more limited in the United States than in other industrialized countries. And because sex remains a contentious topic, with many political ramifications, effective sex education programs are difficult to develop and implement. (For a consideration of the components of successful sex education programs, see the "Directions in Development" feature.)

FIGURE 15-8

PREGNANCY RATES FOR FEMALES AGED 15 TO 19 IN VARIOUS INDUSTRIALIZED COUNTRIES

(*Source:* Alan Guttmacher Institute, 1988.)

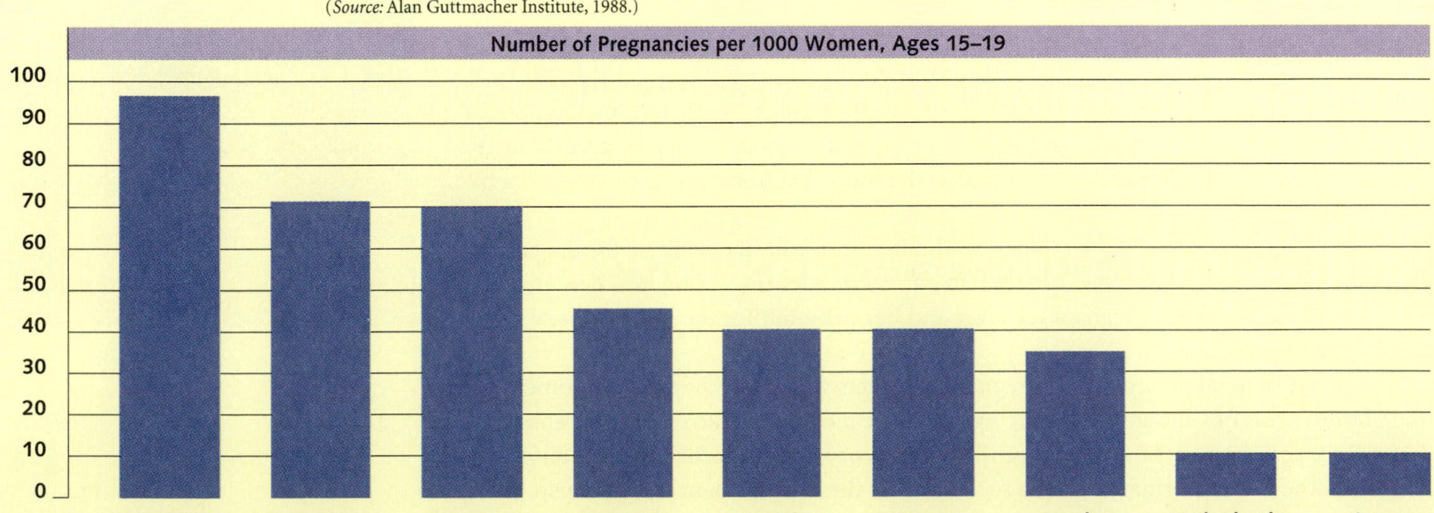

Directions in Development

Preventing Adolescent Pregnancies: Sex Education Programs that Work

According to surveys, almost 90 percent of Americans agree that all children should have sex education. Just what that sex education should consist of, however, is a question that elicits far less agreement.

Some proponents of sex education hold that the only appropriate message is 100 percent abstinence. However, there is little scientific evidence that such a message is effective: When carefully evaluated, the efficacy of programs that teach only abstinence is not conclusively supported (American Psychological Association Public Policy Office, 1996). Particularly for adolescents who are already sexually active, abstinence is not a compelling message.

However, several types of sex education programs are effective. According to recent analyses, delays of 2 or more years in first sexual intercourse have been brought about in junior- and senior-high-school students involved in such programs, compared with stu-

Speaking of Development

Patricia Canessa, Pregnancy Counselor

Born: 1948

Education: University of Chile, B.S. in biology
University of Colombia, M.A. in psychology
Northwestern University, M.A. in psychology
University of Rome, Ph.D. in family therapy

Position: Department director of the Arts of Living Institute

Home: Chicago, Illinois

When a young teenage girl faces pregnancy, it can be a tough world, but for the past 24 years the Arts of Living Institute has helped hundreds of pregnant teenagers, aged 14 to 19, find new lives, raise healthy children, and make the transition from teenager to mother a bit more easily.

Department director Patricia Canessa, who has been with the Institute for the past 10 years, notes that its success rate is attributable to a comprehensive program designed not only for the health of the pregnant teenager and her baby, but for the new mother's social development as well.

Eighty-five to 90 percent of the pregnant teenagers who reach the Institute come from the poorest areas of Chicago and are living below the poverty line, according to Canessa.

"Once the girl comes in with a parent, guardian, or relative who lives in the household, we gather the basic information, and a social worker then performs an extensive psychosocial assessment," Canessa explains.

dents who were not in the programs. Furthermore, such programs reduced unprotected sexual intercourse by 40 percent among adolescents who were already sexually active (Ubell, 1995).

Effective programs make use of the basic concepts of learning theory, including reinforcement and modeling. They teach specific social skills that permit adolescents to say "no" effectively and to anticipate the pressures that they may confront in sexual situations. For instance, students are taught the following things:

- That they will benefit—socially, physically, economically—from avoiding disease and averting unwanted pregnancy.
- How to delay first intercourse. Students learn—and practice, through role-playing with classmates—how to anticipate and avert sexual advances deftly and even pleasantly.
- How to get and use protection—usually condoms—if they are already sexually active.
- How to develop, through practice, confidence that the skills being learned will actually work in real-life situations (Ubell, 1995, p. 19–20).

Effective programs use exercises and games that promote student involvement. For instance, they employ role-playing and involve homework in which teenagers and their parents discuss sex. They also address the realities of caring for a baby. Teenagers often have a

"We need . . . to be aware of potential conditions that might affect the pregnancy, such as a sexually transmitted diesease or a urinary tract infection—two major contributors to low birth weight."

"The target of the program is comprehensive: to change a pattern of dysfunctional behaviors that cross generations, to break a cycle of behavior."

"During the psychosocial assessment we explain the importance of developing the ability to do three things: establish social interactions; develop cognitively through academic accomplishments; and succeed behaviorally in a structured situation such as the school, the family, or the community."

The psychosocial assessment also covers the current living situation, a history of the family, and the precipitating factors that led to the current pregnancy, as perceived by the teenager. A health assessment follows the psychosocial assessment.

"We need to know what the girl has been doing for prenatal care and to be aware of potential conditions that might affect the pregnancy, such as a sexually transmitted disease or a urinary tract infection—two major contributors to low birth weight," Canessa adds.

The teenager's reproductive history and a family health history are also taken. "We follow this with a brief parenting evaluation in which we stress the importance of the father or boyfriend and assess the role he will play in prenatal care, delivery, and parenting. The father can be interviewed either alone or with the girl," Canessa says. "We look at his educational level and his plans in terms of vocation, social development, and engagement in coparenting activities."

Efforts are also made to reintegrate the girl into school. "The target of the program is comprehensive: to change a pattern of dysfunctional behaviors that cross generations, to break a cycle of behavior," says Canessa. "In working with the families, we try to change the mother-daughter relationship so that the daughter-baby relationship is changed as well."

romanticized view of what childrearing is all about. Exercises designed to make adolescents truly understand single parenthood drive home the difficulties involved.

No sex education program can be 100 percent effective. Still, researchers are making advances in producing programs that are increasingly effective. However, such programs are highly sensitive to political demands and pressures, and their implementation depends in part on the nation's political and social climate (Christopher, 1995).

Although adolescent pregnancy and parenthood are difficult problems, some teenagers successfully break the poverty-and-pregnancy cycle. Two key factors for teenage mothers are completing high school and postponing future births. Social programs that help young mothers complete their education and that support them in other basic ways are critically important (Buchholz & Korn-Bursztyn, 1993; Furstenberg et al., 1987; Rauch-Elnekave, 1994).

Review and Rethink

REVIEW

- The functions of dating in adolescence include intimacy, entertainment, and prestige. The ability to achieve intimacy develops gradually during the period.
- Masturbation, once viewed very negatively, is now generally regarded as a normal and harmless practice that continues into adulthood.
- Sexual intercourse is a major milestone that most people reach during adolescence. The age of first intercourse reflects cultural differences and has been declining over the last 50 years.
- Sexual orientation, which is most accurately viewed as a continuum rather than categorically, develops as the result of a complex combination of factors.
- Teenage pregnancy is a major problem in the United States, with negative consequences for adolescent mothers and their children. Effective sex education can reduce the incidence of teenage pregnancy.

RETHINK

- What factors in early and middle adolescence work against the achievement of true intimacy in dating?
- Do you think old social attitudes toward masturbation decreased its incidence? Are modern attitudes toward the practice likely to cause an increase? Why or why not?
- Why is the age of first intercourse declining? What factors contribute to a double standard toward sex for males and females?
- How might the interplay of genetic, physiological, and environmental factors influence sexual orientation?
- Are social programs that help pregnant teenagers to complete high school and to postpone future pregnancies beneficial? Do they serve only pregnant teenagers, or are the benefits broader?

How does the development of self-concept, self-esteem, and identity proceed during adolescence?

1. During adolescence, self-concept differentiates to encompass others' views as well as one's own. Adolescents become more perceptive as their views of themselves grow more organized and coherent, include multiple aspects simultaneously, and regard personal traits more abstractly than before. Sometimes this differentiation can cause confusion as different situations elicit behaviors that reflect a complex, rather than a simple, definition of the self.
2. The differentiation of self-concept permits a similar differentiation in self-esteem. Adolescents are able to evaluate particular aspects of themselves differently. Self-esteem can be affected not only by personal factors, but by gender, socioeconomic status, and ethnicity as well.
3. According to Erik Erikson, adolescents are in the identity-versus-identity-confusion stage, seeking to discover their individuality and identity. Faced with societal pressures to make important life decisions, adolescents may experience confusion and may sometimes exhibit dysfunctional reactions. They may come to rely for help and information more on friends and peers than on adults, and some adolescents may undertake a psychological moratorium to explore various roles and possibilities.
4. In an expansion of Erikson's work, James Marcia finds four identity statuses that are determined by the presence or absence of crisis and commitment. The four stages are identity achievement, identity foreclosure, identity diffusion, and moratorium. People may fall into one category during adolescence, and later in life may reassess their choices and move into a different category.

What dangers do adolescents face as they deal with the stresses of adolescence?

5. Many adolescents have feelings of sadness and hopelessness, and some experience major depression, a psychological disorder with enduring effects. Biological, environmental, and social factors contribute to depression; and there are gender, ethnic, and racial differences in the likelihood of its occurrence. The fact that the incidence of depression is higher among girls than boys may be due to confusing societal expectations for girls and differences in the ways boys and girls react to stress.
6. The rate of adolescent suicide is rising, with suicide now the third most common cause of death in the 15- to 24-year-old bracket. The reasons for this increase are not fully understood, but adolescent stresses and family situations are being examined closely for causal links.
7. Persons who come into contact with adolescents should be aware of the warning signs of suicide, including talk about suicide, school problems, making a will or communicating long-term plans for possessions or pets, depression, eating problems, and dramatic changes in behavior. When suicide is suspected, the proper steps include listening and being actively supportive, finding help, removing hazards, and maintaining close contact.

How does the quality of relationships with family and peers change during adolescence?

8. Adolescents' quest for autonomy often brings confusion and tension to their relationships with their parents, as parents and children work out their changing roles and

strike a new balance of power. In part, the tension can be attributed to differences in parents' and children's definitions of appropriate and inappropriate behavior, but the actual "generation gap" between parents' and teenagers' attitudes is usually small.

9. Peers are important during adolescence because they provide a means of social comparison and offer reference groups against which to judge social success. Relationships among adolescents are characterized by the need to belong, whether to a clique or a crowd. Group membership brings peer acceptance but can limit behavior by imposing stereotypical expectations.

What are gender, race, and ethnic relations like in adolescence?

10. The strict sex cleavage that characterizes gender relations in middle childhood and early adolescence diminishes at puberty. Boys and girls begin to spend time together in groups and, toward the end of adolescence, to pair off.

11. In general, segregation between people of different races and ethnicities increases in middle and late adolescence, even in schools with a diverse student body. Racial and ethnic separation may be due not only to race per se, but also to socioeconomic status, different academic achievement and class assignments, and mutually distrustful attitudes. A very high degree of consistent interaction between adolescents of different races can help alleviate segregation.

What does it mean to be popular and unpopular in adolescence, and how do adolescents respond to peer pressure?

12. Degrees of popularity during adolescence include popular and controversial adolescents (on the high end of popularity) and neglected and rejected adolescents (on the low end). Popular adolescents enjoy a greater number of friendships, activities, and relationships with the opposite sex than their less popular peers.

13. The phenomenon of peer pressure during adolescence is not as simple as often thought. In actuality, adolescents rely on and conform to their peers in areas where they regard their peers as experts, and they rely on and conform to adults in areas of adult expertise. As adolescents grow in confidence, their conformity to both peers and adults declines.

14. Although most do not commit crimes, adolescents are disproportionately involved in criminal activities. Juvenile delinquents can be categorized as undersocialized or socialized delinquents. Undersocialized delinquents are raised with little discipline or with harsh or uncaring parental supervision and begin criminal activity prior to adolescence. In contrast, socialized delinquents know and subscribe to the norms of society and are fairly normal psychologically. They are less likely to be involved in crime beyond adolescence.

What are the functions and characteristics of dating during adolescence?

15. During adolescence, dating has several functions, serving as a way for adolescents to establish intimacy, as a form of entertainment, and even as a means of achieving social prestige.

16. The development of psychological intimacy is difficult at first, due to early adolescents' unwillingness to expose themselves psychologically. True intimacy comes later, as adolescents mature, gain confidence, and take relationships more seriously.

How does sexuality develop in the adolescent years?

17. For most adolescents, masturbation serves as their initiation into sexuality. Past views of masturbation have changed, and today this widespread practice is generally regarded as normal and harmless.

18. Sexual intercourse, which generally begins in the teens, is regarded as a major milestone. The age of first intercourse has declined over the past 50 years, as the double standard that restricted premarital sex exclusively to men and "bad girls" has faded and as the norm of permissiveness with affection has gained ground.

19. Most people's sexual orientation is largely or entirely heterosexual, with between 4 and 10 percent being mostly or exclusively homosexual. Sexual orientation, which should probably be viewed as a continuum rather than as discrete categories, apparently develops out of a complex interplay of genetic, physiological, and environmental factors. Because they face societal disapproval, homosexual adolescents are at greater risk for depression and suicide than heterosexual adolescents.

Why is teenage pregnancy a particular problem in the United States, and what can be done about it?

20. Pregnancy among teenagers is reaching epidemic proportions in the United States, with about 10 percent of girls under age 20 becoming pregnant each year. Adolescent childbirth can have highly negative effects for mother and child. The incidence of both contraception and sex education is comparatively low in the United States, which contributes to the high rate of adolescent pregnancy.

21. Effective sex education holds out the promise of decreasing the incidence of teenage pregnancy. Effective sex education involves more than simple advocacy of abstinence; it also teaches the benefits of avoiding unwanted pregnancies, practical methods of delaying first intercourse and averting sexual advances, and ways to get and use protection.

Key Terms and Concepts

identity-versus-identity-confusion stage (p. 478)
identity achievement (p. 480)
identity foreclosure (p. 480)
identity diffusion (p. 480)
moratorium (p. 481)
cluster suicide (p. 484)
autonomy (p. 487)
generation gap (p. 487)
reference groups (p. 490)
cliques (p. 490)
crowds (p. 490)
sex cleavage (p. 491)
peer pressure (p. 494)
undersocialized delinquents (p. 495)
socialized delinquents (p. 495)
masturbation (p. 498)

Glossary

abstract modeling the process in which modeling paves the way for the development of more general rules and principles of behavior (Ch. 9)

acceleration special programs that allow gifted students to move ahead at their own pace, even if this means skipping to higher grade levels (Ch. 11)

accommodation changes in existing ways of thinking that occur in response to encounters with new stimuli or events (Ch. 1, 5)

acquired immunodeficiency syndrome (AIDS) a sexually transmitted disease, produced by the HIV virus, that has no cure and ultimately causes death (Ch. 13)

active genotype-environment effects situations in which children focus on those aspects of their environment that are most congruent with their genetically determined abilities (Ch. 2)

addictive drugs drugs that produce a biological or psychological dependence in users, leading to increasingly powerful cravings for them (Ch. 13)

adolescence the developmental stage that lies between childhood and adulthood (Ch. 13)

adolescent egocentrism a state of self-absorption in which the world is viewed from one's own point of view (Ch. 14)

adolescent growth spurt a period of very rapid growth in height and weight during adolescence (Ch. 13)

agentic professions occupations associated with getting things accomplished (Ch. 14)

age of viability the point at which an infant can survive a premature birth (Ch. 3)

aggression intentional injury or harm to another person (Ch. 9)

Ainsworth Strange Situation a sequence of staged episodes that illustrate the strength of attachment between a child and (typically) his or her mother (Ch. 6)

alcoholics people who have learned to depend on alcohol and are unable to control their drinking (Ch. 13)

ambivalent children children who display a combination of positive and negative reactions to their mothers; they show great distress when the mother leaves, but upon her return they may simultaneously seek close contact but also hit and kick her; about 12 percent of children fall into the category of ambivalent (Ch. 6)

amniocentesis the process of identifying genetic defects by examining a small sample of fetal cells drawn by a needle inserted into the amniotic fluid surrounding the unborn fetus (Ch. 2)

androgynous a state in which gender roles encompass characteristics thought typical of both sexes (Ch. 9)

anorexia nervosa a severe eating disorder (primarily afflicting women age 12 to 40) in which individuals refuse to eat, while denying that their behavior and appearance, which may become skeletonlike, are out of the ordinary (Ch. 13)

anoxia a restriction of oxygen to the baby, lasting a few minutes, during the birth process, which can produce brain damage (Ch. 3)

Apgar scale a standard measurement system that looks for a variety of indications of good health in newborns (Ch. 3)

artificial insemination a process of fertilization in which a man's sperm is placed directly into a woman's vagina by a physician (Ch. 2)

assimilation the process in which people understand an experience in terms of their current stage of cognitive development and way of thinking (Ch. 1, 5)

associative play play in which two or more children actually interact with one another by sharing or borrowing toys or materials, although they do not do the same thing (Ch. 9)

asthma a chronic condition characterized by periodic attacks of wheezing, coughing, and shortness of breath (Ch. 10)

attachment the positive emotional bond that develops between a child and a particular individual (Ch. 6)

attention-deficit hyperactivity disorder (ADHD) a learning disability marked by inattention, impulsiveness, a low tolerance for frustration, and a great deal of inappropriate activity (Ch. 10)

attributions understandings of the causes behind someone's behavior (Ch. 11)

auditory impairment a special need that involves the loss of hearing or some aspect of hearing (Ch. 10)

authoritarian parents parents who are controlling, punitive, rigid, and cold; their word is law, and they value strict, unquestioning obedience from their children and do not tolerate expressions of disagreement (Ch. 9)

authoritative parents parents who are firm, setting clear and consistent limits, but try to reason with their children, giving explanations for why they should behave in a particular way (Ch. 9)

autobiographical memory memory of particular events from one's own life (Ch. 8)

autonomy independence and a sense of control over one's life (Ch. 15)

autonomy-versus-shame-and-doubt stage the period during which toddlers (ages 18 months to 3 years) develop independence and autonomy if exploration and freedom are encouraged or shame and self-doubt if they are restricted and overprotected (Ch. 6)

avoidant children children who do not seek proximity to the mother; after the mother has left they seem to avoid her when she returns as if they are angered by her behavior; 20 percent of children fall into this category (Ch. 6)

babbling making speechlike but meaningless sounds (Ch. 5)

Bayley Scales of Infant Development a measure that evaluates an infant's development from 2 to 30 months (Ch. 5)

behavior modification a formal technique for promoting the frequency of desirable behaviors and decreasing the incidence of unwanted ones (Ch. 1)

behavioral genetics the study of the effects of heredity on behavior (Ch. 2)

behavioral perspective the approach that suggests that the keys to understanding development are observable behavior and outside stimuli in the environment (Ch. 1)

bicultural identity the maintenance of one's original cultural identity while becoming integrated into the dominant culture (Ch. 11)

bilingualism the use of more than one language (Ch. 11)

blended families remarried couples who have at least one stepchild living with them (Ch. 12)

bonding close physical and emotional contact between parent and child during the period immediately following birth, argued by some to affect later relationship strength (Ch. 3)

Brazelton Neonatal Behavioral Assessment Scale (NBAS) a measure designed to determine infants' neurological and behavioral responses to their environment (Ch. 4)

bulimia an eating disorder that primarily afflicts adolescent girls and young women and is characterized by binges on large quantities of food, followed by purges of the food through vomiting or the use of laxatives (Ch. 13)

case studies extensive, in-depth interviews with a particular individual or small group of individuals (Ch. 1)

centration the process of concentrating on one limited aspect of a stimulus and ignoring other aspects (Ch. 8)

cephalocaudal principle the principle that growth follows a pattern that begins with head and upper body parts and then proceeds to the rest of the body (Ch. 4)

cerebral cortex the upper layer of the brain (Ch. 4)

cesarean delivery a birth in which the baby is surgically removed from the uterus, rather than traveling through the birth canal (Ch. 3)

child abuse the physical or psychological maltreatment or neglect of children (Ch. 7)

child development the field that involves the scientific study of the patterns of growth, change, and stability that occur from conception through adolescence (Ch. 1)

child neglect neglect in which parents ignore their children or act emotionally unresponsive to them (Ch. 7)

chlamydia the most common sexually transmitted disease, caused by a parasite (Ch. 13)

chorionic villus sampling (CVS) a test used to find genetic defects that involves taking samples of hairlike material that surrounds the embryo (Ch. 2)

chromosomes rod-shaped portions of DNA that are organized in 23 pairs (Ch. 2)

chronological (physical) age the actual age of the person taking the intelligence test (Ch. 11)

circular reaction an activity that permits the construction of cognitive schemes through the repetition of a chance motor event (Ch. 5)

classical conditioning a type of learning in which an organism responds in a particular way to a neutral stimulus that normally does not bring about that type of response (Ch. 1, 5)

cliques groups of from 2 to 12 people whose members have frequent social interactions with one another (Ch. 15)

cluster suicide a situation in which one suicide leads to attempts by others to kill themselves (Ch. 15)

cognitive development development involving the ways that growth and change in intellectual capabilities influence a person's behavior (Ch. 1)

cognitive perspective the approach that focuses on the processes that allow people to know, understand, and think about the world (Ch. 1)

cohort a group of people born at around the same time in the same place (Ch. 1)

collectivistic orientation a philosophy that promotes the notion of interdependence (Ch. 9)

communal professions occupations associated with relationships (Ch. 14)

concrete operational stage the period of cognitive development between 7 and 12 years of age, which is characterized by the active, and appropriate, use of logic (Ch. 11)

conservation the knowledge that quantity is unrelated to the arrangement and physical appearance of objects (Ch. 8)

constructive play play in which children manipulate objects to produce or build something (Ch. 9)

continuous change gradual development in which achievements at one level build on those of previous levels (Ch. 1)

control group the group that receives either no treatment or alternative treatment (Ch. 1)

cooperative play play in which children genuinely interact with one another, taking turns, playing games, or devising contests (Ch. 9)

coping the effort to control, reduce, or learn to tolerate the threats that lead to stress (Ch. 13)

coregulation a transitional stage during middle childhood in which children and parents jointly control the children's behavior (Ch. 12)

corpus callosum a bundle of fibers that connects the hemispheres of the brain (Ch. 7)

correlational research research that seeks to identify whether an association or relationship between two factors exists (Ch. 1)

critical period a specific time during development when a particular event has its greatest consequences (Ch. 1)

cross-modal transference the ability to identify a stimulus that has previously been experienced through only one sense by using another sense (Ch. 5)

cross-sectional research research in which people of different ages are compared at the same point in time (Ch. 1)

cross-sequential studies the process by which researchers examine a number of different age groups over several points in time (Ch. 1)

crowds larger groups than cliques, composed of individuals who share particular characteristics but who may not interact with one another (Ch. 15)

crystallized intelligence the store of information, skills, and strategies that people have acquired through education and prior experiences and through their previous use of fluid intelligence (Ch. 11)

cultural assimilation model the model that fostered the view of American society as the proverbial melting pot (Ch. 11)

cycle-of-violence hypothesis the theory that the abuse and neglect that children suffer predispose them as adults to abuse and neglect their own children (Ch. 7)

day-care centers places that typically provide care for children all day, while their parents are at work (Ch. 8)

decentering the ability to take multiple aspects of a situation into account (Ch. 11)

deferred imitation an act in which a person who is no longer present is imitated later by children after they have witnessed the person's actions (Ch. 5)

dependent variable the variable that is measured in an experiment and is expected to change as a result of the experimental manipulation (Ch. 1)

developmentally appropriate educational practice education that is based on both typical development and the unique characteristics of a given child (Ch. 8)

developmental quotient an overall developmental score that relates to performance in four domains: motor skills, language use, adaptive behavior, and personal-social (Ch. 5)

differential emotions theory the theory that emotional expressions not only reflect emotional experiences, but also help in the regulation of emotion itself (Ch. 6)

difficult babies babies who have negative moods and are slow to adapt to new situations; when confronted with a new situation, they tend to withdraw; about 10 percent of all babies belong in this category (Ch. 6)

discontinuous change development that occurs in distinct steps or stages, with each stage bringing about behavior that is assumed to be qualitatively different from behavior at earlier stages (Ch. 1)

disorganized-disoriented children children who show inconsistent, often contradictory behavior, such as approaching the mother when she returns but not looking at her; they may be the least securely attached children of all (Ch. 6)

dizygotic twins twins who are produced when two separate ova are fertilized by two separate sperm at roughly the same time (Ch. 2)

DNA (deoxyribonucleic acid) the substance that genes are composed of that determines the nature of every cell in the body and how it will function (Ch. 2)

dominance hierarchy rankings that represent the relative social power of those in a group (Ch. 12)

dominant trait the one trait that is expressed when two competing traits are present (Ch. 2)

Down syndrome a disorder produced by the presence of an extra chromosome on the 21st pair; once referred to as mongolism (Ch. 2)

easy babies babies who have a positive disposition; their body functions operate regularly, and they are adaptable; about 40 percent of all babies are in this category (Ch. 6)

ecological approach the perspective suggesting that different levels of the environment simultaneously influence individuals (Ch. 1)

ego according to Freud, the part of personality that is rational and reasonable (Ch. 1)

egocentric thought thinking that does not take into account the viewpoints of others (Ch. 8)

embryonic stage the period from 2 to 8 weeks following fertilization during which significant growth occurs in the major organs and body systems (Ch. 2)

empathy an emotional response that corresponds to the feelings of another person (Ch. 6, 9)

enrichment an approach through which students are kept at grade level but are enrolled in special programs and given individual activities to allow greater depth of study on a given topic (Ch. 11)

enuresis a lack of bladder control past the age when most children are toilet trained (Ch. 7)

episiotomy an incision sometimes made to increase the size of the opening of the vagina to allow the baby to pass (Ch. 3)

Erikson's theory of psycholosocial development the theory that considers how individuals come to understand themselves and the meaning of others'—and their own—behavior (Ch. 6)

evocative genotype-environment effects situations in which a child's genes elicit a particular type of environment (Ch. 2)

experiment a process in which an investigator, called an experimenter, devises two different experiences for subjects or participants (Ch. 1)

experimental research research designed to discover causal relationships between various factors (Ch. 1)

fantasy period according to Ginzberg, the period when career choices are made, and discarded, without regard to skills, abilities, or available job opportunities (Ch. 14)

fast mapping the process in which new words are associated with their meaning after only a brief encounter (Ch. 8)

fertilization the process by which a sperm and an ovum—the male and female gametes, respectively—join to form a single new cell (Ch. 2)

fetal alcohol syndrome (FAS) a disorder caused by the pregnant mother consuming substantial quantities of alcohol during pregnancy, potentially resulting in mental retardation and delayed growth in the child (Ch. 2)

fetal monitors devices that measure the baby's heartbeat during labor (Ch. 3)

fetal stage the stage that begins at about 8 weeks after conception and continues until birth (Ch. 2)

fetus a developing child, from 8 weeks after conception until birth (Ch. 2)

field study a research investigation carried out in a naturally occurring setting (Ch. 1)

fixation behavior reflecting an earlier stage of development (Ch. 1)

fluid intelligence the ability to deal with new problems and situations (Ch. 11)

formal operational stage the stage of cognitive development at which people develop the ability to think abstractly (Ch. 14)

functional play play that involves simple, repetitive activities typical of 3-year-olds (Ch. 9)

gametes the sex cells from the mother and father that form a new cell at conception (Ch. 2)

gender the sense of being male or female (Ch. 6)

gender constancy the belief that people are permanently males or females, depending on fixed, unchangeable biological factors (Ch. 9)

gender identity the perception of oneself as male or female (Ch. 9)

gender schema a cognitive framework that organizes information relevant to gender (Ch. 9)

generation gap a divide between parents and children in attitudes, values, aspirations, and worldviews (Ch. 15)

genes the basic unit of genetic information (Ch. 2)

genetic counseling the discipline that focuses on helping people deal with issues relating to inherited disorders (Ch. 2)

genital herpes a common sexually transmitted disease which is a virus and not unlike cold sores that sometimes appear around the mouth (Ch. 13)

genotype the underlying combination of genetic material present (but not outwardly visible) in an organism (Ch. 2)

germinal stage the first—and shortest—stage of the prenatal period which takes place during the first 2 weeks following conception (Ch. 2)

gifted and talented children who show evidence of high performance capability in intellectual, creative, or artistic areas; in leadership capacity; or in specific academic fields (Ch. 11)

goal-directed behavior behavior in which several schemes are combined and coordinated to generate a single act to solve a problem (Ch. 5)

goodness of fit the notion that children's long-term adjustment is dependent on the degree of match between their temperament and the nature and demands of the environment in which they are being raised (Ch. 6)

grammar the system of rules that determine how our thoughts can be expressed (Ch. 8)

habituation the decrease in the response to a stimulus that occurs after repeated presentations of the same stimulus (Ch. 5)

handedness a clear preference for the use of one hand over the other (Ch. 7)

Head Start a program begun in the United States in the 1960s, designed to serve the "whole child" and promote future academic success (Ch. 8)

heteronomous morality the stage of moral development in which rules are seen as unchangeable and never varying (Ch. 9)

heterozygous inheriting different forms of a gene from parents for a given trait (Ch. 2)

holophrases one-word utterances that depend on the particular context in which they are used to determine meaning (Ch. 5)

homozygous inheriting similar genes from parents for a given trait (Ch. 2)

hypothesis a prediction stated in a way that permits it to be tested (Ch. 1)

id according to Freud, the raw, unorganized, inborn part of personality that is present at birth (Ch. 1)

identification the process in which children attempt to be similar to their same-sex parent, incorporating the parent's attitudes and values (Ch. 9)

identity achievement the particular identity to which teenagers commit following a period of crisis during which they consider various alternatives (Ch. 15)

identity diffusion the category in which adolescents consider various identity alternatives but never commit to one, or never even consider identity options in any conscious way (Ch. 15)

identity foreclosure the state of adolescents who prematurely commit to an identity without adequately exploring alternatives (Ch. 15)

identity-versus-identity-confusion stage the period during which teenagers seek to determine what is unique and distinctive about themselves (Ch. 15)

imaginary audience fictitious observers who pay as much attention to adolescents' behavior as adolescents do themselves (Ch. 14)

imminent justice the notion that rules that are broken earn immediate punishment (Ch. 9)

independent variable the variable that is manipulated in the experiment by researchers (Ch. 1)

individualistic orientation a philosophy that emphasizes personal identity and the uniqueness of the individual (Ch. 9)

industry-versus-inferiority stage the period from age 6 to 12 characterized by a focus on efforts to attain competence in meeting the challenges presented by parents, peers, school, clubs and groups, and the other complexities of the modern world (Ch. 12)

infant mortality death within the first year of life (Ch. 3)

infantile amnesia the lack of memory for experiences that occurred prior to 3 years of age (Ch. 5)

infertility the inability to conceive after 12 to 18 months of trying to become pregnant (Ch. 2)

information-processing approaches approaches to cognitive development that seek to identify the ways individuals take in, use, and store information (Ch. 1, 5)

initiative-versus-guilt stage the period during which children age 3 to 6 years experience conflict between independence of action and the sometimes negative results of that action (Ch. 9)

intelligence the capacity to understand the world, think with rationality, and use resources effectively when faced with challenges (Ch. 11)

intelligence quotient (IQ) a score that takes into account a person's mental *and* chronological ages (Ch. 11)

intuitive thought thinking that reflects preschoolers' use of primitive reasoning and their avid acquisition of knowledge about the world (Ch. 8)

in vitro fertilization (IVF) a procedure in which a woman's ova are removed from her ovaries, and a man's sperm are used to fertilize the ova in a laboratory (Ch. 2)

Kaufman Assessment Battery for Children (K-ABC) a children's intelligence test which measures the ability to integrate different kinds of stimuli simultaneously and to use step-by-step thinking; it permits unusual flexibility in its administration (Ch. 11)

Klinefelter's syndrome a disorder resulting from the presence of an extra X chromosome that produces underdeveloped genitals, extreme height, and enlarged breasts (Ch. 2)

kwashiorkor a disease in which a child's stomach, limbs, and face swell with water (Ch. 4)

laboratory study a research investigation conducted in a controlled setting explicitly designed to hold events constant (Ch. 1)

language the systematic, meaningful arrangement of symbols, which provides the basis for communication (Ch. 5)

language-acquisition device (LAD) a neural system of the brain hypothesized to permit understanding of language structure and provide strategies for learning the particular characteristics of a language (Ch. 5)

lateralization the process in which certain functions are located more in one hemisphere of the brain than the other (Ch. 7)

learning disabilities difficulties in the acquisition and use of listening, speaking, reading, writing, reasoning, or mathematical abilities (Ch. 10)

learning theory approach the theory that language acquisition follows the basic laws of reinforcement and conditioning (Ch. 5)

least restrictive environment the educational setting that is most similar to that of children without special needs (Ch. 10)

longitudinal research research in which the behavior of one or more individuals is measured as the subjects age (Ch. 1)

low-birthweight infants infants that weight less than 2,500 grams (about 5½ pounds) at birth (Ch. 3)

mainstreaming an educational approach in which exceptional children are integrated as much as possible into the traditional educational system and are provided with a broad range of educational alternatives (Ch. 10)

marasmus a disease characterized by the cessation of growth (Ch. 4)

masturbation sexual self-stimulation (Ch. 15)

maturation the process of the predetermined unfolding of genetic information (Ch. 1)

memory the process by which information is initially recorded, stored, and retrieved (Ch. 5, 11)

menarche the onset of menstruation (Ch. 13)

mental age the typical intelligence level found for people of a given chronological age (Ch. 11)

mental representation an internal image of a past event or object (Ch. 5)

mental retardation a significantly subaverage level of intellectual functioning that occurs with related limitations in two or more skill areas (Ch. 11)

metacognition the knowledge that people have about their own thinking processes, and their ability to monitor their cognition (Ch. 14)

metalinguistic awareness an understanding of one's own use of language (Ch. 11)

metamemory an understanding about the processes that underlie memory, which emerges and improves during middle childhood (Ch. 11)

mild retardation retardation with IQ scores in the range of 50 or 55 to 70 (Ch. 11)

moderate retardation retardation with IQ scores from around 35 or 40 to 50 or 55 (Ch. 11)

monozygotic twins twins who are genetically identical (Ch. 2)

moral development the changes in people's sense of justice and of what is right and wrong, and in their behavior related to moral issues (Ch. 9)

moratorium the category in which adolescents may have explored various identity alternatives to some degree but have not yet committed themselves (Ch. 15)

motherese a type of speech directed toward infants that is characterized by short, simple sentences (Ch. 5)

multicultural education a form of education in which the goal is to help students from minority cultures develop competence in the culture of the majority group while maintaining positive group identities that build on their original cultures (Ch. 11)

multifactorial transmission traits that are determined by a combination of both genetic and environmental factors in which a genotype provides a range within which a phenotype may be expressed (Ch. 2)

multimodal approach to perception the approach that considers how information that is collected by various individual sensory systems is integrated and coordinated (Ch. 4)

mutual regulation model the model in which infants and parents learn to communicate emotional states to one another and to respond appropriately (Ch. 6)

myelin a fatty substance that helps insulate neurons and speeds the transmission of nerve impulses (Ch. 4, 7)

naturalistic observation studies in which researchers observe some naturally occurring behavior without intervening or making changes in the situation (Ch. 1)

neglected children children who receive relatively little attention, in the form of either positive or negative interactions, from their peers (Ch. 12)

neonates the term used for newborns (Ch. 3)

neurons the basic nerve cells of the nervous system (Ch. 4)

nightmares vivid bad dreams, usually occurring towards morning (Ch. 7)

night terrors intense physiological arousals that cause a child to wake up in an intense state of panic (Ch. 7)

nonnormative life events specific, atypical events that occur in a particular person's life at a time when such events do not happen to most people (Ch. 1)

normative age-graded influences biological and environmental influences that are similar for individuals in a particular age group, regardless of when or where they are raised (Ch. 1)

normative history-graded influences biological and environmental influences associated with a particular historical moment (Ch. 1)

normative sociocultural-graded influences the impact of social and cultural factors present at a particular time for a particular individual, depending on such variables as race, ethnicity, social class, and subcultural membership (Ch. 1)

norms the average performance of a large sample of children of a given age (Ch. 4)

obesity a body weight more than 20 percent above the average weight for a person of a given age and height (Ch. 7)

object permanence the realization that people and objects exist even when they cannot be seen (Ch. 5)

onlooker play action in which children simply watch others at play but do not actually participate themselves (Ch. 9)

operant conditioning a form of learning in which a voluntary response is strengthened or weakened, depending on its association with positive or negative consequences (Ch. 1, 5)

operations organized, formal, logical mental processes (Ch. 8)

overextension the act of using words too broadly, overgeneralizing their meaning (Ch. 5)

parallel play action in which children play with similar toys, in a similar manner, but do not interact with each other (Ch. 9)

passive genotype-environment effects situations in which parents' genes are associated with the environment in which children are raised (Ch. 2)

peer group children who are about the same age and developmental level as one another (Ch. 12)

peer pressure the influence of one's peers to conform to their behavior and attitudes (Ch. 15)

perception the sorting out, interpretation, analysis, and integration of stimuli involving the sense organs and brain (Ch. 4)

permissive parents parents who provide lax and inconsistent feedback and require little of their children (Ch. 9)

personal fables the view held by some adolescents that what happens to them is unique, exceptional, and shared by no one else (Ch. 14)

personality the sum total of the enduring characteristics that differentiate one individual from another, beginning during infancy (Ch. 6)

personality development development involving the ways that the enduring characteristics that differentiate one person from another remain stable or change over the life span (Ch. 1)

phenotype an observable trait; the trait that actually is seen (Ch. 2)

physical development development involving the body's physical makeup, including the brain, nervous system, muscles, and senses, and the need for food, drink, and sleep (Ch. 1)

placenta a conduit between the mother and fetus, providing nourishment and oxygen via the umbilical cord (Ch. 2)

plasticity the degree to which a developing structure or behavior is susceptible to experience (Ch. 4)

pluralistic society model the concept that American society is made up of diverse, coequal cultural groups that should preserve their individual cultural features (Ch. 11)

polygenic inheritance inheritance in which a combination of multiple gene pairs is responsible for the production of a particular trait (Ch. 2)

postmature infants infants still unborn 2 weeks after the mother's due date (Ch. 3)

pragmatics the aspect of language relating to communicating effectively and appropriately with others (Ch. 8)

prelinguistic communication communication through sounds, facial expressions, gestures, imitation, and other nonlinguistic means (Ch. 5)

preoperational stage the stage of cognitive development which lasts from age 2 until around age 7 when children's use of symbolic thinking grows, mental reasoning emerges, and the use of concepts increases (Ch. 8)

preschools (nursery schools) child-care facilities designed to provide intellectual and social experiences for youngsters (Ch. 8)

preterm infants infants who are born prior to 38 weeks after conception (also known as premature infants) (Ch. 3)

primary sex characteristics characteristics that are associated with the development of the organs and structures of the body that directly relate to reproduction (Ch. 13)

principle of hierarchical integration the principle stating that simple skills typically develop separately and independently but are later integrated into more complex skills (Ch. 4)

principle of the independence of systems the principle of growth that suggests that different body systems grow at different rates (Ch. 4)

private speech spoken language that is not intended for others and is commonly used by children during the preschool years (Ch. 8)

profound retardation retardation with IQ scores below 20 or 25 (Ch. 11)

prosocial behavior helping behavior that benefits others (Ch. 9)

proximodistal principle the principle that development proceeds from the center of the body outward (Ch. 4)

psychoanalytic theory the theory proposed by Freud that suggests that unconscious forces act to determine personality and behavior (Ch. 1)

psychodynamic perspective the approach that states that behavior is motivated by inner forces, memories, and conflicts of which a person has little awareness or control (Ch. 1)

psychological maltreatment maltreatment in which parents or other caregivers harm children's behavioral, cognitive, emotional, or physical functioning (Ch. 7)

psychosexual development according to Freud, a series of stages that children pass through in which pleasure, or gratification, is focused on a particular biological function and body part (Ch. 1)

psychosocial development according to Erikson, development that encompasses changes both in the understandings individuals have of themselves as members of society and in their comprehension of the meaning of others' behavior (Ch. 1, 9)

psychosomatic disorders medical problems caused by the interaction of psychological, emotional, and physical difficulties (Ch. 13)

puberty the period of maturation during which the sexual organs mature, beginning earlier for girls than for boys (Ch. 13)

race dissonance the phenomenon in which minority children indicate preferences for majority values or people (Ch. 9)

rapid eye movement (REM) sleep the period of sleep that is found in older children and adults and is associated with dreaming (Ch. 4)

realistic period the stage in late adolescence and early adulthood during which people explore career options through job experience or training, narrow their choices, and eventually make a commitment to a career (Ch. 14)

recessive trait a trait within an organism that is present but is not expressed (Ch. 2)

reciprocal socialization a process in which infants' behaviors invite further responses from parents and other caregivers (Ch. 6)

reference groups groups of people with whom one compares oneself (Ch. 15)

reflexes unlearned, organized involuntary responses that occur automatically in the presence of certain stimuli (Ch. 3, 4)

rejected children children who are actively disliked and whose peers may react to them in an obviously negative manner (Ch. 12)

resilience the ability to overcome circumstances that place a child at high risk for psychological or physical damage (Ch. 7)

rhythms repetitive, cyclical patterns of behavior (Ch. 4)

sample the group of participants chosen for an experiment (Ch.1)

scaffolding the support for learning and problem solving that encourages independence and growth (Ch. 8)

scheme an organized pattern of sensorimotor functioning (Ch. 5)

school day care child-care programs provided by some local school systems in the United States (Ch. 8)

scientific method the process of posing and answering questions using careful, controlled techniques that include systematic, orderly observation and the collection of data (Ch. 1)

scripts general representations in memory of a sequence or series of events (Ch. 8)

secondary sex characteristics the visible signs of sexual maturity that do not involve the sex organs directly (Ch. 13)

secular trend a statistical tendency observed over several generations (Ch. 13)

securely attached children children who use the mother as a kind of home base and are at ease when she is present; when she leaves they become upset and go to her as soon as she returns; about two thirds of children fall into the securely attached category (Ch. 6)

self-awareness knowledge of oneself (Ch. 6)

self-care children children who let themselves into their homes after school and care for themselves until their parents return from work (Ch. 12)

self-concept one's identity, or set of beliefs about what one is like as an individual (Ch. 9)

self-efficacy learned expectations that one is capable of carrying out a behavior or producing a desired outcome in a particular situation (Ch. 12)

self-esteem an individual's overall and specific positive and negative self-evaluation (Ch. 12)

sensation the stimulation of the sense organs (Ch. 4)

sensitive period a specific time when organisms are particularly susceptible to certain kinds of stimuli in their environments (Ch. 1, 4)

sensorimotor stage the initial major stage of cognitive development; can be broken down into six substages (Ch. 5)

separation anxiety the distress displayed by infants when a customary care provider departs; usually begins at about 8 or 9 months of age (Ch. 6)

severe retardation retardation with IQ scores that range from around 20 or 25 to 35 or 40 (Ch. 11)

sex cleavage sex segregation in which boys interact primarily with boys, and girls primarily with girls (Ch. 15)

sexually transmitted disease (STD) a disease that is spread through sexual contact (Ch. 13)

sickle cell anemia a blood disorder that gets its name from the shape of the red blood cells in those who have it (Ch. 2)

slow-to-warm babies babies who are inactive, showing relatively calm reactions to their environment and are generally negative, withdrawing from new situations and adapting slowly; around 15 percent of infants are slow-to-warm (Ch. 6)

small-for-gestational-age infants infants who, because of delayed fetal growth, weigh 90 percent (or less) of the average weight of infants of the same gestational age (Ch. 3)

social comparison the desire to evaluate one's own behavior, abilities, expertise, and opinions by comparing them to those of others (Ch. 12)

social competence the collection of specific social skills that permit individuals to perform successfully in social settings (Ch. 12)

social development the way in which individuals' interactions with others and their social relationships grow, change, and remain stable over the course of life (Ch. 1)

socialized delinquents adolescent delinquents who know and subscribe to the norms of society and who are fairly normal psychologically; they engage in petty crimes but do not continue lawbreaking into adulthood (Ch. 15)

social learning learning by observing the behavior of another person, called a model (Ch. 1)

social problem solving the use of strategies for solving social conflicts in ways that are satisfactory both to oneself and to others (Ch. 12)

social referencing the intentional search for information to help explain the meaning of uncertain circumstances and events (Ch. 6)

social smile smiling in response to other individuals (Ch. 6)

social speech speech directed toward another person and meant to be understood by that person (Ch. 8)

sociobiologists scientists who consider the biological roots of social behavior (Ch. 9)

speech impairment speech that deviates so much from the speech of others that it calls attention to itself, interferes with communication, or produces maladjustment in the speaker (Ch. 10)

Stanford-Binet Intelligence Scale an oral test that consists of a series of problems that get progressively more difficult and that vary according to the age of the person being tested (Ch. 11)

state the degree of awareness an infant displays to both internal and external stimulation (Ch. 4)

status the evaluation of a role or person by other members of a group or society (Ch. 12)

stillbirth the delivery of a child who is not alive, occurring in less than 1 delivery in 100 (Ch. 3)

stranger anxiety the caution and wariness displayed by infants when encountering a strange person; begins at around 6 months of age (Ch. 6)

stress the response to events that threaten or challenge us (Ch. 13)

stuttering substantial disruption in the rhythm and fluency of speech; the most common speech impairment (Ch. 10)

sudden infant death syndrome (SIDS) the unexplained death during sleep of a seemingly healthy baby (Ch. 4)

superego according to Freud, the aspect of personality that represents a person's conscience, incorporating distinctions between right and wrong (Ch. 1)

surrogate mother a woman who agrees to carry a child to term in cases in which the mother who provides the donor eggs is unable to conceive (Ch. 2)

survey research research in which a group of people chosen to represent some larger population are asked questions about their attitudes, behavior, or thinking on a given topic (Ch. 1)

symbolic function the ability to use a mental symbol, a word, or an object to stand for or represent something that is not physically present (Ch. 8)

syntax the combining of words and phrases to form sentences (Ch. 8)

Tay-Sachs disease a disorder for which there is no treatment and which produces blindness and muscle degeneration prior to death (Ch. 2)

teacher expectancy effect the cycle of behavior in which a teacher transmits an expectation about a child and thereby actually brings about the expected behavior (Ch. 11)

telegraphic speech speech in which words not critical to the message are left out (Ch. 5)

temperament patterns of arousal and emotionality that represent consistent and enduring characteristics in an individual (Ch. 2, 6)

tentative period the second stage of Ginzberg's theory, which spans adolescence, in which people begin to think in pragmatic terms about the requirements of various jobs and how their own abilities might fit with them (Ch. 14)

teratogen a factor that produces a birth defect (Ch. 2)

theories explanations and predictions concerning phenomena of interest, providing a framework for understanding the relationships among an organized set of facts or principles (Ch. 1)

theory of mind a child's knowledge and beliefs about the mental world (Ch. 6)

transformation the process in which one state is changed into another (Ch. 8)

treatment a procedure applied by an investigator based on two different experiences devised for subjects or participants (see **experiment**) (Ch. 1)

treatment group the group receiving the treatment (Ch. 1)

triarchic theory of intelligence the model that states that intelligence consists of three aspects of information processing: the componential element, the experiential element, and the contextual element (Ch. 11)

trust-versus-mistrust stage the period during which infants develop a sense of trust or mistrust, largely depending on how well their needs are met by their caregivers (Ch. 6)

ultrasound sonography a process in which high-frequency sound waves scan the mother's womb to produce an image of the unborn baby, whose size and shape can then be assessed (Ch. 2)

underextension the act of using words too restrictively, common among children just mastering spoken language (Ch. 5)

undersocialized delinquents adolescent delinquents who are raised with little discipline or with harsh, uncaring parental supervision; they typically begin criminal activities at an early age (Ch. 15)

universal grammar a similar underlying structure shared by all the world's languages, according to linguist Noam Chomsky's theory (Ch. 5)

very-low-birthweight infants infants who weigh less than 1,250 grams (around 2¼ pounds) or, regardless of weight, have been in the womb less than 30 weeks (Ch. 3)

visual impairment difficulties in seeing that may include blindness or partial sightedness (Ch. 10)

visual-recognition memory the memory of and recognition of a stimulus that has been previously seen (Ch. 5)

Wechsler Adult Intelligence Scale-Revised (WAIS-III) a test for adults that provides separate measures of verbal and performance (or nonverbal) skills, as well as a total score (Ch. 11)

Wechsler Intelligence Scale for Children-III (WISC-III) a test for children that provides separate measures of verbal and performance (or nonverbal) skills, as well as a total score (Ch. 11)

X-linked genes genes that are considered recessive and located only on the X chromosome (Ch. 2)

zone of proximal development (ZPD) according to Vygotsky the level at which a child can *almost*, but not fully, comprehend or perform a task on her or his own (Ch. 8)

zygote the new cell formed by the process of fertilization (Ch. 2)

References

Able, E. L., & Sokol, R. J. (1987). Incidence of fetal alcohol syndrome and economic impact of FAS-related anomalies. *Drug and Alcohol Dependence, 19,* 51–70.

Aboud, F. E., & Skerry, S. A. (1983). Self- and ethnic concepts in relations to ethnic constancy. *Canadian Journal of Behavioral Science, 15,* 14–26.

Achenbach, T. A. (1992). Developmental psychopathology. In M. H. Bornstein & M. E. Lamb (Eds.), *Developmental psychology: An advanced textbook.* Hillsdale, NJ: Erlbaum.

Adams, R. J., Mauer, D., & Davis, M. (1986). Newborns' discrimination of chromatic from achromatic stimuli. *Journal of Experimental child Psychology, 41,* 267–281.

Adams, G. R., Montemayor, R., & Gullotta, T. P. (Eds.). (1996). *Psychosocial development during adolescence.* Thousand Oaks, CA: Sage Publications.j

Adler, P. A., Kless, S. J., & Adler, P. (1992). Socialization to gender roles: Popularity among elementary school boys and girls. *Sociology of Education, 65,* 169–187.

Ainsworth, M. D. (1989). Attachments beyond infancy. *American Psychologist, 44,* 709–716.

Ainsworth, M. D. S. (1973). The development of infant-mother attachment. In B. M. Caldwell & H. N. Ricciuti (Eds.), *Review of child development research* (Vol. 3). Chicago: University of Chicago Press.

Ainsworth, M. D. S., Blehar, M. C., Waters, E., & Wall, S. (1978). *Patterns of attachment: A psychological study of the strange situation.* Hillsdale, NJ: Erlbaum.

Ainsworth, M. D. S., & Bowlby, J. (1991). An ethological approach to personality development. *American Psychologist, 46,* 333–341.

Ainsworth, M. S. (1993). Attachment as related to mother-infant interaction. *Advances in Infancy Research, 8,* 1–50.

Aitken, R. J. (1995, July 7). The complexities of conception. *Science, 269,* 39–40.

Alan Guttmacher Institute. (1988). *Pregnancy rates around the world.* New York: Author.

Alan Guttmacher Institute. (1993a). *Report on viral sexual diseases.* Chicago: Author.

Alan Guttmacher Institute. (1993b). *Survey of male sexuality.* Chicago: Author.

Alan Guttmacher Institute. (1994). *National teenage pregnancy rate.* New York: Author.

Albers, L. L., & Krulewitch, C. J. (1993). Electronic fetal monitoring in the United States in the 1980s. *Obstetrics & Gynecology, 82,* 8–10.

Ales, K. L., Druzin, M. L., & Santini, D. L. (1990). Impact of advanced maternal age on the outcome of preganacy. *Surgery, Gynecology & Obstetrics, 171,* 209–216.

Alessandri, S. M., Sullivan, M. W., Imaizumi, S., & Lewis, M. (1993). Learning and emotional responsivity in cocaine-exposed infants. *Developmental Psychology, 29,* 989–997.

Alexander, G. M., & Hines, M. (1994). Gender labels and play styles: Their relative contributions to children's selection of playmate. *Child Development, 65,* 869–879.

Allen, L. S., Hines, M., Shryne, J. E., & Gorski, R. A. (1989). Two sexually dimorphic cell groups in the human brain. *Journal of Neuroscience, 9,* 497–506.

Allison, A. C. (1954). Protection afforded by sickle cell trait against subtertian malarial infection. *British Medical Journal, 1,* 290–294.

Alloy, L. B., Acocella, J., & Bootzin, R. R. (1996). *Abnormal Psychology: Current perspectives.* New York: McGraw-Hill.

Als, H. (1992). Individualized, family-focused developmental care for the very low-birthweight preterm infant in the NICU. In S. L. Friedman & M. D. Sigman (Eds.), *The psychological development of low birthweight children.* Norwood, NJ: Ablex.

Altemus, M., Deuster, P. A., Galliven, E., Carter, C. S., & Gold, P. W. Suppression of hypothalmic pituitary adrenal axis responses to stress in lactating women. *Journal of Clinical Endocrinology and Metabolism, 80,* 2954–2959.

Ambuel, B. (1995). Adolescents, unintended pregnancy, and abortion: The struggle for a compassionate social policy. *Current Directions in Psychological Science, 4,* 1–5.

American Academy of Pediatrics. (1982). The promotion of breast feeding. *Pediatrics, 72,* 891–894.

American Academy of Pediatrics. (1983). Growth hormone treatment of children with short stature. *Pediatrics, 73,* 891–894.

American Academy of Pediatrics. (1989). *The facts on breastfeeding.* Elk Grove Village, IL: Author.

American Academy of Pediatrics. (1992). The use of whole cow's milk in infancy. *Pediatrics, 89,* 1105–1109.

American Academy of Pediatrics. (1995). Policy statement on length of hospital stay following birth.

American Academy of Pediatrics/American College of Obstetricians and Gynecologists. (1992). *Guidelines for perinatal care.* Elk Grove, IL: Author.

American Academy of Pediatrics Committee on Accident and Poison Prevention. (1990). Bicycle helmets. *Pediatrics, 85,* 229–230.

American Academy of Pediatrics Committee on Drugs. (1978). Effects of medication during labor and delivery on infant outcome. *Pediatrics, 62,* 402–403.

American Academy of Pediatrics Committee on Sports Medicine. (1988). Infant exercise programs. *Pediatrics, 82,* 800–825.

American Academy of Pediatrics Committee on Sports Medicine and Committee on School Health. (1989). Organized athletics for preadolescent children. *Pediatrics, 84,* 583–584.

American Academy of Pediatrics Task Force on Pediatric AIDS. (1991). Education of children with human immunodeficiency virus infection. *Pediatrics, 88,* 645–648.

American Association on Mental Retardation. (1992). *Mental retardation: Definition, classification, and systems of support.* Washington, DC: Author.

American Association of University Women. (1992). *How schools shortchange women: The AAUW Report.* Washington, DC: American Association of University Women Educational Foundation.

American Cancer Society. (1992). *Cancer facts and figures.* New York: Author.

American Cancer Society. (1993). Cancer statistics, 1993. *Cancer Journal for Clinicians, 43,* 7–26.

American College of Obstetricians and Gynecologists. (1994, February). *Guidelines for exercise during pregnancy and the postpartum period.* Washington, DC: American College of Obstetricians and Gynecologists.

American Council on Education. (1995). *The American freshman: National norms for fall 1994.* Los Angeles: University of California–Los Angeles, Higher Education Research Institute.

American Psychiatric Association. (1994). *Diagnostic and statistical manual of mental disorders* (4th ed.). Washington, DC: Author.

American Psychological Association. (1992). Ethical principles of psychologists and code of conduct. Washington, DC: Author.

American Psychological Association. (1993, August 10). A Public Interest Directorate. *Violence and youth: Psychology's response.* Washington, DC: Author.

Amsel, A. (1988). *Behaviorism, neobehaviorism, and cognitivism in learning theory.* Hillsdale, NJ: Erlbaum.

Anand, K. J. S., & Hickey, P. R. (1987). Pain and its effect in the human neonate and fetus. *New England Journal of Medicine, 317,* 1321–1329.

Anand, K. J. S., & Hickey, P. R. (1992). Halothane-morphine compared with high-dose Sufentanil for anesthesia and post-operative analgesia in neonatal cardiac surgery. *New England Journal of Medicine, 326,* 1–9.

Anders, T. F., & Taylor, T. (1994). Babies and their sleep environment. *Children's Environments, 11,* 123–134.

Anderson, D. A. (1994). Lesbian and gay adolescents: Social and developmental considerations. *High School Journal, 77,* 13–19.

Andersson, T., & Magnusson, D. (1990). Biological maturation in adolescence and the development of drinking habits and alcohol abuse among young males: A prospective longitudinal study. *Journal of Youth and Adolescence, 19,* 33–42.

Apgar, V. (1953). A proposal for a new method of evaluation in the newborn infant. *Current Research in Anesthesia and Analgesia, 32,* 260.

Appelbaum, M. (1995, March). Paper presented at the biennial meeting of the Society for Research in Child Development, Indianapolis, IN.

Apter, A., Galatzer, A., Beth-Halachmi, N., & Laron, Z. (1981). Self-image in adolescents with delayed puberty and growth retardation. *Journal of Youth and Adolescence, 10,* 501–505.

Archer, S. L., & Waterman, A. S. (1994). Adolescent identity development: Contextual perspectives. In C. B. Fisher & R. M. Lerner (Eds.), *Applied developmental psychology.* New York: McGraw-Hill.

Archibald, W. P. (1974). Alternative explanations for the self-fulfilling prophecy. *Psychological Bulletin, 81,* 74–84.

Ardila, A., & Rosselli, M. (1994). Development of language, memory, and visuospatial ability in 5- to 12-year-old children using a neuropsychological battery. *Developmental Neuropsychology, 10,* 97–120.

Ards, S., & Harrell, A. (1993). Reporting of child maltreatment: A secondary analysis of the national incidence surveys. *Child Abuse & Neglect, 17,* 337–344.

Arias, R. (1995, January 23). *People Weekly,* 34–39.

Aries, P. (1962). *Centuries of Childhood.* New York: Knopf.

Arnett, J. (1995). The young and reckless: Adolescent reckless behavior. *Current Directions in Psychological Science, 4,* 67–71.

Art of Living. (1995, March 20). *People Weekly,* 69.

Aseltine, R. H., Gore, S., & Colten, M. E. (1994). Depression and the social developmental context of adolescence. *Journal of Personality and Social Psychology, 67,* 252–263.

Asendorpf, J. B., & Baudonniere, P. M. (1993). Self-awareness and other-awareness: Mirror self-recognition and synchronic imitation among unfamiliar peers. *Developmental Psychology, 29,* 88–95.

Asendorpf, J. B., Warkentin, V., & Baudonniere, P. (1996). Self-awareness and other-awareness II: Mirror self-recognition, social contingency awareness, and synchronic imitation. *Developmental Psychology, 32,* 313–321.

Asher, S. R. (1983). Social competence and peer status: Recent advances and future directions. *Child Development, 54,* 1427–1434.

Asher, S. R., Hymel, S., & Renshaw, P. D. (1984). Loneliness in children. *Child Development, 55,* 1456–1464.

Asher, S. R., & Parker, J. G. (1991). The significance of peer relationship problems in childhood. In B. H. Schneider, G. Attili, J. Nadel, & R. P. Weisberg (Eds.), *Social competence in developmental perspective.* Amsterdam: Kluwer.

Asher, S. R., Singleton, L. C., & Taylor, A. R. (1982). *Acceptance vs. friendship.* Paper presented at the meeting of the American Research Association, New York.

Aslin, R. N. (1987). Visual and auditory development in infancy. In J. D. Osofsky (Ed.), *Handbook of infant development.* (2nd ed.). New York: Wiley.

Atken, D. J., Moorman, J. U., & Linn, C. A. (1991). Ready for prime-time: Network series devoted to working women in the 1980s. *Sex Roles, 25,* 677–685.

Attie, I., & Brooks-Gunn, J. (1989). The development of eating problems in adolescent girls: A longitudinal study. *Developmental Psychology, 25,* 70–79.

Atwater, L. E. (1992). Beyond cognitive ability: Improving the prediction of performance. *Journal of Business and Psychology, 7,* 27–44.

Aved, B. M., Irwin, M. M., Cummings, L. S., & Findeisen, N. (1993). Barriers to prenatal care for low-income women. *Western Journal of Medicine, 158,* 493–498.

Aviezer, O., van IJzendoorn, M. H., Sagi, A., & Schuengel, C. (1994). "Children of the dream" revisited: 70 years of collective early child care in Israeli kibbutzim. *Psychological Bulletin, 116,* 99–116.

Axia, G., Bonichini, S., & Benini, F. (1995). Pain in infancy: Individual differences. *Perceptual and Motor Skills, 81,* 142.

Azar, B. (1995, January). "Gifted" label stretches, it's more than high IQ. *APA Monitor,* p. 25.

Azar, B., & McCarthy, K. (1994, October). Psychologists recommend vigilance against aggression. *APA Monitor,* p. 45.

Azuma, S., & Chasnoff, I. (1993). Outcome of children prenatally exposed to cocaine and other drugs: A path analysis of three-year data. *Pediatrics, 92,* 396–402.

Baar, K. (1995, March 29). Time for a fitness pyramid? *The New York Times,* pp. C1, C6.

Babad, E. (1992). Pygmalion—25 years after interpersonal expectations in the classroom. In P. D. Blanck (Ed.), *Interpersonal expectations: Theory, research and application.* Cambridge, England: Cambridge University Press.

Backer, P. (1993, February 28). On turning 13: Reports from the front lines. *The New York Times,* sec. 4, p. 2.

Bahrick, L. E. (1989). Intermodal learning in infancy: Learning on the basis of two kinds of invariant relations in audible and visible events. *Child Development, 50,* 197–209.

Bahrick, L. E., & Pickens, J. N. (1988). Classification of bimodal English and Spanish language passages by infants. *Infant Behavior and Development, 11,* 277–296.

Bailey, W. T. (1994). A longitudinal study of fathers' involvement with young children, infancy to age 5 years. *Journal of Genetic Psychology, 155,* 331–339.

Baillargeon, R. (1987). Object permanence in 3 1/2- and 4 1/2-month-old infants. *Developmental Psychology, 23,* 655–670.

Baillargeon, R., & DeVos, J. (1991). Object permanence in young infants: Further evidence. *Child Development, 62,* 1227–1246.

Baker, D. B. (1994). Parenting stress and ADHD: A comparison of mothers and fathers. *Journal of Emotional and Behavioral Disorders, 2,* 46–50.

Baldwin, W. (1993). The consequences of early childbearing: A perspective. *Journal of Research on Adolescence, 3,* 349–352.

Ball, J. A. (1987). *Reactions to motherhood.* New York: Cambridge University Press.

Baltes, P. B. (1987). Theoretical propositions of life-span developmental psychology: On the dynamics between growth and decline. *Developmental Psychology, 23,* 611–626.

Baltes, P. B., Reese, H. W., & Lipsitt, L. (1980). Life-span developmental psychology. *Annual Review of Psychology, 31,* 65–110.

Bandura, A. (1977). *Social learning theory.* Englewood Cliffs, NJ: Prentice Hall.

Bandura, A. (1978). Social learning theory of aggression. *Journal of Communication, 28,* 12–29.

Bandura, A. (1986). *Social foundations of thought and action.* Englewood Cliffs, NJ: Prentice Hall.

Bandura, A. (1988). Perceived self-efficacy: Exercise of control through self-belief. In J. P. Dauwalder, M. Perrez, & V. Hobbi (Eds.), *Annual series of European research in behavior therapy* (Vol 2). Lisse, The Netherlands: Swets & Zietlinger.

Bandura, A. (1991). Social cognitive theory of moral thought and action. In W. M. Kurtines & J. L. Gewirtz (Eds.), *Handbook of moral behavior and development.* Hillsdale, NJ: Erlbaum.

Bandura, A. (1993). Perceived self-efficacy in cognitive development and functioning. *Educational Psychologist, 28,* 117–148.

Bandura, A., Grusec, J. E., & Menlove, F. L. (1967). Vicarious extinction of avoidance behavior. *Journal of Personality and Social Psychology, 5,* 16–23.

Bandura, A., Ross, D., & Ross, S. (1963). Vicarious extinction of avoidance behavior. *Journal of Personality and Social Psychology, 49,* 521–532.

Bandura, A., & Schunk, D. H. (1981). Cultivating competence, self-efficacy, and intrinsic interest through proximal self-motivation. *Journal of Personality and Social Psychology, 67,* 601–607.

Barinaga, M. (August 9, 1996). New experiments underscore warnings on maternal drinking. *Science, 273,* 738–739.

Barkley, R. A. (1997). Behavioral inhibition, sustained attention, and executive functions: Constructing a unifying theory of ADHD. *Psychological Bulletin, 121,* 65–94.

Barkley, R. A. (1995). *Taking charge of ADHD: The complete, authoritative guide for parents.* New York: Guilford Press.

Barnett, R. C., & Rivers, C. (1992, February). The myth of the miserable working woman. *Working Woman, 2,* 62–65, 83–85.

Barr, H. M., Streissguth, A. P., Darby, B. L., & Sampson, P. D. (1990). Prenatal exposure to alcohol, caffeine, tobacco, and aspirin: Effects on fine and gross motor performance in 4-year-old children. *Developmental Psychology, 26,* 339–348.

Barr, R. G., Konner, M., Bakeman, R., & Adamson, L. (1991). Crying in !Kung San infants: A test of the cultural specificity hypothesis. *Developmental Medicine and Child Neurology, 33,* 601–610.

Barrett, D. E., & Frank, D. A. (1987). *The effects of undernutrition on children's behavior.* New York: Gordon & Breach.

Barrett, D. E., & Radke-Yarrow, M. R. (1985). Effects of nutritional supplementation on children's responses to novel, frustrating, and competitive situations. *American Journal of Clinical Nutrition, 42,* 102–120.

Bartecchi, C. E., MacKenzie, T. D., & Schrier, R. W. (1995, May). The global tobacco epidemic. *Scientific American,* 44–51.

Bates, E., Bretherton, I., & Snyder, L. (1988). *From first words to grammar: Individual differences and dissociable mechanisms.* New York: Cambridge University Press.

Bates, J. E., Marvinney, D., Bennett, D. S., Dodge, K. A., Kelly, T., & Pettit, G. S. (1991). *Children's daycare history and kindergarten adjustment.* Paper presented at biennial meeting of the Society for Research in Child Development, Seattle, WA.

Bates, J. E., Marvinney, D., Kelly, T., Dodge, K. A., Bennett, D. S., & Pettit, G. S. (1994). Child-care history and kindergarten adjustment. *Developmental Psychology, 30,* 690–700.

Bauer, P. J. (1996). What do infants recall of their lives? Memory for specific events by 1- to 2-year-olds. *American Psychologist, 51,* 29–41.

Baumeister, R. F. (Ed.). (1993). *Self-esteem: The puzzle of low self-regard.* New York: Plenum.

Baumeister, R. F., Smart, L., & Boden, J. M. (1996). Relation of threatened egotism to violence and aggression: The dark side of high self-esteem. *Psychological Review, 103,* 5–33.

Baumrind, D. (1971). Current patterns of parental authority. *Developmental Psychology Monographs, 4*(1, Pt. 2).

Baumrind, D. (1980). New directions in socialization research. *Psychological Bulletin, 35,* 639–652.

Bayer, C. L., & Cegala, D. J. (1992). Trait verbal aggressiveness and argumentativeness: Relations with parenting style. *Western Journal of Communication, 56,* 301–310.

Bayley, N. (1949). Consistency and variability in the growth of intelligence from birth to 18 years. *Journal of Genetic Psychology, 75,* 165–196.

Bayley, N. (1969). *Manual for the Bayley Scales of infant development.* New York: The Psychological Corporation.

Beal, C. R. (1994). *Boys and girls: The development of gender roles.* New York: McGraw-Hill.

Beal, C. R., & Belgrad, S. L. (1990). The development of message evaluation skills in young children. *Child Development, 61,* 705–712.

Bear, G. G., & Rys, G. S. (1994). Moral reasoning, classroom behavior, and sociometric status among elementary school children. *Developmental Psychology, 30,* 633–638.

Beardsley, T. (1996, March). Vital data. *Scientific American,* 100–105.

Becahy, R. (1992, August 3). AIDS epidemic. *Newsweek,* 49.

Beckwith, L., & Rodning, C. (1991). Intellectual functioning in children born preterm: Recent research. In L. Okagaki & R. J. Sternberg (Eds.), *Directors of development: Influences on the development of children's thinking.* Hillsdale, NJ: Erlbaum.

Begley, S. (1995, July 10). Deliver, then depart. *Newsweek,* 62.

Behrend, D. A. (1988). Overextensions in early language comprehension: Evidence from a signal detection approach. *Journal of Child Language, 15,* 63–75.

Beilin, H., & Pufall, P. (Eds.) (1992). *Piaget's theory: Prospects and possibilities.* Hillsdale, NJ: Erlbaum.

Bell, A., & Weinberg, M. S. (1978). *Homosexuality: A study of diversities among men and women.* New York: Simon & Schuster.

Bell, C. C., & Jenkins, E. J. (1991). Traumatic stress and children. *Journal of Health Care for the Poor and Underserved, 2,* 175–185.

Bell, C. C., & Jenkins, E. J. (1993). Community violence and children on Chicago's southside. *Psychiatry, 56,* 46–56.

Bell, S. M., & Ainsworth, M. D. S. (1972). Infant crying and maternal responsiveness. *Child Development, 43,* 1171–1190.

Bellack, A. S., Hersen, M., & Kazdin, A. E. (1990). *International handbook of behavior modification and therapy.* New York: Plenum.

Belluck, P. (1995, January 25). At 15, Westinghouse Finalist grasps Holy Grail of math. *The New York Times,* p. A1.

Belmont, J. M. (1995). Discussion: A view from the empiricist's window. Special Issue: Lev S. Vygotsky and contemporary educational psychology. *Educational Psychologist, 30,* 99–102.

Belsky, J., Campbell, S. B., Cohn, J. F., Moore, G. (1996). Instability of infant-parent attachment security. *Developmental Psychology, 32,* 921–924.

Belsky, J., Fish, M., & Isabella, R. (1991). Continuity and discontinuity in infant negative and positive emotionality: Family antecedents and attachment consequences. *Developmental Psychology, 27,* 421–431.

Belsky, J., & Rovine, M. (1987). Temperament and attachment in the Strange Situation: An empirical rapprochement. *Child Development, 58,* 787–795.

Belsky, J., & Rovine, M. (1988). Nonmaternal care in the first year of life and infant-parent attachment security. *Child Development, 59,* 157–167.

Belsky, J., Rovine, M., & Fish, M. (1989). The developing family system. In M. Gunnar (Ed.), *Systems and development: Minnesota Symposium on Child Psychology* (Vol. 22). Hillsdale, NJ: Erlbaum.

Belsky, J., Rovine, M., & Taylor, D. G. (1984). The Pennsylvania Infant and Family Development Project, III: The origins of individual differences in infant-mother attachment: Maternal and infant contributions. *Child Development, 55,* 718–728.

Belsky, J., Steinberg, L., & Walker, A. (1982). The ecology of day care: A critical review. *Child Development, 49,* 929–949.

Bem, S. (1987). Gender schema theory and its implications for child development: Raising gender-aschematic children in a gender-schematic society. In M. R. Walsh (Ed.), *The psychology of women: Ongoing debates.* New Haven, CT: Yale University Press.

Benedict, H. (1979). Early lexical development: Comprehension and production. *Journal of Child Language, 6,* 183–200.

Benenson, J. F. (1994). Ages four to six years: Changes in the structures of play networks of boys and girls. *Merrill-Palmer Quarterly, 40,* 478–487.

Benenson, J. F., & Apostoleris, N. H. (1993, March). *Gender differences in group interaction in early childhood.* Paper presented at the biennial meeting of the Society for Research in Child Development, New Orleans, LA.

Benjamin, J., Li, L., Patterson, C., Greenberg, B. D., Murphy, D. L., & Hamer, D. H. (1996). Population and familial association between the D4 dopamine receptor gene and measures of Novelty Seeking. *Nature Genetics, 12,* 81–84.

Bennet, A. (1992, October 14). Lori Schiller emerges from the torments of schizophrenia. *The Wall Street Journal,* pp. A1, A10.

Benoit, D., & Parker, K. C. H. (1994). Stability and transmission of attachment across three generations. *Child Development, 65,* 1444–1456.

Benson, H. (1993). The relaxation response. In D. Goleman & J. Gurin (Eds.), *Mindbody medicine: How to use your mind for better health.* Yonkers, NY: Consumer Reports Books.

Berenbaum, S. A., & Hines, M. (1992). Early androgens are related to sex-typed toy preferences. *Psychological Science, 3,* 202–206.

Berenbaum, S. A., & Snyder, E. (1995). Early hormonal influences on childhood sex-typed activity and playmate preferences: Implications for the development of sexual orientation. Sexual orientation and human development [Special Issue]. *Developmental Psychology, 31,* 31–42.

Bergeman, C., Chipuer, H., Plomin, R., Pedersen, N., McClearn, G., Nesselroade, J., Costa, P., & McCrae, R. (1993). Genetic and environmental effects on openness to experience, agreeableness, and conscientiousness: An adoption/twin study. *Journal of Personality, 61,* 159–179.

Bergman, J., & Kimberlin, L. V. (1993). Developmental outcome in extremely premature infants. Impact of surfactant. *Pediatric Clinics of North America, 40,* 937–953.

Berk, L. E. (1992). Children's private speech: An overview of the theory and the status of research. In R. M. Diaz & L. E. Berk (Eds.), *Private speech: From social interaction to self-regulation.* Hillsdale, NJ: Erlbaum.

Berk, L. E., & Landau, S. (1993). Private speech of learning disabled and normally achieving children in classroom academic and laboratory contexts. *Child Development, 64,* 556–571.

Berko, J. (1958). The child's learning of English morphology. *Word, 14,* 150–177.

Berkowitz, G. S., Skovron, M. L., Lapinski, R. H., & Berkowitz, R. L. (1990). Delayed childbearing and the outcome of pregnancy. *New England Journal of Medicine, 322,* 659–664.

Berkowitz, L. (1993). *Aggression: Its causes, consequences, and control.* New York: McGraw-Hill.

Berman, A. L., & Jobes, D. A. (1991). *Adolescent suicide: Assessment and intervention.* Washington, DC: American Psychological Association.

Bernal, M. E. (1994, August). Ethnic identity of Mexican American children. Address at the annual meeting of the American Psychological Association, Los Angeles.

Bernstein, G. A., & Borchardt, C. M. (1991). Anxiety disorders of childhood and adolescence: A critical review. *Journal of the American Academy of Child and Adolescent Psychiatry, 30,* 519–532.

Bernstein, N., & Bruni, F. (1995, December 24). She suffered in plain sight, but alarms were ignored. *The New York Times,* pp. 1, 22.

Bersoff, D. M. N., & Ogden, D. W. (1991). APA Amicus Curiae briefs: Furthering lesbian and gay male civil rights. *American Psychologist, 46,* 950–956.

Berthier, N. E. (1996). Learning to reach: A mathematical model. *Developmental Psychology, 32,* 811–823.

Best, C. T. (1994). The emergence of native-language phonological influences in infants: A perceptual assimilation model. In J. C. Goodman & H. C. Nusbaum (Eds.), *The development of speech perception: The transition from speech sounds to spoken words.* Cambridge, MA: MIT Press.

Betancourt, H., & Lopez, S. R. (1993). The study of culture, ethnicity, and race in American Psychology. *American Psychologist, 48,* 1586–1596.

Biemiller, L. (1995, September 22). Berkeley uses British art to track the changes in the meaning of childhood. *Chronicle of Higher Education*, A67.

Bierman, K. L., & Furman, W. (1984). The effects of social skills training and peer involvement on the social adjustment of preadolescents. *Child Development, 55*, 151–162.

Bierman, K. L., Miller, C. L., & Stabb, S. D. (1987). Improving the social behavior and peer acceptance of rejected boys: Effects of social skill training with instructions and prohibitions. *Journal of Consulting and Clinical Psychology, 55*, 194–200.

Biernat, M., & Wortman, C. B. (1991). Sharing of home responsibilities between professionally employed women and their husbands. *Journal of Personality and Social Psychology, 60*, 844–860.

Bigelow, B. J., Tesson, G., & Lewko, J. H. (1996). *Learning the rules: The anatomy of children's relationships.* New York: Guilford Press.

Bijeljac-Babic, R., Bertoncini, J., & Mehler, J. (1993). How do 4-day-old infants categorize multisyllabic utterances? *Developmental Psychology, 29*, 711–721.

Bing, E. D. (1983). *Dear Elizabeth Bing: We've had our baby.* New York: Pocket Books.

Bird, G., & Melville, K. (1994). *Families and intimate relationships.* New York: McGraw-Hill.

Biron, O., Mongeau, J. G., & Bertrand, D. (1977). Familial resemblance of bodyweight and weight/height in 374 homes with adopted children. *Journal of Pediatrics, 91*, 555–558.

Bisanz, J., Morrison, F. J., & Dunn, M. (1995). Effects of age and schooling on the acquisition of elementary quantitative skills. *Developmental Psychology, 31*, 221–236.

Bjorklund, D. F., Schneider, W., Cassel, W. S., & Ashley, E. (1994). Training and extension of a memory strategy: Evidence of utilization deficiencies in the acquisition of an organizational strategy in high- and low-IQ children. *Child Development, 65*, 951–965.

Black, J. E., & Greenough, W. T. (1986). Induction of pattern in neural structure by experience: Implication for cognitive development. In M. E. Lamb, A. L. Brown, & B. Rogoff (Eds.), *Advances in developmental psychology* (Vol. 4). Hillsdale, NJ: Erlbaum.

Blake, J., & Boysson-Bardies, B. de (1992). Patterns in babbling: A cross-linguistic study. *Journal of Child Language, 19*, 51–74.

Blakeslee, S. (1995, August 29). In brain's early growth, timetable may be crucial. *The New York Times*, pp. C1, C3.

Blass, E. M., Ganchrow, J. R., & Steiner, J. E. (1984). Classical conditioning in newborn humans 2–48 hours of age. *Infant Behavior and Development, 7*, 223–235.

Bloch, H. (1989). On early coordinations and their future. In A. de Ribaupierre (Ed.), *Transition mechanisms in child development: The longitudinal perspective* (pp. 259–282). New York: Cambridge University Press.

Bloom, L. (1993). *The transition from infancy to language: Acquiring the power of expression.* New York: Cambridge University Press.

Blount, B. G. (1982). Culture and the language of socialization: Parental speech. In D. A. Wagner & H. W. Stevenson (Eds.), *Cultural perspectives on child development.* San Francisco: Freeman.

Blumberg, B. D., Lewis, M. J., & Susman, E. J. (1984). Adolescence: A time of transition. In M. G. Eisenberg, L. C. Sutkin, & M. A. Jansen (Eds.), *Chronic illness and disability through the life span: Effects on self and family.* New York: Springer.

Blustein, D. L., & Palladino, D. E. (1991). Self and identity in late adolescence: A theoretical and empirical integration. *Journal of Adolescent Research, 6*, 437–453.

Bochner, S. (1996). The learning strategies of bilingual versus monolingual students. *British Journal of Educational Psychology, 66*, 83–93.

Boehm, K. E., & Campbell, N. B. (1995). Suicide: A review of calls to an adolescent peer listening phone service. *Child Psychiatry & Human Development, 26*, 61–66.

Boehm, K. E., Schondel, C. K., Marlowe, A. L., & Rose, J. S. (1995). Adolescents calling a peer-listening phone service: Variations in calls by gender, age, and season of year. *Adolescence, 30*, 863–871.

Bogatz, G. A., & Ball, S. (1972). *The second year of Sesame Street: A continuing evaluation.* Princeton, NJ: Educational Testing Service.

Boismier, J. D. (1977). Visual stimulation and wake-sleep behavior in human neonates. *Developmental Psychology, 10*, 219–227.

Boivin, M., Dodge, K. A., & Coie, J. D. (1995). Individual-group behavioral similarity and peer status in experimental play groups of boys: The social misfit revisited. *Journal of Personality and Social Psychology, 69*, 269–279.

Bolger, K. E., Patterson, C. J., Thompson, W. W., & Kupersmidt, J. B. (1995). Psychosocial adjustment among children experiencing persistent and intermittent family economic hardship. *Child Development, 66*, 1107–1129.

Booth, A., & Edwards, J. N. (1989). Transmission of marital and family quality over the generations: The effect of parental divorce and unhappiness. *Journal of Divorce, 13*, 41–58.

Bootzin, R. R., Manber, R., Perlis, M. L., Salvio, M., & Wyatt, J. K. (1993). Sleep disorders. In P. B. Sutker & H. E. Adams (Eds.), *Comprehensive handbook of psychopathology* (2nd ed.). New York: Plenum.

Bornstein, M. H. (1989a). Sensitive periods in development: Structural characteristics and causal interpretations. *Psychological Bulletin, 105*, 179–197.

Bornstein, M. H. (1989b). Stability in early mental development: From attention and information processing in infancy to language and cognition in childhood. In M. H. Bornstein & N. A. Krasnegor (Eds.), *Stability and continuity in mental development: Behavioral and biological perspectives* (pp. 147–170). Hillsdale, NJ: Erlbaum.

Bornstein, M. H., & Lamb, M. E. (1992a). *Development in infancy: An introduction.* New York: McGraw-Hill.

Bornstein, M. H., & Lamb, M. E. (Eds.). (1992b). *Developmental psychology: An advanced textbook* (p. 135). Hillsdale, NJ: Erlbaum.

Bornstein, M. H., & Ruddy, M. G. (1984). Infant attention and maternal stimulation. In H. Bouma & D. G. Bouwhuis (Eds.), *Attention and performance* (Vol. 10). London: Erlbaum.

Bornstein, M. H., & Sigman, M. D. (1986). Continuity in mental development from infancy. *Child Development, 57*, 251–274.

Bornstein, M. H., & Tamis-LeMonda, C. S. (1989). Maternal responsiveness and cognitive development in children. In M. H. Bornstein (Ed.), *Maternal responsiveness: Characteristics and consequences* (pp. 49–61). San Francisco: Jossey-Bass.

Botvin, G. J., Epstein, J. A., Schinke, S. P., & Diaz, T. (1994). Predictors of cigarette smoking among inner-city minority youth. *Journal of Developmental and Behavioral Pediatrics, 15*, 67–73.

Bouchard, C., Tremblay, A. Despres, J. P., Nadeau, A., et al. (1990, May 24). The response to long-term overfeeding in identical twins. *New England Journal of Medicine, 322*, 1477–1482.

Bouchard, T. J., Jr. (1994, June 17). Genes, environment, and personality. *Science, 212*, 1055–1059.

Bouchard, T. J., Jr., Lykken, D. T., McGue, M., Segal, N. L., & Tellegen, A. (1990, October 12). Sources of human psychological differences: The Minnesota study of twins reared apart. *Science, 250,* 223–228.

Bouchard, T. J., Jr. & McGue, M. (1981). Familial studies of intelligence: A review. *Science, 264,* 1700–1701.

Boulton, M. J., & Smith, P. K. (1990). Affective bias in children's perceptions of dominance relationships. *Child Development, 61,* 221–229.

Bowen, D. J., Kahl, K., Mann, S. L., & Peterson, A. V. (1991). Descriptions of early triers. *Addictive Behaviors, 16,* 95–101.

Bower, B. (1985). The left hand of math and verbal talent. *Science News, 127,* 263.

Bower, T. G. R. (1974). *Development in infancy.* San Francisco: Freeman.

Bower, T. G. R. (1977). *A primer of infant development.* San Francisco: Freeman.

Bowers, K. E., & Thomas, P. (1995, August). Handle with care. *Harvard Mental Health Letter,* 6–7.

Bowlby, J. (1951). Maternal care and mental health. *Bulletin of the World Health Organization, 3,* 355–534.

Boyd, G. M., Howard, J., & Zucker, R. A. (Eds.). (1995). *Alcohol problems among adolescents: Current directions in prevention research.* Mahwah, NJ: Erlbaum.

Boylan, P. (1990). Induction of labor, complications of labor, and postmaturity. *Current Opinion in Obstetrics and Gynecology, 2,* 31–35.

Boysson-Bardies, B. de, Sagart, L., & Durand, C. (1984). Discernible differences in the babbling of infants according to target language. *Journal of Child Language, 11,* 1–15.

Boysson-Bardies, B. de, & Vihman, M. M. (1991). Adaptation to language: Evidence from babbling and first words in four languages. *Language, 67,* 297–307.

Brackbill, Y. (1979). Obstetrical medication and infant behavior. In J. D. Osofsky (Ed.), *Handbook of infant development.* New York: Wiley.

Brackbill, Y., & Broman, S. H. (1979). *Obstetrical medication and development in the first year of life.* Unpublished manuscript.

Braddick, O. (1993). Orientation- and motion-selective mechanisms in infants. In K. Simons (Ed.), *Early visual development: Normal and abnormal* (pp. 163–177). New York: Oxford University Press.

Bradley, R. H., & Caldwell, B. M. (1995). Caregiving and the regulation of child growth and development: Describing proximal aspects of caregiving systems. *Developmental Review, 15,* 38–85.

Bradley, R. H., Whiteside, L., Mundfrom, D. J., Casey, P. H., Kelleher, K. J., & Pope, S. K. (1994). Early indications of resilience and their relation to experiences in the home environments of low-birthweight, premature children living in poverty. *Child Development,* 65, 346–360.

Brady, L. S. (1995, January 29). Asia Linn and Chris Applebaum. *The New York Times,* p. 47.

Branstetter, E. (1969). The young child's response to hospitalization: Separation anxiety or lack of mothering care? *American Journal of Public Health, 59,* 92–97.

Bray, G. A. (1983). Obesity. In N. M. Kaplan & J. Stamler (Eds.), *Prevention of coronary heart disease.* Philadelphia: Saunders.

Bray, G. A. (1990). Exercise and obesity. In C. Bouchard, R. J. Shephard, T. Stephens, J. R. Sutton, & B. D. McPherson (Eds.), *Exercise, fitness, and health: A consensus of current knowledge.* Champaign, IL: Human Kinetics.

Brazelton, T. B. (1973). *The Neonatal Behavioral Assessment Scale.* Philadelphia: Lippincott.

Brazelton, T. B. (1983). *Infants and mothers: Differences in development* (Rev. ed.). New York: Dell.

Brazelton, T. B. (1990). Saving the bathwater. *Child Development, 61,* 1661–1671.

Brazelton, T. B. (1991). Discussion: Cultural attitudes and actions. In M. H. Bornstein (Ed.), *Cultural approaches to parenting.* Hillsdale, NJ: Erlbaum.

Brazelton, T. B., Nugent, J. K., & Lester, B. M. (1987). Neonatal Behavioral Assessment Scale. In J. D. Osofsky (Ed.), *Handbook of infant development* (2nd ed.). New York: Wiley.

Breakwell, G. M. (1992). *Social psychology of identity and the self-concept.* New York: Academic Press.

Bredekamp, S. (Ed.). (1989). *Developmentally appropriate practice in early childhood programs serving children from birth through age 8.* Washington, DC: National Association for the Education of Young Children.

Bregman, J., & Kimberlin, L. V. (1993). Developmental outcome in extremely premature infants. Impact of surfactant. *Pediatric Clinics of North America, 40,* 937–953.

Brennan, K. A., & Shaver, P. R. (1995). Dimensions of adult attachment, affect regulation, and romantic relationship functioning. *Personality and Social Psychology Bulletin, 21,* 267–283.

Brent, D. A., Perper, J. A., Moritz, G., & Liotus, L. (1994). Familial risk factors for adolescent suicide: A case-control study. *Acta Psychiatrica Scandinavica, 89,* 52–58.

Bridges, J. S. (1993). Pink or blue: Gender-stereotypic perceptions of infants as conveyed by birth congratulations cards. *Psychology of Women Quarterly, 17,* 193–205.

Briere, J., Bulkley, J. A., Jenny, C., & Reid, T. (Eds.). (1996). *The APSAC handbook on child maltreatment.* Newbury Park, CA: Sage.

Brislin, R. (1993). *Understanding culture's influence on behavior.* Fort Worth, TX: Harcourt Brace Jovanovich.

Brockington, I. F. (1992). Disorders specific to the puerperium. *International Journal of Mental Health, 21,* 41–52.

Brody, J. E. (1994a, February 2). Fitness and the fetus: A turnabout in advice. *The New York Times,* p. C13.

Brody, J. E. (1994b, April 6). The value of breast milk. *The New York Times,* p. C11.

Brody, L. E., & Benbow, C. P. (1987). Accelerative strategies: How effective are they for the gifted? *Gifted Child Quarterly, 3,* 105–110.

Brody, N. (1993). Intelligence and the behavioral genetics of personality. In R. Plomin & G. E. McClearn (Eds.), *Nature, nurture, and psychology.* Washington, DC: American Psychological Association.

Bronfenbrenner, U. (1979). *The ecology of human development.* Cambridge, MA: Harvard University Press.

Bronfenbrenner, U. (1989). Ecological systems theory. In R. Vasta (Ed.), *Six theories of child development.* Greenwich, CT: JAI Press.

Brooks, J., & Lewis, M. (1976). Infants' responses to strangers: Midget, adult, and child. *Child Development, 47,* 323–332.

Brooks-Gunn, J., Klebanov, P. K., & Duncan, G. J. (1996). Ethnic differences in children's intelligence test scores: Role of economic deprivation, home environment, and maternal characteristics. *Child Development, 67,* 396–408.

Brooks-Gunn, J., & Matthews, W. S. (1979). *He and she: How children develop their sex role identity.* Englewood Cliffs, NJ: Prentice Hall.

Brooks-Gunn, J., Petersen, A. C., & Compas, B. E. (1994). What role does biology play in childhood and adolescent depression? In I. M. Goodyear (Ed.), *Mood disorders in childhood and adolescence.* New York: Cambridge University Press.

Brooks-Gunn, J., & Reiter, E. (1990). The role of pubertal processes. In S. Feldman & G. Elliott (Eds.), *At the threshold: The developing adolescent.* Cambridge, MA: Harvard University Press.

Brooks-Gunn, J., & Ruble, D. (1982). The development of menstrual-related beliefs and behaviors during early adolescence. *Child Development, 53,* 1567–1577.

Brossard, M. A., & Morin, R. (1996, Sept. 15). American voters focus on worries close to home. (Washington Post public opinion poll). *The Washington Post,* pg. A1.

Brouwers, P., Moss, H., Wolters, P., Eddy, J., Balis, F., Poplack, D. G., & Pizzo, P. A. (1990). Effect of continuous-infusion zidovudine therapy on neuropsychologic functioning in children with symptomatic human immunodeficiency virus. *The Journal of Pediatrics, 117,* 980–985.

Brown, B. (1990). Peer groups. In S. Feldman & G. Elliott (Eds.), *At the threshold: The developing adolescent.* Cambridge, MA: Harvard University Press.

Brown, B., Lohr, M., & Trujillo, C. (1983). *Adolescent peer group stereotypes, member conformity, and identity development.* Paper presented at the meeting of the Society for Research in Child Development, Detroit, MI.

Brown, J. D. (1991). Staying fit and staying well: Physical fitness as a moderator of life stress. *Journal of Personality and Social Psychology, 60,* 368–375.

Brown, J. D., & McGill, K. L. (1989). The cost of good fortune: When positive life events produce negative health consequences. *Journal of Personality and Social Psychology, 57,* 1103–1110.

Brown, J. L. (1987). Hunger in the U.S. *Scientific American, 256(2),* 37–41.

Brown, J. L., & Pollitt, E. (February, 1996). Malnutrition, poverty and intellectual development. *Scientific American,* 38–43.

Brown, R. (1973). *A first language.* Cambridge, MA: Harvard University Press.

Brown, R., & Fraser, C. (1963). The acquisition of syntax. In C. N. Cofer and B. Musgrave (Eds.), *Verbal behavior and learning: Problems and processes.* New York: McGraw-Hill.

Brownell, C. (1986). Convergent developments: Cognitive-developmental correlates of growth in infant/toddler peer skills. *Child Development, 57,* 275–286.

Brownell, K. D., & Rodin, J. (1994). The dieting maelstrom: Is it possible and advisable to lose weight? *American Psychologist, 49,* 781–791.

Bruce, M. L., & Hoff, R. A. (1994) Social and physical health risk factors for first-onset major depressive disorder in a community sample. *Social Psychiatry and Psychiatric Epidemiology, 29,* 165–171.

Buchanan, M., & Robbins, C. (1990). Early adult psychological consequences for males of adolescent pregnancy and its resolution. *Journal of Youth and Adolescence, 19,* 413–424.

Buchholz, E., & Korn-Bursztyn, C. (1993). Children of adolescent mothers: Are they at risk for abuse? *Adolescence, 28,* 361–382.

Bukowski, W. M., Newcomb, A. F., & Hartup, W. W. (Eds.). (1996). *The company they keep: Friendships in childhood and adolescence.* New York: Cambridge University Press.

Bullock, J. (1988). Altering aggression in young children. *Early Childhood Education, 15,* 24–27.

Bullock, M. (1995, July/August). What's so special about a longitudinal study? *Psychological Science Agenda,* 9–10.

Bullough, V. L. (1981). Age at menarche. *Science, 213,* 365–366.

Burbules, N. C., & Linn, M. C. (1988). Response to contradiction: Scientific reasoning during adolescence. *Journal of Educational Psychology, 80,* 67–75.

Burchinal, M. R., Roberts, J. E., Nabors, L. A., & Bryant, D. M. (1996). Quality of center child care and infant cognitive and language development. *Child Development, 67,* 606–620.

Burgess, R. L., & Huston, T. L. (Eds.). (1979). *Social exchanges in developing relationships.* New York: Academic Press.

Buriel, R. (1993). Acculturation, respect for cultural differences, and biculturalism among three generations of Mexican American and Euro American school children. *Journal of Genetic Psychology, 154,* 531–543.

Burn, S. M. (1996). *The social psychology of gender.* New York: McGraw-Hill.

Burnham, D. K., & Harris, M. B. (1992). Effects of real gender and labeled gender on adults' perceptions of infants. *Journal of Genetic Psychology, 153,* 165–183.

Burns, B. & Lipsitt, L. P. (1991). Behavioral factors in crib death: Toward an understanding of the sudden infant death syndrome. *Journal of Applied Developmental Psychology, 12,* 159–184.

Bushman, B. J. (1993). Human aggression while under the influence of alcohol and other drugs: An integrative research review. *Current Directions in Psychological Science, 2,* 148–152.

Bushman, B. J., & Geen, R. G. (1990). Role of cognitive-emotional mediators and individual differences in the effects of media violence on aggression. *Journal of Personality and Social Psychology, 58,* 156–163.

Buss, A. H., & Plomin, R. (1984). *Temperament: Early developing personality traits.* Hillsdale, NJ: Erlbaum.

Bussey, K. (1992). Lying and truthfulness: Children's definition, standards, and evaluative reactions. *Child Development, 63,* 1236–1250.

Bussey, K., & Bandura, A. (1992). Self-regulatory mechanisms governing gender development. *Child Development, 63,* 1236–1250.

Butterfield, E., & Siperstein, G. (1972). Influence of contingent auditory stimulation upon non-nutritional suckle. In J. Bosma (Ed.), *Oral sensation and perception: The mouth of the infant.* Springfield, IL: Charles C. Thomas.

Butterworth, G. (1994). Infant intelligence. In J. Khalfa (Ed.), *What is intelligence? The Darwin College lecture series* (pp. 49–71). Cambridge, England: Cambridge University Press.

Button, E. (1993). *Eating disorders: Personal construct theory and change.* New York: John Wiley.

Byne, W., & Parsons, B. (1994, February). Biology and human sexual orientation. *Harvard Mental Health Letter, 10,* 5–7.

Cairns, E., McWhirter, L., Duffy, U., & Barry, R. (1990). The stability of self-concept in late adolescence: Gender and situational effects. *Personality and Individual Differences, 11,* 937–944.

California Task Force to Promote Self-esteem and Personal and Social Responsibility. (1990). *Toward a state of self-esteem.* Sacramento: California State Department of Education.

Calkins, S. D., & Fox, N. A. (1992). The relations among infant temperament, security of attachment, and behavioral inhibition at 24 months. *Child Development, 63,* 1456–1472.

Caminiti, S. (1992, August 10). Who's minding America's kids? *Fortune,* 50–53.

Campbell, F. A., & Ramey, C. T. (1994). Effects of early intervention on intellectual and academic achievement: A follow-up study of children from low-income families. *Child Development, 65,* 684–698.

Campbell, J., Poland, M., Waller, J., & Ager, J. (1992). Correlates of battering during pregnancy. *Research in Nursing and Health, 15,* 219–226.

Campione, J., & Brown, A. (1987). Linking dynamic assessment with school achievement. In C. Lidz (Ed.), *Dynamic assessment.* New York: Guilford Press.

Campos, J. J., Langer, A., & Krowitz, A. (1970). Cardiac responses on the visual cliff in prelocomotor human infants. *Science, 170,* 196–197.

Campos, J. J., & Stenberg, C. (1981). Perception, appraisal, and emotions: The onset of social referencing. In M. E. Lamb & L. R. Sherrod (Eds.), *Infant social cognition: Empirical and theoretical considerations.* Hillsdale, NJ: Erlbaum.

Camras, L. A., Malatesta, C., & Izard, C. E. (1991). The development of facial expressions in infancy. In R. S. Feldman & B. Rime (Eds.), *Fundamentals of nonverbal behavior.* Cambridge, England: Cambridge University Press.

Camras, L. A., & Sachs, V. B. (1991). Social referencing and caretaker expressive behavior in a day-care setting. *Infant Behavior and Development, 14,* 27–36.

Canfield, R. L., & Smith, E. G. (1996). Number-based expectations and sequential enumeration by 5-month-old-infants. *Developmental Psychology, 32,* 269–279.

Caplan, L. J., & Barr, R. A. (1989). On the relationship between category intensions and extensions in children. *Journal of Experimental Child Psychology, 47,* 413–429.

Cardon, L. R., Fulker, D. W., DeFries, J. C., & Plomin, R. (1992). Continuity and change in general cognitive ability from 1 to 7 years of age. *Developmental Psychology, 28,* 64–73.

Cardon, L. R., & Fulker, D. (1993). Genetics of specific cognitive abilities. In R. Plomin & G. E. McClearn (Eds.), *Nature, nurture, and psychology* (pp. 99–120). Washington, DC: American Psychological Association.

Carey, S. (1978). The child as word learner. In M. Halle, G. Miller, & J. Bresnan (Eds.), *Linguisitc theory and psychological reality.* Cambridge, MA: MIT Press.

Carlson, J. S., & Wiedl, K. H. (1992). The dynamic assessment of intelligence. In C. Haywood & D. Tzuriel (Eds.), *Interactive assessment.* New York: Springer-Verlag.

Carlsson-Paige, N., & Levin, D. E. (1994). Power Rangers and aggression. Unpublished study, Lesley College, Cambridge, MA.

Carmody, D. (1990, March 7). College drinking: Changes in attitude and habit. *The New York Times,* p. B7.

Carnegie Council on Adolescent Development. (1995). *Great transitions: Preparing adolescents for a new century.* New York: Carnegie Corporation.

Carnegie Task Force on Meeting the Needs of Young Children. (1994). *Starting points: Meeting the needs of our youngest children.* New York: Carnegie Corporation.

Carr, C. N., Kennedy, S. R., & Dimick, K. M. (1996). Alcohol use among high school athletes. *The Prevention Researcher, 3,* 1–3.

Carr, J. (1995). *Down syndrome.* Cambridge, England: Cambridge University Press.

Carroll, D. (1985). *Living with dying.* New York: McGraw-Hill.

Carson, R. C., Butcher, J. N., & Coleman, J. C. (1988). *Abnormal psychology and modern life* (9th ed.). Glenview, IL: Scott, Foresman.

Carstensen, L. L. (1995). Evidence for a life-span theory of socioemotional selectivity. *Current Directions in Psychological Science, 4,* 151–156.

Case, R. (1991). Stages in the development of the young child's first sense of self. *Developmental Review, 11,* 210–230.

Caspi, A., Henry, B., McGee, R. O., Moffitt, T. E., & Silva, P. A. (1995). Temperamental origins of child and adolescent behavior problems: From age three to age fifteen. *Child Development, 66,* 55–68.

Caspi, A., & Moffitt, T. E. (1991). Individual differences are accentuated during periods of social change: The sample case of girls at puberty. *Journal of Personality and Social Psychology, 61,* 157–168.

Caspi, A., & Moffitt, T. E. (1993). *Continuity amidst change: A paradoxical theory of personality coherence.* Manuscript submitted for publication.

Cassidy, J., & Berlin, L. J. (1994). The insecure/ambivalent pattern of attachment: Theory and research. *Child Development, 65,* 971–991.

Catania, J. A., Coates, T. J., Stall, R., Turner, H., Peterson, J., Hearst, N., Dolcini, M. M., Hudes, E., Gagnon, J., Wiley, J., & Groves, R. (1992). Prevalence of AIDS-related risk factors and condom use in the United States. *Science, 258,* 1101–1106.

Catell, R. B. (1967). *The scientific analysis of personality.* Chicago: Aldine.

Catell, R. B. (1987). *Intelligence: Its structure, growth, and action.* Amsterdam: North-Holland.

Caughy, M. O., DiPietro, J. A., & Strobino, D. M. (1994). Day-care participation as a protective factor in the cognitive development of low-income children. *Child Development, 65,* 457–471.

Centers for Disease Control. (1991, January 9). *Morbidity and Mortality Report,* pp. 183–184.

Ceci, S. J., & Bruck, M. (1993). The suggestibility of the child witness: A historical review and synthesis. *Psychological Bulletin, 113,* 403–439.

Ceci, S. J., & Bruck, M. (1995). *Jeopardy in the courtroom.* Washington, DC: American Psychological Association.

Ceci, S. J., & DeSimone, M. (1992). *Group distortion effects in preschoolers' reports.* Paper presented at the biennial meeting of the American Psychology and Law Society, San Diego, CA.

Ceci, S. J., & Hembrooke, H. (1993). The contextual nature of earliest memories. In J. M. Puckett & H. W. Reese (Eds.), *Mechanisms of everyday cognition* (pp. 117–136). Hillsdale, NJ: Erlbaum.

Center on Addiction and Substance Abuse. (1994). *Report on college drinking.* New York: Columbia University.

Centers for Disease Control (1991). *Preventing lead poisoning in young children: A statement by the Centers for Disease Control.* Atlanta, GA: U.S. Department of Health and Human Services.

Centers for Disease Control. (1994). Figures on average days in hospital for mothers after noncaesarean delivery. Atlanta, GA: Author.

Cernoch, J. M., & Porter, R. H. (1985). Recognition of maternal axillary odors by infants. *Child Development, 56,* 1593–1598.

Chalmers, I., Enkin, M., & Keirse, M. J. (Eds.). (1989). *Effective care in pregnancy and childbirth.* New York: Oxford University Press.

Chao, R. K. (1994). Beyond parental control and authoritarian parenting style: Understanding Chinese parenting through the cultural notion of training. *Child Development, 65,* 1111–1119.

Chase-Lansdale, P. L., Cherlin, A. J., & Kiernan, K. E. (1995). The long-term effects of parental divorce on the mental health of young adults: A developmental perspective. *Child Development, 66,* 1614–1634.

Chase-Lansdale, P., & Owen, M. (1987). Maternal employment in a family context: Effect on infant-mother and infant-father attachment. *Child Development, 58,* 1505–1512.

Chasnoff, I. J., Hunt, C. E., & Kaplan, D. (1989). Prenatal cocaine exposure as associated with respiratory pattern abnormalities. *American Journal of Diseases of Childhood, 143,* 583–587.

Chen, C., & Stevenson, H. W. (1995). Motivation and mathematics achievement: A comparative study of Asian-American, Caucasian-American, and East Asian high school students. *Child Development, 66,* 1215–1234.

Cherlin, A. (1993). *Marriage, divorce, remarriage.* Cambridge, MA: Harvard University Press.

Child Health USA '93. (1993). *Recommended child vaccination schedule* (p. 43). Washington, DC: U.S. Department of Health and Human Services, Public Health Service, Health Resources and Services Administration.

Chin, J. (1994). The growing impact of the HIV\AIDS pandemic on children born to HIV infected women. *Clinical Perinatalogy, 21,* 1–14.

Chira, S. (1994, July 10). Teen-agers, in a poll, report worry and distrust of adults. *The New York Times,* pp. 1, 16.

Chollat-Traquet, C. (1992). *Women and tobacco.* Geneva, Switzerland: World Health Organization.

Chomsky, N. (1968). *Language and mind.* New York: Harcourt Brace Jovanovich.

Chomsky, N. (1978). On the biological basis of language capacities. In G. A. Miller & E. Lennenberg (Eds.), *Psychology and biology of language and thought* (pp. 199–220). New York: Academic Press.

Chomsky, N. (1991). Linguistics and cognitive science: Problems and mysteries. In A. Kasher (Ed.), *The Chomskyan turn.* Cambridge, MA: Blackwell.

Chomsky, N. (1993). On the nature, use, and acquisition of language. In A. I. Goldman (Ed.), *Readings in philosophy and cognitive science* (pp. 511–534). Cambridge, MA: MIT Press.

Christopher, F. S. (1995). Adolescent pregnancy prevention. *Family Relations, 44,* 384–391.

Cicchetti, D., & Beeghly, M. (Eds.). (1990). *Children with Down syndrome.* Cambridge: Cambridge University Press.

Cielinski, K. L., Vaughn, B. E., Seifer, R., & Contreras, J. (1995). Relations among sustained engagement during play, quality of play, and mother-child interaction in samples of children with Down syndrome and normally developing toddlers. *Infant Behavior and Development, 18,* 163–176.

Cipra, B. (1991, October 18). They'd rather switch than fight. Why college students transfer out of science and engineering majors. *Science, 254,* 370–372.

Clark, E. (1983). Meanings and concepts. In J. Flavell & E. Markham (Eds.), *Handbook of child psychology: Cognitive development* (Vol. 3). New York: Wiley.

Clark, J. E., & Humphrey, J. H. (Eds.), *Motor development: Current selected research.* Princeton, NJ: Princeton Book Company.

Clark, K. B., & Clark, M. P. (1947). Racial identification and preference in Negro children. In T. M. Newcomb & E. L. Hartley (Eds.), *Readings in social psychology.* New York: Holt, Rinehart and Winston.

Clarke-Stewart, A. (1993). *Daycare.* Cambridge, MA: Harvard University Press.

Clarke-Stewart, A., & Friedman, S. (1987). *Child development: Infancy through adolescence.* New York: Wiley.

Clarke-Stewart, K. A. (1989). Infant day care: Maligned or malignant? [Special Issue] Children and their development: Knowledge base, research agenda, and social policy application. *American Psychologist, 44,* 266–273.

Clarke-Stewart, K. A., Gruber, C. P., & Fitzgerald, L. M. (1994). *Children at home and in day care.* Hillsdale, NJ: Erlbaum.

Clifton, R. (1992). The development of spatial hearing in human infants. In L. A. Werner & E. W. Rubel (Eds.), *Developmental psychoacoustics* (pp. 135–157). Washington, DC: American Psychological Association.

Cnattingius, S., Berendes, H., & Forman, M. (1993). Do delayed childbearers face increased risks of adverse pregnancy outcomes after the first birth? *Obstetrics and Gynecology, 81,* 512–516.

Coats, E., & Feldman, R. S. (1995). The role of television in the socialization of nonverbal behavioral skills. *Basic and Applied Social Psychology, 17,* 327–341.

Coccaro, E., Bergeman, C., & McClearn, G. (1993). Heritability of irritable impulsiveness: A study of twins reared together and apart. *Psychiatry Research, 48,* 229–242.

Coddington, R. D. (1984). Measuring the stressfulness of a child's environment. In J. H. Humphrey (Ed.), *Stress in childhood.* New York: AMS Press.

Cohen, P., Cohen, J., Kasen, S., Velez, C. N., Hartmark, C., Johnson, J., Rojas, M., Brook, J., & Streuning, E. L. (1993). An epidemiological study of disorders in late childhood and adolescence: I. Age- and gender-specfic prevalence. *Journal of Child Psychology and Psychiatry and Allied Disciplines, 34,* 851–867.

Cohen, S. E. (1996). Prediction of low and normal school achievement in early adolescents born preterm. *Journal of Early Adolescence, 16,* 46–70.

Cohen, S., Tyrell, D. A., & Smith, A. P. (1993). Negative life events, perceived stress, negative affect, and susceptibility of the common cold. *Journal of Personality and Social Psychology, 64,* 131–140.

Cohen, S. E. (1995). Biosocial factors in early infancy as predictors of competence in adolescents who were born prematurely. *Journal of Developmental and Behavioral Pediatrics, 16,* 36–41.

Cohn, J. F., & Tronick, E. Z. (1983). Three-month-old infants' reaction to simulated maternal depression. *Child Development, 54,* 185–193.

Cohn, J. F., & Tronick, E. Z. (1989). Mother-infant face-to-face interaction: Influence is bidirectional and unrelated to periodic cycles in either partner's behavior. *Developmental Psychology, 24,* 386–392.

Colby, A., & Damon, W. (1987). Listening to a different voice: A review of Gilligan's *In a different voice.* In M. R. Walsh (Ed.), *The psychology of women.* New Haven, CT: Yale University Press.

Colby, A., & Kohlberg, L. (1987). *The measurement of moral judgment* (Vols. 1–2). New York: Cambridge University Press.

Cole, M. (1992). Culture in development. In M. H. Bornstein & M. E. Lamb (Eds.), *Developmental psychology: An advanced textbook* (3rd ed.). Hillsdale, NJ: Erlbaum.

Coleman, J. (1961). *The adolescent society.* Glencoe, IL: Free Press.

Coleman, J. C. (1980). Friendship and the peer group in adolescence. In J. Adelson (Ed.), *Handbook of adolescent psychology.* New York: Wiley.

Coles, R., & Stokes, G. (1985). *Sex and the American teenager.* New York: Harper & Row.

Collins, W. A. (1983). Interpretation and inference in children's television. In J. Bryant and D. R. Anderson (Eds.), *Children's understanding of television.* New York: Academic Press.

Colombo, J. (1995). On the neural mechanisms underlying developmental and individual differences in visual fixation in infancy: Two hypotheses. *Developmental Review, 15,* 97–135.

Committee for Rights and Legal Matters. (1989). Corporal punishment in schools. *American Journal of Psychiatry, 146,* 1524.

Committee on Children, Youth, and Families. (1994). *When you need child day care.* Washington, DC: American Psychological Association.

Committee to Study the Prevention of Low Birthweight (1985). *Preventing low birthweight.* Washington, DC: National Academy Press.

Compas, B. E., Hinden, B. R., & Gerhardt, C. A. (1995). Adolescent development: Pathways and processes of risk and reliance. *Annual Review of Psychology, 46,* 265–293.

Comstock, G., & Strasburger, V. C. (1990). Deceptive appearances: Television violence and aggressive behavior. Conference: Teens and television (1988, Los Angeles, California). *Journal of Adolescent Health Care, 11,* 31–44.

Condit, V. (1990). Anorexia nervosa: Levels of causation. *Human Nature, 1,* 391–413.

Condry, J. (1989). *The psychology of television.* Hillsdale, NJ: Erlbaum.

Condry, J., & Condry, S. (1976). Sex differences: A study of the eye of the beholder. *Child Development, 47,* 812–819.

Conel, J. L. (1930/1963). *Postnatal development of the human cerebral cortex* (Vols. 1–6). Cambridge, MA: Harvard University Press.

Conger, J. (1977). *Adolescence and youth* (2nd ed.). New York: Harper & Row.

Conway, M., & Rubin, D. (1993). The structure of autobiographical memory. In A. F. Collins, S. E. Gathercole, M. A. Conway, & P. E. Morris (Eds.), *Theories of memory.* Hillsdale, NJ: Erlbaum.

Cook, S. W. (1984). Cooperative interaction in multiethnic contexts. In N. Miller and M. Brewer (Eds.), *Groups in contact: The psychology of desegregation.* New York: Academic Press.

Cook, W. J., & Wollersheim, J. P. (1976). The effect of labeling of special education students and the perception of contact versus noncontact peers. *Journal of Special Education, 10,* 187–198.

Cook-Deegan, R. (1994). *The gene wars: Science, politics, and the human genome.* New York: Norton.

Coons, S., & Guilleminault, C. (1982). Developments of sleep-wake patterns and non rapid eye movement sleep stages during the first six months of life in normal infants. *Pediatrics, 69,* 793–798.

Cooper, R. P., & Aslin, R. N. (1990). Preference for infant-directed speech in the first month after birth. *Child Development, 61,* 1584–1595.

Cooper, R. P., & Aslin, R. N. (1994). Developmental differences in infant attention to the spectral properties of infant-directed speech. *Child Development, 65,* 1663–1677.

Cooperative Institutional Research Program of the American Council on Education [CIRE]. (1990). *The American freshman: National norms for fall 1990.* Los Angeles: American Council on Education.

Corbin, C. (1973). *A textbook of motor development.* Dubuque, IA: Brown.

Coren, S. (1989). Left-handedness and accident-related injury risk. *American Journal of Public Health, 79,* 1–2.

Coren, S., & Halpern, D. F. (1991). Left-handedness: A marker for decreased survival fitness. *Psychological Bulletin, 109,* 90–106.

Corrigan, R. (1987). A developmental sequence of actor-object pretend play in young children. *Merrill-Palmer Quarterly, 33,* 87–106.

Costa, P. T., Busch, C. M., Zonderman, A. B., & McCrae, R. R. (1993). Correlations of MMPI factor scales with measures of the five factor model of personality. (1986). *Journal of Personality Assessment, 50,* 640–650.

Coulton, C. J., Korbin, J. E., Su, M., & Chow, J. (1995). Community level factors and child maltreatment rates. *Child Development, 66,* 1262–1276.

Cowan, N. (1992). Verbal memory span and the timing of spoken recall. *Journal of Memory and Language, 31,* 668–684.

Cox, M. J., & Cox, R. D. (Eds.). (1985). *Foster care: Current issues, policies, and practices.* Norwood, NJ: Ablex.

Cox, M. J., Owen, M. T., Henderson, V. K., & Margand, N. A. (1992). Prediction of infant-father and infant-mother attachment. *Developmental Psychology, 28,* 474–483.

Crandall, C., & Biernat, M. (1990). The ideology of anti-fat attitudes. *Journal of Applied Social Psychology, 20,* 227–243.

Cratty, B. (1979). *Perceptual and motor development in infants and children* (2nd ed.). Englewood Cliffs, NJ: Prentice Hall.

Cratty, B. (1986). *Perceptual and motor development in infants and children* (3rd ed.). Englewood Cliffs, NJ: Prentice Hall.

Crews, D. (1993). The organizational concept and vertebrates without sex chromosomes. *Brain, Behavior, and Evolution, 42,* 202–214.

Crick, N. R., & Grotpeter, J. K. (1995). Relational aggression, gender, and social-psychological adjustment. *Child Development, 66,* 710–722.

Crockenberg, S. B. (1986). Are tempermental differences in babies associated with predictable differences in caregiving? In J. V. Lerner & A. C. Peterson (Eds.), *Temperament and social interaction in infants and children* (pp. 75–88). San Francisco: Jossey-Bass. (Reprinted from *New Dimensions in Child Development, 30.*)

Crockett, L. J., & Crouter, A. C. (Eds.) (1995). *Pathways through adolescence: Individual development in relation to social contexts.* Hillsdale, NJ: Erlbaum.

Cromwell, E. S. (1994). *Quality child care: A comprehensive guide for administrators and teachers.* Boston: Allyn & Bacon.

Crook, C. K. (1978). Taste perception in the newborn infant. *Infant Behavior and Development, 1,* 52–69.

Crook, C. K. (1987). Taste and olfaction. In P. Salapatek & L. B. Cohen (Eds.), *Handbook of infant perception* (Vol. 1). New York: Academic Press.

Crosby, W. (1991). Studies in fetal malnutrition. *American Journal of Diseases of Children, 145,* 871–876.

Croyle, R. T., & Hunt, J. R. (1991). Coping with health threat: Social influence processes in reactions to medical test results. *Journal of Personality and Social Psychology, 60,* 382–389.

Crystal, D. S., Chen, C., Fuligni, A. J., Stevenson, H. W., Hsu, C., Ko, H., Kitamura, S., & Kimura, S. (1994). Psychological maladjustment and academic achievement: A cross-cultural study of Japanese, Chinese, and American high-school students. *Child Development, 65,* 738–753.

Csikszentmihalyi, M., & Larson, R. (1984). *Being adolescent: Conflict and growth in the teenage years.* New York: Basic Books.

Culbertson, J. L., & Gyurke, J. (1990). Assessment of cognitive and motor development in infancy and childhood. In J. H. Johnson & J. Goldman (Eds.), *Developmental assessment in clinical child psychology: A handbook* (pp. 100–131). New York: Pergamon Press.

Culp, A. M., Clyman, M. M., & Culp, R. E. (1995). Adolescent depressed mood, reports of suicide attempts, and asking for help. *Adolescence, 30,* 827–837.

Cummings, E. M., Iannotti, R. J., & Zahn-Waxler, C. (1989). Aggression between peers in early childhood: Individual continuity and developmental change. *Child Development, 60,* 887–895.

Dainton, M. (1993). The myths and misconceptions of the step-mother identity. *Family Relations, 42,* 93–98.

Daly, M., & Wilson, M. I. (1996). Violence against stepchildren. *Current Directions in Psychological Science, 5,* 77–81.

Daly, T., & Feldman, R. S. (1994). *Benefits of social integration for typical preschool children.* Unpublished manuscript.

Damon, W. (1977). *The social world of the child.* San Francisco: Jossey-Bass.

Damon, W. (1983). *Social and personality development.* New York: Norton.

Damon, W. (1988). *The moral child.* New York: The Free Press.

Damon, W., & Hart, D. (1988). *Self-understanding in childhood and adolescence.* New York: Cambridge University Press.

Damon, W., & Hart, D. (1992). Self-understanding and its role in social and moral development. In M. H. Bornstein & M. E. Lamb (Eds.), *Developmental psychology: An advanced textbook* (3rd ed.). Hillsdale, NJ: Erlbaum.

Daniels, H. (Ed.). (1996). *An introduction to Vygotsky.* New York: Routledge.

Darling, N., & Steinberg, L. (1993). Parenting style as context: An integrative model. *Psychological Bulletin, 113,* 487–496.

Dasen, P. R. (1977). Are cognitive processes universal? A contribution to cross-cultural Piagetian psychology. In N. Warren (Ed.), *Studies in cross-cultural psychology* (Vol. 1). London: Academic Press.

Dasen, P., Inhelder, B., Lavallee, M., & Retschitzki, J. (1978). *Naissance de l'intelligence chez l'enfant Baoule de Cote d'Ivorie.* Bern, Switzerland: Hans Huber.

Dasen, P., Ngini, L., & Lavallee, M. (1979). Cross-cultural training studies of concrete operations. In L. H. Eckenberger, W. J. Lonner, & Y. H. Poortinga (Eds.), *Cross-cultural contributions to psychology.* Amsterdam: Swets & Zeilinger.

Davidson, J. E. (1990). Intelligence recreated. *Educational Psychologist, 25,* 337–354.

Davies, P. T., & Cummings, E. M. (1994). Marital conflict and child adjustment: An emotional security hypothesis. *Psychological Bulletin, 116,* 387–411.

Davis, M., & Emory, E. (1995). Sex differences in neonatal stress reactivity. *Child Development, 66,* 14–27.

Davis-Floyd, R. E. (1994). The technocratic body: American childbirth as cultural expression. *Social Science & Medicine, 38,* 1125–1140.

Davydov, V. V. (1995, April). The influence of L. S. Vygotsky on education theory, research, and practice. *Educational Researcher, 24,* 12–21.

DeAngelis, T. (1994, December). What makes kids ready, set for school? *APA Monitor,* pp. 36–37.

Deary, I. J., & Stough, C. (1996). Intelligence and inspection time. *American Psychologist, 51,* 599–608.

Deaux, K., Reind, A., Mizrahi, K., & Ethier, K. A. (1995). Parameters of social identity. *Journal of Personality and Social Psychology, 68,* 280–291.

Decarrie, T. G. (1969). A study of the mental and emotional development of the thalidomide child. In B. M. Foss (Ed.), *Determinants of infant behavior* (Vol. 4). London: Methuen.

DeCasper, A. J., & Fifer, W. P. (1980). Of human bonding: Newborns prefer their mothers' voices. *Science, 208,* 1174–1176.

DeCasper, A. J., & Prescott, P. (1984). Human newborns' perception of male voices: Preference, discrimination, and reinforcing value. *Developmental Psychobiology, 17,* 481–491.

DeCasper, A. J., & Spence, M. J. (1986). Prenatal material speech influences newborns' perception of speech sounds. *Infant Behavior and Development, 9,* 133–150.

deChateau, P. (1980). Parent-neonate interaction and its long-term effects. In E. G. Simmel (Ed.), *Early experiences and early behavior.* New York: Academic Press.

DeClercq, E. R. (1992). The transformation of American midwifery: 1975 to 1988. *American Journal of Public Health, 82,* 680–684.

DeFrain, J., Martens, L., Stork, J., & Stork, W. (1991). The psychological effects of a stillbirth on surviving family members. *Omega Journal of Death and Dying, 22,* 81–108.

Delaney, C. H. (1995). Rites of passage in adolescence. *Adolescence, 30,* 891–897.

Delemarre-van de Wall, H. (1993). Environmental factors influencing growth and pubertal development. *Environmental Health Perspectives, 101* (Suppl. 2), 39–44.

Demetriou, A., Shayer, M., & Efklides, A. (Eds.). (1993). *Neo-Piagetian theories of cognitive development: Implications and applications for education.* London: Routledge.

Demo, D. H., & Acock, A. (1991). The impact of divorce on children. In A. Booth (Ed.), *Contemporary families.* Minneapolis, MN: National Council on Family Relations.

Denny, F. W., & Clyde, W. A. (1983). Acute repiratory tract infections: An overview. In W. A. Clyde & F. W. Denny (Eds.), Workshop on acute respiratory diseases among children of the world. *Pediatric Research, 17,* 1026–1029.

Dent, J. (1984, March). Laughter is the best medicine. *Reader's Digest, 124,* 38.

De Róiste, A., & Bushnell, I. W. R. (1996). Tactile stimulation: Short- and long-term benefits for pre-term infants. *British Journal of Developmental Psychology, 14,* 41–53.

DeRosier, M. E., Kupersmidt, J. B., & Patterson, C. J. (1994). Children's academic and behavioral adjustment as a function of the chronicity and proximity of peer rejection. *Child Development, 65,* 1799–1813.

Desforges, D. M., Lord, C. G., Ramsey, S. L., Mason, J. A., VanLeeuwen, M. D., West, S. C., & Lepper, M. R. (1991). Effects of structured cooperative contact on changing negative attitudes toward stigmatized social groups. *Journal of Personality and Social Psychology, 60,* 531–544.

Deutsch, F. M., Lussier, J. B., & Servis, L. J. (1993). Husbands at home: Predictors of paternal participation in childcare and housework. *Journal of Personality and Social Psychology, 65,* 1154–1166.

Deutsch, M. (1967). *The disadvantaged child: Selected papers of Martin Deutsch and associates.* New York: Basic Books.

Deveny, K. (1994, December 5). Chart of kindergarten awards. *The Wall Street Journal,* p. B1.

deVilliers, P. A., & deVilliers, J. G. (1992). Language development. In M. H. Bornstein & M. E. Lamb (Eds.), *Developmental psychology: An advanced textbook* (3rd ed.). Hillsdale, NJ: Erlbaum.

deVries, M. W. (1984). Temperament and infant mortality among the Masai of East Africa. *American Journal of Psychiatry, 141,* 1189–1194.

deVries, R. (1969). Constancy of generic identity in the years 3 to 6. *Monographs of the Society for Research in Child Development, 34* (3, Serial No. 127).

Diamond, A. (Ed.) (1991). Frontal lobe involvement in cognitive changes during the first year of life. In K. Gibwon, M. Konner, & A. Patterson (Eds.), *Brain and behavioral development.* Hillsdale, NJ: Erlbaum.

Dickenson, G. (1975). Dating behavior of black and white adolescents before and after desegregation. *Journal of Marriage and the Family, 37,* 602–608.

Dietz, W. H. (1987). Childhood obesity. *Annals of the New York Academy of Sciences, 499,* 47–54.

DiFranza, J. R., & Lew, R. A. (1995, April). Effect of maternal cigarette smoking on pregnancy complications and sudden infant death syndrome. *The Journal of Family Practice, 40,* 385–394.

DiLalla, L. F., Thompson, L. A., Plomin, R., Phillips, K., Fagan, J. F., Haith, M. M., Cyphers, L. H., & Fulker, D. W. (1990). Infant predictors of preschool and adult IQ: A study of infant twins and their parents. *Developmental Psychology, 26,* 433–440.

Dinges, M. M., & Oetting, E. R. (1993). Similarity in drug use patterns between adolescents and their friends. *Adolescence, 28,* 253–266.

Dion, K. K. (1972). Physical attractiveness and evaluations of children's transgressions. *Journal of Personality and Social Psychology, 24,* 207–213.

Dion, K. L., & Dion, K. K. (1988). Romantic love: Individual and cultural perspectives. In R. J. Sternberg & M. L. Barnes (Eds.), *The psychology of love.* New Haven, CT: Yale University Press.

DiPietro, J. A., Hodgson, D. M., Costigan, K. A., & Johnson, T. B. B. (1996). Fetal antecedents of infant temperament. *Child development, 67,* 2568–2583.

Dodge, K. A. (1985a). Facets of social interaction and the assessment of social competence in children. In B. H. Schneider, K. H. Rubin, & J. E. Ledingham (Eds.), *Children's peer relations: Issues in assessment and intervention.* New York: Springer-Verlag.

Dodge, K. A. (1985b). A social information-processing model of social competence in children. In M. Perlmutter (Ed.), *Minnesota Symposia on Child Psychology:* Vol. 18, (pp. 77–126). Hillsdale, NJ: Erlbaum.

Dodge, K. A., Bates, J. E., & Pettit, G. S. (1990, December 20). Mechanisms in the cycle of violence. *Science, 250,* 1678–1683.

Dodge, K. A., & Coie, J. D. (1987). Social information-processing factors in reactive and proactive aggression in children's peer groups. *Journal of Personality and Social Psychology, 53,* 1146–1158.

Dodge, K. A., & Crick, N. R. (1990). Social information-processing bases of aggressive behavior in children. *Personality and Social Psychology Bulletin, 16,* 8–22.

Dodge, K. A., Pettit, G. S., McClasky, C. L., & Brown, M. M. (1986). Social competence in children. *Monographs of the Society for Research in Child Development, 51*(2, Serial No. 213).

Dodge, K. A., & Price, J. M. (1994). On the relation between social information processing and socially competent behavior in early school-aged children. *Child Development, 65,* 1385–1397.

Dolcini, M. M., Coh, L. D., Adler, N. E., Millstein, S. G., Irwin, C. E., Kegeles, S. M., & Stone, G. C. (1989). Adolescent egocentrism and feelings of invulnerability: Are they related? *Journal of Early Adolescence, 9,* 409–418.

Dornbusch, S., Carlsmith, J., Bushwall, S., Ritter, P., Leiderman, P., Hastorf, A., & Gross, R. (1985). Single parents, extended households, and the control of adolescents. *Child Development, 56,* 326–341.

Dornbusch, S. M., Ritter, P. L., & Steinberg, L. (1992). Differences between African Americans and non-Hispanic whites in the relation of family statuses to adolescent school performance. *American Journal of Education, 99,* 543–567.

Douglas, M. J. (1991). Potential complications of spinal and epidural anesthesia for obstetrics. *Seminars in Perinatology, 15,* 368–374.

Douvan, E., & Adelson, J. (1966). *The adolescent experience.* New York: Wiley.

Dove, A. (1968, July 15). Taking the chitling test. *Newsweek,* 32–34.

Dreyer, P. H. (1982). Sexuality during adolescence. In B. B. Woman (Ed.), *Handbook of developmental psychology.* Englewood Cliffs, NJ: Prentice Hall.

Dromi, E. (1987). *Early lexical development.* Cambridge, England: Cambridge University Press.

Dromi, E. (1993). The development of prelinguistic communication: Implications for language evaluation. In N. J. Anastasiow & S. Harel (Eds.), *At-risk infants: Interventions, families, and research* (pp. 19–26). Baltimore: Brookes.

Dryfoos, J. G. (1990). *Adolescents at risk: Prevalence and prevention.* New York: Oxford University Press.

DuBois, D. L., & Hirsch, B. J. (1990). School and neighborhood friendship patterns of blacks and whites in early adolescence. *Child Development, 61,* 524–536.

Duckitt, J. (1994). Conformity to social pressure and racial prejudice among white South Africans. *Genetic, Social, and General Psychology Monographs, 120,* 121–143.

Duff, C. (1994, September 12). Cool pad, fab food, one catch: Mom lives there, too. *The Wall Street Journal,* pp. A1, A8.

Duke, M., & Nowicki, S., Jr. (1979). *Abnormal psychology: Perspectives on being different.* Monterey, CA: Brooks/Cole.

Duke, M. P., & Nowicki, S., Jr. (1986). *Abnormal psychology: A new look.* New York: Holt Reinhart and Winston.

Dukes, R., & Martinez, R. (1994). The impact of gender on self-esteem among adolescents. *Adolescence, 29,* 105–115.

Duncan, G. J., Brooks-Gunn, J., & Klebanov, P. K. (1994). Economic deprivation and early childhood development. *Child Development, 65,* 296–318.

Duncan, P., Ritter, P., Dornbusch, S., Gross, R., & Carlsmith, J. (1985). The effects of pubertal timing on body image, school behavior, and deviance. *Journal of Youth and Adolescence, 14,* 227–236.

Dunham, R. M., Kidwell, J. S., & Wilson, S. M. (1986). Rites of passage at adolescence: A ritual process paradigm. *Journal of Adolescent Research, 1,* 139–153.

Dunn, A. (1995, January 28). Cram schools: Immigrants' tools for success. *The New York Times,* pp. 1, 24.

Dunn, J. (1991). Understanding others: Evidence from naturalistic studies of children. In W. Whiten (Ed.), *Natural theories of mind: Evolution, development and stimulation of everyday mindreading.* Oxford, England: Blackwell.

Dunn, J. F. (Ed.) (1995). *Connections between emotion and understanding in development.* Hillsdale, NJ: Erlbaum.

Dunn, L. M., (1968). Special education for the mildly retarded—Is much of it justifiable? *Exceptional Child, 35,* 5–22.

Dunphy, D. C. (1963). The social structure of urban adolescent peer groups. *Society, 26,* 230–246.

Dweck, C. S. (1991). Self-theories and goals: Their role in motivation, personality and development. In R. Dienstbier (Ed.), *Nebraska Symposium on Motivation:* Vol. 36. Lincoln: University of Nebraska Press.

Dweck, C. S., & Bush, E. S. (1976). Sex differences in learned helplessness: I. Differential debilitation with peer and adult evaluators. *Developmental Psychology, 12,* 147–156.

Eagly, A. H., & Steffen, V. J. (1984). Gender stereotypes stem from the distribution of women and men into social roles. *Journal of Personality and Social Psychology, 46,* 735–754.

Eagly, A. H., & Steffen, V. J. (1986). Gender and aggressive behavior: A meta-analytic review of the social psychological literature. *Psychological Bulletin, 100,* 309–330.

Eakins, P. S. (Ed.) (1986). *The American way of birth.* Philadelphia: Temple University Press.

Eaton, W. O., & Enns, L. R. (1986). Sex differences in human motor activity level. *Psychological Bulletin, 100,* 19–28.

Eaton, W. O., & Yu, A. P. (1989). Are sex differences in child motor activity level a function of sex differences in maturational status? *Child Development, 60,* 1005–1011.

Eaves, L., Silberg, J., Hewitt, J. K., Meyer, J., Rutter, M., Simonoff, E., Neale, M., & Pickles, A. (1993). Genes, personality, and psychopathology: A latent class analysis of liability to symptoms of attention-deficit hyperactivity disorder in twins. In R. Plomin & G. E. McClearn (Eds.), *Nature, nurture, and psychology.* Washington, DC: American Psychological Association.

Eberstadt, N. (1994). Why babies die in D. C. *The Public Interest, 115,* 3–16.

Ebstein, R. P., Novick, O., Umansky, R., Priel, B., Osher, Y., Blaine, D., Bennett, E. R., Nemanov, L., Katz, M., & Belmaker, R. H. (1996). Dopamine D4 recepetor (D4DR) exon III polymorphism associated with the human personality trait of Novelty Seeking. *Nature Genetics, 12,* 78–80.

Eccles, J. S., Amberton, A., Buchanan, C. M., Jacobs, J., Flanagan, C., Harold, R., MacIver, D., Midgley, C., Reuman, D., & Wigfield, A. (1993). School and family effects on the ontogeny of children's interests, self-perceptions, and activity choice. In J. Jacobs (Ed.), *Nebraska Symposium on Motivation, 1992.* Lincoln: University of Nebraska Press.

Eccles, J. S., Wigfield, A., Flanagan, C., Miller, C., Reuman, D., & Yee, D. (1989). Self-concepts, domain values, and self-esteem: Relations and changes at early adolescence. *Journal of Personality and Social Psychology, 57,* 283–310.

Ecenbarger, W. (1993, April 1). America's new merchants of death. *The Reader's Digest,* 50.

Eckerman, C. O., & Oehler, J. M. (1992). Very-low-birthweight newborns and parents as early social partners. In S. L. Friedman & M. D. Sigman (Eds.), *The psychological development of low-birthweight children.* Norwood, NJ: Ablex.

Eden, D. (1990). Pygmalion without interpersonal contrast effects: Whole groups gain from raising manager expectations. *Journal of Applied Psychology, 75,* 394–398.

Eder, R. A. (1990). Uncovering young children's psychological selves: Individual and developmental differences. *Child Development, 61,* 849–863.

Egan, M. C. (1994). Public health nutrition: A historical perspective. *Journal of the American Dietetic Association, 94,* 298–304.

Egeland, B., & Farber, E. A. (1984). Infant-mother attachment: Factors related to its development and changes over time. *Child Development, 55,* 753–771.

Egeland, B., & Hiester, M. (1995). The long-term consequences of infant day care and mother-infant attachment. *Child Development, 66,* 474–485.

Egeland, B., Pianta, R., & O'Brien, M. A. (1993). Maternal intrusiveness in infancy and child maladaptation in early school years. *Development and Psychopathology, 5,* 359–370.

Ehlers, C. L., Frank, E., & Kupfer, D. J. (1988). Social Zeitgebers and biological rhythms: A unified approach to understanding the etiology of depression. *Archives of General Psychiatry, 45,* 948–952.

Eiger, M. S. (1987). The feeding of infants and children. In R. A. Hoekelman, S. Blatman, S. B Friedman, N. M. Nelson, & H. M. Seidel (Eds.), *Primary pediatric care.* St. Louis, MO: Mosby.

Eiger, M. S., & Olds, S. W. (1987). *The complete book of breastfeeding.* New York: Workman; Bantam.

Eimas, P. D., Sigueland, E. R., Jusczyk, P., & Vigorito, J. (1971). Speech perception in infants. *Science, 171,* 303–306.

Einbinder, S. D. (1992). *A statistical profile of children living in poverty: Children under three and children under six, 1990.* Unpublished document, Columbia University, New York, School of Public Health, the National Center for Children in Poverty.

Eisenberg, N., & Fabes, R. (1991). Prosocial behavior and empathy: A multimethod, developmental perspective. In M. S. Clark (Ed.), *Review of personality and social psychology* (Vol. 12). Newbury Park, CA: Sage.

Eisenberg, N., Wolchik, S. A., Hernandez, R., & Pasternack, J. F. (1985). Parental socialization of young children's play: A short-term longitudinal study. *Child Development, 56,* 1506–1513.

Ekman, P., & O'Sullivan, M. (1991). Facial expression: Methods, means, and moues. In R. S. Feldman & B. Rime (Eds.), *Fundamentals of nonverbal behavior.* Cambridge, England: Cambridge University Press.

Elkind, D. (1967). Egocentrism in adolescence. *Child Development, 38,* 1025–1034.

Elkind, D. (1978). The child's reality: Three developmental themes. In Coren, S. & Ward, L. M. (Eds.), Hillsdale, NJ: Erlbaum.

Elkind, D. (1984). *All grown up and no place to go.* Reading, MA: Addison-Wesley.

Elkind, D. (1985). Egocentrism redux. *Developmental Review, 5,* 218–226.

Elkind, D. (1996). Inhelder and Piaget on adolescence and adulthood: A postmodern appraisal. *Psychological Science, 7,* 216–220.

Elkind, D. (1988). *Miseducation.* New York: Knopf.

Endo, S. (1992). Infant-infant play from 7 to 12 months of age: An analysis of games in infant-peer triads. *Japanese Journal of Child and Adolescent Psychiatry, 33,* 145–162.

England, P., & McCreary, L. (1987). *Integrating sociology and economics to study gender and work.* Newbury Park, CA: Sage Publications.

Engler, J., & Goleman, D. (1992). *The consumer's guide to psychotherapy.* New York: Simon & Schuster.

Ennett, S. T., Tobler, N. S., Ringwalt, C. L., & Flewelling, R. L. (1994, September). How effective is Drug Abuse Resistance Education? A meta-anlysis of Project DARE outcome evaluations. *American Journal of Public Health, 84,* 1394–1401.

Enright, M. K., Rovee-Collier, C. K., Fagen, J. W., & Caniglia, K. (1983). The effects of distributed training on retention of operant conditioning in human infants. *Journal of Experimental Child Psychology, 36,* 209–225.

Epperson, S. E. (1988, September 16). Studies link subtle sex bias in schools with women's behavior in the workplace. *The Wall Street Journal,* p. 19.

Epstein, J. A., Botvin, G. J., Diaz, T., Toth, V., et al. (1995). Social and personal factors in marijuana use and intentions to use drugs among inner city minority youth. *Journal of Developmental and Behavioral Pediatrics, 16,* 14–20.

Epstein, K. (1993). The interactions between breastfeeding mothers and their babies during the breastfeeding session. *Early Child Development and Care, 87,* 93–104.

Epstein, L. H. (1992). Exercise and obesity in children. *Journal of Applied Sport Psychology, 4,* 120–133.

Epstein, S. (1994). An integration of the cognitive and the psychodynamic unconscious. *American Psychologist, 49,* 709–724.

Epstein, S., & Meier, P. (1989). Constructive thinking: A broad coping variable with specific components. *Journal of Personality and Social Psychology, 57,* 332–350.

Erikson, E. H. (1963). *Childhood and society.* New York: Norton.

Eron, L. D., Gentry, J., & Schlegel, P. (1994). *Reason to hope: A psychosocial perspective on violence and youth.* Washington, DC: American Psychological Association.

Eron, L. D., & Huesmann, L. R. (1985). The control of aggressive behavior by changes in attitude, values, and the conditions of learning. In R. J. Blanchard and C. Blanchard (Eds.), *Advances in the study of aggression.* New York: Academic Press.

Erwin, P. (1993). *Friendship and peer relations in children.* Chichester, England: Wiley.

Espenschade, A. (1960). Motor development. In W. R. Johnson (Ed.), *Science and medicine of exercise and sports.* New York: Harper & Row.

Eveleth, P., & Tanner, J. (1976). *Worldwide variation in human growth.* New York: Cambridge University Press.

Evinger, S. (1996). How to read race (Categories of race and ethnicity and the 2000 Census). *American Demographics, 18,* 36–42.

Eyer, D. (1992). The bonding hype. In M. E. Lamb & J. B. Lancaster (Eds.), *Birth management: Biosocial perspectives.* Hawthorne, New York: Aldine de Gruyter.

Eyer, D. E. (1994). Mother-infant bonding: A scientific fiction. *Human Nature, 5,* 69–94.

Eysenck, H. J. (1976). Structure of social attitudes. *Psychological Reports, 39,* 463–466.

Fabsitz, R. R., Carmelli, D., & Hewitt, J. K. (1992). Evidence for independent genetic influences on obesity in middle age. *International Journal of Obesity and Related Metabolic Disorders, 16,* 657–666.

Fagot, B. I. (1978). The influence of sex of child on parental reactions to toddler children. *Child Development, 49,* 459–465.

Fagot, B. I. (1979). Sex differences in toddlers' behavior and parental reaction. *Developmental Psychology, 10,* 554–558.

Fagot, B. I. (1987). Toddler's play and sex stereotyping. In D. Bergen (Ed.), *Play as a medium for learning and development.* Portsmouth, NH: Heinemann.

Fagot, B. I. (1991). *Peer relations in boys and girls from 2 to 7.* Paper presented at the biennial meeting of the Society for Research in Child Development, Seattle, WA.

Fagot, B. I., & Hagan, R. (1991). Observation of parent reaction to sex-stereotyped behaviors: Age and sex effects. *Child Development, 62,* 617–628.

Fagot, B. I., & Leinbach, M. D. (1993). Gender-role development in young children: From discrimination to labeling. *Developmental Review, 13,* 205–224.

Fairburn, C. C., Jones, R., Peveler, R. C. et al. (1993). Psychotherapy and bulimia nervosa. *Archives of General Psychiatry, 50,* 419–428.

Fangman, J. J., Mark, P. M., Pratt, L., Conway, K. K., Healey, M. L., Oswald, J. W., & Uden, D. L. (1994). *American Journal of Obstetrics and Gynecology, 170,* 744–750.

Fanshel, D., Finch, S. J., & Grundy, J. F. (1990). *Foster children in a life course perspective.* New York: Columbia University Press.

Fanshel, D., Finch, S. J., & Grundy, J. F. (1992). *Serving the urban poor.* Westport, CT: Praeger.

Fantz, R. (1963). Pattern vision in newborn infants. *Science, 140,* 296–297.

Fantz, R. L. (1961). The origin of form perception. *Scientific American, 138,* 72.

Farhi, P. (1995, June 21). Turning the tables on TV violence. *The Washington Post,* pp. F1, F2.

Farley, C. F. (1993, April 19). CNN/Time national poll. *Time,* 15.

Farrington, D. (1991). Childhood aggression and adult violence: Early precursors and later-life outcomes. In D. Pepler & K. Rubin (Eds.), *The development and treatment of childhood aggression.* Hillsdale, NJ: Erlbaum.

Farver, J. M., & Branstetter, W. H. (1994). Preschoolers' prosocial responses to their peers' distress. *Developmental Psychology, 30,* 334–341.

Farver, J. M., Kim, Y. K., & Lee, Y. (1995). Cultural differences in Korean- and Anglo-American preschoolers' social interaction and play behaviors. *Child Development, 66,* 1088–1099.

Feather, N. T. (1980). Values in adolescence. In J. Adelson (Ed.), *Handbook of adolescent psychology.* New York: Wiley.

Fein, G. G., Gariboldi, A., & Boni, R. (1993). The adjustment of infants and toddlers to group care: The first 6 months. *Early Childhood Research Quarterly, 8,* 1–14.

Feldman, R. S. (Ed.). (1982). *Development of nonverbal behavior in children.* New York: Springer-Verlag.

Feldman, R. S. (Ed.). (1992). *Applications of nonverbal behavioral theories and research.* Hillsdale, NJ: Erlbaum.

Feldman, R. S., Philippot, P., & Custrini, R. J. (1991). Social competence and nonverbal behavior. In R. S. Feldman & B. Rimé (Eds.), *Fundamentals of nonverbal behavior.* Cambridge, England: Cambridge University Press.

Feldman, R. S., & Prohaska, T. (1979). The student as Pygmalion: Effect of student expectation on the teacher. *Journal of Educational Psychology, 4,* 485–493.

Feldman, R. S., & Rimé, B. (Eds.). (1991). *Fundamentals of nonverbal behavior.* Cambridge, England: Cambridge University Press.

Feldman, R. S., & Theiss, A. J. (1982). The teacher and student as Pygmalions: The joint effects of teacher and student expectation. *Journal of Educational Psychology, 74,* 217–223.

Feldman, R. S. (Ed.). (1990). *The social psychology of education.* Cambridge, MA.: Cambridge University Press.

Feldman, S. S., Biringen, Z. C., & Nash, S. C. (1981). Fluctuations of sex-related self-attributions as a function of stage of family life cycle. *Developmental Psychology, 17,* 24–35.

Feldman, S. S. & Rosenthal, D. A. (1990). The acculturation of autonomy expectations in Chinese high schoolers residing in two Western nations. *International Journal of Psychology, 25,* 259–281.

Feldman, W., Feldman, E., & Goodman, J. T. (1988). Culture versus biology: Children's attitudes toward thinness and fatness. *Pediatrics, 81,* 190–194.

Feng, T. (1993). Substance abuse in pregnancy. *Current Opinion in Obstetrics and Gynecology, 5,* 16–23.

Fenson, L., Dale, P. S., Reznick, J. S., Bates, E., Thal, D. J., & Pethick, S. J. (1994). Variability in early communicative development. *Monographs of the Society for Research in Child Development, 59* (5, Serial No. 242).

Fenwick, K., & Morrongiello, B. (1991). Development of frequency perception in infants and children. *Journal of Speech, Language Pathology, and Audiology, 15,* 7–22.

Fernald, A. (1984). The perceptual and affective salience of mothers' speech to infants. In L. Feagans, C. Garvey, & R. Golinkoff (Eds.), *The origins and growth of communication.* Norwood, NJ: Ablex.

Fernald, A. (1989). Intonation and communicative intent in mothers' speech to infants: Is the melody the message? *Child Development, 60,* 1497–1510.

Fernald, A. (1991). Prosody in speech to children: Prelinguistic and linguistic functions. In R. Vasta (Ed.), *Annals of child development* (Vol. 8, pp. 43–80). London: Jessica Kingsley.

Fernald, A., & Kuhl, P. (1987). Acoustic determinants of infant preference for motherese speech. *Infant Behavior and Development, 10,* 279–293.

Fernald, A., Taeschner, T., Dunn, J., Papousek, M., Boysson-Bardies, B. de, & Fukui, I. (1989). A cross-language study of prosodic modifications in mothers' and fathers' speech to preverbal infants. *Journal of Child Language, 16,* 477–501.

Ferrarri, F., Kelsall, A. W., Rennie, J. M., & Evans, D. H. (1994). The relationship between cerebral blood flow velocity fluctuations and sleep state in normal newborns. *Pediatric Research, 35,* 50–54.

Feshbach, S. (1980). Child abuse and the dynamics of human aggression and violence. In J. Gerbner, C. J. Ross, & E. Zigler (Eds.), *Child abuse: An agenda for action.* New York: Oxford University Press.

Festinger, L. (1954). A theory of social comparison processes. *Human Relations, 7,* 117–140.

Field, D. (1987). A review of preschool conservation training: An analysis of analyses. *Developmental Review, 7,* 210–251.

Field, T. (1990). *Infancy.* Cambridge, MA: Harvard University Press.

Field, T., Cohen, D., Garcia, R., & Greenberg, R. (1984). Mother-stranger face discrimination by the newborn. *Infant Behavior and Development, 7,* 19–27.

Field, T., Dempsey, J., & Shuman, H. H. (1983). Five-year follow-up of preterm respiratory distress syndrome and post-term postmaturity syndrome infants. In T. Field & A. Sostek (Eds.), *Infants born at risk: Physiological, perceptual and cognitive processes.* New York: Grune & Stratton.

Field, T., Greenberg, R., Woodson, R., Cohen, D., & Garcia, R. (1984). Facial expression during Brazelton neonatal assessments. *Infant Mental Health Journal, 5,* 61–71.

Field, T., Masi, W., Goldstein, S., Perry, S., & Parl, S. (1988). Infant day/care facilitates preschool social behavior. *Early Childhood Research Quarterly, 3,* 341–359.

Field, T., & Roopnarine, J. L. (1982). Infant-peer interactions. In T. Field, A. Huston, H. Quay, & G. Finley. (Eds.) *Review of human development.* New York: Wiley.

Field, T., & Walden, T. (1982). Perception and production of facial expression in infancy and early childhood. In H. Reese and L. Lipsitt (Eds.), *Advances in child development and behavior.* (Vol. 16). New York: Academic Press.

Field, T. M. (1978). Interaction of primary versus secondary caretaker fathers. *Developmental Psychology, 14,* 183–184.

Field, T. M. (1979). Games parents play with normal and high-risk infants. *Child Psychiatry and Human Development, 10,* 41–48.

Field, T. M. (1981). Infant gaze aversion and heart rate during face-to-face interactions. *Infant Behavior and Development, 4,* 307–313.

Field, T. M. (1982). Individual differences in the expressivity of neonates and young infants. In R. S. Feldman (Ed.), *Development of nonverbal behavior in children.* New York: Springer-Verlag.

Field, T. M. (1987). Interaction and attachment in normal and atypical infants. *Journal of Consulting and Clinical Psychology, 14, 183–184.*

Field, T. M. (Ed.). (1988). *Stress and coping across development.* Hillsdale, NJ: Erlbaum.

Field, T. M. (1990). Alleviating stress in newborn infants in the intensive care unit. In B. M. Lester & E. Z. Tronick (Eds.), *Stimulation and the preterm infant: The limits of plasticity.* Philadelphia: Saunders.

Field, T. M. (1991). Reducing stress in child and psychiatric patients by massage and relaxation therapy. In T. M. Field, P. M. McCabe, & D. Schneiderman (Eds.), *Stress and coping in infancy and childhood* (Vol. 4). Hillsdale, NJ: Erlbaum.

Field, T. M. (Ed.). (1995). *Touch in early development.* Hillsdale, NJ: Erlbaum.

Field, T. M., Woodson, R., Greenberg, R., & Cohen, D. (1982). Discrimination and imitation of facial expressions by neonates. *Science, 218,* 179–181.

Fifer, W. (1987). Neonatal preference for mother's voice. In N. A. Kasnegor, E. M. Blass, & M. A. Hofer, (Eds.), *Perinatal development: A psychobiological perspective. Behavioral biology* (pp. 111–124). Orlando, FL: Academic Press.

Figley, C. R. (1973). Child density and the marital relationship. *Journal of Marriage and the Family, 35,* 272–282.

Fingerhut, L. A. & Kleinman, J. C. (1990). International and interstate comparisons of homicide among young males. *Journal of the American Medical Association, 263,* 3292–3295.

Fingerhut, L. A., & MaKuc, D. M. (1992). Mortality among minority populations in the United States. *American Journal of Public Health, 82,* 1168–1170.

Finkbeiner, A. K. (1996). *After the death of a child: Living with loss through the years.* New York: The Free Press.

First, J. M., & Cardenas, J. (1986). A minority view on testing. *Educational Measurement Issues and Practice, 5,* 6–11.

Fischgrund, J. E. (1996). Learners who are deaf or hard of hearing. In M. C. Wang, M. C. Reynolds, & H. J. Walberg (Eds.), *Handbook of special and remedial education: Research and practice* (2nd ed.). New York: Pergamon Press.

Fishbein, H. D., & Imai, S. (1993). Preschoolers select playmates on the basis of gender and race. *Journal of Applied Developmental Psychology, 14,* 303–316.

Fishel, E. (1993, September). Starting kindergarten. *Parents,* 165–169.

Fisher, C. B., & Fryrberg, D. (1994). Participant partners: College students weigh the costs and benefits of deceptive research. *American Psychologist, 49,* 417–427.

Fisher, C. B., & Lerner, R. M. (1994). *Applied developmental psychology.* New York: McGraw-Hill.

Fiske, S. T., & Taylor, S. E. (1991). *Social cognition* (2nd ed.). New York: McGraw-Hill.

Fivush, R. (Ed.). (1995). *Long-term retention of infant memories.* Hillsdale, NJ: Erlbaum.

Flavell, J. H. (1979). Metacognitive aspects of problem solving. In L. Resnick (Ed.), *The nature of intelligence.* Hillsdale, NJ: Erlbaum.

Flavell, J. H. (1985). *Cognitive development* (2nd ed.). Englewood Cliffs, NJ: Prentice Hall.

Flavell, J. H. (1993). Young children's understanding of thinking and consciousness. *Current Directions in Psychological Science, 2,* 40–43.

Flavell, J. H. (1994). Cognitive development: Past, present, and future. In R. D. Parke, P. A. Ornstein, J. J. Rieser, & C. Zahn-Waxler (Eds.), *A century of developmental psychology.* Washington, DC: American Psychological Association.

Flavell, J. H. (1996). Piaget's legacy. *Psychological Science, 7,* 200–203.

Flavell, J. H., Green, F. L., & Flavell, E. R. (1995). The development of children's knowledge about attentional focus. *Developmental Psychology, 31,* 706–712.

Flavell, J. H., Green, F. L., Flavell, E. R., & Grossman, J. B. (1997). The development of children's knowledge about inner speech. *Child Development, 68,* 39–47.

Fleming, J. E., & Offord, D. R. (1990). Epidemiology of childhood depressive disorders: A critical review. *Journal of the American Academy of Child and Adolescent Psychiatry, 29,* 571–580.

Fletcher, A. C., Darling, N. E., Steinberg, L., & Dornbusch, S. M. (1995). The company they keep: Relation of adolescents' adjustment and behavior to their friends' perceptions of authoritative parenting in the social network. *Developmental Psychology, 31,* 300–310.

Flowers, B. J., & Richardson, F. C. (1996). Why is multiculturalism good? *American Psychologist, 51,* 609–621.

Flum, H. (1994). The evolutive style of identity formation. *Journal of Youth and Adolescence, 23,* 489–498.

Fogel, A. (1980). Peer vs. mother-directed behavior in 1- to 3-month-old infants. *Infant Behavior and Development, 2,* 215–226.

Folkman, S., & Lazarus, R. S. (1980). An analysis of coping in a middle-aged community sample. *Journal of Health and Social Behavior, 21,* 219–239.

Folkman, S., & Lazarus, R. S. (1988). Coping as a mediator of emotion. *Journal of Personality and Social Psychology, 54,* 466–475.

Forslund, M. (1992). Growth and motor performance in preterm children at 8 years of age. *Acta Paediatrica, 81,* 840–842.

Fowler, W. (1990). *Talking from infancy: How to nurture and cultivate early language development.* Cambridge, MA: Brookline Books.

Fowles, D. C. (1992). Schizophrenia: Diathesis-stress revisited. *Annual Review of Psychology, 43,* 303–336.

Fox, N. A., Kimmerly, N. L., & Schafer, W. D. (1991). Attachment to mother/attachment to father: A meta-analysis. *Child Development, 62,* 210–225.

Fox, J. L. (1984). International group suspends Nestlé boycott. *Science, 223,* 569.

Fox, N. A. (1995). Of the way we were: Adult memories about attachment experiences and their role in determining infant-parent relationships: A commentary on van IJzendoorn. *Psychological Bulletin, 117,* 404–410.

Fox, N.A. (Ed.). (1994). *The development of emotion regulation: Biological and behavioral considerations.* (2–3, Serial No. 240). Chicago: Society for Research in Child Development.

Franck, I., & Brownstone, D. (1991). *The parent's desk reference.* New York: Prentice-Hall.

Frankenburg, W. K., Dodds, J., Archer, P., Shapiro, H., & Bresnick, B. (1992). The Denver II: A major revision and restandardization of the Denver Developmental Screening Test. *Pediatrics, 89,* 91–97.

Franzoi, S. L., Davis, M. H., & Vasquez-Suson, K. A. (1994). Two social worlds: Social correlates and stability of adolescent status groups. *Journal of Personality and Social Psychology, 67,* 462–473.

Freedman, D. G. (1979, January). Ethnic differences in babies. *Human Nature,* 15–20.

Frenkel, L. D., & Gaur, S. (1994). Perinatal HIV infection and AIDS. *Clinics in Perinatology, 21,* 95–107.

Freud, S. (1920). *A general introduction to psychoanalysis.* New York: Boni & Liveright.

Freud, S. (1922/1959). *Group psychology and the analysis of the ego.* London: Hogarth.

Fried, P. A., & Watkinson, B. (1990). 36- and 48-month neurobehavioral follow-up of children prenatally exposed to marijuana, cigarettes, and alcohol. *Journal of Developmental and Behavioral Pediatrics, 11,* 49–58.

Friedman, H. S., Tucker, J. S., Schwartz, J. E., Martin, L. R., Tomlinson-Keasey, C., Wingard, D. L., & Criqui, M. H. (1995a). Childhood conscientiousness and longevity: Health behaviors and cause of death. *Journal of Personality and Social Psychology, 68,* 696–703.

Friedman, H. S., Tucker, J. S., Schwartz, J. E., Tomlinson-Keasey, C., Martin, L. R., Wingard, D. L., & Criqui, M. H. (1995b). Psychosocial and behavioral predictors of longevity: The aging and death of the "Termites." *American psychologist, 50,* 69–78.

Friedman, S. L., & Sigman, M. D. (1992). *The psychological development of low-birthweight children.* Norwood, NJ: Ablex.

Friedman, W. J. (1993). Memory for the time of past events. *Psychological Bulletin, 113,* 44–66.

Fromme, K., & Rivet, K. (1994). Young adults' coping style as a predictor of their alcohol use and response to daily events. *Journal of Youth and Adolescence, 23,* 85–97.

Fuchs, D. & Fuchs, L. S. (1994). Inclusive schools movement and the radicalization of special education reform. *Exceptional Children, 60,* 294–309.

Furman, W., & Bierman, K. L. (1983). Developmental changes in young children's conceptions of friendship. *Child Development, 54,* 549–556.

Furnham, A., & Weir, C. (1996). Lay theories of child development. *Journal of Genetic Psychology, 157,* 211–226.

Furstenberg, F. F., Jr., Brooks-Gunn, J., & Morgan, S. P. (1987). *Adolescent mothers in later life.* New York: Cambridge University Press.

Gaddis, A., & Brooks-Gunn, J. (1985). The male experience of pubertal change. *Journal of Youth and Adolescence, 14,* 61–70.

Gadow, K. D., & Sprafkin, J. (1993). Television "violence" and children with emotional and behavioral disorders. *Journal of Emotional and Behavioral Disorders, 1,* 54–63.

Gaertner, S. L., Mann, J. A., Dovidio, J. F., Murrell, A. J., & Pomare, M. (1990). How does cooperation reduce intergroup bias? *Journal of Personality and Social Psychology, 59,* 692–704.

Gagne, F. (1985). Giftedness and talent: Reexamining a reexamination of the definitions. *Gifted Child Quarterly, 29,* 103–112.

Galambos, N. L., & Dixon, R. A. (1984). Toward understanding and caring for latchkey children. *Child Care Quarterly, 13,* 116–125.

Gallagher, J. J. (1994). Teaching and learning: New models. *Annual Review of Psychology, 45,* 171–195.

Gallant, J. L., Braun, J., & VanEssen, D. C. (1993, January 1). Selectivity for polar, hyperbolic, and cartesian gratings in macaque visual cortex. *Science, 259,* 100–103.

Gallup, G. G., Jr. (1977). Self-recognition in primates: A comparative approach to the bidirectional properties of consciousness. *American Psychologist, 32,* 329–337.

Gans, J. E., Blyth, D. A., Elsby, A. B., & Gaveras, C. C. (1990). America's adolescents: How healthy are they? *AMA profiles of adolescent health series* (Vol. 1). Chicago: American Medical Association.

Garbaciak, J. A. (1990). Labor and delivery: Anesthesia, induction of labor, malpresentation, and operative delivery. *Current Opinion in Obstetrics and Gynecology, 2,* 773–779.

Garbarino, J. (1985). *Adolescent development: An ecological perspective.* Columbus, OH: Merrill.

Garbarino, J. (1988). Preventing childhood injury: Developmental and mental health issues. *American Journal of Orthopsychiatry, 58,* 25–45.

Garbarino, J., & Asp, C. (1981). *Successful schools and competent students.* Lexington, MA: Lexington Books.

Garbarino, J., Dubrow, N., Kostelny, K., & Pardo, C. (1992). *Children in danger: Coping with the consequences of community violence.* San Francisco: Jossey-Bass.

Garber, M. (1981). Malnutrition during pregnancy and lactation. In G. H. Bourne (Ed.), *World review of nutrition and dietetics* (Vol. 36). Basel, Switzerland: Karger.

Gardner, H. (1980). *Artful scribbles: The significance of children's drawings.* New York: Basic Books.

Gardner, H., & Hatch, T. (1989). Multiple intelligences go to school. *Educational Researcher, 18*(8), 4–10.

Garland, A. F., & Zigler, E. (1993). Adolescent suicide prevention: Current research and social policy implications. *American Psychologist, 48,* 169–182.

Garner, P. W., Jones, D. C., & Miner, J. L. (1994). Social competence among low-income preschoolers: Emotion socialization practices and social cognitive correlates. *Child Development, 65,* 622–637.

Garner, R., & Alexander, P. A. (1989). Metacognition: Answered and unanswered questions. *Educational Psychologist, 24,* 143–158.

Gaulden, M. E. (1992). Maternal age effect: The enigma of Down syndrome and other trisomic conditions. *Mutation Research, 296,* 69–88.

Gazzaniga, M. S. (1983). Right-hemisphere language following brain bisection: A 20-year perspective. *American Psychologist, 38,* 525–537.

Geary, D. C., Fan, L., & Bow-Thomas, C. C. (1992). Even before formal instruction, Chinese children outperform American children in mental addition. *Cognitive Development, 8,* 517–529.

Gelles, R. J. (1994). *Contemporary families.* Newbury Park, CA: Sage.

Gelles, R. J., & Cornell, C. (1990). *Intimate violence in families.* Beverly Hills, CA: Sage.

Gelman, D. (1994, April 18). The mystery of suicide. *Newsweek,* 44–49.

Gelman, R. (1972). Logical capacity of very young children: Number invariance rules. *Child Development, 43,* 75–90.

Gelman, R., & Au, T. K. (1996). (Eds.). *Perceptual and cognitive development.* San Diego: Academic Press.

Gelman, R., & Baillargeon, R. (1983). A review of some Piagetian concepts. In P. H. Mussen (Ed.), *Handbook of child psychology: Vol 3. Cognitive Development* (4th ed., pp. 167–230). New York: Wiley.

Gelman, R., & Gallistel, C. R. (1978). *The child's understanding of number.* Cambridge, MA: Harvard University Press.

Gelman, S. A., & Kalish, C. W. (1993). Categories and causality. In R. Pasnak & M. L. Howe (Eds.), *Emerging themes in cognitive development. Vol. 2: Competencies.* New York: Springer-Verlag.

Genesee, F. (1994). Bilingualism. In V. S. Ramachandran (Ed.), *Encyclopedia of human behavior.* San Diego: Academic Press.

Gerard, H. B. (1988). School desegregation: The social science role. In P. A. Katz & K. A. Taylor (Eds.), *Eliminating racism: Profiles in controversy.* New York: Plenum.

Gesell, A. L. (1946). The ontogenesis of infant behavior. In L. Carmichael (Ed.), *Manual of Child Psychology.* New York: Harper.

Gibbins, A. (1994, September 2). Childrens' Vaccine Initiative stumbles. *Science, 265,* 1376–1377.

Gibson, E. J., & Walk, R. D. (1960). The "visual cliff." *Scientific American, 202,* (9) 64–71.

Gil, D. G. (1970). *Violence against children: Physical abuse in the United States.* Cambridge, MA: Harvard University Press.

Gilbert, L. A. (1994). Current perspectives on dual-career families. *Current Directions in Psychological Science, 3,* 101–105.

Gilligan, C. (1982). *In a different voice: Psychological theory and women's development.* Cambridge, MA: Harvard University Press.

Gilligan, C. (1987). Adolescent development reconsidered. In C. E. Irwin (Ed.), *Adolescent social behavior and health.* San Francisco: Jossey-Bass.

Gilligan, C., Lyons, N. P., & Hammer, T. J. (Eds.). (1990). *Making connections.* Cambridge, MA: Harvard University Press.

Gilligan, C., Ward, J. V., & Taylor, J. M. (Eds.). (1988). *Mapping the moral domain: A contribution of women's thinking to psychological theory and education.* Cambridge, MA: Harvard University Press.

Ginzberg, E. (1972). Toward a theory of occupational choice: A restatement. *Vocational Guidance Quarterly, 12,* 10–14.

Gjerde, P., Block, J., & Block, J. (1988). Depressive symptoms and personality during late adolescence: Gender differences in the externalization-internalization of symptom expression. *Journal of Abnormal Psychology, 97,* 475–486.

Gladue, B. (1984). Hormone markers for homosexuality. *Science, 225,* 198.

Gladue, B. A. (1994). The biopsychology of sexual orientation. *Current Directions in Psychological Science, 3,* 150–154.

Gleason J. B. (1987). Sex differences in parent-child interaction. In S. U. Philips, S. Steele, & C. Tanz (Eds.), *Language, gender, and sex in comparative perspective.* New York: Cambridge University Press.

Gleason, J. B., Perlmann, R. Y., Ely, R., & Evans, D. W. (1991). The babytalk register: Parents' use of diminutives. In J. L. Sokolov & C. E. Snow (Eds.), *Handbook of research in language development using CHILDES.* Hillsdale, NJ: Erlbaum.

Gleick, E., Reed, S., & Schindehette, S. (1994, October 24). The baby trap. *People Weekly,* 38–56.

Gleitman, L., & Landau, B. (1994). *The acquisition of the lexicon.* Cambridge, MA: Bradford.

Glick, P. (1989). Remarried families, stepfamilies, and stepchildren: A brief demographic analysis. *Family Relations, 38,* 24–27.

Glick, P., Zion, C., & Nelson, C. (1988). What mediates sex discrimination in hiring decisions? *Journal of Personality and Social Psychology, 55,* 178–186.

Glover, J. A., Ronning, R. R., & Reynolds, C. R. (Eds.). (1992). *Handbook of creativity.* New York: Plenum.

Gold, P. W., Gwirtsman, H., Avgerinos, P. C., Nieman, L. K., Gallucci, W. T., Kaye, W., Jimerson, D., Ebert, M., Rittmaster, R., Loriaux, L., & Chrousos, G. P. (1986). Abnormal hypothalmic-pituitary-adrenal function in anorexia nervosa. *New England Journal of Medicine, 314,* 1335–1342.

Goldberg, S. (1983). Parent-infant bonding: Another look. *Child Development, 54,* 1355–1382.

Goldberg, S., & DiVitto, B. (1983). *Born too soon.* San Francisco: Freeman.

Goldsmith, H. H., & Gottesman, I. I. (1981). Origins of variation in behavioral style: A longitudinal study of temperament in young twins. *Child Development, 53,* 91–103.

Goldsmith, H. H., & Harman, C. (1994). Temperament and attachment: Individuals and relationships. *Current Directions in Psychological Science, 3,* 53–57.

Goldstein, A. (1994, August). Paper presented at the annual meeting of the American Psychological Association, Los Angeles.

Goleman, D. (1993, July 21). Baby sees, baby does, and classmates follow. *The New York Times,* C10.

Golinkoff, R. M. (1993). When is communication a "meeting of minds"? *Journal of Child Language, 20,* 199–207.

Golombok, S., Cook, R., Bish, A., & Murray, C. (1995). Families created by the new reproductive technologies: Quality of parenting and social and emotional development of the children. *Child Development, 66,* 285–298.

Golombok, S., & Fivush, R. (1994). *Gender development.* Cambridge, England: Cambridge University Press.

Gongla, P., & Thompson, E. H. (1987). Single-parent families. In M. B. Sussman & S. K. Steinmetz (Eds.), *Handbook of marriage and the family.* New York: Plenum.

Goodman, G. S., & Reed, R. S. (1986). Age differences in eyewitness testimony. *Law and Human Behavior, 10,* 317–332.

Goodman, J. C., & Nusbaum, H. C. (Eds.). (1994). *The development of speech perception.* Cambridge, MA: Bradford.

Goodwin, M. H. (1980). Directive-response speech sequences in girls' and boys' task activities. In S. McConnell-Ginet, R. Borker, & N. Furman (Eds.), *Women and language in literature and society* (pp. 157–173). New York: Praeger.

Goodwin, M. H. (1990). Tactical uses of stories: Participation frameworks within girls' and boys' disputes. *Discourse Processes, 13,* 33–71.

Googans, B., & Burden, D. (1987). Vulnerability of working parents: Balancing work and home roles. *Social Work, 32,* 295–300.

Goossens, F. A., & van IJzendoorn, M. H. (1990). Quality of infants' attachments to professional caregivers: Relation to infant-parent attachment and day-care characteristics. *Child Development, 61,* 832–837.

Goren, G. C., Sarty, M., & Wu, P. Y. K. (1975). Visual following and pattern discrimination of face-like stimuli by newborn infants. *Pediatrics, 56,* 544–549.

Gorman, K. S., & Pollitt, E. (1992). Relationship between weight and body proportionality at birth, growth during the first year of life, and cognitive development at 36, 48, and 60 months. *Infant Behavior and Development, 15,* 279–296.

Gortmaker, S. L., Dietz, W. H., Sobol, A. M., & Welher, C. A. (1987). Increasing pediatric obesity in the United States. *American Journal of the Diseases of Children, 141,* 535–540.

Gortmaker, S. L., Must, A., Sobol, A. M., Peterson, K., Colditz, G. A., & Dietz, W. H. (1996). Television viewing as a cause of increasing obesity among children in the United States, 1986–1990. *Archives of Pediatrics & Adolescent Medicine, 150,* 356–362.

Gottesman, I. I. (1991). *Schizophrenia genesis: The origins of madness.* New York: Freeman.

Gottesman, I. I. (1993). Origins of schizophrenia: Past as prologue. In R. Plomin, & G. E. McClearn (Eds.), *Nature, nurture, and psychology.* Washington, DC: American Psychological Association.

Gottfredson, G. D., & Holland, J. L. (1990). A longitudinal test of the influence of congruence: Job satisfaction, competency utilization, and counterproductive behavior. *Journal of Counseling Psychology, 37,* 389–398.

Gottfried, A. E., & Gottfried, A. W. (Eds.). (1994). *Redefining families.* New York: Plenum.

Gottfriend, A. W., Gottfried, A. E., Bathurst, K., & Guerin, D. W. (1994). *Gifted IQ: Early developmental aspects-The Fullerton Longitudinal Study.* New York: Plenum Publishing.

Gottlieb, G. (1991). Experimental canalization of behavioral development: Theory. *Developmental Psychology, 27,* 373–381.

Gottman, J. M. (1986). The world of coordinated play: Same- and cross-sex friendship in young children. In J. M. Gottman & J. G. Parker (Eds.), *Conversations of friends: Speculations on affective development* (pp. 139–191). Cambridge, England: Cambridge University Press.

Gottman, J. M. (1993). *What predicts divorce? The relationship between marital processes and marital outcomes.* Hillsdale, NJ: Erlbaum.

Gottman, J. M. (Ed.). (1995). *What predicts divorce? The measures.* Hillsdale, NJ: Erlbaum.

Gottman, J. M., Buehlman, K. T., & Katz, L. F. (1992). Factors determining divorce. *Journal of Family Psychology, 1,* 37–43.

Gottman, J. M., & Katz, L. F. (1989). Effects of marital discord on young children's peer interaction and health. *Developmental Psychology, 25,* 373–381.

Gottman, J. M., & Parkhurst, J. (1980). A developmental theory of friendship and acquaintance processes. In W. A. Collins (Ed.), *Development of cognition, affect, and social relations.* Hillsdale, NJ: Erlbaum.

Gottwald, S. R., & Thurman, S. K. (1994). The effects of prenatal cocaine exposure on mother-infant interaction and infant arousal in the newborn period. *Topics in Early Childhood Special Education, 14,* 217–231.

Gould, S. J. (1977). *Ontogeny and phylogeny.* Cambridge, MA: Harvard University Press.

Graber, J. A., Brooks-Gunn, J., Paikoff, R. L., & Warren, M. P. (1994). Prediction of eating problems: An 8-year study of adolescent girls. *Developmental Psychology, 30,* 823–834.

Graber, J. A., Brooks-Gunn, J., & Warren, M. P. (1995). The antecendents of menarcheal age: Heredity, family environment, and stressful life events. *Child Development, 66,* 346–359.

Grady, C. L., McIntosh, A. R., Horwitz, B., Maison, J. M., Ungerleider, L. G., Mentis, M. J., Pietrini, P., Schapiro, M. B., & Haxby, J. V. (1995, July 14). Age-related reductions in human recognition memory due to impaired encoding. *Science, 269,* 218–221.

Graham, E. (1994, September 30). The long goodbye: Starting preschool means "separation." *The Wall Street Journal*, pp. A1, A7.

Graham, E. (1995, February 9). Leah: Life is all sweetness and insecurity. *The Wall Street Journal*, p. B1.

Graham, J. W., Marks, G., & Hansen, W. B. (1991). Social influence processes affecting adolescent substance use. *Journal of Applied Psychology, 76*, 291–298.

Graham, S. (1992). "Most of the subjects were white and middle class": Trends in published research on African Americans in selected APA journals. *American Psychologist, 47*, 629–639.

Graham, S. (1994). Motivation in African Americans. *Review of Educational Research, 64*, 55–117.

Graham, S. (1997). Using attribution theory to understand social and academic motivation in African American youth. *Educational Psychologist, 32*, 21–34.

Grant, C. A., & Sleeter, C. E. (1986). Race, class, and gender in education research: An argument for integrative analysis. *Review of Educational Research, 56*, 195–211.

Grant, V. J. (1994). Sex of infant differences in mother-infant interaction: A reinterpretation of past findings. *Developmental Review, 14*, 1–26.

Grantham-McGregor, S., Powell, C., Walker, S., Chang, S., & Fletcher, P. (1994). The long-term follow-up of severely malnourished children who participated in an intervention program. *Child Development, 65*, 428–439.

Gratch, G., & Schatz, J. A. (1987). Cognitive development: The relevance of Piaget's infancy books. In J. D. Osofsky (Ed.), *Handbook of infant development* (2nd ed.). New York: Wiley.

Grattan, M. P., DeVos, E. S., Levy, J., & McClintock, M. K. (1992). Asymmetric action in the human newborn: Sex differences in patterns of organization. *Child Development, 63*, 273–289.

Greeberg, M. T., Cicchetti, D., & Cummings, E. M. (Eds.) *Attachment in the preschool years: Theory, research, and intervention.* Chicago: University of Chicago Press.

Greenfield, P. (1995, Winter). Culture, ethnicity, race, and development: Implications for teaching theory and research. *SRCD Newsletter.* Chicago: Society for Research in Child Development.

Greenfield, P. M. (1966). On culture and conservation. In J. S. Bruner, R. R. Olver, & P. M. Greenfield (Eds.), *Studies in cognitive growth.* New York: Wiley.

Greenfield, P. M. (1976). Cross-cultural research and Piagetian theory: Paradox and progress. In K. F. Riegel & J. A. Meacham (Eds.), *The developing individual in a changing world: Vol. 1.* The Hague, The Netherlands: Mouton.

Greenglass, E. R., & Burke, R. J. (1991). The relationship between stress and coping among Type A's. *Journal of Social Behavior and Personality, 6*, 361–373.

Gregory, S. (1856). *Facts for young women.* Boston.

Greven, P. (1990). *Spare the child: The religious roots of punishment and the psychological impact of physical abuse.* New York: Knopf.

Grieser, T., & Kuhl, P. (1988). Maternal speech to infants in atonal language: Support for universal prosodic features in motherese. *Developmental Psychology, 24*, 14–20.

Griffith, D. R., Azuma, S. D., & Chasnoff, I. J. (1994). Three-year outcome of children exposed prenatally to drugs. *Journal of the American Academy of Child and Adolescent Psychiatry, 33*, 20–27.

Grolnick, W. S., & Slowiaczek, M. L. (1994). Parents' involvement in children's schooling: A multidimensional conceptualization and motivation model. *Child Development, 65*, 237–252.

Groome, L. J., Swiber, M. J., Atterbury, J. L., Bentz, L. S., & Holland, S. B. (1997). Similarities and differences in behavioral state organization during sleep periods in the perinatal infant before and after birth. *Child Development, 68*, 1–11.

Gross, R. T., Brooks-Gunn, J., & Spiker, D. (1992). Efficacy of comprehensive early intervention for low-birthweight premature infants and their families: The Infant Health and Development Program. In S. L. Friedman & M. D. Sigman (Eds.), *The psychological development of low-birthweight children.* Norwood, NJ: Ablex.

Gross, R. T., McCormick, M. C., Brooks-Gunn, J., Shapiro, S., Benasich, A. A., & Black, G. (1990). Health care use among young children in day care. Results in a randomized trial of early intervention. *Journal of the American Medical Association, 265*, 2212–2217.

Grossman, K. E., Grossman, K., Huber, F., & Wartner, U. (1982). German children's behavior towards their mothers at 12 months and their fathers at 18 months in Ainsworth's Strange Situation. *International Journal of Behavioral Development, 4*, 157–181.

Groves, B., Zuckerman, B., Marans, S., & Cohen, D. (1993). Silent victims: Children who witness violence. *Journal of the American Medical Association, 269*, 262–264.

Grusec, J. E. (1982). Socialization processes and the development of altruism. In J. P. Rushton & R. M. Sorrentino (Eds.), *Altruism and helping behavior.* Hillsdale, NJ: Erlbaum.

Grusec, J. E. (1991). The socialization of altruism. In M. S. Clark (Ed.), *Prosocial behavior.* Newbury Park, CA: Sage.

Grusec, J. E., & Goodnow, J. J. (1994). Impact of parental discipline methods on the child's internalization of values: A reconceptualization of current points of view. *Developmental Psychology, 30*, 4–19.

Guerin, D. W., & Gottfried, A. W. (1994). Developmental stability and change in parent reports of temperament: A 10-year longitudinal investigation from infancy through preadolescence. *Merrill-Palmer Quarterly, 40*, 334–355.

Gullotta, T. P., Adams, G. R., & Montemayor, R. (Eds.). (1995). *Substance misuse in adolescence.* Thousand Oaks, CA: Sage Publications.

Gunnar, M. R., Porter, F. L., Wolf, C. M., Rigatuso, J., & Larson, M. C. (1995). Neonatal stress reactivity: Predictions to later emotional temperament. *Child Development, 66*, 1–13.

Gur, R. C., Gur, R. E., Obrist, W. D., Hungerbuhler, J. P., Younkin, D., Rosen, A. D., Skilnick, B. E., & Reivich, M. (1982). Sex and handedness differences in cerebral blood flow during rest and cognitive activity. *Science, 217*, 659–661.

Gurman, E. B. (1994). Debriefing for all concerned: Ethical treatment of human subjects. *Psychological Science, 5*, 139.

Guthrie, G., & Lonner, W. (1986). Assessment of personality and psychopathology. In W. Lonner & J. Berry (Eds.), *Field methods in cross-cultural research.* Newbury Park, CA: Sage.

Guttman, J. (1993). *Divorce in psychosocial perspective: Theory and research.* Hillsdale, NJ: Erlbaum.

Guyer, B. et al. (1995). Annual summary of vital statistics—1994. *Pediatrics, 96*, 1029–1039.

Haan, N. (1985). Processes of moral development: Cognitive or social disequilibrium? *Developmental Psychology, 21*, 996–1006.

Hack, M., Klein, N. K., & Taylor, H. G. (1995). Long-term developmental outcomes of low-birthweight infants. *The Future of Children, 5*, 176–197.

Haggerty, R., Garmezy, N., Rutter, M., & Sherrod, L. (Eds.). (1994). *Stress, risk, and resilience in childhood and adolescence.* New York: Cambridge University Press.

Haith, M. M. (1980). *Rules that babies look by.* Hillsdale, NJ: Erlbaum.

Haith, M. M. (1986). Sensory and perceptual processes in early infancy. *Journal of Pediatrics, 109(1),* 158–171.

Haith, M. M. (1991a). Gratuity, perception-action integration and future orientation in infant vision. In F. Kessel, M. Bornstein, & A. Sameroff (Eds.), *Contemporary constructions of the child.* Hillsdale, NJ: Erlbaum.

Haith, M. M. (1991b, April). *Setting a path for the 90s: Some goals and challenges in infant sensory and perceptual development.* Paper presented at the biennial meeting of the Society for Research in Child Development, Seattle, WA.

Hakuta, K. U., & Garcia, E. E. (1989). Bilingualism and education. *American Psychologist, 44,* 374–379.

Hales, K. A., Morgan, M. A., & Thurnau, G. R. (1993). Influence of labor and route of delivery on the frequency of respiratory morbidity in term neonates. *International Journal of Gynecology & Obstetrics, 43,* 35–40.

Halford, G. S., Maybery, M. T., O'Hare, A. W., & Grant, P. (1994). The development of memory and processing capacity. *Child Development, 65,* 1338–1356.

Hall, E. G., & Lee, A. M. (1984). Sex differences in motor performance of young children: Fact or fiction? *Sex Roles, 10,* 217–230.

Halliday, M. A. K. (1975). *Learning how to mean—Explorations in the development of language.* London: Edward Arnold.

Hallinan, M. T., & Williams, R. A. (1989). Interracial friendship choices in secondary schools. *American Sociological Review, 54,* 67–78.

Halpern, L. F., MacLean, W. E., & Baumeister, A. A. (1995). Infant sleep-wake characteristics: Relation to neurological status and the prediction of developmental outcome. *Developmental Review, 15,* 255–291.

Halverson, C. F., Jr., Kohnstamm, G. A., & Martin, R. P. (Eds.). (1994). *The developing structure of temperament and personality from infancy to adulthood.* Hillsdale, NJ: Erlbaum.

Hammen, C. (1991). *Depression runs in families.* New York: Springer-Verlag.

Hammer, R. P. (1984). The sexually dimorphic region of the preoptic area in rats contains denser opiate receptor binding sites in females. *Brain Researcher, 308,* 172–176.

Hammond, W. A., & Romney, D. M. (1995). Cognitive factors contributing to adolescent depression. *Journal of Youth & Adolescence, 24,* 667–683.

Hampson, J., & Nelson, K. (1993). The relation of maternal language to variation in rate and style of language acquisition. *Journal of Child Language, 20,* 313–342.

Hanna, E., & Meltzoff, A. N. (1993). Peer imitation by toddlers in laboratory, home, and day-care contexts: Implications for social learning and memory. *Developmental Psychology, 29,* 701–710.

Harkness, S., & Super, C. M. (1985). The cultural context of gender segregation in children's peer groups. *Child Development, 56,* 219–224.

Harlow, H. F., & Zimmerman, R. R. (1959). Affectional responses in the infant monkey. *Science, 130,* 421–432.

Harrington, R., Fudge, H., Rutter, M., Pickels, A., & Hill, J. (1990). Adult outcomes of childhood and adolescent depresssion. *Archives of General Psychiatry, 47,* 465–473.

Harris, M. J., Milich, R., Corbitt, E. M., Hoover, D. W., et al. (1992). Self-fulfilling effects of stigmatizing information on children's social interactions. *Journal of Personality and Social Psychology, 63,* 41–50.

Harris, M. J., & Rosenthal, R. (1986). Four factors in the mediation of teacher expectancy effects. In R. S. Feldman (Ed.), *The social psychology of education.* Cambridge, MA: Cambridge University Press.

Harris, P. L. (1983). Infant cognition. In M. Haith & J. J. Campos (Eds.) & P. H. Mussen (Gen. Ed.), *Handbook of child psychology: Vol. 2. Infancy and developmental psychobiology.* New York: Wiley.

Harris, P. L. (1987). The development of search. In P. Salapatek & L. Cohen (Eds.), *Handbook of infant perception: From perception to cognition* (Vol. 2, pp. 155–207). Orlando: Academic Press.

Hart, B., & Risley, T. R. (1995). *Meaningful differences in the everyday experience of young American children.* Baltimore: Brookes.

Hart, S. N., & Brassard, M. R. (1987). A major threat to children's mental health. *American Psychologist, 42,* 160–165.

Harter, S. (1983). Developmental perspectives on the self-system. In P. H. Mussen (Ed.), *Handbook of child psychology: Vol. 4. Socialization, personality and social development.* New York: Wiley.

Harter, S. (1990a). Identity and self development. In S. Feldman & G. Elliott (Eds.), *At the threshold: The developing adolescent.* Cambridge, MA: Harvard University Press.

Harter, S. (1990b). Issues in the assessment of self-concept of children and adolescents. In A. LaGreca (Ed.), *Through the eyes of a child.* Boston: Allyn & Bacon.

Hartshorne, T. S. (1994). Friendship. In V. S. Ramachandran (Ed.), *Encyclopedia of human behavior.* San Diego: Academic Press.

Hartup, W. W. (1970). Peer relations. In T. D. Spencer & N. Kass (Eds.), *Perspectives in child psychology: Research and review.* New York: McGraw-Hill.

Hartup, W. W. (1983). Peer relations. In P. H. Mussen (Ed.), *Handbook of child psychology* (4th ed., Vol. 4). New York: Wiley.

Hartup, W. W. (1989). Social relationships and their developmental significance. *American Psychologist, 44,* 120–126.

Hartup, W. W. (1992). Friendships and their developmental significance. In H. McGurk (Ed.), *Childhood social development: Contemporary perspectives.* London: Erlbaum.

Hartup, W. W. (1996). The company they keep: Friendships and their developmental significance. *Child Development, 67,* 1–13.

Harvard Mental Health Letter. (1994, February). AIDS and mental health—Part II. *Harvard Mental Health Letter, 10,* 1–4.

Harvey, P. G., Hamlin, M. W., Kumar, R., & Delves, H. T. (1984). Blood lead, behavior, and intelligence test performance in preschool children. *Science of the Total Environment, 40,* 45–60.

Harwood, R. L., Miller, J. G., & Irizarry, N. L. (1995). *Culture and attachment: Perceptions of the child in context.* New York: Guilford Press.

Haskins, R. (1985). Public school aggression among children with varying day-care experience. *Child Development, 56,* 689–703.

Haskins, R. (1989). Beyond metaphor: The efficacy of early childhood education. *American Psychologist, 44,* 274–282.

Hatfield, E., & Sprecher, S. (1986). *Mirror, mirror . . . The importance of looks in everyday life.* Albany: State University of New York Press.

Hattie, J. (1992). *Self-concept.* Hillsdale, NJ: Erlbaum.

Hawton, K. (1986). *Suicide and attempted suicide among children and adolescents.* Newbury Park, CA: Sage.

Hay, D. F. (1984). Social conflict in early childhood. In G. Whitehurst (Ed.), *Annals of child development* (Vol. 1). Greenwich, CT: JAI Press.

Hayne, H., & Rovee-Collier, C. (1995). The organization of reactivated memory in infancy. *Child Development, 66,* 893–906.

Hazell, P. (1993). Adolescent suicide clusters: Evidence, mechanisms and prevention. *Australian and New Zealand Journal of Psychiatry, 27,* 653–665.

Heath, C. (1994, February). Winning at sports. *Parents,* 126–130.

Heatherton, T. F., Polivy, J., & Herman, C. P. (1991). Restraint, weight loss, and variability of body weight. *Journal of Abnormal Psychology, 100,* 78–83.

Hebbeler, K. (1985). An old and a new question on the effects of early education for children from low income families. *Educational Evaluation and Policy Analysis, 7,* 207–216.

Hellige, J. B. (1993). Unit of thought and action: Varieties of interaction between the left and right cerebral hemispheres. *Current Directions in Psychological Science, 2,* 21–25.

Hellige, J. B. (1994). *Hemispheric asymmetry: What's right and what's left.* Cambridge, MA: Harvard University Press.

Hellman, P. (1987, November 23). *Sesame Street* smart. *New York,* 49–53.

Henry, C. S., Stephenson, A. L., Hanson, M. F., & Hargett, W. (1993). Adolescent suicide and families: An ecological approach. *Adolescence, 28,* 291–308.

Hepper, P. G., Scott, D., & Shahidullah, S. (1993). Infant response to maternal voice. *Journal of Reproductive and Infant Psychology, 11,* 147–153.

Herbst, A. L. (1981). Diethylstilbestrol and other sex hormones during pregnancy. *Obstetrics and Gynecology, 58,* 355–405.

Herbst, A. L. (1994). The epidemiology of ovarian carcinoma and the current status of tumor markers to detect disease. *American Journal of Obstetrics and Gynecology, 170,* 1099–1105.

Herek, G. M. (1993). Sexual orientation and military service: A social science perspective. *American Psychologist, 48,* 538–549.

Herrgard, E., Luoma, L., Tuppurainen, K., Karjalainen, S., & Martikainen, A. (1993). Neurodevelopmental profile at five years of children born at < or = 32 weeks gestation. *Developmental Medicine and Child Neurology, 35,* 1083–1096.

Herrnstein, R. J., & Murray, C. (1994). *The bell curve: Intelligence and class structure in American life.* New York: Free Press.

Hetherington, E. M., & Blechman, E. A. (Eds.). (1996). *Stress, coping, and resiliency in children and families.* Hillsdale, NJ: Erlbaum.

Hetherington, E. M., & Clingempeel, W. (1992). Coping with marital transitions: A family systems perspective. *Monographs of the Society for Research in Child Development, 57*(2–3, Serial No. 227).

Hetheringon, E. M., Stanley-Hagan, M., & Anderson, E. (1989). Marital transitions: A child's perspective. *American psychologist, 44,* 303–312.

Hetherington, T. F, & Weinberger, J. (Eds.). (1993). *Can personality change?* Washington, DC: American Psychological Association.

Heward, W. L., & Orlansky, M. D. (1988, October). The epidemiology of AIDS in the U.S. *Scientific American,* 72–81.

Hewett, F. M., & Forness, S. R. (1974). *Education of exceptional learners.* Boston: Allyn & Bacon.

Higher Education Research Institute. (1991). *The American freshman: National norms for fall 1990.* Los Angeles: University of California, Higher Education Research Institute.

Hille, E. T. M., denOuden, A. L., Aauer, L., van den Oudenrijn, C., Brand, R., & Verloove-Vanhorick, S. P. (1994). School performance at 9 years of age in very premature and very low birthweight infants: Perinatal risk factors and predictors at 5 years of age. *Journal of Pediatrics, 125,* 426–434.

Hinde, R. A., Tamplin, A., & Barrett, J. (1993). Social isolation in 4-year-olds. *British Journal of Developmental Psychology, 11,* 211–236.

Hines, M., & Kaufman, F. R. (1994). Androgen and the development of human sex-typical behavior: Rough-and-tumble play and sex of preferred playmates in children with congenital adrenal hyperplasi (CAH). *Child Development, 65,* 1042–1053.

Hirsch, H. V., & Spinelli, D. N. (1970). Visual experience modifies distribution of horizontally and vertically oriented receptive fields in cats. *Science, 168,* 869–871.

Hirshberg, L. (1990). When infants look to their parents: II. Twelve-month-olds' response to conflicting parental emotional signals. *Child Development, 61,* 1187–1191.

Hirshberg, L., & Svejda, M. (1990). When infants look to their parents: I. Infants' social referencing of mothers compared to fathers. *Child Development, 61,* 1175–1186.

Hirsh-Pasek, K., & Michnick-Golinkoff, R. (1995). *The origins of grammar: Evidence from early language comprehension.* Cambridge, MA: MIT Press.

Hocutt, A. M. (1996). Effectiveness of special education: Is placement the critical factor? *The Future of Children, 6,* 77–102.

Hoff-Ginsberg, E. (1986). Function and structure in maternal speech. *Child Development, 22,* 155–163.

Hoffman, L. W. (1989). Effects of maternal employment in the two-parent family. *American Psychologist, 44,* 283–292.

Hoffman, L. W. (1996). Progress and problems in the study of adolescence. *Developmental Psychology, 32,* 777–780.

Holahan, C. J., & Moos, R. H. (1987). Personal and contextual determinants of coping strategies. *Journal of Personality and Social Psychology, 52,* 946–955.

Holahan, C. J., & Moos, R. H. (1990). Life stressors, resistance factors, and improved psychological functioning: An extension of the stress resistance paradigm. *Journal of Personality and Social Psychology, 58,* 909–917.

Holden, G. W., Coleman, S. M., & Schmidt, K. L. (1995). Why 3-year-old children get spanked: Parent and child determinants as reported by college-educated mothers. *Merrill-Palmer Quarterly, 4,* 431–452.

Holland, A., Sicotte, N., & Treasure, L. (1988). Anorexia nervosa: Evidence for a genetic basis. *Journal of Psychosomatic Research, 32,* 561–571.

Holland, J. L. (1973). *Making vocational choices: A theory of careers.* Englewood Cliffs, NJ: Prentice Hall.

Holland, J. L. (1987). Current status of Holland's theory of careers: Another perspective. *Career Development Quarterly, 36,* 24–30.

Holland, N. (1994, August). *Race dissonance—implications for African American children.* Paper presented at the annual meeting of the American Psychological Association, Los Angeles.

Hollenbeck, A. R., Gewirtz, J. L., Sebris, S. L., & Scanlon, J. W. (1984). Labor and delivery medication influences parent-infant interaction in the first post-partum month. *Infant Behavior and Development, 7,* 201–209.

Holman, R. L. (1991, December 21). Exam hell linked to depression. *The Wall Street Journal,* p. 4.

Holmbeck, G. N., Crossman, R. E., Wandrei, M. L., & Gasiewski, E.(1994). Cognitive development, egocentrism, self-esteem, and adolescent contraceptive knowledge, attitudes, and behavior. *Journal of Youth and Adolescence, 23,* 169–193.

Holmes, D. L., Reich, J. N., & Gyurke, J. S. (1989). The development of high-risk infants in low-risk families. In F. J. Morrison, C. Lord, & D. Keating (Eds.), *Psychological development in infancy.* San Diego, CA: Academic Press.

Holmes, J. (1994). *John Bowlby and attachment theory.* New York: Routledge.

Holmes, T. H., & Rahe, R. H. (1967). The social readjustment scale. *Journal of Psychosomatic Research,* 11, 257–261.

Hopkins, B., & Westra, T. (1988). Maternal handling and motor development: An intracultural study. *Genetic Psychology Monographs, 114,* 377–420.

Hopkins, B., & Westra, T. (1989). Maternal expectations of their infants' development: Some cultural differences. *Developmental Medicine and Child Neurology, 31,* 384–390.

Hopkins, B., & Westra, T. (1990). Motor development, maternal expectation, and the role of handling. *Infant Behavior and Development, 13,* 117–122.

Hoptman, M. J., & Davidson, R. J. (1994). How and why do the two cerebral hemispheres interact? *Psychological Bulletin, 116,* 195–219.

Hornik, R., & Gunnar, M. R. (1988). A descriptive analysis of infant social referencing. *Child Development, 59,* 626–634.

Hornik, R., Risenhoover, N., & Gunnar, M. (1987). The effects of maternal positive, neutral, and negative affective communications on infant response to new toys. *Child Development, 58,* 937–944.

Houle, R., & Feldman, R. S. (1991). Emotional displays in children's television programming. *Journal of Nonverbal Behavior, 15,* 261–271.

Howard, A. (1992). Work and family crossroads spanning the career. In Sheldon Zedeck (Ed.), *Work, families and organizations.* San Francisco: Jossey-Bass.

Howe, M. L., & O'Sullivan, J. T. (1990). The development of strategic memory: Coordinating knowledge, metamemory, and resources. In D. F. Bjorklund (Ed.), *Children's strategies: Contemporary view of cognitive development.* Hillsdale, NJ: Erlbaum.

Howes, C. (1987). Social competence with peers in young children: Developmental sequences. *Developmental Review, 7,* 252–272.

Howes, C., Phillips, D. A., & Whitebook, M. (1992). Thresholds of quality: Implications for the social development of children in center-based child care. *Child Development, 63,* 449–460.

Howes, C., Unger, O., & Seidner, L. B. (1989). Social pretend play in toddlers: Parallels with social play and with solitary pretend. *Child Development, 60,* 77–84.

Howes, C., & Wu, F. (1990). Peer interactions and friendships in an ethnically diverse school setting. *Child Development, 61,* 537–541.

Howie, P. W. et al. (1990). Protective effect of breast-feeding against infection. *British Journal of Medicine, 300,* 11.

Hsu, L. K. G. (1990). *Eating disorders.* New York: Guilford Press.

Hubbard, J., & Coie, J. D. (1994). Emotional correlates of social competence in children's peer relationships. *Merrill-Palmer Quarterly, 40,* 1–20.

Hubel, D. H., & Wiesel, T. N. (1979). Brain mechanisms of vision. *Scientific American, 241,* 150–162.

Huesmann, L. R. (1986). Psychological processes promoting the relations between exposure to media violence and aggressive behavior by the viewer. *Journal of Social Issues, 42,* 125–139.

Huesmann, L. R., & Eron, L. D. (Eds.). (1986). *Television and the aggressive child: A cross-national comparison.* Hillsdale, NJ: Erlbaum.

Huesmann, L. R., Eron, L. D., Klein, R., Brice, P., & Fischer, P. (1983). Mitigating the imitation of aggressive behaviors by changing children's attitudes about media violence. *Journal of Personality and Social Psychology, 5,* 899–910.

Humphreys, L. G. (1992). Commentary: What both critics and users of ability tests need to know. *Psychological Science, 3,* 271–274.

Hunt, E., Streissguth, A. P., Kerr, B., & Olson, H. C. (1995). Mothers' alcohol consumption during pregnancy: Effects on spatial-visual reasoning in 14-year-old children. *Psychological Science, 6,* 339–342.

Hunt, J., & Hunt, L. (1975). Racial inequality and self-image: Identity maintenance as identity diffusion. *Sociology and Social Research, 61,* 539–559.

Hunt, M. (1974). *Sexual behaviors in the 1970s.* New York: Dell.

Hunt, M. (1993). *The story of psychology.* New York: Doubleday.

Huston, A. (Ed.). (1991). *Children in poverty: Child development and public policy.* Cambridge, England: Cambridge University Press.

Huston, A. C., & Wright, J. C. (May, 1995). *The effects of educational television viewing of lower income preschoolers on academic skills, school readiness, and school adjustment 1 to 3 years later: Report to Children's Television Workshop.* Lawrence: University of Kansas, Department of Human Development, Center for Research on the Influences of Television on Children.

Hwang, C. P., Lamb, M. E., & Sigel, I. E. (Eds.). (1996). *Images of childhood.* Mahwah, NJ: Lawrence Erlbaum Associates.

Hyde, J. S. (1994). *Understanding human sexuality* (5th ed.). New York: McGraw-Hill.

Iacono, W. G., & Grove, W. M. (1993). Schizophrenia reviewed: Toward an integrative genetic model. *Psychological Science, 4,* 273–276.

Ikels, C. (1989). Becoming a human being in theory and practice: Chinese views of human development. In D. I. Kertzer & K. W. Schaie (Eds.), *Age structuring in comparative perspective.* Hillsdale, NJ: Erlbaum.

Illingworth, R. S. (1973). *Basic developmental screening: 0–2 years.* Oxford, England: Blackwell Scientific.

Infant Health and Development Program (1990, June 13). *Journal of American Medical Association, 263,* 3035–3042.

Insel, P. M., & Roth, W. T. (1991). *Core concepts in health* (6th ed.). Mountain View, CA: Mayfield.

Irwin, E. G. (1993). A focused overview of anorexia nervosa and bulimia: I. Etiological issues. *Archives of Psychiatric Nursing, 7,* 342–346.

Isabella, R. A. (1993). Origins of attachment: Maternal interactive behavior across the first year. *Child Development, 64,* 605–621.

Isaksen, S. G., & Murdock, M. C. (1993). The emergence of a discipline: Issues and approaches to the study of creativity. In S. G. Isaksen, M. C. Murdock, R. L. Firestein, & D. J. Treffinger (Eds.), *The emergence of a discipline* (Vol. 1). Norwood, NJ: Ablex.

Isay, R. A. (1990). *Being homosexual: Gay men and their development.* New York: Avon.

Israeloff, R. (1991, July). First steps. *Parents,* 53–59.

Iwaniec, D. (1995). *The emotionally abused and neglected child.* New York: Wiley.

Izard, C., & Malatesta, C. (1987). Perspectives on emotional development: I. Differential emotions theory of early emotional development. In J. D. Osofsky (Ed.), *Handbook of infant development* (2nd ed.). New York: Wiley.

Izard, C. E. (1977). *Human emotions.* New York: Plenum.

Izard, C. E., Frantauzzo, C. A., Castle, J. M., Haynes, O. M., Rayias, M. F., & Putnam, P. H. (1995). The ontogeny and significance of infants' facial expressions in the first 9 months of life. *Developmental Psychology, 31,* 997–1013.

Jacklin, C. N., Snow, M. E., & Maccoby, E. E. (1981). Tactile sensitivity and muscle strength in newborn boys and girls. *Infant Behavior and Development, 4,* 261–268.

Jackson, L. A., Gardner, P. D., & Sullivan, L. A. (1992). Explaining gender differences in self-pay expectations: Social comparison standards and perceptions of fair pay. *Journal of Applied Psychology, 77,* 651–663.

Jacobsen, L., & Edmondson, B. (1993, August). *American Demographics,* 22–27.

Jacobson, N. S. (1987). Family type, visiting patterns, and children's behavior in the stepfamily: A linked family system. In K. Pasley & M. Ihinger-Tallman (Eds.), *Remarriage and stepparenting.* New York: Guilford Press.

Jacobson, S. W., Fein, G. G., Jacobson, J. L., Schwartz, P. M., & Dowler, J. K. (1985). The effect of intrauterine PCB exposure on visual recognition memory. *Child Development, 56,* 853–860.

Jacoby, L. L., & Kelley, C. M. (1992). A process-dissociation framework for investigating unconscious influences: Freudian slips, projective tests, subliminal perception, and signal detection theory. *Current Directions in Psychological Science, 1,* 174–179.

Jacoby, R., & Glauberman, N. (Eds.). (1995). *The bell curve debate.* New York: Times Books/Random House.

Jadack, R. A., Hyde, J. S., Moore, C. F., & Keller, M. L. (1995). Moral reasoning about sexually transmitted diseases. *Child Development, 66,* 167–177.

Jahoda, G. (1980). Theoretical and systematic approaches in mass-cultural psychology. In H. C. Triandis and W. W. Lambert (Eds.), *Handbook of cross-cultural psychology* (Vol. 1). Boston: Allyn & Bacon.

Jahoda, G., & Lewis, I. M. (1988). *Acquiring culture: Cross-cultural studies in child development.* London: Croom Helm.

Jakobson, R. (1971). Why "Mama" and "Papa"? In A. Bar-Adon & W. F. Leopold (Eds.), *Child language.* Englewood Cliffs, NJ: Prentice Hall.

James, W. (1890/1950). *The principles of psychology.* New York: Holt.

Jamieson, D. W., Lydon, J. E., Stewart, G., & Zanna, M. P. (1987). Pygmalion revisited: New evidence for student expectancy effects in the classroom. *Journal of Educational Psychology, 79,* 461–466.

Janda, L. H., & Klenke-Hamel, K. E. (1980). *Human sexuality.* New York: Van Nostrand.

Jarvik, M. E. (1990, October 19). The drug dilemma: Manipulating the demand. *Science, 250,* 387–392.

Jensen, A. (1969). How much can we boost IQ and scholastic achievement? *Harvard Educational Review, 39,* 101–123.

Jepson, H. A., Talashek, M. L., & Tichy, A. M. (1991). The Apgar score: Evolution, limitations, and scoring guidelines. *Birth, 18,* 83–92.

Johnson, A. M., Wadsworth, J., Wellings, K., & Bradshaw, S. (1992). Sexual lifestyles and HIV risk. *Nature, 360,* 410–412.

Johnson, J. L., Primas, P. J., & Coe, M. K. (1994). Factors that prevent women of low socioeconomic status from seeking prenatal care. *Journal of the American Academy of Nurse Practitioners, 6,* 105–111.

Johnson, S. L., & Birch, L. L (1994). Parents' and children's adiposity and eating style. *Pediatrics, 94,* 653–661.

Johnson, W., Emde, R. N., Pannabecker, B., Stenberg, C., & Davis, M. (1982). Maternal perception of infant emotion from birth through 18 months. *Infant Behavior and Development, 5,* 313–322.

Johnston, C. C. (1989). Pain assessment and management in infants. *Pediatrician, 16,* 16–23.

Jones, S. S., Collins, K., & Hong, H. (1991). An audience effect on smile production in 10-month-old infants. *Psychological Science, 2,* 45–49.

Jones, S. S., & Raag, T. (1989). Smile production in older infants: The importance of a social recipient for the facial signal. *Child Development, 60,* 811–818.

Jost, H., & Sontag, L. (1944). The genetic factor in autonomic nervous system function. *Psychosomatic Medicine, 6,* 308–310.

Julien, R. M. (1991). *A primer of drug action* (4th ed.). New York: Freeman.

Julien, R. M. (1992). *A primer of drug action* (5th ed.). New York: Freeman.

Julien, R. M. (1995). *A primer of drug action* (6th ed.). New York: Freeman.

Juvenile Justice Clearinghouse. (1995). Current statistics on World Wide Web page. Washington, DC.

Juvenile offenders and victims: A focus on violence. (Year). Rockville, MD: Juvenile Justice Clearinghouse.

Kagan, J. (1981). Universals in human development. In R. H. Munroe, R. L. Munroe, & B. B. Whiting (Eds.), *Handbook of cross-cultural human development* (pp. 53–62). New York: Garland.

Kagan, J. (1994). Yesterday's premises, tomorrow's promises. In R. D. Parke, P. A. Ornstein, J. J. Rieser, & C. Zahn-Waxler (Eds.), *A century of developmental psychology.* Washington, DC: American Psychological Association.

Kagan, J., Arcus, D., & Snidman, N. (1993). The idea of temperament: Where do we go from here? In R. Plomin & G. E. McClearn (Eds.) *Nature, nurture, and psychology.* Washington, DC: American Psychological Association.

Kagan, J., Arcus, D., Snidman, N., Feng, W. Y., Hendler, J., & Greene, S. (1994). Reactivity in infants: A cross-national comparison. *Developmental Psychology, 30,* 342–345.

Kagan, J., Kearsley, R., & Zelazo, P. R. (1978). *Infancy: Its place in human development.* Cambridge, MA: Harvard University Press.

Kagan, J., Reznick, S., & Gibbons, I. (1989). Inhibited and uninhibited life of children. *Child Development, 60,* 838–845.

Kagan, J., & Snidman, N. (1991). Infant predictors of inhibited and uninhibited profiles. *Psychological Science, 2,* 40–44.

Kahn, S., Zimmerman, G., Csikszentmihalyi, M., & Getzels, J. W. (1985). Relations between identity in young adulthood and intimacy at midlife. *Journal of Personality and Social Psychology, 49,* 1316–1322.

Kail, R. (1991). Controlled and automatic processing during mental rotation. *Journal of Experimental Child Psychology, 51,* 337–347.

Kaitz, M., Meschulach-Sarfaty, O., Auerbach, J., & Eidelman, A. (1988). A re-examination of newborns' ability to imitate facial expressions. *Developmental Psychology, 24,* 3–7.

Kalmijn, M. (1991). Status homogamy in the United States. *American Journal of Sociology, 97,* 496–523.

Kamerman, S., & Hayes, C. (1982). *Families that work: Children in a changing world.* Washington, DC: National Academy Press.

Kamhi, A. (1986). The elusive first word: The importance of the naming insight for the development of referential speech. *Journal of Child Language, 13,* 155–161.

Kantrowitz, B. (May 16, 1988). Preemies: Intensive care nurseries are outposts on the frontier of life. *Newsweek,* 62–68.

Kaplan, H., & Dove, H. (1987). Infant development among the Ache of Eastern Paraguay. *Developmental Psychology, 23,* 190–198.

Kaplan, R. M., Sallis, J. F., Jr., & Patterson, T. L. (1993). *Health and human behavior.* New York: McGraw-Hill.

Karmel, B. Z., Gardner, J. M., & Magnano, C. L. (1991). Attention and arousal in early infancy. In M. J. S. Weiss & P. R. Zelazo (Eds.), *Newborn attention: Biological constraints and the influence of experience* (pp. 339–376). Norwood, NJ: Ablex.

Katchadourian, H. A. (1987). *Biological aspects of human sexuality* (3rd ed.). New York: Holt, Rinehart & Winston.

Kates, E. (1995). Escaping poverty: The promise of higher education. *Social Policy Report: Society for Research in Child Development, 9,* 1–21.

Katrowitz, B. (1988, May 16). Preemies. *Newsweek,* 62–67.

Katrowitz, B., & Wingert, P. (1990, Winter/Spring). Step by step. *Newsweek Special Edition,* pp. 24–34.

Katz, L. G. (1989, December). Beginners' ethics. *Parents,* 213.

Katz, P. A. (Ed.). (1976). *Towards the elimination of racism.* New York: Pergamon Press.

Kauffman, J. M. (1993). How we might achieve the radical reform of special education. *Exceptional Children, 60, 6–16.*

Kazdin, A. E. (1990). Childhood depression. *Journal of Child Psychology and Psychiatry, 31,* 121–160.

Keating, D. (1980). Thinking processes in adolescence. In J. Adelson (Ed.), *Handbook of adolescent psychology.* New York: Wiley.

Keating, D. (1990). Adolescent thinking. In S. Feldman & G. Elliott (Eds.), *At the threshold: The developing adolescent.* Cambridge, MA: Harvard University Press.

Keating, D. P., & Clark, L. V. (1980). Development of physical and social reasoning in adolescence. *Developmental Psychology, 16,* 23–30.

Keefer, B. L., Kraus, R. F., Parker, B. L., Elliot, R., et al. (1991). A state university collaboration program: Residents' prespectives. Annual Meeting of the American Psychiatric Association (1990, New York, New York). *Hospital and Community Psychiatry, 42,* 62–66.

Kellogg, R. (1970). Understanding children's art. In P. Cramer (Ed.), *Readings in developmental psychology today.* Celmar, CA: CRM.

Kelly, J. A. (1995). *Changing HIV risk behavior: Practical strategies.* New York: Guilford Press.

Kemper, R. L., & Vernooy, A. R. (1994). Metalinguistic awareness in first graders: A qualitative perspective. *Journal of Psycholinguistic Research, 22,* 41–57.

Kessen, W. (1979). The American child and other cultural inventions. *American Psychologist, 34,* 815–820.

Kiecolt-Glaser, J. K., & Glaser, R. (1986). Behavioral influences on immune function: Evidence for the interplay between stress and health. In T. Field, P. McCabe, & N. Schneiderman (Eds.), *Stress and coping* (Vol. 2). Hillsdale, NJ: Erlbaum.

Kiecolt-Glaser, J. K., & Kiecolt-Glaser, R. (1991). Psychosocial factors, stress, disease, and immunity. In R. Ader, D. L. Felten, & N. Cohen (Eds.), *Psychoneuroimmunology.* San Diego, CA: Academic Press.

Kiecolt-Glaser, R., & Kiecolt-Glaser, J. K. (1993). Mind and immunity. In Goleman, D., & Gurin, J. (Eds.), *Mind-body medicine.* Yonkers, NY: Consumer Reports Books.

Kihlstrom, J. F. (1987, September 18). The cognitive unconscious. *Science, 237,* 1445–1452.

Killen, M., & Hart, D. (Eds.). (1995). *Morality in everyday life: Developmental perspectives.* New York: Cambridge University Press.

Kim, U., Triandis, H. C., Kagitçibais, Ç., Choi, S., & Yoon, G. (Eds.). (1994). *Individualism and collectivism: Theory, method, and applications.* Thousand Oaks, CA: Sage.

Kim, J. (1995, January). "You cannot know how much freedom you have here." *Money,* 133.

Kim, Y., & Stevens, J. H. (1987). The socialization of prosocial behavior in children. *Childhood Education, 63,* 200–206.

Kimball, J. W. (1983). *Biology* (5th Ed.). Reading, MA: Addison-Wesley.

Kimble, G. A. (1993). Evolution of the nature-nurture issue in the history of psychology. In R. Plomin & G. E. McClearn (Eds.) (1993). *Nature, nurture, and psychology.* Washington, DC: American Psychological Association.

Kimbrough, R. D., LeVois, M., & Webb, D. R. (1994). Management of children with slightly elevated blood lead levels. *Pediatrics, 93,* 188–191.

Kinsey, A. C., Pomeroy, W. B., & Martin, C. E. (1948). *Sexual behavior in the human male.* Philadelphia: Saunders.

Kitterle, F. L. (1991). (Ed.). *Cerebral laterality: Theory and research.* Hillsdale, NJ: Erlbaum.

Klaus, H. M., & Kennell, J. H. (1976). *Maternal- infant bonding.* St. Louis, MO: Mosby.

Klein, M. C., Gauthier, R. J., Robbins, J. M., Kaczorowski, J., Jorgensen, S. H., Franco, E. D., Johnson, B., Waghorn, K., Gelfand, M. M., Guralnick, M. S. et al. (1994). Relationship of episiotomy to perineal trauma and morbidity, sexual dysfunction, and pelvic floor relaxation. *American Journal of Obstetrics and Gynecology, 171,* 591–598.

Kleinman, A. (1991, July). The psychiatry of culture and culture of psychiatry. *Harvard Mental Health Letter.*

Kleinman, J. C. (1992). The epidemiology of low birthweight. In S. L. Friedman & M. D. Sigman (Eds.), *The psychological development of low birthweight children.* Norwood, NJ: Ablex.

Klinnert, M. (1984). The regulation of infant behavior by maternal facial expression. *Infant Behavior and Development, 7,* 447–465.

Klinnert, M., Campos, J. J., Sorce, J., Emde, R. N., & Svejda, M. (1983). Emotions as behavioral regulators: Social referencing in infancy. In R. Plutchik and H. Kerrman (Eds.), *Emotions in early development: Vol. 2. The emotions.* New York: Academic Press.

Knight, K. (1994, March). Back to basics. *Essence,* 122–138.

Knittle, J. L. (1975). Early influences on development of adipose tissue. In G. A. Bray (Ed.), *Obesity in perspective.* Washington, DC: U.S. Government Printing Office.

Kochanska, G. (1995). Children's temperament, mothers' discipline, and security of attachment: Multiple pathways to emerging internalization. *Child Development, 66,* 597–615.

Kochanska, G. (1997). Mutually responsive orientation between mothers and their young children: Implications for early socialization. *Child Development, 68,* 94–112.

Kohlberg, L. (1966). A cognitive-developmental anaylsis of children's sex-role concepts and attitudes. In E. E. Maccoby (Ed.), *The development of sex differences.* Stanford, CA: Stanford University Press.

Kohlberg, L. (1969). Stage and sequence: The cognitive-developmental approach to socialization. In D. Goslin (Ed.), *Handbook of socialization theory and research.* Chicago: Rand McNally.

Kohlberg, L. (1975). Counseling and counselor education: A developmental approach. *Counselor Education and Supervision, 14,* 250–256.

Kohlberg, L. (1984). *The psychology of moral development: Essays on moral development* (Vol. 2). San Francisco: Harper & Row.

Kolata, G. (1991, May 15). Drop in casual sex tied to AIDS peril. *The New York Times,* pp. A1, A9.

Kolata, G. (1994, August). Selling growth drug for children: The legal and ethical questions. *The New York Times,* pp. A1, A11.

Kolb, B. (1989). Brain development, plasticity, and behavior. *American Psychologist, 44(9),* 1203–1212.

Kolb, B. (1995). *Brain plasticity and behavior.* Mahwah, NJ: Erlbaum.

Kontos, S., Hsu, H., & Dunn, L. (1994). Children's cognitive and social competence in child-care centers and family day-care homes. *Journal of Applied Developmental Psychology, 15,* 387–411.

Kopp, C. B., & Kaler, S. R. (1989). Risk in infancy: Origins and implications. *American Psychologist, 44,* 224–230.

Kornhaber, M., Krechevsky, M., & Gardner, H. (1991). Engaging intelligence. *Emotional Psychologist, 25,* 177–199.

Kotre, J., & Hall, E. (1990). *Seasons of life.* Boston: Little, Brown.

Kozulin, A., & Falik, L. (1995). Dynamic cognitive assessment of the child. *Current Directions in Psychological Science, 4,* 192–196.

Kraemer, H. C., Korner, A., Anders, T., Jacklin, C. N., & Dimiceli, S. (1985). Obstetric drugs and infant behavior: A re-evaluation. *Journal of Pediatric Psychology, 10,* 345–353.

Kroger, J. (1995). The differentiation of "firm" and "developmental" foreclosure identity statuses: A longitudinal study. *Journal of Adolescent Research, 10,* 317–337.

Kryter, K. D. (1983). Presbycusis, sociocusis, and nosocusis. *Journal of the Acoustical Society of America, 73,* 1897–1917.

Kuchuk, A., Vibbert, M., & Bornstein, M. H. (1986). The perception of smiling and its experimental correlates in 3-month-old infants. *Child Development, 57,* 1054–1061.

Kuczynski, L. (1984). Socialization goals and mother-child interaction: Strategies for long-term and short-term compliance. *Developmental Psychology, 20,* 1061–1073.

Kuczynski, L., & Kochanska, G. (1990). Development of children's noncompliance strategies from toddlerhood to age 5. *Developmental Psychology, 26,* 398–408.

Kuhn, D., Garcia-Mila, M., Zohar, A., & Andersen, C. (1995). Strategies of knowledge acquisition. *Monographs of the Society for Research in Child Development, 69,* 210–235.

Kupfermann, I. (1991). Hypothalamus and limbic system: Petidergic neurons, homeostatis, and emotional behavior. In E. R. Kandel, J. H. Schwartz, & T. M. Jessell (Eds.), *Principles of neural science* (3rd ed.). New York: Elsevier.

Kupfersmid, J., & Wonderly, D. (1980). Moral maturity and behavior: Failure to find a link. *Journal of Youth and Adolescence, 9,* 249–261.

Kurtines, W. M., & Gewirtz, J. L. (1987). *Moral development through social interaction.* New York: Wiley.

LaBuda, M., Gottesman, I., & Pauls, D. (1993). Usefulness of twin studies for exploring the etiology of childhood and adolescent psychiatric disorders. *American Journal of Medical Genetics, 48,* 47–59.

Ladd, G. W. (1983). Social networks of popular, average, and rejected children in social settings. *Merrill-Palmer Quarterly, 29,* 282–307.

LaFromboise, T., Coleman, H. L., & Gerton, J. (1993). Psychological impact of biculturalism: Evidence and theory. *Psychological Bulletin, 114,* 395–412.

Lagercrantz, H., & Slotkin, T. A. (1986). The "stress" of being born. *Scientific American, 254(4),* 100–107.

Lamaze, F. (1970). *Painless childbirth: The Lamaze method.* Chicago: Regnery.

Lamb, D. R. (1984). *Physiology of exercise: Response and adaptation* (2nd ed.). New York: Macmillan.

Lamb, M. (1982). The bonding phenomenon: Misinterpretations and their implications. *Journal of Pediatrics, 101,* 555–557.

Lamb, M. (1994). Infant care practices and the application of knowledge. In C. B. Fisher & R. M. Lerner (Eds.), *Applied developmental psychology.* New York: McGraw-Hill.

Lamb, M. E. (1977). The development of mother-infant and father-infant attachments in the second year of life. *Developmental Psychology, 13,* 637–648.

Lamb, M. E. (1982). Paternal influences on early socioemotional development. *Journal of Child Psychology and Psychiatry and Allied Disciplines, 23,* 185–190.

Lamb, M. E. (Ed.). (1986). *The father's role: Applied perspectives.* New York: Wiley.

Lamb, M. E. (1987). Predictive implications of individual differences in attachment. *Journal of Consulting and Clinical Psychology, 55,* 817–824.

Lamb, M. E., Ketterlinus, R. D., & Fracasso, M. P. (1992). Parent-child relationships. In M. H. Bornstein & M. E. Lamb (Eds.), *Developmental psychology: An advanced textbook* (3rd ed.). Hillsdale, NJ: Erlbaum.

Lamb, M. E., Morrison, D. C., & Malkin, C. M. (1987). The development of infant social expectations in face-to-face interaction. *Merrill-Palmer Quarterly, 33,* 241–254.

Lamb, M. E., Sternberg, K. J., Hwang, C. P., & Broberg, A. G. (Eds.). (1992). *Child care in context: Cross-cultural perspectives.* Hillsdale, NJ: Erlbaum.

Lamb, M. E., Thompson, R. A., Gardner, W. P., Charnov, E., & Estes, D. (1984). Security of infantile attachment as assessed in the strange situation: Its study and biological interpretation. *Behavioral and Brain Sciences, 7,* 127–147.

Lambert, W. E., & Peal, E. (1972). The relation of bilingualism to intelligence. In A. S. Dil (Ed.), *Language, psychology, and culture* (3rd ed.). New York: Wiley.

Lampl, M., Cameron, N., Veldhuis, J. D., & Johnson, M. L. (1995, April 21). Patterns of human growth. *Science, 268,* 442–447.

Lander, E. S., & Schork, N. J. (1994, September 30). Genetic dissection of complex traits. *Science, 265,* 2037–2048.

Lang, J. S. (1987, April 13). Happiness is a reunited set of twins. *U.S. News and World Report,* 63–66.

Langer E., & Janis, I. (1979). *The psychology of control.* Beverly Hills, CA: Sage.

Langford, P. E. (1995). *Approaches to the development of moral reasoning.* Hillsdale, NJ: Erlbaum.

Langlois, J. H., Ritter, J. M., Casey, R. J., & Sawin, Douglas, B. (1995). Infant attractiveness predicts maternal behaviors and attitudes. *Developmental Psychology, 31,* 464–472.

Langlois, J. H., Ritter, J. M., Roggman, L. A., & Vaughn, L. S. (1991). Facial diversity and infant preferences for attractive faces. *Developmental Psychology, 27,* 79–84.

Larsen-Freeman, D., & Long, M. H. (1991). *An introduction to second language acquisition research.* London: Longman.

Larson, R. W., Richards, M. H., Moneta, G., Holmbeck, G., & Duckett, E. (1996). Changes in adolescents' daily interactions with their families from ages 10 to 18: Disengagement and transformation. *Developmental Psychology, 32,* 744–754.

Larsson, B., & Melin, L. (1992). Prevalence and short-term stability of depressive symptoms in school children. *Acta Psychiatrica Scandinavica, 85,* 17–22.

Larwood, L., Szwajkowski, E., & Rose, S. (1988). Sex and race discrimination resulting from manager-client relationships: Applying the rational bias theory of managerial discrimination. *Sex Roles, 18,* 9–29.

Lask, B., & Bryant-Waugh, R. (Eds.). (1993). *Childhood onset of anorexia nervosa and related eating disorders.* Hillsdale, NJ: Erlbaum.

Laszlo, J. (1986). Scripts for interpersonal situations. *Studia Psychologia, 28,* 125–135.

Laursen, B., & Collins, W. A. (1994). Interpersonal conflict during adolescence. *Psychological Bulletin, 115,* 197–209.

Lavigueur, A., Tremblay, R. E., & Saucier, J. F. (1995). Interactional processes in families with disruptive boys: Patterns direct and indirect influence. *Journal of Abnormal Child Psychology, 23,* 359–378.

Lazarus, R. S. (1968). Emotions and adaptations: Conceptual and empirical relations. In W. Arnold (Ed.), *Nebraska Symposium on Motivation.* Lincoln: University of Nebraska Press.

Lazarus, R. S. (1991). *Emotion and adaptation.* New York: Oxford University Press.

Lazarus, R. S., & Folkman, S. (1984). *Stress, appraisal, and coping.* New York: Springer.

Leavitt, L. A., & Goldson, E. (1996). Introduction to special section: Biomedicine and developmental psychology: New areas of common ground. *Developmental Psychology, 32,* 387–389.

Leboyer, F. (1975). *Birth without violence.* New York: Knopf.

Lecanuet, J.-P., Fifer, W. P., Krasnegor, N. A., & Smotherman, W. P. (Eds.). (1995). *Fetal development: A psychobiological perspective.* Hillsdale, NJ: Erlbaum.

Lecanuet, J.-P., Granier-Deferre, C., & Busnel, M.-C. (1995). Human fetal auditory perception. In J.-P. Lecanuet, W. P. Fifer, N. A. Krasnegor, & W. P. Smotherman (Eds.), *Fetal development: A psychobiological perspective.* Hillsdale, NJ: Erlbaum.

Lecours, A. R. (1982). Correlates of developmental behavior in brain maturation. In T. Bever (Ed.), *Regressions in mental development.* Hillsdale, NJ: Erlbaum.

Lee, H., & Barratt, M. S. (1993). Cognitive development of preterm low birth weight children at 5 to 8 years old. *Journal of Developmental and Behavioral Pediatrics, 14,* 242–249.

Lee, V. E., Brooks-Gunn, J., Schnur, E., & Liaw, F. (1990). Are Head Start effects sustained? A longitudinal follow-up comparison of disadvantaged children attending Head Start, no preschool, and other preschool programs. *Child Development, 61,* 495–507.

Lefkowitz, M. M. (1981). Smoking during pregnancy: Long-term effects on offspring. *Developmental Psychology, 17,* 192–194.

Legerstee, M. (1990). Infants use multimodal information to imitate speech sounds. *Infant Behavior and Development, 13,* 343–354.

Leigh, B. C., Morrison, D. M., Trocki, K., & Temple, M. (1994). Sexual behavior of American adolescents: Results from a U.S. national survey. *Journal of Adolescent Health, 15,* 117–125.

Leitenberg, H., Detzer, M. J., & Srebnik, D. (1993). Gender differences in masturbation and the relation of masturbation experience in preadolescence and/or early adolescence to sexual behavior and sexual adjustment in young adulthood. *Archives of Sexual Behavior, 22,* 87–98.

Leiter, J., & Johnsen, M. C. (1994). Child maltreatment and school performance. *American Journal of Education, 102,* 154–189.

Lelwica, M., & Haviland, J. (1983). *Ten-week-old infants' reactions to mothers' emotional expressions.* Paper presented at the biennial meeting of the Society for Research in Child Development.

Lenssen, B. G. (1973). Infants' reactions to peer strangers. *Dissertation Abstracts International, 33,* 60–62.

Lepore, S. J., Evans, G. W., & Schneider, M. L. (1991). Dynamic role of social support in the link between chronic stress and psychological distress. *Journal of Personality and Social Psychology, 61,* 889–909.

Lepore, S. J., Palsane, M. N., & Evans, G. W. (1991). Daily hassles and chronic strains: A hierarchy of stressors? *Social Science and Medicine, 33,* 1029–1036.

Leslie, A. M. (1987). Pretense and representation: The origins of "theory of mind." *Psychological Review, 94,* 412–426.

Lester, B. M., & Brazelton, T. B. (Eds.). (1989). *The cultural context of infancy: Vol. 2. Multicultural and interdisciplinary approaches to parent-infant relations* (pp. 39–61). Norwood, NJ: Ablex.

Lester, B. M., & Tronick, E. Z. (1990). Introduction. In B. M. Lester & E. Z. Tronick (Eds.), *Stimulation and the preterm infant: The limits of plasticity.* Philadelphia: Saunders.

Lester, R., & Van Theil, D. H. (1977). Gonadal function in chronic alcoholic men. *Advances in Experimental Medicine and Biology, 85A,* 339–414.

Levano, K. J., Cunningham, F. G., Nelson, S., Roark, M., Williams, M. L., Guzick, D., Dowling, S., Rosenfeld, C. R., & Buckley, A. (1986). A prospective comparison of selective and universal electronic fetal monitoring in 34,995 pregnancies. *New England Journal of Medicine, 315,* 615–619.

LeVay, S. (1993). *The sexual brain.* Cambridge, MA: MIT Press.

Leviton, A., Bellinger, D., Allred, E. N., Rabinowitz, M., Needleman, H., & Schoenbaum, S. (1993). Pre- and postnatal low-level lead exposure and children's dysfunction in school. *Environmental Research, 60,* 30–43.

Lewin, T. (1995, May 11). Women are becoming equal providers: Half of working women bring home half the household income. *The New York Times,* p. A14.

Lewinsohn, P. M., Roberts, R. E., Seeley, J. R., & Rohde, P. (1994). Adolescent psychopathology: II. Psychosocial risk factors for depression. *Journal of Abnormal Psychology, 103,* 302–315.

Lewinsohn, P. M., Rohde, P., & Seeley, J. R. (1994). Psychosocial risk factors for future adolescent suicide attempts. *Journal of Consulting and Clinical Psychology, 62,* 297–305.

Lewis, C., & Mitchell, P. (Eds.). (1994). *Children's early understanding of mind: Origins and development.* Hillsdale, NJ: Erlbaum.

Lewis, C., Wilkins, R., Baker, L., & Woobey, A. (1995). "Is this man your daddy?" Suggestibility in children's eyewitness identification of a family member. *Child Abuse & Neglect, 19,* 739–744.

Lewis, D. O., Yeager, C. A., Loveley, R., et al. (1994). A clinical follow-up of delinquent males: Ignored vulnerabilities, unmet needs, and the perpetuation of violence. *Journal of the American Academy of Child and Adolescent Psychiatry, 33,* 518–528.

Lewis, M., & Bendersky, M. (Eds.). (1995). *Mothers, babies, and cocaine: The role of toxins in development.* Hillsdale, NJ: Erlbaum.

Lewis, M., & Brooks-Gunn, J. (1979). *Social cognition and the acquisition of self.* New York: Plenum.

Lewis, M., Feiring, C., McGuffog, C., & Jaskir, J. (1984). Predicting psychopathology in 6-year-olds from early social relations. *Child Development, 55,* 123–136.

Lewit, E. M., Baker, L. S., Corman, H., & Shiono, P. H. (1995). *The Future of Children, 5,* 35–56.

Leyens, J.-P., Camino, L., Parke, R. D., & Berkowitz, L. (1975). Effects of movie violence on aggression in a field setting as a function of group dominance and cohesion. *Journal of Personality and Social Psychology, 32,* 346–360.

Liaw, F.-R., & Brooks-Gunn, J. (1993). Patterns of low birthweight children's cognitive development. *Developmental Psychology, 29,* 1024–1035.

Liebert, R. M., & Sprafkin, J. (1988). *The early window: Effects of television on children and youth* (3rd ed.). New York: Pergamon Press.

Lightfood, C. (1997). *The culture of adolescent risk-taking.* NY: Guilford Press.

Lin, S. X., & Lasker, J. N. (1996). Patterns of grief reaction after pregnancy loss. *American Journal of Orthopsychiatry, 66,* 262–271.

Lindholm, K. J. (1991). Two-way bilingual/immersion education: Theory, conceptual issues, and pedagogical implications. In R. V. Padilla & A. Benavides (Eds.), *Critical perspectives on bilingual education research.* Tempe, AZ: Bilingual Review Press.

Lindhout, D., Frets, P. G., & Niermeijer, M. F. (1991). Approaches to genetic counseling. *Annals of the New York Academy of Sciences, 630,* 223–229.

Linz, D. G., Donnerstein, E., & Penrod, S. (1988). Effects of long-term exposure to violent and sexually degrading depictions of women. *Journal of Personality and Social Psychology, 55,* 758–768.

Lipka, R. P., & Brinthaupt, T. M. (Eds.). (1992). *Self-perspectives across the life span.* Albany: State University of New York Press.

Lipman, J. (1992, March 10). Surgeon general says it's high time Joe Camel quit. *The Wall Street Journal,* pp. B1, B7.

Lipsitt, L. P. (1986a). Learning in infancy: Cognitive development in babies. *Journal of Pediatrics, 109(1),* 172–182.

Lipsitt, L. P. (1986b). Toward understanding the hedonic nature of infancy. In L. P. Lipsitt & J. H. Cantor (Eds.), *Experimental child psychologist: Essays and experiments in honor of Charles C. Spiker* (pp. 97–109). Hillsdale, NJ: Erlbaum.

Liskin, L. (1985, Nov.–Dec.). Youth in the 1980s: Social and health concerns 4. *Population Reports, 8, No. 5.*

Livingston, R., Adam, B. S., Bracha, H. S. (1993). Season of birth and neurodevelopmental disorders: Summer birth is associated with dyslexia. *Journal of the American Academy of Child and Adolescent Psychiatry, 32,* 612–616.

Livson, N., & Peskin, H. (1980). Perspectives on adolescence from longitudinal research. In J. Adelson (Ed.), *Handbook of adolescent psychology.* New York: Wiley.

Lloyd, B., & Duveen, G. (1991). Expressing social gender identities in the first year of school. *European Journal of Psychology of Education, 6,* 437–447.

Locke, J. L. (1983). *Phonological acquisition and change.* New York: Academic Press.

Locke, J. L. (1993). *The child's path to spoken language.* Cambridge, MA: Harvard University Press.

Locke, J. L. (1994). Phases in the child's development of language. *American Scientist, 82,* 436–445.

Loehlin, J. C. (1992). *Genes and environment in personality development.* Newbury Park, CA: Sage.

Lohr, S. (1996, March 13). Plan to block censorship on Internet; pre-emptory effort at self-policing. (National Consumers League, online services companies begin campaign against Communications Decency Act.) *The New York Times,* p. D4.

Long, T., & Long, L. (1983). *Latchkey children.* New York: Penguin.

Lorenz, K. (1957). Companionship in bird life. In C. Scholler (Ed.), *Instinctive behavior.* New York: International Universities Press.

Lorenz, K. (1966). *On aggression.* New York: Harcourt Brace Jovanovich.

Lorenz, K. (1974). *Civilized man's eight deadly sins.* New York: Harcourt Brace Jovanovich.

Lorenz, K. Z. (1965). *Evolution and the modification of behavior.* Chicago: University of Chicago Press.

Lourenço, O., & Machado, A. (1996). In defense of Piaget's theory: A reply to 10 common criticisms. *Psychological Review, 103,* 143–164.

Lowrey, G. H. (1986). *Growth and development of children* (8th ed.). Chicago: Year Book Medical Publishers.

Lozoff, B., Wolf, A. W., & Davis, N. S. (1985). Sleep problems seen in pediatric practice. *Pediatrics, 75,* 477–483.

Lucas, A., Morley, R., Cole, T. J., Lister, G., & Leeson-Payne, C. (1992). Breast milk and subsequent intelligence quotient in children born preterm. *Lancet, 339,* 261–264.

Lust, B., Hermon, G., & Kornfilt, J. (Eds.). (1994). *Syntactic theory and first language acquisition: Binding, dependencies, and learnability.* Hillsdale, NJ: Erlbaum.

Lust, B., Suner, M., & Whitman, J. (Eds.) (1994). *Syntactic theory and first language acquisition: Cross-linguistic perspectives.* Hillsdale, NJ: Erlbaum.

Luster, T., & McAdoo, H. P. (1994). Factors related to the achievement and adjustment of young African American children. *Child Development, 65,* 1080–1094.

Luster, T., & McAdoo, H. P. (1996). Family and child influences on educational attainment: A secondary analysis of the high/scope Perry preschool data. *Developmental Psychology, 32,* 26–39.

Lykken, D., Bouchard, T., McGue, M., & Tellegen, A. (1993). Heritability of interests: A twin study. *Journal of Applied Psychology, 78,* 649–661.

Lykken, D. T., McGue, M., Tellegen, A., & Bouchard, T. J., Jr. (1993). Emergenesis: Genetic traits that may not run in families. *American Psychologist, 47,* 1565–1577.

Lyon, G. R. (1996). Learning disabilities. *The Future of Children, 6,* 54–76.

Maccoby, E. E. (1980). *Social development: Psychological growth and the parent-child relationship.* New York: Harcourt Brace Jovanovich.

Maccoby, E. E. (1990). The role of gender identity and gender constancy in sex-differentiated development. In D. Schrader (Ed.), *New directions for child development* (No. 47). San Francisco: Jossey-Bass.

Maccoby, E. E., & Jacklin, C. (1974). *The psychology of sex differences.* Stanford, CA: Stanford University Press.

Mackey, M. C. (1990). Women's preparation for the childbirth experience. *Maternal-Child Nursing Journal, 19,* 143–173.

Mackey, M. C., White, U., & Day, R. (1992). Reasons American men become fathers: Men's divulgences, women's perceptions. *Journal of Genetic Psychology, 153,* 435–445.

Mackey, W. E., & Hess, D. J. (1982). Attention structure and stereotype of gender on television: An empirical analysis. *Genetic Psychology Monographs, 106,* 199–215.

MacPhee, D., Kreutzer, J. C., & Fritz, J. J. (1994). Infusing a diversity perspective into human development courses. *Child Development, 65,* 699–715.

MacWhinney, B. (1991). Connectionism as a framework for language acquisition. In J. Miller (Ed.), *Research on child language disorders.* Austin, TX: Pro-ed.

Major, B., & Konar, E. (1984). An investigation of sex differences in pay expectations and their possible causes. *Academy of Management Journal, 27,* 777–792.

Malina, R. M. (1979). Secular changes in size and maturity. *Monographs of the Society for Research in Child Development, 54* (1–2, Serial No. 219).

Malinosky-Rummell, R., & Hansen, D. J. (1993). Long-term consequences of childhood physical abuse. *Psychological Bulletin, 114,* 68–79.

Malinowski, C. I., & Smith, C. P. (1985). Moral reasoning and moral conduct: An investigation prompted by Kohlberg's theory. *Journal of Personality and Social Psychology, 49,* 1016–1027.

Malott, R. W., Whaley, D. L., & Malott, M. E. (1993). *Elementary principles of behavior* (2nd. ed.). Englewood Cliffs, NJ: Prentice Hall.

Mandel, D. R., Jusczyk, P. W., & Pisoni, D. B. (1995). Infants' recogniton of the sound patterns of their own names. *Psychological Science, 6,* 314–317.

Mandich, M., Simons, C. J., Ritchie, S., Schmidt, D., & Mullett, M. (1994). Motor development, infantile reactions and postural responses of preterm, at-risk infants. *Developmental Medicine and Child Neurology, 36,* 397–405.

Mandler, J. M. (1990). A new perspective on cognitive development in infancy. *American Scientist, 78,* 236–243.

Mandler, J. M., & McDonough, L. (1994). Long-term recall of event sequences in infancy. *Journal of Experimental Child Psychology, 59,* 457–474.

Mangelsdorf, S., Gunnar, M., Kestenbaum, R., Lang, S., & Andreas, D. (1990). Infant proneness-to-distress temperament, maternal personality, and mother-infant attachment: Association and goodness of fit. *Child Development, 61,* 820–831.

Maratsos, M. P. (1983). Some current issues in the study of the acquisition of grammar. In P. H. Mussen (Ed.), *Handbook of child psychology* (4th ed., Vol. 3). New York: Wiley.

Marche, T. A., & Howe, M. L. (1995). Preschoolers report misinformation despite accurate memory. *Developmental Psychology, 31,* 554–567.

Marcia, J. E. (1966). Development and validation of ego identity status. *Journal of Personality and Social Psychology, 3,* 551–558.

Marcia, J. E. (1980). Identity in adolescence. In J. Adelson (Ed.), *Handbook of adolescent psychology.* New York: Wiley.

Marcus, G. F. (1996). Why do children say "breaked"? *Current Directions in Psychological Science, 5,* 81–85.

Margolin, G. (1995, January). Paper presented at a conference, "Violence against children in the family and the community: A conference on causes, developmental consequences, interventions, and prevention." Los Angeles: University of Southern California.

Marjoribanks, K. (1994). Cross-cultural comparisons of family environments of Anglo-, Greek-, and Italian-Australians. *Psychological Reports, 74, 49–50.*

Markus, H. R., & Kitayama, S. (1991). Culture and the self: Implications for cognition, emotion, and motivation. *Psychological Review, 98,* 224–253.

Marsh, H. W. (1990). Influences of internal and external frames of reference on the formation of math and English self-concepts. *Journal of Educational Psychology, 82,* 107–116.

Marsh, H. W., & Holmes, I. W. M. (1990). Multidimensional self-concepts: Construct validation of responses by children. *American Educational Research Journal, 27,* 89–118.

Marsh, H. W., & Parker, J. W. (1984). Determinants of student self-concept: Is it better to be a relatively large fish in a small pond even if you don't learn to swim as well? *Journal of Personality and Social Psychology, 47,* 213–231.

Marsh, H. W., & Shavelson, R. (1985). Self-concept: Its multifaceted, hierarchical structure. *Educational Psychologist, 20,* 107–123.

Martin, B. A. (1989). Gender differences in salary expectations. *Psychology of Women Quarterly, 13,* 87–96.

Martin, C. L. (1993). New directions for investigating children's gender knowledge. *Developmental Review, 13,* 184–204.

Martin, G. B., & Clark, R. D. (1982). Distress crying in neonates: Species and peer specificity. *Developmental Psychology, 18,* 3–9.

Martinez, R., & Dukes, R. L. (1991). Ethnic and gender differences in self-esteem. *Youth and Society, 22,* 318–338.

Marx, J. (1995, December 22). A new guide to the human genome. *Science, 270,* p. 1919–1920.

Marx, M. B., Garrity, T. F., & Bowers, F. R. (1975). The influence of recent life experience on the health of college freshman. *Journal of Psychosomatic Research, 19,* 87–98.

Masataka, N. (1993). Motherese in a signed language. *Infant Behavior and Development, 15,* 453–460.

Masters, W. H., Johnson, V., & Kolodny, R. C. (1982). *Human sexuality.* Boston: Little, Brown.

Mastropieri, M. A., & Scruggs, T. E. (1991). *Teaching students ways to remember: Strategies for learning mnemonically.* Cambridge, MA: Brookline Books.

Maternal and Child Health Bureau. (1994). *Child Health USA '93.* Washington, DC: U.S. Department of Health and Human Services.

Mathew, A., & Cook, M. L. (1990). The control of reaching movements by young infants. *Child Development, 61,* 1238–1257.

Mathews, J. J., & Zadak, K. (1991). The alternative birth movement in the United States: History and current status. *Women and Health, 17,* 39–56.

Mathews, J. R., Friman, P. C., Barone, V. J., Ross, L. V., & Christophersen, E. R. (1987). Decreasing dangerous infant behaviors through parent instruction. *Journal of Applied Behavior Analysis, 20,* 165–169.

Matlin, M. M. (1987). *The psychology of women.* New York: Holt.

Matlock, J. R., & Green, V. P. (1990). The effects of day care on the social and emotional development of infants, toddlers, and preschoolers. *Early Child Development and Care, 64,* 55–59.

Matson, J. L., & Mulick, J. A. (Eds.). (1991). *Handbook of mental retardation* (2nd ed.). New York: Pergamon Press.

Mattes, R. D., Maone, T., Wager, P. S., Beauchamp, G., Bernbaum, J., Stallings, V., Pereira, G. R., Gibson, E., Russell, P., & Bhutani, V. (1996). Effects of sweet taste stimulation on growth and sucking in preterm infants. *Journal of Obstetrics, Gynecology, and Neonatal Nursing, 25,* 407–414.

Mayes, L. C., Bornstein, M. H., Chawarska, K., Haynes, O. M., & Grangers, R. H. (1996). Impaired regulation of arousal in 2-month-old infants exposed prenatally to cocaine and other drugs. *Development and Psychopathology, 8,* 29–42.

McAdoo, H. P. (1988). *Black families.* Newbury Park, CA: Sage.

McCabe, M. (1984). Toward a theory of adolescent dating. *Adolescence, 19,* 159–169.

McCall, R. B. (1979). *Infants.* Cambridge, MA: Harvard University Press.

McCartney, K. (1984). Effect of quality of day care environment on children's language development. *Developmental Psychology, 20,* 244–260.

McClearn, G. E. (1993). Behavioral genetics: The last century and the next. In R. Plomin & G. E. McClearn (Eds.), *Nature, nurture, and psychology.* Washington, DC: American Psychological Association.

McClelland, D. C. (1993). Intelligence is not the best predictor of job performance. *Current Directions in Psychological Research, 2,* 5–8.

McCloskey, L. A., Figueredo, A. J., & Koss, M. P. (1995). The effects of systemic family violence on children's mental health. *Child Development, 66,* 1239–1261.

McCormick, M. C. (1992). Advances in neonatal intensive care technology and their possible impact on the development of low-birthweight infants. In S. L. Friedman & M. D. Sigman (Eds.), *The psychological development of low-birthweight children.* Norwood, NJ: Ablex.

McDaniel, K. D. (1986). Pharmacologic treatment of psychiatric and neurodevelopmental disorders in children and adolescents: III. *Clinical Pediatrics, 25,* 198–204.

McDonald, M. A., Sigman, M., Espinosa, M. P., & Neumann, C. G. (1994). Impact of a temporary food shortage on children and their mothers. *Child Development, 65,* 404–415.

McDonald, R. M., & Towberman, D. B. (1993). Psychosocial correlates of adolescent drug involvement. *Adolescence, 28,* 925–936.

McGraw, K. M., & Bloomfield, J. (1987). Social influence on group moral decisions: The interactive effects of moral reasoning and sex-role orientation. *Journal of Personality and Social Psychology, 53,* 1080–1087.

McGue, M. (1993). From proteins to cognitions: The behavioral genetics of alcoholism. In R. Plomin & G. E. McClearn (Eds.), *Nature, nurture, and psychology.* Washington, DC: American Psychological Association.

McGue, M., Bouchard, T., Iacono, W., & Lykken, D. (1993). Behavioral genetics of cognitive ability: A life-span perspective. In R. Plomin & G. E. McClearn (Eds.), *Nature, nurture, and psychology* (pp. 59–76). Washington, DC: American Psychological Association.

McGuffin, P., & Katz, R. (1993). Genes, adversity, and depression. In R. Plomin & G. E. McClearn, (Eds.), *Nature, nuture and psychology* (pp. 217–230). Washington, DC: American Psychological Association.

McGuinness, D. (1972). Hearing: Individual differences in perceiving. *Perception, 1,* 465–473.

McKenna, J. J. (1983). Primate aggression and evolution: An overview of sociobiological and anthropological perspectives. *Bulletin of the American Academy of Psychiatry and the Law, 11,* 105–130.

McKey, R. H., Condelli, L., Ganson, H., Barrett, B. J., McConkey, C., & Plantz, M. C. (1985). *The impact of Head Start on children, families, and communities.* Washington, DC: CSR.

McWhirter, D. P., Sanders, S., & Reinisch, J. M. (1990). *Homosexuality, heterosexuality: Concepts of sexual orientation.* New York: Oxford University Press.

McWhirter, L., Young, V., & Majury, Y. (1983). Belfast children's awareness of violent death. *British Journal of Psychology, 22,* 81–92.

Mead, M. (1942). *Environment and education, a symposium held in connection with the 50th anniversary celebration of the University of Chicago.* Chicago: University of Chicago.

Mehler, J., & Dupoux, E. (1994). *What infants know: The new cognitive science of early development.* Cambridge, MA: Blackwell.

Mehren, E. (1996, Oct. 11). Parents want safety, not family values: A survey discovers that moms and dads are far more interested in the practical matters of daily life. (National Parenting Association report). *Los Angeles Times,* pg. E1.

Meisels, S. J., & Plunket, J. W. (1988). Developmental consequences of preterm birth: Are there long-term deficits? In P. B. Baltes, D. L. Featherman, & R. M. Lerner (Eds.), *Lifespan development and behavior* (Vol. 9). Hillsdale, NJ: Erlbaum.

Meltzoff, A. N. (1981). Imitation, intermodal coordination, and representation in early infancy. In G. Butterworth (Ed.), *Infancy and epistemology.* Brighton, England: Harvester Press.

Meltzoff, A. N., & Moore, M. K. (1977). Imitation of facial and manual gestures by human neonates. *Science, 198,* 75–78.

Meltzoff, A. N., & Moore, M. K. (1989). Imitation in newborn infants: Exploring the range of gestures imitated and the underlying mechanisms. *Developmental Psychology, 25,* 954–962.

Meltzoff, A. N., & Moore, M. K. (1994). Imitation, memory, and the representation of persons. *Infant Behavior and Development, 17,* 83–99.

Mendelson, M. J., Aboud, F. E., & Lanthier, R. P. (1994). Personality predictors of friendship and popularity in kindergarten. *Journal of Applied Developmental Psychology, 15,* 413–435.

Menyuk, P. (1995). *Early language development in full term and premature infants.* Hillsdale, NJ: Erlbaum.

Mercer, C. (1992). *Students with learning disabilities* (4th ed.). Columbus, OH: Merrill.

Mercer, J. R. (1973). *Labeling the mentally retarded.* Berkeley: University of California Press.

Meyer, J. S., Mirochnick, M., Frank, D. A., & Zuckerman, B. S. (1996). Adversity in the newborn infant: Psychological and physiological effects of prenatal cocaine exposure. In R. S. Feldman (Ed.), *The psychology of adversity.* Amherst, MA: University of Massachusetts Press.

Meyer-Bahlburg, H. F. L., Ehrhardt, A. A., Rosen, L. R., Gruen, R. S., Veridiano, N. P., Vann, F. H., & Neuwalder, H. F. (1995). Prenatal estrogens and the development of homosexual orientation. *Developmental Psychology, 31,* 12–21.

Meyerhoff, M. K., & White, B. L. (1986, September). Making the grade as parents. *Psychology Today,* 38–45.

Michael, R. T., Gagnon, J. H., Laumann, E. O., & Kolata, G. (1994). *Sex in America: A definitive survey.* Boston: Little, Brown.

Michel, G. F., & Moore, C. L. (1995). *Developmental psychobiology.* Cambridge, MA: Bradford.

Michel, G. L. (1981). Right-handedness: A consequence of infant supine head-orientation preference? *Science, 212,* 685–687.

Midlarsky, E., & Bryan, J. H. (1972). Affect expressions and children's imitative altruism. *Journal of Experimental Research in Personality, 6,* 195–203.

Miller, B. C. (1992). Adolescent parenthood, economic issues, and social policies. *Journal of Family and Economic Issues, 13,* 467–475.

Miller, C. A. (1987). A review of maternity care programs in western Europe. *Family Planning Perspectives, 19(5),* 207–211.

Miller, D. A., McCluskey-Fawcett, K., & Irving, L. (1993). Correlates of bulimia nervosa: Early family mealtime experiences. *Adolescence, 28,* 621–635.

Miller, J. L., & Eimas, P. D. (1995). Speech perception: From signal to word. *Annual Review of Psychology, 46,* 467–492.

Miller, N., & Brewer, M. (1984). *Groups in contact: The psychology of desegregation.* New York: Academic Press.

Miller, N., & Brewer, M. B. (1990). Social categorization theory and team learning procedures. In R. S. Feldman (Ed.), *The social psychology of education: Current research and theory.* Cambridge, England: Cambridge University Press.

Miller, P. A., Eisenberg, N., Fabes, R. A., & Shell, R. (1996). Relations of moral reasoning and vicarious emotion to young children's prosocial behavior toward peers and adults. *Developmental Psychology, 32,* 210–219.

Miller, W. (1958). Lower-class culture as a generation milieu of gang delinquency. *Journal of Social Issues, 14,* 5–19.

Miller-Bernal, L. (1993). Single-sex versus coeducational environments: A comparison of women students' experiences at four colleges. *American Journal of Education, 102,* 23–54.

Miller-Jones, D. (1989). Culture and testing. *American Psychologist, 44,* 360–366.

Milner, J. (1995, January). Paper presented at a conference, "Violence against children in the family and the community: A conference on causes, developmental consequences, interventions and prevention." Los Angeles: University of Southern California.

Minde, K. (1992). Aggression in preschoolers: Its relation to socialization. *Journal of the American Academy of Child and Adolescent Psychiatry, 31,* 853–862.

Mindell, J. A., & Cashman, L. (1995). Sleep disorders. In A. R. Eisen, C. A. Kearney, & C. E. Schaefer (Eds.), *Clinical handbook of anxiety disorders in children and adolescents.* Northvale, NJ: Aronson.

Miner, D. (1983). *Children and race.* Beverly Hills, CA: Sage.

Minkowski, A. (1967). *Regional development of the brain in early life.* Oxford: Blackwell.

Minorities in Higher Education. (1995). Annual status report on minorities in higher education. Washington, DC: American Council on Education.

Mistretta, C. M. (1990). Taste development. In J. R. Coleman (Ed.), *Development of sensory systems in mammals* (pp. 567–613). New York: Wiley.

Mitchell, J., McCauley, E., Burke, P. M., & Moss, S. J. (1988). Phenomenology of depression in children and adolescents. *Journal of the American Academy of Child and Adolescent Psychiatry, 27,* 12–20.

Mittendorf, R., Williams, M. A., Berkey, C. S., & Cotter, R. F. (1990). The length of uncomplicated human gestation. *Obstetrics and Gynecology, 75,* 73–78.

Mones, P. (1995, July 28). Life and death and Susan Smith. *The New York Times,* p. A27.

Money, J., & Ehrhardt, A. A. (1972). *Man and woman, boy and girl: The differentiation and dimorphism of gender identity from conception to maturity.* Baltimore: Johns Hopkins University Press.

Montemayor, R., Adams, G. R., & Gulotta, T. P. (Eds.). (1994). *Personal relationships during adolescence.* Newbury Park, CA: Sage.

Moon, C., Cooper, R. P., & Fifer, W. P. (1993). Two-day-olds prefer their native language. *Infant Behavior and Development, 16,* 495–500.

Moore, K. L. (1974). *Before we are born: Basic embryology and birth defects.* Philadelphia: Saunders.

Moore, S. M., & Rosenthal, D. A. (1991). Condoms and coitus: Adolescents' attitudes to AIDS and safe sex behavior. *Journal of Adolescence, 14,* 211–227.

Moores, D., & Meadow-Orlans, K. (1990). *Educational and developmental aspects of deafness.* Washington, DC: Gallaudet University Press.

Morbidity & Mortality Weekly Report. (1989). *Progress toward achieving the 1990 national objectives for physical fitness and exercise, 38,* 449–453.

Morelli, G. A., Rogoff, B., Oppenheim, D., & Goldsmith, D. (1992). Cultural variation in infants' sleeping arrangements: Questions of independence. Special section: Cross-cultural studies of development. *Developmental Psychology, 28,* 604–613.

Morgane, P., Austin-LaFrance, R., Bronzino, J., Tonkiss, J., Diaz-Cintra, S., Cintra, L., Kemper, T., & Galler, J. (1993). Prenatal malnutrition and development of the brain. *Neuroscience and Biobehavioral Reviews, 17,* 91–128.

Morrison, A. M., & von Glinow, M. A. (1990). Women and minorities in management. *American Psychologist, 45,* 200–208.

Morrison, F. J. (1993). Phonological processes in reading acquisition: Toward a unified conceptualization. Special Issue: Phonological processes and learning disability. *Developmental Review, 13,* 279–285.

Morse, R. M., & Flavin, D. K. (1992). The definition of alcoholism. *Journal of the American Medical Association, 268,* 1012–1014.

Moses, L. J., & Chandler, M. J. (1992). Traveler's guide to children's theories of mind. *Psychological Inquiry, 3,* 286–301.

Moshman, D., Glover, J. A., & Bruning, R. H. (1987). *Developmental psychology.* Boston: Little, Brown.

Moss, H. A. (1974). Early sex differences and mother-infant interaction. In R. C. Friedman, R. N. Richart, & R. L. Verde Wicle (Eds.), *Sex differences in behavior.* New York: Wiley.

Mounts, N. S., & Steinberg, L. (1995). An ecological analysis of peer influence on adolescent grade point average and drug use. *Developmental Psychology, 31,* 915–922.

Mueller, E., & Vandell, D. (1979). Infant-infant interactions. In J. D. Osofsky (Ed.), *Handbook of infant development.* New York: Wiley.

Murray, A. D., Dolby, R. M., Nation, R. L., & Thomas, D. B. (1981). Effects of epidural anesthesia on newborns and their mothers. *Child Development, 52,* 71–82.

Murray, M. (1995, February 9). Alex: Fun, games, and harsh truths at the age of 10. *The Wall Street Journal,* pp. B1–B2.

Musick, J. (1993). *Young, poor, and pregnant: The psychology of teenage motherhood.* New Haven, CT: Yale University Press.

Mussen, P. H. (1969). Early sex-role development. In D. A. Goslin (Ed.), *Handbook of socialization theory and research,* (pp. 707–732). Chicago: Rand McNally.

Mussen, P. H., & Jones, M. C. (1957). Self-conceptions, motivations, and interpersonal attitudes of late- and early-maturing boys. *Child Development, 28,* 243–256.

Mutryn, C. S. (1993). Psychosocial impact of cesarean section on the family: A literature review. *Social Science and Medicine, 37,* 1271–1281.

Myerhoff, B. (1982). Rites of passage: Process and paradox. In V. Turner (Ed.), *Celebration: Studies in festivity and ritual.* Washington, DC: Smithsonian Press.

Myers, B. J. (1987). Mother-infant bonding: The status of this critical-period hypothesis. In M. H. Bornstein (Ed.), *Sensitive periods in development: Interdisciplinary perspectives.* Hillsdale, NJ: Erlbaum.

Myers, B. J., Britt, G. C., Lodder, D. E., Kendall, K. A. et al. (1992). Effects of cocaine exposure on infant development: A review. *Journal of Child and Family Studies, 1,* 393–415.

Myers, N. A., Clifton, R. K., & Clarkson, M. G. (1987). When they were very young: Almost-threes remember two years ago. *Infant Behavior and Development, 10,* 123–132.

Myklebust, B. M., & Gottlieb, G. L. (1993). Development of the stretch reflex in the newborn: Reciprocal excitation and reflex irradation. *Child Development, 64,* 1036–1045.

Nagel, K. L., & Jones, K. H. (1992). Predisposition factors in anorexia nervosa. *Adolescence, 27,* 381–386.

Nakagawa, M., Lamb, M. E., & Miyaki, K. (1992). Antecedents and correlates of the Strange Situation behavior of Japanese infants. *Journal of Cross-Cultural Psychology, 23,* 300–310.

National Center for Education Statistics (1991). *Digest of education statistics 1990* (pp. 113, 116, 118, 120, 121). Washington DC: U.S. Department of Education.

National Center for Health Statistics. (1993b). *Health United States, 1992.* DHHS Pub. No. (PHS) 92–1232. Hyattsville, MD: Public Health Service.

National Center for Health Statistics. (1993c). *Vital Statistics of the United States. Forthcoming, 1990. Vol. II Mortality, Part A.* Washington, DC: Public Health Service.

National Center for Health Statistics. (1994). Division of Vital Statistics. Washington, DC: Public Health Service.

National Center for Health Statistics (1994). Advance Report of Final Natality Statistics, 1993. *Monthly Vital Statistics Report, Vol. 44.* Washington, DC: Public Health Service.

National Center for Health Statistics. (1993a). Advance Report of Final Natality Statistics, 1991. *Monthly Vital Statistics Report, Vol. 42.* Washington, DC: Public Health Service.

National Center for Missing and Exploited Children. (1995). Child Safety on the Information Highway. [Brochure]. Washington, DC: Author.

National Institute on Alcohol Abuse and Alcoholism. (1990). *Alcohol and Health.* Washington, DC: U.S. Government Printing Office.

National Joint Committee on Learning Disabilities. (1989). *Letter from NJCLD to member organizations. Topic: Modifications to the NJCLD definition of learning disabilities.* Washington, DC: Author.

National Opinion Research Center. (1990). *General Social Surveys 1972–1990: Cumulative Codebook.* Chicago: Author.

National Research Council. (1991). *Caring for America's children.* Washington, DC: National Academy Press.

National Safety Council. (1989). *Accident Facts: 1989 edition.* Chicago: National Safety Council.

National Survey of Families and Households. (1988). *Married fathers with preschoolers.* Washington, DC: U.S. Government Printing Office.

Needleman, H. L., & Bellinger, D. (Eds.). (1994). *Prenatal exposure to toxicants: Developmental consequences.* Baltimore: Johns Hopkins University Press.

Needleman, H. L., Riess, J. A., Tobin, M. J., Biesecker, G. E., & Greenhouse, J. B. (1966, February 7). Bone lead levels and delinquent behavior. *Journal of the American Medical Association, 2755,* 363–369.

Neill, M., & Haederle, M. (1995, June 12). A family's furious race against time. *People Weekly,* 44–47.

Neisser, U., Boodoo, G., Bourchard, T. J., Jr., Boykin, A. W., Brody, N., Ceci, S. J., Haplern, D. F., Loehlin, J. C., Perloff, R., Sternberg, R. J., & Urbina, S. (1996). Intelligence: Knowns and unknowns. *American Psychologist, 51,* 77–101.

Nelson, C. A. (1987). The recognition of facial expressions in the first 2 years of life: Mechanisms of development. *Child Development, 58,* 889–909.

Nelson, C. A. (1995). The ontogeny of human memory: A cognitive neuroscience perspective. *Developmental Psychology, 31,* 723–738.

Nelson, D. G. K., Jusczyk, P. W., Mandel, D. R., Myers, J. et al. (1995). *Infant Behavior and Development, 18,* 111–116.

Nelson, K. (1981). Individual differences in language development: Implications for development and language. *Developmental Psychology, 17,* 170–187.

Nelson, K. (1986). *Event knowledge: Structure and function in development.* Hillsdale, NJ: Erlbaum.

Nelson, K. (1989). Remembering: A functional developmental perspective. In P. R. Solomon, G. R. Goethels, C. M. Kelley, & B. R. Stephens (Eds.), *Memory: An interdisciplinary approach.* New York: Springer-Verlag.

Nelson, K. (1992). Emergence of autobiographical memory at age 4. *Human Development, 35,* 172–177.

Nelson, T. O. (1990). Metamemory: A theoretical framework and new findings. In G. H. Bower (Ed.), *The psychology of learning and motivation.* San Diego, CA: Academic Press.

Nelson, T. O. (1994). Metacognition. In V. S. Ramachandran (Ed.), *Encyclopedia of human behavior* (Vol. 3). San Diego, CA: Academic Press.

Nettles, S. M., & Pleck, J. H. (1990). Risk, resilience, and development: The multiple ecologies of black adolescents. In R. J. Haggerty, N. Garmezy, M. Rutter, & L. Sherrod (Eds.), *Risk and resilience in children: Developmental approaches.* New York: Cambridge University Press.

Neuringer, M. (1993). Cerebral cortex docosahexaenoic acid is lower in formula-fed than in breast-fed infants. *Nutrition Review, 51,* 232–241.

Newcomb, A. F., & Bagwell, C. L. (1995). Children's friendship relations: A meta-analytic review. *Psychological Bulletin, 117,* 306–347.

Newcomb, A. F., Bukowski, W. M., & Pattee, L. (1993). Children's peer relations: A meta-analytic review of popular, rejected, neglected, controversial, and average sociometric status. *Psychological Bulletin, 113,* 99–128.

Newcombe, N., Drummey, A. B., & Lie, E. (1995). Children's memory for early experience. *Journal of Experimental Child Psychology, 59,* 337–342.

Newcombe, N., & Fox, N. A. (1994). Infantile amnesia: Through a glass darkly. *Child Development, 65,* 31–40.

Ney, P. G., Fung, T., & Wickett, A. R. (1993). Child neglect: The precursor to child abuse. *Pre- and Peri-Natal Psychology Journal, 8,* 95–112.

Nihart, M. A. (1993). Growth and development of the brain. *Journal of Child and Adolescent Psychiatric and Mental Health Nursing, 6,* 39–40.

Nisbett, R. (1994, October 31). Blue genes. *New Republic, 211,* 15.

Nisbett, R. E. (1972). Hunger, obesity, and the ventromedial hypothalamus. *Psychological Review, 79,* 433–453.

Noble, G. (1983). Social learning from everyday television. In M. Howe (Ed.), *Learning from television: Psychological and educational research.* New York: Academic Press.

Nolen-Hoeksema, S., & Girgus, J. S. (1994). The emergence of gender differences in depression during adolescence. *Psychological Bulletin, 115,* 424–443.

Nossiter, A. (1995, September 5). Asthma common and on rise in the crowded South Bronx. *The New York Times,* pp. A1, B2.

Notzon, F. C. (1990). International differences in the use of obstetric interventions. *Journal of the American Medical Association, 263,* 3286–3291.

Nowak, R. (1994a, July 22). Genetic testing set for takeoff. *Science, 265,* 464–467.

Nowak, R. (1994b, March 18). Nicotine scrutinized as FDA seeks to regulate cigarettes. *Science, 263,* 1555–1556.

Nowicki, S., & Duke, M. P. (1994). Individual differences in the nonverbal communication of affect: The Diagnostic Analysis of Nonverbal Accuracy Scale. Special Issue: Development of nonverbal behavior: II. Social development and nonverbal behavior. *Journal of Nonverbal Behavior, 18,* 9–35.

Nugent, J. K., Lester, B. M., & Brazelton, T. B. (Eds.). (1989). *The cultural context of infancy: Vol. 1. Biology, culture, and infant development.* Norwood, NJ: Ablex.

Nwokah, E., & Fogel, A. (1993). Laughter in mother-infant emotional communication. *Humor: International Journal of Humor Research, 6,* 137–161.

Nyhan, W. L. (1990). Structural abnormalities. *Clinical Symposia, 42,* 2.

O'Connor, M. J., Sigman, M., & Brill, N. (1987). Disorganization of attachment in relation to maternal alcohol consumption. *Journal of Consulting and Clinical Psychology, 55,* 831–836.

O'Donnell, C. R. (1995). Firearm deaths among children and youth. *American Psychologist, 50,* 771–776.

Ogbu, J. (1992). Understanding cultural diversity and learning. *Educational Researcher, 21,* 5–14.

Ogbu, J. U. (1988). Black education: A cultural-ecological perspective. In H. P. McAdoo (Ed.), *Black families.* Beverly Hills, CA: Sage.

Ogden, C. L., Troiano, R. P., Briefel, R. R., Kuczmarski, R. J., Flegal, K. M., & Johnson, C. L. (1997). Prevalence of overweight among preschool children in the United States, 1971 through 1994. *Pediatrics, 99,* e1.

Ogilvy, C. M. (1994). Social skills training with children and adolescents: A review of the evidence on effectiveness. *Educational Psychology, 14,* 73–83.

O'Leary, S. G. (1995). Parental discipline mistakes. *Current Directions in Psychological Science, 4,* 11–13.

Olewus, D. (1982). Development of stable aggressive reaction patterns in males. In R. Blanchard & C. Blanchard (Eds.), *Advances in the study of aggression* (Vol. 1). New York: Academic Press.

Oliver, M. B., & Hyde, J. S. (1993). Gender differences in sexuality: A meta-analysis. *Psychological Bulletin, 114,* 29–51.

O'Malley, P. M., Johnston, L. D., & Bachman, J. G. (1995). Adolescent substance abuse. Epidemiology and implications for public policy. *Pediatric Clinics of North America, 42,* 241–260.

O'Neill, C. (1994, May 17). Exercise just for the fun of it. *The Washington Post,* p. WH18.

Ono, Y. (1995, October 15). Ads do push kids to smoke, study suggests. *The Wall Street Journal,* pp. B1–B2.

Onslow, M. (1992). Choosing a treatment program for early stuttering: Issues and future directions. *Journal of Speech and Hearing Research, 35,* 983–993.

Osofsky, J. D. (1995). The effects of exposure to violence on young children. *American Psychologist, 50,* 782–788.

O'Sullivan, J. T. (1993). Applying cognitive developmental principles in classrooms. In R. Pasnak & M. L. Howe (Eds.), *Emerging themes in cognitive development* (Vol. 2). New York: Springer-Verlag.

Ozecki, M. (1993, February 28). On turning 13: Reports from the front lines. *The New York Times,* sec. 4, p. 2.

Paikoff, R. L., & Brooks-Gunn, J. (1990). Physiological processes: What role do they play during the transition to adolescence? In R. Montemayor, G. R. Adams, & T. P. Gulotta (Eds.), *From childhood to adolescence: A transitional period?* Newbury Park, CA: Sage.

Paneth, N. S. (1995). The problem of low birth weight. *The Future of Children, 5,* 19–34.

Panneton, R. K. (1985). *Prenatal auditory experience with melodies: Effects on postnatal auditory preferences in human newborns.* Unpublished doctoral dissertation, University of North Carolina, Greensboro.

Papousek, H., & Bernstein, P. (1969). The functions of conditioning stimulation in human neonates and infants. In A. Ambrose (Ed.), *Stimulation in early infancy.* New York: Academic Press.

Papousek, H., & Papousek, M. (1991). Innate and cultural guidance of infants' integrative competencies: China, the United States, and Germany. In M. H. Bornstein (Ed.), *Cultural approaches to parenting.* Hillsdale, NJ: Erlbaum.

Papps, F., Walker, M., Trimboli, A., & Trimboli, C. (1995). Parental discipline in Anglo, Greek, Lebanese, and Vietnamese cultures. *Journal of Cross-Cultural Psychology, 26,* 49–64.

Park, K. A., Lay, K., & Ramsay, L. (1993). Individual differences and developmental changes in preschoolers' friendships. *Developmental Psychology, 29,* 264–270.

Parke, R., Ornstein, P. A., Rieser, J. J., & Zahn-Waxler, C. (1994). The past as prologue: An overview of a century of developmental psychology. In R. D. Parke, P. A. Ornstein, J. J. Rieser, & C. Zahn-Waxler (Eds.), *A century of developmental psychology.* Washington, DC: American Psychological Association.

Parke, R., & Slaby, R. (1983). The development of aggression. In E. M. Hetherington (Ed.), *Handbook of child psychology: Vol. 4. Socialization, personality, and social development* (pp. 547–642). New York: Wiley

Parke, R. D. (1981). *Fathers.* Cambridge, MA: Harvard University Press.

Parke, R. D. (1989). Social development in infancy: A 25-year perspective. In D. Palermo (Ed.), *Advances in child development and behaviors.* New York: Academic Press.

Parke, R. D. (1990). In search of fathers: A narrative of an empirical journey. In I. Sigel & G. Brody (Eds.), *Methods of family research* (Vol. 1). Hillsdale, NJ: Erlbaum.

Parke, R. D., & Sawin, D. B. (1980). The family in early infancy: Social interactional and attitudinal analyses. In F. A. Pedersen (Ed.), *The father-infant relationship: Observational studies in the family setting.* New York: Praeger Special Studies.

Parke, R. D., & Tinsley, B. J. (1987). Family interaction in infancy. In J. D. Osofsky (Ed.), *Handbook of infant development* (2nd ed.). New York: Wiley.

Parmalee, A. H. (1986). Children's illnesses: Their beneficial effects on behavioral development. *Child Development, 57,* 1–10.

Parmalee, A. H., Jr., & Sigman, M. D. (1983). Prenatal brain development and behavior. In P. H. Mussen (Ed.), *Handbook of child psychology* (4th ed., Vol. 2). New York: Wiley.

Parmalee, A. H., Wenner, W., & Schulz, H. (1964). Infant sleep patterns from birth to 16 weeks of age. *Journal of Pediatrics, 65,* 572–576.

Parritz, R. H., Mangelsdorf, S., & Gunnar, M. R. (1992). Control, social referencing, and the infants' appraisal of threat. In S. Feinman (Ed.), *Social referencing and the social construction of reality in infancy.* New York: Plenum.

Parten, M. B. (1932). Social participation among preschool children. *Journal of Abnormal and Social Psychology, 27,* 243–269.

Pascalis, O., deSchonen, S., Morton, J., Deruelle, C. et al. (1995). Mother's face recognition by neonates: A replication and an extension. *Infant Behavior and Development, 18,* 79–85.

Pascoe, J. M. (1993). Social support during labor and duration of labor: A community-based study. *Public Health Nursing, 10,* 97–99.

Patterson, C. J. (1992). Children of lesbian and gay parents. *Child Development, 63,* 1025–1042.

Patterson, C. J. (1994). Lesbians and gay families. *Current Directions in Psychological Science, 3,* 62–64.

Patterson, C. J. (1995). Families of the baby boom: Parents' division of labor and children's adjustment. Special Issue: Sexual orientation and human development. *Developmental Psychology, 31,* 115–123.

Patterson, G. R., DeBaryshe, B. D., & Ramsey, E. (1989). A developmental perspective on antisocial behavior. *American Psychologist, 44,* 339–335.

Pavlov, I. P. (1927). *Conditioned reflexes.* London: Oxford University Press.

Payne, J. S., Kauffman, J. M., Brown, G. B., DeMott, R. M. (1974). *Exceptional children in focus.* Columbus, OH: Merrill.

Pederson, D. R., Moran, G., Sitko, C., Campbell, K., Ghesquire, K., & Acton, H. (1990). Maternal sensitivity and the security of infant-mother attachment: A q-sort study. *Child Development ,61* 1974–1983.

Pedlow, R., Sanson, A., Prior, M., & Oberklaid, F. (1993). Stability of maternally reported temperament from infancy to 8 years. *Developmental Psychology, 29,* 998–1007.

Peplau, L. A., & Cochran, S. D. (1990). A relationship perspective on homosexuality. In D. P. McWhirter, S. A. Sanders, & J. M. Reinisch (Eds.), *Homosexuality/heterosexuality: The Kinsey scale and current research.* New York: Oxford University Press.

Pereira, J. (1994, December 7). Caution: "Morphing" may be hazardous to your teacher. *The Wall Street Journal,* pp. A1, A8.

Pereira-Smith, O., Smith, J. et al. (1988, August). Paper presented at the annual meeting of the International Genetics Congress, Toronto, Canada.

Perez, C. M., & Widom, C. S. (1994). Childhood victimization and long-term intellectual and academic outcomes. *Child Abuse & Neglect, 18,* 617–633.

Perleth, C., Lehwald, G., & Browder, C. S. (1993). Indicators of high ability in young children. In K. Heller, F. J. Monks, & A. H. Passow (Eds.), *International handbook of research and development of giftedness and talent* (pp. 283–310). Oxford, England: Pergamon Press.

Perlmann, R. Y., & Gleason, J. B. (1990, July). *Patterns of prohibition in mothers' speech to children.* Paper presented at the Fifth International Congress for the Study of Child Language, Budapest, Hungary.

Perozzi, J. A., & Sanchez, M. C. (1992). The effect of instruction in L1 on receptive acquisition of L2 for bilingual children with language delay. *Language, Speech, and Hearing Services in Schools, 23,* 348–352.

Perris, E. E., Myers, N. A., & Clifton, R. K. (1990). Long-term memory for a single infancy experience. *Child Development, 61,* 1796–1807.

Perry, C., & McIntire, W. G. (1995). Modes of moral judgment among early adolescents. *Adolescence, 30,* 707–715.

Perry, W. G. (1970). *Forms of intellectual and ethical development in the college years.* New York: Holt.

Petersen, A. (1985). Adolescent development. *Annual Review of Psychology, 39,* 583–607.

Petersen, A. (in press). A longitudinal investigation of adolescents' changing perceptions of pubertal timing. *Developmental Psychology.*

Petersen, A. C. (1988, September). Those gangly years. *Psychology Today,* 28–34.

Petersen, A. C., Compas, B., & Brooks-Gunn, J. (1991). *Depression in adolescence: Implications of current research for programs and policy.* Report prepared for the Carnegie Council on Adolescent Development, Washington, DC.

Petersen, A. C., Compas, B. E., Brooks-Gunn, J., Stemmler, M., Ey, S., & Grant, K. E. (1993). Depression in adolescence. *American Psychologist, 48,* 155–168.

Petersen, A. C., & Crockett, L. (1985). Pubertal timing and grade effects on adjustment. *Journal of Youth and Adolescence, 14,* 191–206.

Petersen, A. C., Sarigiani, P. A., & Kennedy, R. E. (1991). Adolescent depression: Why more girls? *Journal of Youth and Adolescence, 20,* 247–271.

Peterseon, B. E., & Stewart, A. J. (1993). Generativity and social motives in young adults. *Journal of Personality and Social Psychology, 65,* 186–198.

Peterson, L. (1994). Child injury and abuse-neglect: Common etiologies, challenges, and courses toward prevention. *Current Directions in Psychological Science, 3,* 116–120.

Petitto, L. A., & Marentette, P. F. (1991, March 22). Babbling in the manual mode: Evidence for the ontogeny of language. *Science, 251,* 1493–1496.

Petraitis, J., Flay, B. R., & Miller, T. Q. (1995). Reviewing theories of adolescent substance use: Organizing pieces in the puzzle. *Psychological Bulletin, 117,* 67–86.

Phelan, P., Yu, H. C., & Davidson, A. L. (1994). Navigating the psychosocial pressures of adolescence: The voices and experiences of high school youth. *American Educational Research Journal, 31,* 415–447.

Philippot, P., & Feldman, R. S. (1990). Age and social competence in preschoolers' decoding of facial expression. *British Journal of Social Psychology, 29,* 43–54.

Philipott, P., Feldman, R. S., & McGee, G. (1992). Nonverbal behavior skills in an educational context: Typical and atypical populations. In R. S. Feldman (Ed.), *Applications of nonverbal behavioral theories and research.* Hillsdale, NJ: Lawrence Erlbaum Associates.

Phillips, D. A., & Zimmerman, M. (1990). The developmental course of perceived competence and incompetence among competent children. In R. Sternberg & J. Kolligian (Eds.), *Competence considered.* New Haven, CT: Yale University Press.

Phillips, D., McCartney, K., Scarr, S., & Howes, C. (1987). Selective review of infant day care research: A cause for concern. *Zero to Three, 7,* 18–21.

Phillips, D. A., Voran, M., Kisker, E., Howes, C., & Whitebook, M. (1994). Child care for children in poverty: Opportunity or inequity? *Child Development, 65,* 472–492.

Phillips, R. D., Wagner, S. H., Fells, C. A., & Lynch, M. (1990). Do infants recognize emotion in facial expressions?: Categorical and "metaphorical" evidence. *Infant Behavior and Development, 13,* 71–84.

Phillips, S., King, S., & DuBois, L. (1978). Spontaneous activities of female versus male newborns. *Child Development, 49,* 590–597.

Phinney, J., Lochner, B., & Murphy, R. (1990). Ethnic identity development and psychological adjustment in adolescence. In A. Stiffman & L. Davis (Eds.), *Advances in adolescent mental health: Vol. 5. Ethnic issues.* Greenwich, CT: JAI Press.

Phinney, J. S., & Alipuria, L. L. (1990). Ethnic identity in college students from four ethnic groups. *Journal of Adolescence, 13,* 171–183.

Piaget, J. (1932). *The moral judgment of the child.* New York: Harcourt, Brace & World.

Piaget, J. (1952). *The origins of intelligence in children.* New York: International Universities Press.

Piaget, J. (1954). *The construction of reality in the child.* (M. Cook, Trans.). New York: Basic Books.

Piaget, J. (1962). *Play, dreams, and imitation in childhood.* New York: Norton.

Piaget, J. (1983). Piaget's theory. In W. Kessen (Ed.) & P. H. Mussen (Series Ed.), *Handbook of child psychology: Vol 1. History, theory, and methods* (pp. 103–128). New York: Wiley.

Piaget, J., & Inhelder, B. (1958). *The growth of logical thinking from childhood to adolescence* (A. Parsons & S. Seagrin, Trans.). New York: Basic Books.

Piaget, J., & Inhelder, B. (1969). *The psychology of the child* (H. Weaver, Trans.). New York: Basic Books.

Piaget, J., Inhelder, B., & Szeminska, A. (1960). *The child's conception of geometry.* New York: Basic Books. (Original work published 1948.)

Pinker, S. (1989). Resolving a learnability paradox in the acquisition of the verb lexicon. In M. Rice & R. Schiefelbusch (Eds.), *The teachability of language.* Baltimore: Brookes.

Pinker, S. (1994). *The language instinct.* New York: William Morrow.

Pintney, R., Forlands, F., & Freedman, H. (1937). Personality and attitudinal similarity among classmates. *Journal of Applied Psychology, 21,* 48–65.

Pipp, S., Easterbrooks, M., & Brown, S. R. (1993). Attachment status and complexity of infants' self- and other-knowledge when tested with mother and father. *Social Development, 2,* 1–14.

Plomin, R. (1990). The role of inheritance in behavior. *Science, 248,* 183–188.

Plomin, R. (1994a). *Genetics and experience: The interplay between nature and nurture.* Newbury Park, CA: Sage.

Plomin, R. (1994b). Nature, nurture, and social development. *Social Development, 3,* 37–53.

Plomin, R. (1994c). The genetic basis of complex human behaviors. *Science, 264,* 1733–1739.

Plomin, R. (1995, August). Molecular genetics and psychology. *Current Directions in Psychological Science, 4,* 114–117.

Plomin, R., Corley, R., DeFries, J. C., & Fulker, D. W. (1990). Individual differences in television viewing in early childhood: Nature as well as nurture. *Psychological Science, 1,* 371–377.

Plomin, R., DeFries, J. C., & McClearn, G. E. (1990). *Behavioral genetics: A primer.* New York: Freeman.

Plomin, R., & McClearn, G. E. (Eds.). (1993). *Nature, nurture, and psychology.* Washington, DC: American Psychological Association.

Poest, C. A., Williams, J. R., Witt, D. D., & Atwood, M. E. (1990). Challenge me to move: Large muscle development in young children. *Young Children, 45,* 4–10.

Pollitt, E. (1994). Poverty and child development: Relevance of research in developing countries to the United States. *Child Development, 65,* 283–295.

Pollitt, E., Golub, M., Gorman, K., Grantham-McGregor, S., Levitsky, D., Schürch, B., Strupp, B., & Wachs, T. (1996). A reconceptualization of the effects of undernutrition on children's biological, psychosocial, and behavioral development. *Social Policy Report, 10,* 1–22.

Pollitt, E., Gorman, K. S., Engle, P. L., Martorell, R., & Rivera, J. (1993). Early supplementary feeding and cognition: Effects over two decades. *Monographs of the Society for Research in Child Development, 58,* v–99.

Pomerleau, A., Bolduc, D., Malcuit, G., & Cossette, L. (1990). Pink or blue: Environmental gender stereotypes in the first 2 years of life. *Sex Roles, 22,* 359–367.

Pomerleau, O. F., & Pomerleau, C. S. (1989). A biobehavioral perspective on smoking. In T. Ney & A. Gale (Eds.), *Smoking and human behavior.* New York: Wiley.

Ponomarev, D. (1993, February 28). On turning 13: Reports from the front lines. *The New York Times,* sec. 4, p. 2.

Ponsonby, A. L., Dwyer, T., & Couper, D. (1997). Sleeping position, infant apnea, and cyanosis: A population-based study. *Pediatrics, 99,* e3.

Porges, S. W., & Lipsitt, L. P. (1993). Neonatal responsivity to gustatory stimulation: The gustatory-vagal hypothesis. *Infant Behavior and Development, 16,* 487–494.

Porter, F. L., Porges, S. W., & Marshall, R. E. (1988). Newborn pain cries and vagal tone: Parallel changes in response to circumcision. *Child Development, 59,* 495–515.

Porter, R. H., Bologh, R. D., & Makin, J. W. (1988). Olfactory influences on mother-infant interactions. In C. Rovee-Collier & L. Lipsitt (Eds.), *Advances in infancy research* (Vol. 5). Norwood, NJ: Ablex.

Posada, G., Gao, Y., Wu, F., Posada, R., Tascon, M., Schoelmerich, A., Sagi, A., Kondo-Ikemura, K., Haaland, W., & Synnevaag, B. (1995). The secure-base phenomenon across cultures: Children's behavior, mothers' preferences, and experts' concepts. *Monograph of the Society for Research in Child Development,* Serial No. 244.

Potter, M. C. (1990). Remembering. In D. N. Osherson & E. E. Smith (Eds.), *Thinking.* Cambridge, MA: MIT Press.

Poulin-Dubois, D., Serbin, L. A., Kenyon, B., & Derbyshire, A. (1994). Infants' intermodal knowledge about gender. *Developmental Psychology, 30,* 436–442.

Power, T. G., & Parke, R. D. (1982). Play as a context for early learning: Lab and home analyses. In L. M. Laosa & I. E. Sigal (Eds.), *The family as a learning environment.* New York: Plenum.

Prechtl, H. F. R. (1982). Regressions and transformations during neurological development. In T. G. Bever (Ed.), *Regressions in mental development.* Hillsdale, NJ: Erlbaum.

Prentice, A. (1991). Can maternal dietary supplements help in preventing infant malnutrition? *Acta Paediatrica Scandinaica—Supplement, 374,* 67–77.

Prescott, C., & Gottesman, I. (1993). Genetically mediated vulnerability to schizophrenia. *Psychiatric Clinics of North America, 16,* 245–267.

Pressley, M. (1987). Are keyword method effects limited to slow presentation rates? An empirically based reply to Hall and Fuson (1986). *Journal of Educational Psychology, 79,* 333–335.

Pressley, M., Cariglia-Bull, T., Deane, S., & Schneider, W. (1987). Short-term memory, verbal competence, and age as predictors of imagery instructional effectiveness. *Journal of Experimental Child Psychology, 43,* 194–211.

Pressley, M., & Levin, J. R. (1983). *Cognitive strategy research: Psychological foundations.* New York: Springer-Verlag.

Pressley, M., & VanMeter, P. (1993). Memory strategies: Natural development and use following instruction. In R. Pasnak & M. L. Howe (Eds.), *Emerging themes in cognitive development* (Vol. 2). New York: Springer-Verlag.

Price, D. W., & Goodman, G. S. (1990). Visiting the wizard: Children's memory for a recurring event. *Child Development, 61,* 664–680.

Price, R., & Gottesman, I. (1991). Body fat in identical twins reared apart: Roles for genes and environment. *Behavior Genetics, 21,* 1–7.

Prieto, S. L., Cole, D. A., & Tageson, C. W. (1992). Depressive self-schemas in clinic and nonclinic children. *Cognitive Therapy and Research, 16,* 521–534.

Prodromidis, M., Brams, S., Field, T., Scafidi, F., & Rahdert, E. (1994). Psychosocial stressors among depressed adolescent mothers. *Adolescence, 29,* 331–343.

Purdy, M. (1995, November 6). A kind of sexual revolution. *The New York Times,* pp. B1, B6.

Putallaz, M. (1983). Predicting children's sociometric status from their behavior. *Child Development, 54,* 1417–1426.

Putnam, F. (1995, January). Paper presented at a conference, "Violence against children in the family and the community: A conference on causes, developmental consequences, interventions and prevention." Los Angeles: University of Southern California.

Pyryt, M. C., & Mendaglio, S. (1994). The multidimensional self-concept: A comparison of gifted and average-ability adolescents. *Journal for the Education of the Gifted, 17,* 299–305.

Pyszczynski, T., Greenberg, J., & LaPrelle, J. (1985). Social comparison after success and failure: Biased search for information consistent with a self-servicing conclusion. *Journal of Experimental Social Psychology, 21,* 195–211.

Quay, L. C., & Blaney, R. L. (1992). Verbal communication, nonverbal communication, and private speech in lower and middle socioeconomic status preschool children. *Journal of Genetic Psychology, 153,* 129–138.

Quinn, J. B. (1993, April 5). What's for dinner, Mom? *Newsweek,* 68.

Quinn, M. (1990, January 29). Don't aim that pack at us. *Time,* 60.

Quinn, P. C., & Eimas, P. D. (1996). *Perceptual organization and categorization in young infants.* Norwood, NJ: Ablex.

Radetsky, P. (1994, December 2). Stopping premature births before it's too late. *Science, 266,* 1486–1488.

Radke-Yarrow, M., Zahn-Waxler, C., & Chapman, M. (1983). Children's prosocial dispositions and behavior. In E. M. Hetherington, (Ed.), *Handbook of child psychology: Vol. 4. Socialization, personality, and social development* (pp. 469–545). New York: Wiley.

Rahe, R. H., & Arthur, R. J. (1978). Life change and illness studies: Past history and future directions. *Human Stress, 4,* 3–15.

Ramsay, D. S. (1980). Onset of unimanual handedness in infants. *Infant Behavior and Development, 3,* 377–385.

Ramsey, P. G. (1995). Changing social dynamics in early childhood classrooms. *Child Development, 66,* 764–773.

Ranade, V. (1993). Nutritional recommendations for children and adolescents. *International Journal of Clinical Pharmacology, Therapy, and Toxicology, 31,* 285–290.

Randahl, G. J. (1991). A typological analysis of the relations between measured vocational interests and abilities. *Journal of Vocational Behavior, 38,* 333–350.

Rauch-Elnekave, H. (1994). Teenage motherhood: Its relationship to undetected learning problems. *Adolescence, 29,* 91–103.

Rauscher, F. H., Shaw, G. L., Levine, L. J., Ky, K. N., & Wright, E. L. (1994, August). *Music and spatial task performance—A causal relationship.* Paper presented at the annual meeting of the American Psychological Association, Los Angeles.

Ravitch, D. (1985). *The troubled crusade: American education 1945–1980.* New York: Basic Books.

Rayner, K., & Pollatsek, A. (Eds.). (1989). *The psychology of reading.* Englewood Cliffs, NJ: Prentice Hall.

Reinis, S. & Goldman, J. M. (1980). *The development of the brain: Biological and functional perspectives.* Springfield, IL: Charles C. Thomas.

Reiss, I. L. (1960). *Premarital sexual standards in America.* New York: Free Press.

Reiss, M. J. (1984). Human sociobiology. *Zygon Journal of Religion and Science, 19,* 117–140.

Reissland, N. (1988). Neonatal imitation in the first hour of life: Observations in rural Nepal. *Developmental Psychology, 24,* 450–469.

Reitman, V. (1994, February 15). Tots do swimmingly in language-immersion programs. *The Wall Street Journal,* p. B1.

Reschly, D. J. (1996). Identification and assessment of students with disabilities. *The future of Children, 6,* 40–53.

Reynolds, A. J. (1994). Effects of a preschool plus follow-on intervention for children at risk. *Developmental Psychology, 30,* 787–804.

Ricciardelli, L. A. (1992). Bilingualism and cognitive development in relation to threshold theory. *Journal of Psycholinguistic Research, 21,* 301–316.

Ricciuti, H. N. (1993). Nutrition and mental development. *Current Directions in Psychological Science, 2,* 43–46.

Rice, M. L., Huston, A. C., Truglio, R., & Wright, J. (1990). Words from "Sesame Street": Learning vocabulary while viewing. *Developmental Psychology, 26,* 421–428.

Richards, H. D., Bear, G. G., Stewart, A. L., & Norman, A. D. (1992). Moral reasoning and classroom conduct: Evidence of a curvilinear relationship. *Merrill-Palmer Quarterly, 38,* 176–190.

Richards, M. H., & Duckett, E. (1991). Maternal employment and adolescents. In J. V. Lerner & N. Galambos (Eds.), *Employed mothers and their children.* New York: Garland.

Richards, M. H., & Duckett, E. (1994). The relationship of maternal employment to early adolescent daily experience with and without parents. *Child Development, 65,* 225–236.

Richardson, G. A., & Day, N. L. (1994). Detrimental effects of prenatal cocaine exposure: Illusion or reality? *Journal of the American Academy of Child and Adolescent Psychiatry, 33,* 28–34.

Richardson, V., & Champion, V. (1992). The relationship of attitudes, knowledge, and social support to breast-feeding. *Issues in Comprehensive Pediatric Nursing, 15,* 183–197.

Rief, S. F. (1995). *How to reach and teach ADD/ADHD children.* West Nyack, NY: Center for Applied Research in Education.

Riese, M. L. (1987). Temperamental stability between the neonatal period and 24 months. *Developmental Psychology, 23,* 216–222.

Riese, M. L. (1990). Neonatal temperament in monozygotic and dizygotic twin pairs. *Child Development, 61,* 1230–1237.

Rimm, S. B., & Lovance, K. J. (1992). The use of subject and grade skipping for the prevention and reversal of underachievement. Special Issue: Challenging the gifted: Grouping and acceleration. *Gifted Child Quarterly, 36,* 100–105.

Rist, M. C. (1990, January). The shadow children. *The American School Board Journal,* 19–24.

Rizzo, T. A., Metzger, B. E., Dooley, S. L., & Cho, N. H. (1997). Early malnutrition and child neurobehavioral development: Insights from the study of children of diabetic mothers. *Child Development, 68,* 26–38.

Robbins, M. W. (1990, December 10). Sparing the child: How to intervene when you suspect abuse. *New York Magazine,* 42–53.

Robbins, W. J. (1929). *Growth.* New Haven, CT: Yale University Press.

Robertson, S. S. (1982). Intrinsic temporal patterning in the spontaneous movement of awake neonates. *Child Development, 53,* 1016–1021.

Rochat, P., & Goubet, N. (1995). Development of sitting and reaching in 5- and 6-month old infants. *Infant Behavior and Development, 18,* 53–68.

Rodin, J., & Hall, E. (1987). A sense of control. In E. Hall, (Ed.), *Growing and changing.* New York: Random House.

Rodin, J. (1992). Determinants of body fat localization and its implications for health. *Annals of Behavioral Medicine, 14,* 275–281.

Rodman, H., & Cole, C. (1987). Latchkey children: A review of policy and resources. *Family Relations, 36,* 101–105.

Roffwarg, H. P., Muzio, J. N., & Dement, W. C. (1966). Ontogenic development of the human sleep-dream cycle. *Science, 152,* 604–619.

Rogan, W. J., & Gladen, B. C. (1993). Breastfeeding and cognitive development. *Early Human Development, 31,* 181–193.

Rogoff, B., & Chavajay, P. (1995). What's become of research on the cultural basis of cognitive development? *American Psychologist, 50,* 859–877.

Rolfe, S. A. (1994). Does assessment of cognitive functioning in infancy hold the key to early detection of developmental disabilities? A review of research. *Australia and New Zealand Journal of Developmental Disabilities, 19,* 61–72.

Romaine, S. (1994). *Bilingualism* (2nd ed.). London: Blackwell.

Rönkä, A., & Pulkkinen, L. (1995). Accumulation of problems in social functioning in young adulthood: A developmental approach. *Journal of Personality and Social Psychology, 69,* 381–391.

Roodenrys, S., Hulme, C., & Brown, G. (1993). The development of short-term memory span: Separable effects of speech rate and long-term memory. *Journal of Experimental Child Psychology, 56,* 431–442.

Roopnarine, J. (1992). Father-child play in India. In K. MacDonald (Ed.), *Parent-child play.* Albany: State University of New York Press.

Roopnarine, J., & Honig, A. S. (1985, September). The unpopular child. *Young Children,* 59–64.

Roopnarine, J. L., Johnson, J. E., & Hooper, F. H. (Eds.). (1994). *Children's play in diverse cultures.* Albany: State University of New York Press.

Rose, S. A., & Feldman, J. F. (1995). Prediction of IQ and specific cognitive abilities at 11 years from infancy measures. *Developmental Psychology, 31,* 685–696.

Rose, S. A., Feldman, J. F., & Wallace, I. F. (1992). Infant information processing in relation to 6-year cognitive outcomes. *Child Development, 63,* 1126–1141.

Rose, S. A., Feldman, J. F., Wallace, I. F., & McCarton, C. (1991). Information processing at 1 year: Relation to birth status and developmental outcome during the first 5 years. *Developmental Psychology, 27,* 723–737.

Rose, S. A., & Ruff, H. A. (1987). Cross-modal abilities in infants. In J. D. Osofsky (Ed.), *Handbook of infant development* (2nd ed.). New York: Wiley.

Rosemond, J. (1988, September). Taming the TV monster and why that's so important. *Better Homes and Gardens,* 26–27.

Rosen, D. (March 25, 1997). The physician's perspective. *HealthNews,* 3.

Rosen, W. D., Adamson, L. B., & Bakeman, R. (1992). An experimental investigation of infant social referencing: Mothers' messages and gender differences. *Developmental Psychology, 28,* 1172–1178.

Rosenstein, D., & Oster, H. (1988). Differential facial responses to four basic tastes in newborns. *Child Development, 59,* 155–158.

Rosenthal, A. (January, 10, 1996). In vitro child grows up. *The New York Times, A1, B8.*

Rosenthal, D. A., & Shepherd, H. (1993). A six-month follow-up of adolescents' sexual risk-taking, HIV/AIDS knowledge, and attitudes to condoms. *Journal of Community and Applied Social Psychology, 3,* 53–65.

Rosenthal, R. (1987). Pygmalion effects: Existence, magnitude, and social importance. *Educational Researcher,* 37–40.

Rosenthal, R. (1994). Interpersonal expectancy effects: A 30-year perspective. *Current Directions in Psychological Science, 3,* 176–179.

Rosenthal, R., & Jacobson, L. (1968). *Pygmalion in the classroom: Teacher expectation and pupils' intellectual development.* New York: Holt, Rinehart and Winston.

Rosenzweig, M. R., & Bennett, E. L. (1976). Enriched environments: Facts, factors, and fantasies. In L. Petrinovich & J. L. McGaugh (Eds.), *Knowing, thinking, and believing.* New York: Plenum.

Rosnow, R. L., Rotheram-Borus, M. J., Ceci, S. J., Blanck, P. D., & Koocher, G. O. (1993). The institutional review board as a mirror of scientific and ethical standards. *American Psychologist, 48,* 821–826.

Ross Laboratories. (1993). *Ross Laboratories mothers' survey, 1992.* Division of Abbott Laboratories, USA, Columbus, OH. Unpublished data.

Ross, C. E., Mirowsky, J., & Goldsteen, K. (1991). The impact of the family on health. In A. Booth (Ed.), *Contemporary Families.* Minneapolis, MN: National Council on Family Relations.

Ross, R. K., & Yu, M. C. (1994, June 9). Breastfeeding and breast cancer. *New England Journal of Medicine, 330,* 1683–1684.

Rosser, P. L., & Randolph, S. M. (1989). Black American infants: The Howard University normative study. In J. K. Neugent, B. M. Lester, & T. B. Brazelton (Eds.), *The cultural context of infancy: Vol. 1. Biology, culture, and infant development.* Norwood, NJ: Ablex.

Rotenberg, K. J., & Morrison, J. (1993). Loneliness and college achievement: Do Loneliness Scale scores predict college drop-out? *Psychological Reports, 73,* 1283–1288.

Rothbart, M. K., Ahadi, S. A., & Hershey, K. L. (1994). Temperament and social behavior in childhood. *Merrill-Palmer Quarterly, 40,* 21–39.

Rothblum, E. D. (1990). Women and weight: Fad and fiction. *Journal of Psychology, 124,* 5–24.

Rotheram-Borus, M. H., Rosario, M., van Rossem, R., Reid, H., & Gillis, R. (1995). Prevalence, course, and predictors of multiple problem behaviors among gay and bisexual male adolescents. *Developmental Psychology, 31,* 75–81.

Roush, W. (1995, March 31). Arguing over why Johnny can't read. *Science, 267,* 1996–1998.

Rovee-Collier, C. (1993). The capacity for long-term memory in infancy. *Current Directions in Psychological Science, 2,* 130–135.

Rovee-Collier, C., Borza, M. A., Adler, S. A., & Boller, K. (1993). Infants' eyewitness testimony: Effects of postevent information on a prior memory representation. *Memory & Cognition, 21,* 267–279.

Rovee-Collier, C. K. (1984). The ontogeny of learning and memory in human infancy. In R. V. Kail, Jr., & N. E. Spear (Eds.), *Comparative perspectives on the development of memory.* Hillsdale, NJ: Erlbaum.

Rovee-Collier, C. K. (1987). Learning and memory in infancy. In J. D. Osofsky (Ed.), *Handbook of infant development* (2nd ed.). New York: Wiley.

Rovee-Collier, C. K., & Hayne, H. (1987). Reactivation and infant long-term memory. In H. W. Reese (Ed.), *Advances in child development and behavior* (Vol. 20). New York: Academic Press.

Rowe, D. C. (1993). Genetic perspectives on personality. In R. Plomin & G. E. McClearn (Eds.), *Nature, nurture, and psychology.* Washington, DC: American Psychological Association.

Rowe, D. C. (1994). *The effects of nurture on individual natures.* New York: Guilford Press.

Rubenstein, J., Howes, C., & Boyule, P. (1981). A 2-year follow-up of infants in community-based day care. *Journal of Child Psychology and Psychiatry, 22,* 209–218.

Rubin, D. C. (1985, September). The subtle deceiver: Recalling our past. *Psychology Today,* 39–46.

Rubin, D. C. (1986). *Autobiographical memory.* Cambridge, England: Cambridge University Press.

Rubin, D. H., Krasilnikoff, P. A., Leventhal, J. M., Weile, B., & Berget, A. (1986, August 23). Effects of passive smoking on birthweight. *Lancet,* 415–417.

Rubin, K. H., Daniels-Beirness, T., & Hayvren, M. (1982). Social and social-cognitive correlates of sociometric status in preschool and kindergarten children. *Canadian Journal of Behavioral Science, 14,* 338–349.

Rubin, K. H., Fein, G., & Vandenberg, B. (1983). In E. M. Hetherington (Ed.), *Handbook of child psychology: Vol. 4. Socialization, personality, and social development* (pp. 693–774). New York: Wiley

Ruble, D. (1983). The development of social comparison processes and their role in achievement-related self-actualization. In E. T. Higgins, D. N. Ruble, and W. W. Hartup (Eds.), *Social cognition and social development.* New York: Cambridge University Press.

Ruble, D., & Brooks-Gunn, J. (1982). The experience of menarche. *Child Development, 53,* 1557–1566.

Ruble, D. N., Boggiano, A. K., Feldman, N. S., & Loebl, J. H. (1989). Developmental analysis of the role of social comparison in self-evaluation. *Developmental Psychology, 16,* 105–115.

Ruff, H. A. (1989). The infant's use of visual and haptic information in the perception and recognition of objects. *Canadian Journal of Psychology, 43,* 302–319.

Rule, B. G., & Ferguson, T. J. (1986). The effects of media violence on attitudes, emotions, and cognitions. *Journal of Social Issues, 42,* 29–50.

Russell, G., & Radojevic, M. (1992). The changing role of fathers? Current understandings and future directions for research and practice. Special Section: Australian Regional Meeting: Attachment and the relationship of infant and caregivers. *Infant Mental Health Journal, 13,* 296–311.

Russo, R., & Parkin, A. J. (1993). Age differences in implicit memory: More apparent than real. *Memory & Cognition, 21,* 73–80.

Russon, A. E., & Waite, B. E. (1991). Patterns of dominance and imitation in an infant peer group. *Ethology and Sociobiology, 12,* 55–73.

Rusting, R. (1990, March). Safe passage? *Scientific American, 262,* 36.

Rutter, M. (1987). Continuities and discontinuities from infancy. In J. D. Osofsky (Ed.), *Handbook of infant development* (2nd ed.). New York: Wiley.

Rutter M., & Garmezy, N. (1983). Developmental psychopathology. In E. M. Hetherington (Ed.), *Handbook of child psychology Vol. 4. Socialization, personality, and social development.* New York: Wiley.

Rutter, M., Bailey, A., Bolton, P., LeCouteur, A. (1993). Autism: syndrome defintion and possible genetic mechanisms. In R. Plomin and G. McClearn (Eds.), *Nature, nurture, and psychology* (pp. 269–284). Washington, DC: American Psychological Association.

Ryan, A. S. (1997). The resurgence of breastfeeding in the United States. *Pediatrics, 99,* e12.

Saarni, C., & Borg, V. (in press). Television's influence on children's understanding of emotions and social control. In A. Dorr (Ed.), *Television and affect.* Hillsdale, NJ: Erlbaum.

Sacks, M. H. (1993). Exercise for stress control. In D. Goleman & J. Gurin (Eds.), *Mind-body medicine.* Yonkers, New York: Consumer Reports Books.

Sadker, M., & Sadker, D. (1994). *Failing at fairness: How America's schools cheat girls.* New York: Charles Scribner's Sons.

Sagi, A. (1990). Attachment theory and research from a cross-cultural perspective. *Human Development, 1990, 33,* 10–22.

Sagi, A., Donnell, F., van IJzendoorn, M. H., Mayseless, O., & Aviezer, O. (1994). Sleeping out of home in a kibbutz communal arrangement: It makes a difference for infant-mother attachment. *Child Development, 65,* 992–1004.

Sagi, A., Lewkowicz, K. S., Shoham, R., Dvir, R., & Estes, D. (1985). Security of infant-mother, father, metapelet attachments among kibbutz-reared Israeli children. In I. Bretherton and E. Waters (Eds.), Growing points of attachment theory and research. *Monographs of the Society for Research in Child Development, 50(1–2, Serial No. 209)*, 257–275.

Sagi, A., van IJzendoorn, M. H., Aviezer, O., Donnell, F., Koren-Karie, N., Joels, T., & Harel, Y. (1995). Attachments in multiple-caregiver and multiple-infant environment: The case of the Israeli kibbutzim. *Monographs of the Society for Research in Child Development,* SRCD Monograph.

Sagi, A., van IJzendoorn, M. H., & Koren-Karie, N. (1991). Primary appraisal of the Strange Situation: A cross-cultural analysis of preseparation episodes. *Developmental Psychology, 27,* 587–596.

Salber, E. J., Freeman, H. E., & Abelin, T. (1968). Needed research on smoking: Lessons from the Newton study. In E. F. Borgatta & R. R. Evans (Eds.), *Smoking, health, and behavior.* Chicago: Aldine.

Salmon, D. K. (1993, September). Getting through labor. *Parents,* 62–66.

Samaritans. (1989). *Annual report, 1989.* Boston: Author.

Sandberg, S. (Ed.). (1996). *Hyperactivity disorders of childhood.* New York: Cambridge University Press.

Sanderson, C. A., & Cantor, N. (1995). Social dating goals in late adolescence: Implications for safer sexual activity. *Journal of Personality and Social Psychology, 68,* 1121–1134.

Sandler, B. (1994, January 31). First denial, then a near-suicidal plea: "Mom, I need your help." *People Weekly,* 56–58.

Sandyk, R. (1992). Melatonin and maturation of REM sleep. *International Journal of Neuroscience, 63,* 105–114.

Sanoff, A. P., & Minerbrook, S. (1993, April 19). Race on campus. *U.S. News and World Report,* 52–64.

Sanson, A., & diMuccio, C. (1993). The influence of aggressive and neutral cartoons and toys on the behavior of preschool children. *Australian Psychologist, 28,* 93–99.

Sanson, A. V., Smart, D. F., Prior, M., Oberklaid, F., & Pedlow, R. (1994). The structure of temperament from age 3 to 7 years: Age, sex, and sociodemographic influences. *Merrill-Palmer Quarterly, 40,* 233–252.

Sarason, I. G., Sarason, B. R., & Pierce, G. R. (1991). Anxiety, cognitive interference, and performance. *Journal of Social Behavior and Personality, 5,* 1–18.

Sarason, S., Johnson, J. H., & Siegel, J. M. (1978). Assessing the impact of life changes: Development of the Life Experiences Survey. *Journal of Consulting and Clinical Psychology, 46,* 932–946.

Sarnat, H. B. (1978). Olfactory reflexes in the newborn infant. *Journal of Pediatrics, 92,* 624–626.

Savage-Rumbaugh, E. S., Murphy, J., Sevcik, R. A., Brakke, K. E., Williams, S. L., & Rumbaugh, D. M. (1993). Language and comprehension in ape and child. *Monographs of the Society for Research in Child Development, 58*(3–4, Serial No. 233).

Savin-Williams, R., & Demo, D. (1983). Situational and transsituational determinants of adolescent self-feelings. *Journal of Personality and Social Psychology, 44,* 824–833.

Savin-Williams, R. C., & Berndt, T. J. (1990). Friendship and peer relations. In S. Feldman & G. Elliott (Eds.), *At the threshold: The developing adolescent.* Cambridge, MA: Harvard University Press.

Scanlon, J. W., & Hollenbeck, A. R. (1983). Neonatal behavioral effects of anesthetic exposure during pregnancy. In A. E. Friedman, A. Milusky, & A. Gluck (Eds.), *Advances in perinatal medicine.* New York: Plenum.

Scarr, S. (1992). Developmental theories for the 1990s: Development and individual differences. *Child Development, 63,* 1–19.

Scarr, S. (1993). Biological and cultural diversity: The legacy of Darwin for development. *Child Development, 64,* 1333–1353.

Scarr, S., & Carter-Saltzman, L. (1982). Genetics and intelligence. In R. J. Sternberg (Ed.), *Handbook of human intelligence* (pp. 792–896). Cambridge, England: Cambridge University Press.

Scarr, S., Phillips, D., & McCartney, K. (1989). Working mothers and their families. *American Psychologist, 44,* 1402–1409.

Schachter, S., Goldman, R., & Gordon, A. (1968). Effects of fear, food deprivation, and obesity on eating. *Journal of Personality and Social Psychology, 10,* 91–97.

Schaefer, R. T., & Lamm, R. P. (1992). *Sociology* (4th ed.). New York: McGraw-Hill.

Schaffer, H. R. (1971). *The Growth of Sociability.* Hammondsworth, England: Penguin Books.

Schaffer, H. R., & Emerson, P. E. (1964). The development of social attachments in infancy. *Monographs of the Society for Research in Child Development, 29,* No. 94.

Schanberg, S., & Field, T. M. (1987). Sensory deprivation stress and supplemental stimulation in the rat pup and preterm human neonate. *Child Development, 58,* 1431–1447.

Schanberg, S., Field, T. M., Kuhn, C., & Bartolome, J. (1993). Touch: A biological regulator of growth and development in the neonate. *Verhaltenstherapie, 3(Suppl. 1),* 15.

Schatz, M. (1994). *A toddler's life.* New York: Oxford University Press.

Schechtman, V. L., & Harper, R. M. (1991). Time of night effects on heart rate variation in normal neonates. *Journal of Developmental Physiology, 16,* 349–353.

Scheier, M. F., & Carver, C. S. (1992). Effects of optimism on psychological and physical well-being: Theoretical overview and empirical update. *Cognitive Therapy and Research, 16,* 201–228.

Schlicker, S. A., Borra, S. T., & Regan, C. (1994). The weight and fitness status of United States children. *Nutrition Reviews, 52,* 11–17.

Schmidt, U., & Treasure, J. (1993). *Getting better bit(e) by bit(e): A survival kit for sufferers of bulimia nervosa and binge eating disorders.* Hillsdale, NJ: Erlbaum.

Schneider, B. A., Bull, D., & Trehub, S. E. (1988). Binaural unmasking in infants. *Journals of the Acoustical Society of America, 83,* 1124–1132.

Schneider, B. A., Trehub, S. E., & Bull, D. (1980). High-frequency sensitivity in infants. *Science, 207,* 1003–1004.

Schneider, W., & Pressley, M. (1989). *Memory between two and twenty.* New York: Springer-Verlag.

Schneiderman, N. (1983). Animal behavior models of coronary heart disease. In D. S. Kranz, A. Baum, & J. E. Singer (Eds.), *Handbook of psychology and health* (Vol. 3). Hillsdale, NJ: Erlbaum.

Schofield, J. W., & Francis, W. D. (1982). An observational study of peer interaction in racially mixed "accelerated" classrooms. *Journal of Educational Psychology, 74,* 722–732.

Schor, E. L. (1987). Unintentional injuries: Patterns within families. *American Journal of the Diseases of Children, 141,* 1280.

Schorr, L. (1988). *Without our reach: Breaking the cycle of disadvantage.* New York: Anchor Press.

Schulenberg, J. E., Asp, C. E., & Peterson, A. C. (1984). School from the young adolescent's perspective. *Journal of Early Adolescence, 4,* 107–130.

Schulman, M. (1991). *The passionate mind: Bringing up an intelligent and creative child.* New York: Free Press.

Schulman, P., Keith, D., & Seligman, M. (1993). Is optimism heritable? A study of twins. *Behavior Research and Therapy, 31,* 569–574.

Schultz, A. H. (1969). *The life of primates.* New York: Universe.

Schunk, D. H. (1991). Self-efficacy and academic motivation. Special Issue: Current issues and new directions in motivational theory and research. *Educational Psychologist, 26,* 207–231.

Schuster, C. S., & Ashburn, S. S. (1986). *The process of human development* (2nd ed.). Boston: Little, Brown.

Schwebel, M., Maher, C. A., & Fagley, N. S. (Eds.). (1990). *Promoting cognitive growth over the life span.* Hillsdale, NJ: Erlbaum.

Schweinhart, L. J., Barnes, H. V., & Weikart, D. P. (1993). *Significant benefits: The High/Scope Perry Preschool Study through age 27* (Monographs of the High/Scope Educational Research Foundation, No. 10). Ypsilanti, MI: High/Scope Press.

Scruggs, T. E., & Mastropieri, M. A. (1994). Successful mainstreaming in elementary science classes: A qualitative study of three reputational cases. *American Educational Research Journal, 31,* 785–811.

Sears, R. R. (1977). Sources of life satisfaction of the Terman gifted men. *American Psychologist, 32,* 119–129.

Segal, B. M., & Stewart, J. C. (1996). Substance use and abuse in adolescence: An overview. *Child Psychiatry & Human Development, 26,* 193–210.

Segal, J., & Segal, Z. (1992, September). No more couch potatoes. *Parents,* 235.

Segal, N. L. (1993). Twin, sibling, and adoption methods: Tests of evolutionary hypotheses. *American Psychologist, 48,* 943–956.

Segall, M. H., Dasen, P. R., Berry, J. W., & Poortinga, Y. H. (1990). *Human behavior in global perspective.* Boston: Allyn & Bacon.

Seibel, M., & McCarthy, J. A. (1993). Infertility, pregnancy, and the emotions. In D. Goleman & J. Gurin (Eds.), *Mind-body medicine.* Yonkers, N. Y.: Consumer Reports Books.

Seidman, S. N., & Rieder, R. O. (1994). A review of sexual behavior in the United States. *American Journal of Psychiatry, 151,* 330–341.

Seifer, R., Schiller, M., & Sameroff, A. J. (1996). Attachment, maternal sensitivity, and infant temperament during the first year of life. *Developmental Psychology, 32,* 12–25.

Serbin, L. A., Moller, L., Powlishta, K., & Gulko, J. (1991, April). *The emergence of gender segregation and behavioral compatibility in toddlers' peer preferences.* Paper presented at the biennial meeting of the Society for Research in Child Development, Baltimore.

Sesser, S. (1993, September 13). Opium war redux. *New Yorker,* 78–89.

Shafer, R. G. (1990, March 12). An anguished father recounts the battle he lost—trying to rescue a teenage son from drugs. *People Weekly,* 81–83.

Shankaran, S., Cohen, S. N., Linver, M., & Zonia, S. (1988). Medical care costs of high-risk infants after neonatal intensive care: A controlled study. *Pediatrics, 81,* 372–378.

Sharf, R. S. (1992). *Applying career development theory to counseling.* Pacific Grove, CA: Brooks/Cole.

Sharpe, R. (1994, July 18). Better babies: School gets kids to do feats at a tender age, but it's controversial. *The Wall Street Journal,* pp. A1, A6.

Shavelson, R., Hubner, J. J., & Stanton, J. C. (1976). Self-concept: Validation of construct interpretations. *Review of Educational Research, 46,* 407–441.

Shaver, P. R., Hazan, C., & Bradshaw, D. (1988). Love as attachment: The integration of three behavioral systems. In R. J. Sternberg & M. L. Barnes (Eds.), *The psychology of love* (pp. 68–99). New Haven, CT: Yale University Press.

Shaw, D. S., & Vondra, J. I. (1995). Infant attachment security and maternal predictors of early behavior problems: A longitudinal study of low-income families. *Journal of Abnormal Child Psychology, 23,* 335–357.

Shea, J. D. (1985). Studies of cognitive development in Papua New Guinea. *International Journal of Psychology, 20,* 33–61.

Shealy, C. N. (1995). From *Boys Town* to *Oliver Twist*: Separating fact from fiction in welfare reform and out-of-home placement of children and youth. *American Psychologist, 50,* 565–580.

Shearer, E. L. (1993). Cesarean section: medical benefits and costs. *Social Science and Medicine, 37,* 122–123.

Sheingold, K., & Tenney, Y. J. (1982). Memory for a salient childhood event. In U. Neisser (Ed.), *Memory observed.* New York: Freeman.

Shepard, G. B. (1991). A glimpse of kindergarten—Chinese style. *Young Children, 47,* 11–15.

Sherry, B., Springer, D. A., Connell, F. A., & Garrett, S. M. (1992). Short, thin, or obese? Comparing growth indexes of children from high- and low-poverty areas. *Journal of the American Dietetic Association, 92,* 1092–1095.

Shields, J. (1973). Heredity and psychological abnormality. In H. Eysenck (Ed.), *Handbook of abnormal psychology* (pp. 540–603). San Diego: Edits Publishers.

Shiono, P. H., & Behrman, R. E. (1995). Low birth weight: Analysis and recommendations. *The Future of Children, 5,* 4–18.

Shirley, M. M. (1933). *The first two years: A study of twenty-five babies* (Vol. 2). Minneapolis: University of Minnesota.

Shore, C. M. (1994). *Individual differences in language development.* Newbury Park, CA: Sage.

Shostak, M. (1981). *Nissa: The life and words of a !Kung woman.* Cambridge, MA: Harvard University Press.

Shriver, M. D., & Piersel, W. (1994). The long-term effects of intrauterine drug exposure: Review of recent research and implications for early childhood special education. *Topics in Early Childhood Special Education, 14,* 161–183.

Shrum, W., Cheek, N., Jr., & Hunter, S. M. (1988). Friendship in school: Gender and racial homophily. *Sociology of Education, 61,* 227–239.

Shucard, J., Shucard, D., Cummins, K., & Campos, J. (1981). Auditory evoked potentials and sex-related differences in brain development. *Brain and Language, 13,* 91–102.

Shurkin, J. N. (1992). *Terman's kids: The groundbreaking study of how the gifted grow up.* Boston: Little, Brown.

Siegel, B. (1996). Is the emperor wearing clothes? Social policy and the empirical support for full inclusion of children with disabilities in the preschool and early elementary grades. *Social Policy Report, 10,* 2–17.

Siegel, L. A. (1983). The prediction of possible learning disabilities in preterm and full-term children. In T. Field & A. Sostek (Eds.), *Infants born at risk: Physiological, perceptual, and cognitive processes.* New York: Grune & Stratton.

Siegel, L. S. (1989). A reconceptualization of prediction from infant test scores. In M. H. Bornstein & N. A. Krasnegor (Eds.), *Stability and continuity in mental development: Behavioral and biological perspectives.* Hillsdale, NJ: Erlbaum.

Siegler, R. S. (1989). How domain-general and domain-specific knowledge interact to produce strategy choices. *Merrill-Palmer Quarterly, 35,* 1–26.

Siegler, R. S. (1995, April). Paper presented at the biennial meeting of the Society for Research in Child Development, Indianapolis, IN.

Siegler, R. S. (1991). *Children's thinking* (2nd ed.). Englewood Cliffs, NJ: Prentice Hall.

Siegler, R. S. (1994). Cognitive variability: A key to understanding cognitive development. *Current Directions in Psychological Science, 3,* 1–5.

Siegler, R. S. (1995). How does change occur: A microgentic study of number conservation. *Cognitive Psychology, 28,* 225–273.

Siegler, R. S., & Ellis, S. (1996). Piaget on childhood. *Psychological Science, 7,* 211–215.

Siegler, R. S., & Richards, D. (1982). The development of intelligence. In R. Sternberg (Ed.), *Handbook of human intelligence.* London: Cambridge University Press.

Sigman, M. (1995). Nutrition and child development: More food for thought. *Current Directions in Psychological Science, 4,* 52–55.

Sigman, M., Cohen, S. E., Beckwith, L., Asarnow, R., & Parmelee, A. H. (in press). Continuity in cognitive abilities from infancy to 12 years of age. *Cognitive Development.*

Sigman, M., Neumann, C., Jansen, A. A. J., & Bwibo, N. (1989). Cognitive abilities of Kenyan children in relation to nutrition, family characteristics, and education. *Child Development, 60,* 1463–1474.

Sigman, M. D., Cohen, S. E., Beckwith, L., Asarnow, R., & Parmelee, A. H. (1992). The prediction of cognitive abilities at 8 and 12 years of age from neonatal assessments of preterm infants. In S. L. Friedman & M. D. Sigman (Eds.), *The psychological development of low birthweight children.* Norwood, NJ: Ablex.

Signorella, M. L., Bigler, R. S., & Liben, L. (1993). Development differences in children's gender schemata about others: A meta-analytic review. *Developmental Review, 13,* 106–126.

Signorelli, N. (1987). Children and adolescents on television: A consistent pattern of devaluation. *Journal of Early Adolescence, 7,* 255–268.

Signorelli, N. (1990). Children, television, and gender roles: Messages and impact. *Journal of Adolescent Health Care, 11,* 50–58.

Silbereisen, R., Peterson, A., Albrecht, H., & Krache, B. (1989). Maturational timing and the development of problem behavior: Longitudinal studies in adolescence. *Journal of Early Adolescence, 9,* 247.

Silverstein, B., Perdue, L., Peterson, B. & Kelly, E. (1986). The role of the mass media in promoting a thin standard of bodily attractiveness for women. *Sex Roles, 14,* 519–532.

Simmons, R., & Blyth, D. (1987). *Moving into adolescence.* New York: Aldine de Gruyter.

Simmons, R., Brown, L., Bush, D., & Blyth, D. (1978). Self-esteem and achievement of black and white adolescents. *Social Problems, 26,* 86–96.

Simmons, R., & Rosenberg, F. (1975). Sex, sex roles, and self-image. *Journal of Youth and Adolescence, 4,* 229–258.

Simons, K. (Ed.). (1993). *Early visual development normal and abnormal.* New York: Oxford University Press.

Simpson, J. A. (1987). The dissolution of romantic relationships: Factors involved in relationship stability and emotional distress. *Journal of Personality and Social Psychology, 53,* 683–692.

Singer, J. L, & Singer, D. G. (1983). Psychologists look at television. *American Psychologist, 38,* 826–834.

Singer, M. S., Stacey, B. G., & Lange, C. (1993). The relative utility of expectancy-value theory and social cognitive theory in predicting psychology student course goals and career aspirations. *Journal of Social Behavior and Personality, 8,* 703–714.

Singh, G. K., & Yu, S. M. (1995). Infant mortality in the United States: Trends, differentials, and projections—1950 through 2010. *The American Journal of Public Health, 85,* 957–964.

Singleton, L. C., & Asher, S. R. (1979). Racial integration and children's peer preferences. *Child Development, 50,* 936–941.

Skinner, B. F. (1957). *Verbal behavior.* New York: Appleton-Century-Crofts.

Skinner, B. F. (1975). The steep and thorny road to a science of behavior. *American Psychologist, 30,* 42–49.

Skipper, J. K., & Nass, G. (1966). Dating behavior: A framework of analysis and an illustration. *Journal of Marriage and the Family, 28,* 412–420.

Slater, A. (1995). Individual differences in infancy and later IQ. *Journal of Child Psychology and Psychiatry and Allied Disciplines, 36,* 69–112.

Slater, A., Mattock, A., & Brown, E. (1990). Size constancy at birth: Newborn infants' responses to retinal and real size. *Journal of Experimental Child Psychology, 49,* 314–322.

Slobin, D. (1970). Universals of grammatical development in children. In G. Flores D'Arcais & W. Levelt (Eds.), *Advances in psycholinguistics.* New York: American Elsevier.

Smetana, J. (1988). Concepts of self and social convention: Adolescents' and parents' reasoning about hypothetical and actual family conflicts. In M. Gunnar (Ed.), *21st Minnesota Symposium on Child Psychology.* Hillsdale, NJ: Erlbaum.

Smetana, J. (1989). Adolescents' and parents' reasoning about actual family conflict. *Child Development, 60,* 1052–1067.

Smetana, J., Yau, J., & Hanson, S. (1991). Conflict resolution in families with adolescents. *Journal of Research on Adolescence, 1,* 189–206.

Smetana, J. G. (1995). Parenting styles and conceptions of parental authority during adolescence. *Child Development, 66, 299–316.*

Smith, D. (1993). Brain, environment, and personality. *Psychological Reports, 72,* 3–13.

Smith, M. (1990). Alternative techniques. *Nursing Times, 86,* 43–45.

Smith, P. K. (1978). A longitudinal study of social participation in preschool children: Solitary and parallel play reexamined. *Developmental Psychology, 12,* 517–523.

Smith, T. W. (1992). Hostility and health: Current status of a psychosomatic hypothesis. *Health Psychology, 11,* 139–150.

Smotherman, W. P., & Robinson, S. R. (1996). The development of behavior before birth. *Developmental Psychology, 32,* 425–434.

Smuts, A. B., & Hagen, J. W. (1985). History of the family and of child development: Introduction to Part 1. *Monographs of the Society for Research in Child Development, 50*(4–5, Serial No. 211).

Snarey, J. R. (1985). Cross-cultural universality of social-moral development. A critical review of Kohlbergian research. *Psychological Bulletin, 97,* 202–232.

Snow, C. E. (1977). Mother's speech research: From input to interaction. In C. E. Snow & C. A. Ferguson (Eds.), *Talking to children: Language input and acquisition.* London: Cambridge University Press.

Snow, R. (1969). Unfinished Pygmalion. *Contemporary Psychology, 14,* 197–199.

Snyder, M. (1974). The self-monitoring of expressive behavior. *Journal of Personality and Social Psychology, 30,* 526–537.

Snyder, M. (1987). *Public appearances/private realities: The psychology of self-monitoring.* New York: Freeman.

Snyder, R. A., Verderber, K. S., Langmeyer, L., & Myers, M. (1992). A reconsideration of self- and organization-referent attitudes as "causes" of the glass ceiling effect. *Group and Organization Management, 17,* 260–278.

Socolar, R. R. S., & Stein, R. E. K. (1995, January 1). Spanking infants and toddlers: Maternal belief and practice. *Pediatrics, 95,* 105–111.

Sohlberg, S., & Strober, M. (1994). Personality in anorexia nervosa: An update and a theoretical integration. *Acta Psychiatrica Scandinavica, 89 (Suppl. 378),* 1–16.

Sorensen, K. (1992). Physical and mental development of adolescent males with Klinefelter's syndrome. *Hormone Research, 37(Suppl. 3),* 55–61.

Sorensen, T., Nielsen, G., Andersen, P., & Teasdale, T. (1988). Genetic and environmental influences on premature death in adult adoptees. *New England Journal of Medicine, 318,* 727–732.

Souther, W. T., Jones, E. D., & Stanley, J. C. (1993). Acceleration and enrichment: The context and development of program options. In K. A. Heller, F. J. Monks, & A. H. Passow (Eds.), *International handbook of research and development of giftedness and talent.* Oxford, England: Pergamon.

Sparrow, A. (1985). Some practical ideas for meeting the needs of the gifted child in the classroom. *Gifted Education International, 3,* 65–67.

Spearman, C. (1927). *The abilities of man.* London: Macmillan.

Spelke, E. (1987). The development of intermodal perception. In P. Salapatek & L. Cohen (Eds.), *Handbook of infant perception* (Vol. 2). Orlando, FL: Academic Press.

Spelke, E. S. (1991). Physical knowledge in infancy: Reflections on Piaget's theory. In S. Carey & R. Gelman (Eds.), *The epigenesis of mind.* Hillsdale, NJ: Erlbaum.

Spencer, M. B. (1991). Identity, minority development. In R. M. Lerner, A. C. Petersen, & J. Brooks-Gunn (Eds.), *Encyclopedia of adolescence* (Vol. 1). New York: Garland.

Spencer, M. B. & Dornbusch, S. M. (1990). Challenges in studying minority youth. In S. Feldman & G. Elliott (Eds.), *At the threshold: The developing adolescent.* Cambridge, MA: Harvard University Press.

Spiegel, D. (1993). Social support: How friends, family, and groups can help. In D. Goleman & J. Gurin (Eds.), *Mind-body medicine.* Yonkers, NY: Consumer Reports Books.

Spira, A., Bajos, N., Bejin, A., & Beltzer, N. (1992). AIDS and sexual behavior in France. *Nature, 360,* 407–409.

Springer, I. (1991, April 28). Afraid to feel. *Boston Globe Health,* pp. 14, 30.

Springer, S. P., & Deutsch, G. (1989). *Left brain, right brain* (3rd ed.). New York: Freeman.

Squires, S. (1991, September 17). Lifelong fitness depends on teaching children to love exercise. *The Washington Post,* p. WH16.

Sreri, A. O., & Spelke, E. S. (1988). Haptic perception of objects in infancy. *Cognitive Psychology 20,* 1–23.

Sroufe, L. A. (1996). *Emotional development: The organization of emotional life in the early years.* New York: Cambridge University Press.

Stabler, B., Clopper, R. R., Siegel, P. T., Stoppani, C., Compton, P. G., & Underwood, L. E. (1994). Academic achievement and psychological adjustment in short children. *Developmental and Behavioral Pediatrics, 14,* 1–6.

Stack, D., & Muir, D. (1992). Adult tactile stimulation during face-to-face interactions modulates five-month-olds' affect and attention. *Child Development, 63,* 1509–1525.

Stacy, A. W., Sussman, S., Dent, C. W., Burton, D., & Flay, B. R. (1992). *Personality and Social Psychology Bulletin, 18,* 163–172.

Stallone, D. D., & Stunkard, A. J. (1991). The regulation of body weight: Evidence and clinical implications. *Annals of Behavioral Medicine, 13,* 220–230.

Stangor, C., Lynch, L., Changming, D., & Glass, B. (1992). Categorization of individuals on the basis of multiple social features. *Journal of Personality and Social Psychology, 62,* 207–218.

Stanjek, K. (1978). Das Uberreichen von Gaben: Funktion und Entwicklung in den ersten Lebensjahren. *Zeitschrift fur Entwicklungpsychologie und Pedagogische Psychologie, 10,* 103–113.

Stanley, J. C. (1980). On educating the gifted. *Educational Researcher, 9,* 8–12.

Stanley, J. C., & Benbow, C. P. (1983). SMPY's first decade: Ten years of posing problems and solving them. *Journal of Special Education, 17,* 11–25.

Starfield, B. (1991). Childhood morbidity: Comparisons, clusters, and trends. *Pediatrics, 88,* 519–526.

Starfield, B., Katz, H., Gabriel, A., Livingston, G., Benson, P., Hankin, J., Horn, S., Steinwachs, D. (1984). Morbidity in childhood—a longitudinal view. *New England Journal of Medicine, 310,* 824–829.

Staub, E. (1977). A child in distress: The influence of nurturance and modeling on children's attempts to help. *Developmental Psychology, 5,* 124–133.

Steele, C. M. (1992, April). Race and the schooling of black America. *Atlantic Monthly,* 37–53.

Steele, C. M., & Aronson, J. (1995). Stereotype threat and the intellectual test performance of African Americans. *Journal of Personality and Social Psychology, 69,* 797–811.

Steen, R. G. (1996). *DNA and destiny: Nature and nurture in human behavior.* New York: Plenum.

Steers, R. M., & Porter, L. W. (1991). *Motivation and work behavior* (5th ed.). New York: McGraw-Hill.

Stein, J. H., & Reiser, L. W. (1994). A study of white middle-class adolescent boys' responses to "semenarche" (the first ejaculation). *Journal of Youth and Adolescence, 23,* 373–384.

Stein, Z., Susser, M., Saenger, G., & Marolla, F. (1975). *Famine and human development: The Dutch hunger winter of 1944–1945.* New York: Oxford University Press.

Steinberg, J. (August 25, 1996). Why America's ever-fatter kids don't go to gym. *The New York Times,* 14.

Steinberg, L. (1986). Latchkey children and the susceptibility of adolescents to antisocial peer pressure. *Child Development, 58,* 269–275.

Steinberg, L. (1990). Autonomy, conflict, and harmony in the family relationship. In S. Feldman & G. Elliott (Eds.), *At the threshold: The developing adolescent.* Cambridge, MA: Harvard University Press.

Steinberg, L. (1993). *Adolescence.* New York: McGraw-Hill.

Steinberg, L., Dornbusch, S., & Brown, B. B. (1992). Ethnic differences in adolescent achievement: An ecological perspective. *American Psychologist, 47,* 723–729.

Steinberg, L., Lamborn, S. D., Darling, N., Mounts, N., & Dornbusch, S. M. (1994). Over-time changes in adjustment and competence among adolescents from authoritative, authoritarian, indulgent, and neglectful families. *Child Development, 65,* 754–770.

Steinberg L., & Silverberg, S. (1986). The vicissitudes of autonomy in early adolescence. *Child Development, 57,* 841–851.

Steiner, J. E. (1977). Facial expressions of the neonate infant indicating the hedonics of food-related chemical stimuli. In J. M. Weiffenbach (Ed.), *Taste and development.* Bethesda, MD: Department of Health, Education, and Welfare.

Steiner, J. E. (1979). Human facial expressions in response to taste and smell stimulation. *Advances in Child Development and Behavior, 13,* 257.

Steinmetz, S. K. (1987). Family violence. In S. K. Steinmetz & M. Sussman (Eds.), *Handbook of marriage and the family.* New York: Plenum.

Stephan, W. G. (1985). Intergroup relations. In G. Lindzey & E. Aronson (Eds.), *Handbook of social psychology.* Hillsdale, NJ: Erlbaum.

Stephan, W. G. (1986). The effects of school desegregation: An evaluation 30 years after *Brown.* In M. J. Saks & L. Saxs (Eds.), *Advances in applied social psychology.* Hillsdale, NJ: Erlbaum.

Stern, M. & Karraker, K. H. (1989). Sex stereotyping of infants: A review of gender labeling studies. *Sex Roles, 20,* 501–522.

Sternberg, R. J., & Wagner, R. K. (1993). The *g*-ocentric view of intelligence and job performance is wrong. *Current Directions in Psychological Science, 2,* 1–5.

Sternberg, R. J. (1982). Reasoning, problems solving, and intelligence. In R. J. Sternberg (Ed.), *Handbook of human intelligence* (pp. 225–307). Cambridge, England: Cambridge University Press.

Sternberg, R. J. (1985a). *Beyond IQ: A triarchic theory of human intelligence.* New York: Cambridge University Press.

Sternberg, R. J. (1985b). Implicit theories of intelligence, creativity, and wisdom. *Journal of Personality and Social Psychology, 49,* 607–627.

Sternberg, R. J. (1986). Triangular theory of love. *Psychological Review, 93,* 119–135.

Sternberg, R. J. (1987). Liking versus loving: A comparative evaluation of theories. *Psychological Bulletin, 102,* 331–345.

Sternberg, R. J. (1990). *Metaphors of mind: Conceptions of the nature of intelligence.* Cambridge, England: Cambridge University Press.

Sternberg, R. J. (1991). Theory-based testing of intellectual abilities: Rationale for the Sternberg triarchic abilities test. In H. A. H. Rowe (Ed.), *Intelligence: Reconceptualization and measurement.* Hillsdale, NJ: Erlbaum.

Sternberg, R. J. (1995). For whom *The Bell Curve* tolls: A review of *The Bell Curve. Psychological Science, 6,* 257–261.

Sternberg, R. J. (1996). Educating intelligence: Infusing the triarchic theory into school instruction. In R. J. Sternberg and E. Grigorenko, (Eds.), *Intelligence, heredity, and environment.* New York: Cambridge University Press.

Sternberg, R. J., & Grigorenko, E. (Eds.). (1996). *Intelligence, heredity, and environment.* New York: Cambridge University Press.

Sternberg, R. J., Conway, B. E., Ketron, J. L., & Bernstein, M. (1981). Peoples' conceptions of intelligence. *Journal of Personality and Social Psychology, 41,* 37–55.

Stevenson, H. W. (1992, December). Learning from Asian schools. *Scientific American,* 70–75.

Stevenson, H. W., Chen, C., & Lee, S. Y. (1992). A comparison of the parent-child relationship in Japan and the United States. In L. L. Roopnarine & D. B. Carter (Eds.), *Parent-child socialization in diverse cultures.* Norwood, NJ: Ablex.

Stevenson, H. W., & Lee, S. (1990). Contexts of achievement: A study of American, Chinese, and Japanese children. *Monographs of the Society for Research in Child Development, 55,* (1–2, Serial No. 221).

Stevenson, H. W., & Stigler, J. W. (1992). *The learning gap: Why our schools are failing and what we can learn from Japanese and Chinese education.* New York: Summit.

Stevens-Simon, C., & White, M. M. (1991). Adolescent pregnancy. *Pediatric Annals, 20,* 322–331.

Steward, E. P. (1995). *Beginning writers in the zone of proximal development.* Hillsdale, NJ: Erlbaum.

Stipek, D. J., & Hoffman, J. (1980). Development of children's performance-related judgments. *Child Development, 51,* 912–914.

Storfer, M. (1990). *Intelligence and giftedness: The contributions of heredity and early environment.* San Francisco: Jossey-Bass.

Strassberg, Z., Dodge, K. A., Pettit, G. S., & Bates, J. E. (1994). Spanking in the home and children's subsequent aggression toward kindergarten peers. *Development and Psychopathology, 6,* 445–461.

Straus, M. A., & Gelles, R. J. (Eds.). (1990). *Physical violence in American families.* New Brunswick, NJ: Transaction.

Straus, M. A., Gelles, R. J., & Steinmetz, S. K. (1980). *Behind closed doors: Violence in the American family.* Garden City, New York: Anchor Press.

Streissguth, A. P., Barr, H. M., & Sampson, P. D. (1990). Moderate prenatal alcohol exposure: Effects on child IQ and learning problems at age 7-½ years. *Alcohol Clinical and Experimental Research, 54,* 662–669.

Streri, A. (1994). *Seeing, reaching, touching: The relations between vision and touch in infancy.* Cambridge, MA: Bradford.

Sturner, W., Sweeney, K., Callery, R., & Haley, N. (1992). Cocaine babies: The scourge of the '90s. *Journal of Forensic Sciences, 36,* 34–39.

Sugarman, S. (1988). *Piaget's construction of the child's reality.* Cambridge, England: Cambridge University Press.

Sugden, J. (1995, January 23). Sanctuaries for broken children. *People Weekly,* 39.

Sullivan, M. W., Rovee-Collier, C. K., & Tynes, D. M. (1979). A conditioning analysis of infant long-term memory. *Child Development, 50,* 152–162.

Suls, J., & Wills, T. A. (Eds.). (1991). *Social comparison: Contemporary theory and research.* Hillsdale, NJ: Erlbaum.

Sulzer-Azaroff, B., & Mayer, R. (1991). *Behavior analysis and lasting change.* New York: Holt.

Sung, B. L. (1985). Bicultural conflicts in Chinese immigrant children. *Journal of Comparative Family Studies, 16,* 255–270.

Sung, I. K., Borh, B., & Oh, W. (1993). Growth and neurodevelopmental outcome of very low birthweight infants with intrauterine growth retardation: Comparison with control subjects matched by birthweight and gestational age. *Journal of Pediatrics, 123,* 618–624.

Super, C. M. (1976). Environmental effects on motor development: A case of African infant precocity. *Developmental Medicine and Child Neurology, 18,* 561–576.

Super, C. M., & Harkness, S. (1982). The infant's niche in rural Kenya and metropolitan America. In L. Adler (Ed.), *Issues in cross-cultural research.* New York: Academic Press.

Suro, R. (1992, May 26). For women, varied reasons for single motherhood. *The New York Times,* p. A12.

Suskind, R. (1994, September 24). Class struggle: Poor, black, and smart. *The New York Times,* p. A1.

Swanson, L. A., Leonard, L. B., & Gandour, J. (1992). Vowel duration in mothers' speech to young children. *Journal of Speech and Hearing Research, 35,* 617–625.

Tajfel, H. (1982). *Social identity and intergroup relations.* London: Cambridge University Press.

Takahashi, K. (1986). Examining the Strange Situation procedure with Japanese mothers and 12-month-old infants. *Developmental Psychology, 22,* 265–270.

Takahashi, K. (1990). Are the key assumptions of the "Strange Situation" procedure universal? A view from Japanese research. *Human Development, 33,* 23–30.

Tamis-LeMonda, C. S., & Bornstein, M. H. (1993). Antecedents of exploratory competence at 1 year. *Infant Behavior and Development, 16,* 423–439.

Tannen, D. (1991). *You just don't understand.* New York: Ballantine.

Tanner, J. (1972). Sequence, tempo, and individual variation in growth and development of boys and girls aged twelve to sixteen. In J. Kagan and R. Coles (Eds.), *Twelve to sixteen: Early adolescence.* New York: Norton.

Tanner, J. M. (1978). *Education and physical growth* (2nd ed.). New York: International Universities Press.

Tate, D. C., Reppucci, N. D., & Mulvey, E. P. (1995). Violent juvenile delinquents: Treatment effectiveness and implications for future action. *American Psychologist, 50,* 777–781.

Taylor, M. S., Locke, E. A., Lee, C., & Gist, M. E. (1984). Type A behavior and faculty research productivity: What are the mechanisms? *Organizational Behavior and Human Performance, 34,* 402–418.

Taylor, R. J., Chatters, L. M., Tucker, M. B., & Lewis, E. (1991). Developments in research on black families. In A. Booth (Ed.), *Contemporary families.* Minneapolis, MN: National Council on Family Relations.

Taylor, S. E. (1991). *Health psychology* (2nd ed.). New York: McGraw-Hill.

Tegano, D. W., Lookabaugh, S., May, G. E., & Burdette, M. P. (1991). Constructive play and problem solving: The role of structure and time in the classroom. *Early Child Development and Care, 68,* 27–35.

Tellegen, A., Lykken, D. T., Bouchard, T. J., Jr., Wilcox, K. J., Segal, N. L., & Rich, S. (1988). Personality similarity in twins reared apart and together. *Journal of Personality and Social Psychology, 54,* 1031–1039.

Terman, D. L., Larner, M. B., Stevenson, C. S., & Behrman, R. E. (1996). Special education for students with disabilities: Analysis and recommendations. *The Future of Children, 6,* 4–24.

Terman, L. M., & Oden, M. H. (1959). *The gifted group at mid-life: Thirty-five years' follow-up of the superior child.* Stanford, CA: Stanford University Press.

Termine, N. T., & Izard, C. E. (1988). Infants' responses to their mothers' expressions of joy and sadness. *Developmental Psychology, 24,* 223–229.

Terry, D. (1994, December 12). When the family heirloom is homicide. *The New York Times,* pp. A1, B7.

Tesman, J. R., & Hills, A. (1994). Developmental effects of lead exposure in children. *Social Policy Report, 8,* 1–17.

Tharp, R. G. (1989). Psychocultural variables and constants: Effects on teaching and learning in schools. Special Issue: Children and their development: Knowledge base, research agenda, and social policy application. *American Psychologist, 44,* 349–359.

Thelen, E. (1979). Rhythmical stereotypes in normal human infants. *Animal Behavior, 27,* 699–715.

Thelen, E. (1994). Three-month-old infants can learn task-specific patterns of interlimb coordination. *Psychological Science, 5,* 280–285.

Thelen, E. (1995). Motor development: A new synthesis. *American Psychologist, 50,* 79–95.

Thoman, E. B. (1990). Sleeping and waking states in infants: A functional perspective. *Neuroscience and Biobehavioral Review, 14,* 93–107.

Thoman, E. B., & Whitney, M. P. (1989). Sleep states of infants monitored in the home: Individual differences, developmental trends, and origins of diurnal cyclicity. *Infant Behavior and Development, 12,* 59–75.

Thoman, E. B., & Whitney, M. P. (1990). Behavioral states in infants: Individual differences and individual analyses. In J. Colombo & J. Fagen (Eds.), *Individual differences in infancy: Reliability, stability, prediction* (pp. 113–136). Hillsdale, NJ: Erlbaum.

Thomas, A., & Chess, S. (1977). *Temperament and development.* New York: Brunner-Mazel.

Thomas, A., & Chess, S. (1980). *The dynamics of psychological development.* New York: Brunner-Mazel.

Thomas, A., & Chess, S. (1984). Genesis and evolution of behavioral disorders: From infancy to early adult life. *American Journal of Orthopsychiatry, 141*(1), 1–9.

Thomas, A., Chess, S., & Birch, H. G. (1968). *Temperament and behavior disorders in children.* New York: New York University Press.

Thomas, J. (1995). The effects on the family of miscarriage, termination for abnormality, stillbirth and neonatal death. *Child: Care, Health & Development, 21* 413–424.

Thomas, P. (1994, September 6). Washington's infant mortality rate, more than twice the U.S. average, reflects urban woes. *The Wall Street Journal,* p. A14.

Thomas, R. M. (1996). *Comparing theories of child development.* 4th Ed. Pacific Grove, CA: Brooks/Cole Publishing Company.

Thompson, J. K. (Ed.). (1996). *Body image, eating disorders, and obesity: An integrative guide for assessment and treatment.* Washington, DC: American Psychological Association.

Thompson, L. A., Fagen, J. F., & Fulker, D. W. (1991). Longitudinal prediction of specific cognitive abilities from infant novelty preference. *Child Development, 62,* 530–538.

Thompson, R. A., & Limber, S. P. (1990). Social anxiety in infancy: Stranger and separation reactions. In H. Leitenberg (Ed.), *Handbook of social and evaluation anxiety.* New York: Plenum.

Thornburg, K. R., Pearl, P., Crompton, D., & Ispa, J. M. (1990). Development of kindergarten children based on child-care arrangements. *Early Childhood Research Quarterly, 5,* 27–42.

Thorne, B. (1986). Girls and boys together, but mostly apart. In W. W. Hartup & Z. Rubin (Eds.), *Relationships and development* (pp. 167–184). Hillsdale, NJ: Erlbaum.

Thorpe, J. A., Hu, D. H., Albin, R. M., McNitt, J., Meyer, B. A., Cohen, J. R., & Yeast, J. D. (1993). The effect of intrapartum epidural analgesia on nulliparous labor: A randomized, controlled prospective trial. *American Journal of Obstetrics and Gynecology, 169,* 851–858.

Thyssen, S. (1995). Care for children in day-care centers. *Child & Youth Care Forum, 24,* 91–106.

Tobin, J. J., Wu, D. Y. H., & Davidson, D. H. (1989). *Preschool in three cultures: Japan, China, and the United States.* New Haven, CT: Yale University Press.

Tobin-Richards, M. H., Boxer, A. M., & Petersen, A. C. (1983). The psychological significance of pubertal change: Sex differences in perceptions of self during early adolescence. In J. Brooks-Gunn & A. C. Petersen (Eds.), *Girls at puberty.* New York: Plenum.

Toch, T. (1995, January 2). Kids and marijuana: The glamour is back. *U.S. News and World Report, 12.*

Toda, S., & Fogel, A. (1993). Infant response to the still-face situation at 3 and 6 months. *Developmental Psychology, 29,* 532–538.

Tomlinson-Keasey, C. (1985). *Child development: Psychological, sociological, and biological factors.* Homewood, IL: Dorsey.

Tomson, G. O. B., Raab, G. M., Hepburn, W. S., Hunter, R., Fulton, M., & Laxen, D. P. H. (1989). Blood-lead levels and children's behavior: Results from the Edinburgh lead study. *Journal of Child Psychology and Psychiatry, 30,* 515–528.

Topolnicki, D. M. (1995, January). The real immigrant story: Making it big in America. *Money,* 129–138.

Touwen, B. C. L. (1984). Primitive reflexes—conceptual or semantic problem? In H. F. R. Prechtl (Ed.), *Continuity of neural functions from prenatal to postnatal life* (Clinics in developmental medicine, No. 94, pp. 115–125). Philadelphia: Lippincott.

Treasure, J., & Tiller, J. (1993). The aetiology of eating disorders: Its biological basis. *International Review of Psychiatry, 5,* 23–31.

Treffers, P. E., Eskes, M., Kleiverda, G., & van Alten, D. (1990). Home births and minimal medical interventions. *Journal of the American Medical Association, 2624,* 2203, 2207–2208.

Trehub, S. E., Schneider, B. A., Morrongiello, B. A., & Thorpe, L. A. (1988). Auditory sensitivity in school-age children. *Journal of Experimental Child Psychology, 46,* 272–285.

Trehub, S. E., Schneider, B. A., Morrongiello, B. A., & Thorpe, L. A. (1989). Developmental changes in high-frequency sensitivity. *Audiology, 28,* 241–249.

Trehub, S. E., Thorpe, L. A., & Morrongiello, B. A. (1985). Infants' perception of melodies: Changes in a single tone. *Infant Behavior & Development, 8,* 213–223.

Triandis, H., Gontempo, R., Betancourt, H., Bond, M., Leung, K., Brenes, A., Georgas, J., Hui, C. H., Marin, G., Setiadi, B., Sinha, J. B. P., Verma, J., Spangenberg, J., Touzard, H., & de Montmollin, G. (1986). The measurement of ethnic aspects of individualism and collectivism across cultures. *Australian Journal of Psychology, 38,* 257–267.

Triandis, H. C. (1994). *Culture and social behavior.* New York: McGraw-Hill.

Triandis, H. C. (1995). *Individualism and collectivism.* Boulder, CO: Westview Press.

Trickett, P. K., & McBride-Chang, C. (1995). The developmental impact of different forms of child abuse and neglect. *Developmental Review, 15,* 311–337.

Troiano, R. P., Flegal, K. M., Kuczmarski, R. J., Campbell, S. M., & Johnson, C. L. (1995). Overweight prevalence and trends for children and adolescents. The National Health and Nurtrition Examination Surveys, 1963–1992. *Archives of Pediatric and Adolescent Medicine, 10,* 1085–1091.

Tronick, E. Z. (1995). Touch in mother-infant interactions. In T. M. Field (Ed.), *Touch in early development.* Hillsdale, NJ: Erlbaum.

Tronick, E. Z., & Gianino, A. F. (1986). The transmission of maternal depression to the infant. In E. Z. Tronick & T. Field (Eds.), *Maternal depression and infant disturbance.* San Francisco: Jossey-Bass.

Tronick, E. Z., Thomas, R. B., & Daltabuit, M. (1994). The Quechua manta pouch: A caretaking practice for buffering the Peruvian infant against the multiple stressors of high altitude. *Child Development, 65,* 1005–1013.

Tsunoda, T. (1985). *The Japanese brain: Uniqueness and universality.* Tokyo: Taishukan.

Tulving, E., & Thompson, D. M. (1973). Encoding specificity and retrieval processes in episodic memory. *Psychological Review, 80,* 352–373.

Turner, J. S., & Helms, D. B. (1995). *Lifespan Development* (5th ed.). Fort Worth: Harcourt Brace College Publishers.

Turner, P. H., Scadden, L., & Harris, M. B. (1990). Parenting in gay and lesbian families. *Journal of Gay and Lesbian Psychotherapy, 1,* 55–66.

Turner, P. J., Gervai, J., & Hinde, R. A. (1993). Gender-typing in young children: Preferences, behavior, and cultural differences. *British Journal of Developmental Psychology, 11,* 323–342.

Turner, P. J., & Gervai, J. (1995). A multidimensional study of gender typing in preschool children and their parents: Personality, attitudes, preferences, behavior, and cultural differences. *Developmental Psychology, 31,* 759–772.

U.S. Advisory Board on Child Abuse and Neglect. (1995). *A nation's shame: Fatal child abuse and neglect in the United States.* Washington, DC: Superintendent of Documents.

U.S. Bureau of the Census. (1990a). *Current population reports* (pp. 25–917, 25–1095).

U.S. Bureau of the Census. (1990b). *Statistical abstract of the United States: 1990* (110th ed.). Washington, DC: U.S. Government Printing Office.

U.S. Bureau of the Census. (1990c). *Studies in marriage and the family: Single parents and their children.* (Current Population Reports, Series P-23, No. 167). Washington, DC: U.S. Government Printing Office.

U.S. Bureau of the Census. (1991a). *Statistical abstract of the United States: 1991.* (111th ed.). Washington, DC: U.S. Government Printing Office.

U.S. Bureau of the Census. (1991b). *Population Profile of the United States: 1991.* (Current Population Reports, Series P-23, No. 173). Washington, DC: U.S. Government Printing Office.

U.S. Bureau of the Census. (1991c). *Studies in household formation: Remarriage among women in the United States* (Current Population Reports, Series P-23, No. 169). Washington, DC: U.S. Government Printing Office.

U.S. Bureau of the Census. (1992). *Poverty in the United States: 1991.* (Current Population Reports. Series P-60, No. 181). Washington, DC: U.S. Government Printing Office.

U.S. Bureau of the Census. (1993). *Child Health USA.* Washington, DC: U.S. Government Printing Office.

U.S. Bureau of the Census. (1993). *Statistical abstract of the United States* (110th ed.). Washington, DC: U.S. Government Printing Office.

U.S. Bureau of the Census. (1994). *Household statistics, 1993.* (Current Population Reports). Washington, DC: U.S. Government Printing Office.

U.S. Bureau of Labor Statistics. (1993). *Average wages earned by women compared to men.* Washington, DC: U.S. Department of Labor.

U.S. Bureau of Labor Statistics. (1995). *Workforce demographics and makeup.* Washington, DC: U.S. Department of Labor.

U.S. Commission on Civil Rights. (1983). *Statistics of minority groups.* Washington, DC: Author.

U.S. Department of Agriculture. (1992). *Dietary guidelines.* Washington, DC: Author.

U.S. Department of Education. (1988). *James Madison Elementary School: A curriculum for American students.* Washington, DC: Author.

U.S. Department of Education. (1992). *Enrollment projections to the year 2000.* Washington, DC: National Center for Education Statistics.

U.S. Department of Education. (1992, April). *Experiences in child care and early childhood programs of first and second graders.* Washington, DC: National Center for Education Statistics.

U.S. Department of Education, Office of Special Education and Rehabilitative Services. (1987). *Eighth Annual Report to Congress on the Implementation of the Education of the Handicapped Act, 1986.* Washington, DC: U.S. Government Printing Office.

U.S. Department of Health and Human Services. (1990). *Health United States 1989* (DHHS Publication No. PHS 90-1232). Washington, DC: U.S. Government Printing Office.

U.S. Department of Labor. (1992). *Occupational Outlook Handbook.* Washington, DC: U.S. Government Printing Office.

U.S. Surgeon General. (1988). *Report on nutrition and health.* Washington, DC: U.S. Government Printing Office.

USA Weekend, Nov. 25–27, 1995, p. 15.

Ubell, E. (1995, February 12). Sex-education programs that work—and some that don't. *Parade Magazine,* 18–20.

UNESCO. (1990). *Compendium of statistics on illiteracy,* No. 31. Paris: United Nations Educational, Scientific, and Cultural Organization.

Unger, R., & Crawford, M. (1992). *Women and gender.* New York: McGraw-Hill.

Unger, R., & Crawford, M. (1996). *Women and gender: A feminist psychology* (2nd ed.). New York: McGraw-Hill.

Unger, R., Kreeger, L., & Christoffel, K. K. (1990). Childhood obesity. Medical and familial correlates and age of onset. *Clinical Pediatrics, 29,* 368–373.

Ungrady, D. (1992, October 19). Getting physical: Fitness experts are helping shape up young America. *The Washington Post,* p. B5.

United Nations. (1990). *Declaration of the world summit for children.* New York.

United Nations. (1994). *World Social Situation in the 1990s.* New York: United Nations Publications.

University of Michigan. (1994). *Monitoring the future study.* Ann Arbor, MI: University of Michigan.

Urberg, K. A. (1982). The development of the concepts of masculinity and femininity in young children. *Sex Roles, 8,* 659–668.

Vaillant, G. E. & Vaillant, C. O. (1981). Natural history of male psychological health, X: Work as a predictor of positive mental health. *American Journal of Psychiatry, 138,* 1433–1440.

Vaillant, G. E. & Vaillant, C. O. (1990). Natural history of male psychological health, XII: A 45-year study of predictors of successful aging. *American Journal of Psychiatry, 147(1),* 31–37.

van Biema, D. (1995, December 11). Abandoned to her fate. *Time,* 32–36.

Vance, B., Hankins, N., & Brown, W. (1988). Ethnic and sex differences on the Test of Nonverbal Intelligence, Quick Test of intelligence, and Wechsler Intelligence scale for Children–Revised. *Journal of Clinical Psychology, 44,* 261–265.

VandeBerg, L. R., & Streckfuss, D. (1992). Prime-time television's portrayal of women and the world of work: A demographic profile. *Journal of Broadcasting & Electronic Media, 36,* 195–208.

Vandell, D. L., & Hembree, S. E. (1994). Peer social status and friendship: Independent contributors to children's social and academic adjustment. *Merrill-Palmer Quarterly, 40,* 461–477.

VanEvra, J. (1990). *Television and child development.* Hillsdale, NJ: Erlbaum.

van IJzendoorn, M. H. (1995). Adult attachment representations, parental responsiveness, and infant attachment: A meta-analysis on the predictive validity of the adult attachment interview. *Psychological Bulletin 117,* 387–403.

van IJzendoorn, M. H., & Kroonenberg P. M. (1988). Cross-cultural patterns of attachment: a meta-analysis of the Strange Situation. *Child Development, 59,* 147–156.

van IJzendoorn, M. H., & Tavecchio, L. W. C. (1987). The development of attachment theory as a Lakatosian research program: Philosophical and methodological aspects. In L. W. C. Tavecchio and M. H. van IJzendoorn (Eds.), *Attachment in social networks: Contributions to the Bowlby-Ainsworth attachment theory,* 3–31. Amsterdam: North-Holland.

Van Manen, S. & Pietromonaco, P. (1993). *Acquaintance and consistency influence memory from interpersonal information.* Unpublished manuscript. University of Massachusetts at Amherst.

Van Riper, C. (1972). *Speech correction: Principles and methods.* Englewood Cliffs, NJ: Prentice Hall.

VanTassel-Baska, J. (1986). Effective curriculum and instructional models for talented students. *Gifted Child Quarterly, 30,* 164–169.

VanTassel-Baska, J., Olszewski-Kubilius, P., & Kulieke, M. (1994). A study of self-concept and social support in advantaged and disadvantaged seventh- and eighth-grade gifted students. *Roeper Review, 16,* 186–191.

Vaughn, B. E., Lefever, G. B., Seifer, R., & Barglow, P. (1989). Attachment behavior, attachment security, and temperament during infancy. *Child Development, 60,* 728–737.

Vaughn, B. E., Stevenson-Hinde, J., Waters, E., Kotsaftis, A., Lefever, G. B., Shouldice, A., Trudel, M., & Belsky, J. (1992). Attachment security and temperament in infancy and early childhood: Some conceptual clarifications. *Developmental Psychology, 28,* 463–473.

Vaughn, V., McKay, R. J., & Behrman, R. (1979). *Nelson textbook of pediatrics* (11th ed.). Philadelphia: Saunders.

Verbrugge, L. M. (1985). Gender and health: An update on hypotheses and evidence. *Journal of Health and Social Behavior, 26,* 156–182.

Vercellini, P., Zuliani, G., Rognoni, M., Trespidi, L., Oldani, S., & Cardinale, A. (1993). Pregnancy at 40 and over: A case-control study. *European Journal of Obstetrics, Gynecology, & Reproductive Biology, 48,* 191–195.

Vernberg, E. M. (1990). Psychological adjustment and experiences with peers during early adolescence: Reciprocal, incidental, or unidirectional relationships? *Journal of Abnormal Child Psychology, 18,* 187–198.

Vihman, M. M. (1991). Early syllables and the construction of phonology. In C. A. Ferguson, L. Menn, & C. Stoel-Gammon (Eds.), *Phonological development: Models, research, implications* (pp. 69–84). Hillsdale, NJ: Erlbaum.

Vincze, M. (1971). Examinations on the social contacts between infants and young children reared together. *Magyar Pszichologiai Szemle, 28,* 58–61.

Vitaro, F., & Pelletier, D. (1991). Assessment of children's social problem-solving skills in hypothetical and actual conflict situations. *Journal of Abnormal Child Psychology, 19,* 505–518.

Volling, B. L., & Belsky, J. (1992). The contribution of mother-child and father-child relationships to the quality of sibling interaction: A longitudinal study. *Child Development, 63,* 1209–1222.

Volling, B. L., & Feagans, L. V. (1995). Infant day care and children's soccial competence. Infant Behavior and Development *18,* 177–188.

Volling, B. L., Mackinnon-Lewis, C., Rabiner, D., & Baradaran, L. P. (1993). Children's social competence and sociometric status: Further exploration of aggression, social withdrawal, and peer rejection. *Development and Psychopathology, 5,* 459–483.

Vondra, J. I., Barnett, D., & Cicchetti, D. (1990). Self-concept, motivation, and competence among preschoolers from maltreating and comparison. *Child Abuse and Neglect, 14,* 525–540.

Vurpillot, E. (1968). The development of scanning strategies, and their relation to visual differentiation. *Journal of Experimental Child Psychology, 6,* 632–650.

Vygotsky, L. S. (1962). *Selected psychological investigations.* Moscow: Izdstel'sto Akademii Pedagogicheskish Nauk SSR.

Vygotsky, L. (1976). *Mind in society.* Cambridge, MA: Harvard University Press.

Vygotsky, L. S. (1930/1978). *Mind in society: The development of higher mental processes.* Cambridge, MA: Harvard University Press.

Vygotsky, L. S. (1979). *Mind in society: The development of higher mental processes.* Cambridge, MA: Harvard University Press. (Original works published 1930, 1933, and 1935)

Vygotsky, L. S. (1986). *Thought and language* (A. Kozulin, Trans.). Cambridge, MA: MIT Press. (Original work published 1934)

Wachs, T. D. (1992). *The nature of nurture.* Newbury Park, CA: Sage.

Wachs, T. D. (1993). The nature-nurture gap: What we have here is a failure to collaborate. In R. Plomin & G. E. McClearn (Eds.), *Nature, nurture, and psychology.* Washington, DC: American Psychological Association.

Wachs, T. D. (1996). Known and potential precesses underlying developmental trajectories in childhood and adolescence. *Developmental Psychology, 32,* 796–801.

Wadsworth, B. J. (1971). *Piaget's theory of cognitive development.* New York: Longman.

Wagner, R. K., & Sternberg, R. J. (1985). Alternate conceptions of intelligence and their implications for education. *Review of Educational Research, 54,* 179–223.

Wagner, R. K., & Sternberg, R. J. (1986). Tacit knowledge and intelligence in the everyday world. In R. J. Sternberg & R. K. Wagner (Eds.), *Practical intelligence: Nature and origins of competence in the everyday world.* Cambridge, England: Cambridge University Press.

Wagner, R. K., & Sternberg, R. J. (1991). *Tacit knowledge inventory.* San Antonio, TX: Psychological Corporation.

Wagner, W. G., Smith, D., & Norris, W. R. (1988). The psychological adjustment of enuretic children: A comparison of two types. *Journal of Pediatric Psychology, 13,* 33–38.

Walden, T. A., & Baxter, A. (1989). The effect of context and age on social referencing. *Child Development, 60,* 1230–1240.

Walden, T. A., & Ogan, T. A. (1988). The development of social referencing. *Child Development, 59,* 1230–1240.

Walker, D. K., Palfrey, J. S., Handley-Derry, M. H., & Singer, Judith, D. (1989). Mainstreaming children with handicaps: Implications for pediatricians. *Journal of Developmental and Behavioral Pediatrics, 10,* 151–156.

Walker-Andrews, A. S., & Grolnick, W. (1983). Infants' discrimination of vocal expressions. *Infant Behavior and Development, 6,* 491–498.

Walker-Andrews, A. S., & Lennon, E. (1991). Infants' discrimination of vocal expressions: Contributions of auditory and visual information. *Infant Behavior and Development, 14,* 131–142.Wallace, I. F., Rose, S. A., McCarton, C. M., Kurtzberg, D., & Vaughan, H. G., Jr. (1995). Relations between infant neurobehavioral performance and cognitive outcome in very low birthweight preterm infants. *Developmental and Behavioral Pediatarics, 16,* 309–317.

Waller, N. G., Kojetin, B. A., Bouchard, T. J., Jr., Lykken, D. T., & Tellegen, A. (1990). Genetic and environmental influences on religious interests, attitudes, and values: A study of twins reared apart and together. *Psychological Science, 1,* 138–142.

Wallerstein, J. S., & Blakeslee, S. (1989). *Second chances.* New York: Ticknor & Fields.

Wallerstein, J. S., & Blakeslee, S. (1990). *Second chances: Men, women, and children a decade after divorce.* Boston: Houghton Mifflin.

Wallis, C. (1994, July 18). Life in overdrive. *Time,* 42–50.

Walster, H. E., & Walster, G. W. (1978). *Love.* Reading, MA: Addison-Wesley.

Walters, E., & Gardner, H. (1986). The theory of multiple intelligences: Some issues and answers. In R. J. Sternberg & R. K. Wagner (Eds.), *Practical intelligence.* Cambridge, England: Cambridge University Press.

Wang, M. C., Peverly, S. T., & Catalano, R. (1987). Integrating special needs students in regular classes: Programming, implementation, and policy issues. *Advances in Special Education, 6,* 119–149.

Wang, M. C., Reynolds, M. C., & Walberg, H. J. (Eds.). (1996). *Handbook of special and remedial education: Research and practice* (2nd ed). New York: Pergamon Press.

Wang, Z. W., Black, D., Andreasen, N. C., & Crowe, R. R. (1993). A linkage study of Chromosome 11q in schizophrenia. *Archives of General Psychiatry, 50,* 212–216.

Warrick, P. (1991, October 30). What the doctors have to say. *The Los Angeles Times,* p. E4.

Watanabe, T. (1992, September 14). A lesson for Japan's kids: Play! *The Los Angeles Times,* p. v111.

Waterman, A. (1982). Identity development from adolescence to adulthood: An extension of theory and a review of research. *Developmental Psychology, 18,* 341–358.

Waterman, A., & Waterman, M. (1981). A longitudinal study of changes in ego identity status during the freshman year at college. *Developmental Psychology, 5,* 167–173.

Watson, J. B., & Rayner, R. (1920). Conditioned emotional reactions. *Journal of Experimental Psychology, 3,* 1–14.

Weber, K. S., Frankenberger, W., & Heilman, K. (1992). The effects of Ritalin on the academic achievement of children diagnosed with attention-deficit hyperactivity disorder. *Developmental Disabilities Bulletin, 20,* 49–68.

Webster, R. A., Hunter, M., & Keats, J. A. (1994). Peer and parental influences on adolescents' substance use: A path analysis. *International Journal of the Addictions, 29,* 647–657.

Wechsler, D. (1975). Intelligence defined and undefined. *American Psychologist, 30,* 135–139.

Wechsler, H., Davenport, A., Dowdall, G., Moeykens, B., & Castillo, S. (1994, December 7). Health and behavioral consequences of binge drinking in college. A national survey of students at 140 campuses. *JAMA. Journal of the American Medical Association, 272,* 1672–1677.

Wechsler, H., Isaac, N. E., Grodstein, F., & Sellers, D. E. (1994). Continuation and initiation of alcohol use from the first to the second year of college. *Journal of the Study of Alcohol, 55,* 41–45.

Weed, K., Ryan, E. B., & Day, J. (1990). Metamemory and attributions as mediators of strategy use and recall. *Journal of Educational Psychology, 82,* 849–855.

Wegman, M. E. (1993). Annual summary of vital statistics—1992. *Pediatrics, 92,* 743–754.

Weinberg, R. A. (1989). Intelligence and IQ: Landmark issues and great debates. *American Psychologist, 44(2),* 98–104.

Weiner, B. (1994). Integrating social and personal theories of achievement striving. *Review of Educational Research, 64,* 557–573.

Welker, W. J. (1991). Is sparing the rod a wise, or ill-advised, strategy? *Pediatric News, 25,* 5.

Wellman, H. M. (1990). *The child's theory of mind.* Cambridge, MA: MIT Press.

Wellman, H. M., & Gelman, S. A. (1992). Cognitive development: Foundational theories of core domains. *Annual Review of Psychology, 43,* 337–375.

Wells, A. S., & Crain, R. L. (1994). Perpetuation theory and the long-term effects of school desegregation. *Review of Educational Research, 64,* 531–555.

Wenar, C. (1994). *Developmental psychopathology: From infancy through adolescence* (3rd ed.). New York: McGraw-Hill.

Wender, E. H. (1995). Attention-deficit hyperactivity disorders in adolescence. *Journal of Developmental and Behavioral Pediatrics, 16,* 192–195.

Wentzel, K. R., & Asher, S. R. (1995). The academic lives of neglected, rejected, popular, and controversial children. *Child Development, 66,* 754–763.

Werner, E. E. (1972). Infants around the world: Cross-cultural studies of psychomotor development from birth to 2 years. *Journal of Cross-Cultural Psychology, 3,* 111–134.

Werner, E. E. (1993). Risk resilience, and recovery: Perspectives from the Kauai Longitudinal Study. *Development and Psychopathology, 5,* 503–515.

Werner, E. E. (1995). Resilience in development. *Current Directions in Psychological Science, 4,* 81–85.

Werner, E. E., & Smith, R. S. (1992). *Overcoming the odds: High risk children from birth to adulthood.* Ithaca, NY: Cornell University Press.

Werner, L. A., & Marean, G. C. (1996). *Human auditory development.* Boulder, CO: Westview Press.

Wertsch, J. V., & Tulviste, P. (1992). L. S. Vygotsky and contemporary developmental psychology. *Developmental Psychology, 28,* 548–557.

Westen, D. (1990). Psychoanalytic approaches to personality. In L. A. Previn (Ed.), *Handbook of personality: Theory and research.* New York: Guilford Press.

Wheeden, A., Scafidi, F. A., Field, T., Ironson, G., (1993). Massage effects on cocaine-exposed preterm neonates. *Journal of Developmental and Behavioral Pediatrics, 14,* 318–322.

Whitbourne, S. K., Zuschlag, M. K., Elliot, L. B., & Waterman, A. S. (1992). Psychosocial development in adulthood: A 22-year sequential study. *Journal of Personality and Social Psychology, 63,* 260–271.

Whiting, B. B., & Edwards, C. P. (1988). *Children of different worlds: The formation of social behavior.* Cambridge, MA: Harvard University Press.

Wideman, M. V., & Singer, J. F. (1984). The role of psychological mechanisms in preparation for childbirth. *American Psychologist, 34,* 1357–1371.

Widom, C. S. (1989). Does violence beget violence? A critical examination of the literature. *Psychological Bulletin, 106,* 3–28.

Wiederhold, W. C. (Ed.). (1982). *Neurology for non-neurologists.* New York: Academic Press.

Wierson, M., & Forehand, R. (1994). Parent behavioral training for child noncompliance: Rationale, concepts, and effectiveness. *Current Directions in Psychological Science, 3,* 146–150.

Wierson, M., Long, P. J., & Forehand, R. L. (1993). Toward a new understanding of early menarche: The role of environmental stress in pubertal timing. *Adolescence, 28,* 913–924.

Wilcox, A., Skjaerven, R., Buekens, P., & Kiely, J. (1995, March 1). Birth weight and perinatal mortality: A comparison of the United States and Norway. *The Journal of the American Medical Association, 273,* 709–711.

Williams, B. C. (1990). Immunization coverage among preschool children: The United States and selected European countries. *Pediatrics, 86,* 1052–1056.

Williams, B. C., & Miller, C. A. (1992). Preventive health care for young children: Findings from a 10-country study and directions for United States policy. *Pediatrics, 89,* Supplement.

Willows, D. M., Kruk, R. S., & Corcos, E. (Eds.). (1993). *Visual processes in reading and reading disabilities.* Hillsdale, NJ: Erlbaum.

Wilson, M. N. (1989). Child development in the context of the black extended family. *American Psychologist, 44,* 380–385.

Wilson, R. S. (1983). The Louisville twin study: Developmental synchronies in behavior. *Child Development, 54,* 298–316.

Windle, M. (1994). A study of friendship characteristics and problem behaviors among middle adolescents. *Child Development, 65,* 1764–1777.

Wineburg, S. S. (1987). The self-fulfillment of the self-fulfilling prophecy. *Educational Researcher, 16,* 28–37.

Winner, E. (1986, August). Where pelicans kiss seals. *Psychology Today,* 24–35.

Winner, E. (1989). Development in the visual arts. In W. Damon (Ed.), *Child development today and tomorrow.* San Francisco: Jossey-Bass.

Wisnia, S. (1994, June 27). On the right track. *The Washington Post,* p. D5.

Witelson, S. (1989, March). *Sex differences.* Paper presented at the annual meeting of the New York Academy of Science, New York.

Wolf, A. M., Gortmaker, S. L., Cheung, L., & Gray, H. M. (1993). Activity, inactivity, and obesity: Racial, ethnic, and age differences among schoolgirls. *American Journal of Public Health, 83,* 1625–1627.

Wolff, P. H. (1963). Observations of the early development of smiling. In B. M. Foss (Ed.), *Determinants of infant behaviour* (Vol. 4). London: Methuen.

Wong, B. Y. L. (1996). *The ABCs of learning disabilities.* New York: Academic Press.

Wood, J. (1989). Theory and research concerning social comparisons of personal attributes. *Psychological Bulletin, 106,* 231–248.

Wood, W., Wong, F. Y., & Chachere, J. G. (1991). Effects of media violence on viewers' aggression in unconstrained social interaction. *Psychological Bulletin, 109,* 371–383.

Woolfolk, A. E. (1993). *Educational psychology* (5th ed.). Boston: Allyn & Bacon.

World Conference on Education for All. (1990, April). *World Declaration on Education for All and Framework for Action to Meet Basic Learning Needs.* Preamble, p. 1. New York.

World Factbook. (1994). Washington, DC: The Central Intelligence Agency.

World Food Council. (1992). *The global state of hunger and malnutrition. 1992 Report* (Table 2, p. 8). New York: Author.

World Health Organization. (1993). *The HIV/AIDS Pandemic: 1993 Overview* (Document WHO/GPA/EVA/93.1, Global Program on AIDS). Geneva, Switzerland: Author.

World Health Organization. (1995). First annual report on global health. Geneva, Switzerland: Author.

Worobey, J., & Bajda, V. M. (1989). Temperament ratings at 2 weeks, 2 months, and 1 year: Differential stability of activity and emotionality. *Developmental Psychology, 25,* 257–263.

Wright, J. C., Huston, A. C., Reitz, A. L., & Piemyat, S. (1994). Young children's perceptions of television reality: Determinants and developmental differences. *Developmental Psychology, 30,* 229–239.

Wright, R. (1995, March 13). The biology of violence. *New Yorker,* 68–77.

Wynn, K. (1992, August 27). Addition and subtraction by human infants. *Nature, 358,* 749–750.

Wynn, K. (1995). Infants possess a system of numerical knowledge. *Current Directions in Psychological Science, 4,* 172–177.

Xiohe, X., & Whyte, M. K. (1990). Love matches and arranged marriages: A Chinese replication. *Journal of Marriage and the Family, 52,* 709–722.

Yankelovich, D. (1974, December). Turbulence in the working world: Angry workers, happy grads. *Psychology Today, 8,* 80–87.

Yarrow, L. (1990, September). Does my child have a problem? *Parents,* 72.

Yarrow, L. (1992, November). Giving birth: 72,000 moms tell all. *Parents,* 148–159.

Yarrow, M. R., Scott, P. M., & Waxler, C. Z. (1973). Learning concern for others. *Developmental Psychology, 8, 240–260.*

Yee, M., & Brown, R. (1994). The development of gender differentiation in young children. *British Journal of Social Psychology, 33,* 183–196.

Yell, M. L. (1995). The least restrictive environment mandate and the courts: Judicial activism or judicial restraint? *Exceptional Children, 61,* 578–581.

Yelland, G. W., Pollard, J., & Mercuri, A. (1993). The metalinguistic benefits of limited contact with a second language. *Applied Psycholinguistics, 14,* 423–444.

Yerkes, R. M. (1923). *A point scale for measuring mental ability: A 1923 revision.* Baltimore, MD: Warwick & York.

Young, H., & Ferguson, L. (1979). Developmental changes through adolescence in the spontaneous nomination of reference groups as a function of decision context. *Journal of Youth and Adolescence, 8,* 239–252.

Youniss, J. (1989). Parent-adolescent relationships. In W. Damon (Ed.), *Child development today and tomorrow.* San Francisco: Jossey-Bass.

Youniss, J., & Haynie, D. L. (1992). Friendship in adolescence. *Journal of Developmental and Behavioral Pediatrics, 13,* 59–66.

Yuill, N., & Perner, J. (1988). Intentionality and knowledge in children's judgments of actor's responsibility and recipient's emotional reaction. *Developmental Psychology, 24,* 358–365.

Zahn-Waxler, C., & Radke-Yarrow, M. (1990). The origins of empathic concern. *Motivation and Emotion, 14,* 107–130.

Zahn-Waxler, C., Robinson, J. L., & Emde, R. N. (1992). The development of empathy in twins. *Developmental Psychology, 28,* 1038–1047.

Zaidel, D. W. (1994). Worlds apart: Pictorial semantics in the left and right cerebral hemispheres. *Current Directions in Psychological Science, 3,* 5–8.

Zaporozhets, A. V. (1965). The development of perception in the preschool child. *Monographs of the Society for Research in Child Development, 30,* 82–101.

Zarbatany, L., Hartmann, D. P., & Rankin, D. B. (1990). The psychological functions of preadolescent peer activities. *Child Development, 61,* 1067–1080.

Zelazo, N., Zelazo, P. R., Cohen, K., & Zelazo, P. D. (1993). Specificity of practice effects on elementary neuromotor patterns. *Developmental Psychology, 29,* 686–691.

Zelazo, P. R. (1983). The development of walking: New findings on old assumptions. *Journal of Motor Behavior, 2,* 99–137.

Zelazo, P. R., Zelazo, N. A., & Kolb, S. (1972). "Walking" in the newborn. *Science, 176,* 314–315.

Zeskind, P. S., & Ramey, D. T. (1981). Preventing intellectual and interactional sequels of fetal malnutrition: A longitudinal, transactional, and synergistic approach to development. *Child Development, 52,* 213–218.

Zevon, M., & Corn, B. (1990). Paper presented at the annual meeting of the American Psychological Association, Boston.

Zhang, J., Dawson, V. L., Dawson, T. M., & Snyder, S. H. (1994, February 4). Nitric oxide activation of poly(ADP-Ribose) synthetase in neurotoxicity. *Science, 263,* 687–689.

Zhang, Y., Proenca, R., Maffel, M., Barone, M., Leopold, L., & Friedman, J. M. (1994, December 1). Positional cloning of the mouse *obese* gene and its human homologue. *Nature, 372,* 425–432.

Zigler, E. (1994). Early intervention to prevent juvenile delinquency. *Harvard Mental Health Letter,* 5–7.

Zigler, E., & Styfco, S. J. (1994). Head Start: Criticism in a constructive context. *American Psychologist, 49,* 127–132.

Zigler, E., Styfco, S. J., & Gilman, E. (1993). The national Head Start program for disadvantaged preschoolers. In E. Zigler & S. J. Styfco (Eds.), *Head Start and beyond: A national plan for extended childhood intervention* (pp. 1–41). New Haven, CT: Yale University Press.

Zill, N. (1983). *Marital disruption and the child's need for psychological help.* Washington, DC: National Institute for Mental Health.

Zillman, D. (1993). Mental control of angry aggression. In D. M. Wegner & J. W. Pennebaker (Eds.), *Handbook of mental control.* Englewood Cliffs, NJ: Prentice Hall

Acknowledgments

Photographs

About the Author Page xxiv, Courtesy of Robert Feldman

Chapter 1 Page 5 Hank Morgan, Rainbow; p. 9 (top) Jeff Greenberg, Picture Cube, Inc.; (bottom) M. Grecco, Stock Boston; p. 11 H. Dratch, The Image Works; p. 15 Todd Buchanan, New York Times Pictures; p. 18 Lewis Hime, Corbis-Bettman; p. 19 Corbis-Bettman; p. 21 (top)Jon Eirkson, Simon & Schuster/PH College; (bottom) Archive Photos; p.22 Ken Heyman, Black Star; p. 23 Everett Collection; p. 27 Christiana Dittman, Rainbow; p. 31 (a) Alexander Tsiaras, Stock Boston; (b) Mary Kate Denny, PhotoEdit; (c) LeDuc, Monkmeyer Press; p. 34 Courtesy of Donald J. Hernandez, Ph.D.

Chapter 2 Page 45 Jan Sonnenmair; p. 46 D.W.Fawcett, Photo Researchers, Inc.; p. 48 (top) L. Willatt, E. Anglan Regional Genetics Service/Science Photo Library, Photo Researchers, Inc.; (bottom) Peter Menzel, Stock Boston; p. 49 Aaron Haupt, Stock Boston; p. 51 Corbis-Bettman; p. 54 Bill Longcore, Photo Researchers, Inc.; p. 56 SIU Biomed Comm, Custom Medical Stock Photo; p. 58 Courtesy of Lopa Malkin Wani; p. 63 Peter Glass, Monkmeyer Press; p. 65 (left) Douglas Mason, Woodfin Camp & Associates; (right) Lance Nelson, The Stock Market; p. 69 Courtesy of Sandra Scarr, KinderCare Learning Centers, Inc., Alabama; p. 71 Jason Burns/ACE Phototake NYC; p. 73 Steve Allen, The Image Bank; p. 76 John Chiasson, Gamma-Liaison, Inc.

Chapter 3 Page 83 Comstock; p. 84 (left) Comstock; (right) M. Greenlar, The Image Works; p. 86 Henry Schleichkorn, Custom Medical Stock Photo; p. 89 Byron, Monkmeyer Press; p. 91 Bill Stanton, Rainbow; p. 92 Lawrence Migdale, Stock Boston; p. 93 (top) P. Bouhous, Sygma; (bottom) Charles Gupton, Stock Boston; p. 94 Courtesy of Kathy McKain; p. 97 Susan Leavines, Photo Researchers, Inc.; p. 98 Ansell Horn, Phototake NYC; p. 99 Lawrence Migdale, Stock Boston; p. 108 Laura Dwight; pp. 109 & 110 Tiffany M. Field, Ph.D.

Chapter 4 Page 119 Lawrence Migdale/PIX; p. 124 (left and right) Comstock; p. 126 Ed Bock The Stock Market; p. 129 (left) Laura Elliot, Comstock; (center) L.J.Weinstein, Woodfin Camp & Associates; (right) Laura Dwight; pp. 131, 132 Laura Dwight; p. 133 Nubar Alexanian, Woodfin Camp & Associates; p. 136 J. Kenneth Whitt; p. 138 (top) Jose L. Pelaez, The Stock Market; (bottom) Stuart Cohen, Comstock; p. 141 Bob Daemmrich, The Image Works; p. 143 (top) Wally McNamee, Woodfin Camp & Associates; p. 143 (bottom) Mark Richards, PhotoEdit, courtesy of Joe Campos & Roseanne Kermoian; p. 146 Dion Ogust, The Image Works; p. 147 Michelle Bridwell, PhotoEdit

Chapter 5 Page 153 Patrick Segal, Sygma; p. 160 Owen Franken, Stock Boston; p. 161 David Sanders, *The Arizona Daily Star;* p. 164 The Granger Collection; p. 167 Carolyn Rovee-Collier; p. 168 Laura Dwight; p. 169 Laura Dwight; p. 171 Robert Brenner, PhotoEdit; p. 172 Courtesy of Ellen Sackoff, Bill Mitchell Photography; p. 176 Dr. Laura Ann Petitto, McGill University; p. 179 Laura Dwight; p. 180 Laura Dwight, PhotoEdit

Chapter 6 Page 189 David J. Sams, Stock Boston; p. 190(top right, left, bottom right) Dr. Carroll Izard; (bottom left) Dr. Murray L. Barr; p. 192 (top)Shackman, Monkmeyer Press; (bottom) Comstock; p. 195 Fredrik D. Bodin, Stock Boston; p. 197 Harlow Primate Laboratory, University of Wisconsin; p. 198 (left, center, right) William Hamilton, Johns Hopkins University; p. 199 Keren Su, Stock Boston; p. 201 Collins, Monkmeyer Press; p. 202 Stacy Pick, Stock Boston; p. 205 Elizabeth Hathon, Stock Market; p. 210 Goodwin, Monkmeyer Press; p. 211 (left) Corbis-Bettman, Springer/Bettman Film Archive; (right) Photofest; p. 213 Lawrence Migdale/PIX; p. 214 Courtesy of Melinda Rauch

Chapter 7 Page 223 Stephen Ferry, Gamma-Liaison, Inc.; p. 224 David Young-Wolff, Photo Edit; p. 226 Laura Dwight; p. 226 Courtesy of Dr. M. E. Raichle, research based upon *Nature, Vol. 331*, pp. 585-589, 1988; p. 231 Laura Dwight; p. 232 Tannenbaum, Sygma; p. 233 Geoff Tompkins/Science Photo Library, Photo Researchers, Inc.; p. 234 Chris Priest/Science Photo Library, Photo Researchers, Inc.; p. 235 Jeff Albertson, Stock Boston; p. 237 Monkmeyer Press; p. 238 Courtesy of David Kurtz, Ph.D.; p. 244 Margaret Miller, Photo Researchers, Inc.

Chapter 8 Page 251 Jacques Chenet, Woodfin Camp & Associates; p. 252 Corbis-Bettman; p. 256 (left & right) Laura Dwight; p. 259 Al Cook, Stock Boston; p. 260 Catherine Karnow, Woodfin Camp & Associates; p. 261 Courtesy of A. R. Luria and Dr. Michael Cole; p. 266 (left) Billy E. Barnes, PhotoEdit; (right) Goodwin, Monkmeyer Press; p. 270 (top) Jacques Chenet, Woodfin Camp & Associates; (bottom) Collins, The Image Works; p. 272 (top) Alain Evrard, Photo Researchers, Inc.; (bottom) Courtesy of Yolanda Garcia; p. 274 Laura Dwight; p. 276 R. Termine/CTW, Everett Collection

Chapter 9 Page 283 Photofest; p. 285 Rick Browne, Stock Boston; p. 287 (left) Ursula Markus, Photo Researchers, Inc.; (right) Laura Dwight; p. 289 (left) Spencer Grant, Stock Boston; (right) Ed Wheeler, The Stock Market; p. 290 (left) Michael Newman, PhotoEdit; (right) Laura Dwight; p. 292 Reuters/Sue Ogrocki, Archive Photos; p. 294 Collins, Monkmeyer Press; p. 297 Brady, Monkmeyer Press; p. 298 Tim Davis, Photo Researchers, Inc.; p. 305 Catherine Ursillo, Photo Researchers, Inc.; p. 306 Kopstein, Monkmeyer Press; p. 307 Albert Bandura, D. Ross, and S. A. Ross, Imitation of film-mediated aggressive models. *Journal of Abnormal and Social Psychology; 66*, 1963, p. 8; p. 308 Courtesy of Joy D. Osofsky

Chapter 10 Page 319 Jose Azel, Aurora & Quanta Productions; p. 320 Arthur Tilley, FPG International; p. 321 Ken Heyman, Woodfin Camp & Associates; p. 324 (left) Tom McCarthy, Rainbow; (right) David Young-Wolff, PhotoEdit; p. 325 Lester Sloan, Woodfin Camp & Associates; p. 328 Kopstein, Monkmeyer Press; p. 329 John Eastcott/YVA Momatiuk, Stock Boston; p. 330 Gary Landsman, The Stock Market; p. 331 Bonnie Kamin, PhotoEdit; p. 332 Courtesy of Kathryn C. Montgomery, photo by Rich Reinhard; p. 334 Brent M. Jones, Stock Boston; p. 336 Ken Schles

Chapter 11 Page 343 Frank Siteman, Stock Boston; p. 345 Lawrence Migdale/PIX; p. 348 (top)Penny Tweedie, Woodfin Camp & Associates; (bottom) Laura Dwight; p. 350 Bob Daemmrich, The Image Works; p. 353 Bob Daemmrich, Stock Boston; p. 358 Bernard Wolf, Monkmeyer Press; p. 364 Courtesy of Lauro Cavazos; p. 366 Corbis-Bettman; p. 375 Richard Hutchings, Photo Researchers, Inc.; p. 376 Russell D. Curtis, Photo Researchers, Inc.

Chapter 12 Page 383 Lori Grinker, Contact Press Images; p. 386 Robert Houser, Comstock; p. 388 Frank Siteman, Stock Boston; p. 389 Merrim, Monkmeyer Press; p. 391 Laura Dwight; p. 394 Bob Daemmrich, Stock Boston; p. 396 Bill Horsman, Stock Boston; p. 398 Jonathan Nourak, PhotoEdit; p. 402 Phil Borden, PhotoEdit; p. 403 Comstock; p. 405 (left) Corbis-Bettman; (right) Melchoir DiGiacomo, Boys Town; p. 406 Courtesy of Sam Schmidt

Chapter 13 Page 415 Marty Katz; p. 416 Thomas S. England, Photo Researchers, Inc.; p. 418 (top) C/B Productions; (bottom) Dana White, PhotoEdit; p. 421 Express Newspapers, Archive Photos; p. 424 John Eastcott, Photo Researchers, Inc.; p. 430 (top) Collins, Monkmeyer Press; (bottom) SIU, Photo Researchers, Inc.; p. 432 Courtesy of Doreen Branch; p. 434 Jacques Chenet, Woodfin Camp & Associates; p. 435 ChromoSohm/Sohm, Stock Boston; p. 436 Roger Mastroianni; p. 437 Michael A. Keller Studios Ltd., The Stock Market

Chapter 14 Page 445 Photo by Adam Fernandez; p. 449 Christopher Brown, Stock Boston; p. 453 Jerry Bauer, Courtesy of Harvard Graduate School of Education; p. 458 Ken Straiton, The Stock Market; p. 461 Jose L. Pelaez, The Stock Market; p. 466 Courtesy of Dr. Henry Klein; p. 467 Bob Daemmrich, The Image Works; p. 468(top) Bill Stanton, Rainbow; (bottom) Miro Vintoniv, Stock Boston

Chapter 15 Page 475 Torleif Svensson, The Stock Market; p. 481 G&M David de Lossy, The Image Bank; p. 483 Paul Kern.UPI, Corbis-Bettman; p. 487 Lawrence Migdale, Stock Boston; p. 488 David Young-Wolf, PhotoEdit; p. 489 Laura Dwight; p. 490 Bob Daemmrich, Stock Boston; p. 492 Bob Daemmrich, Stock Boston; p. 494 Ron Chapple, FPG International; p. 494 Yoav Levy, Phototake NYC; p. 499 Paula Lerner, Woodfin Camp & Associates; p. 501 Evan Johnson, Impact Visuals Photo & Graphics, Inc.; p. 502 Courtesy of Patricia Canessa

Figures and Tables

Chapter 1 Figure 1-1 C.B. Kopp/J.B. Krakow, *Child Development in the Social Context,* (p. 648) © 1982 by Addison-Wesley Publishing Company, Inc. Reprinted by permissions of Addison-Wesley Longman, Inc.

Chapter 2 Figure 2-2 Copyright 1995, USA Weekend. Reprinted with permission; Figure 2-5 Kimball, J.W. (1983) *Biology* (5th ed.) Reading, MA: Addison-Wesley. Reproduced with permission of The McGraw-Hill Companies; Figure 2-7 Bouchard, T.J. & McGue, M. (1981). Familial studies of intelligence: A review. *Science, 264,* 1700-1701. Reprinted with permission of Dr. Matt McGue and Dr. Thomas J. Bouchard; Figure 2-8 Tellegen, A. et al. (1988). Personality similarity in twins reared apart and together. *Journal of Personality and Social Psychology, 54,* 10311-1039. Copyright © 1988 by the American Psychological Association. Adapted with permission; Figure 2-9 From: *Schizophrenia Genesis* by Gottesman. Copyright © 1991 by Irving I. Gottesman. Used with Permission of W.H. Freeman and Company; Figure 2-10 Robbins, W.J. (1929). *Growth.* New Haven, CT: Yale University Press. Reprinted with permission of Yale University; Figure 2-11 Moore, K.L. (1974). *Before we are born: Basic embryology and birth defects.* Philadelphia: Saunders; Table 2-2 Kagan, J., Arcus, D., & Snidman, N. (1993). The idea of temperament. Where do we go from here? In Plomin, R., & McCleary G. E. (eds.), *Nature, nurture, and psychology.* Washington, DC: American Psychological Association. Copyright © 1993 by the American Psychological Association. Adapted with permission.

Chapter 3 Figure 3-3 Reprinted with permission of the publishers from *Infancy* by Tiffany Field, Cambridge, Mass: Harvard University Press, Copyright © by the President and Fellows of Harvard College; Figure 3-4 Notzon, F.C. (1990). International differences in the use of obstetric interventions. *Journal of the American Medical Association, 263* (24), 3286–3291; Figure 3-5 National Center for Health Statistics. (1993). Advance Report of Final Natality Statistics, 1991. *Monthly Vital Statistics Report, Vol. 42.* Washington, DC: Public Health Service; Figure 3-6 The World Factbook. The Central Intelligence Agency: Washington, DC, 1994; Figure 3-7 Courtesy of Dr. Tiffany Field; Table 3-1 Adapted from Apgar, V. (1953) A proposal for a new method of evaluation in the newborn infant. *Current Research in Anesthesia and Analgesia, 32,* 260. Used with permission of Waverly, Baltimore, MD; Table 3-2 Adapted with permission from *Preventing low birthweight;* Copyright 1985 by the National Academy of Sciences. Courtesy of the National Academy Press, Washington, DC; Table 3-3 From Caminiti, S. (1992, August 10) Who's minding America's kids? *Fortune,* pp. 50-53. © 1992 Time Inc. All rights reserved; Table 3-5 From Eckerman, C.O. & Oehler, J.M. (1992). Very low birthweight newborns and parents as early social partners. In Friedman, S.L. & Sigman, M.B., *The psychological development of low birthweight children.* Norwood, NJ: Ablex.

Chapter 4 Figures 4-1 From Cratty, B.J. (1979). *Perceptual and motor development in infants and children.* All rights reserved. Reprinted by permission of Allyn & Bacon; Figure 4-3 Bornstein, M.H., & Lamb, M.E. (eds.). (1992). *Development in Infancy: An introduction* (3rd. ed.) New York: McGraw-Hill. Reproduced with permission of the McGraw Companies; Figure 4-5 Reprinted from Roffwarg, H.P., Muzio, J.N., & Dement, W.C. (1966). Ontogenic development of the human sleep-dream cycle. *Science, 152,* 604-619. Copyright 1966 American Association for the Advancement of Science; Figure 4-6 Shirley, M.M. (1933). *The first two years: A study of twenty-five babies, Vol. 2. Institute of Child Welfars Monograph No. 7.* Minneapolis: University of Minnesota; Figure 4-7 World Food Council. (1992). *The global state of hunger and malnutrition. 1992 Report.* Table 2, p. 8. New York: World Food Council; Figure 4-8 Einbinder, S.D. (1990). A statistical profile of children living in poverty: Children under three and children under six. Unpublished document from the National Center for Children in Poverty. New York: Columbia University School of Public Health; Figure 4-9 Used with permission of Ross Products Division, Abbott Laboratories, Columbus, OH 43216. From Mother's Survey © 1993 Ross Products Division, Abbott Laboratories; Figure 4-11 Adapted from The origin of form perception, by R. L. Fantz. Copyright © 1961 by *Scientific American.* All rights reserved.; Table 4-2 Adapted from: Thoman, E.B., & Whitney, M.P. (1990). Behavioral states in infants: Individual differences and individual analyses. In J. Columbo, & J. Fagen (Eds), *Individual differences in infancy: Reliability, stability, prediction.* Hillsdale, NJ: Erlbaum; Table 4-4 *Manual for the Bayley Scales of infant development.* Copyright ©1960 by the Psychological Corporation. Reproduced by permission. All rights reserved. "Bayley Scales of Infant Development" is a registered trademark of The Psychological Corporation.

Chapter 5 Figure 5-6 Bornstein, M.H. & Lamb, M.E. (Eds). (1992). *Development in Infancy: An Introduction* (3rd ed.) New York: McGraw-Hill. Reproduced with permission of the McGraw-Hill Companies; Figure 5-7 Gleason, J.B., Perlmann, R.Y., Ely, R., & Evans, D.W. (1991). The babytalk registry: Parents' use of diminutive. In J.L. Sokolov, & CE. Snow (Eds), *Handbook of Research in Language Development using CHILDES.* Hillsdale, NJ: Erlbaum; Figure 5-8 Fernald, A., Taeschner, T., Dunn, J., Papousek, M., Boysson-Bardies, B., & Fukui, I. (1989). A cross-language study of prosodic modifications in mothers' and fathers' speech to preverbal infants. *Journal of Child Language, 16,* 477-501. Reprinted with the permission of Cambridge University Press; Table 5-4 *Bayley Scales of Infant Development.* Copyright ©1969 by The Psychological Corporation. Reproduced by permission. All rights reserved. "Bayley Scales of Infant Development" is a registered trademark of The Psychological Corporation; Table 5-5 Adapted from Benedict, H. (1979). Early lexical development: Comprehension and production. *Journal of Child Language, 6,* 183-200. Copyright 1979. Reprinted by permission of Cambridge University Press; Table 5-6 Brown, R. & Fraser, C. (1963). The acquisition of syntax. In C.N. Cofer and B. Musgrave (Eds.), *Verbal behavior and learning: Problems and processes.* New York: McGraw-Hill; Table 5-7 Blount, B.G. (1982). Culture and the language of socialization: Parental speech. In D.A. Wagner and H.W. Stevenson (Eds.), *Cultural perspectives on child development.* San Francisco: Freeman.

Chapter 6 Figure 6-3 Reprinted with permission. ©1993 *American Demographics* , Ithaca, New York; Figure 6-4 Adapted from Bell, S. M., & Ainsworth, M. D. (1972). Infant crying and maternal responsiveness. *Child Development, 43,* 1171-1190. Reprinted with permission of the Society for Research in Child Development, Inc. University of Michigan, Ann Arbor; Figure 6-4 Adapted from Tomlinson-Keasey, C. (1985). *Child development: Psychological, sociological and biological factors.* Homewood, IL: Dorsey Press. Reprinted with the permission of Dr. Carol Tomlinson-Keasey; Figure 6-5 U.S. Bureau of the Census. (1993). Child Health USA. Washington, DC; Table 6-1 Adapted from Waters, E. (1978). The reliability and stability of individual differences in infant-mother attachment. *Child Development, 49,* 480-494. Reprinted with permission of the Society for Research in Child Development, Inc. University of Michigan, Ann Arbor; Table 6-2 Adapted from Thomas, A., Chess, S., and Birch, H.G. (1968). *Temperament and behavior disorders in children.* New York: New York University Press. Reprinted with permission of Alexander Thomas, M.D.

Chapter 7 Figure 7-1 Lowrey, G.H. (1986). *Growth and development of children* (8th ed.). Chicago: Year Book Medical Publishers; Figure 7-3 Elkind, D. (1978). The child's reality: Three development themes. In Coren & Ward. Hillsdale, NJ: Erlbaum; Figure 7-4 Needleman, H.L., Reiss, J.A., Tobin, M.J., Biesecker, G.E., & Greenhouse, J.B. (1996, February 7). Bone lead levels and delinquent behavior. *Journal of the American Medical Association, 275,* 363-369. Used by permission. American Medical Association; Figure 7-5 Reprinted with permission of the American Humane Association, Englewood, CO; Table 7-2 Adapted with permission from Charles C. Corbin, *A textbook of motor development.* Copyright © 1973 Times Mirror Higher Education Group, Inc., Dubuque, Iowa. All rights reserved.

Chapter 8 Figure 8-5 Adapted from Berko, J. (1958). The child's learning of English morphology. *Word, 14,* 150-177; Figure 8-6 Hart, B., Risley, R. T, (1995). *Meaningful differences in the everyday experience of young American children.* Paul H. Brookes Publishing, P.O. Box 10624, Baltimore, MD 21285-0624; Figure 8-7 Based on table 5-2, p. 192 in : Tobin, J.J., Wu, D.Y.H., & Davidson, D.D.(1989). *Preschool in three cultures: Japan, China, and the United States.* New Haven: Yale University Press. Reprinted with permission of Yale University Press; Figure 8-8 Huston, A.C. & Wright, J.C. (May, 1995). *The effects of television viewing of lower-income preschoolers on academic skills, school readiness, and school adjustment one to three years later.* Unpublished report. Center for Research on the Influences of Television on Children (CRITC). Lawrence, KS: University of Kansas; Table 8-1 Pinker, S. (1994). *The language instinct.* New York: William Morrow.

Chapter 9 Figure 9-1 Adapted from: Farver, J.M., Kim, Y.K., & Lee, Y. (1995). Cultural differences in Korean- and Anglo-American preschooler's interaction and play behaviors. *Child Development, 66,* 1088-1099. Reprinted with permission of the Society for Research in Child Development, Inc., University of Michigan, Ann Arbor; Figure 9-3 Adaptation of analysis of violent content of broadcast and cable television stations on Thursday, April 7, 1995. Washington, DC: Center for Media and Public Affairs; Figure 9-6 ©UNESCO 1990. Reproduced by permission of UNESCO; Table 9-2 Walters, E., & Gardner, H. (1986). The theory of multiple intelligences: Some issues and answers. In R.J. Sternberg & R.K. Wagner (eds.), *Practical Intelligence.* Cambridge University Press. Copyright 1986. Reprinted with the permission of Cambridge University Press.

Chapter 10 Figure 10-1 Derived from Barrett, D. E., & Radke-Yarrow, M. (1985). Effects of nutritional supplementation on children's responses to novel, frustrating, and competitive situations. *American Journal of Clinical Nutrition, 42,* 102-120. © American Journal of Clinical Nutrition. American Society for Clinical Nutrition; Figure 10-2 From Cratty, B.J. (1989). *Perceptual and motor development in infants and children.* (2nd ed.). Englewood Cliffs, NJ: Prentice-Hall; Figure 10-3 From Schor, E.L. (1987). Unintentional injuries: Patterns within families. *American Journal of the Diseases of Children, 141,* 1280. Used by permission. American Medical Association; Table 10-1 From *Child Safety on the Information Highway* by Lawrence J. Magid. (1995). Reprinted with permission of the National Center for Missing and Exploited Children (NCMEC). Copyright ©NCMEC 1994. All rights reserved; Table 10-2 Wallis, C. (1994, July 18). Life in overdrive. *Time,* p. 42-50. ©1994 Time, Inc. Reprinted by permission.

Chapter 11 Figure 11-2 Dasen, P., Ngini, L. & Lavallee, M. (1979). Cross-cultural training studies of concrete operations. In L.H. Eckenberger, W.J. Lonner, & Y.H. Pootinga (Eds.), *Cross-cultural contributions to psychology.* Amsterdam: Swets & Zeilinger; Figure 11-3 U.S. Bureau of the Census. (1991). Population Profile of the United States: 1991. *Current Population Reports,* Series P-23, No. 173. Washington, DC: U.S. Government Printing Office; Figure 11-4 UNESCO (1990). Compendium of statistics on illiteracy, No. 31. Paris; Figure 11-5 U.S. Bureau of the Census (1993) Washington, DC; Figure 11-6 Stevenson, H.W. and Lee, S. (1990). Contexts of achievement: A study of American, Chinese and Japanese children. *Research in Child Development, No. 221, 55,* Nos. 1-2. Reprinted with permission of the Society for Research in Child Development. University of Michigan, Ann Arbor; Figure 11-7 Weschler Intelligence Scales for Children (WISC-III); Table 11-1 U.S. Department of Education (1988). James Madison Elementary School: A curriculum for American students. Washington, DC; Table 11-2 Walters, E. & Gardner, H. (1986). The theory of multiple intelligences: Some issues and answers. In R.J. Sternberg and R.K. Wagner (Eds.), *Practical intelligence.* Cambridge University Press. Copyright 1986. Reprinted with permission of Cambridge University Press.

Chapter 12 Figure 12-1 Shavelson, R., Hubner, J.J., & Stanton, J.C. (1976). Self-concept: Validation of construct interpretations. *Review of Educational Research,* 46, 407-441; Figure 12-3 Adapted from Dodge, K.A. (1985). A social information processing model of social competence in children. In M. Perlmutter (Ed.), Minnesota Symposia on Child Psychology (Vol. 18), 77-126. Hillsdale, NJ: Erlbaum; Figure 12-4 From Figure 10-2 in Suro, R. (1992, May 26). For women, varied reasons for single motherhood. The New York Times, A12. Copyright ©1992 by The New York Times Company. Reprinted by permission; Table 12-1 Zarbatany, L., Hartmann, D.P. & Rankin, B.D. (1990). The psychological functions of preadolescent peer activities. *Child Development, 61,* 1067-1080. Reprinted with permission of the Society for Resarch in Child Development. University of Michigan, Ann Arbor; Table 12-2 Shealy, C.N. (1995). From *Boys Town* to *Oliver Twist:* Separating fact from fiction in welfare reform and out-of-home placement of children and youth. *American Psychologist, 50,* 565-580. Copyright ©1995 by the American Psychological Association. Adapted with permission.

Chapter 13 Figure 13-1 From Cratty, B.J. (1989). *Perceptual and motor development in infants and children.* (2nd. ed.). Englewood Cliffs, NJ: Prentice Hall; Figure 13-2 Adapted from Eveleth, P. & Tanner, J. (1976).*Worldwide variation in human growth.* New York: Cambridge University Press. Copyright 1976. Reprinted with permission of Cambridge University Press; Figure 13-3 Tanner, J.M. (1978) *Education and physical growth* (2nd. ed.). New York: International Universities Press; Figure 13-4 Adapted from Silverstein, B., Perdue, L., Peterson, B., & Kelly, E. (1986). The role of mass media in promoting a thin standard of bodily attractiveness for women. *Sex Roles, 14,* 519-532. Copyright Plenum Publishing Corporation; Figure 13-5 Lazarus, R.S., & Folkman, S. (1984). *Stress, appraisal, and coping.* ©1984 by Springer Publishing Company, Inc., New York, New York, 10012. Used by permission; Figure 13-6 Adapted from O'Malley, P.M., Johnston, L.D., & Bachman, J.G. (1995). Adolescent substance abuse. Epidemiology and implications for public policy. *Pediatric Clinics of North America, 42,* 241-260. Used by permission. W.B. Saunders Company; Figure 13-7 Reprinted with permission from *Journal of Studies on Alcohol, 55,* 41-45, 1994. Copyright by Alcohol Research Documentation, Inc., Rutgers Center of Alcohol Studies, Piscataway, NJ 08855; Figure 13-9 Adapted from Alan Guttmacher Institute (1993). Sexually transmitted diseases (STDs) in the United States. New York: Alan Guttmacher Institute; Table 13-1 Rahe, K.H., & Arthur, R.J. (1978). Life change and illness studies: Past history and future directions. *Journal of Human Stress, 4,* 3-15. Reprinted with permission of the Helen Dwight Reid Educational Foundation. Published by Heldref Publications, 1319 Eighteenth St., N.W., Washington, D.C. 20036-1802; Table 13-2 Benson, H. (1993). The relaxation response. In D. Goleman & J. Guerin (Eds.). *Mind-body medicine: How to use your mind for better health.* Yonkers: Consumer Reports Publications. Reprinted with the permission of Dr. Herbert Benson.

Chapter 14 Figure 14-1 Bayley, N. (1949). Consistency and variability in the growth of intelligence from birth to eighteen years. *Journal of Genetic Psychology, 75,* 165-196. Reprinted with permission of the Helen Dwight Reid Educational Foundation. Published by Heldref Publications, 1319 Eighteenth St., NW, Washington, DC 20036-1802. Copyright ©1949; Figure 14-3 Crystal, D.S., Chen, C., Fuligni, A.J., Stevenson, H.W., Hsu, C., Ko, H., Kitamura, S., & Kimura, S. (1994). Psychological maladjustment and academic achievement: A cross-cultural study of Japanese, Chinese, and Amrerican high school students. *Child Development, 65,* 738-753; Figure 14-5 From Astin, A.W., Korn, W.S. & Berz, E.R. (1990). *The American freshman: National norms for Fall, 1990.* Los Angeles: Higher Education Research Institute, UCLA; Table 14-1 Kohlberg, L. (1969). Stage and Sequence: The cognitive developmental approach to socialization. In D. Goslin (Ed.), *Handbook of socialization research.* Chicago: Rand McNally. Reprinted with permission of David. A. Goslin, President, American Institute for Research, Washington, DC; Table 14-2 Gilligan, C. (1982). *In a different voice: Psychological theory and women's development.* Cambridge, MA: Harvard University Press; Table 14-3 National Center for Education Statistics (1991). Digest of education statistics 1990. Washington, DC: National Center for Education Statistics, U.S. Department of Education, pp. 113, 116, 118, 120, 121; Table 14-4 Reprinted with permission of Scribner, a Division of Simon & Schuster from *Failing at fairness: How America's schools cheat girls* by Myra & David Sadker. Copyright ©1994 by Myra & David Sadker.

Chapter 15 Figure 15-1 Source: AMA profiles of Adolescent health, *America's Adolescents: How Healthy Are They?* American Medical Association, copyright 1990; Figure 15-2 Boston Samaritans (1991). Boston, MA; Figure 15-3 Steinberg, L., & Silverberg, S.B., (1986) Influences on marital satisfaction during middle stages of the family life cycle. *Journal of Marriage and the Family, 49,* 751-760. Copyrighted 1986 by the National Council on Family Relations, 3989 Central Ave., NE, Suite 550, Minneapolis, MN 55421. Reprinted by permission; Figure 15-4 Larson, R.W., Richards, M.H., Moneta, G., Holmbeck, G., & Duckett, E. (1996). Changes in adolescents' daily interactions with their families from ages 10 to 18: Disengagement and transformation. *Developmental Psychology, 32,* 744-754; Figure 15-5 Brown, B., Lohr, M., & Trujillo, C. (1983). *Adolescent peer group stereotypes, member conformity, and identity development.* Paper presented at the meeting of The Society for Research in Child Development, Detroit, MI; Figure 15-6 Adapted from Michael, R.T., Gagnon, J.H., Laumann, E.O., & Kolata, G. (1994). *Sex in America: A definitive study.* Boston: Little Brown; Figure 15-7 Adapted from Alan Guttmacher Institute (1988). *Pregnancy rates around the world.* New York: Alan Guttmacher Institute; Table 15-1 From *Childhood and society* by Erik H. Erikson. Copyright 1950. ©1963 by W.W. Norton & Company, Inc., renewed ©1978, 1991 by Erik H. Erikson. Reprinted by permission of W.W. Norton & Company, Inc.; Table 15-2 Adapted from Marcia, J.E. (1980). Identity in adolescence. In J. Adelson (Ed.) *Handbook of adolescent psychology.* New York: Wiley. Copyright ©1990. Reprinted by permission of John Wiley & Sons, Inc.

Name Index

Subject Index